Under the Editorship of

DAYTON D. MCKEAN

UNIVERSITY OF COLORADO

Norman D. Palmer • Howard C. Perkins

UNIVERSITY OF PENNSYLVANIA

INTERNATIONAL

RELATIONS

The World Community in Transition

THIRD EDITION

INDIAN EDITION

CBS

CBS Publishers & Distributors Pvt. Ltd.

New Delhi • Bengaluru • Chennai • Kochi • Kolkata • Mumbai
Hyderabad • Nagpur • Patna • Pune • Vijayawada

ISBN: 81-239-1346-X

First Indian Edition: 1985
Reprint: 1999, 2001

This edition has been reprinted in India by arrangement with Houghton Mifflin Company, Boston, USA

Published by **Satish Kumar Jain** and produced by **Varun Jain** for
CBS Publishers & Distributors Pvt. Ltd.,
4819/XI Prahlad Street, 24 Ansari Road, Daryaganj, New Delhi - 110002
delhi@cbspd.com, cbspubs@airtelmail.in • www.cbspd.com
Ph.: 23289259, 23266861, 23266867 • Fax: 011-23243014

Corporate Office: 204 FIE, Industrial Area, Patparganj, Delhi - 110 092
Ph: 49344934 • Fax: 011-49344935
E-mail: publishing@cbspd.com • publicity@cbspd.com

Branches:

- ***Bengaluru:*** 2975, 17th Cross, K.R. Road, Bansankari 2nd Stage, Bengaluru - 70 • Ph: +91-80-26771678/79 • Fax: +91-80-26771680 E-mail: cbsbng@gmail.com, bangalore@cbspd.com
- ***Chennai:*** No. 7, Subbaraya Street, Shenoy Nagar, Chennai - 600030 Ph: +91-44-26681266, 26680620 • Fax: +91-44-42032115 E-mail: chennai@cbspd.com
- ***Kochi:*** Ashana House, 39/1904, A.M. Thomas Road, Valanjambalam, Ernakulum, Kochi • Ph: +91-484-4059061-65 Fax: +91-484-4059065 • E-mail: cochin@cbspd.com
- ***Kolkata:*** 6-B, Ground Floor, Rameshwar Shaw Road, Kolkata - 700014 Ph: +91-33-22891126/7/8 • E-mail: kolkata@cbspd.com
- ***Mumbai:*** 83-C, Dr. E. Moses Road, Worli, Mumbai - 400018 Ph: +91-9833017933, 022-24902340/41 • E-mail: mumbai@cbspd.com

Representatives:

- Hyderabad: 0-9885175004
- Patna: 0-9334159340
- Jharkhand: 0-9811541605
- Nagpur: 0-9021734563
- Pune: 0-9623451994
- Uttarakhand: 0-9716462459

Printed at: Srk Graphics

TO THE MEMORY OF

Howard C. Perkins

CO-AUTHOR, COLLEAGUE, FRIEND

PREFACE

More than two decades have passed since the authors of this book began to prepare the first edition. At that time — the early postwar years — the atomic age was in its infancy, and the space age had not begun. The United States and the Soviet Union had emerged from the travail of World War II as the only superpowers, and were already eyeing each other with doubts and suspicions. The cold war was just becoming a salient feature of international relations. Western Europe was still in disarray, not having recovered from the physical and psychological shocks of World War II. Germany and Japan were occupied countries, bereft of their former sovereign status. China had not yet passed under Communist control. The newly emerging nations of South and Southeast Asia and the Middle East were just beginning to face their problems of national unity, survival, development, and international status. The era of African independence was still in the future. The Organization of American States had not yet given more definite form to the movement for inter-American cooperation, and the Alliance for Progress was not even a dream.

When the first edition was in its final stages of preparation, twenty years of Democratic administration in the United States came to an end, and General Dwight D. Eisenhower, heading a Republican administration, entered the White House. A few weeks later the Stalin era of Soviet politics, which had lasted for more than a quarter of a century, ended with the death of the dictator, to be followed by an uncertain period of collective leadership, personal jockeying for power within the murky recesses of the Kremlin, de-Stalinization, and a new look in Soviet domestic and foreign policy. While the second edition was being readied for the press, the Suez and Hungarian crises of 1956 burst, almost simultaneously, upon the world scene, creating vast apprehensions, great confusion, strange alliances, and presaging new departures of uncertain direction and import.

The third edition is going through its final stages during a period of growing confusion and uncertainty, within as well as between nations and international systems. The struggle in Vietnam and the Soviet occupation of Czechoslovakia are darkening the hopes for world peace and are frustrating international cooperation on many vital fronts. The United States is a nation divided over racial and foreign policies; the leaders of the Soviet Union are on the defensive because of pressures from within, the growing independence of the East European states, and the split with Communist China; and Communist China, approaching the end of the Maoist era and trying to recover from the adverse effects of the Red Guard excesses and the Great Cultural Revolution, is in a militant mood. The gap between the "have" and "have-not" nations of the North and South, the developed and developing worlds, is growing greater, rather than less, and the problems of the developing countries — a description which may unhappily prove to be inaccurate — are mounting inexorably. The Development Decade, so bravely launched in the early 1960's, is ending in growing frustration. Movements for cooperation in Western Europe seem to be stymied by the recalcitrance of De Gaulle and the different assessments and priorities of the West European states. The encouraging steps toward African unity are foundering on the rocks of personal and nationalistic rivalries. Mounting atomic stockpiles in the arsenals of nuclear powers and the danger of further nuclear proliferation are grim reminders of the precariousness of the "balance of terror" and deterrence strategies on which the peace of the world seems to depend. Problems of race and color are clearly being accentuated. In many countries — Communist and non-Communist, developed and underdeveloped alike — the generation gap seems to be greater than ever, and a vast wave of protest and unrest on the part of students and other young people is challenging the existing political and social leadership and perhaps even the underlying political and social canons and institutions. As Walter Lippmann has pointed out, "the word revolution carries with it today a far deeper meaning than it did when many of us were young."

More than ever, therefore, the study of international relations, as the subtitle of this book suggests, is a study of "the world community in transition." This third edition attempts to give due attention to underlying trends and major developments in international relations, as well as to basic principles and practices. It also attempts to give due recognition to the new trends in the study of international relations, including greater emphasis on interdisciplinary, comparative, behavioral, and quantitative methods and theoretical approaches. Since this is primarily a basic text in the field, it tries to take account of the revolutionary developments in both the international scene and the study of international relations in a manner consistent with its basic purpose: to provide a comprehensive, balanced, non-argumentative, *teachable* introduction to international relations, clearly and logically organized and intelligibly written.

A basic text should be neither a compendium of current events nor an abstract essay in one particular approach or in general theory. The authors believe that it should deal primarily with the substance of international relations, without neglecting theory and methodology, and above all that it should be truly a text in international relations and not primarily a manual for the study of the subject. Writing a text in such an amorphous and rapidly changing field as international relations has always presented very special difficulties. In view of the present state of international relations research, and the profound changes which are under way in the international system — changes whose nature and impact can only be dimly foreseen — such a venture may be downright hazardous, or even foolhardy. Clearly there is widespread disagreement regarding the proper scope of the field, and regarding method and theory.

This text is designed to meet a variety of needs. It has enough substance and breadth to serve as a basic text for either a one-term or a one-year course. The first half deals essentially with the principles, instruments, institutions, and techniques of international relations, and the second with contemporary world politics. However it is used, it can — and should — be supplemented by a variety of readings and exercises, in accordance with the tastes and interests of the instructors, who, it is hoped, will bear in mind the needs and backgrounds of their students and will be familiar with new developments in the field. This book can also be used for supplementary and reference purposes in advanced courses, and it should have some value for anyone who is interested in a substantive and comprehensive analysis of the basic principles of international politics and the salient aspects of contemporary international life.

With each edition our debts of gratitude multiply. We are indebted to friends and professional colleagues in many institutions for their encouragement, interest, and concrete help; to the students in our classes, graduate and undergraduate, over many years, who provided the laboratories in which we tested our ideas and who made it all worthwhile; to the staffs of several excellent libraries in this country and abroad; to authors, publishers, and artists, for their kindness in allowing us to reprint passages, maps, charts, and cartoons; and to seminal thinkers and writers in the field of international relations, whose contributions have in various ways enriched our thinking and influenced our work. We are particularly grateful to Dr. Dayton D. McKean of the University of Colorado, general editor of the Houghton Mifflin publications in political science, and to the editors, artists, and technicians of the Houghton Mifflin Company, who, though nameless here by mandate of "the code," have given of their experience, skill, and patience to the making of this book.

The prolonged illness, followed by the untimely death, of Dr. Howard C. Perkins deprived me of his invaluable cooperation during the preparation of the third edition; and since he was one of my oldest and closest friends and for many years my colleague in the Political Science Department at the University of Pennsylvania, his passing was a personal as well as a professional loss to me. A meticulous scholar, he set standards which neither of us ever fully attained, but which neither of us could ever disregard. It is only fitting that his name has been retained as one of the authors of the book, and that this edition is dedicated to his memory.

NORMAN D. PALMER

Leopard Lake
Berwyn, Pennsylvania

CONTENTS

PART FOUR *Conflict and Change in the Postwar World*

PART FIVE *Formulations of the National Interest*

PART SIX *The Future of the World Community in the Nuclear and Space Age*

The Study of International Relations

Almost two centuries ago Tom Paine spoke the mind of many people when he said: "These are times that try men's souls." What would he say today, were he here to see the frightful weapons of the atomic age, the deterioration of international relations, and the failure of the most powerful states to devise formulas for living together without the ever-present threat of war? He would certainly see, as does every thinking man, that thoughtful attention to the problems of international life has become mandatory for our security, welfare, and, indeed, our survival.

The crisis of our age is no temporary one. It is probable that we are living in one of the great transition periods of human history. The real international crisis of our time, says E. H. Carr, "is the final and irrevocable breakdown of the conditions which made the nineteenth-century order possible."[1] It is not only that "the foundations are shaking," as one writer describes the "world revolution" of our time, but also that new political forms and relationships are emerging.

International relations today have become truly *international,* and are characterized by a high degree of interaction and interdependence. Clearly the international system is changing in innumerable ways. Old actors are playing new and often reduced roles, and new actors, of uncertain quality and prospects, are appearing constantly. We may be witnessing not only major changes within the system, but a systemic change that in time may produce a new pattern of international relations altogether.

Much of international relations in the period since World War II has centered around the search for a new international system to replace the old order that was shattered in two world wars and to work out a new pattern of relationships in a world dominated by two superpowers, divided between Communist and non-Communist and between have and have-not nations, and altered beyond recognition by the emergence of many new states and by the technological changes consequent upon the nuclear and space age.

Present Nature of the Study

The study of international relations, like the world community itself, is in transition. In a rapidly changing and increasingly complex world it encompasses much more than the relations among nation-states and international organizations and groups. It includes a great variety of transitional relationships, at various levels, above and below the level of the nation-state, still the main actor in the international community. Both the

[1] E. H. Carr, *The Twenty Years' Crisis, 1919–1939,* 2d ed. (London, 1946), pp. 236–237.

content of and the approaches to the subject are expanding as scholars apply the insights and techniques of many disciplines, and the tools of modern technology, to the problems of international affairs. Traditional approaches, of a historical, descriptive, and analytical nature, are being supplemented — and sometimes supplanted — by other approaches, which attempt to give greater order and form to the vast amounts of data available and being accumulated for international relations research and to use the data in both applied research and in theoretical analysis. These new approaches have already made a significant impact on the study of international relations. They are designed to bridge the gap between theory and practice, to provide better tools for analysis of the increasingly complex data of international life, and to apply the findings and techniques of the behavioral sciences and other disciplines to international relations research.

In this introduction we shall look at some of these new dimensions as well as underscore some of the major themes and conflicting trends of which the student of international relations will need to be aware.

Is International Relations a Discipline? Although the study of international relations has emerged from its earlier status as a poor relation of political science and history, it is still far from being a well-organized discipline. It lacks a clear-cut conceptual framework and a systematic body of applicable theory; and it is heavily dependent upon other and for the most part better-organized disciplines. But it does have certain features which set it apart from other disciplines, and, above all, it has a particular approach to the problems with which it deals.

Some behaviorally-oriented students insist that international relations is on the way to becoming a science, or at least that this should be the object of all those who are trying to give greater meaning and significance to the field. Measured by any rigid test, international relations is clearly not a science, nor is it even a discipline, if one accepts C. Dale Fuller's definition that this requires "a body of data systematized by a distinctive analytical method and capable of permitting predictions with exactitude."[2] However, Stanley Hoffmann has argued that it is possible to distinguish the field of international relations for analytical purposes, and that therefore it "should be treated as an autonomous discipline."[3] In practice it is being so treated in many programs featuring both teaching and research. Hence the question "Is international relations a discipline?" admits of no more than a pragmatic answer. Applying Morton Kaplan's criteria that "a discipline implies a set of skills and techniques; a body of theory and of propositions; and a subject matter,"[4] international relations, as a field of study and research, may be regarded as a discipline. Certainly it has a distinctive methodology, distinctive theories (if not a general theory), and a distinctive subject matter, however fluctuating and ill-defined its boundaries may be.

Impact of the International Environment. The study of international relations is still too subjective in character and content, too likely to be perverted from its real purpose by proponents of a utopian or a power-political approach — to mention only the extreme "schools." In its early stages, as Carr has pointed out in one of the basic works in the field, it was "markedly and frankly utopian," for "the passionate desire to prevent war determined the whole initial

[2] *Training of Specialists in International Relations* (Washington, D.C.: American Council on Education, 1957), p. 26.

[3] Introduction in Stanley Hoffmann, ed., *Contemporary Theory in International Relations* (Englewood Cliffs, N.J.: Prentice-Hall, 1960), p. 1.

[4] Morton A. Kaplan, "Is International Relations a Discipline?" *The Journal of Politics,* XXIII (August, 1961), 464.

course and direction of the study."[5] But the failure of the League of Nations and of the "collective security" system, observed Carr, "clearly revealed the inadequacy of pure aspiration as the basis for a science of international politics, and made it possible for the first time to embark on serious and critical analytical thought about international problems."[6]

The disillusionment of the two decades of aggression and war gave impetus to a "realistic" school of international politics; here the emphasis was on power politics and the virtual inevitability of war. Then, after World War II a newly-born optimism swung the pendulum back toward the utopian approach. Observers hopefully assumed that the major non-Fascist states would cooperate in peace as they had in war, and that the United Nations would provide a means for cooperation in averting threats to the peace and in building a better world. Actually, of course, these assumptions were based more on hope than on a realistic appraisal of the world scene. Overenthusiastic champions of the United Nations gave the impression that the new organization had more authority than it actually possessed and that it somehow operated above the plane of power politics.

With the widening gulf between the Communist and non-Communist worlds, and particularly with the disillusioning events in Korea after June, 1950, the realists again seemed to be in the ascendant. It was difficult to be optimistic in the period of the cold war, which coincided with the loss of the American nuclear monopoly and the development of thermonuclear weapons by both the superpowers. However, certain trends of the 1950's and 1960's, including the "new look" in Soviet foreign policy after the death of Stalin in 1953, the limited détente between the United States and the Soviet Union, the change from bipolarity to multipolarity and the emergence of polycentrism within and outside the Communist world, and the growing recognition of a common stake in survival, encouraged a cautious but widespread optimism. This was tempered by a sober realization that international relations must continue to operate under conditions of "protracted conflict" and "permanent crisis." It was clearly a time for neither optimism nor pessimism, but for clear-headed realism. This was easy to prescribe but difficult to achieve; for too often what was regarded by some as realism was considered by others to be the height of unreason and unreality. And too often "realistic" definitions and attempted applications of policies in support of the "national interest" led to *cul de sacs* of nationalism, narrowly conceived, rather than to cooperative measures for international development.

Today, "international relations bids fair to replace economics as the dismal science. Forecasts and projections from analyses of any number of aspects of the world situation inescapably create an atmosphere of 'If you think things are bad now, wait until a little later.' "[7] But a student of international relations can be a realist without succumbing to the darkest despair. In fact, he can even be to some extent an optimist, at least to the degree that Winston Churchill once described himself as such, because "there isn't much point in being anything else."

"International Politics" or "International Relations"? These terms are often used almost interchangeably. Some modern students, however, particularly those who specialize in the study of political behavior, hold that there ought to be a distinction in usage, and that the failure on the part of writers and practitioners of international af-

[5] Carr, p. 8.
[6] *Ibid.*, p. 9.

[7] Charles A. McClelland, *College Teaching of International Relations: Problems of Organization and Collaboration*, a report on applied and experimental studies of undergraduate college education in international relations (1962), p. 30.

fairs and diplomacy to make a distinction has contributed to a semantic confusion in the study of international relations today. Briefly stated, these students insist that international politics should deal with the politics of the international community in a rather narrow sense, centering on diplomacy and the relations among states and other political units, whereas international relations is a term properly embracing the totality of the relations among peoples and groups in the world society. Those who subscribe to this broader and more nebulous term differ on the role of international politics in international relations; some of them would assign it a major role, while others would subordinate it to various cultural, social, and psychological forces in the world environment.

Most students would agree that the term "international politics" is used primarily to "describe official political relations between governments acting on behalf of their states,"[8] although at least one political scientist has asserted, rather cryptically, that " 'international politics' today is not conducted between or among nations, nor in its most important phases even between states."[9] The term "international relations" is broader and less easily circumscribed.

As Stanley Hoffmann has suggested, "the discipline of international relations is concerned with the factors and activities which affect the external policies and the power of the basic units into which the world is divided";[10] and these include a wide variety of transnational relationships, political and nonpolitical, official and unofficial, formal and informal.

This description should be broad enough. It should not be necessary to go far beyond it, as does Trygve Mathiesen, and to claim that the term is in effect synonymous with "international affairs" and embraces "all kinds of relations traversing state boundaries, no matter whether they are of an economic, legal, political, or any other character, whether they be private or official," and "all human behavior originating on one side of a state boundary and affecting human behavior on the other side of the boundary."[11]

The authors of this volume recognize that "international relations" is a broader term than "international politics," and that its study is being enriched by the wider and more versatile approaches and methods currently being pursued; but they also believe that the new insights and techniques should be employed to understand better the "core" as well as to explore the peripheries of the field. They acknowledge, however, that one can work fruitfully in the peripheries of a field without neglecting its central focus. While the historian, the economist, the geographer, the sociologist, the psychologist, the anthropologist, and other specialists make their distinctive and indeed indispensable contributions, the fact remains that the working relationships of states are conditioned most of all by the enactments and engagements of governments, however much these may be predetermined by underlying conditions and forces. Moreover, the use of "international relations" to mean essentially "international politics" is by no means a deliberate effort to exclude the nonpolitical.

Content of the Study. Contemporary international relations is a study of "the world community in transition." Since the study of international relations is not itself a well-organized discipline with a coherent and integrated body of material, it is not at all surprising that approaches to the subject vary greatly. Much depends upon the orientation, training, and interests of those who

[8] John Hanessian, Jr., "The Study and Teaching of International Relations: Some Comments on the Current Crisis," *SAIS Review*, X (Summer, 1966), 29.

[9] Herbert J. Spiro, *Politics in Africa: Prospects South of the Sahara* (Englewood Cliffs, N.J.: Prentice-Hall, 1962), p. 12.

[10] Hoffmann, p. 6.

[11] *Methodology in the Study of International Relations* (Oslo, 1959), pp. 1, 2.

teach and write in the field. History and political science are the disciplines from which international relations has emerged, and approaches natural to these two older disciplines are still common. In introductory courses the necessary historical background — or at least as much of it as can be compressed within rigid space limitations — may be presented as a separate section or it may be woven into the textual material at various places on a basically analytical framework. In general, it may be said that in Britain, and in countries influenced directly by the British pattern of education, introductory courses in international relations are usually courses in the history of recent international affairs, whereas in the United States the analytical approach seems to be preferred. One variation or adaptation of this is the problem approach, which is common in government policy-making and is employed to a considerable extent in the university teaching of international relations in the United States.[12] A related approach is the use of case studies of various kinds. Neither of these is popular in European universities, where the study of international relations is still heavily theoretical, legalistic, and institutional, with emphasis on legal norms, jurisprudence, and history.

Many of the basic principles and underlying factors of international relations have not altered, but the international environment has changed and is still changing. The changes are a result of the modifications in the state system, the vast technological developments of our time, the increasingly influential role being played by non-Western societies, and the "revolution of rising expectations" which is affecting, directly or indirectly, the majority of the underprivileged peoples of the world. Thus in the study of international relations old and new elements must be interwoven. The focus is still the nation-state system and interstate relations; but the actions and interactions of many organizations and groups and of many subterranean forces and factors also have to be considered.

In a report published in 1947 by the Council on Foreign Relations, Grayson Kirk, on the basis of surveys and conferences dealing with the study of international relations in American colleges and universities, concluded that "five ingredients" were usually "combined according to the individual taste of the instructor" in the basic course in the subject. These ingredients were: (1) the nature and operation of the state system; (2) factors which affect the power of a state; (3) the international position and foreign policies of the great powers; (4) the history of recent international relations; and (5) the building of a more stable world order.[13] Seven years later Vincent Baker, reporting on a survey under the auspices of the Carnegie Endowment for International Peace, found that "the following ingredients seem now to appear in most courses": (1) the nature and principal forces of international politics; (2) the political, social, and economic organization of international life; (3) the elements of national power; (4) the instruments available for the promotion of the national interest; (5) the limitation and control of national power; (6) the foreign policy of one or more major powers and occasionally of a small state; and (7) the historical ingredient as a background for other factors and as a history of recent international events. Other trends noted by Baker were

[12] The International Studies Group of the Brookings Institution, which was headed by Leo Pasvolsky until his death in 1953, did much to promote the growing interest in the problem approach, especially through the sponsorship of several seminars, the publication of a number of problem papers, and its volumes on *Major Problems of United States Foreign Policy*.

[13] *The Study of International Relations in American Colleges and Universities* (Harper, for the Council on Foreign Relations, 1947), pp. 27–29. See also Russell H. Fifield, "The Introductory Course in International Relations," *American Political Science Review*, XLII (December, 1948), 1189–1196.

the growing concern with theory, the increased emphasis on the policy-making process, a tendency to draw more heavily upon other disciplines, and the more frequent use of case studies of various types.[14]

By 1962 the trends discerned earlier had gained greater prominence. A report issued in that year, for example, called for undergraduate courses in international relations to stress such themes as "the ways by which governments attempt to maintain sovereignty and security of nations and . . . the patterns of behavior which arise in pursuit of these objectives"; "the profound effects on all types of international relations brought about by the spread and growth of science and technology"; "the network of interactions generated by the continuing increases in world population, the growth of the production and consumption of material resources, the changing social and technical arrangements in the producing, distributing, and consuming processes, and the concomitant shifts and adjustments of nations between the poles of isolation and international collaboration as they face these economic and social situations"; "the civilized accomplishments, past and present, of the peoples of Asia and Africa"; and "the psychological responses to international situations . . ."[15]

This list calls attention to the widening dimensions of the study of international relations, resulting largely from the impact of the behavioral sciences upon the field. "During the past fifteen years we have witnessed in the United States an explosion of scholarly activity directed towards making the study of international relations more rigorous and systematic."[16]

The study of international relations along multidimensional lines can be challenging and well worthwhile, but it has definite limitations for the undergraduate student. In fact, at the beginning level it may easily be carried too far, giving greater satisfaction and enlightenment to the behaviorally-oriented teacher than to the increasingly bewildered student. Hedley Bull, an unabashed advocate of the "classical approach," has expressed himself quite forcefully on this point:

> Whatever virtues one might discern in the scientific approach, it is a wholly retrograde development that it should now form the basis of undergraduate courses of instruction in international politics. . . . The student whose study of international politics consists solely of an introduction to the techniques of systems theory, game theory, simulation, or content analysis is simply shut off from contact with the subject, and is unable to develop any feeling either for the play of international politics or for the moral dilemmas to which it gives rise.[17]

Without going all the way with Mr. Bull, the authors of this book believe that a basic undergraduate course in international relations should still emphasize substance more than method, and the actual conduct of international relations more than model-building or simulation exercises. But they see no real dichotomy between a thorough grounding in the fundamentals of the subject and rigorous methods of investigation and analysis. They hope and assume that a standard text will be supplemented by a wide variety of readings and exercises and demonstrations that will illuminate the expanding dimensions of the field and illustrate many of the newer techniques and approaches. Certainly teachers of undergraduates should not fight their methodological battles at the expense of their students, nor concentrate so much on their pet theories and approaches

[14] Vincent Baker, "The Introductory Course in International Relations: Trends and Problems," Universities and World Affairs Document No. 62, Carnegie Endowment for International Peace, November 1, 1954.

[15] McClelland, pp. 24–26.

[16] Hanessian, p. 27.

[17] "International Theory: The Case for a Classical Approach," *World Politics,* XVIII (April, 1966), 368.

that they neglect the real dimensions of the field, substantive as well as methodological.

Although the beginning student in international relations can be expected to become familiar with the interdisciplinary approach in only a general way, the basic text and other materials which he uses should incorporate some of the results of this kind of research. The broader approach, however, should not become so diffuse as to obscure the central core of the study; "whereas international relations as a field of study is now conceived in such broad terms as 'all social relations that transcend national boundaries,' the focus of the introductory course may be said to be 'the political processes of international society.' "[18]

One of the reasons for the wide range of approaches to the study of international affairs and for the absence of an agreed-upon frame of reference is the lack of a basic theory. Many scholars of a theoretical bent of mind have made significant contributions to the formulation of such a theory, and many practitioners of diplomacy have called attention to the need for further work in this field.[19] Former Secretary of State Dean Acheson, for example, has declared that "an applicable body of theory" is necessary for the conduct of a more effective foreign policy. The beginning course should not be primarily a course in theory — some teachers would disagree with this view — but it should have some theoretical content, and it should challenge the student to probe for the limitations and the possibilities of some of the theories that have been advanced.

Theory is closely allied to philosophy, and in international relations a philosophy is perhaps even more important than a theory. The subject deals with important aspects of human nature and conduct, with the behavior and standards of groups, with the principles and forces underlying and motivating national and international actions, with ideological considerations, with ends and means, and with values and value judgments and hypotheses. All of these and many related considerations are of deep concern to the social philosopher. Thus a philosophy of international relations, as Feliks Gross has observed, "may be an appropriate term for this area of ideology, visions, values, principles, future plans and solutions in the area of foreign politics."[20]

One obvious way to keep abreast of current trends in international relations research is to consult professional journals in the field, such as *World Politics* (published by the Center of International Studies, Princeton University), the *Journal of Conflict Resolution* (published by the Center for Research in Conflict Resolution, University of Michigan), *International Studies Quarterly* (the organ of the International Studies Association), *International Journal* (the organ of the Canadian Institute of International Affairs), *International Affairs* (the organ of the Royal Institute of International Affairs), *Europa Archiv* (the organ of the Deutsche Gesellschaft für Auswärtige Politik), and *International Studies* (the organ of the Indian School of International Studies).

Any student of international relations should also have some knowledge of the most important writings and the distinctive contributions of eminent scholars in the field. Among these — to mention only scholars who are still living — are E. H. Carr,

[18] Baker, p. 7.

[19] See especially Kenneth W. Thompson, "Toward a Theory of International Politics," *American Political Science Review*, XLIX (September, 1955), 733–746. This article is a report of a weekend conference on theoretical approaches to international relations, attended by Robert Bowie, Dorothy Fosdick, William T. R. Fox, Walter Lippmann, Hans J. Morgenthau, Reinhold Niebuhr, Paul N. Nitze, Don K. Price, James B. Reston, Dean Rusk, Kenneth W. Thompson, and Arnold Wolfers.

[20] Feliks Gross, *Foreign Policy Analysis* (New York: Philosophical Library, 1954), p. 88.

Hans J. Morgenthau, Quincy Wright, Robert Strausz-Hupé, Kenneth Thompson, William T. R. Fox, Karl Deutsch, Morton Kaplan, J. David Singer, Thomas Schelling, Charles A. McClelland, Richard C. Snyder, Harold Guetzkow (the last seven are prominently identified with the new quantitative and behavioral approaches), Walter Lippmann, George F. Kennan, and Raymond Aron. This list is, of course, highly selective and very inadequate. It could be expanded almost indefinitely, especially by adding the names of scholars who are no longer living or of living scholars who have contributed mainly to some special aspect of international relations, such as diplomatic history, international law, international organization, or area studies, or by correcting the American bias of the above list by adding more non-American scholars.

Approaches to International Relations Theory

As Hedley Bull has pointed out, "Two approaches to the theory of international relations at present compete for our attention: (1) the classical approach, that derives from philosophy, history, and law, that holds that general propositions cannot be accorded more than tentative and inconclusive status . . . ; (2) the scientific approach, whose devotees aspire to a theory of international relations whose propositions are based either upon logical or mathematical proof, or upon strict, empirical procedures of verification."[21] Actually, there are many varieties and combinations of these two approaches. Scholars who are more concerned with substance than with method, including most of the older generation, tend to favor the first approach, whereas those who are particularly absorbed in methods and techniques, embracing a large proportion of younger scholars, prefer the latter. But the two approaches are not necessarily incompatible, and many scholars manage to combine them without difficulty and with fruitful results. Some "true believers" are quite impatient with any approaches which do not fit into their doctrinal — or methodological — faith, but most students of international affairs would agree with Morton Kaplan, one of the leading proponents of the scientific approach, that "None of us has achieved such success with his methods that he should be prepared to read others out of court."[22]

As a result of the new approaches, the study of international relations has become increasingly interdisciplinary, behavioral, comparative, and "scientific." The obvious purpose has been to place the study within a broader and more meaningful theoretical framework, and to give it more adequate methodological and conceptual tools.

New Emphasis on Theory. Much of this "new look" is due to the contributions of the behavioral sciences. These contributions, as Karl W. Deutsch has noted, "are no longer a mere matter of programs for the future. A large volume of such contributions has been made in such topics as international communications, public opinion and propaganda, the effect of contacts among persons of different backgrounds of culture, language, race, or nationality, the behavior of small groups of negotiators or committee members, the social and political effects of the growth of towns and industry, the development of intergroup prejudices, conflicts, the realistic and stereotyped perception of foreign countries and peoples, the formation of policies, the making of decisions, and many others."[23] The "traditional" approach to international relations was anchored mainly in political science, with heavy borrowings from history, economics, and law.

[21] Bull, p. 360.

[22] Kaplan, p. 476.

[23] "The Place of Behavioral Sciences in Graduate Training of International Relations," *Behavioral Science*, III (July, 1958), 280.

Behavioral approaches are now common in all these disciplines, but the contributions of other fields of the social sciences, notably sociology, psychology, and anthropology, are also particularly noteworthy. Almost all problems and processes in international relations have to be analyzed within an interdisciplinary framework.

The new interest in theory, both normative and empirical, general and analytical, may be a sign that a discipline of international relations is at last beginning to emerge. "There is a time," wrote Deutsch, "in which the science goes through a philosophic stage in its development; the emphasis is on theory, on general concepts, and on the questioning of the fundamental assumptions and methods by which knowledge has been accumulated."[24] The study of international relations is going through such a "philosophic stage," which may therefore be a sign that it is becoming more truly a "discipline." All efforts to develop a "general theory" have fallen far short of the announced objective, but they have nevertheless helped to meet one of the most obvious deficiencies in the practice as well as the study of international relations, namely, the lack of a theoretical base.[25]

More progress has been made in the development of more specific and analytic theories. Three examples are system, game, and communications theory. Others are power, decision-making, strategy, equilibrium, and field theories.

System Theory. The concept of systems seems to provide a useful basis for both theoretical and practical analysis. It embraces general system theory, which, like most theories in international relations research, has been borrowed from other disciplines, and the concept of international systems, subsystems, and subordinate state systems, past or present. One student of international systems, James Rosenau, "has suggested that systemic research be pursued not only in terms of local, national, and international systems — that is, actors and their relational pattern as a focal point — but also in terms of issue areas."[26]

The general conception of an international system, and of international systems, forms the framework of many current studies in the field of international relations. "Almost all of Karl W. Deutsch's writing," for example, "has been oriented by the theory of systems and by system analysis techniques."[27] The same orientation is manifest in Raymond Aron's *tour de force, Peace and War: A Theory of International Relations.*[28] As Aron observed, there "has never been an international system including the whole of the planet"; but the postwar period, when "for the first time humanity is living one and the same history," has witnessed the emergence of a kind of global system.[29] It is

[24] Karl W. Deutsch, *The Nerves of Government* (New York: The Free Press of Glencoe, 1963), p. 3.

[25] See J. W. Burton, *International Relations: A General Theory* (Cambridge, England, 1965). Some students of international relations, belonging to both the "classical" and "scientific" schools, feel that the pendulum is swinging again away from theory, toward what Michael Haas has called a "brute empiricism," "hyper-factualism," and "anti-theoretical positivism." "International Relations Theory," unpublished manuscript to be included in Michael Haas and Henry S. Kariel, eds., *Approaches to the Study of Political Science* (San Francisco: Chandler Publishing Co., 1968), p. 47.

[26] Wolfram F. Hanrieder, "The International System: Bipolar or Multibloc?" *The Journal of Conflict Resolution,* IX (September, 1965), 302. See also James Rosenau, "The Functioning of International Systems," *Background,* VII (November, 1963).

[27] Charles A. McClelland, *Theory and the International System* (New York: The Macmillan Company, 1966). McClelland's book is a good illustration of the prevalence, and the utility, of the system approach.

[28] Raymond Aron, *Peace and War: A Theory of International Relations* (Garden City, N.Y.. Doubleday & Company, 1966). See especially Chapters IV ("On International Systems"), V ("On Multipolar and Bipolar Systems"), and XIII ("The Heterogeneity of the Global System").

[29] *Ibid.,* pp. 162, 371, 374, 381.

characterized by great heterogeneity and is perhaps too loose to be properly designated a system. An international system, in the words of Stanley Hoffmann, "is a pattern of relations between the basic units of world politics, which is characterized by the scope of the objectives pursued by these units and of the tasks performed among them, as well as by the means used in order to achieve those goals and perform those tasks."[30] One of the leading systems analysts, Morton Kaplan, suggests that six international systems may be identified: the balance of power, the loose bipolar, the tight bipolar, the universal, the hierarchical, and the unit veto systems, ranging in degree of integration from the unit veto to the hierarchical.[31] This classification, which Kaplan has refined in various ways, has been a central theme in the discussion of system theory and classification; it has also provoked strong criticism.

Other studies have developed the idea of international subsystems and subordinate state systems, usually related to geographical regions. Michael Haas has identified and discussed twenty international subsystems, ten in Europe (divided chronologically from 1649 to 1963), six in Asia (covering the years 1689 to 1964), and five in Hawaii (between 1738 and 1898).[32] Richard Rosencrance has devoted an entire volume to nine European subsystems, over the period 1740 to 1960, in one of the best-known studies of international systems.[33] Michael Brecher has looked at Southern Asia as a "subordinate state system," and Leonard Binder has taken a similar approach to the Middle East as a "subordinate international system."[34]

Game Theory. International politics is often described as a "game," in which the rules, while generally known and observed, are often changed and sometimes openly violated. Game theory attempts to provide models for studying world politics. A common version is the so-called zero-sum game, in which one party loses what the other wins. A more appropriate model in international relations, however, is the multiparty non-zero-sum game; for, as J. K. Zawodny reminds us, "We must recognize that some types of international conflict today can be resolved only by situations in which neither side loses and in which sometimes both sides may win."[35] The applicability of this observation to international negotiations and to crises in contemporary international relations is obvious, if often disregarded.

Game theory owes a heavy debt to the seminal work of John von Neumann and Oskar Morgenstern, *The Theory of Games and Economic Behavior*,[36] which expounded "the mathematics of probability and of decisional sequences" under "conditions of incomplete information."[37] It has been applied to many fields of the social sciences, with modifications to make it more relevant to the particular fields. In international relations it is often used as a basis of theoretical and applied analysis.[38] But, as Morton Kaplan

[30] "International Systems and International Law," *World Politics*, XIV (October, 1961), 207.

[31] See *System and Process in International Politics* (New York: John Wiley & Sons, 1957).

[32] "Approaches to the Analysis of Systemic Factors," Chapter 9 of *International Conflict: A Prolegomenon to Peace Research* (unpublished manuscript), p. 103.

[33] *Action and Reaction in World Politics* (Boston: Little, Brown and Company, 1963).

[34] Michael Brecher, "International Relations and Asian Studies: The Subordinate State System of Southern Asia," *World Politics*, XV (January, 1963); Leonard Binder, "The Middle East as a Subordinate International System," *World Politics*, X (April, 1958).

[35] Z. K. Zawodny, ed., *Man and International Relations* (San Francisco: Chandler Publishing Co., 1967), II, 699.

[36] 2d ed. (Princeton, N.J.: Princeton University Press, 1947).

[37] Deutsch, *The Nerves of Government*, p. 53.

[38] Two outstanding examples are Thomas C. Schelling, *The Strategy of Conflict* (Cambridge,

points out, "it has only limited applicability to most problems of international politics."[39] One of the reasons for this is suggested by Karl W. Deutsch: "Game theory usually assumes that most games have an end but international politics resembles rather an unending game in which no great power can pick up its marbles and go home."[40]

Communications Theory. Communications theory attempts to give salience and meaning to the revolution in communications which has profoundly changed the nature of human contacts and social relations, to a greater or lesser degree, in all parts of the world. "The 20th century breakthrough in communications ranks with the great forces which have shaped mankind's progress through history. Its impact on human behavior and on world affairs already exceeds that of the atom bomb. In the relatively brief span of four decades, modern communications technology has changed the way of life of the developed societies, rent centuries-old customs and traditions in the developing ones, and substantially altered the relationships between the two. . . . In spite of these far reaching changes, it appears certain that we stand merely at the threshold of a world transformed by electronics, a world in which further developments in communications will magnify both our opportunities for progress and our problems."[41]

In international relations, as in other aspects of human endeavor, the great advances in communications are bound to have profound consequences, for good or for ill. They provide the instruments and the techniques for the transmission of information and ideas, of skills and technology, and for closer contacts among peoples, within as well as between nations. They are useful for the promotion of education and propaganda, national objectives and international cooperation, economic, social, and political development, and also, unfortunately, political regimentation and control. Various agencies for political recruitment, mobilization, and socialization, such as political parties, may be analyzed in terms of communications theory. A study of the flow of communications within nations and across national frontiers may throw light on internal dynamics and transnational relations. As Charles A. McClelland notes, "three areas of international relations" which "appear to be particularly amenable to consideration from the standpoint of communication" are cross-cultural relations, public opinion and attitudes, and decision-making processes in the area of "statecraft."[42] "Communications theorists deal less with the structural or gaming aspects of statements and behavior than with the gross flow of goods, persons, and messages across territorial boundaries. By constructing maps of mail flow, airline traffic, trade, exchanges of diplomats, and other instances of state interaction one can observe communication models, clusters, and isolates."[43] Communications, in short, should be considered in theory as well as in application, in accordance with the ends which are sought and the values which are held as

---

Mass.: Harvard University Press, 1960); and Anatol Rapoport, *Fights, Games and Debates* (Ann Arbor: University of Michigan Press, 1960).

[39] "The New Great Debate: Traditionalism vs. Science in International Relations," *World Politics*, XIX (October, 1966), 14.

[40] Deutsch, *The Nerves of Government*, p. 69.

[41] *Modern Communications and Foreign Policy*, Report of the Subcommittee on International Organizations and Movements, Committee on Foreign Affairs, U.S. House of Representatives (Washington, D.C.: Government Printing Office, 1967), pp. 1R, 2R.

[42] *Theory and the International System*, pp. 120–136.

[43] Haas, "International Relations Theory," p. 31. See Karl W. Deutsch, *Nationalism and Social Communication* (Cambridge, Mass.: The M.I.T. Press, 1953); and Karl W. Deutsch, "Shifts in the Balance of Communications Flows: A Problem of Measurement in International Relations," *Public Opinion Quarterly*, XX (Spring, 1956), 143–160.

well as with the media and techniques that are available at a given time.

Methods of Analysis and Data Processing. In international relations research, interest in methods and techniques, many quite novel, has increased even more markedly than interest in theory. In part, this has been a natural consequence of the "behavioral revolution" that has dominated international relations research, at least in the United States, in recent years, and in part it reflects the efforts to give a more "scientific" base to the study of international affairs. Doubtless it has also been stimulated by the new interest in quantitative approaches, emphasizing empirical data and mathematical and statistical methods, and often involving the use of high-speed electronic computers. Sophisticated analyses of many international problems are now being made by the techniques of operations research, data processing, content analysis, factor analysis, multivariate analysis, regression analysis, structural-functional analysis, model-building, simulation, and survey research. Ingenious methods of data collection have been developed, and vast amounts of such data are being used for purposes of cross-cultural and comparative research by the use of aggregate analysis, made feasible by computers and other techniques for handling aggregate data.[44] Long lists of indicators and other characteristics of political systems have been made available in several bulky compendia, notably Arthur S. Banks and Robert B. Textor, *A Cross-Polity Survey* (The M.I.T. Press, 1963) and Bruce M. Russett *et al., World Handbook of Political and Social Indicators* (Yale University Press, 1964). Valuable data from these and other collections and projects, including the Yale Political Data Program, the Almond-Verba five-nation study which led to the publication of *The Civic Culture* (Princeton University Press, 1963), election statistics, public opinion polls, etc., are readily available to scholars in universities participating in the Inter-University Consortium for Political Research.

No doubt many of the advocates of the "new" quantitative and behavioral approaches resort too often to mathematical formulas and symbols and statistical methods, use unintelligible jargon, become obsessed with techniques to the neglect of substance, and so divorce themselves from reality that their work seems to have little relevance or meaning. Hedley Bull, an English defender of the "classical approach," argues that "What is of value in the contribution of theorists who adopt a scientific approach can be accommodated readily enough within the classical approach."[45] This view errs as much in one direction as the following assertion by an exponent of the "scientific approach" does in another: "Tomorrow, due to influences as different as the impact of computer technology and governmental interest and support in international relations research, the study of international relations may become a scientific discipline specializing in data-processing and analysis of international system phenomena and providing routine reports and advice on foreign policy alternatives available to national governments."[46]

The differences between these two approaches are by no means so sharp or so absolute as these statements would suggest. The study and practice of international relations require a variety of methods and techniques, as well as a framework of theory and theories, most of which, if properly used, will draw upon "classical," "scientific," and many other approaches.

[44] See Michael Haas, "Aggregate Analysis," *World Politics,* XIX (October, 1966).

[45] Bull, p. 377.

[46] McClelland, *Theory and the International System,* p. 136.

Current Themes

Although the current emphasis is increasingly on interdisciplinary approaches, much of international relations teaching and research is still weighted heavily in favor of some more established discipline, notably history, political science, law, and economics, and to an increasing extent sociology, social psychology, and cultural anthropology. Even today many courses in the subject are hardly more than courses in political geography, human ecology, international organizations and institutions, comparative political systems, or political behavior. Some critics of the "new look" in the subject complain that the most "far out" of the new courses in international relations deal almost exclusively with such esoteric approaches as general theory or quantitative methodology, often presented in statistical and mathematical terms.

Supplementing the general approaches are a variety of more specific ones that give a distinctive flavor to almost every basic text in the field. Most introductory texts, for example, give special emphasis to one or more of the following themes:

Power. When E. H. Carr wrote his classic work, *The Twenty Years' Crisis,* first published in 1939, his "deliberate aim" was to counteract "the glaring and dangerous defect of nearly all thinking . . . about international politics in English-speaking countries from 1919 to 1939 — the almost total neglect of the factor of power."[47] After World War II this factor was no longer neglected. Indeed, it has become perhaps the central theme in the study of international relations. Quite obviously it has practical as well as theoretical relevance. Power seems to be a major determinant of the policies of the leading states of the world and of international relations generally. Moreover, the concept of power has been widened markedly by research in various disciplines, while at the same time its limitations are also being more generally recognized. As applied to the study of international relations, however, the emphasis is on such old concepts as the balance of power, elements of national power, and the power equation in its practical application to international politics.

International Institutions and Organizations. The existence of the United Nations, the most comprehensive of all international organizations, of regional arrangements such as NATO and the OAS, and other organizations of an international or regional character has insured the continued popularity of the institutional emphasis. Doubtless too much attention is often given to a description of the structure and operation of the many different kinds of international institutions and organizations, governmental and nongovernmental, and too much emphasis is placed on procedure rather than on substance or operational behavior; but the institutional approach, if broadly conceived, opens up many promising avenues, especially if it includes the nation-states, the main "actors" in the world community, and if it emphasizes process as well as framework.

International Systems. A more sophisticated approach, and one that is currently very popular, is to study international relations in terms of international systems. As has been noted, it involves the elaboration of system theory or theories that may be applied to a wide variety of international phenomena, as well as the development of typologies of systems in the international community. International systems may be studied historically or from the point of view of contemporary world politics. We may, for example, consider ancient China, classical Greece, imperial Rome, Renaissance Italy,

[47] These words appear in the Preface to the second edition, p. vii.

Mughal India, or nineteenth-century Europe as international systems. Contemporary international systems may be constructed on the basis of concepts, such as bipolarity or multipolarity or other versions of polarity, or of regions, such as continents or geographic areas of greater or lesser extent. Different regions are often considered as international subsystems or as subordinate state systems.

Integration and the Community Approach. A functioning international system requires a high degree of integration, and is most effective if it is undergirded by a supporting community structure. Integration is one of the central themes in the interdisciplinary approach to international relations. Studies of past and present tendencies toward integration as well as toward conflict in the international community may suggest factors that have an important bearing on contemporary diplomacy and political behavior. Many scholars, such as Karl W. Deutsch, Amitai Etzioni, and Ernst Haas, and groups of scholars in cooperative projects have analyzed experiments in integration, successful and unsuccessful, past and contemporary.[48] Deutsch, "probably the first academic exponent of a community approach to international subsystems," concluded that "most cases of successful integration occurred in the premodern era" and is rather dubious about the possibilities of integration under existing conditions. Etzioni would disagree, for he believes "that conditions are ripest in modern times for the formation of transnational structures, inasmuch as a higher level of economic, political and administrative skill is attainable."[49] Certainly the theme of integration in the international community merits thoughtful study.

Conflict, Conflict Management, and Conflict Resolution. Much of international relations is concerned with conflict, its management and resolution. In these vital areas the contributions of the behavioral sciences and of quantitative methods of analysis have been particularly fruitful. One major collection of readings, featuring contributions from psychology and other behavioral sciences, takes integration and conflict as the two guiding concepts and considers conflict on three levels: intrapersonal conflict, interpersonal and intergroup conflict, and nation-state conflict.[50] In a well-known work Thomas Schelling draws upon game theory and other quantitative techniques in analyzing *The Strategy of Conflict*. One of the most useful periodicals in the field of international relations is entitled *The Journal of Conflict Resolution*. Conflict management is a term which embraces a multitude of techniques for the control, if not always the resolution, of international conflicts. It is closely related to crisis management, which Alastair Buchan has called "the new diplomacy" and for which Herman Kahn has identified no fewer than 44 separate measures which may be taken in response to a crisis situation.[51]

War and Peace. Almost all issues and studies in international relations lead, directly or indirectly, to questions of war and peace, questions which today more than

[48] See Karl W. Deutsch, *Nationalism and Social Communication* (New York: John Wiley & Sons, 1953), Karl W. Deutsch, *Political Community at the International Level* (Garden City, N.Y.: Doubleday & Company, 1954), Deutsch *et al., Political Community and the North Atlantic Area* (Princeton, N.J.: Princeton University Press, 1957); Amitai Etzioni, *Political Unification* (New York: Holt, Rinehart & Winston, 1965); and Ernst Haas, *The Uniting of Europe* (Stanford, Calif.: Stanford University Press, 1958).

[49] Michael Haas, "Approaches to the Analysis of Systemic Factors," p. 24.

[50] Zawodny, ed., *Man and International Relations*, Vol. I: Conflict; Vol. II: Integration.

[51] Alastair Buchan, *Crisis Management — The New Diplomacy* (Paris, 1966); Herman Kahn, *On Escalation* (New York: Frederick A. Praeger, 1965).

ever involve human survival. In this respect, at least, the study of international relations is one of the most vital of all human endeavors and calls for interdisciplinary research of the most sophisticated kind.

War has been a recurrent phenomenon throughout human history. In the twentieth century, in spite of the high hopes of the early years, it has been just as frequent and much more virulent than ever before. Even in the nuclear age, which has thus far at least avoided the ultimate catastrophe of total war, few years have been free of war in some parts of the world. However fearful the prospects may be, "thinking about the unthinkable," to use the words of Herman Kahn, is absolutely necessary. Almost all conceivable methods of preventing World War III, and of limiting, if not preventing, lesser armed conflicts have been examined and have found ardent supporters.

A vast literature already exists on the subjects of disarmament and arms control. Some 1400 peace organizations are devoted to research or activities relating to problems of war and peace.[52] These range in size and importance from well-established organizations such as the Carnegie Endowment for International Peace to small movements with limited resources but large ideas and aims, and include many associations for peace research (e.g., the International Peace Research Society and the Committee to Study the Organization of Peace) as well as a number of peace research institutes (e.g., the Institute for International Order, its affiliate, the Fund for Education Concerning World Peace Through World Law, and the World Peace Through World Law Institute at Duke University). Several journals, such as *Current Thought on Peace and War,* publish the results of recent studies in the field. The impact of all of these programs cannot be accurately assessed, but they certainly provide a mine of information for the student of international affairs.

Ideologies. In the twentieth century, with aggressive totalitarianisms and deep-seated conflicts between political, economic, and social systems, ideological issues have become the burning realities of international life. It is apparent that at the present time much of international relations centers on ideological issues which complicate and obstruct efforts to emphasize long-range problems and needs. Many commentators have pointed to the difficulty of identifying the ideological components in today's international tensions and crises, which obviously have other aspects as well; but to overlook the ideological elements in current world crises would be to miss some of their underlying motivations and essence.

Nationalism, Imperialism, and Colonialism. Nationalism is certainly one of the most powerful forces in the world today, especially in non-Western countries and areas. It helps to explain the almost paranoic sensitivity of leaders and peoples of former colonies to any infringements, real or imagined, on their newly-won independence. It is also an element in the appeals of Charles de Gaulle to French grandeur and glory, and to the response which he receives from many Frenchmen. Although imperialism and colonialism in their traditional forms seem to be declining, they survive in many parts of the world and in many minds and policies. Peoples who have been or are now victims of these "isms" know something of the tragedies they can cause. Moreover, new forms of imperialism are appearing. One is Communist imperialism; another is the economic and cultural predominance of major powers that is often described as "neo-imperialism." An awareness of these forces is central to an understanding of many of the

[52] See *International Peace/Disarmament Directory,* 3d ed. (Yellow Springs, Ohio: Lloyd Wilkie, Publisher, 1963); and Arthur Herzog, *The War-Peace Establishment* (New York: Harper & Row, 1965).

stresses apparent in the international relations of our time.

The National Interest. In recent years, especially in the United States, a major school of historians and students of world affairs has emphasized the concept of national interest as a central theme for the conduct of national policies. Obviously the leaders of every nation are expected to promote the national interest, but interpretations of that interest may vary greatly, and consciously or unconsciously policy-makers may be diverted from their true objective. Much of the controversy in the United States over American policies in Vietnam centered around fundamentally divergent views of what constituted the national interest in this difficult situation. Here is a theme which may be useful in assessing the history and conduct of a nation's foreign policy.

Decision-Making and Policy Formation. This approach is in a way a counterweight to excessive concern with the institutional aspects of international relations. It is especially popular in the United States, where increasing attention is being given to the decision-making and governmental processes.[53] It offers a useful method for getting behind the surface of announced policies by nation-states or international agencies in an attempt to explain these policies. Clearly, decisions are made at various levels and in different ways in different political and international systems. A study of the total political process, on a national, international, or comparative basis, provides a broader setting for a detailed analysis of decision-making and policy formation.

National Character. This approach illustrates the possibilities of a broadly based analysis of the distinctive attributes of peoples and social groups, especially those that compose the national units of modern international society. While it is difficult and perhaps even dangerous to attempt to generalize about such a nebulous thing as national character, it is a necessary task for those who are concerned with the mainsprings of thought and behavior of nation-states. Despite a lack of precise and reliable tests and standards, useful work is being done in studying national character by techniques as varied as those employed in the past by such seasoned writers and observers as Alexis de Tocqueville, or those of social and cultural anthropologists such as Geoffrey Gorer, Ruth Benedict, and Margaret Mead, or those used by specialists in attitudinal research and political behavior.

Political and International Behavior. Studies of political behavior have thrown light not only on national character but also on other aspects of national motivation and response. Such studies, for example, can help to explain the reactions and policies of the Soviet Union and why the Russians behave like Russians and not like Americans or Japanese. In a sense these studies represent a useful extension of research in individual and small-group behavior to the national and international arena. This new interest in interdisciplinary research and in the applications of the behavioral sciences to international problems has prompted a leading American psychologist who has been interested in these studies to suggest that "a new discipline seems to be emerging — the social psychology of international affairs."[54]

Political-Strategic Studies. With so much of international relations centering around such problems of national security and defense as preparation for and protec-

[53] See Richard C. Snyder, H. H. Bruck, and Burton Sapin, *Foreign Policy Decision Making: An Approach to the Study of International Politics* (New York: The Free Press of Glencoe, 1962).

[54] Herbert C. Kelman, ed., *International Behavior: A Social-Psychological Analysis* (New York: Holt, Rinehart & Winston, 1965), p. vii.

tion against both conventional and unconventional warfare, bilateral and multilateral security arrangements, alliance diplomacy, and arms control and disarmament measures, it is natural that many studies in the field give special attention to political-strategic approaches and analyses. Many articles and books are devoted to these subjects, as are research institutes such as the Rand Corporation, the Hudson Institute, the Institute of War and Peace Research at Columbia University, the Foreign Policy Research Institute at the University of Pennsylvania, and the Institute of Strategic Studies in London.

Alliance Systems and Alliance Politics. In the postwar years bilateral and multilateral alliances and other security arrangements have proliferated, and alliance politics, which embraces political-strategic aspects and diplomatic and other relationships, has become a prominent feature of international relations. This was especially true when alliance systems were flourishing, as they seemed to be in the 1950's and early 1960's. Even though most of the major multilateral alliançes, including NATO, the Warsaw Pact, SEATO, and CENTO, now are in disarray and have lost much of their original purpose and momentum, the politics of NATO and other alliance systems remains an important new dimension in the study of contemporary international relations.

Arms Control and Disarmament. Closely related to national security and indeed to human survival in the nuclear age is the question of arms control and disarmament, which are not necessarily synonymous terms, although they are often bracketed in international negotiations and scholarly research. Few questions have received more attention, and few have led to such limited results. The Disarmament Commission of the United Nations, the General Assembly itself, and the Eighteen Nation Disarmament Committee at Geneva have conducted lengthy deliberations on these subjects. The United States has a large Arms Control and Disarmament Agency, a semi-autonomous agency within the Department of State, and many other governments have similar agencies.

Allied with arms control and disarmament are questions of the peaceful uses of atomic energy, with which the International Atomic Energy Agency and most governments are deeply concerned; the enforcement and extension of the Nuclear Test Ban Treaty of 1963; and the prevention of the proliferation of nuclear weapons. On all of these matters there is a vast documentation and a great deal of scholarly research and practical investigation.

Demographic Studies. Many observers of what Arnold Toynbee and others have called "the human situation" believe that the two most pressing questions in the world today are those of food and people, which are in many respects interrelated. The population explosion is certainly one of the most significant phenomena of the contemporary world. Some of the predictions regarding future rates of population expansion indicate that population control is of paramount importance today and more especially in the immediate future. The United Nations, its Population Commission, and some of its specialized agencies are all actively concerned with this question, as are an increasing number of scholars, policy-makers, and informed citizens in many lands. Centers and programs of demographic studies exist in many countries, and frequent conferences, large and small, official and unofficial, discuss population problems and their possible solution. Demographic factors must be included in any balanced course in international relations, and demographic studies have a place in international relations research.

Economic Factors. Food, as has been mentioned, is a matter of pressing importance for man's future. While it is more than an economic question, it obviously has significant economic aspects, as do many international issues. In fact, no student of international affairs can afford to neglect the theory and the practice of international and comparative economics. Of particular relevance are economic planning and development, rates of exchange, tariffs, exchange controls, commodity agreements, international trade, balance of payments, foreign aid, disparities between developed and underdeveloped economies, international investment, international economic agencies such as the World Bank and International Monetary Fund, and many other UN-affiliated agencies and regional economic agencies.

In economics as in politics there are marked differences in approach, especially between Communist and non-Communist and between developed and underdeveloped nations. The Marxist-Leninist approach to international relations is basically an economic one — witness Marx's theory of economic determinism and Lenin's theory of imperialism — and many non-Communists are also inclined to emphasize the economic aspects of international life. Almost every problem can be analyzed from an economic point of view, even though few problems are wholly economic.

Conflicting Trends

As we reflect upon the present state of the world, and as we embark on a general survey of existing conditions and trends, we must keep alert for the appearance of many paradoxes and inconsistencies. Among the conflicting trends which confront and perhaps confuse the student of international relations are the following:

1. Objectivity — subjectivity. Objectivity, we have said, is important for the student of international relations. Without it, how can the great problems of the world be fairly analyzed and appraised? Yet one society may accept without question certain goals and values which may be anything but acceptable to other societies. "The problems of international relations," observes Quincy Wright, "usually concern the divergence of the subjective truths accepted by different societies and regarded by each to be objective truth."[55] In the Communist world objectivity is deliberately repudiated. It is a "bourgeois" value which must not stand in the way of political and doctrinal purity. We, on the other hand, must resolve to be as objective as possible, to make allowances for our own preconditioning and prejudices, and to apply rigid standards to our analyses of international problems and phenomena, without abandoning the basic values and principles that we associate with the democratic way of life. This is indeed a big order.

2. Realism — idealism. The issue of realism versus idealism has occupied the attention of philosophers and men of affairs throughout history; and it has a continuing application to international problems. Much of the difference of opinion on current issues of foreign policy or of national behavior centers on this dilemma. The recent debates on the national interest, for example, have raised questions on the meaning of realism and idealism and their relative roles and validity as touchstones of foreign policy. Actually, both are of great importance in national and international affairs, and the differences are perhaps of degree rather than of kind. For this reason the idealists like to talk about "the reality of idealism" and the realists like to insist that they are the true idealists. Undoubtedly, extreme devotees of either position have done a great deal of harm in the world; realism can degenerate into *machtpolitik,* and idealism into an ivory tower mentality and a blind disregard of realities.

[55] Quincy Wright, *The Study of International Relations* (New York: Appleton, Century-Crofts, 1955), p. 20.

3. Nationalism — internationalism. Here we encounter one of the most obvious dichotomies of the present day. To an increasing degree this is one world; but it is also many worlds, and economic, social, and cultural differences, not to mention political issues, tend to obstruct the development of a real sense of world community. Nationalism is still a major factor in the contemporary world, especially among peoples who have recently won political independence and are now struggling to achieve economic and social emancipation, or who are still living in a dependent political status. Yet nationalism may become an ever more anomalous phenomenon, and internationalism may represent the "wave of the future." Perhaps, as Leslie Lipson has contended, "modern internationalism . . . is a reaction to the declining adequacy of nationalism."[56]

4. National security — international cooperation. As long as the nation-state system is the prevailing form of political organization, the emphasis must continue to be on national security rather than on international cooperation. To be sure, these two goals are not necessarily incompatible, and the popularity of military alliances and regional associations suggests that the one goal can often be reached only by the use of means which lead to the other. But no major nation can afford to gamble its national security on the assumption that all nations will cooperate in their own self-interest; it must keep its own guard up while at the same time it is trying to be a cooperative member of the international community. The presence of powerful states or groups of states which seem to be willing to cooperate only on their own terms, or which seem to be emphasizing their desire for peace and international cooperation as a front for activities which threaten the peace and security of other nations not of the same mind is, of course, an additional reason for the primacy given to national security, defined as the maximum possible reliance on a state's own resources and the support of its allies.

5. Force — consent. The relative importance of force and consent in international conduct, as in national and even personal affairs, is difficult to ascertain. Even the most peace-loving state has to mix the two. Totalitarian states are expert users of the "carrot-stick" technique. Democratic states, if they adhere to their own best traditions, must seek as wide an area of agreement and of consent as possible, but they can by no means avoid the use of force or be oblivious to its use by other states. Indeed, the role of force and consent is one of the underlying themes that call for special attention, for it has never been carefully studied or even understood.[57]

6. Cooperation — conflict. Closely related to the issues of national security versus international cooperation and of force versus consent is that of the respective roles of cooperation and conflict in international affairs. It is clear that innumerable instances of both tendencies occur daily. Examples of conflict are more newsworthy, and they do involve basic questions of war and peace and of national and human survival; but cooperation is more common than conflict, and the opportunities for promoting it in fundamental ways are being constantly explored. As has been noted, the findings in many disciplines — as in psychology and psychiatry and other branches of the behavioral sciences — have thrown new light on the causes of cooperation and conflict in international

[56] *The Great Issues of Politics* (Englewood Cliffs, N.J.: Prentice-Hall, 1954), p. 351.

[57] For a stimulating discussion of this point, see Louis J. Halle, *Civilization and Foreign Policy* (New York: Harper, 1955), Chapter VII; and A. Appadorai, *The Use of Force in International Relations* (Bombay, 1958).

affairs as well as in individual and group behavior.

7. Collectivism — individualism. The trend toward collectivism — one of the strongest trends of the past century — has been in keeping with the prevailing patterns of human society in most parts of the world at most periods of history. Only in the Western world in relatively modern times has the individual *qua* individual been the focus of national and international policy, and even in this area the idea has encountered many reverse tendencies. Americans, brought up on the principles of the rights of man and the importance of the individual, have difficulty in understanding other societies where the emphasis has been upon the group and upon the subordination of individuals in the mass to the interests of the favored few. They also seem to be baffled because even within their own country the state is playing an expanding role in their private lives, and in most parts of the world collectivism seems to fit in with the desires as well as with the needs of the people. The concept of the welfare state, for example, which is viewed with considerable suspicion in America, has very favorable connotations in most other areas. Yet at the same time the independence movements in non-Western lands outside the Communist orbit have been profoundly influenced by Western ideas of human freedom, and leaders of these movements have repeatedly insisted that one of their chief aims is to promote human freedom and dignity. Arnold Toynbee has suggested that in attempting to appeal to peoples in non-Western societies the West should emphasize spiritual rather than material factors. "We should put our main stress on the West's respect for individual freedom. That has universal appeal."[58] This is a mass age, however, and the individual will have difficulty in maintaining his freedom of maneuver and even his dignity under the impact of the growing collectivism.

8. Plenty — want. One of the great paradoxes of our time is the presence of human want on a colossal scale at a time when man has developed the scientific skill and the capacity to provide a tolerable standard of existence for everyone. The paradox assumes gigantic proportions when it is considered in global and in human terms. "This planet of ours," wrote an eloquent French student of human affairs, "is like a nightmare ocean liner. In the first-class, a few well-fed passengers live luxuriously in spacious quarters, while on the decks and in the holds all the rest of the passengers are herded together in hunger and misery. Who can fail to see the dynamite in this situation? The ocean liner is one world, but a unified world does not necessarily mean a world at peace. It is only too obvious that the people on the decks and in the holds could mutiny, and by the weight of numbers could easily overwhelm and enslave the first-class passengers. Our world is that ocean-going liner, headed toward an unknown destiny common to all on board."[59] A substantial improvement in the life conditions of the majority of mankind would seem to be a prerequisite for a peaceful world. It is already a scientific possibility, but no formula has yet been devised for dealing with the political and other problems involved.

9. Humanity — inhumanity. In many respects there has been a steady improvement in moral standards and in social responsibility. Toynbee has predicted that the twentieth century will be remembered longest because for the first time in history the welfare of the whole human race became an object of international policy. Unfortunately

[58] Press conference in New York, reported in the *New York Times*, November 4, 1954

[59] R. L. Bruckberger, *Image of America* (New York: The Viking Press, 1959), pp. 271, 272.

there is another side to the picture. The twentieth century has also been an iron age, and it has witnessed brutalization of the human spirit and some of the worst examples of man's inhumanity to man. Particularly disturbing have been the prevalence of racial persecution, purges, mass murders, and a growing callousness in countries which were supposedly among the most civilized. But inhumanity knows no boundaries, and it persists as an affront to the professions of statesmen, the avowed goals of nations, and the teachings of all of the great religions.

10. The promise of an unprecedented era of human progress — the danger of mass annihilation. Mankind has come to a fork in the road as a consequence of recent technological developments. For the first time "power without limit" seems to be attainable, with all of its potentialities for human betterment or destruction. This is perhaps the greatest paradox of this age of paradoxes — that inherent in the limitless possibilities of the atomic age are limitless dangers.

Purpose of the Study

The student of international relations should pursue his study with a sensible appraisal of its limitations and possibilities, its goals and objectives. He cannot have the assurance of an engineer; he is not a scientist working through the laws of the physical world. Instead, he is endlessly concerned with emotions, personalities, traditions, motivations, and a host of other intangible and changing factors. At the same time he must never regard himself as a mere observer or onlooker — as one who finds the unfolding story of politics among nations "interesting" but without profit as a means to help men shape their future. He must not be discouraged by the defeatists who deprecate the study of international relations because it has not yet revealed sufficiently effective means to prevent tensions and conflicts among nations or because it has not made it possible accurately to predict the course of events.

Why study international relations? The answer is that in this increasingly interdependent world its study is essential for human survival and human progress. It reveals how men and nations tend to act in given circumstances and so tells us what conditions should be encouraged and what conditions discouraged if we are to promote international harmony and well-being.[60] The serious student will see that national interests are interpreted by states alone and not by the "organized conscience of mankind," that propaganda can poison as well as inspire, and that it can upset all expectations regarding the actions of a nation, that states can move in countless ways to implement their policies through economic, political, and cultural pressures, that national power is a *sine qua non* of survival but that it is varied and changeable in its form and measure, that the actions of nature and of forceful personalities can wreck the most painstaking calculations of wise men, that the road to world peace may not lead altogether through the field of politics, that race, history, language, and culture may devise wholly irrational but supremely effective ties, that democracy and dictatorship can be both constructive and destructive, that problems of poverty and overpopulation are not to be solved by generalized prescriptions, and that technical assistance has its limitations as well as its promise. He will see that full stomachs will not inaugurate the brotherhood of man or a worldwide rise in physical or educational standards banish conflict from the earth, but that without a minimum standard of toler-

[60] A UNESCO report of 1954 answers the same question very simply: "The case for a teaching of international relations is a part of the case for a teaching of the social sciences in general. That case rests at bottom upon an article of faith: namely, that the better the world is understood by the better people in it, the better for the world will it be." C. A. W. Manning, *The University Teaching of Social Sciences: International Relations* (Paris, 1954), p. 84.

able existence for the world's people international cooperation — perhaps even human survival — will be constantly in jeopardy. He will learn that war deferred is a kind of peace, perhaps the only peace that nations will ever know. Above all, he should gain a sense of realism — a realization that the road to a better order is filled with obstacles of infinite complexity, that it can be traversed only by men who see the horizon ahead as well as the soil below.

A careful and thinking student will come to understand the subjectivity of his own analyses. He will observe that the diagnosis of the ills of the world is not a particularly difficult task and that most people can achieve it to their own satisfaction. He will discover that prescribing the cure is a somewhat more difficult task but by no means a baffling one. He may then be shocked by the resolute unwillingness of the patient to take the cure. When and if the cure finally comes it will have to be acceptable to a great many sovereign patients, most of whom have long been convinced that the impairment of their sovereignty is far more likely to be fatal than any of the grave afflictions to which they have long been accustomed. The student will learn that acceptability conditions every proposal for international action, and that it so screens every venture that the only surviving ones are those possessing the rare quality of mutual self-interest, mutually perceived.

The study of international relations is not a science with which we solve the problems of international life. At its best it is an objective and systematic approach to those problems. Every man who believes that the human race has been endowed with capabilities above those of the lower animals must concede that we have an obligation to ourselves and our posterity to use our minds to attempt to escape in the future the miseries and harassments so frequently experienced in the past, and to make the necessary adjustments to changing conditions. One such line of effort pertains to the conditions of the world society in which we live; we call it the study of "international relations."

Students of international relations must always strive for objectivity, balance, and perspective. They must carry on their work in the face of obstacles of prejudice, ignorance, emotionalism, and vested interest — often including their own. Since the world is their laboratory, and since a healthy combination of realism and idealism must underlie their approach to the subject, they must beware of "simple" solutions to complex problems, and they must also shun the thesis of the "inevitability" of war, the "wave of the future" approach, and all such encouragements to disaster. They must look with understanding on the world as it is, and at the same time keep their eyes on the world as it should be; but they must never mistake the ideal for the actual, or conclude that what "must" be will in fact occur.

They must reconcile themselves to the fact that many of the problems of international relations are unsolvable under present conditions. "The plain fact is that we are living in a very complicated and dangerous world. There are few if any easy, just and completely satisfying solutions to the great problems that face us today."[61] Not all of these problems, however, constitute major threats to peace and security, and those which are unsolvable and dangerous may take on a different complexion and decline in importance with the passage of time, even if they are never really "solved." Basic agreement may never be reached between the Communist and the non-Communist worlds, but this does not mean that war is therefore inevitable, or that this particular fissure in the international community must exist indefinitely. The problem of war may never be solved, but there is hope that it can be kept under control and that *total* war in the atomic age, with all of its frightful consequences, can be

[61] Editorial, *New York Times*, November 22, 1949. This editorial observation of 1949 is just as applicable today.

avoided. For many issues it may be impossible to devise a genuine solution, for they may be so complicated and have so many ramifications that they may baffle the most experienced and far-sighted statesmen. The only possible course in some instances may be to keep the problems under control as much as possible, to do everything that can be done within the range of practicable alternatives to deal with them, and to worry along with them as circumstances permit. "The limits of foreign policy," to use the title of a book by a former member of the State Department's Policy Planning Staff, are often narrower than most people realize. Another former high official in the State Department, writing in the early postwar period, explained the limits in this way:

> Justice Holmes used to remark that there are some statements to which the only answer is, "Well, I'll be damned." There are also, in this world, some situations posing policy problems where any answer that can conceivably be advanced can be conclusively demonstrated to be wrong. There are occasions when it is quite simple to make out a strong case against a particular line of action, and all that can be said in its favor is that an even stronger case can be made against any other course. That is life in this imperfect world. It will do no good to be hysterical or morose about it.[62]

This homely philosophy is badly needed as a guide to the study of international relations. It helps to explain why, to paraphrase the famous statement of Oxenstierna, the world is governed with so little wisdom, and why the policy-makers and practicing diplomats often seem so much less brilliant than writers and speechmakers without responsibility for conducting the world's affairs.

SUGGESTIONS FOR FURTHER READING

ARON, RAYMOND. *Peace and War: A Theory of International Relations.* Garden City, N.Y.: Doubleday & Company, 1966. A major work, combining historical and systems approaches.

BANKS, ARTHUR S. and ROBERT B. TEXTOR, *A Cross-Polity Survey.* Cambridge, Mass.: The M.I.T. Press, 1963. A valuable reference work for comparative analysis.

BOASSON, CHARLES. *Approaches to the Study of International Relations.* Assen, The Netherlands, 1963.

BOULDING, KENNETH E. *Conflict and Defense: a General Theory.* New York: Harper & Row, 1962. A publication of the Center for Research in Conflict Resolution at the University of Michigan.

BURTON, J. W. *International Relations: A General Theory.* Cambridge, England, 1965.

CARR, E. H. *The Twenty Years' Crisis, 1919–1939,* 2nd ed. London, 1946. One of the most influential works on international relations; first published in 1939.

CLAUDE, INIS L., JR. *Power and International Relations.* New York: Random House, 1962.

DEUTSCH, KARL. *The Analysis of International Relations.* Englewood Cliffs, N.J.: Prentice-Hall, 1968. A concise commentary by a leading communication and integration theorist.

———. *The Nerves of Government.* New York: The Free Press of Glencoe, 1963. Especially Chapter 9, "Communication Models and Decision Systems."

FARRELL, R. BARRY, ed. *Approaches to Comparative and International Politics.* Evanston, Ill.: Northwestern University Press, 1966. Especially the contribution by Oliver Benson entitled "Challenges for Research in International Relations and Comparative Politics."

FISHER, ROGER D., ed. *International Conflict*

[62] Francis H. Fifield, "Foreign Policy and the Democratic Process," *Department of State Bulletin,* XVII (December 28, 1947), 1254.

and Behavioral Science; the Craigville Papers. New York: Basic Books, 1964. Papers prepared for a conference in 1961, sponsored by the American Academy of Arts and Sciences.

FOX, WILLIAM T. R. *The American Study of International Relations.* Columbia, S.C.: The University of South Carolina Press, 1968. Six essays by a leading scholar in the field.

———, ed. *Theoretical Aspects of International Relations.* Notre Dame, Ind.: University of Notre Dame Press, 1959

GUETZKOW, HAROLD *et al. Simulation in International Relations: Developments for Research and Teaching.* Englewood Cliffs, N.J.: Prentice-Hall, 1963.

HARRISON, HORACE V., ed. *The Role of Theory in International Relations.* Princeton, N.J.: D. Van Nostrand Co., 1963. Includes contributions by William T. R. Fox, Hans J. Morgenthau, Kenneth Thompson, and Quincy Wright.

HERZ, JOHN H. *Political Realism and Political Idealism: A Study in Theories and Realities.* Chicago: University of Chicago Press, 1951. A penetrating approach to a fundamental problem in international relations.

HOFFMANN, STANLEY, ed. *Contemporary Theory in International Relations.* Englewood Cliffs, N.J.: Prentice-Hall, 1960. An excellent collection of readings.

———. *The State of War: Essays in the Theory and Practice of International Politics.* New York: Frederick A. Praeger, 1965.

KAPLAN, MORTON. *System and Process in International Politics.* New York: John Wiley, 1957. An influential analysis of international systems.

KELMAN, HERBERT C., ed. *International Behavior: A Socio-Psychological Analysis.* New York: Holt, Rinehart & Winston, 1965. One of the best collections of essays on socio-psychological approaches to international relations.

KIRK, GRAYSON. *The Study of International Relations in American Colleges and Universities.* New York: Council on Foreign Relations, 1947.

KNORR, KLAUS, and SIDNEY VERBA, eds. *The International System: Theoretical Essays.* Princeton, N.J.: Princeton University Press, 1961.

KUHN, HAROLD W., ed. *Game Theory, Bargaining and International Relations.* A special issue of *The Journal of Conflict Resolution,* VI (March, 1962).

LERCHE, CHARLES O., JR. and ABDUL A. SAID. *Concepts of International Politics.* Englewood Cliffs, N.J.: Prentice-Hall, 1963.

LERNER, MAX. *The Age of Overkill: A Preface to World Politics.* New York: Simon and Schuster, 1962.

LISKA, GEORGE. *International Equilibrium.* Cambridge, Mass.: Harvard University Press, 1957.

MCCLELLAND, CHARLES A. *Theory and the International System.* New York: The Macmillan Company, 1966. A paperback based on recent research.

MCNEIL, ELTON P., ed. *The Nature of Human Conflict.* Englewood Cliffs, N.J.: Prentice-Hall, 1965. Essays featuring interdisciplinary approaches.

MANNING, C. A. W. *The University Teaching of Social Sciences: International Relations.* Paris, 1954. A report for UNESCO.

MATHIESEN, TRYGVE. *Methodology in the Study of International Relations.* Oslo, 1959.

MODELSKI, GEORGE A. *A Theory of Foreign Policy.* New York: Frederick A. Praeger, for the Center of International Studies, Princeton University, 1962

OLSON, WILLIAM C. and FRED A. SONDERMAN. *The Theory and Practice of International Relations,* 2d ed. Englewood Cliffs, N.J.: Prentice-Hall, 1966.

Rapoport, Anatol. *Fights, Games and Debates.* Ann Arbor: University of Michigan Press, 1960.

ROSENAU, JAMES N., ed. *International Politics and Foreign Policy: A Reader in Research and Theory.* New York: The Free Press of Glencoe, 1961. One of the most widely used collections of readings, featuring behavioral approaches.

ROSECRANCE, RICHARD N. *Action and Reac-*

tion in World Politics. Boston: Little, Brown and Company, 1963. A survey of nine European international systems, historically considered.

RUSSELL, F. M. *Theories of International Relations.* New York: Appleton-Century, 1936. Still a useful historical treatment.

RUSSETT, BRUCE M. *et al. World Handbook of Political and Social Indicators.* New Haven: Yale University Press, 1964. A valuable compendium of comparative quantitative data.

SCHELLING, THOMAS C. *The Strategy of Conflict.* Cambridge, Mass.: Harvard University Press, 1960. An influential study.

SCOTT, ANDREW M. with WILLIAM A. LUCAS and TRUDI M. LUCAS. *Simulation and National Development.* New York: John Wiley & Sons, 1966.

SINGER, J. DAVID. *Human Behavior and International Politics: Contributions from the Social-Psychological Sciences.* Chicago: Rand McNally & Co., 1965.

———, ed. *Quantitative International Politics: Insights and Evidence.* New York: The Free Press of Glencoe, 1967. Vol. VI of the International Yearbook of Political Science Research.

SNYDER, RICHARD C. and JAMES A. ROBINSON. *National and International Decision-Making.* New York: Institute for International Order, 1961.

"Theory and Reality in International Relations," *Journal of International Affairs,* XXI (1967). An excellent collection of essays by leading authorities.

TOMA, PETER A. and ANDREW GYORGY, eds. *Basic Issues in International Relations.* Boston: Allyn & Bacon, 1967. A collection of readings.

VAN DYKE, VERNON, ed. *The Teaching of International Politics.* Ames: The State University of Iowa, 1955. Contains outlines for courses in international relations, and an excellent bibliography.

WALTZ, KENNETH N. *Man, the State and War.* New York: Columbia University Press, 1959.

WRIGHT, QUINCY. *The Study of International Relations.* New York: Appleton-Century-Crofts, 1955. Still one of the most comprehensive and profound surveys of the subject.

ZAWODNY, J. K. *Guide to the Study of International Relations.* San Francisco: Chandler Publishing Co., 1966. A useful manual for ready reference.

———, ed. *Man and International Relations.* 2 vols. San Francisco: Chandler Publishing Co., 1967. Vol. I: Conflict; Vol. II: Integration. An interdisciplinary collection of readings, featuring contributions of social psychologists.

PART ONE

THE PATTERN OF INTERNATIONAL LIFE

1 The State System and Its Corollaries

"World community" is something of a poet's term. It raises visions of a neighborhood that reaches to the ends of the earth, of all peoples united in peace and goodwill, of a brotherhood of man. It is the stuff that dreams are made of.

But in another sense the world community is a historic reality. It is made up of all people everywhere — most of whom live in "sovereign" states that must "co-exist" on the same planet. Through sheer necessity these states have relations with each other — relations to promote their well-being and security. These relations and the universal pattern of their conduct put the stamp of a community on the collectivity of some one hundred and thirty sovereign states and their dependent areas. Added to these is a vast array of international organizations, of which the most important are the United Nations and its specialized agencies, and regional organizations such as the Organization of American States and the North Atlantic Treaty Organization.

Throughout most of what is called "modern" history the nation-state system has been the dominant pattern of international political organization in the Western world, and more recently it has spread to other parts of the world as well. Nation-states have been, and still are, the major actors on the international scene. In Toynbee's terms the nation-state system entered its "time of troubles" long ago, and it may be in its final stages of dominance. It is becoming increasingly inadequate in the light of the growing interdependence of peoples and the imperatives of the nuclear and space age. But while many observers criticize it as obsolete and on its way out, the system has shown a remarkable capacity for adaptation and survival.

It is therefore premature to say, as does Herbert Spiro, that " 'International politics' today is not conducted between or among nations, nor in its most important phases even between states."[1] Probably Charles Malik is correct in concluding that "The ultimate units in a world suddenly brought together are cultures and not nations,"[2] for a large part of the activities of the world community takes place on the intercultural, supranational, sub-national, and interregional rather than on the international level. Yet the nation-state system still forms the political basis and the political framework of international life. Consequently, it is here that the study of the world community and of international relations must begin.

1 *Politics in Africa: Prospects South of the Sahara* (Englewood Cliffs, N.J.: Prentice-Hall, 1962), p. 12.

2 Address at annual meeting of the American Political Science Association, Washington, D.C., September 10, 1953.

The State System

What is variously called the state system, the Western state system, the nation-state system, and the national state system may be described rather simply: It is the pattern of political life in which people are separately organized into sovereign states that interact with one another in varying degrees and in varying ways. The heart of the "problem" of the state system lies in the conflict between the theory of legal omnipotence and the fact of unavoidable concession and accommodation. To defend its sovereignty, its national honor, and its material interests, each state organizes its coercive resources: it builds up its "national power." When peaceful persuasion is inadequate it may use more forcible means, even to employing all of its strength in total war. Conflicts of interest often do lead to war, and it is natural that they should do so when each state is legally free to set its own course, or when in fact it is able to do so regardless of legal theory.

In analyzing the nation-state system it is necessary to discuss the nature of the state, the differences among states, the classifications of states in power-political terms, the historical evolution of the state system, and some important characteristics of the system.

The State. The term "state" is an imprecise one. According to one definition it is "any body of people occupying a definite territory and politically organized under one government." The essential components of a state, as this definition suggests, are people, land, and a government.

The terms "state," "government," and "nation" differ in meaning. A government is "the established form of political administration" of a state. A "nation" may be a "body of inhabitants of a country united under a single independent government," and in this sense the word is virtually synonymous with "state." But a "nation" may also be "any aggregation of people having like institutions and customs and a sense of social homogeneity and mutual interest." Thus several nations may be present in one state, or a nation may extend beyond the borders of a single state. The state is a legal entity, and the term "state" is essentially a legal one. Strictly speaking, "nation" is a sociocultural term, and it may be used without implications of legal or political integrity. In general, writers commonly use "state," "nation," and "country" interchangeably to avoid the excessive use of one word — not because the three words mean exactly the same thing.

Differences Among States. Vast differences exist among states in population, size, resources, culture, economies, government, military power, and almost every other conceivable respect. According to international law, however, all states are equal and sovereign. The United Nations, for example, as Article 2 of the Charter proclaims, "is based on the principle of the sovereign equality of all its Members." But in actuality there are many inequalities and many degrees of dependence among states.

Differences in population and area are particularly striking. The combined population of all other nations in the Western Hemisphere is only slightly greater than that of the United States, and — taking the less populous states — the combined population of more than half of the nations of the earth is less than that of the Soviet Union. Some seventy states have fewer people each than New York City; this list includes such important states as Chile, Greece, New Zealand, Sweden, and Switzerland. On the other hand, more than one-third of all the people in the world live in India and China. Size presents the same contrasts. Aside from tiny units which hardly deserve the designation of states — such as Andorra, Liechtenstein, Monaco, Nauru, and San Marino — Luxembourg is smaller than Rhode Island, and Lebanon is smaller than Connecticut. At the other extreme, covering more than a million square miles each, are India, Australia. Brazil, the United States, China, Canada and the U.S.S.R., in rising order of size. Russia alone, with approximately eight and a half million square miles, covers one-sixth of the land area of the world; and the member states of the Commonwealth occupy nearly one-fourth of the earth's surface.

Contrasts among states in other respects are also great. In national wealth and material resources the differences are truly startling. United Nations statisticians have estimated that the nineteen richest countries, with sixteen per cent of the world's population, have sixty-six per cent of the world's income, while the fifteen poorest countries have more than half the world's population and less than one-tenth of its income. If we may take national budgets as the measure of wealth, we note that some states expend less than one-half cent for every one hundred dollars spent by the United States. The budget of the city of New York is larger than that of most of the states of the world. The national income of India, with a population of more than half a billion, is smaller than that of Britain with less than one-ninth as many people. In some states the resources are largely agricultural, in others mineral, and in others technological or commercial; in only a few are they relatively well-balanced. Cultures show the same lack of uniformity, with marked differences in history, tradition, religion, language, ethical codes, social patterns, and economic and political ideologies. Some states have a high degree of racial, cultural, and religious homogeneity; others have very little.

One state may have a government headed by a parliament, a cabinet, and a queen, while another may have a parliament without a king or queen but with a president. Some may have a president with a congress, some a president, an army, and no congress, others a pyramidal soviet form, and still others a plural executive or some other arrangement. More important than form, some governments are high-handed and dictatorial, others just and democratic; some are dictatorial and honest, others democratic and corrupt. Governments are variously monarchies or republics, federal or unitary in form, but these terms imply nothing about representative institutions and the rights of individuals. Some states, like the United States, have a written constitution that is brief and general; some, like Mexico and India, have one that is long and definitive; some, like Great Britain, have no written constitution at all in the usual meaning of the term.

Power Classification of States. For the student of international relations the most common and perhaps the most useful way of classifying states is in terms of national power. Although the power position of a state is the result of many variables and intangibles, certain yardsticks can be employed. At best, however, these are an unsatisfactory basis for classification. It is particularly difficult to avoid assessing the power of a state in terms of its past position or its power potential. Sweden was once a major power but clearly is not one now; India seems to possess the human and natural resources and the qualities of mind and spirit to become a major power, but she has not yet attained that status. The rating of states in terms of national power does not, of course, imply any superiority or inferiority in levels of culture or in overall contributions to civilization.

The most conventional classification of states, speaking in power-political terms, is that of "great powers" or "major powers" and "small powers" or "lesser powers." We shall have many occasions to use this terminology, but it will be necessary to speak also of "world powers," "superpowers," "middle powers," and powers of uncertain status. Writers use the term "world powers" in two different senses: (1) to refer to those countries which have — or had — worldwide possessions and interests; and (2) to refer to those countries which have both worldwide commitments and extraordinary military power. Several European states, notably France, the Netherlands, Belgium, and Portugal, were once world powers under the first definition, but today they would no longer qualify for such a classification. The United States is clearly a world power according to the second definition. In some respects Britain, once the greatest of the world powers, may still be so classified, although her possessions, commitments, and power have declined drastically.

The term "superpowers" is one which has come into rather general use in the post-World War II period. Today only two nations, the United States and the Soviet Union, can properly be described as superpowers. They are also, of course, the only major nuclear powers.

The term "great power" or "major power" is sanctified by long historical usage and is still meaningful today. As is pointed out in the next section of this chapter, the list of great powers has varied widely over the past few centuries. Today the list is rather limited. In addition to the two superpowers, only Great Britain deserves to be classified as a great power, and even this is debatable. In some respects four other states — France, the Federal Republic of Germany, Communist China, and Japan — seem to qualify as great powers, but at present none of them has a clear claim to this status.[3]

Perhaps France and Communist China should be classified as "middle powers." This category is a particularly useful one, for certainly some states which are not great powers exercise far more influence in international relations than the majority of the small countries. They may exercise local or regional superiority and have an effective power-in-being that is substantial. India, for example, may clearly be regarded as a middle power; the same title may be bestowed, with less certainty, upon Argentina, Brazil, Canada, Italy, Mexico, and perhaps also on Spain, Turkey, and Pakistan. Conceivably Yugoslavia should be classed as a middle power, since it has a sizable area and population, an important geographical position, and a strong and relatively independent government.

Small powers, in the words of Martin Wight, "are Powers with the means of defending only limited interests, and of most of them it is true that they possess only limited interests."[4] This is a large and rather nondescript category, embracing all the states of the world except the great and middle powers and those temporarily of uncertain status. Wight may be wrong in asserting that most small powers "possess only limited interests," although he is correct in a technical sense. Some small powers, indeed, have shown a universality of interests and a breadth of vision beyond those of most great powers. Many of them play a surprisingly active and influential role in world affairs. Individually they are small and weak, but they often gain collective strength through membership in regional arrangements such as the Arab League and the OAS, through participation in "voting blocs" or "caucusing groups" at the United Nations — the Asian-African Group is the outstanding example — and at international conferences, through conciliatory or mediatory roles in international diplomacy, and through policies of "nonalignment" with the great "power blocs."

The classification of "powers of uncertain status" is reserved for only two states — Germany and Japan. Germany remains divided. The major victor nations in World War II have been unable to agree on the terms for a peace treaty for her. Part of the

[3] For a concise commentary on "the series of changes in the membership of the ring of 'great powers,'" see Arnold J. Toynbee, "Peace, Empire, and World Government," *Saturday Review*, L (April 29, 1967), 19–21.

[4] *Power Politics* (London, 1946), p. 11.

former German national territory has been incorporated into Poland, and in the former zones of occupation two allegedly independent states have come into existence. In April, 1952, after more than six and a half years of military occupation, the peace treaty for Japan went into effect, and that country was readmitted into the family of nations despite the bitter opposition of the Soviet-dominated world. Since their re-emergence as sovereign states both West Germany and Japan have made impressive economic progress. They are beginning to pursue more active political as well as economic policies abroad. In the recent past they have been great powers, and they still have vast power potentials.

The State System since Westphalia

Scholars commonly designate 1648, the date of the Treaty of Westphalia, as the time when the state system began to take on its modern form. States had existed before Westphalia, and they had conducted relations with each other, but they had done so on quite a different basis. The ancient world had known a succession of sprawling dynastic empires and tiny city-states, and it had known the vast Roman Empire, which had encompassed the civilized Western world. But it had never known a national state or a system of independent states resting upon something akin to the theory of sovereignty. Notable changes had come by the eve of Westphalia: England, France, and Spain had arrived as national states, and others were well on the way; the Roman Church had failed in its long effort to assert and make good its universality; the Holy Roman Empire was doomed in both fact and theory; and Machiavelli, Bodin, Grotius, and a host of other theorists had together provided defense and justification for the independent secular state.[5]

The Peace of Westphalia. The Thirty Years' War, although stemming from the Protestant-Catholic schism begun by the Protestant Reformation and intensified by the Catholic Counter-Reformation, also involved dynastic rivalries of the Hapsburgs and the Bourbons as well as certain issues among German princes. After a long, destructive struggle, the exhausted contenders accepted a religious and political settlement that paved the way for a semblance of European stability. The Treaty of Westphalia may be said to have formalized the nation-state system through its recognition that the empire no longer commanded the allegiance of its parts and that the pope could not everywhere maintain his authority, even in spiritual matters. Henceforth German princes were to rule as they saw fit, and they were to be free to choose Calvinism, Lutheranism, or Roman Catholicism. Holland and Switzerland were recognized as independent republics. The enlargement of Brandenburg began an expansion that produced the kingdom of Prussia and, eventually, the German Empire. France and Sweden also were given additional territory. One historian has summarized the results of the Peace of Westphalia as follows: "By 1648 the state system was fully established in Europe. The Empire was an empty shell. The claim of the pope to temporal sovereignty in Europe was, as an effective force, a thing of the past."[6] Henceforth the states of Europe were "on their own."

As of 1648 the roll of European states read something like this: England, France, Spain, and Sweden were the great powers. England had not been a party to the Thirty Years' War and was largely unaffected by it; France was about to enter a period of continental dominance; Spain was beginning a long period of decline; Sweden, in control of the Baltic area, was only momentarily a first-rate military power. Russia had not yet

[5] See Frederick L. Schuman, *International Politics; the Western State System and the World Community*, 6th ed. (New York: McGraw-Hill Book Company, 1958), pp. 62–69.

[6] Warren O. Ault, *Europe in Modern Times* (Boston: D. C. Heath & Company, 1946), p. 110. See also Schuman, p. 74.

emerged as a strong state. Poland, large and populous, was too poorly governed to count for much in international politics. Italy, a conglomeration of petty states, was only a geographical expression. The Ottoman Empire, important for strategic rather than military reasons, had exhausted its expansive force and was soon to decay. Germany, nominally unified as part of the Holy Roman Empire, was actually disunited, although some of the larger states — Brandenburg, Bavaria, and Saxony — wielded considerable influence. The emperor was also r er of the Hapsburg dominions, but he never succeeded in making a nation of them. The most important of these were Austria, Spain, and the Spanish Netherlands. The independent small powers were Denmark (which then included Norway), Holland, Portgual, and Switzerland.

While it is true that the state system that came into being at Westphalia still remains unchanged in its basic pattern — which is simply the concurrent existence of many "sovereign" states in one world — it is also true that the passing of time has brought many developments which have affected the system. These include the rise of representative government, the Industrial Revolution, population changes, the growth of international law, the evolution of diplomatic method, the increase in the economic interdependence of states, the setting up of procedures for the peaceful settlement of disputes, the expansion of the state system to the non-Western world, and many others. These will be discussed elsewhere. Here, to bring our account of the state system down to the present time, we shall briefly note the course of balance of power politics and the appearance of new states.

Westphalia to Utrecht. The international relations of the years between the

European States after the Peace of Westphalia, 1648

Peace of Westphalia in 1648 and the Treaty of Utrecht in 1713 were dominated by the ambition of Louis XIV (1643–1715) to establish French hegemony on the continent of Europe and by the rivalries of Great Britain, France, Holland, and Spain for colonial supremacy in the Western Hemisphere. Britain provided the chief link between the two areas of conflict, for she joined with continental states to preserve the balance of power in Europe and so reduce the capacity of France to fight on the seas and overseas.

Louis XIV possessed a magnificent army and a consuming urge to use it. He was remarkably successful in extending his power and his domains; but at length a coalition of powers, headed by Britain and Austria, stopped him in the War of the Spanish Succession (1701–13). France suffered heavy losses by the Treaty of Utrecht (1713); while she managed to keep a Bourbon on the throne of Spain, she was forced to pledge that France and Spain would never be united. She lost Nova Scotia to Britain. Austria was given Naples, Sardinia, Milan, and the Spanish Netherlands; and Britain won Gibraltar and Minorca from Spain, as well as certain trading rights. The Treaty of Utrecht also gave further impetus to the unification of Prussia, later the pivot of the European balance, and the agreement made it clear that Sweden, Russia, and Poland could no longer resolve issues in the east without involving the west. In fact, it is not too much to say that after Utrecht no European state could act without reckoning with the others.

Utrecht to Vienna. The balance of power set up at Utrecht was often imperiled during the next hundred years, but it was not destroyed. No state was able to establish permanent hegemony over Europe. By 1733 France had recovered enough to fight the War of the Polish Succession, by which she forced the Hapsburgs to cede to her the duchy of Lorraine. After five years of peace she undertook to partition Austria, only to be thwarted by the courage of Maria Theresa in the War of the Austrian Succession (1740–48). The primacy of France and Austria, which permitted or forced them to clash whenever a continental issue arose, was disturbed by the development within Prussia of a powerful military machine. Fearing Frederick the Great (1740–86) and his fine army, France reversed her strategy and concluded an alliance with Austria.

Russia, likewise becoming alarmed by Frederick, also joined the coalition against Prussia, whereupon, seeing in these alliances an increase in French strength, England quickly jumped on the scales to counterbalance the combination against Prussia. In 1756 the Seven Years' War began when Frederick invaded Saxony. Only the defection of Russia gave him victory, as he was considerably outnumbered by the forces arrayed against him. His ally, Britain, won a clearer victory in North America, virtually eliminating France from the New World.

The defeat of Austria, France, and Spain in the Seven Years' War, together with the exhaustion of Prussia, left no state powerful enough to dominate Europe: the balance of power had been restored. The next threat was precipitated by the French Revolution. When the revolutionists sought to carry the new gospel of liberalism to the rest of Europe, they touched off a conflagration that was to last for twenty-three years. The war was several years old when the "Little Corporal" strode onto the scene, asserted his mastery of France, and set out upon the conquest of Europe. At the pinnacle of his power Napoleon held the Continent under tribute, and Russia was his ally. For a time Britain fought alone. Then, as "Liberty, Equality, Fraternity" deteriorated into aggressive French nationalism, vigorous rival nationalisms sprang up under the heel of Napoleon's conquering armies. British naval supremacy, "General Winter" in Russia, and the combined might of Britain, Russia, Prussia, Austria, and Sweden finally brought about the defeat of the Corsican adventurer and the end of the most formidable of all French attempts to conquer Europe.

Since the period from Westphalia to the rise of Napoleon had been regarded as one of relative peace and stability, it is not surprising that the representatives of the nations meeting at Vienna in 1814–15 sought to reestablish the old system. They decreed that eight states should be accorded diplomatic recognition as first-rate powers: Great Britain, Russia, Austria, Prussia, France, Sweden, Portugal, and Spain — the last three as a gesture to tradition. The deliberations were dominated by four states — Britain, Russia, Austria, and Prussia. At the opening of the Congress France had held the position of a vanquished nation, but through the sheer brilliance of Talleyrand's diplomacy she emerged as a major power with considerable influence in continental Europe. To protect the Continent against new ventures in French imperialism the Congress erected a *cordon sanitaire* between France and her neighbors; and to restore the balance of the state system it invoked the principles of compensation and "legitimacy," usually ascribed to Prince Metternich of Austria.

Between Utrecht and Vienna one old European state had passed from the scene and a new state had appeared in the Western Hemisphere; Poland had been divided and absorbed by Prussia, Russia, and Austria, and the United States had been born of the American Revolution. England, Prussia, Russia, Austria, and France remained as major powers; Spain, Holland, Portugal, and Sweden had definitely become lesser powers.

Vienna to Versailles. The years between 1815 and 1914, sometimes referred to as the period of the *Pax Britannica,* were disturbed only twice by major conflicts in which the status of great powers was involved. In the first of these, the Crimean War (1854–56), the Russian threat to dominate Constantinople and the Straits was blocked by Britain and France. The second, the Franco-Prussian War (1870–71), did not immediately disturb the overall balance of power in the European system, but it did mark the displacement of France by a unified Germany as the leading power on the Continent.

The rise of Germany was due to Prince Otto von Bismarck (1815–98), who welded the states of the German Confederation into the German Empire through a policy of "blood and iron." The empire was proclaimed on January 18, 1871, at Versailles. Operating somewhat differently, Count Camillo di Cavour (1810–61) performed the same services for the new state of Italy, which was proclaimed in early 1861, with Victor Emmanuel of Sardinia-Piedmont as king. Thus the decline in the power of France and Austria, plus the shrewd diplomacy of Bismarck and Cavour, led to the addition of two new major states to the European system.

In the Balkans, the decline in Turkish strength permitted realization of the dreams of independence among Slavs in the nineteenth and early twentieth centuries. Greece, Montenegro, Rumania, Serbia, Bulgaria, and, finally, Albania became the sovereignties which were to make nationalism in the Balkans a constant threat to the peace of Europe and to the conflicting designs of the great powers.

Overseas, a group of new states joined the United States of America in the Western Hemisphere. The removal of Ferdinand VII from the throne of Spain by Napoleon furnished the occasion for the assumption of sovereign power by some of Spain's American colonies, a course eventually followed by all the rest. Brazil declared her independence of Portugal in 1822, with the son of the Portuguese king as emperor; the monarchy remained until 1889, when a republican form of government was established. During these years the United States of America was growing steadily. By the sixties she had population and resources sufficient to wage one of the most colossal wars of the century. Certainly an important power by the end of the Civil War, she was recognized as one of the major world powers after the Spanish-American War in 1898.

In the Far East, Japan emerged from feudalism in 1867–68 with the overthrow of the shogun. Copying the techniques of the Western world, she was able to parry the imperialistic thrusts of the European powers and to build a strong nation-state. As a result of her victory over China in 1894–95, her alliance with Great Britain in 1902, and her defeat of Russia in 1904–5, she was admitted to equality with the major powers.

By the outbreak of war in 1914, then, there were eight major powers, all but two located on the continent of Europe. Their power interests were varied. Germany, Austria, and Italy had combined in the Triple Alliance (1882), born of German desire to maintain the status quo of 1871, Austrian fear of Russia, and Italian displeasure with French imperialistic policy in northern Africa. Italian designs on Austrian sovereignty over parts of unredeemed Italy, however, made her susceptible to counter-offers and at best an unreliable member of the combination. Great Britain, France, and Russia had teamed together in the Triple Entente (1907), a product of French desire for both revenge and security against Germany, English fear of a rapidly growing industrial Germany, and Russian designs in the Balkans. The United States, untested in world combat, was a potential counterweight to any undue tipping of the scales by an unfriendly continental combine. Consequently Britain worked to find an opening in the wall of isolationism of the United States in world affairs. She had achieved limited success by 1900; but she had won greater success with Japan by 1902, when she concluded the Anglo-Japanese Alliance, aimed at the maintenance of stability in the Far East. Thereafter Japan carefully watched the moves of the great powers. Willing to expand in any direction, but sensing the greatest potentialities in Manchuria, she adjusted her policies to those of warring European states to achieve regional gains in the Far East. She gave little thought to the balance of power in Europe.

During World War I the German Empire, the Austro-Hungarian monarchy, and the tsarist regime in Russia collapsed. Although a member of the Triple Entente, Italy entered the war in 1915 on the Allied side and at the Paris Peace Conference in 1919 was rewarded with some, but not all, of the territory promised to her in secret wartime treaties.

Versailles to the Present. After the Treaty of Versailles and other peace treaties with the defeated states, only the United States, Britain, and Japan could be described as major powers. The United States retreated from her brief but decisive intervention in Europe into isolationism. Britain, facing growing challenges in her colonial possessions and finding it increasingly difficult to play her traditional role in the balance of power game, experimented first with a Labor government and then, in the growing darkness of the 1930's, with a coalition government and a weak Conservative regime, whose only reaction to the growing menace of fascism was a policy of appeasement. Japan, after a brief experiment with a "democratic" government headed by a commoner and civilian, fell under the control of a military fascism which, beginning with the Manchurian incident of 1931, started a "march of aggression" in the Far East. Italy, where political weaknesses and internal discontent had enabled Mussolini and the Fascists to seize power, assumed the posture of a great power, but after 1933 she was overshadowed by a resurgent Germany led by Hitler. Russia, under Communist rule, became a formidable, unorthodox, and disturbing factor on the world scene.

World War II involved three totalitarian states with varying patterns of fascism in a major conflict with another totalitarian state, the Soviet Union, the three major democratic states of the Western world, and China. France was soon occupied, but Britain and the Soviet Union withstood the German assaults. After the Japanese attack on Pearl Harbor in December, 1941, the total might of the United States was mobilized against the Fascist powers. The result was the destruction of nazism in Germany, fascism in Italy, and military-fascism and the emperor system in Japan.

Out of the fires of war only the United States emerged with enhanced power, although the Soviet Union rapidly recovered from the wartime trials and devastation. France and Britain, although gravely weakened, continued to play a major role in international life. In China the Nationalists lost out to the Communists, who have brought China to at least the threshold of great power status. After several years of military occupation, Germany (that is, West Germany) and Japan re-emerged as sovereign nations, and, for all the suspicions arising from the past and their continuing military weakness, they are well on the way to becoming again major powers.

Since World War II the "European" state system has become worldwide. Europe is still its center in a qualified sense, but none of the most powerful states of the world today — unless West Germany is included in this list — is a wholly European power. The state system has been substantially enlarged in membership, especially by the emergence of new states in Asia and Africa, and middle and even lesser powers have been playing an increasingly active and influential role, far out of proportion to their actual strength.

It may be argued that the very changes which have enlarged and apparently consolidated the state system have effected a fundamental alteration in the nature of the state system itself. Indeed, many students of international affairs believe that "the systemic revolution has undermined the nation-state as the primary force on the world's political stage" and that "the passing of the nation-state system constitutes the true revolution of our times."[7] This obituary is probably premature. Perhaps, as Max Lerner has opined, "it is not the nation-state that is dying, but its untrammeled sovereignty and the historic pattern of relations between nation-states. . . . It is a total system that is passing."[8] The system is clearly in transition, and it may be in its sunset period, but there seems to have been little change in its basic design, which is the co-existence of a large number of states, including some of preeminent military power, all subject to the drive of their special interests and emotions, all subscribing to the theory of sovereignty, and all impelled to develop national power as the instrument of their national policies. There is much wisdom in the following advice by Benjamin Akzin: "For the present century, and probably for a good many centuries to come, nations are here to stay. Rather than dream about their disappearance, it is better to learn how to live with them."[9] It is therefore necessary to study the nation-state system in transition, whether the process is one of revitalization or decline.

Corollaries of the State System

Certain features of the state system are inseparable from it, not adjuncts of it. We might call them *corollaries.* The first is the concept of sovereignty, the second is the doctrine of nationalism, and the third is the principle of national power. Sovereignty is the legal theory that gives the state unique

[7] Robert Strausz-Hupé, James E. Dougherty, and William R. Kintner, *Building the Atlantic World* (New York: Harper & Row, 1963), pp. 25, 304.

[8] Max Lerner, *The Age of Overkill* (New York: Simon and Schuster, 1962), p. 19.

[9] Benjamin Akzin, *State and Nation* (London, 1964), p. 207.

and virtually unlimited authority in all domestic matters and in its relations with other states. Nationalism is that psychological or spiritual quality which, although it may involve some earthy considerations, unites the people of a state and gives them the will to champion what they regard as their national interests. National power is the might of a state; it provides the capabilities for getting done the things that the state wills to be done. It is a complex of many elements, both tangible and intangible. In the following sections we shall examine the first two corollaries. The components of national power will be discussed in Chapters 2 and 3.

Sovereignty

The concept of sovereignty, like the doctrine of nationalism, is indissolubly associated with the nation-state system. It is, said Professor McIlwain, the "central formula under which we try to rationalize the complicated facts of our modern political life."[10] Some understanding of this concept is essential to the purposeful study of international relations.

The Meaning of Sovereignty. As interpreted by earlier writers — Bodin, Hobbes, Locke, Rousseau — and by modern political scientists — Jellinek, Duguit, Kelsen, and Laski — sovereignty has assumed many different guises. Moreover, it has frequently changed its content, its laws, and even its functions during the modern period.[11] It has been invoked to justify absolute rule, and it has given rise to the concept of "popular sovereignty." It has often been regarded as a major stumbling block to hopes and plans for supranational organization and cooperation, the rock on which so many hopes for peace have foundered.

"Few political conceptions," observed Professor McIlwain, "have been the subject of so much discussion amongst us in the last hundred years."[12] "No word in political science," declared Professor Coker, "is used with a greater variety of meanings."[13] Because of this semantic confusion and because of the difficulties in adapting the concept of sovereignty into the realities of the modern world, some political scientists contend that the concept is obsolete, or even dangerous, and that it should be discarded altogether.

The father of the modern theory of sovereignty was the sixteenth-century French political thinker, Jean Bodin (1530–96). His *De la République,* published in Paris in 1576, contained the first systematic presentation of his theory. Sovereignty, wrote Bodin, is "the supreme power over citizens and subjects, unrestrained by law." Thus sovereignty was identified from the outset with royal absolutism; and the sovereign monarch, whose power was absolute and unlimited, restrained by no human authority whatsoever, was equipped to resist the universalist claims of the papacy and the Empire on the one hand and the decentralizing, almost anarchic tendencies of feudalism on the other. Writing less than half a century later, Hugo Grotius, who believed that states should be subject to the law of the international community, nevertheless gave a similar definition of the term in his famous work *De Jure Belli ac Pacis:* Sovereignty is "that power whose acts . . . may not be made void by the acts of any other human will."

Recent political theorists have, in general, given similar definitions of this much-de-

[10] C. H. McIlwain, *Constitutionalism and the Changing World* (New York: Cambridge University Press, 1939), p. 47. This volume contains three stimulating essays, "Sovereignty," "A Fragment on Sovereignty," and "Whig Sovereignty and Real Sovereignty."

[11] Quincy Wright, *A Study of War,* (Chicago: University of Chicago Press, 1942), II, 898–899.

[12] McIlwain, p. 47.

[13] Francis Coker, "Sovereignty," *Encyclopaedia of the Social Sciences* (New York: The Macmillan Company, 1937), XIV, 268. Used by permission of The Macmillan Company.

bated concept. Here are three examples from distinguished authorities: Oppenheim: "Sovereignty is supreme authority, an authority which is independent of any other earthly authority." Willoughby: "Sovereignty is the supreme will of the state." Kelsen: "In its original and only specific meaning, sovereignty means supreme authority."

One might add, in the interests of narrowing the definition and at the risk of incurring the wrath of those political philosophers who hold that the state is not sovereign or even that sovereignty does not apply to the state at all, that sovereignty is the supreme authority, and particularly the ultimate coercive power, which the state possesses, and which other institutions do not. Various writers on political theory have also insisted that every legally recognized state is by definition sovereign, that otherwise it could not be called a state. This is not to overlook the fact that some states by virtue of their power, size, location, and so on, obviously have greater influence and greater freedom of action than others. It is simply a reminder that just as every state is legally equal to any other, so it is legally sovereign.[14] Most writers on international law do not believe that sovereignty is incompatible with the existence of a body of definite regulations which civilized states generally accept and which are supported by recognized sanctions. We shall return to the limitations on sovereignty during this discussion and again in the chapter on international law.

The Source of Sovereignty. The source of sovereignty in a state is often difficult, if not impossible, to locate in any meaningful way. The problem was a relatively easy one to solve in an absolute state, where sovereignty resided in the "Sovereign Monarch," as Bodin believed; but it became an increasingly baffling one with the evolution of nonmonarchical forms of government, especially those of a federal type. If, as Bodin insisted, sovereignty was absolute and indivisible, it certainly had to reside in some specific place or person in the governmental structure.

Frequently attempts are made to locate the seat of sovereignty by distinguishing between legal sovereignty and popular sovereignty, but even efforts to identify the legal sovereign are not too successful. It is often claimed, for example, that in England sovereignty rests with "the King in Parliament" — presumably meaning the House of Commons; but this statement is subject to all kinds of qualifications. Even in the modern versions of absolute states, the totalitarian states, the location of sovereignty is not easy to determine. Where, for instance, does sovereignty reside in the Soviet Union? In the Communist Party? In the Politburo? In "the toiling majority," as Soviet dialecticians hold? In "the multi-national Soviet people," as Vyshinsky declared?[15]

---

[14] This interpretation, like nearly every approach to questions of sovereignty, will be challenged by many political scientists. The following statement by Robert Strausz-Hupé and Stefan Possony indicates that they are in sharp disagreement: "It must be recognized that there are degrees of sovereignty and self-determination. A fully sovereign nation is one which has sufficient power to be master of its decisions. In the past, there were many nations who were sovereign in the true sense of the word. Today, there are probably only two or three, but certainly not more than five or seven." *International Relations* (New York: McGraw-Hill Book Company, 1950), p. 709. Small nations in particular, according to these writers, lack sovereignty. But while small states may be subject to more practical restrictions on their freedom of action, they do not thereby lose their sovereignty. Sovereignty is the supreme authority which all states, large or small, possess. See Alfred Verdross-Drossberg. "The Study of International Law in German-Speaking Countries," in *Contemporary Political Science,* UNESCO Publication No. 426, pp. 601–603; and F. S. Hinsley, *Sovereignty* (New York: Basic Books, 1966).

[15] For a good summary of Soviet views on the source of sovereignty in the Soviet state, see Julian Towster, *Political Power in the U.S.S.R., 1917–1947* (New York: Oxford University Press, 1948), pp. 46–69. Dr. I. H. Qureshi, former Minister of Education of Pakistan, has advanced an interesting thesis about the source of sovereignty in an Islamic state: "Progress and Islamic ideals can be reconciled in a threefold definition of sovereignty in an Islamic state: (1) the legal sovereign shall be the

There is little point under present conditions in attempting to locate the exact source of sovereignty in a state. As Sabine and Shephard pointed out, "all these attempts to fix sovereignty in a particular element of the state . . . are futile. . . . Hence the attempt to find a tangible sovereign is nothing but an attempt to force modern political institutions into a mold of thought which applied to an altogether different state of facts."[16]

Can Sovereignty Be Divided or Limited? Clearly sovereignty, in its meaning of absolute, unlimited, and indivisible authority, is incompatible with international law, perhaps with any law. The implications of this interpretation, not only for the future of international law but also for the hopes for peace and the prospects of more effective international cooperation, are obvious. According to the champions of sovereignty, argued Jacques Maritain, "the sovereign State — each individual sovereign State — is by right *above* the community of nations and possessed of absolute independence with regard to this community." Therefore "no international law binding the States can be consistently conceived. Furthermore, this absolute independence is inalienable (*unrenounceable*), because by virtue of its nature the state is a monadic entity which cannot cease to be sovereign without ceasing to be a state. As a result, no day can dawn — as long as the States behave consistently with their so-called Sovereignty — on which they could possibly give up their supreme independence in order to enter a larger political body, or a world society."[17] Hans Morgenthau holds that "the conception of a divisible sovereignty is contrary to logic and politically unfeasible . . . a significant symptom of the discrepancy between the actual and pretended relations existing between international law and international politics in the modern state system."[18] He is one of the school of political scientists that holds that sovereignty is indivisible, that limitations on sovereignty or the surrender of part of a state's sovereignty in the interests of international cooperation are both theoretically untenable and practically impossible.

From the theoretical and historical point of view those who insist that sovereignty is by its very nature indivisible and incompatible with international law are absolutely correct. Therefore, either a new interpretation must be evolved or the whole concept must be scrapped; for unless the concept of sovereignty under law and of limitations on sovereignty can be established and put into practice, there is little hope for developing a legal basis for a peaceful international society. Certainly one can make a strong case for the proposition that "from the standpoint of international law the concept of absolute sovereignty is no longer valid."[19]

Clyde Eagleton, an eminent American authority on international law, took a sane and realistic view of this difficult problem:

> Sovereignty cannot be an absolute term. It is just as foolish to say that sovereignty must be surrendered or eliminated as to say that it must be absolute and unrestrained. . . . The problem is not one of asking whether we should throw off a thing called sovereignty; it is rather one of asking with regard to what

Muslim law; its definition shall be in the hands of the legislature; (2) the political sovereign shall be the people who will elect and dismiss their governments; (3) the real sovereign will be basically the principles of Islam, brought into the public forum and discussed at length." "Sovereignty in the Islamic State," an address at the All-Pakistan Political Science Conference, Peshawar, April 10, 1951, in I. H. Qureshi, *Pakistan: An Islamic Democracy* (Lahore, n.d.), pp. 26–27.

[16] Hugo Krabbe, *The Modern Idea of the State* (New York: Appleton, 1927), p. xxvii.

[17] Jacques Maritain, *Man and the State* (Chicago: University of Chicago Press, 1951), pp. 50–51.

[18] Hans J. Morgenthau, *Politics Among Nations*, 3d ed. (New York: Alfred A. Knopf, 1962), p. 326.

[19] S. C. Rath, "National Sovereignty in the Present Day World," *The Indian Journal of Political Science*, XXV (July–September–December, 1964), 29–30.

matters would we gain by having an international control, and in which matters would we gain more by reserving control to ourselves?[20]

One might argue that states often enter into bilateral or multilateral commitments which in effect limit their sovereignty, or that proposals such as the United Nations plan for the international control of atomic energy and the Schuman Plan in its original form involve some real surrender of sovereignty. But obviously neither of these plans is a real test case: the former has never been implemented, and the European Coal and Steel Community and the European Economic Community, as they now function, are less independent of the member states than M. Schuman first proposed.[21]

In the strict sense of the term there are no truly supranational organizations in the world today, if the word "supranational" is taken to mean a genuine surrender of sovereignty by member states. But in the present interdependent world no state, however powerful, can attempt to shape its future without giving due heed to outside pressures and commitments; and most states are bound to other states by many formal as well as informal ties. Few persons would insist that states that participate in various kinds of international agreements thereby lose their status as sovereign states, whatever may happen to the theoretical fullness of their sovereignty.

Some students of political science and international law have attempted to distinguish between internal sovereignty, which is absolute and indivisible, and external sovereignty, which is subject to limitations. Indeed, both Bodin and the English political theorist John Austin (1790–1859) were primarily concerned with the internal aspects of sovereignty. In his study *Mandates under the League of Nations* Quincy Wright declared: "From the point of view of Municipal law, sovereignty is a unity incapable of division or limitation, from the point of view of international law it is susceptible to analysis, division and limitation. . . . External sovereignty or status exists insofar as a state can change, by unilateral action, the jural relations with other states, and must be distinguished from internal sovereignty or independence."[22] Wright also distinguished between "partial" and "full" sovereignty, and between "political" and "legal" sovereignty. Elsewhere he suggested that the three aspects of national sovereignty that "are in most need of limitation" are "the power of self-judgment in international controversies, the power to prepare and use armed force in international relations, and the power to impose arbitrary barriers to international trade."[23]

In his *Recent Theories of Sovereignty* H. E. Cohen pointed out that "international

[20] *The Forces That Shape Our Future* (New York: New York University Press, 1945), p. 174.

[21] "Since the governments in effect remain in the saddle the diminution in sovereignty is, at least at the outset, not far beyond that entailed in a close concert of nations pursuing agreed-upon objectives and sufficiently committed so that it is difficult to turn back. . . . Sovereignty is . . . curtailed in the EEC, but it is not as a result of turning power over to an international or supranational body of administrators as Schuman seemed to be suggesting in his first proposal for a coal and steel community. Sovereignty has been curtailed as a result, first, of accepting a broad commitment to follow common policies moving towards economic and eventually political integration. Secondly, sovereignty has been restricted by institutional arrangements that expose each member to more readily applied pressures from the others and subsequently to the possibility of having a decision imposed by some combination of the other member countries." Irving B. Kravis, *Domestic Interests and International Obligations* (Philadelphia: University of Pennsylvania Press, 1963), pp. 361, 362.

[22] Quincy Wright, *Mandates Under the League of Nations* (Chicago: University of Chicago Press, 1930), pp. 289, 291.

[23] "Fundamental Problems of International Organization," *International Conciliation,* No. 369 (April 1941), pp. 469–472.

law finds room for the concepts of joint sovereignty, divided sovereignty, and the sovereignty of international corporations."[24] And it also finds room for the principle of sovereignty under law.[25] A clear example of this is the text of Article 14 of the Draft Declaration on Rights and Duties of States, prepared by the International Law Commission of the United Nations. This article reads: "Every State has the duty to conduct its relations with other States in accordance with international law and with the principle that the sovereignty of each State is subject to the supremacy of international law." Perhaps, as one of the leading students of sovereignty, Hans Kelsen, insisted, the writers of this article might have been wise if they avoided the use of the term "sovereignty" in this connection, especially since they did not define it "in a way compatible with international law"[26]; but here again we see a conscious attempt to assert the principle of sovereignty under law, in external as well as in internal affairs.

The idea of accepting, or even encouraging, limitations on sovereignty has been expressed so frequently, sometimes in surprising quarters, that it has become commonplace today.[27] Taken at their face value, these statements suggest that the leaders and peoples of virtually all non-Communist states may be prepared to surrender part of their sovereignty for certain common ends. But such statements can hardly be taken at their own value, for actions say more authoritatively than words that no major voluntary surrender of sovereignty has yet been made in order to achieve these ends.

Western Europe has produced some of the most ardent champions of national sovereignty outside of the Communist world, and also some of its most vigorous critics. This difference is reflected in the very diverse views of General Charles de Gaulle and Paul-Henri Spaak. De Gaulle is an outspoken opponent of all efforts to diminish France's sovereignty in any way. In 1960 he referred to "sovereign statehood and national independence" as "the incontestable foundations of all French politics," and he has adhered to this position consistently in his statements and policies. To Spaak, one of the great spokesmen for European unity, such a position is antediluvian and runs counter to the course which he believes Europe and the world must take in the interests of mutual cooperation for survival and human betterment. At the *Pacem in Terris* conference in New York in February, 1965, he declared flatly: "We must renounce absolute national sovereignty."

Those who advocate world government or effective federation on a regional basis are the talking champions of the pooling of sovereignty and the creation of suprana-

[24] H. E. Cohen, *Recent Theories of Sovereignty* (Chicago: University of Chicago Press, 1937), p. 85.

[25] Perhaps Bodin may be resting more peacefully than this statement suggests. For, as C. H. McIlwain pointed out in his significant essay on "Whig Sovereignty and Real Sovereignty," Bodin distinguished clearly between absolute power and arbitrary power and between fundamental law and ordinary law. Professor McIlwain wrote: "Bodin's conception of a republic and of the sovereign authority in it can only be understood in light of this fundamental distinction between constituent law and ordinary legislation." McIlwain, p. 73.

[26] "The Draft Declaration on Rights and Duties of States," *The American Journal of International Law*, XLIV (April, 1950), 276.

[27] The constitutions of a few nation-states contain provisions for the surrender of sovereignty under certain conditions and for certain stated objectives. Article 24 of the Basic Law of the Federal Republic of Germany states that the Parliament "will consent to such limitations upon its sovereign powers as will bring about and secure a peaceful and lasting order in Europe and among the nations of the world." The Draft Constitution of Ghana of 1960 contained the following arresting provision: ". . . in the confident expectation of an early surrender to a union of African states and territories, the people now confer on the Parliament the power to provide for the surrender of the whole or of any part of the sovereignty of Ghana."

tional agencies with real powers; but there are grounds for serious doubt whether they always mean what they say. Many of the people who enthusiastically endorse world government in public opinion polls begin to hedge and qualify their stand when it comes even to preliminary steps to implement their declared position. Either they do not know the consequences of the movements they advocate or they are in favor of the surrender of some sovereignty by *other* states and peoples but not by their own.

Soviet Views on Sovereignty. Spokesmen of the Soviet Union strongly object to the idea of any limitation on sovereignty. Confronted, according to their doctrine, with the perpetual threat of capitalist encirclement, Soviet leaders are sensitive to any such attempts, real or imaginary. Nothing arouses their wrath quite so much as a suspicion that their absolute sovereignty is being threatened. This view is unquestionably one of the main reasons for their insistence on the principle of great-power unanimity in the Security Council of the United Nations, and for their refusal even to consider any limitations on the right of veto.

Thus E. A. Korovin, an authority on the Soviet view of international law, declared: "No really democratic state will agree to limitations on its sovereignty other than those which are voluntary, reciprocal, fair and freely consented to. It will have nothing to do with limitations on its sovereignty that are unilateral and imposed from without."[28] This position seems reasonable enough, and indeed almost platitudinous; but the Soviet Union's constant insistence on her unlimited sovereignty conveys the impression that she is really determined to avoid all limitations, even those which are "voluntary" and "reciprocal." Thus her attitude is a major obstacle to all efforts toward effective international cooperation in areas where some concessions in sovereignty are necessary.

The reasons for Soviet emphasis on the sovereignty of the state have been well summarized as follows:

> So long as the U.S.S.R. is compelled to remain an island encircled by capitalism, any restriction on Soviet sovereignty must needs entail concessions of a more or less serious character to the political and economic principles opposed to her own and to the social groups guided thereby. . . . Under these circumstances, any restriction of sovereignty . . . would delay the advent of socialist revolutions and reduce the number of the Soviet's potential allies.[29]
>
> The Soviet state . . . regards sovereignty, not as a manifestation of unrestricted arbitrary power, but as the principle of self-determination in domestic and foreign affairs. . . . The principle of sovereignty serves as a legal barrier defending nations from imperialistic encroachment, from military and economic aggression.[30]

Interpretations of this kind are the stock in trade of Soviet experts on international law. They were expressed in the authorita-

[28] Quoted in Kazimierz Szczerba and Alexander von Schelting, "International Relations in Soviet Sociological and Legal Doctrine," in *Contemporary Political Science,* UNESCO Publication No. 426, p. 555. "Soviet Jurisprudence recognizes the idea of limitations on sovereignty even though it is seldom put into practice. In his report to the XIIth Party Congress (1923) J. Stalin, speaking of the Union of Soviet Republics in a common federation, stated that 'any union implies some restriction of the previous rights of those who join together.' Addressing the League of Nations Council, on January 23, 1936, the Soviet delegate declared: 'Only a state free from any international commitments enjoys absolute sovereignty and the right to do whatever it pleases. . . . On February 10, 1946, at a session of the UN Security Council, M. Vyshinsky, chief of the Soviet delegation, answered in the affirmative on being asked whether the United Nations statute 'restricted the sovereignty of sovereign states.' " *Ibid.*

[29] Szczerba and Von Schelting, p. 554.

[30] E. A. Korovin, quoted in "Anglo-Soviet Debate on Sovereignty," *Current Readings on International Relations No. 4* (Reading, Mass.: Addison-Wesley Press, 1948), pp. 4, 7. See also Oliver J. Lissitzyn, "International Law in a Divided World," *International Conciliation,* No. 542 (March, 1963), p. 18.

tive Soviet manual, *The Law of the Soviet State,* edited by Andrei Vyshinsky, and they are repeatedly declaimed before the organs and agencies of the United Nations. It is important to bear in mind that the concept of unlimited sovereignty is inseparable from the Soviet theory of international law — a theory which, "if logically pursued in practice, would make the application of the generally accepted rules of international law between her and other States to a large degree impossible."[31]

Should the Concept of Sovereignty Be Discarded? Any analysis of the concept of sovereignty is bound to be a study in contradictions. Sovereignty, in its literal sense, means supreme authority, yet it must be limited under present conditions. It is absolute and indivisible, yet it must be qualified and divided. It is incompatible with international law, yet it must be reconciled with international law. It is historically associated with a period of absolutism, yet it is still regarded as an essential characteristic of a nation-state — perhaps *the* essential characteristic — in a period of many different patterns of government. It is a fairly rigid and inflexible theory, yet it must be applied to an evolving pattern of interstate relations.

Faced with these contradictions, many political theorists have reached the conclusion that the term "sovereignty," and perhaps the doctrine as well, should be abandoned. As early as 1916, in *The Problem of Sovereignty,* Harold J. Laski, a political pluralist, predicted: "The sovereignty of the state will pass, as the divine right of kings has had its day"; and in *A Grammar of Politics* he wrote: ". . . it would be of lasting benefit to political science if the whole concept of sovereignty were surrendered."[32] Jacques Maritain concluded a challenging interpretation of sovereignty with the flat assertion: "The two concepts of Sovereignty and Absolutism have been forged together on the same anvil. They must be scrapped together."[33] John Scholte Nollen is equally positive that sovereignty is an anachronism in the modern world: "The first piece of old lumber that must be discarded in this new day is the obsolete idea of 'sovereignty.' "[34] Carl J. Friedrich argues that "both 'state' and 'sovereignty' " in current usage "are symbols of totalitarian government" and are "fraught with implications that are incompatible not only with democracy but with the essence of Christianity."[35]

Confronted by this imposing array of accusers, one might conclude that the wisest and simplest solution would be to banish the offending term. Yet "sovereignty," for all its vagueness and variety of definitions, describes a cardinal feature of the nation-state system for which there is no remotely acceptable synonym. Hence students of politics will continue to speak of it, with or without a careful definition of the particular ways in which they use the term. At the end of his careful study of theories of sovereignty, H. E. Cohen came to the conclusion that "the theory of sovereignty will persist as a term defining power or the status of

[31] L. B. Schapiro, "The Soviet Concept of International Law," in G. W. Keeton and Georg Schwarzenberger, eds., *The Year Book of World Affairs, 1948* (London, 1948), p. 309. For summaries of Soviet authorities on the concept of sovereignty, see the above and Szczerba and Von Schelting. See also T. A. Taracouzio, *The Soviet Union and International Law* (New York: The Macmillan Company, 1935), pp. 26–47, and E. A. Korovin, "The Contribution of the USSR to International Law," *Soviet Press Translations,* III, No. 21 (December 1, 1948), 655–664.

[32] Harold J. Laski, *The Problem of Sovereignty* (Cambridge, Mass.: Harvard University Press, 1916), p. 209; and *A Grammar of Politics* (New Haven: Yale University Press, 1925), pp. 44–45.

[33] Maritain, p. 53.

[34] "Sovereignty?" in Stuart Gerry Brown, ed., *Internationalism and Democracy* (Syracuse: Syracuse University Press, 1949), p. 48.

[35] *The New Belief in the Common Man* (Boston: Little, Brown and Company, 1942), p. 79. See also Georges Scelle, *Manuel élémentaire de droit international public* (Paris, 1943), pp. 73 ff.

that power, or as a term defining a legal order, or the status of parts within that order or the totality of that order." Even if the word "sovereignty" disappears with changes in terminology, Cohen believed that "the substance of sovereignty will remain so long as the problems of social control divide men into rulers and ruled, into leaders and led."[36] Perhaps he should have revised the last part of his prediction to read: "so long as the nation-state system remains the prevailing pattern of international society." Those who view sovereignty with suspicion may find some consolation in E. H. Carr's timely reminder that the concept of sovereignty "is likely to become in the future even more blurred and indistinct than it is at present. . . . It was never more than a convenient label."[37] Yet for the time being, the notion of sovereignty is indispensable to the study of international relations.

Nationalism

"For students of international politics, an understanding of nationalism is as indispensable as the possession of a master key to a person seeking to enter all the rooms in a building. Indeed, the *total* behavior of the state system in our day may largely be explained in terms of *national* hopes, *national* fears, *national* ambitions, and *national* conflicts."[38] If nationalism is unmentioned in any serious discussion of international problems, it is because its significance is assumed. As Carlton J. H. Hayes said: "So much is nationalism a commonplace in the modes of thought and action of the civilized populations of the contemporary world that most men take nationalism for granted. Without serious reflection they imagine it to be the most natural thing in the universe and assume that it must always have existed."[39]

The leaders of every state regard the national interests, as interpreted by themselves alone, as paramount, and loyalty to the state as superior to every other earthly obligation. Sometimes, in fact, nationalism takes precedence over moral and religious beliefs, as was the case in Nazi Germany; or it may become fused with such beliefs, as seems to be true in Israel and Pakistan today. It has become a kind of secular religion alongside other religious faiths, but in our day it has sometimes actually replaced supernatural religion. Arnold Toynbee characterized it as "the real if unavowed religion of 'post-modern' Western society." In its most virulent form it has commanded virtually the total allegiance of men, and some of the most inhuman acts of this age have been wrapped in the mystical and religious trappings of nationalism.

The Meaning of Terms. Among the terms that we need to clarify before we can undertake an intelligent discussion of the evolution and importance of nationalism are *nation, nation-state, nationality, national self-determination, patriotism,* and *chauvinism.* The related concept of *sovereignty* has been examined at some length in this chapter. Other chapters will deal with imperialism, which has often been closely associated with nationalism, with economic nationalism, one of the most important and pervasive aspects of the whole subject, and with nationalism in different countries and regions, especially in Asia and Africa.

The word *nation* has had many meanings, some with no relation to the state system. In modern times the word *nation* has been used in several senses, on the basis of differ-

[36] Cohen, pp. 147, 148.

[37] *The Twenty Years' Crisis, 1919–1939,* 2d ed. (London, 1946), p. 230.

[38] Walter R. Sharp and Grayson Kirk, *Contemporary International Politics* (New York: Rinehart, 1944), p. 93. Italics in original.

[39] Carlton J. H. Hayes, *The Historical Evolution of Modern Nationalism* (Peterborough, N.H.: The Richard R. Smith Co., 1931), p. 289. Used by permission of The Macmillan Company.

ent theories and interpretations.[40] One of the most satisfactory definitions was advanced by Ernest Barker more than forty years ago:

> A nation is a body of men, inhabiting a definite territory, who normally are drawn from different races, but possess a common stock of thoughts and feelings acquired and transmitted during the course of a common history; who on the whole and in the main, though more in the past than in the present, include in that common stock a common religious belief; who generally and as a rule use a common language as the vehicle of their thoughts and feelings; and who, besides common thoughts and feelings, also cherish a common will, and accordingly form, or tend to form, a separate state for the expression and realization of that will.[41]

In his famous lecture at the Sorbonne in 1882, *"Qu'est-ce qu'une nation?,"* Ernest Renan emphasized the intangible ties which bind people together into a nation. "What constitutes a nation," he said, "is not speaking the same tongue or belonging to the same ethnic group, but having accomplished great things in common in the past and the wish to accomplish them in the future."

A nation, as noted earlier, is not necessarily the human and physical incarnation of a state. In fact, even in a modern sense we may conceive of a state's being composed of several nations, although perhaps the term *nationalities* should be used in this connection. Indeed, we often speak of the multinational state. But in modern parlance the terms *nation* and *state* are used almost interchangeably, and the major political units which exist today may appropriately be called *nation-states*. As Hans Morgenthau suggests, "the nation needs a state. 'One nation — one state' is thus the political postulate of nationalism; the nation-state is its ideal."[42]

Nationality, one of the main sources of nationalism, may be defined as the distinctive quality of a group which has a common origin and tradition. It may imply either national character and the spirit of belonging to a nation or a group of people possessed of such a spirit. The latter connotation is very common today. Thus the sociologist Louis Wirth defines a nationality as "a people who, because of the belief in their common descent and their mission in the world, by virtue of their common cultural heritage and historical career aspire to sovereignty over a territory or seek to maintain or enlarge their political or cultural influence in the face of opposition."[43] Frederick Hertz defined it as "a community formed by the will to be a nation."[44] It is "nothing material or mechanical," observed Arnold J. Toynbee, "but a subjective psychological feeling in a living people."[45]

National self-determination means "the right of individuals to determine the sovereign state to which they would belong and the form of government under which they would live."[46] It is the principle by which nationalities justify their efforts to acquire "nationhood" in the form of "statehood"; within states, exalted and strengthened by sovereignty, they hope to find a new prestige and a new security. This right was

[40] See Louis L. Snyder, *The Meaning of Nationalism* (New Brunswick, N.J.: Rutgers University Press, 1954), Chapter II, "The Concept of the Nation." See also Pierre Renouvin, "The Contribution of France to the Study of International Relations," in *Contemporary Political Science,* UNESCO Publication No. 426; and Akzin, Chapter 3, "The Phenomenon of the Nation."

[41] *National Character and the Factors in Its Formation* (London, 1927), p. 17.

[42] Morgenthau, p. 160.

[43] Louis Wirth, "Types of Nationalism," *American Journal of Sociology,* XLI (May, 1936), 723.

[44] *Nationality in History and Politics,* 3d ed. (London, 1951), p. 12.

[45] *Nationality and War* (London, 1915), p. 13.

[46] Hayes, p. 10.

strongly championed by Woodrow Wilson, and it has inspired many movements, successful and unsuccessful, for national independence.

Patriotism is a familiar concept, commonly defined as love of country. From the historical point of view it is not necessarily associated with the nation-state. The addresses of Pericles to the Athenians, of Hannibal to the Carthaginians, of Cicero to the Romans are among the greatest examples of patriotic oratory. Today, however, patriotism, like nationalism, is associated almost exclusively with loyalty to the nation-state. It is capable of inspiring some of the finest of human sentiments, but it can become as intense and as narrow as that which prevailed among the city-states of ancient Greece — and infinitely more dangerous. In its exaggerated form it is known as *chauvinism*.

The Concept of Nationalism. The foremost modern students of nationalism, including Carlton J. H. Hayes and Hans Kohn, admitted that no satisfactory single definition is possible. Perhaps the most revealing clue to its nature is Hayes's statement that nationalism consists of "a modern emotional fusion and exaggeration of two very old phenomena — nationality and patriotism";[47] or, as Hans Kohn put it, "nationalism is first and foremost a state of mind, an act of consciousness."[48] In the twentieth century, as he observed in a subsequent work, nationalism became "the common form of political life all over the earth," but "everywhere nationalism differs in character according to the specific historic conditions and the peculiar social structure of each country" and because of the "stress upon national sovereignty and cultural distinctiveness" has become "a deeply divisive force." When it "spread to Eastern Europe and later to Asia . . . nationalism tended toward the closed society, in which the individual counted for less than the strength and authority of the national whole."[49]

Although he pointed out that "nationalism cannot be defined adequately in simple terms," Professor Louis L. Snyder advanced the following statement as "least objectionable":

> . . . nationalism, a product of political, economic, social, and intellectual factors at a certain stage in history, is a condition of mind, feeling, or sentiment of a group of people living in a well-defined geographical area, speaking a common language, possessing a literature in which the aspirations of the nation have been expressed, attached to common traditions and common customs, venerating its own heroes, and, in some cases, having a common religion.[50]

"Nationalism," said Snyder, "is neither wholly logical nor rational. Its roots lie in the illogical, irrational, and fantastic world of the unconscious." It is "in part a psychological response to grave threats of insecurity." Since it "is not innate instinct, but rather a socially conditioned, synthetic sentiment," it can hardly be understood without reference to the findings of psychology and

[47] Carlton J. H. Hayes, *Essays on Nationalism* (New York: The Macmillan Company, 1926), p. 6.

[48] Hans Kohn, *The Idea of Nationalism* (New York: The Macmillan Company, 1944), p. 10. Used by permission of The Macmillan Company. "The most essential and the only indispensable condition for the rise and growth of any nationalism is a living and active corporate will." Hans Kohn, "Nationalism and Internationalism in the Nineteenth and Twentieth Centuries," *Rapports — I. Grands Thèmes*, XIIe Congrès International des Sciences Historiques (Ferdinand Berger & Söhne, Horn and Vienna, 1965), p. 191.

[49] *Prophets and Peoples: Studies in Nineteenth Century Nationalism* (New York: The Macmillan Company, 1946), p. 4. Used by permission of The Macmillan Company. See also Hans Kohn, *Nationalism: Its Meaning and History* (Princeton, N.J.: D. Van Nostrand Co., 1955); Boyd C. Shafer, *Nationalism: Myth and Reality* (New York: Harcourt, Brace, 1955); and Snyder, *The Meaning of Nationalism*.

[50] Snyder, pp. 196–197.

psychoanalysis.[51] Here we have clear evidence of the importance of studying international relations from the points of view of all the behavioral sciences.[52]

The Dangers of Nationalism. In its origins modern nationalism was associated with democracy and liberty, and for some time it was believed that the relationship was more than a historical one. Now we know that nationalism, far from always promoting democracy and liberty, often places these blessings in jeopardy; that it has proved on occasion to be wholly compatible with autocracy and totalitarianism; that it tends, unless carefully watched, to restrict the area of human freedom, not to enlarge it. In a sense we should perhaps be grateful that nationalism and liberty are not necessarily coterminous; for the former may well be an ephemeral phenomenon in history, whereas we hope that the latter will long endure.

Because nationalism tends to degenerate into ever more intolerant forms and because it has been a major cause of war, it is generally condemned as an evil force. In the final chapter of his *Essays on Nationalism,* entitled "Nationalism: Curse or Blessing," Hayes distinguished between nationalism as a historical fact and nationalism as a belief. As a belief, he asserted, nationalism has been "a curse and nothing but a curse." Rabindranath Tagore, the Indian poet and philosopher, held that nationalism was a great menace because it called for a "strenuous effort after strength and efficiency" and thereby "drains man's energy from his higher nature where he is self-sacrificing and creative."[53] Arnold Toynbee's ten-volume work *A Study of History* contains many references to crimes committed in the name of the nation-state and of nationalism during the last three or four hundred years. Many students of nationalism have commented on its apparent tendency to exclusiveness and its incompatibility with international cooperation. Thus Vladimir Solovyev, a Russian philosopher of the nineteenth century, wrote about nationalism: "In its extreme form it destroys a nation, for it makes it the enemy of mankind."[54]

[51] *Ibid.*, pp. 89–110.

[52] An outstanding study which applies new techniques in the behavioral sciences to the analysis of nationalism is Karl W. Deutsch, *Nationalism and Social Communication: An Inquiry into the Foundations of Nationality* (New York: John Wiley & Sons, 1953). See also Karl W. Deutsch, *An Interdisciplinary Bibliography on Nationalism* (Cambridge, Mass.: The M.I.T. Press, 1956); and Karl W. Deutsch and William Foltz, eds., *Nation-Building* (New York: Atherton Press, 1963).

[53] Rabindranath Tagore, *Nationalism* (London, 1917), p. 110.

[54] From one of a series of articles on "The National Question in Russia," written about 1880; quoted in Kohn, *Prophets and People,* p. 205.

Justus in the Minneapolis Star

Whistling Past the Graveyard

Instruments and Symbols of Nationalism. Among the most powerful instruments for the propagation of nationalism are schools, the press, and the radio. In a totalitarian state these instruments are deliberately used to serve the state. Even in the free world nationalistic propaganda is widespread. The controls are more indirect, arising more out of the folkways and mores of the various societies than out of the pressures from governments, but they are nevertheless powerful. Most Americans, for example, would be surprised at the amount of nationalistic propaganda to be found in present-day textbooks in use in all schools, from the primary grades to the most advanced levels. But "when honest efforts are made to secure objectivity in history textbook writing, they meet with stiff resistance from powerful interest groups in most national communities. Under the guise of patriotism, such groups exert pressure upon ministries of education, school boards, and teachers in order to prevent a balanced treatment of the nation's relations with other countries."[55] Texts have been criticized as "un-American" because they gave too favorable treatment to unicameralism, social security, and, of course, the United Nations. A number of superpatriots have charged that UNESCO has become an organization for propagating ideas of world government which, if carried out, would strip the United States of her sovereignty. In some instances, as in Los Angeles, this campaign generated local pressures to prevent instruction in the public schools on the work of UNESCO.

Nationalism is propagated by the use of symbols and "social myths." Among the commonly used symbols have been patriotic slogans and songs, flags, uniforms, shrines and monuments, public spectacles, pageantry, and ritualism. Such symbols may serve very worthy ends — certainly love of country and belief in it are among the finest of human sentiments. But these same symbols may and do serve dangerous masters when they are used to deceive and to enslave, to instill hatred of other peoples and a false sense of the nation's "glory" and "destiny." "Integral nationalism has surpassed all its predecessors in rites and ceremonies, in mysticism and devotion, and likewise in intolerance."[56] This has been especially true of totalitarian nationalism. Fascist Italy, Nazi Germany, Communist Russia, and Communist China have demonstrated that the ugly face of despotism can be "glorified" by the cosmetics of nationalism.

Types or Stages of Nationalism. Although nationalism cannot be accurately defined, it does have divers forms which can be analyzed in different ways. One approach is to attempt to classify its types and stages. It has been described as "good" and "bad," constructive and destructive, material and spiritual, conscious and subconscious (or unconscious). Hans Kohn has drawn a most useful distinction between (1) nationalism in the Western world and (2) nationalism outside the Western world. This distinction calls attention to the very different forms which nationalism has assumed, and it helps to explain "the process of cultural influence and resistance in non-European areas."[57] Nationalism may also be studied on a country-by-country basis. But the most common and perhaps still most valuable approach is the chronological. This is followed in a number of rewarding studies by historians and students of international relations.[58]

[55] Sharp and Kirk, p. 121.

[56] Hayes, *Historical Evolution*, p. 299.

[57] Snyder, p. 121. See also pp. 118–120 for a summary of "the Kohn dichotomy" in outline form.

[58] The most complete analysis of the origins of nationalism is Kohn's *The Idea of Nationalism.* Among the best summaries of the historical evolution of nationalism are Hayes, *The Historical Evolution of Modern Nationalism;* Shafer, *Nationalism: Myth and Reality;* Kohn, *Nationalism: Its Meaning and History;* Kohn, *The Age of National-*

Many years ago Hayes described five principal successive types or stages of nationalism, which he labeled humanitarian, Jacobin, traditional, liberal, and integral. The first four types originated in the eighteenth century and took distinctive form in the period of the French Revolution and Napoleon and during the nineteenth century. Integral nationalism, primarily a growth of the twentieth century, has characterized the policies of totalitarian states, although some of its chief exponents were not conscious supporters of totalitarianism, and more than traces of it can be found in the policies of supposedly democratic states. A somewhat similar classification of the stages in the development of nationalism — though one which suggests an earlier development of the concept — is presented in Quincy Wright's monumental work, *A Study of War*.[59] Wright discussed in succession medieval, monarchical, revolutionary, liberal, and totalitarian nationalism. However, neither Hayes nor Wright singled out economic nationalism as one of the major types, although both were well aware of its importance, especially in connection with their fifth stage.

Professor Snyder discerned four stages in the chronology of nationalism. These he labeled integrative nationalism (1815–71), disruptive nationalism (1871–90), aggressive nationalism (1890–1945), and contemporary nationalism (since 1945). During the first stage nationalism was a unifying force, and found concrete expression in the unification of Italy and of Germany; during the second, subject nationalities of Austria-Hungary and other multinational states clamored for independence; during the third, "nationalism became virtually identical with aggressive imperialism," and the "collision of opposing national interests" led to two world wars; during the early years of the contemporary stage "political nationalism asserted itself in the form of widespread revolts again European masters," and communism "in its Stalinist form took on the trappings of nationalism in the Soviet Union."[60]

Nationalism During the French Revolution and the Napoleonic Era. While the roots of nationalism go far into the past, modern nationalism is a development of the past two centuries and is indissolubly associated with the nation-state system. "Modern nationalism," in the opinion of Hans Kohn, "originated in the seventeenth and eighteenth centuries in northwestern Europe and its American settlements. It became a general European movement in the nineteenth century,"[61] and "in the twentieth century it has become a world-wide movement."[62]

It is possible, of course, to find evidences of national feeling in the period when various nations were taking form; certainly the English, French, and Dutch were often motivated by real sentiments of nationality before 1500. As Quincy Wright indicates, this early "nationalism" was monarchical, for the concept of the nation as the body of citizens had little meaning. It was the French Revolution which, almost for the

---

ism: The First Era of Global History (New York: Harper & Row, 1962); and Kohn, "Nationalism and Internationalism in the Nineteenth and Twentieth Centuries."

[59] See the section on the evolution of nationalism in the chapter entitled "Nationalism and War," II, 1004–1009.

[60] Snyder, pp. 116–117. Snyder summarizes many classifications of nationalism by scholars in various disciplines. See Chapter V, "Classifications of Nationalism." For additional classifications, see Max Sylvius Handman, "The Sentiment of Nationalism," *Political Science Quarterly*, XXXVI, No. 1 (1921), 107–114; Harry Elmer Barnes, *The History of Western Civilization*, (New York: Harcourt, Brace, 1935), II, 453–456; Wirth, "Types of Nationalism"; and George Orwell, *England Your England and Other Essays* (London, 1953), pp. 55–62.

[61] Kohn, *Prophets and Peoples*, p. 3.

[62] Kohn, *Nationalism: Its Meaning and History*, Preface, p. 4.

first time, introduced the concept of popular democracy resting on the will of the people and on the rights of man and of the citizen.

The revolutions of the late eighteenth century — the Industrial, the American, and the French — were the seed-beds of most of the forms of nationalism of modern times. The period of the French Revolution and the Napoleonic Wars was particularly fruitful for the evolution of nationalism. This force became so strong that it could not be curbed; in a sense it turned against its creators, for it diverted the revolution into channels which were not charted, and it stimulated a reaction in other peoples of Europe against their French conquerors.

What was the character of the nationalism that emerged from the French Revolution? In some respects it was revolutionary and democratic. To it Professor Hayes applied the term "Jacobin"; but, as he admits, it was democratic in only a limited and functional way. Inevitably, Jacobin nationalism became more and more militaristic, and a creed that was democratic in origin provided an opportunity for the dictatorship of Napoleon, who, though himself not a nationalist, had raised the banner of nationalism and under it had led the armies of France over much of Europe, extinguishing the liberties of many other peoples in the course of his triumphal progress. Eventually he fell victim to the very force of nationalism "which his wars aroused abroad and which he did not understand."[63]

The nationalism which Napoleon evoked among his enemies was chiefly what Hayes has called "traditional nationalism." It was aristocratic, evolutionary, and conservative — the very antithesis of Jacobin nationalism. It sought to preserve rather than to destroy or change. But precisely because it regarded Jacobin nationalism with aversion, even with horror, it became itself as violent as the Jacobin variety in defense of the status quo as established by the Congress of Vienna.

63 *Ibid.*, p. 27.

Nationalism in the Nineteenth Century. The nineteenth century was the great age of nationalism, both in theory and in practice. More and more accepted as almost the natural order of things, nationalism developed a more popular base and won important victories. In Europe its greatest practical achievements were the unification of Germany and of Italy. Other European states, such as Greece and Belgium, won nationhood as a result of nationalistic uprisings, and agitation elsewhere, notably in Poland, Ireland, and the Austro-Hungarian Empire, demonstrated the intensity of national feelings. Nationalism, until then almost exclusively a European phenomenon, spread to other continents. The Spanish and Portuguese colonies in the New World won their independence, while in Asia the stirrings of national consciousness presaged the upheaval that is now revolutionizing the largest of the continents. In Japan, nationalism was becoming a powerful force by the turn of the century; it was one of the Western products which the Japanese adopted in order to build a state powerful enough to resist Western imperialism.

The nationalism of the greater part of the nineteenth century was linked with most of the other great movements and tendencies of that period; democracy, romanticism, industrialism, imperialism, and especially liberalism. In the generation following the Congress of Vienna liberal nationalism found solid support in the middle classes, whose power was growing with expanding industrialism. Reflecting the new democratic spirit astir in most countries, it championed individual and national freedom. This kind of nationalism, like so many of its exponents, was high-minded and pacifist; yet in a Europe still controlled by reactionaries these goals could not be achieved by peaceful means. Liberal nationalism failed in that "it could not realize its ideal of basing the state system of Europe on the principle of nationality without sacrificing its ideal of pacifism. . . . So fighting became the practical means of transforming cultural into political nationalism."[64]

As the nineteenth century waned, so too did liberal nationalism. "The changing concept and meaning of nationalism between 1840 and 1890 is striking: at the latter time nationalism had ceased to be regarded as a democratic-revolutionary movement of the people; it became a predominantly conservative or reactionary movement, frequently representing the upper classes against the people, and it was strongly opposed to all internationalism. Its ideal was by the end of the century an exclusive, self-centered, closed society." Furthermore, "economy and biology entered the conceptual arsenal of nationalism, which until then had been political and cultural."[65]

The late nineteenth and early twentieth centuries brought growing rivalries among the great powers — rivalries for trade, for industrial, military, and naval supremacy, for allies, and for colonies in the great imperialist scramble. More and more the state assumed functions previously outside its scope. The reasons for this portentous development were at least two: in the first place, there was a growing demand for the protection of the economic and social interests of the individual; and, second, the state began to require more from its people as the price of maintaining its prestige and status in the face of pressures from within and rivalries from without. In the twentieth century its activities in some instances extended to the all-encompassing operations of monolithic totalitarianism.

Nationalism in the Twentieth Century. In the halcyon years before the outbreak of World War I, many people believed that whereas the nineteenth century had been an age of nationalism, the twentieth century would be an age of internationalism. These hopes have obviously not been realized. Instead, in the twentieth century nationalism has assumed particularly virulent forms. It has continued to shape the international politics of the Western world; it has become a worldwide phenomenon, attaining new heights of emotionalism and significance in the newly emergent states of Asia and Africa; and it has achieved a curious kind of linkage with international communism.

Nationalism was one of the underlying causes of the First World War, as Sidney B. Fay and other students of the origins of the war demonstrated. It was, in fact, both a cause and a product of the war. This point was brought home by Professor Hayes:

> Nationalism paved the way of statesmen and prepared the mind of peoples for the World War. . . . Its immediate cause was the murderous activity of a secret nationalistic society of Jugoslavs. Its fighting was done by "nations in arms," whose morale was sustained by nationalist propaganda. . . . Its most obvious immediate result was the triumph of the principle of national self-determination in central and eastern Europe. The last of the non-national empires on the continent were shattered — the Austrian, the Russian and the Ottoman — and from their ruins were constructed new or enlarged national states. . . . The World War not only issued from nationalism but led to a more intense nationalism. In Europe the newest national states almost instantly passed from liberal pronouncements to illiberal conduct and speedily vied with older national states in establishing nationalist tariffs, armies, schools, and other agencies of propaganda and in discriminating socially if not legally against dissident minorities.[66]

1. Totalitarian Nationalism. In the years following World War I the facade of internationalism, built across the world stage

[64] Carlton J. H. Hayes, "Nationalism," *Encyclopaedia of the Social Sciences* (New York: The Macmillan Company, 1937), XI, 245. Used by permission of The Macmillan Company.

[65] Kohn, "Nationalism and Internationalism in the Nineteenth and Twentieth Centuries," pp. 201, 206.

[66] Hayes, "Nationalism," p. 247.

by the League of Nations and by such agreements as the Locarno and Kellogg pacts, proved to be frail indeed. Fascism gained power in Italy only three years after Versailles, in Germany and Japan in the early thirties, and in Spain in 1936. In fascism the world witnessed the first lush flowering of modern totalitarianism, bringing a form of nationalism more powerful, more encompassing, more brutal, and more dangerous than any previous variety. "Though this fascist nationalism took various forms in different countries, according to their national traditions and social structures, it represented in all its forms a total repudiation of the liberal ideas of the seventeenth and eighteenth century revolutions, of the rights of the individual and of the desirability of a rational international order based upon the equality of men and nations. . . . Nationalism in its fascist period . . . assumed far beyond anything known in the period before 1914, an absolutist and extremist self-assertiveness, glorifying war between nations or races as the supreme and final meaning of life and history."[67] Eventually this type of nationalism culminated in World War II.

Since the defeat of the Axis powers in World War II, fascism has faded before another form of totalitarian nationalism, Communist totalitarianism. To speak of communism as a form of totalitarian nationalism may seem to be a contradiction in terms, since communism, unlike fascism, is presumably an international and not a national gospel. In practice, however, both within and outside the Communist world, communism has become increasingly nationalistic. The Soviet rulers have posed as champions of nationalism in Asia and as enemies of colonialism and imperialism, and they have had considerable success in identifying communism with nationalistic aspirations. Native Communist leaders have identified themselves with nationalist movements, or they have made profitable use of them; they have scored notable successes in Indo-China, Korea, and, above all, China. The Chinese Communists succeeded in taking over the nationalist revolution that had been under way ever since it had overthrown the Manchu dynasty in 1911–12; and they still pose as national leaders who favor independence from foreign exploitation and domination.

During World War II, when German armies were occupying the western part of Russia, the Russian people were exhorted to rise up in defense of "Mother Russia" — not of communism or world revolution. Soviet rulers have constantly warned of the danger of "foreign encirclement." In the postwar years the Soviet government encouraged the nationalism of Russia's many minorities, permitting their cultural, political, and economic institutions to be "national" in form as long as they are "proletarian" in spirit and substance. In the satellite states of Eastern Europe it encouraged dissident nationalist groups even while extinguishing the liberties and independence of those countries.

When Tito was denounced by the Cominform for his heresies, and when he assumed a position of open defiance of the Kremlin, a startling phenomenon appeared: a Communist state which was apparently more nationalist than Communist. Since his open break with the rest of the Communist world, Tito has relied primarily on Yugloslav nationalism, but in part also on increasing assistance from non-Communist states. Elsewhere in the Communist world communism has gone national.[68] Indeed, polycentrism within the Communist orbit has been one of the major new developments in contemporary international relations.

2. Integral Nationalism. The kind of

[67] Kohn, "Nationalism and Internationalism in the Nineteenth and Twentieth Centuries," p. 210.

[68] See William G. Carleton, "Is Communism Going National?" *The Virginia Quarterly Review*, XXV (Summer, 1949), 321–334; and Kohn, *Nationalism: Its Meaning and History*, p. 90.

nationalism which has been begotten by the totalitarian states seems to be so phenomenal and so all-pervasive that some authorities believe that it is fundamentally different from anything known before and that it represents the characteristic form of nationalism of the twentieth century. Hans Morgenthau has insisted that there is a basic difference between the nationalism of the nineteenth century and the "nationalistic universalism" of today:

> To call by the same name what inspired the oppressed and competing nationalities of the nineteenth century and what drives the superpowers of the mid-twentieth century into deadly combat, is to obscure the fundamental change which separates our age from the preceding one. The nationalism of today, which is really a nationalistic universalism, has only one thing in common with the nationalism of the nineteenth century — the nation as the ultimate point of reference for political loyalties and actions. But here the similarity ends. For the nationalism of the nineteenth century the nation is the ultimate goal of political action, the endpoint of the political development beyond which there are other nationalisms with similar and equally justifiable goals. For the nationalistic universalism of the mid-twentieth century the nation is but the starting point of a universal mission whose ultimate goal reaches to the confines of the political world. While nationalism wants one nation in a state and nothing else, the nationalistic universalism of our age claims for one nation and one state the right to impose its own valuations and standards of action upon all the other nations.[69]

Morgenthau presents an interesting thesis, but why should nationalism connote exclusively the totalitarian type? It could be argued that Morgenthau's "nationalistic universalism" is not nationalism at all but a peculiar interpretation of the foreign policy objectives of the superpowers.

[69] Morgenthau, p. 337.

Unique though it is, totalitarian nationalism has stemmed from the age of nationalism and of the nation-state system.[70] It is the extreme and perhaps logical end-product of what Hayes and others, borrowing from Charles Maurras and Maurice Barres, have called "integral nationalism," the characteristic form of the twentieth century. Maurras himself once described integral nationalism as "the exclusive pursuit of national policies, the absolute maintenance of national integrity, and the steady increase of national power — for a nation declines when it loses military might."[71]

3. Nationalism and Internationalism Since World War II. The twentieth century has thus proved to be another age of nationalism. Not only has nationalism expanded to the emerging countries of Asia and Africa; it survives in the Western world where it bedevils efforts to formulate common defense or economic policies and surges in time of crisis. The reactions in Britain and France

[70] What Sharp and Kirk wrote in 1940 about fascist nationalism can be applied to totalitarian nationalism in general: "Today, with the democratic countries definitely on the defensive against the menace of fascist aggression, a superficial view of the situation might easily lead to the assumption that fascist nationalism has little or nothing in common with the national state of mind now prevalent under democracy. But a more thorough examination of the factors that have produced fascism, considered along with the historic connection between democracy and the principle of nationality, suggests that the seeds of fascist internationalism are inherent in a state system which has made of national sovereignty a political fetish." Sharp and Kirk, p. 143.

[71] Quoted in Hayes, *Historical Evolution*, p. 165 "Charles Maurras (1868–1952) and Maurice Barrès (1862–1923) first formulated clearly the principle of integral nationalism which rejected humanitarian liberalism as old-fashioned in favor of exclusive national self-interest and speedy decisive action." Kohn, *Nationalism: Its Meaning and History*, p. 74. See a brilliant essay on "Charles Maurras: The Politics of Hate," written by D. W. Brogan in 1944 and reprinted in his *French Personalities and Problems* (New York: Alfred A. Knopf, 1947), pp. 117–128. Another excellent essay in the same volume deals with "Maurice Barrès: The Progress of a Nationalist."

during the Suez crisis of 1956 and in the United States during the Cuban crises of 1961 and 1962 evinced deep nationalistic emotions. General de Gaulle is an unabashed champion of French nationalism, and for the people of both East and West Germany the reunification of the German nation remains an aspiration that refuses to fade despite years of division.

At the same time the twentieth century is also an era of increasing interdependence and internationalism. This is particularly true of the period since the end of World War II. "The nationalism of the post-1945 era is in many ways different from that of 1900. It regards itself as compatible with international or supranational organizations; it knows of the interdependence brought about by recent technological changes. . . . Nationalism has assumed again in most countries, and not only in the 'new' countries, the populist and revolutionary character which it had before 1848."[72]

Today, as Professor Kohn has observed, "we are living in the age of pan-nationalism on all continents." It is therefore hardly surprising that nationalism has assumed so many different forms. These range from Communist patterns and ultra-nationalistic forms to constructive associations of national and international trends and movements.

What role will nationalism play in future years? "Undoubtedly, it is a divisive force in a world growing more and more interdependent, a force capable of producing bitter tensions and one-sided, selfrighteous judgments that threaten the rational solution of international conflicts." But "today the possibility is growing that . . . the age of nationalism and of warring nation-states" may be transformed "into an age of an uneasy but on the whole peaceful coexistence of nationalism with their various civilizations, traditions, and ideologies, which, like everything in history, are subject to change and transformation."[73]

Great Destructive-Constructive Forces

We have attempted an analysis of the nature and evolution of the nation-state system and of two of its corollaries — sovereignty and nationalism. We have noted that sovereignty is the legal theory which sustains the state and the state system, and that nationalism is the moving spiritual or emotional force of the state. Both have been invoked to strengthen the authority of absolute monarchs, and both have tended to encourage rather than retard the totalitarian movements of our own day. They have led to wars and to international anarchy; they are perhaps the most formidable barriers to international peace and the building of a true world community.

On the other hand, the doctrines of sovereignty and nationalism have given strength and cohesion to the prevailing pattern of international society. They have been flexible doctrines, evolving through the years as conditions have changed and giving rise to many schools of interpreters. They have been used in the interests of democracy and liberalism, as well as in those of absolutism and totalitarianism. Actually they are neither moral nor immoral doctrines. There is nothing inherently evil about them. They are not vast cosmic forces moving inexorably to encompass the doom of mankind. D. W. Brogan called nationalism "this great destructive, constructive force," and the same label could be attached to sovereignty. If uncontrolled or misused, both can lead to tyranny and war; but if directed to constructive purposes they can evoke some of the finest of human sentiments for the service of worthy ends. They are vital parts of the machinery that men have created to regulate their relations; and they reflect rather than constitute the really basic problems in international affairs.

[72] Kohn, "Nationalism and Internationalism in the Nineteenth and Twentieth Centuries," pp. 219–220.

[73] *Ibid.*, pp. 239, 240.

SUGGESTIONS FOR FURTHER READING

AKZIN, BENJAMIN. *State and Nation.* London, 1964. A perceptive study by an Israeli scholar.

CARR, E. H. *International Relations Between the Two World Wars, 1919–1939.* London, 1948.

Nationalism and After. New York: The Macmillan Company, 1945. Foresees a regional nationalism.

CHAMBERS, FRANK P. *This Age of Conflict: The Western World, 1914 to the Present,* 3d ed. New York: Harcourt, Brace and World, 1962.

COHEN, H. E. *Recent Theories of Sovereignty.* Chicago: University of Chicago Press, 1937.

COX, RICHARD H., ed. *The State in International Relations.* San Francisco: Chandler Publishing Company, 1965. Varied readings on the attributes, purposes, and forms of states.

DEUTSCH, KARL W. *An Interdisciplinary Bibliography on Nationalism, 1935–1953.* Cambridge, Mass.: The M.I.T. Press, 1956. A useful list of interdisciplinary research on nationalism, but obviously not up-to-date.

Nationalism and Social Communication. New York: John Wiley & Sons, 1953. A difficult but important interdisciplinary analysis. Excellent bibliography.

DEUTSCH, KARL W. and WILLIAM FOLTZ, eds. *Nation-Building.* New York: Atherton Press, 1963. Based on a panel discussion at the annual meeting of the American Political Science Association, September, 1962.

GROSS, FELIKS. *European Ideologies: A Survey of 20th Century Political Ideas.* New York: Philosophical Library, 1948.

HAYES, CARLTON J. H. *Essays on Nationalism.* New York: The Macmillan Company, 1926.

The Historical Evolution of Modern Nationalism. New York: The Macmillan Company, 1948. A seminal work.

Nationalism: A Religion. New York: The Macmillan Company, 1960.

HAYES, CARLTON J. H., MARSHALL W. BALDWIN, and CHARLES W. COLE. *History of Europe.* 2 vols. New York: The Macmillan Company, 1949. Good on the rise of the state system and on modern international relations.

HINSLEY, F. H. *Sovereignty.* New York: Basic Books, 1966.

HOLBORN, HAJO. *The Political Collapse of Europe.* New York: Alfred A. Knopf, 1951. Argues that the old European order passed with World War II.

HOLLAND, WILLIAM, ed. *Asian Nationalism and the West.* New York: The Macmillan Company, 1953. An international symposium based on papers and reports of the 11th conference of the Institute of Pacific Relations.

JOUVENEL, BERTRAND DE. *Sovereignty: An Inquiry into the Political Good.* Chicago: University of Chicago Press, 1957.

KOHN, HANS. *The Age of Nationalism: The First Era of Global History.* New York: Harper & Row, 1962. A survey of the period 1789–1961.

American Nationalism. New York: The Macmillan Company, 1957.

The Idea of Nationalism. New York: The Macmillan Company, 1944. A study of the origins of nationalism, by a leading authority.

Nationalism: Its Meaning and History. Princeton, N.J.: D. Van Nostrand Co., 1955. An excellent brief introduction.

Prophets and Peoples: Studies in Nineteenth Century Nationalism. New York: The Macmillan Company, 1946.

KOHN, HANS and WALTER SOKOLSKY. *African Nationalism in the Twentieth Century.* Princeton, N.J.: D. Van Nostrand Co., 1964.

LASKI, HAROLD J. *The Problem of Sovereignty.* Cambridge, Mass.: Harvard University Press, 1916. A statement of the pluralist approach.

MARITAIN, JACQUES. *Man and the State*. Chicago: University of Chicago Press, 1951. Chapter 2: "The Concept of Sovereignty."

Nationalism. New York: Augustus M. Kelley, Publishers, 1966. Report of a Study Group of the Royal Institute of International Affairs, London.

AL-RAZZAZ, MUNIF. *The Evolution of the Meaning of Nationalism*. Garden City, N.Y.: Doubleday & Company, 1963. Gives special attention to Arab nationalism.

SCHUMAN, FREDERICK. *International Politics; the Western State System and the World Community*, 6th ed. New York: McGraw-Hill Book Company, 1958.

SETON-WATSON, HUGH. *Nationalism and Communism; Essays, 1946–1963*. New York: Frederick A. Praeger, 1964.

SHAFER, BOYD. *Nationalism: Myth and Reality*. New York: Harcourt, Brace, 1955.

SILVERT, K. H., ed. *Expectant Peoples; Nationalism and Development*. New York: Random House, 1963.

SNYDER, LOUIS L. *The Meaning of Nationalism*. New Brunswick, N.J.: Rutgers University Press, 1954. A comprehensive survey of various approaches to the study of nationalism.

———. *The New Nationalism*. Ithaca: Cornell University Press, 1968.

"Sovereignty in the Present Day World," *The Indian Journal of Political Science*, XXV (July–September–December, 1964), Section I. A series of 12 articles.

2 National Power: Land and Its Resources

Like sovereignty and nationalism, national power is a vital and inseparable feature of the state system. Power of some kind is the means by which states implement their policies, domestic as well as foreign. All states possess power, but very different amounts and kinds of power. We must therefore approach an analysis of power in international relations with the realization that we are dealing with a complex subject.

Our discussion here will center on three aspects of national power. First, we shall answer the question why states are so much concerned with power, why the cultivation of national power is a corollary of the nation-state system. Second, we shall consider the various forms of national power. Third, we shall point out the elements or factors of national power, indicating why some states are strong and others weak. The first two of these we shall discuss only briefly, reserving most of our attention for an analysis of the factors of national power, both tangible and intangible.

The Corollary of National Power

To say that states possess power is to say what everybody knows and what many people deplore. Yet power is an essential element of politics; "the struggle for power," says Morgenthau, "is universal in time and space and is an undeniable fact of experience."[1] Some writers insist that "power politics" is a redundancy — that there is no politics without power. This seems to be particularly the case in international relations. But the "power" aspects of international politics are often characterized as an evil which should be minimized, or even exorcised, if international cooperation and world peace are to be achieved. In his address at the ceremonies in San Francisco commemorating the twentieth anniversary of the signing of the United Nations Charter, on June 26, 1965, Secretary-General U Thant declared:

> The greatest obstacle to the realization of the Charter is the inescapable fact that power politics still operates, both overtly and covertly, in international relations. The concept of power politics, whether as the instrument of nationalism or of ideological extremism, is the natural enemy of international order as envisaged in the Charter. It is also an expensive, and potentially disastrous, anachronism.

Yet states are inexorably driven to the struggle for power simply because they wish to survive. As Reinhold Niebuhr has pointed out, there is "no possibility of drawing a sharp line between the will-to-live and the

[1] Hans J. Morgenthau, *Politics Among Nations*, 3d ed. (New York: Alfred A. Knopf, 1962), p. 33.

will-to-power."[2] Of course power may be mobilized beyond the peaceful requirements of states, and it may be abused and misused, but the wrongful use of power does not in itself destroy the need of states to possess power; in fact, the evil use of power by some states is the best reason why other states must have power.

Viewed historically, the fact of state power antedated the formulation of the theory of sovereignty. What Bodin and other political philosophers did was to recognize a *fait accompli* and offer ethical justification for what had already happened. Once states had assumed the obligation of promoting the welfare of their peoples and, of course, of their rulers, they rejected all external controls and endeavored to marshal whatever strength was felt to be necessary to implement policies designed to serve the state, or, at least, the dominant group within the state. But sovereignty did more than underwrite the past and the present; its affirmation of the omnipotence of the state amounted to a clear declaration of the right and duty of states to be strong enough to maintain themselves. It served notice that thenceforth states would be weak at their own peril: a sovereignty that disallowed the means of its own preservation would be no sovereignty at all. Not only had national power become legally correct; the conditions of international life made it mandatory. Predatory forces outside the state posed a constant threat, and what is perhaps more important, interests within the state — king, nobles, the clergy, or the rising commercial classes — demanded policies tailored to their own taste and profit and often were able to commit the power of the state to the execution of those policies. National power is too effective to lie around unused; there is seldom a dearth of those who would use it, perhaps in good causes, perhaps in bad.

The authority of the state differs from every other earthly authority in that it alone has no theoretical limit. All other organizations — industrial corporations, labor unions, churches, fraternal orders, patriotic societies, professional bodies, and the like — have sanctions of their own, often very effective ones. But only the state — not the government, by any means — knows no limits to its rights of coercion. In this respect the state is *sui generis* — in a class by itself. All other organizations may come up against legal barriers built and manned by the state. That the state should set the limits of power exercised by internal groups follows logically from the fact that the state itself creates, validates, and sustains the legal framework into which they must fit. "State power," wrote one authority, "towers above the power exercised by smaller pluralistic groupings in that it controls the system of law which is set up and perpetuated by state organs."[3] It might be added that the security function of the state may require that its power also tower above the power of those states that would assail it. And, as Bertrand Russell remarked, "nothing but lack of military force limits the power of one state over another."[4]

The legal justification of a state's power is to be found in the concept of sovereignty; the ethical defense is to be sought in the responsibility imposed on the state for seeing to the security of its people and their interests. The nature of power, its propensity to rush into and occupy every nook and crevice, is to be explained partly by the diligence of states in striving to enhance their security — power being regarded as the best assurance of security in the present nation-state system — and partly by a natural impulse to power. In his interesting study of

[2] *Moral Man and Immoral Society* (New York: Charles Scribner's Sons, 1933), p. 42.

[3] Herman Heller, "Political Power," *Encyclopaedia of the Social Sciences* (New York: The Macmillan Company, 1937), XII, 301. Used by permission of The Macmillan Company.

[4] Bertrand Russell, *Power* (New York: W. W. Norton & Company, 1938), p. 180.

power, Russell said that "every man would like to be God, if it were possible; some few find it difficult to admit the impossibility."[5] Whether, among states, the urge to power is to be attributed primarily to this same impulse to omnipotence or simply to political realism hardly warrants debate — the pattern of international life points the way to the grave for the impotent.

There is, however, another side to the picture. About half a century ago a distinguished English student of international relations, G. Lowes Dickinson, pointed out the "absurdity" of the reliance of every state on power. In answer to the question "Why must the State be strong?" he found that the usual answer is "to defend itself from attack." He then commented in these words:

> This looks sound enough. But meantime people in every other country are reasoning in precisely the same way. So that the doctrine, looked at all round, amounts to this: "The only way to keep the peace is for every State at the same time to be stronger than every other." The maxim thus becomes a flat absurdity as soon as every nation adopts it. But every nation does adopt it; with the result that you get an endless competition in armaments, an increasing strain, mental, moral, and physical, and finally, and in consequence of that strain, a breakdown into war. This is the plain truth of the matter.[6]

Forms of National Power

According to Professor Hans J. Morgenthau, power in a political context means "the power of man over the minds and actions of other men."[7] Georg Schwarzenberger defined it as the "capacity to impose one's will on others by reliance on effective sanctions in case of non-compliance."[8] He distinguished it from both influence and force by regarding it as containing a threat not present in influence and yet stopping short of the actual use of force. This distinction is uncommon if not unique; most authorities use the word to cover the whole range of pressures on thought and conduct, from those without the shadow of a threat to those involving total war. It is consistent with this use to speak of the power of an example, the power of public opinion, and the power of the sword. It is in this inclusive sense that we shall use the word.

As E. H. Carr pointed out, "in its essence, power is an indivisible whole"; and, while it must be somehow divided to permit an intelligible discussion, all theoretical divisions must be made with the realization that "it is difficult in practice to imagine a country for any length of time possessing one kind of power in isolation from the others."[9] Thus a state having the industrial establishment to sustain great military power is likely to be in a position to make effective use of devices of economic coercion, and military and economic power give strength to moral suasion, even when there is no suggestion of their use. Since military power is the ultimate and most violent kind of force that may be invoked, its use naturally implies parallel efforts to paralyze the enemy's economy, weaken his morale, and turn third states against him. The absence of war, on the other hand, does not mean the absence of all coercion. Even friendly states try to induce each other to pursue certain policies, just as friendly individuals do, and they may use milder forms of economic pressure without disrupting their good relations.

For purposes of analysis national power may be divided in a number of ways, all of

[5] *Ibid.*, p. 11.

[6] Reprinted by permission of Dodd, Mead & Company and Allen & Unwin, Ltd., from *The Choice Before Us* by G. Lowes Dickinson (copyright 1919), pp. 90–92.

[7] Morgenthau, p. 101.

[8] *Power Politics* (New York: Frederick A. Praeger, 1951), p. 14.

[9] E. H. Carr, *The Twenty Years' Crisis*, 2d ed. (London, 1946), p. 108.

them more or less arbitrary. Carr divided it into three categories: military power, economic power, and power over opinion. The paramount importance of military power lies in the fact that it is the end-argument, the last word, the final court of appeal. "Every act of the state, in its power aspect, is directed to war, not as a desirable weapon but as a weapon which it may require in the last resort to use."[10] Thus national power is in the final analysis military power, but military power is a complex of many elements. "The enemy's capacity to wage war must be viewed, therefore, within the context of his over-all political power, and that political power must be seen in the context of the society as a whole, with regard to the sources of that power."[11]

Economic power is inseparable from military power, for it is one of its basic components; to say that under conditions of modern warfare economic power is military power is only a slight exaggeration. But economic power is not limited to its part in the building of a military machine. Control of markets, raw materials, credits, and transportation is another form.

Power over opinion — now usually spoken of as propaganda, though perhaps not quite the same thing — encompasses the building of national morale at home, psychological warfare abroad, and the fight for moral leadership everywhere. It too is inseparable from other forms of national power, for it is always used to stimulate domestic production, fighting spirit, and the willingness to sacrifice; and it is used abroad to recruit allies and weaken the enemy. Thus it seeks to influence opinion both at home and abroad, and in some instances world opinion as well — although it is probably true, as Walter Trohan has claimed, that in many instances what is called "world opinion is a mythical thing, largely manufactured in foreign offices in various nations to advance their own policy."[12] Carr wrote that power over opinion is "not less essential for political purposes than military and economic power."[13] Closely related to it is political warfare.

Diplomacy also may be regarded as a form of national power, although some writers prefer to list it as an element. It may be argued that diplomacy provides only a channel for intercourse among states — that its effectiveness depends upon a state's military, economic, and propaganda resources; but this contention seems hardly valid. Diplomacy may make effective use of the power of a state, or it may tend to neutralize that power. Through astute diplomacy a relatively weak state, in power-political terms, may enhance its influence and position in world affairs out of proportion to its actual power. The wit and wisdom of a Talleyrand or a Franklin may give a state an influence unwarranted by all other factors. When this happens, diplomacy is certainly both a source and a form of national power.

So that we may better understand the nature of national power, we shall devote the remainder of the present chapter and all of the following one to an examination of its elements or ingredients. Then in the five succeeding chapters we shall describe the ways in which various forms of power — diplomacy, propaganda, and political warfare, economic policy, imperialism and colonialism, and war — are used as instruments of national policy.

The Elements of National Power

Everyone can see that atom bombs and armies make for power, and most people can readily understand that cotton and rubber do the same. Power becomes less tan-

[10] *Ibid.*, p. 109.

[11] Gene Sharp, "'The Political Equivalent of War' — Civilian Defense," *International Conciliation*, No. 515 (November, 1965), p. 22.

[12] Walter Trohan, "Report from Washington," *Chicago Tribune*, January 10, 1966.

[13] Carr, p. 132.

gible, however, when we speak of it in terms of geography, technology, and morale. Nevertheless, these are highly important elements of national power. All elements, moreover, are interrelated; for instance, oil without engineers is almost valueless, and so is radio without ideas. The interdependence of all the elements is so complete that actually power is indivisible. Furthermore, the separate elements of national power defy statistical calculation, and even if we could assign a figure to each one the grand total of these values would still fail to give us a correct appraisal of national power. Professor William Ebenstein explained this by noting that important qualitative factors are involved:

> In the field of international relations, the central problem of the strength of a nation is essentially a problem of qualitative judgment and measurement, as national power is more than the sum total of population, raw materials and quantitative factors. The "alliance potential" of a nation, its civic devotion, the flexibility of its institutions, its technical "know-how," its capacity to endure privations — these are but a few qualitative elements that determine the total strength of a nation.[14]

We shall here forego any attempt to measure national power. Instead we shall simply discuss its elements so that we may better understand the great differentials in power that partially explain the differing roles which states play in world politics. We shall divide power into seven component elements. Two of these — those relating to land and its resources — we shall discuss in the present chapter. The remaining five, which relate to people, their ways of doing things, and their ways of thinking, we shall examine in the following chapter. Four of the elements — geography, raw materials and natural resources, population, and technology — are tangible, and can to some extent be assessed in quantitative terms. The remaining three — ideologies, morale, and leadership — are intangible, but nonetheless important. Many other elements, such as military power and the quality of a nation's diplomacy, could also be examined. Diplomacy, as has been pointed out, will be considered as an instrument of national policy. In terms of potential, military power is not so much an element, in a basic sense, as an end-product of more fundamental aspects of national power, whereas in terms of power-in-being it is a tangible but unreliable index of a nation's real power.

Geography

The importance of geography to a study of international relations has long been recognized. History has often been characterized as geography in motion. Napoleon once said that "the foreign policy of a country is determined by its geography." This may be an exaggeration, but there can be no question that geographical factors have had a decisive effect upon civilizations and upon national development. The "shrinking" of the world with modern means of transportation and communication has increased interdependence among peoples and has brought them into closer contact in a variety of ways. A basic knowledge of political, economic, and human geography, as well as of physical geography, is essential to an understanding of the present-day world.

In this section, after a brief comment on maps and map projections, we shall refer to the geographic factors of size, location, climate, shape, topography, and boundaries. We shall also consider the significance of geographic factors in the air age, and we shall also discuss geopolitics, which is the application of geography for particular purposes and in particular ways.

[14] "Toward International Collaboration in Political Science: A Report on the UNESCO Project, 'Methods in Political Science,'" *American Political Science Review*, XLII (December, 1948), 1183–1184.

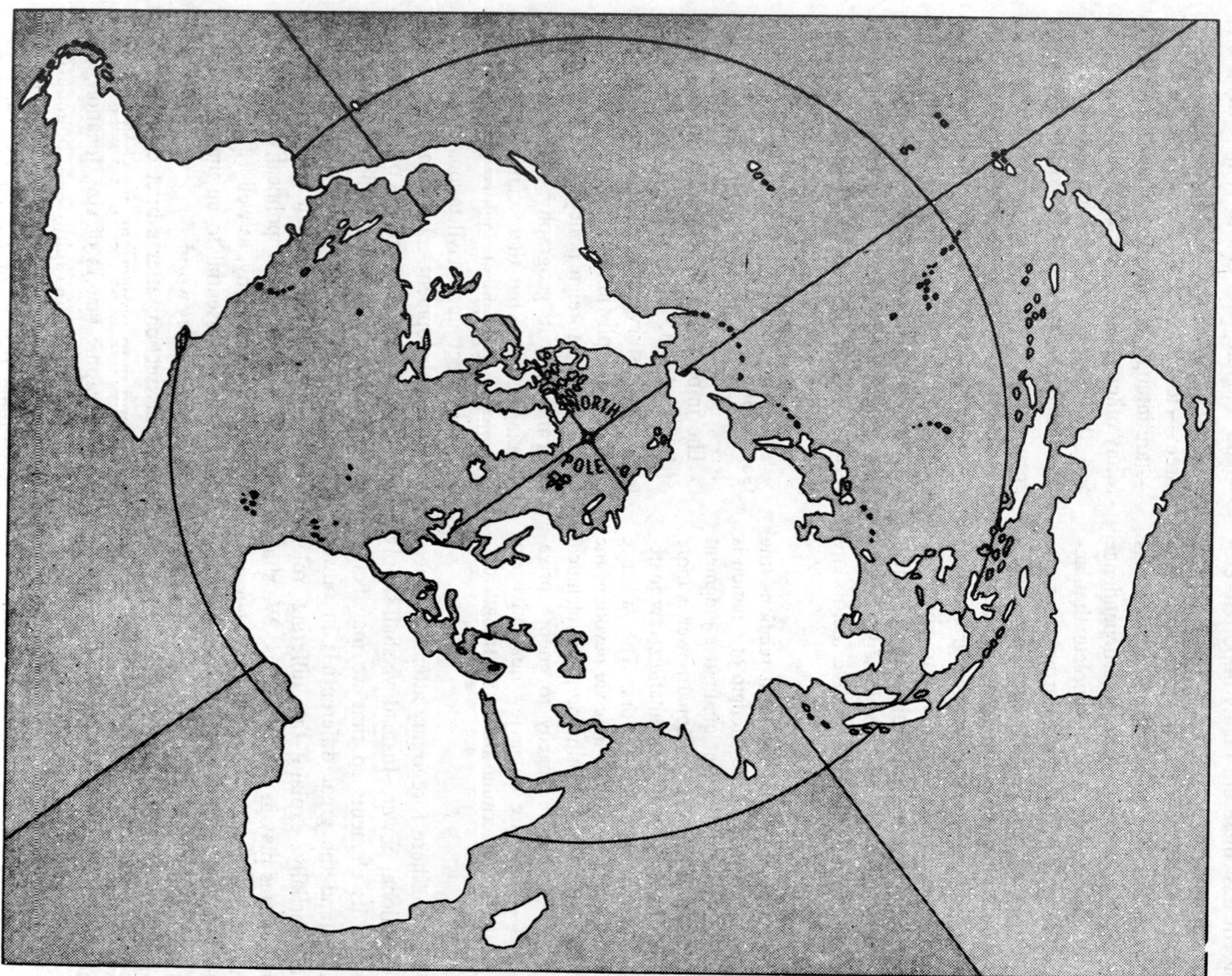

Russell H. Lenz. Adapted by permission from the Christian Science Monitor

Azimuthal Equidistant Projection, Centered on North Pole

Maps and Map Projections. Maps are indispensable tools for the study of international relations, and a knowledge of different types of map projections and the uses and limitations of each type can be of great value. Most of us were brought up in a Mercator world; that is to say, we were taught to think of the world as it looks on maps using the Mercator projection. On this familiar projection meridians of longitude and parallels of latitude are shown as straight lines crossing each other at right angles. This type of projection is still the best map for surface navigation, for by it a compass course between any two points can be shown by a straight line. But it does not show the relative size of different parts of the world, and the distortions become greater the farther one moves away from the Equator. For this reason Greenland on a Mercator map looks even larger than South America, although actually it is only about one-tenth as large. The United States seems to be isolated from all countries outside the Western Hemisphere by great oceans and by the distant Arctic regions. This is an increasingly unfortunate misconception. For a long time the oceans have been as much highways as barriers, and in the air age the Arctic regions have become the shortest avenue between the United States and many places in Europe, the Soviet Union, and Asia.

For the air age different map projections are needed.

> The map which shows us the actual relationships of the earth's areas from any given point is one with a rather frightening name. It is called an 'Azimuthal Equidistant' projection. In simple language, that merely means a map which is centered on a definite spot on the globe, and on which the distance to any or all other points on the globe can be accurately measured. On this map, the straight line connecting the center of the map with any other point on the globe is really a 'great circle,' which is the shortest distance between those two points.[15]

There are of course many different maps of this type but the most common is one on which the North Pole is the center.

Many other types of map projections have been developed to meet particular needs. Equal-area maps are useful for comparing areas or the distribution of, say, population or raw materials and natural resources. For studying hemispheres the orthographic projection is usually satisfactory. The Royal Geographic Society, the National Geographic Society, and other professional associations of geographers have acquired great ingenuity in adapting the basic types of map projections to special purposes. We should remember that no map is wholly satisfactory, and that the purpose for which a map is to be used may determine to a large degree the proper type of projection.[16]

Size. The land area of a state is in itself an element of power, small or great. Its mere size implies little about its capacity to sustain a large population, as witness the Sahara Desert on the one hand and Belgium or Japan on the other. Whether it can be too small to exert effective power depends upon a host of other factors, as, for instance, location, fertility, rainfall, the temper of its people, the nature of its technology, and the quality of its leadership. Thus Japan was not too small to defeat Russia in the Russo-Japanese War of 1904–5. Russia's immensity was a handicap, for it impeded the concentration of her armies and supplies in distant Siberia. For the same reasons it was

[15] *Maps — and How to Understand Them*, 2d ed. (Consolidated Vultee Aircraft, 1943), pp. 11–12.

[16] See Richard Edes Harrison and Robert Strausz-Hupé, "Maps, Strategy, and World Politics," in *The Smithsonian Institution Report for 1943* (Washington, D.C.: Government Printing Office, 1944), pp. 253–258; and two publications by the National Geographic Society: Wellman Chamberlin, *The Round Earth on Flat Paper: Map Projections Used by Cartographers;* and Gilbert Grosvenor, *Map Services of the National Geographic Society.*

an initial disadvantage for her when Hitler attacked in June, 1941. On the other hand, size operated to her eventual advantage in Napoleon's invasion in 1812 and again in World War II by permitting long retreat, complicating the enemy's supply problem, and precluding effective occupation. She was able to trade space for time, just as China did when Japan attacked in 1937. Although size certainly affects the conduct of both defensive and offensive warfare, the extent of that effect is obviously related to other factors, such as efficiency of transportation, the disposition of troops, the weather, and the foresight of diplomatic and military leaders. Short of war, great size may in itself be an asset, for the difficulties of occupation may discourage invasion. Here, size as a factor is related to population, military installations, transportation routes, and so on. Also, short of war, it may be a liability, for it adds to the difficulty of achieving national unity, effective administration, and cultural integration.

Location. Perhaps more important than size is location. This does much to fix a particular type of economy upon an area and people. Thus lumbering, hunting and trapping, grazing, crop culture, mining, commerce, and manufacturing are, in part, the result of location. In turn, the economy does much to determine the culture, as mining gives rise to mining towns, and commerce and manufacturing to cities. Location in the sense of spatial relationship to other land bodies and to other states also profoundly affects a state's culture and economy and both its military and economic power. Location tends to make a state a land power or a sea power, with attendant overall advantages and disadvantages, depending upon whether it accepts the thinking of Mackinder or that of Alfred T. Mahan, one the great theorist of geographical determinism and the other of naval power.[17] England's insularity gave her partial exemption from the continental struggles of medieval Europe and contributed to her early leadership in constitutional government, literature, and industry. North America became French and English, and Central and South America became Spanish and Portuguese, partly because those continents lie generally westward of the colonizing powers. Hawaii became American partly because of its location, and certain other areas became British for the same reason, always in combination with other factors.

Location also figures in the diplomacy and strategy of war. It may help to determine whether a state finds its land a battleground or a generally respected buffer area. The strategic assets of Finland, Norway, and Denmark, for instance, brought war to those peace-loving countries in 1939–40. The Low Countries are another case in point. Except for the jealousies of Germany, France, and England, they would probably have long since been swallowed by Germany or France. On the other hand, just as they may in part owe their continued existence to their location, their very position has at times brought invasion when the neighboring great powers went to war. The realization that France and Great Britain would spring to their defense in case of German aggression added immensely to their power, but the need to accommodate themselves to the leadership of France and Britain detracted from it. Somewhat the same relationship exists between Canada and the United States, except that the geographical position of Canada — location again — permits far greater freedom of action. In such relationships, the

[17] Mackinder's theories are discussed later in this chapter. His most important work was *Democratic Ideals and Reality*, published in 1919. Mahan wrote several books on the history of naval warfare and the theories of naval power. Perhaps the most significant was his *The Influence of Sea Power upon History, 1660–1783*, published in 1890.

stronger state also both gains and loses in power.

Climate and Weather. Location is one of the determinants of climate, as it makes a land mass equatorial, polar, or something between; but of course altitude, rainfall, and winds also help to determine climate. In turn, climate is one of the determinants of culture and of economy, along with natural resources, political organization, and religion. Climate has a direct effect on the health and energy of a people. It is not a coincidence that almost all of the major powers are located in the temperate zones. Continuous extremes of heat or cold are alike unfavorable for energy, productive capacity, and national strength. Excessive heat is enervating, even though the people who live in tropical and semi-tropical areas do not require much protection from the weather and may have natural sources of food close at hand. Excessive cold forces human beings to burn too much of their energy in resisting its effects. Generally speaking, temperatures around 68 to 70 degrees Fahrenheit, with considerable seasonal variation, appear to be best for energetic and healthful living. Excessive aridity or rainfall is a handicap to effective human existence. Some sections of the earth's surface are virtually uninhabitable, or are inhabited by only a few persons per square mile, because they are deserts or because they are covered with dense tropical forests, which thrive on abundant rainfall. Examples are the Sahara Desert region, covering an area about as large as the United States, and the Amazon Basin. In large parts of South and Southeast Asia the rhythm of life is determined to a large extent by the monsoons. If the summer monsoon brings enough rain, but not too much, the people of India, for example, will fare relatively well; but if too much or too little rain comes, thousands suffer and many die.

Increasing attention is being given to the possibility of climate and weather control on a large scale. "When one considers that the capability of large-scale weather control automatically includes the possessor's national and international control, to a very great extent, over agricultural yields, water supply, health, electrical power, lines of communication, the course and intensity of storms and hurricanes, and military aspects of national defense, the political and other implications are truly terrifying."[18] Some commentators have speculated that scientific weather control is possible, and that it will add a new dimension to international politics. This point of view was reflected in a striking article by an American naval officer, who wrote: "When precise and extensive control of atmospheric processes and patterns is achieved, a new force — a fantastic force — in power politics will be born. This force might be christened 'atmospolitics.' It might be defined as 'the science of international relations in terms of the physical atmosphere and politics.' And there can be no question as to its future zenith position in the realm of power politics."[19]

Shape and Topography. The shape of a state's area may add to or detract from its vulnerability to attack; it may make for long or short coast lines or boundaries, good ports or no ports, ease or difficulty of access to centers of population and trade, and efficiency or inefficiency in administration and military operations. Closely related to configuration is topography, for rivers may provide good ports and access where configuration would otherwise deny them. Good rivers may afford transportation throughout a state; and, on the other hand, as interna-

[18] William J. Kotsch, "Weather Control and National Strategy," *U.S. Naval Institute Proceedings*, LXXXVI, (July, 1960), p. 76.

[19] *Ibid.*, p. 80

tional boundary lines they may invite commercial problems with another state. Topography has given good ports to Europe but almost none to Africa. The fall of rivers may be adequate for the production of enormous energy, and rivers and lakes may provide the means for extensive irrigation. Mountains may bar invaders, but perhaps trade as well. They may foster national unity, but they may also prevent it. They may cut a land off from the travel path of the world, as in Bolivia, or they may make of it a meeting ground for travelers of all nations, as in Switzerland. As a prime determinant of climate and rainfall, topography has an obvious and important bearing on economy and culture. Together with land size, location, and configuration, it provides the geographical setting of the national state, and, like the others, is a significant element of power, military and economic.[20]

The following observations about the Soviet Union may serve to illustrate the significance of topographic factors:

(1) While the U.S.S.R. has the longest frontiers of any nation in the world, these frontiers do not offer easy access to the seas or, with some exceptions, to contiguous lands. She has four seacoasts, widely separated: on the Baltic, on the Black Sea, on the Pacific Ocean, and on the Arctic Ocean. None of these seacoasts provides free or easy access to the great ocean highways of the world, although her occupation of southern Sakhalin and the Kuriles after World War II gave her a protected outlet to the North Pacific area. The land frontiers in the west offer excellent protection in the Karelian Isthmus, the Pripet Marshes, and the Carpathian Mountains, and the gaps between make contact with Europe relatively easy. Elsewhere the borders of Russia run through some of the most remote and inaccessible desert and mountain areas in the world.

(2) Much of the area of the U.S.S.R. is tundra, forest, or desert, made more forbidding by vast distances and harsh climate.

(3) The great European Plain extends in a broadening path through European Russia and beyond the Urals into Soviet Asia. Parts of the plains and steppes of Russia are ideally suited to large-scale agriculture. The Ukraine is one of the finest wheat-producing regions in the world. The Urals are not a major barrier, contrary to a common assumption, and the broad lands of Siberia are being developed at a rapid rate.

(4) The river systems of European Russia are great highways of transportation and commerce, having an importance far greater than the river systems of the United States or other countries which have relatively well-developed railroad networks and highways. The Dniester, the Dnieper, and the Don flow into the Black Sea. The Volga, the largest river in Europe, on which many important cities — Kalinin, Yaroslavl, Gorki, Syzran, Saratov, Volgograd (formerly Stalingrad) — are located, ends in the great landlocked Caspian Sea. Siberia has four of the largest rivers in the world, but three of them — the Ob, the Yenisei, and the Lena — pass through bleak, barren, and thinly settled tundra areas to empty into the Arctic Ocean, and the fourth — the Amur — which forms the boundary between U.S.S.R. and Manchuria for hundreds of miles, veers northward at Khabarovsk and empties into the Sea of Okhotsk near the northern tip of Sakhalin.

Boundaries. Boundaries may be either natural or artificial; that is, they may be determined by such natural features as mountains, rivers, and coastlines, or by strictly nonphysical considerations. Most boundaries between states are sharply delineated, although they have often been changed; but there are still some undefined frontiers.

[20] A detailed analysis of the influence of geography on the power status of all major states is presented in Harold and Margaret Sprout, eds., *Foundations of National Power,* (Princeton, N.J.: Princeton University Press, 1945). A revised edition was published by D. Van Nostrand Co. in 1951.

Problems and disputes arising from boundaries seem to be always with us. Consider the tension and friction that now exist with regard to the frontiers between North and South Korea, North and South Vietnam, India and Pakistan in the Kashmir area, India and China, China and the Soviet Union, Israel and some of the Arab states, East and West Germany, Ethiopia and Somalia. The boundaries drawn in the post-World War I treaties were based largely on ethnic considerations, although in some instances historical or strategic concepts were given precedence. Thus the "historic frontiers" of Bohemia determined the westernmost boundaries of Czechoslovakia, even though this meant placing thousands of people of Germanic stock in the "Sudetenland" of the new Slavic state; and Poland, which was resurrected after more than a century of death, was given a corridor to the Baltic, even though this corridor separated Germany proper from eastern Germany and was itself inhabited almost entirely by Germans. After World War II the major boundary problem — the borders of Germany — was never settled, and the other frontiers defined in the peace treaties emphasized political and strategic more than ethnic factors. By Russian pressure the boundaries of Poland were pushed westward, and some 8,000,000 Germans were forced out of the areas occupied by the new Poland. In several instances, as in Korea, Vietnam, Kashmir, and Israel, boundaries were determined by the cease-fire lines fixed by truce agreements. These may prove to be anything but permanent dividing lines, and they are potent sources of conflict. Ethnic considerations were important in the division and eventual disposition of the disputed area of Trieste.

The "Science" of Geopolitics. It was left to Nazi Germany to make the most of geographic influences on world politics. In doing so the Germans developed what they regarded as the science of geopolitics. "Geopolitics, to take a convenient definition, is the science of the relationship between space and politics which attempts to put geographical knowledge at the service of political leaders. It is more than political geography, which is descriptive. It springs from national aspirations, searches out facts and principles which can serve national ends."[21]

The beginnings of the "science" are lost in the past, but there is an obvious indebtedness to Immanuel Kant (1724–1804), the father of modern geography. A century later Friedrich Ratzel (1844–1904) formulated a general theory of the influence of geographic factors on states, which he compared to organisms that must grow or die. Rudolf Kjellén (1864–1922), admittedly a disciple of Ratzel, accepted some of his master's theories, modified others, added some of his own, and then gave the name "geopolitics" to what he had. To him the state was an organism and as such more than a legal entity; it must grow and expand as geography and nature permitted and invited. The rules of growth constituted the new science, and although it involved biological and social sciences it was essentially a mass of theories based on geographic determinism. Kjellén's *The Great Powers* became the acknowledged bible of German geopoliticians.[22]

The two most notable geopoliticians have both been geographers, one a Scot, Sir Halford Mackinder (1869–1947), and the other a German, Karl Haushofer (1869–1946). Mackinder first publicized his theories in a famous paper on "The Geographical Pivot of History," which he read at a meeting of the Royal Geographic Society in London on January 25, 1904. While the Versailles Peace Conference was sitting, he published his *Democratic Ideals and Reality*, in which he declared that a new world order must be based upon an understanding of geography

[21] William H. Hessler, "A Geopolitics for Americans," *U.S. Naval Institute Proceedings*, LXX (March, 1944), 246.

[22] Thorsten V. Kalijarvi *et al.*, *Modern World Politics*, 3d ed. (New York: Thomas Y. Crowell Company, 1953), p. 292.

and its influences. He contended that the so-called Heartland, bounded by the Volga River, the Arctic Ocean, the Yangtze River, and the Himalaya Mountains, dominated the world geographically and could do so politically; its position was invulnerable because world politics was in the long run a struggle between continental and oceanic peoples, and the Heartland was safe from sea power. Clearly he believed in the superiority of land power over sea power, in contrast to the views of the famous American exponent of sea power, Captain Alfred Thàyer Mahan, whose best-known work, *The Influence of Sea Power Upon History, 1600–1783*, published in 1890, may also be described as a geopolitical treatise. Mackinder's famous dictum runs this way: "Who rules eastern Europe commands the Heartland. Who rules the Heartland commands the World-Island [Eurasia-Africa]. Who rules the World-Island commands the world." Thus, he added, Germany and Russia together could dominate the world; fortunately, they had been divided in World War I, but they might not always be so.

Mackinder's geopolitical theories seem to have been tailor-made for Dr. Karl Haushofer, geographer, geologist, historian, Far Eastern traveler, and major general in World War I. After his war service Haushofer worked secretly with other former members of the German General Staff on a series of geographic studies designed to contribute to

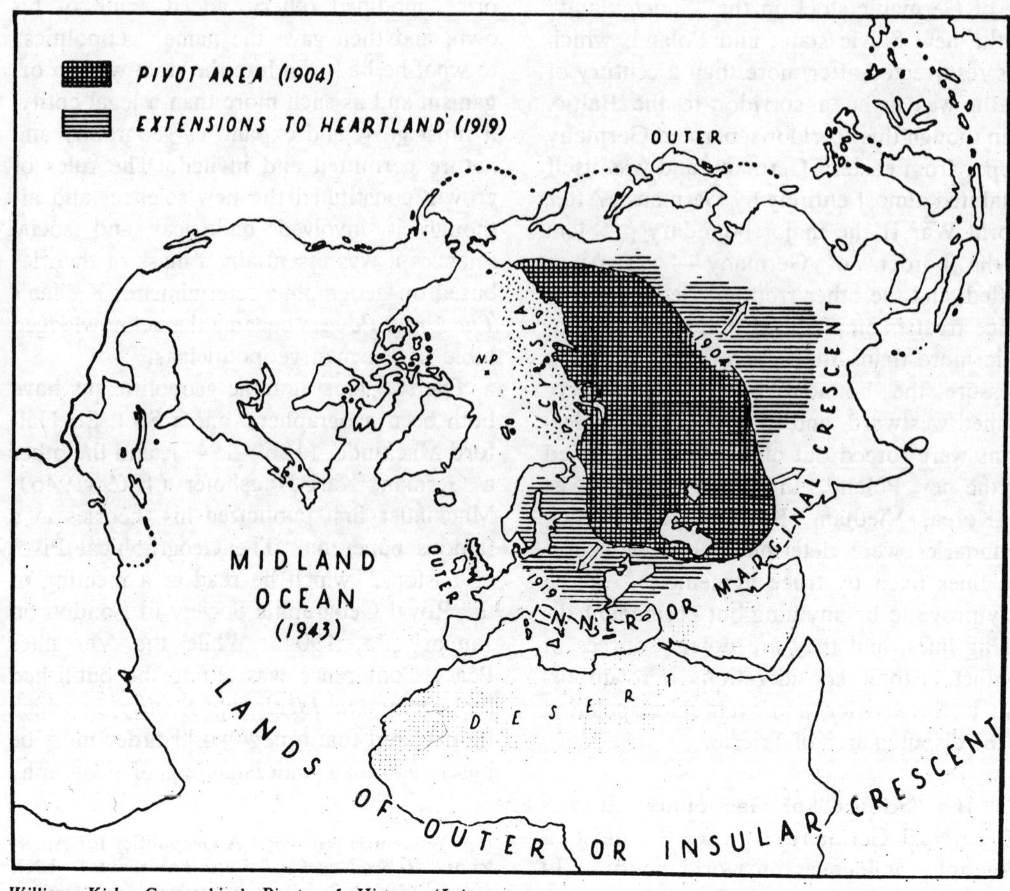

William Kirk, Geographical Pivots of History *(Leicester, England, 1956), p. 6.*

Mackinder's Concept of Pivot Area and Heartland, 1904–1943

German success in another war effort. Through a former student, Rudolf Hess, he became acquainted with Adolf Hitler, and on Hitler's coming to power he induced him to subsidize an Institute of Geopolitics in Munich. The Institute built up a vast storehouse of information on the geography and resources of the states that Germany was eventually to attack. Haushofer became an important adviser to Hitler, but he fell from grace when he advised against the invasion of Russia in 1941. Following Mackinder's Heartland theory, he argued for a German-Russian-Japanese bloc, and predicted that German armies would fail if they sought to swallow the vast lands of Russia. Haushofer was sent to the Dachau concentration camp in 1944; released at the end of the war in 1945, he returned to Munich a bitter old man and committed suicide less than a year later.

The geopolitics developed by Haushofer and his associates may be presented as a series of five major concepts:[23]

(1) For military reasons, a state should be economically self-sufficient.

(2) Germany is a dynamic state with a mission to rejuvenate the world, and her master race, through world domination, will bring peace and a higher civilization. Germany, thus commissioned, is entitled to living room (*Lebensraum*); and weaker states, colonial empires, and large land-monopolizing states must give way. States accepting Germany's leadership will gain new morality and health; others will resist Germany's destiny with futility and disaster.

(3) All areas German by language, race, and economic interest must be brought under German rule. The United States might for a time head a Pan-America, Japan a Pan-Asia, but Germany would rule Europe and Africa and, eventually, the world.

(4) By dominating the world's greatest island — Afro-Eurasia — Germany will occupy an impregnable economic and military position; from this base she could eventually dominate the world. Sea power would be circumvented by land marches.

(5) Boundaries are temporary things, subject to change in Germany's interest, and very useful in starting wars.

Dr. Haushofer and his school attempted to demonstrate that geopolitics was a science. In the minds of some of its proponents during the Nazi era it became a fantastic thing, combining geographic determinism with economics, anthropology, racism, psychology, romanticism, and mysticism.

During World War II the Heartland theory was criticized and revised by Nicholas J. Spykman, Professor of International Relations at Yale University and a leading American geopolitician. He held that Mackinder had exaggerated the potentialities of the Heartland and underestimated those of the Inner Crescent, which he renamed the Rimland and defined as the "intermediate region . . . between the heartland and the marginal seas . . . a vast buffer zone of conflict between sea power and land power." He declared that Mackinder's dictum was false, and should be replaced by the following: "Who controls the Rimland rules Eurasia; who rules Eurasia controls the destinies of the world."[24] On the other hand, Robert Strausz-Hupé, who first criticized many aspects of Mackinder's doctrines,[25] later declared: "Sir Halford Mackinder's concept of the 'heartland' is today, no less

[23] Based upon a summary of Haushofer's concepts by Derwent Whittlesey in "Haushofer: Geopolitician," in E. M. Earle, ed., *Makers of Modern Strategy* (Princeton, N.J.: Princeton University Press, 1943), pp. 398–406. See also Andreas Dorpalen, *The World of General Haushofer* (New York: Farrar and Rinehart, 1942).

[24] Nicholas J. Spykman, *The Geography of the Peace*, edited by Helen R. Nicholl (New York: Harcourt, Brace, 1944), pp. 41–43.

[25] *Geopolitics: The Struggle for Space and Power* (New York: G. P. Putnam's Sons, 1942).

than when it was first presented in 1904, the fundamental axiom of world politics."[26]

Current Applications of Geopolitics. In 1943 Mackinder was asked to prepare an article for the American journal *Foreign Affairs,* assessing the validity of his Heartland concept in the light of the revolutionary changes in the world political situation and in warfare during the forty years that had elapsed since he first enunciated the principle. His answer was given in an article entitled, "The Round World and the Winning of the Peace." The Heartland idea, he contended, was "more valid and useful today than it was either 20 or 40 years ago"; it still provided "a sufficient physical basis for strategic thinking." The advent of the air age had not changed the fundamental bases of strategy. He gave more specific attention to those parts of the world which he had originally included in the "Outer or Insular Crescent." He believed that the control of Eastern Europe and the Heartland still offered a single power a chance for world domination, but he viewed the problem of winning the peace as one of finding a balance between the power constellations of the Heartland and of the North Atlantic Basin. He also gave particular attention to "the mantle of vacancies," the tropical forest lands of South America and Africa, and the monsoon lands of India and China.[27]

Geopolitical analysis, as Mackinder believed, can throw much light upon some of the major problems and attitudes to be found in present-day international relations. To cite two examples only, it helps to explain the importance of the Middle East to the rest of the world and the concern of the United States in the power situation in Eurasia. The Middle East, although important for historical, cultural, and religious reasons, is one of the crossroads of the world today because of its geographic and strategic location and because of its wealth in oil. Situated at the junction of three continents, it occupies a key position in the Inner Crescent or Rimland, and is a potential zone of rivalry and conflict between the power controlling the Heartland and the insular or "offshore" powers. If the Soviet Union controlled this vital area, the entire world balance of power would be upset. With respect to American interest in Eurasia, Spykman wrote more than two decades ago that "the situation at this time . . . makes it clear that the safety and independence of this country can be preserved only by a foreign policy that will make it impossible for the Eurasian land mass to harbor an overwhelmingly dominant power in Europe and the Far East."[28]

The strategic view of the world held by Mahan, Mackinder, Haushofer, Spykman, and other geopolitical thinkers of the preatomic era may seem to be quite inapplicable, or at least rather old-fashioned, in the age of nuclear and thermonuclear bombs, of ICBM's and space satellites. In a sense this is certainly true; but one should remember that these thinkers often adjusted their views in accordance with changing conditions and their own evolving ideas, and they always conceived of their principles as dynamic, not static. Surely they would have adapted their theories to the realities of the nuclear age.

Geopolitics is by no means outdated, although some of the past concepts and applications associated with it clearly are.[29] Un-

[26] Robert Strausz-Hupé, *The Balance of Tomorrow* (New York: G. P. Putnam's Sons, 1945), p. 262.

[27] See Mackinder, "The Round World and the Winning of the Peace," *Foreign Affairs,* XXI (July, 1943). See also W. Gordon East, "How Strong Is the Heartland?" *Foreign Affairs,* XXVIII (October, 1950), and Charles Kruszewski, "The Pivot of History," *Foreign Affairs,* XXXII (April, 1954).

[28] Spykman, pp. 58–60.

[29] See Albert H. Rose, *A Geography of International Relations* (Dayton, Ohio: University of Dayton Press, 1965), p. 9; and William Kirk, *Geographical Pivots of History* (Leicester, England, 1965), p. 24.

doubtedly "the struggle for space and power" over the vast land and sea regions of the world, and perhaps in outer space as well, will be a central theme in the international relations of the future.

Natural Resources

The study of natural resources involves some definitions, a series of classifications, and, in the mind at least, a distribution map. We must note the sources of energy and their relation to industrial strength, and, in these respects, observe the position of the United States in particular. We must appraise the well-being of states in terms of food supply and the national power of states in terms of their total assets in natural resources.

Natural Resources and Raw Materials. We must first make it clear that natural resources and raw materials are not the same thing. Waterfall and fertility of soil are natural resources, but they are obviously not raw materials. Natural resources may be defined as gifts of nature of established utility; they would include, for example, most minerals, flora and fauna, and, as mentioned, waterfall and fertility of soil. Some of these, like minerals and forests, are commonly both natural resources and raw materials. On the other hand, some raw materials must themselves be produced, as rubber, hides, and cotton. When these are domesticated products, they should not be regarded as natural resources. With some validity they could even be discussed under technology.

"Resource" implies asset, and what constitutes an asset varies from time to time and place to place. Unknown coal deposits are not an asset, but only potentially so; oil and natural gas and a thousand other things are not assets in a primitive society, just as cottonseed was no asset a hundred years ago in the United States. Even today sea water in itself has little inherent value, but we hear of scientific probings that may result in its becoming a useful source of certain minerals and of unlimited quantities of pure water. Raw materials, too, possess only potential rather than actual utility. Sometimes the conversion of raw materials into finished products is long, complicated, and costly, as in the production of radium from pitchblende, or in the famous two-billion-dollar job of making the first atom bomb. The point is that even when states have raw materials they must add labor, technology, and capital to convert potential utility into actual utility.

The gifts of nature not only may fail to be natural resources at a given time or place but may even be grave liabilities. Forests may have to be destroyed and animal life obliterated, clay or granite or coal may impede agriculture, and oil or salt may complicate the problem of water supply. Furthermore, even when their usefulness has been fully established, natural resources may perform a positive disservice for a state, for natural wealth may invite aggression, as historians can testify with many examples.

The Classification of Raw Materials. Raw materials may be divided into three groups: vegetable products, animal products, and minerals. Vegetable products include most foodstuffs, cotton, rubber, jute, flax, some oils, wood pulp, sisal, hemp, some fertilizers, barks, roots, all kinds of wood, certain dyestuffs, kapok, bamboo, seeds, charcoal, nuts, and the ingredients of many chemicals, drugs, and paint and varnish products. Unlike his position in respect to minerals, man is not altogether dependent upon the original bounty of nature for his vegetable products. Although many of them are peculiar to certain climates and soils, some of them can be produced in areas to which they are not indigenous.

Animal products include some foodstuffs — such as meat, poultry, fish, milk, and eggs — wool, hides, silk, tallow, some oils, furs, feathers, ivory, the ingredients of certain drug products, and much else. Within limits, man can also expand and diversify his resources in animal products.

Minerals, the products of inorganic processes, may be subdivided into various groups, as chemists and mineralogists would do. A common classification divides minerals into metals, nonmetals, and fuels. In international relations particular attention is given to minerals which are classified as critical or strategic. Some minerals have general and well-known usefulness; others have such highly specialized utility that we must take the word of metallurgists on their present and potential importance.

Synthetics may reduce or remove the reliance on what were regarded as essential raw materials, as in the cases of synthetic rubber, industrial alcohol, nylon, rayon, leather substitutes, various plastics, and even foodstuffs. The development of new alloys and new pharmaceutical products, the reuse of oils and fats, and the conquest of mountains of old rubber and tin cans — all contributed during World War II to stretching limited supplies of essential raw materials, and, incidentally, demonstrated the interdependence of raw materials and technology as elements of national power.

Foodstuffs and Agricultural Products. Foodstuffs are, of course, a vital element in a nation's strength. Most Americans are only vaguely conscious of this, for they suffer more from over-eating than from under-eating. The United States and Russia are fully self-sufficient, France is nearly so, Germany and Great Britain — especially Britain — normally require substantial imports, and Italy and Japan, which have lower standards of living, are almost self-sufficient. Western Europe as a whole is dependent upon imports for about half of its food.

In most parts of the world food is a major problem, one closely related to effective utilization of human resources. Most of the underdeveloped countries have to import large amounts of food even to sustain their people at low standards of living. In all of these countries the proportion of world population is greater than the proportion of the world's food production. In most of them the average diets are nutritionally inadequate.

Malnourished people cannot produce as much as well-fed ones, and they are potent sources of dissatisfaction and unrest. Dr. Raymond W. Miller said: "Hunger is the most important factor in the world today. The real challenge of the twentieth century is the race between men and starvation."[30] And it is by no means certain that the race is being won. Rapid population growth, natural disasters, increasing pressure on arable land, civil wars and political instability, international tensions and suspicions, ignorance and superstition, corrupt or incapable leadership, and a thousand and one natural and man-made causes greatly hamper all efforts to win the grim race.

Basic foodstuffs such as rice, wheat, and corn are essential for national as well as for individual survival and for economic as well as for physical development. Three other agricultural products — cotton, wool, and rubber — are hardly less essential in terms of national power than coal, iron ore, and petroleum; they play a major role in the economies of many states and areas and in international relations in general. All have innumerable industrial uses, and all have been subjects of various international agreements.

The United States, generally speaking, is not heavily dependent on foreign trade, but some of her basic producers are, as for instance, the cotton-growers of the South. Exports of cotton are even more important for countries like Egypt and Pakistan, which

[30] Quoted in *Together We Are Strong,* Dept. of State Pub. 4614, Commercial Policy Series 144 (Washington, D.C.: Government Printing Office, 1952), p. 33.

have to rely on them to provide the foreign exchange with which to buy a great variety of essentials. American wool-growers need a foreign market, but the producers of certain other countries, such as Australia, are even more dependent on outside markets.

The economies of Malaysia and Indonesia, countries which occupy critically important areas in the non-Communist world, would collapse if foreign markets for their rubber were not available. The peoples of these lands are painfully conscious of their dependence on world market conditions, and they have experienced the serious effects of great fluctuations in the world price of raw rubber and of exclusion from normal markets, as well as the heady effects of abnormally high prices during the Korean War. They are concerned about the rapid development of substitutes for rubber and of the production of synthetic rubber, especially in the United States, their chief market. The United States, however, is mindful of the consequences to Malaysia's and Indonesia's internal politics of any reduction in their export revenues. Nor has the United States forgotten the critical situation which arose when the Japanese occupied the rubber-producing regions of Southeast Asia during World War II. Thus her concern with insuring supplies of natural rubber or for developing adequate capacity for producing synthetic rubber or acceptable substitutes conflicts with her desire to encourage the expansion of international trade and to help the underdeveloped countries to find markets for their products and strengthen their economies.

Animal Products. Many of the world's peoples are vegetarians, by choice or by necessity; but animal products are important, and often major, sources of food for many millions, especially outside of the torrid zone. In 1964, for example, Americans ate an average of 174.8 pounds of meat per person. In the same year, according to the Food and Agriculture Organization of the United Nations, the world catch of fish was 113.8 billion pounds. Poultry is another major source of food, and in some countries seems to be the favored kind of edible animal product. Tandoori chicken is a well-known dish in overwhelmingly vegetarian India, and chicken (a term often used to include older and tougher species) is a staple in both the gourmet and regular fare of many countries. Eggs are an important product — or by-product — of poultry. The milk of cows and other milk-producing animals is an especially valuable food for children in many lands. It is a staple item of innumerable school lunches and in powdered form is distributed widely in underdeveloped countries, especially by UNICEF.

Minerals. The development of mechanized warfare has meant that only states with substantial industry — both qualitative and quantitative — may be great military powers. Since minerals are the sinews of industry, it is evident that a wealth of mineral resources is a necessary condition of impressive military strength. Studies of international relations in recent years have given much attention to minerals as a factor in national power. While statistics are abundant, they must be used with some caution.[31]

[31] This is true even of the voluminous data presented in two standard sources, the *Statistical Abstract of the United States* and the *Statistical Yearbook of the United Nations*, both issued annually. See the following valuable publications issued under the auspices of Resources for the Future: B. C. Netschert and Hans H. Lansberg, *The Future Supply of the Major Metals: a Reconnaissance Survey* (Baltimore: The Johns Hopkins Press, 1961); and James F. McDivitt, *Minerals and Men* (Baltimore: The Johns Hopkins Press, 1965). For United States minerals, see also *Resources for Freedom*, Report of the President's Materials Policy Commission (Washington, D.C.: Government Printing Office, 1952); and *Minerals Yearbook*, issued annually by the Government Printing Office and prepared by the Bureau of Mines, U.S. Department of the Interior.

LEADING NATIONS IN THE PRODUCTION OF SELECTED METALLIC ORES

Ferroalloys

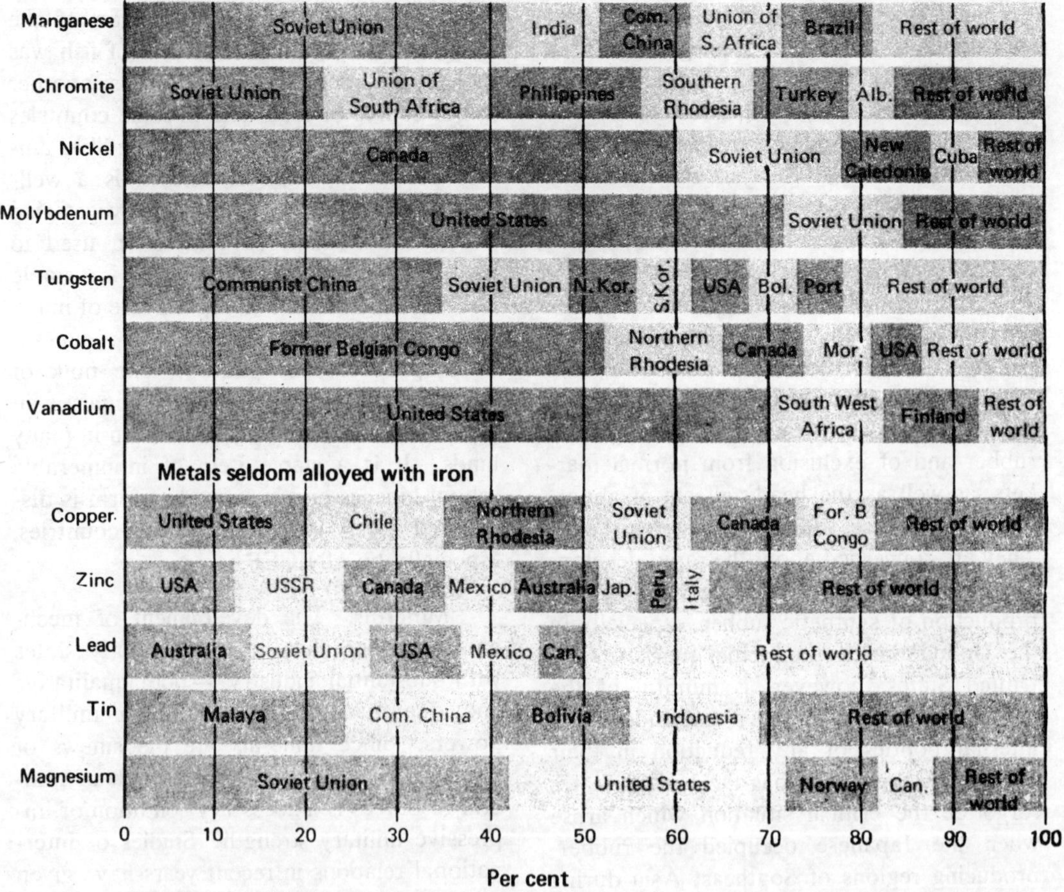

From The Geography of Economic Activity *by R. S. Thoman. Copyright ©1962 by McGraw-Hill, Inc. Used by permission of McGraw-Hill Book Company.*

Figures on the U.S.S.R., for instance, are both fragmentary and unreliable, and for Communist China the problem of reliable data seems almost insolvable. For another thing, ore production and reserves indicate nothing about a country's technology; all the ore may be shipped abroad. Also, the possession of vast mineral resources does not imply that these are always available; thus the extensive holdings of the British and French overseas may be kept from the mills of Britain and France by transportation difficulties, by local unrest, or by enemy action. Finally, essential civilian demands may affect the proportion of mineral output that can be allocated to military goods. Nevertheless, great importance must be attached to statistics on both mineral production and reserves.

While the unfavorable mineral position of Germany, Italy, and Japan may be used to explain why they launched World War II, it may have more validity in explaining why they lost the war. Germany had an exportable surplus of no important mineral and adequate supplies of only coal and potash, and she partially or completely relied on imports for every other basic mineral. Italy had an exportable surplus of only sulphur and mercury, adequate supplies of bauxite (aluminum ore), lead, and zinc, and a total lack of many other minerals, including the basic ones of coal, iron, and oil.

Japan exported phosphates; she had adequate supplies of copper, graphite, and noncoking coal; she was partially or totally dependent in everything else.[32]

Statistics on mineral resources reveal the advantageous position of the Soviet Union and the United States, thus partially explaining the military preeminence of those states. The United States ranks first among world producers of crude petroleum, copper, aluminum, salt, and gypsum; second in the production of coal, iron ore, and zinc; and third in the production of lead. It has to import 100 per cent of its tin, 92 per cent of its manganese, and 84 per cent of its bauxite. The Soviet Union is the world's largest producer of coal, iron ore, manganese, and chromite; and the second largest producer of petroleum, copper, lead, aluminum, bauxite, asbestos, gold, and natural gas. It has to import all of its tin. No other country is even close to self-sufficiency in most of the major minerals. Canada is the leading producer of aluminum and nickel, Jamaica of bauxite, the Congo (Kinshasa) of cobalt and industrial diamonds, South Africa of gold, Mexico of silver, Malaysia of tin, and China of tungsten.

[32] These lists have been taken from Walter Sharp and Grayson Kirk, *Contemporary International Politics* (New York: Rinehart, 1944), pp. 66–69.

The Distribution of Raw Materials. No country in the world today is close to self-sufficiency in essential raw materials, and all states are therefore heavily dependent on foreign sources of supply. This dependence, which varies greatly from state to state, raises vital questions concerning the accessibility of these materials, control of the sea lanes or other routes from the sources of supply, exchange and balance of payments

MANY COUNTRIES ARE DEPENDENT ON A SINGLE EXPORT COMMODITY

Single Export Commodity as a Percent of Total Exports (1957-59 Average)

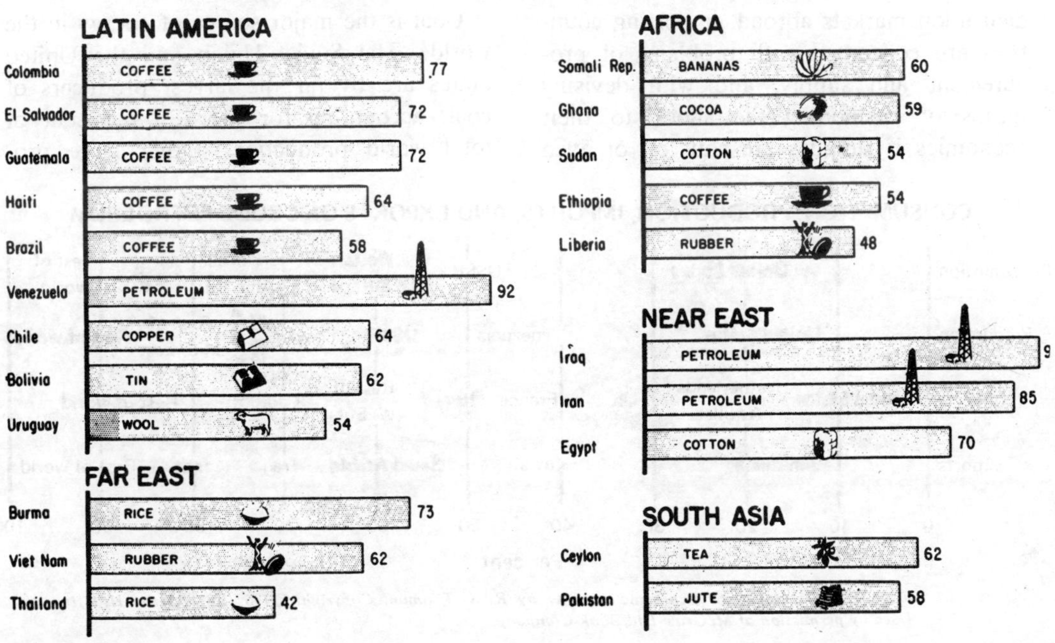

Department of State

problems, relations between states needing the materials and states possessing them, trade restrictions and other barriers to international commerce, and significant security and policy issues. Some countries are heavily dependent on finding foreign markets for one or a few basic products, and their entire economies and political systems are affected by the world price and demand. Unfortunately, world price and demand may fluctuate in an unpredictable fashion, thus creating serious problems for the countries whose economies are at the mercy of conditions beyond their control.

Oil is the chief export of Saudi Arabia, Iran, Kuwait, Iraq, Venezuela, and several other countries, tin of Malaysia and Bolivia, coffee of Brazil, Colombia, El Salvador, Guatemala, Haiti, and Ethiopia, rice of Burma and Thailand, jute of Pakistan, rubber of Indonesia and Liberia, and tea of Ceylon. Nearly every state is dependent in some degree on the export of raw materials. This is true even of the United States, especially is the cases of wheat, cotton, and tobacco.

Whereas producing countries are dependent upon markets abroad, importing countries are concerned with problems of procurement and supply, and with devising means of cushioning the shock to their economies if supplies are shut off or even seriously curtailed because of depletion, bad diplomatic relations, or a general international crisis. The United States, which is far less dependent on imports of raw materials than many other countries, is concerned with problems of this sort, and devotes a great deal of time, energy, and money to stockpiling and to developing substitute products and alternative sources of supply. Countries for whom foreign trade and imports of raw materials and foodstuffs are matters of life and death, such as Britain and Japan, must make every effort to assure themselves of an adequate flow of imports under any and all circumstances.

Major Sources of Energy. The sources of energy today range from the oldest, human and animal power, to atomic and solar energy. Manpower is still a chief source of energy in most parts of the world, although in the highly developed countries it is overshadowed by the energy-producing machines of man's creation. It is of major importance in underdeveloped countries, as is the energy provided by bullocks, water buffalo, oxen, horses, and other draft animals.

Coal is the major source of energy in the world. The Soviet Union and the United States are by far the largest producers of coal, accounting for over 35 per cent of total world production. Other large pro-

CONSUMPTION, PRODUCTION, IMPORTS, AND EXPORTS OF CRUDE PETROLEUM

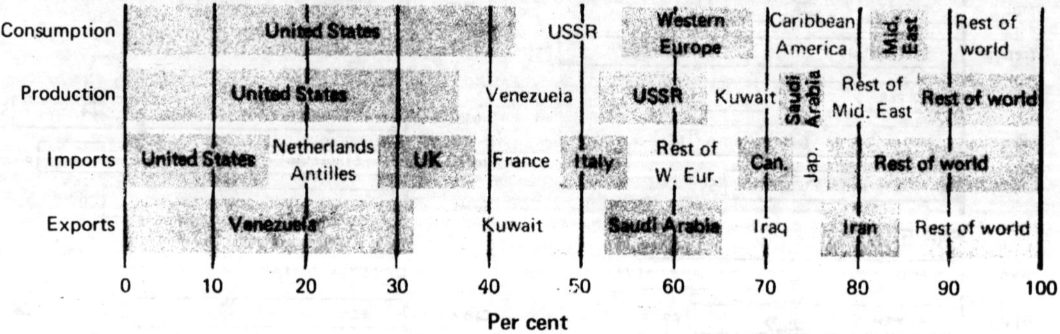

From The Geography of Economic Activity *by R. S. Thoman. Copyright © 1962 by McGraw-Hill, Inc. Used by permission of McGraw-Hill Book Company.*

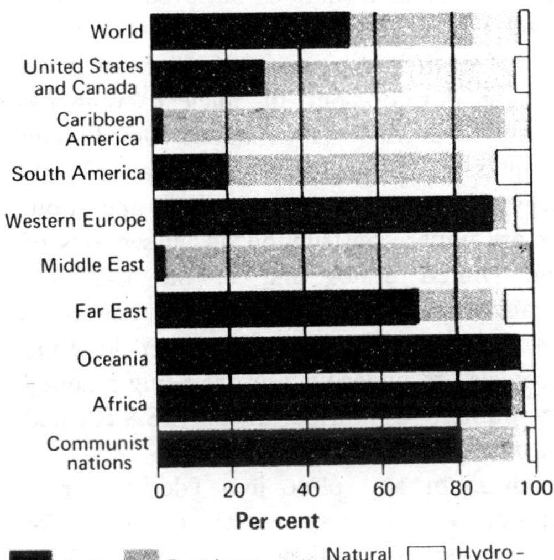

in many underdeveloped countries, such as India, where vast multipurpose river-valley development schemes are being brought into operation. It is of potential significance in many parts of Africa. The waters of many rivers are providing increasing amounts of hydroelectric power, but some great rivers, such as the Amazon and the Orinoco in

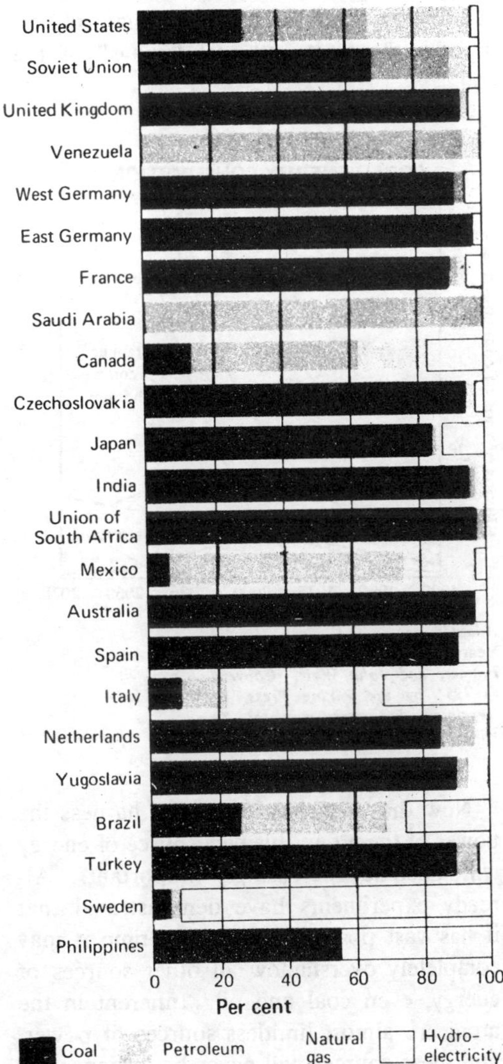

Both charts from The Geography of Economic Activity *by R. S. Thoman. Copyright ©1962 by McGraw-Hill, Inc. Used by permission of McGraw-Hill Book Company.*

ducers are Communist China, East and West Germany, Great Britain, Poland, Czechoslovakia, India, France, Japan, Australia, and South Africa. In the United States more than three-fifths of the production is mined in three states — West Virginia, Pennsylvania, and Kentucky.

Oil, now the major source of energy in the United States, ranks second in world importance. World output is now more than 30 million barrels a day, and reserves are estimated at about 350 billion barrels. In 1967 oil production was 8.8 billion barrels in the United States (over one-third of which was produced in Texas), 5.6 billion in the U.S.S.R., 3.5 billion in Venezuela, 2.3 million in Kuwait, 2.6 million in Saudi Arabia, and 2.6 million in Iran. Iraq and Libya were also important oil-producing states. The United States, of course, was the world's largest consumer of oil. Most of the free world's imported oil comes from the Middle East and from Venezuela. Much of this business is controlled by huge American, British, Dutch, and French companies.

Water power, especially hydroelectric power, is important in some industrial states, such as Japan and the United States, and

South America, the Yukon in North America, and the Mekong in Southeast Asia are largely unharnessed.

Natural gas is used extensively in areas where it is available in quantity. It is abundant, and is piped for long distances, in both the United States and the Soviet Union. In the United States some 25 billion cubic feet are piped daily over a 710,000-mile system. In Pakistan attempts to find oil, disappointing in their main object, have led to discoveries of major fields of natural gas, in both the west and east "wings" of the country.

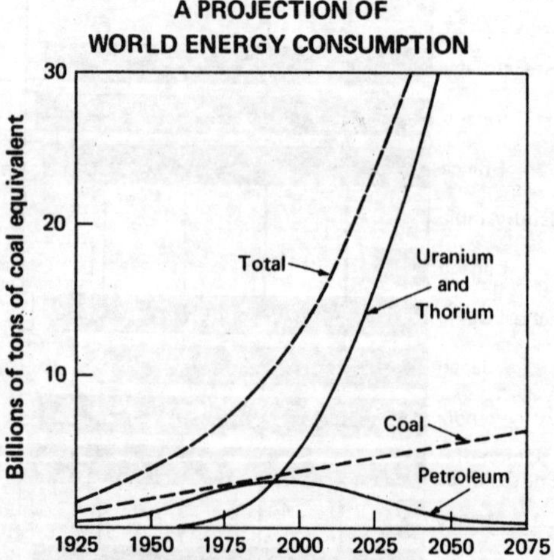

Adapted from The Next Hundred Years *by Harrison Brown, James Bonner, and John Weir. Copyright © 1957 by the Viking Press, Inc. Reprinted by permission of The Viking Press, Inc.*

Now that man has learned to harness the power of the atom, this new source of energy will become increasingly important. Already experiments have demonstrated that it has vast possibilities, and in time it may completely overshadow all other sources of energy, even coal and oil. Inherent in the atom are almost limitless sources of power, and these sources will never be in danger of depletion, as are coal, oil, and natural gas. The implications of the utilization of atomic energy can hardly be grasped; this is a development which may revolutionize not only the economies of nations but even the character of human life on this planet.[33]

Although heavy emphasis has been given to the development of nuclear weapons, many countries have made considerable progress in the peaceful uses of atomic energy. Nuclear power plants are in operation, or are under construction, in all sections of the United States and in the U.S.S.R., France, Britain, and many other countries. Dual-purpose power and water-desalting projects are under way or are being planned in southern California, in the U.S.S.R., and in Israel.

Uranium and plutonium (derived from uranium) are now the chief sources of atomic energy. Minerals containing substantial amounts of uranium are available in many parts of the world, and further exploration may unearth limitless quantities. At present the main supplies of pitchblende, from which most uranium is now derived, come from Canada and the Congo (Kinshasa). Uranium-bearing carnotite has been found in several of the western states of the United States. Other significant known deposits of uranium-bearing minerals are located in several countries of Europe, in the northern regions of European Russia, in Soviet Asia where it borders on Iran and Afghanistan, in China, Japan, Australia, and South Africa. Monazite sands containing thorium, another important source of atomic energy, can be obtained in several parts of the world. The largest deposits of suitable quality are in India and Brazil.

In time an even greater source of energy may be captured and may supplement atomic or fuel power. This is solar energy. In 1955, the science editor of the *New York Times* speculated as follows on this subject:

> On a single day the land areas of the temperate and tropical zones are flooded with more energy from the sun than the human race has utilized in the form of fuel, falling

[33] This is further discussed in Chapter 24.

water, and muscle since it came out of the trees over a million years ago. The whole amount of coal, petroleum, and natural gas left in the earth is the energy equivalent of only 100 days of sunshine. In fact there is more energy in the small fraction of radiation received from the sun than in all the uranium in the world.[34]

Large-scale utilization of solar energy is not yet a practical possibility, but its potentialities stagger the imagination.

Iron and Steel. The U.S.S.R., the United States, France, and Communist China are the largest producers of iron ore, and the United States, the U.S.S.R., West Germany, Japan, and Great Britain of pig iron and steel. Major sources of iron ore are the Mesabi Range in Minnesota, the Urals in the U.S.S.R., Lorraine in France, northern China and Manchuria, Labrador, northern Sweden, Bihar and West Bengal in India, and Bolivar in Venezuela.

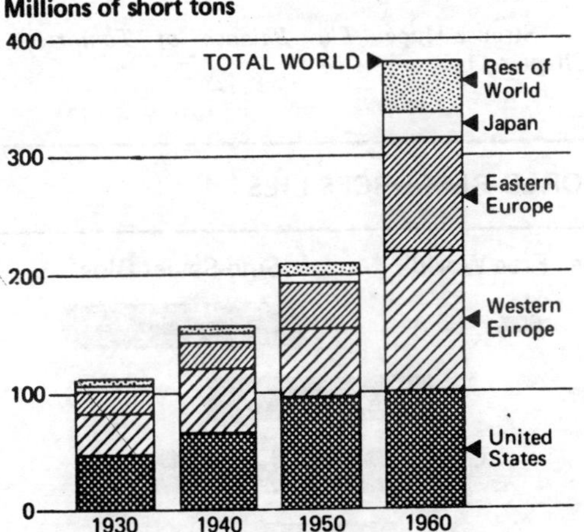

James F. McDivitt, Minerals and Men *(Baltimore: The Johns Hopkins Press, 1965), p. 31.*

According to United Nations experts, world steel production will exceed 600 million tons annually in a few years, and will be more than 700 million tons by 1975. In 1965 it passed the 500 million ton mark. Of this amount, 26 per cent (131.5 million tons) was produced in the United States, 20 per cent (100 million tons) by the Soviet Union, 9 per cent (45.4 million tons) by Japan, 8 per cent (40.6 million tons) by West Germany, and 6 per cent (30.2 million tons) by the United Kingdom.[35] Other important producers are France, Belgium-Luxembourg, Italy, Canada, Poland, Czechoslovakia, and India. Since steel production is often taken as an indicator of a nation's economic strength and capability, these figures are of particular significance for a student of international relations.

The Industrial Strength of the Superpowers. Modern industry is based upon coal, iron ore and steel, and petroleum. Coal and oil are the chief sources of energy, and iron and steel are vital to the transportation and construction industries and to a machine- and tool-using economy. The great powers of today are those nations which are relatively well off in these essentials and have the advanced technological base which possession of them makes possible.

The quantity, quality, and relative accessibility of coal, iron ore, and oil have made the United States the industrial giant of modern times. By far the greatest producer and consumer of oil, she imports substantial quantities from Venezuela and lesser amounts from the Middle East; and she exports some oil to Europe and the Far East. She is holder of the largest known reserves of coal in the world, and also is the largest consumer. She has the capacity to produce well over 100,000,000 tons of steel a year.

The Soviet Union has some of the world's largest oil reserves, and is obtaining large amounts of petroleum from the Baku fields, the Ural Mountains, and elsewhere in the

[34] Waldemar Kaempffert, "Science in Review," *New York Times,* November 6, 1955, p. E9.

[35] "World Output Sets a Record," *Steel Facts,* No. 191 (April, 1966), p. 8.

vast reaches of the U.S.S.R., as well as from Rumania. And the Middle East, with probably the greatest oil reserves in the world, lies next door. Coal and iron ore also are abundant in the Urals and in other parts of the Soviet Union. The main problems facing the Soviet Union in exploiting her resources effectively are those of distance, transportation, and the general level of the technology.

No other country approximates the industrial strength of the two superpowers, although Great Britain, the countries of the European Economic Community, collectively considered, and Japan are also industrial giants. Britain, the first nation to experience the impact of the Industrial Revolution, was for a century or more indisputably the greatest industrial power. She is still in the forefront by virtue of "know-how," large supplies of coal and iron ore, her position as banker and center of the sterling area and the Commonwealth, her overseas connections, and the skills of her people. The countries associated in EEC, if considered as a single unit, would comprise the third most powerful industrial complex in the world. Western Germany, in particular, after an amazing recovery, is once more a formidable industrial power. Japan still has a strong technological base, which can again give her great strength if she can solve the problems of finding markets for her products and assuring herself of adequate supplies of raw materials and foodstuffs. In recent years she has enjoyed perhaps the highest rate of industrial growth in the world.

"Heartlands of Heavy Industry." At the present time there are only three great "heartlands of heavy industry," although there are several other centers of growing industrial strength which may become of real significance within a relatively short time.[36] The key questions are adequate sources of essential materials, financial strength, and a satisfactory political situation. One great heartland comprises the northern and northeastern sections of the United States, roughly from Chicago through the industrial centers of New England, and includes the great industries of Ohio, Penn-

[36] Strausz-Hupé, *The Balance of Tomorrow*, Chapter 11.

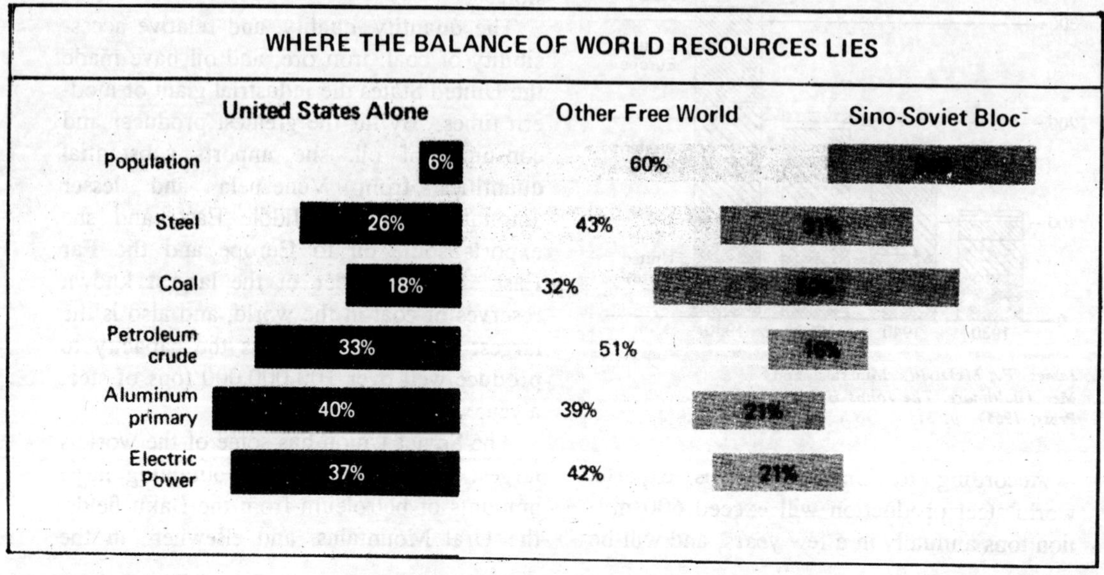

Department of State

sylvania, and New York. Another is Western Europe. Perhaps this could more properly be divided industrially into two heartlands, one covering England and the other covering the industrial complex in West Germany, the Benelux countries, and eastern France. The continental heartland utilizes the iron ore of Lorraine and the Rhineland area, the coal of the Ruhr, Belgium and the Saar, and the steel plants of the Ruhr, Lorraine, Belgium, Luxembourg, and the Saar. A third major complex, also divided into several centers, is in the Soviet Union. Before World War II the main industrial centers in Russia were in the Ukraine and the Urals. Since the war much of the industrial strength of the Ukraine has been restored, and the Ural Mountain region has remained a major center as well; but other industrial concentrations now exist in the vicinity of Moscow, Gorki, and other cities of European Russia, and at several places in Soviet Asia.

Potentially another great heartland of industry is in the Far East; it combines the technological capacity and skill of the Japanese with the raw materials, including coal and iron ore, and the developing industries of north China and Manchuria. The development of this heartland, however, is now being retarded by political difficulties. The second most significant heartland in Asia, outside Soviet Russia, is in eastern India, where coal and iron ore and some petroleum as well are available.

The Position of the United States. Economically the United States seems to be in a dominating and almost impregnable position. With only about six per cent of the population and seven per cent of the land area of the globe, she has some forty per cent of the entire world's productive capacity. With the possible exception of the Soviet Union, she is more nearly self-sufficient in vital minerals and raw materials than any other country. With respect to the three most vital current sources of industrial strength, coal, iron ore, and petroleum, she is in a particularly enviable position.

There is, however, another side to this picture. The United States is in reality far from self-sufficient in the vital materials of modern industry. She is wholly deficient in such essentials as tin, natural rubber, industrial diamonds, and quartz crystals. She has to rely on foreign sources for virtually all of her manganese, chromite, nickel, and bauxite. She now has to import substantial quantities of several vital minerals which she once possessed in sufficient supply: copper, zinc, and lead.

Manganese and chromite, materials that are essential for steel production and for certain other processes in which no substitutes are satisfactory, illustrate some of the problems of America's raw materials situation. The chief source of these materials is the Soviet Union; but in view of Soviet restrictions and the political difficulties involved, the United States has to look elsewhere for them. At present India and South Africa are the chief suppliers of manganese. Most chromite comes from South Africa, the Philippines, Rhodesia, and Turkey.

In attempting to avert any serious emergency that might arise from a shortage of "critical and strategic materials" the United States government has given much attention to stockpiling, to research on substitutes and synthetics, and to the development of domestic sources of those essential materials that are in short supply. An exhaustive study of this whole problem was conducted by the President's Materials Policy Commission. Its report, made in 1952, is a detailed analysis of the position of the United States in the raw materials field, with extensive recommendations of measures which should be taken to ensure supplies adequate for any emergency.[37]

[37] See *Resources for Freedom*, Vol. I.

Something like seventy materials are now classed as "critical and strategic." Of these materials "over forty are not produced in the United States in sufficient quantities to mention; of those produced in this country in any significant amounts, only eight are available to meet one-half of . . . peace-time requirements. Thirteen are not available in the entire Western Hemisphere!"[38]

Relation to National Power. The possession of rich natural resources does not make a state prosperous, but it is essential to great national power. Advantageous geography, fertile soil, or mineral deposits can contribute to economic power, for they can create dependence by other states. By producing the wealth which permits investments, by supplying essential goods, or by affording a remunerative market, a state may gain economic power, and its capacity to do so is vastly enhanced by if not entirely dependent upon natural resources of one kind or another. Thus an important element of military power is also an element of economic power — additional evidence of the inseparability of the two.

Two observations remain to be made in our discussion of raw materials. One is that financial interests in the more powerful states often control important sources of raw materials in underdeveloped areas, thus adding further to the resources of the leading states. This is true with oil, iron ore, copper, lead, zinc, tin, and rubber. The second observation is that colonial possessions did not provide the vast supplies of raw materials which one might too readily assume. In only eight minerals — including none of the basic three of coal, iron ore, and oil — did the total

[38] Norman J. Padelford and George A. Lincoln, *International Politics: Foundations of International Relations* (New York: The Macmillan Company, 1954), pp. 33–34.

STRATEGIC MATERIALS FROM OTHER FREE NATIONS ARE ESSENTIAL TO U.S. INDUSTRY

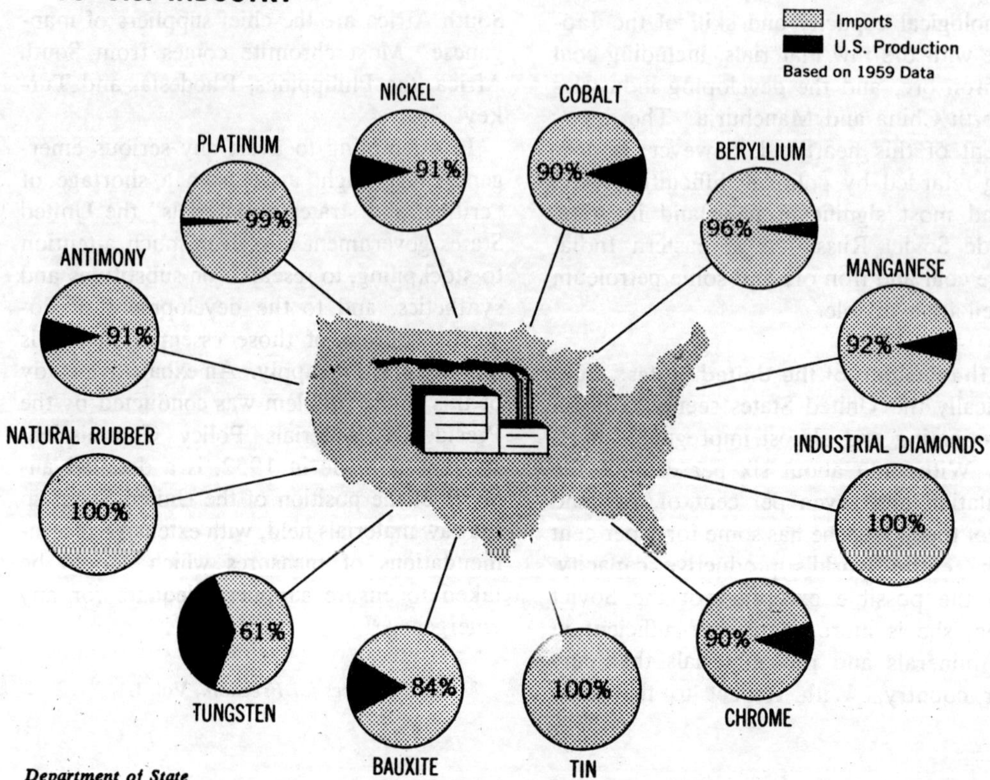

Department of State

colonial production before the war amount to as much as ten per cent of the world's output.[39]

The study of natural resources and raw materials discloses that even the greatest of the great powers fall far short of economic sufficiency, but that at the same time there is an astounding concentration of the basic raw materials in the hands of a few states. These few states, therefore, have vast superiority in this important element of national power.

SUGGESTIONS FOR FURTHER READING

BARNETT, HAROLD J. and CHANDLER MORSE. *Scarcity and Growth.* Baltimore: The Johns Hopkins Press, for Resources for the Future, 1963.

BIDWELL, PERCY. *Raw Materials: A Study of American Policy.* New York: Council on Foreign Relations, 1958.

BROWN, HARRISON, JAMES BONNER, and JOHN WEIR. *The Next Hundred Years.* New York: The Viking Press, 1957. Deals with raw material availabilities, food production potentials, energy resources, and population trends.

CARR, E. H. *The Twenty Years' Crisis, 1919–1939,* 2d ed. London, 1946.

CLAUDE, INIS L., JR. *Power and International Relations.* New York: Random House, 1963.

COHEN, SAUL B. *Geography and Politics in a Divided World.* New York: Random House, 1963.

COLE, J. P. *Geography of World Affairs,* 3d ed. Baltimore: Penguin Books, 1964.

DORPALEN, ANDREAS. *The World of General Haushofer.* New York: Farrar and Rinehart, 1942.

EAST, W. GORDON and A. E. MOODIE. *The Changing World: Studies in Political Geography.* Cleveland: World Book Company, 1956. Contributions by 20 specialists. Regional treatment within a world framework.

FISHER, JOSEPH I. and NEAL POTTER. *World Prospects for Natural Resources.* Baltimore: The Johns Hopkins Press, for Resources for the Future, 1964. The subtitle is "Some projections of demand and indicators of supply to the year 2000."

[39] Sharp and Kirk, pp. 65–66.

FISHER, JOSEPH I. and ROGER REVELLE. *Natural Resources Policies and Planning for Developing Countries.* UN Conference on the Application of Science and Technology for the Benefit of Less Developed Areas. Geneva, 1963.

FRYER, D. W. *World Economic Development.* New York: McGraw-Hill Book Company, 1965.

GINSBURG, NORTON. *Atlas of Economic Development.* Chicago: University of Chicago Press, 1961. Basic data presented in graphic fashion.

GYORGY, ANDREW. *Geopolitics, The New German Science.* Berkeley: University of California Press, 1944.

JACKSON, W. A. D. *et al. Politics and Geographic Relationships.* Englewood Cliffs, N.J.: Prentice-Hall, 1964.

JARRETT, HENRY, ed. *Science and Resources; Prospects and Implications of Technological Advance.* Baltimore: The Johns Hopkins Press, for Resources for the Future, 1959.

KIRK, WILLIAM. *Geographical Pivots of History.* Leicester. England, 1965.

LANDSBERG, HANS H. *Natural Resources for U.S. Growth; a Look Ahead to the Year 2000.* Baltimore: The Johns Hopkins Press, for Resources for the Future, 1964

LANDSBERG, HANS H., LEONARD L. FISCHMAN and JOSEPH I. FISHER. *Resources in America's Future.* Baltimore: The Johns Hopkin Press, for Resources for the Future, 1963 A formidable tome of over 1,000 pages.

McDIVITT, JAMES F. *Minerals and Men.* Baltimore: The Johns Hopkins Press, for Resources for the Future, 1965. Carries the intriguing subtitle: "An exploration of the world of minerals and its effect on the world we live in."

MACKINDER, HALFORD J. *Democratic Ideals and Reality.* New York: Holt, 1919. The fullest exposition of the theories of a famous geopolitician. A new edition, with a foreword by Edward Mead Earle, was issued in 1942.

MAHAN, ALFRED T. *The Influence of Sea Power on History, 1660–1783.* Boston: Little, Brown and Company, 1890.

Minerals Yearbook. Issued annually, in several volumes, by the Bureau of Mines, U.S. Department of the Interior. One volume consists of "Area Reports: International."

NETSCHERT, BRUCE C. and HANS H. LANDSBERG. *The Future Supply of the Major Metals: A Reconnaissance Survey.* Baltimore: The Johns Hopkins Press, for Resources for the Future, 1961.

NETSCHERT, BRUCE C. and S. H. SCHURR. *Atomic Energy Application; a Preliminary Survey.* Baltimore: The Johns Hopkins Press, for Resources for the Future, 1957.

Proceedings of the United Nations Conference on New Sources of Energy. Solar Energy, Wind Power, and Geothermal Energy. Rome, 21–31 August 1961. Vol. I, General Sessions (UN Sales No. 63.I.2). Vol. II, Geothermal Energy (UN Sales No. 63.I.16). Vol. III, Solar Energy — Part One (UN Sales No. 63.I.29). Vol. IV, Solar Energy — Part Two (UN Sales No. 63.I.30).

PUTNAM, P. C. *Energy in the Future.* Princeton, N.J.: D. Van Nostrand Co., 1953.

Resources for Freedom, Report of the President's Materials Policy Commission. 5 vols. Washington, D.C.: Government Printing Office, 1952.

ROSE, ALBERT H. *A Geography of International Relations.* Dayton, Ohio: University of Dayton Press, 1965.

SPROUT, HAROLD and MARGARET SPROUT. *The Ecological Perspective on Human Affairs, with Special Reference to International Politics.* Princeton, N.J.: Princeton University Press, 1965. An enlarged version of an essay entitled "Man-Milieu Relationship Hypotheses in the Context of International Politics," circulated by the Center of International Politics at Princeton University in 1956.

———, eds. *Foundations of National Power,* 2d ed. Princeton, N.J.: D. Van Nostrand Co., 1951. A basic collection of readings in international relations, emphasizing the factors of national power.

SPYKMAN, NICHOLAS J. *America's Strategy in World Politics: The United States and the Balance of Power.* New York: Harcourt, Brace, 1942.

———. *The Geography of the Peace,* edited by Helen R. Nicoll. New York: Harcourt, Brace, 1944.

STILL, HENRY. *Will the Human Race Survive?* New York: Hawthorn Books, 1966. A scientist and engineer believes that human ingenuity can more than keep up with the growth of population.

STRAUSZ-HUPÉ, ROBERT. *Geopolitics: The Struggle for Space and Power.* New York: G. P. Putnam's Sons, 1942.

THOMAN, RICHARD S. *The Geography of Economic Activity.* New York: McGraw-Hill Book Company, 1962.

WEIGERT, HANS W. *German Geopolitics.* New York: Oxford University Press, 1941.

WEIGERT, HANS W., VILHJALMUR STEFANSSON, and RICHARD EDES HARRISON, eds. *Compass of the World.* New York: The Macmillan Company, 1944.

WEIGERT, HANS W. and VILHJALMUR STEFANSSON, eds. *New Compass of the World.* New York: The Macmillan Company, 1949. Most of the contributions to this and the preceding volume place heavy emphasis on political geography and geopolitics.

ZIMMERMANN, ERICH W. *Introduction to World Resources,* edited by Henry L. Hunker. New York: Harper & Row, 1964. An edited and updated version of a classic work, *World Resources and Industries.*

3 National Power: People and Their Genius

We have spoken of geography and natural resources under the heading of "Land and Its Resources." To complete our view of national power we must now examine the people who inhabit the land, their numbers and kinds, and the traditions, mental processes, and moral concepts that together make up that "peculiar character or inherent nature" that is known as genius. It must be understood, of course, that the genius of a people is not a thing apart from the physical setting in which the people live. Whether we speak of technology, ideologies, morale, or leadership — and we shall here regard these as the components of genius — the compelling influence of geographic factors and of the generosity or parsimony of nature is always present. Furthermore, each of the seven elements into which we divide national power has an interrelationship with every other one, and in some instances that interrelationship all but effects an identification.

Population

Perhaps the most striking fact about today's world is the number of people inhabiting it. The total population is estimated to be about 3,500,000,000, and it is expected to double by the end of the century. Are there any limits to this human growth as it relates to the space and resources available on this planet? Obviously this question poses problems of human survival and of man's future. Here, however, we shall discuss population as an element of national power by considering the "population explosion" and its implications, trends in population growth, the present distribution of the world's peoples, the relation of numbers to national power, the quality and character of a nation's population, the efforts to achieve population control and the obstacles in the way, and the problem of population and food supply.

The Population Explosion. During the past 150 years increases in population have been so rapid that they may accurately be described as revolutionary. Most demographic experts believe that because of famines, epidemics, and wars the population of the world showed relatively little growth for some centuries before 1650 A.D. From 250,000,000 some 2,000 years ago, it reached half a billion only by about 1620, the year the Pilgrims landed on Plymouth Rock. It did not reach one billion until shortly before the American Civil War. Since then the "revolution" has occurred: in a century the world increase has amounted to more than 200 per cent, and more recently the "revolution" has become an "explosion." Daily more than 135,000 people are added to the world's population, each year more than 50,000,000. Put in another way, every day a small city is added, every month a new Chicago, every year a new France, every decade a new India. "And every time your pulse beats in your wrist, three more babies are born."[1]

The reasons for this phenomenal increase are clear. They are associated with the industrial and technological revolution of modern times, which has brought about great changes in political, economic, and social organization. New technology has made possible an immense increase in the food supply, and, along with improvements in medical knowledge and in popular education, it has produced a marked decline in death rates, a rise in birth rates, and a lengthening of the span of life.

Demographers who have charted the future pattern of population growth offer startling estimates. The world population may reach seven billion by the year 2000. Some predict that by the year 2240 the population will be over 20 billion, and around 100 billion by the end of the twenty-third century. Harrison Brown has suggested that if population continues to expand at present rates, "in 730 years human beings will cover the land areas of the earth and will be so tightly packed that each of us will be able to own on the average but one square foot of land." "By the year 3500," according to an estimate issued by the Editorial Division of *Newsweek*, "the weight of human bodies on the earth's surface will equal the weight of the world itself. By the year 6000, the solid mass of humanity would be expanding outward into space at the speed of light."[2]

It should be remembered, of course, that all of these figures are at best scientific guesses, and that population trends are based on three assumptions which may not be valid, namely that future trends of birth and death rates will be an orderly continuation of past trends, that there will be no international migration on a scale large enough to affect the predictions, and that there will be no major war.

Trends in Population Growth. Population growth appears to be related to the stages of economic development.[3] In the first stage, that of an essentially agricultural society, both birth and death rates are high, the people are young, and the number is usually expanding rapidly. Most of the peoples of Asia and, in fact, most of the underdeveloped areas of the world belong to this classification. In the second stage, that of countries in an early phase of industrial development, birth rates are still high but death rates are decreasing; invariably the population is a young and rapidly increasing one. The Soviet Union is now in this stage, and presumably will continue to be for some time to come. The third stage, that of the industrially mature nations, is characterized by low birth rates as well as low death rates. Hence there is a larger percentage of older people, and the population may be stationary, declining, or at best growing very slowly and beginning to level off. "The list of countries facing the likelihood of future population decline," says Dudley Kirk, "is a roster of the nations that have led the world in material progress.[4]

[1] *News Pointer*, issued by the Educational Division of *Newsweek*, April, 1964, p. 4.

[2] *Ibid.*, p. 2.

[3] In analyzing these three stages and their implications, a study of population pyramids would be helpful. See, for instance, Frank W. Notestein *et al.*, *The Future Population of Europe and the Soviet Union* (New York: Columbia University Press, 1944).

[4] "Population Changes in the Post-War World," *American Sociological Review*, IX (February, 1944), 30. Some authors disagree, the theory of cycles and of decline in the industrial state is challenged by Joseph S. Davis in "Fifty Million More Americans," *Foreign Affairs*, XXVIII (April, 1950), 412–426.

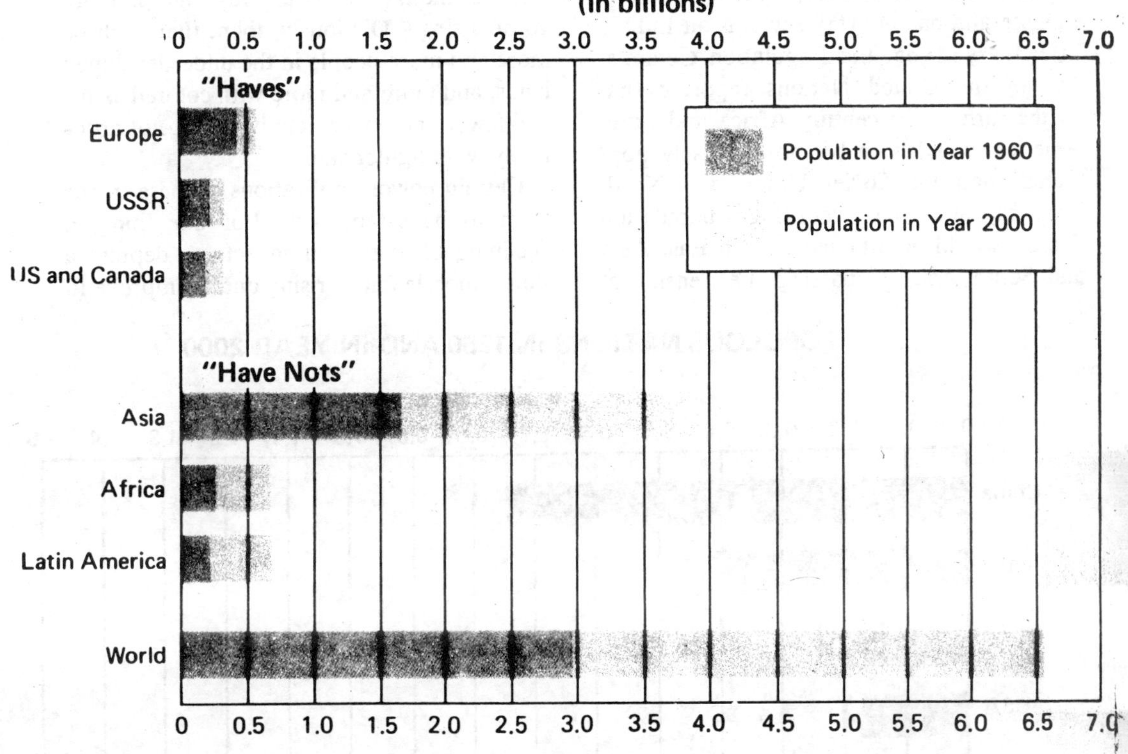

Population Reference Bureau

Most of the countries of the world are experiencing a much more rapid rate of population increase than demographic experts predicted, even a few years ago; but the increase is relatively much greater in underdeveloped countries, which can least afford to have such rapidly expanding numbers, than in the developed countries, where larger numbers can be accommodated at increasing standards of living. This is clearly one of the main reasons why the economic gap between the "rich" and the "poor" nations is widening, not narrowing — a most explosive fact in contemporary international relations. Whereas nearly one-half of the world's people in 1960 lived in developed countries, by the year 2000 the ratio will apparently be between one-fourth and one-fifth.

According to United Nations figures, which probably err on the conservative side, the rate of population growth in 1964 was 3.2 per cent or higher in Latin America and Africa, 2.4 per cent in Asia, 1.2 per cent in Europe (excluding the U.S.S.R.), 1.6 per cent in the U.S.S.R., and 1.4. per cent in the United States. Among the larger states which were experiencing a growth rate of 2 per cent or higher were Communist China, India, Pakistan, Indonesia, and Brazil. Large states with a growth rate of 1.5 per cent or less included the United States, Japan, Great Britain, France, West Germany, and Italy.

Despite Latin America, the center of population is shifting ever eastward. Population growth will be less in the West (except in Latin America) than in Asia and Africa, which already have two-thirds of the inhabitants of the globe. Indeed, about one-third of the world's people live in China and India together; one out of every five persons is a Chinese and one in every seven is an Indian. In January, 1965, the Population Commission of the United Nations reported that by the turn of the century Africa and Latin America would both be more densely populated than the Soviet Union and North America, and that "very high population density would be attained . . . in East Asia and South Asia, surpassing the density of Europe, though this is already high and will go on rising." Obviously, then, there will be more and more people in the underdeveloped lands, and more and more with colored skins, and fewer and fewer, relatively but not absolutely, with lighter skins.

Certain power implications of these trends seem to be established. For one thing, a declining birth rate often acts to depress a state's morale and a rising one to improve it.

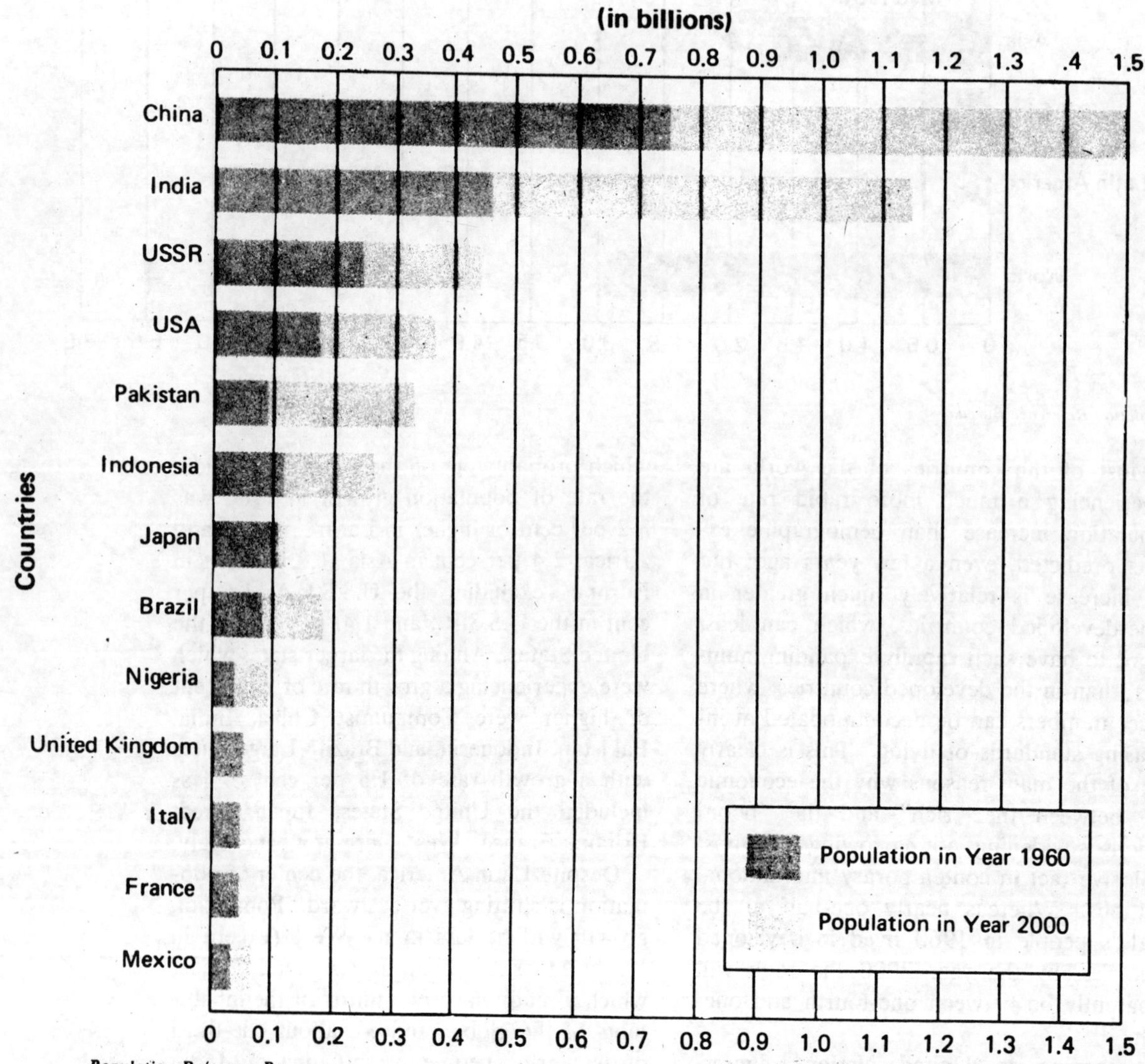

Population Reference Bureau

Growing populations usually seem to have more spirit and vitality than static or declining ones. With more certainty we can say that countries of rapidly rising population have a larger proportion of young people — hence a greater economic and military potential. A rising birth rate, however, may also mean too many mouths, a lowered standard of living, a reduction in personal efficiency, and a consequent decrease in national power. A constant or declining birth rate will probably mean the growth of the nonproducing consumer class, for old people will become an increasingly larger proportion of the population.

Overpopulation is a relative term, but where it exists in fact — i.e., where population is too large in relation to levels of development and food supply — it creates all kinds of economic, social, and political problems and pressures. As Aldous Huxley pointed out, "overpopulation leads to insecurity and unrest." "Given this fact," Mr. Huxley argued, "the probability of overpopulation leading through unrest to dictatorship becomes a virtual certainty. It is a pretty safe bet that twenty years from now, all the world's overpopulated and underdeveloped countries will be under some form of totalitarian rule." Even if one does not agree with Mr. Huxley's gloomy prediction, he can hardly avoid agreeing that the dangers to which Mr. Huxley refers are real ones.

Now, what are the power implications of these population trends? They are uncertain at best. Professor Quincy Wright concluded that "today the character of the influence of a particular population change is so dependent on other factors that it is impossible to predict from a study of population phenomena alone what international policies or occurrences to expect."[5]

[5] "Population Trends and International Relations," in Hans W. Weigert, Vilhjalmur Stefansson, and Richard Edes Harrison, eds., *Compass of the World* (New York: The Macmillan Company, 1944), pp. 427–428.

Present Distribution of Population. A map showing present-day population distribution reveals a few areas of dense population and many large regions with relatively few inhabitants. The most thickly populated areas are: China, in the southeast around Canton, along the Yangtze Valley and well into the interior, and in northeastern China; India, particularly in the valleys of the Ganges and the lower Brahmaputra; Japan; Java; Egypt along the Nile River; Western Europe, especially in northern Italy, Germany, Belgium, Holland, and England; and the eastern part of the United States, roughly from lower Connecticut to Washington, D.C. There are numerous empty areas of almost continental proportions: northern Siberia, inner Asia, the interior of the Arabian Peninsula, the interior of Borneo, western New Guinea, most of Australia, the Sahara Desert, southwest Africa, the great Amazon River region, Patagonia, the American southwest, most of Canada and Alaska, not to mention Antarctica, Greenland, or the northern part of the Scandinavian Peninsula. Although a demographic map of the world shows only ten per cent of the land area of the globe inhabited or under cultivation, it by no means follows that there is much room left for human settlement. Because of climate, terrain, or aridity, most of the still sparsely populated areas are not suited to large populations, unless water, power (especially thermonuclear power), human toil, and ingenuity can make larger areas useful for human habitation and sustenance.[6]

Population and National Power. Large populations may be a source of weakness or a source of strength in the modern world. The test is whether a state can utilize its human resources effectively, can support them at tolerable standards of living, and

[6] This point of view is strongly championed in Henry Still, *Will the Human Race Survive?* (New York: Hawthorn Books, 1966).

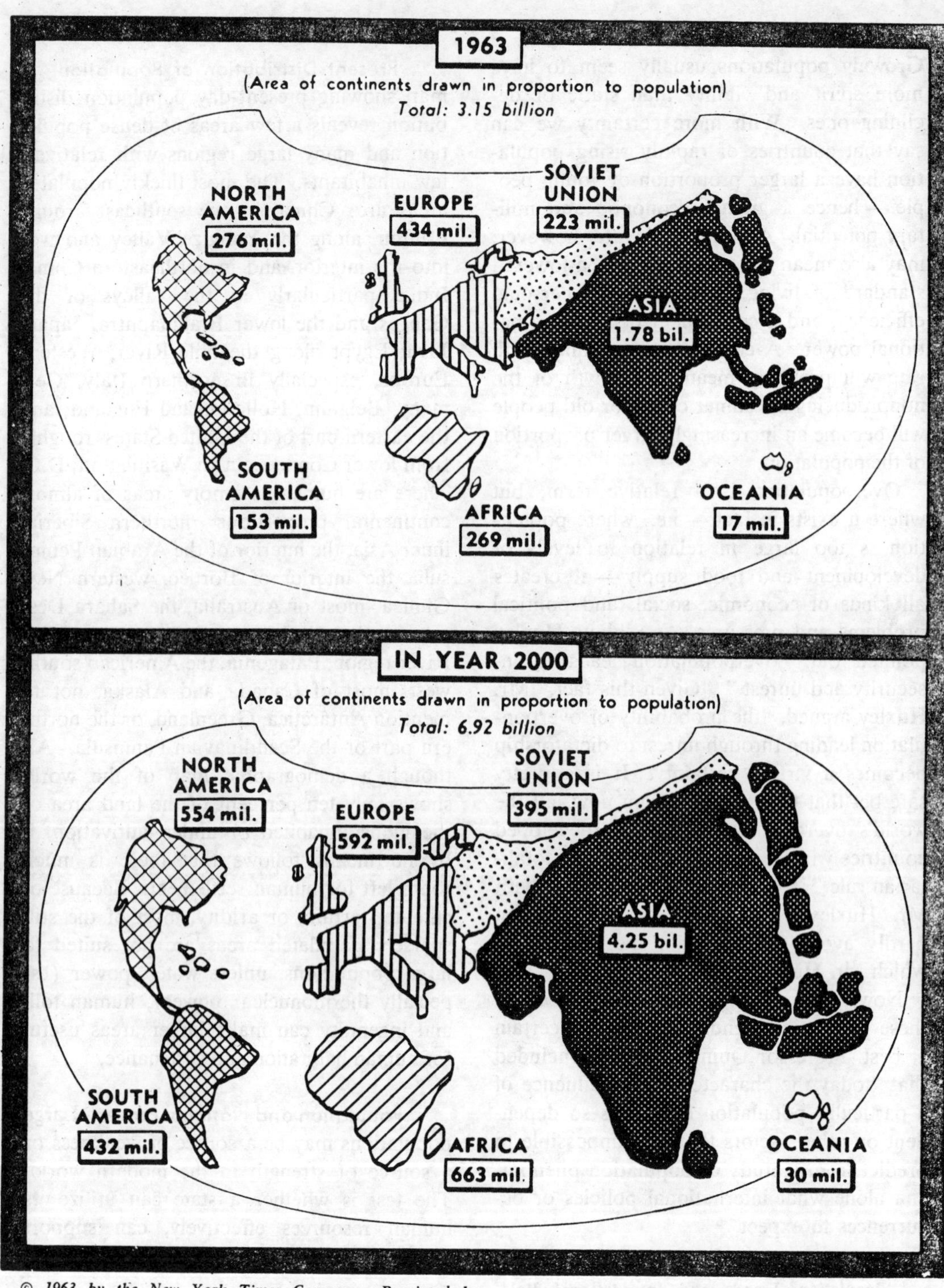

World Population—The Picture in Late 1963 and a Look Toward 2000

can provide constructive outlets for their talents and energies. In developed countries large numbers are usually a source of strength, whereas in underdeveloped lands the opposite is usually the case.

A casual glance at the power status of some populous states today might suggest that population has nothing to do with power. The answer is that a populous state may or may not make the most of its population, but that only a populous state can be a major power, by almost any definition. China and India, by far the most populous states, are certainly not regarded as the most powerful; but they are potentially major powers, and the influence of China, in particular, seems to be growing rapidly. The next most populous states, the Soviet Union and the United States, are the two superpowers. The next three states in order of population, Pakistan, Indonesia, and Japan, are not among the major powers, but Japan once had this status and may regain her former position if her present political and economic progress continues. West Germany, next in size, is becoming increasingly powerful and influential. Britain and France have smaller populations than all of these states — and also than Brazil, Nigeria, and Italy, none of which is more than a regional power — but they clearly have a world status far higher than their numbers would indicate.

Quality and Character of Population. The total number of people in a state is clearly a factor of major importance; so too are the quality and character of the population. These involve such considerations as age and sex distribution; trends in birth rates; standards of living, health, and literacy; productive capacity and skills; customs and beliefs; moral and religious codes and standards; and vigor and morale. They also involve the relative proportions of people living in rural and urban areas, changing patterns of life and thought, sectional and regional differences and characteristics, racial and minority group composition, class or caste structure, and degree of social mobility. In short, it is important to know not only how many people live in a state but what kind of people they are, what they are doing, and what they are striving to become. Some information can be gained through quantitative studies, at least in countries where fairly reliable statistics are available; but the kind of sophisticated analysis that is called for raises many questions about intangibles, and above all it leads into the nebulous but vital area of national character.

Age distribution is greatly affected by the stage of economic development, as we have noted. A mature industrial society will have a relatively large number of older people, whereas a society in the early stage of industrial development will have a relatively large number of young people. For military and economic purposes it is important to have large numbers of people within the ages of maximum physical and productive effectiveness, say between 18 and 45. The Population Commission of the United Nations reported that in 1960 the percentage of people 65 years of age or older in the more developed countries was 8.3, whereas it was only 3.3 in less developed regions.

In the United States the increasing number of older people is having a great effect on the entire structure of American life and thought, whereas in China and India and other underdeveloped countries the profitable use of the rising number of younger people in an economy characterized by far greater unfilled needs than capabilities is a particularly urgent problem.

The vigor, energy, and productive capacity of a people are definitely related to their standards of living, their health, their levels of education, and their economic incentives. These factors account for the vast differences between the majority of the people in underdeveloped countries, whose energies are sapped by inadequate nourishment, poor health (including various kinds of wasting diseases and chronic maladies), illiteracy, and lack of economic opportunity, and people in the more highly developed countries. Doubtless there are also other factors of importance, such as climate, the character of a people, and social and religious values and attitudes. Figures of life expectancy are particularly revealing. In some of the more developed countries, such as Norway, Sweden, the Netherlands, Denmark, and Israel, the normal life expectancy is now 70 years or over for men, and about four years higher for women; and in several more, including the United States, Japan, Canada, Switzerland, Czechoslovakia, Australia, and New Zealand, the figure is 67 or more for men and over 70 for women. On the reverse side of the shield are the underdeveloped areas, where life expectancy figures may be below 40 years and infant mortality is particularly high (along with maternal deaths in childbirth). Indians, for example, are proud — and justly so — that since independence the life expectancy in India has been raised from 27 to about 40 years; but this is still a shockingly low figure, and suggests the magnitude of the problems remaining.

The racial character of a population is also of great importance. Migrations of peoples throughout the centuries have produced a vast intermingling and miscegenation. In spite of all the nonsense about pure and superior races, there is probably no such thing as a pure race at the present time; but the degree of racial intermixture varies greatly. A few countries, such as Japan, are still relatively homogeneous; but most are multiracial and many are multilingual. A study of the racial composition of a national group throws much light upon national character and behavior, and provides clues for the analysis of national power. The United States has often been called a melting-pot, but parts of the country are inhabited largely by peoples of a single or a few ethnic backgrounds, and there has not yet been a high degree of "melting" between white and black Americans. In the Republic of South Africa a sharp distinction is drawn among the black Africans who constitute the great majority of the total population, the "coloreds" — people of Indian origin and others with colored skins who are not classed as black Africans — and the small minority of white people, who are mostly of Dutch (Boer) or English stock.

Population Control. A great deal of attention is now being devoted to the "population explosion" and it implications. The main channels of action to deal with the population problem are fairly clear. They include combined efforts at more economic development and more effective measures for birth control, or "family planning," to use a more comprehensive term.

Thus far birth control has never been practiced on a large scale, and there are formidable reasons — of religion, ignorance, human nature, economics, and politics — for this. The list of countries which have embarked on birth control programs is growing every year. President Ayub Khan of Pakistan has called population "our problem number one." Both Pakistan and India have included family planning programs in their five-year plans. Communist China, which began a birth control program in 1956 but abandoned it two years later, has recently been conducting a campaign against early marriages. Various organs and agencies of the United Nations, especially the Population Commission, have been studying birth control techniques and have been calling attention to the importance of extending their use. Two private American foundations, Ford and Rockefeller, have helped to develop and finance birth control experiments, especially in India. Until recently the United States refrained officially from more than cautious and indirect encouragement of birth control programs, largely because the subject is a delicate political issue; but President Johnson expressed a definite interest in such programs, and the Agency for International Development and other United States agencies working abroad have actively supported research and planning in this field. Even the Roman Catholic Church, long a staunch and unyielding opponent of birth control in any form other than the "rhythm method," has given evidence of modifying its position, although Pope Paul VI's encyclical letter, *Humanae Vitae,* of July 29, 1968, sternly reaffirmed the Church's ban on all mechanical and chemical measures of birth control.

Perhaps the greatest obstacle of all is ignorance and custom. In spite of all the publicity efforts, only a few people in underdeveloped areas, where the need for family planning is most urgent, are familiar with birth control techniques, and even fewer are really interested in trying them. "In the practical affairs of life, where human labor is still the main force of a primitive society, many parents in Asia and Africa consider their myriad children as necessary helpers in the fields, as defenders against feuding tribes, and as security for old age. 'To preach birth control to an underdeveloped country is a joke,' says the sociologist Germaine Tillion."[7]

Even in the relatively few countries which have endorsed and publicized methods of birth control, very little actual control has been apparent. Japan is the one conspicuous exception. It achieved a drastic reduction in the birth rate by legalizing abortions in 1948 and followed with a program which resulted in a widespread use of contraceptives.

The real incentives to voluntary limitation of the size of families seem to come from increasing economic development and a growing desire for a better standard of living. This has been the experience in almost all of the industrially mature countries, and doubtless the pattern will be repeated elsewhere, as other countries enter more fully into the industrial age.

[7] *News Pointer,* April, 1964, p. 4.

Population and Food Supply. We have already listed food and people as perhaps the greatest "problems" of the twentieth century. A United Nations report on world standards of living, released in 1952, stated: "While one-third of the world is maintaining increasingly higher standards of living, two-thirds of the world are living under conditions which are getting worse." Thirteen years later a special report concluded: "The amount of food, housing and employment available to each Asian has shown little improvement over the years and in some cases has actually declined." The Food and Agriculture Organization calculates that, whereas food production has increased by some nine per cent since the end of World War II, population has increased by twelve per cent. Fortunately, the picture is beginning to look a little brighter; but the stark fact remains that two-thirds of the people of the globe do not now get enough to eat, and every month there are four million more mouths to fill than the month before.

This rather grim situation has evoked dire predictions from a group of social thinkers who might be termed Neo-Malthusians. They predict that unless and until men stop wasting natural resources and, in addition, place drastic checks on their "happy-go-lucky procreation," they are doomed to an endless cycle of wars and to pestilence, disease, and famine, as Malthus warned more than a hundred and fifty years ago. This was the theme of a widely read book by William Vogt, *Road to Survival,* published in 1948. A somewhat more moderate but still alarming view has been expressed by Fairfield Osborn in *Our Plundered Planet* (1948) and *The Limits of the Earth* (1953). The main conclusion of these works is that all prospects for vast increases in the production of food are utterly inadequate to meet the needs of a rapidly expanding population. "The infinitely tragic fact," writes Osborn, "is that starvation is at present the only controlling factor to constantly increasing human numbers in a vast portion of the world." But he does not believe "that this must always be so."[8] He thinks it may be easier to keep population in check by means of birth control than to increase production to keep pace with an uncontrolled growth in population.

In a paper first presented to the American Chemical Society in 1964, Dr. Raymond Ewell, a chemical economist, warned that "the world is on the threshold of the biggest famine in history," because in the "three poor continents, Asia, Africa, and Latin America, the production of food . . . is lagging behind the population growth." "This," he added, "is the greatest and most nearly insoluble problem in the history of the world. And it is almost here." To avert this disaster Dr. Ewell emphasized the usual two prescriptions: increase agricultural and other production, and reduce population growth by birth control.[9]

FAO studies have suggested that it should be possible for the production of food and other basic necessities to keep well ahead of the growth of population and thereby to make higher standards of living for more people. In a study entitled *The Geography of Hunger,* Josué de Castro, former chairman of the Executive Council of FAO, contended that the answer lay not in the elimination of "surplus people" but in an "economy of abundance." Remarkable progress has been made in discovering new sources of food as well as of energy, and there is no reason to believe that there are not even more promising sources still untapped. The Neo-Malthusian prophecies of gloom may prove to be amply justified, but man's ingenuity in response to desperate human needs may yet prevail:

> . . . the world is still both a prodigious storehouse and a prodigious mechanism of production. The ingenuity and energy of man can turn up resources at present unknown and man can, if he will, go on reaping an abundant harvest from the chemistry of sun, earth, and water. . . . And finally, there are the possibilities of science's reaching beyond present known resources and changing the whole concept of what constitutes a resource. Science is not satisfied that animals, grains, vegetables, fruit, and fish are the only things man can eat. . . . The world faces, as it always has, an endless struggle to feed itself, today and tomorrow. . . . But there is no reason for energetic and ingenious men to despair.[10]

Technology

From the time that the first man sharpened a stick or wielded a rock to crack a clam shell or a skull, technology has played a part in the lives of people. The first advances were slow, and it was by accident that man learned to make fire, build steps, fashion weapons, and snare his game. Progress by accident was the rule until far into historical times, and it is by no means altogether absent today. Sooner or later, however, men began an active search for new ways of doing things, and today we speak with deep respect of "research" in many fields of science. Industries, universities, foundations, and governments are engaged in a ceaseless quest for new knowledge. The results are apparent everywhere — in agriculture, industry, medicine, administration, education, transportation, finance, and, of course, the science of warmaking.

Technology is often defined as applied science. Technological change "reflects the actual adoption of new methods and prod-

[8] *The Limits of the Earth* (Boston: Little, Brown and Company, 1953), pp. 214–215.

[9] Dr. Ewell's paper was reprinted in the *Philadelphia Inquirer,* October 25, 1966.

[10] "Malthusian Mischief," *Fortune,* XLV (May, 1952), 210, 211. The *Fortune* article refers to an interesting paper by Dr. Edgar Taschdjian in the August, 1951, issue of the *Bulletin of Atomic Scientists* in which he asserted that other promising sources of human food were wood and cellulose, plankton (sea-borne micro-organisms), Chlorella (a green alga), and Euglena ("half-plant, half-animal").

ucts; it is the triumph of the new over the old in the test of the market and the budget."[11] Moreover, it "involves a complex social process including many elements: science, education, research and development under private and public auspices, management, technology, production facilities, workers, and labor organizations."[12] It has already ushered in the age of computers, automation, and atomic and space technology.

"The extraordinary predominance of technology," as Robert L. Heilbroner pointed out, "is the decisive characteristic of modern times. The political and ideological agonies of our age are not without parallels in the past. What gives them their 'modern' character . . . is above all the technological attributes of the situation to which they now apply. The conduct of peace as well as war, the most routine flow of the economic process, even the intimate details of social existence must cope, at every instant, with the magnifying presence of a gigantic and dynamic technological foundation for contemporary life."[13]

Thus the scale and rate of technological change are relatively new phenomena; and "we are still only entering upon this age of technological predominance."[14] The impact on international relations, as on almost every aspect of "the human situation," will obviously be profound.

If writers on international relations seem to be too quick to measure technological advances in terms of war, it is not because they are unaware of the tremendous contributions of science to human welfare and happiness. It is because they are dealing with national states that still believe that only power can bring security, and because military effectiveness is the supreme test of power. Hence, we must be interested here, not in technology and the good life, but in technology and power. We need only to recall that our subject is "National Power."

Basic Technology. Less obviously related to warmaking than the technology of the manufacture and use of weapons is the technology of building the basic economy of a state. It is nonetheless an essential preliminary, for only an industrialized state can even begin to produce the highly mechanized weapons of modern warfare. We must remember that technology is a very broad term, that it goes far beyond iron and steel and machinery, that it means organized knowledge whether in agriculture, bookkeeping, or chemistry. In every field men have made advances in their ways of doing things, developing in each one highly specialized techniques. All these are inextricably interwoven, and all contribute to a state's industrial potential. Together they make up what the speech-makers call "know-how."

Only when a technological base has been achieved can a state produce the weapons of modern warfare. Then technology carries on further to convert the productive facilities of the nation into the making of the instruments of war. Blueprints are translated into armies, guns, ships, planes, bombs, missiles, and countless other items of defense and destruction. The point to remember is that immense technological progress must have taken place before the specialized technologies of modern war could be devised, expanded, and utilized. Even then they must continue to rest upon the technologies of peace, with added impetus to time-saving innovations and large-scale production. The majority continue in their old employments because they are doing jobs that sustain war industries, but many take up the spe-

[11] John T. Dunlop, "Introduction: Problems and Potentials," in John T. Dunlop, ed., *Automation and Technological Change* (Englewood Cliffs, N.J.: Prentice-Hall, 1962), p. 4.

[12] From "Final Report of the Twenty-first American Assembly," in Dunlop, p. 176.

[13] "The Impact of Technology: The Historic Debate," in Dunlop, p. 7.

[14] *Ibid.*, pp. 7–8.

cialized technologies of war-goods production. So complete is the dedication of the resources and manpower of the state to the business of making war that this is one of the reasons why we speak of "total war."

War Technology. We cannot undertake here to list the weapons of war and the special tools that are needed to produce them. Their number, variety, and complexity are almost infinite. We must, however, call attention to other kinds of technology that are vital in war and, indeed, oftentimes in peace as well. There must be efficient methods of mobilizing and training both workers and fighting men, of sustaining both public and military morale, of selling bonds, of conserving and allocating scarce materials and food, of organizing transportation, banking, and taxation, of combatting subversive activities, of guarding health, of settling labor disputes, of utilizing weather study, and on and on. Technology extends to every human enterprise in which there is some consciousness of method. It is vital on the fighting front as well as on the home front, for in the military operations area great numbers of men and vast quantities of supplies must be handled with maximum efficiency. There, perhaps even more than on the home front, it is tied in with the element of leadership.

Our emphasis here on basic technology must not let us forget for an instant that the "pay-off" is in the military establishment. Indeed, some writers deal exclusively with the production of war goods when they discuss technology as an element of national power. Indispensable as is a broad, basic technology, it must eventuate in war production. Professor Ralph Turner had this beginning-to-end continuity in mind when he wrote that "every action from finding minerals in the earth and extracting them from it, through every process of manufacturing metals and shaping them, to all movements of metals to and upon the area of combat form a *grand technological sequence*. The organization and maintenance of this sequence is the central problem of waging total war. Subsidiary actions of all kinds support this sequence and facilitate its operation."[15]

The contribution of economic production to the victory of the United Nations in World War II is so well known that it needs no emphasis here. Hanson W. Baldwin wrote that "American production and construction, which reached Wellsian proportions, can be said to have been directly responsible for the victory over Germany and Japan," a victory that was won in spite of the fact that the enemy "was often on a par with us, or even superior to us" in "training for combat, in will-to-fight, in leadership, in tactics, and in the quality of . . . equipment."[16] But, he added, "we could build an airfield or a pipeline in a fraction of the time the enemy needed; and we could turn out ten tanks to his one." In making these judgments Baldwin acknowledged the importance of other elements that contributed to the Allied victory.

Atomic and Space Technology. One of the greatest achievements of modern science and technology has been the harnessing of the power of the atom. The atomic bomb itself was the product of minds of many countries and of innumerable experiments in basic and applied research over many years. It could not have been developed without raw materials from many parts of the world. And above all, it could have been made only in a country which had the financial, economic, and human resources, the technological skills, and the advanced technological structure to launch such a gigantic experiment in time of war. Nor could the H-bomb have been made in a country which did not

[15] "Technology and Geo-Politics," *Military Affairs,* VII (Spring, 1943), 9.

[16] America at War," *Foreign Affairs,* XXIV (January, 1946), 241.

possess the necessary finances, skills, and facilities. Only a few countries — those with complex and well-developed technologies — can hope to pioneer in the nuclear field. But atomic reactors are now being built, or soon will be built, in a number of countries which are by no means among the industrial giants of the present day; and as the major atomic powers make available to other states usable supplies of atomic materials, atomic energy may become rather generally available for peaceful uses — and potentially, at least, for military uses as well. Among the many unanswered questions which the advent of the atomic age has raised are those of its implications for world politics and of its effect on the relative power position of states.

Just as uncertain are the implications of man's ventures into outer space, which began with the launching by the Russians of Sputnik I in October, 1957. The engines and instruments for space vehicles — powerful rockets and booster systems, communication and weather satellites, computers and other electronic and communication devices, etc. — and the continuing program for the scientific exploration of the solar system, with a manned landing on the moon as the immediate target — these and many other startling developments represent a tremendous technological challenge and achievement. Both the United States and the Soviet Union are spending several billions of dollars each year and are allocating vast resources to their space programs. Space science and technology promise "to bring about revolutionary changes in man's life on earth."[17] They have both military and civil applications. They hold forth great prospects for human welfare, and they also have great potential for human destruction. "Capabilities in outer space have become an important reflection of national power."[18] International cooperation is essential to ensure the peaceful use of outer space by all nations and the prevention of its use. for launching weapons of mass destruction.

Because of the fundamental importance of atomic and space technology and its implications, an entire chapter of this volume is devoted to the larger question. Here we shall essay a brief analysis of the power-political aspect.

Technological Position of the United States. The United States is the technological giant of the modern world — indeed, of all time. Whatever other peoples and nations may think of the United States and of her policies, they are acutely aware of her tremendous power, both actual and potential. The circumstances which gave the United States this unique preeminence have often been explored. They include: a fortunate geographical location and historical experience; a large and well-endowed land mass; a highly developed economy based on the effective utilization of natural resources; mastery of the techniques of mass production; great inventive skill and incentives to progress; stable political institutions and a high degree of national unity; relative freedom — at least until recently — from the troubles and vicissitudes of other parts of the world; a relative absence of class distinctions; and a skilled and energetic people. American industry today accounts for about forty per cent of the world's productive capacity.

But American resources, however great, are by no means inexhaustible. To keep up the level of her technology, and to expand it to meet expanding needs, the United States must develop a long-range program for training needed scientists and technical personnel, as well as perfect her techniques of

[17] "Final Report of the Twentieth American Assembly," in Lincoln P. Bloomfield, ed., *Outer Space: Prospects for Man and Society* (Englewood Cliffs, N.J.: Prentice-Hall, 1962), p. 193.

[18] *Ibid.*, p. 196.

mass production and distribution. Furthermore, she is lagging in basic research. She has, in fact, always given far more attention to applied than to basic research. Yet the relationship between the two is often close indeed, and much basic research, even if a large part of it seems to lead nowhere, is a prior condition of significant practical results. "What takes place in the laboratories today, shapes the world of tomorrow. Every scientific advance translated into improved technology changes, and in some instances may revolutionize, the distribution of political power over the globe."[19]

Nor has the United States government yet developed a well-coordinated program of scientific research and development in the tools of war, even though the need was amply demonstrated by wartime experience. The story of the work of the Office of Scientific Research and Development, under Dr. Vannevar Bush, has been told in a series of excellent volumes.[20] Research is now being continued and actively promoted by several government agencies, including the Office of Defense Mobilization, the Atomic Energy Commission, the National Aeronautics and Space Administration, and the National Science Foundation. But when this is balanced against estimated future needs — and against the present Russian program — it becomes evident that the United States is not doing enough to encourage young Americans to undertake scientific training.

[19] *Foundations of National Power* (Revised outline for course in Foundations of National Power, published by the Bureau of Naval Personnel in July, 1947), p. 21.

[20] Among these are J. C. Boyce, ed., *New Weapons for Air Warfare* (Boston: Little, Brown and Company, 1947); L. R. Thiesmeyer and J. Burchard, *Combat Scientists* (Boston: Little, Brown and Company, 1947); J. Burchard, ed., *Rockets, Guns and Targets* (Boston: Little, Brown and Company, 1948); and I. Stewart, *Organizing Scientific Research for War* (Boston: Little, Brown and Company, 1948). See also James P. Baxter, *Scientists Against Time* (Boston: Little, Brown and Company, 1946).

Technology and Society. Two aspects of the relationship of technology to the social order must be kept in mind by those observers who see in Western industry the answer to the Communist threat. The first relates to governments and technology. Germany, under several different types of regimes, including that of the Nazis, became the leading industrial state of continental Europe. The Soviet Union developed a solid technological base in the short space of hardly more than a generation, and she did so without the incentives of the free enterprise system and without extending substantial freedoms to the great mass of her people. Japan, in an amazingly short time, acquired many of the techniques of industrial production and military organization from the West without effecting a major reorientation in her attitudes or institutions. The experience of these and other states suggests that technology is no monopoly of the Western world or of democratic states.

The second aspect relates to the truism that "technological progress is a function of the entire economy and social system of a country." This lesson has been driven home again and again by those who have been engaged in programs of economic development and technical assistance in underdeveloped countries. Equipment and methods have to be suited to the political, economic, and social environment of the "host" country, and the people of that country have to want the innovations as well as learn how to use them. "The social condition for the origin of science," Professor John Macmurray has observed, "is that a particular society wants to strike out upon a new path in its *social* behavior instead of maintaining its traditional way of behaving."

Technology in war also has its quantitative measure. It is not enough that one plant can make planes and another precision instruments, any more than it is enough that one man can raise wheat and another can fly a bomber. Here it is that population and raw materials clearly become elements of national power. And here it is that better technologies add to the strength of the state.

As technologies enable a state to expand production and extend the variety and quality of goods produced, they add strength to its economy and hence to its economic power. The essence of economic power is other states' dependence, whether for markets, raw materials, labor, or capital, and the greater the dependence the greater the power. British industrial domination of a century ago gave power to the empire; Germany's scientific and technological achievements gave her power in more recent times; and the efficiency of the United States in the making of machinery and in mass-production techniques gives her power today. These are instances of economic power through technology — not quite the same as the power of Malaysian rubber, Iranian and Arabian oil, and Canadian nickel and wood pulp, which exemplify the power of natural resources.

Ideologies

Thus far we have been considering tangible and material factors of national power. Now we must turn to factors that are no less important, although they are more difficult to isolate and define. These are the elements of ideology, morale, and leadership.

Meaning and Nature of Ideologies. The word "ideology" is now a common one in the vocabulary of international politics. We are told that the main issues that divide nations and peoples are basically ideological in nature, and that conflicting ideologies are a major cause of war. But what is an ideology? How does it differ from an idea, or a doctrine, or a belief? What gives it its pervasiveness, its power? Why is it a disturbing element in world affairs?

One of the most satisfactory attempts at definitions is as follows: "An ideology is a cluster of ideas, about life, society, or government, which originate in most cases as consciously advocated or dogmatically asserted social, political, or religious slogans or battle cries and which through continuous usage and preachment gradually become the characteristic beliefs or dogmas of a particular group, party, or nationality."[21] "An ideology," according to Raymond Aron, "presupposes an apparently systematic formalisation of facts, interpretations, desires, and predictions."[22] It is a system of ideas — usually a closed system — put together in some logical way.

Interpreted in such a broad and generic sense, the term "ideology" can be applied to a great variety of the moving ideas of our time, including many of the "isms" — nationalism, anti-imperialism, totalitarianism, communism, fascism, nazism, Marxism, socialism, liberalism, collectivism, and so on through a long list. Democracy also is in many respects an ideology; the same is true of the major religions, notably the proselytizing ones such as Islam and Christianity. Ideologies may be classified in a variety of ways. Hans Morgenthau discusses certain "typical ideologies of foreign policies" under three headings: (1) ideologies of the status quo, such as peace and international law; (2) ideologies of imperialism; and (3) those ideologies which appear to be somewhat ambiguous, such as the principle of national self-determination.[23]

Some of the ideologies which we have just listed are hardly ideologies at all, but rather umbrella terms which cover a multitude of

[21] Richard C. Snyder and H. Hubert Wilson, *Roots of Political Behavior* (New York: American Book Company, 1949), p. 511.

[22] Raymond Aron, *The Opium of the Intellectuals* (Garden City, N.Y.: Doubleday & Company, 1957), p. 307.

[23] Hans J. Morgenthau, *Politics Among Nations*, 3d ed. (New York: Alfred A. Knopf, 1954), pp. 90–96.

idea systems and patterns. Thus there are many ideologies of totalitarianism and even more of democracy. Christianity, too, considered in its ideological aspects, clearly has many varieties of ideologies. Perhaps the most powerful and most pervasive ideology of the twentieth century is nationalism; some writers hold that there are many varieties of it, and others that it is not an ideology at all. Is peace an ideology as Morgenthau believes? Is capitalism?

We speak of the American type of democracy — or even the American Creed, the American Way of Life, or the American Dream — but what precisely do these terms imply? No one ideology, not even the general ideology of democracy, can be regarded as the motivating force of American political behavior and the major determinant of American national character. This does not mean that there is no point in attempting to ascertain the permanent sources of national character and conduct.[24] These are reflected in the great documents of American freedom, especially the Declaration of Independence and the Bill of Rights of the Constitution. They are examined perceptively in many important works, including those of foreign observers. In his classic study *An American Dilemma* Gunnar Myrdal wrote: "America, compared to every other country in Western civilization, large or small, has the most explicitly expressed system of general ideals in reference to human interrelations." He found the "ideological roots" of the system in the European philosophy of Enlightenment, in Christianity, and in English law.

The term "ideology" was apparently coined only about a century and a half ago. According to Webster's *New International Dictionary* it was first used by Destutt de Tracy (1754–1836). Others have ascribed it to Jeremy Bentham or Napoleon. Although ideological factors have been a persistent element of social and political life throughout centuries of history, they were seldom of decisive importance before the twentieth century. In recent years, however, acquiring strength and inclusiveness and called ideologies, they have injected passionate new drives into international relations.

"Ours is not the first age," noted Joseph Roucek, "which has produced new systems of ideas, and which has been marked by ideological conflicts. But no age, with the exception of the time of the religious wars of the sixteenth century, has seen such a variety of doctrines; without any exception no age has seen the struggle of ideologies run so deeply and in such complex patterns."[25]

In the modern era "ideologism" became an important factor in international relations after the Bolshevik Revolution in Russia. The Bolsheviks emphasized ideological factors, and Western reactions to the consolidation of Communist control over a major state also had strong ideological overtones. The struggle between "communism" and "democracy" — or, as the Soviets described it, between "socialism" and "capitalism" — became a central theme in international relations. The rise of fascism and nazism further complicated the international ideological picture. World War II was in part an ideological conflict, as World War I had also been. Since World War II ideologies have had a powerful impact. The cold war may be viewed as an ideological conflict as well as a test of strength and will between the Soviet Union and the Western democracies. The Third World of newly emerging states has been a cockpit of ideological pressures. Communism, socialism, and liberal democracy have all exerted a powerful appeal, as have nationalism and anti-colonialism.

[24] Snyder and Wilson, pp. 553–694. The chapters here indicated are entitled "The American Ideology" and "The American Character."

[25] "Ideology as a Means of Social Control," *American Journal of Economics and Sociology*, III (April, 1944), 364.

The significance of ideologies in world politics today lies in the fact that in some instances they have become linked to national power. Just as power became the instrument of ambitious nationalism, it has now become the tool of ideologies. Without power of some kind, an ideology — even one which aspires to universalism — is a passive, harmless pattern of related ideas. What makes communism the dread of the free world is not the gospel of Marx and Lenin; it is Soviet and Chinese power associated with and sustaining the Communist ideology. Without power communism would be an impotent psychosis.

The "Ideologization of World Politics." Certainly the ideologization of world politics" is a phenomenon of the contemporary era. While this development has often produced a new cohesiveness within nations and groups of nations, it has generally exerted a disturbing and dangerous influence. Ideologies, in fact, are fertile sources of international conflict, and they greatly complicate the task of the peaceful resolution of all conflicts. At a time when the existing split between the Communist and the non-Communist worlds constitutes one of the major threats to peace, this point hardly needs elaboration. Ideologies are essentially irrational; they have a considerable emotional content; they can be used to obscure the real facts of a situation or the real motives of ambitious leaders; they can be appealed to by extremists and thus can make reasonable approaches and compromises difficult or even impossible; they frustrate efforts to find areas of agreement; they make it hard to deal with international problems without undue sacrifice of national honor or prestige; they turn international conferences into propaganda forums instead of opportunities for the accommodations of diplomacy. When strongly held ideologies come into conflict with other strongly held ideologies, international crises are bound to occur, and "solutions" are bound to become all the more elusive.

One of the most ominous trends of recent times has been the urge of totalitarian ideologies to universalism. This urge rests upon a gross perversion of the "One World" concept, for it envisages not interdependent states motivated by sentiments of mutual helpfulness but a single pattern of thought, emotions, and loyalties to which all men and nations must conform. Because ideologies of this kind can evoke fanatical support they must be regarded as instruments of national policy.

Ideologies may be "good" as well as "bad," for they give strength to worthy causes, unity to nations, and a sense of common interest to peoples in many parts of the world. One can argue that any progress toward effective international cooperation and realization of the goals of human brotherhood — in itself, perhaps, an ideology — must depend upon an ideological motivation. Although it is impossible to avoid the conclusion that the growing ideologization of world politics is on the whole an alarming development, it must be realized that love of a free world is also a powerful ideology, and that many great states have resolved that it shall remain stronger than any of its rivals.

The End of Ideology? In spite of the apparent "ideologization of world politics," some observers have talked of "the end of ideology." This is the title of a well-known book by an American sociologist, Daniel Bell, published in 1960. For the Western world, and especially for the United States, argued Professor Bell, "ideology which was once the road to action, has become a dead end." His subtitle referred to "the exhaustion of political ideas in the fifties." He was apparently convinced that the ideological fires in the Western world had largely cooled;

and while they still burned vigorously elsewhere, in time they might subside, and more pragmatic ideas and considerations would become predominant.

Other Western observers have also advanced the view that the age of ideologies may be coming to an end. In 1957 Raymond Aron, for example, wrote: ". . . it seems to me that the battle of ideologies belongs to the past, though Leninism, whether Stalinist or not, is bound to conduct a vigorous counter-offensive in the next few years. The wars of secular religions are ending. The wars of Great Powers animated by incompatible beliefs are not yet over."[26] One might point out that "incompatible beliefs," like "secular religions," contain strong ideological elements, but perhaps they are less likely to lead to conflict because of ideological emotionalism. The main issues in the world today, and such major disputes as those between China and the Soviet Union, Israel and the Arab states, and India and Pakistan, are not primarily ideological, although ideological factors are obviously present.

In many countries it may be true that political ideas and ideologies have lost their old appeal, but in international politics this seems to be less true. Even in the Western world ideological factors continue to shape national and international policies and popular attitudes and reactions, and in the non-Western world they continue to be pervasive and moving forces. Clearly it is premature to speak of "the end of ideology" in international affairs; but, as Zbigniew Brzezinski observed, while "the end of ideology may not yet be at hand, . . . the relevance of several ideologies seems to be ending."[27]

Morale and National Character

Morale. Morale is a thing of the spirit, made up of loyalty, courage, faith, and the impulse to the preservation of personality and dignity. It has been described as a healthy frame of mind characterized by fidelity to a cause.[28] In political usage it commonly pertains to a large group or even a nation. Morale alone cannot produce raw materials, food, and the weapons of war, but it can provide the "drive" that leads to more raw materials, more food, and so on. It can make men and women work harder, sacrifice more, and fight harder. It can evoke that last ounce of strength, that tightening of the belt, that willingness to compromise domestic differences, that impulse to service "above and beyond the call of duty" that has so often been the margin of victory.

Morale is certainly related to ideologies and even to ideas. We have earlier discussed the importance of nationalism as a determinant of loyalties and conduct. History is replete with hero stories of men who died fighting for their king, for their religion, for freedom, for democracy, for national unity, for fascism, for nazism, or for communism; in fact, sometimes history seems wholly made up of men fighting and dying for what were to them holy and righteous causes. Devotion is not the whole of morale, but it is a large part of it. Other conditions may have to be added — hope, means, health, etc. Essentially a thing of the mind and spirit, morale defies precise analysis.

Within limits, national morale can be manufactured, or at least stimulated, by various propaganda techniques. State propaganda in time of peace is usually prosaic: obey the law, pay your taxes, vote, join the Navy and see the world, drive carefully and save a life, and don't pick flowers or start a fire in the national parks. In wartime the tempo is vastly accelerated, and the propaganda machines are thrown into high gear to call forth the maximum fighting efficiency of which the country is capable. Conversely, the morale

[26] Aron, p. xviii.

[27] "Tomorrow's Agenda," *Foreign Affairs,* XLIV (July, 1966), 668.

[28] See J. A. Ulio, "Military Morale," *American Journal of Sociology,* XLVII (November, 1941), 321–330.

of the leaders and people in enemy countries must be weakened.

Morale is by no means entirely the product of the techniques of propaganda. It is partly that, but it is also the result of the impact on the public spirit of incidents and events. In wartime it may be lowered by the loss of a great battle, the death of a key leader, the sinking of ships, the defection of an ally, additions to the enemy's strength, new conscription demands, the announcement of a staggering budget, and the like. It may also be affected by reverses on the home front: crop failures, floods, sabotage, strikes, industrial and railroad accidents, epidemics, and so on. Even good news can produce bad effects; a single spectacular victory in the field may bring a premature relaxation of effort.

Morale is closely related to leadership; it is strongly influenced by personality, by success and failure, and by dramatic words and daring actions. Words alone sometimes work miracles. American history is filled with dramatic phrases that whipped the nation into a fighting mood: "I have just begun to fight"; "Damn the torpedoes — full steam ahead"; "Remember the Maine"; "We must make the world safe for democracy." World War II produced no single ringing call to arms, but several phrases caught on and contributed to America's high morale: "Arsenal of Democracy"; "Remember Pearl Harbor"; "Sighted sub; sank same"; MacArthur's "I shall return"; and General McAuliffe's reply of "Nuts" to a German demand for the surrender of an isolated unit in the Battle of the Bulge. Other words, including those of Winston Churchill and Franklin D. Roosevelt, together with many unforeseen incidents of war, have affected national morale for better or for worse, and they have often done so without benefit of well-oiled machinery.

We must not regard morale-building as something exclusively in the domain of national leaders. In a democratic country it is everybody's business. In World War II thousands of persons made notable contributions. Acting through clubs and organizations of every kind, and often alone, these persons worked long and hard to awaken others to consciousness of the great issues involved and to the need for the best efforts of everyone. True, they frequently used the established techniques, but the motivation was often spontaneous.

National Character. Morale seems to be related to what we call "national character," but the relationship is not clear. We tend to think of the Chinese in terms of cosmic unchangeability, of the Germans in terms of thoroughness, discipline, and efficiency, of the Russians in terms of relentless persistence, of all Latins in terms of esthetic instinct and volatility, of Americans and Canadians in terms of resourcefulness and inventiveness, and of the English in terms of dogged common sense. Whether these characterizations are correct and, if so, to what extent they are acquired traits are questions that we gladly surrender to the sociologists. What concerns us here is the part that national character plays in morale. Why, for instance, did the Finns fight so heroically in 1939 and the Greeks in 1940, whereas French resistance collapsed so completely in 1940? Why did Germany fold up so neatly in 1918 and fight almost to the last ditch in 1945? Or take the miracle of Dunkirk in the spring of 1940, one of the most dramatic pages in world history, and the thundering challenge of Winston Churchill that electrified the world and expressed the resolve of every Englishman: "We shall fight on the beaches, we shall fight on the landing grounds, we shall fight in the fields and in the streets, we shall fight in the hills; we shall never surrender." What have we here? National character, morale, or both?

Some writers list national character as one of the elements of national power, as does Professor Hans J. Morgenthau in his *Politics*

Among Nations. It may be regarded as one of the major determinants of national morale, although, of course, it is broader than morale. But where it is more than the basis of morale, it may help to explain some other elements, as American "resourcefulness and ingenuity" help to explain the advanced state of American technology. At other times it may account in part for the cohesiveness of a population, or for the effectiveness of leadership. National character may be thought of as climate, morale as weather.

Culture. The relationship of morale and national character to the general educational and cultural achievements of a people is difficult to determine. One may reason that the members of an advanced society have clear advantages over those of a backward society: they are better qualified to devise new weapons and to improve their production techniques, to organize morale-building propaganda, to train their leaders, to recruit strength through diplomacy, to enlist financial assistance, and in many other ways to utilize their resources. He may believe that the people of an advanced society have a better realization that there are ups and downs in every war, that the last battle counts most, and that the miseries of submission may be worse than the horrors of war. On the other hand, he may contend that backward peoples are less dependent on "critical raw materials," on a smoothly functioning factory system, on the continued flow of the comforts and luxuries of life, and on the uninterrupted efficiency of a complex administrative system. He may argue that people on the lowest cultural level can gain new hope in ways that are closed to members of a more progressive society—from "signs," "tokens," rituals, and the assurances of "wise men."

Emphasis on culture — at least "modern culture" — as an important factor in morale and national character does not appear to be justified by history. Backward peoples have at times been easy victims of conquest; at other times they have fought with incredible valor and ferocity. Advanced peoples have the same contradictory record: witness the fighting France of 1914 and the defeatist France of 1940; and the capitulating Germany of 1918 and the fighting Germany of 1945. Until further studies have been made, it seems hardly correct to regard cultural differences as a significant factor in the determination of national character and morale.

Leadership

The importance of leadership in general probably needs to be called to nobody's attention, but two aspects of it as an element of national power may be somewhat less obvious. The first of these is the extent to which it overlaps other elements of power, and the other is the range of activities in which able leadership is essential to the realization of maximum power.

Leadership is interrelated with the other elements of national power because it is one of the measures of the extent to which those elements are utilized. Without leadership people cannot even constitute a state; without it there can be no well-developed or integrated technology; and without it morale is totally useless, if indeed it can exist at all. While leadership must be presumed if potential elements of national power are to be effectively used, it varies so greatly in quality that it may be regarded as a distinct factor or element.

Leadership in Total War. Gone are the days when effective leadership in time of war meant the authority to conscript or hire men, requisition supplies, and ride and fight well. Since the advent of total war, virtually every resource of the state must be guarded, developed, and utilized. Even in a democratic state the ultimate control of all war potential is in the hands of the duly constituted leaders of the state. Theirs is the responsibility for the maximum utilization of everything that can be made to contribute to national power in terms of ability to wage war. The range is staggering: food supply, raw materials of industry, industry itself, transportation, communications, public health, national morale, and war financing, plus the creation and maintenance of a vast military establishment, which itself has truly colossal problems of organization, supply and transport, health, strategy, morale, and, it hopes, of occupation and military government. Total war is total partly because it calls for total resources, total organization, and total effort, and often what is close to the assumption of total power by the government. Upon the political leaders of the state falls the final responsibility for the coordination of all the energies of the state.

Specialized Leadership. But it is not enough to have competent leaders of the state, regardless of the authority they may possess. There must also be leaders of great ability to direct the many phases of the national effort which the political leaders must control and coordinate but in which they have no special qualifications for technical direction. Perhaps of first importance in time of war would be the men at the top posts in the military and naval establishments, but the government also has vital need of bringing the leaders in many fields to the support of the war effort. When William Green and Philip Murray promised that the American Federation of Labor and the Congress of Industrial Organizations would back the war effort to the limit, they were offering skill in the leadership of organized labor that existed nowhere in the government itself. So it was when spokesmen of industry, finance, education, farming, transportation, and other specialized groups pledged their support. Leadership is an elastic term, susceptible of various uses, but in the sense in which it is an element of national power it must include many persons upon whose qualities of leadership depends the development of the military potential.

Leadership in Diplomacy. Although the supreme test of a state's power is its effectiveness in waging war, most states are technically in a state of peace much more of the time than they are engaged in war. The United States, for example, has been at peace with all other nations of the world just about ninety per cent of the time between the Declaration of Independence and the present. Even in times of peace, however, states possess power. One measure of that power is the effectiveness of the state's diplomacy, which in turn is in part the measure of the competence of leadership.

Diplomacy can serve the interests of a state by protecting its people abroad; by constant vigilance in the search for new opportunities for trade; by facilitating established commercial intercourse; by the accumulation of a wide range of information on the geography, resources, techniques, culture, military establishment, diplomatic interests, and people of a foreign state; and, in general, by promoting respect and goodwill for the state and by keeping its leaders "informed." All of this is, of course, more or less routine, quite different from what we might call "power diplomacy." States making their diplomacy an instrument of power must maintain constant alertness and keep their ablest men in the foreign office. They must exploit to the limit "the art of bringing the different elements of national power to bear with maximum effect upon those points in the international situation which concern the national interest most directly."[29]

Diplomatic effectiveness, like military effectiveness, is a combination of various elements of national power. Both of them

[29] Morgenthau, p. 139. Diplomacy as an instrument of national power is discussed in Chapter 4.

are likely to be measured by the skill or genius of individuals. An astute diplomacy often achieves successes out of keeping with a state's power potential, just as brilliant generalship may win victories that upset all sober calculations. One might conclude that diplomatic and military talents ought to be regarded as more or less distinct elements of national power. One would then have to add still other elements, such, perhaps, as financial talent, which may be of such an order as to constitute the margin of victory. It seems much simpler to give leadership a definition broad enough to include all these special fields, and to regard it in this comprehensive sense as one of the elements of national power.

The Appraisal of National Power

We have presented national power as made up of seven elements: geography, natural resources, population, technology, ideologies, morale and national character, and leadership. We have not given special attention to military power, either potential or in-being, because this is a product of the other factors and represents the application of these factors to perhaps the most obvious and striking manifestation of a nation's power. Before concluding the discussion, it is necessary to make a few observations that should be kept in mind if national power is to be correctly understood

Relativity of Power. National power, like nearly everything else in this world of ours, is relative. A man with a million dollars is not rich in a group of multimillionaires; a man of forty is old to a child of ten and youthful to an octogenarian. Similarly, with power the absolute has little meaning. Fifty divisions, three hundred war vessels, two thousand planes — all these may represent overwhelming might against one opponent and miserable inadequacy against another. Power, however impressive on paper, is always to be measured in terms of the power of other states.

Changes in Power. Power is subject to continuous change. Absolute power may change for many reasons. A state's economic and political position and power may change fundamentally over a period of time. Much of human history is the story of "the rise and fall" of nations and other political entities. A state may increase or decrease the size of its military forces; morale may go down or up; leaders may be changed; raw materials may become less or more abundant; technological processes may be improved; new instruments and weapons of war may be invented; plagues, floods, and earthquakes may lower production, destroy supplies, kill workers, and depress morale; alliances may be formed or broken — all these and countless other changes may affect one or more of the elements of power and thereby alter a state's power potential. A change in absolute power will very likely produce a change in relative power as well.

A change in a state's relative power — the only important measure of power — may come with no perceptible change in its absolute power. The explanation is simple: the absolute power of another state or other states has changed more rapidly. One example will illustrate. At the beginning of World War I the British navy was undisputed mistress of the seas; at the close of World War II a stronger British navy was only second-rate, because the United States had greatly expanded her naval power.

Attention to Power. Leaders of states are, of course, aware of the essential elements of power and of their interdependence. If they are power-conscious, they try to bring about the maximum utilization of each of the elements within their respective states. Yet all the power-consciousness in the world cannot effect a precise measurement of power. Since power is relative, states would need to have detailed information on other states, and this is never complete. Arms of the same size are not necessarily of equal effectiveness, and the same rule must apply to all weapons. Transportation efficiency may upset apparent equality in raw materials, and an abundance of oil can hardly be measured against adequate supplies of iron ore. Much depends on where military action is to take place, on morale, on the attitude of outside states, and on the caprices of nature. Many variable factors, both quantitative and qualitative, prevent mathematical calculations from being accurate. All of these considerations add enormously to the burdens of leaders who must see to the security of the state.

When the warnings of statesmen are not enough, high taxes and excited commentators often help to remind people that we are living in a world in which states still feel that their best assurance of security lies in their own strength. As long as that is true, regardless of the fervent wishes of some peoples to live in peace, states must be expected to protect themselves with whatever power they can muster. If the United Nations, or some more viable and effective international organizations or arrangements, can eventually provide security for all, the need for reliance on national power, as now understood, may pass. Until that time statesmen will remain deeply conscious of the elements of national power. To ask them to do less is to ask them to ignore the lessons of history and to blind themselves to their paramount obligation.

SUGGESTIONS FOR FURTHER READING

ALMOND, GABRIEL A. *The American People and Foreign Policy*. New York: Harcourt, Brace, 1950. A study of national attitudes and characteristics.

APPLEMAN, PHILIP. *The Silent Explosion*. Boston: Beacon Press, 1965.

ARON, RAYMOND. *The Opium of the Intellectuals*. Garden City, N. Y.: Doubleday & Company, 1957. The concluding pages discuss the question: "The end of the ideological age?"

BARKER, SIR ERNEST. *National Character and Factors in Its Formation*. London, 1948. Reissue of a notable work.

BAXTER, JAMES PHINNEY, III. *Scientists Against Time*. Boston: Little, Brown and Company 1946.

BELL, DANIEL. *The End of Ideology; on the Exhaustion of Political Ideas in the Fifties*. New York: The Free Press, 1960. An arresting thesis which has provoked both interest and controversy.

BENEDICT, RUTH. *The Chrysanthemum and the Sword; Patterns of Japanese Culture*. Boston: Houghton Mifflin Company, 1946. An excellent study of Japanese national character.

BERELSON, BERNARD, *et al. Family Planning and Population Programs*. Chicago: University of Chicago Press, 1966. A summary of family planning programs actually under way throughout the world.

BOURGEOIS-PICHAT, JEAN. "Population Growth and Development," *International Conciliation*, No. 556 (January, 1966). A textual and tabular analysis, based largely on the material submitted to the United Nations World Population Conference, held in Belgrade in August–September, 1965.

BROWN, HARRISON. *The Challenge to Man's Future*. New York: The Viking Press, 1954.

BROWN, HARRISON, JAMES BONNER, and JOHN WEIR. *The Next Hundred Years; Man's Natural and Technological Resources*. New York: The Viking Press, 1957.

BURNS, EDWARD MCNALL. *Ideas in Conflict: The Political Theories of the Contemporary World*. New York: W. W. Norton & Company, 1960. Deals with theories of liberalism and democracy, collectivism, conservatism, and world conflict and world order.

Castro, Josué de. *The Geography of Hunger.* Boston: Little, Brown and Company, 1952.

Chandrasekhar, Sripati. *Hungry People and Empty Lands.* London, 1954. By a well-known Indian demographer.

Chisholm, Brock. *Prescription for Survival.* New York: Columbia University Press, 1957. By the former head of the World Health Organization.

Cottrell, Fred. *Energy and Society.* New York: McGraw-Hill Book Company, 1955.

Darwin, Sir Charles G., *The Problem of World Population.* Cambridge, England, 1958.

Demographic Yearbook. Statistical Office, United Nations. A voluminous collection of statistical data, issued annually.

Ebenstein, William. *Today's Isms,* 4th ed. Englewood Cliffs, N.J.: Prentice-Hall, 1964. Concise analyses of totalitarian communism, totalitarian fascism, democratic capitalism, and democratic socialism.

The Future Growth of World Population. United Nations, Population Studies No. 28, 1958.

Gould, Jay M. *The Technical Elite.* New York: Augustus M. Kelley, Publishers, 1966. Documents the growing importance of technology in human affairs.

Hauser, Philip M., ed. *The Population Dilemma.* Englewood Cliffs, N.J.: Prentice-Hall, 1963. A collection of papers prepared for the 23rd American Assembly, held in May, 1963.

ed. *Population and World Politics.* New York: The Free Press, 1958. Contributions by 12 outstanding experts.

"World Population Problem," *Headline Series* No. 174. New York: Foreign Policy Association, 1965.

Hsu, Francis L. K. *Americans and Chinese: Two Ways of Life.* New York: H. Schuman, 1953.

Kelman, Herbert C., ed. *International Behavior: A Social-Psychological Analysis.* New York: Holt, Rinehart, and Winston, 1965. Contains good discussions of ideologies, leadership, national character, etc.

Lasswell, Harold D. and Abraham Kaplan. *Power and Society.* New Haven: Yale University Press, 1950.

McCormack, Arthur. *The Population Explosion and World Hunger.* London, 1963.

Mead, Margaret, ed. *Cultural Patterns and Technical Change.* Paris, 1950.

And Keep Your Powder Dry. New York: William Morrow & Co., 1965. A new expanded edition of a study of American character, first published in 1942.

Notestein, Frank W. *et al. The Future Population of Europe and the Soviet Union.* New York: Columbia University Press, 1944.

Ogburn, William F., ed. *Technology and International Relations.* Chicago: University of Chicago Press, 1949.

Organski, Katherine, and A. F. K. Organski. *Population and World Power.* New York: Alfred A. Knopf, 1961.

Riesman, David. *The Lonely Crowd: A Study of the Changing American Character.* New Haven: Yale University Press, 1950.

Roucek, Joseph S., ed. *Contemporary Political Ideologies.* New York: Philosophical Library, 1960.

Strausz-Hupé, Robert. *The Balance of Tomorrow.* New York: G. P. Putnam's Sons, 1945. Meaning power balance, especially industrial power.

Vogt, William. *People! Challenge to Survival.* New York: William Sloane Associates, 1960. A call for vigorous action in the interests of human survival, by the author of *The Road to Survival,* published in 1948.

World Population and Food Supplies. American Society of Agronomy, Special Publication No. 6., 1961.

PART TWO

INSTRUMENTS FOR THE PROMOTION OF THE NATIONAL INTEREST

4 Diplomacy as an Instrument of National Policy

Sometime during his service as the top American military commander in the China-Burma-India theater, General "Vinegar Joe" Stilwell recorded his thoughts as a "Deck-Hand Diplomat":

> A brief experience with international politics confirms me in my preference for driving a garbage truck. This is admittedly not the proper approach to the matter of international politics. It is a very serious business. A lot of Big Figures indulge in it, and a host of little ones trail along. Those who make the grade are of course interested to dignify and even glorify the profession, which can be done in the wink of the eye by using the term "diplomacy" — a word we usually utter on a hushed and respectful note. The term "diplomat" to the average American evokes a vision of an immaculately dressed being — pin stripe pants, spats, cutaway and topper — and a coldly severe and superior manner which masks the lightning-like play of the intellect that guides the Ship of State, moves the pieces on the board with unerring precision, and invariably turns up in Washington without his shirt. Or rather our shirt.[1]

More than a quarter of a century before General Stilwell wrote these words, a man of a wholly different background, Joseph Stalin, had paid his respects to the art of diplomacy in these words:

> A diplomat's words must have no relation to actions — otherwise what kind of diplomacy is it? Words are one thing, actions another. Good words are a mask for the concealment of bad deeds. Sincere diplomacy is no more possible than dry water or wooden iron.[2]

General Stilwell had encountered almost as many difficulties with American diplomatic representatives and Chinese officials as he had with the jungles of Burma or from the Japanese. Moreover, he also reflected a deep-rooted American conviction that whenever representatives of the United States engage in negotiations with foreign diplomats they come out on the short end of the deal. Stalin, on the other hand, expressed the traditional attitude of modern dictators toward diplomacy, namely, that it is a means of concealing a nation's real aims and of providing a smoke screen for actions of a vastly different character. The two Joes, in short, took a cynical view of the art of diplomacy.

[1] Joseph W. Stilwell, *The Stilwell Papers*, arranged and edited by Theodore H. White (New York: William Sloane Associates, 1948), p. 256.

[2] Quoted in David Dallin, *The Real Soviet Russia* (New Haven: Yale University Press, 1944), p. 71.

The Nature of Diplomacy

While the sentiments of Stilwell and Stalin have some justification, they do not suggest the real nature of diplomacy, which consists of the techniques and procedures for conducting relations among states; it is, in fact, the normal means of conducting international relations. In itself diplomacy, like any machinery, is neither moral nor immoral; its use and value depend upon the intentions and abilities of those who practice it.

Diplomacy functions through a labyrinth of foreign offices, embassies, legations, consulates, and special missions all over the world. It is commonly bilateral in character, but as a result of the growing importance of international conferences, international organizations, regional arrangements, and collective security measures, its multilateral aspects have become increasingly significant. It may embrace a multitude of interests, from the simplest matter of detail in the relations between two states to vital issues of war and peace. When it breaks down, the danger of war, or at least of a major crisis, is very real.

Definition. No general definition of diplomacy can be very satisfactory or very revealing. The *Oxford English Dictionary* calls it "the management of international relations by negotiation," or "the method by which these relations are adjusted and managed." A charming characterization, though vague and inadequate, is given in Sir Ernest Satow's *Guide to Diplomatic Practice,* a work which has been the bible of British diplomats for many years. "Diplomacy," wrote Sir Ernest, "is the application of intelligence and tact to the conduct of official relations between the governments of independent states."[3] Since the eminent author of these lines is no longer living, we cannot ask him this impertinent but timely question: If intelligence and tact are lacking in the relations between states, is diplomacy impossible?

[3] Sir Ernest Satow, *Guide to Diplomatic Practice* (London, 1922), I, 1.

Foreign Policy and Diplomacy. A necessary distinction to bear in mind is that between foreign policy and diplomacy. The foreign policy of a state, as J. R. Childs has said, is "the substance of foreign relations," whereas "diplomacy proper is the process by which policy is carried out."[4] Policy is made by many different persons and agencies; but presumably on major matters in any state, whatever its form of government, it is made at the highest levels, though subject to many different kinds of controls. Then it is the purpose of diplomacy to provide the machinery and the personnel by which foreign policy is executed. One is substance; the other is method.

One of the most astute students and practitioners of diplomacy in the twentieth century, Harold Nicolson, is particularly insistent on calling attention to this distinction. In some cases, however, his efforts to be very precise in this matter seem to raise further questions. For example, in his interesting study, *The Congress of Vienna,* Nicolson wrote:

> It is useful, even when dealing with a remote historical episode, to consider where diplomacy ends and foreign policy begins. Each of them is concerned with the adjustment of national to international interests. Foreign policy is based upon a general conception of national requirements. . . . Diplomacy, on the other hand, is not an end but a means; not a purpose but a method. It seeks, by the use of reason, conciliation and the exchange of interests, to prevent major conflicts arising between sovereign states. It is the agency through which foreign policy seeks to attain its purpose by agreement rather than by war. Thus when agreement becomes impossible diplomacy, which is the instrument of peace, becomes inoperative; and foreign policy, the final sanction of which is war, alone becomes operative.[5]

[4] J. R. Childs, *American Foreign Service* (New York: Holt, 1948), p. 64.

[5] *The Congress of Vienna: A Study in Allied Unity, 1812–22* (New York: Harcourt, Brace, 1946), p. 164.

The last sentence tends to destroy the nice distinction between diplomacy and foreign policy which Mr. Nicolson makes; and it is misleading in that it suggests that diplomacy ceases to function when major international crises arise, especially if they lead to war. The object of diplomacy, as of foreign policy, is to protect the security of a nation, by peaceful means if possible, but by giving every assistance to the military operations if war cannot be avoided. Diplomacy does not cease to function, as Nicolson suggests, in time of war; although it necessarily plays a different role in wartime, the work of diplomats, as of foreign ministers, may even expand. The diplomacy of the two world wars of this century provides convincing support for this contention.

Functions of Diplomats

A diplomat is at times spoken of as the eyes and ears of his government in other countries. His chief functions are to execute the policies of his own country, to protect its interests and its nationals, and to keep his government informed of major developments in the rest of the world. In an address before the America-Japan Society in Tokyo, on November 22, 1938, Joseph C. Grew, United States Ambassador to Japan, commenting on the work of the professional diplomat, thus explained the "supreme purpose and duty of an ambassador":

> He must be, first and foremost, an interpreter, and this function of interpreting acts both ways. First of all he tries to understand the country which he serves — its conditions, its mentality, its actions, and its underlying motives, and to explain these things clearly to his own government. And then, contrariwise, he seeks means of making known to the government and the people of the country to which he is accredited the purposes and hopes and desires of his native land. He is an agent of mutual adjustment between the ideas and forces upon which nations act.[6]

[6] *Ten Years in Japan* (New York: Simon and Schuster, 1944), p. 262.

The work of a diplomat may be broken down into four basic functions: (1) representation, (2) negotiation, (3) reporting, and (4) the protection of the interests of the nation and of its citizens in foreign lands. These functions, as we shall see, are closely interrelated.

Representation. A diplomat is a formal representative of his country in a foreign state. He is the normal agent of communication between his own foreign office and that of the state to which he is accredited. In the eyes of many citizens of the country in which he is stationed, he *is* the country he represents, and that country is judged according to the personal impression he makes. The diplomat must cultivate a wide variety of social contacts, with the ranking officials of the foreign office and of the foreign government in general, with his fellow diplomats, with influential persons in all walks of life, and with articulate groups in the country. Social contacts can be enjoyable, stimulating, and profitable; they can also be hard on the stomach as well as on the pocketbook, trying to the diplomat's patience as well as to his intelligence. Whatever else they may be, they seem to be an inescapable adjunct of the important duty of representation. Although these contacts have tended to become less formal, they have at the same time broadened in scope. Ambassador Grew, a career diplomat of long experience, referred to them as "the X-Ray language vibrating beneath the surface of the spoken and the written word," which is simply a diplomat's way of saying that a trained mixer-observer-auditor can often pick up information or intelligence of great value in — or from — conversations at social functions.

Negotiation. Virtually a synonym for diplomacy, negotiation is par excellence the pursuit of agreement by compromise and direct personal contact. Diplomats are by definition negotiators. As such, they have duties that, as described by Mr. Childs, include "the drafting of a wide variety of bilateral and multilateral arrangements embodied in treaties, conventions, protocols, and other documents of a political, economic, and social nature. Their subject matter ranges from the creation of an international security organization, through territorial changes, establishment of rules to govern international civil aviation, shipping and telecommunications, and the adjustment of international commercial relationships, to such particular matters as immigration, double taxation, waterway rights, tourist travel, and exchange control. Almost the entire gamut of human activities is covered."[7]

Because of the developments in communications and the increasing resort to multilateral diplomacy, as well as for other reasons, diplomats do not play as great a role in international negotiations as they once did. Most agreements between states are still bilateral and are concluded through negotiations between the foreign offices by the use of ordinary diplomatic channels. But the major international agreements, especially those of a multilateral character, are usually negotiated directly by foreign ministers or their special representatives, often at international conferences. Diplomats also have less latitude than they once enjoyed; they are now bound more closely to their foreign offices by detailed instructions and constant communication by cable, diplomatic pouch, and transoceanic telephone; but, although their stature has been somewhat reduced, they are more than glorified messenger boys at the end of a wire, and the value of the personal factor in diplomacy is still very great.

Reporting. Reports from diplomats in the field are the raw material of foreign policy. These reports cover nearly every conceivable subject, from technical studies to appraisals of the psychology of nations. Diplomats must, above all, be good reporters; if they have the ability to estimate trends accurately, if they keep an eye out for all useful information, and if they present the essential facts in concise and intelligible form, they may be worth a king's ransom. According to a publication of the United States Department of State on the American Foreign Service, diplomats are expected to "observe, analyze, and report on political, social and economic conditions and trends of significance in the country in which they are assigned. Some major subjects of these reports are legislative programs, public opinion, market conditions, trade statistics, finance, production, labor, agriculture, forestry, fishing, mining, natural resources, shipping, freights, charters, legislation, tariffs and laws."[8] American diplomats alone prepare thousands of reports of this sort every year.

Protection of Interests. Although a diplomat is expected to get along with the authorities of the state to which he is accredited — that is, he must be *persona grata* to the government of a state — he is also expected at all times to seek to further the best interests of his own country. However selfish this approach may seem to be, it is the bedrock of the practice of diplomacy. While it is assumed that the interests of each state will be so interpreted that they will harmonize with those of the international community, it is not the function of the diplomat to make the interpretation. His duty is to look after the interests of his country as interpreted by the policy-makers back home and in accordance with treaties, other international agreements, and principles of international law. He also has the more specific duty of attempting to assist and protect businessmen, seamen, and all other nationals of his own country who are living or traveling in the country in which he is stationed or who happen to have interests there. He seeks to prevent or

[7] Childs, p. 70.

[8] *The Foreign Service of the United States*, Dept. of State Pub 3612, Foreign Service Series 6 (Washington, D.C.: Government Printing Office, August 11, 1946).

correct practices which might discriminate against his country or its citizens.

Classification of Diplomats and Consuls

Thus far we have used the word "diplomats" in a loose and rather general sense to include all members of the foreign services of all nations, and particularly those acting as chiefs of mission. Not all diplomacy, however, is carried on by diplomats. In a sense every citizen of a state who travels in another country is a diplomat, sometimes not a very good or skilful one. In a professional sense, diplomats include two main groups: diplomatic officers and consular officers. All the diplomatic functions which have just been described are performed, to a greater or lesser degree, by both groups; but, generally speaking, diplomatic officials specialize in representation and negotiation, whereas consular officials are particularly concerned with the protection of the interests of the nationals of their country. Reporting is an important function of both groups.

Diplomatic Personnel. The top positions in the diplomatic service are held by the chiefs of mission, most of whom have the rank of ambassador or minister. The various ranks of the diplomats who form the diplomatic hierarchy are still based on the rules agreed upon at the Congress of Vienna in 1815. The number of ambassadors, the highest diplomatic officers, has greatly increased in recent years. The United States, for example, refused to appoint any ambassadors until 1893, because it was felt that this title was too suggestive of monarchical diplomacy. Until very recently the United States had more ministers than ambassadors abroad, but today there are only a few ministers in the American Foreign Service.

Ambassadors and ministers together constitute only a fraction of the total number of diplomats, most of whom are career officials or noncareer specialists. Unlike the upper diplomatic hierarchy, there is no agreed-upon basis for classifying all these lesser diplomats, but at least three ranks are widely recognized. These are (1) counselors of embassy or legation, who rank highest among diplomatic staff members; (2) secretaries of an embassy or legation, usually ranked as first, second, and third secretaries; and (3) attachés, who may be junior career officers or noncareer persons serving in a diplomatic capacity on a temporary basis — including commercial, agricultural, military, naval, air, petroleum, cultural, press, and other attachés.

Within this generally accepted framework the foreign service of each country has many distinctive features. The Foreign Service Act of 1946 divided the American Foreign Service into five main categories: (1) Chiefs of Mission, divided into four classes for salary purposes; (2) Foreign Service Officers, the elite corps of the American Foreign Service, divided into seven classes (a top category of career ministers, plus Classes I–VI); (3) Foreign Service Reserve Officers, in six classes, who are assigned to the Service on a temporary basis (no more than four consecutive years); (4) Foreign Service Staff Officers and Employees, in 22 classes, who perform "technical, administrative, fiscal, clerical, or custodial" duties; and (5) Alien Clerks and Employees.[9] Personnel of the United States Foreign Service, nearly half of whom are alien employees, number over 20,000.

In the United Kingdom a new Diplomatic Service, comprising some 6,400 civil servants, was created on January 1, 1965, to absorb the personnel in the former Foreign Service, Commonwealth Service, and Trade Commission Service. This new Service has its own grade structure, comparable to the grades of the Administrative Class, the Executive Class, and the Clerical Classes of the Home Civil Service.

[9] As a result of amendments to the Foreign Service Act of 1946 there are now ten classes of Foreign Service Officers, eight of Foreign Service Reserve Officers, and ten of Foreign Service Staff Officers and Employees.

Consular Duties and Personnel. Consuls are a part of the foreign service of a country. They often perform diplomatic as well as consular functions, but their duties are different from those of the diplomatic service. They form a separate branch of the foreign service, even though diplomatic and consular officials are interchangeable in most foreign services at the present time. Historically, the consular service is older than the diplomatic, since it is concerned largely with two general functions which were of importance long before the rise of the nation-state system and the beginnings of organized diplomacy. These functions pertain to commercial and business relations and to services to nationals.

The specific duties under the first general function include many activities in the promotion of trade: periodical and special reports; replies to trade inquiries; settlement of trade disputes; certification of invoices of goods shipped to the country the consular official represents; enforcement of provisions of treaties of commerce and navigation, and of regulations regarding plant and animal quarantine, sanitation and disinfectants, etc.; protection and promotion of shipping; entrance and clearance of ships and aircraft; and other duties related to international commerce.

The second function refers to the varied work of consuls in many of the above respects but also to their work in helping nationals who live or are traveling in the country to which the consul is sent. These duties include welfare and whereabouts cases; funeral arrangements, and settlement of estates of nationals dying abroad; services to nationals who for any reason run afoul of local authorities or violate the laws of the foreign country; protection and relief of seamen (a very special function); notarial services; services to veterans; and the like.

Consuls are usually divided into five classes: (1) consuls general; (2) consuls; (3) vice consuls of career; (4) vice consuls not of career; and (5) consular agents. The first three classes are career foreign service officers who are assigned to duties as consuls general, consuls, or vice consuls; the last two are noncareer officers, who may be promoted from the ranks of the clerical staff or who, in the case of some consular agents, may not even be citizens of the country which they represent. Consuls general have supervisory powers over a large consular district or several smaller districts — but not necessarily over a whole country — and over the consular officials within their area.

Diplomatic Rules and Procedures

Diplomacy is still conducted largely on the basis of an intricate code that has evolved over many centuries. The unwritten rules of the game are as important as the written regulations, such as those laid down in the famous Règlement of 1815, in the Convention on Diplomatic Officers and the Convention on Consular Officers adopted by the American nations at Havana in 1928, in the Vienna Convention on Diplomatic Relations of 1961, "the first major international effort to regulate the wide field of diplomatic relations and immunities,"[10] and in the Vienna Convention on Consular Relations of 1963.

Matters of procedure and protocol[11] have often bulked very large in diplomatic relations; indeed, in past centuries the relations between sovereigns and the fate of nations sometimes seemed to be affected by what Diplomat X said to Diplomat Y, or who preceded whom and who sat where at a formal

[10] K. Ahluwalia, "Vienna Convention on Diplomatic Relations, 1961," *The Indian Journal of International Law*, I (July & October, 1961), 599. For a detailed consideration of the whole subject of diplomatic and consular procedure, see Satow; and Graham H. Stuart, *American Diplomatic and Consular Practice*, 2d ed. (New York: Appleton-Century-Crofts, 1952).

[11] "Protocol" has two meanings in diplomatic usage. As used above, it means what might be called diplomatic etiquette. In its other sense, it refers to a preliminary memorandum to be used as the basis for a later treaty or convention.

diplomatic function. If diplomats violated the code, the consequences to their country as well as to themselves might be unfortunate.

Appointment and Reception of Diplomats. Each state appoints its diplomatic representatives in its own way, but appointments are generally followed by certain internationally recognized procedures. As a rule, the nomination of a diplomat will be publicly announced only after the country to which he is to be sent has given its approval. The approval is called *agrément,* and the procedure of determining upon it is known as *agréation.* No country is obligated to accept a foreign representative who for any reason is *persona non grata* to it; in fact, there have been many cases in which the *agrément* has been refused.

Ordinarily, before proceeding to his new post, a diplomat will spend some time in his own capital. There he will confer with the head of the state, the foreign minister and other officials in the foreign office, and the diplomatic representatives in his own capital from the country to which he is soon to proceed. He will study the past relations between the two countries; he will be briefed by experts in the appropriate geographical office or offices; and before leaving to assume his new post he will be furnished with important papers, including diplomatic passports for himself and his family and staff, and a letter of credence.

The letter of credence is a diplomat's formal commission. It is signed by the head of the state and is addressed to the head of the state to which the diplomat is accredited. As soon as he arrives at his new post he will immediately get in touch with the foreign minister to request an audience with the head of the state in order that he may present his letter of credence. The ceremony of presentation may be accompanied by the most elaborate ritual and formality. Essentially, it consists of a brief speech by the envoy, and another in the same vein by the head of the state as he accepts the letter of credence. Usually copies of both speeches are exchanged in advance so that there will be no surprises during the formal ceremony. The diplomat next confers with the foreign minister and other influential leaders of the government, and visits his colleagues of the diplomatic corps, who return his visit in due course. Then the real work of the diplomat begins.

Termination of a Diplomatic Mission. The termination of a diplomatic mission may come about in a number of ways. The diplomat may, of course, resign.[12] A mission may be terminated by the recall or dismissal of an envoy. He may be recalled by his own government on its own volition, or his recall may be asked for by the government of the state to which he is accredited. In the latter case, the request for his recall may be made because he has himself become *persona non grata* in the country, or because the relations between the states concerned have become so strained that recall is demanded, possibly as a preliminary to actual hostilities. If recalled by his own government, the diplomat may be brought home "for consultation" — a practice which is particularly common when relations between states are strained — or in order to be transferred to another post or as a preliminary step to dismissal. An envoy is rarely sent home on direct orders of

[12] A diplomat may resign because of disagreement with the policy of his own government. Thus in the fall of 1945 General Patrick Hurley resigned as American Ambassador to China, and immediately leveled a vitriolic blast at the Foreign Service Officers in China and in the Office of Far Eastern Affairs in the State Department, who he claimed had sabotaged the announced policies of the United States in the Far East. Arthur Bliss Lane resigned as American Ambassador to Poland because of the "betrayal" of Poland at the Yalta Conference and the failure of the United States to seek to hold the Soviet Union to the Yalta Agreements. Once he was free to state his views, Lane did so at once, particularly in a powerful book entitled *I Saw Poland Betrayed* (Indianapolis: The Bobbs-Merrill Co., 1948).

a foreign government, because almost invariably that government will request the diplomat's own government to recall him and this will be done as a matter of course. Obviously, if his own government refuses to honor the request for his recall, the foreign government will thereupon hand the offending diplomat his passport and dismiss him forthwith. The most famous case of this kind in American diplomatic history was the dismissal of Lord Sackville-West by President Cleveland in 1888.[13]

A more recent instance in which an ambassador became *persona non grata* to the government to which he was accredited was that of George F. Kennan, American Ambassador to the Soviet Union, in 1952. Kennan made a speech in Berlin on September 19 in which he said that an American's life in Moscow was not much different from that of American diplomats interned in Germany after Pearl Harbor. The Soviet government asked for Kennan's recall on the ground that he had engaged in "slanderous attacks hostile to the Soviet Union." The United States replied that "Ambassador Kennan's statement accurately and in moderate language described the position of foreign diplomats accredited to the Soviet Government." Kennan was nevertheless recalled. The incident demonstrates how one government may reject the charges and allegations of another government and at the same time recognize the right of that government to have an envoy who is acceptable to it.

Consular Officials. Much less formality attends the work of consular officials, but they must in the first instance be approved by the government of the state to which they are to be sent. When a consular officer is appointed he receives a commission signed by the head of the state. An *exequatur* is a consul's official authorization to discharge his duties at his assigned post. It is "in fact an executive order of the foreign government which recognizes the official character of the consular officer and grants him the privileges or immunities conferred upon his office by treaty, law or custom and permits him to exercise his official duties."[14]

Regular foreign service personnel are largely exempt from the formalities which are required of top diplomatic and consular officials. They do not have to be accredited. All they need are diplomatic passports and visas of the governments of the countries to which they have been assigned.

Diplomatic and Consular Privileges and Immunities

Certain privileges and immunities are extended to diplomats which are not granted to private citizens. The reason for this special status is largely twofold: (1) diplomats are personal representatives of their heads of state and also, in effect if not in form, of the governments and hence of the people of their own countries; (2) in order to carry out their duties satisfactorily, they must be free of certain restrictions which local laws would otherwise impose. Ordinarily they enjoy exemption from direct taxes and customs duties, from the civil and criminal jurisdiction of the countries to which they are accredited, and, in fact, from the laws of the foreign state in general. They themselves, their families, and the members of their staff are personally inviolable. Embassies and legations, with all furnishings and their archives, are regarded as part of the national territory of the states which diplomats represent and are therefore immune from molestation by officials of the states or the local governmental units in which the properties are actually located. The same rights and privileges were extended to officials of the League

[13] See *Foreign Relations of the United States* (Washington, D.C.: Government Printing Office, 1888), II, 1667–1718; J. B. Moore, *Digest of International Law* (Washington, D.C.: Government Printing Office, 1906), IV, 536–548.

[14] Stuart, p. 346.

of Nations and delegates to it; and they are now similarly granted to the United Nations.

Consuls are not generally accorded as many rights and privileges as diplomats, and their status is regulated more by agreements between governments or by courtesy privileges than by well-established rules of international law. In certain instances they are extended all the privileges and immunities of diplomats, usually when they perform diplomatic as well as consular functions. On the other hand, noncareer consuls receive few if any immunities. Almost invariably consular offices and archives are regarded as the property of the nations which the consuls represent and are therefore in a sense extraterritorial. Consuls are usually exempt from local taxes and customs duties, but, except for the giving of testimony in civil cases, they are customarily held to be subject to the laws of the state of their residence.

There are, of course, many variations and exceptions to the generally recognized status of diplomatic and consular officials as here described. The Vienna conventions of 1961 and 1963, to which reference has already been made, constituted an effort to state the commonly accepted rules regarding the status of such officials, but even these conventions have not received universal acceptance. Moreover, cases are always arising in which diplomats or consuls are alleged to have abused their privileges, or in which a state is alleged to have violated the immunities of these representatives or their residences. Some cases are relatively minor—as, for example, traffic violations involving no injury to persons — but they may cause bad feeling on the part of local officials or the populace, or both, and even on the part of the governments concerned. The United States granted full diplomatic privileges and immunities to United Nations officials and delegates over the protests of articulate groups in the country and in Congress. Since Soviet embassies, legations, and consulates seem to be headcenters for subversive and espionage activities, there is considerable feeling that strong measures should be taken, including search of the premises if necessary, although this would be impossible under existing agreements. According to international law diplomatic and consular officials are strictly forbidden to engage in espionage.[15]

The Origins of Modern Diplomacy

The beginnings of organized diplomacy may be traced to the relations among the city-states of ancient Greece. By the fifth century B.C., Nicolson states, "special missions between the Greek city-states had become so frequent that something approaching our own system of regular diplomatic intercourse had been achieved."[16] Thucydides told us much about diplomatic procedure among the Greeks, as, for instance, in his account of a conference at Sparta in 432 B.C. in which the Spartans and their allies considered what action should be taken against Athens.

The Romans did little to advance the art of diplomacy by negotiation, but they did make important contributions to international law. In the Eastern Roman Empire, which was established after Constantine had moved his capital to the city that honored his name for many centuries, diplomatic methods were employed with great effect. The Eastern emperors had marked success in playing off potential rivals against each other, and the reports of their representatives at foreign courts gave them information which they were able to utilize to their advantage. Their representatives therefore became skilled diplomats and trained observers, thus extending the practice of diplomacy to include accurate observation and reporting as well as representation.

Until the late eighteenth or early nineteenth century diplomacy more often meant

[15] For a detailed commentary on diplomatic and consular privileges and immunities, see Stuart.

[16] Harold Nicolson, *Diplomacy* (London, 1939), p. 21.

the study and preservation of archives than the act of international negotiation. This concept was especially prevalent in the Middle Ages. "It is no exaggeration to say that it was in the Papal and other chanceries, under the direction and authority of successive 'masters of the rolls,' that the usages of diplomacy as a science based upon precedent and experience first came to be established."[17]

Modern diplomacy as an organized profession arose in Italy in the late Middle Ages. The rivalries of the Italian city-states and the methods which their rulers used to promote their interests are described in masterful fashion in Machiavelli's *The Prince*. The Holy See and the Italian city-states developed systems of diplomacy at an early date. It is possible that the Holy See was the first to utilize the system of permanent representation which is the characteristic feature of modern diplomacy; but the first known permanent mission was that established at Genoa in 1455 by Francesco Sforza, Duke of Milan. During the next century Italian city-states established permanent embassies in London and Paris and at the court of the Holy Roman Emperor; a British ambassador was assigned to residence in Paris; and Francis I of France "devised something like a permanent diplomatic machinery."

For nearly three centuries, however, the machinery appears to have been neither adequate nor standardized. Diplomacy was still the diplomacy of the court; its object was to promote the interests of the sovereign abroad by various means, direct or devious, fair or foul; and its standards were low and ill-defined. The ambassador, then as now, was deemed to be the personal representative of his chief of state in a foreign country. An affront to him was an affront to the chief of state himself and hence to the nation that he symbolized. In the absence of well-defined rules of procedure, frequent disputes — sometimes so bitter as to lead to duels or even to wars — arose from questions of precedence and immunity. Ambassadors who attempted to entertain in a style befitting the dignity of their sovereigns often found themselves in dire financial straits, especially if the sovereigns whose dignity they were trying to enhance by sumptuous display neglected to pay them salaries.

By the seventeenth century permanent missions were the rule rather than the exception, and diplomacy had become an established profession and a generally accepted method of international intercourse. The rise of nationalism and the nation-state system made some such machinery essential, especially after the Peace of Westphalia of 1648 had crystallized and formalized the state system. Diplomats from all European countries, as well as noblemen and other courtiers from all parts of France, graced the court of Louis XIV, and gave it that pomp and splendor which dazzled his contemporaries and set a pattern for decades to come. Many other monarchs of Europe tried, not too successfully, to ape the "Sun King" and to establish their own courts of Versailles.

The diplomacy of the courts entered its golden age in the eighteenth century. The game came to be played according to well-understood rules, with a great deal of glitter on the surface and much incompetence and intrigue beneath. Diplomats represented their sovereigns, and often were merely the willing tools in the great contests for empire and for European supremacy that were waged in that century. Strong rulers like Peter the Great of Russia and Frederick the Great of Prussia used diplomacy and force, as the occasion seemed to demand, to achieve their ends. The same comment might be made of important ministers of state, men like Pitt the Elder and Vergennes.

By the late eighteenth century the Industrial, American, and French revolutions had ushered in a new era of diplomacy, and indeed of history. Captains and kings passed

[17] *Ibid.*, p. 27.

from the scene in many lands, and the voice of the people began to be heard. The unassuming figure of Benjamin Franklin in the streets of Paris and London, representing a nation in the making, symbolized the coming era of more democratic diplomacy. To attempt to represent a nation rather than a ruler, and to attempt to feel the pulse of a people rather than of the king alone, imposed far more complicated duties on the diplomat. Indeed, it called for a new kind of diplomat, but the remuneration remained so inadequate that the diplomatic profession was still largely confined to those who had other sources of income. Inevitably, this meant that so-called democratic diplomacy was still carried on by representatives of the aristocracy of wealth and often of rank.

As diplomacy became less formal and restricted, its rules became more standardized and more generally accepted. The Congress of Vienna made particularly important contributions in this respect. To place diplomacy on a more systematic and formal basis, the Congress laid down certain rules of procedure which are still commonly observed. These rules were embodied in the Règlement of March 19, 1815, and in regulations of the Congress of Aix-la-Chapelle in 1818. The diplomatic hierarchy thus established consisted of four ranks or classes of representatives: (1) ambassadors, papal legates, and papal nuncios; (2) envoys extraordinary and ministers plenipotentiary; (3) ministers resident, later merged with the second rank; and (4) chargés d'affaires. The vexing question of precedence in a particular country was neatly solved by providing that the order of priority within each rank should be on the basis of the length of service in that country rather than on the more subjective basis of the relative importance of the sovereign or country the diplomat represented. The ambassador who was senior in terms of length of service in a country should be the *doyen* or dean of the diplomatic corps in that country. Since the papacy, as a general practice, changed its representatives less frequently than most states, many of the deans at foreign capitals were papal representatives.

Conditions of the New Diplomacy

The new diplomacy of the nineteenth century, then, demanded new methods as well as new personnel. These methods were defined in many international agreements, and became an intricate and generally observed code. Under the aegis of the Holy Alliance and the Concert of Europe, buttressed by the operations of the balance of power system, the game was played according to the new rules with a fair degree of success. The system broke down in the twentieth century, but while it endured it provided the framework for the practice of diplomacy. It should be noted, however, that Europe was still thought to be the center of all the world that mattered, and that no important European state challenged the bases of the system. Diplomats were gentlemen who observed the rules of the game and understood each other.

Harold Nicolson, whose delightful little book *Diplomacy* has become a classic on the subject, has called attention to three developments of the nineteenth and twentieth centuries which have greatly affected the theory and practice of diplomacy. These are (1) the "growing sense of the community of nations," (2) the "increasing appreciation of the importance of public opinion," and (3) the "rapid increase in communications."[18] The first two developments have clearly enlarged the diplomat's functions and enhanced his importance. The result has been the "world-wide intermeshing" of the foreign offices and diplomatic posts through which most of the formal contacts between states are now maintained. As the number of international organizations, groupings, and conferences increased, multilateral diplomacy took on added significance. The impact of public opinion on diplomacy

[18] P. 70.

is now generally recognized, but until the era of the new diplomacy that impact seemed to be slight. Today it is demonstrable that the policy-makers of all nations, including those of totalitarian states, are very sensitive to currents of public sentiment: witness the time and effort that are devoted to educational and propaganda work. One of the main functions of diplomatic representatives is reporting on the attitudes of the people in the countries to which they are accredited.

The third development, the rapid increase in communications, has in many respects reduced the status of diplomats and opened up more convenient channels of international negotiation. It has become possible for the foreign minister or head of the government to direct virtually all important negotiations. If he so desires, he can bypass the regular diplomatic representatives. As a matter of fact, more and more the major international issues are being handled outside normal diplomatic channels. Roosevelt and Churchill talked by transatlantic telephone and exchanged views by direct correspondence and by special agents, such as Harry Hopkins. United Nations representatives of the U.S.S.R. and the United States met privately in a New York hotel room to arrange the ending of the Berlin blockade. Diplomacy by conference, as we shall see, and other multilateral procedures are becoming more and more popular. For these reasons there is some basis for Lord Vansittart's lament that although high-ranking diplomats are more numerous than ever "they have lost stature" and "are increasingly mouthpieces." But a study of the memoirs of practicing diplomats of recent years will show that their role is still a great one. Some may complain that not enough attention was given to their reports and recommendations, or that they were occasionally bypassed on important matters, but all give a picture of manifold and useful activities. There seems to be little danger that the diplomat will become the victim of technological unemployment.

Democratic Diplomacy

By the early twentieth century the term "democratic diplomacy" had come into common use. It seemed to symbolize a new order in world affairs — one in which governments were fast losing their aristocratic leanings and their aloofness, and peoples were speaking to peoples through democratic representatives and informal channels. Actually, the new order was not so different from the old as it seemed in the atmosphere of hope that ushered in the present century. While diplomacy remained a rather esoteric profession, carried on by men of wealth and influence and power, it was conducted with the assistance of a growing number of career officers, the elite guard of diplomacy, whose standards of competence and training were being steadily raised. Diplomacy was thus being put more generally on a professional and nonpolitical basis.

Dangers of Democratic Democracy. On the whole, experience in democratic diplomacy has been disappointing. Too often it has been associated with the diplomacy of the market place, or even plebiscitary diplomacy — that is, with conditions under which important and delicate negotiations between states cannot possibly be conducted with success. In a brilliant chapter in his *Diplomacy* Nicolson calls attention to some of the evils of democratic diplomacy.[19] The first and "most potent source of danger," he declares, "is the irresponsibility of the sovereign people." The second is ignorance, arising not so much from a lack of facts as from the failure of the ordinary citizen "to apply to the general theory of foreign affairs that thought and intelligence which he devotes to domestic matters." In other words, foreign affairs are too *foreign* to the citizens of a state, and their implications are not adequately grasped. Even more dangerous than ignorance, Nicolson continues,

[19] Chapter IV.

"are certain forms of popular knowledge." The willingness of partially informed people to make quick and positive conclusions and judgments on even the most complex issues of foreign policy is a constant source of embarrassment to those who must weigh all the evidence and accept responsibility for the eventual decisions. "Cracker-barrel philosophers" and "Monday morning quarterbacks" always seem to have all the answers; responsible statesmen, like trained football coaches, seldom do.

Two other serious dangers in democratic diplomacy, according to Nicolson, are those of delay and of imprecision. In a democracy public opinion sets the limits within which the foreign policy of the country must operate. On the whole this is a healthy condition, but it may prevent the leaders of a nation from taking positive action at the opportune moment and thereby may hamper the effectiveness of diplomacy as "the first line of defense." Democratic states have often been criticized for following policies of "too little and too late," and the failure to act in time often seems to have caused greater crises at a later date. A case in point was the unwillingness of the American people to support President Roosevelt's plea of 1937 for the "quarantine" of aggressor states. In large part this failure has stemmed from the reluctance or unwillingness of the people to support strong measures which involve great risks. Leaders of democratic nations seldom launch foreign policies, however essential they may deem them to be to the welfare and security of their country, until and unless they are reasonably confident of popular understanding and support. On the other hand, the historian can suggest instances in which the people's urge to action has been restrained by the chief executive. Thus the American public seemed to be far more belligerent than President McKinley in 1898; and President Wilson refused to capitulate to a momentary war fever after the sinking of the *Lusitania.*

Imprecision became a common vice of the new diplomacy. Perhaps in no profession has the gulf between words and meaning been more marked. Diplomats were trained to be masters of double talk. The language of diplomacy, as well as its ritual and practice, became smooth stilted, and incomprehensible to the uninitiated. When diplomats were allowed to make public addresses they were encouraged to say as little as possible but in the most pleasing fashion. If for any reason a diplomat was charged with the task of making a public statement of policy, it was usually necessary to read carefully between the lines to understand what he meant. Anyone who has listened to such addresses will realize that the art has not been lost. In the present war of semantics, in which diplomats of totalitarian states are particularly skilled, the confusion of meaning is equally marked, although the language used has become much less refined. The "language of politeness," stilted and circuitous as it was, was nevertheless much preferable to the "language of the fishmarket" in which many diplomatic exchanges, especially those of a public nature, are now conducted. Actually, as K. M. Panikkar, a skilled Indian scholar-diplomat, remarked, the "language of politeness" was "fully understood by the persons to whom it was addressed," whereas today "the language of diplomacy has become abusive and is addressed over the heads of governments to the masses."[20]

As related to democratic diplomacy imprecision suggests, in Nicolson's words, the "tendency of all democracies (and especially of Anglo-Saxon democracies) to prefer a vague and confirming formula to a precise and binding definition." Consider, for example, the Kellogg-Briand Pact of 1928 — in which most of the states of the world renounced war as "an instrument of national

[20] Lecture on "The Theory and Practice of Diplomacy" at the Delhi School of Economics, Delhi, India, August 18, 1952.

policy" — or the countless general and almost meaningless resolutions adopted by the Assembly of the League of Nations and the United Nations General Assembly, or statements of "policy" that have emanated from the highest circles in democratic countries.

The Demand for Open Diplomacy. Democratic diplomacy came to be associated in the popular mind with open rather than secret negotiations. Secrecy connoted undercover, shady dealings; it was held to be incompatible with true democracy. It had been a cardinal feature of the old diplomacy and was the rule, rather than the exception, in the nineteenth century. The Congress of Berlin of 1878 represented a high-water mark of the practice of secret diplomacy. The demand for open diplomacy reached a climax at the time of the First World War, and it was given classic expression in the first of Wilson's famous Fourteen Points, as presented in his message to Congress of January 8, 1918: "Open covenants of peace, openly arrived at, after which there shall be no private international understandings of any kind but diplomacy shall proceed always frankly and in the public view."

The principle of open diplomacy was embodied in the Covenant of the League of Nations and later in the Charter of the United Nations. It became a shibboleth to which all statesmen paid lip service, but often lip service only. The principle was based at once on a well-founded distrust of secret diplomacy and on a naive misconception of the nature and functions of diplomacy. As a matter of fact, open diplomacy, as popularly defined, is an impossibility. Negotiations between states call for a high degree of compromise and finesse. They can seldom be conducted in the white glare of publicity with any useful results. The major issues involved, however, can and should be publicly declared and discussed, and the decisions and agreements which are reached by negotiation can and should be subjected to the most searching public scrutiny. There is an important distinction between negotiations — that is, diplomacy — and final decisions — that is, policy. Those who decry the evils of secret diplomacy usually mean that the secrecy but not the diplomacy should cease. Some have expressed the view that "open covenants" are certainly desirable but that they can hardly be "openly arrived at." Even Wilson came to believe that people had taken his famous phrase too literally. "When I pronounced for open diplomacy," he wrote to the Senate in 1918, "I meant, not that there should be no private discussions of delicate matters, but that no secret agreements should be entered into, and that all international relations, when fixed, should be open, aboveboard, and explicit."

Secret Diplomacy vs. Secret Agreements. Secret treaties have left an evil legacy throughout modern history. In the secret treaties of World War I the Allies made sweeping promises to Italy and other states in order to win their neutrality or their participation in the struggle — promises which bedeviled the Paris Peace Conference and which conflicted with the principles the Allied nations professed to hold. Many treaties of alliance and friendship have contained secret provisions — for example, the *Entente Cordiale* between Britain and France in 1904. The secret provisions of the Yalta Agreements of 1945 caused an international sensation when they became known. The secrecy was later defended on grounds of wartime necessity and expediency; but it is widely felt that the price was much too high. "The clandestine treaties themselves," as DeWitt C. Poole observed, "may not directly do the chief harm, but rather the poisoning suspicion and fear that are bred internationally, frequently beyond all real need, by rumors which inevitably leak out."[21]

[21] DeWitt C. Poole in Francis J. Brown, Charles Hodges, and Joseph S. Roucek, eds., *Contemporary World Politics* (New York: John Wiley & Sons, 1940), p. 423.

The evil of secret treaties, as of secret diplomacy in general, is the deliberate concealment of the end products of negotiations, not of the negotiations themselves. Most international diplomacy is necessarily carried on in secret; at least, very little publicity is given to it. The United Nations, for instance, provides a forum for the airing of grievances and the "open" consideration of major issues. As a forum it is a convenient vehicle for propaganda and enlightenment. But these activities are not diplomacy in any real sense of the word. The United Nations plays an important role in international diplomacy, but not through its operation as a world forum; its real diplomatic work is done in committees and in discussions, both formal and informal, behind the scenes.

Statesmen of democratic countries are constantly faced with the question of how much should be told, and when and in what manner. They must weigh the obvious value of keeping the public informed of major developments in foreign affairs against considerations of national security and the effect upon the negotiations in progress, and upon the other countries concerned, of telling too much too soon. A frequent complaint in the United States is that the people are not given the information necessary to make intelligent decisions in vital matters of foreign policy, or that if enough information is given, it is usually after decisions have been made. Too often, it is charged, the people are asked to approve what are really accomplished facts. Even members of Congress feel that at times they have to vote without full knowledge of the pertinent facts. The general feeling in the United States on this issue was well expressed in the report of the Task Force on Foreign Affairs of the Hoover Commission: "In case of doubt, it is far better, national security permitting, to give too much information too soon rather than too little and too late."[22]

Democratic Diplomacy: An Assessment. The rise of democratic or popular diplomacy — a manifestation of the increasing participation of the people in the affairs of government — can be traced at least to the late eighteenth century, but it became a dominant trend only after the First World War. It has been largely responsible for the decline of diplomacy in the more conventional and more formal sense, a decline that has been deplored by many students of international affairs and modern society, including Walter Lippmann, Harold Nicolson, Hans Morgenthau, and Sisley Huddleston.[23] Many observers argue that unless there can be a return to some of the traditions and practices of more conventional and less public diplomacy, the prospects for world peace are dim. Huddleston, whom Harry Barnes called "the ablest journalist who concentrated on international affairs between the two World Wars," was well aware of the defects of the pre-1914 type of diplomacy, but he regarded post-World War I diplomacy as infinitely worse — indeed, as the very negation of real diplomacy. "We must return to the more discreet and competent methods of professional diplomacy." he insisted, and abandon "the limitless idiocies of popular diplomacy"; but, he stated, "nothing short of a miracle will enable us to bring about those reforms in diplomatic practice which might prevent popular diplomacy from continuing its fatal trend toward world ruin."[24]

The shortcomings of democratic diplomacy are largely in the formulation of policies and in their implementation, and its virtues primarily in its objectives. In a

[22] *Task Force Report on Foreign Affairs*. Appendix H. Prepared for the Commission on Organization of the Executive Branch of the Government (Washington, D.C.: Government Printing Office, 1949), p. 134.

[23] Walter Lippmann, *Essays in the Public Philosophy* (Boston: Little, Brown and Company, 1955); Harold Nicolson, *Diplomacy* and *The Evolution of Diplomatic Method* (New York: The Macmillan Company, 1955); Hans J. Morgenthau, *Politics Among Nations*, 3d ed. (New York: Alfred A. Knopf, 1961), Chapters 31 and 32; Sisley Huddleston, *Popular Diplomacy and War* (Peterborough, N.H.: The Richard R. Smith Co., 1954)

[24] Huddleston, pp. 256, 261.

democratic state the people, by and large, determine those objectives. Diplomacy serves their interests as the people understand and express those interests. That they are at times in error in conceiving what is best for themselves, that special groups can sometimes manipulate public opinion or government itself to their selfish ends, does not destroy the premise upon which all democratic government rests — that its purpose is to promote the welfare of the people who sustain it, and that, generally speaking, the people know and serve their own interests better than do leaders who lack the controls of democratic processes. An active free press and freedom of speech exert a continuous pressure on public officials for information, and interested citizens and organized private interests are constantly alert in their own behalf. Constitutional procedures for the ratification of treaties and for the appropriation of money also help to make the course of democratic diplomacy a matter of public knowledge. As we have suggested, open diplomacy can be carried to a point where it possesses very real disadvantages. Democratic processes serve the people best when they make it possible to hold leaders to a strict accountability for results and objectives but not to an obligation to negotiate on the television screens of a million homes and bars.

Totalitarian Diplomacy

The rise of totalitarian states in the twentieth century introduced new and disturbing problems into international relations. These states were ruthless dictatorships; they presented a fundamental challenge to human freedoms everywhere by their subordination of the individual to the collective will — determined in fact by a few men at the top — by their worldwide propaganda to disguise or hide aggressive policies, and by their contemptuous rejection of the traditions of the supposedly civilized world. They utilized modern techniques of military, political, and psychological power to expand their dominions, to gain control of other states, and to subvert other regimes. They invoked strange doctrines of racial superiority, mysticism, materialism, and militarism in furtherance of their ends. They used diplomacy as an instrument of national policy, but in doing so they degraded its language and its practice. Diplomats became agents of conquest, double-dealing, and espionage, whose business was not to work for peaceful international relations but to provoke dissension rather than understanding — to make the leaders and peoples of other nations weak and blind and divided in the face of the growing totalitarian menace. As Lord Vansittart complained, the object of totalitarian diplomacy, contrary to that of the traditional diplomacy of the eighteenth and nineteenth centuries, "is thoroughly calculated to create and maintain *bad* relations."[25]

Diplomatic representatives of totalitarian states used most of the established rules of procedure, but they conformed to the generally accepted standards of international conduct only when this suited the schemes of their masters. In fact, modern dictators openly boasted that treaties and other international obligations, whether bilateral or multilateral in nature, would be broken at will. They looked upon all gestures of friendship by other nations as evidences of weakness, or of appeasement, or of sinister intentions. At every opportunity they made the League of Nations, and later the United Nations, instruments of their propaganda. They used their embassies as centers of espionage, as the Germans and Russians did in Canada, Great Britain, the United States, and Latin America.

In dealing with totalitarian states the old techniques of diplomacy seemed to be of little use. Diplomats were restricted in their movements in the capitals of these states;

[25] "The Decline of Diplomacy," *Foreign Affairs,* XXVIII (January, 1950), 179. Italics in original.

they had little access to officials of the government and almost none to the people; and they were viewed with suspicion and dislike. Negotiations with representatives of totalitarian states at international conferences and in foreign capitals have frequently degenerated into endurance contests, usually ending in complete frustration. Again and again, as on the questions of the international control of atomic energy and the settlement of problems relating to Germany, real possibilities for acceptable compromise have apparently arisen, only to be shattered at the last moment by a dictator's intransigence. When agreements have been reached they have often been violated, in spirit or in letter, or in both, or evaded by unilateral definitions which destroyed the essence of the "understanding."

In the 1930's, after repeated rebuffs in the field of diplomacy, the democratic nations finally realized that appeasement of a Fascist state only whetted its appetite. In the postwar period, frustrations in diplomacy led to the cold war and a generally unhappy state of international relations. The democratic states soon discovered that to conduct the cold war was difficult, expensive, exhausting, and nonsensical, and that in a climate of "neither war nor peace" democratic diplomacy was particularly ineffective. The Soviets apparently believed that there was a wide no-man's-land between diplomacy and war in the conventional sense of armed hostilities, and that they could operate in this no-man's-land until the "capitalist" nations collapsed from internal weakness and external pressure.

But even the Soviets soon found the cold war singularly unproductive. Soon after the death of Stalin in 1953 the cold war seemed to be giving way to "cool war" or "cold peace," largely as a result of the various "new looks" in the Soviet Union under Khrushchev and his successors, and of basic changes in the international situation. The Soviet leaders have used the technique of the smile instead of the frown; they have been more accessible and more friendly; they have relaxed many restrictions; they have been willing to engage in apparently endless negotiations on many subjects and have even made real concessions in a few instances, such as on the Austrian state treaty and the nuclear test ban treaty; they have publicly declared their desire to achieve a lessening of international tensions and a settlement of the major issues that divide the Communist and non-Communist worlds. They have apparently abandoned, or at least pushed into the background, the doctrine of inevitable conflict. They seem to be giving priority to their internal problems and to relations with Communist China, the East European states, and the states of the Third World. But the evidence is unconvincing that they have abandoned any of their basic tenets or altered the substance and objectives of their foreign policy. "No one can say with certainty whether the present peace [featured by an apparent lessening of tensions between the two superpowers and a high degree of polycentrism within both the Communist and non-Communist worlds] is really the end of the cold war or just an interval between two offensives."[26]

Diplomacy by Conference

The normal channels of diplomacy are the foreign offices and the diplomatic and consular establishments; but often these channels are either bypassed for one reason or another or used in a decidedly subordinate role. As an alternative, states have had increasing resort to "diplomacy by conference." In the postwar period international conferences have proliferated as never before. Although this is by no means a new technique — there were international conferences of a sort in the ancient world — it became really popular after the First World War under the stimulus of the League of Nations and the

[26] *Die Zeit* (Hamburg), June 3, 1966.

quest for regional and collective security. Since World War II it has become so common as to constitute a new development in international relations.[27]

Perhaps the first great conferences of modern times were those which ended the Thirty Years' War and led to the Peace of Westphalia of 1648. Representatives of France and the Catholic states of the Holy Roman Empire met in Munster, and representatives of Sweden and the Protestant states of the Empire in Osnabruck. These two conferences, which lasted more than four years, finally produced two treaties, collectively known as the Treaty of Westphalia. In the nineteenth century important conferences were held in Vienna (1814–15), Paris (1856), and Berlin (1878). The most famous of all twentieth-century conferences was the Paris Peace Conference of 1919, but there were others of significance in the interwar years — the Washington Conference of 1921, the Locarno Conference of 1925, and the Geneva Disarmament Conference, which met intermittently from 1932 to 1937. During World War II several major conferences brought the leaders of the allied countries together for consultation and major decisions, and the San Francisco Conference, which opened before V-E Day and closed before the surrender of Japan, drafted the Charter of the United Nations.

Six thousand to ten thousand sessions of international conferences are now held each year. Some deal with highly technical subjects and are attended by relatively few persons, mostly experts in their fields. Others are general international meetings, attended by hundreds of persons, including many foreign ministers or diplomats of the highest rank. Most numerous of all are the conferences held under the aegis of the United Nations and its agencies, which now sponsor more than five thousand meetings each year. The time and effort involved in the preparation and staffing of these conferences are staggering. This work is one of the chief functions of the Secretariat of the United Nations — especially of its Department of Conferences and General Services — and of important divisions of every foreign office. International negotiations are also a heavy burden on the foreign ministers and other top policy-makers. James F. Byrnes served as secretary of state for 562 days, and he spent 350 of these, or 62 per cent of the time, attending various international conferences.

That diplomacy by conference meets a real need seems to be proved by its growing popularity. For the personal observation of a qualified authority one might cite the comments of Lord Maurice Hankey, a member of Lloyd George's War Cabinet, who wrote in 1946 that this type of diplomacy had come to stay and that the "best hope" for the prevention of war "appears to lie in the judicious development of diplomacy by conference."[28] "My personal experience," he added, "is that the most important elements of success in diplomacy by conference are elasticity of procedure, small numbers, informality, mutual acquaintance and if possible, personal friendship among the principals, a proper perspective between secrecy in deliberation and publicity in results, reliable secretaries and interpreters."[29] On the other hand, a veteran in international conferences, former Secretary of State Dean Acheson, has pointed out that in the postwar years the international conference has to a large extent "ceased to be an instrument for ending conflict and has become one for continuing it. . . . In short, the international

[27] See Elmer Plischke, *Conduct of American Diplomacy* (Princeton, N.J.: D. Van Nostrand Co., 1950), pp. 361–363, 384–388; William Sanders, "Multilateral Diplomacy," *Department of State Bulletin*, XXI (August 8, 1949), 163.

[28] Lord Maurice Hankey, *Diplomacy by Conference* (New York: G. P. Putnam's Sons, 1946), pp. 38, 39. The term "Diplomacy by Conference," incidentally, goes back at least to 1920, when Lord Hankey used it as the subject of a lecture.

[29] *Ibid.*, pp. 37–38

conference has been so used for political warfare that it is not likely to be useful now, except for registering, and for getting peripheral consent to, adjustments reached elsewhere, when adjustment is possible."[30]

Personal Diplomacy

Summit and Near-Summit Diplomacy. The direct participation of foreign ministers, prime ministers, and even heads of states in diplomatic negotiations is not a recent innovation, but it has become increasingly common in recent years. Major and fateful decisions affecting the whole course of the war and the postwar international order were made during the several personal meetings between Churchill and Roosevelt, beginning with the rendezvous in August, 1941, that resulted in the Atlantic Charter, during the conferences of these two men with Chiang Kai-shek at Cairo (November, 1943), and with Stalin at Teheran (December, 1943) and at Yalta (February, 1945). These were followed by the Potsdam Conference of July-August, 1945, in which the main participants were Churchill (replaced by Attlee after the General Elections of July), Stalin, and Truman. The only postwar meeting at this level was the "summit" conference in Geneva in July, 1955, attended by the President of the United States and the prime ministers of France, the United Kingdom, and the U.S.S.R. A second effort to hold a similar conference in 1960 broke down on the eve of the scheduled opening. Meetings of prime ministers of Asian and African countries have been frequent, either by an exchange of visits on a bilateral basis or at major international conferences, such as the Asian-African Conference at Bandung in 1955, and the conferences of nonaligned states in Belgrade in 1961 and in Cairo in 1964. African prime ministers and heads of states have frequently participated in conferences held under the auspices of the Organization of African Unity.

The foreign ministers of the Big Three of the war period — the U.S.S.R., the United Kingdom, and the United States — held an important meeting in Moscow in the fall of 1943 and again in December, 1945. Together with the foreign minister of France they met several times in the postwar period as the Council of Foreign Ministers to attempt to draft peace treaties for the defeated Axis states. They met again in Berlin in February, 1954, to attempt to resolve the deadlock on German unification, and in Geneva in October, 1955, to consider the same question, plus the problems of European security, German rearmament, disarmament, and other pressing issues. As the cold war developed, and as the ties that bound the North Atlantic Community became stronger, at least in a formal sense, the American secretary of state and the foreign ministers of Great Britain and France met on numerous occasions to discuss matters of common interest. They continued to hold consultations in the more relaxed international atmosphere that developed as a result of the "new look" in Russia. Before the October, 1955, meeting in Geneva with Molotov, for example, they met in New York for preliminary discussions. More recently, because of the uncooperative attitude of General de Gaulle, the French foreign minister has seldom met with his British and American counterparts. The opening of sessions of the United Nations General Assembly and top-level meetings of various regional arrangements and organizations, such as NATO, the Organization of American States, the Organization of African Unity, and the Council of Europe, provide foreign ministers of many states with opportunities to meet and exchange views.

Personal Agents and Direct Contact. Personal diplomacy may take many other forms, but invariably it has the effect of by-

[30] "Meetings at the Summit: A Study in Diplomatic Method," address at the University of New Hampshire, May 8, 1958.

passing the normal channels of diplomacy or of using them only to a limited degree. Heads of states have often relied on personal representatives to handle delicate problems in international relations. The use of executive agents has been common for many decades. Henry Wriston's study of *Executive Agents in American Foreign Relations* shows that they have been employed in American diplomatic relations from colonial times. Wilson's reliance on Colonel House and Roosevelt's on Harry Hopkins are the best-known examples of this practice. *The Intimate Papers of Colonel House* and Robert Sherwood's *Roosevelt and Hopkins* provide excellent case studies of this type of diplomacy. Heads of states have sometimes preferred to consult personal favorites rather than their foreign ministers on major questions of diplomacy. Thus, as Lord Vansittart stated, "a rival Foreign Office was run by Lloyd George: it consisted of Lord Lothian." Vansittart, who was Permanent Under Secretary of the British Foreign Office and then Chief Diplomatic Adviser to the Prime Minister, confesses that "as Chief Diplomatic Adviser I saw Chamberlain only thrice in three years, and never once alone."[31]

Another practice of heads of states, less frequently used except by certain practitioners, is the direct approach to their opposite numbers in other countries. Churchill and Roosevelt developed this practice to a fine art, especially by use of the transatlantic telephone. They also corresponded directly, or sent messages to each other by personal emissaries and confidants. When Harry Hopkins was in England on wartime missions, he often spent weekends with Churchill and was therefore able to convey Roosevelt's views and get Churchill's in return with a maximum of frankness and a minimum of formality. When the American President tried to appeal directly to the heads of the Axis powers, however, he got nowhere. He sent repeated messages to Hitler just before the attack on Poland precipitated World War II, and to Mussolini just before Italy stabbed France in the back in June, 1940; but the answer of each of the dictators was made in angry public speeches and in armed attacks. On the eve of Pearl Harbor, Roosevelt tried to appeal directly to the Emperor of Japan to do his best to avert war. The Japanese answer was delivered, not by Kurusu and Nomura in Washington but by Japanese planes over Pearl Harbor. The personal diplomacy of Churchill and Roosevelt led to some unfortunate results in their dealings with Stalin. Roosevelt, in particular, was convinced after the Yalta meeting that Stalin was a reasonable man and that he could get along with him and induce him to accept necessary compromises. Before his death in April, 1945, FDR had reason to doubt that Stalin intended to abide by the Yalta Agreements.

Advantages and Disadvantages. The advantages of this kind of summit or near-summit diplomacy are obvious. In an increasingly interdependent world it is useful for top leaders to meet their counterparts in other countries. Presumably this will provide opportunities for fruitful exchange of views and more realistic assessments of the character and concerns of other leaders. Sometimes — although no doubt very rarely — such meetings can help to remove misunderstandings between nations and to clear roadblocks to international agreement. If heads of states, prime ministers, and foreign ministers are to assume major responsibility for foreign policy decisions, they should gain as much experience as they can in international diplomacy. This experience should make them more aware of the realities of international life and better qualified to discharge the awesome responsibilities that devolve on them.

On the other hand, the disadvantages

[31] Lord Vansittart, "The Decline of Diplomacy," *Foreign Affairs*, XXVIII (January, 1950), 186.

of this kind of diplomacy are even more obvious. Top leaders have many responsibilities and preoccupations. They do not have time to participate in tedious international meetings or to prepare adequately for such meetings. They may be more influential if they remain relatively aloof from the hurlyburly of bilateral and multilateral negotiation. This is presumably true of foreign ministers, and it is even more true of prime ministers and heads of states.

Most practicing diplomats and students of diplomacy view with strong misgivings the increasing tendency of heads of states, prime ministers, and foreign ministers to participate directly in international diplomacy.[32] They point out that the function of the top officials of a state is policy-making, not negotiation — a task that should be left to professional diplomats. They cite the experience of Woodrow Wilson, who insisted on attending the Paris Peace Conference in 1919 against the advice of his diplomatic advisers and whose stature as the spokesman of a new order in world affairs, as well as his health, was undermined as a result.[33] They insist that personal diplomacy on the highest level, or the use of personal favorites in more delicate negotiations, is often characterized by incompetence and is based on subjective considerations which may affect the vital interest of a state. "The practice," complained Lord Vansittart, who spoke from bitter experience, "is an essay in omniscience, and it is only sometimes successful, because everyone needs advice."[34] Harold Nicolson also had a marked distaste for the participation of top policy-makers in international negotiations; to him it indicated a misunderstanding of their functions and of the important distinctions between foreign policy and diplomacy. He believed that foreign ministers should keep to policy-making, leaving the work of negotiation to the professional diplomatist; that they may take a dislike to each other which would affect all their relationships; and that with responsibilities in worldwide problems their time is needed in their home offices. Visits of an accredited representative to the foreign office, unlike those of a foreign minister, "arouse no public expectation, inspire no Press indiscretions, and if sterile lead to no public disappointment."[35] Sisley Huddleston shared this view: "In foreign affairs, in particular, a president, a prime minister, or any other high functionary of the state entrusted with the most vital responsibilities, should, first and last, make, as it were, an abstraction of himself."[36] Speaking reflectively on the same theme, Dean Acheson remarked:

> For high international negotiation, whether or not in conferences, it is not necessary that chiefs of state or heads of government be

[32] In the fifteenth century Philip de Commines, "the father of modern history," observed: "It is the highest act of imprudence for two great princes, provided there is any equality in their power, to admit of an interview, unless it be in their youth, when their minds are wholly engaged and taken up with entertainments of mirth and pleasure." Under any other circumstances personal meetings were undesirable. "Though their persons should be in no danger (which is almost impossible), yet their heartburnings and animosities will certainly augment. It were better, therefore, that they accommodated their differences by the mediation of wise and faithful ministers." Quoted in Lindsay Rogers, "Of Summits," *Foreign Affairs,* XXXIV (October, 1955), 143. This is a review article of *The Memoirs of Philip de Commines, Lord of Argenton,* edited, with Life and Notes, by Andrew H. Scoble (London, 1856).

[33] Whether Wilson was wise in deciding to attend the Paris Peace Conference as an active participant is still a matter of opinion; a strong case can be made in support of his decision, as well as against it.

[34] Vansittart, p. 187.

[35] Nicolson, *Diplomacy,* p. 101. Secretary of State Dulles was a firm believer in the kind of personal diplomacy permitted by his peripatetic propensities. His Democratic critics spoke of him as an "unguided missile," and scholars too felt that Dulles was too much of the time up in the air or abroad. See, for example, Henry M. Wriston, "The Secretary of State Abroad," *Foreign Affairs,* XXXIV (July, 1956), 523–540.

[36] Huddleston, p. 230. Huddleston's relevant chapter bears the unequivocal title, "The Menace of Intimate Top-Level Conferences."

involved. Indeed, it is better that they should not be. The makers of ultimate decisions must be insulated a little from the negotiators themselves. They must remain more detached. Neither their prestige nor their judgment should be caught up by the ebb and flow of the struggle in the negotiating chamber.[37]

Some experienced diplomats disagree with this view. Lord Hankey, for instance, believes that the solution of difficult problems may require "resources beyond those of the most competent and qualified diplomatist." He contends that some questions can be settled only in conferences by persons who, along with other qualifications, are "alone in a position to make real concessions" and that "nowadays, when governments are often responsible to parliaments elected on the widest franchise, it is no longer advisable to rely entirely on intermediaries."[38]

Propaganda and Diplomacy

One of the first rules of the old diplomacy was that a diplomat must not attempt to interfere in any way in the internal affairs of the country to which he was accredited. If he did so, he usually met the fate of a Citizen Genêt or of a Lord Sackville-West. Both Genêt and Sackville-West were dismissed from their Washington posts for taking a hand in American internal politics; and Sackville-West had done no more than indicate a presidential election preference in a supposedly private letter that he had been tricked into writing.

The new diplomacy has developed various instruments and techniques of formal and informal penetration. One of the most pervasive of these is propaganda. The use of the radio, the press, and other methods of making a direct appeal to peoples rather than to governments through formal channels is becoming a commonplace approach. Propaganda, in the words of George V. Allen, former Assistant Secretary of State for Public Affairs, has become "a conscious weapon of diplomacy."[39] As Mr. Allen admits, the technique is not a new one. "The Duke of Wellington doubtless addressed messages to Napoleon through the press of his day, and Cyrus the Great probably started bizarre rumors for his purposes." Woodrow Wilson tried to appeal over the heads of the rulers of Germany to the German people. His famous Fourteen Points, which were eventually accepted as the basis of the armistice and the peace negotiations, were enunciated, not through diplomatic channels but in a message to Congress. When Wilson attempted to appeal to the Italian people to bring pressure on Orlando and the Italian government in connection with debates at the Paris Peace Conference, his efforts backfired. In other instances outside appeals to peoples to repudiate their rulers have served only to consolidate support for the ruling group in the state or to make the people resentful of "interference."

The State Department deliberately intervened in the Italian elections of 1948, in which great issues affecting the balance of power between the Communist and the non-Communist worlds seemed to be at stake. Allen has thus described the campaign:

> By press, motion picture, and radio we tried our level best, through open propaganda methods, to persuade the Italian voter that democracy, although offering no immediate paradise, was a surer method of progress [than communism]. The Voice of America transmitted short-wave radio programs in the Italian language every day, beamed toward the people of Italy, extolling the advantages of democracy. Americans of Italian origin were encouraged to write to their relatives in Italy, counseling them to vote democratic. We arranged for American newsreels, showing the American way of life

[37] "Meetings at the Summit: A Study in Diplomatic Method," address at the University of New Hampshire, May 8, 1958.

[38] Hankey, p. 38.

[39] George V. Allen, address at Duke University, Durham, North Carolina, December 10, 1949; *Department of State Bulletin, XXI* (December 19, 1949), 941–943.

and American aid to Italy, to be shown in every Italian theater for several weeks prior to election day.[40]

Mr. Allen ought to have added that James Dunn, United States Ambassador to Italy, assiduously met almost every ship bringing American supplies to Italian ports, and on each occasion made a public address on the aid which the American people were extending to the people of Italy.

The use of the direct approach in diplomacy, by resort to all the instruments of propaganda, has been most fully developed in totalitarian states. Much of Fascist and Nazi diplomacy was conducted in this manner; hence the functions of regular diplomats were rather different from those of the conventional type. The Russians have been adept in the same techniques. In the Italian elections of 1948, for example, Radio Moscow was even more vocal than the Voice of America, and all the agents of communism, inside and outside Italy, were apparently instructed to join in the chorus. When in the spring of 1948 General Walter Bedell Smith, American Ambassador to the Soviet Union, was engaged in presumably secret exploratory conversations with Soviet Foreign Minister Molotov on matters relating to Germany, Radio Moscow announced these conversations to the world in such a manner as to create the impression that the United States was trying to reach a basis of agreement with the U.S.S.R. without the knowledge of her other wartime allies, and perhaps even at their expense. When the Soviet Union decided that, in view of the success of the Berlin airlift and the stronger Allied measures in Western Germany, the blockade of Berlin was not achieving its intended purpose and should therefore be abandoned, Russia's willingness to negotiate an ending of the blockade was conveyed not through the Russian Foreign Office, via Ambassador Panyushkin in Washington or Ambassador Smith in Moscow, but through a cable from Stalin to an American newspaperman in Paris, who had addressed certain questions to him. But the chief vehicles of Russian diplomacy by propaganda are the radio and the press. Indeed, there is some basis for Lord Vansittart's flat statement that "Communist radio is Communist diplomacy."

There can be no question of the magnitude of the propaganda activities of the governments of modern states, especially totalitarian states and all major powers, but there can be all kinds of doubts concerning the relation of these activities to diplomacy. Do they supplement the efforts of diplomats or do they interfere with normal diplomatic procedures? Can the objectives of a state be furthered simultaneously by propaganda barrages for all the world to hear and by diplomacy, which for the most part works quietly behind the scenes? Is propaganda an arm of diplomacy or has diplomacy become the arm of propaganda? What is the connection between the foreign office of a state and its propaganda agency or agencies? In the United States, for example, what are the relative functions and responsibilities of the Department of State and the United States Information Agency? Whatever the answers to these questions, the relation of propaganda to diplomacy is obviously a matter of great importance in modern world politics.

The new and intimate connection between propaganda and diplomacy has altered the nature of the relations between states and has to a considerable degree weakened diplomacy in the traditional sense. Yet in an age of mass communications, of growing literacy, and of bitter war for the minds of men, it seems inevitable, if regrettable, that propaganda will rise in importance as "a conscious weapon of diplomacy," and therefore that diplomacy, viewed in this light, will increase in power and significance as an instrument of national policy.

New Dimensions in Diplomacy

Twentieth-century diplomacy, then, has been characterized by new techniques, new

[40] *Ibid.*, p. 942.

practices, and new types of diplomats. Three developments, themselves reflections of the broadening scope of democratic diplomacy and the emergence of totalitarian democracy, are particularly striking: (1) the increasing incidence of public multilateral negotiations; (2) the expansion of diplomatic activity into the cultural and educational fields; and (3) the multiplication of informal channels of contact among peoples and nations.

There has been, as Kenneth W. Thompson has pointed out, a "novel, revolutionary and worldwide institutionalizing of diplomacy."[41] This has led to the growing importance of what has been called "parliamentary diplomacy," a type of multilateral negotiation which, as Dean Rusk has explained, involves "a continuing organization," a "regular public debate exposed to the media of mass communication," "rules of procedure which govern the process of debate," and "formal conclusions, ordinarily expressed in resolutions." "Typically, we are talking about the United Nations and its related organizations, although not exclusively so, because the same type of organization is growing up in other parts of the international scene."[42]

Much of this new diplomacy is conducted in a "goldfish-bowl" atmosphere, a fact which horrifies devotees of the classical patterns of diplomacy. "Diplomacy," wrote James Reston in 1958, "which started in the royal court, and moved then to the cabinets of world governments, has moved once more into the headlines of the world's press. It is a bad way to conduct diplomacy."[43] This way can lead to the excesses of "plebiscitary diplomacy."

Even on the formal level the dimensions of diplomacy have widened markedly. Diplomacy is no longer confined to political and economic relations, or to relations between governments and top political representatives. Its activities now embrace the whole field of educational and cultural relations. While this is still, as Charles Frankel termed it, "the neglected aspect of foreign affairs," it is receiving increasing attention and is becoming increasingly important. It requires the cooperation of many people in both official and unofficial positions, and it gives greater depth to a nation's relations with other states. It means that diplomacy is not just governments dealing with governments, but also peoples speaking to peoples.

An interesting glimpse of the dimensions of educational and cultural affairs is provided by former Senator William Benton, who was put in charge of these affairs in the State Department in 1945. He soon found that his was really a pioneering task:

> When I joined the post-war State Department, I was to be in charge of the new diplomacy. This included the war-spawned activities of the OIAA, the OWI, the OSS and other vibrant overseas agencies. It encompassed all of the Department's informational activities, domestic as well as international, including what became "The Voice of America." I was also in charge of American participation in UNESCO and, indeed, of all the Department's so-called cultural activities, including the exchange of professors and students. Further — believe it or not — I was responsible for nothing less than the re-education of Germany and Japan.[44]

The dimensions of diplomacy have also been widened by "the rapid growth of informal relations between states," a development which is new in scope although not in essence. "The advent of informal penetra-

[41] *American Diplomacy and Emergent Patterns* (New York: New York University Press, 1962), p. 203.

[42] "Parliamentary Diplomacy — Debate *vs.* Negotiation," *World Affairs Interpreter,"* XXVI (Summer, 1955), 121–122.

[43] "The Narcotic Force of Tricky Slogans," *New York Times,* January 12, 1958.

[44] "Education as an Instrument of American Foreign Policy," address at annual meeting of the American Academy of Political and Social Science, April 16, 1966.

tion on a large scale adds an important new dimension to international politics."[45] In a pioneering study of this phenomenon, Andrew M. Scott distinguished five main types of informal penetration or access: (1) informal governmental access, "achieved by agents of a governmental organization"; (2) quasi-governmental access, including the activities of some journalists, scholars, or representatives of companies such as United Fruit or Aramco, "whose operations may occasionally have an almost governmental character"; (3) nongovernmental access, including "the activities of missionaries, tourists, students, teachers, journalists, researchers, engineers, businessmen, and the like"; (4) informal access by an international organization "to the people or processes of a nation by virtue of its operations there"; and (5) informal access by a nation through the medium of an international organization.[46] This phenomenon of informal penetration or access has aspects and implications far beyond the scope of diplomacy, but it also clearly involves types of diplomatic relations and practices which were virtually unknown in the days of the old diplomacy.

Important as these developments are, the conventional forms of diplomacy provide the means by which the nations of the world continue to carry on much of their formal business and regulate most of their official contacts. "Sometimes," as Sir William Hayter, himself an experienced diplomat, observed, ". . . oppressed with the futility of much of diplomatic life, the fatiguing social round, the conferences that agree on nothing, the dispatches that nobody reads, you begin to think that diplomacy is meaningless. . . . But . . . it does seem to me that States will always need to organize their relationships with each other. . . ."[47] Diplomacy remains a central mechanism for conducting the world's work, and as such, it is a major instrument of national policy and of international relations.

SUGGESTIONS FOR FURTHER READING

CAMBON, JULES M. *The Diplomatist.* London, 1931.

CECIL, A. *Metternich, 1773–1859: A Study of His Period and Personality.* New York: The Macmillan Company, 1933.

COOPER, SIR ALFRED DUFF. *Talleyrand.* New York: Harper, 1932.

CRAIG, G. A., and FELIX GILBERT. *The Diplomats, 1919–1939.* Princeton, N.J.: Princeton University Press, 1953. Contributions by 17 authors.

DENNETT, RAYMOND and JOSEPH E. JOHNSON, eds. *Negotiating with the Russians.* Boston: World Peace Foundation, 1952.

FOSTER, J. W. *The Practice of Diplomacy.* Boston: Houghton Mifflin Company, 1906.

FRANKEL, CHARLES. *The Neglected Aspect of Foreign Affairs: American Educational Policy and Cultural Policy Abroad.* Washington, D.C.: The Brookings Institution, 1966.

FRIEDRICH, CARL J. *Foreign Policy in the Making.* New York: W. W. Norton & Company, 1938.

GIBSON, HUGH. *The Road to Foreign Policy.* Garden City, N.Y.: Doubleday, Doran, 1944.

GREW, JOSEPH C. *Turbulent Era: A Diplomatic Record of Forty Years, 1904–1945,* edited by Walter Johnson. 2 vols. Boston: Houghton Mifflin Company, 1952.

HANKEY, MAURICE. *Diplomacy by Conference.* New York: G. P. Putnam's Sons, 1946.

[45] Andrew M. Scott, *The Revolution in Statecraft: Informal Penetration* (New York: Random House, 1965), p. 156.

[46] *Ibid.*, p. 17.

[47] *The Diplomacy of the Great Powers,* (New York: The Macmillan Company, 1966), pp. 73–74.

HAYTER, SIR WILLIAM. *The Diplomacy of the Great Powers.* New York: The Macmillan Company, 1966. Interesting comments by a former diplomat on British, French, Soviet, and American diplomacy.

HILL, DAVID J. *A History of Diplomacy in the International Development of Europe.* 3 vols. London, 1924.

HUDDLESTON, SISLEY. *Popular Diplomacy and War,* edited by Harry Elmer Barnes. Peterborough, N.H.: The Richard R. Smith Co. 1954.

IKLÉ, FRED C. *How Nations Negotiate.* New York: Harper & Row, 1964. A study of the strategies and tactics of negotiation.

KENNAN, GEORGE F. *American Diplomacy, 1900–1950.* Chicago: University of Chicago Press, 1951.

FITZSIMONS, M. A. and STEPHEN D. KERTESZ, eds. *Diplomacy in a Changing World.* Notre Dame, Ind.: University of Notre Dame Press, 1959. Excellent collection of articles by scholars and practicing diplomats.

LALL, ARTHUR. *Modern International Negotiation.* New York: Columbia University Press, 1967.

LONDON, KURT. *How Foreign Policy Is Made.* Princeton, N.J.: D. Van Nostrand Co., 1949.

MORGENTHAU, HANS J. *Politics Among Nations,* 3d ed. New York: Alfred A. Knopf, 1960. Contains stimulating and unconventional comments on diplomacy.

MOWAT, R. B. *A History of European Diplomacy, 1914–1925.* London, 1927.

NICOLSON, HAROLD. *The Congress of Vienna, A Study in Allied Unity: 1812–1822.* New York: Harcourt, Brace, 1946.

——— *Diplomacy,* 3d ed. New York: Oxford University Press, 1963.

——— *The Evolution of Diplomatic Method.* New York: The Macmillan Company, 1955. Significant insights into the theory and practice of diplomacy by a leading authority.

——— *Peacemaking,* 1919. New York: Harcourt, Brace. 1939.

PANIKKAR, K. M. *The Principles and Practice of Diplomacy.* Delhi, 1952. Lectures at the Delhi School of Economics.

PETRIE, SIR CHARLES. *Diplomatic History, 1713–1933.* New York: The Macmillan Company, 1949.

——— *Earlier Diplomatic History, 1492–1713.* New York: The Macmillan Company, 1949.

PLISCHKE, ELMER. *Conduct of American Diplomacy,* 2d ed. Princeton, N.J.: D. Van Nostrand Co., 1961.

——— *Summit Diplomacy.* College Park, Md.: Bureau of Governmental Research, University of Maryland, 1958. A study of the personal diplomacy of the Presidents of the United States.

SATOW, SIR ERNEST. *Guide to Diplomatic Practice.* 2 vols. London, 1922. A classic work in the field.

SEYMOUR, CHARLES, ed. *The Intimate Papers of Colonel House.* 4 vols. Boston: Houghton Mifflin Company, 1926–28.

SHERWOOD, ROBERT E. *Roosevelt and Hopkins,* rev. ed. New York: Harper, 1950.

STUART, GRAHAM H. *American Diplomatic and Consular Practice,* 2d ed. New York: Appleton-Century-Crofts, 1952.

THAYER, CHARLES W. *Diplomat.* New York: Harper, 1959. A comprehensive commentary on the procedures and practices of diplomacy, in its widest dimensions, by a former American diplomat.

THOMPSON, KENNETH W. *American Diplomacy and Emergent Patterns.* New York: New York University Press, 1962. Contains good discussion of "the old and new diplomacy," "parliamentary and personal diplomacy," and "diplomacy in a changing world."

United Nations Conference on Diplomatic Intercourse and Immunities. Vienna, March 2–April 14, 1961. Washington, D.C.: Government Printing Office, 1962.

WEBSTER, SIR CHARLES. *The Art and Practice of Diplomacy.* London, 1952.

WRISTON, HENRY M. *Diplomacy in a Democracy.* New York: Harper, 1956.

——— *Executive Agents in American Foreign Relations.* Baltimore: The Johns Hopkins Press, 1929.

YOUNG, SIR GEORGE. *Diplomacy, Old and New.* New York: Harcourt, Brace, 1921.

5 Propaganda and Political Warfare as Instruments of National Policy

Throughout history statesmen have used the devices of propaganda, at home and abroad, but only in recent years have they begun to suspect that there can be a great deal of science in the art of persuasion. Only in the past half-century have states established permanent agencies for the systematic exploitation of the possibilities of propaganda as an instrument of national policy. Today no state can safely ignore these possibilities.

The most important development of modern times in terms of the potentialities of propaganda has been the revolution in communications and transportation. The expansion in educational facilities and techniques likewise contributed enormously, and so did the coming of cheaper and better mail service. The appearance of the "penny press" in Europe and America in the nineteenth century meant that for the first time the propagandist could exploit a "mass" medium. Low-priced magazines and books have re-enacted this revolution for the twentieth century. Motion pictures, radio, and television have opened still other channels to the influence of propaganda.

Coincidentally with the growth in means of affecting the attitudes of people came an expanded need. The extension of the franchise in many nations gave large numbers of voters a share in the formation of government policy. These voters often became divided along political, economic, sectional, or class lines into groups whose conflicting interests had to be reconciled before an effective national policy could emerge. Propaganda, therefore, has been increasingly needed both to create some semblance of unified opinion at home and to exert influence abroad in behalf of national policies.

In the twentieth century propaganda has become a major instrument of national policy. Moreover, it has been developed by totalitarian states into an evil science. An analysis of the techniques used by the Fascists in Italy, the Nazis in Germany, and the Communists in Russia, China, and elsewhere would be a depressing exercise in the application of psychological principles to group manipulation. A study of Mussolini's capacity for exhibitionism, of Goebbels' vast propaganda machine, and of Communist successes in confusing issues, in using "upside-down language," in exploiting weaknesses in opponents, and in pulling all the stops from "peace offensives" to "hate campaigns" not only would illustrate the staggering power of the propaganda weapon in the hands of the totalitarians but also would drive home the conviction that George Orwell's 1984 is unhappily not far removed from present-day realities.

Neither propaganda nor political warfare should be regarded as comprising a fixed list of devices or as instruments to be used at some precise stage in the changing relationships of states. On the contrary, states are always finding new propaganda approaches and improvising new forms of political warfare, and they may employ both propaganda and political warfare in times of ostensible peace as well as in times of open hostility. Moreover, propaganda may itself be a weapon of political warfare, and so may any one of the so-called instruments of economic warfare. But the use of propaganda by no means implies a state of political warfare, and political warfare may or may not take the form of propaganda. States frequently wish to influence other states, both friendly and unfriendly, and to do this they often employ propaganda; occasionally they seek to exert greater pressures and may employ some of the devices of political warfare.

We shall devote the remainder of this chapter to an analysis of how states utilize these instruments to promote their national interests. The first section of this chapter will define propaganda, describe its various techniques and devices, and trace its development into a major instrument of national policy from the pre-World War II period to the present. The second section will define psychological and political warfare and discuss some of the forms each may take.

The Nature and Techniques of Propaganda

Definition. The word *propaganda* was first given general currency by the Roman Catholic Church to refer to the dissemination of its doctrines. More recently, after being taken over by the Marxists, it has been so used and misused that it defies exact definition. The reason for this difficulty in analysis stems from the figurative meanings, the malicious connotations, and the overtones of bias and partial or complete falsity which have become attached to it. For accuracy, the *method* of propaganda must be separated from the *aims* for which it is used. In the most general terms "any attempt to persuade persons to accept a certain point of view or to take a certain action" is propaganda. This definition is especially useful because it makes propaganda "morally neutral." To persuade per se is neither "good" nor "bad"; moral judgments must be directed to the purposes of the persuasion. Confusion arises from the failure to separate procedures from motives.

The meaning of propaganda may become clearer if we note its relationship to education. An authoritative handbook states: "Propaganda is the manipulation of symbols to control controversial attitudes; education is the manipulation of symbols (and of other means) to transmit accepted attitudes (and skills)."[1] Other writers doubt that a line can be drawn between propaganda and education. They point out that to speak of "accepted attitudes" is to raise questions such as: accepted by whom? how is acceptance signified?

For the purposes of the present study the broad field of propaganda will for the most part be narrowed to mean only organized efforts by governments or members of governments to induce either domestic groups or foreign states to accept policies favorable — or at least not unfavorable — to their own. This definition takes into account the fact that the size of the group to be propagandized varies with the object of the propagandist— all appeals are not to the "masses." We shall exclude the whole realm of "unofficial" propaganda, such as that issuing from individuals, business interests,

[1] Harold D. Lasswell and Dorothy Blumenstock, *World Revolutionary Propaganda* (New York: Alfred A. Knopf, 1939), p. 10.

and a host of special-purpose organizations. With the exception of totalitarian states, and others in wartime, most of these channels are beyond the direct control of governments.

Methods and Techniques. The science — or perhaps it is an art — of propaganda is similar to the arts of advertising and selling, and like the advertiser and salesman the propagandist must study his market and tailor his product to suit the demand. He must analyze the preconceptions, the fears, the desires, and the weaknesses of the group to be approached in order to use the most promising technique to achieve his purpose. The total number of available techniques is large. One handbook lists as many as seventy-seven;[2] but these may be grouped under four general headings: (1) Methods of Presentation; (2) Techniques for Gaining Attention; (3) Devices for Gaining Response; and (4) Methods of Gaining Acceptance.

1. *Methods of Presentation.* The propagandist seldom presents his materials in such a way as to assert both the pros and cons of an issue. His approach is more like that of a trial lawyer who carefully organizes his argument to prove one side of the case. He may keep to the truth but not to the whole truth. He usually omits evidence contrary to his view. The Nazis, for example, claimed that their interest in Czechoslovakia was the return of the Sudeten Germans. What they failed to say was that the Sudeten area contained key mountain defenses and important industries, and that they really wanted not part but all of Czechoslovakia.

Perhaps the classic example of propaganda by omission and distortion is the Ems dispatch of 1870. The French ambassador Benedetti was negotiating at Ems with King William of Prussia on the critical question of whether a Hohenzollern prince was to become king of Spain. At one point the King received a French proposal which he could not accept, whereupon he informed Benedetti that he had nothing more to say on the matter until he received further information. Neither the ambassador in his offer, nor the King in his reply, meant to be offensive. When Bismarck, who wanted war with France, learned of the proceedings at Ems from a dispatch sent by the King, he edited the dispatch in such a way that it appeared that Benedetti had offended the King with his proposal, and that William, in turn, had broken off negotiations. The dispatch was then released to the press. Both nations felt insulted, and Bismarck's propaganda by partial truth brought about the result he desired — the Franco-Prussian War.[3]

Sometimes the propagandist may resort to lying or to the use of faked documents and incidents. Thus Hitler exploited a fantastic story that the Jews were plotting an international conspiracy to rule the world. He "proved" his charges by citing the infamous *Protocols of the Wise Men of Zion.* This amazing masterpiece of fraudulence started with a book published in 1864 as a satire on Napoleon III in which the author, Maurice Joly, proclaimed the coming of an "anti-Christ" who would stop at nothing to gain domination of the world. Four years later a German, Hermann Godsche, wrote a lurid novel entitled *Biarritz,* which described twelve rabbis convening in a cemetery at Prague from all corners of the earth, rejoicing over their conquest of the world. At the turn of the century a group of the tsar's secret police, planning a revolutionary movement and needing a scapegoat for Russia's misfortunes, combined the basic elements of the two books into the fabulous *Protocols* — a highly successful work if it is to be

[2] D. Lincoln Harter and John Sullivan, *Propaganda Handbook* (Philadelphia: Twentieth Century Publishing Company, 1953), p. 3.

[3] A. J. Butler, trans., *Bismarck, the Man and the Statesman: Being the Reflections and Reminiscences of Otto, Prince von Bismarck, Written and Dictated by Himself after his Retirement from Office* (New York: Harper, 1898), II, 100 ff.

judged by its purpose. It eventually fell into the hands of one Alfred Rosenberg, a Russian of German extraction, who took it to Germany after the Bolshevik Revolution. Rosenberg became a top Nazi and the book a bible of Nazidom.

It must not be thought that deception is exclusively the product of totalitarian regimes, or that it has served only "bad" purposes. Benjamin Franklin, trying to win support for the American Revolution both abroad and in the colonies, forged letters showing how the British, by purchasing bales of scalps, encouraged the Indians to slaughter colonists. Lincoln must have known better when in his Gettysburg Address he implied that there had been conceded in 1776 an equality of men that was denied in 1861. McKinley did not deal with Congress or the country with full candor when in his war message of 1898 he failed to give due attention to the latest proposals of Spain. FDR has been criticized even by friendly historians for "deceiving" the American people about the seriousness of the war threat in the months before Pearl Harbor. Truth in itself may be effective propaganda. Churchill's "blood, sweat, and tears" speech was a completely honest characterization of the struggle ahead; his address merely put into eloquent words the great challenge to the British spirit. The later plea for "austerity" was another instance of effective truth.

Faked incidents are a convenient and often-used excuse for starting a war. On September 18, 1931, a small bomb happened to explode a few miles north of Mukden, Manchuria. Within three days the Japanese Kwantung Army had occupied strategic points throughout the province. Apparently the explosion was part of an elaborate plan to bring about war with China. The sinking of the battleship *Maine* in Havana harbor in 1898 may have been the work of Cuban revolutionists who wanted American intervention.

2. *Techniques for Gaining Attention.* Once his purpose has been formulated, the propagandist must attract attention to his cause. The notes, protests, official speeches, and declarations of a statesman in power will reach the government circles of foreign nations, but other means may be needed to reach the masses of the people. One of the more popular methods by which this is achieved is a show of strength. The Roman stunt of parading armies to impress observers has continued in popularity down to the present. The Nazis used this technique a great deal, and the Russians and Chinese Communists still do. With the advent of modern navies a variation on this same theme has been the naval demonstration. Since 1945, however, the most awesome demonstrations of power have been the tests of atomic and hydrogen bombs. Several states have thus effectively called attention to their nuclear developments.

Nations are resourceful in their attempts to attract favorable attention to their ways of life. Embassies usually contain certain staff members called "cultural attachés" who use lectures, colorful folders, travel guides, posters, and movies to glorify the home country. The United States Information Agency, with personnel in many countries, "tells America's story abroad." The British Council, a semi-official organization with close ties with the British Foreign Office, performs a similar function for Britain. Compared with the propaganda machine of the Soviet Union, with reported annual expenditures of between one and two billion dollars, the overseas information programs of the democratic states are puny indeed. By way of comparison, the total budget of the United States Information Agency for the fiscal year 1965 was only $165 million.

In addition to the normal methods of calling attention to themselves, countries sometimes devise special ones. The *Alliance Française,* formed in 1883, established centers of French learning throughout the world; it heightened the prestige and influence of France abroad and in addition served as an adjunct to French diplomacy. The Olympic Games in Berlin in 1936 featured a gigantic propaganda display by the host country, Nazi Germany. In more recent Olympic Games the Russians have attempted to prove that their system can develop athletes superior to those from capitalist countries. President Sukarno of Indonesia built a huge stadium, which Indonesia could ill afford, in Djakarta, and he sought to gain a great deal of propaganda mileage by staging "Games of the New Emerging Forces."

Visits of statesmen or monarchs to foreign countries are a way of indicating solidarity of interests and friendship. Tsar Alexander III's trip to France in 1893 was an important step in the completion of the Dual Alliance between Russia and France. The visits of English and Dutch royalty to the United States after World War II received friendly publicity in the American press and undoubtedly influenced both the President and Congress. In recent years heads of states have become ubiquitous features of the international landscape, and foreign ministers shuttle from country to country so frequently that many of them have become international commuters.

A favorable impression may be created by deeds as well as by words. Indeed, no words can be more effective than "the propaganda of the deed." Constructive policies will probably attract favorable attention even if the propaganda agencies fail to give them the Hollywood or the Madison Avenue treatment. Although major efforts are made to "sell" countries' aims and policies as an advertising man sells soap or automobiles, there may be deep wisdom in the Gandhian conviction that "good ideas sell themselves." Certainly there is a close and significant relation between the success of propaganda and the soundness of policies and aspirations. Neither honest information nor ballyhoo is a substitute for solid performance, at least in the long run.[4]

3. *Devices for Gaining Response.* Advertisers rely upon fear of social disapproval, desire for prestige, pride in possession, and other normal emotions to gain one response: the purchase of goods or services. In a similar manner the propagandist attempts to appeal to certain basic emotions — patriotism, love of justice, right of self-defense, and others — in order to gain special responses. A common device is the slogan — a short, catchy phrase used to incite action. Thus "No Taxation without Representation," *"Liberté, Egalité, Fraternité,"* and "Bread for the Workers, Land for the Peasants, and Peace for All" became the battle cries of revolutions. The *Maine* and Pearl Harbor were "remembered" to remind Americans of the causes for which they were fighting. Texans fought their war for independence from Mexico with the cry "Remember the Alamo!"

Closely akin to the slogan is the symbolic device — the pictorial or graphic representation. The Romans carried the *fasces* to symbolize might, the Christians bore the cross as a symbol of faith, and the French tricolor came to represent the revolutionary cause. Today each nation is represented by a flag and, in addition, often by an animal, such as the British lion, the American eagle, or the Russian bear. It may have its national anthem, its national hero, and its national flower.

The most effective symbol in recent history has been the swastika. Unlike many symbols, it had no intrinsic meaning either for the party which first used it or for the nation

[4] See Leo Cherne, "The Loin Cloth or the Rajah?" *Saturday Review*, September 17, 1955, p. 14. Cherne's article is one of seven in a symposium entitled, "What Do We Say to the World?" See also Victor Lasky, "Can Propaganda Make Friends?", the seventh article in the same symposium, pp. 19–20, 48.

which later adopted it, yet it won fanatical devotion and rallied a people as few symbols have ever done. An aid to the strength of its hold on Germans was its extreme simplicity, which allowed anyone to draw it. It was copied over and over — on the streets, in the schoolroom, on the walls — until it at last became a mystic, almost religious symbol of faith. The words, threats, and promises of Hitler became associated with the swastika, and the German people came to revere the symbol and, through it, the person of *Der Fuehrer*.

Often a person, like Hitler in Germany, becomes the symbol or personification of an idea. When Benjamin Franklin visited France, plainly dressed, carefully unpretentious, a fur cap atop his unpowdered hair, he was to the French "the embodiment of the ideals of Rousseau and the personification of the American cause"[5] — a representation which won many friends for his country. Other national heroes, particularly Washington, Jefferson, and Lincoln, have become symbols of American democracy. The tendency to associate a man with a certain idea is common in political cartoons. Often the person in power represents the nation. During World War II Churchill personified Great Britain, Stalin the Soviet Union, and Roosevelt the United States.

Times of great stress provide fruitful opportunities for propaganda, because usual attitudes and behavior patterns are then unsettled. Economic dislocation and insecurity — as in the Great Depression — incline men to accept any system which promises order and security. The effectiveness of the Soviet "peace" propaganda in the post-World War II years lies in the fact that people — especially Europeans — are sick of war and intensely want to believe that they can co-exist with communism. Fertile soil for American propaganda is provided by the fear of Soviet domination. Everywhere the propagandist capitalizes on existing attitudes and tries to manipulate them in such a way as to get responses that will further his purposes.

4. *Methods of Gaining Acceptance*. The establishment of a *rapport* or liaison between propagandist and "propagandee" is one of the successful ways of gaining acceptance for a program. In the attempt to convince men of his regard for their welfare the propagandist may stress his similarity to them. Many an American politician has been elected because he appealed to the voters as a "man of the people." The emphasis is usually on the candidate's humble origins. The idea was expressed most succinctly by Mrs. Calvin Coolidge, who once declared: "We're just plain folks." This kind of appeal is not peculiar to the United States, as can be seen in the case of Señora Eva Perón. When she displayed her fabulous jewels and furs to the people from whose ranks she had risen she would explain that it was for them that she had taken the jewels from the "oligarchs." For years this somehow made sense to the *descamisados* ("shirtless ones") in the Argentine nation.

History is filled with examples of the "plain folks" technique on the national level, but in international affairs the propagandist usually resorts to exploiting more inclusive common characteristics, such as race and religion. The expansion of Russian influence into the Balkans during the last two centuries has been continually cloaked in Pan-Slavism. Russia also posed as the defender of the Greek Orthodox Church. Hitler's use of the Aryan myth and Pan-Germanism is a more recent example of this type of appeal. The Japanese based their "Co-Prosperity Sphere" and "Asia for the Asiatics" slogans on the appeal of common interests.

Another approach used by the propagandist to make his cause more readily acceptable is the invocation of the higher sanctions of God, justice, and history. Pope Urban II launched the Crusades with the

[5] Thomas A. Bailey, *A Diplomatic History of the American People*, 4th ed. (New York: Appleton-Century-Crofts, 1950), p. 15.

cry *"Deus vult"* ("God wills it"). In most wars both sides ask Divine blessing for their cause. The "lessons of history" are often used by propagandists to lend force to their arguments. In America, isolationists have misquoted George Washington's dictum on alliances in his Farewell Address to fortify their sentiments and to influence foreign policy. The Russians, combining history with a pseudo-religious fervor, quote Marx and Lenin to give sanction to current policies. The propagandist may in these ways strive to give his aims a more universal appeal.

One of the chief limitations to the effectiveness of propaganda is the sharp competition for the attention, response, and acceptance of those to whom it is directed. Propaganda efforts are seldom free from counterpropaganda. Yet even where the channels of information are state-controlled or where strict censorship prevails, it is well-nigh impossible in this technological age to seal off a country from the rest of the world. Censorship in a greater or lesser degree is practiced by most states today; it is all-encompassing in totalitarian states and is very extensive in many other countries during periods of national emergency.

Since under normal conditions the propagandist must battle against other lines of propaganda, he often attempts to discredit his opposition. The Russians portray the Americans as the "capitalist-imperialist warmongers of Wall Street." The Allies in World War I referred to the Germans as "the Boche" or "Huns." Propagandists frequently try to associate their opponents with something bad. The Russians have paraded before the world the unsolved Negro problem in the United States. In American politics the Democrats are linked with two world wars as the "War Party" while, on the other hand, the Republicans are labeled the "Depression Party." Competition is almost always present to restrict the effectiveness of propaganda.

Specialists in the fields of propaganda, public opinion, and pressure-group tactics have added immensely to the scientific stature of their studies in recent years. While we cannot here turn aside to explore the nature of their researches and conclusions, we must point out that earlier judgments in this field must be regarded as subject to constant re-evaluation. The present discussion will undertake only to suggest the role of propaganda in recent years and to note its gradual adoption as an important instrument of national policy.

Propaganda in the Dictator States before World War II

The Soviet Union. "Propaganda," wrote Lenin in 1905, "is of crucial importance for the triumph of the Party." Twelve years later he remarked that the revolution had succeeded "because it knew how to combine force with persuasion."[6] The Bolsheviks soon put into practice the Marxian view that every phase of society should contribute to the indoctrination of the individual. They disseminated propaganda through party workers, the local soviets of towns and villages, and the army. Eventually they addressed appeals to everybody — peasants, workers, soldiers, intelligentsia, racial minority groups, all showing how the utopian Soviet state, free of classes, conflict, and capitalism, provided everything for everybody "according to his need." Their aims were to consolidate the dictatorial control of the government and party, to gain adherents to their program, and to make the people willing to sacrifice, suffer, and die for Mother Russia.

The Soviet leaders proved to be masters both in developing propaganda devices and in adapting techniques to specific situations. First of all, Communist propaganda has al-

[6] Quoted in Saul K. Padover and Harold D. Lasswell, "Psychological Warfare," *Headline Series*, No. 86 (Foreign Policy Association, March–April, 1951), p. 24.

ways had a vocabulary of its own. Such terms as "proletariat," "communism," "socialism," "toiling masses," and "revolution," for example, had a favorable meaning, while "capitalism," "bourgeoisie," "classes," "imperialism," and "parliamentarianism" became the epithets that Communists used in speaking of their enemies. They continuously diverted public dissatisfaction from themselves, and blamed all the nation's troubles upon "decadent bourgeoisie" and "counterrevolutionary influences." They made good use of slogans such as the traditional "Workers of the World, Unite" and of symbols such as the Red Star and the Hammer and Sickle.

Besides the propaganda machinery existing within the Soviet Union after 1918, the Communists promoted the Third International (the Comintern).[7] Dominated from the start by the People's Commissariat for Foreign Affairs, the Comintern was a useful medium for directing the activities of Communist parties throughout the world and for exerting pressure on foreign governments to follow policies favorable to the Soviet Union. Until 1935, with only minor parliamentary representation, if any, Communists in other states generally followed policies of opposition to other parties, hoping to clog the wheels of government or to incite revolution. This was the case in Germany before the fall of the Weimar Republic, when Communists cooperated on several occasions with the Nazis in the hope of defeating the hated Social Democrats; they believed that if a reactionary government came into power the proletariat would arise. After 1935, however, Communist parties in Europe followed the Moscow directive for a "People's Front," i.e., cooperation with "liberal" groups against the Nazi threat. Thus the Soviet Union had the advantage of tentacles stretching throughout the world – a most effective aid to foreign policy.

Nazi Germany. After their defeat in 1918 the German people had been subjected to propaganda — chiefly from military sources — insisting that the German army had never been defeated. Germany collapsed, according to this thesis, because alien and radical elements of the population had been easy prey for Allied propaganda. A few other ideas circulated among the people: the Versailles Treaty had been unjustly imposed upon them; the leaders of the Weimar Republic had betrayed their country; the "Jew-Communists" were the cause of their grievances; they, the *Herrenvolk* ("master race"), needed *Lebensraum* ("living space"). Hitler and his followers exploited these ideas, made appeals, to both labor and capitalist segments of society, enrolled unemployed youths in the Storm Troops, and finally maneuvered themselves into power, owing much of their success to propaganda.[8]

One of Hitler's first official acts was to establish a National Ministry of Popular Enlightenment and Propaganda, headed by Joseph Goebbels, who defined his job as the achievement of "one single public opinion." Whatever affected the minds of the people fell under the jurisdiction of at least one of Goebbels' thirty-one departments. The National Chamber of Culture had great powers of control and censorship over literature, movies, music, and the graphic arts, carefully and forcefully suppressing anything "incompatible with the cultural aims of National Socialism."

[7] The Third International was organized by the Communist Party to bring about a worldwide revolution. The famous Trotsky-Stalin fight was over this issue; Stalin wanted the energies of Communists to be devoted to the consolidation of party gains in Russia; Trotsky advocated the promotion of revolution outside Russia. Although Stalin's view prevailed, the Third International remained an instrument of Russian foreign policy until it was dissolved in 1943.

[8] Fritz Morstein Marx, *Government in the Third Reich*, 2d ed. (New York: McGraw-Hill Book Company, 1936), p. 99.

Hitler obtained fanatical support for himself by invoking the *Fuehrerprinzip* (the idea of a great leader) — a not too difficult task in postwar Germany. Before 1923 (the year of the Munich Beer Hall *Putsch*) Hitler had ridiculed the masses, calling them stupid, cowardly, and worthless. He had praised instead the "elite," the "intelligent group in society," and he had said that his party — and eventually the state — must be led by a "forceful minority."[9] After 1923, however, he realized where his potential strength lay. Thenceforth there was no criticism of the masses — only praise and admiration of their power, and the constant assertion that the Nazis were working for them. This approach had by 1933 attracted a large following of people who identified themselves with National Socialism. And where intellectual identification had not yet been achieved, Hitler was willing to accept physical, symbolic demonstrations of acceptance. Hence the "German salute" or "salute of the free man" was required of all civil servants in 1933. Early in 1934 it became compulsory for all Germans to salute one another with "Heil Hitler," for it was "a task of popular enlightenment to introduce the German salute among all sections of the German people as the expression of German solidarity."[10] The omnipresence of the swastika and the use of slogans such as "One people, one state, one *Fuehrer*" seemed to demonstrate the solidarity of the German nation.

It would be a gross oversimplification to credit the creation of this semblance of unity and power to the personality and words of Hitler alone. The Nazis were well schooled in the use of propaganda, but mere words were accented by blackjacks, bullets, and the Gestapo. The chain of diplomatic victories which went from the Saar plebiscite (1935) to the absorption of Czechoslovakia (1938–39) and the Soviet-German pact (1939) gave the Germans a feeling of superiority, supported not by murky theories of race but by the sight of Europe cowering before Nazi military strength. In addition, the large production of war materiel, the building of fortifications, and the construction of internal improvements created a false prosperity that provided full employment and created the impression that the economy was flourishing. For a time Hitler was able to carry out his threats and to match words with deeds.

Fascist Italy. Mussolini's propaganda machine was much older than Hitler's organization, and it developed many techniques which the Nazis copied. The appeal of fascism was exerted on all groups within the country: on the army and navy (to win the guarantee of a strong government); on the monarchists (to gain support for the monarchy); on the "Irridentists" (to bribe the "patriots" and the enemies of the Versailles Treaty); on the clerics (to enlist the support of the church); and on the malcontents in general (to pick up the hungry, the unhappy, and any loose ends). In consolidating his own power, Mussolini appealed to the people with the "plain folks" technique, often stressing his low background and distributing pictures of himself, toiling at some humble task. But his role was that of *Il Duce* ("the leader"). In other words, he was the common man become a Caesar.

Mass appeals were issued in many forms. For the general public *Il Duce* painted glorious pictures: Italy as a resurrected Roman Empire; the Fascist legions as great as Caesar's; the Adriatic as an Italian lake and the Mediterranean as an Italian sea. Slogans were used to inspire the people; symbols such as the *fasces* were used to signify glory; and badges and fancy uniforms were used to give a feeling of importance and status to soldiers and others. The system of incentives, rewards, and coercions employed was

[9] Serge Chakhotin, *The Rape of the Masses* (New York: Alliance Book Corp., 1940), p. 248.

[10] Morstein Marx, p. 96.

strikingly similar to that of the Soviet Union, from whom the Fascists, as well as the Nazis, were willing to learn.

Propaganda and World War II

The outbreak of World War II found the totalitarian states provided with well-staffed and well-equipped propaganda machines. The democracies had no comparable organizations. Britain, however, had learned the importance of propaganda and psychological warfare in World War I, and the United States had substantial resources in money and ideas. Together they proved that unfettered ingenuity can be far more potent than standardized thinking such as characterized Nazi Germany, Fascist Italy, and Imperial Japan. With the worldwide cooperation of the Communists after June, 1941, they were able to wage war on the propaganda front with better results than the Axis.

Germany. As the German people had already been subjected to years of vituperation against the British, the French, the "Jew-Communists," and "Jew-Niggers," the Nazi leaders had no problem in whipping up hatred against their enemies. Censorship, manipulation of information, and indoctrination along Nazi lines had been so long in operation that there was less difficulty in winning war support in Germany than in the democracies. The Nazis had little to worry about on the home front; they could devote most of their energies to psychological warfare against the enemy.

America was the target of a mighty propaganda drive by the Axis. As far back as 1933 hundreds of American Fascist groups, calling themselves by such all-American names as "Crusaders for Americanism," "Christian Fronters," and "American Guards," had blossomed forth. The goal of these "bunds" was to align groups — economic, religious, or ethnic — against one another, and their chief line of attack was to pit gentile against Jew. Thus in America, as in Germany, "Jew-Communists" were blamed for the country's economic and social ills. Furthermore, the New Deal, or "Jew Deal," as it was often termed, was pictured as a gigantic plot to rob "one hundred per cent Americans" of their independence. Two official German organizations, the *Weltdienst* and the *Deutscher Fichte-Bund,* took on the task of supplying Axis agents in America with anti-Semitic posters, pamphlets, and bulletins. This material was reprinted in such patriotic-sounding papers as Father Coughlin's *Social Justice,* William Dudley Pelley's *Liberator,* and Gerald Winrod's *Defender.* The outbreak of the war brought the formation of something new on the propaganda scene: various "Committees," such as the "America First Committee" and the "Make Europe Pay War Debts Committee," which were soon infiltrated by Nazis and used to foster isolationist sentiment in the country in the hope of preventing America from aiding the Allies.

Nazi propaganda within Europe was at first successful because Goebbels was able to exploit two basic human emotions — hope and fear.[11] Initial successes on the battlefield raised visions of quick victory and struck fear into the hearts of enemy soldiers and people. German propagandists were later thrown on the defensive, and their earlier and well-remembered boasts and misrepresentations then undermined their prestige and effectiveness. Toward the end, fear of defeat rather than hope of victory was used to rally the German nation to fight on.

Japan. In planning their psychological warfare the Japanese collaborated with the Germans, and the patterns of propaganda reflected more than a casual similarity.[12]

[11] Ernst Kris *et al., German Radio Propaganda* (New York: Oxford University Press, 1944), pp. 479 ff.

[12] See Peter De Mendelssohn, *Japan's Political Warfare* (London, 1944). Although no clear distinction is made between propaganda and political warfare, the book is mainly about the former.

For example, the favorite themes of the Nazis were the God-like *Fuehrer,* for whom it was the greatest possible honor for citizens to die, the *Herrenvolk* concept, the New Order for Europe, and scapegoats — Jews, Communists, Catholics. The Japanese had the God-Emperor, to whom they pledged their lives, the "Son of Heaven" idea, the new "Greater East Asia Co-Prosperity Sphere," and scapegoats — the "red-haired barbarians of the West" (British, Americans, and other Western "imperialists").

Although the Japanese did not employ psychological warfare in support of military offensives on as grand a scale as did Germany in her attack on France, they nonetheless took propaganda wherever they went. Their promises of a "Greater East Asia" and their tales of Japanese victories won many Asian supporters, who believed that Japan would give them greater freedom and opportunity than would be possible under Western "imperialism." Cut off from the United States by six thousand miles of Pacific Ocean and by faulty short-wave transmission, the Japanese were unable to reach the American people with any sustained campaign of political, psychological, or cultural warfare. Even in the Hawaiian Islands, nearly 2500 miles closer to Japan, with one-third of its population of Japanese descent and with a mixture of nationalities which seemed to offer fertile soil for racial tensions and for espionage and sabotage, Japanese efforts were notably unproductive. Against American troops in the Southwest Pacific, however, the Japanese scored propaganda as well as military victories. They were particularly adept in their efforts to induce homesickness among soldiers through the broadcasts of "Tokyo Rose," the Asian sister of "Axis Sally" of Berlin, who played songs of home while describing the latest American military defeats. In the jungles, the Japanese soldiers were masters of tactical psychological warfare: strange noises and fake attacks gave the G.I.'s little rest.

Great Britain. Propaganda activities were deemed of sufficient importance by the British to warrant a director of cabinet rank, and on September 1, 1939, Parliament set up a Ministry of Information. While its scope was not as broad as that of the German Propaganda Ministry, it was nevertheless efficient in maintaining tight censorship over mail and news and in carefully editing press releases. In addition, it managed the Overseas Services of the British Broadcasting Corporation and directed a large staff in the conduct of psychological warfare operations. The big job at home, of course, was to keep up the morale of the populace in spite of such disasters as the repeated bombing of London. The bulk of British war propaganda work, however, was done not alone but in conjunction with the United States. It must therefore be regarded as an important part of what is here described under United States propaganda.

The United States. The United States waged her war of ideas chiefly through the Office of War Information (OWI), set up in 1942. To the OWI, headed by Elmer Davis, fell the tremendous responsibility of conducting propaganda and psychological warfare abroad. It established outposts in foreign countries, operated several foreign-language radio stations in Europe, printed many pamphlets, and supplied the armed forces with personnel trained in propaganda techniques. The United States and Britain set up a joint psychological warfare division in the Supreme Headquarters of the Allied Expeditionary Force (SHAEF) in the European Theater of Operations (ETO). This PWD-SHAEF, as it was called, had as its primary purpose the destruction of German morale. Headed by Brigadier General Robert A. McClure, a direct chain of command led from Supreme Headquarters to the battlefield, where every Allied army had psychological warfare teams, often at regimental and company levels. These teams usually had at their disposal mobile radio broadcasting systems, with public-address facilities, radios, mobile printing presses, and ready-made leaflets. In the last months of the war some commanding generals put loudspeakers on their forward tanks for the purpose of persuading the enemy to surrender.

The United States, Great Britain, and the U.S.S.R. all maintained "white" or openly identified radio stations, which broadcast news and advice to the Germans. Although listening to forbidden stations — "black listening" — was punishable by imprisonment or death, many Germans risked the penalties, according to postwar surveys. The main reason for this was that the Propaganda Ministry's lies of German successes had caught up with it. Particularly after Stalingrad, few thinking Germans were willing to accept the Goebbels version of anything. In addition to the "white" stations, there were the "black" stations — Allied stations posing as German. Their primary purpose was to confuse the enemy and make him turn to Allied broadcasts to learn the truth. Finally, there were the "grey" stations, which laid no claim to being either Allied or German.

Although their propaganda naturally gained in effectiveness as their mighty war machine took form and then gained momentum, the Allies were not completely successful in their propaganda and psychological warfare efforts; nor were they immune to enemy tactics. One of the moot questions of the war was the advisability of the "unconditional surrender" dictum.[13] The original top-level plans had not called for psychological warfare against either Germany or Japan. According to one observer's views, the men in the higher echelons of command in Washington consistently overestimated the solidarity of the Japanese nation. This led to the bringing of Russia into the war in the Far East and to the dropping of atomic bombs — developments which might have been avoided by greater understanding of the actual Japanese weaknesses and by more intensive psychological warfare.[14] Only in the last weeks of the war were intensive efforts made to weaken Japanese morale by propaganda as well as by aerial and naval attacks. Day after day throughout the summer of 1945, broadcasts over Radio Saipan drove home a message of betrayal and defeat to the Japanese people and soldiers. Almost every day this powerful station named a number of major Japanese cities, one of which, it added, would be the target of the next mass assault by American B–29's based in the Marianas and on Iwo Jima. After the war it was learned that political warfare of this sort, coupled with the growing power of the Allied forces in the western Pacific, had contributed immensely to the weakening of Japanese morale. In spite of their strict discipline as a people and as a nation, as evidenced by their devotion to the Emperor and the traditions of Imperial Japan, by their unwillingness to surrender in battle, and by their "Kamikaze" pilots, the Japanese proved to be vulnerable to psychological as well as military warfare.

Perhaps another major error was the failure to differentiate between the Nazi regime and ordinary German citizens. Goebbels felt that had such a distinction been made it would have ripped the German nation apart. "If I were on the enemy side," he said, "I should from the very first day on have adopted a slogan of fighting against Nazism, but not against the German people."[15] After the "unconditional surrender"

[13] Daniel Lerner, *Sykewar: Psychological Warfare Against Germany* (New York: Geo. W. Stewart, 1949), pp. 329 ff.

[14] Ellis M. Zacharias, *Secret Missions* (New York: G. P. Putnam's Sons, 1946), pp. 387–388 and *passim*. See also U.S. Strategic Bombing Survey, *Japan's Struggle to End the War* (Washington, D.C.: Government Printing Office, 1946).

[15] Louis P. Lochner, ed., *The Goebbels Diaries, 1942–1943* (New York: Doubleday & Company, 1948), p. 147.

formula had been agreed upon in 1943, most Germans apparently believed that they were left with no alternative to resisting to the last. The testimony of Allied experts in psychological warfare and of Germans in the postwar years was virtually unanimous that this formula strengthened the determination of the Germans to resist and thus assisted Hitler in his last desperate months.

Propaganda since World War II

In the years since World War II propaganda has become a major element of international relations. It permeates these relations and the conducting of them, from bilateral and multilateral diplomacy to political warfare and various forms of military action. It has become a major component of the so-called cold war between the Communist and non-Communist states, especially between the Soviet Union and the United States, both in direct relations and in competitive policies toward the emerging nations of the Third World. It has been a prominent feature of the Sino-Soviet dispute. It has been carried on in "hot" as well as "cold" wars, such as those in Korea and in Vietnam.

Soviet Propaganda. There are several reasons why the Soviet Union leads the West, including the United States, in the use of propaganda. The most obvious one is longer experience. First used to consolidate the Revolution of 1917 and then to spread Communist ideology throughout the world, the Soviet propaganda machine gained momentum during the depression of the 1930's, the Spanish Civil War, and the period just before World War II. Another reason is the place of propaganda in the total Soviet system. It is an integral part of its national and international policy.

At the end of the war the Communist Party of the Soviet Union was in possession of a propaganda machine second to none in history — the Administration of Agitation and Propaganda (*Agitprop*). The head of this mighty organization had one of the biggest jobs in the Soviet Union, commanding more than 1,400,000 full-time professional propagandists, all of whom had to be loyal party members.[16] In addition to the *Agitprop* staff were the 250 employees of the Foreign Office whose job was to prepare propaganda specifically for foreign consumption. The Foreign Office and the Soviet diplomatic missions abroad were centers of propaganda — and also of political warfare and espionage — as well as of diplomacy. TASS, an agency of the Soviet Government, had a monopoly of the dissemination of Russian news abroad. VOKS — the All-Union Society for Cultural Relations with Foreign Countries — was active in promoting cultural exchange programs in many countries, in encouraging the formation of Soviet Friendship Societies, and in maintaining liaison with such camouflaged propaganda organizations as the World Federation of Trade Unions and the Cominform, and with fellow-traveling groups and individuals. And in her propaganda activities the Soviet Union was for a time obediently aided by her satellites and by Communist parties throughout the world.

Between 1945 and 1947 Soviet propaganda aimed primarily at encouraging the growth of "People's Democracies" and, conversely, at lessening the power and influence of the United States abroad. Accordingly, emphasis was placed on the superiority of the Soviet way of life, the decadence of capitalism, and the cruelties of capitalist-imperialist exploitation. Backed by active Communist subversive groups and by Soviet power, the propaganda offensive was part of an overall drive to acquire satellites in Eastern Europe and to spread communism westward into Europe and eastward into China. In 1947, however, the United States inaugu-

[16] Richard L. Brecker, "The New Arm of Diplomacy," *The American Foreign Service Journal*, XXVIII (August, 1951), 23–25; and Padover and Lasswell, p. 24.

rated the "containment policy" with the speech of President Truman on March 12, soon followed by the offer of aid that eventually produced the Marshall Plan. As these policies took concrete form, *Izvestia* charged that West Germany's "military potential is being completely restored and will have to serve as a weapon in the aggressive policy of the American monopolies."[17] Just a week later *Pravda* declared that the United States had contrived the "military and economic enslavement of Turkey" and had deprived that country of her "political independence" so that she might be used as a "strategic and military springboard for the U.S.A."[18]

In 1949 the Russians launched a new major propaganda offensive, "a more vigorous and consistent struggle for peace" against the "instigators of a new war," as Foreign Minister Molotov explained it. The main purpose of the new drive, which *Bolshevik* termed "a holy conflict," was to convince the people of the Soviet Union — and whomever else could be convinced — that the Soviet Union was fighting with all her strength for peace, the abolition of atomic weapons, and disarmament. To support the new "peace offensive" the "Partisans of Peace" were organized on a worldwide scale, complete with an official organ of their own. The "Partisans" climaxed their campaign with the Stockholm Peace Appeal, to which, it was claimed, 300,000,000 signatures of people throughout the world were affixed. The United States took no formal notice of the "offensive"— although some Americans signed the Appeal — for this would have implied that the U.S.S.R. was indeed the foremost exponent of world peace. But her failure to do so gave *Agitprop* "proof" that America was against peace.[19]

Soviet propaganda techniques were further illustrated in the case of Korea. Soon after the end of World War II the Soviet press was replete with statements insisting that the Korean people resented the United States and admired the Soviet Union. Much attention was given to the comparison of the position of the North Koreans, with "extensive political rights and unlimited opportunity to develop their economy and culture," with the wretched lot of South Korea, where the American forces had lingered on to exploit the people long after Soviet troops had left.[20] Pursuing this theme, the Soviet press and radio featured stories of Soviet-Korean friendship, the corruption of Syngman Rhee and his "puppet government," and abuses of "the American expansionists," who wished to convert Korea into a colony of Wall Street and "a military and political springboard" for America. By June, 1950, there was at least one article a day in Soviet papers describing American abuses, Korean resentment, and the desire of Koreans to unite *immediately*. When the Korean War did break out, the Communist world was well prepared for it — militarily and psychologically.

Since the death of Stalin in 1953, Soviet propaganda has given greater emphasis to the themes of peaceful co-existence — apparently even the doctrine of the inevitability of conflict between Communist and non-Communist states has been shelved, if not abandoned — and the reduction of international tensions. Since 1955 the Soviet "peace offensive" has been directed particularly to the peoples of underdeveloped countries, and has taken the form of economic assistance programs, cultural exchanges, and intense political activity. Since the late 1950's the growing split with Communist China has led

[17] July 21, 1948: reprinted in *Soviet Press Translations*, III, No. 15 (September 1, 1948), 453.

[18] July 28, 1948, *Translations*, III, No. 15 (September 1, 1948), 484–486.

[19] An account of various Soviet "peace offensives" in the postwar period, and of Soviet propaganda techniques during the era of the "new look," is given in Chapter 21.

[20] *Pravda*, February 23, 1949, *Translations*, III, 229–232.

to a fantastic propaganda barrage in both the Soviet Union and Communist China against the other. In the meantime, in spite of all the propaganda about the peaceful co-existence of different systems, the organs of Soviet propaganda have continued to foment discontent in newly emerging nations, to denounce the policies of the United States and other "capitalist" nations, to create dissension among the NATO allies, to attack military alliances generally, and to exploit any weakness and division within the non-Communist world.

American Propaganda. After World War II the Office of War Information and other groups working on propaganda and psychological warfare were abolished, and their functions devolved upon offices in the State Department which in the course of the next three years administered the Fulbright Act and other educational exchanges and a reduced information program abroad.

As the cold war became more intense, it began to dawn on Americans, including members of Congress, that the United States was handicapped by the lack of a major weapon: propaganda and counterpropaganda. To rectify this situation, the Smith-Mundt Act of 1948 provided for the establishment of an Office of International Information and an Office of Educational Exchange "to promote a better understanding of the United States, and to increase mutual understanding between the people of the United States and the people of other countries." In January, 1952, the two Offices were consolidated into the International Information Administration, still in the Department of State. In 1953, however, the President, by a reorganization plan, established the United States Information Agency as a separate organization within the executive branch. Since its creation USIA has been the main official propaganda instrument of the United States abroad, but many other agencies and departments of the government are engaged in one way or another in information and propaganda activities.

According to a presidential memorandum to the director of USIA, dated January 25, 1963, the mission of the Agency "is to help achieve U.S. foreign policy objectives by (a) influencing public attitudes in other nations, and (b) advising the President, his representatives abroad, and the various departments and agencies on the implications of foreign opinions for present and contemplated U.S. policies, programs and official statements."

Organizationally, USIA is divided into four major categories, the executive level, media services, geographic offices, and overseas operations. The media services are broadcasting (the "Voice of America"), motion pictures, television, press and publications, and information. The installations abroad operate under the label "United States Information Service" (USIS). In 1964 there were 239 USIS mission posts, branch posts and subposts, reading rooms, binational centers and cultural centers in 105 countries.

In 1964 USIA serviced over 226 film centers in some 106 countries, and distributed films in more than 50 languages. It provides weekly newsreels and feature programs on TV film to television stations in many countries. In Washington it prepares a variety of printed matter for Agency use. It transmits some of this material to more than 100 USIS posts via radioteletype — a daily service known as the wireless information file. It publishes a monthly Russian-language magazine, *America Illustrated,* and a bimonthly Arabic-language magazine, *Al Hayat Fi America.* It has sizable printing plants in Manila, Beirut, and Mexico City. It distributes millions of leaflets, pamphlets, posters, newspaper and magazine features, photographs, cartoon strips, and other information material to more than 10,000 newspapers and magazines in non-Communist countries. In 1962 it maintained 174 libraries in 85 countries, supplemented by 79 reading rooms and 160 USIS-supported binational centers around the world. It has a major book translation and book distribution program, including low-priced books and materials for the teaching of English as a foreign language.

The most famous branch of USIA is the "Voice of America." In 1963 it was broadcasting directly around the clock in 36 languages, for approximately 796 hours a week. Many of its broadcasts are beamed directly at the peoples of the Soviet Union, Eastern Europe, and Communist China. It has many transmitters at home and abroad, and nine overseas relaying stations, including million-watt installations in Munich, the Philippines, and Okinawa. It also supports RIAS (Radio in the American Sector) in West Berlin, which broadcasts to East Berlin and East Germany. Programming emphasizes factual news and commentary; the broadcasters include musicians, actors, statesmen, religious leaders, and thousands of ordinary citizens of the United States and foreign countries.

Unlike the Soviet Union, the United States has been slow to recognize the importance of propaganda as an instrument of national policy. One reason for this is that only since World War II has the United States assumed global responsibilities in peacetime. A further explanation of the belated realization of a need for an American propaganda organization in times of peace lies in the strong tradition of free speech. Just before World War II, when the United States became a battleground for competing propagandists, censorship or suppression was not considered; the government merely forced the identification of the origin of the propaganda and tried "to keep all channels of communication flowing as freely as possible."[21] Even today large segments of the American population and their representatives in Congress remain unconvinced that propaganda and the expense it entails are necessary.[22]

Psychological and Political Warfare

Since 1890 Europe and the rest of the world have been in a state of war, or of preparation for war, much of the time. Peace has become an uneasy truce in which the supporters of various ideologies jockey for the most favorable positions. As the relations between states have assumed this uncertain status, old-style diplomacy has proved ineffective and inadequate. Two instruments which have come into increasing use, operating in the twilight zone between diplomacy and war, are psychological and political warfare. During World Wars I and II they were important supplements to the military efforts, and since World War II they have been chiefly identified with the cold war and with other conflict situations in a troubled world.

Psychological Warfare. "Definitions of psychological warfare vary from narrow usage during World Wars I and II as an adjunct to military force in time of war, to the broad concepts underlying establishment of the Psychological Strategy Board by President Truman in 1951, and President Eisenhower's appointment of C. D. Jackson as his psychological warfare adviser early in

[21] Charles A. H. Thomson, *Overseas Information Service of the United States Government* (Washington, D.C.: The Brookings Institution, 1948), p. 2. This book contains an excellent study of the problems and achievements in the formation of postwar propaganda agencies.

[22] For an analysis of the suggested goals for a United States propaganda program, see *The U.S. Ideological Effort: Government Agencies and Programs,* study prepared by the Legislative Reference Service, Library of Congress, for the Subcommittee on International Organizations and Movements of the Committee on Foreign Affairs, House of Representatives, 88th Cong., 1st Sess. (Washington, D.C.: Government Printing Office, 1964). See also "Communications Crisis: What Can Persuaders Do?" *Printers' Ink,* September 14, 1962.

1953."[23] Eisenhower obviously associated psychological warfare with "the struggle for the minds of men." Professor Paul Linebarger, author of a basic book on the subject, defined psychological warfare in the broad sense as "the application of parts of the science of psychology to further the efforts of political, economic, or military actions," and in the narrow sense as "the use of propaganda against an enemy, together with such other operational measures of a military, economic, or political nature as may be required to supplement propaganda."[24] Roland I. Perusse has identified eighteen terms which have been associated with psychological warfare or which have been used as synonyms for it. These are: cold war, war of ideas, struggle for the minds and wills of men, war for the minds of men, thought war, ideological warfare, nerve warfare, political warfare, international information, overseas information, campaign of truth, propaganda, international propaganda, propaganda warfare, war of words, indirect aggression, agitation, and international communication.[25]

Political Warfare. It is easier and less hazardous to cite examples of political warfare than it is to define the term. In general, it embraces the means — short of war — which a state takes to weaken a specific enemy or specific enemies. The persuasion of friendly diplomacy is not political warfare; neither is propaganda which does not seek to impair or limit another state's freedom of action. On the other hand, diplomacy or propaganda which has the intent to coerce must be regarded as political warfare. Economic measures must be so characterized when they are aimed at a particular state. Thus a given act may or may not be political warfare. The distinction lies in its purpose. An embargo conceived solely to conserve domestic resources of a commodity is quite different from an embargo imposed to deprive an unfriendly state of essential imports, regardless of the fact that both may apply to exports to all states. Political warfare does not end with the coming of military conflict; indeed, it is then likely to be accentuated and to lead to all sorts of diplomatic, propaganda, and economic measures to weaken the enemy. Whether political warfare always involves intervention in the affairs of the state or states against which it is directed hinges upon the definition of intervention.

Political warfare is by no means a recent innovation in the conduct of relations between states. The strategy of the Trojan horse has been practiced throughout history. The more dramatic devices of modern political warfare have included the following: propaganda to confuse and divide; the support of minority groups and "fifth column" agents to disrupt the normal processes of the enemy state; the encouragement of revolt to overthrow the existing government; the use of sabotage to wreck industry and transport; and the resort to assassination to remove key leaders and demoralize the population.

World War I. The most direct method of undermining the war production of an enemy country — or of a neutral country supplying an enemy — is through sabotage, or the destruction of machinery or materials. During World War I the German government employed a vast network of secret agents in America whose chief job was to sabotage production intended for the Allied powers. The Germans were blamed — probably rightly — for hundreds of mysterious explosions and fires throughout the United States;

[23] Roland I. Perusse, "Psychological Warfare Reconsidered," in William E. Daugherty and Morris Janowitz, *A Psychological Warfare Casebook* (Baltimore: The Johns Hopkins Press, 1958), p. 28.

[24] *Psychological Warfare,* 2d ed. (Washington, D.C.: Combat Forces Press, 1954), p. 40.

[25] Perusse, pp. 26–27.

the most famous explosion, that on Black Tom Island, near the Statue of Liberty, resulted in an estimated loss of $30,000,-000.[26] These and other instances of sabotage by the Central Powers were a major factor in turning American public opinion against Germany — an example of political warfare boomeranging.

The ultimate triumph of the Allies was in part due to their effective waging of political warfare. Through British control of the cable lines and through lurid atrocity stories the Allies won their greatest political victory of the war: the active participation of the United States on their side. Many other factors were, of course, involved. During the last year of the conflict the Allies capitalized on the propaganda value of Wilson's Fourteen Points — particularly the one on "self-determination." Numerous agreements were entered into with the Slavic peoples of Austria-Hungary, and these led to the establishment of "governments-in-exile," desertions at the front to the Allies, and the eventual disintegration of the Austro-Hungarian Empire. Another notable success of Allied political warfare was the negotiation of the so-called secret treaties, aimed at building a winning alignment against the Central Powers. By this means Italy was detached from the Triple Alliance and brought into the war on the side of the Allies.

The Nazi Assault on Austria. A great deal might be written on political warfare during the years between the two world wars. This might include the efforts of the Allies to bolster and encourage the counterrevolutionary forces in Russia; the worldwide agitation of the Comintern, including the promotion of uprisings in Bavaria, Saxony, Hungary, and China; the assassination of French Prime Minister Barthou in 1934 and of Leon Trotsky in 1940; the intervention of Fascist and Communist forces in Spain; and the Nazi penetration of Latin America. Here, however, we shall briefly describe only the dramatic Nazi assault on Austria, a notable instance of political warfare.

Even before Hitler assumed power Austria had her own Nazi party. The Austrian Nazis maintained a close liaison with their comrades in Germany, using German propaganda, funds, and tactics. Hitler regarded them as members of his own party who would fight with him to return Austria to the Greater Reich. In July, 1931, he appointed his hatchet man, Theo Habicht, special "Inspector of Austria." After Hitler's assumption of power in 1933 the connection between the two Nazi organizations was no longer disguised. German newspapers began printing "evidence" of mistreatment of the Austrian Nazis, German stations broadcast a deluge of anti-Austrian programs, and German airplanes dropped propaganda leaflets in flights over the Austrian border. In July, 1934, the Nazis assassinated Chancellor Engelbert Dollfuss and attempted to set up a government under Habicht and Rintelen. The *putsch* was soon put down, and the Austrian Nazi Party was outlawed.

By 1938 the Nazis were ready to try again. This time their plan was a model of thoroughness. Before it had been executed in March, 1938, the secretary-general of the Austrian Nazi Party, one Dr. Tavs, had outlined it in writing. Here is what he had to say:

> At the beginning of March, 1938, a sudden wave of terrorism will break out over Austria. Acts of violence will be committed everywhere. Simultaneously, infernal machines will explode along the principal railway lines. Immediately after, leaflets will be distributed announcing to the whole of Austria, but especially to foreign countries, that the Austrian Communists are the instigators of this terrorism. It will be described as a

[26] John Price Jones and Paul Merrick Hollister, *The German Secret Service in America, 1914–1918* (Boston: Small, Maynard & Co., 1918); see also Henry Landau, *The Enemy Within* (New York: G. P. Putnam's Sons, 1937).

visible symbol of the deep-rooted indignation and hostility of the working classes against Dr. Schuschnigg's government. These "communist" pamphlets are intended to prove that Austria is faced with an imminent Bolshevik uprising. Further acts of terrorism, more particularly a staged attack upon the German legation, will confirm this impression.

At the moment when serious breaches of public order have reached their culmination, Austrian S.A. and S.S. will come forward. Collisions will occur between Nazis, on the one side, and paid *agents-provocateurs,* on the other. The world must be made to think that Austria is on the brink of a terrible civil war. At that moment pressing demands will be made for the immediate removal of the veto on the Nazi party and for sanction to be given to its militant section, on the ground that the Nazis are willing to help the State defend itself against a Bolshevist attack. Simultaneously, the Nazis' confidence-men in the army, police and *gendarmerie* will persuade their comrades that it is futile to proceed against the Nazis, even if the Schuschnigg government gives the order to do so. They will explain that armed intervention in Austria by the Third Reich is at hand and that the "Austrian Legion" will actually at the same time march on Austria in five columns. The invasion of the "Austrian Legion" will be covered by divisions of armored cars. Berlin will tell the world that intervention is necessary in order to prevent Germans from shedding German blood in Austria.[27]

When Mussolini allied himself with Hitler in 1936, Chancellor Kurt Schuschnigg, who succeeded Dollfuss, made a last-minute attempt to prevent the *Anschluss* by holding a plebiscite; but when this brought an ultimatum from Nazi Germany, Schuschnigg yielded. In March, 1938, Austria was occupied by German troops. Thus the tactics of political warfare outlined by Dr. Tavs led to the intended result, almost exactly as he had predicted.

[27] Eugen Lennhoff, *The Last Five Hours of Austria* (New York: Frederick A. Stokes Co., 1938), pp. 68–69.

Germany and World War II. Simultaneously with her preparations for war Germany made elaborate plans for political warfare. In World War II, as in the previous war, she tried to prevent the United States from aiding or joining the Allies. To this end the Germans employed disruptive propaganda, especially rumors and lies; they created artificial movements and exploited genuine movements; they used bribery, blackmail, and threats. These activities had as their purposes the division of the American people by stirring up class, racial, and religious hatreds, the undermining of confidence in the Roosevelt Administration, the obstruction of preparations for war, and the creation of powerful Fascist groups to act as a "fifth column." Nevertheless, the Japanese attack on Pearl Harbor brought about far greater unity in America than had been present at any time during World War I, and Germany was unable to repeat the political warfare successes of World War I in the United States.

The fall of France in 1940 attested to the internal weaknesses of that country as well as to the power of Germany's military machine, but political warfare was also an important contributing factor. Propaganda had been particularly effective in France because of the bitter party strife and the existence of strong pacifist elements. The "phony war" or *sitzkrieg* during the winter of 1939–40 had given ample time for disillusionment and for the disintegration of morale, a process accelerated by Pierre Laval's urging of peace[28] and by the work of the Communists. Until June, 1940, industrial mobilization and war production were greatly slowed down by Communist workers.[29] Once the invasion of France began, Nazi fifth columnists started operating behind French lines,

[28] J. P. T. Bury, *France, 1814–1940* (Philadelphia: University of Pennsylvania Press, 1949), p. 291.

[29] André Maurois, *Why France Fell* (London, 1941), p. 52.

disrupting communications and directing German fire on troop concentrations. While it is true that "the defeat of the French forces was a military defeat,"[30] it was nevertheless hastened by political and psychological warfare.

The Allies and World War II. The Western states gradually built up a war machine to match that of the Axis; and at the same time they used political warfare with great success. In 1941, for instance, they supported a movement in Yugoslavia which overthrew the pro-German government and forced Hitler to declare war against Yugoslavia. In the following year the American representative in North Africa, Robert Murphy, organized a coup in Algiers which so embroiled the Vichy authorities that they were unable to prevent the landing of Allied forces. The invasion of Italy was skilfully coordinated with the announcement of an Italian armistice by Marshal Badoglio, Mussolini's successor, in order to hamper resistance.[31] Support of the Free French and of other governments-in-exile, as well as of resistance movements in the various occupied countries, helped the Allies immensely. Representatives of the United States Office of Strategic Services and other Allied agents, operating mainly from Switzerland, were in constant touch with dissident elements inside Nazi Germany. They gave tangible support to the movement which led to the abortive attempt on Hitler's life in 1944, and they had some success in their efforts to weaken German morale, especially during the last months of the war when the military situation of Germany was obviously deteriorating.[32]

After World War II. One of the most portentous developments of the postwar era has been the absorption of a large number of countries into the Soviet orbit. The changes in the political orientation of the governments of Eastern Europe came about through no accident, coincidence, or spontaneous "people's movements"; they were the results of well-planned Soviet political warfare. In every case the general pattern of political conquest has been the same. First the Communist Party of a given country convinced the other parties that some sort of coalition government should be formed. Once this was done, the Communists saw to it that they received key positions in the department of the interior, enabling them to gain control of the police force. Finally came the coup in which Communists seized control of the government and, with a Communist-dominated police force and with a Soviet army usually nearby, there was little resistance.

The uprisings in East Berlin in June, 1953, and in Hungary in October–November, 1956, were evidences that the Soviet hold in the "satellite" states of Eastern Europe was by no means absolute. Although these uprisings were crushed, the myth of a monolithic Communist bloc, under the firm direction of the Soviet Union, was shattered. More recent developments, especially the Sino-Soviet rift and the signs of growing independence in Eastern Europe, have revealed the limitations as well as the capabilities of Soviet political warfare. They have also raised anew the question of the extent to which the United States and other Western countries should attempt to carry on political and psychological warfare on the other side of the "iron curtain."[33]

Difficulties confronting the Soviet Union within the Communist world, especially with

[30] Bury, p. 294.

[31] Lerner, pp. 326–328.

[32] See Allen W. Dulles, *Germany's Underground* (New York: The Macmillan Company, 1947).

[33] A strong case for "taking the offensive against the main enemy on the decisive front of Eastern Europe and Russia itself" is presented in Edmond Taylor, "Political Warfare: A Sword We Must Unsheathe," *The Reporter*, September 14, 1961, pp. 27–31.

Communist China, and the apparent relaxation of tensions between the two superpowers, have blunted but not diverted Soviet efforts, by divers techniques of diplomacy, propaganda, and political and psychological warfare, to win support in the underdeveloped nations. In this Third World the Soviets have carried on vigorous political, economic, cultural, and psychological offensives. They have skilfully exploited native feelings of anti-imperialism and nationalism; they have used all the techniques of infiltration, subversion, insurgency, and insurrection that are designed to lead to civil conflict and "wars of national liberation." Clever Soviet propaganda, abounding in all sorts of mass appeals, thousands of well-trained Communist agitators and organizers, plus ample funds and materials add up to a powerful cold war machine — one that works best in underdeveloped, dependent, or "exploited" countries.

Even in the period of "the relaxation of tensions" between the superpowers, and even while they have been concentrating more and more on their position within the Communist world and on relations with the countries of the Third World, the Soviet spokesmen have not neglected the cold war against the Western powers, especially the United States. They have tried to undermine the position and influence of the Western "capitalist" nations in the underdeveloped countries, and to exploit weaknesses and divisions within Western Europe and the North Atlantic Alliance. They have held forth prospects of economic and political cooperation in resolving the problems of Europe and have played down military threats as inducements to pry European allies from the United States.

The Chinese Communists have entered the field of political and psychological warfare with a vengeance. They have carried on militant campaigns in underdeveloped countries, especially in Southeast Asia, directed against the Soviet Union as well as against Western nations. They have accused the Soviets of "revisionism," of betraying the Communist revolution, and even of unprincipled collaboration with the archenemy, the United States. Even more than the Russians they have encouraged "wars of national liberation," and they have insisted that Mao Tse-tung's strategy of revolutionary warfare is adaptable to almost all revolutionary situations.[34] By resorting to military action against India, a nonaligned country with which they were presumably on friendly terms, they apparently sought to humiliate a potential rival for influence in the Third World and to demonstrate Chinese power as a warning to those leaders who might not suitably respond to Chinese overtures. At a time when the Soviet Union seems to have become less aggressive in its political and propaganda offensive, Communist China has emerged as a militant and increasingly powerful advocate of revolutionary strategy and tactics, at home and abroad.

It is clear that non-Communist states cannot — and indeed probably should not — match the Communists in the field of political and psychological warfare. Admittedly, the United States and the other Western democracies have two great handicaps in their struggle against aggressive communism. One of these, as we have noted, consists of the restraints on political warfare imposed by the principles of free government. The other is the lack of coordination among themselves. Nevertheless, they also have immense resources: stable and popular governments, natural wealth, technological skills, and a developing consciousness of the imperatives of the situation. Fortified by these, they are moving to defend themselves. They are employing some of the techniques of political and psychological warfare to reduce the potentialities of other states for aggressive action.

[34] See Tang Tsou and Morton H. Halperin, "Mao Tse-tung's Revolutionary Strategy and Peking's International Behavior," *American Political Science Review*, LIX (March, 1965), 80–99

SUGGESTIONS FOR FURTHER READING

ATKINSON, JAMES D. *The Politics of Struggle: The Communist Front and Political Warfare.* Chicago: Henry Regnery Co., 1966.

BARGHOORN, FREDERICK C. *Soviet Foreign Propaganda.* Princeton, N.J.: Princeton University Press, 1964.

———. *The Soviet Image of the United States: A Study in Distortion.* New York: Harcourt, Brace, 1950. Analysis of Russian propaganda techniques.

BARRETT, EDWARD W. *Truth Is Our Weapon.* New York: Funk & Wagnalls Company, 1953. By a former Assistant Secretary of State for Public Affairs.

CARR, E. H. *Propaganda in International Politics.* New York: Farrar and Rinehart, 1939.

CARROLL, WALLACE. *Persuade or Perish.* Boston: Houghton Mifflin Company, 1948.

CHASE, ALAN. *Falange: The Axis Secret Army in America.* New York: G. P. Putnam's Sons, 1943.

CHOUKAS, MICHAEL. *Propaganda Comes of Age.* Washington, D.C.: Public Affairs Press, 1964. Summarizes recent findings about the effects of propaganda.

CLEWS, JOHN C. *Communist Propaganda Techniques.* London, 1964.

DAUGHERTY, WILLIAM E. and MORRIS JANOWITZ. *A Psychological Warfare Casebook.* Baltimore: The Johns Hopkins Press, 1958.

DULLES, ALLEN W. *Germany's Underground.* New York: The Macmillan Company, 1947. By the wartime head of the U.S. Office of Strategic Services in Europe, later Director of the Central Intelligence Agency.

DUNN, FREDERICK S. *War and the Minds of Men.* New York: Harper, 1950.

DYER, MURRAY. *The Weapon on the Wall: Rethinking Psychological Warfare.* Baltimore: The Johns Hopkins Press, 1959.

ELLUL, JACQUES. *Propaganda: The Formation of Men's Attitudes,* translated by Konrad Kellen and Jean Lerner. New York: Alfred A. Knopf, 1964. Discusses techniques of the "propaganda of integration" typical of twentieth-century mass society.

GORDON, D. L. and ROYDEN DANGERFIELD. *The Hidden Weapon: Story of Economic Warfare.* New York: Harper, 1947.

HEILBRUNN, OTTO. *The Soviet Secret Services.* New York: Frederick A. Praeger, 1956. Activities of Soviet spies during World War II.

HOETTL, WILHELM. *The Secret Front.* London, 1953.

HOLT, ROBERT T. *Radio Free Europe.* Minneapolis: University of Minnesota Press, 1958. A detailed study of a significant private propaganda broadcasting enterprise. Discusses role of RFE during Polish and Hungarian uprisings of 1956.

HUNTER, EDWARD. *Brain-Washing in Red China.* New York: Vanguard Press, 1951. The techniques of re-education.

INKELES, ALEX. *Public Opinion in Soviet Russia.* Cambridge, Mass.: Harvard University Press, 1950. A study of communications media rather than of the content of public opinion.

KINTNER, WILLIAM R. *The Front Is Everywhere.* Norman: University of Oklahoma Press, 1951.

KRIS, ERNST *et al. German Radio Propaganda.* New York: Oxford University Press, 1944. Broadcasting at home after the war.

LANDAU, HENRY. *The Enemy Within.* New York: G. P. Putnam's Sons, 1937.

LASSWELL, HAROLD D. *Propaganda Technique in the World War.* New York: Alfred A. Knopf, 1927.

LASSWELL, HAROLD D. and DOROTHY BLUMENSTOCK. *World Revolutionary Propaganda.* New York: Alfred A. Knopf, 1939.

LENIN, V. I. and J. STALIN. *Lenin and Stalin on Propaganda.* London, 1942.

LERNER, DANIEL, ed. *Propaganda in War and Crisis.* Geo. W. Stewart, 1951.

LIFTON, ROBERT JAY. *Thought Reform and the Psychology of Totalism.* New York:

W. W. Norton & Company, 1961. A study of "brainwashing" in Communist China, based on nearly two years of psychiatric investigation in Hong Kong.

LINEBARGER, PAUL M. A. *Psychological Warfare*, 2d ed. Washington, D.C.: Combat Forces Press, 1954.

MARKEL, LESTER *et al. Public Opinion and Foreign Policy*. New York: Harper & Company, for the Council on Foreign Relations, 1949. An analysis of the influence of public opinion and propaganda abroad.

MARTIN, L. JOHN. *International Propaganda: Its Legal and Diplomatic Control*. Minneapoplis: University of Minnesota Press, 1958. An analysis of the propaganda activities of the Soviet Union, Great Britain, and the United States, and the possible legal and diplomatic controls over undesirable international propaganda.

MOCK, JAMES R. and CEDRIC LARSON. *Words That Won the War*. Princeton, N.J.: Princeton University Press, 1939.

RANSOM, HARRY HOWE, ed. *An American Foreign Policy Reader*. New York: Thomas Y. Crowell Company, 1965. Section IV contains selections on "The Propaganda Instrument."

RAVINES, EUDOCIO. *The Yenan Way*. New York: Charles Scribner's Sons, 1951. A former Communist agent's account of Kremlin moves in South America.

SCOTT, JOHN. *Political Warfare: A Guide to Competitive Coexistence*. New York: The John Day Company, 1955.

SELZNICK, PHILIP. *The Organizational Weapon: A Study of Bolshevik Strategy and Tactics*. New York: McGraw-Hill Book Company, 1952.

SETON-WATSON, HUGH. *The Pattern of Communist Revolution, a Historical Analysis*. London, 1953.

SUMMERS, ROBERT E. *America's Weapons of Psychological Warfare*. Bronx, N.Y.: H. W. Wilson Co., 1951.

WHITAKER, URBAN G., JR., ed. *Propaganda and International Relations*. San Francisco: Chandler Publishing Co., 1960.

WHITTON, JOHN BOARDMAN, ed. *Propaganda and the Cold War*. Washington, D.C.: Public Affairs Press, 1963.

WHITTON, JOHN B. and ARTHUR LARSON. *Propaganda: Toward Disarmament in the War of Words*. Dobbs Ferry, N.Y.: Oceana Publications, 1964. From the World Rule of Law Center at Duke University.

ZACHARIAS, ELLIS M. *Secret Missions*. New York: G. P. Putnam's Sons, 1946. By a noted and controversial expert in naval intelligence.

6 Economic Instruments of National Policy

States differ greatly in the measure of control that they impose on economic activities within their borders and on their economic relations with other states. Under totalitarian regimes the control may be almost complete. In democratic states a very considerable freedom may normally be permitted. Both control and freedom are policies consciously adopted by states in pursuit of their national interests.

A state may adopt economic policies designed to promote its domestic welfare without having any intention to injure another state. A protective tariff may be levied to encourage home manufactures, and adulterated goods may be excluded to protect the public health. But a state may also adopt economic policies clearly intended to injure another state. Because every state is in some degree dependent on other states — it must import or export or both — it is to some extent responsive to pressures which other states may bring to bear on it, just as it may itself bring pressures to bear on other states. Whenever economic policies are shaped to promote national ends — whether or not they are intended to injure other states — they are economic instruments of national policy.

Economic instruments are in constant use in furtherance of national policy. In times of peace all states have objectives which must be pursued whenever possible, such as raising the standard of living, promoting foreign sales, expanding employment, conserving natural resources, advancing technology, and improving health. Economic instruments may also be used when a state is preparing to go to war or is fearful of being attacked. It may wish to conserve certain goods and to stockpile others, or it may seek to impede the war preparations of the threatening state or states. Finally, war itself changes the nonviolent conflict of "near war" into a struggle that calls into play all the resourcefulness of the state in mobilizing its economic power as well as its military power. The state may then resort to the most drastic economic controls in order to husband its own resources and to reduce the warmaking effectiveness of the enemy.

"Economic weapons" must not be assumed to mean the weapons of "economic warfare." Many of the operations of full-scale war are aimed at the destruction of the economic assets of the enemy: factories, railroads, harbors, warehouses, supplies, dams, power installations, ships, and the like. Some writers call this destruction "economic warfare,"[1] but the instruments employed are

[1] For instance, David L. Gordon and Royden Dangerfield in *The Hidden Weapon* (New York: Harper, 1947).

obviously military rather than economic. Indeed, in this sense much of modern warfare is economic. Economic instruments, on the other hand, are nonviolent in nature; they represent manipulations of a state's economic policy in an effort to advance the national interest. They reflect policy choices which lie within the right of the state under the law of peace, although their use may of course lead to reprisals and to armed conflict.

Economic instruments may serve either good purposes or bad ones; they may be used to secure desperately needed markets or to relieve widespread unemployment or, on the other hand, they may be used to establish foreign control, as during the rise of the "new imperialism," or to expand the power of an aggressor, as in Nazi Germany. Much as we may rail against "nationalistic" economic policies, it is difficult to distinguish between what a state ought to do in legitimate furtherance of its national interests and what, in the interest of a sound international economy and a regime of "live and let live," it ought to refrain from doing. The issues are highly subjective.

In our discussion of the economic instruments of national policy we shall first sketch the evolution of the international economy down to World War II. We shall see that at times states have carried on their trade relations with comparative freedom but that at other times they have imposed formidable barriers against each other. Next we shall see that the very nature and motivations of world trade reveal an interdependence that makes it possible for individual states to disturb the entire international economy through nationalistic practices. It is, of course, the *international* character of the modern economy that makes all states vulnerable to economic weapons in the hands of other states. Finally, we shall describe some of the more important economic instruments that are at the disposal of states which have the will and the strength to use them.

The Rise and Decline of International Trade

The modern period of world trade may be dated from 1800. At that time foreign trade began to expand rapidly in volume, and the export of capital greatly increased. Perhaps the most important of the factors accounting for this growth was the development of industrialism in response to power technology. Other factors were the American Revolution and, somewhat later, the Wars of Independence in Latin America, which opened vast areas to trade with all nations; a rapid increase in population, largely a result of the Industrial Revolution; and a mass migration to the countries of the Western Hemisphere. The migrants naturally retained their taste for European goods, and to get them they had to produce for export. The so-called invisible imports and exports (services and capital funds), which had been negligible in amount, rose immensely in importance; today they are a significant part of international trade.

Due to these factors, the composition of world trade shifted in emphasis from a primary reliance on spices, precious metals, and certain textiles to industrial raw materials, agricultural products, machinery, and other components of a modern trade pattern. In this process England rapidly became the virtual linchpin of the new system.

Nineteenth-Century Liberalism. The sharp upward turn in world trade was accelerated by a shift in the prevailing view of national trade policy. The mercantilist doctrine of the seventeenth and eighteenth centuries had held that the true wealth of a state consisted of precious metals, and that to get these the state should try to achieve a permanent excess of exports over imports. But the Manchester economists began to emphasize the absurdity of all states fighting for a balance of trade favorable to themselves. They insisted that trade could be advantageous to both parties — that every transaction did not necessarily produce a gainer and a loser.

Rather, if each state were free to produce the goods for which it was best suited, each would find its place and all could prosper. But, they reasoned, natural advantage could be utilized only if trade were exempt from undue restraints.

This was Manchesterian liberalism or laissez faire; it was the gospel of free trade. That it should appear first in England was altogether natural, for England's priority in the Industrial Revolution gave her a competitive advantage in foreign markets and forced her to rely increasingly on imports of raw materials. By 1846 Britain had swung to a free trade policy, where she stayed, officially at least, until the Great Depression of the 1930's. France followed in 1860 but had lost the faith by 1892. Germany, Russia, and the United States clung to protective policies, but these entailed no such barriers as mercantilism. Belgium and The Netherlands adopted free trade in principle and in practice. Thus, although the world economy of the period between 1800 and World War I was hardly on a laissez faire or a free trade basis, it was conducted with substantially fewer restraints than had existed before or have been present since. And during these years the total of the world's foreign commerce increased more than twenty-seven times, or by a tenfold amount on a per capita basis.

Four states together controlled fully half of the world's trade on the eve of World War I: the United Kingdom (17 per cent), the United States (15 per cent), Germany (12 per cent), and France (7 per cent).[2] No other state had as much as 3 per cent of the total. The foreign trade of the United States was increasing more rapidly than that of any other nation.

[2] Franz Eulenburg, "International Trade," *Encyclopaedia of the Social Sciences* (New York: The Macmillan Company, 1937), VIII, 194. Used by permission of The Macmillan Company. See also William B. Ashworth, *A Short History of the International Economy, 1850–1950* (London, 1952), Chapter VI.

Foreign Exchange and Foreign Investment. With this phenomenal growth in foreign trade there developed an intricate system of balancing imports against exports so that very little money had to be sent from one country to another. The total which a country owed — covering imports, loans, interest on investments, payments to foreign shipowners and insurance agents, gifts to institutions and individuals abroad, and many other items — was compared to the sums which were due the country from other states. If the sums did not match or "balance," the difference was called the "balance of payments." Since countries used different currencies, they had to find a common standard of value. This was the international gold standard. As nearly all countries had a fixed gold content for their units of currency, currencies could be evaluated in terms of gold content. The rate at which a particular currency could be exchanged for that of another country was subject to fluctuations, depending in part upon its need of foreign exchange. When the rate became too high to make it feasible to buy foreign exchange, a country could pay off its balance and reduce the exchange rate by shipping gold.

This system worked very well up to World War I. British bankers specialized in the handling of foreign exchange and made London the financial center of the world. The pound sterling, with its sound gold basis, became an international currency.

While foreign trade was rising to new heights, international investment was following a similar course. Perhaps the first great international banking house was that of the Fuggers of Augsburg in the sixteenth century. Other banking firms engaged in overseas finance from time to time during the seventeenth and eighteenth centuries, but by the second half of the eighteenth century the Dutch bankers had acquired something like a monopoly in foreign investments. English interests took the leadership soon after the Napoleonic Wars and retained it for more than a century. France became a large-scale exporter of capital in the 1860's, Germany in the 1890's. Smaller exporters were the Netherlands, Belgium, Switzerland, and Sweden. The United States did not become an important lender until after World War I.

These foreign investments fell into two general categories: direct investment in productive enterprises and loans to governments and their subdivisions. The British preferred the first, and they made sure that their investments promoted the prosperity of British industry. The Germans also invested heavily in private ventures. The French, on the other hand, reflecting the conservatism of the small investor and fear of Germany, leaned more toward direct loans to governments, particularly to those where debtor-creditor relationships might pay political dividends. Paris became the largest market in the world for the securities of foreign governments. By 1914 about one-fourth of the national wealth of Britain was in foreign investments; with France the figure was about 15 per cent; that of all other countries was smaller. American foreign investments at the time amounted to $2.5 billion, whereas $6 billion in American securities were held by foreign interests.

Effects of World War I. On the whole, the international economy of the years before World War I appeared to operate reasonably well. The century between Waterloo and Sarajevo was without a major international war. Trade and investment seemed to prosper. States tried to promote their interests and those of their nationals, but economic rivalry did not become bitter and nationalistic. Backward areas received the gains and suffered the losses of imperialism. Two authorities have summarized the state of affairs as follows: "Until 1914 the international economy was organically so integrated that prices of goods and services and the financial side of the national economies in general harmonized fairly well with the distribution of real resources and the composition of national output. Change was orderly and gradual, and in the main it was toward higher living standards within a world possessing a common ideology."[3]

Economic historians are not in agreement on whether the world economy had begun to unravel in 1914, but unravel during the war it certainly did. "The war tore a gaping rent in the intricate fabric of the international economy that hasty stitching in the twenties and extensive patching in the thirties quite failed to mend."[4] It disrupted the old competitive economy. The blockade, government controls and purchasing, inter-Allied coordination, concentration on military production, enforced liquidation of foreign investments, huge inter-Allied loans and credits, new taxes, and many other manipulations of finance and trade all operated to throw the international economy completely out of gear. The peace and the postwar years brought other obstacles which tended substantially to impede the return to "normalcy": the job of restoring the ruined industries and lands of the battle areas; reparations and the shackling of German productivity; enormous war debts and woefully unbalanced national budgets; low consumer purchasing power and unemployment; scarcity of food and raw materials; inflation; capital shortages; a wrecked transport system; and a Europe that needed desperately to buy but had too little to sell.

In a sense the interwar period may be divided into two parts. From 1918 to 1930 states sought to restore the economy in the image of that which had existed before the war. After the onset of the Great Depression they turned from essentially negative measures to drastically positive ones. The result was the economic nationalism that must be accounted one of the major under-

[3] Norman S. Buchanan and Friedrich A. Lutz, *Rebuilding the World Economy* (New York: The Twentieth Century Fund, 1947), p. 36.

[4] *Ibid.*, p. 27. See also Ashworth, pp. 186–189.

lying causes of World War II. It is still with us in the postwar years.

The concentration of gold holdings in the United States and the inflation of European currencies seriously disturbed the operation of the international gold standard; and they made it increasingly difficult for European countries to control their fluctuating exchange rates. The United States, little affected by the war, tried to pretend that nothing had changed. She sought to revive her trade; she loaned money; she expected repayment. It worked for a while, and Americans lived high; but "when the gong sounded the close of business on the New York Stock Exchange on October 29, 1929, it signalized more than the loss of thousands of personal fortunes: it signalized the end of a superficial effort to reassemble a global economy that had been deeply scarred and damaged."[5]

The Great Depression. The United States could hardly be blamed for the Great Depression, but she could not avoid responsibility for certain unwise steps that were taken to meet the emergency. Outstanding among these was the passage of the Smoot-Hawley Tariff Act of 1930, the highest tariff ever imposed by the United States and the highest tariff in the world at the time, approached only by that of Spain. Furthermore, the United States, unlike Spain, was a powerful creditor nation, in a unique position to exert an influence for good or ill in international economic relations. Her deliberate ignoring of the recommendations of the World Economic Conference of 1927 for the lowering of tariffs had most unhappy consequences. "Such action," warned over a thousand American economists in a statement protesting the proposed tariff bill, "would inevitably provoke other countries to pay us back in kind by levying retaliatory duties against our goods," and "would inevitably inject a great deal of bitterness into our international relations."[6]

Put into nontechnical language, the basic difficulties of the early 1930's were three: productive capacity so far exceeded purchasing power that some goods were sold on credit and some factories worked at less than full capacity; the free price system could not bring prices down to those of countries that had suffered a serious deflation; and investment capital sought short-term speculative gains as a consequence of the general political instability. Frantically, states fell back on the traditional nostrums — liquidation, lower prices, wage reductions, and credit restrictions — but with little effect on their sagging economies. Furthermore, as people lost faith in the futile and essentially negative programs of their governments, they observed the apparent success of authoritarian regimes in stabilizing their economies. Russia and Germany appeared to worry little about deficit financing and adverse trade balances, and they seemed to have little unemployment. In those states the government took matters into its own hands and "bent the price system to its iron will with subsidies, quotas, state enterprise, and an outburst of deficit financing." Other states, desperately seeking to rehabilitate their national economies, felt driven to do through state controls what they had not been able to do by coaxing and pump-priming.

When a state undertakes to control the domestic economy, it is forced willy-nilly into restrictions on foreign trade. To sustain prices and encourage industry it must protect both against foreign competition. When it tries to promote exports and at the same time restricts imports, it soon faces countermeasures by other states and is often forced to use many of the conventional weapons of economic warfare and to improvise new ones. Furthermore, it will to some ex-

[5] Buchanan and Lutz, p. 30; see also Ashworth, pp. 202–203.

[6] The text of this statement is given in the *New York Times,* May 5, 1930.

tent take account of ideological differences, for governments, unlike private traders, have both economic and political objectives, and they cannot wholly separate the two. Trade thereupon takes on a political complexion which further compromises the international economy. Finally, since trade is no longer generally free it comes increasingly to rest upon explicit agreement; it presumes an understanding which is most easily made by two parties, thus fostering bilateralism and tending to militate against the multilateralism that is fundamental to a sound world economy.

Increasing economic difficulties during the Great Depression led one nation after another to impose restrictions upon imports and exports by such devices as quotas, licenses, clearing agreements, and higher tariffs. Even Britain, the traditional home of free trade, yielded in 1932 to the demands of the Dominions for imperial preferences. In general this system was based on lower tariffs within the Empire-Commonwealth and higher tariffs on products from other countries. There were many attempts to organize economic "blocs" in the 1930's and early 1940's, usually on regional lines. Nazi Germany built up such a bloc in southeastern Europe; instead of being an arrangement among equals, it was designed to promote German autarchy. Japan tried to use her economic as well as her military power to further her aspirations in Manchuria and later in all of East Asia. Argentina took the initiative in plans to create a regional trading bloc in a large part of South America; one result of this effort was the River Plate Conference of 1941, "the first meeting of its kind ever held in South America,"[7] at which representatives of Argentina, Brazil, Bolivia, Paraguay, and Uruguay considered regional economic interests.

[7] John C. Campbell, "Nationalism and Regionalism in South America," *Foreign Affairs,* XXI (October, 1942), 140.

The Decline of Trade. One of the many unhappy consequences of the mounting restrictions on trade and other adverse economic trends, such as the disastrous fall in prices, was a serious decline in international trade. According to a League of Nations report, the total value of world trade, estimated at 68.6 billion dollars in 1925, had fallen to 24.1 billion dollars by 1933. Later in the decade the value rose appreciably, but much of this was due to the rearmament effort of the major powers and to the rise in prices which resulted from increased military budgets. World War II, of course, completely altered the pattern of international trade, and in this way carried into the postwar period the struggle between economic nationalism and the ideal of a relatively free world trade.

The Basis and Nature of International Trade

Trade occurs among nations "precisely because there are differences in costs of production between countries."[8] Some commodities or goods cannot be produced in particular countries at all; they can be produced in other countries only at a comparatively high cost; and they can be produced in still other countries at a comparatively low cost. Consequently, the first group of states must trade rather than produce; the second group finds it advantageous to trade rather than produce; and the third group sees that it can obtain goods which it cannot produce, or which it can produce only at high cost, by selling its cheaply produced goods to the states where production of those goods is more costly or perhaps impossible. Since the natural endowments of countries differ, as do other factors of production, the classification of states into these three groups differs in respect to specific products.

[8] Walter Krause, *International Economics* (Boston: Houghton Mifflin Company, 1965), p. 6.

The Factors of Production. Perhaps the most obvious difference among states in the factors of production is in natural resources and geographic position. Some states are favored with minerals, fertile soil, natural flora and fauna, climatic advantages, and general topographic amenability, or with some of these assets; other states are poor in some or even virtually all of them. In some states labor is abundant; in others it is scarce and relatively expensive. For historic or natural reasons, or a combination of them, some states have a high proportion of skilled labor; in others the proportion is low. For similar reasons, the working population of some states may have special aptitudes, as the silver workers of Mexico, the textile makers of Guatemala, and the precision-instrument workmen of Switzerland. Advanced countries, with ample capital, are able to develop and maintain industrial processes unknown to underdeveloped states. One producing state may be located near populous areas and potential markets, whereas some states, favorably situated in other respects, may be unable to bear the added burden of transportation. Collectively these factors are of tremendous importance because, to repeat our point, "fundamentally, *international trade occurs because of international differences in costs.*"[9]

From this it seems to follow that from a purely economic point of view a country will profit most when it specializes in the area of its greatest comparative advantage. When a particular country enjoys no such advantage, theoretically its greatest economic gain will come from specialization in those products in which it is burdened with the least comparative disadvantage.

Obstructions to Specialization. Despite the theory of international production, states often specialize only to a limited extent and at times they seek to specialize in areas in which they are at a substantial natural disadvantage. Three of the factors limiting specialization are of particular importance.

For one thing, the cost of transportation, already mentioned, may operate to change a lower comparative production cost to a higher comparative delivered cost. For another, many industries are subject to the law of diminishing returns. In other words, after a certain output has been reached the per-unit cost of additional production may rise to the point where comparative disadvantage begins. The added cost may appear with the opening of new mines, the construction of new factories, the fertilization or irrigation of new land, the importation or training of additional technicians or workers, or the borrowing of needed capital.

The third factor, and the one which here concerns us most, is the employment of economic devices in the implementation of national policy. These may include tariffs, bounty systems, dumping, exchange controls, cartels, intergovernmental commodity agreements, and many other impediments to the operation of the natural law of supply and demand. Practices of this sort give rise to charges of "economic nationalism" — that is, to charges that states are using the control of economic policy to gain for themselves a share of the world's income that would go to other states if the international economy were permitted to operate on a more freely competitive basis. Such practices are therefore alleged to be "unfair," "selfish," "arbitrary," and "aggressive."

International Trade and the American Economy. The United States is now one of the few nations in the world that approaches self-sufficiency. Nature is largely responsible for this. She has given the United States a stimulating climate, great expanses of fertile soil, vast mineral resources, adequate rainfall, favorable geography, and the attractions to lure resourceful and vigorous people from all parts of the world, but chiefly from Eu-

[9] *Ibid.*, p. 8. Italics in original.

rope. Added to a great political heritage from England, these gave Americans so much more to work with and for — and be it remembered that they have been willing to do both — that they would have been degenerate indeed if they had not built a rich and powerful nation.

For all the beneficence of nature, the United States is not self-sufficient. She imports all of her consumption of several vital minerals, more than three-fourths of her needs in such basic minerals as tin, chromite, mica, asbestos, manganese, platinum, antimony, and cobalt, and from a fourth to three-fourths of her requirements in additional minerals, as, for instance, mercury, aluminum, lead, copper, tungsten, and zinc. Among heavy imports of nonminerals are bananas, cocoa, coffee, tea, rubber, silk, newsprint, wool, jute and Manila fibers, and medicinals. The list might be extended. The crux of the matter is that "the United States does not import an *average* of 4 per cent of *every* item it uses, but it imports *all* or a *large proportion* of *particular* items."[10]

Imports provide about 4 per cent of the American national income and exports about 5 per cent. These figures may seem trifling, especially when compared with the Netherlands' 50 and 43, Norway's 42 and 24, Switzerland's 34 and 28, or Canada's 21 and 21. But America must export if she is to import, and she must export to sustain certain domestic industries, such as those related to the production of rice, wheat, cotton, dried fruits, and tobacco, as well as the automotive, agricultural machinery, and machine tool industries. In these the export figure is not 5 per cent of production but often 30 or 40 per cent or more.

American foreign trade may also be appraised in terms of jobs for Americans. As long ago as 1947 a report issued by the House Committee on Foreign Affairs calculated that the number of jobs within the country attributable to exports was in excess of 3,350,000. In a number of major industries the percentage was between 10 and 20. With the United States the situation may not be, as with some countries, "trade or die," but foreign trade nevertheless means added comforts to virtually all Americans and a decent livelihood for several millions. Beyond this there is an international aspect. The American national income is now about one-half of the world's total; and the world economy as a whole is quite dependent upon the American economy. When the Great Depression shattered American prosperity it also destroyed the prosperity of many other countries. Between 1929 and 1932 American imports dropped by about 69 per cent, and exports fell in an almost identical ratio.

World Prosperity and National Policy. The economic interdependence of states is one of the basic conditions of international life. "No country is now economically independent; in the long run it needs trade with the rest of the world in order to survive."[11] Some countries would face disaster if cut off from outside food supplies for their people or from raw materials for their industry; some would be ruined if they could not export manufactured goods or raw materials; and others would remain backward and primitive for generations if they could not import capital for the development of their natural resources.

From this interdependence it is common practice to reach the facile conclusion that the use of economic controls as instruments of national policy ought to be abandoned forthwith. Certain difficult questions must be answered, however, before the careful student of international relations can be brought to believe that free trade would lead easily to improved well-being everywhere.

[10] Krause, pp. 21–22. Italics in original. Most of the statistics in this section are taken from Krause.

[11] Eulenburg, p. 200.

In the first place, some states appear to be so dependent on the export of one or a few products that their prosperity hinges on the maintenance of prices. Thus Bolivia relies on tin, Brazil on coffee, Chile on copper, Cuba on sugar, Indonesia on rubber and tin, Pakistan on cotton and jute, Thailand on rice and rubber, and a number of states in the Near East on oil. In the second place, how is a state to determine at what point it should forego assistance to domestic interests? At what point is the balance of the internal economy disturbed? At what point the international economy? When do economic considerations give way to political ones? Finally, how do we answer that recurrent question: how to get some one hundred and thirty sovereign states to accept what some or most of them believe to be for the best interests of all?

Most persons deeply concerned with the effect of national measures on world prosperity and world peace believe that some modest controls must be available to underdeveloped and one-product states; but in general they are convinced that the best interests of most states would be served by a drastic modification of nationalistic economic practices. Although this judgment appreciably limits the area within which these practices may be pursued, it still leaves room for a great many subjective appraisals.

The Economic Arsenal

Before looking at economic instruments we should understand a number of conditions that may accompany their use. First, although these are usually employed by the government of a state, some of them — or at least some forms of them — may be used by persons within a state without actual participation by the government itself. Thus cartels may be controlled to the advantage of one state by private groups within the state, and informal boycotts may be imposed by an aroused public. Second, economic coercion may be used for ends that are essentially political rather than economic. Arms embargoes and economic sanctions are familiar examples. Third, the devices of economic pressure are often so intimately interrelated that the use of one leads to the use of another and then still another, and so on. Moreover, when directed toward a particular state they invite retaliation, with the result that economic warfare may ensue. Finally, some but not all economic instruments become useless in time of actual war; others become much more important. Thus protective tariffs or export bounties become useless in the face of an effective naval blockade. On the other hand, preemptive buying and the taking over of enemy assets are commonly employed only in the event of a war or of a crisis which approaches a state of war.

1. The Tariff, Trade and Payments Agreements

Definitions. A customs tariff is a duty or tax imposed upon imported or exported goods. Duties on exports are uncommon; in the United States they are prohibited by the Constitution — a provision originally insisted upon by the southern states to prevent the burdening of their great staples. The first duties on imports, levied in ancient times, were devised to provide state revenue. A tariff imposed for this purpose is known as a revenue tariff; one designed to protect domestic industries against foreign competition is called a protective tariff. States may impose some duties for revenue and others for protection, and the same tariff may serve both purposes. Generally speaking, however, a tariff low enough to avoid discouragement of imports will yield more revenue than a higher, discouraging tariff, and an extremely high tariff may stop importation altogether. Protective tariffs first became important when the mercantilism of the sixteenth and seventeenth centuries gave a powerful impetus to economic nationalism. It is not too much to say that they have been a significant factor in power politics for more than two hundred years.

Purposes. Although it is conceivable that a tariff may operate to reduce the economic strength of a state — as when essential goods are kept out of a country or when the protection is so great that it encourages waste and inefficiency — tariff policy is usually formulated with the enhancement of the state's economic power in mind. Or it might be more accurate to say that theoretical considerations in behalf of the strengthening of the economy can always be advanced to support a tariff policy. A tariff for revenue requires only the positive justification of a need for income, but a protective tariff calls for further defense. It may be imposed to limit competition and protect domestic producers; in this case the real motive may be increased profits for local industry, better wages, or the promotion of manufactures to improve the economic position of the state in its relations with foreign states. If national well-being and security are the objectives, the tariff may afford a general protection or it may seek to foster a particular industry, as, for instance, when high tariffs were used after World War I to remedy the weakness which the war had revealed in the American chemical industry.

Tariffs may be used to strengthen the economy by discouraging the importation of luxury goods or encouraging the production of essential civilian goods, or they may be used to advance military preparedness by adding to the profit margin on war goods. They may be used to discourage imports and thus conserve foreign exchange or reduce a balance of payments deficit. They may be used as an even more positive weapon of foreign policy through the enactment of high tariff schedules in order to give the state a position from which it might bargain, or through their use as an instrument of retaliation. High tariffs beget high tariffs, and it is a common occurrence to have one state try to breach the tariff wall of another state by penalizing its export business. Tariffs and other restrictive devices that aim to further the prosperity of one country at the expense of another represent what is known as a "beggar-my-neighbor" policy. This "is not a game of solitaire; it is as many-handed as there are governments concerned with their countries' foreign trade balances."[12] Its importance is further indicated by the fact that a revision of tariff policy has often been prescribed in the terms of peace following war.

Recent Trends. The general trend of tariff rates has been almost constantly upward since the early seventeenth century. During the first decades of the twentieth century the "free list" shrank more and more, rates continued to climb, and in the interwar period many of the larger states aspired to as much self-sufficiency as they could manage. The Great Depression, with its unstable currencies and falling price levels, further encouraged the building of trade barriers. One significant reversal of the trend came with President Roosevelt's vigorous support of Secretary Cordell Hull's Trade Agreements Program that made possible the first genuine departure from a high tariff policy in recent American history. Some gains toward the relaxation of trade restraints were made elsewhere, notably in the Oslo Protocol of 1930, but the general trend toward economic nationalism was undeniable.

Government participation in trade is largely a development of the past three decades. The Great Depression gave it impetus, for governments then sought desperately to find some way to reinvigorate the very sickly international trade. Sometimes they worked out agreements for the actual exchange or barter of particular commodities, usually on a bilateral basis, but more

[12] Carroll and Marion Daugherty, *Principles of Political Economy* (Boston: Houghton Mifflin Company, 1950), II, 1100.

commonly they established credits in favor of each other, with these to be consumed by exports. If the exchange left a balance one way or the other, this would be liquidated by further trade or by payments in gold or foreign exchange. The actual buying and selling were usually carried on by private interests. Such was the common pattern of what we call bilateral trade agreements or — in the case of credit establishment — bilateral payments or clearing agreements. World War II, like World War I, may be explained partly in terms of the economic policies which made effective political collaboration impossible.

The grip of governments on international trade was further tightened by the military demands of World War II; actually during the war "most foreign trade was either controlled or carried on directly by governments."[13] With the close of the war, shortages of foreign exchange, the breakdown in production and transportation, and the shortage of certain commodities, plus many political uncertainties, seemed to require that governments continue their controls over foreign trade. The United States tried to encourage a general return to a freer economy, but economic and political conditions prevented anything like a hearty response to American urgings, even in the other democratic states. Instead, governments continued to rely on bilateral trade and payments agreements. Sometimes the agreements were multilateral, notably in the instance of the payments agreements engineered by Germany. Since all such arrangements can be utilized to reduce the share of outside countries in world trade, they can be significant instruments of discrimination.

The American Trade Agreements Program and GATT. Since World War II the trend toward protectionism and economic nationalism has continued, as exemplified in the economic policies of state trading nations and underdeveloped countries, in the demands of business interests in industrially advanced states, in imperial preference, in the efforts of many states to discourage imports and foster exports and to secure a "favorable balance of trade." Regional trading blocs, notably the European Common Market and the Central American Common Market, are seeking to lower trade barriers among the member countries, but they also aim to apply a common external tariff in dealings with other states.

Two major efforts to reverse the trend toward protectionism have been the American Trade Agreements Act, first passed in 1934 and renewed several times since that date, and the General Agreement on Tariffs and Trade (GATT), negotiated under the auspices of the United Nations in 1947 and extended in several later negotiations. The Trade Agreements Program and GATT have achieved substantial reductions in tariff duties and have contributed greatly to freeing the channels of world trade by uniting most of the important trading countries in bilateral and multilateral negotiations and agreements; but both have been subject to continuous sniping from protectionists, and both have been weakened by many concessions and loopholes. The "escape clause," the "peril point" provision, and the "national security clause," which have been added to the Trade Agreements Act since 1947, have made it possible to protect adversely affected American industries; but these provisions, if too generously interpreted and applied, could greatly hamper the operation of the entire program. In order to accommodate many of its signatories GATT had to be modified to permit special concessions to new nations, to states in balance of payments difficulties, and to regional trading groups. The problem of reconciling the obligations of members of the European Common Market to GATT and to their regional economic or-

[13] John Parke Young, *The International Economy*, 4th ed. (New York: The Ronald Press Company, 1963), p. 322.

ganization has been a major stumbling-block.[14]

2. International Cartels

Definition. A cartel may be defined as "an association of independent enterprises in the same or similar lines of business which exists for the purpose of exercising some sort of control over competition."[15] It is spoken of as an international cartel "if the members are domiciled under more than one government or do business across national frontiers." It is not to be confused with a trust, a merger, a pool, a trading association, a corner, or a ring. The essence of a cartel is the contractual arrangement existing among independently owned businesses; "cartel," in fact, is derived from *charta,* meaning a contract. The purpose is to exert a monopolistic influence on the market, or, as cartel members prefer to put it, "to regulate the market." Its interest is usually in the seller's market, not the buyer's; and it generally comes into being only when most of the enterprises which had been competing with each other agree to enter it. It may be a loose association based on informal understandings or a strong one based on explicit contractual agreements. The government of a state may participate, but it does not commonly do so. On the basis of the means by which cartels seek to influence the market, they may be divided into three general types: those which fix prices, those which limit production, and those which divide the sales territory. All have the objective of fixing prices. Beyond these three general types all sorts of combinations are possible, including those allocating portions of a total fixed production, those using a central selling agency or syndicate, and those pooling and dividing all profits.

History. Something not unlike the modern cartel was used by certain industries and trading groups as early as the Middle Ages, and even more closely related organizations existed in England in the late eighteenth century and in Germany and France in the early nineteenth century, but the term itself did not come into common usage until the 1870's in Germany. The cartel movement reached its greatest development in Germany, and that country is still considered "the classic land of the cartel." A number of conditions help to explain this: more favorable laws respecting cartels; closer government control of business; a strong German tendency toward mutual organization; and the slower trend toward corporate undertakings, itself a natural consequence of the diversities among the many German states.[16] Cartels were eventually forbidden by law in England, the United States, France, Austria, and many other countries; they were encouraged in Germany and Italy, and at least tolerated in Russia, Spain, Rumania, and Norway.

German cartels of the 1870's are usually regarded as having sprung from the economic depression of the times, as an effort to prevent drastic cuts in prices. They flourished again during the two decades before World War I without benefit of the economic crisis in which they attained their first popularity. Set back by the war and the dislocations of the postwar period, they again became highly significant forces in world trade during the 1930's. According to a League of Nations estimate, at least 32 per cent of all international trade in 1937 was under some form of marketing control, but this calculation takes no account of the effect of cartels in re-

[14] For further comments on GATT, see Chapter 14, pp. 358–359 and Chapter 19, pp. 537–541.

[15] Charles R. Whittlesey, *National Interest and International Cartels* (New York: The Macmillan Company, 1946), p. 1. Used by permission of The Macmillan Company. See also Krause, p. 213.

[16] Robert Liefmann, "Cartel," *Encyclopaedia of the Social Sciences* (New York: The Macmillan Company, 1937), III, 236. Used by permission of The Macmillan Company.

stricting the volume of trade.[17] Two years later, in 1939, the United States Department of Justice listed 179 international cartels, an enumeration incomplete because cartels are often highly secret arrangements. During World War II it was naturally expected that cartels would present a major problem for years to come.[18] Even in Western Europe, the traditional stronghold of cartels, this method of interlocking business organizations and operations across national boundaries has largely given way to other forms of association, and it has, moreover, been overshadowed by the formation of the European communities, which are sometimes erroneously described as gigantic international governmental cartels.

Areas of Operation. Cartels are almost nonexistent in some industries, notably agriculture. They operate best in those in which mass production is possible and qualitative differences are unimportant, and in which exclusiveness is protected by patent rights. Ervin Hexner in his *International Cartels*[19] presented about a hundred case studies of cartels, which he grouped into eight categories: foodstuffs and related products, steel and ferro-alloys, nonferrous metals, nonmetallic minerals, raw materials not otherwise classified, chemical and pharmaceutical materials, other manufactured goods, and services. Americans have been most conscious of the cartels in the chemical and electrical industries, and it is against these that they have directed much of their criticism.

"The Wicked Cartellist." Contrary to the traditional European attitude, American public opinion has been definitely hostile to cartels or at least to the word "cartel." Professor C. R. Whittlesey declared that "the word 'cartel' has become less a name than an epithet," and he quoted the editor of the London *Economist* as saying that in the United States "the wicked cartellist has taken the place of the wicked arms manufacturer in popular demonology."[20] This aversion was by no means the exclusive property of the man in the street; it has been shared by some representatives of business, both big and small, and by such poles-apart thinkers as Henry A. Wallace and Eric A. Johnston. Suspicions that cartels are a weapon of Big Business might seem to be allayed by the resolutions of condemnation enacted by the National Association of Manufacturers.

Cartels and National Security. Although it may be contended that even free societies resort to cartel-like practices in time of war — as the United States certainly did in World War II — and therefore that free states themselves confess the inadequacy of the competitive system, two important weaknesses in this line of thinking must be pointed out. First, it assumes that maximum military power is the principal objective of the state, a condition that is rarely true. It does not even follow that maximum economic power is produced by wartime regimentation, but, as economic power is then secondary and as the two kinds of power are inseparable anyway, it does not matter what happens to economic power per se. Second, wartime integration merely utilizes the potentials accumulated during the years of peace; generally speaking, it does not create them. It does not follow that they would have achieved equal vitality in a highly cartelized system.

Are international cartels a menace to world peace and a threat to American security? The accusation here includes a num-

[17] Corwin D. Edwards *et al.*, *A Cartel Policy for the United Nations* (New York: Columbia University Press, 1945), p. 11.

[18] *Ibid.*, pp. 10–11.

[19] *International Cartels* (Chapel Hill: University of North Carolina Press, 1945).

[20] Whittlesey, p. 4.

ber of more or less specific charges. First, cartels foster wars by dividing loyalties and creating a profit interest that rises above patriotism. Second, cartels can deprive a state of vital war materials by their restrictions on production and distribution. Third, cartels can be instruments of espionage and sabotage by serving as undercover agencies and by transmitting scientific information to potential enemies. Fourth, cartels may exploit third countries to the detriment of "legitimate" foreign investment interests. Fifth, cartels are the special tool of totalitarian states and therefore should be discouraged.[21]

The threat of cartels to American security was the theme that ran through Joseph Borkin and Charles A. Welsh's *Germany's Master Plan: The Story of Industrial Offensive*.[22] The book was a scathing indictment of the whole system of cartels, and since its authors were men of established competence, its conclusions must be seriously pondered. Summarized, these asserted that "armed with patents, German cartels launched a shrewd and well-planned industrial offensive on a world scale. They laid siege to the business interests of the world, achieving conquests at a whole series of industrial Munichs, while the . . . industrial strength of the United Nations . . . drained away." And "if Germany keeps its cartel system it will be eternally armed for war even though we destroy every plane and tank that Hitler has built." The main target of *German's Master Plan* was the fabulous I. G. Farben Industries, which, with its vast physical plant of mines, factories, and railroads, its skilled research staff, its labor force of 350,000, its cartel agreements with powerful industries in other countries — including, in the United States, Standard Oil of New Jersey, Alcoa, Dow Chemical, E. I. duPont, Pennsalt International, Hercules Powder, and Remington Arms — and its subordination of profits to nationalistic aims, became the driving power of the Nazi war machine. Its fields of operation were so broad and its range of products so vast that "the best-qualified investigators cannot name them all"; its functions were "as unlimited as the scientific application of physics and chemistry to raw materials."[23]

Professor Whittlesey found the accusations of *Germany's Master Plan* unconvincing. He believed that cartels may encourage international cooperation as well as exalt and arm nationalism, and that there was an understandable eagerness to charge against cartels the sins for which nazism was responsible. He argued that cartels are two-way information channels. Admitting that the Germans gained valuable scientific information from American sources through cartels, he said that the United States also got vital information from Germany, and he pointed to the oil-hydrogenation process which led to a great expansion in the production of TNT and to a cut of 80 per cent in costs. He cited the opinion of American chemical manufacturers that the "know-how" which the United States got from the Germans exceeded anything the Germans got from the Americans. Cartels, he argued, are merely instruments, usable for both good and bad purposes. National security "is perhaps the weakest ground on which to attack cartels."[24]

3. Intergovernmental Commodity Agreements

Definition. What is known as the intergovernmental commodity agreement is a device for assuring a particular state a definite share in the world market. It is entered into because of general overproduction in a

[21] *Ibid.*, pp. 36–54.

[22] Joseph Borkin and Charles A. Welsh, *Germany's Master Plan: The Story of Industrial Offensive* (New York: Duell, Sloan and Pearce, 1943). Copyright, 1943, by Joseph Borkin and Charles A. Welsh.

[23] *Ibid.*, p. 39.

[24] Whittlesey, p. 36.

specific commodity and to avoid the ruinous competition that may accompany a buyer's market. Such agreements may take a variety of forms; perhaps the most important are those which set up a buffer stock agency,[25] those which allot export quotas, and those which fix production quotas. When arrangements like any of these are set up by private interests, they are commonly regarded as cartels.

When a commodity is produced by more than one country, efforts by a single country to keep up world prices are usually foredoomed to failure. When one state restricts exports or limits production the producers of some other state will rush into the market. For this reason the Stevenson rubber restriction scheme of 1922, supported only by the British Empire, collapsed in the face of increased production in the Netherlands East Indies. A more effective agreement was concluded in 1934, subscribed to by producers of 90 per cent of the world's rubber. An American effort to bolster the domestic price of cotton only weakened the position of American producers in the world market; within ten years, 1928–38, their contribution to foreign cotton consumption shrank from 47 per cent to 20 per cent.[26] Actually, surplus production, if it exists at all, is likely to embarrass all producing states, and unilateral efforts at control often lead to international commodity agreements.

Areas of Use. Intergovernmental controls in the past have applied to wheat, sugar, tea, coffee, beef, timber, tin, rubber, wool, cotton, and other primary commodities. At the present time there are seventeen international commodity groups. Five are autonomous councils that report to the UN; they deal with wheat, tin, sugar, coffee, and olive oil, and except for the olive oil council they administer price control agreements. In addition there are the six FAO-subsidiary study groups and six independent study groups, each concerned with a special commodity such as rice, cocoa, rubber, wool, cotton, or lead-zinc.[27]

That the commodity agreements have not been used with manufactured goods may require an explanation. Several points must be advanced: agricultural crops and minerals are far more standardized than manufactured goods; a country is far more likely to be dependent upon a single crop or a single mineral than upon a single manufactured product — hence the public welfare is more vitally concerned; industrial commodities are more commonly produced by a few persons or interests — so few that they can readily combine in a private agreement, whereas the producers of minerals and particularly crops are so numerous that they can act effectively only through the government; and finally, agricultural and mineral production responds more slowly to changes in short-term demand than does industrial production. All this means that certain minerals and agricultural products are specially suited to be the subjects of intergovernmental commodity agreements.

Proper Use. International agreements of this kind have escaped the bitter criticism that has been directed against cartels. In general, the judgment seems to be that they may serve a commendable purpose in some contingencies but must be carefully super-

[25] Under the buffer stock scheme, an intergovernmental agency establishes a minimum price at which it will buy all of the commodity offered and a maximum price at which it will sell any amount wanted; the scheme entails no export or production quotas. See Krause, pp. 235–236, 238–240.

[26] Buchanan and Lutz, p. 263.

[27] See "Special Report on Aid for Free World Growth," *Economic World*, August–September, 1960, p. 2. For details regarding the International Wheat Agreement of 1962 and the International Coffee Agreement of the same year, see Krause, pp. 245–249.

vised, and that care must be taken lest they become permanent. The United States has participated in a number of such agreements, as in the Inter-American Coffee Agreement of 1940 and the International Wheat Agreement of 1949. Nevertheless, here and there warnings are sounded against them. One such warning came from the Committee on Cartels and Monopoly of The Twentieth Century Fund, a private American research organization, which pointed to the danger of commodity agreements becoming "not an umbrella for emergencies" but "a concrete shelter for permanent residence" for "inefficient producers." "The aim of commodity agreements," said the Committee, "should be to end the need for commodity agreements."[28] When they do not end with their legitimate purpose they become unwarranted barriers to international trade, though instruments of national policy.

4. Dumping

Definition and History. Dumping means the sale of goods for export at prices lower than those charged domestic buyers. Jacob Viner called it "the foreign trade parallel of local price cutting in internal trade, as defined in American legal usage."[29] It first became a systematic and important trade practice about 1890, when it came into extensive use by German cartels and by the rising American trusts. The United States Steel Corporation, the International Harvester Company, and the Standard Oil Company had become leading practitioners of dumping by World War I.[30] French, Belgian, Canadian, and, to a lesser extent, British concerns also resorted to systematic dumping. During the interwar period anti-dumping legislation and the eventual stabilization of currencies operated to reduce its importance. Nor has it been a significant problem in the years following World War II, although the Soviet Union has resorted to it occasionally, with generally disturbing results.

Purposes, Operation and Effects. Sporadic dumping may take place to move a temporary overstock, to build goodwill in a depressed market, to introduce a new commodity, to weaken or remove a competitor in the foreign market, or in retaliation against dumping in the producer's domestic market. Dumping may be used for the purpose of obtaining foreign exchange, as the Germans and the Japanese used it on the eve of World War II to finance their military preparations and presumably also to enlarge their factories, train skilled workers, and permit technological research. It may be used as an instrument of economic warfare. Apparently Soviet dumping of tin, rubber, wheat, rice, and other products was a part of its "economic offensive" against the non-Communist world, although it may also have been employed as a means of obtaining needed foreign exchange or of disposing of surplus stocks obtained in barter arrangements with underdeveloped countries such as Burma.

Long-term dumping is practiced in order to enable the producer to gain the economies of large-scale production. Something approaching monopolistic control of the domestic market is almost necessary to long-term dumping, for only in the largest plants are fixed charges likely to be an important part of total production costs. Tariffs are also a significant encouragement, as they help toward monopoly by giving protection against foreign competition. Perhaps most important are export bounties; in fact, Viner went

[28] George W. Stocking and Myron W. Watkins, *Cartels or Competition?* (New York: The Twentieth Century Fund, 1948), p. 450.

[29] Jacob Viner, "Dumping," *Encyclopaedia of the Social Sciences* (New York: The Macmillan Company, 1937), V, 275. Used by permission of The Macmillan Company.

[30] *Ibid.*, p. 275.

so war as to write that "systematic long time dumping is not conceivable under competitive conditions in the absence of export bounties."[31]

The net effect of dumping for the exporting country seems to be that it may stabilize production and maintain employment, it may induce an expansion in production facilities, and it may or may not reduce prices on the home market. For the importing country sporadic dumping may divert or ruin local competitive industries, more than offsetting the gain to consumers. Long-term dumping may, of course, retard industrial maturity, and so may prevent the realization of the national economic potential.

5. Preemptive Buying

Definition. The purchase of goods in a neutral country to prevent their coming into the hands of the enemy is called preemption or preemptive buying; "the whole substance of the principle of pre-emption lies in the diversion of supplies from the enemy irrespective of commercial considerations."[32] It may be employed when states are technically at peace but fearful of hostilities, but it would be nonsensical to buy "irrespective of commercial considerations" except when national welfare may be served. Consequently, preemptive buying is peculiar to times of war and crisis. Stockpiling, no matter how great, is not in itself preemptive buying; purchasing so qualifies only when controlled by the motive of depriving the enemy of needed goods.

World War II. Much earlier than the Allies, the Nazis revealed an awareness of the importance of preemption. Soon after World War II began, German agents in the Baltic and Balkan areas were given "unlimited resources" and instructed to buy at "any price obtainable and relieve the sellers of the problems of delivery"; consequently, while the British haggled over prices and delivery schedules, worked with too little money, and persisted in all sorts of bureaucratic red tape, the Germans succeeded in "buying up everything worth having in the Balkans and in the Baltic States."[33] With the setting up of the United Kingdom Commercial Corporation in 1940 British buying practices improved, but political developments in the Balkans soon eliminated Hungary and Rumania from the market entirely and Yugoslavia in large part. The Nazis repeated their successes in Spain and Portugal, and Britain repeated her failures. Later the combined resources of Britain and the United States, plus Britain's hindsight wisdom, led the Allies to significant preemptive buying, especially in Spain, Sweden, Turkey, and Latin America.

Problems. Preemptive buying is by no means a simple and easy operation. Often the prices are driven to fantastic heights, domestic interests may intervene to obstruct a buying program, and, as in the case of Britain, price discrimination against one's Commonwealth partners may enormously complicate the problems. Further difficulties may appear respecting the availability of goods in the right currency and in the transport of purchased goods. Yet the gains of preemptive buying are so obvious that one may say that it has become a conventional weapon of true economic warfare.

6. Control of Enemy Assets

Definition. Most of the financial interests of foreign nationality in a particular state are owned by individuals, not by the foreign state as such. It is a state's seizure of these assets that is referred to as "control of enemy

[31] *Ibid.*, p. 276. See also Krause, p. 130.

[32] Paul Einzig, *Economic Warfare* (London, 1941), p. 49.

[33] *Ibid.*, pp. 51, 52.

assets." These assets are usually in the form of credits, debts, funds on deposit, insurance policies, stocks and bonds, monetary claims, and patent rights, although, of course, they may be in ships, real estate, art treasures, or something else.

History. According to Edwin M. Borchard, confiscation of enemy assets was probably common until the thirteenth century, at which time these assets began to acquire a degree of immunity, often resting upon a reciprocal basis as provided for in treaties.[34] By 1914 the rule of immunity was "deemed impregnable"; it was "not the result of any outburst of humanitarian sentiment, but rested upon a sound development in political and legal theory which emphasized the essential distinction between private property and public property, between enemy owned property in one's own jurisdiction and in enemy territory, and between combatants and noncombatants."[35] The United States did not authorize the confiscation of enemy property in any war before October, 1917, when the Trading with the Enemy Act was passed. Even this was intended to set up a system of trusteeship rather than to legalize confiscation, but some of the practices actually used cannot be described except as confiscation. The Treaty of Versailles following World War I asserted the right of the Allied states to appropriate German private property in all areas under their respective jurisdictions, with the proceeds of sale to be used to pay claims against Germany or her nationals, and with Germany to compensate her citizens for their assets thus confiscated. The other peace treaties had similar provisions. In practice the Allied states followed no common policy; some compensated German nationals in full, some in part, and some not at all. The United States adopted a complicated program of conditional full restitution.

World War II. In 1940 the United States again invoked the legislation of 1917. On the day on which the Nazis invaded Denmark and Norway, President Roosevelt "froze" Danish and Norwegian assets in the United States. The purpose was to defend the interests of innocent neutrals rather than to deprive Hitler of potential gains; the assets of nationals of Axis states themselves were not frozen in the United States until more than a year later. Meantime, the freeze had been extended to the Low Countries, France, and the Balkan and Baltic states. When the United States entered the war, in December, 1941, the only new action required was prohibiting communication with the enemy territory and appointing an Alien Property Custodian to assume control of enemy assets.

The job of administering the controls was a sizable one. Two authorities have estimated that more than eight billions of dollars in assets were subject to freezing and that other transactions subject to control amounted to just as much more. Local banks and other financial institutions, already familiar with their clients' business, did most of the scrutinizing and checking. Probably the most serious problem was to distinguish between innocent neutral assets — which were to be free for use in legitimate trade — and Axis assets concealed behind foreign dummies. "Cloaking," as it was called, had become widespread among German firms long before the war. The usual form was to set up an establishment in a country likely to remain neutral, giving it a good front but no real authority and employing neutrals in the foreign agencies. I. G. Farben did this. Although the purpose of earlier cloaking may have been the evasion of taxes and controls at home, later cloaking "must have been

[34] Edwin M. Borchard, "Alien Property," *Encyclopaedia of the Social Sciences* (New York: The Macmillan Company, 1937), I, 636. Used by permission of The Macmillan Company.

[35] *Ibid.*, p. 636.

known to the Nazi government, and tacitly approved or actively encouraged by them to camouflage German penetration and protect German interests from seizure or sanctions in the event of war."[36] The Alien Property Custodian uncloaked at least sixty German enterprises. The favorite sanctuaries for dummy companies were Switzerland, Liechtenstein, and Spain. That Americans are not above the use of cloaking for their own purposes, whatever those may be, is a conclusion that seems warranted by the fabulous tonnage of the merchant marine of Panama.

The "defrosting" of foreign assets is a trivial matter in an analysis of economic warfare; it is something like collecting the scrap iron after a great battle. Complicated by the cloaking problem, it was handled during and after World War II largely by putting on the government of each liberated country the responsibility for safeguarding the welfare of its nationals. The snarls of private finances were baffling indeed; they required the retention of some controls for several years after the close of the war.

7. Loans and Grants

Loans and gifts of all kinds — dressed up in a wide range of names and forms — date from many centuries ago, but they have become everyday occurrences in the modern world. The objective of the lender or donor may be specific or general, and the means taken to reach it may be direct or indirect. At times deals have been as bald as the purchase of military assistance, and at other times gifts have been as overtly without *quid pro quo* as disaster relief. Loans between governments almost always provide for the shipment of goods of a stated amount rather than the transfer of money or securities; in such transactions the lending government is clearly promoting domestic industry, and it may be strengthening an ally or making a friend as well. Often the rate of interest — as with many American loans since World War II — has been so low as to constitute a partial gift. Postwar rehabilitation loans were significant and perhaps expected consequences of World War I and World War II. Sometimes the granting of a loan involves commitments to policy changes on the part of the borrower. The Anglo-American Financial Agreement of 1946 provided for a loan of $3.75 billion at 2 per cent interest and a British promise to achieve full convertibility by July 15, 1947, if possible. The development of an acute dollar crisis in Britain prevented her from complying. The principal American foreign aid programs of recent years have included Lend-Lease, UNRRA, Truman Doctrine assistance, the Marshall Plan, the Mutual Security Program, including military assistance and Point Four, Export-Import Bank loans, and development loans. Most of these are discussed in Chapter 22.

States may also support international economic agencies and programs for the purpose of advancing national interests — such, for instance, as the United Nations Expanded Program of Technical Assistance, the International Bank for Reconstruction and Development, the International Monetary Fund, the International Development Association, the International Finance Corporation, the Inter-American Development Bank, the Organization for Economic Cooperation and Development, and the European Coal and Steel Community.

Some states have resorted to expropriation and repudiation, but these devices, although they have undoubted economic effects, are essentially political. In some instances they have amounted to nothing more than compulsory grants — that is, to confiscation. When handled by an honest government, expropriation can be an entirely ethical device similar to the exercise of eminent domain. Repudiation may be justified in very exceptional cases. Recent instances of expropriation include the acts of Mexico in taking

[36] Gordon and Dangerfield, p. 146.

over the railway system in 1937 and the oil industry in 1938, Iran's nationalization of the British-owned oil industry in 1952, Guatemala's assumption of ownership of certain banana lands in 1953, Egypt's nationalization of the Suez Canal in 1956 and the seizures of foreign properties by Castro's Cuba in 1959 and 1960, which amounted more to confiscation than to expropriation. The most famous instance of repudiation in recent times occurred when the Bolshevik regime in Russia refused to assume the foreign debts incurred by the monarchy.

8. Barter Agreements

For political as well as for economic reasons states sometimes enter into barter agreements, whereby they commit themselves to exchange certain goods in stipulated quantities or of stipulated value. Totalitarian states may obtain needed commodities from satellite countries in exchange for products of greater or lesser value. Thus Nazi Germany developed fairly extensive markets in Eastern Europe and the Balkans in return for products ranging all the way from manufactured goods to Hartz Mountain canaries. It also temporarily caused embarrassment to Great Britain and improved its relations with Argentina by accepting substantial quantities of Argentine beef at a favorable price to Argentina in return for shipments to this key South American country. Totalitarian states may also seek to promote their objectives in underdeveloped countries by barter arrangements, some of which seem attractive to these countries as a means of obtaining materials needed for economic development or to dispose of surpluses of raw materials. Examples are the rice-rubber deals between Communist China and Ceylon, the Soviet agreement with Burma to accept rice in exchange for products Burma needed (the Burmese were eventually rather disillusioned by this arrangement), and various barter agreements between the Soviet Union and some of the new African states, notably Guinea. Such arrangements are not uncommon between nontotalitarian states, especially among underdeveloped countries and states in which an unfavorable balance of payments limits the supply of foreign exchange, thereby necessitating this type of trade.

9. Exchange Controls

Nature. Exchange controls, which are invoked because a country's supply of foreign exchange is not equal to the demand, operate to establish a rationing system. If this is to be effective, the government or some designated control authority must have a complete or virtual monopoly of foreign exchange. The control authority receives the foreign exchange (all or perhaps a stipulated fraction) which is due the country's exporters for goods sold abroad. It also sells to importers the foreign exchange which they need for buying abroad. By putting the selling price high enough, and by paying exporters for their foreign exchange according to a classified schedule, the control authority is able to stimulate certain exports and to discourage certain imports. There may be enough difference between buying and selling prices to pay the government a profit.

In addition to controlling trade and making a profit for the government, exchange controls may serve to prevent the flight of capital from a country, to maintain overvalued currencies, and to protect domestic programs by insulating a national economy. "It is because of this insulating effect that exchange control has long been a leading weapon in the economic arsenal of those countries which are committed to the idea of national planning."[37]

Operation. The "sterling area" — those countries whose currencies are linked to the British pound — is far and away the

[37] Krause, p. 163.

THE WORLD'S MAJOR CURRENCY AREAS

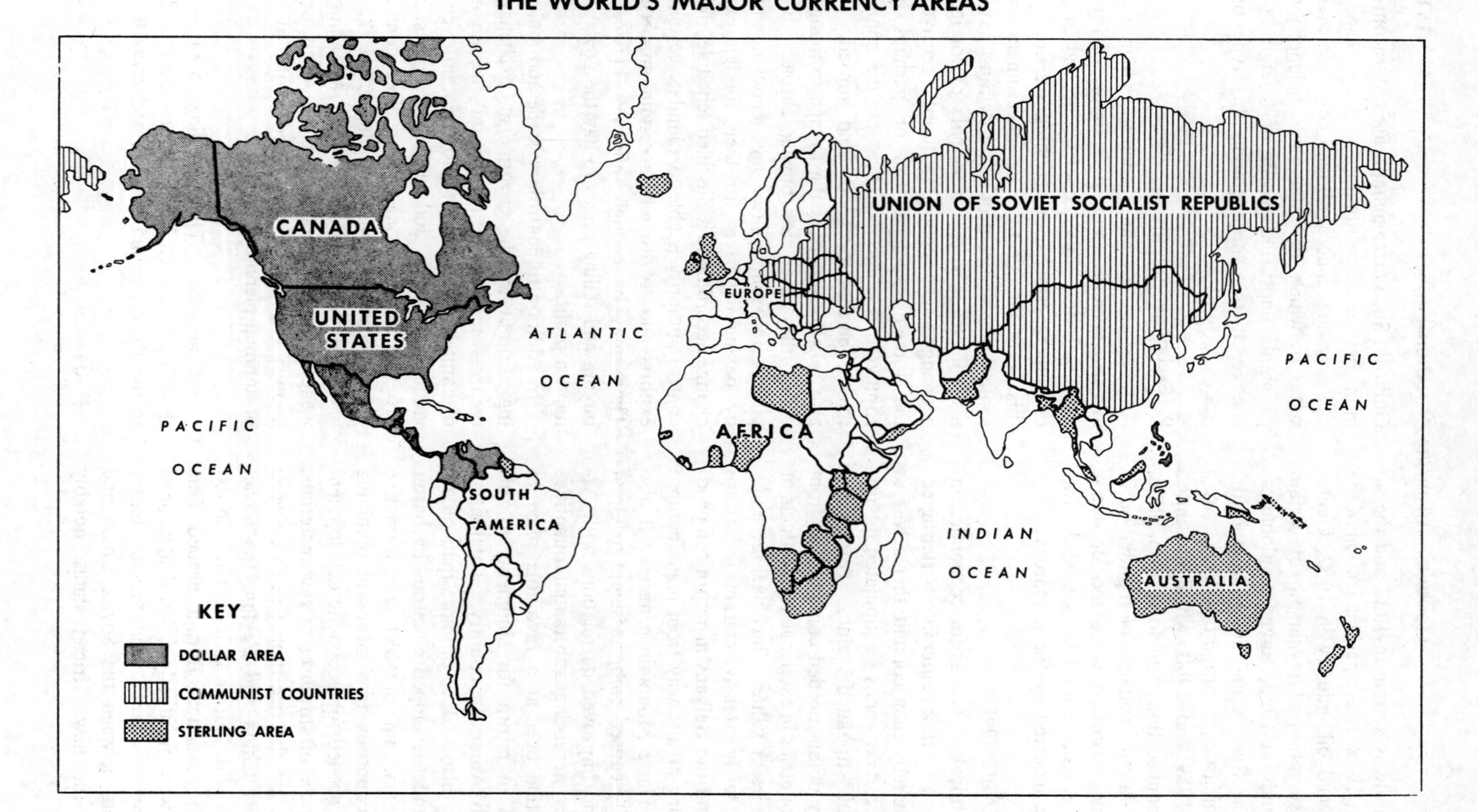

most important user of exchange controls. It embraces about one-third of the world's population and conducts approximately one-half of the world's total volume of trade and finance.

We shall here illustrate the working of exchange controls by noting the system employed for nearly twenty-five years by Argentina, an even older user than the sterling area. Exchange controls were instituted in Argentina in 1931 in response to two adverse developments: the dwindling of exchange reserves because of the depression and the monetary difficulties of Argentina's best customer, Great Britain, which produced an exchange-rate instability between the pound and the peso. The Argentine system, which featured a multiple exchange rate and the co-existence of a controlled exchange market and a free exchange market, was substantially modified in December, 1955, following the overthrow of Perón.

All of Argentina's major exports were handled through the controlled exchange market. The exchange which came into the country was held by the government, which compensated the exporter at one of nine rates, depending upon the product exported. In practice most exchange receipts were converted at one of three rates. Most of the leading exports, including beef, wheat, and corn, were converted at the "basic export rate" of 5.00 pesos per dollar; others, generally those more difficult to market, at the "preferential export rate" of 7.50 pesos; and still others, limited in volume, at the "free" rate of 13.95 pesos. This meant that the exporter of products classified under the second of the three rates was, in effect, paid a 50 per cent subsidy as a means of encouraging the export of goods in that class. Exporters under the 13.95 classification were paid an even larger subsidy. The "free" rate was so designated because free market transactions took place at that figure. These involved only exchange derived from specific sources — tourist receipts, ocean freights, and imports of capital — and represented one-fifth or less of the country's foreign transactions.

Foreign exchange was sold to importers at one of three rates. Exchange for preferred imports (coal, coke, fuel oil, and crude petroleum) could be bought at the rate of 5.00 pesos for a dollar, for "essential imports" at 7.50 pesos per dollar, and for nonessential and luxury imports at 13.95 pesos per dollar. By these differentials the importation of essential goods was promoted while the importation of luxuries was discouraged.

Since Argentina was an important trading country, and since most of the foreign exchange was purchased at the 5.00 rate and sold at the 7.50 rate, the government realized a handsome profit. Under a free economy, of course, this profit would have gone to domestic producers and traders. The income which the government derived was used "to service or to purchase foreign investments situated within the country and to finance new domestic projects, in lieu of dependence, to equivalent extent, upon outright taxation or public borrowing."[38]

10. Quotas and Licenses

When a government wishes to impose a more direct control over imports it may use the quota system. By this it may fix a quota on each country separately or it may establish an overall or global quota. The purpose may be to protect domestic producers or to make sure that imports do not exceed exports — that there is no unfavorable balance of trade. It has been increasingly used during the past thirty years to keep the total value of imports within predetermined limits. The use of quotas in export trade is limited to wartime, when it reduces the amount of goods which a neutral may buy to transship to an enemy of the

[38] *Ibid.*, p. 185. This discussion of exchange controls in Argentina is based on Krause, pp. 184–189.

exporting state. Perhaps the most rigid control over imports is attained by the licensing system. When this is in force, each new importation of goods requires a separate license, and thus the government can effect a continuous limitation to accord with the state's changing economic position. As quota and licensing systems are an even more overt interference with the flow of trade than tariffs, they are more likely to invite retaliation. Nevertheless, they were used in increasing measure during the interwar years, with France perhaps the leading practitioner.

The United States uses the quota system in a limited but important way. Having adopted the principle of domestic price supports in consequence of the Great Depression, she foresaw that these supports would be meaningless unless American producers were protected against imports from lower-producing-cost countries. Under the controls adopted, the importation of certain goods is subject to quota limits or even to complete exclusion. These quantitative restrictions are usually imposed in addition to import tariffs. Cotton imports were put under the quota system in 1939 and wheat and wheat flour imports in 1941.

Interestingly enough, the United States sugar quota is largely designed to aid friendly countries. Indeed, American producers of beet and cane sugar, who could easily supply all the sugar needs of the American economy, are directly hindered by the sugar imports. For some years the United States purchased Cuban sugar at substantially above the world price. When all sugar imports from Cuba were cut off after Castro came into power, the American sugar quotas were revised, to the benefit of other sugar-exporting countries, like India.

Employment of a quota is an illiberal trade practice, and it tends to encourage an uneconomic use of labor and resources, but it is apparently unavoidable if a state feels committed to the support of certain interests in its economy and of certain foreign countries which can obtain a greater share of the market in specified products under a quota system. Such a system, however, may in some cases impose considerable hardship on foreign producers, and it raises prices at home.

A quota should be distinguished from an international commodity agreement, which, as has been indicated, is a multilateral, not a bilateral, understanding to curtail ruinous competition among the producers of basic commodities, to ensure that producers in all participating countries receive a fair share of the world markets, and to take positive and concerted steps to expand foreign markets.[39]

Other Economic Instruments

State Trading. State trading is a highly restrictive practice invariably engaged in by totalitarian governments and used by most governments on special occasions and with a limited number of commodities.[40] It simply means that the government itself becomes a direct participant in trade. Since it is then in a position to control the volume, direction, and timing of foreign trade, it is also in a position to exert powerful economic and political pressures. In Communist countries state trading is more than a device; it is the basic pattern of the international trading activities. Since it is such a major and such a divisive component of the international economy today, it is considered more fully in Chapter 19.

Subsidies. Subsidies are payments made to encourage production at home or sales abroad. Although their net effect on international commerce is the same as that

[39] See Krause, Chapter 8; and Stephen Enke and Virgil Salera, *International Economics*, 3d ed. (Englewood Cliffs, N.J.: Prentice-Hall, 1957), pp. 226, 259–269.

[40] See Enke and Salera, Chapter 21; and Young, Chapter 21.

of tariffs, they have advantages in special situations. Thus subsidies have been used to promote the expansion of the American merchant marine, an objective that would be hard to achieve by means of the tariff. They also forestall the grant of special tariff concessions that may have been agreed to in a preferential agreement, and, strange as it may seem, they have been used by the United States to prevent the growth of an embarrassing surplus in the Treasury, as in the sugar bounty in the McKinley Act of 1890. "A subsidy may be thought of as a weapon of offense in international economic rivalry or warfare, whereas a protective tariff is a defensive weapon."[41] As an offensive weapon, subsidies facilitate dumping, which a tariff could not do.

Blacklists. Another device, blacklisting, was extensively used by the United States just before her entry into World War II. To prevent firms and individuals in Latin America from shipping supplies to the Axis countries, the American government, in July, 1941, published a "Proclaimed List of Certain Blockaded Nationals" with whom Americans were forbidden to have commercial relations and whose assets in the United States were frozen. The original list contained the names of 1,800 corporations and individuals. Five months later it was extended to inhibit Latin American trade with Japan, and one month after that it was expanded to cover Axis connections in neutral Europe. These blacklists, it must be noted, applied to private concerns and persons, not to states as such.

The Arab League has long maintained a blacklist of foreign firms which have any economic dealings with Israel. In recent years the United States has made a rather ineffectual effort to discourage trade with the Castro regime by maintaining a blacklist of foreign shipping firms which are engaged in trade with Cuba.

Valorization. The term "valorization" has come to be applied to any governmental measure for raising the price of a commodity, but in its original meaning it referred to an action taken by a government to raise the price of a commodity "above a level regarded as uneconomically low but not above the price that would in the long run be set by free competition." It was designed as a temporary measure to stabilize prices over a short period of lessened demand or bumper production. It was usually accomplished by purchasing and withholding from the market or by limiting production. Supposedly the government itself derives no direct profit. The best known instances of valorization have been in Brazilian coffee, Ecuadorian cacao, Mexican henequen, British rubber, Cuban sugar, and Egyptian cotton. Valorization has declined in importance in recent years, for the tendency has been to replace it with the more effective multilateral intergovernmental commodity agreements.

Embargoes and Boycotts. The embargo may be used to prohibit the shipment of all goods or certain goods to a particular country or group of countries, and the boycott, which is the reverse of the embargo, may be used to stop imports. Both the embargo and the boycott may be unofficial or official — that is, they may be imposed by private groups or public sentiment or by governments. On the eve of World War II there was an unofficial but widespread movement in the United States to discourage the purchase of Japanese goods. After the war the Battle Act imposed a qualified embargo on shipments to Communist China. Purchase regulations may effect a kind of indirect and partial boycott. Legislation of 1933 stipulated that, with exceptions under certain conditions, materials and supplies for government use must be of American production. This "Buy Ameri-

[41] Daugherty and Daugherty, II, 1104. See also Young, pp. 608–610, 777–779.

can" mandate raises the cost of government purchases, bestows favors on some American industries, and, of course, discriminates against foreign producers and reduces the volume of world trade. Beginning in 1934 various laws have given a similar protection to American shipping. The usual provision — which applied to Marshall Plan aid and Mutual Security assistance — is that at least fifty per cent of the goods sent abroad on aid programs or purchased by loans from American government agencies must be shipped in American-flag vessels.

The Role of Economic Instruments

The weapons that we have described are not all of those which states have in their economic arsenals. Indeed, governments are so resourceful in their improvisation of instruments of economic coercion that new ones are constantly appearing. The use of economic instruments to injure other states can be far more readily condemned than abolished; it presents one of the truly grave issues in contemporary international relations. In the first place, the sovereignty of states interposes a formidable barrier between the idea of free and easy trade relations and its attainment. In the second place, as we have already observed, it is difficult to draw a sharp line between a state's obligations to its own people and its obligations — if any — to the world community. Nevertheless, along with the growing economic nationalism of the past thirty years there has developed a conviction on the part of many statesmen that the well-being of the whole world requires that vigorous action be taken to reduce the barriers to world trade and finance and to limit the means by which states can by unilateral action impose their wishes on other states. Consequently, although the trend today is strongly in the direction of economic nationalism, efforts toward economic internationalism also are being made. We shall examine the present stage of these conflicting trends in Chapter 19.

SUGGESTIONS FOR FURTHER READING

ALLEN, ROBERT LORING. *Soviet Economic Warfare.* Washington, D.C.: Public Affairs Press, 1960.

ASHWORTH, WILLIAM B. *A Short History of the International Economy, 1850–1950.* London, 1952. Excellent background material.

BELL, PHILIP W. *The Sterling Area in the Postwar World.* London, 1956.

CLARK, COLIN. *The Conditions of Economic Progress,* 2d ed. London, 1951.

COPPOCK, JOSEPH D. *International Economic Instability: The Experience after World War II.* New York: McGraw-Hill Book Company, 1962.

DAVIS, J. S. *International Commodity Agreements: Hope, Illusion, or Menace.* New York: The Committee on International Economic Policy, 1947.

EINZIG, PAUL. *Economic Warfare.* London, 1941.

ELLSWORTH, P. T. *The International Economy,* 3d ed. New York: The Macmillan Company, 1964.

ENKE, STEPHEN and VIRGIL SALERA. *International Economics,* 3d ed. Englewood Cliffs, N.J.: Prentice-Hall, 1957.

HABERLER, GOTTFRIED. *A Survey of International Trade Theory.* International Finance Section, Princeton University, 1961.

———. *The Theory of International Trade.* New York: The Macmillan Company, 1936. A classic statement.

JENSEN, FINN D. and INGO WALTER, eds. *Read-*

ings in International Economic Relations. New York: The Ronald Press Company, 1966.

KENEN, PETER. *International Economics.* Englewood Cliffs, N.J.: Prentice-Hall, 1964.

KINDLEBERGER, CHARLES P. *International Economics.* Homewood, Ill.: Richard D. Irwin, 1963.

KRAUSE, WALTER. *International Economics.* Boston: Houghton Mifflin Company, 1965.

MASON, EDWARD S. *Controlling World Trade: Cartels and Commodity Agreements.* New York: McGraw-Hill Book Company, 1946.

MILLER, J. PERRY. *Competition, Cartels and Their Regulation.* Amsterdam, 1961.

ROOT, FRANKLEN R., ROLAND L. KRAMER, and MAURICE D'ARLIN. *International Trade and Finance.* Cincinnati: South-Western Publishing Co., 1959.

SNIDER, DELBERT A. *Introduction to International Economics.* Homewood, Ill.: Richard D. Irwin, 1963.

STOCKING, GEORGE W. and MYRON W. WATKINS. *Cartels in Action.* New York: The Twentieth Century Fund, 1946. Subtitled: "Case studies in international business diplomacy."

———. *Cartels or Competition?* New York: The Twentieth Century Fund, 1946.

VANEK, JAROSLAV. *International Trade: Theory and Economic Policy.* Homewood, Ill.: Richard D. Irwin, 1962.

WHITTLESEY, CHARLES R. *National Interest and International Cartels.* New York: The Macmillan Company, 1946.

YOUNG, JOHN PARKE. *The International Economy,* 4th ed. New York: The Ronald Press Company, 1963.

7 Imperialism and Colonialism

The defenders of modern imperialism and colonialism long pleaded their case in terms of the White Man's Burden. They rationalized that it was the obligation of advanced nations to help the people of "backward" nations — to civilize and "Christianize" them, to teach them the dignity of labor, and to impress upon them the beauties of their own concepts of law and order. They argued that colonialism was a necessary prelude to the emergence of most of the free and independent states of the world and to the twentieth-century awakening of Asia and Africa. They talked a great deal about roads, medicine, schoolhouses, trade, and self-government. There is much truth in what they said.

The critics used quite another vocabulary. Their indictment was filled with such words as war, brutality, exploitation, misery, hatred, and degradation. They insisted that the struggle for empire led only to the urge to create greater and still greater empires and that the appetite of empire builders knew no limits. They too spoke much truth.

Imperialism and colonialism have long been employed as instruments of national policy. They are closely related parts of the phenomenon that we are about to examine. The subject is a timely one, for most of the Western world and part of the Eastern are anxiously weighing the threat of Communist imperialism, the Communists are still inveighing against Western imperialism, and vast areas of Asia and Africa are charging most of their woes to the colonialism of the once-great colonial powers and to so-called neo-colonialism, in its various forms.

We shall note first the use of terms, then the relation of imperialism to nationalism, and then the motives of imperialism. After this we shall quickly review the march of imperialism, examine its balance sheet, and then close with some observations on the manifestations and significance of colonialism and the process of de-colonialization in the postwar era.

What Is Imperialism?

Imperialism can be discussed, denounced, defended, and died for, but it cannot be defined in any generally acceptable way. It means different things to different people. Let us note some of these differences as they appear in the definitions of a number of able writers on the subject:

> Imperialism is a policy which aims at creating, organizing, and maintaining an empire; that is, a state of vast size composed of various more or less distinct national units and subject to a single centralized will. (Moritz Julius Bonn)[1]

[1] Moritz Julius Bonn, "Imperialism," *Encyclopaedia of the Social Sciences* (New York: The Macmillan Company, 1937), VII, 605. Used by permission of The Macmillan Company.

> *Imperialism* is . . . employment of the engines of government and diplomacy to acquire territories, protectorates, and/or spheres of influence occupied usually by other races or peoples, and to promote industrial, trade, and investment opportunities. (Charles A. Beard)[2]

> Imperialism . . . means domination of non-European native races by totally dissimilar European nations. (Parker T. Moon)[3]

It will be seen that Bonn imposed a quantitative measurement and presumably ruled out the possibility of a "small imperialism." Beard excluded all except economic motivations, and he made direct government action an inseparable part of imperialism. Moon injected the test of racial difference. The definitions of Hans Morgenthau, Joseph Schumpeter, E. M. Winslow, and Lenin suggest additional qualifications.[4] Morgenthau scrapped the conditions of exclusive economic motivation, size of operation, and difference of race; he defined imperialism altogether in terms of the expansion of a state's power beyond its borders. Schumpeter deprived imperialism of all conscious motivation and definable objectives. He regarded it as an "atavistic force, ancient in inception, decadent and self-conscious in an age of rationalism, yet still powerful enough to lord it over its rival, the upstart capitalism."[5] Winslow reversed Schumpeter and saw both organization and specific objectives in the imperialist operation, and he made it evil by definition. Lenin asserted the traditional view of communism, in which imperialism is not only entirely economic but also a rather precise stage in the development of international capitalism.

It would be futile to attempt to reconcile these definitions — and a host of others — but it may be possible to make a number of helpful observations. The first and most obvious one is that "imperialism" is a highly subjective word — that writers define it pretty much as they please. Second, imperialism has become more of an epithet than anything else: the Russians use it to stigmatize the policies of the Western states, the anti-Communist powers use it to blacken Soviet policies, and the "uncommitted world" uses it to condemn the policies of both the Communist and non-Communist worlds. As Raymond L. Buell remarked many years ago, "every unjustifiable demand made by one government upon another — every aggressive war — is called imperialistic. Imperialism is a word which indeed covers many sins."[6] Third, it seems that if there is any consensus in common usage certain occasional qualifications ought to be disregarded. Thus, what commonly passes for imperialism seems to warrant these assertions: (1) it may have powerful noneconomic motivations — it may, as a matter of fact, be without expectation of economic gain; (2) it may pertain to a very limited operation — a

[2] Charles A. Beard, *American Foreign Policy in tne Making, 1932–1940: A Study in Responsibilities* (New Haven: Yale University Press, 1946), p. 113n.

[3] Parker T. Moon, *Imperialism and World Politics* (New York: The Macmillan Company, 1926), p. 33. Used by permission of The Macmillan Company.

[4] Hans J. Morgenthau, *Politics Among Nations,* 3d ed. (New York: Alfred A. Knopf, 1954), pp. 44–47; Joseph A. Schumpeter, *Imperialism and Social Classes,* edited by Paul M. Sweezy (Oxford, 1951), pp. 6, 7; E. M. Winslow, *The Pattern of Imperialism: A Study in the Theories of Power* (New York: Columbia University Press, 1948), pp. 3, 237; and E. Varga and L. Mendelsohn, eds., *New Data for V. I. Lenin's "Imperialism, the Highest Stage of Capitalism"* (U.S.S.R., n.d.), p. 194.

[5] Winslow, p. 229. Joseph A. Schumpeter was a distinguished German economist who spent his later years at Harvard. His "Zur Soziologie der Imperialismen," published as an essay in 1919, was, together with another essay, published in book form in 1951 by Basil Blackwell of Oxford. Paul M. Sweezy, editor of this edition, notes in his introduction (p. vii) that Schumpeter's work on imperialism "has apparently been almost totally ignored by Anglo-American social scientists."

[6] Raymond L. Buell, *International Relations,* rev. ed. (New York: Holt, 1929), p. 305.

"vast empire" need not be contemplated at all; (3) it need not involve a difference of race — there may very well be imperialism within a single race; and (4) it may be planned or unplanned. Furthermore, imperialism may be with or without high regard for the welfare of the inhabitants of the area in question, it may be developmental or exploitative, and it may promote the capacity for self-government or ruthlessly suppress all impulses in that direction. Finally, it may be economically profitable for the imperialist country, or it may be decidedly unprofitable.

Shorn of the special conditions which individual writers attach to it, imperialism comes close to being what Charles Hodges called it many years ago: "a projection externally, directly or indirectly, of the alien political, economic, or cultural power of one nation into the internal life of another people. . . . it involves the imposition of control — open or covert, direct or indirect — of one people by another."[7] "The object of imperialism," added Professor Hodges, "is to affect the destinies of the backward people in the interest of the more advanced from the standpoint of world power." It seems that "backward" must here be interpreted in a power sense, for history furnishes many examples of peoples being held in bondage by stronger but culturally less advanced peoples.

"Economic imperialism" and "cultural imperialism" would appear to be very special kinds of imperialism, if, indeed, they should be called imperialism at all. Foreign trade and foreign investments are everywhere, and some aspects of the cultures of many states find their way into many other states. All these exert some influence; hence if mere influence is to constitute imperialism the word is almost meaningless. If there is to be a pragmatic test it must center on the freedom of the "influenced" people to muddle in their own way through their own problems, economic and cultural pressures included.

Professor William L. Langer made much this same point in protest against the fuzzy use of the word "imperialism":

> Some may argue that imperialism is more than a movement toward territorial expansion and that financial imperialism in particular lays the iron hand of control on many countries supposedly independent. But if you try to divorce imperialism from territorial control you get nowhere. . . . If imperialism is to mean any vague interference of traders and bankers in the affairs of other countries, you may as well extend it to cover any form of influence. You will have to admit cultural imperialism, religious imperialism, and what not. Personally, I prefer to stick by a measurable, manageable concept.[8]

It further appears that there have been both good and bad imperialisms. Therefore, unless one wishes to argue that it is *ipso facto* bad, imperialism itself must be regarded as amoral. This is not to say that the good balances the bad, but merely that imperialism, like the tariff or propaganda, is an instrument of the state, available for good purposes or bad.

These observations suggest that imperialism pertains to a relationship in which one area and its people are subordinate to another area and its government. Thus construed, imperialism in essence always involves subordination; it is a power relationship without moral implications of any kind.

What Is Colonialism?

The classic study of imperialism is J. A. Hobson's *Imperialism: A Study,* first published in 1902. Although Hobson failed to define imperialism, he did have this to say of colonialism: "Colonialism, in its best sense, is a natural overflow of nationality;

[7] Charles Hodges, *The Background of International Relations* (New York: John Wiley & Sons, 1932), pp. 421, 422.

[8] William L. Langer, "A Critique of Imperialism," *Foreign Affairs,* XIV (October, 1935), 107.

its test is the power of colonists to transplant the civilization they represent to the new natural and social environment in which they find themselves."[9] Later writers also have attributed to colonialism something of the parent-and-offspring relationship that Hobson had in mind. Winslow spoke of it as the "occupation of virgin territory in which conflict was incidental, or even unnecessary, and subordinate to the desire of Europeans to find a new place to live."[10] Townsend and Peake chose not to use "imperialism" because "it has come to connote a particular kind of colonial rule — generally exploitative — which has often characterized this modern movement, but not always."[11] Winslow had aversions of the same kind; "imperialism," he felt, "quite properly suggests something more organized, more military, more self-consciously aggressive, bent on objectives above and beyond" those of colonialism.

These distinctions in theory tend to break down in practice. It is sometimes impossible to draw a line between the "overflow of nationality" on the one hand and the "projection . . . of the . . . power of one nation into the internal life of another people" on the other hand. Hobson recognized this inaccuracy of terms when he said that "the 'colonial' party in Germany and France is identical in general aim and method with the 'imperialist' party in England." And President Sukarno of Indonesia certainly had imperialism in mind when in his opening address at the Bandung Conference of 1955 he said: "I beg of you not to think of colonialism only in the classic form which we . . . knew. Colonialism has also its modern dress in the form of economic control, intellectual control, and actual physical control by a small but alien community within the nation." The Bandung Conference itself disclosed a total lack of agreement on the meaning of colonialism. This historic gathering of the representatives of twenty-nine countries of Asia and Africa solemnly resolved that "colonialism in all its manifestations is an evil which should speedily be brought to an end," but whereas the spokesmen of Pakistan, the Philippines, Thailand, Turkey, Iraq, and Ceylon voiced apprehensions concerning Soviet colonialism, the representatives of the "uncommitted world," led by Nehru of India, denied that there was such a thing as Soviet colonialism. While the delegates could all agree that colonialism was "an evil," they could not agree on what it was or where it existed.

The most significant thing about imperialism and colonialism is not that they cannot be precisely defined or that they cannot always be distinguished from each other; it is that both terms refer to a superior-inferior relationship, and that hundreds of millions of people, particularly in Asia and Africa, have resolved to abandon their historic role as inferiors and to assert their equality with the people of the former colonial powers. In current practice the two terms are used almost interchangeably. We shall not try to preserve the distinction in the present discussion.

Imperialism and Nationalism

Imperialism is almost universally charged to nationalism, already indicted for most of the sins of the world community. "Modern imperialism," wrote one authority, "was born with the break up of mediaeval universalism . . . [when] the rise of national self-consciousness brought a desire for expression in a wider sphere." The new states sought to extend their boundaries and create empires by the conquest of lands usually inhabited by peoples considered heathen, and "they more or less consciously tried to foist upon

[9] J. A. Hobson, *Imperialism: A Study,* 3d ed. (London, 1938), p. 7.

[10] Winslow, p. 4.

[11] Mary E. Townsend, with the collaboration of Cyrus H. Peake, *European Colonial Expansion Since 1871* (Philadelphia: J. B. Lippincott Co., 1941), p. 9.

the natives their own social and cultural systems by 'Hellenizing the barbarians' in a particular and national rather than in a universal way." In doing so, "rivalries waxed strong; each modern nation wanted to extend its newly established nationality overseas in a New Spain, a New Holland, a New France, or a New England by sending out colonists or by assimilating in some degree the native races." Out of these endeavors emerged the Spanish Empire, "the first realization of modern imperialism." It was Spain's monopolistic exploitation of her colonies that "forced competitors along the path of imperialism." Later, after the imperialist recession which lasted until about 1870, "protectionism as a combination of national sentiment, lust for power and individual greed again became rampant," and the "new imperialism" was launched.[12]

So many other writers have charged nationalism with responsibility for the evils of imperialism that the indictment is commonly taken as proved. It has obvious plausibility: nationalism in the form of desire to exalt a state and to add to its prestige drives men into carrying their flag, their culture, their language, and their institutions into every power-weak area on earth; and it compels governments to justify, defend, and champion the economic ventures of their nationals in foreign lands, especially weak ones. "Just as romantic nationalism clothed the crass materialism of expansion with a beautiful idealism, the concept of 'the white man's burden,' with humanitarianism and uplift of the 'little brown brothers,' so materialism with its 'economic necessity' advanced the national arguments of 'surplus population,' outlets for capital and bursting overproduction."[13] During the last years of the nineteenth century "Darwin's catchwords — the struggle for existence and the survival of the fittest — which he himself always refused to apply to the social organism, were snapped up by others who were less scrupulous, and soon became an integral part of popular and even official thought on foreign affairs. It . . . supplied a divine sanction for expansion."[14] Professor Hans Kohn spoke of imperialism and nationalism as "interlocked":

> Imperialism is for the most part a later phase in the process begun by nationalism. Nationalism strives to unite the members of one nation, politically and territorially, in a State organization. When that is accomplished the struggle for the possession of the earth proceeds further. . . . imperialism then inflames the nationalism of the oppressed peoples or fractions. Thus imperialism and nationalism are interlocked.[15]

Buell had in mind the same relationship when he said that "paradoxical as it may seem, pure nationalism has forced governments into the path of imperialism."[16]

Winslow entered a somewhat lonely dissent from the view that imperialism has been begotten of nationalism. He observed that it is much older than nationalism, which is certainly true, and that it was not "a product of popular mass revolt against absolutism such as produced democracy, industrialism, and nationalism, but the opposite" — which is a curious assertion, for nationalism long existed under absolutism. His case against imperialism as an offspring of nationalism, however, is stronger than the which-was-first argument. He held that the two are based on fundamentally different concepts:

> Nationalism has within it the same feeling as has democracy, that of mutuality, but imperialism is an exclusive concept. Wherever the spirit of exclusiveness creeps into a na-

[12] Bonn, pp. 606, 607, 609.
[13] Townsend, p. 37.
[14] Langer, p. 109.
[15] *Nationalism and Imperialism in the Hither East* (New York: Harcourt, Brace, 1932), p. 49
[16] Buell, p. 315.

tion, as it well may, it is a sign that the nation is losing the attributes of nationalism, internationalism, and democracy and is setting forth on the ancient business of telling "foreigners" what to do and what not to do, which is the path of empire. . . . nation-building and empire-building by no means involve the same set of attitudes; in fact, they involve attitudes which are essentially opposed to each other, and which find their opposite expressions in popular rather than scholarly reactions.[17]

Winslow's thesis is more interesting than convincing. If nationalism and imperialism are antithetical, if states lose their nationalism when they take to imperialism, there never was a Spanish nationalism, a Russian nationalism, or even an English nationalism, and Americans have been losing their nationalism for at least half a century. And since when has nationalism prescribed democracy? Or democracy prescribed anti-imperialism? Langer declared that enfranchisement and free education brought the "rank and file" of the British public into the "political arena," where "colonial adventure and far-away conflict satisfied the craving for excitement." "The upper crust of the working class," he continued, "was easily converted to the teaching of imperialism and took pride in the extension of empire." Hobson "was keenly aware of the relationship between democracy and imperialism" and held it to be one of the "contributory explanations of the phenomenon" of imperialism.[18]

The Motives of Imperialism

Because the fruits of imperialism — the subordinate areas variously called possessions, colonies, protectorates, semi-protectorates, and dependent states — have long been regarded as valuable to the controlling state, they have been eagerly sought. To some extent they have been the badge of status in international society. Consequently, imperialistic rivalries have been a fertile source of interstate conflict, they have figured importantly in the international economy, they have often been an expression of belligerent nationalism, and they have been a major or a contributing cause of many of the great wars of the past three centuries.

The motives and techniques of modern imperialism were enormously varied and complex. The leading motives appear to have been the following:

1. Economic Gain. This includes conquest for the sake of loot, the quest for competition-free markets and sources of raw materials, the search for virgin fields of investment for the capitalists of imperial powers, and the urge to secure certain strategic raw materials. At times imperialism may have provided goods that could not be obtained otherwise; at other times it merely made it possible to get them at a lower price or with less likelihood of interruption by war. While the nineteenth-century imperialist's declaration that "trade follows the flag" is not verified by statistics, as we shall see, nevertheless he believed it, and in any event he found in imperialism a shortcut around foreign exchange difficulties. Some British Whigs of the eighteenth and early nineteenth centuries and some American statesmen of the nineteenth century insisted that "colonies do not pay," but until recently states have generally assumed otherwise.

2. National Prestige. Many defenders of imperialism have believed that a state must achieve its "manifest destiny" or its "place in the sun." Generations of Englishmen gloried in the boast that "the sun never sets on the British Empire."[19] Not Texans

[17] Winslow, p. 7.

[18] Langer, p. 108.

[19] English workers of the nineteenth century at times preferred to speak of "the Empire on which the sun never sets and wages never rise."

alone, but many other people are intoxicated by dimensions. Benito Mussolini loved to move his hand over the map of those expanses of African desert and hill land that he had brought under the Italian flag. His chest expanded with his dominions. Indiscriminate Americans applauded the acquisition of territory that at the turn of the century made their country a world power, quite apart from any information or conviction about its intrinsic worth. More recently we have come to the sober realization that land for flag-flying may mean responsibility and expense rather than grandeur, but an analysis of imperialism shows that the desire for land and still more land has often been a product of aggressive nationalism.

A study of the motivations of French imperialism in Eastern Asia concluded that the values which the French sought were far less tangible than those of land. The author's conclusions are unequivocal:

> The taproot of French imperialism in the Far East from first to last was national pride — pride of culture, reputation, prestige, and influence. This was the constant factor which ran through the kaleidoscope of episodes of missionary dedication and daring, of naval coups, and of private adventures. . . . One need not discount the genuineness of the religious zeal which sustained the program of the Société des Missions Etrangères over two centuries or challenge the validity of the liberal religious revival under Louis Philippe to see in both of them an expression of supreme confidence in the superiority of French spirit and culture. . . . French honor was enlisted to vindicate the inherent superiority of its national culture and could permit no challenge of it to go unanswered.[20]

Speaking of imperialism generally, Hans Kohn made the following observation on its noneconomic impetus:

> Besides the economic urge, psychological motives played a great role in imperialism — the lust for adventure and for power, the added prestige and glory which seemed to accrue from a vast colonial empire not only to the governing classes but even to the masses of the colonizing nations, the new sentiment of pride and superiority which animated even the lowest members of the white races in their dealings with the "backward" races.[21]

3. The White Man's Burden. In the past, at least, many members of "advanced" Western societies believed that their state had a moral obligation to carry the blessings of their own religion and civilization to "backward" peoples. In their view, the white man had a duty to uplift his less fortunate brothers, usually in the yellow man's Asia or in the black man's Africa. Many of these people were wholly sincere, as is proved by the countless missionaries, soldiers, and administrators who braved the perils of the strange and unknown. Few will question the sincerity of Rudyard Kipling,[22] the poet of British imperialism, or perhaps of President William McKinley, who announced that in answer to his prayer for guidance God told him "to take them all [the Philippine Islands], and to educate the Filipinos, and uplift and civilize and Christianize them, and by God's grace do the very best we could by them, as our fellowmen for whom Christ also died." The conquest of Latin America is a classic example of imperialism in behalf of a religious mission, for

[20] John F. Cady, *The Roots of French Imperialism in Eastern Asia* (Ithaca: Cornell University Press, 1954), pp. 294–295.

[21] *Force or Reason: Issues of the Twentieth Century* (Cambridge, Mass.: Harvard University Press, 1937), p. 80.

[22] E. L. Godkin, English-born editor of the anti-imperialist New York *Nation,* once wrote of Kipling: "I think most of the current jingoism on both sides of the water is due to him. He is the poet of the barrack-room cads." Rollo Ogden, ed., *Life and Letters of Edwin Lawrence Godkin* (New York: The Macmillan Company, 1907), II, 30–31.

the Catholic sovereigns of Spain and Portugal were at least as religious as they were mercenary. Thousands of humble priests went willingly to do God's work in the wilderness, and the motive which impelled them was in most cases genuine. It is true, of course, that many a consecrated soul has unwittingly served the cause of militarism or economic exploitation, but it also is true that millions of people have been sincerely committed to the idealism of the White Man's Burden, particularly during the greatest age of imperialism, from 1870 to 1914.

Joseph Chamberlain, next to Disraeli perhaps Britain's leading exponent of imperialism, declared in 1893 that "it is our duty to take our share in the work of civilization in Africa," and John Bright, possibly the chief spokesman of the opposition, did not see how Britain could withdraw from India until that country had been made secure against discord and anarchy. Albert J. Beveridge, often regarded as the ablest defender of imperialism in the American Senate during the debates on the treaty of peace with Spain, thus interpreted America's responsibility: "God has made us adepts in government that we may administer government among savage and servile people."

Raymond L. Buell, one of the foremost students of imperialism, declared years ago that "it would be a gross perversion of fact to say that European and American imperialism was originally inspired by a desire to better the lives of the people whom it forcibly subjugated"; but, he added, "there have been a number of instances where governments have established political control for humanitarian purposes." He cited the occupation of New Zealand in 1833 to stop the debauching and robbing of the natives by white men; the assumption by the British Government of direct rule in India in 1858, partly to end the abuses of indirect administration by the British East India Company; the assertion of British jurisdiction over certain Pacific islands in 1872 to stamp out the slave traffic; and the fact that "thousands of Americans supported the war against Spain in 1898 because of their belief that Spain was pursuing a policy of oppression and exploitation in Cuba and Puerto Rico."[23]

4. **National Defense.** Imperialism may serve national defense in a number of ways: by providing areas and bases for the defense of the state or its lines of communication, by providing much-needed markets and sources of essential raw materials, and by providing populations from which troops and laborers may be drawn. States have often sought to protect themselves by gaining control of outlying or border areas, either by completely subordinating the areas or by winning influence over nominally independent states, called buffer states. Moves of this sort are designed to fix broad belts of insulation around states by keeping enemies far from their borders, and sometimes by installing defenses within the protective belt itself. Thus through most of the nineteenth century England relied upon the buffer states of Afghanistan, Persia, and Tibet for the defense of India against Russia.

The acquisition and retention of sources of raw materials bring economic motivation and military motivation very much together. One has only to note the importance that some states attached to their colonial sources of oil, rubber, tin, and other raw materials to be convinced that certain products play an important role in imperialism. Colonies may also be valuable as reservoirs of manpower. During World War I France drew nearly 500,000 troops and more than 200,000 laborers from her colonies, while England drew nearly 400,000 troops from India.[24] Because of the entirely different character of World War II, colonial troops

23 Buell, p. 318.
24 *Ibid.*, p. 313.

were used mostly to defend their homelands, when used at all. Nevertheless, casualties among British colonials exceeded 200,000.

5. Surplus Population. Statesmen have at times supported imperialism because they saw in colonies an outlet for a population growing with embarrassing rapidity. Economic interests may profit, too, for emigrating nationals promise to be good customers. Actually, however, overpopulated states have found little relief in emigration to their colonies. Englishmen have gone to the Dominions in great numbers; but they have shown less interest in moving to colonial possessions. Of nearly 20,000,000 Europeans who emigrated between 1880 and 1940, nearly 17,000,000 went to the free nations of the Western Hemisphere.[25] Between 1925 and 1933, while Japan was trying to justify her designs on China with the population-pressure argument, less than four per cent of her population increase of that period migrated to her own colonies.[26] During the last decade of her colonial empire, 1904–13, Germany sent only one out of 24,000 of her annual population increment to her colonies — in absolute numbers, about thirty persons a year.[27] All imperialist states have failed completely to win as much enthusiasm for home as for flags in those faraway places with strange-sounding names.

6. The Marxist-Leninist View. The Communists have their own interpretations of imperialism. They apply the term to a phase in the expansion of capitalism, but, of course, not to their own expansionism. There is thus a sharp distinction between Leninist imperialism, which is a Communist theory to explain the inherent and progressive iniquity of capitalism, and Soviet imperialism, which is a term applied by anti-Communists to the pattern of subversion and subjugation carried on by the Soviet Union.

The Leninist theory of imperialism rests upon the assumption that all political action springs from economic motives. Consequently, when capitalistic societies find that they have reached a point where the production of goods is so great that domestic markets are no longer adequate, they bring political forces into play in order to achieve the subordination of outside areas so that these may be held as controlled markets for surplus products and surplus investment capital. Therefore capitalism is itself the cause of imperialism.

While some of the Marxists believed that capitalistic states turned to imperialism more or less as a matter of choice, Lenin held that capitalism led inevitably to imperialism. "If it were necessary to give the briefest possible definition of imperialism," he wrote, "we should have to say that imperialism is the monopoly stage of capitalism."[28] He severely criticized Kautsky for his "wrong and un-Marxian" contention that imperialism was the "preferred" policy of capitalist states rather than an unavoidable one.[29] The difference in the propaganda value of the two theories was immense, for in the Leninist view there was no stopping the worldwide imperialism out of which would come the proletarian revolution.

The March of Imperialism

What might be called modern imperialism may be divided into the old imperialism, for which we might set the somewhat arbitrary dates of 1492 to 1763, and the new imperialism, extending from about 1870 to the pres-

[25] H. Arthur Steiner, *Principles and Problems of International Relations* (New York: Harper, 1940), pp. 145–146.

[26] Grover Clark, *The Balance Sheets of Imperialism: Facts and Figures on Colonies* (New York: Columbia University Press, 1936), p. 10.

[27] *German Statistical Year Book, 1915,* cited in L. S. Amery, *The German Colonial Claim* (London, 1939), p. 79.

[28] Varga and Mendelsohn, p. 192.

[29] *Ibid.*, p. 200.

ent or at least until World War II. Between these two periods there was a full century of comparative quiet in the rivalry of states in the building of colonial empires. This is not to say that imperialism itself disappeared, for if we use the term to signify a relationship rather than a process it must be said to have continued in many areas. The dates of the old imperialism and the new are literally the periods of imperialist expansion.

The impetus of the old imperialism was the emerging nationalism, its philosophy was mercantilism, and its tools were the innovations of more advanced technological societies that gave Europeans almost complete assurance of victory over non-European peoples. Gunpowder was the most persuasive among the tools, but printing and banking also conferred immense advantages, as did advances in the building of ships, roads, and fortifications and in the science of navigation. The principal gainer was Britain, but Spain, Portugal, and the Netherlands also won great colonial empires. The New World was the foremost area of imperialist activity, but Africa and Asia figured too.

The Imperialist Recession. The imperialist recession, which began in 1763 and lasted for a little more than a century, brought some expansion to counterbalance immense losses. France conquered Algeria, England took possession of the southern tip of Africa, New Zealand, and Australia. The reverses included the colonies lost to England by the American Revolution and the vast areas lost to Spain and Portugal in the Latin American Wars of Independence.

The relapse of imperialism calls for an explanation. Of first importance, the Industrial Revolution turned the attention of the more progressive states and their speculators to the prospect of juicy profits from the sale to home consumers of the products of the newly invented machinery. Also, much of the time Spain and England were using their energies to resist the efforts of their colonial subjects to achieve independence, leaving little strength for aggressive action. Moreover, Spain was a decadent empire, having used her fabulous treasure chest of colonial gold and silver in foreign wars and in maintaining an extravagant court rather than in building a solid economy, and England had already had her fingers burned in the American War of Independence. France, virtually bankrupt, experienced the savage ordeal of the French Revolution and the Napoleonic Wars. Napoleon's ambitions for overseas dominions were ended by the defeat of his fleet at Trafalgar. By 1820 France had recovered enough to dream again of an expanding empire. Germany and Italy had not yet entered the ranks of national states.

The New Imperialism. The impetus of the new imperialism, beginning about 1870, was well summarized by Professor Parker T. Moon:

> . . . an anti-imperialist, free-trade Europe was converted to imperialism, rather suddenly in the seventies and eighties, when England began to feel the competition of other industrial rivals, when manufacturing nations began to raise protective tariff walls around their own markets and to compete bitterly for foreign markets, when steamships and railways provided facilities for world commerce and conquest, when greedy factories and hungry factory towns called out for raw materials and foodstuffs, when surplus capital, rapidly accumulating, sought investments in backward countries, when the doctrine of economic nationalism triumphed over the old individualistic liberalism.[30]

Imperialist control was established in many ways. At times it was asserted through complete military conquest; and at other times it took the form of negotiations between representatives of two supposedly

[30] Moon, pp. 56–57.

equal but actually unequal "states," wherein "empire builders" through the use of "gold, gimcracks, or gunpowder" induced native leaders to make their marks on or otherwise signify their assent to a treaty, of which they may not have had the remotest understanding. In addition to these techniques of military conquest and fraud, imperialists devised others: the mere threat of force, demoralization through economic penetration, and the undermining of the established regime by friends of an outside state, as in Hawaii. Colonies have also passed as the spoils of war in which the colonies suffered no direct conquest, as was the case when Guam was acquired by the United States. They have passed by sale, as in the famous Louisiana Purchase. Plebiscites, held on quite a number of occasions to determine to what state a particular area should be joined, have been used in a few instances to permit a small population to choose its allegiance as a colony or possession, as with the Ionian Islands, St. Bartholomew, and the Danish West Indies. Recent history offers a political oddity in the form of "independent" states agreeing by plebiscite to subordinate themselves to another state, the Soviet Union.

1. *Great Britain.* The Industrial Revolution that a century earlier had begun to turn would-be English colonists into factory workers had by 1870 stocked warehouses with a surplus of manufactured goods. Sale abroad was possible, but it was not easy in competing industrial states, particularly those with high tariff walls, like the United States and Germany. It was easier in English colonies, where England could manipulate the tariff, control the currency, and, if she wished, post "No Hunting" signs for outsiders. There, too, she might acquire a protected source of supply of some of the commodities that she already regarded or was coming to regard as necessary: cotton, rubber, cocoa, coffee, tea, sugar, iron, hemp, oil, phosphates, and nitrates. Furthermore, her transportation, communication, and banking facilities were ready, and industrialization had produced an abundance of surplus capital, eager for dividends and unafraid of a sea voyage. The English spirit was ready, too, or in any event was soon readied. Greed, patriotism, nationalism, jingoism, militarism, navalism, Christianity, humanitarianism, adventure, and the simple desire to eat every day — all of these whipped Englishmen into a state of mind in which they were willing to accept the imperialist program announced by Disraeli in 1872. Even Gladstone's Liberal Party was won over in the course of the next dozen years. In the hands of friendly theorists, imperialism became a holy mission — in fact, a patriotic and profitable holy mission. The British accretions of the new imperialism amounted, in Africa alone, to more than two and a half million square miles, with a population of nearly fifty millions. The gains elsewhere, principally in southeastern Asia, were small. In 1914 the British Empire, despite its losses, was still the world's largest and richest.

2. *France.* France acclaimed the imperialistic program of Jules Ferry in the early eighties, and within forty years had planted the tricolor on nearly three million square miles of soil and sand. Her prizes, too, were largely in Africa, with lesser ones in Southeast Asia, especially Indo-China. These geographically impressive conquests, plus some trivial, scattered acreage, added to the surviving crumbs of her former empire, gave her the world's second largest empire on the eve of World War I.

3. *Germany.* Bismarck, father of the German Empire, reluctantly turned from continental politics to imperialism. Within six years (1884–90) he acquired Togoland, Kamerun (the Cameroons), German South-West Africa, and German East Africa, with a total of nearly a million square miles, plus a portion of New Guinea, the leasehold of Kiaochow and extensive economic rights in the Shantung Peninsula in China, and scattered groups of islands in the Pacific. Germany had been late in entering the struggle for colonies, and all the swashbuckling and

conniving of Kaiser William II could not produce a first-rate colonial empire.

Germany lost her colonies as a result of World War I and ceased to be a colonial power. In the Nazi period Hitler annexed Austria, occupied the Sudetenland in Czechoslovakia, and in a short span invaded and occupied most of the nations in Europe. These actions were partly imperialist in purpose, although they were occasioned by many other factors. Hitler clearly had visions of a Greater Reich, extending far beyond the boundaries of Germany herself.

4. *Italy*. The kingdom of Italy, like Germany a new arrival among national states, shared the appetite of her neighbors. Although she lacked the strength to gain very much, she was able to carve out three colonies in Africa: Eritrea on the Red Sea, Italian Somaliland on the eastern tip of Africa, and Libya in North Africa. Libya was a unification of Tripoli and Cyrenaica, taken from Turkey in the Italo-Turkish War of 1911–12. Italy tried to absorb Ethiopia and thus unify her East African colonies, but she suffered a crushing military defeat at the hands of the Ethiopians at Aduwa in 1896. Later, just before World War II, she tried again, succeeded, organized Italian East Africa, and then soon lost everything.

5. *Belgium*. The little country of Belgium was put on the road to imperialism through a venture of Leopold II, who early in the days of the new imperialism staked out for himself the Congo Free State, an empire-size tract in the heart of Africa. Acquired as a personal possession by the King in the 1880's, it became a Belgian colony in 1908 when the Belgian government, responding to outside criticism of Leopold's abuse of the Congo natives, forced the King to relinquish his proprietorship.

6. *Japan*. While Japan was rapidly becoming industrialized, she was also learning to play Western games. Of the Western culture imported on the breakdown of her isolation in the second half of the nineteenth century, she rejected democracy but accepted industrial capitalism, militarism, and imperialism. Supported by an astonishing industrial development, she began her career of militarism and imperialism in 1894 with a war on China. With victory hers, she annexed Formosa and the Ryukyu Islands and forwarded the eventual absorption of Korea, completed in 1910. With success in a second imperialistic conflict, the Russo-Japanese War of 1904–05, she annexed southern Sakhalin, acquired a leasehold on Port Arthur on the Liaotung Peninsula, and eliminated Russian influence from Korea and southern Manchuria. Such was her position when she entered World War I as an ally of Great Britain. During World War I she took advantage of the preoccupation of the Western powers with the conflict in Europe to move into the Shantung Peninsula and to demand far-reaching concessions from China, especially in the Twenty-One Demands of 1915.

In the 1930's, as military fascism triumphed at home, Japan embarked on a policy of carving out a "Greater East Asia Co-Prosperity Sphere" on the Asian mainland. In 1931 she invaded Manchuria, and in 1937 China proper. Soon after Nazi troops attacked Poland in September, 1939, thus precipitating World War II, Japan moved into Southeast Asia and the islands of the South Pacific and the West Central Pacific, and threatened India and Australia. Japan's dreams of empire ended with her defeat in 1945.

7. *Russia*. The imperialism of Russia differed from the imperialistic expansion that had in turn sliced up North and South America, Africa, and much of Asia. As Professor Frederick L. Schuman said, "it represented the spreading out over contiguous territory of a land-hungry agrarian population, rather than an imperialism of commerce, sea power, and investments over the ocean highways."[31] Like the expansionism of the United States in

[31] *International Politics*, 4th ed. (New York: McGraw-Hill, 1948), p. 528.

continental America, that of Russia was unquestionably predatory but presumably was aimed at the absorption of new areas into the state itself and not at a permanent colonialism. She manifested some interest in the African scramble, particularly in Ethiopia, but she gained nothing there, nor, indeed, did she ever possess any noncontiguous territory, except coastal islands, after the sale of Alaska in 1867. Her continental gains between 1850 and 1914 amounted to more than a million square miles, plus an additional two millions in spheres of influence in Persia, Manchuria, and Mongolia.

During the interwar years the Soviet Union concentrated on domestic problems and on building up her industrial and military strength. She made no serious effort toward territorial expansion, and indeed posed as an ardent champion of the liberation of subject peoples and of anti-imperialism. She did put some pressure on Turkey in 1939, she dabbled in Iranian politics, she had a brief period of success in getting her foot in the Chinese door, and she fought a "semi-war" with Japan over Manchuria, but she brought no additional land or people under her control.

After World War II, however, the threat of Soviet imperialism gave rise to the cold war, grave international tensions, rearmament, and the proliferation of anti-Communist alignments. At a time when the imperialism of the traditionally great imperialist powers — notably Britain, France, and the Netherlands—retracted from or were expelled from vast areas of Asia and Africa, the imperialism of the Soviet Union expanded until it encompassed virtually all of Eastern Europe and parts of Asia. The Soviet Union annexed 264,000 square miles of land with a population of more than 24,000,000; and she acquired as satellites parts or all of eleven countries to the extent of more than five million square miles with a population in excess of 731,000,000. Even before this expansion, by her own official census of 1939 Russians comprised only 58 per cent of the population of the Soviet Union.[32]

The threat of further Soviet aggressions and of a still further expanded imperialism became a major anxiety of much of the non-Communist world. This was not the restless expansionism of tsarist Russia, working within the concept of co-existence. Rather, it was believed "the Soviet Union proceeds unswervingly toward the goal of world revolution, with all that this may imply for the free world."[33] In a vital way its motivation differs from that of pre-Communist Russia:

> The distinctive feature of Soviet as compared with traditional Russian motivation . . . is its dynamism. Part of Russia plus part of Marx formed a mixture far more explosive than either ingredient, and helped make a revolution that is still at work in the ferment of our century. Its driving force is enshrined in Lenin's doctrine of the vanguard of revolution: the party must never wait passively for the "inexorable laws of history" to destroy capitalism. Rather it must tirelessly push forward to exploit every weakness, every advantage. History has to be shoved.[34]

This picture of an expansionist and imperialist Soviet Union may have been overdrawn. World communism is an aggressive international movement, and in the postwar years it has expanded territorially beyond the confines of the world's largest state to embrace the world's most populous state, the

[32] See "The Only Empire That Never Stops Growing," *U.S. News and World Report,* May 25, 1956, pp. 40–47.

[33] Christian A. Herter in C. Grove Haines, ed., *The Threat of Soviet Imperialism* (Baltimore: The Johns Hopkins Press, 1954), p. xv. This volume consists of twenty highly competent papers, together with summaries of general discussions, from a conference on "The Problem of Soviet Imperialism," sponsored by the School of Advanced International Studies and held in Washington in August, 1953.

[34] George A. Morgan, "The Motivation of Soviet Policy Toward the Non-Soviet World," in Haines, p. 35.

states of Eastern Europe, and North Korea and North Vietnam. Whether this process should be described as imperialism may well be questioned. In any event, more recently the influence of the Soviet Union within the Communist world, especially in Communist China and most of the states of Eastern Europe, has materially declined.

8. *Other States.* Austria-Hungary, too, felt the urge to imperialism, but like Russia she found an outlet through expansion into contiguous territory rather than in overseas conquest. The lesser powers of Europe — Spain, Portugal, the Netherlands, and Denmark — lacking capital and power to compete with major powers, kept the colonies they had acquired earlier, but only Spain and Portugal made efforts — feeble ones — to expand their holdings, with some modest successes in Africa. Thus five lesser powers — these four plus Belgium — possessed colonies at the outbreak of World War I, but of these only one was of great economic value — the rich Netherlands East Indies, which antedated the new imperialism.

Special Rights and Spheres of Influence. While European states were thus engaged in extending their control over huge parts of the earth in an obvious form of imperialism, some of them were also advancing their interests in remote regions through somewhat more subtle methods. Seeking special rights in states still nominally independent, several of them acquired "leaseholds" in China; Britain, France, Germany, Russia, and Japan established spheres of influence in China, as did Britain, France, Germany, and Italy in Turkey and Britain and Russia in Persia. In some cases, spheres of influence preceded annexation, as was often the case in Africa; in other cases, as in Turkey, they were later completely extinguished. The advantage sought was economic or military, and the form of control was variously tariff regulation, financial supervision, or military occupation. The United States carefully avoided this subtle kind of imperialism in non-American areas, and, in fact, in 1899–1900 she sponsored the Open Door in China to protect American interests against monopoly-minded powers.

American Imperialism

The story of American imperialism may be divided into three parts: continental expansion, overseas expansion, and intervention. The first of these may be disposed of rather quickly, if we disregard the rights of the Indians and think of legal titles as belonging to those European states which staked out generally recognized claims. Most of the territory was acquired by purchase or by other voluntary procedures, but some of it was gained by conquest, notably the Mexican Cession in 1848. Happily, the precedent had been established that possession and settlement should be followed by full political equality as soon as feasible. Consequently, American continental imperialism was short-lived; and it now seldom occurs to anybody to think of it as imperialism.[35]

Overseas Expansion. The many noncontiguous areas which have come under the American flag have been acquired through a variety of processes. Alaska and the Virgin Islands were purchased; the Hawaiian Islands and the Canal Zone were acquired by the voluntary acts of *de facto* governments, although there was chicanery in both in-

[35] Professor Dexter Perkins denied that imperialism was present in American continental expansion, saying that "it is important to draw a clear distinction between expansion and imperialism." He would rule out imperialism from the beginning because of the expectation of incorporation, whereas the definition used in this book would terminate imperialism with the fact of incorporation. The difference is unimportant in this instance, but it would be substantial in the event of long-delayed incorporation. *The American Approach to Foreign Policy* (Cambridge, Mass.: Harvard University Press, 1952), pp. 30–31. Chapter II of this work is a brief and sensible answer to the question: "Is there an American imperialism?"

stances; Puerto Rico, Guam, and the Philippines went to the United States as fruits of victory in the Spanish-American War of 1898, even though the transfer of the Philippines carried some compensation to Spain. Nobody knows just why Alaska was bought, but few people seem to regret it. With the other acquisitions the motives concerned national defense, trade economics, nationalism, and humanitarianism. The Canal Zone, of course, was leased for the building of a canal, regarded as necessary to American defense and American commerce. Many other bits of land, mostly uninhabited islands in the Pacific, have been picked up from time to time. Except for the Philippine Republic, all these areas are politically subordinate to the United States, although some of them now have a large measure of self-government. The Philippines have been independent since 1946, Alaska and Hawaii became states in 1959, and Puerto Rico now enjoys a very special status as a commonwealth associated with the United States.

While imperialism is still present, a number of extenuating considerations should be noted. For one thing, many of these areas are so small that they can never achieve independence and keep it. Furthermore, though not always conspicuously successful in all respects, American imperialism has been comparatively enlightened and beneficent. Finally, "American rule over other peoples has always been rule with an uneasy conscience"[36] — an observation which really means that the American people have been imperialistic less by choice than by real or imagined imperatives. On the positive side, it can hardly be questioned that American control has brought material and cultural advantages to the peoples of these areas beyond what would have been likely under the displaced regimes.

Intervention and the Monroe Doctrine. American intervention in the Western Hemisphere may be thought of as defense imperialism. To understand it we must first examine the Monroe Doctrine. This was first asserted in President James Monroe's address to Congress, in December, 1823, which declared, among other things, that the United States would oppose the transfer of any land on the American continent from one European state to another, the acquisition or further expansion of American holdings by a European state, or the interference by European states in the political affairs of the independent states of the New World. Monroe was prompted to take this position by the threatening actions of the Holy Alliance and by the evident coincidence of British and American interests. The declaration was merely an announcement of executive policy and did not take hold of the American mind until late in the century when it became a basic principle of the nation's foreign policy. The newly born states of Latin America welcomed Monroe's pronouncement. Only much later, when danger of Spanish reconquest had passed and they themselves had grown in strength and national consciousness, did they begin to resent the imperialistic implications of the Doctrine. Latin American states have never quarreled with its objective of preventing foreign intervention in the Western Hemisphere, but the Doctrine did not shield them from the United States herself. Indeed, expanded and formalized by the Roosevelt Corollary in 1904, the Doctrine became the juridical basis of American interventions.

The Caribbean Policy. American imperialism of the early twentieth century in the general Caribbean area soon came to be spoken of as resting on what some writers call the Caribbean Policy and others the Panama Policy. This was simply the resolution of the United States to defend the Isthmus and its approaches, even, if need be, by violating the sovereignty of Caribbean republics. The first step was the establishment of a protectorate over Cuba in 1901, while the

[36] *Ibid.*, p. 32.

United States was still in military occupation of the island as a result of the Spanish-American War. Here the motivation to imperialism was complex: Isthmian defense, determination to end a long-continued nuisance, economics, and humanitarianism. The next step in defense imperialism, the imposition of a protectorate on the new Republic of Panama in 1903, was a means to the single end of canal-building and defense.

Here, in the Canal Zone, we have the diplomacy of American imperialism in its most ruthless form. The Spanish-American War made the United States a world power and an interoceanic canal a necessity. When Colombia delayed the ratification of a lease on an Isthmian strip in her province of Panama — as she had a perfect right to do — President Theodore Roosevelt stormed in, used the navy to support a revolt hatched in the United States — though not by government officials — precipitately recognized the independence of Panama, and in general did enough to warrant his later declaration that "I took Panama."

National defense was also the reason for the interventions in the Dominican Republic (1905), Nicaragua (1913), and Haiti (1915), although in these cases Canal defense was conceived not only in terms of naval and military installations but also in terms of preventing the occupation of Caribbean areas by another great power. This possibility became real when the Hague Permanent Court of Arbitration, in ruling on the claims of blockading powers to preferential treatment in the payment of debts — an outgrowth of the Venezuela blockade of 1902 — put a premium on the use of force in the collection of international debts.

Appraisal. American defense imperialism has been comparatively mild. It has been professedly temporary and rarely exploitative; furthermore, it was almost everywhere terminated by Franklin D. Roosevelt. Going even further, at the Buenos Aires Conference of American States in 1936 Roosevelt renounced the "right" of intervention. Even before 1936, the famous Clark Memorandum of 1928 — a commentary on the Monroe Doctrine prepared by Under Secretary of State J. Reuben Clark — had declared that intervention could not be justified by the Doctrine but implied that it might well be necessitated by considerations of national security.

In 1948 the principle of nonintervention was incorporated in the Charter of the Organization of American States, to which the United States adhered. In the following years many Latin Americans criticized the United States for alleged deviation from Roosevelt's Good Neighbor Policy. During the Kennedy era the United States was accused by Latin American critics of violating the nonintervention principle by its policies towards Castro's Cuba, especially in the Bay of Pigs incident in 1961. Later the same charge was leveled against the Johnson administration because of unilateral intervention by the United States in the Dominican Republic in 1965. Criticisms of American economic and financial "imperialism" and fear of the "Colossus of the North" have been hardy perennials in United States-Latin American relations.

Finally, we should note the charges of imperialism that Communists hurl at the United States in great profusion. They accuse her of imperialism in Japan because of the security arrangements which the Americans and the Japanese have established, and they accuse her of imperialism virtually everywhere because of her foreign aid programs and her sponsorship of mutual security arrangements. Neither charge deserves much serious attention on its own merits; nevertheless, both can still be used effectively as propaganda.

The Balance Sheet of Imperialism

The student of imperialism must do more than contemplate motives and techniques and measure loot. His natural humanitarianism will quickly lead him to ask about its effects on native peoples; his business sense will lead him to ask if imperialism really pays in dollars and cents, or, more often, in pounds, francs, and guilders; and, we hope, his interest in international relations will lead him to ask how imperialism is related to the larger field of world politics.

Effects on Native Peoples. A few facts will suggest the staggering possibilities for the abuse of the native inhabitants of the "backward" areas subjected to imperialistic control. As late as the mid-1920's half the world's land area and one-third of the human race had a colonial status.[37] European states possessed colonies with twice their own total population and twenty times their own area. To put it another way, the area of the colonial empires of the world in the 1920's was roughly eight times the size of the United States, and their population was more than five times that of the United States.

As profit from colonies usually depended upon the use of native labor, and as colonial peoples were strangers to capitalistic propaganda on the dignity of labor, imperialist powers were hard driven to find ways of forcing natives to till the soil, dig for gold, gather rubber, hunt for ivory, or collect coconuts. But the colonial powers were equal to the occasion, and through slavery, forced labor, heavy taxation, and the confiscation of land they succeeded in getting the work done. Sometimes the natives were forced to give a share of their crops or their time to the government; sometimes troops directed forced labor; sometimes a hut tax or poll tax was imposed, payable only in labor or in certain products; sometimes native chieftains were rewarded according to their success in mobilizing their tribesmen for labor; and sometimes laborers were imported from strange and distant lands. Punishment was equally varied: lashing, mutilation, death, separation from wife and family, confiscation of land, or exclusion from hunting grounds.

Imperialist powers have also debauched their colonials in order to obtain revenue. At one time about half the revenue from French West Africa came from taxes on hard liquor. The British profited from the encouragement of gambling and opium smoking in the Far East. There have been no serious charges of debauchery or brutality in American colonies and protectorates, although on one or two occasions United States occupation forces have engaged in bloodletting on a scale to shock the American public. Everywhere there was sharp discrimination against the natives and in favor of white men. Lest we be too quick to conclude that depravity is peculiar to white men, however, we should remember that African chieftains were often equally ruthless with the natives, that black men were collectors of other black men to be sold into slavery, and that the yellow men of Japan and more recently of China have proved amazingly resourceful in the techniques of human torture and abuse. Morality is certainly not a matter of race, and the brutalities of imperialism suggest the disheartening conclusion that it may have little to do with "culture" or with what passes for Christianity.

Even before World War I colonial regimes made some contributions to the welfare of their dependent populations. Most of them undertook to set up public schools and encourage missionaries, and some of them sought to use natives in local government. Nevertheless, except for the United States, the expenditures on education in colonial areas were pitifully small. About eighty per cent of the educational work was done by missionaries,[38] American colonies again excepted. For one thing, imperialist powers learned that education did not make for docility; rather, the reverse was true.

The Philippines remain the most notable instance in which a major colony has been carefully led along the road to complete independence by an imperialist power. The evolution of certain English colonies into

[37] Moon, p. 513.

[38] Buell, p. 353.

"Dominions" is somewhat comparable, although here the granting of independence has not been wholly voluntary. In the postwar era the colonial powers, with varying degrees of preparation and grace, have given independence to most of their colonial possessions. The immediate aftermath of independence has often been a heady experience, but most of the peoples formerly under colonial rule are already discovering that the tasks of economic viability, social cohesion, and political development are even more difficult than the winning of political independence.

The Profits of Imperialism. The answer to the question whether imperialism and colonies have "paid" is complex. In the first place, what is the imperialist power trying to buy? Certainly the United States has never sought to buy an income; instead, it has bought Canal defense, continental security, and the opportunity to do a bit of chest-thumping. Other colonial powers also have bought intangibles, often defense in the form of strategic areas, sometimes merely land to appease an aggressive nationalism. All these, of course, cannot be reckoned in dollars and cents; they may be essentials or trinkets, priceless or valueless.

If, for instance, the incentive to French imperialism after 1880 was the "persistent urge to enhance national prestige and to vindicate French cultural superiority," as one careful student asserts, how well did the investment pay? It is obviously impossible to say, except to note the same writer's observation that "it may prove to be one of the tragedies of the decline of Western influence in Asia that France could not admit the possibility of cultural or political equality with herself, much less the outright surrender of colonial possessions, without seeming to repudiate not only her position as a world power but also the very rationale of her role in world affairs."[39] It is interesting to observe the further judgment that "French politicians after World War II were thus denied the easy rationalization of the eventual surrender of their colonial empire in Indo-China in terms of the vindication of French ideals," whereas "Americans could see in the emancipation of the Philippines a vindication of the principle of 'government by the consent of the governed," and the British accepted the independence of India as fulfillment of the concept of a commonwealth of equal partners. . . ."[40] It might be added that British grace in granting independence to India was largely *ex post facto*.

A major difficulty in a purely economic appraisal of imperialism arises from the fact that often the expenditure is public and the income private. That is to say, a state may use its army and navy, build ports and roads, pay public officials and other necessary personnel, and even offer production subsidies, while the profits from all business enterprises may go into the pockets of private investors, merchants, shippers, and manufacturers. The government's balance sheet may be in the red, and still the colony may be a rich prize for a limited few, with some of the profits undoubtedly trickling through to the general population of the imperialist power. It may be impossible to determine whether the improvement of a state's economic well-being warrants the taxation required to sustain a colonial empire. In any event, imperialism in the sense of physical control of distant territories by a colonial power is largely a thing of the past. Whether colonies did or did not "pay," whatever the standards or tests of profit and loss may have been, is becoming more and more a question of academic interest only.

Hobson's *Imperialism*. Perhaps the ablest pioneer in the study of the economics of imperialism was John A. Hobson (1858–1940), an English writer of the liberal school. Early in the twentieth century he

[39] Cady, pp. 295–296.

[40] *Ibid.*, p. 295.

concluded that colonies gave no assurance of the control of raw materials, that they formed no trading areas of substantial value, that they gave negligible relief to population pressures, and, in general, that they made little or no contribution to the economic welfare of the colonizing state. His test of the good and bad of imperialism was largely an exercise in comparative economic statistics; thus tested, imperialism was "a depraved choice of national life, imposed by self-seeking interests which appeal to the lusts of quantitative acquisitiveness and of forceful domination surviving in a nation from early centuries of animal struggle for existence." "The laws which, operative throughout nature, doom the parasite to atrophy, decay, and final extinction," declared Hobson, "are not evaded . . . by rendering some real but quite unequal and inadequate services to 'the host.' "[41]

Although Hobson later gave more attention to the political causes of imperialism, he never abandoned his conviction that economic causes were paramount. The impact of his *Imperialism* was immense: "No other book has been so influential in spreading the doctrine of economic imperialism," and Hobson's theory has had "a more direct and apparent influence on the writing of history, at least in the English language, than that of Marx and the Marxists."[42] The qualification is well made, for among Asians the generally accepted theories of imperialism are those of Lenin and Mao Tse-tung.

Clark's *Balance Sheets*. Later students followed Hobson's lead in checking the ledgers to see if imperialism paid. The results of such enterprises, tolerantly remarked a later scholar, "may not be very satisfactory or conclusive from a broad economic point of view, because, as in the case of tariffs, there are a number of questions that cannot be answered statistically, but, so far as it goes, drawing up balance sheets of imperialism is a salutary exercise."[43] For the most part these salutary exercises dealt with single colonies or with the colonies of a single imperialist power; but in 1936 Grover Clark published the results of a comprehensive appraisal, subsidized by the Carnegie Endowment for International Peace. His ambitious project, completed just before Mussolini, Hitler, and World War II rang the curtain down on the old imperialist order, rates today as the broadest analysis of the economics of both winning and maintaining colonies.

In the preface to *The Balance Sheets of Imperialism* Clark asserted that three main claims had been made about the value of colonies: they provided important outlets for population; they made possible valuable trade opportunities that would not otherwise be available; and they added to the security of the colonizing state by assuring it of raw materials in both war and peace. He added that "the actual record . . . demonstrates conclusively that each of these three claims is essentially fallacious."[44] This is not to say that individuals did not profit; and of course it is true that states might buy an improved military position and, at a heavy cost, provide some degree of emotional satisfaction, people being what they are.

[41] Hobson, pp. 367, 368.
[42] Winslow, pp. 94, 106.

[43] *Ibid.*, p. 55.
[44] Clark, pp. 9–17. George Padmore entered the following dissent from Clark's conclusions: "From a purely imperialistic point of view, Belgian colonial policy has been most profitable. According to Mr. Robert Godding, Colonial Minister in the exiled wartime Belgian government, 'during the war, the Congo was able to finance all expenditures of the Belgian Government in London, including the diplomatic service as well as the cost of our armed forces in Europe and Africa, a total of some £40 million. In fact, thanks to the resources of the Congo, the Belgian Government in London had not to borrow a shilling or a dollar, and the Belgian gold reserve could be left intact.' " Cited in George Padmore, "Comparative Patterns of Colonial Development in Africa: 3. The Belgian System," *United Asia,* VII (March, 1955), 89.

Kohn's *Reflections*. The Communist leaders of the Soviet Union and Red China have succeeded so well in their campaign to make imperialism and colonialism wholly odious things and to heap unrelieved guilt on the Western powers that many westerners, like most Asians, have come to accept the indictment as proved. It is therefore refreshing to have a scholar of the stature of Hans Kohn declare that "Western speakers should not put themselves on the defensive, but state the facts as they are." He himself stated some of the facts in a brief paper entitled "Reflections on Colonialism."[45]

Professor Kohn declared that Americans themselves are in part responsible for propagating the curious idea "that colonial 'empires' are established by sea powers, whereas expansion into contiguous land masses does not produce 'empires' or colonialism." The American reaffirmation of this fifteenth-century judgment was made to defend the morality of expansion into the West and Southwest in the course of the nineteenth century. Later, with Soviet coaching, the people of Asia have accepted this view; in consequence, the United States and her allies are colonial powers but not so the Soviet Union. Kohn denies the charge that "Western imperialism introduced poverty, wars, racial discrimination, and economic exploitation into Asia and Africa." Those conditions have existed from time immemorial. "As far as historical memory goes" Asian peoples have enslaved other Asian people, and African tribes have exterminated or enslaved other African tribes. Western imperialism, though guilty of "many injustices and cruelties . . . has awakened and vitalized lethargic civilizations." The standards of justice now used in condemning imperialism are products of the West — "developed by the Western world and only by the Western world."

[45] Hans Kohn, "Reflections on Colonialism," Chapter 1 in Robert Strausz-Hupé and Harry W. Hazard, eds., *The Idea of Colonialism* (New York: Frederick A. Praeger, 1958), pp. 2–16.

Colonialism, continued Kohn, has nothing to do with race or race superiority, "one of the most bewildering myths of the present time." He pointed out that rule by one people of another is an old story in Europe and that resentment of it has been manifested as strongly there as in Asia and expressed in "the very same words which are now used in Africa and Asia by the anticolonialist leaders."[46]

The Principle of Trusteeship

The story of imperialism — or colonialism, or whatever word may be used — is not one of unrelieved exploitation and abuse. The civilized world, in fact, has come a long way since the early sixteenth century, when the states of Europe began to extend their control into America, Asia, and Africa with "no principles of law, policy, or morality to restrain them."[47] Progress was for a long time very slow, with only enlightened individuals like Bartolomé de las Casas and Francis de Victoria raising their voices in behalf of the oppressed peoples of other lands. It was not until the late eighteenth century that humanitarianism became organized and effective. One of the first tangible results was legislation against the slave trade. In 1837 a British Parliamentary committee asserted what was in substance the principle of trusteeship, and by mid-century "the eventual self-determination of colonies was viewed with equanimity by nearly all British statesmen."[48] The United States occupied Cuba and the Philippines at the close of the Spanish-American War with the promise to grant them independence in due course. Nevertheless, "the principle that dependencies are a trust of civilization had influenced theory

[46] *Ibid.*, pp. 7, 10–12.

[47] Quincy Wright, *Mandates under the League of Nations* (Chicago: University of Chicago Press, 1930), p. 6.

[48] Quincy Wright, "Mandates," *Encyclopaedia of the Social Sciences* (New York: The Macmillan Company, 1937), X, 88. Used by permission of The Macmillan Company.

more than practice when the [First] World War broke out . . . but the principle . . . was beginning to have effects in practice."[49]

The endeavors of the imperialist powers to put into effect the principle of trusteeship related to a number of aspects of colonial life: land ownership, native labor, imported labor, foreign capital, education, health and preparation for self-government. Some efforts were made to break up the large plantations on which natives worked and to encourage private ownership of small land tracts. Higher wages, better working conditions, and controls on the involuntary movement of workers were substituted for more drastic methods of persuasion in some colonies. Some states entered into agreements to modify the severity of the conditions under which laborers were obtained in large numbers from China or elsewhere for service in colonial areas. In a few instances, notably that of the Basel Mission Trading Company, which had interests in Africa and India, dividends were limited to a given percentage, with profits above that figure to be expended in behalf of the colonials. Governments in some cases appropriated money for education: between one and four per cent of the budgets of British colonies in West Africa were so expended about the time of World War I, and American contributions in the Philippines and Puerto Rico ranged from thirty to forty per cent. Various missionary bodies spent far more than governments. Medicine, too, was long the province of missionaries, although late in the nineteenth century army physicians were sent to many colonies. The work of William Gorgas in Panama and that of Walter Reed in Cuba are perhaps the best-known instances of the rendering of medical service by an imperialist power. The training of local personnel for handling the lower administrative posts was a conspicuous feature of British colonial government, and the coaching of Cuba, the Philippines, and Puerto Rico for self-government was a declared policy of the United States from the time of the separation of those lands from Spain.

Despite these contributions and many others, the record of service by imperialist states was not impressive. The encouraging thing about it was its acceleration: there was clearly a growing sense of responsibility. Furthermore, it must be remembered that in respect to certain aspects of government service and policy all states, even the most advanced, have been doing no more than groping their way forward at home during the past few decades. This is true in labor relations, control of foreign capital, vocational training, and education, sanitation and health, and, in a formal sense at least, in preparation for citizenship. The imperialist states have enough to answer for without being charged with criminal offenses for being products of their own times.

Imperialism has often encountered powerful resistance in the homelands of the great imperialist powers. Anti-imperialist associations of various kinds sought to influence government policy in Great Britain, Germany, and the United States. Newspapers too raised a cry against colonialism or against some of the abuses which it permitted. The press of Great Britain was especially critical, and it is to be given much of the credit for the distinct improvement in the treatment of colonial populations which began about 1910. But long before national reform made any significant modification in colonial practices the idea of international responsibility had taken root. The international conferences of Berlin in 1885 and Brussels in 1890 gave concrete form to the growing conviction that the control of backward areas was a trust for the benefit of the natives and for the good of the world. As Allied statesmen looked forward to the drafting of the peace terms that would end World War I, they saw that some form of international supervision

[49] Wright, *Mandates under the League of Nations*, pp. 10, 11.

of colonial peoples not yet ready for independence would please the idealists and at the same time somewhat assuage the feelings of the Germans and Turks who were about to be shorn of their colonies. The Mandates System which emerged from the Paris Peace Conference of 1919 was the answer to the rising demand for international guardianship. This system, administered by the League of Nations, and its successor, the Trusteeship System, administered by the United Nations, have removed many of the evils of the old imperialism. They are further discussed in Chapter 14.

Colonialism Today

In 1959 British Prime Minister Harold Macmillan said in a speech in Moscow: "Imperialism is an epoch in history, not a present reality." Even Jawaharlal Nehru sometimes spoke in a similar vein, although in 1954 he declared: "We talk about the crisis of the time and many people do it in different ways. Probably in the United States of America the crisis of the time is supposed to be communism versus anti-communism. Maybe so to some extent. Well, the crisis of the time in Asia is colonialism versus anti-colonialism."[50] Professor D. W. Brogan and others have frequently referred to "the post-imperial age."[51] Certainly the great colonial empires have passed into history.

Early in 1963 an American newspaper surveyed the remnants of colonial empires and found that "there are still 99 dependent areas, U.N. trust territories and South Africa's League of Nations mandate." More than one-fourth of these "bits and pieces" of colonialism were less than 50 square miles in area. Only nine of these territories were larger than 100,000 square miles, and by 1966 five of these had become independent or were on the verge of independence. The United Nations Trusteeship Council has almost run out of business, even though the task of decolonization is still unfinished. It has only two trust territories under its jurisdiction: New Guinea, administered by Australia; and the Strategic Trust Territory of the Pacific Islands, administered by the United States. "With few exceptions, only the hard core now remains."[52] "For all practical purposes, there are really only two Western colonial powers left: Portugal, with its huge Angola and Mozambique possessions in Africa, and South Africa, whose large South West Africa mandate was handed to it by the League of Nations after World War I."[53]

But if the colonial age is over, the "colonial hangover" continues. "To the still smarting 'old' colonial powers of the West, there is a new colonialism in the Soviet Union's comparatively recent acquisitions on shores as widespread as the Baltic and the Pacific." Some of Communist China's expansionist and aggressive policies, especially along its borders, are labeled by critics as "Red imperialism." One of the favorite terms in the lexicon of Communist propaganda against the West is the term "imperialism" or "colonialism." Above all, the peoples formerly under colonial rule harbor bitter memories of real or alleged indignities and exploitation of the recent past and are still suspicious of the designs of the former colonial powers. "To the newly independent nations of Asia and Africa, . . . colonialism is anything that involves the white man dominating the dark, the big powers preva.ing

[50] Quoted in *Indiagram*, issued by the Embassy of India, Washington, D.C., No. 526 (August 31, 1954).

[51] See, for example, two articles by Professor Brogan: "The Post-Imperial Age," *New Republic*, December 17, 1956; and "The End of Empire," *Saturday Evening Post*, November 29, 1958.

[52] "Issues Before the Seventeenth General Assembly," *International Conciliation*, No. 539 (September, 1962), p. 61. See also "Issues Before the 22nd General Assembly," *International Conciliation*, No. 564 (September, 1967), p. 55.

[53] Warren Unna, "Western Colonialism Dwindles to 99 Bits and Pieces," *Washington Post*, January 27, 1963.

over the small."[54] To peoples in these new nations the Communist charges of "neo-colonialism" seem to have some real basis in fact. "The genesis of 'neo-colonialism' might be described in horse-breeding terms as by Communism out of Embarrassment. . . . The 'neo-colonialist' argument is that the imperialists, though surrendering political power, retain real control by economic, military, or cultural means, or by a combination of all three. Thus 'trade and aid,' which a disinterested witness might easily see as mainly benefiting the new nation, becomes, in the words of President Nasser, 'a veil to dominate the resources of nations and to exhaust them for the benefit of exploiters.' "[55] When he was still President of Ghana, Kwame Nkrumah, in obvious imitation of Lenin's classic *Imperialism, the Highest Stage of Capitalism*, wrote a little book entitled *Neo-Colonialism: The Last Stage of Imperialism*.[56] Thus "neo-colonialism" is regarded as a new and more insidious form of imperialism, widely prevalent and particularly pernicious and dangerous.[57]

The United Nations has been a main forum for the continuing struggle against "colonialism in all its manifestations," to use the words of the final communiqué of the Bandung Conference of 1955. Although the majority of the original members of the UN came from the Western world, more than one-half of its members today are states that have attained independence since the end of World War II, most of them located in Asia and Africa. The former colonial powers and their supporters have been increasingly put on the defensive in the organs and agencies of the United Nations.

The assault on colonialism reached a climax in 1960, when 17 new members were admitted and when the General Assembly passed a historic Declaration on the Granting of Independence to Colonial Countries and Peoples.[58] The declaration condemned "the subjection of peoples to alien subjugation, domination, and exploitation" and called for "immediate steps . . . to transfer all powers to the peoples of [dependent] territories, without any conditions or reservations." A special committee for the implementation of the declaration was created. Soon known as the Committee of 24, it has become the General Assembly's "overseer of decolonization," and a significant organ of the UN system.

More and more, in the United Nations and in other forums, anti-colonialism has become a complex struggle against vestiges or any revival of the old types of imperialism, against "neo-colonialism," and for the acceleration of the process of de-colonization. Indeed, as Mario Rossi noted, " 'colonialism' refers today far less to colonies than to the process of decolonization, which represents one of the most complex and threatening problems facing humanity."[59]

While the vast imperialist recession of the postwar years and the labors of many organs and agencies of the UN have enormously reduced the territorial limits of imperialism and the harshness of imperialist practices, the problem of still-dependent peoples seems to have risen to new heights of harassment.

[54] *Ibid.*

[55] Review of Brian Crozier, *Neo-Colonialism* (London, 1964), in *NATO Letter*, XIII (October, 1965), 29.

[56] New York: International Publishers Co., 1965. It has been alleged that this book caused the United States to turn down a $3 million loan to Ghana and to send a sharp note of protest to Nkrumah.

[57] The term "neo-colonialism" has also been used, although not very frequently, to refer to certain policies of Communist states. In his State of the Union message in 1963, for example, President Kennedy charged that "as older colonialism recedes . . . the neo-colonialism of the Communist powers stands out more starkly than ever."

[58] General Assembly Res. 1514 (XV), 14 December 1960, adopted by a vote of 89 to 0 with 9 abstentions (including France, the United Kingdom, and the United States).

[59] *The Third World* (New York: Funk & Wagnalls, 1963), p. 60.

Aroused spokesmen of these peoples — some of the loudest come from now-liberated lands — may inveigh against colonialism in all its forms, but they too often accept the Leninist theory of imperialism and speak from resentment and frustration rather than from sober judgment.

The great ages of imperialism are over. Whether the present era may more properly be characterized as the post-colonial era or as "the last stage of imperialism," the major battles against imperialism have been won or are in the process of being won, and a new relationship is being forged between former colonial powers and the peoples of recently dependent areas. But for millions of people in the former colonial areas and in areas still not free, the main external struggle is still, as Nehru described it some years ago, "colonialism versus anti-colonialism."

SUGGESTIONS FOR FURTHER READING

ADAM, THOMAS R. *Modern Colonialism: Institutions and Policies.* Garden City, N.Y.: Doubleday & Company, 1955.

BUELL, RAYMOND L. *The Native Problem in Africa.* 2 vols. New York: The Macmillan Company, 1928.

CADY, JOHN F. *The Roots of French Imperialism in Eastern Asia.* Ithaca: Cornell University Press, 1954.

CHARMIAN, C. E. *The Trusteeship System of the United Nations.* New York: Frederick A. Praeger, 1956.

CLARK, GROVER. *The Balance Sheets of Imperialism.* New York: Columbia University Press, 1936.

CROZIER, BRIAN. *Neo-Colonialism.* London, 1964. A critical analysis.

EASTON, STEWART C. *The Rise and Fall of Western Colonialism.* New York: Frederick A. Praeger, 1964. Subtitled: "A Historical Survey from the Early Nineteenth Century to the Present."

EGERTON, HUGH E. *A Short History of British Colonial Policy,* rev. ed. London, 1932.

FIELDHOUSE, D. K. *The Colonial Empires.* New York: Delacorte Press, 1966. An interpretation of "the entire history of modern colonialism."

FURNIVAL, J. S. *Colonial Theory and Practice.* London, 1948. A classic work.

HAILEY, LORD. *The Future of Colonial Peoples.* Princeton, N.J.: Princeton University Press, 1944.

HAINES, C. GROVE, ed. *The Threat of Soviet Imperialism.* Baltimore: The Johns Hopkins Press, 1954. Contributions by several competent scholars.

HALL, H. DUNCAN. *Mandates, Dependencies and Trusteeships.* New York: Carnegie Endowment for International Peace, 1948.

HANCOCK, W. K. *Wealth of Colonies.* London, 1950.

HOBSON, J. A. *Imperialism: A Study,* 3d ed. London, 1938. A classic work, originally published in 1902.

KOEBNER, R. and H. D. SCHMIDT. *Imperialism.* London, 1964. Traces various meanings of the term "imperialism."

KOLARZ, WALTER. *Russia and Her Colonies.* New York: Frederick A. Praeger, 1953.

LANGER, WILLIAM L. *The Diplomacy of Imperialism, 1890–1902,* 2d ed. 2 vols. New York: Alfred A. Knopf, 1951. A major work.

LENIN, V. I. *Imperialism, the Highest Stage of Capitalism.* New York: International Publishers Co., 1933.

MERK, FREDERICK. *Manifest Destiny and Mission in American History.* New York: Alfred A. Knopf, 1963.

MOON, PARKER T. *Imperialism and World Politics.* New York: The Macmillan Company, 1926. Still one of the best analyses of the subject.

NADEL, GEORGE H. and PERRY CURTIS, eds. *Imperialism and Colonialism.* New York:

The Macmillan Company, 1964. A collection of readings.

Nkrumah, Kwame. *Neo-Colonialism: the Last State of Imperialism.* New York: International Publishers Co., 1965. An impassioned political argument.

Panikkar, K. M. *Asia and Western Dominance.* New York: The John Day Company, 1954. A highly critical account of "the Vasco da Gama epoch of Asian history," by a well-known Indian scholar-diplomat.

Perkins, Dexter. *The American Approach to Foreign Policy.* Cambridge, Mass.: Harvard University Press, 1952. Chapter II, "Is There an American Imperialism?"

Pratt, Julius W. *America's Colonial Experiment.* Englewood Cliffs, N.J.: Prentice Hall, 1950. A survey of American colonialism and imperialism.

Priestley, Herbert I. *France Overseas: A Study of Modern Imperialism.* New York: Appleton-Century, 1938.

Snyder, Louis L., ed. *The Imperialist Reader: Documents and Readings on Modern Expansionism.* Princeton, N.J.: D. Van Nostrand Co., 1962. Characteristics, techniques, arguments for and against, and historical evolution of modern imperialism. Last two parts deal with "The Twilight of Western Imperialism" and "The Emergence of Communist Imperialism."

Stalin, Josef. *Marxism and the National and Colonial Question.* London, 1936.

Strausz-Hupé, Robert and Harry W. Hazard, eds. *The Idea of Colonialism.* New York: Frederick A. Praeger, 1958. Essays by 17 authorities, prepared for the Foreign Policy Research Institute, University of Pennsylvania.

Townsend, Mary E., with the collaboration of Cyrus H. Peake. *European Colonial Expansion since 1871.* Philadelphia: J. B. Lippincott Co., 1941.

Winslow, E. M. *The Pattern of Imperialism.* New York: Columbia University Press, 1948. Challenges the thesis that imperialism is economic in origin.

8 War as an Instrument of National Policy

War needs no documentation to prove its horrors. It destroys and ruins lives beyond number; it makes anything like normal existence impossible; it imposes immense burdens on national economies and imperils the freedoms of everyone; it endangers man's very existence on this planet. It is the great curse of the international society, the endemic disease of the nation-state system. As the *ultima ratio* of power, it is always lurking in the background of international politics. The problem of war, as Edward M. Earle declared, is "the greatest unresolved riddle in politics,"[1] and the coming of total war and the nuclear and space age has given it a new and greater urgency.

The study of war differs in form from the study of other instruments of national policy. With respect to diplomacy, propaganda, political warfare, and economic instruments we were concerned with the many techniques and devices available to states that care to use them; but we are not here concerned with such military considerations as strategy, tactics, and logistics. Instead we shall note the various approaches to the study of war, inquire into the causes of war, determine what functions war has performed so well that states have been and still are unwilling to surrender their right to use it, and evaluate some of the many suggested ways by which wars might be avoided.

Approaches to the Problem of War

There is, of course, nothing new about the problem of war. Wars and rumors of war have filled the pages of history. It is quite unnecessary to review the gloomy record. It suggests that war, and not peace, is the "normal" condition of "civilized" human society. This conclusion seems to be substantiated by the elaborate documentation of the types and frequency of wars throughout history in Quincy Wright's classic two-volume work, *A Study of War*. In 1960 a Norwegian statistician, with the use of a computer, "announced that in 5,560 years of recorded human history there have been 14,531 wars, or . . . 2.6135 a year," and that "of 185 generations of man's recorded experience . . . only ten have known unsullied peace."[2] In the twentieth century the incidence of wars has not abated, and potentially, and sometimes actually, their scale has increased tremendously.

In spite of the fearful lessons of two

[1] Edward M. Earle, "The Influence of Air Power upon History," *Yale Review*, XXXV (Summer, 1946), 592.

[2] "On War as a Permanent Condition," *Time* Essay, *Time*, September 24, 1965.

global wars and the even more frightful prospects of a nuclear holocaust, limited wars of varying types have been as frequent since 1945 as during most of the more martial periods of pre-nuclear history. *Time's* essay "On War as a Permanent Condition," in the issue of September 24, 1965, reported that fighting was then going on in the Indian subcontinent, in Yemen, in the Sudan, and in the Congo; and that in Cyprus, in the Malacca Straits, in Angola, and in the Dominican Republic armed forces "kept their powder dry and their gunsights blackened." It listed 40 wars since 1945, but the list included the Cuban missile crisis of 1962, a major confrontation between the United States and the Soviet Union which did not lead to military hostilities, and several examples of guerrilla wars or civil disturbances. It pointed out that 22 of the 40 crises involved Communists, eight were anti-colonial struggles, and three were "outright land grabs"; that in only three cases — Britain and France in Suez and Russia in Hungary in 1956, and the United States in Cuba in 1961 —"have nuclear-armed nations indulged in high-handed power plays in the past 20 years"; and that in only one crisis have nuclear powers opposed each other directly. The experience in the postwar years has been discouraging and alarming to all who are concerned with keeping the peace, although nuclear exchanges have been avoided and the importance of preventing a recurrence of total war in the nuclear era has been increasingly recognized. But over man's future hang the shadow of the atomic cloud and the haunting fear that his institutions — and his imagination — are inadequate to cope with the problems of human survival.

On the other hand, Professor Arnold Toynbee insists that war is not man's normal condition. In support of this contention he calls attention to the fact that whereas before the reign of the Emperor Augustus the Romans were seldom at peace, for 265 years, from 31 B.C. to 235 A.D., peace was generally preserved, with insignificant and temporary interruptions; that prior to the invasion by Nazi Germany in 1940 Norway, the land of the Vikings, "had been at peace for 126 years without a break"; and that whereas "during the millennium ending in 221 B.C., the Chinese world was as full of wars as the contemporary Mediterranean world, . . . since the political unification of China in 221 B.C., China has normally been at peace down to this day, with some exceptional bouts of internal disorder of the kind that punctuated the shorter lived Roman peace."[3]

Nevertheless, if war is not "the normal condition of man," it does seem to have been a recurring phenomenon in almost all parts of the world at almost all periods of history. "It is doubtless safe to say," declared Raymond Fosdick, "that half the tragedies in the long story of the human race have been due to the inability of men to find any method except organized slaughter as a means of solving their rivalries and antagonisms."[4] War has occurred with alarming frequency under all forms of political and social order; "recourse to war appears to follow no particular pattern in terms of race, form of government, social order, or stage of development after the appearance of warfare and property interests some five thousand years ago."[5]

Obviously any approach to the problem of war, like war itself, is likely to become bogged down in technicalities and in contradictions. The complexities and ramifications of the subject can be better understood from an analysis of some of the more detailed

[3] Arnold J. Toynbee, "War Is Not the Normal Condition of Man," *New York Times Magazine*, November 7, 1965, pp. 122, 124.

[4] Raymond Fosdick, "We Need New Words and New Faiths," *New York Times Magazine*, December 19, 1948.

[5] Charles Hodges, "Why War?" in F. J. Brown, Charles Hodges, and J. S. Roucek, *Contemporary World Politics* (New York: John Wiley & Sons, 1940), p. 25.

studies, such as Quincy Wright's *A Study of War* and the third volume of Pitirim Sorokin's *Social and Cultural Dynamics*. The possible approaches to the study of war are numerous. Wright suggests the following: the legalistic, the technological, the sociological, the psychological, the biological, the ideological, and the synthetic.[6] Another fruitful approach would be the historical; as we have already suggested, it is a sad but undeniable fact that much of human history can be written in terms of wars and the preparations for and the consequences of wars. The literature on the major wars of history is enormous. One student has estimated that filing cases filled with records of World War II would reach from New York to Chicago.

What is War?

Before we continue with our analysis of the problem of war, it may be well to attempt a few simple definitions. What is war? How does it differ from other "nonamicable modes of settlement" such as police actions, the application of sanctions, blockades, and boycotts? Mussolini refused to admit that Italy's attack on Ethiopia in 1935–36 was war. Technically, the military operations that began in Korea in June, 1950, were not war, although they involved major military units and brought heavy casualties. Today the term "war" is used in many different ways. We have become accustomed to speaking of cold war, hot war, limited war, total war, conventional war, unconventional war, civil war, guerrilla war, preventive war, political warfare, propaganda war, psychological warfare, and so on. The Communists often use such terms as "imperialist wars" and "wars of national liberation." Wars may be limited in various ways — in geographical scope, in weaponry (conventional rather than unconventional), in duration, in size of contending forces, in degree of actual commitment, in frequency, and in intensity. Total war may refer to total commitment, but in the nuclear age it usually refers to a war fought by many combatants, including the superpowers, with all the arsenals of atomic and other unconventional weapons. In other words, in contemporary parlance total war refers to World War III. In our time the term "war" has been extended to include many kinds of hostile acts besides the direct use of armed force, and the borderlands between war and peace are becoming more and more blurred.[7] The spectrum of human conflict is indeed a wide one.

Most authorities, however, still define war in a relatively narrow sense. According to the *New English Dictionary* it is a "hostile contention by means of armed forces, carried on between nations, states, or rulers, or between parties in the same nation or state; the employment of armed forces against a foreign power, or against an opposing party in the state." After presenting this relatively direct and simple definition the same dictionary devotes six and a half columns of fine print to various interpretations and usages of the term "war."

Hoffman Nickerson, in the *Encyclopaedia Britannica,* states that "war is the use of organized force between two human groups pursuing contradictory policies, each group seeking to impose its policy upon the other." This is a broader and somewhat more general definition than the first. Concerning the qual-

[6] See Appendix III, "Approaches to the Study of War," in Quincy Wright, *A Study of War* (Chicago: University of Chicago Press, 1942), I, 423–437.

[7] "Lewis Richardson attempted to arrange all 'deadly quarrels' in a single series from those in which one man was killed (murder) to those in which 10 million were killed (World War II). Such episodes would not normally be called war unless casualties amounted to at least one thousand." Quincy Wright, "History of the Concept of War," in T. S. Rama Rao, ed., "Studies in the History of the Law of Nations," *The Indian Year Book of International Affairs,* 1964, Part II (Madras: The Indian Study Group of International Law and Affairs, University of Madras, 1964), p. 117. See also Lewis Richardson, *The Statistics of Deadly Quarrels* (Pittsburgh: Boxwood Press, 1960).

ifying clause, Nickerson explains rather cryptically that it applies even to the party which is trying to resist aggression, since this party is trying to impose upon the aggressor its policy of retaining its freedom and independence.

One of the most famous and at the same time one of the most often misquoted commentaries on war is that of the great German student of war, Karl von Clausewitz. "War," wrote Clausewitz, "is only a part of political intercourse, therefore by no means an independent thing in itself . . . war is nothing but a continuation of political intercourse with an admixture of other means."[8] This statement — it can hardly be called a definition — reflects a rather cynical view of international relations, but it is useful in calling attention to the broader setting in which the nature of war must be examined;[9] and, ironically, it seems to have a particular relevance to the present condition of "neither war nor peace."

Quincy Wright examined many formal definitions of war and many characteristics of it. In the broadest sense he defined war as "a *violent contact* of *distinct* but *similar* entities," and in a narrower and more exact sense as "the *legal condition* which equally permits two or more *hostile groups* to carry on a *conflict* by *armed* force."[10] He also distinguished between "war in the material sense" and "war in the legal sense." In the material sense the boundaries between war and peace are not clearly demarcated; war, in other words, "is a phenomenon distinguished not by *qualitative* but by *quantitative* differences." In the legal sense, as defined in recent international law, war is "a legal condition or state" and there is a sharp line between war and peace.[11]

Professor Wright discerned various stages in the nature and position of war over the centuries:

> History suggests that war has at times been considered (1) a customary reaction to circumstances jeopardizing group solidarity and security, (2) a legitimate instrument of state policy, (3) an indispensable means for maintaining justice, (4) a legitimate procedure for settling quarrels between sovereigns, (5) an inevitable condition of the coexistence of sovereign states, and (6) an illegitimate form of state behaviour. While most of these conceptions have been held by some members of most human groups, the first is characteristic of primitive societies, the second of ancient

[8] *On War,* translated by O. J. Matthijs Jolles (New York: Modern Library, 1943), Book VIII, Chapter 6, p. 596.

[9] "While modern war is waged on the diplomatic, economic, and propaganda fronts, as well as on the military front, and while in the broadest sense, the art of war co-ordinates all these elements to the purpose of victory, yet in the narrower sense used in the discipline, the art is confined to the military aspect. This embraces the organization, discipline, and maintenance of the morale of the armed forces on land, sea, and air; the invention, development, and procurement of weapons; the provision of transport and the movement of forces; the conversion of policies into military objectives, such as enemy territory to be occupied, enemy forces or resources to be destroyed, and civilian or neutral interests or morale to be attacked; and the strategy of campaigns and tactics of battles, sieges, blockades, or air raids to achieve these objectives. The larger problems of military policy, such as determination of the national policy it is to serve; the preparation of national opinion, economy, and institutions for war; the co-ordination of military preparation and action with diplomacy, policy, and government; the co-ordination of national military action with that of allies; the determination of specific war aims and peace terms; and the conduct of diplomacy, propaganda, and economic relations with enemy, neutral, and allied countries lie in the realm of international politics and diplomacy. Yet the conduct of war is so closely related to these activities that the art of war cannot entirely ignore them. It is in fact subordinate to the art of politics." Quincy Wright, *The Study of International Relations* (New York: Appleton-Century-Crofts, 1955), pp. 149–150.

[10] Wright, *A Study of War* I, 8; II, 685. Italics in original. For various definitions of war, see Quincy Wright, "Changes in the Conception of War," *The American Journal of International Law*, XVIII (October, 1924); and "History of the Concept of War," pp. 116–118.

[11] Wright, "History of the Concept of War," pp. 116–118. Italics in original.

societies, the third of medieval societies, the fourth in the first stage of modern society, the fifth in international law prior to World War I, and the sixth in the new international law elaborated in general conventions since that war.[12]

War in the Modern Period

No period of human history has been free of war, whether of tribe against tribe or of nation against nation. Fortunately, it is not necessary for our purposes to attempt a historical survey of the wars of the past. The results of many of these wars are amply recorded in the pages of history, but the issues which precipitated them are often buried with the bones of the victims.

The general tendency of warfare in the modern period — since about 1500 — has been to become more terrible in almost every respect. This tendency has been aggravated by the development of new and vastly more powerful weapons, the evolution of total war, especially as practiced by ruthless modern totalitarian regimes, and by many other concomitants of the age of industrialism, of militarization, and of ideological struggle on an unprecedented scale. Quincy Wright noted: "War has during the last four centuries tended to involve a larger proportion of the belligerent states' population and resources and, while less frequent, to be more intense, more extended, and more costly."[13]

In his seminal work *A Study of History* Arnold Toynbee presented an arresting analysis of the trend of war in modern times. By the latter part of the eighteenth century, he argued, war "was manifestly on the wane, not so much because wars were less frequent . . . as because they were being conducted with more moderation." The fundamental reason for this phenomenon, he believed, was that war "had ceased to be a weapon of religious fanaticism and had not yet become an instrument of national fanaticism." From about the time of the French Revolution, according to Toynbee, we have been in the period of "nationalistic internecine warfare, reinforced . . . by the combined 'drive' of energies generated by the recently released forces of Democracy and Industrialism." Moreover, "this is a typical pattern of a time of troubles: a breakdown, a rally and a second relapse."[14] This analysis, though gloomy, is helpful in that it seems to give perspective to the troubles of our own days. It seems quite clear that the roots of these troubles extend far back into the past, as Toynbee forces us to realize, and that the seeds of some of the rankest plants of the twentieth century, such as total war and modern totalitarianism, are to be found in the Industrial and French revolutions, which were thought to herald a new and happier order for men.

Although one might be heartened by Quincy Wright's analysis, which noted a development from "the first stage of modern society" when war was considered to be "a legitimate procedure for settling quarrels between sovereigns," to the later stages, when it changed from "an inevitable condition of the coexistence of sovereign states" to "an illegitimate form of state behavior,"[15] unhappily it must be admitted that even in international law the status of war is still indeterminate. Thus, the last half-century has witnessed the paradox of a growing movement for the outlawing of war and for building the institutions of peace on a sounder basis and at the same time no diminution in the frequency of war.

Modern warfare has made science and technology its handmaidens, with revolution-

[12] *Ibid.*, p. 120.

[13] Wright, *A Study of War*, I, 248. See Professor Wright's analysis of the fluctuations of war in modern history, pp. 235 ff.

[14] Arnold J. Toynbee, *A Study of History* abridgment of Vols. I–VI by D. C. Somervell (New York: Oxford University Press, 1947), pp 283–284, 552–553.

[15] Wright, "History of the Concept of War," p 120.

ary effect. Vannevar Bush, who headed the Office of Scientific Research and Development in the United States during World War II, declared that the technological innovations of World War I "made mechanized warfare possible," that the scientific developments of World War II "rendered conventional military practice obsolete," and that "over the horizon now loom radiological and biological warfare, new kinds of ships and planes, an utterly new concept of what might be the result if great nations again fly at each other's throats. It is this which makes the thinking hard."[16]

The Causes of War

Much thought and study have been devoted to the causes of particular wars, and of war in general; but even experts differ sharply on these questions, and to the masses of the people the whole subject is a very confused one. Some of the confusion arises from a failure to distinguish between the immediate and the underlying causes of wars. Professor Sidney B. Fay, writing in the 1920's, found the distinction useful in his pioneer work on *The Origins of the World War.* After a careful study of the available documents from the archives of the belligerent powers and other original materials, Fay concluded that "the greatest single underlying cause of the War was the system of secret alliances which developed after the Franco-Prussian War." Other underlying causes which he singled out for special mention were militarism, nationalism, economic imperialism, and the newspaper press.[17] These and many other causes have been emphasized by other students of diplomacy. Quincy Wright summarized some of the manifold approaches to this problem:

> Writers have declared the cause of World War I to have been the Russian or the German mobilization; the Austrian ultimatum; the Sarajevo assassination; the aims and ambitions of the Kaiser; Poincaré, Izvolsky, Berchtold, or someone else; the desire of France to recover Alsace-Lorraine or of Austria to dominate the Balkans; the European system of alliances; the activities of the munition-makers, the international bankers, or the diplomats; the lack of an adequate European political order; armament rivalries; colonial rivalries; commercial policies; the sentiment of nationality; the concept of sovereignty; the struggle for existence; the tendency of nations to expand; the unequal distribution of population, of resources, or of planes of living; the law of diminishing returns; the value of war as an instrument of national solidarity or as an instrument of national policy; ethnocentrism or group egotism; the failure of the human spirit; and many others.[18]

Some of these causes are immediate and some are basic; some refer to specific events or activities, while others call attention to deep-seated forces and underlying trends. Each of these aspects would be well worth careful investigation and appraisal. Volumes have been written on almost every one of them. The abundance of materials should not be surprising, for a study of the causes of war leads into the most baffling labyrinths of international affairs.

Among the most exhaustive analyses of the causes of war have been those sponsored by the Conference on the Cause and Cure of War and by the Social Science Research Committee of the University of Chicago. Both studies were made over a period of several years in the interwar period. In the *Findings* of the Conference on the Cause and Cure of War, published in 1925, more than 250 causes were itemized, under four headings: political, economic, social and psychological. Professor Quincy Wright summarized the findings of the Committee in a

[16] *Modern Arms and Free Men* (New York: Simon and Schuster, 1949), pp. 3, 16.

[17] *The Origins of the World War* (New York: The Macmillan Company, 1929), I, 32–49. Used by permission of The Macmillan Company.

[18] Wright, *A Study of War,* II, 727–728.

series of lectures published under the title *Causes of War and Conditions of Peace.* The causes of war were portrayed as being in a sense the obverse of the conditions of peace. Professor Wright related them to the following aspects of the world situation: "(1) a state of opinion violently hostile to the existing state of affairs; (2) inadequacy of international organization to deal with conflicts; (3) inadequate system of law; (4) unstable equilibrium of material forces." He also emphasized the fact that economic and political factors entered powerfully into every one of these considerations.[19]

In the two formidable volumes which he devoted to *A Study of War,* Wright pointed out that the causes of war could be approached from many different angles. "War," he wrote, "has politico-technological, juro-ideological, socio-religious, and psycho-economic causes";[20] and a substantial section of his work was built around this rather technical classification. Tell A. Turner, in a book entitled *The Causes of War and the New Revolution,*[21] listed forty-one causes of war, under these headings: economic, dynastic, religious, and sentimental. Professor Charles Hodges, in a textbook in international relations published in the early 1930's, drew up an elaborate chart listing twenty-one causes of war under four "primary causes": social, political, strategic, and economic. The social causes were grouped under five subheadings: religious, racial, cultural, chauvinistic, and fear. The political causes were broken down into monarchic, domestic, nationalistic, imperialistic, diplomatic, and juridic. The strategic causes related to territory, disarmament, armament, world position, and vital interests. Under economic causes were grouped population, commercial policy, foreign investment, indemnities, and neutral rights.[22] Obviously, even the subheadings are general rather than specific in character, and would require an extended breakdown and analysis in any meaningful study of war. In truth, it would seem that of the listing of causes of war there is no end.

It should be pointed out, however, tnat many commentators, sometimes with considerable objectivity and sometimes with none, have stressed one factor, or at most a very few factors, as the major cause of war. Thus Communist dialecticians distinguish between certain kinds of wars, such as imperialist wars, revolutionary wars, and wars of national liberation; the seeds of war, they allege, are inherent in capitalism and in imperialism, which Lenin described as capitalism in its last desperate stages.

Wickham Steed expressed the belief that fear is the chief cause of war. "The feeling of insecurity," he wrote many years ago, "and the fears which it engenders, are undoubtedly the strongest potential causes of war in the world today." These causes seem to be closely associated with the prevailing pattern of international society, composed as it is of a large number of "sovereign" states and lesser political units, with no adequate number of "sovereign" states and lesser political units, with no adequate regulatory devices or agencies for peaceful readjustment on a supranational level. Here, perhaps, we come close to a major cause of modern war. "There is a cause of wars between sovereign states," declared Arnold Brecht, "that stands above all others — the fact that there are sovereign states, and a very great many of them."[23] In quoting this comment Professor

[19] Quincy Wright, *Causes of War and Conditions of Peace* (New York: Longmans, Green & Co., 1935). See also Clyde Eagleton, *Analysis of the Problem of War* (New York: The Ronald Press Company, 1937), pp. 55–56.

[20] Wright, *A Study of War,* II, 739.

[21] Boston: Marshall Jones Co., 1927.

[22] *The Background of International Relations* (New York: John Wiley & Sons, 1932), p. 555.

[23] "Sovereignty," in Hans Speier and Alfred Kahler, eds., *War in Our Time* (New York: W. W. Norton & Company, 1939), p. 58.

Wright supplied a very useful addendum: "Perhaps it would be no less accurate to attribute war to the fact that there are no sovereign states but a great many that want to be."[24] The same eminent authority also suggested that wars occur because of the absence of an effective system of law and of international organization to control the use of force among nations.

Clearly, then, the causes of war are many and varied, and they may be analyzed in many different ways, all of which are likely to be at the same time useful and artificial. Under present conditions much of the difficulty can be associated with the nation-state system, and with the generally anarchic framework of contemporary international relations. We should remember, however, that wars have occurred under all types of political organization from the earliest recorded history of man. This is not to say that man is by nature warlike; it suggests, rather, that man has never been successful in evolving political, economic, and social institutions of which the war institution has not been a part. This failure is particularly tragic in the era of nuclear and biological weapons and of modern totalitarianisms.

It is well to remember also that the roots of the war system are deeply imbedded in human society and institutions, and that there is no simple or single explanation for such a complex phenomenon as war. "A war, in reality," as Quincy Wright has pointed out, "results from a total situation involving ultimately almost everything that has happened to the human race up to the time the war begins."[25] War occurs, of course, only where there is a profound conflict of interests, "material or ideal, actual or traditional";[26] but doubtless the distinguished Catholic historian Don Luigi Sturzo was correct in stating: "War does not arise merely from differences of ideas nor from a clash of interests. Both these factors are overshadowed by a long-range psychological preparation and conditioning."[27]

The causes of war are related to war as an instrument of national policy in that they tend to establish the objectives of national policy. Agitation for the recovery of lost territory may become so strong that the leaders of a state are driven to accept the recovery as an objective of state policy; and they may find no way to attain that objective except by war. Militarism, nationalism, or the press may whip the people of a state into such a state of frenzy that they may demand a spectacular feat of arms. Imperialists, investment interests, or traders in foreign goods may foster the conviction of national economic insecurity or of national humiliation unless stipulated concessions be extorted from a foreign country. Munition makers may point to the preparations of another state and urge a country into preventive war. Invariably, when "something" causes a war between states it does so because the "something" has become identified with the national policy of one or more of the states.

The Functions of War

The recurrence of war throughout history surely cannot be explained in terms of human cussedness or original sin. Unless war served some useful purpose, or at least unless rulers, governments, and peoples fancied that it did, it would not have become such a hardy perennial of the international society. Some social institutions came into being and then passed rather quickly from the scene, as the conditions which gave rise to them changed; others, like slavery, persisted for centuries but then lost much of their former utility and gradually assumed less formidable

[24] Wright, *A Study of War*, II, 896.

[25] *Ibid.*, I, 17.

[26] Alvin Johnson, "War," in *Encyclopaedia of the Social Sciences* (New York: The Macmillan Company, 1937), XV, 341. Used by permission of The Macmillan Company.

[27] *Nationalism and Internationalism* (New York: Roy Publishers, 1946), p. 2[illegible].

proportions; others have endured throughout all ages of civilization. War belongs to the third group; and no matter how bitterly men may attack it, or how convincingly they may prove that its costs far exceed the values gained from it, it will survive as long as the rulers of mankind are unable to agree on an acceptable alternative to it. The hard fact is that, as Clyde Eagleton pointed out, "war is a method of achieving purposes."[28]

The evidence contradicts those persons who in their hatred of war loudly insist that war has never "paid." It does not sustain assertions like the following: "The most unfortunate thing about war is that it accomplishes nothing. All the effort that goes into it is wasted; all its sacrifices are vain. The issues between nations, over which they go to war, still remain when the war is done; war does not settle anything."[29] On the contrary, the evidence points inescapably to the conclusion that war has often paid — and, moreover, that it has paid not only for bad men working in bad causes but often for good men in good causes. For that reason it persists as an instrument of national policy. The attack on war must rest not upon misconceptions of its utility but upon the realization that it is an inhumane and barbarous way of achieving even good ends — that it should never be available to bad causes and never necessary to good ones. It has been a clumsy, costly, and indeed a rather stupid means of achieving certain ends and its frequent use has been a humiliating confession of man's inability to find more civilized means.

The point that we wish to emphasize here, however, is that war has persisted because of its social utility — that it has performed functions for which there have been no other workable procedures. While these functions tend to overlap, and while it is difficult to distinguish between primary and secondary functions and between proper and improper ones, we shall characterize them and discuss them as the major function and the minor functions.

Major Function: The Righting of Wrongs and the Enforcement of Rights

It seems indisputable that war has performed functions that have been socially desirable, and that it has made contributions quite beyond the capabilities of any other means. Professor Eagleton noted that "for centuries, war has been regarded as a means of remedying unjust situations, of settling disputes, of enforcing rights."[30] Professor Shotwell added that "war has been used as an instrument against criminal aggression as much as it has been the instrument of aggression itself. It has played a beneficent role in history as well as a criminal one." He then asked two pointed questions: "Where would this nation be now, or for that matter any other civilized nation, if it had not met oppression with force and asserted its determination to maintain as against the world those institutions which embody its political career? Are we of this generation to take the strange position that, after having made thorough use of the war tool to establish liberty, to secure democracy and to create our modern states, we are now to deny ourselves these uses?"[31]

The student of history can point to countless instances in which war was the means by which peoples escaped from oppression which to them had become intolerable. The American Revolution ended a regime which the colonists had come to regard as denying the natural rights of man; the French Revolution overturned a corrupt and autocratic

[28] Eagleton, p. 5.

[29] Willard Waller, "War in the Twentieth Century," in Willard Waller, ed., *War in the Twentieth Century* (New York: Dryden Press, 1940), p. 31.

[30] Eagleton, p. 5.

[31] James T. Shotwell, *War as an Instrument of National Policy* (New York: Harcourt, Brace, 1929), pp. 15, 16.

monarchy; the Latin American Wars of Independence removed the heavy hand of Spain and gave to Latin Americans the opportunity to build their own lives and fortunes; the American Civil War ended once and for all the question of national unity and it brought the abolition of Negro slavery; wars in the Balkans brought release from Turkish misrule; and the Spanish-American War gave Cubans relief from the tyrannical rule of Spain, and Americans relief from the constant nuisance of bloodshed and conspiracy on their doorstep. Who is to say that in these and many other cases war did no "good"? Who is to say that war produces only evil, that it is never rightfully accepted as a proper course of action, that it may not again serve to rescue the oppressed and bring better lives to many people?

Although the Communists do not attempt to glorify war itself, they appear to believe that they cannot achieve their final goals without war, and they preach the inevitability of conflict with the capitalist world. Lenin, in a famous passage, predicted "a series of frightful collisions between the Soviet Republic and the bourgeois states." Stalin declared that "capitalism can only be overthrown by means of revolution which will take the form of protracted and violent struggle to the death." Mao Tse-tung wrote: ". . . the central task and the highest form of revolution is to seize political power by force, to solve problems by war. . . . Political power emerges only from among the guns. Yes, we do uphold the revolutionary "omnipotence of war.' . . . This is not bad. It is good, it is Marxist. . . . The whole world must be recreated with guns."[32] These views are in accord with the familiar Marxist distinction between just and unjust wars.

There are many people today who would actually prefer war to any existing alternative. These are by no means only the would-be conquerors or the fanatics of our time. Millions of poverty-stricken, ignorant, and isolated people, living under almost intolerable conditions, might welcome another war in the hope of bettering their lot in life; in any event, they have little or nothing to lose, and to them life is cheap. Many living in the Soviet-dominated states of Eastern Europe, as well as refugees from this area, feel that war offers the only hope of regaining their lands and their freedom; they can see no endurable future except through the holocaust of war, and no reassuring messages over the Voice of America can convince them that there is any other hope. Presumably Chiang Kai-shek and his followers would welcome an American military involvement with Communist China, or even World War III, as a possible means of destroying the Communist regime and of enabling them to return to the Chinese mainland. In short, while it is doubtless true that the masses of mankind long desperately for peace, and that this longing is shared by most of their political leaders, this feeling is by no means universal.

We must draw a distinction between war of an earlier time and that of today. War was the instrument of kings, and later, of peoples, for the destruction of the power of local tyrants and the unification of states. It is impossible to see how the same desirable ends could have been achieved by any means except war. Professor Shotwell says that "to eliminate this privilege at any earlier stage of political development [before World War I] might have endangered the whole process of internal evolution, for liberty within the state, so slowly and so hardly won, had still to be maintained against possible external foes."[33] Today the picture is changed, but only in part. Internal security seldom requires more than police action — although

[32] Quoted by Shen-Yu Dai, "Mao Tse-tung and Confucianism" (Unpublished dissertation, University of Pennsylvania, 1952), pp. 114, 131, from Mao Tse-tung, *Selected Writings of Mao Tse-tung* (Harbin, Manchuria, 1948).

[33] Shotwell, p. 14.

no state would surrender the right to make war on its own rebellious elements — but has the external aspect changed? Can states safely renounce or abandon the right to make war?

It is easy to argue that the misery and abuse which have produced war should not have existed, or to insist that some other remedy should have been found. Both contentions must be readily granted. The fact remains, however, that the conditions did exist and that the people concerned saw no alternative — if, indeed, there was one. Short of long-suffering submission, which few persons would defend, it seems difficult or impossible to avoid the conclusion that resort to war has at times in the past been the only hopeful course and that on many occasions the hope has been warranted. The judgment appears unavoidable that war has demonstrated real utility in the righting of wrongs and the enforcement of rights.

The Minor Functions of War

We shall give particular attention to two of the minor functions of war, and only passing mention to a number of alleged functions. The distinction between the major function and the first minor function, as we use the terms, is imprecise. There are many occasions in which military force has not been used to right a wrong or enforce a right and yet has profoundly affected the course of history. A case in point would be the conquest of the New World. It is such instances that we have in mind here.

The Reconstruction and Modernization of the Political and Social Order. In his significant book *War as an Instrument of National Policy,* Professor James T. Shotwell, one of the great modern crusaders for peace, asserted frankly: "War . . . has been the instrument by which most of the great facts of political national history have been established and maintained. It has played a dominant role in nearly all political crises; it has been used to achieve liberty, to secure democracy, and to attempt to make it secure against the menace of its use by other hands." "The map of the world today," wrote Shotwell, "has been largely determined upon the battlefield. The maintenance of civilization itself has been, and still continues to be, underwritten by the insurance of army and navy ready to strike at any time where danger threatens."[34] Professor Quincy Wright developed this same theme: "War has been the method actually used for achieving the major political changes of the modern world, the building of nation-states, the expansion of modern civilization throughout the world, and the changing of the dominant interests of that civilization."[35]

It may be superfluous to remind anyone that the great states of modern times have been the products of war, often of many wars. England, France, Spain, Russia, China, Japan, and the United States acquired their domains and their territorial integrity through war. Civilization and Christianity were carried to the New World by conquest. The resources of weaker lands and peoples have been made available to the stronger powers through exploitation made possible by the might of arms. Markets, too, have been opened by the British Royal Navy, by the ships of Commodore Perry in Japan, and by the fleets and soldiers of many states in a hundred lands. The technological progress of mankind has involved the use of raw materials from every section of the globe, and many of these have been surrendered at sword's point. The White Man's Burden of Rudyard Kipling and William McKinley was carried by men with a Bible and some trinkets in a satchel and guns in their hands. In

[34] *Ibid.*, p. 15.

[35] Wright, *A Study of War*, I, 250; see also the section on "The Political Utility of War," II, 853–860. Wright explained that war may be "a valuable instrument of policy" under certain "conditions of law, of military technology, of foreign policy, and of international relations."

short, war has been a chief maker of the modern world — its states, its industries, its morality, and its cultural pattern.

Admittedly, the world of today is not as most of us would have it. Can it not therefore be argued that in making the world as it is war has performed a disservice rather than a service, that it can be credited with no useful function? Is not the nation-state system, itself the product of war, the greatest obstacle to peace? The answer is that the absence of war as we have known it could not possibly have meant the evolution of a cooperative, peaceful world. The alternative to the building of powerful states would have been the continuation of a decentralized order of things, the persistence of literally thousands of quarreling, backward centers of population. Man's use of war — often the only instrument that he knows — has given us the modern world.

The Exaltation of Moral and Spiritual Qualities. Evidence abounds that in the past many persons have thought that war contributed to the attainment of higher moral and spiritual qualities. Some appear to have believed that the sacrifices of war were a form of atonement for past sins, others that suffering called attention to unrealized blessings, and still others that bloodshed and deprivation showed the superficiality of the materialistic ambitions that had led people to neglect spiritual values. Sentiments of this kind seem to be less common in more recent times — or at least less frequently expressed.[36] Perhaps they have been a casualty of total war.

We shall limit our example to a single crisis in American history, noting only what one editor had to say about the moral and spiritual values of war when the Civil War was getting under way:

> The impulses, emotions and purposes that have moved . . . men for the last week have done more to elevate them than all the sermons of all the ministers of America could do in a century. They have grown better, larger, nobler, purer men for this experience. Verily war is a means of grace to them. . . . So, bowed with sadness that it must be, we bend to the necessities of war, believing that it is best for us. Honorable war is better than dishonorable peace. We believe that when this struggle passes by, we shall be a better and stronger nation for it. The medicine is harsh, but who will dare to say that it is not needful? Let it come, then; and may God in his mercy make it the blessing to us which he means it to be![37]

The sentiments expressed by the *Daily Republican* were by no means universal. Some editors took sharp exception to them, declaring that war could only debase and harden men.[38] Nevertheless, the evidence is clear that in the United States on the eve of the Civil War an articulate segment of public opinion believed that war had or might have moral and spiritual functions. These sentiments, of course, are by no means peculiar to Americans. They have been expressed in other democratic states; and nobody needs to be reminded of the extent to which spokesmen of totalitarian states extolled the virtues of war during the 1930's and early 1940's.

Other Functions. Some writers, particularly Germans, have insisted that war is a necessary process for weeding out weak and inferior peoples, leaving room for the growth and development of strong peoples. Early in World War II it was "an official credo of several powerful nations . . . that war, else-

[36] Some more restrained sentiments on this subject may be found in A. Lawrence Lowell, *Public Opinion in War and Peace* (Cambridge, Mass.: Harvard University Press, 1923), p. 267; and Henry M. Wriston, *Prepare for Peace* (New York: Harper, 1941), p. 13.

[37] "War as a Means of Grace," editorial in Springfield, Mass., *Daily Republican,* April 20, 1861; reprinted in Howard C. Perkins, ed., *Northern Editorials on Secession* (New York: Appleton-Century, 1942), II, 1066–1067.

[38] See Perkins, II, 1063–1096.

where than on the battlefield, makes such peremptory demands upon a nation that it revitalizes the productive and creative processes of the whole of society."[39] One of the better-known proponents of this line of thinking was General Friedrich von Bernhardi. His famous pamphlet *Germany and the Next War,* published in 1914, is full of such passages as the following:

> We are accustomed to regard war as a curse, and refuse to recognize it as the greatest factor in the furtherance of culture and power. . . . War is a biological necessity of the first importance, a regulative element in the life of mankind which cannot be dispensed with, since without it an unhealthy development will follow, which excludes every advancement of the race, and therefore all real civilization. . . . Without war, inferior or decaying races would easily choke the growth of healthy budding elements, and a universal decadence would follow.[40]

Declarations of this sort require no serious refutation, particularly in an age of mechanized warfare. Addiction to the military life, the chance possession of essential war materials, and the overall capacity to wage war are certainly not adequate criteria for separating "healthy budding elements" from "inferior or decaying races." By Bernhardi's own standards, Germans have twice been proved to be the kind of "race" that should be removed as an impediment to civilization, a totally nonsensical judgment.

Other writers have also advanced controversial views of the functions of war: that foreign wars are sometimes essential to unity and peace at home; that war may provide a less painful outlet for surplus population than starvation and disease; that it has stimulated inventions; and that it has produced a veritable revolution in industrial and agricultural production. Probably all of these claims can be verified in some instance or other, but in nearly every case they seem to magnify what was gained and to minimize what was paid.

Approaches to Peace

The reading of history with its never-ending recital of wars that were long and bloody and often futile, together with the realization of how many ruined lives they entailed, must lead the reader to raise the question: Wasn't there some other way out? He must conclude that in many instances war could have been prevented by patience, information, and fair dealing. But what course was open to leaders of states who possessed those assets, who sincerely wished to avoid war but at the same time believed that fundamental interests were at stake? We must recognize that in many instances they did find a way out; one can readily imagine that the history of wars that might have been would be far bloodier than the history we actually have. But what about the wars that were fought? Could they have been averted by some means? Were there not practicable alternatives?

We shall here consider a number of suggested ways by which war might be prevented. One such list was published a number of years ago by John Foster Dulles. Although prepared before the outbreak of World War II, Dulles' "False or Inadequate Solutions" may still be regarded as a thoughtful and useful compilation. We shall examine these in their original order, together with Dulles' critical comments, after which we shall note other approaches that also have gained support.

Dulles' "False or Inadequate Solutions"[41]

1. Education as to the horrors of war. The weakness of this approach to peace is

[39] Jesse D. Clarkson and Thomas C. Cochran, *War as a Social Institution: The Historian's Perspective* (New York: Columbia University Press, 1941), p. 180.

[40] Pp. 11, 18, 20.

[41] *War, Peace and Change* (New York: Harper, 1939), pp. 72–99. Dulles also presented some interesting proposals for the prevention of war (pp. 100 ff.).

that it relies primarily upon emotion. Preaching the violence and suffering of war appeals to people who are concerned about their welfare and that of their friends and families. It is "ineffective as a mass influence because . . . war as it becomes totalitarian ceases to be a selfish pursuit." The emotions of wartime lead people to make precisely the kind of sacrifices that normally they would hate most to make, for sacrifice becomes the measure of patriotism. Moreover, devotion to the country's cause is not left to chance; "when critical times arise, control of mass emotions tends to pass into official hands."

2. Education to the Fact that "War Does Not Pay." The inadequacy of this approach is also explained by the fact that "war is represented as a sacrificial act." Giving war this character "cuts the ground from under those who would stop war by emphasizing the risks to persons which are inherent in it." Furthermore, "we cannot gain our goal by persuading people that self-interest is the primary consideration, in terms of which all else must be judged"; "the remedy is not to be found in deprecating unselfishness and extolling material or personal selfishness as the desirable standard of human conduct."

3. Isolation and Economic Internationalism. The purpose here is evidently to show the fallacy of isolation and of economic internationalism as two opposite approaches to peace and to suggest that something like a middle course is preferable to either.

Those who favor isolation argue that contacts produce conflicts; therefore to avoid conflicts, avoid contacts. As Dulles saw it, the weakness of the argument is twofold. First, it is difficult or impossible to isolate nations against ideas, and "the precipitant of modern war is primarily ideology, and . . . economic contacts are seldom its cause." Second, "the refusal of certain nations to facilitate economic intercourse with others may take a form which will itself be a contributing cause of war because it gives rise to a sense of repression and confinement." When states feel "shunned or isolated" by the isolationist policies of other states, "they tend to develop emotional reactions and attitudes" and become "abnormally sensitive"; consequently, they "are apt to strike out against others who are weaker than themselves."

Economic internationalism is an unsatisfactory approach to peace for several reasons. "It may be artificially stimulated [as by credit] to a point where a reaction becomes inevitable which causes isolation more complete or more repressive than would otherwise have been the case." A debtor state may be driven to economic regimentation, autarchy, and an exaggerated nationalism. The creditor state may become irritated and resort to "aspersions" on the debtor state. Furthermore, ill will may arise against an exporting state because an importing state's domestic interests may be adversely affected by "obnoxious imports." Finally, since too much foreign trade may make a country dependent upon others and thus subject to embarrassment if the trade should be cut off, "a large measure of economic independence is desirable."

4. Renunciation of War. The outstanding formal effort to outlaw war by international agreement was the Kellogg-Briand Pact, or the Pact of Paris, of 1928. The pact, eventually adhered to by more than sixty nations, condemned "recourse to war for the solution of international controversies" and renounced war "as an instrument of national policy." While the pact is of some importance in the development of international law, it was powerless to prevent even small conflicts like the Italo-Ethiopian war, and it was ignored by the Nazi and Fascist leaders whose actions precipitated World War II. Dulles put his finger on the weakness of the Pact of Paris when he pointed out that it sought to "realize a desirable result without taking any of the steps essential to achieve it." "So long as force is the only mechanism for assuring international changes," concluded Dulles, "then a purported renunciation of force is a nullity. Far from being sacred, it would be iniquitous, even if it were practicable, thus to put shackles on the dynamic peoples and condemn them forever to acceptance of conditions which might become intolerable."

5. The League of Nations. The Covenant of the League was "well conceived and susceptible of practical, constructive evolution." Article 19 authorized the Assembly to "advise the reconsideration by Members of the League of treaties which have become inapplicable and the consideration of international conditions whose continuance might endanger the peace of the world." Here was the germ of peaceful change, without which change by violent means becomes inevitable. The dominant members of the League, however, mistakenly conceived peace as the preservation of the status quo and the League as an instrument for that purpose. In fact, "true 'peace' means merely the avoidance of one particularly obnoxious *method* of change by facilitating a less obnoxious method — that 'security' can be attained only at the price of insecurity." As the Treaty of Versailles had been drawn up in an atmosphere of emotion and so embodied many injustices, only a willingness to promote peaceful change could prevent an eventual breakdown of peace itself. Largely because France and her European allies felt that their safety and even their existence would be imperiled by a slight concession which might lead to a whole series of concessions, the League Covenant became, for "all practical purposes, an alliance to perpetuate rigidly the post war status. 'Sanctity of treaties' became the League slogan, and those seeking change were branded as potential 'aggressors.'" The League was further incapacitated for its proper role by the refusal of the United States to join, by the withdrawal of certain dissatisfied powers, and by Britain's disengagement of her foreign policy from the framework of the League. The failure of the League was thus due not so much to its structural defects as to the unwillingness of its members to utilize the instrumentalities which the Covenant had created and put into their hands.

6. Nonrecognition of the Fruits of Aggression. This approach is "essentially another variant of the doctrine that peace means a rigid and unchanging world structure." In a practical sense it holds an intermediate position between the Pact of Paris and the League of Nations. All three aimed at preserving the status quo. The Pact of Paris involved no sanctions whatever, or at least no formal sanctions; the League provided the possibility of severe economic and military sanctions, nonrecognition imposed only the comparatively gentle sanctions of diplomatic disapproval, with a possible embarrassment or disruption of trade relations.

This approach has several weaknesses. Nonrecognition is not calculated to deter a major power; it will influence only weak powers, especially those under the influence of some major power. It is not a policy which can be consistently and continuously applied, for it is based upon the absurd assumption that changes brought about by force are not changes at all. Such changes could accumulate to the point where the political relations of the states of the world would be hopelessly confused. We can condemn the use of violence in domestic society, for provision is made there for peaceful evolution and change, but we cannot "indiscriminately carry forward moral judgments of aggression into a society within which neither political nor ethical solutions are operative." Finally, "there are too few nations which have so controlled their own conduct that their officially expressed moral indignation rings true to others." Nonrecognition, when applied under circumstances of this kind, "serves as an irritant rather than a pacificator."

7. Armament. This approach to peace is supported by two theories. The first of these, and one officially presented by a number of states at the Hague Peace Conference, held that the more frightful war became "the less likelihood there was of its becoming a reality." While this argument appears to have some validity, two interrelated considerations make the theory unworkable and dangerous. For one thing, as we have noted before, the prosecution of war has shifted "from an operation motivated by selfishness to an operation motivated by unselfishness"; the effect of this change is, of course, to arouse a sacrificial spirit among people which in part disregards or even embraces the frightfulness of modern war. Second, "the creation of vast armament in itself calls for a condition midway between war and peace. Mass emotion on a substantial scale is a prerequisite." Moreover, "a sense of peril from abroad must be engendered." Once these conditions have been brought about, "we have gone a long way on the path toward war" and "it is dangerous to rely upon reasoning as to consequence to restrain against the small additional transition necessary to the actual attainment of war." A third consideration must also be added: the effect on the internal standard of living and on domestic tranquillity of huge expenditures for armaments.

The second theory of peace through armament was supported by France during the years following World War I. This called for heavy armaments for the status quo powers and disarmament for the states which would soon be seeking to revise the status quo in their own favor. The peace treaties saw to it that Germany, Austria, Hungary, Bulgaria, and Turkey were disarmed and forbidden to rearm. Two errors underlie this approach. First, it assumes that the classification of powers will be permanent, an assumption soon invalidated in this instance by the switch of Italy from the presumably satisfied powers to the dissatisfied powers. This was accomplished under the aggressive leadership of Mussolini. The theory also presumes the absence of national dynamics, a condition that will never exist. In addition, the success of this approach is contingent upon the continuous maintenance of superior armaments by the status quo countries. Actually, however, imagined security invariably leads to carelessness and to opposition to the cost of "needless" military establishments. A false sense of security eventually prompts these states to undo the very conditions on which they are dependent for the continuance of peace. Dissatisfied states are not so deluded about their national interests. War always comes again.

8. Disarmament. If armaments are conducive to war, should it not follow that disarmament is the road to peace? This appears not to be the case. "If limitation of armament comes, it will be a result rather than a cause of peace." It is more realistic to argue that "so long as the force system prevails, then armament has a utility" and that "so long as it has utility, so long will armament survive and the greater the utility, the greater will be the armament (subject to limitations of finance)." Armament limitation has been agreed upon in a few instances, but only for short periods of time when conflict between the participating states seemed impossible. While disarmament cannot be the means of obtaining peace, vast armaments do produce economic waste and emotional aberrations which become precipitating causes of war. We are unlikely ever to have "armament placed permanently on a non-competitive basis unless we first demote force from its role of supreme arbiter of change."

9. Sanctions. In his discussion of the weaknesses of sanctions, Dulles apparently had in mind both police force action and the operation of general collective security organizations. If "public force serves as deterrent to individual acts of violence [within states] . . . why should we not in the international field adopt a similar procedure?" The idea is right, but it requires some important qualifications. Domestic order is possible because the state provides peaceful means for resolving conflicts between individuals — not because the state is always prepared to suppress violence among a substantial part of the population. As long as peaceful procedures are available to them, most people will accept these alternatives to force. A police force can deal effectively only with "marginal and usually abnormal elements" which do not accept the social forms agreeable to most of the people. "We must in the international field look upon sanctions as adapted only to play a comparable role." Sanctions cannot themselves be "a primary method of avoiding violence. This task is one to be achieved by the creation of a balanced form of world society. Until this is achieved it is premature to consider sanctions. When it is achieved, the role of sanctions will have shrunk to small dimensions and the problem of their form will be one of manageable proportions." As it is, "the premature development of sanctions" has led to their discrediting in many quarters.

Sanctions also have two other weaknesses. First, they may operate as a challenge to states. "Thus the dynamic nations, feeling themselves to be the likely subject of sanctions by the status quo nations, are spurred on to build up their armament and attain economic self-sufficiency." When states react in this manner, the result is the accentuation of nationalism and the encouragement of the very policies which the sanction concept was supposed to prevent. Another weakness of this approach is that it encourages the tendency toward undeclared wars. This comes about because the invocation of sanctions is contingent upon the announcement by some high authority of the existence of a state of war. In an effort to avoid commitment, the authority can pretend to see no war when none has been declared. The failure to declare war can thus disrupt the whole system of sanctions.

Mr. Dulles concluded his analysis of "false and inadequate solutions" with these words: "Most peace efforts have had only ephemeral results because they are limited to striking directly at an undesired manifestation. There is a failure to deal with causes which, if unaltered, inevitably produce that which we would avoid."

Mr. Dulles' analysis revealed some of the weaknesses of nine frequently suggested approaches to peace. His discussion was somewhat academic and theoretical, and was, of course, far from exhaustive. Other aspects of some of these approaches will be examined elsewhere in this book.

Two frequently proposed approaches to peace do not appear in Mr. Dulles' list. These are the development of international law and the establishment of world government. We shall therefore explore their adequacy as ways to avoid war. We shall also give special attention to a remarkable document, *Pacem in Terris,* and to the new role of the Vatican in world affairs. First, however, we shall give some further consideration to one of the most persistent of all proposals — disarmament and the limitation of armaments.

The Limitation of Armaments

The struggle for the limitation of armaments — often called disarmament, although technically there are considerable differences between the two terms — has been motivated by the belief that the building up of armed strength by one state leads to belligerence on the part of that state and to feelings of insecurity on the part of other states, which then desperately augment their own strength or resort to preventive war. It is also motivated by a desire to reduce the staggering budgets which result from competition in armaments. Sir Edward Grey, British Foreign Minister on the eve of World War I, declared that the increase in armaments "produces a consciousness of the strength of other nations and a sense of fear. Fear begets suspicion and distrust and evil imaginings of all sorts, till each Government feels that it would be criminal and a betrayal of its own country not to take every precaution, while every other Government regards every precaution of every other government as evidence of hostile intent."[42] A report issued by the American Friends Service Committee in 1951 expressed essentially the same view: "In the realm of arms, one nation's common sense is another nation's high blood pressure. Our arms create fear in Russia; Russian arms create fear in us. By seeking to deter the Russians by military might, we are inevitably forced to plunge the world into an arms race, and arms races are not conducive to security. Indeed, each new measure and countermeasure adopted by the principals in the name of defense has the effect of intensifying insecurity in both countries."[43]

There has long been a consciousness of an inverse relationship between disarmament and security, and security has almost always won out. Unless some system can be evolved whereby nations will actually be more secure with less armed strength, disarmament will indeed remain a "pipe dream." It was no mere accident that instead of evolving formulas for reducing "the staggering burden of armaments" the First Hague Conference issued a Convention for the Pacific Settlement of International Disputes and established a Permanent Court of Arbitration. The Second Hague Conference, presumably called for the same purpose as the first, dropped the question of disarmament from its agenda. Very early in the prolonged discussions of arms limitation in the League of Nations, the question of security was raised, particularly by France; it persisted throughout the lifetime of the League. There is much justification for Professor Eagleton's rather contemptuous comments on the efforts of the League to bring about disarmament: ". . . the League held hundreds of meetings in an impressive effort to reach agreement. Yet its whole history can be summed up in the change of the name of one of its committees, which started as a committee on the Reduction of Armaments, and ended as a committee on Arbitration, Security, and Disarmament. The latter order of words represents the evolution of the thinking of the League."[44]

The discussions of armament reduction in the United Nations have followed a similar pattern. Indeed, the need for security has become all the greater in the age of the "iron curtain" and the atomic bomb. It accounts for the strong insistence on the development of effective methods of inspection and control before any nation is willing to reduce its armed strength; it is one of the major reasons for the failure of the efforts of the Atomic Energy, Conventional Armaments, and Disarmament Commissions. Of the five principles which were laid down for the guidance of the new Disarmament Commission in the Assembly resolution of January 11, 1952, three were concerned with security.

The point of view which has determined the policy of all great powers was succinctly described by Leo Pasvolsky:

> My reading of history convinces me that there is more risk and danger in a continuing disparity of armed strength than in efforts to

[42] *Twenty-Five Years, 1892–1916* (New York: Stokes, 1925), I, 89. Used by permission of Sir Cecil Graves, K.C.M.G., M.C., and Messrs. Hodder & Stoughton, Ltd.

[43] *Steps to Peace: A Quaker View of U.S. Foreign Policy* (Philadelphia: American Friends Service Committee, 1951), pp. 13–14.

[44] Eagleton, *International Government,* rev. ed. (New York: The Ronald Press Company, 1948), p. 395.

correct that disparity. . . . there are perhaps twenty or thirty different lines of action that must be pursued, domestically and internationally, to give us a reasonable expectation of peace and security. But I am also satisfied that none of these will suffice unless we are sufficiently strong militarily to deter the aggressor, if possible, or have a better chance of defeating him if that should become necessary.[45]

American policy was well stated in the 1948 report of President Truman's Air Policy Commission:

> . . . the United States must have a double-barrelled policy abroad. It must work to achieve world peace through support and development of the United Nations. At the same time it must prepare to defend itself for the possibility that war may come. Not being able to count on the creation, within the future for which it now has to prepare, of a world settlement which would give it absolute security under law, it must seek the next best thing — that is, relative security under the protection of its own arms.[46]

There is no more tragic spectacle in our time than that of great nations squandering their resources, mortgaging their future, and imperiling the lives of their citizens in a costly and perhaps catastrophic arms race. Such a race saps economic and human resources, diverts creative energies from peaceful pursuits to purposes of destruction, heightens international tensions, and accentuates the feeling that the world is headed toward disaster. Is there no way to reverse this alarming trend? The dilemma which faces us was candidly stated by Raymond Fosdick: "There may be little logic in our course, because, by an ironical but demonstrable law, nations which have armed themselves to preserve the peace have seldom avoided war. But logical or illogical, there is nothing else we know how to do."[47] It does not necessarily follow, however, that failure to rearm will enhance the prospects of preserving the peace; indeed, under conditions such as those which exist at the present time, unilateral or regional disarmament by the non-Communist states alone might well be the height of folly.

International Law

To contend that wars of the past or the present could have been prevented by prohibitory law is to misunderstand the whole nature of international law or, indeed, of law in general. "No topic," says E. H. Carr, "has been the subject of more confusion in contemporary thought about international problems than the relationship between politics and law." He adds that "international law is a function of the political community of nations" and that it "can have no existence except in so far as there is an international community which, on the basis of a 'minimum common view,' recognizes it as binding." To put it another way, "law proceeds on the assumption that the question has been satisfactorily disposed of."[48] Seen in this light, international law merely registers agreement already reached; it does not seek to impose a rule of action on a world of dissenting states. It is, in fact, made by states; it expresses agreement, not compels it. Hence, states jealous of their sovereignty — that is, all states — have not "outlawed" war for the simple reason that they have regarded it as an indispensable instrument of national policy.

The outlawing of war has seemed to commend itself particularly to Americans, but it

[45] "The United Nations in Action," *Edmund J. James Lectures on Government* (Urbana: University of Illinois Press, 1951), p. 82.

[46] *Survival in the Air Age: A Report by the President's Air Policy Commission* (Washington, D.C.: Government Printing Office, 1948), p. 6.

[47] "We Need New Words and New Faiths," *New York Times Magazine*, December 19, 1948, p. 35.

[48] *The Twenty Years' Crisis, 1919–1939*, 2d ed. (London, 1946), pp. 170, 178, 172.

has had almost universal appeal. The high-water mark of this kind was represented by the famous Kellogg-Briand Pact of 1928. Since it required nothing but the acceptance of the principles it enunciated, nations were quite willing to sign it; sixty-one did so. It contained no provisions for enforcement; it had no teeth. It had little legal significance, although it stated an important principle and although efforts were made to amend the Covenant of the League of Nations to bring it into harmony with the new pledge.[49] The pact did not outlaw war, in spite of a rather widespread popular assumption that it did exactly that.[50] The signatories simply *condemned* recourse to war and *renounced* war as an instrument of *national* policy. Presumably, war could still be used as an instrument of *international* policy, and, as an American interpretation which was accepted by all the other signatories made perfectly clear,[51] it did not limit in any way the right of self-defense. Since every nation could decide "whether circumstances require recourse to war in self-defense," and since no nation would admit that it was engaged in an aggressive war, this reservation alone reduced the Kellogg Pact to a document of no more than symbolic importance. Events were soon to prove that war could not be prevented by paper pledges.

Nevertheless, international law has performed enormous services for peace. One of these has been the establishment of procedures for the peaceful settlement of international disputes. Behind every sane and peaceful international order must be a legal framework. The greater the number of disputes that are submitted to the arbitrament of law, the less the likelihood that some issue which originally would admit of a judicial approach will be allowed to grow and become a cause of war.

As noted in Chapter 10, various procedures for the peaceful settlement of international disputes have been developed, and often employed. These procedures are spelled out in the Charter of the United Nations; the General Assembly and other UN organs and agencies, notably the International Law Commission, have given a great deal of attention to their strengthening and implementation. In these efforts international law plays a major role. The ILC, for example, has even undertaken the formidable task of codifying the law of treaties, and the General Assembly has established a Special Committee on Principles of International Law Concerning Friendly Relations and Co-operation Among States.[52]

Another notable contribution of international law has been the development of the laws of war. Indeed, "the law of nations has contented itself, until our own day, with efforts to ameliorate the horrors of war by making rules for its conduct."[53] The Hague Conferences of 1899 and 1907 formulated elaborate codes for land and naval warfare,

[49] See *Report of the Committee for the Amendment of the Covenant of the League of Nations in Order to Bring It into Harmony with the Pact of Paris,* League of Nations, 1930, Vol. 2; and *Records of the Eleventh Assembly,* First Committee, pp. 131–132.

[50] In 1937 Professor Clyde Eagleton wrote: "International lawyers are unable to find in the Treaty any binding rule against war; one of them even goes so far as to assert that this treaty for the first time in history makes war legal. This is so, he argues, because international law had never before admitted war to be legal, but had accepted it as an unavoidable fact, whereas the Pact of Paris admits all wars of self-defense as legal, and then makes it possible to call any war a war of self-defense. This exception, of course, vitiates the Treaty." *Analysis of the Problem of War,* pp. 84–85.

[51] This statement read as follows: "There is nothing in the American draft of an anti-war treaty which restricts or impairs in any way the right of self-defense. That right is inherent in every sovereign state and is implicit in every treaty. Every nation is free at all times and regardless of treaty provisions to defend its territory from attack or invasion and it alone is competent to decide whether circumstances require recourse to war in self-defense."

[52] See below, p. 285.

[53] Clyde Eagleton, *International Government,* p. 389.

and for the rights of belligerents and of neutrals in time of war. There was even some attempt to draft regulations for aerial warfare. Under the conditions of twentieth-century warfare the international law of neutrality has a very limited applicability; it cannot prevent the use of such weapons as the submarine and the atomic bomb, or the bombardment of industrial targets. But the rules of war are still being elaborated and are still generally obeyed. During World War II violations of these rules, even by Germany and Japan, were the exception rather than the rule, although the violations were often serious ones.

Although Hugo Grotius — the first great writer on international law — viewed war as a necessary evil, he tried to distinguish between a "just" and an "unjust" war, and he wanted to limit the "lawful" justification of war to self-defense and to the punishment of aggressor states. In recent years some attempts have been made to return to the concepts of Grotius, to limit the resort to war to certain well-defined situations, and to ban "unjust" wars. In the postwar period an effort has been made to revise or rewrite international law by declaring that "aggressive war" is a crime and that individuals as well as states can come within the purview of the law. Neither effort is wholly new. The records of both the League and the United Nations contain scores of proposed definitions of "aggression" and impassioned speeches in support of various proposals; but seldom have so much effort and so many words been expended with such limited results. Both the Covenant and the Charter contain strong provisions for dealing with acts of aggression, but nowhere do they attempt to define aggression.[54] In the UN the task is left to the Security Council, and, since the passage of the Uniting for Peace Resolution in 1950, to the General Assembly in certain cases. It is up to them to determine when an act of aggression has occurred.

The most concerted effort to make aggressive war a crime in international law was made in the Nuremberg and Tokyo War Crimes Trials. The defendants were accused of "crimes against peace," "war crimes," and "crimes against humanity." An "International Military Tribunal," composed of judges from the United States, Britain, France, and the U.S.S.R., acting under the authority of a charter agreed upon by these four powers, sentenced a number of Nazi and Japanese political and military leaders to death, and others to terms of imprisonment ranging from a few years to life. It exonerated a few. "Various questions were raised by this procedure: could these four victor nations declare international law on behalf of the community of nations, and would it be *ex post facto* law? Is aggressive war a crime? Are individuals subjects of international law, and can they appear before an international court?" Nevertheless, the principles of the Nuremberg trials were approved by fifty-five members of the General Assembly of the UN in December, 1946, and the International Law Commission of the UN has been attempting to translate them into rules of law. "Thus the precedent at Nuremberg seems well on its way to acceptance as a rule of law."[55] This may indeed represent a significant extension of international law and a step in the development of a stronger legal basis for international relations.

The usefulness of international law in the prevention of war does not lie in an unenforceable renunciation or prohibition. Rather, it lies in a persistent effort to close the gaps, to define the rights and duties of states more precisely, to register agreement

[54] See Clyde Eagleton, "The Attempt to Define Aggression," *International Conciliation*, No. 264 (November, 1930); and Quincy Wright, "The Concept of Aggression in International Law," *The American Journal of International Law*, XXIX (July, 1935).

[55] Eagleton, *International Government*, pp. 118-119.

on as many areas of the law as states can be brought to approve. In such a way, norms of international conduct will be established and the number of occasions for political decisions will be constantly reduced. For the foreseeable future, international law will not by itself prevent recourse to war as an instrument of national policy, but it may reduce the frequency of such recourse.

World Government

Most of the proposed alternatives to war call for the strengthening and more effective use of procedures which have already been evolved, especially through such agencies as the League of Nations in the interwar period and the United Nations today. Since no procedures yet devised have been fully effective, however, it is only natural that other and more far-reaching "solutions" should also be considered. Most of the current proposals which might be placed in this category call for some kind of world government, on a regional or global scale. These proposals start with the thesis, which may be wholly correct, that there is no hope of averting war as long as the nation-state system is the prevailing pattern of international society; therefore it logically follows that this increasingly anachronistic system must be replaced by effective supranational institutions to which the nation-states would surrender at least the most vital of their present powers. The experience of the United States in evolving a federal union after the unsatisfactory years under the Articles of Confederation is often cited as a historical parallel to indicate possible lines of development.

An eloquent statement of the case for "a world state embracing the whole of society," which would by definition make international law "an impossibility," was made in 1965 by the leading historian of civilizations, Professor Arnold Toynbee:

> Since civilization has become global now and since the whole surface of our planet has become a single arena for warmaking purposes, the world state that we have to build must be on a literally worldwide scale. . . . The obstacle is not organizational or technological; it is psychological.[56]

This is a stirring appeal, a long look ahead which raises one's sights and forces him to face the magnitude of the problem of the future political organization of mankind. But without inquiring into the validity of the historical comparison, it is doubtful that the remedy is a practicable one, even if the diagnosis is correct. As long as the nations of the world so jealously guard their "sovereign rights" — the Soviet Union is particularly sensitive on this point, but all other countries hold essentially the same point of view — there is little prospect that they can be persuaded or forced to surrender their rights to supranational agencies. The difficulty with any and all proposals for world government is that they would take us from where we are to where they think we should be, across bridges that have not been built to a heavenly city that does not exist. Perhaps we can and should move in the direction toward which they are pointing; but, if so, we must move slowly from our present encampment, building roads and bridges to the future as we go along. No political leader in his right mind would advocate the abandonment of national sovereignty unless he was absolutely convinced that some larger association would actually work. As Professor Shotwell tersely stated the issue: "Humanity cannot afford to trust its wistful hopes to anything, however promising, that may betray it in the hour of crisis."[57]

An incisive analysis of "the illusion of world government" has been made by Reinhold Niebuhr, who is both a distinguished theologian and a realistic commentator on world affairs. "The fallacy of world government," he said, "can be stated in two simple propositions. The first is that governments

[56] Toynbee, "War Is Not the Normal Condition of Man," p. 127.

[57] Shotwell, p. 4.

are not created by fiat (though sometimes they can be imposed by tyranny). The second is that governments have only limited efficacy in integrating a community."[58] He declared that the idea of world government "assumes that constitutions can insure the mutual trust upon which community rests," and he observed that "no group of individuals has ever created either government or community out of whole cloth." The present sharp division of the world makes impossible the success of such a venture, for neither the Russians nor we are ready "at the moment, to submit our fate to a world authority without reservation, so long as the possibility remains that such an authority could annul a system of law and justice to which we are deeply committed." Even if a world government were established, Niebuhr contended, it could not create a genuine community "for the simple reason that the authority of government is not primarily the authority of law nor the authority of force, but the authority of the community itself. Laws are obeyed because the community accepts them as corresponding, on the whole, to its conception of justice." To put it another way, "the police power of a government cannot be a pure political artifact. It is an arm of the community's body. If the body is in pieces, the arm cannot integrate it." Moreover, if a world government were established, it would be more likely to be established by force than by consent. It would, in other words, probably be a world imperium of a totalitarian nature rather than a voluntary union of the free.

Pacem in Terris

One of the most eloquent and potentially most influential statements to be issued in recent years was the famous encyclical, or circular letter, *Pacem in Terris,* issued from the Vatican by Pope John XXIII on April 10, 1963, just two months before his death.[59] Addressed not just to Catholics but to "all men of good will," the Pope's encyclical might be regarded, in Vice President Hubert Humphrey's words, as "a public philosophy for the nuclear era" and as an important tract for the times. It contained the expected general precepts — for example, that "Love, not fear, must dominate relationships between individuals and between nations," and that the road to peace lies not "in equity of arms, but in mutual trust alone" — but it also referred quite specifically to some of the difficult problems of international relations, particularly in Part III, "Relations Between States," and in Part IV, "Relationship of Men and of Political Communities with the World Community."

The following brief excerpts illustrate the range of the encyclical. One section commented on "The Evolution of Economically Underdeveloped Countries": "It is vitally important . . . that the wealthier states, in providing various forms of assistance to the poorer, should respect the moral values and ethnic characteristics peculiar to each, and also that they should avoid any intention of political domination." Another section emphasized the "Insufficiency of Modern States to Ensure the Universal Common Good": "It can be said . . . that at this historical moment the present system of organization and the way its principle of authority operates on a world basis no longer corresponds to the objective requirements of the universal common good." The encyclical also expressed confidence that "Men are becoming more and more convinced that disputes that arise between states should not be resolved by recourse to arms, but rather by negotiation," and that "all human beings . . . are becoming more consciously aware that they are living members of a world community." The entire document was thus

[58] "The Illusion of World Government," *Foreign Affairs,* XXVII (April, 1949), 379–388.

[59] The full text of this document was printed in the *New York Times,* June 11, 1963.

a mosaic of moral preachments, hopeful assertions, and penetrating comments on pressing current problems in the international community and on the nature and needs of present-day international relations.

It is, of course, impossible to evaluate the impact, if any, of a statement of this kind. Certainly it attracted worldwide attention, and has been referred to perhaps as often as any single document of the 1960's.[60] Along with the Second Vatican Council, which opened on October 11, 1962, and closed on December 8, 1965, it seemed to mark the Catholic Church's willingness to join, and indeed to take a leading part, in ecumenical dialogue and to assume a real initiative in encouraging efforts looking toward international cooperation and the preservation of peace.

This new initiative was dramatically highlighted by the visit of John XXIII's successor, Pope Paul VI, to New York on October 4, 1965 — the first visit of a reigning pope to the Western Hemisphere — for the purpose of addressing the General Assembly of the United Nations. His address was not in itself a dramatic one, but the presence of the supreme pontiff of the Roman Catholic Church before the Assembly, reminding its members that for many persons throughout the world the UN was "the last hope of concord and peace" and urging all nations to seek peace, was an unprecedented event of historic significance.

The Future of War as an Instrument of National Policy

The student of world affairs must not conclude too quickly that no gains have been made against the menace of war as an instrument of national policy, or that none can be made. A more hopeful approach would be to see to it that we have fewer and fewer wars and smaller and smaller ones, and that in particular another global war is averted. If, as seems to be the case, states cannot now safely abandon war as an instrument of national policy, perhaps they can be brought to use it more sparingly and only in morally defensible ways. Progress in disarmament, the development of international law, constructive work in international organizations, the improvement and utilization of the techniques of peaceful settlement and collective security, education for international understanding — these and other approaches may help to remove the scourge of war. This means, in short, that the realistic approach to the prevention of war is a piecemeal one. Eventually there may appear other assurances of security which will permit the total relinquishment of war as an instrument of national policy.

One distinguished authority on international relations, Edward M. Earle, suggested the possible consequences of the rejection of the piecemeal approach:

> It will, of course, be said that realistic grappling with Mars is Utopian. The charge might have some justification were we to hope for the eternal banishment of violence from human affairs. It is not Utopian if we consider that the problem is primarily one of removing specific causes of friction between the great powers and the adjudication of disputes, as they arise, through diplomatic negotiations and through the United Nations. . . . Every war which is averted will be a war not fought, and every war not fought is a contribution to the long-range problem of reducing the area within which armed conflict operates in politics. The alternative is to assume that war is inevitable, to take less than the necessary measures to deal with recurring crises, to drift into catastrophe, and thus "to commit suicide in anticipation of death."[61]

[60] A notable International Convocation on the Requirements of Peace, sponsored by the Center for the Study of Democratic Institutions, held in New York City on February 17–20, 1965, took *Pacem in Terris* as its central theme. Follow-up regional conferences were held in 1966.

[61] Earle, pp. 592–593.

Realistic workers for peace will have to dismiss, though with genuine reluctance, various idealistic and religious approaches which call for a higher degree of perfectibility than can reasonably be expected of man and his social institutions. As long as the ideals of pacifism and passive resistance are confined to a small minority of high-souled men and women they do not provide security against the danger of war. "Passive resistance destroys the means, but it does not achieve the end; it offers no substitute for the means which it eliminates. . . . there are still many, whether persons or nations, who are willing to take advantage of their fellows, and who can only be restrained from doing so by the exercise of superior force. Passive resistance removes this superior force and leaves the criminal, who is willing to use force, in undisputed control."[62]

To recognize the essential futility of pacifism and piety in building effective safeguards against war is not to deny that the job calls for morality and idealism, but it also calls for the realization that certain social functions have been performed by war because men and governments have devised no peaceful means for their performance.

If a careful student of war were to be asked whether he would abolish all war if he could, he would probably reply by inquiring whether the abolition of war also meant the abolition of all the oppression, injustices, and abuses which so often lead to war. If told that it did not, he might understandably decide that he would perform no service to humanity by decreeing that war should go. Now and then war has brought men closer to "justice" than any available peaceful recourse could have done. The door to war cannot be barred so long as the door to justice is thereby also barred.

Nevertheless, it must be recognized that war today has potentialities for destruction beyond the range of human comprehension. The coming of the nuclear and the space age has ushered in "the age of overkill." President Kennedy predicted that "A full scale nuclear exchange, lasting less than 60 minutes, could wipe out more than 300 million Americans, Europeans, and Russians, as well as untold numbers elsewhere." Dr. Albert Einstein, one of the pioneers of the nuclear age, once remarked: "I do not know the weapons with which World War III will be fought, but I can assure you that World War IV will be fought with sticks and stones." These statements, if somewhat hyperbolic, dramatize a ghastly truth, which mankind will ignore at its peril — namely, that for the first time in history man has at his disposal weapons powerful enough to annihilate countless millions of people and perhaps to destroy civilization as we have known it. For this reason, as President Eisenhower declared, "there is no alternative to peace." "War in our time," according to Eisenhower, "has been an anachronism. Whatever the case in the past, war in the future can serve no useful purpose." Yet, as Senator Fulbright and others have emphasized, one must "think the unthinkable," including even the possibility of thermonuclear war.[63] Hence the importance of all efforts to reduce international tensions, to curtail the atomic arsenals of atomic powers and to prevent nuclear proliferation, and to deal with fundamental problems of human misery and unrest as well as with crises as they arise. In the meantime, until more fundamental readjustments in the international system and in man's thinking are made, an uneasy peace may be maintained by such old techniques as the balance of power and by such a curren phenomenon as "the balance of terror."

"No problem is more important . . . ,

[62] Eagleton, *Analysis of the Problem of War*, p. 69.

[63] See Herman Kahn, *On Thermonuclear War* (Princeton, N.J.: Princeton University Press 1960), and *Thinking About the Unthinkable* (New York: Horizon Press, 1962).

writes Professor Stanley Hoffmann, "than that of knowing to what extent the invention of nuclear weapons opened a totally new phase of history — of knowing whether the 'state of war' was drastically transformed . . . or whether, on the contrary, the traditional competition persists, although at a higher level of risk and with new rules."[64] The evidence is mounting that "the state of war" has indeed been transformed by the advent of nuclear weapons, but that at the same time "the traditional competition persists." This is perhaps the central paradox of our age, and it presents new challenges and new threats to the conventional ways of conducting international affairs.

The task of peoples and of statesmen everywhere is to do everything in their power to find alternatives to the war system. Now that the atomic age is here, this task is indeed the central problem of international relations. But alternatives to war will be workable only when they take over the defensible functions of war and, above all, when they are utilized by reasonable men with a will to keep the peace.

[64] *The State of War: Essays on the Theory and Practice of International Politics* (New York: Frederick A. Praeger, 1965), p. viii.

SUGGESTIONS FOR FURTHER READING

ADLER, M. J. *How to Think about War and Peace.* New York: Simon and Schuster, 1944.

ANGELL, NORMAN. *The Great Illusion.* New York: G. P. Putnam's Sons, 1933.

ARON, RAYMOND. *The Century of Total War.* Garden City, N.Y.: Doubleday & Company, 1954.

———. *On War.* Garden City, N.Y.: Doubleday & Company, 1959.

———. *Peace and War: A Theory of International Relations.* Garden City, N.Y.: Doubleday & Company, 1967. An important work originally published in Paris in 1962.

BALLIS, W. B. *The Legal Position of War: Changes in Its Practice and Theory from Plato to Vattel.* The Hague, 1937.

BARNETT, FRANK R., WILLIAM C. MOTT, and JOHN C. NEFF. *Peace and War in the Modern Age: Premises, Myths, and Realities.* Garden City, N.Y.: Doubleday & Company, 1965. A Doubleday Anchor Original.

BERNARD, L. L. *War and Its Causes.* New York: Holt, 1946.

BUSH, VANNEVAR. *Modern Arms and Free Men.* New York: Simon and Schuster, 1949.

CANTRIL, HADLEY, ed. *Tensions That Cause Wars.* Urbana: University of Illinois Press, 1950.

CARR, E. H. *The Twenty Years' Crisis, 1919–1939,* 2d ed. London, 1946.

CLARKSON, JESSE D. and THOMAS C. COCHRAN, eds. *War as a Social Institution: The Historian's Perspective.* New York: Columbia University Press, 1941. Edited for the American Historical Association.

CLAUSEWITZ, KARL VON. *On War,* translated by O. J. Matthijs Jolles. New York: Modern Library, 1943.

CURTIS, LIONEL. *World War, Its Cause and Cure.* New York: G. P. Putnam's Sons, 1946.

DURBIN, E. F. M. and J. BOWLBY. *Personal Aggressiveness and War.* New York: Columbia University Press, 1939.

EAGLETON, CLYDE. *Analysis of the Problem of War.* New York: The Ronald Press Company, 1937.

EARLE, EDWARD M., ed. *Makers of Modern Strategy: Military Thought from Machiavelli to Hitler.* Princeton, N.J.: Princeton University Press, 1943. Part 4.

FALLS, CYRIL. *A Hundred Years of War.* London, 1953.

FRIEDRICH, CARL J. *Inevitable Peace.* Cambridge, Mass.: Harvard University Press, 1948.

GELBER, LIONEL. *Reprieve from War: A*

Manual for Realists. New York: The Macmillan Company, 1950.

GROB, FRITZ. *The Relativity of War and Peace: A Study in Law, History, and Politics*. New Haven: Yale University Press, 1949.

HALPERIN, MORTON H. *Limited War in the Nuclear Age*. New York: John Wiley & Sons, 1963.

HOFFMANN, STANLEY. *The State of War: Essays on the Theory and Practice of International Politics*. New York: Frederick A. Praeger, 1965.

HOWE, FREDERIC C. *Why War*. New York: Charles Scribner's Sons, 1916. A readable presentation of the thesis of economic causation by a prominent reformer-journalist of an earlier day.

KAHN, HERMAN. *On Escalation: Metaphors and Scenarios*. New York: Frederick A. Praeger, 1965.

———. *On Thermonuclear War*. Princeton, N.J.: Princeton University Press, 1960.

———. *Thinking About the Unthinkable*. New York: Horizon Press, 1962.

LARSON, ARTHUR, ed. *A Warless World*. New York: McGraw-Hill Book Company, 1963.

MARTIN, KINGSLEY. *War, Peace and Human Nature*. Bombay, 1959.

MILLIS, WALTER and JAMES REAL. *The Abolition of War*. New York: The Macmillan Company, 1963.

MONTROSS, LYNN. *War Through the Ages*. New York: Harper, 1944.

NEF, JOHN U. *War and Human Progress*. Cambridge, Mass.: Harvard University Press, 1950.

NICKERSON, HOFFMAN. *Can We Limit War?* London, 1932.

OSGOOD, CHARLES. *An Alternative to War and Surrender*. Urbana: University of Illinois Press, 1962. An ingenious plan for "Graduated Reciprocation in Tension-Reduction."

PEAR, T. H., ed. *Psychological Factors in War and Peace*. New York: Philosophical Library, 1951.

Perspectives on Peace: 1910–1960. New York: Frederick A. Praeger, for the Carnegie Endowment for International Peace, 1960. Papers by 12 eminent authorities, commemorating the 50th anniversary of the Carnegie Endowment.

PRESTON, RICHARD A., S. F. WISE, and H. O. WERNER. *Men in Arms: A History of Warfare and Its Interrelationships with Western Society*. New York: Frederick A. Praeger, 1956.

ROPP, THEODORE. *War in the Modern World*. Durham, N.C.: Duke University Press, 1959. An excellent summary of military history and literature.

SHOTWELL, JAMES T. *War as an Instrument of National Policy*. New York: Harcourt, Brace, 1929. Mostly on the Kellogg-Briand Pact.

SMITH, LOUIS. *American Democracy and Military Power*. Chicago: University of Chicago Press, 1951.

SPAULDING, OLIVER L., JR., HOFFMAN NICKERSON, and JOHN W. WRIGHT. *Warfare, A Study of Military Methods from Earliest Times*. New York: Harcourt, Brace, 1925.

STRACHEY, ALIX. *The Unconscious Motives of War; a Psychological Contribution*. London, 1957.

TATE, MERZE. *The Disarmament Illusion: The Movement for a Limitation of Armaments to 1907*. New York: The Macmillan Company, 1942. A scholarly study.

TOYNBEE, ARNOLD J. *War and Civilization*. New York: Oxford University Press, 1951.

VAN SLYCK, PHILIP. *Peace: The Control of National Power*. Boston: Beacon Press, for the Fund for Education Concerning World Peace Through World Law, 1963.

WALLER, WILLARD, ed. *War in the Twentieth Century*. New York: Dryden Press, 1940.

WALTZ, KENNETH. *Man, the State and War*. New York: Columbia University Press, 1959.

WHEELER-BENNET, JOHN W. *The Pipe Dream of Peace: The Story of the Collapse of Disarmament*. New York: William Morrow & Co., 1935.

WRIGHT, QUINCY. *Problems of Stability and Progress in International Relations*. Berkeley: University of California Press, 1954.

———. *A Study of War*. 2 vols. Chicago: University of Chicago Press, 1942. A work of outstanding scholarship. Also available in a one-volume unabridged edition (1600 pages, published in 1964), and in an abridged edition by Louise Leonard Wright (448 pages, published in 1964).

WRIGHT, QUINCY *et al.*, eds. *Preventing World War III: Some Proposals*. New York: Simon and Schuster, 1962. An international symposium.

WYNNER, EDITH and GEORGIA LLOYD. *Searchlight on Peace Plans*. New York: E. P. Dutton & Co., 1944.

PART THREE

THE CONTROLS OF INTERSTATE RELATIONS

9 The Balance of Power

"Sovereignty" and "power" are perhaps the two most frequently used words in the vocabulary of writers on international relations. This emphasis seems to suggest that states may do pretty much as they please — that the nation-state system is not a system at all but, instead, a polite label for international anarchy, as some critics have contended. Nevertheless, it is true that most states are on friendly terms with most other states most of the time. This condition implies that some restraints or controls must be in fairly continuous operation. We shall discuss some of these in this chapter and the five following ones.

The observer who fancies himself a "realist" may insist that all states are driven by an urge to enlarge their territory and enhance their prestige, and that only military power in the hands of other states restrains them. The economic determinist may emphasize the interdependence of states; the legalist may think in terms of the rights and duties fixed by international law; and the idealist may be convinced that such goodwill and harmony as exist must be attributed to religion, to the fundamental decency of men, and to a world "public opinion."

To point out the importance of national power to the security of a state is not to argue that all states are aggressive and predatory, or that they would be if they had the strength. It is rather to say that states must be strong because some state or states may spurn all other controls and because a state's own power is its last line of defense. National power is therefore the most important of all controls in interstate relations. Much that has been written in the earlier chapters of this book is a commentary on that statement. National power can be used for peacekeeping or peacemaking as well as for warmaking; it has, in fact, proved to be the only effective instrument for halting aggression. It should be noted that the balance of power, which we are about to discuss, involves only the utilization or arrangement of national power in a special way, and that the same is true of collective security.

Our attention to national power, to the balance of power, to collective security, to procedures for peaceful settlement, to international law, and to international organization as institutionalized approaches to the control of interstate relations does not mean that other controls may not be of equal or even greater significance. Most of them, however, are too intangible for measurement or appraisal; they include moral convictions, humanitarianism, pacifism, toleration, enlightened self-interest and many other ways of thinking that normally lead people and states to prefer to live in peace rather than in anarchy.

Nature of the Balance of Power

The great period of the theory and practice of the balance of power began shortly after 1500, and its rise to prominence coincided with the emergence of the nation-state system and with the Age of Discoveries. Increasingly, and especially after the Treaty of Westphalia of 1648, it became a cardinal feature of international relations. As Quincy Wright pointed out, "While other factors have had an influence, the concept of the balance of power provides the most general explanation for the oscillations of peace and war in Europe since the Thirty Years' War."[1] The classical period of the European balance of power system was from 1648 until the end of the Napoleonic era in 1815.[2]

The principle of the balance of power was most fully applied in the eighteenth and nineteenth centuries and was even written into several treaties of the eighteenth century. It is still a basic principle in international relations, and doubtless will continue to be as long as the nation-state system is the controlling pattern of world politics. Under present conditions it operates far less efficiently and satisfactorily than in previous centuries when Europe was the main arena of international politics and when the nation-state system was not subject to the strains and stresses which characterize the second half of the twentieth century; but one could make a case for the assertion that "the idea of 'balance of power' is still the central theoretical concept in international relations."[3]

Definitions. Just what is meant by the phrase "the balance of power"? The term has been used in so many different ways that it almost defies definition. As Inis L. Claude has observed, "The trouble with the balance of power is not that it has no meaning, but that it has too many meanings."[4] Professor A. F. Pollard, simply by consulting a good dictionary, concluded that there were several thousand possible meanings of the phrase, as analyzed word by word.[5] The essential idea is simple enough: it is "equilibrium" of the type represented by a pair of scales. When the weights in the scales are equal, balance results. Applied to a world of sovereign states, uncontrolled by effective supranational agencies, the concept of the balance of power assumes that through shifting alliances and countervailing pressures no one power or combination of powers will be allowed to grow so strong as to threaten the security of the rest.

The balance of power may be described in a number of ways. Georg Schwarzenberger spoke of it as an "equilibrium" or "a certain amount of stability in international relations" that under favorable conditions is produced by an alliance of states or by other devices.[6] He asserted that the balance of power "is of universal application wherever a number of sovereign and armed States co-exist,"[7] whereas Hans Morgenthau described it as "only a particular manifestation of a general social principle."[8] G. Lowes Dickinson clarified two uses of the term "balance": "It means, on the one hand, an equality, as

[1] Quincy Wright, *A Study of War* (Chicago: University of Chicago Press, 1942), II, 758.

[2] See Edward V. Gulick, "Our Balance of Power System in Perspective," *Journal of International Affairs*, XIV (1960), 10–11.

[3] Glenn H. Snyder, "Balance of Power in the Missile Age," *Journal of International Affairs*, XIV (1960), 21.

[4] Inis L. Claude, Jr., *Power and International Relations* (New York: Random House, 1962), p. 13.

[5] "The Balance of Power," *Journal of the British Institute of International Affairs*, II (March, 1923), 51–64.

[6] Georg Schwarzenberger, *Power Politics*, 2d rev. ed. (New York: Frederick A. Praeger, 1951), p. 178.

[7] *Ibid.*, p. 181.

[8] Hans J. Morgenthau, *Politics Among Nations*, 3d ed. (New York: Alfred A. Knopf, 1960), p. 167.

of the two sides when an account is balanced, and on the other hand, an inequality, as when one has a 'balance' to one's credit at the bank." He added, significantly, that "the balance of power theory professes the former, but pursues the latter."[9]

One of the most cogent of modern definitions was offered by Professor Sidney B. Fay in his article on the subject in the *Encyclopaedia of the Social Sciences:* "It means," said Professor Fay, "such a 'just equilibrium' in power among the members of the family of nations as will prevent any one of them from becoming sufficiently strong to enforce its will upon the others."[10] In his *Politics Among Nations* Professor Hans J. Morgenthau stated quite frankly that he would use the term in four different senses: "(1) as a policy aimed at a certain state of affairs, (2) as an actual state of affairs, (3) as an approximately equal distribution of power, (4) as any distribution of power"; but he added that "whenever the term is used without qualification, it refers to an actual state of affairs in which power is distributed among several nations with approximate equality."[11]

Characteristics. Having suggested the essential nature of the balance of power, we may now observe a number of its characteristics.

First, the term itself suggests equilibrium — balance — but every student of history knows that almost the only certain thing about history is that it is subject to constant, ceaseless change, to shifting political patterns and power relationships — in short, to disequilibrium. The concept, may, however, be discussed in terms of equilibrium theory, which is concerned, among other things, with international disequilibrium as well as with equilibrium.[12]

Second, in practice balance of power systems have proved to be temporary and unstable. As Deutsch and Singer pointed out, "No balance-of-power system has lasted longer than a few centuries, and most of the original powers contending in such systems have survived as independent powers only for much shorter periods."[13]

Third, the balance of power, according to Nicholas J. Spykman, is not "a gift of the gods" but is achieved by "the active intervention of man."[14] States cannot afford to wait until it "happens"; if they wish to survive, Spykman added, "they must be willing to go to war to preserve a balance against the growing hegemonic power of the period." Thus we are dealing with a diplomatic contrivance, not with a matter of historical causation.

Fourth, the balance of power has generally tended to favor the status quo, but again the lessons of history are instructive, for they reveal that a policy which disregards the forces making for change is doomed to eventual failure. To be effective, a balance of power policy must be changing and dynamic.

Fifth, it is difficult for a nation to tell when a balance of power has been achieved. As any overall comparison in power terms is a rough one at best, a real balance of power can seldom exist, and it probably would not be recognized as such if it did exist. The only real test, presumably, is that of war,

[9] *The International Anarchy, 1904–1914* (New York: Century, 1926), pp. 5–6.

[10] (New York: The Macmillan Company, 1937), II, 395. Used by permission of The Macmillan Company.

[11] Morgenthau, p. 167, n. 1. See also Professor Claude's discussion of "Morgenthau and the Balance of Power," in *Power and International Relations,* pp. 25–37.

[12] See George Liska, *The International Equilibrium* (Cambridge, Mass.: Harvard University Press, 1957).

[13] Karl W. Deutsch and J. David Singer, "Multipolar Power Systems and International Stability," *World Politics,* XVI (Apr. 1964), 403.

[14] Nicholas J. Spykman, *America's Strategy in World Politics* (New York: Harcourt, Brace, 1942), p. 25.

and resorting to war not only upsets the balance but also creates the very conditions which a balance of power policy is supposedly designed to prevent.

Sixth, another characteristic of the balance of power is that it offers both an objective and a subjective approach. Martin Wight has suggested that the difference is that between the historian and the statesman: "The historian will say that there is a balance when the opposing groups seem to him to be equal in power. The statesman will say that there is a balance when he thinks that his side is stronger than the other. And he will say that his country *holds* the balance, when it has freedom to join one side or the other according to its own interests."[15] The historian, in other words, takes the objective view, whereas the statesman takes the subjective. The latter is perhaps the more realistic approach, for, as Spykman has declared, "the truth of the matter is that states are interested only in a balance of power which is in their favor. Not an equilibrium, but a generous margin is their objective."[16] Hence nations which play the balance of power game seek not a balance, but an imbalance — in their favor. The result, of course, may be political as well as mathematical absurdity.

Professor Quincy Wright, whose often-quoted work *A Study of War* contains one of the best contemporary analyses of the theory and practice of the balance of power, described the manner in which statesmen have exploited the doctrine:

> Each of the powers . . . especially the great powers, has been interested not only in preserving but also in augmenting its relative power; consequently, there has never been wholehearted devotion to the balance of power principle among them. Each statesman considers the balance of power good for others but not for himself. Each tries to get out of the system in order to "hold the balance" and to establish a hegemony, perhaps eventually an empire, over all the others.[17]

Seventh, the balance of power has not been primarily a device for preserving the peace. At times it has had this effect, in particular areas or on the state system as a whole. It could be argued, for example, that it was a major factor in preserving the peace, with relatively minor interruptions, for a century following the Congress of Vienna. On the other hand, it has also tended to increase tensions between nations and to precipitate wars. There is some point to the claim that the balance of power system "in the final analysis rests upon war,"[18] implying not so much that it inevitably leads to war as that participants in the system must be willing to resort to war, if necessary, in order to prevent an upsetting of the basic balance. In any event, it should be recognized that the primary purpose of the balance of power is to maintain the independence of states, and not to preserve the peace.[19] Presumably in the nuclear age the first objective cannot be achieved without the second; but in previous periods this generalization would not necessarily have been valid.

Eighth, the balance of power game is obviously one for the great states. Although small ones are vitally concerned in the outcome, they are more often victims, or at best spectators, rather than players. As Spykman observed, "unless they can successfully combine together," they "can only be weights in a balance used by others."[20] Collectively, they may be able to exert some influence upon even the most powerful states, as is illus-

[15] *Power Politics* (London, 1946), p. 46.

[16] Spykman, p. 21

[17] Wright, II, 757–758.

[18] Gulick, p. 18.

[19] This point is a controversial one, which has provoked considerable disagreement among students and practitioners of balance of power techniques. See Claude, pp. 51–66; and Gulick, pp. 17–18.

[20] Spykman, p. 20.

trated by the international roles played by the Arab League, the Organization of American States, or the caucusing groups in the United Nations. Individually, they may be important factors in regional balances, and they may try to maintain their independence or improve their bargaining positions by exploiting great power rivalries and conflicts of interest. Nepal, for example, may be said to be following a kind of Himalayan balance of power policy vis-à-vis its giant neighbors, India and Communist China.

Ninth, the balance of power seems to be a policy that is suitable neither for democracies nor for dictatorships. Unless geographical, political, military, and other considerations are peculiarly favorable, a democracy is a reluctant player and a poor leader in the balance of power game. It is deeply concerned with power politics only in periods of crisis. A dictatorship, on the other hand, is usually interested in dominating the contest, in establishing rules to suit its own convenience, and in gathering in all the rewards.

Tenth, many commentators insist that the balance of power is largely inoperative under present conditions. They point out that it functioned well only when it was confined to the European state system, and that with the expansion of the state system to an international scale where the balance, to the extent that it exists at all, is bipolar or multipolar, it is impossible for any nation or international organization to play the role of balancer or for the system to function along its classical lines. They also argue that the nuclear and space age has relegated balance of power techniques to diplomatic history, or that at best "the balance of power is not suitable to our era beyond its function as a transitional device."[21] There is merit in these arguments, but the fact is that the balance of power game continues to be played, with nation-states as the chief actors. A persistent question in contemporary international politics is whether "a new balance of power" may be in the making,[22] or whether the whole concept is outmoded. Certainly new forces and patterns are developing, and though still in their formative stages, they may make former preoccupation with balance of power seem inconsequential indeed.

The Role of Balancer. The balance of power is a dangerous game even for the great powers. The risks are great and the outcome uncertain. The most desirable role for a great power to play is that of holder of the balance, and not that of major participant in the balance itself. This is a role which England has filled more often than any other state, though with varying degrees of success. Morgenthau cites two early examples of this traditional feature of British foreign policy. Henry VIII "is reported to have had himself painted holding in his right hand a pair of scales in perfect balance, one of them occupied by France, the other by Austria, and holding in his left hand a weight ready to be dropped in either scale." William Camden, writing of England in the time of Queen Elizabeth I, stated that "France and Spain are as it were the Scales in the Balance of Europe and England the Tongue or the Holder of the Balance."[23]

In the eighteenth and nineteenth centuries Britain, by virtue of her sea power, her semidetachment from the Continent, her industrial and political strength, her astute diplomacy, and other factors, was able to develop an effective balance of power policy and to act as a real balancer of the European state

[21] Gulick, p. 19.

[22] This is a theme which is explored in various articles in the *Journal of International Affairs,* XIV (1960), a special issue on the general topic "A New Balance of Power?"

[23] Morgenthau, p. 196. The latter quotation is from William Camden, *Annales of the History of the Most Renowned and Victorious Princess Elizabeth, Late Queen of England* (London, 1635), p. 196.

system; but the rise of new great powers on the continent of Europe and in America and the Far East in the late nineteenth and early twentieth centuries ended her enjoyment of this unique position. At the present time no real balancer exists; indeed, under modern conditions it is doubtful that any nation can hope to succeed to England's former role. If this is true, then one of the outstanding aspects of the balance of power system in its classical period has disappeared, perhaps forever. In fact, those who believe that a balancer is essential to a balance of power system would argue that the system itself has lost its effectiveness.

A Bipolar or Multipolar World? In the absence of a balancer, balance of power policies have tended toward the polarization of power, usually around the strongest members of rival alliances or groupings. Historical proof of this tendency need not be sought, for it obviously was one of the central features of international politics in the years following World War II when the Soviet Union and the United States, at opposite poles and dominating "satellite" and allied nations, created that simple balance which is generally regarded as the most dangerous and unstable form of the balance of power. The bipolarity of power was made even more dangerous by the absence of other power centers, by the ideological differences between Communist and democratic systems, and by the growing nuclear arsenals which each of the superpowers was accumulating.

The common result of these tendencies of the balance of power system toward polarization has been the establishment of a new balance by the intervention of outside states, the enlargement of the area affected by the balance, and the beginning of a new cycle of rivalries and wars. Quincy Wright called attention to this tendency of the system "to make each civilization the cockpit of the next." His interpretation is arresting:

> The balance of power having reached a state of polarization within a given situation, each faction tries to draw in states from the outside. As a result, when economic and social contacts have sufficiently progressed, a larger balance of power, dominated by states of a different civilization, has developed around the original area. The states of the original area, even though utilizing more advanced military techniques, remain divided by historic animosities and are unable to defend their civilization as a unit. Consequently, the civilization is overwhelmed. . . . The disintegrating Holy Roman Empire was the cockpit for wars of all Europe in the seventeenth century. Europe, still intent upon its balance of power, has been and promises to continue to be the cockpit of wars involving the United States, Japan, Russia, and the British Empire. With a world balance of power established among these states, this process can no longer continue without interplanetary wars.[24]

Once bipolarity exists, it tends to become rigid as well as unstable, and a peaceful transition to a complex balance — one involving many states — becomes difficult. Most authorities would agree with DeWitt C. Poole that a good balance of power must be complex.[25] When the principle was most effective, as on the continent of Europe in the eighteenth century, a complex or multiple balance existed. One of the great questions of our day is whether other centers of power will arise in the world in time to transform the bipolar balance of the present into a multiple balance in the future, without resort to war.

Apparently this process of evolution is already under way. The stark bipolarity of the immediate postwar years seems to be yielding to a more complex balance. Polycentrism has become a marked feature of politics within and without the Communist world. In the formerly monolithic Communist bloc there are now at least two "Romes," Moscow

[24] Wright, I, 382–383.

[25] "Balance of Power," *Life*, September 22, 1947, p. 77.

and Peking, and even the so-called satellite states of Eastern Europe are showing signs of following more independent policies, sometimes in defiance of the Soviet Union. Yugoslavia has been a nonaligned Communist state for some years; Albania has identified herself with Communist China against the Soviet Union; and Rumania is trying to develop independent links with the non-Communist world and is openly demanding a relaxation of Soviet controls over COMECON and the Warsaw Pact. The countries of Western Europe have staged a remarkable economic, political, and psychological recovery and are working out new and more independent patterns of relationships with both the United States and the U.S.S.R. The United States is still the dominant member of the NATO alliance, but other members are demanding a larger role and a greater voice in decision-making on vital issues.

Only recently has Asia entered the balance of power picture in any significant way. Today Communist China, independent India, and Japan, while not great powers, play major roles in international politics, and several other Asian states, including Indonesia, Pakistan, the Arab states as a group, and Turkey, are not without influence in the councils of the nations. Moreover, several Asian states are deliberately trying to follow policies of "nonalignment" or "independence" in world affairs. Individually, the more than 35 independent African states which have emerged in the postwar years are too weak to exert much influence on the course of international affairs, but to the extent that they can cooperate on matters of common interest, especially through the Organization of African Unity and the Asian-African Group in the United Nations (with the African members now acting as a distinct sub-group), they are definitely factors in the existing world balance of power. These nations, as well as those of Latin America, comprise a Third World that may be contributing importantly to the evolution of a more complex balance of power than existed in the early years of the postwar period.

While a more complex balance of power, such as exists in a multipolar system, is generally regarded as more conducive to international stability and peace than a bipolar balance, this may not prove to be the case in fact, or if it does, the difference may turn out to be minimal. As Karl Deutsch and J. David Singer pointed out, "If we are chiefly interested in rapid de-escalation — that is, in partial or complete disarmament — a multipolar world may prove more intractable than a bipolar one." Moreover, "A multipolar world, though often more stable in the short run than a bipolar one, has its own problem of long-run political stability." On the other hand, "If we are merely concerned . . . with preventing any rapid escalation of the two-power arms competition between the United States and the Soviet Union, a shift toward a multipolar world may appear preferable." Furthermore, "both in the short and long run the instability of tight bipolar systems appears to be substantially greater. It seems plausible that, *if the spread of nuclear weapons could be slowed down or controlled,* a transition from the bipolar international system of the early 1950's to an increasingly multipolar system in the 1960's might buy mankind some valuable time to seek some more dependable bases for world order.[26]

Historical Significance. Historically, the concept of the balance of power has been of great significance only for limited periods. It was particularly successful in Europe from the sixteenth century to the nineteenth. When it was then extended to a world scale — a development which began after 1815 at the latest and received great impetus from

[26] Deutsch and Singer, pp. 403, 406. Italics in original. See also Morton Kaplan, Arthur L. Burns, and Richard M. Quandt, "Theoretical Analysis of the 'Balance of Power,'" *Behavioral Science,* V (July, 1960), 240–252.

the rise of non-European states, notably the United States and Japan — it proved to be less than adequate. Even in its heyday in Europe, moreover, it was, as Robert Strausz-Hupé pointed out, "but one of the many delicate balances" that regulated the equilibrium.[27]

The balance of power system, even in its most fully developed form, has been definitely limited in its operations. Although in the Western world in the modern period of history it has been a main regulator of interstate relations, even there it has been by no means a single system, possibly not a system at all. Within that area there have been many sub-systems, or local balances of power, which often affected the major power picture. Thus we can speak of an Italian balance of power in the fifteenth century, or later of a balance of power in the Western Hemisphere, or in the Balkans, or even in the Germanies. For some decades, especially in the eighteenth century, there seemed to be two major balances in Europe, one in the west, the other in the east. Local balances, however, usually had implications which directly affected the general pattern of great power relations; this was obviously true in the Balkans and the Germanies. Where the interrelations were less direct, the autonomous character of the balances was usually of a temporary nature, as in fifteenth-century Italy; or they were in areas which, during a period of autonomous development, were on the periphery of the zones of great power conflicts, as in Eastern Europe until late in the eighteenth century, or in the Western Hemisphere until the present century.

Historical Evolution of the Balance of Power

The concept of the balance of power has been present wherever and whenever the multiple-state system has existed. It was known and applied in the ancient world, most conspicuously in the city-states of Greece, but also in Egypt, Babylonia, India, and China; indeed, David Hume, in his famous essay "Of the Balance of Power," called it "a prevailing notion of ancient times." This fact, he argued, should be no occasion for surprise; for, as he explained:

> The maxim of preserving the balance of power is founded so much on common sense and obvious reasoning, that it is impossible it could altogether have escaped antiquity, where we find, in other particulars, so many marks of deep penetration and discernment. If it was not so generally known and acknowledged as at present, it had, at least, an influence on all the wiser and more experienced princes and politicians.[28]

Balance of power principles were recognized and exalted, in theory and in practice, by Hindu rulers and commentators well before the beginnings of the Christian era. Indeed, Heinrich Zimmer referred to balance of power as the "principal Hindu formula for the management of foreign alliances and coalitions." The *mandala,* or circle of states theory of the ancient Hindus, which is described at length in Kautilya's *Arthaśastra,* a political classic of perhaps the fourth century B.C., may be characterized as a version of the balance of power theory.[29] Chinese statesmen also spoke and acted in terms of the balance of power.[30]

Like most students of the subject, Hume believed that the theory and practice of the balance of power in the ancient world found their most complete expression in the politics of Greece and in the Hellenistic era which followed the conquest of Greece by Alexander. Greek political commentators,

[27] *The Balance of Tomorrow* (New York: G. P. Putnam's Sons, 1945), p. 22.

[28] *Essays and Treatises on Several Subjects* (London, 1788), I, 305.

[29] See Kautilya's *Arthaśastra,* translated by Dr. R. Shamasastry, 5th ed. (Mysore, 1956), pp. 344–348.

[30] See Ssu-yü Têng and John K. Fairbank, *China's Response to the West* (Cambridge, Mass.: Harvard University Press, 1945), pp. 29–33.

including Thucydides, Demosthenes, and Aristotle, were well aware of the principle.

The term "balance of power," therefore, may be regarded as one of the oldest in international relations theory. But with the coming of the Roman world-state its importance declined sharply. Nor did this concept mean much during the confused period that followed the decline and eventual collapse of the Roman Empire, or in the Middle Ages in general, with some exceptions. The idea of balance, on the interstate level, was foreign to scholastic thinkers and to the whole spirit of the medieval world. Actually, as Quincy Wright said, it "scarcely existed anywhere as a conscious principle of international politics before 1500."[31]

Fifteenth and Sixteenth Centuries. The real beginning of the balance of power system dates from the late fifteenth century, when the political and secular basis of the modern world was being laid. The rivalries among the princes of northern Italy — the Medici, the Visconti, the Sforzas, and many others — and among Spanish, French, and German rulers who attempted to intervene in Italian politics, seemed to represent a conscious application of the system. In this area the modern study of statecraft and diplomacy, of political science and international relations, had its origin, and here the doctrine of the balance of power began to be formulated and consciously applied. The first explicit statement of the doctrine in early modern times is usually credited to Bernardo Rucellai (1449–1514), brother-in-law of Lorenzo de Medici.[32] It was further elaborated by a more famous Florentine historian, Niccolo Machiavelli (1469–1527), whose classic essay *The Prince* analyzed the methods employed by successful princes in the city-states of northern Italy. About that time, too, Venice, a once-mighty city-state, was seeking to act as balancer between France and the Empire, leading Queen Mary of Hungary to say of the Venetians: "You know how they fear the power of the one and of the other of the two princes [Charles V and Francis I] and how they are concerned to balance their power."[33]

In the sixteenth century the concept of the balance of power was applied to a larger theater than the Italian peninsula. From that time until the rise of non-European powers to dominance in our own day, the concept has been a key to European politics. Morgenthau stated that "the alliances Francis I concluded with Henry VIII and the Turks in order to prevent Charles V of Hapsburg from stabilizing and expanding his empire are the first modern example on a grand scale of the balance of power operating between an alliance and one nation intent upon establishing a universal monarchy."[34]

England is regarded as the classic example of a country which long followed a balance of power policy. In the sixteenth century she attempted to hold the balance between France and the Holy Roman Empire; but occasionally, for her own good reasons, she supported the stronger side against the weaker — certainly a flagrant violation of the principles of the balance of power. Even Wolsey, sometimes called the originator of this historic English policy, violated these principles when, because of his overweening ambition to become pope, he led England into alliances with Charles V at a time when the Empire was stronger than France. The

[31] Wright, II, 758.

[32] Carl J. Friedrich, *Foreign Policy in the Making* (New York: W. W. Norton & Company, 1938), p. 123. Some historians believe that the famous French diplomat and writer Philippe de Comines, a contemporary of Rucellai, first formulated and defined the doctrine. Edward V. Gulick, *The Balance of Power* (The Pacifist Research Bureau, 1943), p. 15. Friedrich (p. 123) suggests that the idea may have originated "with papal diplomacy."

[33] *Papiers d'État du Cardinal de Granvelle* (Paris, 1841–52), IV, 121; quoted in Morgenthau, p. 195.

[34] Morgenthau, p. 188.

battle of Pavia in 1525, and the territorial concessions which Francis was forced to make for his release from captivity, nearly destroyed the balance of power in Europe in an early stage of its evolution. Thereafter, to right the balance, England swung over to a strongly pro-French policy.

The famous English philosopher Francis Bacon, writing during the reign of Queen Elizabeth (1558–1603), clearly analyzed the doctrine of the balance of power. In his essay "Of Empire" he pointed to some of its essential features. "First, for their neighbors," he wrote, "there can no general rule be given (the occasions are so variable), save one which ever holdeth — which is, that princes do keep due sentinel, that none of their neighbors do overgrow so (by increase of territory, by embracing of trade, by approaches, or the like) as they become more able to annoy them than they were." To illustrate his point, Bacon cited the two earliest modern examples of the operation of the balance of power: among the city-states of Italy in the fifteenth century, and among Francis I, Henry VIII, and Charles V in the early sixteenth century; and he said of them, "there was such a watch kept that none of the three could win a palm of ground, but that the other two would straightways balance it."[35]

Seventeenth Century. The Thirty Years' War (1618–48) can be analyzed from many points of view, including that of the balance of power. Cardinal Richelieu, for instance, sought not a real balance but one in favor of France. To weaken the Empire, in Europe as a whole as well as in the Germanies, he encouraged rival alliances, at first with the diplomatic and financial support of France and later with her military participation as well. The alliance of France with Sweden suggested new potentialities for an old doctrine. In the first place, it aligned a staunchly Catholic country, whose policy was being shaped by a Prince of the Church, with a Protestant nation whose great ruler, Gustavus Adolphus, was regarded as the champion of Protestantism in Europe. In the second place, it associated the balance of power in Western Europe with the new regional balance that had developed in the northern and northeastern sections of the continent.

The Treaty of Westphalia of 1648 firmly established the nation-state system and clearly delineated the general pattern of international relations. As a result, the balance of power began to play an even greater role than before. When the ambitions of Louis XIV of France (1643–1715) threatened to destroy the balance, he faced a series of wars against various coalitions of powers, with England and the Netherlands spearheading the opposition to him. For a time, before the nation awoke to the danger, England under Charles II was actually in alliance with France. The reaction to the alliance, and to Louis' political, religious, and economic policies, however, was so strong that Charles and James II, his ardently Catholic brother, who succeeded him, could not prevent England's reversion to her now-traditional balance of power role. "Louis XIV made the fatal mistake of threatening both the commercial interests of the maritime powers and the continental balance of power."[36] As a result he provoked a series of alliances against him, in which England joined with continental powers to frustrate Louis XIV's dreams of continental hegemony and to counter his threat to the European balance.

Eighteenth Century. The Treaty of Utrecht of 1713, which closed the War of the Spanish Succession, in which an English-led coalition had defeated Louis XIV, expressly

[35] Quoted in Morgenthau, p. 188.

[36] Carl J. Friedrich and Charles Blitzer, *The Age of Power* (Ithaca: Cornell University Press, 1957), p. 185.

stated that its provisions for the division of the Spanish inheritance between Bourbons and Hapsburgs were made *ad conservandum in Europa equilibrium*. This phrase is frequently regarded as the first formal incorporation of the doctrine of the balance of power in an international agreement. The same principle, stated in greater detail, was embodied in several other treaties within the next half-century.

The eighteenth century, especially the period from the Treaty of Utrecht (1713) to the first partition of Poland (1772), has been acclaimed as the golden age of the balance of power, in theory as well as in practice. During that period most of the literature of the balance of power appeared; and the princes of Europe accepted the balance of power as the supreme principle for their guidance in the conduct of foreign affairs. One must conclude that here was a kind of thread running through the maze of alliances and counter-alliances, the frequent shifts in alignments, and the devious maneuverings which marked the foreign policies of the great powers of that century. The evidence is abundant. In the first place, an analysis of the causes of the "diplomatic revolution" between the Peace of Aix-la-Chapelle in 1748 and the outbreak of the Seven Years' War in 1756 supports the conclusion. It is also sustained by the career of Frederick the Great of Prussia (1740–86), an acknowledged master of the balance of power, who both wrote of his specialty and practiced it in his subtle intrigues and military ventures. Finally, one may cite the three partitions of Poland, in 1772, 1793, and 1795, as evidences of the application of balance of power principles, particularly that of compensations of territory. The treaty of 1772 between Austria and Russia explicitly stated that "the acquisitions . . . shall be completely equal, the portion of one cannot exceed the portion of the other."

In this period a multiple balance of power existed, involving England, France, Prussia, Austria, and Russia; and much of the political history of the eighteenth century between the Treaty of Utrecht and the outbreak of the French Revolution and the Napoleonic Wars could be written around the varying relations among these five powers.

The eighteenth century, as we have noted, produced a prolific literature on the balance of power. By this time the concept had assumed great significance as the basis of international conduct, but it had not yet been exposed to criticism that challenged its fundamental assumptions. It was not surprising, then, that many British writers and statesmen testified to its merits, including two of the greatest of British philosophers, Edmund Burke and David Hume, and the elder and younger Pitts. Continental writers paid less attention to the doctrine, and ascribed less merit to it; but several important rulers, notably Frederick the Great, wrote about it as well as practiced it. All of them linked the idea of the balance of power with natural law and other prevailing conceptions of "the age of reason." As Carl J. Friedrich said, "incredible as it may seem today, the theorists of the balance in the seventeenth and eighteenth centuries saw it as a 'beautiful design.' " "At that period," he added, "men were seeing 'natural balances' everywhere"; they believed in the " 'pre-established harmony' of the universe," and felt that "a harmonious society would result if each person pursued his own interests."[37]

Toward the close of the century revolutionary events in France seemed to the rulers of Europe to conjure up new and serious threats to the stability of institutions everywhere. The states united in the first coalition against republican France, in 1792, proclaimed that "no power interested in the maintenance of the balance of power in Europe could see with indifference the Kingdom of France, which at one time formed so im-

[37] Friedrich, *Foreign Policy in the Making*, p. 119.

portant a weight in this great balance, delivered any longer to domestic agitations and to the horrors of disorder and anarchy which, so to speak, have destroyed her political existence."[38]

Nineteenth Century. The rise of Napoleon Bonaparte confronted Britain and other nations of Europe with a threat that they disposed of only after many years of war. The Allies formed one coalition or alliance after another, but Napoleon seemed able to shatter them all. Finally, British sea power and finances, combined with the nationalism that Napoleon himself had evoked in Europe, brought Allied success and the restoration of the balance of power. The victors promised in the Convention of Paris of April 23, 1814, to "put an end to the miseries of Europe, and to found her repose upon a just redistribution of forces among the nations of which she is composed." The ensuing conference, the famous Congress of Vienna of 1814–15, sought to establish a new balance of power in Europe, based upon the principles of legitimacy and, as far as possible, the preservation of the status quo. "The Vienna arrangements proved to be the last major peace settlement which could be based unanimously and consistently on an avowed balance of power policy."[39]

A notable extension of the balance of power doctrine was revealed by the British foreign minister, George Canning, in a speech on December 12, 1826, before the House of Commons. "Is the balance of power a fixed and unalterable standard," he asked, "or is it not a standard perpetually varying, as civilization advances, and as new nations spring up, and take their place among established political communities?" After citing some historical evidence to support his point, Canning defended his refusal to resort to war to restore the balance in Europe after the French invasion of Spain in 1823, as Britain had been invited to do by the Congress of Verona of 1822. He said:

> Was there no other mode of resistance, than by a direct attack upon France — or by a war to be undertaken on the soil of Spain? What, if the possession of Spain might be rendered harmless in rival hands . . . ? Might not compensation for disparagement be obtained . . . by means better adapted to the present time? If France occupied Spain, was it necessary, in order to avoid the consequences of that occupation — that we blockade Cadiz? No. I looked another way — I saw materials for compensation in another hemisphere. Contemplating Spain . . . I resolved that if France had Spain, it should not be Spain *"with the Indies."* I called the New World into existence, to redress the balance of the Old.[40]

The final sentence of Canning's statement has often been quoted by American historians, for it raises the question of Canning's part in the origin of the Monroe Doctrine. In any case, it suggests a highly important step in the evolution of the balance of power system: the beginning of its gradual extension to a worldwide system.

The interest of statesmen in the extension of the balance of power to include areas outside the major European states was also disclosed by the intervention of the great powers in the politics of the Balkans. Alarmed by the growing incapacity of Turkey and the rising influence of Russia in the Balkan Peninsula, Austria, France, and Great Britain banded together in 1854, declaring "that the existence of the Ottoman Empire in its present extent, is of essential importance to the balance of power among the states of Europe." The Crimean War followed. Later, the Congress of Berlin of 1878, called by the great powers of Europe, forced Russia to

[38] Quoted in Morgenthau, p. 188.

[39] Gulick, "Our Balance of Power System in Perspective," p. 11.

[40] *Speeches of the Right Honourable George Canning* (London, 1836), VI, 109–111. Italics in original.

revise the Treaty of San Stefano which she had imposed upon defeated Turkey at the close of the Russo-Turkish War of 1877–78. The action of the European powers must be explained as another attempt to prevent a great power from gaining a position of dominance in the Balkan cockpit.

With the Concert of Europe and its related alliances and arrangements a new multiple balance of power existed on the continent of Europe throughout most of the century following the Congress of Vienna. Two of the most brilliant practitioners were Metternich in the first half of the century and Bismarck in the latter part.

Meantime, however, while the doctrine of the balance of power was being cherished and practiced its assumptions were being seriously challenged. Foremost among the critics were the political philosophers of the Manchester school in Great Britain. These men espoused laissez faire, nonimperialist, and often pacifist ideals. John Bright and Richard Cobden, the outstanding spokesmen of this school, repeatedly condemned the balance of power as a mechanical and almost satanic doctrine. Cobden in his *Political Writings* declared that ". . . the balance of power is a chimera! It is not a fallacy, a mistake, an imposture — it is an undescribed, indescribable, incomprehensive nothing; mere words, conveying to the mind not ideas, but sounds."[41]

For a substantial part of the century following the Congress of Vienna Britain held the enviable position of balancer. This *Pax Britannica* was made possible by a favorable combination of circumstances at home and abroad: England's leadership in the Industrial Revolution, in international finance, and in world trade; her navy, which gave her control of the seas and free access to her widespread possessions and to the markets of the world; and the post-Napoleonic situation in Europe, which gave Britain no formidable challenger to her unique position until the rise of Germany. The growth of the United States and Japan, the emergence of Germany, and the increasing competition for the markets and underdeveloped areas of the world, heralded the beginning of the end of England's political and industrial leadership, and, indeed, even of her naval supremacy. The rise of the United States and Japan furthermore served notice that the extension of the balance of power system, so dramatically begun by Canning, had reached around the world.

Twentieth Century. With the completion of the Triple Entente by the Anglo-Russian understanding of 1907 Europe was divided into two armed camps — that of the Triple Alliance and that of the Triple Entente. The complex balance of power of the previous century had become an alarmingly simple one. Moreover, England had been forced to emerge from her "splendid isolation," to abandon her role of balancer, and to become a member of one of the rival alliances. English statesmen, nevertheless, continued to follow balance of power policies, although they often eschewed them in theory.[42]

The delicate balance in the Balkans persisted, and its threatened disturbance in 1914 produced a titanic conflict of the great powers. An authoritative statement on the point came from Tsar Nicholas II of Russia on

[41] *Political Writings* (New York: Appleton, 1867), I, 258.

[42] A classic statement of the British balance of policy was made by Sir Eyre Crowe in a memorandum in January, 1907, when he observed that Britain followed a policy of seeking to maintain an equilibrium on the continent of Europe "by throwing her weight now in this scale and now in that, but ever on the side opposed to the political dictatorship of the strongest single State or group at a given time." "Memorandum by Sir Eyre Crowe on the Present State of British Relations with France and Germany, Jan. 1, 1907," in G. P. Gooch and Harold Temperley, eds., *British Documents on the Origins of the War, 1898–1914* (London, 1926–38), III, 403.

August 2, 1914, when, in a telegram to King George V of England, he thus referred to Austria's ultimatum to Serbia:

> Object of that action was to crush Servia and make her a vassal of Austria. Effect of this would have been to upset balance of power in Balkans, which is of such a vital interest to my Empire as well as to those Powers who desire maintenance of balance of power in Europe. . . . I trust your country will not fail to support France and Russia in fighting to maintain balance of power in Europe.[43]

In the interwar period, from 1919 to 1939, the balance of power doctrine was still followed, although in theory it conflicted with the search for collective security and with the principles underlying the League of Nations. In fact, it proved stronger than collective security, inside or outside the League, and it provoked a series of alliances and counter-alliances, military preparations and rivalries, which, as was to be expected, eventually broke down in aggression and war. After World War II, as we shall explain later in this chapter, conditions seemed to be peculiarly unfavorable for the operation of the old system. Despite this, the balance of power remained and still remains a basic concept in international relations.

Devices for Maintaining the Balance of Power

The balance of power is an uncertain regulator, for it creates an equilibrium that is at best temporary and improvised. Even under ideal conditions its operation requires great skill and finesse and possibly a ruthless disregard of moral concepts and human welfare. As in any perfected game, it has developed rules, techniques, and devices of its own. Among these the following may be singled out for special emphasis:

[43] Quoted in *Ibid.*, XI, 276.

1. Alliances and Counter-Alliances. These have been the most commonly employed devices of the balance ot power system. Whenever one nation threatened the balance in Europe, other states formed coalitions against it, and were always able, at times after an exhausting war or series of wars, to curb the power of the overly ambitious nation. Ad hoc or temporary alliances of a constantly shifting character have been standard practices in modern European history. After the Triple Alliance had been formed in 1882, portending significant changes in the European balance, a rival alliance — the Triple Entente — was slowly forged in dual agreements over a period of seventeen years (1891–1907), first between France and Russia, then between France and England, and finally between England and Russia.

Alliances are often divided into two kinds, offensive and defensive. Both are concerned with the balance of power, for an offensive alliance seeks to upset the balance in favor of its members and a defensive alliance aims at restoring the balance or at tipping it in favor of the states which make up the alliance. The balance of power which figures so importantly in national policies may be the world balance or it may be a strictly regional balance. Although it is conceivable that two or more states should form an alliance to discourage aggression when they could not hope to defeat it, such a move would probably be regarded as the first step toward a really effective alignment. It is not too much to say that balance of power considerations, whether regional, hemispheric, or worldwide, are a controlling factor in virtually every alliance of states. Hence the study of power alignments leads at once to the balance of power.

The first prerequisite of an effective alliance is, of course, power enough to achieve the purpose for which it was formed. The second prerequisite is a common fundamental interest between or among the allying states. Other conditions, such as strategy, geography, common ideologies, cultural similarities, and complementary economies, help to make alliances relatively stable and even long-lived, but they are not prerequisites of an effective alliance for a temporary purpose. Thus alliance with the Soviet Union was a cornerstone of United States foreign policy during World War II; despite geographical separation and all sorts of ideological and cultural differences, the two states were able to cooperate with each other, with Great Britain, and with other states so effectively that together they carried to a successful termination the most colossal military operation in history. "The Strange Alliance" was a joining of unlikes, kept together only because of desperate urgency, but its temporary effectiveness admits of no doubt.

The question whether alliances tend to promote wars is an old one. Of course offensive alliances bring wars — at least the successful ones do, for that is their purpose. These alliances are usually to be condemned, but purely defensive alliances are quite another matter. The difficulty is that the nature and purposes of an alliance may be open to the most divergent interpretations. Every alliance is defensive from the point of view of those states which participate in it, and aggressive from the point of view of those states which are opposed to it. This terminological inexactitude makes most alliances suspect. No amount of declaiming will prevent aggression-minded states from combining for their evil purposes. The would-be victims must have the right to combine in defense, and no amount of declaiming will prevent them from doing so. To another charge — that defensive alliances do not defend — the reply must be that sometimes they do, sometimes they do not. When they fail to serve their purpose it is not because the idea is bad, but because they are poorly implemented or lack sufficient power.

2. **Compensations.** This common device usually entails the annexation or division of territory. Examples include: the division of the Spanish possessions, in Europe and outside, among Bourbons and Hapsburgs in the Treaty of Utrecht; the partitions of Poland; the revision of the territorial arrangements of the Treaty of San Stefano at the Congress of Berlin; and the territorial losses of the defeated powers after World Wars I and II. Territorial compensations have frequently been made by strong powers at the expense of weaker ones, and almost invariably by victor nations at the end of a war. They were employed on a large scale during the great age of the new imperialism, from 1870 to 1914, as evidenced by the distribution of colonial territories and the delineation of spheres of influence in China and elsewhere among the European powers. When compensations do not relate directly to territorial areas, the principle is the same. "The bargaining of diplomatic negotiations, issuing in political compromise," for instance, as Morgenthau stated, "is but the principle of compensations in its most general form, and as such it is organically connected with the balance of power."[44]

3. **Armaments and Disarmament.** All major powers place great emphasis on military preparedness and other means of national defense. This policy may lead to an armaments race, to intensified rivalries among the major powers, and to an ever more dangerous and uncertain state of affairs. Moreover, improvements in weapons and methods of warfare may place an added premium on the offensive, which may at least temporarily favor would-be aggressors.

In theory, a more stable balance of power could be created by ending armaments races and by proportionate reduction of armaments by rival powers. Although repeated efforts

[44] Morgenthau, p. 180.

have been made to achieve reductions, the only outstanding exception to the record of continued failures and postponements is the Washington Naval Treaty of 1922, and even this famous treaty was limited in application and duration. Various kinds of disarmament have been proposed from time to time — quantitative and qualitative disarmament, arms-building holidays (as the Washington Naval Treaty), revision of the rules of war ("disarmament not of materials but of methods," as Quincy Wright put it), even moral disarmament (rather "moral rearmament"); but the results of all of these well-intentioned efforts have been disappointing. Perhaps the real reason for this record of substantial failure was suggested by that wise Spanish philosopher-statesman-litterateur, Salvador de Madariaga: "The problem of disarmament is not the problem of disarmament. It is really the problem of the organization of the World Community."[45] In essence, it is the problem of the maintenance of the balance of power.

4. Intervention and Nonintervention. These devices have been employed by countries in the position of balancer, most often Great Britain. Enjoying considerable freedom of choice, they have been able to utilize different methods for maintaining the European balance. Intervention may range all the way from slight deviations from neutrality, in the traditional sense, to full-scale military participation in a major war. Nonintervention suggests the kind of policy usually followed by small states and also by those great powers which are satisfied with the political order and can follow peaceful methods to preserve the balance. There is considerable justification for Talleyrand's remark that "non-intervention is a political term meaning virtually the same thing as intervention"; the record of the Non-Intervention Committee during the Spanish Civil War, for instance, may be cited in support of it. Nonintervention also suggests neutrality, to the extent that such a policy is possible, or guarantees of neutrality for certain states, of efforts to localize wars or protect the "rights" of neutrals in time of war. It is particularly emphasized by small states seeking means of protection or even of survival in a world dominated by great powers. It has been a cardinal principle of the inter-American system in recent years, on the insistence of the Latin American states, and it has been repeatedly espoused by statesmen of the newly emerging nations of Asia and Africa, most of whom are following varying forms and patterns of neutrality and nonalignment.

Unfortunately, few nations have ever enjoyed the position which George Washington sought for the United States, "when we may choose peace or war, as our interest, guided by justice, shall counsel." But, as Quincy Wright stated, "Whether taking the characteristic American form of profiting by other people's wars, the characteristic British form of divide (the continent of Europe) and rule (elsewhere), or the characteristic Scandinavian form of peace at almost any price, neutrality has assumed a balance of power, and the neutral has shaped its policy accordingly."[46]

5. Buffer States. The balance of power is especially precarious in a bipolar world without buffer zones and neutral areas, and with the rival powers in direct contact with each other. To some extent, despite signs of a trend toward a more complex balance, this situation prevails today; but the two superpowers, the Soviet Union and the United States, are widely separated by land and ocean barriers, even though an "iron curtain" is all that separates their allies in Europe, and though American troops are almost face to face with Russian soldiers in

[45] *Disarmament* (New York: Coward-McCann, 1929), p. 56.

[46] Wright, II, 783–784.

areas as widely separated as the Bering Strait and Germany. Buffer states are of great importance because of their cushioning effect between great powers; they may be neutral or neutralized states, satellite states, or dependent territories, or they may be actively associated with one of two or more aggregations of power in a relatively honorable role.

One of the most important buffer zones in the world is that which separates the Soviet Union from the major non-Communist powers. This is an area of weak states, vast distances, formidable geographic barriers, rising nationalisms, and conflicting interests among the great powers. It is an area of never-ending interest to the geopoliticians; it constitutes a large part of the Inner Crescent of Sir Halford Mackinder and of the Rimland of Nicholas J. Spykman. Of tremendous importance today, it may be of even greater significance in the future. If Russia should break through one of the weak points in the buffer zone — through the Straits to the Mediterranean and possibly beyond, through Iran to the Persian Gulf and the Indian Ocean, through Afghanistan to the Punjab and the plains of the Indian subcontinent and the Indian Ocean, through Manchuria and Korea to the China seas and the Pacific — if any one of these developments, not impossible in peacetime and highly probable in the event of war, should occur, the effects on the balance of power would be incalculable.

6. Divide and Rule. This is a time-honored policy, not necessarily associated with the balance of power; for instance, it was employed by the Romans to maintain their control over scattered peoples, and by imperialist nations to keep native populations in subjection. But it has also been a device of the balance of power system. Perhaps the outstanding examples in modern times are the traditional policy of France vis-à-vis Germany ever since the seventeenth century, the historic policy of England toward the Continent — to divide, and in a sense to rule — and the policy of the Soviet Union toward the rest of Europe. This doubtless accounts in part for the persistent opposition of the U.S.S.R. to all plans and proposals for the closer political and economic integration of Western Europe.

Collective Security and the Balance of Power

A system of collective security has often been pictured as a pattern of international relations which is able to dispense with the balance of power and thereby to elevate the nature and tone of the world society. When nations are bound together in an international organization or association, and when they really cooperate to preserve the peace, so the argument runs, there will be no need for alliances, burdensome armaments, shady territorial deals, political manipulations and rivalries, instability, or war, all of which, it is charged, are inherent in the balance of power system. The record of attempts at collective security to date teaches a different lesson, namely, that short of effective world government such efforts are certain to be associated with balance of power policies and cannot operate unless a foundation of "power politics" exists. Quincy Wright was quite justified in asserting that "the relations of the balance of power to collective security have, therefore, been at the same time complementary and antagonistic."[47] "Until world opinion is more unified than it is likely to be for a long time," Wright believed, "collective security must rely upon a balance of power which maintains such general stability that a localizing of policing actions is possible."[48]

The three outstanding examples of systems of collective security in modern times have been the Concert of Europe, the League of Nations, and the United Nations. What has

[47] *Ibid.*, II, 781.

[48] Quincy Wright, *Problems of Stability and Progress in International Relations* (Berkeley: University of California Press, 1954), p. 106.

been the relation of these organizations to the balance of power?

1. The Concert of Europe. This was the most successful application of an idea which had been entertained for centuries and had prompted many earlier experiments in international cooperation — the idea of a "Concert of Powers." The alliance system which emerged from the Congress of Vienna, centered in the Quadruple and Holy Alliances and extended and applied at a series of international conferences in the years following 1815, was presumably based on just such a concert, and was, in fact, called the Concert of Europe. The great powers were expected to cooperate harmoniously to prevent hostile groupings of powers; hence it was conceived to be on a different and perhaps a higher plane than the balance of power.

The Concert of Europe was a loose relationship among the major European powers which came into being soon after the Napoleonic Wars and lasted until World War I, with the second half of the nineteenth century as the time of its greatest effectiveness. Thus it was a controlling mechanism in Europe during one of the periods of the most successful operation of the balance of power. Within its broad framework the states of Europe played the power game according to traditional rules, which for a time concealed the basic changes which were occurring in the relations of states. On occasion the Concert helped to prevent major conflicts on the Continent or in peripheral or colonial areas where the interests of various European states appeared to be divergent. On the whole, it was most successful in dealing with the Balkan area; although it did not prevent serious wars, such as the Crimean War of 1854–56 and the Russo-Turkish War of 1877–78, it did succeed, for several decades, in localizing wars in the Balkans, and in resolving the conflicting interests of the great powers there without resort to war. The Congress of Berlin of 1878 subjected the Concert of Europe to a critical test. In the late nineteenth century the Concert collapsed, for its foundations had not been seen as secure as its proponents had fancied. Its existence had been possible only under peculiarly favorable conditions, but with the rise of Germany, the growth of imperialistic rivalries, and the division of Europe into two armed camps with opposing alliances, the Concert disintegrated into a mêlée of contending states. Instead of superseding the balance of power, it had been dependent upon a balance which for a time had made great power cooperation both desirable and possible.

2. The League of Nations. It was the hope of Woodrow Wilson and other founders of the League of Nations that the League would provide a system of international cooperation and collective security which would supplant the balance of power, nurturing in its place a true "community of power." In the second of his Four Principles of February 11, 1918, Wilson expressed his firm conviction that "peoples and provinces are not to be bartered about from sovereignty to sovereignty as if they were mere chattels and pawns in a game, even the great game, now forever discredited, of the balance of power."[49] From its outset the reality was but a faint shadow of the hope. The League concept implied universality; yet the United States and several smaller nations refused to join, and Germany and Soviet Russia were not allowed to do so until a later date. The concept also implied that if the League's authority was challenged, enforcement machinery would be automatically invoked and members would abide by their obligations in the Covenant; yet the League functioned haltingly, even in minor political disputes,

[49] Ray S. Baker and William E. Dodd, eds., *The Public Papers of Woodrow Wilson, War and Peace* (New York: Harper, 1927), I, 631. See also Claude, pp. 75–87, for a commentary on "the Wilsonian critique" of the balance of power. For a fuller analysis see Edward H. Buehrig, *Woodrow Wilson and the Balance of Power* (Bloomington: Indiana University Press, 1955).

and proved to be impotent in the face of flagrant acts of aggression by powerful member states. Several efforts to strengthen the League's collective security principles by regional security arrangements, notably in the Locarno Pacts, and by a solemn renunciation of war in the Kellogg-Briand Pact of 1928, proved to be no more than momentary stimulants.

With the coming of the worldwide depression after 1929, the rise of Hitler to power in Germany, and the succession of open challenges by the totalitarian aggressors, beginning with Japan's invasion of Manchuria in 1931, the League's impotence and inadequacies became painfully evident. Although it had been able to throw a cloak of internationalism and of collective security over the world of nation-states, it had never actually supplanted the balance of power, except in theory. It had become involved in a peculiarly unstable balance, and again collective security had failed to find a path out of the maze of the balance of power. Indeed, many careful observers came to believe with the British diplomat Lord D'Abernon that "the balance of power is a condition for an effective League of Nations" and with a distinguished authority on international law, L. Oppenheim, that "the existence of the League of Nations makes a balance of power not less, but all the more necessary, because an omnipotent state could disregard the League of Nations."[50]

3. The United Nations. While the Allied powers were waging war against the Axis in World War II, they also were laying the foundations of a new international organization. Leaders in many nations studied the lessons of the League of Nations and also those which they had learned during the bitter harvest of depression, aggression, and global war. The United Nations which they set up was in many respects a stronger organization, more closely geared to the realities of the international scene, than the League had been. In some features, however, concessions to realities seemed to weaken it as an instrument of collective security; for example, the great powers were given a privileged status and through use of the veto in the Security Council they could paralyze almost any action that the UN might wish to take. Again the Charter sanctioned and even encouraged steps for "individual and collective self-defense" outside the UN (Article 51); and it approved regional arrangement which could buttress but could also, in effect, bypass the UN (Articles 52–54). It would be difficult to determine whether regional arrangements and understandings, such as the Rio Treaty of 1947 and the Organization of American States, the Arab League, and the Brussels Treaty and the North Atlantic Pact, tend to strengthen the United Nations system of collective security or to furnish current examples of the prevalence and persistence of the balance of power.

The United Nations, like the League of Nations, was launched with high expectations on the part of many of its founders. One of the most distinguished of these, the American Secretary of State, Cordell Hull, on his return from the Moscow Conference of 1943, where the Soviet Union had agreed for the first time to join in the establishment of a new international organization at the end of hostilities, declared: "As the provisions of the Four-Nation Declaration are carried into effect, there will no longer be need for spheres of influence, for alliances, for balance of power, or any other of the special arrangements through which, in the unhappy past, the nations strove to safeguard their security or promote their interests."[51] Regrettably, this buoyant prediction was as

[50] L. Oppenheim, *International Law,* edited by R. F. Roxburgh (New York: Longmans, Green & Co., 1920–21), I, 94.

[51] *Memoirs* (New York: The Macmillan Company, 1948), II, 1314–1315. Used by permission of The Macmillan Company.

naive and groundless as Wilson's reference, a quarter of a century before, to "the great game, now forever discredited, of the balance of power." The UN, like the League, is based on the sovereignty of the members of the nation-state system, and does not operate in a vacuum. It is profoundly affected by its milieu, by contemporary international society, and especially by the nature of great power relations. Since these relations are still based in large measure on balance of power considerations, and since many aspects of the foreign policies of the great powers seem to operate outside the UN and to revolve around the fact of bipolarity and efforts to create a more complex balance, it is clear that the UN is likewise involved in a balance of power situation.

International Law and the Balance of Power

These examples seem to validate Quincy Wright's conclusion, already quoted, that "the relations of the balance of power to collective security have . . . been at the same time complementary and antagonistic." The same statement may be made about the balance of power and international law. L. Oppenheim called the balance of power "an indispensable condition of the very existence of International Law." "A law of nations," he argued, "can exist only if there be an equilibrium, a balance of power, between the members of the Family of Nations. . . . As there is not, and never can be, a central political authority above the sovereign States that could enforce the rules of the Law of Nations, a balance of power must prevent any member of the Family of Nations from becoming omnipotent."[52] Oppenheim's approach is typical of that of many authorities on international law. They are obviously thinking of a stable balance — which is in itself something of a contradiction in practice if not in theory — and are assuming that international law would have to continue to operate in a world of sovereign states. But perhaps most present-day students believe that international law, like international society, must move out of an era in which balance of power considerations are predominant and into another era in which really effective international organization and genuine collective security will exist. Perhaps, indeed, as Quincy Wright insisted, "International law . . . tends to convert the system of balance of power into a system of collective security."[53]

Even in an international society in which law predominated over politics, however, balance of power considerations would by no means be neglected. Wright himself fully appreciated this fact: "The difference between a world regime of law and a world regime of power politics," he wrote in 1954, "is not that the latter rests on balance of power and the former on union of power, but rather that the latter rests on a simple balance and the former on a complex balance." Hence, "if a law-governed world is to develop peacefully from the present situation, statesmen must seek to make the balance more complicated."[54]

The Balance of Power Today

We have already indicated some of the contradictions inherent in the assumptions of the balance of power and in its practical operation. Now we must consider the question: Does the concept have any validity today? The answer would seem to be twofold: (1) the conditions of the modern world are peculiarly unfavorable to the balance of power system, but (2) it is still a central theoretical concept and operational principle in international relations, and it still exists, if only by default.

Unfavorable Conditions. The balance of power worked best on the European con-

[52] Oppenheim, I, 93–94.

[53] Wright, *A Study of War*, II, 765.

[54] Wright, *Problems of Stability and Progress*, pp. 270, 271.

tinent in those periods of modern history in which a number of states of approximately equal strength, with policies controlled by a limited number of persons, competed with each other according to well-established and generally recognized rules. After the French Revolution, and particularly after the expansion of the European balance to a world system, conditions became less favorable for the successful adjustment of a balance among nations. The impact of new forces — nationalism, industrialism, democracy, mass education, new methods and techniques of warfare, the growing importance of public opinion, developments in international organization and international law, the growing economic interdependence of nations and peoples in a shrinking world, the disappearance of colonial frontiers, the emergence of many new nations, the advent of the nuclear and space age — all these and many other forces that have shaped our contemporary world made the balance of power at once too simple and too difficult a policy.

Other conditions unfavorable to its operation are: (1) the confusing bipolar-multipolar pattern of power at the present time and the disappearance of the balancer of the system; (2) the sudden, although perhaps only temporary, increase in the power of the offensive over the defensive, and the character and the frightening implications of total war — implications which would make even the most ruthless proponent of the balance of power hesitate before taking the risk of precipitating a worldwide struggle to right the balance; (3) the growing importance of ideological considerations and other less tangible but nevertheless important elements of power; and (4) the increasing disparities in the power of states, with the superpowers becoming more and more powerful and the lesser states becoming weaker, at least in relative terms.[55] "In short," as Professor Inis L. Claude, Jr. observed, "all the most fundamental tendencies affecting the political realm in recent generations run counter to the requirements of a working system of balance of power. There is nothing to indicate that the global setting is likely to become more, rather than less, appropriate to the operation of a balance system."[56]

The United States or the U.S.S.R. as Balancer? Neither the United States nor the Soviet Union can hope to succeed to Britain's former position as holder of the balance. They are the rival poles around which the bipolar-multipolar balance of the latter half of the twentieth century revolves. Although this is a role which neither power is particularly qualified to fill, there is no escaping the fact of their overwhelming predominance and its serious implications. If the restoration of Western Europe, the strengthening of the British orbit, the development of potentially major states such as China and India, and other long-term forces could be accelerated, a more complex balance of power might come into being. If so, the Soviet Union and the United States might be freed from some of the consequences of their own strength and conflicting ideologies. As it is, neither country is well prepared to play the balance of power game, for the simple reason that the power of either alone is incomparably greater than that of any possible combination of other states. Moreover, one of the characteristics of the balance of power, as noted earlier, is that it is unsuitable as a conscious policy for either democracies or dictatorships.

Although some American statesmen have spoken of the balance of power without disapproval — Jefferson once expressed the hope "that a salutary balance of power may ever be maintained among nations," and even Wilson, to whom the concept was anathema, believed that an attempt to dominate the

[55] Wright, *A Study of War,* II, 760–766, 859–860.

[56] Claude, pp. 92–93.

continent of Europe was a threat to freedom everywhere — the United States has throughout most of her history prided herself on keeping out of "Europe's quarrels" and has developed a strong anti-balance of power tradition. She is saddled with historical, constitutional, and psychological handicaps — one might call them glorious handicaps — which seem to rule out the overt and covert manipulations that an active pursuit of a balancing role would require.

The handicaps of the Soviet Union are of a different nature. They include the traditional aloofness and suspicion of the Russian leaders and a theory of government and of society which assumes the implacable hostility of the non-Communist world and the necessity for expansion of influence and power to the utmost possible limits, with the ultimate goal of the overthrow of capitalism and the establishment of the dictatorship of the proletariat, by means of world revolution. Hence Soviet Russia is not interested in regulating the balance of power; she is interested in undermining and eventually destroying the present balance and — if she holds to Communist objectives — the society out of which it has developed.

The League and the UN as Balancers? When the League of Nations was being formed, some of its founders hoped that it would be able to act as a balancer among the great powers. General Jan C. Smuts expressed this hope as early as 1919. In *The League of Nations: A Practical Suggestion,* written as the Peace Conference was about to open in Paris, he said that "the League will have to occupy the great position which has been rendered vacant by the destruction of so many of the old European empires and the passing away of the old European order."[57] Obviously this hope remained unfulfilled. Today, however, the suggestion is sometimes advanced that the United Nations could act as the regulator of interstate relations; usually the suggestion is expressed in terms of collective security, but occasionally it is applied to a balance of power approach. In 1949 Quincy Wright wrote:

> The UN, with all the great powers participating, may succeed as a balancer where the League of Nations failed. . . . If the UN should itself develop sufficient independent power to serve as balancer, the conditions for decentralization of power might exist. . . . If the UN could act as a balancer even though its independent power is inadequate to enforce its own law, it might reduce the intensity of the rivalry between the United States and the USSR, so that other regions of the world could organize independent power, thus further stabilizing the equilibrium.[58]

This possibility, however desirable, seems so remote as to be hardly worth considering. The "ifs" in Professor Wright's statement are certainly large ones. Moreover, as he himself admitted in the same article, the task of the UN is "much more difficult" than that of the League "because the conditions of the world have deteriorated."

Six years later he still believed that the United Nations could have a significant effect upon the balance of power, although the "ifs" remained:

> Even if amendment of the Charter remains for a long time impossible because of the veto, even if the United Nations, for a long time or indefinitely, lacks the power to coerce the more powerful states by its own efforts, still it may, by throwing what weight it has always on the side of law, give an assurance of predominance to that side. . . . If the United Nations itself were able to play

[57] Quoted in Frank M. Russell, *Theories of International Relations* (New York: Appleton-Century, 1936), p. 345.

[58] "Modern Technology and the World Order," in William F. Ogburn, ed., *Technology and International Relations* (Chicago: University of Chicago Press, 1949), pp. 192, 193.

a more vigorous role in world politics, the old dilemma between supporting international law and maintaining the balance of power may be solved.[59]

Unfortunately, however, the UN has not been able to play the "more vigorous role in world politics" that Professor Wright had in mind. Nor does there seem to be much prospect that the UN can ever play such a role. It can and does have a useful influence in mitigating the conflicts and tensions that threaten the peace, and in laying the foundations of a more viable world order; but as an instrument of the nation-state system it lacks the power, authority, and status to be an effective regulator or balancer of an international system which still rests more on balance of power considerations than on considerations of genuine collective security or genuine supranationalism.

Is the Balance of Power Obsolete? Those who believe that the age of nationalism and sovereignty is ending may logically contend that the concept of the balance of power, which has been intimately associated with nationalistic policies, is an outworn shibboleth of a dying phase of world history. Some students of society are convinced that the international relations of the future will be conducted between supranational groupings of states on principles other than that of the balance of power. Others hold that the ideological factor in world politics has become so potent in our time — consider, for example, the ideological implications of the cold war — that it has superseded nationalism. This view was expressed in 1947 by Professor William G. Carleton, in a challenging article in the *Yale Review:*

> . . . anyone called upon to answer the crucial question in international relations today would be, I think, on safe ground in saying that, from the rise of national states and up to about now, the chief element in international relations has been nationalism and the national balance of power. But he should warn the questioner not to be misled by this historic fact . . . . because this middle of the twentieth century may be witnessing the epoch-making shift in the foundation of international politics from the nationalistic balance of power to ideology, evidence of which we shall ignore at our peril.[60]

Professor Carleton suspected that ideologies were cutting across national boundaries, supplanting the ties of nationalism with those of a common ideology and thus undermining the balance of power concept. It is difficult to conceive of such a transformation. In fact, some more recent commentators have expressed the view that ideology is declining in importance in international relations.[61] Ideologies and the balance of power concept are not necessarily antithetical; actually both have operated in the past to intensify nationalism and are doing so today, but both can also be reconciled with a fundamentally different type of interstate relationship. On the other hand, it is true that where the foreign policy of a state is highly flavored by ideology, that state is usually not much interested in the balance of power and is poorly equipped to pursue it.

Again we return to the question: Does the balance of power have any validity under present conditions? We have seen that its importance in other periods of history has varied greatly, and that it has been invoked more effectively by some countries than by others. We have also seen that the conditions under which it worked best have largely disappeared, and that it is not well adapted to the international scene today. Many eminent authorities maintain that logically, if

59 Wright, *Problems of Stability and Progress,* p. 271.

60 "Ideology or Balance of Power?" *Yale Review,* XXXVI (Summer, 1947), 602. Copyright, Yale University Press.

61 See Daniel Bell, *The End of Ideology* (New York: The Free Press, 1960).

not actually, it is an obsolete concept. As long ago as 1938 Carl J. Friedrich wrote: "The value of the idea of the balance is, under present conditions, rather slight, both for the purpose of explanation and as a guide to action. New difficulties have been added to the old vagueness. . . . One could damn the principle today for not offering any solution at all, either in the light of justice, or of clarity, or even of understanding."[62] Five years later Quincy Wright asserted positively: "If democracy and human liberty are to survive, the nations that espouse these principles must find some device other than the balance of power to give them political security. . . . The balance of power as the structure of world politics is incompatible with democracy, with free enterprise, with welfare economy, and with peace."[63]

Both Friedrich and Wright, being realistic students of world politics, admit that the balance of power is still a basic element in international relations. As Friedrich remarked, it "may yet be preferable to the international anarchy which is prevailing at present"; but, he added, "it is a sorry concession to the foibles of human nature and the world at large."[64]

The reason for the remarkable survival powers of the balance of power is obvious: as yet the nations and peoples of the world have not been willing to create any effective substitute. Such a substitute can probably be found only through world organization on the supranational level, backed by a world public opinion and a worldwide acceptance of the principles of international law. This prospect is distressingly remote. Quincy Wright, who would dearly love to write the obituary of the balance of power, felt impelled to warn that "*gradual* transition from a balance-of-power system to a juridical and co-operative international system is not likely and that states may find themselves in serious difficulties if they pursue policies adapted to the latter type of order before enough of them do so actually to establish that type of order."[65]

Balance of Power or Balance of Terror?

The existing balance of power, which seems to be evolving from a simple to an increasingly complex balance, is obviously an unstable one, which will continue to threaten to break down into global war until a more stable balance develops or until other curative factors begin to have effect. The two sides in the cold war seem to have arrived at an atomic or hydrogen stalemate. The effect of this development of weapons of mass destruction upon the balance of power cannot be precisely determined, but the new weapons certainly enhance the perils to people everywhere, and they may make old-fashioned adherence to balance of power politics as antiquated as the cannon that were such mighty weapons in the Crimea, at Gettysburg, and at Sedan.

Commenting on the "summit" conference at Geneva in the summer of 1955, shortly before the conference took place, Max Ascoli wrote:

> The trouble with the balance of power with which the democracies as well as the Communists are stuck is that it is actually a balance of terror and not of power. It does not lend itself to registering shifts and changes in the international equilibrium. Therefore it stands to reason that the first objective of the negotiations should be that of

[62] Friedrich, *Foreign Policy in the Making*, p. 132.

[63] "International Law and the Balance of Power," *The American Journal of International Law*, XXXVII (January, 1943), 138.

[64] Friedrich, *Foreign Policy in the Making*, p. 138.

[65] Wright, *A Study of War*, II, 1947. In May, 1967, a leading West German newspaper observed: "In the past the balance of power has often been the assurance of an uncertain peace. The balance will also remain the prime condition of progress in detente until controlled disarmament is possible in the East and in the West." *Die Welt*, May 3, 1967.

> moving steadily from a balance of immeasurable terror to one of usable power. It is to be expected that both sides will earnestly engage in the search for practical ways to reduce armaments, for each is pursuing aims incompatible with the constant threat of reciprocal annihilation.[66]

But not even a conference on the highest level, followed by long months of negotiations on disarmament, collective security, and more specific problems, could produce basic agreements between the Communist and non-Communist states on ways of reducing the danger of atomic-hydrogen warfare.

Whatever the imperatives of the atomic age, the game of international politics is still being played according to pre-atomic rules; and, whether obsolete or not, balance of power techniques and concepts are still very much in evidence. In fact, the prevailing grand strategy of dealing with the Soviet Union may be described as a herculean effort to create a sufficient array of power to discourage her from embarking on campaigns of aggression or from attempting to hasten the "inevitable" world revolution. In other words, this strategy seems predicated on the assumption that the balance of power has been drastically altered in the postwar period, and that every effort must be made to restore some kind of balance. Some of the great champions of European unity, such as Winston Churchill and Paul-Henri Spaak, have frankly invoked time-honored principles of the balance of power. Speaking in the Consultative Assembly of the Council of Europe in September, 1953, Spaak declared: "I am, therefore, concerned . . . that if we are ever to agree with the Russians, as I believe we must do if peace is to be assured, such agreements can only be reached on the basis of concrete facts and particularly on that of the balance of power."

[66] "Toward Geneva," *The Reporter*, XII (June 30, 1955), p. 8.

A Final Appraisal. Dag Hammarskjold, former Secretary-General of the United Nations, once predicted that "The increasing danger of destruction will sooner or later force us out of a system of balance of power into a system of true and universal co-operation," but in another connection he pointed out that "We are still in the transition between institutional systems of international co-existence and constitutional systems of international co-operation."[67] In such a transitional stage, with the prospects for the development of "constitutional systems of international co-operation" discouragingly remote, balance of power considerations still have a significant place.

The concept of the balance of power, then, is still a meaningful one, although it has lost much of its validity. It is an important concept in international politics, and in its heyday it was a basic feature of the nation-state system. Its operation was by no means wholly destructive. It did sometimes help to preserve the independence of various states, and to prevent a single nation from becoming all-powerful. But, although the philosophers of the eighteenth century thought of it as a "beautiful design," it was full of contradictions and inconsistencies, even in theory. And it was sounder in theory than in practice. If it averted some wars, it led to greater ones. As long as the nation-state system is the prevailing pattern of international society, balance of power policies will be followed in practice, however roundly they are damned in theory. In all probability they will continue to operate, even if effective supranational groupings, on a regional or world level, are formed. If so, their normal tendencies toward war may be counteracted, and they may then contribute to the evolution of that "just equilibrium" which in theory they were always designed to create but in fact seldom achieved.

[67] Dag Hammarskjold, *Perspectives on Peace, 1910–1960* (New York: Frederick A. Praeger, 1960), p. 65.

SUGGESTIONS FOR FURTHER READING

BUEHRIG, EDWARD H. *Woodrow Wilson and the Balance of Power.* Indiana University Press, 1955.

CLAUDE, INIS L., JR. *Power and International Relations.* New York: Random House, 1962. One of the best contemporary discussions of the balance of power. See especially Chapter 2, "The Balance of Power as an Ambiguous Concept," and Chapter 3, "A Critique of the Balance of Power."

COBDEN, RICHARD. *The Political Writings of Richard Cobden.* 2 vols. New York. Appleton, 1867. See "Balance of Power."

FOX, WILLIAM T. R. *The Super-Powers: The United States, Britain, and the Soviet Union; Their Responsibility for Peace.* New York: Harcourt, Brace, 1944.

FRIEDRICH, CARL J. *Foreign Policy in the Making: The Search for a New Balance of Power.* New York: W. W. Norton & Company, 1938.

FRIEDRICH, CARL J. and CHARLES BLITZER. *The Age of Power.* Ithaca: Cornell University Press, 1957. Especially Chapter VII, "Toward a New Balance of Power."

GAREAU, FREDERICK H., ed. *The Balance of Power and Nuclear Deterrence.* Boston: Houghton Mifflin Company, 1962. "Fourteen excerpts on the balance of power and eight selections of the newer doctrine plus appropriate commentary."

GELBER, LIONEL. *Peace by Power.* New York: Oxford University Press, 1942.

———. *Europe's Classical Balance of Power: A Case History of the Theory and Practice of One of the Great Concepts of European Statecraft.* Ithaca: Cornell University Press, 1955. A thorough and systematic study.

GULICK, EDWARD V. *The Balance of Power.* The Pacifist Research Bureau, 1943. By one of the leading authorities on the balance of power.

HERZ, JOHN H. *International Politics in the Atomic Age.* New York: Columbia University Press, 1959.

HINSLEY, F. H. *Power and the Pursuit of Peace.* Cambridge, England, 1963. Parts I and II contain an excellent historical analysis of the balance of power.

HOLBORN, HAJO. *The Political Collapse of Europe.* New York: Alfred A. Knopf, 1951.

LANGER, WILLIAM L. *European Alliances and Alignments, 1871–1890,* 2d ed. New York: Alfred A. Knopf, 1950.

LARUS, JOEL, ed. *Comparative World Politics.* Belmont, Calif.: Wadsworth Publishing Co., 1964. Chapter 3, "Balancing Power with Power," has selections on Hindu as well as Western concepts of the balance of power.

LISKA, GEORGE. *The International Equilibrium.* Cambridge, Mass.: Harvard University Press, 1957.

MANSERGH, NICHOLAS. *The Coming of the First World War.* New York: Longmans, Green & Co., 1949. A good discussion of the balance of power in operation.

MORGENTHAU, HANS J. *Politics Among Nations,* 3d ed. New York: Alfred A. Knopf, 1960. Contains four chapters on the balance of power.

"A New Balance of Power?" *Journal of International Affairs,* Vol. XIV, No. 1 (1960). A special issue, featuring articles by several specialists, on the role and significance of the balance of power in the nuclear and space age.

ORGANSKI, A. F. K. *World Politics.* New York: Alfred A. Knopf, 1958. Contains unconventional interpretations of balance of power.

PENROSE, E. F. *The Revolution in International Relations: A Study in the Changing Nature and Balance of Power.* London, 1965. Especially Chapter I, "Political Doctrines and Balance of Power."

SCHWARZENBERGER, GEORG. *Power Politics,* 2d rev. ed. New York: Frederick A. Praeger, 1951.

SEABURY, PAUL, ed. *The Balance of Power.* San Francisco: Chandler Publishing Co., 1965. A collection of readings, beginning with Kautilya and Aristotle, and stressing the balance of power after World War II.

SPYKMAN, NICHOLAS. *America's Strategy in World Politics.* New York: Harcourt, Brace, 1942.

STRAUSZ-HUPÉ, ROBERT. *The Balance of Tomorrow.* New York: G. P. Putnam's Sons, 1945. Chapter 17.

TAYLOR, A. J. P. *The Struggle for Mastery in Europe, 1848–1918.* New York: Oxford University Press, 1954.

WIGHT, MARTIN. *Power Politics.* Royal Institute of International Affairs, 1946. "Looking Forward" Pamphlets No. 8.

WOLFERS, ARNOLD B. *Britain and France Between Two Wars.* New York: Harcourt, Brace, 1940.

WRIGHT, QUINCY. *Problems of Stability and Progress in International Relations.* Berkeley: University of California Press, 1954.

———. *The Study of International Relations.* New York: Appleton-Century-Crofts, 1955.

———. *A Study of War.* 2 vols. Chicago: University of Chicago Press, 1942. Vol. II contains a valuable discussion of the balance of power.

10 Collective Security and Peaceful Settlement

Collective security and the peaceful settlement of international disputes have been commonly regarded as the most promising of all the approaches to peace. The first seeks to confront would-be aggressors with the concerted power of states determined to keep the peace; it involves a commitment to go to war if necessary, recognizing that the immediate peace is thereby jeopardized but assuming that future peace will be more secure if it has been clearly demonstrated that crime among nations does not pay. The peaceful settlement of disputes, on the other hand, aims at the prevention of war by the use of noncoercive or at least nonviolent procedures. The machinery of collective security has never been satisfactorily developed; there is, in fact, only the vaguest sort of agreement on what kind of machinery is called for. By contrast, the techniques for peaceful settlement have been well developed and well marked; they are available for all who would use them. Because these two general approaches are sometimes thought to go hand in hand and at other times to exclude each other, we must clarify their relationship to each other before we discuss them separately.

What Is the Relationship?

Some authorities hold that collective security includes measures for peaceful settlement; others, conversely, that the machinery for peaceful settlement, if it is to be adequate, must include regional arrangements and even broader agreements for collective security and defense. Still others, however, insist that the two approaches, far from being complementary, are antagonistic and even mutually exclusive, and that one of the great weaknesses of the United Nations — as earlier of the League of Nations — is that its member states have attempted to make it an instrument serving both purposes. These points of view can hardly be reconciled, especially as they affect the emphasis in approach to the problem of war. The differences among them are highly significant. We must therefore note the current support for some of these views.

The UN View. The founders of the United Nations incorporated elaborate provisions for both approaches into the Charter. Chapter VI (Articles 33–38) deals with the Pacific Settlement of Disputes and Chapter VII (Articles 39–51) with Action with Respect to Threats to the Peace, Breaches of the Peace, and Acts of Aggression. This juxtaposition cannot be explained as a mere coincidence. Apparently the framers of the Charter believed the two approaches to the prevention of war to be complementary. Later statements by UN officials have generally been of the same tenor. Thus Secretary-General Trygve Lie, in his annual report to the General Assembly in the fall of 1951, stated:

> I believe that the development of a strong and effective United Nations collective security system combined with renewed efforts at mediation and conciliation, can improve the chances of ameliorating and, in time, settling the great political conflicts that most endanger world peace today. The greater the ability of the United Nations to foil attempts to solve conflicts of national interest by force, the more likely will it be that those conflicts can be settled by negotiation.

Another statement, made by Benjamin V. Cohen, an American delegate to the General Assembly, may be regarded as typical:

> The pacific settlement of disputes is a chief function of the United Nations; most of our time here in the political field is devoted to it. Some have expressed the fear that by emphasizing collective measures we are in some sense detracting from pacific settlement. . . . My Government regards pacific settlement and collective measures as inseparable parts of collective security under the Charter. . . . If we succeed in building an effective security system, there will be less likelihood that an aggressor will risk the penalties bound to follow aggression. The object of effective security is to relieve the world of the scourge of war and the fears of war. Thus by building collective security we can release the constructive energies of the world for the constructive tasks of peace and human welfare. We can open up new possibilities for pacific settlement and the processes of peaceful change.[1]

In a sense, the UN itself is the most important agency for collective security *and* peaceful settlement that has ever been created. But even though it seeks to promote all possible means "to maintain international peace and security," there is no unanimity of opinion among its members on the relative emphasis that should be placed on particular means or on relative priorities.

The View of Western Powers. Whenever they have had the opportunity, in the United Nations or elsewhere, spokesmen for the United States have endorsed the UN position. But, speeches in the United Nations notwithstanding, it is clear that the United States and other major powers of the Western world are now placing first emphasis on various forms of security programs and arrangements. They are relying more upon heavy expenditures and elaborate plans for national defense and for regional measures for "individual or collective self-defense," to use the language of Article 51 of the Charter, than upon the more general and more nebulous safeguards provided for in the Charter. In other words, they seem to be more concerned with security than with peaceful settlement; and in the field of security they seem to attach more significance to individual and regional than to collective security in its true and broader meaning. They regard this course not as a matter of preference but of necessity; in the face of present dangers they can see no alternative.

After the First World War the French placed primary emphasis on security, the British on peaceful settlement. In the early days of the League of Nations delegates from most of the member states spoke hopefully of the possibilities of arbitration and disarmament, without showing realistic appreciation of the relation of these two approaches to security; but as the international atmosphere darkened in the late twenties and early thirties concern for security pushed all subordinate questions more and more into the background. In the United Nations security considerations have been more prominent from the beginning; today they seem to be dominant, whatever the Charter may say. They are never far from the thoughts of delegates, and outside the UN they are obviously matters of major concern.

1 The text of Mr. Cohens' statement is given in the *Department of State Bulletin,* XXVI (January 21, 1952), 98–102.

What Is the UN's Primary Function? Some member states of the UN, and many organizations and individuals in most if not all the nations of the world, believe that the emphasis on collective security rather than peaceful settlement, both in the UN and outside it, reflects a deplorable absorption in the present power struggle and a kind of hysterical and unbalanced approach to world problems. They hold that unless it is corrected it will make constructive work on the part of the UN impossible, and may even lead to the complete impotence of the UN and to another war. A well-known Quaker report entitled *Steps to Peace,* prepared for the American Friends Service Committee by a special working party and published in 1951, asked the following questions: "May not the most important function of the United Nations in an armed world be as an agency through which peaceful settlement can be continuously sought? Is it possible to keep this central function uppermost and have it unhindered by continuing discussions of the collective measures which the majority will take against the minority if and when the political conflict erupts into a military conflict?"[2] In the opinion of the Quaker group the primary function of the UN is peaceful settlement, and anything that makes it more difficult for the UN to fulfill this function is unwise and should be avoided.

These misgivings call attention to dangers in the present trends of national and international policies, and they point to a "higher way" toward a peaceful world. They tend, however, to be unrealistic and even escapist in nature. The failure to recognize the relation between the activities and functions of the League of Nations and the power-political system within which it was forced to operate gave an air of unreality and impotence to the deliberations at Geneva. The same clouds of unreality hang low over the United Nations and tend to obscure the view of the world in which the organization is trying to function. It is hard to see how the United Nations, which is itself a product of the nation-state system and not a truly supranational organization, can remain aloof from the conflicts of national interests and of power politics which exist today or may arise in the future. If the UN does not place continued emphasis on collective measures to deal with acts of aggression and other threats to the peace, it will not only abdicate some of its major responsibilities but it will also in all probability weaken its usefulness and influence in the field of negotiation and peaceful settlement. It has already played a significant, if limited, role in several peacekeeping operations, including the stationing of UN forces along the borders of Israel (UNEF) and the protracted and expensive operations in the Congo (ONUC).[3]

Thus far we have considered the relationship between collective security and peaceful settlement, and we have summarized very different views regarding that relationship. We next turn to a more detailed analysis of the nature of these two broad approaches to the prevention of war and the maintenance of peace, and we shall examine the measures available or being developed for implementing them.

Collective Security

"Since World War II the concept of collective security has been persistently advocated and attacked, defended and criticized; it has figured prominently in the theoretical and ideological debate concerning the management of international relations. Moreover, there has been recurrent movement toward and away from translation of the collective security principle into a working system."[4] Few terms are more popular to-

[2] *Steps to Peace: A Quaker View of U.S. Foreign Policy* (Philadelphia: American Friends Service Committee, 1951), pp. 42–43.

[3] For case studies of UNEF and ONUC, see David Wainhouse *et al., International Peace Observation* (Baltimore: The Johns Hopkins Press, 1966), pp. 277–291, 405–413.

[4] Inis L. Claude, Jr., *Power and International Relations* (New York: Random House, 1962), p. 150.

day in the Western world than "collective security"; and few are used in such vague and diverse ways. There is considerable point to Charles B. Marshall's tongue-in-cheek observation that collective security is a "generalized notion of all nations banding together in undertaking a vague obligation to perform unspecified actions in response to hypothetical events brought on by some unidentifiable state."[5]

When General MacArthur, who had just been relieved as commander of the United Nations forces in Korea, where presumably the principle of collective security was meeting its greatest test, was asked in the course of hearings before the Senate Armed Services and Foreign Relations Committees in May, 1951, to indicate his attitude toward this principle, he replied: "What do you mean by 'collective security'?" This question must be answered before we can assess the true significance and possibilities of collective security in international affairs.

The Nature of Collective Security. Although it appears to be simple and almost self-explanatory, the concept is in reality a complex and elusive one. It has been defined by Georg Schwarzenberger as "machinery for joint action in order to prevent or counter any attack against an established international order."[6] It clearly implies collective measures for dealing with threats to peace. In a sense Ernest A. Gross, United States Deputy Representative to the United Nations, stated a truism when he declared: "There is no alternative to collective action for the achievement of security. The opposite of collective security is complete insecurity."[7] But not all collective action is collective security.[8] Very few ventures in collective action are designed to carry as far as collective security; of those that are, most are in fact limited by the vague and general nature of the commitments and by the unwillingness of the states concerned to take sufficiently vigorous action to deal with major emergencies. Some efforts of this sort may in truth be better described as pointed toward noncollective insecurity.

Whereas collective action may mean the limited collaboration of a few states on an ad hoc basis, collective security implies far-reaching commitments and obligations on the part of the majority of the states of the world, including all or at least most of the great powers. It is clearly incompatible with neutrality and with a balance of power policy except under most unusual conditions of balanced stability over a period of time. As Quincy Wright explained, "The relations of the balance of power to collective security have . . . been at the same time complementary and antagonistic." Hence there is no necessary contradiction between Professor Wright's assertions, on the one hand, that the principles of collective security are "not antithetic but supplementary" to those of the balance of power and that "International organization to promote collective security is . . . only a planned development of the natural tendency of balance of power policies," and, on the other hand, that "the fundamental assumptions of the two systems are different."[9]

Under usual circumstances collective security and a balance of power policy are incom-

[5] In Ernest W. Lefever, ed., *Ethics and United States Foreign Policy* (Cleveland: Meridian Books, 1957), pp. 38–39.

[6] Georg Schwarzenberger, *Power Politics* (New York: Frederick A. Praeger, 1951), p. 494.

[7] Address at the University of Virginia, July 13, 1951; printed in the *Department of State Bulletin*, XXV (July 30, 1951).

[8] See Arnold Wolfers, "Collective Defense versus Collective Security," in Arnold Wolfers, ed., *Alliance Policy in the Cold War* (Baltimore: The Johns Hopkins Press, 1959), pp. 49–74.

[9] *Constitutionalism and World Politics*, University of Illinois Bulletin, Vol. 49, No. 32, (December, 1951), p. 10; *The Study of International Relations* (New York: Appleton-Century-Crofts, 1955), p. 163; and *A Study of War* (Chicago: University of Chicago Press, 1942), II, 781. See also Claude, pp. 123–133, 144–149, for a good discussion of the similarities and differences between collective security and the balance of power.

patible because the object of the one is to align all other states against an offending or warmaking state, whereas the other contemplates the maintenance of such an equilibrium of power that no state will dare undertake a resort to arms. The substance of the first is a world front against a possible aggressor; the substance of the second is two approximately equal and opposing fronts. Collective security also implies a far greater degree of systematization than does balance of power. "Balance of power is a system only by courtesy; while the accusation that it amounts to anarchy is too strong, it is assuredly a most unsystematic system. . . . Collective security, on the other hand, represents the urge for systematization, the institutionalization of international relations."[10]

A collective security system, to be effective, must be strong enough to cope with aggression from any power or combination of powers, and it must be invoked if and as aggression occurs. "The principle of collective security requires that states identify their national interest so completely with the preservation of the total world order that they stand ready to join the collective action to put down any aggressive threat by any state, against any other state anywhere."[11] It involves a willingness to apply sanctions as and when necessary, and even to go to war. As Stanley Baldwin, himself anything but a stout-hearted champion of collective security in spite of his professions, declared in April, 1939: "Collective security will never work unless all the nations that take part in it are prepared simultaneously to threaten with sanctions and to fight, if necessary, an aggressor."

Such a system must be far more than an alliance. "The typical instrument of advance commitment in the balance system is an alliance, which collectively envisages a broader arrangement, usually involving obligations of common action undertaken in the constitutional document of a general international organization."[12] It calls "upon nations to go beyond aligning themselves with each other to meet the threats emanating from common national enemies and to embrace instead a policy of defense directed against aggression in general or, more precisely, against any aggression anywhere."[13] It must be open to those states which are willing to accept its obligations in good faith. It must not be directed against any specific power or combination of powers. The decisive tests would seem to be whether the system is strong enough, whether the states associated in it abide by the obligations to the fullest extent necessary in times of crises, and whether all, or at least most, of the great powers adhere to it. It should be emphasized that such a system involves acceptance of the view that the national interests of the participating states can in grave emergencies best be defended by collective action, even at the cost of limitations on the freedom of decision of the individual states. As Professor Friedmann explains:

> A successful system of collective security does not necessarily presuppose a complete abandonment of national independence or individuality. It does, however, require the submission of the individual national will to collective decisions . . . and in order to be effective it requires the international control of military forces and vital weapons, which is certainly not possible without a severe restriction of national sovereignty.[14]

This is asking for a more binding commitment than the states of the world are willing

[10] Claude, pp. 147, 148.

[11] *Ibid.*, p. 146.

[12] *Ibid.*, p. 128.

[13] Arnold Wolfers, "Collective Security and the War in Korea," *Yale Review*, XLIII (June, 1954), 482.

[14] W. Friedmann, *An Introduction to World Politics* (Toronto, 1951), p. 57. Used by permission of the author, Macmillan and Company, Ltd., London, and St. Martin's Press, N.Y.

to assume, a fact which explains why collective security is so generally subscribed to in principle and so universally ignored in practice. "In any event," as Professor Claude has pointed out, "the doctrine of collective security requires a more thoroughgoing renunciation of the free hand in foreign policy, a more nearly complete acceptance of advance commitment to participate in sanctions against any aggressor, on behalf of any victim, under any circumstances, than leaders of states are prepared to acknowledge as either necessary or desirable or permissible, given their obligations to the states which they represent. . . . states are not prepared to do, or convinced that they should do, the things that an operative system of collective security would require them to do."[15]

Collective Security and Regional Arrangements. It is often stated that regional arrangements for collective defense and for other purposes establish a collective security system. This is seldom if ever true, not so much because such arrangements are geographically too limited as because they are not sufficiently binding in character and do not represent such an aggregation of military strength that they can deal with any other power or combination of powers. The North Atlantic Treaty Organization alone among regional arrangements past or present may possibly be such an aggregation of strength; but even if it possesses adequate might, it will not provide real collective security unless its members voluntarily assume more binding obligations than they were willing to accept in the North Atlantic Treaty. NATO in fact seems to be moving in the other direction. Largely as a result of De Gaulle's noncooperative policies, its entire organizational and command structure has been curtailed, and the future of the organization itself is very much in question.

Regional arrangements, however, could conceivably be an important part of a broader collective security system. This point was stressed by the Collective Measures Committee of the United Nations, established under the Assembly's Uniting for Peace Resolution of November, 1950, in its first report to the Assembly in October, 1951. Regional arrangements, the report stated,

> constitute an important aspect of the universal collective security system of the United Nations. . . . There should be a mutually supporting relationship between the activities of such arrangements or agencies and the collective measures taken by the United Nations. Thus, collective self-defense and regional arrangements or agencies may, within the limits of their constitutional status, provide effective forces and facilities in their respective areas in order to carry out the Purposes and Principles of the Charter in meeting aggression.[16]

The exact relationship between regional arrangements and the United Nations has never been clarified. Presumably the former are supplementary to the UN system and do not supersede it; but the final wording of a UN resolution of January 12, 1952, suggested that many of the member states of the UN viewed their obligations to regional arrangements as superior to those of the Charter. Before giving the resolution final approval, the Assembly accepted an amendment proposed by Argentina and Chile which made it clear that obligations under regional agreements and arrangements such as the Rio Treaty of 1947 and the Organization of American States, provided for at the Bogotá Conference in 1948, had prior-

[15] Claude, p. 204. See also Kenneth W. Thompson, "Collective Security Reexamined," *American Political Science Review,* XLVII (September, 1953); Howard C. Johnson and Gerhart Niemeyer, "Collective Security: The Validity of an Ideal," *International Organization,* VIII (February, 1954); and Ernst B. Haas, "Types of Collective Security: An Examination of Operational Concepts," *American Political Science Review* XLIX (March, 1955).

[16] U. N. Document A/1891.

ity over the recommendations of the General Assembly.[17]

Collective Security and Disarmament. The relationship between collective security and disarmament has received little attention. For the most part they have been regarded as separate approaches to the problem of war and peace. While it has not yet appeared feasible to link the two in an interdependent way in a practicable measure for maintaining peace, it may be well to observe their theoretical relationship. A forceful statement of this was made in January, 1952, by Benjamin V. Cohen of the United States delegation to the General Assembly:

> I should like to stress the fact that there is an intimate relationship between a program of collective security and a program of disarmament. The two, by their nature, go hand in hand. In the disarmament field, we look to the day when no nation will have armed forces or armaments which could pose a threat to a neighbor. In the collective-security field, we look to the day when nations will not rely so much on their own forces as on the United Nations for their security. If states are assured that in case of attack they will not stand alone, they will need fewer arms for their defense. As progress is made in disarmament, the task of building collective security becomes simpler. The two march together. . . . Disarmament and collective security are the two great enterprises for peace that this General Assembly has before it.[18]

If a substantial reduction of armaments could be achieved, this might make the task of developing a collective security system a simpler and more feasible one, always assuming that the force which can be mustered for collective security purposes is greater than that available to a would-be aggressor. If the arms race continues, and particularly if the nuclear giants add to their already great capacity to "overkill" and other nations enter the nuclear club, the hopes and prospects for effective collective security will grow increasingly less.

Collective Security and the League System. As an instrument for the development and enforcement of collective security the League of Nations was severely handicapped and indeed virtually impotent from the start. The failure of the United States to join, the rise of the Soviet Union outside the League system, the reluctance of Great Britain to assume international obligations, and later the open defiance of Japan, Italy, and Germany — all these combined to destroy any hopes that the League would be effective in major international crises. From the beginning it was not sufficiently broad in membership; it never included all the great powers, and those which belonged were by no means stout champions of collective security. France and the Soviet Union may appear to be exceptions to this judgment; but France was interested in security against Germany rather than in a genuine and universal security system, and Russia was primarily concerned with security against the rising menace of fascism. Although Litvinov and other Soviet delegates spoke eloquently and often of the need for collective security, Russia would have been prevented by her ideological orientation from joining in good faith with capitalist states in implementing a permanent system of collective security. Presumably the members of the League were committed to undertake measures of collective security, if necessary, under Article 16 of the Covenant. The article, however, was never really implemented. Many of the League members had misgivings about it from the outset, and from time to time resolutions interpreting the obligations of the members under it were

[17] See *New York Times*, January 13, 1952. The text of the Assembly's resolution of January 12, 1952, may be found in United Nations, *Resolutions Adopted by the General Assembly during the 6th Session, Nov. 6, 1951–Feb. 6, 1952*, p. 2.

[18] *Department of State Bulletin*, XXVI (January 21, 1952), 101–102.

adopted. Most of these resolutions were of a limiting and restrictive nature. Together with unilateral interpretations of its meaning and the general failure of League members to pay more than lip service to it, they took the heart out of the article.

At no time did the League assume even the external appearance of an effective security organization. In some of the disputes brought before it, especially in the early years, it rendered useful service, but in every major case involving open defiance of the Covenant by a great power the League's security structure proved unequal to the test. From the Manchurian crisis in 1931–32 to the series of acts of aggression by Nazi Germany which culminated in the attack on Poland and the beginning of World War II, the absence of any effective security system was tragically revealed in one act of international banditry after another. In the Manchurian crisis, which began the march of aggression by the totalitarian powers, the League sent a commission to the Far East to make a firsthand investigation, discussed the question at length in Assembly meetings, usually at the insistence of the victim of aggression, China, and finally, early in 1932, passed a resolution branding Japan as the aggressor. This step, which provoked Japan to withdraw from the League, helped to keep the record straight, but it was not followed by any concerted action against the aggressor — only by ineffective protests and fulminations.

In the history of the League the most extensive effort to give teeth to the Covenant and to make the embryonic provisions for collective security work was made during the Ethiopian crisis of 1935–36. When Italian forces invaded the independent African state, the matter was immediately brought to the attention of the League; and when Italy refused to suspend hostilities the Council of the League, in spite of Italian protests, voted to impose sanctions against Italy. The Italo-Ethiopian War thus became the chief test case — indeed, the only real one — of the effectiveness of the League's security system. As all the world knows, the League failed in this crucial test. With strong moral support but little official cooperation from the United States, the members of the League did not apply sanctions "automatically, simultaneously and comprehensively," but "haltingly, gradually and piecemeal."[19] Oil sanctions were never applied, and the Suez Canal remained open to Italian ships. When the tragicomic farce was over, Mussolini had added Ethiopia to his dominions and the weakness of the League as an instrument of security had been clearly revealed. Haile Selassie, the diminutive but dignified Emperor of Ethiopia, appearing before the League's Assembly, spoke more as the voice of international conscience than as the fugitive ruler of a backward African state. He reminded the delegates that Mussolini's successful defiance of the League had not only resulted in the loss of independence of his country but had also dealt a body blow to the hopes for world peace. Gently but firmly he warned the hushed gathering that there would be more Ethiopian incidents and still more until the totalitarian states dominated the world or until the peace-loving nations united to resist further acts of aggression, even at the risk of war.

The gloomy prophecies of Haile Selassie proved all too correct. Not long after Italy's occupation of Ethiopia came the Nazi conquest of Austria, then the surrender to Hitler at Munich, then the obliteration of Czechoslovakia, and then the invasion of Poland that began World War II. After 1936 the League as such made no further attempts of any consequence to arrest the alarming course of events. The year 1936 was "the year of decision." England and France, after the dismal failure of appeasement, began frantically to rearm. The United States was still influenced by the delusions of isolation, although she protested strongly against the

[19] Schwarzenberger, p. 498.

acts of aggression, and although President Roosevelt, after 1937 at least, did his best to arouse the country to the possible dangers to it from unchecked aggression by the Axis powers. The Soviet Union, unable to gain support for collective security, developed a deep-seated suspicion and distrust of the policies of the major Western states, and turned more and more to alternative courses in diplomacy and to an accelerated defense program at home. In March, 1939, soon after the Nazi occupation of Czechoslovakia, Stalin made this bitter but accurate remark: "The non-aggressive states, primarily England, France and the United States . . . have rejected the policy of collective security, the policy of collective resistance to the aggressors, and have taken up a position of non-intervention, a position of 'neutrality.' " "The policy of non-intervention," he warned, "means conniving at aggression, giving free rein to war, and, consequently, transforming the war into a world war." Within six months after Stalin had uttered this warning, the series of acts of aggression, of the "little wars," had culminated in World War II. The feebleness of the attempts at collective security had brought forth bitter fruit.

From the experience of the League of Nations we may conclude that half-hearted efforts in the direction of collective security are almost certain to be unavailing. The League never did develop a security system worthy of the name — in spite of Article 16 of the Covenant, emphasis on security in the interwar period, and the extensive discussions of the principle of collective security in the 1930's. The failure of the League in this vital respect was due to no absence of machinery but to the vacillations and myopia of what Stalin called "the non-aggressive states," particularly the major democratic nations, and to their unreadiness and unwillingness to take the risks which an effective system of collective security necessarily entailed. "The League experience might be summarized as an abortive attempt to translate the collective security idea into a working system. The failure of collective security in this period was not so much the failure of the system to operate successfully as its failure to be established."[20]

Collective Security and the United Nations. The price of the failure to provide collective security after World War I was World War II. It was too high a price, and during the second global conflict within a single generation much more careful preparation was made for a postwar order. Even before V-J Day the states of the world, again with the major states bearing the primary responsibility, were confronted with the same choice they had faced after November, 1918 — the choice, as Hans Kohn once described it, "between making the post-war system of law and order genuinely work or else seeing the frail structure relapse into the chaotic anarchy which had begotten not only the war of 1914–1918 but one war behind another before that."[21] What choice did they make in 1945? Did they profit from the lessons of experience? Did they this time lay the foundations for a really effective collective security system, and erect a strong edifice on these foundations?

1. *Provisions of the Charter.* At first glance it may seem that the foundations were well laid. The provisions of the Charter of the United Nations for collective action are much more extensive and apparently much more far-reaching than those of the Covenant of the League of Nations. Furthermore, the UN system has been buttressed by regional arrangements and agreements, some of which, notably those existing in Western Europe, the Atlantic Community, and the Western Hemisphere, establish strong regional security systems which are presumably

[20] Claude, p. 155.

[21] Quoted in Arnold J. Toynbee, ed., *Survey of International Affairs 1935, II, Abyssinia and Italy* (London, 1936), p. 6.

consistent with and supplementary to the UN system.

Article 1 of the UN Charter calls for "effective collective measures for the prevention and removal of threats to the peace, and for the suppression of acts of aggression or other breaches of the peace," and Chapter VII of the Charter points out in great detail what these "effective collective measures" may be. If the Security Council finds that an act of aggression or other threat to the peace has occurred, and if the parties concerned do not comply with such measures as the Council shall deem necessary, the UN body may call upon the member states to take any of a wide variety of nonmilitary and, if necessary, military measures against the offending state or states. Article 43 provides that "All Members of the United Nations . . . undertake to make available to the Security Council, on its call or in accordance with a special agreement or agreements, armed forces, assistance, and facilities . . . necessary for the purpose of maintaining international peace and security." Article 45 stipulates that "Members shall hold immediately available national air-force contingents for combined international enforcement action." Article 47 provides for a Military Staff Committee "to advise and assist the Security Council on all questions relating to the Security Council's military requirements for the maintenance of international peace and security, the employment and command of forces placed at its disposal, the regulation of armaments, and possible disarmament." Here again problems of security and disarmament are related.

Article 49 states that "The Members of the United Nations shall join in affording mutual assistance in carrying out the measures decided upon by the Security Council." The famous Article 51 specifically recognizes "the inherent right of individual or collective self-defense if an armed attack occurs against a Member of the United Nations," but it also plainly states that "measures taken by Members in the exercise of this right . . . shall not in any way affect the authority and responsibility of the Security Council . . . to take at any time such action as it deems necessary in order to maintain or restore international peace and security." Chapter VII of the Charter thus clearly envisions collective action of a far-reaching nature, and the members of the UN, by adhering to the Charter, accepted a commitment to abide by and give full support to the decision of the Security Council.

Until the Korean crisis developed in 1950, the potentialities of the United Nations for collective action against aggression were largely untested; but because of the very nature of the organization it was obvious from the beginning that it could not become an effective instrument of collective security without radical changes in the Charter. Even the preliminary planning necessary to put into effect the measures provided for in Chapter VII was by no means adequate, and many of the provisions of this chapter have remained a dead letter. The Military Staff Committee held lengthy sessions in secret, but was unable to agree on the nature, employment, and command of the forces which member states were expected to place at the disposal of the Security Council. In point of fact these forces were nonexistent, in spite of the obligations under Article 43, the strong reaffirmation of these obligations in the General Assembly's Uniting for Peace Resolution of November, 1950, and the replies of many member states to the inquiries regarding the steps they were taking to make armed forces available. They are still nonexistent.

It could hardly be expected that an organization "based on the principle of the sovereign equality of all its Members," and in which the great states had a special position to the extent that they were largely exempt from the provisions of Chapter VII of the Charter by virtue of their veto power in the Security Council, could satisfy the tests of an effective collective security system. No amount of praise of the United Nations could gloss over its basic limitations in this respect. Collective security would be meaningful only if it applied to great as well as lesser powers, and only if all, or at least most, of the major powers cooperated to the fullest extent in supporting it. The United Nations was based on a very different concept. As Georg Schwarzenberger observed, "collective security as understood at Dumbarton Oaks and San Francisco, meant collective security against danger to peace from the middle powers and small states and collective insecurity in the face of aggression by any of the world powers." This was exactly the opposite of what was needed. "When minor parties to a dispute thought that the Security Council might act," adds Schwarzenberger, "the need for collective action did not arise. When the contingency arose, the world power which backed the aggressor or was itself held by the other members of the Security Council to be the culprit made action impossible."[22] There is much truth, therefore, in the following observations by Professor Claude: "The League of Nations failed to establish a universal collective security system; the United Nations began by declining to make the effort. . . . In the final analysis, the United Nations has never been intended or expected to apply the principle of collective security on a universal scale."[23]

2. *UN Action in the Korean Crisis.* But what about Korea? Did not the concerted action of the United Nations in the Korean crisis prove that collective security under the UN was possible? The Seventh Report of the Commission to Study the Organization of Peace, issued in July, 1951, stated: "The enforcement action undertaken by the United Nations, under its resolutions of June 25 and 27, 1950, is historic in the sense that it marks the first time that the organized community of nations, in accordance with the principle of collective security, has employed armed force against an aggressor." Assistant Secretary of State John D. Hickerson declared in October, 1950: "Korea has become a tremendous spur to the U. N. efforts to build an effective system of collective security.[24] Let us examine briefly the role of the United Nations in the Korean affair, with the object of determining whether this did in fact, as Benjamin V. Cohen hoped, "mark the beginning of the progressive development of an effective collective-security system."[25]

In resolutions of June 25 and 27 and in subsequent recommendations in early July the Security Council took prompt action to deal with the attack on the Republic of Korea from the northern part of the country. It found that aggression had occurred, it called upon the members of the United Nations to send troops and other assistance to Korea, and it asked the President of the United States to designate a supreme commander of UN forces. Thus the Council demonstrated that even though it had no armed forces at its disposal, as provided for in Article 43 of the Charter, it was not impotent in the face of open aggression. The demonstration, however, was not a conclusive one. That the Council was able to agree on positive action at all was due only to a series of unusual circumstances, including the temporary self-imposed absence from the Council of the representative of the Soviet Union, and the presence of substantial units of American air, land, and naval forces in Japan, the Ryukyus, and adjacent waters. If the Council had not acted promptly, and if sufficient strength to meet the first on-

[22] Schwarzenberger, pp. 510, 515.
[23] Claude, pp. 165, 172.

[24] Address in New York, October 21, 1951; text in the *Department of State Bulletin,* XXV (November 5, 1951), 732–735.
[25] Statement to Political and Security Committee of General Assembly of the United Nations, January 2, 1952; text in the *Department of State Bulletin,* XXVI (January 21, 1952), 98–102.

slaughts of the surprise attack had not been available and immediately ordered into action, in all likelihood the UN would have been faced with a *fait accompli* in Korea before it had proceeded beyond the discussion stage. As soon as Jacob Malik assumed the presidency of the Security Council on August 1, 1950, a complete stalemate developed. This continued throughout the entire month of August, while Malik was president; thereafter, with the Soviet representative in vigilant attendance, the Council was virtually impotent.

Because of this situation, and because of the clear lesson in Korea that the UN's procedures for collective security needed strengthening, the Fifth Session of the General Assembly, in the fall of 1950, endorsed proposals which seemed to herald a considerable shift in emphasis or even a major change in the character of the United Nations. The proposals, first outlined specifically by the American Secretary of State, Dean Acheson, were known at first as the Acheson Plan, but in amended form became the Uniting for Peace Resolution, adopted by the Assembly on November 3.

3. *The Uniting for Peace Resolution.*[26] This historic measure was a three-part affair, but only Resolution A, the longest and most important of the three parts, is customarily referred to in comments on the Uniting for Peace Resolution. After a lengthy preamble, Resolution A contained four significant provisions. The first called for immediate consideration by the General Assembly of any situation involving an act of aggression or other threat to the peace, if the Security Council failed to exercise "its primary responsibility"; if the Assembly were not in session at the time, an emergency meeting could be held within twenty-four hours. The second part established a Peace Observation Committee of fourteen designated members, including the Soviet Union. The third in effect recommended that the members of the UN fulfill their obligations under Article 43 of the Charter. In it the General Assembly recommended

> . . . to the State Members of the United Nations that each Member maintain within its national armed forces elements so trained, organized and equipped that they could promptly be made available, in accordance with its constitutional processes, for service as a United Nations unit or units, upon recommendation by the Security Council or General Assembly, without prejudice to the use of such elements in exercise of the right of individual or collective self-defense recognized in Article 51 of the Charter.

Part four of Resolution A established a Collective Measures Committee of fourteen members and instructed it "to study and make a report to the Security Council and the General Assembly, not later than 1 September 1951, on methods . . . which might be used to maintain and strengthen international peace and security in accordance with the Purposes and Principles of the Charter." In a final and more general section Resolution A recognized "that enduring peace will not be secured solely by collective security arrangements," and urged the members of the UN to cooperate in other important ways.

Resolution B urged the Security Council to "devise measures for the earliest application of Articles 43, 45, 46, and 47 of the Charter regarding the placing of armed forces at the disposal of the Security Council by the States Members of the United Nations and the effective functioning of the Military Staff Committee." Resolution C recommended that the permanent members of the Security Council "meet and discuss, collectively or otherwise . . . all problems which are likely to threaten international peace and hamper the activities of the United Nations, with a view to their resolving fundamental differences and reaching agreement in accordance with the spirit and letter of the Charter."

[26] For a discussion of the legal aspects of the Uniting for Peace Resolution see below, Chapter 14.

The Uniting for Peace Resolution was a conscious effort to develop and implement the security provisions of the United Nations Charter. It "was clearly put forward as a device for making the United Nations a collective security system."[27] Since its adoption, more attention has been given to problems of implementation than ever before; in this sense it has indeed been a major landmark in the progress toward an effective collective security system. The Peace Observation Committee is ready to function as needed; some of its members have been given specific assignments. The Collective Measures Committee has made some significant reports, which have been carefully considered by the General Assembly and which have indicated areas for further exploration. The Assembly itself has passed a resolution on collective security as a result of its consideration of the first report of the committee, and has instructed the committee to continue its work. Nothing of any importance has been done to carry out Resolutions B and C of the Uniting for Peace Resolution.

A year after the adoption of the Uniting for Peace Resolution only twenty-nine states had given even generally affirmative responses to inquiries regarding their plans for maintaining UN units within their armed forces; twenty-two had not even deigned to reply. Almost every one of the states expressing a willingness to implement the recommendation simply pointed to certain units of their armed forces which were then engaged in overseas operations, particularly in Korea. The United States referred to her forces in Europe and in Korea and tried to gloss over her evasiveness by diplomatic double-talk: "After termination of hostilities in Korea and after the United States forces have been withdrawn, the extent to which the United States will maintain armed forces which could be made available for United Nations service will be reviewed."[28] If any such review has been made since 1953, when the truce in Korea entered into effect, the results are not apparent.

4. *Reports of the Collective Measures Committee.* The first report of the Collective Measures Committee, approved for submission to the General Assembly on October 3, 1951, was a pioneer study in the sense that it constituted the "first systematic attempt by the United Nations to study the whole field of collective security."[29] It analyzed a wide variety of political, economic, and military sanctions which might be applied in dealing with acts of aggression. "In respect to each sanction, the report outlines basic considerations which should underlie a decision of the United Nations to apply collective measures; it considers national action which should be taken by cooperating states; the extent to which the coordination of national action is necessary; and the techniques and machinery that should be established to make the imposition of a particular sanction most effective."[30] It also explored the relationship between collective and regional security arrangements and summarized the replies of the members of the UN to the committee regarding the organizing and earmarking of United Nations units within their armed forces.

In 1952 the Collective Measures Committee continued its analysis of the developing situation in Korea, studied how best it could assist member states of the UN to coordinate their efforts to implement the Assembly's Uniting for Peace and collective security resolutions, and considered "the nature of the machinery that the United Nations should have for the future in order to continue its

[27] Claude, p. 167.

[28] Joseph J. Sisco, "The U. N. and Collective Security," *Department of State Bulletin,* XXV (November 12, 1951), 772.

[29] *Ibid.*, p. 774.

[30] *Ibid.*, p. 773.

progressive development as a collective-security organization." In its second report to the Assembly, in the fall of 1952, the committee made useful suggestions on all of these important matters; but the General Assembly "watered down the very mild recommendations proposed by its Collective Measures Committee so as to make absolutely clear that each state would act just as it chose in a particular situation."[31] Since then the committee has been largely inactive and wholly ineffective, except perhaps in a long-range educational sense.

5. *Lessons of the Korean Experience.* In the opinion of an official of the United States State Department, "the collective effort against aggression in Korea, the pragmatic adaptation of the Charter in the security field by means of the 'Uniting for Peace' resolution, and the more undramatic, yet no less significant analyses made by the Collective Measures Committee" — plus, it may be added, the continued concern of the General Assembly, the Secretariat, and other UN agencies with the whole problem of collective security — "represent concrete progress toward a goal which has eluded man for over 2,000 years."[32] We may endorse this statement without suggesting that the "concrete progress" under UN auspices has been very great. From the experience of collective action in Korea and from our study of the efforts of the United Nations to profit from this experience, we can find nothing that forces us to change our original conclusion, namely that the United Nations, by its very nature, was not, is not now, and never can be an effective instrument for collective security.

In actual fact, the operations in Korea never even remotely assumed the aspects of a collective security effort. To be sure, in a symbolic way, and to some extent in actuality, the action was a collective one. Besides the United States, fifteen or more member states of the UN sent armed forces to Korea, and nearly fifty countries provided various kinds of material assistance. More than sixty nations, including some not in the United Nations, endorsed the UN's recommendation of a strategic embargo against Communist China. But in spite of this brave front, Korea was primarily a Korean and American effort; the other military units were of small size; most member states of the UN cooperated only in a token fashion — an ambulance unit, a medical team, a hospital ship, and the like; some members not only did not cooperate, but bitterly attacked all the actions of the UN in and regarding Korea and gave active support to the forces which the UN had branded as aggressors. Under such conditions real collective security could hardly be hoped for; it was, in fact, impossible.

Even the most sanguine interpreters of the Korean experience could not claim much for it beyond the fact that the action had compelled the United Nations to consider more seriously and more realistically the whole problem of collective security. Secretary of State Acheson, in an address of June 29, 1951, declared: "Korea's significance is not the final crusade. It is not finally making valid the idea of collective secruity. It is important, perhaps, for the inverse reason that in Korea we prevented the invalidation of collective security."

Korea did "not establish the practicability or reality of collective security. . . . Instead of being a case of nations fighting 'any aggressor anywhere' and for no other purpose than to punish aggression and to deter potential aggressors, intervention in Korea was an act of collective military defense against the recognized number-one enemv of the United

[31] Reprinted by permission from Philip E. Jacob and Alexine L. Atherton, *The Dynamics of International Organization: The Making of World Order* (Homewood, Ill.: Dorsey Press, 1965), p. 75. See also Stanley H. Hoffmann, "Sisyphus and the Avalanche: The United Nations, Egypt and Hungary," *International Organization,* XI (Summer, 1957).

[32] Sisco, p. 774.

States and of all the countries which associated themselves with its action."[33]

Pitfall or Bulwark? The lessons of historical experience, especially the action taken under the aegis of the League of Nations and the United Nations, have shown that in spite of all the official and unofficial statements about it — and, as we have noted, "collective security" is one of the most popular terms in the jargon of international diplomacy today — nothing like an effective collective security system has ever been developed. Such examples of collective action involving the use of sanctions as the League's efforts to prevent Italian aggression in Ethiopia and the United Nations operations in Korea are few and far between, and cannot properly be regarded as real tests of collective security. It is difficult to test something which does not exist. The tests for real collective security, which were mentioned earlier in this discussion, indicate that the acceptance by states of far more binding commitments than they are now ready or willing to enter into is a stern prerequisite. "Such a policy," as Arnold Wolfers observed, "would constitute a radical break with tradition."[34]

Because of these considerations the student of international politics must regard collective security as one of those desirable goals which under present conditions are distant and unattainable, perhaps "illusive myths."[35] Quincy Wright concluded that it will be reached "only when the balance of power has been so stable that attention has been diverted from it" and perhaps only when there has been created "a democratic organization of the world able to supersede the balance of power as the basis of security."[36] Georg Schwarzenberger believed that "until the day when the Western and Eastern worlds no longer consider each other as *the* potential aggressor, collective security, as envisaged under the Charter of the United Nations, must remain a dead letter."[37]

Hans Morgenthau regards collective security as not only an unworkable but an unwise and dangerous principle, chiefly because in his view it means that under it no war could be localized, that every war would become a world war.[38] Walter Lippmann, in many of his newspaper columns, articles, and books has questioned the desirability as well as the practicability of a collective security system; he holds that in the absence of a true international community, and in the presence of grave threats to the freedom and survival of democratic and peace-loving nations, to concentrate on the establishment of such a system would divert attention from present dangers, weaken more practical and promising arrangements for cooperation in defense and in other matters, lead some states to put too much reliance upon such a system while others were giving only lip service to it, and in general be foolhardy and perhaps disastrous. An inadequate collective security system, Lippmann contends, is worse than no "system" at all. His views are well summarized in the following quotation:

> The trouble with collective security is . . . that when the issue is less than the survival of the *great* nations, the method of collective security will not be used because it is just as terrifying to the policeman as it is to the law-breakers. It punishes the law-enforcing states, at least until they have paid the awful price of victory, as much as the law-breaking

[33] Wolfers, p. 492. See also Leland M. Goodrich, "Korea: Collective Measures Against Aggression," *International Conciliation,* No. 494 (October, 1953).

[34] Wolfers, p. 482.

[35] F. J. Brown, Charles Hodges, and J. S. Roucek, *Contemporary World Politics* (New York: John Wiley & Sons, 1939), p. 3.

[36] Wright, II, 781, 783.

[37] Schwarzenberger, p. 529.

[38] Hans J. Morgenthau, *Politics Among Nations,* 3d ed. (New York: Alfred A. Knopf, 1964), pp. 417–418.

states. . . . It proposes to achieve peace through law by calling upon great masses of innocent people to stand ready to exterminate great masses of innocent people. No world order can be founded upon such a principle; it cannot command the support of civilized men.[39]

Moreover, as Professor Claude noted, there is a growing feeling that "the effort to create a collective security system is not an appropriate response to the problem of managing international power relations in the present era. . . . In certain basic respects the doctrine of collective security is obsolete —it envisages a system which might have been feasible in an earlier period of international relations, but can hardly be expected to operate effectively in the setting which has been produced by the transformations of recent years. . . . The threat of nuclear war . . . poses new problems which make collective security appear as irrelevant to the management of power relations as machine guns have become to the frustration of great-power aggression."[40]

In the general parlance of today, however, the term "collective security" is used in a narrower and at the same time a less specific sense. Almost any form of international cooperation and of collective action in dealing with threats to the peace and open acts of aggression is called collective security. This is particularly true of efforts of the United Nations to give effect to Chapter VIII of the Charter, to the Uniting for Peace Resolution, and to the recommendations of the Collective Measures Committee. Certainly if peace is to be maintained, it must be through collective action; but, as has been emphasized, there is a vast difference between most forms of cooperative action and real collective security. Because of this vague and general use, the term should be viewed with caution by serious students of international affairs, for attached to the impressive terminology there may be a minimum of substance. "Collective security" may be a pitfall for the naive and the unwary rather than a bulwark for the strong and the free.

This does not mean that the concept of collective security is a meaningless one today, or that it has made no impact on the theory and practice of international relations. Professor Claude, in spite of his references to "the irrelevance of collective security," concluded his excellent discussion of the whole subject with these words:

> This is not to say that the persistent ideological popularity of collective security is wholly meaningless, or that recurrent endorsements of the doctrine by statesmen can be explained away as exercises in hypocrisy. While the urge to create a *system* of collective security has been discarded, the *doctrine* has left a considerable deposit. The proposition that international aggression is legally and morally reprehensible, the idea that any aggression is everybody's business, the view that a general international organization should concern itself with all disturbances of the peace, the notion that potential aggressors should be forewarned of the solidarities with which they may be confronted — such basic propositions as these, attributable in large part to the doctrinal impact of collective security, have become embedded in twentieth-century thinking about international relations. In this limited but impor-

[39] *New York Herald Tribune,* January 15, 1951. Commentators of the "revisionist" school have been much more scathing in their criticisms of the concept of collective security. Harry Elmer Barnes, for example, a perennial and indefatigable "revisionist," charged that the free world "conducts its foreign policy under the slavish domination of, and in complete conformity with, the most sinister and dangerous Communist dogma which has thus far gained general acceptance — the myth of collective security which, following the Geneva Protocol and the Briand-Kellogg policy, Litvinov sold to League of Nations liberals in the 1930's. . . . This can produce only that strange and menacing paradox of 'perpetual war for perpetual peace.' ". Foreword to Sisley Huddleston, *Popular Diplomacy and War* (Peterborough, N. H.: The Richard R. Smith Co., 1954).

[40] Claude, pp. 192, 194. Claude devotes a section of one chapter (pp. 190–204) to the subject: "The Irrelevance of Collective Security."

tant sense, collective security has been "adopted."[41]

Peaceful Settlement

Now that we have considered the relationship between collective security and peaceful settlement, the nature of the so-called collective security that is so frequently extolled and so seldom sought after in practice today, and the tests of a truly effective security system, we shall turn to the methods for the pacific settlement of international disputes.

Collective security and peaceful settlement may be regarded as opposite sides of the same coin or as very different, and indeed antithetical, methods for achieving the same ultimate goals. The former view was apparently taken by the framers of the United Nations Charter. Paragraph 1 of Article 1 of the Charter states that the purposes of the United Nations are "To maintain international peace and security, and to that end: to take effective collective measures for the prevention and removal of threats to the peace, and for the suppression of acts of aggression or other breaches of the peace, and to bring about by peaceful means . . . adjustment or settlement of international disputes or situations which might lead to a breach of the peace." Thus in the Charter itself collective security and peaceful settlement are linked in the very first paragraph of the very first article.

A related view is that methods of peaceful settlement are included in the procedures which are needed to establish a genuine collective security system. This was the American view expressed by Benjamin V. Cohen, which has already been quoted, that "My Government regards pacific settlement and collective measures as inseparable parts of collective security under the Charter."[42]

A rather different view is held by most of the nonaligned states, which now constitute more than one-half of the total membership of the United Nations. Spokesmen of these states have been inclined to play down any efforts to enforce the peace or to take collective measures against any state, except against states such as South Africa and Portugal which in their opinion are guilty of grave offenses against human rights and fundamental human freedoms, and to give priority, amounting at times almost to a monopoly, to measures for peaceful settlement. This point of view was well expressed by Madame Pandit, a representative of perhaps the leading nonaligned state and an avowed champion of reliance on peaceful means toward peaceful ends, in a debate in the First Committee of the UN General Assembly in 1953: "The Indian delegation," she declared, "considered that there were no international problems, however complex, which could not be settled by peaceful negotiation. The United Nations should devote itself to the study of measures for the peaceful settlement and conciliation of disputes. . . . It was more urgent and constructive than the study of coercive measures."[43]

Although peaceful settlement is closely related to collective security, as we have seen, it is based upon a different set of assumptions and procedures. It emphasizes negotiation, conciliation, arbitration, and other amicable methods rather than sanctions and other nonamicable procedures. Instead of seeking to build "situations of strength" — to use a term of which Dean Acheson was fond — which may act as a deterrent to aggression or would place the peace-loving states in a more advantageous position if aggression occurs, it emphasizes recourse to all possible methods of amicable settlement and the avoidance of coercive policies or practices that may jeopardize the chances of agreement. It is altogether possible, of course, that negotia-

[41] *Ibid.*, p. 204.
[42] See above, p. 239.

[43] United Nations, *Official Records of the General Assembly*, 7th Sess., First Committee, Summary Records of Meetings; 575th Meeting, 12 March 1953, p. 454.

tion and other methods of peaceful settlement will be effective in dealing with the most critical problems only if "situations of strength" exist — i.e., only if there is some approximation to a balance of power between the nations which are interested in preserving peace and order and the potential aggressor or aggressors.

In origin the methods of peaceful settlement are very old indeed. The earliest existing treaty dates back to about 3000 B.C.; carved in stone, it records the successful arbitration of a boundary dispute between Egyptian kings. The Greeks developed the mechanism for the peaceful settlement of disputes to a degree not surpassed until our own time. In the modern period no well-developed machinery existed until the present century, although certain procedures were widely used in the nineteenth century, or even slightly earlier. Jay's Treaty of 1794, for example, is often described as the beginning of the extensive use of arbitration in modern times.

Some of the landmarks in the evolution of the machinery for peaceful settlements in the last half-century or so are the Hague conventions of 1899 and 1907 for the Pacific Settlement of International Disputes; the Covenant of the League of Nations and the Statute of the Permanent Court of International Justice; the Protocol for the Pacific Settlement of International Disputes (the so-called Geneva Protocol) of 1924, which never went into effect; the General Act for the Pacific Settlement of International Disputes, which was adopted by the Assembly of the League of Nations in 1928 — one of the most significant and comprehensive attempts to develop a system for peaceful settlement; the Inter-American Arbitration and Conciliation treaties drafted at the Washington Conference of 1929 and soon ratified by most of the American republics; the Charter of the United Nations and the Statute of the International Court of Justice; the studies and recommendations of various UN agencies, notably the "Little Assembly," the Collective Measures Committee, the International Law Commission, and the Secretariat; and the Charter of the Organization of American States, and the Pact of Bogotá adopted at the Ninth Inter-American Conference in 1948. We shall have occasion to discuss some of these landmarks at greater length, especially the work of the UN and of regional arrangements such as the OAS.

The Chief Methods of Pacific Settlement. The Charter of the United Nations lists the chief methods of pacific settlement as negotiation, enquiry, mediation, conciliation, arbitration, judicial settlement, and resort to regional agencies or arrangements (Article 33). These conventional devices may be divided into two main categories: (1) those based on persuasion, with no binding force; and (2) those which have a binding character by virtue of the fact that the parties commit themselves in advance to accept the findings of a neutral board or court. Negotiation, good offices, enquiry, mediation, and conciliation fall within the first category; arbitration and judicial settlement fall within the second. The object of the procedures included in the first category is to bring about settlements based on the mutual agreement of the parties to disputes; the object of the procedures in the second category, technically known as procedures for international adjudication, is to reach, on the basis of objective principles of international law and equity, decisions binding on the parties which agreed to submit their disputes to such adjudicatory tribunals.

Naturally, in view of the nature of the sovereign state system and the political aspects of most international disputes, procedures looking to mutual agreement are resorted to much more frequently than those leading to binding decisions. "The reasons are to be found in the continuing reluctance of states to entrust to anyone else a final power of decision over their conduct, no matter how limited or precisely prescribed that power might be."[44] Moreover, the machinery for adjudication is less elaborate, the "law" is less precise and less generally accepted, and many of the issues which cannot be resolved by the various procedures leading to mutual agreement are regarded as primarily political in nature, and hence beyond the competence or jurisdiction or arbitral tribunals or international courts.

1. *Negotiation.* Most disputes which arise between states are settled through the normal channels of diplomacy — that is, by negotiations between diplomatic representatives. These efforts may be supplemented by meetings of foreign ministers or even of heads of states; by international conferences; or by resort to machinery provided by the UN or by a regional organization such as the OAS. But the first step whenever a dispute arises is invariably direct negotiation. This is the very heart of diplomacy, and is the main way in which relations between nations are carried on. It has been dealt with at some length in Chapter 4. Unfortunately, the relatively few instances in which this procedure fails are likely to be the most serious ones, involving real threats to peace and security, for the devices of diplomacy tend to break down in crisis situations. Hence, in order to avert serious consequences other methods for the peaceful settlement of disputes have been developed.

2. *Good Offices and Mediation.* If a third party offers to be of service in attempting to compose differences between two other states, it is said to tender its "good offices." If the offer is accepted by the disputing states, good offices may lead to mediation. The difference between the two is that in good offices the third party acts simply as a friendly "go between," whereas a mediator may make suggestions of his own. In 1905 President Theodore Roosevelt tendered his good offices to Japan and Russia to end the Russo-Japanese War. The offer was accepted, but he actually became a mediator, for he exerted a direct influence in averting a threatened impasse in the negotiations and in bringing about ultimate agreement. Russia and Japan were not bound in any way to accept his suggestions, but they saw fit to do so. The same procedure was followed in 1965 and 1966 by Premier Kosygin of the Soviet Union, whose expressed willingness to extend his good offices to India and Pakistan in an effort to assist these two countries to resolve some of the differences between them led, about three and a half months after the armed hostilities of September, 1965, to the Tashkent Conference. Kosygin, unlike President Roosevelt at the Portsmouth Conference of 1905, attended the meetings at which the leaders of the two countries conferred, and apparently he played a decisive behind-the-scenes role in getting President Ayub Khan and Prime Minister Lal Bahadur Shastri to reach the agreement known as the Tashkent Declaration. This was another instance of strong and effective mediation.

The United Nations has also performed many useful services in the field of mediation, either through individual mediation or through one of its agencies. Examples of the use of individual mediators would be the rather effective roles of Count Folke Bernadotte and Ralph Bunche in the delicate negotiations which led to an armistice between Israel and the Arab states, of Dr. Frank Graham in connection with the Kashmir dispute, and of the Secretary-General himself in a series of crises. Dag Hammarskjold was particularly effective in this role. "This 'preventive diplomacy,' as Hammarskjold called it, was skillfully applied in such divergent situations as the long complex of Middle Eastern crises and the always festering problem of Berlin, and even outside the UN family in arranging with Chinese Communists for release of American fliers who had come down in Chinese territory."[45] In the Berlin crisis representatives of the six

[44] Jacob and Atherton, p. 270.

[45] *Ibid.*, p. 310.

nonpermanent members of the Security Council, under the leadership of Dr. Juan Bramuglia of Argentina, tried without much success to play the role of mediators. In 1948 and 1949 the General Assembly of the United Nations appointed a Conciliation Committee headed by the president of the Assembly to meet with the big powers and with representatives of the four Balkan states immediately concerned with the controversies in that area. This effort led to agreements in principle for the cessation of hostilities, but the agreement was not implemented until later efforts under other auspices were made. The United Nations has also appointed mediation or conciliation commissions to seek settlements of critical issues through negotiations with states directly involved in various disputes. Outstanding examples are the commissions appointed to assist in the resolution of differences between India and Pakistan over Kashmir, between the Netherlands and the Indonesian Republic, and between Israel and the Arab States.[46]

The tender of good offices may thus be made by one or more states, or by individuals acting in an official capacity, such as the head of a state or officers of the principal organs of the United Nations. The tender of good offices or of mediation is never to be regarded as an unfriendly act, and the parties to a dispute are not bound to accept the offer or to regard suggestions of a mediator as binding. Small neutral powers, especially Switzerland, have often assisted in arranging terms of peace between belligerents through good offices or mediation. The UN Good Offices Committee for Indonesia and its successor, the UN Commission for Indonesia, performed notable service in helping to settle the many disputes between the Dutch government and the self-proclaimed Indonesian Republic in the period following World War II.

3. *Enquiry and Conciliation*. Closely related to and often more effective than good offices and mediation are enquiry and conciliation. The First Hague Conference recommended the use of commissions of enquiry. The Second Hague Conference renewed this suggestion, and provisions for such commission have been incorporated into many bilateral and multilateral treaties. The Assembly of the League of Nations strongly endorsed the idea in 1922. In spite of all this, however, the use of commissions of enquiry has "upon the whole . . . been negligible."[47]

A commission of enquiry investigates the facts of a dispute, but largely confines itself to a statement of the facts and a clarification of the issues. Although it may also present conclusions and recommendations, these are in no sense binding on the disputants. This technique was successfully employed in the Dogger Bank incident of 1904, when the Russian Baltic Fleet fired upon some British fishing vessels in the North Sea, sinking two of them. The explanation offered was that the Russians thought that the British vessels were Japanese torpedo boats! A commission of enquiry, accepted by both Great Britain and Russia, found the Russian action unwarranted; and on the basis of the report the Russian government apologized and paid a substantial indemnity.

Conciliation differs from enquiry in that it assumes an obligation on the part of third parties to take the initiative in the search for agreement. A conciliation commission may advance proposals, ask for compromise or concessions, and, in general, actively seek to effect an understanding between the contending parties. Conciliation is scarcely to be distinguished from mediation; the usual difference is that mediation is commonly performed by an individual and conciliation by a committee, commission, or council.

Conciliation is often held to be an especially constructive approach to those disputes which are not justiciable in nature but also

[46] See *ibid.*, pp. 309–313.

[47] Edwin D. Dickinson, *Law and Peace* (Philadelphia: University of Pennsylvania Press, 1951), p. 71.

are not so exclusively political — that is, involving delicate questions of national interest and prestige — that they can be dealt with only by diplomatic or power-political means. Since many kinds of disputes fall into this in-between zone, the possibilities of conciliation would seem to be great, even though they have not been utilized to the full.

In 1913 Secretary of State William Jennings Bryan negotiated treaties with some thirty states providing for permanent boards or commissions of enquiry, and for a "cooling off" period while investigations were under way. Although the machinery provided for in the Bryan treaties was never utilized, the principles and procedures they embodied were incorporated in a number of later conventions, such as the Central American Treaty of 1923, the Locarno Treaties of 1925, and, in many respects, the Covenant of the League of Nations and the Charter of the United Nations. In the mid-1920's 52 conciliation treaties were entered into, 35 of them without reservations.[48] Substantial progress has been made in establishing conciliation procedures and machinery on a regional basis, especially in the Inter-American System. In general, "The development of international organizations, with specific and continuing responsibilities for conciliation on either a regional or global scale, has been the most vital factor in promoting a peaceful settlement of disputes."[49]

The United Nations has been trying to call attention to these opportunities and to suggest procedures for appointing and utilizing commissions of conciliation;[50] it has itself already made successful use of such commissions, as, for example, in dealing with the problem of Palestine. Some members of the UN think that the organization should pioneer more boldly in this field, both in handling disputes which are brought before it and in providing well-developed machinery for enquiry and conciliation. In January, 1948, for example, the Lebanese delegation submitted to the Interim Committee of the General Assembly a proposal for the establishment of a Permanent Committee of Conciliation. This committee would do all it could to assist parties to a dispute to reach a friendly settlement, and if no agreement could be reached it would submit "a detailed report on the reasons for the disagreement" and would "formulate proposals which it deems fair and legal for the pacific settlement of the dispute."[51]

Many private organizations, especially those which tend to regard the UN as either primarily or almost wholly an agency for peaceful settlement, have urged more general resort to conciliation. This method, they argue, has greater flexibility than arbitration or judicial settlement, and can be adapted to a greater variety of issues. At the same time, they reason, it facilitates the settlement of potentially explosive questions through the use of disinterested and competent third parties or commissions, and thus helps to keep them out of the political arena in which conflicting national interests, coercive techniques, and ideological antagonisms make any kind of amicable settlement difficult.

4. *Arbitration and Judicial Settlement.* Arbitration differs from conciliation in a number of ways. In particular, it is a judicial process, whereas conciliation is an attempt at accommodation. Conciliation recommends, arbitration decides; conciliation is friendly counsel, arbitration is binding decree. Conciliation can take into account national honor

[48] Clyde Eagleton, *International Government*, rev. ed. (New York: The Ronald Press Company, 1948), p. 236.

[49] Jacob and Atherton, p. 282; see also pp. 282–292.

[50] See, for example, a memorandum on "Elaboration of Procedural Suggestions as to Procedure for Peaceful Settlement," submitted to the Interim Committee of the General Assembly by China and the United States in June, 1948; U. N. Document A/AC. 18/SC/2/2, June 16, 1948.

[51] The text of this proposal was published in U. N. Document A/AC. 18/15, January 28, 1948.

and "face"; arbitration must keep to the letter of the law, regardless of the cost or embarrassment to the contending parties.

Judicial settlement, or adjudication, is in a sense a form of arbitration, one in which a permanent court is the arbitral tribunal. As explained in a statement by the Legal Section of the Secretariat of the League of Nations, "arbitration is distinguished from judicial procedure in the strict sense of the word by three features: the nomination of the arbitrators by the parties concerned, the selection by these parties of the principles upon which the tribunal should base its findings, and finally its character of voluntary jurisdiction. The boundary between the two kinds of judicial procedure can not be definitely fixed."[52] Because it is less impromptu than arbitration and requires permanent tribunals, judicial settlement assures "a larger measure of jurisdictional and procedural consistency. It should also assure a somewhat more favorable climate for the progress of the law from precedent to precedent."[53]

"The submission of disputes to arbitration is a time-honored practice among states. It was undertaken in medieval times and even by the Greek city-states."[54] The nineteenth century added some four hundred examples of successful arbitration to the precedents set by the arbitrations under the famous Jay's Treaty of 1794 between Great Britain and the United States. The most celebrated case involved the settlement of the *Alabama* claims controversy. The *Alabama* was a cruiser built in Liverpool for the Confederacy during the American Civil War. It inflicted heavy damages on Northern shipping, and, according to the American government, its use prolonged the war. After extended and none-too-friendly negotiations, Great Britain agreed to an American proposal to arbitrate the points in dispute. A tribunal specified in the Treaty of Washington of 1871, composed of five jurists appointed by the President of the United States, the Queen of England, the King of Italy, the President of Switzerland, and the Emperor of Brazil, met in Geneva and awarded the United States direct damages amounting to $15,500,000.

The United States stood as the foremost champion of arbitration during the nineteenth century, but in the present century her interest has slackened. Although she did participate in some eighty-five arbitrations up to the end of World War I, in several cases she refused to arbitrate, or she delayed action for many years. The United States Senate, more because of jealousy over its prerogatives in treaty-making than because of any hostility to the principle of arbitration, rejected a number of arbitration treaties between 1890 and 1914, or so emasculated them by amendment that they were withdrawn.[55] After World War I, however, the United States did agree to arbitrate a number of cases. For example, "Hundreds of 'mixed claims' between the United States and Mexico were brought before a General Claims Commission set up in 1923 to settle cases that had arisen during a long period of friction and revolutionary development in Mexico."[56]

Attempts to create permanent courts of arbitration, and thereby to provide machinery for the judicial settlement of disputes, date from the First Hague Conference of 1899, which established the Permanent Court of Arbitration. Actually, this was neither permanent nor a court but a panel of arbitrators whose names were on file at The Hague, to be drawn upon if disputing states so chose. Despite its limitations, the Permanent Court

52 Permanent Court of International Justice, Advisory Commission of Jurists, *Documents Presented to the Commission Relating to Existing Plans for the Establishment of a Permanent Court of International Justice,* p. 113.

53 Dickinson, p. 73.

54 Jacob and Atherton, p. 271.

55 W Stull Holt, *Treaties Defeated by the Senate* (Baltimore: The Johns Hopkins Press, 1933), pp. 154–162, 204–212.

56 Jacob and Atherton, p. 272.

was utilized successfully in fifteen cases before 1914, including the Venezuelan debt controversy of 1904 involving Germany, Great Britain, and Italy, and the Newfoundland fisheries dispute between Great Britain and the United States. Although still in existence today, the "Hague Court" has been little used since the opening of the Permanent Court of International Justice in 1922.

From 1907 to 1917 a Central American Court of Justice, "which may be called the first real international court ever to be established,"[57] functioned with some success in eight cases. It was wrecked by the refusal of the United States, one of the sponsoring powers, to accept the decision of the Court in 1917 regarding the Bryan-Chamorro Treaty between the United States and Nicaragua."[58]

The most elaborate permanent courts for the judicial settlement of disputes have been, of course, the Permanent Court of International Justice, which functioned in the interwar period in loose association with the League of Nations, and its successor, the International Court of Justice, which was brought into being in 1946 as one of the principal organs of the United Nations. Although the two courts were given different names and derived their authority from different statutes, the present International Court of Justice regards itself as a continuation of the older court. The Carnegie Peace Palace at The Hague has been the seat of both courts.

Since the time of the First Hague Conference many attempts have been made to secure the consent of states to the compulsory adjudication of disputes. These attempts have met with only limited success, for the nature of the state system is not conducive to really binding limitations on the separate states, to put it mildly. Usually agreements to resort to adjudication have been hedged about by reservations in areas involving "vital interests," "matters of domestic concern," or "national honor" — reservations which are obviously so general and so all-inclusive that when interpreted unilaterally they can make the original commitments virtually meaningless. Thus the Hague Convention for the Pacific Settlement of Disputes called for resort to arbitration "in so far as circumstances permit."

A real advance in the prospects for compulsory adjudication was made by the Permanent Court of International Justice and the International Court of Justice. Paragraph 1 of Article 36 of the Statute of the former court, also used almost verbatim in the same article in the Statute of the present International Court of Justice, read as follows: "The jurisdiction of the Court comprises all cases which the parties refer to it and all matters specifically provided for in treaties and conventions in force." In general, therefore, the jurisdiction originally conferred was voluntary; but in fact both courts were given a wide compulsory jurisdiction through "treaties and conventions in force" and through the so-called Optional Clause, also contained in Article 36 of both statutes. This clause provided that states could of their own accord accept the compulsory jurisdiction of the Court "in all legal disputes concerning: (a) the interpretation of a treaty; (b) any question of international law; (c) the existence of any fact which, if established, would constitute a breach of an international obligation; (d) the nature or extent of the reparation to be made for the breach of an international obligation." More than half the states of the world, including all the major non-Communist powers, have accepted the Optional Clause, though in some cases, as with the United States, with devastating reservations.[59]

[57] Eagleton, p. 227.

[58] See Manley O. Hudson, *The Permanent Court of International Justice* (New York: The Macmillan Company, 1943), Chapter III.

[59] See *Compulsory Jurisdiction of the International Court of Justice*, Dept. of State Pub. 3540, International Organization and Conference Series II, 31 (June, 1949). This publication contains the texts of the declarations of the 3[illegible] states which had accepted the Optional Clause up to June,

Pacific Settlement and Regional Arrangements. The United Nations Charter commends the settlement of disputes between nations not only by the conventional methods and through the normal channels of diplomacy but also by resort to "regional agencies or arrangements, or other peaceful means (Article 33)." It also provides that "the Members of the United Nations entering into such arrangements or constituting such agencies shall make every effort to achieve pacific settlement of local disputes through such regional arrangements or by such regional agencies before referring them to the Security Council (Article 52)."

The charters of all regional arrangements contain some provision for the pacific settlement of disputes among the participating states in the spirit of the United Nations Charter. As would be expected, such provisions are most elaborate in the most fully developed regional agency of the present time, the Organization of American States. The Charter of the OAS devotes an entire chapter to the "Pacific Settlement of Disputes" (Chapter IV), and a special treaty, known as the Pact of Bogotá,[60] contains elaborate provisions for peaceful settlement. The eight chapters of the Pact are entitled as follows: (1) General Obligation to Settle Disputes by Pacific Means; (2) Procedures of Good Offices and Mediation; (3) Procedures of Investigation and Conciliation; (4) Judicial Procedure; (5) Procedure of Arbitration; (6) Fulfillment of Decisions; (7) Advisory Opinions; (8) Final Provisions.

"Under the Pact of Bogotá, every American state is obligated to settle *all* its disputes by peaceful means." Various organs and agencies of the OAS, notably the Meeting of Consultation of Ministers of Foreign Affairs and the Council, have been authorized to act on behalf of the organization in dealing with inter-hemispheric disputes. "While the pattern of OAS action has been pragmatic . . . , it has tended to emphasize: first, a mutual accommodation among the protagonists themselves; second, a process of independent fact-finding by investigators accountable to the OAS directly . . . ; third, direct mediation or conciliation by an OAS body . . . ; fourth, a judgment of responsibility directed against one of the parties if the OAS suggestions for settlement were rejected; fifth, the imposition of sanctions in case the states continued to be recalcitrant."[61] This list suggests that, if necessary, the OAS may move from procedures for peaceful settlement to those of collective action, a process also clearly envisaged in Chapters VI and VII of the United Nations Charter.

In general, the OAS has been rather successful in dealing with "the practice of fomenting revolutions against neighboring governments, the most persistent precipitant of Inter-American conflict in recent years,"[62] and it has even resorted at times to sanctions — against the Dominican Republic in the last days of the Trujillo regime and against Cuba after the majority of the member states of the OAS were convinced of the reality of Castro's alignment with the Soviet Union. But in other aspects of the Cuban case and in reactions to unilateral United States intervention in the Dominican Republic in 1965, many OAS members have demonstrated a reluctance to apply sanctions against a mem-

1949. The declaration of the United States, dated August 14, 1946, listed the following reservations: "*Provided,* that this declaration shall not apply to:

a. disputes the solution of which the parties shall entrust to other tribunals by virtue of agreements already in existence or which may be concluded in the future; or

b. disputes with regard to matters which are essentially within the domestic jurisdiction of the United States of America as determined by the United States of America; or

c. disputes arising under a multilateral treaty, unless (1) all parties to the treaty affected by the decision are also parties to the case before the Court, or (2) the United States of America specially agrees to jurisdiction."

[60] See William Sanders, "Bogotá Conference," *International Conciliation,* No. 442 (June, 1948).

[61] Jacob and Atherton, pp. 290, 291.

[62] *Ibid.,* p. 289.

ber state, whatever the provocation. They are very sensitive to any violation, real or alleged, of the principle of nonintervention, and they are rather dubious about collective action by the OAS, which to them smacks of "collective intervention."

Pacific Settlement and the United Nations. One of the major objectives of the United Nations, as we have seen, is "to bring about by peaceful means, and in conformity with the principles of justice and international law, adjustment or settlement of international disputes or situations which might lead to a breach of the peace" (Article 1). Hence, if all other efforts and procedures fail, or if the services of the international organization are needed at any stage of a controversy, the whole machinery of the United Nations is presumably available. The Security Council may "call upon the parties to settle their disputes" by the means provided for in Article 33, may investigate any dispute, may "at any stage of a dispute . . . recommend appropriate procedures or methods of adjustment," and may keep abreast of "any procedures for the settlement of the dispute which have already been adopted by the parties." Article 37 provides that if the parties to a dispute "fail to settle it by the means indicated" in Article 33, "they shall refer it to the Security Council," which may take such action as it considers necessary. If it cannot bring the parties immediately concerned to a settlement, or if its recommendations are not followed and the Council feels that there has developed a "threat to the peace, breach of the peace, or act of aggression," then it may decide that it has exhausted the possibilities of Chapter VI (containing Articles 33–38: Pacific Settlement of Disputes) and that it has become necessary to use its powers under Chapter VII (containing Articles 39–51: Action with Respect of Threats to the Peace, Breaches of the Peace, and Acts of Aggression). If so, it may resort to "measures not involving the use of armed force" (Article 41) or, if necessary, call upon member nations to use their armed forces (Article 42).

The provisions of Chapter VI of the Charter are more elaborate than the comparable ones in the Covenant of the League of Nations. Together with the provisions for judicial settlement contained in the Statute of the International Court of Justice, they seem to open the way to new and impromptu procedures by UN agencies if the stipulated modes of settlement are unavailing, although Professor Clyde Eagleton observed that "it can be debated whether the Charter of the UN represents any advance over the methods for the settlement of disputes of the League of Nations, especially as regards legal or judicial settlement."[63]

Be this as it may, the UN has continued the detailed consideration of the procedures for peaceful settlement which was carried on by the League. Most of this work has been undertaken by a Subcommittee of the Interim Committee of the General Assembly, by the Interim Committee, by the International Law Commission, by the International Court of Justice, and by the Secretariat.

An Evaluation

Collective security and the peaceful settlement of international disputes are only two of the approaches to the problem of preventing war. While some writers regard them as contradictory, and while they can in theory be separately pursued, perhaps the most common view is that they are logical components of a single program. The supporters of this view find it difficult to conceive of a collective security arrangement that does not provide some alternative — some machinery for peaceful settlement — to the prompt and automatic employment of armed force. Indeed, some alternative seems necessary, for, although force alone may be called for to stop an aggressor, peace without accommodation may be only an uneasy truce.

[63] Eagleton, p. 432.

The devices of collective security and peaceful settlement are disparaged by the enthusiasts who would remake the world in a single great constitutional convention of all nations or in an overnight purification of the minds and hearts of men. These people are not to be satisfied with a day-by-day or month-by-month avoidance of war; they seek a new order in which war will be both physically and theoretically impossible. They would in one unrealistic leap cover the ground which supporters of collective security and peaceful settlement would traverse more slowly and with expected halts and perhaps reverses. Some of them come close to repudiating "settlement" and urging what amounts to collective suppression.

Believers in international law as an approach to peace are far more patient with collective security and peaceful settlement. Indeed, peaceful settlement is, in a sense, the basis of the international law prescription. Advocates of this approach seek an expansion of the area in which judicial processes can be made to operate and a contraction of the area in which political processes must be resorted to. Thus they would change the emphasis within "peaceful settlement." In doing so, they would keep in mind the true nature of law — that it registers agreement already reached rather than seeks to institute rules of idealistic conduct. For the most part they would utilize collective security as an interim measure, hoping to find its importance diminishing as international law slowly grows to its potential stature.

In spite of its obvious limitations and some conspicuous failures, peaceful settlement has a rather encouraging record. It provides a framework for the resolution of international conflicts, or at least for keeping them from becoming major threats to the peace. It seems to embrace an honest recognition of the realities of international politics, in which it plays an active and constructive role. While it is concerned with disputes arising out of past and present tensions, it looks to the future and is wholly compatible with other and more hopeful patterns of international relations. In time, it may help to bring into being a really effective system of collective security. Together with collective security, it may lead to a world order based on justice under law.

SUGGESTIONS FOR FURTHER READING

BOURQUIN, MAURICE, ed. *Collective Security.* Paris, 1936. Issued under the auspices of the International Institute of Intellectual Co-operation. A record of the proceedings of the 7th and 8th International Studies Conferences, Paris, 1934, and London, 1935.

BRIERLY, J. L. *The Law of Nations,* 6th ed., edited by Sir Humphrey Waldock. New York: Oxford University Press, 1963. Chapter VIII contains a summary and appraisal of international procedures for peaceful settlement.

CHEEVER, DANIEL S. and H. FIELD HAVILAND, JR. *Organizing for Peace: International Organization in World Affairs.* Boston: Houghton Mifflin Company, 1954.

CLAUDE, INIS L., JR. *Power and International Relations.* New York: Random House, 1962. Especially Chapter 2, "Collective Security: An Alternative to the Balance of Power?" and Chapter 3, "A Critique of Collective Security."

———. *Swords into Plowshares.* New York: Random House, 1959.

———. "The United Nations and the Use of Force," *International Conciliation,* No. 532 (March, 1961).

Collective Security: Shield of Freedom, rev. ed. Bangkok, 1963. A SEATO publication. Deals with collective security pacts involving 41 nations of the non-Communist world.

DE CONDE, ALEXANDER, ed. *Isolation and Security*. Durham, N.C.: Duke University Press, 1957. Contains essay by Kenneth W. Thompson on "Isolation and Collective Security."

DUNN, F. S. *Peaceful Change: A Study of International Procedures*. New York: Harper, for Council on Foreign Relations, 1937.

EAGLETON, CLYDE. *International Government*, rev. ed. New York: The Ronald Press Co., 1948. Chapter IX: "Pacific Settlement of Disputes."

FELLER, A. H. *United Nations and World Community*. Boston: Little, Brown and Company, 1952.

GOODRICH, LELAND M. *Korea: A Study of U.S. Policy in the United Nations*. New York: Council on Foreign Relations, 1956.

GOODRICH, LELAND M. and ANNE P. SIMONS. *The United Nations and the Maintenance of International Peace and Security*. Washington, D.C.: The Brookings Institution, 1955.

HAAS, ERNST and ALLEN S. WHITING. *Dynamics of International Relations*. New York: McGraw-Hill Book Company, 1956. Good discussion of collective security.

HOGAN, WILLARD N. *International Conflict and Collective Security*. Lexington: University of Kentucky Press, 1955. A study of the "principle of concern" as the basis for a system of collective security.

HUDSON, MANLEY O. *By Pacific Means*. New Haven: Yale University Press, 1935.

———. *International Tribunals, Past and Future*. Washington, D.C.: The Brookings Institution, 1944.

JACKSON, ELMORE. *Meeting of Minds: A Blueprint for Peace Through Mediation*. New York: McGraw-Hill Book Company, 1952.

JESSUP, PHILIP C. *A Modern Law of Nations*. New York: The Macmillan Company, 1948. Chapters 7 and 8.

LARUS, JOEL, ed. *From Collective Security to Preventive Diplomacy: Readings in International Organization and the Maintenance of Peace*. New York: John Wiley & Sons, 1965. Part One deals with "Collective Security and the League" and Part Three with "Collective Security and the United Nations."

LATHAM, EARL, ed. *The Philosophy and Policies of Woodrow Wilson*. Chicago: University of Chicago Press, 1958. Especially the chapter by Robert E. Osgood, "Woodrow Wilson, Collective Security, and the Lessons of History."

LIE, TRYGVE. *In the Cause of Peace*. New York: The Macmillan Company, 1954.

LISSITZYN, OLIVER J. *The International Court of Justice*. New York: Carnegie Endowment for International Peace, 1951.

MACIVER, ROBERT M. *The Nations and the United Nations*. New York: Manhattan Publishing Company, for the Carnegie Endowment for International Peace, 1959.

MACLAURIN, JOHN. *The United Nations and Power Politics*. London, 1951.

MANGONE, GERARD J. *A Short History of International Organization*. New York: McGraw-Hill Book Company, 1954.

MANNING, C. A., ed. *Peaceful Change: An International Problem*. New York: The Macmillan Company, 1937.

MARTIN, A. *Collective Security: A Progress Report*. Paris, 1952. A useful and comprehensive study published under the auspices of UNESCO.

MITRANY, DAVID. *The Problem of International Sanctions*. London, 1925.

———. *A Working Peace System*. London, 1944.

RAPPARD, WILLIAM. *The Quest for Peace*. Cambridge, Mass.: Harvard University Press, 1940.

SLATER, JEROME. *A Revaluation of Collective Security: The OAS in Action*. Columbus: Ohio State University Press, 1965. A pamphlet containing two general chapters on "The Theory of Collective Security" and "Collective Security Revaluated."

STROMBERG, ROLAND N. *Collective Security and American Foreign Policy; from the League of Nations to NATO*. New York: Frederick A. Praeger, 1963.

THANT, U. *Toward World Peace; Addresses and Public Statements, 1957–1963*. New York: Thomas Yoseloff, 1964.

WOLFERS, ARNOLD, ed. *Alliance Policy in the*

Cold War. Baltimore: The Johns Hopkins Press, 1959. Chapter III, "Collective Defense versus Collective Security."

WRIGHT, QUINCY. *Problems of Stability and Progress in International Relations*. Berkeley: University of California Press, 1954.

———. *The Study of International Relations*. New York: Appleton-Century-Crofts, 1955.

———. *A Study of War*. 2 vols. Chicago: University of Chicago Press, 1942.

11 International Law

We have seen that balance of power policies, collective security arrangements, and procedures for the pacific settlement of disputes operate to fix the relationship of states to each other. To the extent that they operate effectively they are stabilizing factors in interstate relations. More general and continuous than these controls is international law. In theory this law is common to all states. It incorporates the experience of many centuries during which peoples have lived side by side and have done business with each other; it may properly be spoken of as the moral code of states, for it is the body of rules upon which they have agreed so that they may survive.

Many writers have quarreled with the term "international law," saying that it implies the existence of a law over states. They contend that in reality international law is a law *among* states — not *over* them. The difference is a fundamental one, for it involves the basic nature of the state system. Indeed, international law must be studied with the realization that it not only presumes the sovereignty of states but also seeks to preserve sovereignty — that, in general, it has been the friend rather than the enemy of sovereignty.

To fix international law in its proper relationship to the state system and to the conduct of international politics, we shall offer some definitions of that law, examine certain aspects of it, note its sources and development, review codification and the international legislative process, observe the changing position of individuals under it, and discuss some of its limitations and possibilities.

The Nature and Content of International Law

Definitions. We might do well to begin our brief study of international law by noting some definitions which distinguished writers have used. Oppenheim, a standard authority, spoke of it in 1905 as "the name for the body of customary and conventional rules which are considered legally binding by civilized states in their intercourse with each other." He added that it is "a law for the intercourse of states with one another, not a law for individuals" and that it is "a law *between*, not above, the single states."[1] Ellery C. Stowell, writing in 1931, offered this definition: "International law embodies certain rules relating to human relations throughout the world, which are generally observed by mankind and enforced primarily through the agency of the governments of the independent communities into which humanity is divided."[2] In 1948 Philip C. Jessup wrote that

[1] L. Oppenheim, *International Law* (New York: Longmans, Green & Co., 1905), I, 2.

[2] *International Law* (New York: Holt, 1931), p. 10n.

international law is "generally defined as law applicable to relations between states," but he declared that "there has welled up through the years a growing opposition to this traditional concept." He was so confident that individuals are becoming more and more subject to international law that he outlined a "modern law of nations" based upon the hypothesis that the law of nations is applicable to individuals in their relations with states and even to certain interrelationships of individuals.[3] He also called attention to the growing importance of "transnational law" as a result of the proliferation of agencies of an official and nonofficial nature and of practices which cut across national lines.[4]

> The recent trend in the West, particularly in the United States, is toward a less technical view of the law. The increasingly influential school of international law created by Myres S. McDougal of Yale University regards law as a process of decision into which all relevant factors, and not merely technical norms, enter. It virtually identifies law with policy and calls the study of law "a policy science."[5]

While Dr. Jessup's and Professor McDougal's views of the expanding nature of international law are certainly warranted by the developments of our time, we must continue to regard that law as primarily "the body of rules accepted by the general community of nations as defining their rights and the means of procedure by which those rights may be protected or violations of them redressed," to use Professor Charles G. Fenwick's excellent definition.[6]

Unfortunately, however, "the general community of nations" is split in many ways, and traditional international law, which is after all a product of Western civilization, is regarded with great suspicion in Communist countries and with significant reservations in the developing countries of Asia and Africa.

The Communist States and International Law. The Communists tend to regard traditional international law, as we have defined it, as an instrument of the capitalist, imperialist West, designed to preserve the status quo. A standard Soviet definition of international law was given in 1948 by A. Y. Vyshinsky, who called it "the sum total of the norms regulating relations between states in the process of their struggle and cooperation, expressing the will of the ruling classes of these states and secured by coercion exercised by states individually or collectively."[7] This definition was also presented in the textbook on international law published in 1957 by the Institute of State and Law of the Soviet Academy of Sciences, with the addition of a reference to "peaceful coexistence" as coming within the purview of international law. Although Y. Korovin in 1961 went so far as to insist that "Contemporary international law may be defined as the international code of peaceful co-existence,"[8] a year later a statement by G. I. Tunkin, head of the Treaty and Legal Department of the Soviet Ministry of Foreign Affairs, reaffirmed the more typical Soviet view that

[3] Philip C. Jessup, *A Modern Law of Nations* (New York: The Macmillan Company, 1948), pp. 15–16. Used by permission of The Macmillan Company.

[4] Philip C. Jessup, *Transnational Law* (New Haven: Yale University Press, 1956).

[5] Oliver J. Lissitzyn, "International Law in a Divided World," *International Conciliation*, No. 542 (March, 1963), p. 59. See also Myres S. McDougal *et al.*, *Studies in Public World Order* (New Haven: Yale University Press, 1960); and Myres S. McDougal "International Law, Power and Policy: A Contemporary Conception," *Recueil des Cours*, Vol. 82 (1953–I), 137.

[6] Charles G. Fenwick, *International Law* (New York: Century, 1924), p. 34.

[7] "Mezhdunarodnoie Pravo i Mezhdunarodnaia Organizatsiia," *Sovetskoie Gosudarstvo i Pravo*, No. 1 (1948) p. 22; quoted in Lissitzyn, pp. 16–17.

[8] "International Law Today," *International Affairs*, July, 1961, p. 19. See also Y. Korovin, F. I. Kozhevnikov, and G. P. Zadorezhnyy, "Peaceful Co-existence and International Law," *Izvestiya*, April 18, 1962.

international law reflects "the struggle and cooperation of states, and, first of all, of states of the two systems."[9] "It is this Soviet stress on antagonism rather than cooperation as the primary characteristic of the relations between the states of 'the two systems' that sets narrow limits to the role of international law in world affairs."[10]

A great deal of stress is laid on the study of international law in the Soviet Union. In 1946 the Central Committee of the Communist Party of the Soviet Union directed that special attention should be given to it. Interest in the subject has been especially marked since the Twentieth Congress of the CPSU in 1956. From this time, until early 1962, "more works on international law are said to have appeared in the Soviet Union than in the first forty years of the existence of the Soviet state."[11] In 1957 a Soviet Association of International Law was formed. At the same time, the Institute of State and Law of the Soviet Academy of Sciences published a standard textbook in international law, an important volume which has been translated into several languages, including English.[12]

Soviet officials as well as scholars profess to attach great importance to international law, but their approach to it is highly secretive and colored by their Marxist-Leninist orientation. They give great weight to certain traditional principles, notably sovereignty, nonintervention, and the territorial inviolability and equality of states; and they emphasize such so-called new principles as nonaggression, self-determination, peaceful co-existence, and general and complete disarmament. "Modern international law," asserted Tunkin in 1962, "is anti-colonial in its direction."[13]

The Soviet Union insists that "unequal" treaties are not binding, but it has not hesitated to enter into a large number of bilateral and multilateral treaties with "capitalist" states.[14] In spite of impressions to the contrary, it has lived up to most of its treaty commitments, especially in nonpolitical fields; but its violation of treaties of high political significance have been frequent. While it has rather generally adhered to a policy of routine observance of international law, "the fact remains that, in general, the influence of the Soviet bloc has been strongly exerted against the extension of the judicial function in the international community" and that "Communist ideology and public order stand in the way of the gradual evolution of mankind toward the rule of law in world affairs."[15]

Attitudes toward international law appear to reflect the difference in the ideologies and policies within the Communist world, "from the relative moderation of the Yugoslav government at one end of the spectrum to the intransigence of the Communist regime in mainland China at the other."[16]

The official position of the Chinese Communists toward international law is still in the process of formulation. In general, like the Soviet leaders, they follow the Marxist-Leninist approach, with perhaps even more emphasis on the struggle between systems and on the political rather than the legal approach to foreign affairs. "When it becomes necessary to raise legal questions, the Chinese government sometimes makes skillful use of traditionally accepted international

[9] "XXII S'ezd KPSS i Zadachi Sovetskoi Nauki Mezhdunarodnogo Prava," *Sovetskoie Gosudarstvo i Pravo*, No. 5 (1962), pp. 12–13; quoted in Lissitzyn, p. 17.

[10] Lissitzyn, p. 17.

[11] *Ibid.*, p. 14.

[12] Academy of Sciences of the U.S.S.R., Institute of State and Law, *International Law* (Moscow, n.d.).

[13] "XXII S'ezd KPSS i Zadachi Sovetskoi Nauki Mezhdunarodnogo Prava," p. 11; quoted in Lissitzyn, p. 18.

[14] In the first 40 years of its existence, the Soviet Union entered into 2,516 treaties and agreements. J. F. Triska and R. M. Slusser, *The Theory, Law and Policy of Soviet Treaties* (Stanford, Calif.: Stanford University Press, 1962), p. 4.

[15] Lissitzyn, pp. 29, 34.

[16] *Ibid.*, p. 35.

rules, suiting them to its own characterization of the facts of the situation. At other times, the generally accepted rules are sidestepped by a varying combination of orthodox and Marxist argument. Like the Soviet Union, the Chinese People's Republic has chosen an extremely nationalist and conservative formulation of state sovereignty as the most effective legal safeguard of her freedom of action."[17] Even more than the Soviet Union, the People's Republic emphasizes the absolute primacy of national over international law, the theme of peaceful co-existence, and the doctrine of agreement that considers no obligations under international law valid unless accepted by both "camps." While the Chinese Communists do appear to accept some of the traditional principles of international law, their "emphasis on state sovereignty, the emphasis on intentions rather than obligations, and the softening of legal rules with political generalizations are part of a conscious assault on international law as we know it."[18]

The New States and International Law. The developing nations of Asia and Africa evidence a distrust of traditional international law, a belief that the traditional norms are not binding on them, and a strong desire for the development of international law to meet the needs of the modern world. These nations, like the Communist countries, want to be sure that international law does not become an instrument for the preservation of the status quo which may stand in the way of measures to promote de-colonization, self-determination, human rights, and the social use of natural resources, and they are inclined to give more emphasis to the "progressive development of international law" than to its codification. Unlike the Communists, they have a positive view toward international law and in most instances they are inclined to accept, or at least to abide by, its traditional norms. Most of them are quite ready to join international organizations, become parties to multilateral conventions and treaty arrangements, and play as active a role as possible in international life. Yet, while they have a deep appreciation of the importance of international law, there is among the developing nations, as Oliver Lissitzyn has pointed out, "a perceptible current of discontent with traditional international law,"[19] and a feeling expressed by Judge Radhabinod Pal, a distinguished Indian jurist who wrote a famous dissent in the Tokyo War Crimes Trials and who was a member of the International Law Commission of the United Nations, that they ought not "to be bound by rules of international law which they have not helped to create and which very often ran counter to their interests."[20] "There is also," to return to Professor Lissitzyn's analysis, "a desire to incorporate in it [international law] certain principles that have been usually regarded in the West as political rather than legal and that, by their very generality and flexibility of application, lend themselves to manipulation. The non-Western nations tend to use such principles as weapons in their effort to do away with the remnants of Western domination in both political and economic spheres."[21] The new states, for example, place great stress on the concept of self-determination, which they advance vigorously in their anti-colonial crusades and in their efforts to assert their economic and social, as well as political, independence. This orientation is reflected in the Declaration on the Granting of Independence to Colonial Countries and Peoples, adopted by the General Assembly of the UN

[17] Anthony R. Dicks, "Chinese Attitudes To International Law (I)," a memorandum dated October 9, 1964, privately distributed by the Institute of Current World Affairs, New York, p. 16.

[18] *Ibid.*, p. 16.

[19] Lissitzyn, p. 38.

[20] Quoted in "Future Role of the International Law Commission in the Changing World," *United Nations Review*, IX (September, 1962), p. 31.

[21] Lissitzyn, p. 39.

in December, 1960, which affirmed that "all peoples have the right to self-determination," and in the frequent assertions by new states of their sovereignty in the economic sphere. It also explains the tendencies to challenge the status quo and to seek legal justification for such a challenge, even if it may lead to the use of force against recalcitrant colonialists. This attitude has been encouraged and supported by Communist countries, and viewed with misgivings, or worse, by most Western states, whether colonial powers or not.

The Indian occupation of Goa, by military means, in 1961 brought out the differences in view on this important issue. To India, as to most of the states of Asia and Africa and to the Communist states, the occupation of Goa was a regrettable necessity, a case of decolonization and not of aggression, in keeping with the General Assembly's anti-colonial declaration of 1960 and wholly justified in international law. To most Western countries the action was a flagrant violation of the United Nations Charter and of international law, and was particularly regrettable because it had been taken by a country which had symbolized policies of nonviolence and a scrupulous observance of high standards of international conduct and morality. Whatever its justification under traditional international law, India and her supporters argued that, if necessary, international law must be revised to bring such actions within its purview and to take into account the interests of emerging states of the non-Western world.

Public and Private International Law. The international law we have defined is at times spoken of as "public international law." This is to distinguish it from what is known as "private international law," a branch of the law which deals entirely with the relations of persons living under different legal systems. Occasions for the application of private international law arise when justice requires that the law of some outside jurisdiction — not necessarily a foreign state — be applied in a particular case. For example, to cite a famous English situation, when couples left England to be married in Scotland, where the marriage laws were less stringent, the question arose whether the validity of the marriage should be determined by English law or by Scottish law. The English courts held that the laws of Scotland should apply. Frequently the nationality of a person is the issue. As Professor Edwin D. Dickinson stated, "there is a host of problems concerning the adjudication and regulation of matters of private right and duty which arise uniquely from the continuing movement of persons or things from one nation to another and from the increasing ease with which relationships of agreement, family, property, enterprise, or the like may be consummated across national frontiers."[22] Differences in law have long presented annoying problems in such matters as bills and notes, sales, carriers, shipping, and the like. It might be added that "private international law" is a term more current in Europe than in the United States. American lawyers commonly use "conflict of laws" to mean the same thing, but this term is also used in relation to the laws of states of the United States.

Other Branches of International Law. Two other branches of international law should be mentioned. One of these is admiralty law, which is the law of maritime commerce. It somewhat resembles private international law in that in large part it is concerned with differences between separate national jurisdictions. In the United States, for instance, the system of admiralty or maritime law which prevails by general consent in all commercial states has no inherent force of its own; it is operative only to the extent

[22] Edwin D. Dickinson, *Law and Peace* (Philadelphia: University of Pennsylvania Press, 1951), p. 59.

that it has been adopted by American customs or law. Another branch of international law is administrative law. It consists of the body of rules growing out of the regulations adopted by international administrative agencies, as, for example, the Universal Postal Union. There is, of course, no direct national aspect to such "law," but presumably it will be observed by those states which have accepted the obligations of membership in the relevant administrative union, and it may provide cases and precedents to which national courts will give due heed.

Finally we should mention what is called "international comity." The term itself has been the subject of much controversy. It was earlier held that when the courts of one state gave force to the laws of another state in order to render justice to the parties involved, they did so as a matter of comity or grace. More recently the conviction has grown that a state is bound by its own rules on the conflict of laws or by international law to grant recognition and protection to foreign-created rights. Some writers would abandon the term entirely as it has been applied in private international law. It is used in public international law to explain the practices which states more or less consistently observe, even though they are not legally bound to do so. As practices based on comity tend to become legally binding custom, the scope of international comity is thereby diminished. Comity thus influences the growth of international law.

The Subject Matter of International Law. International law proper — that is, public international law — is commonly divided into the law of war and the law of peace. Hugo Grotius called his great pioneering work *On the Law of War and Peace;* Oppenheim's classic treatise consisted of one volume on peace and one on war. The conventional view was that public international law is made up of two separate and distinct branches, with the law of war being necessary to regulate the rights and obligations of belligerents and neutrals when the law of peace is no longer applicable. But in an era of protracted conflict the boundary lines between war and peace are becoming more obscured, and the new techniques and new weapons of destruction have made conventional laws of war inadequate, if not obsolete.

Some understanding of the subject matter of international law may be gained by reading the International Law Commission's listing of twenty-five topics in the field, prepared at an early stage of the Commission's work: (1) Subjects of international law; (2) Sources of international law; (3) Obligations of international law in relation to the law of States; (4) Fundamental rights and duties of States; (5) Recognition of States and Governments; (6) Succession of States and Governments; (7) Domestic jurisdiction; (8) Recognition of acts of foreign States; (9) Jurisdiction over foreign States; (10) Obligations of territorial jurisdiction; (11) Jurisdiction with regard to crimes committed outside national territory; (12) Territorial domain of States; (13) Regime of the high seas; (14) Regime of territorial waters; (15) Pacific settlement of international disputes; (16) Nationality, including statelessness; (17) Treatment of aliens; (18) Extradition; (19) Right of asylum; (20) Law of treaties; (21) Diplomatic intercourse and immunities; (22) Consular intercourse and immunities; (23) State responsibility; (24) Arbital procedure; (25) Laws of war.[23] Every one of the twenty-five topics raises fundamental questions of international conduct and obligations and has been the subject of careful examination and discussion. It will be noted

[23] The topics are listed in *The American Journal of International Law*, XLIV (January, 1950), Supplement (Official Documents), pp. 5–6. Two of the topics, "Diplomatic intercourse and immunities" and "Pacific settlement of international disputes," are discussed in other chapters.

that the "laws of war" is only one item — and the last one — on the list; yet it is in itself of such scope that Professor Edwin M. Borchard has stressed its importance and described it as "the vast complex of rules governing the relations of belligerents and neutrals in time of war."[24]

Increasingly, in recent years, there has been a marked tendency to attempt to develop principles of international law to apply to questions which in the past would probably have been regarded as outside the scope of international law. An outstanding example is the effort of the UN General Assembly and a Special Committee of the Assembly to develop "principles of international law concerning friendly relations and co-operation among states."

The advent of the space age has moved international law, like man himself, beyond the territorial sphere. In 1959 the General Assembly created a Committee on the Peaceful Uses of Outer Space; in September, 1963, this committee was urged to continue its "efforts to find solutions in the legal field in order to match the continuous scientific and technological progress in outer space."[25] Three months later the General Assembly unanimously adopted a Declaration of Legal Principles Governing the Activities of States in the Exploration and Use of Outer Space,[26] in which it was stated that outer space and celestial bodies are not subject to national appropriation and are free for exploration and use by all states. It also recommended that consideration be given to incorporating principles governing space activities "in international agreement form, in the future as appropriate."

In addition to the international law of outer space and the growing efforts to develop what may be called an international criminal law, as illustrated by the Nuremberg and Tokyo War Crimes Trials and the Genocide Convention, many other fields of international law are expanding in scope and significance or are being developed effectively for the first time. These include such relatively technical fields as international constitutional law, international administrative law, international labor law, international commercial law, international corporation law, international anti-trust law, international tax law, and international economic development law. These new fields, as Professor Wolfgang Friedmann has pointed out, "are developing from a far-reaching interpenetration between public and private law," and may in fact be evolving "the form and authority of new international norms."[27]

The subject matter of international law is expanding rapidly in volume as well as in scope. This is illustrated by the formidable achievements in the codification of international law and in the development of international legislation, which are discussed later in this chapter. The number of treaties and other international instruments, the major source of international law, is increasing year by year. Major — perhaps *the* major — contributors to international law are, of course, the United Nations and its affiliated agencies. "Despite the U.N.'s political paralysis, its various subgroups have probably created more international law in the past 20 years than enacted in all previous history."[28]

The Laws of War. Until recently international law has not even attempted to prohibit or "outlaw" war, for such an effort would leave states no means for redressing wrongs where the law of peace afforded no

[24] "International Law," *Encyclopaedia of the Social Sciences* (New York: The Macmillan Company, 1937), VII, 168. Used by the permission of The Macmillan Company.

[25] U. N. Document A/AC. 105/PV.20, October 10, 1963, p. 6.

[26] General Assembly Res. 1962 (XVIII), December 13, 1963.

[27] Wolfgang Friedmann, *The Changing Structure of International Law* (New York: Columbia University Press, 1964), pp. 152–187 (Chapter 2: "New Fields of International Law")

[28] *Time,* May 28, 1965.

remedy. To deny states the right of self-help when no other help is available would be no furtherance of justice; and such an unrealistic attempt to control conduct by rule-making would bring all law into contempt. Although war itself may in some instances be lawful, and necessarily so, it does not follow that warring states are without obligations. Hence the laws of war.

Laws of war on land and sea have been formulated in various codes and conventions, notably in the conventions drafted at the Hague conferences of 1899 and 1907 and in many Geneva conventions. Among the aspects of warfare dealt with in these documents are the following: privateering, blockade, prize courts, the care of sick and wounded, protection for medical personnel and facilities, the qualifications of lawful combatants, the treatment of prisoners, forbidden weapons and agencies, the powers of military commanders in occupied enemy territory, the status of spies, the beginning of hostilities, the use of merchant vessels as warships, naval bombardments, the use of submarine mines, the right of capture in maritime warfare, the rights and duties of neutrals, and the use of poison gases. On some of these subjects the agreements were largely nullified by sweeping reservations; on others the agreements were never ratified. In some instances, as is the case with the convention on the treatment of prisoners of war,[29] the law is detailed and explicit. Nevertheless, a substantial part of the laws of war is still based on custom and usage.

The laws of war have helped to humanize warfare — if such a thing is possible — and even by the totalitarian states they have been more generally observed than disregarded; but they have not availed to prevent the most inhuman practices, such as unrestricted submarine warfare and the use of flame-throwers, napalm, and atom bombs. They have never been adequately revised to cover the new and more terrible weapons of destruction that were developed during World Wars I and II and in intervening years; nor have they been adapted to meet the needs of the atomic age.

Before the First World War an important offshoot of the laws of war was the laws of neutrality. Among the subjects with which these were concerned were the forms of neutrality and of neutralization, the proclamation of neutrality, and especially the relations between neutral states and belligerent states and between states and individuals. Specific problems involving the rights and duties of neutrals included the maintenance of the inviolability of the territorial jurisdiction of neutrals; the obligation of neutrals not to permit the use of their territory as a base for military operations; the regulation of the rights of asylum and of internment; the conditions under which enemy ships may enter and leave neutral ports; the obligation of a neutral state not to furnish military assistance to any belligerent or to permit enlistment of troops for a belligerent state; and the neutral's obligation to enforce its neutrality laws and to exercise "due diligence" in preventing violations of its status.

Traditional laws of neutrality lost much of their meaning as a result of the practices of the combatants in World War I. In many cases where they should have been honored they were flagrantly disregarded; and in others, relating to the use of such new weapons as the airplane and the submarine, they appeared to be largely inapplicable. Woodrow Wilson sternly insisted on the rights of the United States as the greatest neutral state. His adamant position in this matter led to strained relations with Great Britain over interference with American ships, goods, and nationals and to the American declaration of war upon Germany, since Germany's use of the submarine was to the President a clear violation of America's rights as a neu-

[29] James Wilford Garner, "Laws of Warfare," *Encyclopaedia of the Social Sciences* (New York: The Macmillan Company, 1937), XV, 363. Used by permission of The Macmillan Company.

tral. Traditional laws of neutrality must be listed among the casualties of World War I. They have never been satisfactorily revised since that time, and during World War II they seemed quite anachronistic. One of the important questions in present-day international law is whether laws of neutrality can be meaningful in times of total war and whether the nations can agree on a thorough revision of previous codes. Perhaps even more important is the question of the relationship of neutrality to collective security. Writing before World War II, Philip C. Jessup declared that "it may well be argued that in the present or future condition of world solidarity, neutrality is an antisocial status."[30] The point is still debatable.

The Laws of Peace. Most of the aspects of public international law which we shall consider come under the heading of the laws of peace, not of war and neutrality. The subject matter of the international law of peace is varied in the extreme. It embraces the bulk of the matters with which the international lawyer usually deals. To illustrate, we may refer to "six grand aspects or divisions of the subjects" which are discussed by Professor Dickinson in a brief chapter on "The Law of Nations." The first is the law relating to the nation-state, "the traditional and principal subject of law in the international system," with particular attention to "its birth, recognition, life, and death." If the law of recognition were better defined, many vexatious political differences could perhaps be avoided. The second aspect deals with nationality and "the principles which determine human allegiance to the nation, including the severance of allegiance and the protection of nationals abroad." Third comes "the law of the national domain or homeland, including such earthy business as acquisitions, transfers, boundaries, internal authority and external responsibility." The fourth and fifth aspects cover the laws of jurisdiction and of intercourse and agreements. Finally, number six relates to the settlement of disputes. On each of these aspects a vast literature exists, and in these areas international law is rather well developed. At the same time, however, as Dickinson pointed out, there are in the law that has been generally agreed upon "characteristic weaknesses," "important gaps," and "extraordinary paradoxes." That "the deficiencies observed in various divisions of the law of nations are no more than varying aspects of the same thing" is due to the character of the international society. "The law has developed among the members of an organized community of basically dissimilar subjects." After all, "are not subservience to politics, evasions of reality, exaltation of sovereignty and all the rest" natural among sovereign states?[31]

International Law and Municipal Law. International law is largely but not altogether concerned with relations between states, whereas municipal law controls relations between individuals within a state and between individuals and the state. The two kinds of law are similar in their sources — chiefly custom and express agreement — with, however, substantial differences in legislative machinery. They differ altogether in their judicial processes. Both are usually applied by national courts, which results in complete decentralization of the judicial function in international law and effective centralization in municipal law. What is true of the judicial function is also true of the executive function. As in tort in domestic law, traditional international law always depended for its enforcement upon the initiative of the injured party. Most municipal law, on the other hand, is enforced by a responsible executive unknown to international law.

[30] Philip C. Jessup, "Neutrality," *Encyclopaedia of the Social Sciences* (New York: The Macmillan Company, 1937), XI, 364. Used by permission of The Macmillan Company.

[31] All the quotations used in this paragraph have been taken from Dickinson, Chapter II.

The relationship of international law to municipal law was once a matter of controversy. The principal question at issue was this: in the event of a conflict between international law and domestic law, must a national court apply international law? Oppenheim held that in such a case the national courts neither may nor could apply the law of nations, for "the latter lacks absolutely the power of altering or creating rules of municipal law."[32] Clyde Eagleton, on the other hand, insisted that "to admit that international law is ultimately dependent upon domestic law and courts, or that municipal law may override international law, would be to deny international law outright, and no state makes such a denial"; the "decisions of the courts putting its [the state's] own law above international law are not final, but may be reviewed and reparation may be demanded by an international tribunal."[33] He further pointed out that after World War I the constitutions of Germany and Austria specifically made international law a part of municipal law, and that court decisions have achieved the same result in the United States. Eagleton wrote much later than Oppenheim, and time may in part account for their different interpretations, for earlier writers were much more awed by sovereignty than more recent ones.

The Sources of International Law. The sources of international law are three in number — treaties, custom, and general principles of law. Thus the Statute of the International Court of Justice (Article 38) stipulates that the Court shall apply

(*a*) international conventions, whether general or particular, establishing rules expressly recognized by the contesting states;

(*b*) international custom, as evidence of a general practice accepted as law:

(*c*) the general principles of law recognized by civilized nations;

(*d*) . . . judicial decisions and the teachings of the most highly qualified publicists of the various nations, as subsidiary means for the determination of rules of law.

It should be noted that (*d*) merely indicates means by which (*b*) and (*c*) may be determined.

The question of law as fixed by treaty or convention is a fairly objective one, but even this presents at least two difficulties. One is the matter of interpretation, and the other is that of knowing just when a rule agreed to by some states but not by all becomes international law.

Custom or customary law is often difficult to prove. The task here is to show that a particular rule has been accepted in practice by the community of states, even though the various states have never reached an explicit understanding to that effect. The rule must be proved, if at all, by the presentation of evidence. Generally speaking, this evidence comes from judicial decisions, diplomatic correspondence, state papers, and the findings of research societies and private scholars.

The "general principles of law" have been variously spoken of as justice, common sense, and right reason. Yet they must not be regarded as entirely subjective — that is, as something which each individual determines for himself. Instead, they may be thought of as principles common to the great legal systems of the world. They can be determined with some degree of objectivity, and they make it possible for judges to fill in the gaps between the rules of "positive law" — the term applied to law based upon practice or express assent.

The Enforcement of International Law. Traditional international law did little more than recognize a right of self-help on the part of injured states. While world public opinion has long exerted some pressure on states to observe the rights of other states

[32] Oppenheim, I, 26.

[33] Clyde Eagleton, *International Government*, rev. ed. (New York: The Ronald Press Co., 1948), pp. 48–49.

and of individuals, no international organization intervened to enforce the law. Supposedly states were morally bound to exhaust the means of peaceful settlement of disputes before resorting to forcible measures; they might or might not be bound by law to do so. If they were bound, it was only with their own consent, as given in treaty or convention. If peaceable means failed, they could with complete legality resort to coercive ventures, including war. Each state was the judge in its own cause. Moreover, while states possessed a right of action in behalf of themselves and their citizens, no right of action was lodged anywhere in the international community when a state mistreated its own nationals.

Until recently the community of states has had little machinery for enforcing its own laws; and it has relied upon member states for enforcement. States or their citizens injured by the action of a particular state had the right to expect satisfaction in the courts of the offending state, in which international law was applied. If redress was not afforded by these courts, the injured state or the state whose citizens had been injured could resort to diplomatic or economic pressures, to reprisals, or even to war. Thus under traditional international law self-help, or, more formally, unilateral action, was the ultimate means of enforcement. To the many kinds of compulsion which a state might use against another state and, more recently, which the organized international community might use against a state, we apply the term "sanctions."

Is International Law True Law? Some writers, especially those of the Austinian school, insist that what is called international law is not law at all but a branch of international morality. Others declare that the matter is one of definition, while still others staunchly defend the validity of the term. The average man would probably assume that where there is violence and obvious injustice there is no law. Against this assumption it must be pointed out that international law, unlike domestic law, is very limited in scope, and that the greater portion of international relations has not come within its jurisdiction at all. While it may be true that it *should* govern all the relations of states, traditional international law in reality has applied only to those subjects on which states have agreed that it should apply. Economic discriminations, imperialism, and war may have often revealed greed and the will to aggression, but they were not necessarily violations of international law.

It is also argued at times that international law is not true law because it is not binding. Admittedly it is impossible to reconcile the dogma of sovereignty with the idea of a law to which states must submit whether they like it or not. Some authorities have dodged this contradiction by supporting what is called the theory of consent — that is, by insisting that states cannot be bound without their own consent but once consent has been given they are bound without infringement of their sovereignty because the limitations were voluntarily accepted. More generally, it is held that states enter the community of nations with the assumption that they accept its laws, and that the continued *general* observance of certain rules of conduct implies a tacit acceptance of those rules. The theory of tacit consent does not answer the question whether a state may be bound against its will and, if so, what happens to the doctrine of sovereignty. J. L. Brierly, an English authority, argued that the views of Jean Bodin and Thomas Hobbes, the great champions of absolute and indivisible sovereignty, have been misunderstood, and that those worthies never meant to underwrite international anarchy as some of their followers have done.[34] He added that "the doctrine was developed for the most part by political theorists who were not interested in, and paid little regard to, the relations of states with

[34] J. L. Brierly, *The Law of Nations*, 6th ed., edited by Sir Humphrey Waldock (New York: Oxford University Press, 1963), pp. 7–16, 45.

one another, and in its later forms it not only involved a denial of the possibility of states being subject to any kind of law, but became an impossible theory for a world which contained more states than one." In practice individual states may be bound by international law even against their will, but that law must rest upon the general consent of the community of nations.

What is called the Austinian definition holds that law is a rule of conduct issued by a superior authority to persons over whom it has jurisdiction. By such a definition international law is not true law, for neither the United Nations nor any other international organization has jurisdiction over persons or even in any real sense over states. This view no longer enjoys much support.

Some writers who persist in measuring international law by national law believe that the absence of centralized legislative, judicial, and executive authority disqualifies international law as true law. The status of international law is thus frequently impugned by persons who feel that it cannot be true law because "it is not enforced." The assumption of nonobservance — admittedly not quite the same thing as nonenforcement — has been pretty well demolished by jurists from the time of John Bassett Moore to the present; and the assumption of a necessary inviolability reveals unawareness of the very nature of jural law. Quincy Wright had this to say on the point of enforcement:

> A considerable failure of realization is . . . to be expected of any rule of jural law. Its status as law depends not only on objective observation that persons and official agencies within the society generally conform to the rules but also on subjective assumption of a duty to conform by such persons and agencies. If that assumption is generally made in the society, the rule may be valid law even though its imperfect observance and enforcement makes it ineffective.[35]

[35] Quincy Wright, *The Study of International Relations* (New York: Appleton-Century-Crofts, 1955), p. 220.

The answer to the question here raised thus depends upon definitions; but, as Eagleton complacently remarked, "the theorist who wishes to deny to the law of nations the title of true law does not in the least affect the actual conduct of affairs in that society, nor the fact that those affairs are regulated by rules as well enforced and obeyed as those of domestic law."[36]

The Origin and Development of International Law

Like many other institutions of modern times, international law had its beginnings in the prehistoric world. Historians suggest that tribal communities must have been driven to some sort of understandings about places of habitation, water holes, hunting areas, trespass, warfare, and perhaps intermarriage. At first these inter-group relations were conducted on the assumptions that war and conflicts of interests were normal conditions and that peace was to be achieved only by express agreement. Friendly relations between tribal groups were not unknown, however, and as states emerged in the ancient world certain peoples, perhaps especially the Hebrews and the Hindus, asserted ideals of justice and order in the relations of states. The increasing respectability of commerce added a personal interest in law and order and thus contributed to peaceful relations among trading peoples.

Pre-Grotian International Law. The distinctive feature of the political organization of ancient Greece in the time of its greatness was the supremacy of local loyalties and law. It was in relations among the city-states that the Greeks made their greatest contribution to the law of nations, but they also furthered orderly interstate or international relations through their belief that these relations should be based upon certain rules. In their inter-city-state relations they acknowledged rules of warfare and diplomatic

[36] Eagleton, p. 53.

immunity, they made considerable use of arbitration, and they evolved a system of maritime law. With a greater genius for government and administration, the Romans extended the authority of Rome by conquest and alliance until they achieved what we speak of as a world-state. Their contributions, like those of Greece, sprang from the effort to regulate the relations of peoples and areas which did not qualify as "states," and their legacy to international law was the ideal of a common citizenship and impartial justice everywhere, the idea of a universal law, and the breaking down of the old isolationism and the old contempt for foreigners. To aid them in the government of conquered areas, Roman jurists formulated the principles of the *jus gentium,* or law of peoples, a body of rules and usages believed to be applicable to all peoples and resting upon natural justice. These principles survived the chaotic centuries that followed the fall of Rome and toward the close of the Middle Ages were accepted as part of the emerging international law. In this manner the way was prepared for the modern belief that definite legal principles should control the relations of states.

With the rise of Britain, France, Portugal, and Spain as nation-states, international relations in the modern sense of the term began to develop. Regulations became imperative for the conduct of war, the preservation of neutrality, the use of the seas in both peace and war, and the fixing of boundaries in colonial claims. Agreements were made between states by treaty and conference. A law of neutrality also took form, the principles of Roman law respecting private property were applied to boundary lines and colonial claims, and a law of war was slowly formulated.[37]

Writers long ago began to point out that in the agreements of states, in the principles of Roman law, in practice and custom, and in what they called "natural law" there was a growing body of rules of conduct that states were approving by observance and commitment. Thus while international law was made by the actions and agreements of rulers, it was collected and systematized by scholars through researches in the past and current relations of states. "International law as now practised by the states of the world," wrote Pitman B. Potter a number of years ago, "is largely the product of private scholarship, taken over later by the states more or less in spite of their natural instincts."[38]

Perhaps the first of the important writers was Legnano, an Italian, whose study of the rules of war was written in 1360, although not published until 1477. No outstanding writer appeared in the fifteenth century, but at least six legal scholars produced notable works on international law in the sixteenth century. The most important of these were Vitoria, a Spaniard who "laid down the principle that the nations formed a com-

[37] The progressive character of international law is well illustrated in the evolution of maritime codes. The earliest of these known today was that of the island of Rhodes, dating from the third or second century B.C. The Rhodian Sea Law, imitatively named after the earlier code, was formulated during the later Roman Empire as a guide to Roman practice; it embraced both old and new principles. The Italian codes were written in the eleventh century, and by the close of the thirteenth century many cities of the Mediterranean had their own compilations of maritime customs. In the early twelfth century the Rolls of Oléron, showing the influence of the Rhodian Sea Law, was accepted by many countries of Europe; as late as 1779 it was approved by the state of Virginia. The famous *Consolato del Mare* (Consulate of the Sea) was compiled in Barcelona about 1340: it exerted great influence in Italy and the western Mediterranean. Successive codifications by the Hanseatic League between 1447 and 1592 were much observed by the countries of North Europe. The last of the great maritime codes was the French *Ordonnance de la Marine,* issued in 1681 after ten years of preparation. It was widely observed in England, which has never had a maritime code of its own, and it was cited in American admiralty courts as late as the twentieth century. A significant feature of most of these compilations was the indebtedness of each to earlier formulations.

[38] *An Introduction to the Study of International Organization,* 5th ed. (New York: Appleton-Century-Crofts, 1948), p. 58.

munity based upon natural reason and social intercourse";[39] Suárez, also a Spaniard, who "first distinguished between reason and custom as sources of international law, a distinction followed ever since";[40] and Gentilis, a British subject of Italian extraction, who added historical and legal precedents to natural reason and natural law as sources of international law. Gentilis is remembered today for his *De jure belli,* but probably even more as the direct forerunner of the man destined to become known as the "Father of International Law," Hugo Grotius.

Grotius (1583–1645) and Natural Law. Hugo Grotius was born in Holland in 1583. He took the degree of doctor of laws at the University of Leyden at the age of fifteen. In 1609 he published *Mare liberum,* wherein he argued for freedom of the seas, a view then not generally held. Later he went to Paris, where he lived for ten years and where in 1625 he published the work which has given him permanent fame, *De jure belli ac pacis,* or *On the Law of War and Peace.* It is significant that this notable work appeared in the midst of the bloody Thirty Years' War. He issued an enlarged and revised edition in 1631 and later three other editions with little change. A total of sixty-four editions had been issued by 1928.

With *De jure belli ac pacis,* particularly Part II, "the science of the modern Law of Nations commences . . . because in it a fairly complete system of International Law was for the first time built up as an independent branch of the science of law."[41] One authority describes it as having four main characteristics. First, Grotius would hold states to the same rules which regulate the lives of individuals and make the violation of them a crime subject to punishment. Second, basing his judgment upon researches in the Scriptures, ancient history, and the classics, he formulated the "law of peace" which became the foundation of his whole system. Third, he argued that states may properly punish other states which violate the law. Fourth, he accepted natural law — or right reason — as the primary basis for determining rules for the rightful conduct of states.[42]

Grotius is much admired today for his earnest desire to bring nations to accept the principles of humanity. Indeed, in our esteem for international conduct based on moral principles and in our growing conviction that peace-loving states must accept the obligation to punish lawless states, we are closer to the spirit and mind of Grotius than were the men of the nineteenth century with their glorification of sovereignty.

The natural law or law of nature to which Grotius appealed was made up of those rules of conduct which arose from the attempt to reason out the way by which men and states could best get along with each other. Grotius defined it as "the dictate of right reason which points out that a given act, because of its opposition to or conformity with man's rational nature, is either morally wrong or morally necessary, and accordingly forbidden or commanded by God, the author of nature."[43] In a sense it was a theoretical approach; it sought to assert what ought to be the law rather than to list the rules to which men and states had actually committed themselves by custom or agreement. To these latter we apply the term "positive law." While Grotius did not ignore positive law, which he called "voluntary law," he kept it distinct from the rules which he took from natural law, and he felt it to be of minor importance. He did not originate the concept of natural law, for that was very old, but his formulation of the rules of state con-

39 Fenwick, p. 50.

40 Eagleton, p. 31.

41 Oppenheim, I, 76.

42 Cornelius van Vollenhoven, "Hugo Grotius," *Encyclopaedia of the Social Sciences* (New York: The Macmillan Company, 1937), VII, 177. Used by permission of The Macmillan Company.

43 Book I, Chapter I, Section X.

duct which he felt rested upon or sprang from natural law won such acceptance by other legal writers that it dominated thinking on international law for two centuries.

Zouche (1590–1660) and Positivism. Twenty-five years after the appearance of Grotius' *De jure belli ac pacis,* Richard Zouche, an Oxford professor of civil law, published a little book in which he asserted views quite opposite from those of Grotius.[44] Whereas Grotius had emphasized natural law and minimized customary law, Zouche reversed the order. As the first important champion of the customary law or positivist school of thought he is sometimes spoken of as the "Second Founder of the Law of Nations." Zouche also contributed to the name "international law," for instead of using Grotius' term, *jus gentium* or law of nations, he used *jus inter gentes* or law between nations, thus supplying the "inter" for the term "international law," first used by Jeremy Bentham a century and a half later.[45]

The Three Schools of Thought. For nearly two centuries after Grotius had published his monumental work in 1625, roughly during the seventeenth and eighteenth centuries, writers tended to divide into three schools of thought: the naturalists, who took their cue from Grotius but often went far beyond him to deny all positive law; the positivists, who rejected Grotius' natural law and supported Zouche's customary law, some even outdoing Zouche and denying all natural law; and the so-called Grotians, who accepted both natural and customary law, althought most of them accepted more customary law than had Grotius.

[44] This little volume bears the fascinating title of *Juris et judicii fecialis, sive, juris inter gentes, et quaestionum de eodum explicatio, qua, quae ad pacem et bellum inter diversos principes aut peretis exhibentur.*

[45] Oppenheim, I, 81.

The Ascendancy of Positivism. During the nineteenth century international law lost much of its subjective character, and the distinguished names associated with it came to be those of compilers of treatises rather than of philosophers and moralists. The positivist way of thinking slowly rose in prominence until its methods had won general although not exclusive or universal acceptance. This development seemed to reflect the growing secularism of the times, with its emphasis on the practical rather than the idealistic. Perhaps another factor was the rising popularity of written constitutions, as in the United States and the new republics of Latin America. Commerce and representative government were driving men to insist on the precise terms of their rights and obligations, with these to be measured by custom and statute rather than by some uncertain law of nature.

The writers of the first two-thirds of the century showed the influence of Grotius, for while most of them were positivists they were unable to exclude completely all assumptions based on natural law, sometimes using it merely to fill the gaps in positive law. As scholars in considerable number delved into archives, they narrowed the field in which positive law was lacking; and as states more and more frequently entered into law-making treaties they lessened the need for appeals to natural law. Consequently, by the last third of the nineteenth century positivism had become the prevailing school of thought.

The Codification of International Law

Legal scholars of the past half-century have tended to accept the separation of positive law and natural law that was in progress during the nineteenth century. Although many books and articles continued to be written on the rules of conduct that ought to be embraced and practiced by states, these came to be regarded more as ethics and less as law. Yet they gave a real impetus to the making of international law, for they often stimulated the making of international agreements on subjects not already covered by law. The most significant developments have taken the form of an expanded interest in the collection and systematization of existing law and of organized efforts to translate ideas of improved interstate relations into the law of nations by multilateral agreements. To these developments, commonly known as codification and international legislation, we must turn for a better understanding of the progress that is now being made in international law. We shall see that the difference between the two, though clear in theory, often becomes completely vague in practice. To formulate a code means to systematize the law in a certain field, a process which entails filling in the gaps. States ratifying the code are therefore in a position of approving new law — that is, they are sharing in a legislative process. Professor Eagleton said that "the codification of international law, if it means anything at all, means systematic legislation."[46]

Beginnings. While proposals for codification date from the late eighteenth century, it was not until the 1860's that the earliest attempts were actually made, the first being a précis formulated in 1861 by an Austrian jurist. Two years later, in 1863, Francis Lieber (1800–1872) prepared *A Code for the Government of Armies,* which in revised form was used by the Union armies in the Civil War and by Germany in the Franco-Prussian War. In 1868 Bluntschli (1808–81) produced a more comprehensive codification, declaring that his intention was "to formulate clearly the existing ideas of the civilized world." In 1872 an American, David Dudley Field (1805–94), issued a *Draft Outline of an International Code,* and an Italian jurist, Pasquale Fiore (1837–1914), published in 1889 a code covering the whole field of international law.[47] While in more recent years many scholars have published excellent treatises on international law, the preparation of codes, with their more formal arrangement and definitive treatment, has become almost entirely the work of private associations and of international conferences and commissions of jurists.

Institutional Codification. The year 1873 was a memorable one in the science of international law, for it saw the founding of the *Institut de Droit International* and the Association for the Reform and Codification of the Law of Nations, which in 1895 changed its name to the International Law Association. The *Institut* has issued a number of draft codes, perhaps the most important being the *Manual of the Laws of War on Land,* published in 1880. A compilation of fifty-six "resolutions" and "views" of the *Institut* was published in 1916 by James Brown Scott, director of the Division of International Law of the Carnegie Endowment for International Peace. The International Law Association, like the *Institut,* has concentrated upon the statement of law on particular topics. The American Society of International Law, founded in 1905, publishes a journal of notable excellence, *The American Journal of International Law,* but it does not emphasize codification.

The American Institute of International Law, on the other hand, has devoted its energies almost exclusively to the drafting of codes, particularly as they embody practices in the Western Hemisphere. Founded in 1912 through the efforts of Alejandro Alvarez of Chile and James Brown Scott of the United States, this organization was

[46] Eagleton, p. 207.

[47] Published in an English translation by Edwin M. Borchard in 1915 as *International Law Codified.*

closely associated with the Union of American Republics and its Commission of Jurists, and it enjoyed the financial support of the Carneigie Endowment for International Peace. In June, 1950, the Inter-American Council of Jurists acknowledged the "notable contribution" of the Institute and asked for its continued cooperation. The Institute's part in the codification of "American international law" — the very existence of which some writers have denied — has largely taken the form of making recommendations to the official organs of the Inter-American System. A German organization, the *Institut für Internationales Recht* at Kiel, also gave a great deal of attention to codification. Finally, a number of draft conventions were issued by Harvard University's Research in International Law, set up in 1926 to aid the League of Nations in the work of codification. The first three of the Harvard Research drafts related to nationality, responsibility of states, and territorial waters.

Early Official Codification. Meantime, official codification began when the representatives of twelve states, assembled at Geneva in 1864, endeavored to describe existing practice in respect to the care of the wounded in battle. Meeting on the invitation of the Tsar of Russia at Brussels in 1874, representatives of the leading powers drew up a draft code of the rules of war on land, but it was never ratified. More ambitious ventures in codification were undertaken by the famous Hague Conferences of 1899 and 1907. The first of these approved a code of the laws and customs of war on land and adapted to maritime war the principles formulated in the Geneva Convention of 1864 for the care of the sick and wounded in land warfare. The conference of 1907 adopted conventions on the codification of the rights and duties of neutrals and on certain phases of the conduct of naval warfare. Both conferences also accepted many conventions that embodied new rules of international law. On an average, the conventions were ratified by more than half the states participating in the conferences, but at least one was ratified by none at all. In 1900 the United States Government published *The Laws and Usages of War at Sea,* thus supplementing Lieber's rules of warfare on land; but this, of course, was a unilateral action. In 1909 the leading maritime powers sent delegates to a conference in London to work out a code of warfare on the sea, but the resulting Declaration of London was ratified by only a few states. World War I soon prevented other efforts. Thus, as Professor Fenwick says, "until the creation of the League of Nations, attempts at codification were haphazard and infrequent."[48]

Codification of "American International Law." Proposals for undertaking codification of "American international law" were made at the Inter-American Conferences of 1889–90 in Washington and of 1902 in Mexico City, but no work was actually begun. The Third Conference, however, meeting in 1906 in Rio de Janeiro, approved a convention for setting up a Commission of Jurists to draft codes of international public and private law. When the commission finally met in 1912 it agreed upon a report on extradition and set up six committees to study subjects for codification. Then World War I intervened, and in the immediate postwar period the Latin American states became engrossed in the League of Nations. Moreover, the United States welcomed the respite from the insistence of her neighbors that the American republics write into American international law a categorical renunciation of the right of intervention.

The commission, revitalized by the Fifth Inter-American Conference at Santiago in 1923, submitted twelve projects of codification to the Havana Conference of 1928. But Yankee intervention was again the bogey.

[48] Fenwick, p. 209.

"It was at Havana," says Professor Bemis, "that the United States made its last defense of the interventions still unliquidated in the Caribbean."[49] The clash was between the United States insistence on recognition of international *duties* and the Latin American insistence on international *rights*. Although the United States again engineered defeat of the doctrine of nonintervention, she ratified a resolution condemning aggression and she joined in the approval of projects for codifying public international law on the status of aliens, treaties, diplomatic officers, consular agents, maritime neutrality, asylum, and rights and duties of states in event of civil strife. The Havana Conference also approved the Bustamante Code of private international law and invited the American republics to ratify it. The United States declined to do so, pleading the division of jurisdiction inherent in federalism. The Sixth Conference also directed the Commission of Jurists to continue its work.

Actual work on codification languished, but when the United States accepted the Doctrine of Absolute Nonintervention at Buenos Aires in 1936 it seemed that the American republics might regain their interest. Yet the Mexico City Conference of 1945 "recognized that the frequent attempts to codify international law up to that time had largely failed."[50] At the Ninth Inter-American Conference, held at Bogotá in 1948, the machinery was again revised, this time as part of the general reorganization of the Inter-American System. An Inter-American Council of Jurists was made one of the three responsible to the governing body (the Council), and the Inter-American Juridical Committee was made the permanent committee of the Inter-American Council of Jurists. All other juridical agencies were abolished. One of the four departments of the general secretariat — the Pan American Union — is the Department of International Law and Organization which has begun the publication of the *Inter-American Juridical Yearbook* "to present a survey of the development of inter-American regional law during the current year" and continues the issuance of the *Law and Treaty Series*.

Holding its first meeting in Rio de Janeiro in May and June, 1950, the Council of Jurists approved a draft statute which included a detailed plan for development and codification. This statute directed the new Council of Jurists to "establish relations of mutual cooperation with the International Law Commission of the United Nations."[51] Although the Judicial Committee continues its work on the projects set up at Rio, one might well make the observation that has been made so often in the past on the codification of international law — the American republics have really not accomplished very much, but they quite clearly have made a good start.

Codification by the League of Nations. Although the Covenant of the League contained nothing on codification, sentiment mounted in favor of such action until in 1924 the Assembly and Council set up a Committee of Experts to begin the task. After years of preparatory work, a Codification Conference met at The Hague in 1930 to consider three subjects: nationality, territorial waters, and the responsibility of states for damage caused in their territory to the person or property of foreigners. One convention and three protocols were adopted, but the delegates clung tenaciously to the practices of their respective governments, and the one big venture of the League of

[49] Samuel F. Bemis, *The Latin American Policy of the United States* (New York: Harcourt, Brace, 1943), p. 252.

[50] Edward O. Guerrant, *Roosevelt's Good Neighbor Policy* (Albuquerque: University of New Mexico Press, 1950), p. 80.

[51] The draft Statutes of the Inter-American Council of Jurists are printed in *Annals of the Organization of American States*, II, No. 3 (1950). 278–290.

Nations into the codification of international law accomplished almost nothing.

Codification by the United Nations. Unlike the League Covenant, the United Nations Charter specifically provides for the codification of international law. Accordingly, the General Assembly early created a seventeen-member ad hoc Committee on the Progressive Development of International Law and Its Codification, and assigned to it the duty of studying methods by which the Assembly could discharge its obligation under Article 13 of the Charter of "encouraging the progressive development of international law and its codification." In its report to the Assembly in September, 1947, the committee recommended the creation of an International Law Commission, to which would be assigned the dual task of studying subjects of law not yet highly developed and the "precise formulation of the law in matters in which there was extensive practice, precedent, and doctrine."[52]

The committee also recommended that the commission be instructed "to survey the whole field of customary international law together with any relevant treaties with a view to selecting topics for codification, having in mind previous governmental and non-governmental projects," and it further recommended that the International Law Commission "consider ways and means of making the evidence of customary international law more readily available by the compilation of digests of State practice, and by the collection and publication of the decisions of national and international courts on international law questions."[53] The committee observed that its responsibility involved the two duties of "progressive development" (of new law) and "codification" (of existing law), but at the same time it marked a distinction between the two areas of its labors — a distinction which many authorities regard as purely theoretical. It suggested that conclusions in respect to codification should be submitted to the Assembly in the form of multipartite conventions, which, whether accepted or not, would have value as formulations by a distinguished tribunal. The General Assembly established the International Law Commission on November 21, 1947, adopted a statute for its government, and later elected fifteen members of the commission for three-year-terms. In 1956 the membership was increased to 21, and in 1961 to 25.

The most notable achievements of the ILC toward the "progressive development of international law and its codification" have been the preparation of a Declaration on the Rights and Duties of States, the formulation of some but not all of the principles of law underlying the Nuremberg War Crimes Trials, and the drafting of a Law of Treaties. The basic rights of states, the commission found, include independence, equality in law, jurisdiction over their own territories, and self-defense; duties include the peaceful settlement of international disputes and the observance of human rights and fundamental personal freedoms. The Nuremberg Principles assert that both individuals and governments are to be held responsible for "crimes against peace," "war crimes," and "crimes against humanity." Neither of the two formulations has been approved by enough states to give it the status of international law.

Codification of the Law of Treaties is a most ambitious undertaking. The draft of 73 articles has been considered by the General Assembly, has been submitted to the member states for comment, and will doubtless occupy the attention of the ILC, the Sixth Committee of the General Assembly, and the members of the United Nations for some years to come. Other topics on which

[52] *International Organization,* I (September, 1947), 492.

[53] *Yearbook of the United Nations 1946–1947* (New York: United Nations, 1947), p. 259.

codification may be attempted are state responsibility for the violation of treaties, which was specifically excluded from the Law of Treaties, and the succession of states and governments. Still other matters on the agenda of the ILC which may lead to legal codification are the question of special missions, the relations between states and intergovernmental organizations, the right of asylum, and the regime of the high seas (and historic bays).

For some years the Soviet Union has urged that the ILC and the General Assembly should codify the principles of peaceful coexistence among states. This proposal has been enthusiastically endorsed by many of the new nations of Asia and Africa, but it has been looked upon with considerable doubt and suspicion by the Western powers, largely because such principles would seem to be more political than judicial and because of the peculiar twist which the Communist states have given to the concept of peaceful co-existence. The Seventeenth Session of the General Assembly, on December 18, 1962, adopted a compromise resolution,[54] recognizing the paramount importance in the "progressive development of international law and its codification" of the following seven principles: (1) refraining from the use or threat of force; (2) peaceful settlement of international disputes; (3) nonintervention in matters within the domestic jurisdiction of another state; (4) sovereign equality of states; (5) equal rights and self-determination of peoples; (6) cooperation among states in accordance with the UN Charter; and (7) fulfillment in good faith of obligations assumed in accordance with the Charter. The Eighteenth Session of the General Assembly, in 1963, decided to establish a Special Committee on Principles of International Law Concerning Friendly Relations and Co-operation Among States to study the first four principles and prepare a report on its conclusions and recommendations.[55]

At the request of the General Assembly the ILC considered the advisability of establishing an international criminal tribunal, and in 1950 it reported that such a court was both desirable and feasible. In 1951 the Assembly suggested that the commission attempt a definition of aggression, but after much discussion the ILC reported that a precise definition was impracticable.

As has been noted, the UN's work in developing and codifying international law has not been confined to the ILC. The Secretariat has drafted conventions on certain aspects of the status of the UN, and the International Court of Justice has prepared an agreement on its own status in the Netherlands. The Human Rights Commission drafted the Universal Declaration of Human Rights, two covenants on human rights, and the Convention on Genocide.

The United States has declined to approve the formulation of the Nuremberg Principles, has deferred action on the draft statute for an international criminal court, has refused to support any of several projected drafts of a covenant or covenants on human rights, has taken no action on the Genocide Convention, has substantial reservations concerning many of the articles in the Law of Treaties, and is very dubious indeed regarding the desirability of attempting to codify such nebulous and politically "loaded" principles as those embodied in the General Assembly resolution of December, 1962. Believing many of these efforts premature, she is unwilling to see the sincere commitments of a few states abused by the expediency of states not yet prepared to put law above politics. Indeed, as "international law is ultimately enforceable only through the consent of sovereign states,"

[54] General Assembly Res. 1815 (XVII), December 18, 1962.

[55] General Assembly Res. 1966 (XVIII), December 16, 1963.

law-observing states may understandably consider that "measures which out-run that consent may weaken those doctrines that have finally gained general acceptance."[56]

International Legislation

The acknowledged sources of international law came to be custom and treaties: custom because it disclosed what states had already agreed to in practice, and treaties because they involved express consent. Custom is not always easy to ascertain, for it involves deciding when a practice has become a custom and has achieved something like general acceptance. Consequently, it is not a satisfactory basis for making law. It is therefore upon treaties that the making of new international law has largely depended. But this method too has been unsatisfactory. Historically treaties have usually been bilateral, with a specific *quid pro quo,* with hallowed rights of nonratification, reservation, interpretation, and termination, and often with an implicit exclusiveness. More recently states have turned away from conventional treaties for the making of international law and instead have tended to use what is known as international legislation.

The Nature of International Legislation. Here is a term that must be used with care. Eagleton said that while it "may be used in a general sense, the process is of course far from being really legislative."[57] If international legislation were true legislation, states would automatically be bound by the enactments of a properly constituted international legislative body, just as individuals within a state are bound by laws to which they have not given their express assent. But no international body has ever been set up with a status comparable to that of national legislatures. On the contrary, states almost invariably regard agreements arrived at by treaty or conference as valid and binding only when they have been expressly ratified "in accordance with the respective constitutional processes" of the signatory states. This is true even of most actions taken by any of the organs and agencies of the United Nations, an organization of almost universal membership. While some public international organizations make exceptions to the rule of express assent, the exceptions are few and usually relate to less important matters. Nevertheless, despite its inaccuracy and the protests of some writers, we do use the term "international legislation," having in mind a wide participation in formulating principles of rights and duties rather than a perfect analogy to the national legislative process.

International legislation does not imply a specific procedure. States — or, rather, the representatives of states — may reach an agreement by any one of a number of means or combinations of means. Whatever device is used to reach an understanding, however, that understanding must be ratified by each individual state in order to be binding on that state. Even then the state is not necessarily bound, for the agreement may provide that a certain number of ratifications are required to make it effective, even for ratifying states.

While international legislation closely resembles the conventional multilateral treaty process — that is, negotiations or conference followed by ratification of agreements reached — there are certain important differences. More generally, it seeks to assert rules of law rather than to compromise differences, and it is commonly open to accession by all interested states. While it is still subject to all the obstacles that capricious sovereignty may devise — failure to ratify, nullifying reservations, and unilateral termination — there is some evidence that states are now feeling a stronger moral obligation to accept the "legislation" in good faith. Ten years before the founding of the UN Manley O. Hudson declared that international legis-

[56] "Issues Before the Tenth General Assembly," *International Conciliation,* No. 504 (September, 1955), p. 143.

[57] Eagleton, p. 190.

lation was more important than international jurisprudence as a source of "currently developing international law." That judgment would certainly be valid today.

The Evolution of the Legislative Process. The Congress of Vienna of 1815 "may be taken to have inaugurated the process of international legislation."[58] Agreements of continuing importance were reached at Vienna on the classification of diplomatic agents and on the free navigation of the international rivers of Europe. Another notable conference, that of Paris of 1856, approved a declaration on the abolition of privateering which became securely fixed in international law. International legislation on telegraphic matters dates from 1865, on postal matters from 1874, and on weights and measures from 1875. During these years technological changes in communications and transportation were creating problems of general concern that could be handled only by what amounted to almost continuous international legislative activity. This commonly took the form of ad hoc conferences which, becoming somewhat standardized and regularized and at times being supplemented by the maintenance of permanent offices, led inevitably toward a more general form of permanent international organization. The Hague Conferences of 1899 and 1907 may be said to have represented a transitional step from ad hoc conferences and specialized international organizations toward the League of Nations, the first great experiment of an organization open to all states and without a special-purpose character.

International Legislation by the League of Nations. The League of Nations ushered in a new era of legislative effort. In its first dozen years the League produced more international legislation than had issued from all sources during the entire century before World War I or than was currently being issued from all other sources combined. The subjects were almost as broad as human interest. They included communications and transit; slavery; pacific settlement of disputes; the traffic in opium, women and children, arms, and obscene publications; buoyage and lighting of coasts; counterfeiting; uniformity of bills of exchange; and labor. Under the persuasion of the League's Secretariat states came to feel more and more bound to follow signature with ratification and while the international legislative process was by no means perfected, considerable improvement certainly took place during the lifetime of the League.

Professor Hudson found at least sixteen different names for the understandings reached between or among states since the founding of the League. Alphabetically these were as follows: act, agreement, arrangement, convention, covenant, declaration, final act, general act, pact, plan, protocol, regulation, rule, scheme, statute, and treaty. It is significant that he included them all in the monumental collection to which he gave the name *International Legislation.* Although his compilation, covering the period from 1919 to 1949, fills eight volumes, it is a selective and not an exhaustive one, as will be gathered from the fact that before its termination the *League of Nations Treaty Series* had reached two hundred volumes.

International Legislation by the UN. Within the UN the legislative procedure operates in this fashion: The General Assembly directs one of the commissions or agencies to prepare a "draft statute" — the term varies — on a particular subject. A committee of the agency does the work, keeping at it until the agency approves a report for submission to the General Assembly. This body may approve the draft statute or it may send it back to the agency for revision. If approved, the

[58] Manley O. Hudson, "International Legislation," *Encyclopaedia of the Social Sciences* (New York: The Macmillan Company, 1937), VIII, 175. Used by permission of The Macmillan Company.

statute is sent to member states for ratification. We shall review some examples of legislation in a later chapter of the UN.

The volume of international legislation has become so great that merely keeping a record of it is a problem. Hudson's *International Legislation,* already mentioned, includes only the texts of agreements registered with the League. That these texts are in print is insufficient in itself, for it is often important to know which ones are still in force, what revisions have been made, what states were bound by a particular agreement at a particular date, etc.[59] The *United Nations Treaty Series,* issued by the Secretariat, contains texts of treaties, conventions, and the like entered into by member states since the Charter became effective. By 1967, 568 volumes in this *Series* had been published. Other agreements — those antedating the Charter and those between nonmember states — may or may not be included, depending upon the acceptance of the Secretariat's invitation to submit them. There is considerable support for the proposal to have the Secretariat undertake the all-inclusive publication of international legislation — truly a formidable enterprise.[60]

[59] The question of participation in multilateral treaties concluded under the auspices of the League of Nations by states which had not been in existence before the demise of the League was considered on several occasions by the General Assembly of the United Nations, and was studied carefully by the International Law Commission in 1963. Later in the same year the Eighteenth Session of the Assembly, in accordance with the recommendations of the ILC, designated itself the appropriate organ of the UN to exercise the powers vested in the League Council under general multilateral treaties, and agreed that these treaties should be opened for ratification to all members of the UN or specialized agencies, or to states which were parties to the Statute of the International Court of Justice.

[60] Salo Engel, "On the Status of International Legislation," *The American Journal of International Law,* XLIV (October, 1950), 739. The World Peace Through World Law Center, a private organization supported largely by dues from members, mostly lawyers, in more than one hundred countries, has announced its intention to undertake a compilation of all major treaties now in effect.

The Limitations and Possibilities of International Law

Our review of international law should include some mention of the ways in which, according to eminent authorities, it must be improved and developed if the states of the world are to establish an international order of justice and lasting peace. The limitations listed here should not be regarded as implying a program upon which scholars are agreed. Rather, some are emphasized by one writer and some by another. But together they suggest the chief inadequacies of international law as it now exists. These limitations consist of the following: (1) the incompleteness of the legislative function; (2) various and serious limitations in the judicial function; (3) the lack of effective enforcement; (4) limitations on the scope and functions of international law; and (5) widespread misunderstanding of the nature and purpose of the law. Basically, all the limitations of international law are inherent in the present character of international society, in which the concept of a legal order is not generally accepted but is, in fact, regarded as actually inapplicable in the most vital areas of international relations.

The Legislative Function. We have already noted that the two chief sources of international law have been custom and treaty. Since much of the customary law has been codified, and since the frequency of international conferences has provided states with abundant opportunity to insist upon giving their express assent to international obligations, treaties have become the chief source of international law. Within the past century the multilateral treaty, frequently negotiated at a conference of many states, has become increasingly important. Nevertheless, even states participating insist upon a right to accept or reject the negotiated agreement; and they may individually qualify the agreement or may ratify and then ignore or repudiate it. Such right of independent action rests upon the doctrine of sovereignty.

Codification presents some of the same difficulties as lawmaking, even when the word is used to mean simply transformation of customary law into statute law. To assemble the customary law on a given subject and to organize it into a coherent whole often involves agreement upon interpretation and the filling of gaps. In these matters states frequently disagree, and when they do agree they are legislating, that is, making new law, at least in details. Indeed, as legal authorities and the UN itself recognize, codification and legislation cannot always be differentiated.

The Judicial Function. The problem of the judicial function is more complex. To state this problem as briefly as possible, it may be said to be made up of the limitations arising from the following conditions:

1. *The nature of international judicial machinery.* International law, for the most part, is enforced by national courts. Thus, an individual injured in a foreign state may seek redress in the local courts, which presumably will apply local law enacted to meet the international law requirement of justice to aliens. If the injured person feels that he has been denied justice he may appeal to his own government, which in turn may resort to negotiation, to some form of international adjudication, or, as a last recourse, even to nonamicable pressures. Until the founding of the Permanent Court of International Justice as part of the League of Nations system, international adjudication was always performed by a specially chosen individual or body, with a new "court" for each dispute. The Permanent Court of International Justice and its successor under the United Nations, the International Court of Justice, have provided an established court, but other difficulties remain. For one thing the ICJ is not the highest in a real hierarchy of courts, and so there is necessary uniformity of law only in those matters on which the International Court has spoken and in which its decisions have been accepted. Furthermore, the International Court of Justice is not bound by the doctrine of *stare decisis* — that is, the obligation to follow precedents — and national courts are technically free to ignore each other's rulings on international law and even the decisions of the International Court of Justice itself. It is this "combination of hierarchial organization and of the rule of *stare decisis,*" stated Hans Morgenthau, speaking of national courts, that "produces one system of jurisprudence throughout the judicial system, one body of coherent law ever ready to go into action at the request of whoever claims to need the protection of the law." And, added Morgenthau, "nothing in the international sphere even remotely resembles this situation."[61] Professor J. L. Brierly, a member of the International Law Commission, however, noted that "precedents are taking their proper place in the system . . . creating for international law an ampler stock of detailed rules, testing its abstract principles by their fitness to solve practical problems, and depriving it of the too academic character which has belonged to it in the past."[62]

2. *The lack of compulsory jurisdiction.* International law does not require any state to submit its disputes to an international tribunal against its will. Consent to judicial process may be given on a particular occasion, or it may be given in advance to cover all or certain stipulated classes of disputes, but in theory consent is always a prerequisite. States, either singly or in collaboration, may of course condemn a state and even punish it, but the form of judicial process is not present unless the state so condemned or acted against has consented to the procedure

[61] Hans J. Morgenthau, *Politics Among Nations,* 3d ed. (New York: Alfred A. Knopf, 1954), p. 293.

[62] Brierly, p. 64.

used. The Optional Clause, which is contained in the statutes of both the Permanent Court of International Justice and the International Court of Justice, was devised to bring states closer to compulsory jurisdiction, but states are free to accept or ignore the Optional Clause (whence its name), and the Clause itself limits compulsory jurisdiction to certain types of legal disputes and is operative only when both — or all — parties to a dispute have accepted it. Furthermore, the acceptance of the Optional Clause has often been attended by many and significant reservations, those of the United States being perhaps the most far-reaching. Thus there is nowhere in international law anything like real compulsory jurisdiction, either outside the UN or in it.

3. *The ambiguity of the law.* The uncertainty about what the law is arises in part from the lack of a judicial hierarchy and from the doubtful character of the rule of *stare decisis,* which we have already described. But it is also due in part to the vague and general terms in which international agreements are frequently expressed. This vagueness is probably unavoidable, for states shy away from precise stipulations and find refuge in agreements that may later be interpreted to their own liking. The ambiguity of the law also arises in part from uncertainty about the customary law and doubt whether repeated violations by other states have operated to annul the law or have left its binding character unimpaired. Important, too, is the fact that there is no repeal process for international law comparable to that for national law.

The ambiguity of the law also directly affects the limitations of jurisdiction. This situation arises in part from the conviction that positive law must be supplemented by what is very close to natural law. Torsten Gihl said that "the risk of surprises owing to the tribunals' deciding by rules of their own invention can hardly fail to deter states from having recourse to international tribunals."[63] As we have already pointed out, the Statute of the International Court of Justice authorizes the Court to apply "the general principles of law recognized by civilized nations." While such a grant of power may be unavoidable, it is certainly true that the "general principles" cannot be ascertained with complete objectivity.

4. *Subjects as judges.* Another serious defect in the judicial function has been that the subjects of international law have also been its judges. By this we mean that individual states — the principal subjects — or their agencies possess the right to interpret the law which they are under obligation to enforce. Being in the position of both subject and judge, they are able to exploit every ambiguity and technicality to their own advantage. This has been true even under the League and the UN, for only those disputes that somehow reached the Permanent Court of International Justice or the International Court of Justice have been adjudicated by an international tribunal.

5. *The limitation of justiciable disputes.* So long as states are not subject to compulsory jurisdiction, it is clear that they have the right to say which disputes they will submit to international judicial process and which ones they will not. Generally speaking, they distinguish between "justiciable" and "nonjusticiable" disputes. Some international lawyers have contended that the two groups are really different in nature — that the first is made up of those for which rules of law exist and the second of those for which there is no applicable law. Other authorities insist that the distinction is unreal. Brierly, for instance, called it "imaginary" and analyzed it as follows:

> International law then is never formally or intrinsically incapable of giving a decision, on the basis of law, as to the rights of the parties to any dispute, and if that is so, we

[63] *International Legislation* (New York: Oxford University Press, 1937), pp. v–vi.

must look for the difference between justiciable and non-justiciable disputes elsewhere. Probably to-day most writers would regard it as depending upon the attitude of the parties: if, whatever the subject-matter of the dispute may be, what the parties seek is their legal rights, the dispute is justiciable: if, on the other hand, one of them at least is not content to demand its legal rights, but demands the satisfaction of some interest of its own even though this may require a change in the existing legal situation, the dispute is non-justiciable.[64]

The distinction between justiciable and nonjusticiable disputes is unknown to domestic law. M. A. Weightman called attention to the significance of this difference in one area of personal and state action — steps taken in self-defense: "In municipal law the legality of measures taken in self-defense is universally acknowledged to be a proper subject for judicial determination. No such determination has of course ever been attempted in the international sphere, and indeed publicists have declared — and diplomats have insisted loudly — that recourse to self-defense must be left to the unfettered judgment of the state which believes that it is being attacked." Weightman pointed out, however, that this means only that "no determination of legality can be made in advance" and that "the measures taken are capable of subsequent legal appreciation and, by extension, of judicial interpretation."[65]

The Executive Function. The limitations of the executive function are more obvious than those of the legislative or judicial, for international law does not provide for international enforcement agencies of any kind. Rather, it gives injured states certain rights of action but confers on nobody the obligation to act. Thus states may legally undertake certain actions to obtain a redress of grievances; but if they fail to take action the injury remains unredressed. Collective law enforcement, as by the UN, may be attempted with complete legality, but such collective action is not a requirement of traditional international law. It is a voluntarily and specially assumed obligation. Moreover, even UN action is commonly inaugurated by the complaint of a state; it is by no means as automatic as in national law. And, despite the Charter's grant of authority to the Security Council to "call" upon member states for armed forces to support its decisions, the Korean crisis of 1950 found the Council inviting aid from all sources rather than stipulating contributions of UN members. Law enforcement was still a matter of national choice. Nevertheless, both the Covenant of the League and the Charter of the UN declare certain offenses to be the concern of all states. But this brave assertion applies only to offenses of a war-threatening character, with enforcement in the hands of sovereign states. Despite the UN Charter, wrote Philip C. Jessup, "the traditional legal foundations of unilateralism remain largely unshaken," and he quoted Elihu Root as saying that "if the law of nations is to be binding . . . there must be a change in theory, and violations of the law of such a character as to threaten the peace and order of the community of nations must be deemed to be a violation of the right of every civilized nation to have the law maintained and a legal injury to every nation."[66]

The Narrow Range of International Law. In discussing what he calls one of the "most serious shortcomings of the present system," Brierly asserted that "it is because the demands that international law makes on states are on the whole so light that its rules in general are fairly well observed." He pointed, for example, to the whole field of economic relations as one in which the

64 Brierly, p. 367.

65 "Self-Defense in International Law," *Virginia Law Review*, XXXVII (December, 1951), 1115.

66 Jessup, *A Modern Law of Nations*, p. 11.

individual states have exclusive jurisdiction over matters which often provide the causes of international disputes. Other areas he mentioned are immigration, naturalization, a state's treatment of its own nationals, and the choice in a form of government. "Law will never play a really effective part in international relations," declared Brierly, "until it can annex to its own sphere some of the matters which at present lie within the 'domestic jurisdictions' of the several states."[67]

Actually, the range of international law is far greater than may be assumed from a short discussion of its place in international relations. To say that certain areas of interstate relations are at present *outside* the scope of international law is not to minimize the number and importance of those already *inside*.

Furthermore, as Jessup has observed, it is "the fundamental tenet of traditional international law that it is a law only between states, not between individuals or between individuals and states." To provide a legal basis for the redress of wrongs to individuals, we have long employed Vattel's fiction that a state is injured when one of its citizens is injured, and the state alone has had a right of action. Only the state may collect damages and then may compensate the citizen if it wishes. Admittedly, there have long been exceptions to the rule that international law is a law only between states, notably in the case of piracy.

Individuals as Subjects of International Law. After World War II the Nuremberg War Crimes Trials raised in dramatic fashion the question of the liability of individuals under international law — specifically, could the Nazi war leaders be properly tried and punished by an international tribunal for "war crimes," "crimes against the peace," and "crimes against humanity"? Even in the Allied countries several objections were raised: international law had no application to individuals; the accused could not be held personally accountable for acts performed on direction from authorized spokesmen of the German state; the "law" was in the nature of *ex post facto*. Nevertheless, by the London Agreement of August 8, 1945, Great Britain, France, the U.S.S.R., and the United States set up an International Military Tribunal, adopted a charter for its guidance, and then proceeded to the trial of the alleged offenders.

The General Assembly affirmed the principles laid down in the charter of the Nuremberg Tribunal and later requested the International Law Commission to "formulate the principles of international law recognized in the Charter of the Nürnberg Tribunal and in the judgment of the Tribunal." The commission prepared the formulation, but it declined to express any "appreciation" of the principles of international law involved, saying that such action was beside the point after the General Assembly's affirmation. The commission listed seven principles, which, to summarize, declared the responsibility of individuals under international law, denied the immunity of high government officials and of persons acting under orders when a moral choice was open, and noted the crimes punishable under international law.[68] The legality of the Nuremberg Trials and Judgment remains in dispute, but the fact also remains that a number of Nazi war criminals were hanged.

The Convention on the Prevention and Punishment of Genocide, approved by the General Assembly in December, 1948, alluded to a possible "international penal tribunal," and an Assembly resolution of the same date invited the International Law Commission to study the need and feasibility of "a Crime Chamber of the International Court of Justice." As yet no action has been taken, and despite much discussion an international criminal law does not yet exist.

Philip Jessup held that the expansion of

[67] Brierly, pp. 74, 75.

[68] *International Organization*, IV (November, 1950), 714–721.

international law to include individuals should have high priority if we are to develop what he termed "a modern law of nations."[69] Hans Kelsen also declared his belief in the importance of personal liability: "One of the most effective means to prevent war and to guarantee international peace is the enactment of rules establishing individual responsibility of the persons who as members of government have violated international law by resorting to or provoking war."[70] Quincy Wright observed that "juristic opinion is divided as between advocates of the old and the new international law," and well it might be, for the new law "in principle changes the world society from a system of sovereign states to a world union in which the United Nations protects human rights, punishes international crimes, and enforces its law against both states and individuals."[71] From the legal point of view and in the short run, says Wright, realizing the new international law "concerns the amendment, interpretation, implementation, and supplementation of the United Nations Charter," while "from the factual point of view" its realization "lies in the realm of international politics, international organization, international economics, international education, and international communications."[72]

International Law and World Peace. We should remember that international law is only one aspect of international relations, and by no means the most important one. The great issues of international politics, those most clearly involving issues of peace or war, are largely outside its purview. This is not because many of these issues do not lend themselves to judicial settlement, but because the states of the world will generally not submit them to judicial settlement. Matters of national honor and prestige are too closely involved. International law, moreover, is still in a very primitive stage of development. Professor Dickinson, a friendly critic, described it this way: ". . . as regards its institutions and procedures of adjustment the law of nations has been a jungle law imperfectly ameliorated by a fragmentary and hesitant progress in the direction of legal order."[73] In Professor Brierly's judgment, "the system is still at what we may describe as the *laissez-faire* stage of legal development." Nevertheless, it represents a positive attempt to build an international legal order, in the absence of which peace and sanity in the international community are in constant jeopardy.

We must not regard international law as an alternative to diplomacy. Clearly, diplomacy too is essential to the family of nations; in fact, as we have seen, it is the usual method of conducting interstate relations, including the adjustment of differences and disputes. Even if one argues, as some writers do, that international law now provides rules that are adequate for the solution of all disputes among nations, he must concede that there remains the need for diplomacy to bring nations to seek settlement by law and to accept it. If one argues that diplomacy must take up where law leaves off — that is, that there are justiciable and nonjusticiable disputes — then there falls to diplomacy the whole area of "political" differences among states.

Increasing attention is being given to the study of international law, on both official and unofficial levels. Interest on official levels is illustrated by the growing number of courses in international law in law schools throughout the world, the expanding number and activities of societies of international law, and the voluminous literature on the subject.

[69] *A Modern Law of Nations*, p. 2.

[70] Hans Kelsen, *Peace Through Law* (Chapel Hill: University of North Carolina Press, 1944), p. 71; see also "Collective and Individual Responsibility in International Law with Particular Regard to the Punishment of War Criminals," *California Law Review*, XXXI (1943), 530 ff.

[71] Wright, pp. 229, 230.

[72] *Ibid.*, p. 231.

[73] Dickinson, p. 76.

Ministries of external affairs and other governmental departments maintain staffs of experts in international law, and the United Nations is actively interested in research in the field, especially through its International Law Commission. Many of the member states, especially the newer states, have asked the UN for assistance in undertaking and developing programs of training and cooperation in the field, and the UN is considering the establishment of a training and research institute. At its Eighteenth Session the General Assembly created a Special Committee on the Teaching, Study, Dissemination and Wider Appreciation of International Law. This committee is charged with formulating a program for action by the UN and other agencies, especially during the Decade of International Law which will be inaugurated in the near future.

We must not expect either too little or too much of international law. Persons who have little faith in it point to the occasions on which it has been violated with impunity and to the continuance of war in international society. Faithfulness to the law occurs in countless routine, undramatic matters, and its violations often appear in highly publicized, dramatic incidents. War itself, even when resorted to in violation of law, must not be regarded as flaunting all international law but only as representing the failure of that law to perform what is actually its ultimate service.

Professor Josef L. Kunz has warned against what he describes as the swing from overestimation to underestimation of international law. He recalls that at the close of World War I "there was everywhere, in victors, neutrals, and vanquished, not only the will to achieve a better world through international law, but also the firm conviction that it could be done." After World War II came the flowering of the new "realism" with its emphasis on politics and power. International law was not even mentioned in the Dumbarton Oaks Proposals, and it barely escaped exclusion from the UN Charter. Whereas the Permanent Court of International Justice was busy in its early years, the International Court of Justice has had very little business. Kunz protested against this "underestimation" of international law; he declared that the law is not "sterile" and that it must necessarily play an important role in international relations.[74] That "realism" and regard for international law are not mutually exclusive is proved by the writings of many distinguished contemporary authorities. Professor Dickinson, for example, followed a rather severe critique of international law with a volume of essays entitled *Law and Peace,* in which he affirmed his faith in international law as a realistic approach to peace.[75]

Belief in international law as a basis of enduring peace was also expressed by Senator Robert A. Taft. Although he supported and voted for the UN Charter, he confessed that he was "never satisfied." He objected to "peace and security" as the basis for enforcement action of the Security Council; these, he believed, were not "synonymous with justice." He contended that the veto power in the Security Council of the United Nations "completely dispels the idea that any system of universal law is being established, for surely nothing can be law if five of the largest nations can automatically exempt themselves from its application."[76] "It seems to me," he wrote, "that peace in this world is impossible unless nations agree on a definite law to govern their relations with each other and also agree that, without any veto power, they will submit their disputes to adjudica-

[74] "The Swing of the Pendulum: From Overestimation to Underestimation of International Law," *The American Journal of International Law,* XLIV (January, 1950), 135–140.

[75] "International Law: an Inventory," *California Law Review,* XXXIII (December, 1945), 506–542; see also, the same author's *Law and Peace.*

[76] Robert A. Taft, *A Foreign Policy for Americans* (Garden City, N.Y.: Doubleday & Company, 1951), pp. 39, 40.

tion and abide by the decision of an impartial tribunal. . . ."[77]

Distinguished scholars who point to the development of international law as the most hopeful road to world peace rarely lose sight of the interrelationship of law and power. They are constantly aware that the development of international law into an effective guarantee of a peaceful world order will require a revision of some fundamental concepts and a change in some traditional relationships and practices. Kelsen asserted categorically that "it is the essential characteristic of the law as a coercive order to establish a community monopoly of force"; in 1944 he proposed a Permanent League for the Maintenance of Peace, "with compulsory jurisdiction" for an international court and with the four guarantor states — the United States, Great Britain, China, and the Soviet Union — as "the power 'behind the law.' "[78] Jessup declared that "until the world achieves some form of international government in which a collective will takes precedence over the individual will of the sovereign state, the ultimate function of law, which is the elimination of force for the solution of human conflicts, will not be fulfilled."[79]

Of necessity, all plans and programs for world government emphasize the necessity of strengthening and expanding the scope of international law, for world government is obviously impossible without world law. Prominent international lawyers have been active in most world government movements, and particularly in the preparation of constitutions or other "blueprints" for world order. An outstanding example of such a "blueprint" is the well-known work by Grenville Clark and Louis Sohn, entitled *World Peace Through World Law.*[80]

Professor Dickinson's approach was more cautious and perhaps more realistic. He was sure that for a long time to come we are not going to have "an international constitutional convention." In the meantime he would have us avoid the "immediate and inescapable choice between panaceas for global salvation and the disintegration of all civilization" which the forecasters of doom offer us and instead "use and develop the institutions at hand to better advantage." While he admitted that "world law has yet to assure the order and decency which exclude violence and supplant anarchy," he was convinced that "there is a vast body that is useful, indeed indispensable, and contained in its practices and principles are great potentialities of growth." The law in custom, he wrote, is "tough law," but it "grows glacially." It needs "invigoration and extension." He advanced suggestions for the expansion and improvement of the law and of what may be called the international judicial system, but he took care to warn that labors on this front should be accompanied by accommodation at the highest levels. "Every day of peace is a time for the extension of law" — a time for moving forward on "a vast and complicated front."[81]

There is, of course, validity in sensible realism. Americans have learned in domestic affairs that to be enforceable law must enjoy the support of a substantial proportion of the citizens. To attempt to write off the world's woes by making laws against them would be just as futile as to expect the U.S.S.R. to abandon her present foreign policy if somehow the Western states contrived to trick her into surrendering her veto power in the Security Council. The intent to cooperate must be present. The logical order is the will before the law, not after.

With a consciousness of the defects and limitations of international law — the inadequacies of the legislative, judicial, and executive functions, the narrowness of its range, and the too-frequent misunderstanding of its

[77] *Ibid.*, p. 40.
[78] Kelsen, *Peace Through Law*, p. 66.
[79] Jessup, *A Modern Law of Nations*, p. 2.
[80] 2d ed. (Cambridge, Mass.: Harvard University Press, 1960).

[81] The quoted passages appear in Dickinson, *Law and Peace*, Chapter IV.

nature and of its proper role — the men and women who seek a world of peace and order see that law as an index to their progress. Offering no formula by which the putting of words on paper can compel states to follow a course of justice and friendship, international law does provide almost the only means by which states can register and secure the gains which they make toward a better international order.

SUGGESTIONS FOR FURTHER READING

Academy of Sciences of the U.S.S.R., Institute of State and Law. *International Law*. Moscow, n.d. An English edition of a standard Soviet treatise.

BISHOP, W. W. JR. *International Law, Cases and Materials.* Englewood Cliffs, N.J.: Prentice-Hall, 1953.

BRIERLY, J. L. *The Law of Nations*, 6th ed., edited by Sir Humphrey Waldock. New York: Oxford University Press, 1963. One of the best-known and clearest expositions of the subject.

———. *The Outlook for International Law.* New York: Oxford University Press, 1944.

BRIGGS, HERBERT. *The International Law Commission.* Ithaca: Cornell University Press, 1965. A legal analysis of the Commission's stature, methods, procedures, and achievements.

———. *The Law of Nations: Cases, Documents and Notes*, 2d ed. New York: Appleton-Century-Crofts, 1952.

CLARK, GRENVILLE and LOUIS SOHN. *World Peace Through World Law*, 2d ed. Cambridge, Mass.: Harvard University Press, 1960. A much-discussed legal "blueprint" for world government.

CORBETT, P. E. *Law and Society in the Relations of States.* New York: Harcourt, Brace, 1951.

———. *The Study of International Law.* Garden City, N.Y.: Doubleday & Company, 1955.

DICKINSON, EDWIN D. *Law and Peace.* Philadelphia: University of Pennsylvania Press, 1951. An incisive discussion of law as a means to peace.

FENWICK, CHARLES G. *International Law*, 4th ed. New York: Appleton-Century-Crofts, 1965.

FRANKLIN, C. M. *The Law of the Sea: Some Recent Developments.* Washington, D.C.: Government Printing Office, 1961.

FRIEDMANN, WOLFGANG. *The Changing Structure of International Law.* New York: Columbia University Press, 1964.

GIHL, TORSTEN. *International Legislation: An Essay on Changes in International Law and in International Legal Situations*, translated by S. J. Charleston. New York: Oxford University Press, 1937.

GLUECK, SHELDON. *The Nuremberg Trial and Aggressive War.* New York: Alfred A. Knopf, 1946.

GREEN, L. C. *International Law Through the Cases.* New York: Frederick A. Praeger, 1951.

HACKWORTH, GREEN H. *Digest of International Law.* 8 vols. Washington, D.C.: Government Printing Office, 1940–44. Continued John Bassett Moore, *A Digest of International Law*, published in 8 vols. by the Government Printing Office in 1906.

HENKIN, LOUIS. *How Nations Behave: Law and Foreign Policy.* New York: Frederick A. Praeger, for the Council on Foreign Relations, 1968.

HUDSON, MANLEY O. *International Legislation, 1910–1945.* 9 vols. New York: Carnegie Endowment for International Peace, 1931–52. The standard collection.

HYDE, CHARLES C. *International Law, Chiefly as Interpreted and Applied by the United States*, 2d ed. 3 vols. Boston: Little, Brown and Company, 1945.

JESSUP, PHILIP C. *A Modern Law of Nations.* New York: The Macmillan Company, 1948. Forceful presentation of the case for extending the boundaries of international law, particularly by bringing individuals within its purview.

———. *Transnational Law.* New Haven: Yale University Press, 1956.

KAPLAN, MORTON and NICHOLAS DE B. KATZENBACH. *The Political Foundations of International Law.* New York: John Wiley & Sons, 1961.

KEETON, GEORGE W. and GEORG SCHWARZENBERGER. *Making International Law Work,* 2d ed. London, 1946.

KELSEN, HANS. *The Law of the United Nations.* New York: Frederick A. Praeger, 1950.

———. *Principles of International Law.* New York: Rinehart, 1952.

LARSON, ARTHUR. *When Nations Disagree: A Handbook of Peace Through Law.* Baton Rouge: Louisiana State University Press, 1961.

LAUTERPACHT, H. *International Law and Human Rights.* New York: Frederick A. Praeger, 1950. A significant study by a noted authority.

LISSITZYN, OLIVER J. "International Law in a Divided World," *International Conciliation,* No. 542 (March, 1963). Emphasizes the attitudes of the Soviet Union and the less developed nations toward international law.

MCDOUGAL, MYRES S. *Law and the Public Order in Space.* New Haven: Yale University Press, 1963.

MCDOUGAL, MYRES S. *et al. Studies in World Public Order.* New Haven: Yale University Press, 1960. Reflects the approach of the senior author to law as a "policy science."

MCDOUGAL, MYRES S. and WILLIAM T. BURKE. *Public Order of the Oceans.* New Haven: Yale University Press, 1962.

MCDOUGAL, MYRES S. and FLORENTINE P. FELICIANO. *Law and Minimum World Public Order.* New Haven: Yale University Press, 1961.

MANGONE, GERARD. *The Elements of International Law: A Casebook.* Homewood, Ill.: Dorsey Press, 1963.

NUSSBAUM, ARTHUR. *A Concise History of the Law of Nations,* 2d ed. New York: The Macmillan Company, 1954. A comprehensive historical survey.

OPPENHEIM, L. *International Law,* edited by H. Lauterpacht. 2 vols. Vol. I ("Peace"), 8th ed. New York: David McKay Company, 1955. Vol. II ("Disputes, War and Neutrality"), 7th ed. New York: David McKay Company, 1952. A classic in the field, first published by Longmans, Green and Co. in 1905.

RÖLING, B. V. A. *International Law in an Expanded World.* Amsterdam, 1960.

SCHWARZENBERGER, GEORG. *Manual of International Law,* 3d ed. London, 1952.

SOHN, LOUIS. *Cases and Other Materials on World Law: The Interpretation and Application of the Charter of the United Nations and of Constitutions of Other Agencies of the World Community.* Brooklyn, N.Y.: The Foundation Press, 1950.

STONE, JULIUS. "The International Court and the World Crisis," *International Conciliation* No. 536 (January, 1962).

———. *Legal Controls of International Conflict.* New York: Rinehart, 1954.

———. *Question for Survival: The Role of Law and Foreign Policy.* Cambridge, Mass. Harvard University Press, 1961.

SVARLEIN, OSCAR. *An Introduction to the Law of Nations.* New York: McGraw-Hill Book Company, 1955.

SYATAUW, J. J. G. *Some Newly Established Asian States and the Development of International Law.* The Hague, 1961.

TRISKA, J. F. and R. M. SLUSSER. *The Theory, Law, and Policy of Soviet Treaties.* Stanford, Calif.: Stanford University Press, 1962.

VYSHINSKY, ANDREI. *Law of the Soviet State* New York: The Macmillan Company, 1948

WRIGHT, QUINCY. *Contemporary International Law: A Balance Sheet.* Garden City, N.Y.: Doubleday & Company, 1955. In the Doubleday Short Studies in Political Science.

———. *International Law and the United Nations.* New York: Asia Publishing House, 1960.

Yearbook of the International Law Commission.

12 The Evolution of International Organization

One of the promising developments of the twentieth century in interstate relations has been the proliferation of international organizations. For the first time in history permanent organizations of a nearly universal type have emerged. Perhaps the word "permanent" may seem hardly justified, for the League of Nations lasted for only about a quarter of a century, with an effective period of barely fifteen years, and the future of the United Nations, after more than two decades of active existence, is still very uncertain.

Associated with today's general international organization — the UN — are many lesser ones, some of which, as the specialized agencies, are equally broad in membership but more limited in function, while others, as the Economic Commission for Europe, are both regional and specialized. Outside the UN structure, regional organizations of a general character, as the Organization of American States and the North Atlantic Treaty Organization, and some more specialized in function, as the Organization for Economic Cooperation and Development and the South Pacific Commission, are also numerous and active. In addition to the scores of public international organizations, concerned with almost every conceivable aspect of international relations, hundreds of private international organizations (the so-called nongovernmental organizations), such as the International Red Cross or Rotary International or the International Chamber of Commerce, play useful although less publicized roles.

Before the League of Nations

The great burgeoning of international organizations has come only in the present century, when the complexity of the world society has created a need for them. While they have an obvious indebtedness to the conferences, nonpermanent associations, international public unions, and other nineteenth-century ventures into the institutionalization of interstate relations, their roots go far back into the past.

From the Beginning to Westphalia. Prototypes of today's organizations are to be found in ancient and medieval history, and the modern pattern of international organization has been evolving ever since the nation-state system emerged several centuries ago, and especially since the Congress of Westphalia of 1648.

Professor Pitman B. Potter distinguished six special forms of international organization — diplomacy, treaty negotiation, international law, conference, administration, and adjudication — and one general form, international federation.[1] This classification actually relates more to procedures in international intercourse than to varieties of international organizations. The term "international organization" is defined as "any cooperative arrangement instituted among states, usually by a basic agreement, to perform some mutually advantageous functions implemented through periodic meetings and staff activities."[2] In this well-developed sense few examples of international organizations can be found until the modern period, whereas, according to Professor Potter's conception, international organization has existed in at least primitive form throughout most of recorded history.

Long before the golden age of ancient Greece interstate relations of a sort existed in many parts of the known world, including China, India, Mesopotamia, and Egypt. Contracts between rulers and kingdoms were not uncommon, and there was a fair area of agreement on diplomatic practices, commercial relations, treaties of alliance, codes of warfare, and terms of peace. "The treaties of the past are the first steps toward international organization."[3]

Although local loyalties prevented the Greeks from achieving a true national unity, the procedures and patterns in use among their city-states, as well as their theories of interstate relations, appear strikingly modern. In some ways ancient Greece seems much like the modern world in miniature. Treaties, alliances, diplomatic practices and services, arbitration and other methods for peaceful settlement of disputes, rules of war and peace, leagues and confederations, and other means for regulating interstate relations were well known and widely used.

The Roman contribution to international organization was of a different sort. After the final defeat of Carthage and the conquest of all the Mediterranean world and of most of Western and Central Europe, Rome established a kind of universal empire; the inclusiveness of this empire and its remoteness from other centers of power, such as China and India, precluded interstate relations. The idea of international organization was therefore foreign to the Romans. Nevertheless, the Romans contributed legal, military, and administrative techniques, and they established the basis of the *jus gentium* which in later centuries became a fertile source of international law.

During the late Roman period the foundations of the Christian church were firmly established. As Rome declined, the church asserted its claims to temporal as well as spiritual authority. Through the papacy, the Holy Roman Empire, and the strong appeal of "the faith," the church of the Middle Ages provided a kind of universalism which helped to counteract the decentralizing tendencies of feudalism and other forms of political fragmentation and continued to exert an appeal long after the church itself had split. The Council of Constance, "the most spectacular international congress of history," assembled in 1414 to attempt to resolve rival claims to the papacy and thereby to shape the political as well as spiritual fortunes of Europe. While it was nearly everywhere defeated in its aspirations to temporal power, and while it does not command even the spiritual allegiance of a good part of the civilized world, the Roman church has remained to this day the most powerful of all international nongovernmental organizations.

Throughout the Middle Ages alliances and associations of political, commercial, and religious areas and groups were frequently formed. An outstanding association for the

[1] "International Organization," *Encyclopaedia of the Social Sciences* (New York: The Macmillan Company, 1937), VIII, 180–181. Used by permission of The Macmillan Company.

[2] Daniel S. Cheever and H. Field Haviland, Jr., *Organizing for Peace: International Organization in World Affairs* (Boston: Houghton Mifflin Company, 1954), p. 6.

[3] Gerard J. Mangone, *A Short History of International Organization* (New York: McGraw-Hill Book Company, 1954), p. 14.

promotion of trade, which became a kind of political organization as well, was the Hanseatic League. Possibly the most famous confederation of the medieval period was that developed from a treaty among the Swiss cantons of Uri, Schwyz, and Unterwalden in 1315. Joined by five other cantons before the end of the fourteenth century, it became the nucleus of the modern state of Switzerland.

Westphalia to Vienna. With the breakdown of the medieval system and the coming of the Protestant Reformation, the Catholic Renaissance, the Age of Discoveries, an expanded trade and commerce, and the present state system in the fifteenth, sixteenth, and seventeenth centuries, international relations assumed a new meaning and character. The theories, practices, and institutions of modern international society began to take shape, although they did not become crystallized and fully developed until the nineteenth and twentieth centuries. Machiavelli described the practices which prevailed in the relations of the city-states of northern Italy in the late fifteenth and early sixteenth century, and he gave a new realism to the study of interstate relations. Bodin in the sixteenth century formulated the legal concept of sovereignty, generally regarded as the most basic of the attributes of the nation-state. Grotius, writing while the Thirty Years' War was raging, laid the foundation for the evolution of a "law of nations." Denying that sovereignty, or sovereigns, were absolute, he argued that "there are laws for the community valid both in respect to war, and during war."

The Congress of Westphalia was a notable milestone in the development of international organization, as it was in the evolution of the modern state system. The significance of this great Congress has been well described by Gerard Mangone:

> No international organization was established by the Peace of Westphalia in 1648. . . . But the joining of practically every European state in a diplomatic conference signaled the opening of a new era in international relations. . . . As an international assembly, the Congress of Westphalia bore little resemblance to the intricate organization of twentieth-century peace conferences. . . . Of the greatest importance to international organization, however, were the gathering of hundreds of envoys in a diplomatic conference which represented practically every political interest in Europe and the achievement by negotiation, rather than by dictation, of two great multilateral treaties which legalized the new order of European international relations.[4]

During the dynastic and colonial struggles of the eighteenth century, alliances, coalitions, diplomacy, wars, conferences, and peace settlements became commonplace techniques of international relations. The conference system, which has been perhaps the most conspicuous feature of modern international organization, was developed to a high degree. In the seventeenth and eighteenth centuries some of the best-known early plans and proposals for peaceful relations and for international organization were advanced. These included the "Grand Design" of Henry IV of France and the Duc de Sully (early seventeenth century), William Penn's proposal of a "Parliament of Europe" in his *Essay Toward the Present and Future Peace of Europe* (1693), the Abbé de Saint-Pierre's *Project to Bring Perpetual Peace in Europe* (1712), Jeremy Bentham's "Plea for an Universal and Perpetual Peace" in his *Principles of International Law* (1793), and Kant's famous proposal of the same nature in his essay "Perpetual Peace" (*Zum ewigen Frieden,* 1795).[5]

[4] Mangone, pp. 21, 22.

[5] See Edith Wynner and Georgia Lloyd, *Searchlight on Peace Plans* (New York: E. P. Dutton & Co., 1944); Gerard J. Mangone, *The Idea and Practice of World Government* (New York: Columbia University Press, 1951); Hans Kohn, *World Order in Historical Perspective* (Cambridge, Mass.: Harvard University Press, 1943).

Vienna to Versailles. The Congress of Vienna (1814–15) met to deal with the European political problems which remained after the defeat of Napoleon. The rulers of Europe succeeded only partially and temporarily in their attempt to restore the old order, but unwittingly they laid the foundations of a political and international system which for a century shaped the course of European and to some extent of world affairs.

The central agency for enforcing the Vienna settlement was the Quadruple Alliance of Austria, Great Britain, Prussia, and Russia, which became a quintuple alliance in 1818 with the addition of France. "This development was a landmark in the history of international organization for several reasons. First, the alliance, though forged in war, was continued after hostilities to enforce the peace. Second, periodic conferences were instituted when the great powers agreed to renew their meetings at fixed intervals. Third, despite the suspicions of the smaller powers it was generally agreed that the maintenance of peace depended on this sort of big-power collaboration. These notions were carried over into both the League and the UN."[6] Out of the experience of the years that followed the Congress of Vienna emerged the informal pattern of conferences and consultations and occasional concerted action which is known as the Concert of Europe. It scored a resounding success at the Congress of Berlin in 1878, which dealt with Turkey and the so-called eastern question. It was, however, unable to cope with the nationalistic rivalries and other divisive tendencies which eventually led to World War I.

The conference system, which had been a significant feature of eighteenth-century diplomacy, was the main instrument for international collaboration in the century after the Congress of Vienna. Conferences were held with increasing frequency, especially after the middle of the century. According to one tabulation, the number in each decade from 1840 through 1909 was, respectively, 9, 22, 75, 149, 284, 469, and 1,082.[7] Relatively few of these were primarily political conferences like the Congress of Paris of 1856 or the Congress of Berlin of 1878. Many more dealt with administrative or technical questions.

One of the most promising developments in the history of international organization was the emergence of a multitude of international administrative agencies or public international unions in the latter half of the nineteenth and the early twentieth centuries. They arose in response to the growing need for cooperation in economic and social problems which could not be handled satisfactorily by states alone or without planned coordination. Among the organizations set up were the European Commission for the Danube (1856); the International Geodetic Association (1864); the International Bureau of Telegraphic Administrations (1868); the Universal Postal Union (1875); the International Bureau of Weights and Measures (1875); the International Copyright Union (1886); the International Office of Public Health (1903); and the International Institute of Agriculture (1905).[8] Some of these are still in existence; others have given over their functions to UN agencies. One of the UN affiliates — the Universal Postal Union — has been described as "one of the most significant international organizations in the history of nations."[9]

Outstanding among the conferences of the years prior to World War I were the Hague Peace Conferences of 1899 and 1907. The story of these relates primarily to the development of international law, but it is also of significance in the evolution of international organization. The First Hague Conference

[6] Cheever and Haviland, p. 35.

[7] See James A. Joyce, *World in the Making: The Story of International Cooperation* (New York: H. Schuman, 1953), p. 92.

[8] See Mangone, *A Short History*, pp. 67–90.

[9] *Ibid.*, p. 78.

attempted to place arbitration procedures on a more formal and more generally acceptable basis. In its Convention for the Pacific Settlement of International Disputes it established a Permanent Court of Arbitration. While this was neither permanent nor a court — as has often been remarked — it did offer the services of a panel of members, and it had an Administrative Council and an International Bureau. At the Second Hague Conference the American Secretary of State, Elihu Root, advocated the acceptance of compulsory arbitration for certain types of disputes and "the development of The Hague tribunal into a permanent tribunal." Neither objective was achieved, but before World War I the United States and a few other states entered into several treaties of arbitration, and a few cases were submitted to the Permanent Court of Arbitration. The Court was actually never very active. Nominally it still exists, although it has long since been overshadowed by the world courts associated with the League of Nations and the UN.

The League of Nations

A permanent general international organization of a nearly universal character came into existence for the first time after World War I. This development marked another stage in the history of international organization. The new era owed much to the experience and experiments, including the many abortive plans and projects, of the past. "Modern international organization," stated Mangone, "with its wide array of institutions, evolved from the conferences of the preceding centuries."[10] In the new world of the twentieth century the older techniques were not adequate, but they did provide the foundations upon which the present complex structure of international organization has been built.

Setting Up the League

The idea of an association of nations was an old one, dating back at least to Sully's Grand Design of the early seventeenth century, but the coming of war in 1914 naturally gave it a new impetus. Formulation of a charter or constitution for a world organization began in 1916. The Covenant that finally emerged after long and bitter argument provided for a League of Nations with three main organs: the Assembly, the Council, and the Secretariat. Perhaps next in importance were the Permanent Court of International Justice, the International Labor Organization, and the Technical Organizations.

Assembly members were to present for discussion "any circumstance whatever affecting international relations which threatens to disturb international peace or the good understanding between nations upon which peace depends." The Assembly's function, however, was not to act but to confer, advise, and deliberate. Here it was that small states were expected to have their say. The Council was planned as the executive organ of the League. Although the great powers wished to have its membership restricted to themselves, they had to give way and admit a limited number of smaller states. Thus the Council was designed to consist of five great powers with permanent seats and four lesser powers with nonpermanent seats. The failure of the United States to join the League kept the membership of the Council at eight until two nonpermanent seats were added in 1922. Germany was given a permanent seat in 1926 and the Soviet Union was granted one in 1934; and the number of nonpermanent seats was eventually increased to eleven. The Council was to direct the work of the Secretariat, arrange for international conferences, receive reports from the subsidiary organs of the League, determine which reports should be submitted to the Assembly, deal with disputes among League members, and supervise the observance of the mandates, the Minorities Treaties, and other agreements. Upon it rested primary responsibility for safeguarding the peace of the world.

[10] *Ibid.*, p. 61.

The Secretariat was a permanent civil service headed by a Secretary-General. Its work was to assist all organs of the League by providing services of many kinds: clerical, research, drafting, publication, coordination, registration of treaties, keeping of records, arrangement of meetings, and the like. It came to have a staff of about seven hundred persons, working through eleven "sections" and numerous "services" and offices."

The Statute of the Permanent Court of International Justice was completed in December, 1920. By the start of World War II fifty-one states had become members of the Court. For a period of nearly twenty years, until World War II interrupted its work, this Court functioned with "surprising success," according to Manley O. Hudson, one of its judges.[11] During the period of its activity the Court tried sixty-five cases and handed down thirty-two judgments, twenty-seven advisory opinions, and several hundred orders.[12]

Although the International Labor Organization was regarded as one of the main organs of the League of Nations, it had — and still has — a large measure of autonomy. In 1940 it moved its headquarters to Montreal, and it continued to function throughout World War II. It became a specialized agency of the UN in December, 1946.

The League structure also contained three so-called Technical Organizations: the Economic and Financial Organization, the Communications and Transit Organization, and the Health Organization. Each had its standing committees and each held general conferences from time to time, "thus resembling the League as a whole with its Council and Assembly."[13] All relied upon a similarly named section of the Secretariat for continuous administrative and secretarial assistance.

The Pacific Settlement of Disputes

The Covenant of the League may be said to have contemplated three approaches to the settlement of international differences. First, and very important, states were expected to do everything possible to reach a solution by direct negotiation, making every possible use of the traditional devices of diplomacy, conciliation, and arbitration. It is by these means that the vast majority of disputes have always been settled. Second, states were urged to accept the jurisdiction of the Permanent Court of International Justice, with minimum reservations. The Optional Clause was devised to induce states to commit themselves to the authority of the Court. Third, the Covenant charged the Council with the ultimate responsibility for keeping the peace — or for punishing violators — when all other means had failed or, indeed, if other means had been left untried.

The most conspicuous feature of the Council's handling of disputes was the extreme flexibility of its procedure. The constant objective was not to observe a ritual but to bring the parties into agreement. To that end the Council might resort to any or all of many devices: it might urge direct negotiation, clarify points of law with jurists or the Court, defer proceedings, utilize committees of the Council or of League agencies, call upon the Secretariat for information, attempt only partial settlement in the first instance, turn the dispute over to the Assembly, or contrive still other devices. The entire process was informal and conciliatory, often with private sessions, usually without recorded votes, and always with representatives of all parties sitting as regular or ad hoc members of the Council.

The Promotion of Collective Security

During the fifteen years following the setting up of the League, five major efforts

[11] Manley O. Hudson, "The World Court," in Harriet E. Davis, ed., *Pioneers in World Order* (New York: Columbia University Press, 1944), p. 67.

[12] Hudson, pp. 69–70.

[13] Pitman B. Potter, *An Introduction to the Study of International Organization* (New York: Appleton-Century, 1935), p. 349.

were made to establish systems of collective security, and four of these were made under the aegis of the League. All five will be briefly examined.

Draft Treaty of Mutual Assistance. This proposal was approved by the Assembly in 1923. According to its terms, within four days of the outbreak of hostilities the League Council would name the aggressor and indicate the measures of financial or military assistance to be furnished the victim of aggression, but military aid was to be required only of states in the same hemisphere as the aggressor. Disarmament was linked with security; unless a state agreed to limit or reduce its armaments and had already taken real steps to do so, it would receive no general assistance. "The peg upon which all else hangs is disarmament."[14] Largely because of British opposition to the hemisphere feature, the plan collapsed.

The Geneva Protocol. The Draft Treaty, together with the coming to power of more liberal governments in Britain and France under MacDonald and Herriot and the general easing of the political situation by the adoption of the Dawes Plan with its modification of reparations terms, led to the famous Geneva Protocol of 1924. Signatory states were required to accept the compulsory jurisdiction of the World Court in all disputes covered by the Optional Clause. Nonlegal disputes were to be submitted to the Council, and the failure of a state to accept the jurisdiction of the Court or the unanimous report of the Council would be accounted an act of aggression. Before the year ended, however, MacDonald fell from power, Britain rejected the Protocol, and it failed of ratification by the necessary number of states.

The Locarno Treaties. The Geneva Protocol led more or less directly to the Locarno Treaties, which some historians believe carried the League of Nations to the zenith of its prestige. The represenatives of seven states met at the Swiss village of Locarno in October, 1925, and drew up seven agreements, known as the Locarno Treaties: (1) a Five-Power Treaty, signed by Belgium, France, Germany, Great Britain, and Italy, guaranteed the Franco-German and Belgian-German frontiers and the permanent demilitarization of the Rhineland; Belgium, France, and Germany promised not to resort to war except in self-defense or after "flagrant breach" of the agreements on the demilitarized Rhineland zone or in fulfillment of League obligations, and they further agreed to settle all disputes by peaceful means; (2–5) conventions between Germany on the one hand and Belgium, Czechoslovakia, France and Poland separately, on the other hand, pledged arbitration of disputes; (6–7) pacts between France and Czechoslovakia and between France and Poland provided for mutual assistance against unprovoked aggression by Germany. As part of the general understanding, insisted upon by France, Germany was to join the League of Nations.

The Pact of Paris. The Locarno agreements were everywhere taken as heralding a new and better day in international relations. "The spirit of Locarno" was still manifest in 1928, when the Pact of Paris, also called the Kellogg-Briand Pact, the Kellogg Pact, and, officially, the General Treaty for the Renunciation of War, was signed. The pact mentioned no sanctions, it asserted no positive obligation to seek a peaceful settlement, and, technically at least, it did not outlaw war. It merely "condemned" and "renounced" war, whatever that may mean in diplomatic parlance. Moreover, reservations excluded wars of self-defense and permitted each state to be its own judge. The Pact, signed on August 27, 1928, was eventually ratified by nearly every state in the world. The Soviet Union was the first to ratify. The pact was

[14] Frances Kellor, *Security Against War* (New York: The Macmillan Company, 1924), II, 738.

the only one of the five major efforts to achieve security by collective action before 1935 in which the United States joined, and it was the only one entirely outside the League.

The General Act of 1928. The popularity of the Locarno agreements prompted the League to attempt the further development of interrelated arbitration, nonaggression, and mutual assistance pledges. Using the various Locarno treaties as models, an Assembly committee drafted a series of formal agreements "to serve as a standardized multilateral system of conciliation for all disputes, of arbitration for those of a legal nature and of arbitral procedure for other disputes."[15] The Assembly collected these into a General Act and opened it to accession in September, 1928. By 1935 twenty-three states had acceded to the act — hardly an impressive proportion of the total number of states. Regarded by some persons as the League's most important single effort to establish a system of collective security, it probably remains the least known.

The Limitation of Armaments

The commitment of the League to the principle of the reduction of armaments was equivocal from the start, despite the fact that the carrying out of a disarmament program was one of the chief purposes of its founding.[16] The League Council early set up the Permanent Advisory Committee to formulate a reduction program, but the committee soon demonstrated the futility of expecting a group of military men to sponsor disarmament. About a year later the Council created the Temporary Mixed Commission, a larger body with a civilian majority. Before it went out of existence in 1924 the TMC had been largely responsible for four ventures in disarmament. The first was Lord Esher's plan for fixing land forces according to national needs. This was rejected. The second was the effort to extend the principles of the Washington Conference Treaty of 1922 to nonsignatory powers. This too failed. The third, an indirect approach that would institute collective security as a basis for the reduction of armaments, led to the Draft Treaty of Mutual Assistance. This also was rejected. The fourth venture produced the Geneva Protocol, another indirect approach, one which sought to extend the area of compulsory arbitration and impose sanctions against aggressor states, thus creating an atmosphere of security in which disarmament projects might hopefully be undertaken. This too was rejected. The League took no hand in the Washington Conference of 1921–22, the Geneva Conference of 1927, or the London Conference of 1930.

The establishment of the Preparatory Commission (PC) for a Disarmament Conference by the Council in 1925 put the League on the long road that led to its supreme attempt at limiting national armaments — the Geneva Disarmament Conference. The job assigned to the PC was to prepare a provisional draft treaty dealing with all the principal questions relating to disarmament. After six years of work, marked by sharp differences, considerable acrimony, and frequent pessimism, the draft treaty was finally completed. The Council set the opening date of the conference as February 2, 1932, and the place as Geneva.

Viewed from the outside, from the arena of world politics, the prospects of the Geneva Conference were almost hopeless. The Great Depression was at hand, and in attempting to do something about it the London Economic Conference had just collapsed. Germany had defaulted on her reparations and President Hoover had asked for a year's moratorium on all intergovern-

[15] Denys P. Myers, *Handbook of the League of Nations* (Boston: World Peace Foundation, 1935), p. 288.

[16] Benjamin H. Williams, *The United States and Disarmament* (New York: McGraw-Hill Book Company, 1931), pp. 238–239.

mental debts. Japan had begun her invasion of Manchuria. Germany had just concluded a customs union with Austria, to the consternation of France and other countries, and she was openly threatening to break the Versailles Treaty if denied arms equality with the leading powers. Hitler was rising, and indeed came into power while the conference was in session. The Fascists in Italy and the Communists in Russia were scheming to use the conference for demagogic ends. France was determined that effective security arrangements must precede disarmament, and Britain and the United States were not prepared to commit themselves unreservedly to the defense of European frontiers. In this sombre atmosphere the World Disarmament Conference at Geneva dragged on intermittently for twenty-eight months before it adjourned, never to meet again. Its collapse marked the end of disarmament efforts by the League of Nations.

The League was proving impotent to insure the peace, and states were falling back on their own right arms to protect themselves against the growing threat from Germany, Italy, and Japan. "The letters of FAILURE, written large over the portals of successive disarmament conferences during the two decades after Versailles, became letters of impending catastrophe for all the Western world."[17]

The Mandates System

The mechanism set up by the League for the administration of the colonial areas taken from Germany and Turkey by the Allied and Associated Powers was the Mandates System. To supervise it the League established the Permanent Mandates Commission, with authority to receive reports from the mandatory powers, hear petitions, and make recommendations to the League Council, where alone positive action could be taken.

The fourteen mandated regions were divided into three groups, known as A, B, and C. The A mandates applied to those areas which, with some supervisory assistance, might be expected to reach statehood within a comparatively short period of time. Of the five in this group — all Turkish — Iraq, Palestine, and Transjordan were mandated to Great Britain and Syria and Lebanon to France. The B mandates applied to areas where greater assistance would be required and where independence would probably be long delayed. The six areas of the B group were all former German colonies in Africa. Great Britain was given supervision over Tanganyika and a part of Togoland and the Cameroons; Belgium, over Ruanda-Urundi. In the A and B classes the mandatory powers were to assert no special economic advantages over other states, and they were to discharge their obligations with the moral, cultural, and economic welfare of the natives as the first consideration.

Of the five C mandates, huge but sparsely populated German South-West Africa was entrusted to the contiguous Union of South Africa; Western Samoa went to New Zealand; German New Guinea and the German South Pacific islands to Australia; the German North Pacific islands to Japan; and Nauru jointly to Great Britain, Australia, and New Zealand. These areas were to be administered as integral parts of the mandatory states, with self-determination only a remote possibility.

The chief weapon which the Mandates Commission could use in support of its authority was publicity. When, through constant observation and inquiry, it found a mandatory state guilty of improper practices or incompetent administration, publication of the facts usually produced quick removal of the evils. Among the matters subject to its scrutiny were the slave trade, the arms and liquor traffic, the building of fortifica-

[17] Frederick L. Schuman, *International Politics*, 6th ed. (New York: McGraw-Hill Book Company, 1958), p. 255.

tions, the training of natives for military purposes, freedom of conscience and religion, land tenure, wages, health, and the economic equality of trading states.

Within ten years Britain had chaperoned Iraq into the League of Nations, an accomplishment that may have been due more to British insistence than to any conviction of the Mandates Commission that statehood was actually warranted.[18] Syria was proclaimed a republic in 1944, but the last French occupation forces were not withdrawn until 1946. Lebanon became independent soon after the beginning of World War II; Transjordan and Palestine had to wait until the close of the war. All B and C mandates were still under the supervision of the Permanent Mandates Commission when, on April 18, 1946, the Trusteeship Council of the UN assumed the functions of the Mandates Commission. All former Class B mandates have since been incorporated into independent states.

The Protection of Minorities

The protection of minorities' rights was entrusted to the League of Nations and became the specific responsibility of the Council. In undertaking to set up appropriate machinery, the Council tried to keep two objectives in mind: the protection of minorities for both humanitarian and political reasons and the safeguarding of the sensibilities of the states in which the minorities lived. The procedure agreed upon was a compromise between international supervision and meticulous regard for sovereignty.

Statistically, the League's record in the handling of minority complaints was rather impressive. By 1935 it had examined nearly four hundred petitions, and of the 271 examined during the last five years of that period 192 were regarded as "finished." It seems beyond question that the League reduced the oppression of minorities, discouraged the aggressive intercession of outside states, asserted the interest of the whole international community in the welfare of minorities, and established usable precedents for the attack on minority problems.

Nevertheless, it may be doubted that the League effected any final solutions; it certainly did not silence the complaints of discrimination. Devoted to removing tensions that might provoke war, the system never gave a straightforward answer to the important question whether it sought to lead minorities into an eventual assimilation by the preponderant ethnic group or, on the other hand, sought to protect and promote the cultural individuality of the different minorities. The first of these objectives was naturally preferred by dominant ethnic groups, the second by minority groups.

The Nonpolitical Activities of the League

The League's work in "all spheres of human activity where there were common international interests to be served" has come to be spoken of as its "nonpolitical activities." The program was amazingly broad and its success so impressive that it is universally regarded as the League's outstanding achievement.

The Economic and Financial Organizations. The most important agencies of this organization were the Financial Committee and the Economic Committee. The Financial Committee advised the Council on financial matters in general, on financial assistance to governments, and on financial problems which might be solved by international action. The Economic Committee did the preliminary work on a number of major international conferences, notably the World Economic Conference of 1927 and the Monetary and Economic Conference of 1933. It engaged in studies and on occasion held special conferences on a wide range of problems of an economic nature: eco-

[18] Rupert Emerson, "Iraq: The End of a Mandate," *Foreign Affairs*, XI (January, 1933), 355–360.

nomic statistics, customs formalities, the standardization of commercial practices, tariffs, tourists, arbitration of commercial disputes, whaling, crop exports, currency stabilization, restrictive trade devices, cartels, animal diseases, unfair competition, and economic nationalism.

The Communications and Transit Organization. To implement Article 23 of the Covenant, "to make provision to secure and maintain freedom of communications and of transit and equitable treatment for the commerce of all members of the League," the autonomous Communications and Transit Organization was created and provided with a constitution in 1920. Among its interests were the following: the freedom of international transit, the collection of transit statistics, press facilities and the accuracy of reporting, the simplification of passports and other travel documents, regulations concerning international waterways, discrimination against foreign shipping in ports, regulations pertaining to buoyage and other maritime signals, the use of inland waterways, tonnage measurement, the codification of the permanent obligations of states regarding railway transport, the uniformity of highway traffic regulations, the transmission of electric power across state lines, calendar reform (this involved the study of 185 schemes), the stabilization of Easter, the coordination of national public works programs, and oil pollution of the sea.

The Health Organization. Fulfilling a promise in Article 23 of the Covenant that the League "will endeavor to take steps in matters of international concern for the prevention and control of disease," the Health Organization was set up in 1923 and equipped with a Health Committee and a secretariat. It cooperated closely with governments, performing an incalculable service in reporting on epidemics and their spread, helping to improve national health work, conducting technical conferences, studying medical resources, assisting in the interchange of information, promoting the standardization of biological products, drafting sanitation projects, and organizing action against malaria, cancer, tuberculosis, syphilis, smallpox, heart disease, leprosy, rabies, and other afflictions. It performed notable work in combating infant mortality, collecting statistics, fixing dietary standards, and controlling plagues. It received substantial assistance from the Rockefeller Foundation. By the mid-1930's the labors of the Health Organization had assumed great proportions and they had become perhaps the least criticized phase of League activity.

Refugee Care. World War I created the problem of the care and resettlement of millions of war prisoners and displaced persons. By 1934 the League had provided assistance to nearly four millions of these, the largest groups being Russians, Greeks, and Armenians. Although the resettlement of a million persons still remained to be accomplished in 1934, the work seemed well on the way to completion when it was complicated by Hitler's expulsion of the Jews. The driving force behind the resettlement of refugees from 1920 to 1930 was Dr. Fridtjof Nansen, acting as High Commissioner for Refugees. On his death in 1930 the Nansen International Office for Refugees was established in his honor. The contribution of the League to refugee relief was largely that of coordination, with funds being provided by states with refugees and by private charitable groups.

Intellectual Cooperation. The League Council in 1922 appointed an International Committee on Intellectual Cooperation, which as its first task sought to assist intellectuals in devastated areas. The International Institute of Intellectual Cooperation, set up at Paris in 1926, assumed the functions of an executive organ for League activities in this field. It sought to coordinate "international collaboration with a view to promoting the progress of general civilization and human knowledge, and notably the development and diffusion of science, letters, and arts."[19] Some of the ventures in intellectual cooperation were aimed directly at building public opinion against war, such as the use of conferences, lectures, and published materials to urge collective security, support of the League, moral disarmament, the study of public affairs, and the elimination of inflammatory material from textbooks and radio broadcasts.

The League's program of good works extended into other areas of cooperation: control of the opium traffic, the promotion of child welfare, the extinction of slavery, prison reform, the prohibition of traffic in women, the suppression of trade in obscene publications, and various relief projects.

Secretary of State Cordell Hull, writing in 1939, said that "the League of Nations has been responsible for more humanitarian and scientific endeavor than any other organization in history,"[20] and Arthur Sweetser, analyzing the nonpolitical achievements of the League, declared in 1940 that "the experience has been deeply valuable, for it marks a phase in the slow transition of mankind from international anarchy to the world community."[21]

The League after Fifteen Years

The discerning observer of 1935 must have suspected that the League of Nations was doomed. True enough, he could have pointed to a host of impressive achievements in nonpolitical cooperation, but the drive for collective security had taken the League from one qualified commitment to another, each reflecting on the adequacy of the others and all lacking visible means of enforcement. Despite increasing collaboration, the United States was still outside the League; and the resignations of Japan and Germany would become effective during the year. Disarmament efforts had come to a halt, and the great powers were about to begin a race for naval strength, with all treaty limitations abandoned. Reparations was a dead letter, and so was the restriction on German rearmament. The League Council had stood impotently if not silently by when Japan had invaded Manchuria and laid her plans for the conquest of China proper. Mussolini had found his excuse for the subjugation of Ethiopia, and his legions were ready to intervene in Spain. Hitler could no longer be ignored, for he was already the master of Germany and had begun the marshalling of Germany's strength to execute the plans of *Mein Kampf*. The Nazi underground had shackled Austria.

In December, 1934, Italian and Ethiopian troops had clashed at Wal Wal, some fifty miles within Ethiopian territory. Both sides appealed at once to the League of Nations. Not until September of the following year did the Council take up the dispute. The Italians recited a tale of abuse by the Ethiopians and declared that League states were really under no obligation to observe the Covenant when dealing with a backward and uncivilized state such as Ethiopia; and when the Ethiopians, in turn, presented their case to the Council the Italians walked out to avoid contamination from the representatives of a "barbarous" state. Sanctions against Italy were approved by the votes of fifty-one states, but as their effective use depended upon the full support of Britain and France the attitude of those powers was decisive. Both of them, but particularly France, wanted to be able to count on Italian support against possible aggression by Hitler's Germany. Out of British retreat and French desperation came the infamous

[19] Myers, p. 184.

[20] Warren O. Ault, *Europe in Modern Times* (Boston: D. C. Heath & Company, 1946), p. 643.

[21] "The Non-Political Achievements of the League," *Foreign Affairs*, XIX (October, 1940), 192.

Hoare-Laval Plan. In a pact signed in December, 1935, the two foreign ministers agreed to delay oil sanctions, to avoid military sanctions, and to offer to placate Mussolini by giving him about two-thirds of Ethiopia. When the plan was prematurely disclosed, Hoare was forced to resign. In effect, so too was the League.

The Manchurian affair of 1931 had dealt the League a savage blow, but not necessarily a fatal one. To check Japan was one thing — she was a power of the first rank, she operated far from the bases of the other great powers, and Russia was not then a member of the League; to check Italy was another — she was a third-rate power, she was far more vulnerable, and the Soviet Union was in the League and was urging effective sanctions. While the United States, outside the League, discouraged the imposition of sanctions by her uncertain attitude and so must bear some of the guilt, "French and British anxiety to avoid war with Italy at almost any cost proved to be the decisive factor."[22] From the blow of the Ethiopian War the League never recovered. It took virtually no hand in the Spanish Civil War. The Loyalists made several appeals to it, but it did nothing beyond giving moral support to the nonintervention formula and later helping to supervise the withdrawal of foreign volunteers. The League played no significant part in the events leading to the surrender at Munich in 1938 and to the outbreak of World War II less than a year later. It maintained a shadowy existence until 1946, when it was formally dissolved.

The United Nations

From the earliest stages of World War II people everywhere assumed that some kind of world organization would be established after the final victory of the Allied powers. The statesmen of the West hoped that the nations would profit from the League experience and that the generation which had reaped the bitter fruits of two world wars, a worldwide depression, mass extermination on a scale unprecedented in history, and threats to human freedom everywhere would be more earnestly committed than ever before to the building of a stronger and more equitable international order in which a new world organization would play a central role. The organization which emerged was, of course, the United Nations.

Laying the Foundations

The Charter of the United Nations was signed by representatives of fifty nations in the city of San Francisco on June 26, 1945. During the war many meetings, conferences, and declarations had laid the foundation for the United Nations and had prepared the way for final agreement on the terms of the Charter. The planning which went on was necessarily conducted in private, mostly by "experts" on a national rather than an international scale, and was overshadowed by the wartime activities. A great deal of planning was also done on a concerted basis at several international conferences. The most important of these conferences, and their main results, were the following:

1. *The Atlantic Charter, August 14, 1941.* This is often referred to as marking the birth of the United Nations. In this document Prime Minister Churchill and President Roosevelt, meeting on a battleship in the North Atlantic, laid down eight general principles "on which they base their hopes for a better future for the world."

2. *The Declaration of the United Nations, January 1, 1942.* In this declaration, issued a few weeks after Pearl Harbor and using the name later adopted for the new international organization, twenty-six nations agreed to cooperate in war and in peace.

3. *The Casablanca Conference, January, 1943.* Churchill and Roosevelt, meet-

[22] C. Grove Haines and Ross J. S. Hoffman, *The Origins and Background of the Second World War* (New York: Oxford University Press, 1943), p. 385.

ing with French representatives in the North African city of Casablanca, planned the invasion of Sicily and Italy, agreed on an "unconditional surrender" formula, talked over terms of peace, and discussed the role of their countries in the postwar period.

4. *The Food and Agriculture Conference of May–June, 1943,* at Hot Springs, Virginia. Representatives of forty-four nations studied the problems of feeding millions of displaced persons, and laid the groundwork for activities that led to the establishment of the Food and Agriculture Organization in late 1945.

5. *The Moscow Conference, October–November, 1943.* In this important conference the foreign ministers of Great Britain, Russia, and the United States, and the Chinese ambassador to Russia, on behalf of their governments, pledged that "their united action" would be "continued for the organization and maintenance of peace and security," and declared that they recognized "the necessity of establishing at the earliest practicable date a central international organization, based on the principle of the sovereign equality of all peace-loving states and open to membership by all such states, large and small." This declaration was particularly significant in that it marked the first time that the Soviet Union had agreed in specific terms to the establishment of a world organization after the war.

6. *The Teheran Conference, November, 1943.* This was the first of two meetings of Churchill, Roosevelt, and Stalin. In a joint statement they promised "that large and small nations would be invited to join a world organization."

7. *The Bretton Woods Conference, July, 1944,* "the financial half of the Conference in San Francisco." Representatives of forty-four nations, acting on the assumption that no peace could last if economic and financial chaos prevailed, drew up agreements establishing two important institutions: (1) the International Bank for Reconstruction and Development, and (2) the International Monetary Fund. Both are now actively functioning as specialized agencies of the United Nations.

8. *The Dumbarton Oaks Conference in Washington, D. C., September–October, 1944.* Here representatives of China, Great Britain, the U.S.S.R., and the United States drafted "Proposals for a General International Organization," the first draft of the United Nations Charter. These Proposals were briefer than the final Charter, particularly in respect to economic and functional organization, but the basic resemblance between the two documents was striking.

9. *The Yalta Conference, February, 1945.* Meeting in the Crimea for their second and final conference, Churchill, Roosevelt, and Stalin not only drafted plans for the occupation and control of defeated Germany and for keeping order in liberated Europe and made fateful decisions in secret agreements regarding Eastern Europe and the Far East but also agreed on the "veto" formula later embodied in the UN Charter and called for a full-scale United Nations Conference to convene in San Francisco on April 25, 1945.

10. *The Mexico City Conference, February–March, 1945.* Representatives of twenty American republics — the United States and all the Latin American countries except Argentina — here discussed questions of inter-American defense and cooperation, including the conditions under which Argentina could resume her full participation in inter-American affairs; and they adopted the "Act of Chapultepec" — a far-reaching understanding on the defense of the Americas — and prepared for the forthcoming San Francisco Conference.

11. *Committee of Jurists' Meeting, Washington, D. C., April, 1945.* Jurists from forty-four nations drew up a "Draft Statute and Report," which in amended form became the Statute of the International Court of Justice.

12. *The San Francisco Conference, April 25–June 26, 1945.* This was the cul-

mination of the steps leading to the emergence of the United Nations. The proceedings and records of the San Francisco Conference — the United Nations Conference on International Organization — have been published in fifteen volumes, and voluminous commentaries have been written upon both the conference and the Charter.[23]

The conference "was organized in four Commissions and twelve Committees, most of the actual work being done in the Committees. A Coordination Committee and a Committee of Jurists put the pieces together into a final document; there was a Steering Committee to guide the work and resolve problems; and above all were the Big Five meetings in the penthouse on top the Hotel Fairmont."[24]

At San Francisco the principles of national sovereignty and of great-power unanimity were written into the Charter. China and France, as well as the "Big Three," were given permanent seats on the Security Council, and the voting formula agreed upon at Yalta, giving the permanent members of the Council a veto on all important questions, was incorporated into Article 27. Temporary flurries arose over innumerable issues, large and small, such as the admission of the Ukraine and Byelorussia, Argentina, and Poland, the relative powers of the General Assembly and the Security Council, and voting procedure in the Security Council. Spokesmen of smaller powers, notably Herbert Evatt of Australia, took strong exception to the favored position of the great powers in the new organization. But the delegates made the necessary compromises, accepted many imperfections, and in the end created the United Nations.

On July 28, less than five weeks after the Charter had been signed, the United States approved American membership in the UN by a vote of 89 to 2. To many persons, recalling the refusal of the Senate to ratify the Covenant of the League of Nations, this vote symbolized America's new role in world affairs. Within another three months the Charter had been ratified by all of the permanent members of the Security Council and by a majority of the signatories; and on October 24, 1945, the United Nations was formally declared in being.

The Charter

The Charter of the United Nations clearly reveals the purposes and general nature of the new organization. This remarkable document contains more than ten thousand words, with 111 Articles divided into 19 Chapters. Article 1 states the broad purposes of the UN: "to maintain international peace and security," "to develop friendly relations among nations," "to achieve international cooperation in solving international problems of an economic, social, cultural, or humanitarian character, and in promoting and encouraging respect for human rights and for fundamental freedoms for all," and "to be a center for harmonizing the actions of nations." Article 2 declares that the UN is "based on the principle of the sovereign equality of all its Members," a statement well worth remembering. The bulk of the Charter is devoted to the provisions creating and controlling the principal organs. These are the General Assembly, the Security Council, the

[23] An excellent account of the San Francisco Conference, and of the origins of each provision of the Charter, is given in Leland M. Goodrich and Edvard Hambro, *Charter of the United Nations: Commentary and Documents,* 2d rev. ed. (Boston: World Peace Foundation, 1949). The basic documents of the San Francisco Conference were published in 15 volumes in 1945–46 by the United Nations Information Office, in cooperation with the Library of Congress, under the title *Documents of the United Nations Conference on International Organization, San Francisco, 1945.* A selection of these documents was published in one volume of 992 pages by the U.S. State Department in 1946: *The United Nations Conference on International Organization, San Francisco, California, April 25–June 26, 1945: Selected Documents,* Pub. 2490, Conference Series 83.

[24] Clyde Eagleton, *International Government,* rev. ed. (New York: The Ronald Press Company, 1948), pp. 300–301.

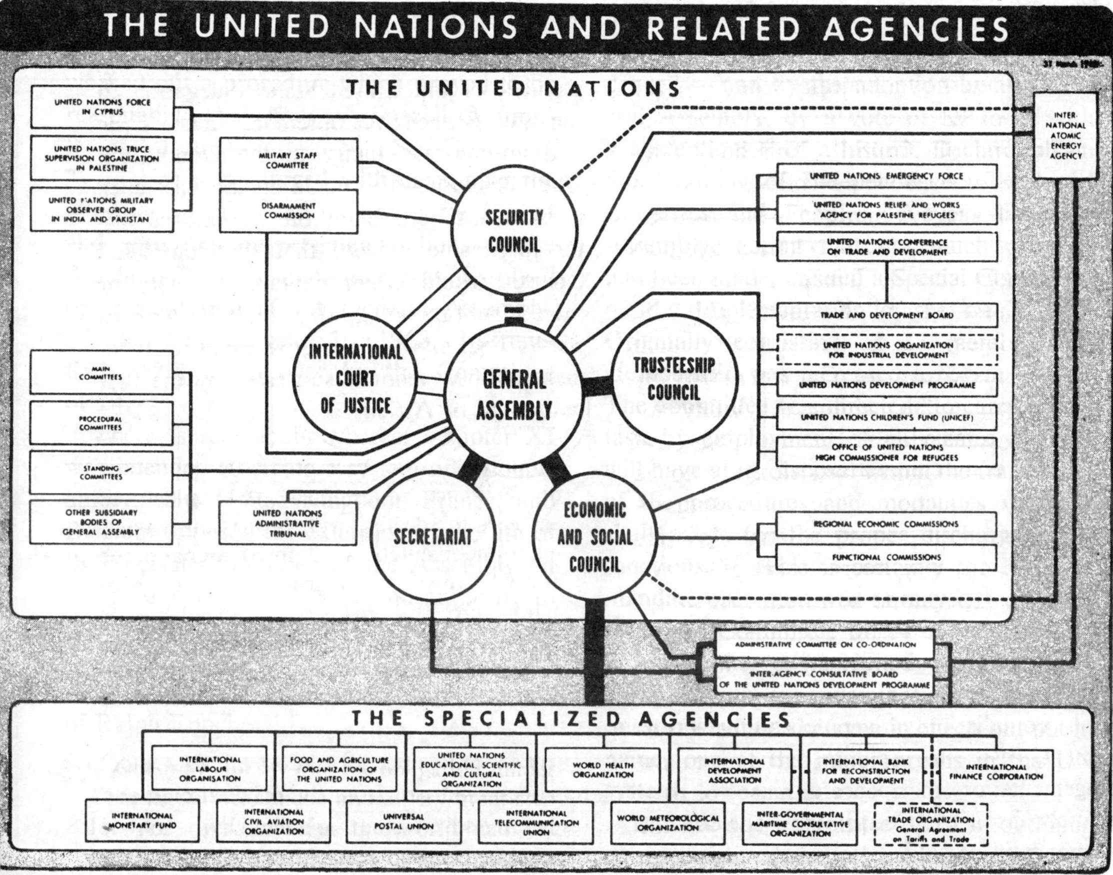

United Nations

Economic and Social Council, the Trusteeship Council, the International Court of Justice, and the Secretariat. The original members of the UN were the states represented at San Francisco, plus Poland, a total of fifty-one; but, according to Article 4 of the Charter, membership was "open to all other peace-loving states . . . able and willing to carry out these obligations" — a provision which has evoked sharp differences in interpretation.

The General Assembly. This body consists of all members of the UN, with each state having one vote and a maximum of five representatives. Its duties are to "discuss," "make recommendations," "consider," "call the attention," "notify," "initiate studies," and "receive and consider." Except in a limited field, it works largely through recommendations and advice to member states and to the Security Council; and it may not even make recommendations on matters already before the Security Council unless that body so requests.

The Assembly, however, was given broad supervisory and investigative responsibilities. It possesses authority in respect to UN finances, certain matters relating to non-self-governing territories, the election of members of the Security Council, the Economic and Social Council, and the Trusteeship Council; on the recommendation of the Security Council it admits states to membership in the UN; and it shares with the Security Council the duty of electing judges to the International Court of Justice. Decisions on important questions are made "by two-thirds majority of the members present and voting" and on all other matters by a majority vote.

The Security Council. This body originally consisted of eleven members of the UN, each having one representative. In 1965 the Council was expanded to fifteen, five permanent members — China, France, the U.S.S.R., the United Kingdom, and the United States — and ten nonpermanent members elected by the General Assembly for two-year terms, without eligibility for immediate re-election.

The Security Council was designed to be the UN's only action agency; it was therefore charged with primary responsibility for the "maintenance of international peace and security." If parties to a dispute fail to exhaust the procedures for pacific settlement, the Security Council may call upon them "to seek a solution by negotiation, inquiry, mediation, conciliation, arbitration, judicial settlement, resort to regional agencies or arrangements, or other peaceful means of their own choice." The Council may also ask the members of the United Nations to apply such measures as "complete or partial interruption of economic relations and of rail, sea, air, postal, telegraphic, radio, and other means of communication, and the severance of diplomatic relations"; and it may even "take such action by air, sea or land forces as may be necessary," using the "armed forces, assistance, and facilities" that UN member states are pledged to provide.

Articles 51–54 in a sense qualify the authority of the Security Council. Article 51 states that "nothing in the present Charter shall impair the inherent right of individual or collective self-defense if an armed attack occurs against a Member of the United Nations, until the Security Council has taken the measures necessary to maintain international peace and security." This article has figured prominently in debates on the North Atlantic Pact, the Rio Treaty, and other regional arrangements for collective defense. According to Harold E. Stassen, a leading member of the United States delegation to the San Francisco Conference, this "basic and important" change in the Dumbarton Oaks Proposals was made on the insistence of the United States and other countries "after it became evident that the completed Charter would either contain the veto or there would be no Charter at all."[25] Articles 52–54 deal expressly with regional arrangements. Their tenor is suggested by the first paragraph of Article 52:

> Nothing in the present Charter precludes the existence of regional arrangements or agencies for dealing with such matters relating to the maintenance of international peace and security as are appropriate for regional action, provided that such arrangements or agencies and their activities are consistent with the Purposes and Principles of the United Nations.

Economic and Social Council. ECOSOC has been enlarged from the original eighteen to twenty-seven states of the UN, each of which has one representative with one vote. It has been established as the chief coordinating agency of the UN in promoting the following important objectives:

> (a) higher standards of living, full employment, and conditions of economic and social progress and development;
> (b) solutions of international economic, social, health, and related problems; and international cultural and educational cooperation; and
> (c) universal respect for, and observance of, human rights and fundamental freedoms for all without distinction as to race, sex, language, or religion.

The Council's instruments are studies, recommendations, conferences, and coordination activities, carried out by special com-

[25] Address at the Model General Assembly of the United Nations, Rutgers University, New Brunswick, New Jersey, March 30, 1949.

mittees and by regional and functional commissions. It is charged with coordinating the activities of the specialized agencies "through consultation with and recommendations to such agencies and through recommendations to the General Assembly and to the Members of the United Nations." It is authorized to deal directly with nongovernmental organizations.

The Trusteeship Council. Chapter XI of the Charter — "Declaration Regarding Non-Self-Governing Territories" — opens with these words: "Members of the United Nations which have or assume responsibilities for the administration of territories whose people have not yet attained a full measure of self-government recognize the principle that the interests of the inhabitants of these territories are paramount." These words constitute the most specific recognition of the rights of native peoples that has ever been incorporated into a major international document.

Chapter XII provides for an international trusteeship system, to apply to territories which come within the following categories: "(a) territories now held under mandate; (b) territories which may be detached from enemy states as a result of the Second World War; and (c) territories voluntarily placed under the system by states responsible for their administration." The objectives of the system are declared to be: the furtherance of international peace and security; the promotion of all the interests of the inhabitants of trust territories, including progress toward self-government or independence; the encouragement of respect for human rights and for fundamental freedoms without distinction of race, sex, language, or religion; and the insurance of equal treatment for UN members and their nationals in all respects in the trust areas. Except for certain strategic areas, which are the direct concern of the Security Council, the functions of the United Nations with regard to trust territories are performed by the General Assembly and, more immediately, by the Trusteeship Council.

The International Court of Justice. The Statute of the Court adopted at the San Francisco Conference was similar to the Statute of the earlier Permanent Court of International Justice. The changes were "comparatively trivial, and mostly for adaptation to the United Nations system."[26] The new Court is an integral part of the United Nations, whereas the Permanent Court of International Justice had been associated only indirectly with the League of Nations.

Members of the UN are *ipso facto* parties to the Statute of the Court, and other states may become parties to it. UN members pledge themselves to comply with the decisions of the Court, although they retain the right to use other tribunals. The General Assembly and the Security Council, and the other organs and specialized agencies of the UN, if authorized by the Assembly, may request advisory opinions. The Court itself consists of fifteen distinguished jurists, representing the major legal systems of the world. Its seat, like that of the earlier court, is at The Hague.

The Secretariat. Articles 97–101 of the Charter establish a Secretariat resembling that of the League of Nations. Its administrative head, the Secretary-General, is aided by several Deputy Secretaries-General in his direction of a staff of about four thousand advisers, experts, administrators, and clerks. Many of these are assigned to other organs and organizations of the UN. The Secretary-General is authorized to "bring to the attention of the Security Council any matter which in his opinion may threaten the maintenance of international peace and security." He and his staff are required to take an oath of loyalty to the principles of the UN, and they are enjoined from seeking or receiving in-

[26] **Eagleton, p. 346.**

structions from any state or from any authority "external to the Organization." More than two-thirds of the regular UN budget, which in 1967 was in excess of $130,000,000, is spent on the Secretariat.

Comparison of the UN with the League of Nations

The United Nations is not a super-state, nor is it a form of world government in any real sense of the term. It does not seek to supplant the normal channels of international relations or to supersede bilateral or multilateral arrangements of a local or regional character. Moreover, since the UN was designed to *maintain* peace rather than to *make* it, its emphasis is on accommodation rather than on coercion. Thus in its basic character the UN is very much like the League of Nations: both were set up as associations of sovereign states with only limited powers.

One important practical difference is that the League had as continuous members only two of the five great powers of the time, whereas both of the superpowers of the post-World War II period have been members of the UN since its inception. Since the United States never joined the League, and since Germany and Japan withdrew before the Soviet Union entered, the League of Nations never possessed the array of the world's power that is now present in the United Nations.

Professor Eagleton insisted that "although there is a resemblance between the two systems in structure and general appearance, fundamental differences show, when added up, that the United Nations is quite different in concept and character" from the League.[27] The most crucial point of difference is in the position of the great powers, which have been given a privileged position within the UN Security Council. The UN Charter was realistic enough to forswear any intention to provide for committing any great power to war against its will. Thus the UN is spoken of as based on "the principle of great power unanimity."

The UN has a number of general advantages over the League. It is a more flexible system, and more comprehensive in scope; in particular, its provisions and agencies for economic, social, and humanitarian advancement are more extensive and more definite. It gives greater latitude to the operation of regional organizations and to other agencies and agreements. The division of functions between the General Assembly and the Security Council of the UN is much more precise than that between the Assembly and the Council of the League. The General Assembly is more of a general directing agency under the Charter than was the Assembly under the Covenant, while the Security Council has been given greater responsibility for the maintenance of international peace and security than the League Council possessed. In spite of the veto in the Security Council, the voting procedure in UN organs is much less rigid than in the agencies of the League, where the unanimity rule generally prevailed.

Despite the differences, it is probably correct to regard the UN as basically similar to the League. This would seem to raise the question why it was necessary to set up a new organization. Could not the old one have been revamped and revitalized? If so, certainly a great deal of labor would have been saved, and many legal questions involving succession would have been avoided. The answer is that the League bore the stigma of failure, that it had unhappy memories for the Russians — they had been thrown out of it — and that it had been a party issue in the United States. The UN, it was hoped, could start with a clean slate.

Setting Up the UN Machinery

The Charter entered into force on October 24, 1945, but as early as November–December, 1944, even before the San Fran-

[27] "Covenant of the League of Nations and Charter of the United Nations: Points of Difference," *Department of State Bulletin,* August 19, 1945. Reprinted as Dept. of State Pub. 2442.

cisco Conference, representatives of fifty-two nations had laid the foundations of the International Civil Aviation Organization. From October 16 to November 1, 1945, delegates from forty-two states met in Quebec to establish the Food and Agriculture Organization. During the first two weeks of November representatives of forty-four nations met in Paris to draft a constitution for the United Nations Educational, Scientific and Cultural Organization. Between January 10 and February 15, 1946, the General Assembly met for the first time and began the real work of general organization.

Other organizational meetings were held in rapid order. The Security Council first met on January 17, 1946, in London. The Boards of Governors of the International Bank for Reconstruction and Development and of the International Monetary Fund held a preliminary joint meeting on March 8 near Savannah, Georgia. The inaugural session of the International Court of Justice convened on April 3 at The Hague. The Atomic Energy Commission held its first meeting on June 14; and an International Health Conference, with representatives from sixty-one nations, convened in the same month to draft a constitution for a World Health Organization. From these beginnings international meetings and conferences under UN auspices soon became a regular occurrence.

The General Assembly. The General Assembly has held regular annual sessions. The First, Third, and Seventh Sessions were held in two parts; most of the others have been continuous meetings of several weeks' duration, usually from September or October into December. Undoubtedly the most unproductive session was the Nineteenth, which was a victim of the impasse over the issue of voting rights of members more than two years in arrears in payment of dues. This session met intermittently from December 1, 1964, to February 18, 1965, but it was able to conduct only the absolute minimum of business required to keep the organization going. It was resumed briefly in September, 1965.

Two special sessions — one in 1947 and another in 1948 — considered the Palestine question. A third was called in 1961, following the Franco-Tunisian clash at Bizerte, and a fourth in 1963 to consider the UN's financial dilemma. Up to 1968 five brief emergency special sessions had been held: two in November, 1956, on the Suez and Hungarian crises; one in August, 1958, on the Lebanon-Jordan question; one in September, 1960, on the situation in the Republic of the Congo (Leopoldville); and one in June–July, 1967, on the Arab-Israeli conflict.

As its First Session the Assembly established six main committees to deal with problems covering the entire range of the work of the United Nations: (1) Political and Security; (2) Economic and Financial; (3) Social, Humanitarian, and Cultural; (4) Trusteeship; (5) Administrative and Budgetary; and (6) Legal. The chairmen of these committees, together with the president and seven vice presidents of the Assembly, constituted a general or steering committee. The first Assembly also elected the nonpermanent members of the Security Council and the members of the Economic and Security Council, approved the recommendation of the Security Council that Trygve Lie of Norway be appointed Secretary-General, participated in the election of the fifteen judges of the International Court of Justice, established the Atomic Energy Commission, provided for the organization of the Secretariat, approved the constitution of the International Refugee Organization, set up the International Children's Emergency Fund, assumed various functions of UNRRA[28] and the League of Nations, took over certain assets of the League, authorized the creation of specialized agencies responsible to the

[28] The United Nations Relief and Rehabilitation Administration (UNRRA), despite its name, had no administrative relationship to the United Nations organization.

Economic and Social Council, and established a number of special committees, ad hoc committees, and subcommittees. In addition, the First Session took a great many other steps to complete its organization, select its working personnel, and effect coordination with other organs and agencies of the UN and with outside bodies.

In later sessions the General Assembly has further elaborated its machinery, mostly by the addition of committees and commissions to enable it to carry out its constantly expanding functions. It has retained the six main committees and added a seventh — the Ad Hoc Political Committee — to share the heavy burden of work which fell on the Political and Security Committee. It has established a special Committee on the Balkans, a Conciliation Commission for Palestine, an International Law Commission, a Commission on Korea, a Peace Observation Commission, and a Collective Measures Committee. It set up the United Nations Relief and Works Agency for Palestine Refugees to aid and resettle the more than 800,000 people who became refugees as a result of the Israeli-Arab conflicts, and the United Nations Korean Reconstruction Agency to assist war-damaged Korea.

The political role of the General Assembly has expanded well beyond the intentions of the framers of the Charter, largely as a result of the virtual impotence of the Security Council in the face of great power differences. This has been particularly marked since the Korean War and the passage of the Uniting for Peace Resolution in November, 1950. The comparative increase in the Assembly's power at the expense of the Security Council has altered the character of the UN as an instrument for the maintenance of peace and security. The Assembly still can only make recommendations in this field, but its recommendations may have considerable weight.

The Second Session of the Assembly voted to create an Interim Committee to meet whenever circumstances required during the interval between the Second and Third Sessions. The committee functioned so satisfactorily that some expectation developed that it might become permanent. Indeed, it became known as the Little Assembly. But after 1948 its use declined until by 1950 or 1951 it had ceased to operate altogether. The Assembly itself, through longer sessions and regular and special committees and commissions, took over the work of the Interim Committee.

The Security Council. This key organ of the UN has been in continuous session since it was organized in January, 1946. As authorized in the Charter, it has adopted its own rules of procedure. The presidency rotates among the members of the Council, changing the first of every month. To assist it in discharging its functions in the security field, three agencies were made directly responsible to the Council: (1) the Military Staff Committee, provided for in Article 47 of the UN Charter and established in early 1946; (2) the Commission on Conventional Armaments, set up in 1947; and (3) the Atomic Energy Commission, created by the Assembly in 1946. In January, 1952, the latter two commissions were merged into a Disarmament Commission. The work of these agencies will be described in the following chapter. Unfortunately, none has been very active or very effective.

The Security Council has set up other committees and commissions as occasion has required. One was the Good Offices Committee for Indonesia, replaced in January, 1949, by the UN Commission for Indonesia, which performed useful work as mediator in negotiations between representatives of the Dutch government and leaders of the Indonesian Republic. Others are the Commission on India and Pakistan, the Truce Commission on Palestine, and the Technical Committee on Berlin Currency and Trade.

Although the Security Council was envisioned as the central agency of the United Nations, it has not been able to play its expected role. The reason is clear. Instead of great power unanimity, on which the United Nations was predicated, the postwar years have brought major rifts and disagreements among the most powerful states of the world. Under these circumstances, the Security Council, in which five permanent members possess an individual veto, has been unable to function effectively. Since the Korean War and the return of the Russian representative to the Security Council on August 1, 1950, the Council has faded into the background, and its place has been taken in considerable measure by the unwieldy General Assembly, which was not designed to play a major role in the security field.

The Economic and Social Council. Normally the Economic and Social Council has met at least twice a year. During 1946 and 1947 its sessions were devoted largely to organizational matters and to working out operating relationships with various specialized agencies, but in 1948 it began to deal primarily with substantive questions. Since its mandate covers virtually the whole field of international nonpolitical activities, it always has a very crowded agenda.

Because ECOSOC serves as coordinator for an elaborate network of commissions, specialized agencies and committees, plus a number of agencies financed by voluntary contributions from member governments, much of the time of ECOSOC members is devoted to a review of the work of these agencies and commissions. They are also charged with consideration of solutions relating to problems within their purview, consultation with many nongovernmental organizations, and supervision of the several conferences of a general or specialized nature that are held under the auspices of ECOSOC each year.

Functional and Regional Commissions under ECOSOC. ECOSOC oversees nine functional and four regional commissions.[29] The functional commissions are: (1) Transport and Communications; (2) Statistical; (3) Fiscal; (4) Population; (5) Social, with a close connection with the International Children's Emergency Fund; (6) Human Rights, with subcommittees on Freedom of Information and of the Press; (7) Status of Women; (8) Narcotic Drugs; and (9) International Commodity Trade. The following regional commissions are now in existence: (1) the Economic Commission for Europe, with headquarters in Geneva; (2) the Economic Commission for Asia and the Far East, with headquarters in Bangkok; (3) the Economic Commission for Latin America, with headquarters in Santiago; and (4) the Economic Commission for Africa, with headquarters in Addis Ababa.

In 1951 the whole rather cumbersome structure of committees and commissions under the Economic and Social Council was subjected to a searching review. ECOSOC considered proposals for the elimination of most of its subordinate agencies, with the work of these bodies to be taken on by ECOSOC itself, by groups of experts, and by the Secretariat.[30] These proposals were not adopted, but the problem of coordination of an intricate pattern of agencies and commissions is still a baffling one.

Specialized Agencies and other UN-affiliated Functional Agencies. Eleven specialized agencies are now fully organized and affiliated with the Economic and Social Council. These are as follows, with alphabetical designation, date of formation, and headquarters also noted:

1. Universal Postal Union (UPU, 1875, Berne)
2. International Labor Organization (ILO, 1919, Geneva)

[29] The Economic, Employment and Development Commission, created in 1946, was abolished in 1951.

[30] We are indebted to Dr. H. W. Singer of the Economic and Social Affairs Department of the UN Secretariat for this information.

3. International Telecommunication Union (ITU, 1934, Geneva)
4. International Bank for Reconstruction and Development (IBRD, 1944, Washington)
5. International Monetary Fund (IMF, 1944, Washington)
6. International Civil Aviation Organization (ICAO, 1944, Montreal)
7. Food and Agriculture Organization (FAO, 1945, Rome)
8. United Nations Educational, Scientific and Cultural Organization (UNESCO, 1945, Paris)
9. World Health Organization (WHO, 1946, Geneva)
10. World Meteorological Organization (WMO, 1947, Lausanne)
11. Intergovernmental Maritime Consultative Organization (IMCO, 1947, London)

The International Refugee Organization (IRO), established in 1947 and affiliated with the UN as a specialized agency in 1948, was dissolved in 1951. Its successor — the Office of High Commissioner for Refugees — was not authorized to assume operational responsibilities, and with its limited budget, staff, and functions, plus the further handicap of the rather unsympathetic attitude of many governments, it has been unable to cope with the grave and continuing refugee problem.

In March, 1948, at the end of the International Conference on Trade and Employment, representatives of fifty-two nations signed the charter for an International Trade Organization (ITO) and established an Interim Commission. This commission (with headquarters in Geneva) is still functioning, but the ITO charter has not yet been approved by a sufficient number of states, and current prospects are not bright.

Many of the functions envisioned for the ITO have been carried on by the contracting parties to the General Agreement on Tariff and Trade (GATT). Twenty-three states participated in the negotiations which led to the conclusion of GATT in 1947. GATT has sponsored several major rounds of tariff negotiations among its members, which now number more than sixty. These negotiations affect well over half of all the world's trade.

At the International Conference on Trade and Development in 1964 the establishment of an ITO, apparently to be a new organization with a new charter, was strongly advocated; but this proposal ran afoul of the fundamentally divergent positions of the developing, advanced, and Communist state-trading countries. Instead, the conference itself was institutionalized and given a permanent organ, the Trade and Development Board, with three permanant committees and other subsidiary organs, and a permanent secretariat "within the United Nations Secretariat."

Three of the specialized agencies — the Universal Postal Union, the International Telecommunication Union, and the ILO, the one surviving agency of major importance associated with the League of Nations — are considerably older than the UN. Some of the specialized agencies, perhaps most of them, have absorbed or are working closely with much older organizations in the same field.

Other important functional organizations which are not specialized agencies but still have some affiliation with the United Nations are the United Nations Children's Fund (UNICEF, 1946, New York); the Office of the United Nations High Commissioner for Refugees (1951, Geneva); the International Atomic Energy Agency (IAEA, 1957, Vienna); the United Nations Development Program (UNDP, 1966, New York), formed by consolidating the Expanded Programme of Technical Assistance (EPTA, 1950, New York) and the Special Fund (1959, New York); the International Development Association (IDA, 1960, Washington), an affiliate of the International Bank for Reconstruction and Development which makes loans to underdeveloped countries on more flexible terms than those of the IBRD; and the International Finance Corporation (IFC, 1957, Washington), another IBRD affiliate which makes loans to private industrial enterprises without government guarantee.

Since they are concerned with all the basic economic and social problems of mankind, the specialized agencies and other UN-affiliated functional agencies have a great role to play in fostering international cooperation and in improving the life conditions of the people of the world. We are often inclined to take for granted such inestimable benefits as international mail service; improved labor standards; facilities for international communication by telegraph, telephone, cable, and radio; weather data from all parts of the world; more adequate food production and distribution; assistance in long-term reconstruction programs; reasonable foreign exchange procedure; high safety standards for international air travel; improved economic and cultural relations and educational facilities; assistance in fighting epidemics and plagues; and generally improved health standards.

Nongovernmental Organizations. Article 71 of the Charter states that "the Economic and Social Council may make suitable arrangements for consultations with nongovernmental organizations which are concerned with matters within its competence." To carry out this provision ECOSOC established three categories of nongovernmental organizations ("a," "b," and "c"), and appointed a committee to study applications for recognition from such organizations. Category "a" is designed to include "organizations which have a basic interest in most of the activities of the Council, and are closely linked with the economic or social life of the areas which they represent." There are at present nine organizations in this category: the World Federation of Trade Unions, the International Confederation of Free Trade Unions, the International Co-operative Alliance, the American Federation of Labor, the International Chamber of Commerce, the International Federation of Agricultural Producers, the Inter-Parliamentary Union, the International Organization of Employers, and the World Federation of United Nations Associations. Category "b" consists of "organizations which have a special competence but are concerned specifically with only a few of the fields of activity covered by the Council." There are about eighty-five organizations in this category. Category "c" contains more than a hundred organizations which have been placed on a register by the Secretary-General of the United Nations and have a consultative status on an ad hoc basis.

Altogether there are something like a thousand international nongovernmental organizations. Their general nature and importance are indicated in the following illuminating comment:

> These bodies are composed of private or unofficial groups in different countries which have formed a joint organization to promote some common interest. A large proportion of the people of the world are connected with one or more of these organizations, for they include in their membership nearly all the large churches, trade unions, businessmen's associations, co-operative societies, farmers' groups, and women's organizations, as well as numerous professional, scientific, humanitarian, and social reform organizations. They deal with almost every possible subject from theology to the Olympic games, from child welfare to astronomy, from cancer to the problems of labor, from aviation to women's rights. . . . Surely the time has come for the students and teachers of international affairs to realize that international nongovernmental organization is a great unexplored continent in the world of international affairs and that expeditions should be sent in search of the great riches to be found there. For it is there that one finds the most positive and constructive elements working for world unity.[31]

[31] Lyman C. White, "Peace by Pieces — The Role of Nongovernmental Organizations," *The Annals* of the American Academy of Political and Social Science, CCLXIV (July, 1949), 88, 95. See also the same author's *International Non-Governmental Organizations* (New Brunswick,

The Trusteeship Council. While the First Session of the General Assembly was in progress in the spring of 1946, all states which held class "B" and class "C" mandates under the League of Nations, with the notable exception of the Union of South Africa, announced their intention of placing their mandates under the international trusteeship system provided for in Chapters XII and XIII of the UN Charter. Although the drafting of agreements for the territories in question proved to be a difficult matter, on December 13, 1946, the Assembly finally approved eight trusteeship agreements. The Soviet Union voted against approval of all of them, holding that they violated the Charter in three respects: (1) "the states directly concerned," which had to approve the agreements, had never been identified; (2) the agreements made the trust territories integral parts of the administering states; and (3) the agreements failed to provide for approval by the Security Council of military arrangements in the trust territories. For these reasons the Soviet Union announced that she would not participate in the work of the Trusteeship Council; but her abstention lasted only until 1948.

The United States submitted a "strategic trusteeship" agreement for the former Japanese-mandated islands in the Pacific — the Marshall, Caroline, and Mariana Islands — to the Security Council; and in April, 1947, to the surprise of those who expected a Soviet veto, the Council approved the agreement.

The Trusteeship Council had completed most of its or ·nizational work by the end of the spring session in April–May, 1948. By the end of 1949 visiting missions had been sent to all of the trust territories under the International Trusteeship System. In the fall of 1950 the General Assembly placed Somaliland under the Trusteeship Council. Italy was thereby made a nonvoting participant in the meetings of the Trusteeship Council; since she was not a member of the UN, she could not be a full-fledged member.

Normally the Council, composed of equal numbers of members which administered trust territories and those which did not, met in regular sessions twice a year to examine reports by administering authorities, to consider petitions from inhabitants of trust territories, to review the reports of visiting missions, and to handle related matters. Reduced to only eight members, it now meets less frequently, for its work has been sharply curtailed. Of the original eleven trust territories, only two remain.

The International Court of Justice. The first session of the Court, held from April 3 to May 6, 1946, was devoted wholly to administrative and organizational matters. Although the services of the Court have not been used as often as was hoped, it has handed down a series of decisions and advisory opinions. In the period 1946–62, 34 disputes were brought before the Court, but for jurisdictional or other reasons no decisions were rendered in nearly half of these cases. The decisions have included a series of rulings in the Corfu Channel dispute between Great Britain and Albania; three ambiguous rulings in a dispute between Colombia and Peru over the right of asylum for Haya de la Torre, a well-known Peruvian political leader; a ruling that it did not have the authority to deal with Britain's charge against Iran in the oil nationalization issue; a judgment favorable to Norway in a fisheries dispute with Great Britain; an opinion favorable to the United States on the rights of American citizens in Morocco; and a ruling that Portugal had transit rights across Indian territory to its territorial enclaves north of Bombay for private persons, civil officials, and goods, but not for military personnel and supplies.

N.J.: Rutgers University Press, 1951), a study of nongovernmental organizations up to 1945. Dr. White was secretary of the Committee on Non-Governmental Organizations of ECOSOC.

By the end of 1962 the Court had given 13 advisory opinions. These included opinions on reparations for injuries suffered in the service of the UN; on the competence of the General Assembly in the admission of new members to the UN; on the interpretation of the peace treaties with Bulgaria, Hungary, and Rumania; on the international status of South-West Africa and South Africa's obligations as the mandatory power; on reservations to the Convention on Genocide; and on the legal authority of the General Assembly to apportion the expenses of the United Nations Emergency Force (UNEF) and the United Nations Operations in the Congo (ONUC) among the members as "expenses of the organization" within the meaning of Article 17 (2) of the Charter (the most controversial of all the Court's advisory opinions).

Other questions are now pending. Less than half of the member states of the UN — but including all of the Big Five except the Soviet Union — have accepted the compulsory jurisdiction of the Court in certain types of legal disputes. In 1948 Switzerland, not a member of the United Nations, became a party to the Statute of the Court.

The Secretariat. Much of the day-to-day work of the United Nations is done by the Secretariat, an international civil service drawn from many countries, with headquarters in New York City and a branch in the former seat of the League of Nations at Geneva. Three-fourths of the Secretariat's staff of more than four thousand persons normally work at UN headquarters in New York, in a thirty-nine story skyscraper of glass and steel which rises high above the East River in a rather unlovely section of the city at the foot of 42nd Street. Affiliated agencies of the UN employ more than ten thousand other persons.

The directing head of the Secretariat is the Secretary-General. Trygve Lie of Norway was the first occupant of this important post. His support of the UN action in Korea, however, aroused the ill will of the Russians, and in the fall of 1952 he resigned in order to remove a source of East-West friction. After a long deadlock the General Assembly on April 7, 1953, approved Dag Hammarskjold, a Swedish minister of state, as his successor. When Hammarskjold was killed in a plane crash in Africa on September 18, 1961, U Thant of Burma became acting Secretary-General; and on November 30, 1962, he was appointed Secretary-General for a term of office expiring in 1966. In 1966 he agreed somewhat reluctantly to serve another term.

There are now eight major departments in the Secretariat: (1) Security Council Affairs; (2) Economic Affairs; (3) Social Affairs; (4) Trusteeship and Information from Non-Self-Governing Territories; (5) Public Information; (6) Conference and General Services; (7) Administrative and Financial Services; and (8) Legal Department. On January 1, 1955, a rather thorough reorganization of the top command of the Secretariat, directed by Hammarskjold in the interests of efficiency and economy, went into effect. Ralph J. Bunche and Ilya S. Tchernychev were made Under Secretaries-General without portfolio, and five appointments were made of Under Secretaries-General with portfolio.

Besides the headquarters office in New York and the Geneva office, the Secretariat provides the staffs for small field services for the regional commissions, for several UN-affiliated agencies, and for information centers in more than forty cities throughout the world.

The Secretariat performs a multitude of undramatic but necessary and exacting tasks. It arranges for and services the meetings of the organs and agencies of the UN, a herculean job in itself. It prepares studies and background materials for meetings. It acts as the executive agent and provides secretarial services for the other principal organs, except the International Court of Justice. It provides information, through all available media and in as many countries as possible, on the purposes and activities of the UN.

The Present-Day Role of International Organizations

We have seen that some forms of international organization have existed throughout most of recorded history, and that most of the techniques and procedures that are customarily employed by the complex international organizations of today have been developed over a long period of time and in many parts of the world. The nineteenth century, in particular, developed techniques such as the administrative unions which have been of central importance to twentieth-century international organization. But nothing like the present complex pattern has ever existed before.

The formation of the League of Nations marked the beginning of a new era in the history of international organization; and the United Nations, essentially like the League, is even more comprehensive and more active — and, let us hope, more permanent. As we have noted, scores of organs, agencies, and commissions are affiliated with the United Nations system. There is hardly a phase of international life that does not come within its purview. It is limited in power by its very nature, but it is certainly not limited in the scope of its interests. Although it is by all odds the most comprehensive international organization in history, it does not embrace all the major organizations of the present day. Some of these, notably regional arrangements such as the North Atlantic Treaty Organization and the Organization of American States, are in many respects more powerful than the United Nations, although they are geographically and functionally more limited. Thus a study of present-day international organization must cover even more than the UN system; but some knowledge of this system is clearly a *must* for those who wish to understand how the world's work is being done.

SUGGESTIONS FOR FURTHER READING

ARNE, SIGRID. *United Nations Primer,* rev. ed. New York: Rinehart, 1948. Describes the steps leading to the San Francisco Conference of 1945.

BAILEY, SYDNEY D. *Secretariat in the United Nations,* rev. ed. New York: Frederick A. Praeger, 1964.

———. *The General Assembly of the United Nations; a Study of Procedure and Practice,* rev. ed. New York: Frederick A. Praeger, 1965.

BENTWICH, NORMAN and ANDREW MARTIN. *A Commentary on the Charter of the United Nations.* New York: The Macmillan Company, 1950.

BRIERLY, J. L. *The Covenant and the Charter.* New York: The Macmillan Company, 1947.

CECIL, LORD ROBERT. *A Great Experiment.* New York: Oxford University Press, 1941.

CHASE, EUGENE. *The United Nations in Action.* New York: McGraw-Hill Book Company, 1950.

CHEEVER, DANIEL S. and H. FIELD HAVILAND, JR., *Organizing for Peace: International Organization in World Affairs.* Boston: Houghton Mifflin Company, 1954. Detailed analyses of the League of Nations and the United Nations; also considerable attention to regional systems.

EAGLETON, CLYDE. *International Government,* rev. ed. New York: The Ronald Press Company, 1948.

Everyman's United Nations, 8th ed. New York: United Nations, 1968.

FRIEDRICH, CARL J. *Inevitable Peace.* Cambridge, Mass.: Harvard University Press, 1948.

GOODRICH, L. M. and E. I. HAMBRO. *Charter*

of the United Nations: Commentary and Documents, 2d rev. ed. Boston: World Peace Foundation, 1949. Still one of the best commentaries on the UN Charter.

HEMLEBEN, S. J. *Plans for World Peace Through Six Centuries.* Chicago: University of Chicago Press, 1943.

HOWARD-ELLIS, C. *The Origin, Structure and Working of the League of Nations.* Boston: Houghton Mifflin Company, 1928.

JOYCE, JAMES A. *World in the Making: the Story of International Cooperation.* New York: H. Schuman, 1953.

KELSEN, HANS. *The Law of the United Nations.* London, 1950. A formal analysis of the legal problems contained in the UN Charter.

KOHN, HANS. *World Order in Historical Perspective.* Cambridge, Mass.: Harvard University Press, 1943.

LEONARD, L. LARRY. *International Organization.* New York: McGraw-Hill Book Company, 1951.

LISSITZYN, OLIVER J. *The International Court of Justice.* New York: Carnegie Endowment for International Peace, 1951.

LUARD, EVAN, ed. *The Evolution of International Organization.* London, 1966.

MANGONE, GERARD J. *A Short History of International Organization.* New York: McGraw-Hill Book Company, 1954. A useful survey.

MARBURG. THEODOR. *Development of the League of Nations Idea.* 2 vols. New York: The Macmillan Company, 1932.

POTTER, PITMAN B. *An Introduction to the Study of International Organization,* 5th ed. New York: Appleton-Century-Crofts, 1948.

RAPPARD, W. E. *The Quest for Peace.* Cambridge, Mass.: Harvard University Press, 1940.

RUSSELL, RUTH B. *A History of the United Nations Charter.* Washington, D.C.: The Brookings Institution, 1958. A detailed and definitive record of the efforts between 1940 and 1945 to fashion a world organization, with particular attention to the role of the United States.

SCHWEBEL, S. M. *The Secretary-General of the United Nations.* Cambridge, Mass.: Harvard University Press, 1952.

United Nations Conference on International Organization: Selected Documents. Washington, D.C.: Government Printing Office, 1945.

United Nations Publications. See Appendix.

VANDENBOSCH, AMRY and WILLARD N. HOGAN. *The United Nations: Background, Organization, Functions, Activities.* New York: McGraw-Hill Book Company, 1952.

WALTERS, F. P. *A History of the League of Nations.* 2 vols. New York: Oxford University Press, 1952. The best history of the League.

WATKINS, JAMES T. and J. WILLIAM ROBINSON. *General International Organization.* Princeton, N.J.: D. Van Nostrand Co., 1956. A collection of 65 key documents.

ZIMMERN, SIR ALFRED. *The League of Nations and the Rule of Law.* London, 1936.

13 The United Nations: Political and Security Issues

The United Nations has been charged with vast responsibilities for the maintenance of international peace and security. According to Article I of the Charter, it is expected "to take effective collective measures for the prevention and removal of threats to the peace, and for the suppression of acts of aggression or other breaches of the peace, and to bring about by lawful means, and in conformity with the principles of justice and international law, adjustment or settlement of international disputes or situations which might lead to a breach of the peace." The procedures available for the discharge of these stupendous obligations are laid down in the Charter in elaborate detail, particularly in Articles 33–51. The chief responsibility rests with the Security Council, but the General Assembly has played an increasingly significant role in this field.

The UN also has great responsibilities in dealing with what are called "security problems." These relate not to one state's charges of aggression or other misconduct against another state but to the UN's obligation to promote conditions of general security so that breaches of the peace by any state will become less likely, and so that effective sanctions can be invoked if breaches do occur. More particularly, its responsibilities pertain to the performances of three specifically assigned security duties: (1) the placing of military forces at its disposal, (2) the regulation of armaments, and (3) the international control of atomic energy.

We shall examine in this chapter the UN's record in the handling of both political and security problems.

Political Issues

The most difficult task of the United Nations has been the adjustment of political disputes. In evaluating its work in this field certain broad considerations should be borne in mind. In the first place, it should be recalled that the Charter imposes primary responsibility on the Security Council but that under certain conditions the General Assembly may take a hand. We shall observe this in a number of instances. Second, it should be remembered that the Security Council is bound to no specific procedure; it is authorized to use any or all of several indicated ways of reaching a settlement, or it may devise ways of its own. Its preference is to induce the disputing parties to settle their differences by direct negotiation. Third, the distinction between political disputes and legal disputes should be kept in mind, but it should not be overemphasized. Generally speaking, political disputes go to the Security Council and/or the General Assembly and legal disputes to the International Court of Justice, but any attempt to divide all disputes into these two categories would lead to confusion.

The so-called peacekeeping operations have been perhaps the most dramatic and the most highly publicized of the multifarious activities of the United Nations. The "operations undertaken to date can be classified into four categories, although these are by no means clearly delineated: (1) observer groups to supervise cease-fires and truce lines, (2) military forces interposed between armies and used to patrol frontiers, (3) military forces with a mandate to curtail military conflict by all necessary means, and to assist in maintaining internal order, and (4) a military presence to prevent the expansion of a communal conflict. Examples of the first type include operations undertaken in the Balkans (1946–47); Indonesia (1947–49); Palestine (1947–64); Kashmir (1948–64); Lebanon (1958); West Irian (1962–63); and Yemen (1963–64). UNEF [the patrol on the Israeli border] is an example of the second; ONUC [the operation in the Congo] of the third; and UNFICYP [the Cyprus force] of the fourth."[1]

The record of the United Nations in dealing with the large number of political disputes brought before it has been varied. While no spectacular successes have been scored, the UN, as we shall see, has contributed, directly or indirectly, to the settlement of several controversies which might otherwise have become serious threats to world peace. A detailed analysis of almost any one of the disputes would require several volumes.[2] Here we can only summarize a few of them, after first pointing out the distinctive and interesting features of the "cases" to be reviewed.

1. Iran. This was the first dispute taken to the UN. It was settled entirely by direct negotiation on the urging of the Security Council.

2. Indonesia. Here the original complaint was brought by a Communist state. It was the first instance of the use of special commissions. After an early reluctance the defendant state cooperated to effect a satisfactory settlement.

3. Greece. This dispute was marked by persistent Communist aggression, repeated use of the veto, and substantial Assembly participation.

4. Kashmir. The India-Pakistan dispute produced the first important use of a personal mediator. The Security Council, which retained exclusive jurisdiction, was unable to accomplish anything beyond a continued truce.

5. Palestine. In this instance the dispute did not originate as a complaint. It involved a reversal of United States policy, concurrent action by the Security Council and the Assembly, and two special sessions of the Assembly. UN mediation helped to produce a cease-fire and an armistice but no final settlement.

6. Korea. Communist aggression in

[1] "Issues Before the Nineteenth General Assembly," *International Conciliation,* No. 550 (November, 1964), pp. 21–22. Julius Stone has suggested that the third category of operations could be subdivided according to the mandate given to the peacekeeping forces: "mere symbolic presence or interposition," "mere peacekeeping or 'policing' function," and "policy-enforcing function." "Legal Bases for the Establishment of Forces Performing United Nations Security Functions," a paper prepared for the Oslo Conference on United Nations Security Forces, February, 1964; quoted in *ibid.*, p. 21, n.9.

[2] More detailed accounts of these disputes may be found in the official records of the Security Council and the General Assembly. Excellent summaries are given in the annual *Yearbook of the United Nations;* in the pertinent issues of the *United Nations Bulletin* (until July, 1954), the *United Nations Review* (July, 1954 to May, 1964), and the *United Nations Chronicle* (since May, 1964); and in the annual reports of the President to the Congress on the activities of the United Nations and the participation of the United States therein (pursuant to the United Nations Participation Act of 1945). Also see *International Organization,* published quarterly by the World Peace Foundation.

Korea prompted the UN's first use of military sanctions. This has been the only test to date of the collective security provisions of the Charter. The results were inconclusive, as we noted in Chapter 10.

7. *Suez.* This crisis produced strange realignments in the Security Council, the first resort to the Uniting for Peace Resolution of 1950, and the first major peacekeeping operation by the UN (UNEF).

8. *Hungary.* By a fateful coincidence, the Hungarian and Suez crises reached a climax at approximately the same time. In Hungary, unlike Suez, UN efforts to compel a great power to suspend military operations and withdraw its forces proved to be unavailing. Hungary proved once again that the UN is particularly impotent in dealing with events inside the Communist world.

9. *The Congo.* Here the UN undertook its most massive operation, both in peacekeeping and in nation-building assistance. Undoubtedly it helped the Congo to survive in the difficult first years of independence. But the cost to the UN was very great, including an insupportable financial burden, the death of Secretary-General Dag Hammarskjold, bitter differences among UN members, and other stresses which jeopardized the future of the organization.

10. *Cyprus.* In the Cyprus crisis the United Nations undertook a limited operation, without incurring heavy financial obligations, which helped to avert a major clash on the troubled island. It has, however, had little success in its efforts to allay tensions between Greek and Turkish Cypriots, or between Greece and Turkey over the Cyprus issue.

11. *Arab-Israeli War, 1967.* In this crisis the United Nations was involved in many ways. Before the fighting, at Nasser's insistence, the United Nations Emergency Force was withdrawn, and after the ceasefire most of the refugees receiving assistance from the United Nations Relief and Works Agency were living in territories occupied by Israel. Although these developments, plus the differing positions of the United States and the Soviet Union and the reluctance of Israel to permit the UN any significant political role, left the world organization with a reduced role and a diminished presence in this part of the world, it was even more obvious than previously that the UN was about the only agency which was at least partially acceptable to both Israel and the Arab states.

1. Iran

On January 19, 1946, two days after the Security Council met for the first time, and before it could agree on matters of organization and procedure, Iran formally charged the Soviet Union with interference in her internal affairs and asked the Council to investigate and attempt to effect a settlement. Differences involved the continued presence of Russian troops in Iran, the alleged support by the Soviet Union of a revolt in the Iranian province of Azerbaijan, and the Russian demand for oil concessions in Iran.

Although the U.S.S.R. "categorically opposed" any discussion of the charges whatsoever, the Council the next day voted to ask the two governments to settle their differences by direct negotiation and to report to the Council on the progress of their consultations. On March 19 the Iranian government declared that the Soviet Union was "continuing to interfere in the internal affairs of Iran through the medium of Soviet agents, officials, and armed forces," and was maintaining troops in Iran beyond the period stipulated in the Tripartite Treaty of 1942, under which Allied troops had been stationed in Iran during World War II. When, on March 27, 1946, the Council voted down a Soviet motion to postpone consideration until April 10, Andrei Gromyko walked out of the Council chamber.

After examining Iranian and Soviet statements on the facts of the case, the Council on April 4 decided to defer further consideration of the Iranian appeal until May 6.

Shortly after this step had been taken, Gromyko returned to the Council table and demanded that the question be dropped from the Council's agenda. This was followed by a message from the premier of Iran agreeing to drop the complaint, the announcement of an agreement between the contending countries for a joint oil company, and an unsolicited opinion from Secretary-General Trygve Lie that the Council no longer had jurisdiction in the matter. On May 23 Moscow and Teheran announced that evacuation of Soviet troops from Iran had been completed on May 9. In spite of these developments the Council decided to keep the question on its agenda for an indefinite period, but it has taken no further action regarding it.

2. Indonesia

Negotiations between the Netherlands government and Indonesian leaders, begun in 1945, led to the Linggadjati Agreement, formally signed on March 25, 1947, for the establishment of a United States of Indonesia within the framework of the Kingdom of the Netherlands. Each side soon charged that the other had violated this agreement, and on July 20, 1947, Dutch troops began military action against the so-called Indonesian Republic. This action was immediately brought to the attention of the Security Council by Australia and India, and on August 1, 1947, the Council called on both parties to cease hostilities and to settle their differences by peaceful means.

To assist in the settlement the Council set up a Committee of Good Offices, composed of representatives of Australia, Belgium, and the United States, with Dr. Frank P. Graham as the first American member. After negotiations aboard the U.S.S. *Renville* under the auspices of the UN committee, Dutch and Indonesian negotiators signed, on January 17, 1948, a truce plan and a set of principles to serve as a basis for settlement. Despite the strenuous efforts of the committee, negotiations for the political implementation of the *Renville* agreement dragged on through the rest of 1948.

In December Dutch troops resumed military operations. The United States formally requested an emergency session of the Security Council to deal with the new situation. The Council issued a cease-fire order and passed several resolutions; but for weeks the Dutch government refused to comply with these resolutions, even re-enforced as they were by pressure of world public opinion, by official remonstrances from several nations, and by the resolutions of an Asian conference convened in New Delhi by the Indian Prime Minister, Jawaharlal Nehru.

The United Nations Commission for Indonesia, which had replaced the Committee of Good Offices, was finally able to effect an agreement under which Dutch troops evacuated Jogjakarta, leaders of the Indonesian Republic were released from their confinement, and hostilities were brought to a halt. In July, 1949, the Indonesian government returned to Jogjakarta, and on the twenty-third of that month Republican and Federalist leaders announced that they had reached an agreement on the creation of a United States of Indonesia. A round-table conference at The Hague, held shortly afterwards and attended by representatives of the Dutch government, Indonesian Republicans and Federalists, and the UN Commission for Indonesia, confirmed the general terms of the understanding and outlined the steps by which the transfer of sovereignty should be effected. Both Dutch and Indonesians, encouraged by the UN commission, implemented these far-reaching agreements in good faith. As a result, a new state — the Republic of Indonesia — was born.

3. Greece

Cases involving the political independence and territorial integrity of Greece were on the agenda of the Security Council almost continuously from 1946 to 1951. In January, 1946, the Soviet Union charged that the presence of British troops in Greece constituted a threat to peace. After some debate the Council adopted a resolution saying that it had heard the statements in the matter and considered the incident closed.

In August, 1946, the Ukrainian Soviet Socialist Republic complained of internal conditions in Greece and of incidents along the Greek-Albanian frontier, allegedly provoked by Greek troops. A proposal that the Council establish a commission to investigate the facts relating to the alleged border incidents was vetoed by the Soviet member.

On December 3, 1946, Greece contended that her neighbors to the north were aiding Greek guerrillas and were, in fact, promoting civil war, and asked the Council to order an on-the-spot investigation. The Council unanimously voted to create a Commission of Investigation. On May 27, 1947, eight of the eleven members of the commission reported to the Security Council that "Yugoslavia, and to a lesser extent, Albania, and Bulgaria" had "supported the guerrilla warfare in Greece." With only the Soviet and Polish members dissenting, the commission proposed the establishment of a new "watchdog" commission. With the Council's approval the commission thereupon appointed a Subsidiary Group to keep the Council informed of activities along the Greek border.

From June 27 to August 29, 1947, the Security Council discussed the report of the Commission of Investigation. The debates were filled with bitter attacks by the Soviet Union on Greece, and all attempts of the Council to act in defense of Greece were frustrated, several times by Soviet vetoes. On September 15, by a vote of 9 to 2, the Council removed the Greek question from its agenda in order that it might be placed before the General Assembly.

At the Second Session of the Assembly the case was discussed at length. On October 21, by a vote of 40 to 6, with 11 abstentions, the Assembly made a number of recommendations to Greece and her neighbors, and established an eleven-nation Special Committee on the Balkans (UNSCOB). Poland and the U.S.S.R., named as members of the committee, declined to participate in its work, and Albania, Bulgaria, and Yugoslavia consistently refused to allow it access to their territories or even to recognize its existence; but in spite of this noncooperation UNSCOB persisted in its work. Through personal observation groups along Greece's northern frontier, from testimony obtained from scores of interviews, and from other sources, it accumulated overwhelming evidence of large-scale aid to Greek guerrillas from Greece's northern neighbors. In 1948 it submitted reports to the General Assembly.

During the Third Session of the Assembly, in the fall of 1948, the First Committee spent more time on the Greek problem than on any other, but the spirited opposition of the Soviet bloc prolonged the debate and confused the issues. The year 1949 brought considerable improvement in the situation, due in large measure to the fact that Yugoslavia's aid to the Greek guerrillas had practically ceased after the Tito "split" and Yugoslavia's expulsion from the Communist bloc. A further improvement was signified by the restoration of diplomatic relations between Greece and Yugoslavia on November 28, 1950.

On December 1, 1950, after hearing UNSCOB's report, the General Assembly adopted three resolutions pertaining to Greece. Two dealt with old questions of the repatriation of members of the Greek armed forces and Greek children. In a further move to bring about repatriation the Assembly established a standing committee and urged the International Committee of the Red Cross and the League of Red Cross Societies to continue their efforts to return Greek nationals.

In 1951 UNSCOB asked the General Assembly to take note of the "changed but continuing threat to Greece, [and to] consider the advisability of maintaining United Nations vigilance of the Balkans in the light of the present nature of the threat to Greece in that area." The Assembly voted to terminate the Special Committee on the Balkans, and set up a subcommission of the Peace Observation Commission, with authority to send observers to any area of international tension in the Balkans.

4. Kashmir

Kashmir was one of the more than five hundred princely states whose status was left undetermined when the Dominions of India and Pakistan came officially into existence on August 15, 1947. Shortly afterwards fighting broke out in Kashmir (officially, the state of Jammu and Kashmir), a predominantly Muslim state ruled by a Hindu maharaja. The maharaja asked the Government of India to send troops into Kashmir to assist him in re-establishing his authority, and announced that the state would accede to the Union of India. The Indian Government accepted the accession, dispatched troops to Kashmir, and pledged that "as soon as law and order have been restored in Kashmir and its soil cleared of the invader, the question of the state's accession should be settled by a reference to the people."

On January 1, 1948, India filed a complaint with the Security Council of the United Nations, charging that the Government of Pakistan was providing assistance to raiders who were attacking the state of Kashmir. Pakistan denied these charges and brought a number of counter-allegations against India. The Security Council voted to establish a United Nations Commission on India and Pakistan (UNCIP). After weeks of investigation UNCIP, on August 13, 1948, presented to the Governments of India and Pakistan a resolution calling for a cease-fire and truce agreement, withdrawal from Kashmir of Pakistani and Indian troops, and a plebiscite to determine the future status of the state. On December 11 it submitted more specific proposals to the two governments for a plebiscite to be supervised by an administrator nominated by the Secretary-General of the United Nations. India and Pakistan agreed to these proposals and to a cease-fire and truce arrangement, effective January 1, 1949.[3] Fleet Admiral Chester W. Nimitz of the United States was appointed by Trygve Lie as plebiscite administrator, a choice approved by all parties concerned. Admiral Nimitz spent several weeks in India and Pakistan, but was unable to secure agreement on the conditions under which the plebiscite should be held.

Through UNCIP agreement was reached on the demarcation of a permanent cease-fire line in July, 1949, but no progress was made in arrangements for the withdrawal of armed forces or for a plebiscite. After its proposal of arbitration had been rejected by India, the commission recommended that the Security Council name an individual to replace the five-member commission and through him continue the efforts to bring the two governments together on the unresolved issues.

On March 14, 1950, the Council asked both parties to prepare and carry out within a five-month period a program of demilitarization. Sir Owen Dixon of Australia was appointed to assist in reaching this objective. In September, however, Dixon reported that he had been unable to make any progress toward demilitarization or arrangements for a plebiscite and requested that he be relieved of his assignment.

In February, 1951, the Council again brought up the question of Kashmir, and in March it appointed Dr. Frank Graham of the

[3] A United Nations Military Observers Group, headed until his death in January, 1966, by General Nimmo, an Australian, has been in Kashmir since 1949. It is charged with ensuring the observance of the cease-fire and truce agreement, and its presence in that beautiful but hotly contested area has been a powerful deterrent to violence.

United States to the position left vacant by Dixon. During months of patient investigations Dr. Graham made a variety of specific proposals regarding demilitarization, and the Security Council discussed the issue at length; but all these efforts led to no basic agreement. The question of a plebiscite was not even discussed. Neither India nor Pakistan replied officially to Dr. Graham's fifth report, submitted in 1953.

The "India-Pakistan question" remained largely dormant on the agenda of the Security Council until 1957, when at the insistence of Pakistan the Council spent 28 unproductive meetings on the matter. The question was revived again in 1962 — the number of Council meetings devoted to Kashmir passed the hundred mark — and in 1964, after extensive talks between India and Pakistan had broken down and had left Indo-Pakistan relations at an even lower ebb than usual. The consideration by the Council consisted largely of lengthy statements by representatives of India and Pakistan and abortive efforts by Council members to persuade the two countries to reach an amicable agreement on Kashmir.

Prospects for agreement on Kashmir seemed more remote than ever when Indo-Pakistan confrontations in 1965 — first in the Rann of Kutch and then, in August and September, in Kashmir itself — led to a three-week war between India and Pakistan. After some military maneuvering, the controversy over the Rann of Kutch was referred to an arbitral tribunal, consisting of one representative nominated by India, one by Pakistan, and one, who served as chairman, by the Secretary-General of the United Nations. The Kashmir problem proved more intractable. During August the Security Council held several meetings to consider the question, and it followed the developments in that area closely, aided by remarkably revealing reports by General Robert H. Nimmo, chief military observer of the UN Military Observers' Group for India and Pakistan (UNMOGIP). On September 1 the Secretary-General appealed to the heads of both governments to respect the cease-fire agreement, which had been in effect for more than 16 years. But by this time the mounting tensions had led to open warfare, and the efforts of the UN were directed to a cessation of hostilities. The Security Council issued several calls for an immediate cease-fire and a withdrawal of armed forces. In the second week of September the Secretary-General went to South Asia to confer with President Ayub Khan and Prime Minister Shastri. On September 20 the Security Council "demanded" a cease-fire and a withdrawal of armed forces to positions held prior to August 5, 1965, to take effect on September 22. Both India and Pakistan — with some reluctance, especially in the case of Pakistan — acceded to this "demand".

After the termination of hostilities a strengthened UNMOGIP observed the cease-fire line in Kashmir, and a second group, known as the UN India-Pakistan Observation Mission, performed a similar function along the 1000-mile stretch of frontier between India and West Pakistan where fighting had also taken place. On November 25 the Secretary-General announced the appointment of Brigadier General Tulio Marambio of Chile as his military representative in India and Pakistan.

Both India and Pakistan submitted frequent complaints of violations of the cease-fire to the Security Council. The Kashmir question, of course, remained on the Council's agenda. While the Council, the Secretary-General, and other UN agencies and representatives were helpful in bringing about a cease-fire and in preventing a renewal of hostilities, they could not persuade India and Pakistan to resolve the issues, notably the Kashmir question, which had bedeviled their relations since independence and which, on two occasions, had led them to war.

5. Palestine

Around the historic land of Palestine, "a center of international rivalry intermittently since the beginning of human history," some of the thorniest problems to confront the United Nations have gathered. The rival claims of Jews and Arabs "have created a dilemma of infinite complexity. Few issues of modern times have taxed statesmanship so heavily; few have offered a greater challenge to an international organization."[4]

The Palestine question was first brought before the United Nations by Great Britain on April 2, 1947, in a letter requesting the Secretary-General to call a special session of the General Assembly to create and instruct a special committee to prepare recommendations for the future government of Palestine. Some action was necessary, as Britain had announced her intention to terminate the mandate that she had assumed at the close of World War I. Accordingly, the first special session convened on April 28, 1947. After lengthy debates in the First Committee, the Assembly, over the violent opposition of the Arab states, appointed a committee of eleven members, not including any of the permanent members of the Security Council, gave it "the widest powers to ascertain and record facts, and to investigate any questions and issues relevant to the problem of Palestine," and instructed it "to submit such proposals as it may consider appropriate for the solution of the problem of Palestine."

The United Nations Special Committee on Palestine (UNSCOP) held its first meeting at Lake Success on May 26, spent six weeks in Palestine, and concluded its report in Geneva on August 31. Its report to the General Assembly contained eleven general principles unanimously agreed upon by the committee, a majority plan for the partition of Palestine, with economic union, and a minority plan for a federal state. On November 29, in a tense plenary session, the General Assembly adopted by the required two-thirds vote the plan for the partition of Palestine, with economic union, and an international area for Jerusalem. It then named a commission to implement the recommendations.

For once the United States and Russia had agreed on a major political issue. Both supported the partition plan, and the United States was largely responsible for its adoption by the General Assembly. Jewish leaders hailed the action of the Assembly as a great victory; but Arab spokesmen warned that such a plan would never be accepted, and the increasing tempo of violence in the Holy Land gave weight to their warnings. The Palestine Commission soon reported to the Security Council that it could not "discharge its responsibilities on the termination of the Mandate" unless assisted by armed force. Until early March, 1948, the United States continued its firm support of the partition proposal; then, on March 19, Warren R. Austin, the American representative in the Security Council, without previous warning to the British or any other government, formally proposed that the Security Council instruct the Palestine Commission to suspend its efforts to implement the partition plan. He urged, instead, that a temporary trusteeship for Palestine under the Trusteeship Council of the UN be established and that a special session of the General Assembly be called to consider this new proposal.

Although Secretary-General Trygve Lie pointed out that a trusteeship for Palestine might be even more difficult to implement peacefully than the partition plan, he issued a call for a special session of the General Assembly, to meet on April 16. On April 17 the Security Council requested all groups in Palestine to desist from acts of violence. and on April 23 it established a Truce Commission. The special session of the Assembly — the second special session to consider the Palestine problem — showed little enthusiasm for the "Draft Trusteeship Agreement for Palestine" which the United States submitted on April 20. Instead it passed an in-

[4] *The United States and the United Nations: Report by the President to the Congress for the Year 1947*, Dept. of State Pub. 3024, International Organization and Conference Series III, 1 (February, 1948), pp. 42, 44.

nocuous resolution, instructed UNSCOP to terminate its activities, established the office of United Nations Mediator for Palestine, and appointed Count Folke Bernadotte of Sweden to that office.

At midnight on May 14, 1948, at the expiration of the British mandate, the new state of Israel was proclaimed. This action, plus other developments of April and May, led to renewed hostilities in Palestine and to attempted invasion of the Holy Land by Egyptian troops. A cease-fire order of the Security Council, issued on May 29 and vigilantly supervised by Count Bernadotte and military observers from Belgium, France, and the United States, produced a truce of four weeks. Thereafter fighting resumed, with the armed forces of Israel quickly gaining the advantage over the combined Arab armies. In mid-July a stronger cease-fire order of the Security Council was generally observed, except in the Jerusalem area, until well into October, when serious fighting broke out in the Negev in southern Palestine. On September 16 Count Bernadotte finished his last and most definite plan for a settlement in Palestine. Two days later he was murdered in Jerusalem. Dr. Ralph Bunche, an American who had been Count Bernadotte's chief assistant, was named acting mediator. His efforts, reinforced by two strong resolutions of the Security Council in November, met with only partial success throughout the remainder of 1948, but early in 1949 Egypt and Israel agreed to suspend hostilities and to undertake armistice negotiations.

On December 11, 1948, the General Assembly voted to establish a Conciliation Commission to assume the functions of the mediator and the Truce Commission. At the second part of the Third Session, held in the spring of 1949, Israel was admitted to the United Nations as the fifty-ninth member, in spite of the bitter opposition of the Arab states. Lengthy negotiations between Israel and the Arab states, conducted by Dr. Bunche mostly on the island of Rhodes, resulted in four general armistice agreements being signed between February 24 and July 20, 1949. On August 11, the Council declared that these superseded the truce directed by the Council on July 15, 1948, and it relieved the mediator of further responsibility to the Council. Later negotiations at Lausanne failed to bring agreement on final terms of peace.

Twice in succeeding years the uneasy truce forged by UN efforts dissolved into warfare. The crises of 1956 and 1967 were so significant, and the role of the UN in relation to them so important, that they are given separate consideration in this chapter.

6. Korea

The Early Korean Problem. The failure of the United States and the U.S.S.R. to agree on steps to implement the wartime promise of independence for Korea "in due course" led the United States, on September 17, 1947, to submit the Korean question to the General Assembly. That body, over the protests of the Soviet bloc, voted to establish a United Nations Temporary Commission on Korea, with authority to observe elections for a national assembly, which, in turn, would establish a national government for Korea. The commission was welcomed in the American zone, but was denied all access to North Korea, which was under Soviet control. It observed the elections of May 10, 1948, in South Korea and reported that they were "a valid expression of the free will of the electorate in those parts of Korea which were accessible to the Commission." On August 15 the "National Government of Korea" was proclaimed, with Syngman Rhee as president, and the United States military government was declared to be terminated.

On December 12, 1948, the Assembly adopted a resolution providing for a new commission of seven members to continue to function in Korea. On the same day it recognized the Republic of Korea as the only legal government in the entire country. The United States extended recognition on January 1, 1949, and thirty-one other states followed suit. The Soviet Union withheld recognition and employed the veto to prevent the new republic from becoming a member of the United Nations. Instead, she sponsored the "Democratic People's Republic of Korea" in North Korea, proclaimed in September, 1948. This government also claimed to be the only legal one in Korea.

The General Assembly in the December resolution had recommended that the occupying powers "withdraw their occupation forces from Korea as early as practicable." The United States announced the complete withdrawal of her forces on June 29, 1949. The United Nations Commission on Korea verified this in its report of July 28, 1949, but it had not been allowed access to North Korea and so was in no position to substantiate the Soviet claim of withdrawal as of December, 1948.

At the Fourth Session of the General Assembly the Korean commission was continued with a more comprehensive mandate to observe and report on developments which might result in armed conflict, as well as to note steps toward representative government and to seek to facilitate the removal of barriers to economic, social, and other friendly intercourse caused by the division of Korea.

Invasion and Early UN Action. On the morning of Sunday, June 25, 1950, armed forces from North Korea began an assault in great force across the 38th parallel upon the Republic of Korea. This action precipitated the greatest international crisis since the end of World War II.

United States Ambassador John J. Muccio, who was in Seoul, reported the attack to the Department of State, where it was received on Saturday, June 24 at 9:26 P.M. Eastern Daylight Time. The United States Government at once contacted the United Nations, and at 3:00 A.M. on June 25 it requested an immediate meeting of the Security Council. When the Council met at 2:00 P.M. of the same day, it already had before it the report of the United Nations Commission on Korea, which confirmed the attack. The commission's cable to Secretary-General Lie stated that the situation was "assuming character of full-scale war."

At its meeting on June 25 the Security Council passed by a 9 to 0 vote (Yugoslavia abstained and the Soviet Union was absent) a United States resolution which noted "with grave concern the armed attack upon the Republic of Korea," stated that the Security Council "determines that this action constitutes a breach of the peace," called for the immediate cessation of hostilities and the withdrawal of North Korean forces to the 38th parallel, and requested "all members to render every assistance to the United Nations in the execution of this resolution and to refrain from giving assistance to the North Korean authorities."[5]

On June 27 the Security Council took a momentous step — it adopted a more specific United States-sponsored resolution *recommending* assistance to the Republic of Korea from all member nations. Fifty-three states pledged their moral support, and a smaller number promised direct assistance. On July 7 the Council set up a Unified Command under the UN flag, with General MacArthur of the United States as supreme commander.

It should be noted that the Security Council could take this action only because of a unique combination of circumstances. First, the Soviet Union had been boycotting the Council since January because it had voted against a U.S.S.R. proposal to exclude the representatives of Nationalist China and seat those of the Chinese Communist regime. Consequently there was no Soviet veto. Second, American occupation forces in Japan and other bases were readily available.

[5] U. N. Document S/1501 (1950).

Moscow charged that the Security Council's resolution of June 27 was illegal (1) because it had been adopted by six votes, the seventh vote being that of the "Kuomintang representative," who, the Soviet Union contended, had no right to represent China, and (2) because the provision of the United Nations Charter required the concurrence of the five permanent members on all substantive decisions. On August 1 the U.S.S.R. sent her representative, Jacob Malik, back to the Security Council to assume his turn as president. From that time on further attempts to deal with the Korean question in the Security Council were effectively blocked.

Beginning in September, 1950, increasing demands were made to ensure that should another "breach of the peace" occur sole reliance need not be placed on the Security Council. The next time the Russians might not be absent. Consequently the Assembly, on November 3, 1950, after considerable debate, adopted the famous Uniting for Peace Resolution, generally credited to American Secretary of State Dean Acheson. The nature of this resolution, which greatly expanded the political role of the General Assembly, is described in Chapters 10 and 14.

After the Korean Communists had nearly succeeded in occupying the whole of the Korean Peninsula, the UN forces began to fight their way back from the Pusan area to the 38th parallel. The United States pressed for a decision that would authorize crossing of the parallel and entering North Korea. The Assembly approved on October 7 by a vote of 47 to 5, with 7 abstentions. The representative from India expressed strong dissatisfaction with the decision, saying that it might very well lead to an enlargement of the war. In spite of this warning United Nations forces crossed the 38th parallel and soon had pushed northward close to the Yalu River, which divides Korea from Manchuria.

The Chinese Enter the War. On November 5, 1950, with United Nations forces very thinly deployed far up in northern Korea, organized Chinese Communist forces intervened on a large scale. Gen. MacArthur reported that "a new war" had begun and that his forces were being attacked by a considerable portion of the Chinese armed forces.

With United Nations forces retreating before the onslaught of the Chinese Communists and the United States pressing for Peking's condemnation as an aggressor, twelve Arab-Asian nations, under India's leadership, offered proposals on December 14 with the objective of attaining a cease-fire in Korea and ultimately negotiating other outstanding issues in the Far East. The resolution was adopted and a Group on Cease-Fire was set up. Its first proposals were rejected by the People's Republic on December 21 with the blunt announcement that it considered all resolutions passed by the United Nations without the participation of the People's Republic of China "as illegal and null and void."

The Cease-Fire Group, not entirely dismayed, drafted a set of principles designed to clarify the United Nations position on the stand by the Chinese Communists. On January 13, 1951, this draft of principles was sent to Peking. When the People's Republic replied by offering a set of counterproposals, the Indian Government, through its ambassador in Peking, made another effort to clarify points of difference. The reply of the Chinese Communist Government to this new overture again brought mixed reactions.

Two resolutions expressing these divergent opinions were introduced in the General Assembly. A United States resolution declared that the Security Council had "failed to exercise its primary responsibility for the maintenance of international peace and security in regard to Chinese Communist intervention in Korea" and asked that the Chinese People's Republic be condemned as an aggressor. The resolution also made provision for a Committee on Additional

Measures which would consist of the same membership as the Collective Measures Committee. On February 1 the United States resolution passed by a vote of 44 to 7, with 9 abstentions, over the protests of most of the Arab-Asian representatives.

While the debate raged, so did the fighting. Early in 1951, after serious reverses in the previous November and December, United Nations forces began to advance again; but April brought another heavy North Korean-Chinese counterattack, and a virtual stalemate developed at the 38th parallel. With the prospects for a negotiated peace appearing very slim, the Committee on Additional Measures noted that a considerable number of states had already imposed an embargo on war material to China and suggested that this might be extended to include more states. By September fifty-one members and thirteen nonmember states had complied with a General Assembly resolution of May 17 embodying this suggestion.

Truce Talking. On June 23, 1951, with the UN forces again advancing, Jacob Malik proposed in a radio broadcast that, as a first step toward settling the conflict in Korea, the belligerents should begin discussions for a cease-fire and an armistice providing for the common withdrawal of forces from the 38th parallel. On July 10 delegations from the United Nations Command and from the North Korean-Chinese commanders opened negotiations in Kaesong, one of the few towns below the 38th parallel still in Communist hands. Because of alleged violations of the neutral zone around Kaesong by the United Nations, the North Koreans and the Chinese suspended negotiations on August 23 but agreed to resume them on October 25 at Panmunjom, not far from Kaesong.

Ostensibly only one issue stood in the way of a settlement, but this issue was a very large one — the exchange of prisoners. Close to 200,000 were involved. There was, in addition, a principle at stake. The United Nations insisted that no prisoner in its hands should be forced against his wishes to return to Communist areas. The Communist thesis was that since the Geneva Convention on Prisoners of War (1929) provided for general repatriation the United Nations' stand was contrary to international law. A matter of prestige was also involved as far as the Chinese and North Koreans were concerned, and they repeatedly stated that only torture and starvation could have forced any of their men to prefer to stay with the Western "imperialists." The Communists' strongest bargaining point was their holding of some 12,000 United Nations prisoners.

Marked by another momentarily promising peace effort by the Arab-Asian group in late 1952 and by another suspension in late 1952 and early 1953, the truce negotiations limped on until the Soviet "peace offensive" in the spring of 1953 introduced a more hopeful note. An armistice agreement was finally reached on July 27, 1953. It provided for a political conference within three months to formulate terms of a final peace settlement and for the voluntary repatriation of the prisoners of war under the supervision of the Neutral Nations Repatriation Commission. In a hostile atmosphere and in the face of many complications the commission attempted to carry out its task. On January 21, 1954, the Indian guards at Panmunjom released the prisoners on both sides who had refused repatriation.

Korea is no longer a battleground, but the scars of more than three years of fighting remain. Moreover, the Korean question is still unresolved. The Geneva Conference of 1954 wrestled with it without making any appreciable progress. The United Nations is giving assistance in rehabilitation efforts, but a Neutral Nations Supervisory Commission was withdrawn in 1956. The commission was forbidden access to North Korea, and was even regarded with suspicion in the territory of the Republic of Korea. A Military Armistice Commission has been in existence since 1953, and at frequent and often stormy meetings in its headquarters in Panmunjom in the demilitarized zone it has considered alleged violations of the truce and other matters arising from the "temporary" armistice agreement, which has not led to a peace settlement. There seems to be little prospect that the long-delayed political conference will be held or that the people of Korea will soon be given a chance to work out their own destiny in a united country.

7. Suez

In late October and early November, 1956, the United Nations became involved in two major world crises that erupted almost simultaneously in Hungary and in Egypt. Although the height of the Suez crisis almost coincided with that of the tragic events in Hungary, it began months earlier and involved the United Nations at an earlier stage. On July 26, 1956, apparently in response to the public withdrawal of American and British support for the proposed High Dam at Aswan, President Nasser announced that his government would nationalize the Suez Canal Company. This dramatic announcement led to a month of bitter protests by the British and French governments, frenzied diplomatic activity, meetings in London of twenty-two of the major users of the Suez Canal, the establishment of a Suez Canal Users Association by eighteen of the participants in the London deliberations, tensions between the United States and its two major allies, and warnings of the deterioration of the situation along the Jordan-Israel armistice demarcation line.

From late September, when the British and French governments asked it to take up the Suez question, the Security Council of the UN held several meetings, some closed sessions, and the Secretary-General conferred with British, French, and Egyptian representatives in an effort to find areas of agreement so that negotiations among these three powers could be held. The Council also considered complaints by Jordan and Israel of alleged violations of the Arab-Israel Armistice Agreements of 1949. When Israeli forces launched an attack across the Sinai Peninsula on October 29, a United States resolution calling for the immediate cessation of hostilities and the withdrawal of Israeli forces was defeated in the Security Council by the negative votes of Britain and France. Following the British-French air attack on Egypt, begun on October 31, the Council adopted a Yugoslav proposal to call an emergency special session of the General Assembly, under the Uniting for Peace Resolution of 1950. "Thus by an irony of fate the resolution designed by the West as a barrier against Communist aggression was first invoked by Yugoslavia with the support of the USSR, against two Western powers."[6]

The first emergency special session, which convened on November 1, adopted a United States resolution calling for an immediate cease-fire and withdrawal of all foreign troops from Egyptian soil. On November 4 it endorsed recommendations of the Secretary-General for the creation of "an emergency international force." In the next few days plans for a United Nations Emergency Force (UNEF) were quickly worked out, and on November 15 the first contingent of the force arrived in Egypt. By that time a general cease-fire was in effect (as of midnight of November 6–7), and the Suez question had been transferred from the emergency special session to the regular session of the General Assembly. In the next few weeks the Secretary-General made vigorous efforts to build up the UNEF, and the Assembly pressed the British, French, and Israeli authorities to withdraw their troops from Egypt. The British and French promptly complied — the last of their forces left Egypt on December 22 — but Israel delayed for over two months in an effort to get

[6] "Issues Before the Twelfth General Assembly," *International Conciliation,* No. 514 (September, 1957), p. 36.

satisfactory assurances regarding freedom of navigation in the Strait of Tiran and the Gulf of Aqaba.

In the early weeks of 1957 salvage and clearance operations, under the general direction of the United Nations, were undertaken with remarkable dispatch and success. By April 24 the Canal was fully reopened. The Security Council and the Secretary-General were helpful in furthering efforts to reach some agreement with Egypt over the future regime of the Canal. In accordance with an Egyptian declaration of April 24, individual users of the Canal worked out arrangements with the Egyptian government, which, however, persisted in its ban on vessels to and from Israel.

The UNEF patrolled the armistice demarcation line — on the Egyptian side only, for Israel steadfastly refused to permit it to operate on the Israeli side — until 1967. It was financed by voluntary contributions, loans, and special assessments. Since several members of the UN refused to pay these assessments, and since the expenses ran to some $20,000,000 a year, the UNEF operation was a major reason, second only to the UN's Congo role, for the mounting financial crisis which has threatened the financial solvency and even the future of the world organization. In May, 1967, at the insistence of President Nasser, UNEF's operations were suddenly terminated.

8. Hungary

Hungary, like most of the other states of Eastern Europe, was profoundly affected by the process of de-Stalinization which began to sweep through the Communist world after the Twentieth Congress of the CPSU in the spring of 1956. Inspired by the success of the Poles in resisting Soviet pressure, Hungarian students and intellectuals in Budapest organized demonstrations of sympathy for the Poles, and of protest against Soviet domination of their own country and against repressive domestic policies. They demanded the appointment of Nagy, who had been premier from 1953 to 1955 and who was regarded as a champion of more liberal policies, as premier and a variety of other concessions and reforms. Instead, on October 23, the state security police opened fire on a crowd of demonstrators, killing many of them. As a Special Committee of the UN General Assembly reported a few weeks later, "In so far as any one moment can be selected as the turning point which changed a peaceful demonstration into a violent uprising, it would be this moment."[7] Within a few hours Soviet tanks appeared in the streets of Budapest, and fighting spread throughout the country and soon developed into a struggle between the majority of the Hungarian people and Soviet troops. On October 24 Imre Nagy was appointed premier, but on the following day this action was balanced by the appointment of Soviet-dominated János Kádár as First Secretary of the Communist Party.

The Hungarian case was first brought before the Security Council by France, the United Kingdom, and the United States on October 28. At that meeting the case was debated for nearly six hours, but no specific action was taken, or even proposed. When it was next discussed, on November 2, several events had made the issue more urgent and more confusing. Israeli, French, and British forces had invaded Egypt, the Soviet Union had offered "to enter into appropriate negotiations . . . on the question of the presence of Soviet troops on the territory of Hungary," and Premier Nagy had appealed for the support of the Security Council in obtaining the withdrawal of Soviet troops. Two days of inconclusive discussion in the Security Council preceded an all-out attack by Soviet forces, the flight of Nagy to the Yugoslav Embassy, and the assumption of

[7] General Assembly, Official Records, 11th Sess., 1957, Suppl. No. 18, *Report of the Special Committee on the Problems of Hungary* (A/3592), para. 56.

power by Kádár. These dramatic events led to more positive action in the UN. When a resolution calling on the Soviet Union "to withdraw all of its forces without delay from Hungarian territory" was defeated by a Soviet veto, the Council promptly voted to call an emergency special session of the General Assembly under the Uniting for Peace Resolution.

During this emergency special session and the eleventh regular session which followed, while resistance to the Soviet-backed Kádár regime in Hungary was being ruthlessly and systematically crushed, the General Assembly discussed the Hungarian question at great length, although with great caution, and adopted no fewer than ten resolutions on this question. The Soviet Union paid no attention to any of these resolutions, and the Kádár regime refused to permit UN observers, or even the Secretary-General himself, to visit Hungary to investigate the conditions at first hand. A Special Committee appointed by the Assembly on January 10, 1957, composed of representatives of Australia, Ceylon, Denmark, Tunisia, and Uruguay, was also denied access to Hungary; but it studied all available documents and other materials and interviewed over one hundred witnesses. Its scathing report,[8] made public on June 20, was described by a Pakistani newspaper as "a massive indictment of the Soviet Union's action in brutally suppressing by armed forces a national movement for freedom."[9]

After considering the report of the Special Committee the Eleventh Session of the General Assembly, on September 14, 1957, passed a resolution, by a vote of 60 to 10, with 10 abstentions, condemning the Soviet actions in Hungary and the continued defiance of the Assembly. The resolution empowered the president of the Assembly, Prince Wan of Thailand, to take such steps as he thought appropriate, as the Special Representative of the Assembly on the Hungarian question, toward implementing the Assembly resolution on Hungary. At the Twelfth Session Prince Wan was obliged to report that his efforts had been unproductive.

Indignation against the Soviet Union and the Kádár regime was heightened by the news that on June 16, 1958, Imre Nagy and other members of his former government who had been arrested by Soviet authorities and interned in Rumania in the previous November, after leaving the Yugoslav Embassy under a promise of safe conduct, had been executed. Upon the receipt of the news the Special Committee on the Problem of Hungary held an emergency meeting, condemned the executions, and in mid-July issued a Special Report.[10]

The Fourteenth Session of the Assembly appointed Sir Leslie Munro of New Zealand as Special Representative, and deplored "the continued disregard" by the Soviet Union and the Hungarian Government of the General Assembly resolutions. To subsequent sessions of the Assembly Sir Leslie reported that he had received no cooperation from the Hungarian or Soviet authorities, and he urged the Assembly to maintain its vigilant interest in developments in Hungary. The Hungarian question remains on the Assembly's agenda and on the consciences of many of its members, but no effective action has been possible. The case illustrates the weakness of the United Nations, and the limitations of UN efforts, in the fact of opposition and noncooperation by the member states most directly involved, especially if one of them is a major power.

9. The Congo

The Congo had hardly become independent, on June 30, 1960, before it seemed to be on the verge of disintegration. Belgium, the former occupying power, rushed troops back to protect her nationals and her

[8] For complete reference, see footnote 10, below.

[9] *Morning News* (*Karachi*), June 26, 1957.

[10] U. N. Document A/3849, July 14, 1958.

enormous interests. On July 11, Moise Tshombe, the President of Katanga, the richest province, announced Katanaga's secession. On behalf of the central government President Joseph Kasavubu and Premier Patrice Lumumba appealed for military aid, first to the United States and then to the United Nations. Acting promptly, the Secretary-General, using for the first time his powers under Article 99 of the Charter "to bring to the attention of the Security Council any matter which in his opinion may threaten the maintenance of international peace and security," called a meeting of the Security Council on July 13. After receiving a vague mandate from the Council, the Secretary-General proceeded to organize a United Nations Operation in the Congo (ONUC), under the field command of Dr. Ralph Bunche as Special Representative.

ONUC was handicapped in its efforts to help to restore order without direct intervention in internal Congolese affairs. For some months it was not permitted to take effective action against the secessionist provinces of Katanga and South Kasai, and it tried to stay out of the struggle between President Kasavubu and Premier Lumumba. Lumumba was responsible for appeals for assistance to individual foreign states, notably Ghana, the People's Republic of China, and the Soviet Union, thus bringing the cold war to the Congo. On September 5 he was dismissed by Kasavubu.

These developments placed fresh strains on the already tenuous consensus in the Security Council. When a Soviet veto on September 17, 1960, seemed to preclude any further Council action, the Congo question was referred to the fourth emergency special session of the General Assembly. After heated debate the Assembly requested the Secretary-General to continue his efforts "to assist the Central Government of the Congo" and created a Conciliation Commission of Asian and African representatives. In November the Fifteenth Session of the Assembly accepted the Kasavubu delegation, instead of a Lumumba delegation, as the rightful representative of the central government of the Republic of the Congo. A few days later Lumumba was arrested. On January 17 he was transferred to the Katanga authorities, who announced within a month that he had been killed by hostile tribesmen while trying to escape.

This announcement aroused worldwide indignation and protest. It was followed by a further deterioration of the military and political situation in the Congo. Lumumba's Vice Premier, Antoine Gizenga, established a rival government in Stanleyville, the capital of Orientale province, and began to extend his control into other sections of the Congo. ONUC was further handicapped by clashes with the ANC, the Congolese "national army," and by antagonism between President Kasavubu and Rajeshwar Dayal, who in September had succeeded Bunche as Special Representative. In May, 1961, Mr. Dayal submitted his resignation. By that time the political situation in the Congo had improved, ONUC had increased its forces to nearly 20,000 men, including some 5,000 Indian troops, and the UN "had put into the field its largest civilian team to date, in a technical assistance effort of unmatched proportions";[11] it had also made substantial funds available for the Congo's economic development. On August 2, 1961, a "government of national unity," headed by Cvrille Adoula, was formed. At about the same time the Secretary-General expressed the view that "the grievous stage" in the Congo "is past."

This hope was somewhat premature. The stability and unity of the Congo were far from secure. Before the end of 1961 UN forces were involved in military operations against the Katangese, who were supported by hundreds of foreign mercenaries. On Sep-

[11] "Issues Before the Sixteenth General Assembly," *International Conciliation,* No. 534 (September, 1961), p. 51.

tember 17 Secretary-General Dag Hammarskjold was killed in a plane crash in Northern Rhodesia, as he was en route to a meeting with Tshombe to "try to find peaceful methods of resolving the present conflict." Although Tshombe, in the "Kitona Declaration" of December 20, promised to recognize the "indivisible unity" of the Congo Republic, he could not be persuaded to agree to specific proposals to implement this declaration. His continued intransigence posed a standing threat to Congolese unity. In December, 1962, and January, 1963, ONUC troops occupied Elisabethville and other important cities in Katanga. By mid-January Tshombe announced that he was ready to end Katanga's secession, and he announced his "temporary withdrawal" from Congolese politics and left for Paris.

In February, 1963, the Secretary-General reported that the UN had "largely fulfilled" its mandates "to maintain the [Congo's] territorial integrity and . . . political independence," and "to prevent the occurrence of civil war." In July he announced his intentions to withdraw all UN forces from the Congo by the end of the year. While the date of departure of the UN forces was postponed to the end of June, 1964, it was clear that their withdrawal was prompted less because they were no longer needed than because their continued presence was strongly disapproved of by leading members of the UN, including the Soviet Union and France, and was imposing a crushing financial burden on the UN.

Ironically, to the extent that conditions in the Congo after the withdrawal of the UN forces improved, the improvement was due in large measure to the efforts of Moise Tshombe, who in July, 1964, returned to the Congo and became premier of the central government. He found conditions in a chaotic state. In Orientale province a new revolt, led by a "National Liberation Committee," led to such excesses that in December, with the approval of the Tshombe regime, American and Belgian paratroops were dropped on Stanleyville in an effort to rescue as many white refugees as possible. Thereafter the rebellion was brought under control, and in 1965 Tshombe scored a decisive electoral victory. In less than a year, however, he was again in the political wilderness. On March 22, 1966, President Joseph D. Mobutu assumed all national legislative powers, and on May 19 Tshombe was formally deprived of his parliamentary seat, accused of treason, and in March, 1967, sentenced to death *in absentia.* On June 30, 1967, a plane carrying Tshombe was hijacked in mid-air over the Mediterranean and forced to land in Algeria. For weeks, while new disturbances rocked the Congo, the Algerian government delayed a decision on the request of the government of the Congo to extradite Tshombe to the Congo, for whatever fate might befall him.

While the situation in the Congo is still precarious, the country seems to have survived the birth pangs of independence. For this the United Nations deserves a fair share of the credit. But the cost to the UN was a heavy one, in commitment, expense, and implications. The Congo operation "was the most complex and protracted operation ever authorized, financed, and administered by an international organization." It was "a novel enterprise that preoccupied politicians from three dozen states for four years and seriously jeopardized the future of the United Nations."[12]

10. Cyprus

After the Congo experience, it seemed rather doubtful that the United Nations would ever again be able to undertake another major peacekeeping operation. It can try to be helpful in the resolution of political disputes, and it can coordinate and to some extent direct military and economic efforts to

[12] Ernest W. Lefever, *Crisis in the Congo: A United Nations Force in Action* (Washington, D.C.: The Brookings Institution, 1965), p. 171.

keep the peace and contribute to nation-building activities; but it cannot expect to mount a Congo-like operation unless its members provide the necessary support.

In the Cyprus crisis, which reached a climax shortly before ONUC ceased its operations in the Congo, the United Nations, and especially its Secretary-General, played a successful but limited role. After December, 1963, tension between Greek and Turkish Cypriots accelerated alarmingly and in turn seriously strained relations between Greece and Turkey, two NATO allies. On February 15, 1964, when representatives of Greece, Turkey, the two Cypriot communities, and the United Kingdom (which had controlled Cyprus as a crown colony from 1925 to 1960) failed to reach agreement at a conference in London, the United Kingdom and Cyprus brought the issue before the Security Council. On March 4 the Council recommended the establishment of a peacekeeping force and the appointment of a mediator. Mindful of the Congo experience, the Council suggested that all the costs be met by the states providing contingents, by the Government of Cyprus, and by voluntary contributions. In April the UN force (UNFICYP), under an Indian general who reported directly to the Secretary-General, relieved the British troops on Cyprus. Because of its limited numbers and its limited authority, UNFICYP was unable to stop the fighting or to disarm the irregular forces.

After the Cypriot house of representatives passed a bill providing for conscription on June 1, Turkey threatened to invade the island. A further complication was introduced by the return to Cyprus of General Grivas, leader of the Greek Cypriots in their revolt against the British in the 1950's, whose staunch advocacy of *enosis* (union with Greece) brought him into conflict with President Makarios. In early August, when Turkish jet fighters carried out air strikes against Greek Cypriot forces, Greece warned that unless the air strikes were stopped immediately, Greece would assist Cyprus "by all the military means available to it." The Government of Cyprus protested to the Security Council, which called for an immediate cease-fire and the cooperation of all concerned in the restoration of peace. Reprimanded by Greece for undertaking military operations without obtaining Greece's consent, President Makarios appealed to the Soviet Union for help, apparently without much success.

All kinds of plans and proposals for solving the Cyprus question have been advanced, but none has been acceptable to both Greek and Turkish Cypriots and their supporters. The United Nations force has been helpful, in spite of the difficulties which it has encountered, in preventing a major explosion on Cyprus, and the UN has done what it can to persuade the powers most directly concerned to avoid intervention and to resolve their differences peacefully.

11. The Arab-Israeli War, 1967

In the fall of 1966 and throughout the first five months of 1967 tension along Israel's borders increased markedly. Israel blamed the attacks of Arab terrorists and warned her Arab neighbors, and so informed the members of the UN Security Council, that Israel could not remain inactive in the face of continued "aggressive" acts against her territory. The Arab states alleged that Israel was becoming increasingly militant and aggressive.

In mid-May the U.A.R. and Syria proclaimed a state of emergency and began to mobilize forces along Israel's borders. On May 18 the U.A.R. formally requested the UN Secretary-General to withdraw the United Nations Emergency Force (UNEF), which had been stationed along her 117-mile frontier with Israel since 1956. Although he expressed "grave misgivings" about this move and its "implications for peace," U Thant promptly complied with the U.A.R.'s request, which obviously amounted to a demand. The positions occupied by UNEF were promptly taken over by the "Palestine Liberation Organization," which was in fact a part of the armed forces of the U.A.R.

On May 22 U Thant left for Cairo to confer with UN representatives in the Middle East and with President Nasser and other high officials of the U.A.R. Before he could meet with Nasser on May 24 the U.A.R. leader announced the closing of the Straits of Tiran and therefore of the Gulf of Aqaba to Israeli shipping, and President Eshkol of Israel called on the UN to act without delay in asserting the right of free navigation in these waters, so vital to Israel. The Security Council held "an urgent meeting . . . to consider the extremely grave situation in the Middle East." In his report to the Council, on May 27, U Thant appealed for a breathing spell, and suggested the revival of the Egyptian-Israeli Mixed Armistice Commission, which had ceased to function when Israel withdrew from it in 1956. On May 29 and June 3 the Security Council held two more inconclusive meetings on the Middle East crisis.

From the outbreak of fighting on June 5 until June 14 the Security Council was in almost continuous session. On June 6 it unanimously adopted a resolution calling for an immediate cease-fire. Similiar resolutions were passed on June 7 and 9, but by that time the war was virtually over. Israel by "blitzkrieg" tactics had definitely gained a military victory, destroying a large part of the planes, tanks, and other military equipment which the Soviet Union and other Communist states had provided to the U.A.R., Syria, and Jordan over several years. Both sides agreed to a cease-fire, which became effective on June 10, although charges of violations were made immediately by both Israel and the Arab belligerents to the Security Council.

On June 13 a Soviet resolution condemning Israel for "aggressive activities" was defeated in the Security Council, which did, however, adopt a resolution calling on Israel to "ensure the safety, welfare and security of the inhabitants of the area where military hostilities have taken place" and to facilitate the return of Arab civilians in areas occupied by the Israelis.

Frustrated in the Security Council, the Soviet Union on June 17 invoked the Uniting for Peace Resolution of 1950 and asked the Secretary-General to call an emergency session of the General Assembly, which for the next month became the main forum for UN consideration of the issues involved in the Middle East confrontation. Unhappily it was an unproductive and often unpleasant session, marked by a trial of strength between the United States and the Soviet Union (which in the emergency session in 1956 had worked together in dealing with the Suez crisis) and illustrating again the ineffectiveness of the UN when the superpowers are in open disagreement. Both the main Soviet draft resolution, introduced by Premier Aleksei N. Kosygin himself on June 19, and a United States draft resolution were quickly shelved. The debate was stormy. Israel showed that she was in no mood to abandon the areas she had occupied militarily, including that part of Jerusalem which had been controlled by Jordan, and, as the *New York Times* observed on July 9, "the Arabs in the U.N. still seem fixed on the idea that by some diplomatic magic they can win unconditional diplomatic surrender from a power that was victorious everywhere in the field."[13] Almost the only substantive resolution to be approved after a month of wrangling was one calling upon Israel to "desist forthwith" from all measures altering the status of the city of Jerusalem.

On July 21 the emergency session ended, "with the Arabs frustrated and bitter, Israel holding its gains while urging negotiations, the United States confident but not complacent — and the Soviet Union smarting under

[13] *New York Times Weekly Review,* July 23, 1967.

a diplomatic reverse." Questions arising from the Arab-Israeli war were again referred to the Security Council, but here also great power differences and the intractability of the Arab states and Israel made effective action difficult.

The fighting reduced the United Nations' status and role in the Middle East. Instead of UNEF, a few UN observers were permitted on both sides of the Suez Canal, along the fragile cease-fire line between Israel and the U.A.R. Israel, which now controlled the area where most of the refugees who were receiving assistance from the United Nations Relief and Works Agency (UNRWA) lived, asked UNRWA to continue its work; but in general Israel's policy seemed to be to keep the UN at arm's length. The Arab states were resentful because they felt they had not received adequate support in the UN. But even though its influence in Israel and neighboring Arab countries was lessened, "the United Nations remains . . . the only effective mediatory instrument accepted by both sides in this bitter and continuing dispute, and this may yet prove to be the decisive factor in determining the nature of its new role."[14]

Other Political Disputes

Many other political issues have come before the Security Council or the General Assembly, or both. In some cases, as in the Soviet blockade of Berlin in 1948–49 and the fighting in Yemen between "royalists" and "rebels," supported rather substantially by Saudi Arabia and the U.A.R. respectively, the UN's efforts to resolve the disputes have been quite ineffectual. In major crises, such as the disputes between Indonesia and the Netherlands over West Iranian and between Indonesia and Malaysia, the direct confrontation between the United States and the Soviet Union over Cuba in October, 1962, and the crisis in the Dominican Republic in May, 1965, the UN has played a useful, but peripheral, role. On other delicate issues, such as the *apartheid* policies of the Republic of South Africa and Portuguese policies in Angola and Mozambique, the General Assembly has passed strong condemnatory resolutions and other UN agencies have gone on record in a similar vein, but stronger action in the form of economic sanctions or military measures has not been attempted. Other important political questions have come before the Security Council or General Assembly without effective UN action. Among these have been the following: a complaint by Syria and Lebanon in 1946 about the slowness of Britain and France in withdrawing troops from their territories; measures against the Franco regime in Spain; charges by India that South Africa was discriminating against the sizable Indian population in that country; a request by Egypt for the assistance of the Security Council in forcing Britain to evacuate her troops from the Suez Canal area and to terminate the joint Anglo-Egyptian rule in the Sudan; a complaint of the Nizam of Hyderabad against India; the events leading to the Communist coup in Czechoslovakia in February, 1948; complaints of violations of human rights in Bulgaria, Hungary, Rumania, and the U.S.S.R.; a charge by Nationalist China that the Soviet Union was aiding the Chinese Communists; an allegation by Communist China that the United States had committed "armed aggression" against her; British claims against Iran during the dispute over oil nationalization; and complaints by Arab-Asian countries against French policies in North Africa.

Security Issues

Chapter VII of the United Nations Charter defines the broad area of "security problems." There provisions, contained in two articles, relate particularly to military security. Article 47 provides for the setting up of a Military Staff Committee, to be composed of the chiefs of staff of the five permanent

[14] *Ibid.*

members of the Security Council (the Big Five) or their representatives, "to advise and assist the Security Council on all questions relating to the Security Council's military requirements for the maintenance of international peace and security, the employment and command of forces placed at its disposal, the regulation of armaments, and possible disarmament"; and Article 26 places upon the Security Council final responsibility for formulating plans "for the establishment of a system for the regulation of armaments." We shall discuss the attempts to implement these provisions and to deal with the problems raised by the development of weapons of mass destruction under three heads: armed forces for the United Nations; the regulation and reduction of armaments; and the control of atomic energy.

1. Armed Forces for the United Nations

The Military Staff Committee was established by the Security Council on January 25, 1946, in accordance with the provisions of the Charter. It was then specifically directed to undertake an examination of the military aspects and implications of Article 43, paragraph 1 of which reads as follows: "All members of the United Nations, in order to contribute to the maintenance of international peace and security, undertake to make available to the Security Council, on its call and in accordance with a special agreement or agreements, armed forces, assistance, and facilities, including the rights of passage, necessary for the purpose of maintaining international peace and security." This was certainly a large order: it was designed to give "teeth" to the UN. While Article 43 did not call for a real international police force it did provide that strong national contingents should be made available to the Security Council.

Most of the twenty-five meetings held in 1946 were devoted to consideration of the basic principles which should govern the organization of the national contingents and to work on a standard form of agreement to be used in negotiations between the Security Council and member states of the UN for the provision of "armed forces, assistance, and facilities." On April 30, 1947, the committee submitted a lengthy report to the Security Council. It revealed that little progress had been made by the military experts of the Big Five and that serious differences of opinion had arisen between the representatives of the Soviet Union and the other members of the committee. The Soviet member insisted that under Article 43 each of the Big Five should make available to the Council armed forces of exactly the same strength and type. While the Western powers also favored a balanced force, with a comparable overall contribution by each of the Big Five, they favored different contributions in land, sea, and air components. Later various estimates showed the major powers to be far apart in their views of the strength and approximate composition of the armed forces which in their opinion should be made available by their nations to the Security Council.

> Since mid-1947 the project of creating a collection of military contingents subject to the direction of the Security Council has been virtually abandoned. The Military Staff Committee has maintained a shadowy existence, holding periodic meetings to assert its formal identity but apparently abstaining from any substantive consideration of this central issue. Formal demands for new efforts to give effect to Article 43 have been made from time to time, but the issue has never been genuinely reopened. The scheme for a collective security force to be placed at the disposal of the Security Council is dead but not forgotten.[15]

The Uniting for Peace Resolution of November, 1950, recognized that the UN could not implement Article 43. According to this, the General Assembly's Collective Measures

[15] Inis L. Claude, Jr., "The United Nations and the Use of Force," *International Conciliation*, No. 532 (November, 1961), p. 347.

Committee, rather than the Security Council's Military Staff Committee, would prepare for the application of sanctions. The military units to be at its disposal, however, would not be true United Nations forces but "national armed forces elements" made available by previous agreement — in effect, a return to the League of Nations system of voluntary contributions. A few states, mostly small ones, have earmarked units of their armed forces for possible UN use, but the response of most UN members to the proposal was "characterized in the main by vague approval but polite refusal to undertake any specific commitments."[16] The Collective Measures Committee produced three reports — in 1951, 1952, and 1954 — but it has been largely inactive since these years.

Beginning with the Korean action in 1950, military operations have been carried on under the UN flag on several dramatic occasions. The Korean case represented a departure, unlikely to be repeated, from the conception that the UN would not attempt to apply the principle of collective security to crises involving great powers. In the Gaza Strip and in the Congo the UN undertook its first peacekeeping operations — under Chapter VI and not Chapter VII of the Charter. In these instances it mobilized military units from several of its member states — with the great powers excluded from a major role — with results which were generally regarded as helpful in dealing with critical situations but which imposed such strains on the UN itself that the desirability or capacity of conducting further peacekeeping operations was very much in question. In Cyprus the UN was also able to establish a peacekeeping force at a critical stage of affairs on that troubled island; but this operation was limited, and most of the expenses were met by the United States, the states which provided troops, and voluntary contributions.

[16] *Ibid.*, p. 369, n.42. For a summary of the responses of the member states, see the first two reports of the Collective Measures Committee: General Assembly, *Official Records*, 6th Sess., 1951, Suppl. No. 13, pp. 22–23, 27–43; 7th Sess., 1952, Suppl. No. 17, p. 21.

2. Disarmament and Arms Control[17]

Article 11 of the United Nations Charter authorizes the General Assembly to consider "the principles governing disarmament and the regulation of armaments"; Article 26 makes the Security Council, with the assistance of the Military Staff Committee, responsible for the formulation of "plans . . . for the establishment of a system for the regulation of armaments"; and Article 47 provides for the creation of the Military Staff Committee, "to advise and assist the Security Council on all questions relating to," *inter alia,* "the regulation of armaments, and possible disarmament." In general, however, the Charter did not emphasize the functions or responsibilities of the UN in the vital areas of disarmament and arms control. "The Charter's provisions may be interpreted as a sober recognition of the facts that disarmament is peculiarly dependent upon agreement among the major powers, and that the potential role of international agencies in bringing about such accord is sharply limited."[18]

But the UN could hardly ignore what has

[17] Technically, as some specialists insist, there is a sharp distinction between disarmament and arms control. Disarmament measures are designed to reduce existing levels of armaments, conventional and/or unconventional. Some advocates of disarmament stress the ultimate — or even the early — goal of general and complete disarmament (GCD). Advocates of arms control, on the other hand, generally stop far short of this goal. They are more concerned with a balance of armaments at tolerable levels, which will be adequate for security purposes but which will not exacerbate international tensions. Obviously this would normally involve a reduction of armaments, but not necessarily so, at least for some countries. Students of military strategy and national security invariably talk about arms control; pacifists and other peace workers want disarmament, as completely and as promptly as possible. The latter are more likely than the former to give the United Nations a central role in disarmament efforts.

[18] Claude, p. 332.

been termed "the most urgent and vital issue confronting the world," and it has been almost continuously involved, either directly or peripherally, in disarmament negotiations. At its first session, in 1946, the General Assembly established, first, an Atomic Energy Commission, and then a Commission on Conventional Armaments, both directly responsible to the Security Council. In 1952 these two commissions were merged into a single Disarmament Commission, which has sometimes been the main theater of disarmament and arms control negotiations, and which at other times has been largely ignored.

The Control of Atomic Energy

> We are here to make a choice between the quick and the dead. That is our business.
>
> Behind the black portent of the new atomic age lies a hope which, seized upon with faith, can work our salvation. If we fail, then we have damned every man to be the slave of Fear. Let us not deceive ourselves: We must elect World Peace or World Destruction.

With these vigorous words Bernard M. Baruch, United States representative on the Atomic Energy Commission of the United Nations, opened his address at the first session of the commission on June 14, 1946. A year before, when the final touches were being put on the United Nations Charter, the statesmen at San Francisco had been unaware that a new era was soon to be born. Less than two months later, however, the terrifying secret was disclosed when atomic bombs were dropped on the Japanese cities of Hiroshima (August 6) and Nagasaki (August 9), with devastating effect.

Realizing that atomic control could not be accomplished on the national level, the President of the United States and the Prime Ministers of Great Britain and Canada, representing the governments which had collaborated during the war in the development of the atomic bomb, met in November, 1945, and issued an Agreed Declaration urging that international action for the control of atomic energy be taken under the auspices of the United Nations. The Soviet Union endorsed the declaration. In January, 1946, the General Assembly established the Atomic Energy Commission, composed of one representative of each of the states on the Security Council and one from Canada. The Council was to issue directives to the AEC, approve its reports, recommendations, and rules of procedure, and transmit such of these as it chose to other UN agencies.[19] In the same resolution the Council instructed the commission to proceed "with the utmost dispatch" to its work and to make specific proposals.

When the AEC met in New York on June 14, after some months' delay, two basic plans were presented to it — the United States plan, presented by Bernard Baruch, and the Soviet proposals, presented by Andrei Gromyko. The United States plan was based largely on the Acheson-Lilienthal Report, which had been drafted in the spring of 1946; it proposed the creation of an International Atomic Development Authority empowered to control "all phases of the development and use of atomic energy, starting with raw materials." The plan further provided that after some effective system of international control had been put into effect, by specifically defined stages, the production of atomic bombs should cease and all existing stockpiles should be destroyed or otherwise disposed of according to the terms of the agreement. The UN would exclusively control and operate all means for the production of atomic energy. The veto was to be inapplicable when the Security Council considered action against states engaged in illegal production. The United States then made a formal offer of potentially tremendous sig-

[19] The official records of the United Nations Atomic Energy Commission, the Disarmament Commission, the Security Council, and the General Assembly, and the *Yearbook of the United Nations,* contain detailed accounts of the consideration of questions relating to the international control of atomic energy by the United Nations.

nificance: to surrender her secrets regarding the manufacture of atomic bombs and to destroy the bombs in her possession. She would do this, however, only after the UN had acquired control of all atomic facilities.

The Soviet proposals were fundamentally different in character and implications. The U.S.S.R. wanted a convention for the immediate outlawing of the production and use of atomic bombs, and the destruction of all existing stockpiles within a brief period. She would accept day-to-day inspection within prescribed limits. As these suggestions were elaborated it became clear that they meant that the Security Council would have to handle cases in this field in the same way as any other threats to peace — in other words, that the veto would apply to enforcement against violators; that inspection would be largely — but not altogether — restricted to scheduled visits to stipulated plants; and that member states could own and operate atomic facilities subject to the regulations of a control commission. Atomic weapons would be outlawed as the instant controls legally entered into force, regardless of when they went into actual operation.

These early exchanges crystallized the issues that have persisted throughout the UN's efforts to set up effective controls in the use of atomic weapons. These issues are (1) the general operation of the control system; (2) the timing of inspection and controls as against the destruction of stockpiles; (3) inspection procedures; and (4) the use of the veto in enforcement actions.

Early in its deliberations the AEC established a Working Committee, a Committee on Controls, a Legal Advisory Committee, and a Scientific and Technical Committee. These committees considered the technical aspects of the United States and Soviet proposals, and in general found the American proposals to be more feasible. This position was also taken by the AEC — with the usual dissenting votes of the two Communist members. The commission specifically endorsed the proposal for an international control agency and, in its Third Report to the Security Council, submitted on May 17, 1948, warned that "Unless effective international control is established, there can be no lasting security against atomic weapons for any nation, whatever its size, location or power." The Third Session of the General Assembly, in the latter part of 1948, endorsed the majority plan of the AEC as a feasible and effective system for the international control of atomic energy, and in effect made it the United Nations plan, but one without the remotest chance of implementation.

The Commission for Conventional Armaments. On October 29, 1946, the Soviet Foreign Minister, V. M. Molotov, introduced into the General Assembly a resolution calling for a general reduction of armaments by the nations of the world and for a prohibition of the production and use of atomic energy for military purposes. A draft presented by the United States became the basis for a resolution which the General Assembly passed, by unanimous vote, on December 14, 1946. Besides urging the Atomic Energy Commission to expedite its work, the resolution requested the Security Council to accelerate as much as possible the implementation of Article 43 of the Charter and to formulate practical measures for the regulation and reduction of armaments. Three months later the Council, pursuant to the mandate of the General Assembly, established the Commission for Conventional Armaments, composed of representatives of the members of the Security Council. The commission was instructed to present to the Council proposals for the regulation and reduction of "conventional" armaments. It was specifically enjoined from considering plans for the control of atomic bombs or other weapons of mass destruction, which came within the province of the Atomic Energy Commission.

The discussion within the commission and

later in the Security Council revealed a fundamental difference of approach. The position of the U.S.S.R., supported by Poland, was that immediate reduction of armaments was a "first and indispensable step" in restoring world confidence and that proposals for the prohibition of atomic weapons should also be considered by the commission. The position of the United States, endorsed by all other members of the commission and the Council, was, as stated by Secretary of State Marshall on September 17, 1947, "that a workable system for the regulation of armaments cannot be put into operation until conditions of international confidence prevail."

After attempting for months to agree on a formulation of basic principles, the Commission for Conventional Armaments, on August 12, 1948, adopted a resolution embodying the views of the United States, and five days later it approved a draft progress report to the Security Council. The Soviet Union opposed the resolution and prevented the draft report from becoming official. The Soviet delegate introduced a resolution calling for the total prohibition of atomic weapons and for the reduction of armaments by the permanent members of the Security Council by one-third within one year. The debate on this proposal led to the passage, on November 19, 1948, of a different kind of resolution, approved by forty-three members of the General Assembly, with only the Soviet bloc in active opposition. This resolution affirmed the view that "the reduction of conventional armaments and armed forces can only be attained in an atmosphere of real and lasting improvement in international relations"; but at the same time it urged the Security Council to continue its study of the problem through the Commission for Conventional Armaments, and suggested that the commission "devote its first attention to formulating proposals for the receipt, checking and publication, by an international organ of control within the framework of the Security Council, of full information to be supplied by Member States with regard to their effectives and their conventional armaments." When, in early 1949, the commission submitted plans for carrying out the Assembly's suggestion, the Soviet Union prevented their adoption by the Security Council.

On June 6. 1950, Secretary-General Trygve Lie asserted that efforts toward the control of armaments had been "virtually a complete failure," but he called upon the UN members for further efforts. Later in the same year, in an address to the General Assembly, President Truman suggested that the Commission for Conventional Armaments and the Atomic Energy Commission be merged. The General Assembly thereupon established a Committee of Twelve to consider the advisability of such a course and to report to the Sixth Session about a year later. On November 8, 1951, just before the report of the Committee of Twelve, Britain, France, and the United States submitted proposals for the reduction of all armaments, including atomic weapons. The proposals embraced the earlier American ideas of national arms inventories, international verification of inventories, accompanied by regulation and "balanced reduction" with everything to move along together on a stage-to-stage basis. It was this set of proposals that gave Mr. Vyshinsky his historic sleepless night: according to his account, he laughed all night. By November 16 he had recovered sufficiently to reply to the tripartite proposals.[20]

In spite of the opposition of the Soviet bloc, the General Assembly, on January 11, 1952, voted to merge the Commissions for Conventional Armaments and Atomic Energy into a single Disarmament Commission, to be composed, like its predecessors, of the eleven members of the Security Council, plus Canada.

[20] A. Y. Vyshinsky, "Speeches Delivered at the Plenary Meetings of the Sixth Session of the United Nations General Assembly," *Information Bulletin* of the Embassy of the U.S.S.R., December, 1951, pp. 35–36.

The Disarmament Commission and Its Subcommittee. The new commission was no more effective than its predecessors. In April, 1952, the United States submitted a working paper on the "Essential Principles for a Disarmament Program."[21] These were summarized under five points: inventory and verification; the calculation of limits and reductions for all armed forces and all armaments; the determination of national armament programs through negotiations among states; the fixing of methods for implementing disarmament; and agreement upon a disarmament timetable. The Soviet representative, Jacob Malik, presented an alternative program. This differed from earlier Soviet proposals largely in that it gave considerable attention to bacteriological warfare, which the U.S.S.R. charged the United States with waging in Korea.

On June 28, 1952, the United States, the United Kingdom, and France proposed in the Disarmament Commission that China, the Soviet Union, and the United States accept troop quotas of 1,500,000 men, France a quota of 800,000 and Britain one of 700,000, and that all other states have smaller forces. As was to be expected, the Soviet Union rejected this proposal. Her two major criticisms were that it did not specify in what proportion military strength was to be divided among armies, navies, and air forces and did not deal concretely with limitations on weapons, atomic as well as conventional.

On November 28, 1953, the General Assembly provided for a Subcommittee of Five of the Disarmament Commission to "seek in private an acceptable solution." From May 13 to June 22, 1954, the subcommittee held nineteen secret meetings in London.[22] It considered various new proposals, but it was unable to find anything approaching "an acceptable solution." During the latter half of 1954 the subcommittee did not meet, but in the spring of 1955, at the behest of the General Assembly, it held many sessions. On May 10, 1955, the Soviet delegate, Jacob Malik, presented what was in many respects the most comprehensive and most significant of the scores of proposals which the Soviet Union had advanced in relation to the atomic weapons.[23]

The Geneva Meetings of 1955. Several events in 1953 had seemingly created a more hopeful atmosphere for the efforts to reach agreement on disarmament, and at least one event — the Russian explosion of a hydrogen bomb — gave these efforts an even greater urgency. In his first foreign policy speech, on April 16, 1953, President Eisenhower proposed the limitation of armaments and the international control of atomic energy with "adequate safeguards, including a practical system of inspection under the United Nations." On December 8, in a dramatic address before the General Assembly of the United Nations, he further proposed that "the governments principally involved . . . begin now and continue to make joint contributions of normal uranium and fissionable materials to an atomic energy agency." At first the leaders of the Soviet Union shunned the President's "atoms-for-peace" plan, but later they agreed to give it serious attention. One of the consequences of the detailed con-

[21] The working paper is summarized in *Report to the President by the Deputy United States Representative on the United Nations Disarmament Commission*, Dept. of State press release, January 14, 1953, No. 24.

[22] The records of seventeen of these meetings were made public later in 1954. For a summary of the proceedings in the subcommittee, see *The Record on Disarmament: Report of U. S. Deputy Representative to Disarmament Commission on London Meeting of Subcommittee of Five and on Disarmament Commission Meetings — July, 1954*, Dept. of State Pub. 5581. International Organization and Conference Series III (September, 1954), p. 102.

[23] The text of the Soviet proposal of May 10, 1955, is given in the *New York Times*, May 12, 1955. For texts of documents submitted by the United States to the Subcommittee of Five between February 25 and May 9, see *New York Times*, May 14, 1955.

sideration of the proposal by the United Nations was the convoking of an international conference on the peaceful uses of atomic energy. At Geneva in the summer of 1955, for the first time representatives of the Soviet Union as well as of the Western atomic powers revealed many of the secrets of their progress in the development of this fabulous new source of energy.

Questions relating to disarmament were also discussed at the "summit" meeting in July, 1955 — held at Geneva just before the UN conference — and all four principals advanced different plans. Premier Faure stressed what he called "positive disarmament" and proposed that money saved from military budgets be used for underdeveloped areas. Sir Anthony Eden suggested that atomic inspection — the main stumbling block to agreement on disarmament measures — begin in a demilitarized zone which he proposed to create between Eastern and Western Europe, and that inspection then be gradually extended to the rest of the world. Marshal Bulganin presented a plan modeled on the Soviet proposal of May 10, with emphasis on a step-by-step reduction of nuclear weapons and a limitation on troops for each country, and also with a reference to the necessity for "effective international control." President Eisenhower contributed the most imaginative idea when he proposed that the Soviet Union and the United States immediately "give to each other a complete blueprint of our military establishments from beginning to end" and "provide within our countries facilities for aerial photography." His was an unprecedented and bold proposal which was enthusiastically received throughout the non-Communist world, but there seemed to be little possibility that it could ever be implemented.

At the close of the "summit" conference the Big Four jointly suggested that the subcommittee of the UN Disarmament Commission meet again on August 29, and they instructed their foreign ministers, at their meeting in October, "to take note of the proceedings in the Disarmament Commission, to take account of the views and proposals advanced by the heads of government at this conference and to consider whether the four governments can take any further useful initiative in the field of disarmament." Neither the UN Disarmament Commission and its Subcommittee of Five nor the Big Four foreign ministers, however, were able to translate the hopes of the heads of government into comforting reality.

In September, 1957, the Subcommittee of Five held its final session, and in November of the following year, after the Soviet Union had announced that it would no longer participate in the work of the Disarmament Commission or its subcommittee unless the commission was enlarged to include all members of the UN, the General Assembly voted to reconstitute the commission along these lines.

Discussions Outside the Disarmament Commission. For the next few years the most significant discussions on disarmament and arms control were held outside of the enlarged Disarmament Commission. One forum was the Ten-Nation Disarmament Committee, set up by the foreign ministers of Britain, France, the United States, and the Soviet Union and consisting of representatives of their own countries as well as of Bulgaria, Canada, Czechoslovakia, Italy, Poland, and Rumania. This committee met several times in the spring of 1960, but it came to an abrupt end in late June when the Communist bloc members withdrew. At the opening of the Fifteenth Session of the General Assembly in September, attended by many heads of government, Khrushchev submitted proposals for disarmament similar to those that had been presented by the Soviet delegate to the Ten-Nation Committee; he proposed that the committee be enlarged to include Ghana, India, Indonesia, Mexico, and the U.A.R. Another forum had become available in the fall of 1958 when the Soviet Union and the United States, after suspending nuclear tests, joined in an international conference of experts on the cessation of these tests. During the next two years agreement was reached on most of the articles in a proposed nuclear test ban treaty; but the conference finally reached a stalemate because of disagreement over control arrangements and the Soviet proposal on March 21, 1961, for a *troika* administrative board. On August 31 the Soviets announced that they had decided to resume nuclear testing, and in the following April the United States followed suit. By this time the question of a ban on nuclear testing had been transferred to the newly created Eighteen-Nation Disarmament Committee (ENDC).

The formation of this new committee was agreed upon in direct talks between Soviet and American representatives in the summer of 1961 and announced in a "Joint Statement of Agreed Principles for Disarmament Negotiations."[24] It was composed of the members of the Ten-Nation Disarmament Committee (except France, which refused to participate), plus Brazil, Burma, Ethiopia, India, Mexico, Nigeria, Sweden, and the U.A.R. — in other words, five Warsaw Pact states, four NATO countries (not counting France), and eight nonaligned countries. Since its first meeting in March, 1962, it has considered both disarmament and arms control questions and the cessation of nuclear tests. In 1962 both the United States and the Soviet Union presented to ENDC detailed proposals that formed the basis of negotiations for the following two years and more.[25] In many respects the two drafts were strikingly similar. Each called for general and complete disarmament of conventional and nuclear weapons in three stages, the establishment of peacekeeping machinery, and the creation of an international Disarmament Organization. "Beneath these similarities, however, lie radically different prescriptions for each stage of the disarmament process."[26]

First Steps: the Long Road Ahead. In 1963 and 1964 a more hopeful atmosphere was created by three agreements which represented almost the only concrete results of nearly twenty years of intermittent negotiations, in the United Nations and outside, through both multilateral and bilateral diplomacy. On June 20, 1963, the United States and the Soviet Union signed an agreement to establish a direct communications link (the so-called hot line); on August 5, at a conference in Moscow, representatives of the United States, the United Kingdom, and the Soviet Union signed a partial nuclear test ban treaty; and on April 20, 1964, the United States and the Soviet Union announced that they had agreed to reduce their production of fissionable materials used in nuclear weapons.

Although opinion in the United States was sharply divided, and although it was a very modest and limited step along the long and difficult road to effective measures of disarmament and arms control, the nuclear test ban treaty was hailed throughout most of the world as a historic development and a significant reversal of the trend toward mounting armaments and nuclear proliferation. The treaty was open to all states. By October 10, 1963, over one hundred nations had signed. There were, however, two conspicuous nonsigners — France and Communist China. France began to develop a nuclear capability in 1960. Communist China exploded her first nuclear device in October, 1964, and less than three years later she tested a hydrogen bomb. Thus only three

[24] The text of this statement is contained in U. N. Document A/4879, September 20, 1961.

[25] U. N. Documents DC/203, June 5, 1962; and DC/207, April 12, 1963.

[26] "Issues Before the Nineteenth General Assembly," *International Conciliation*, No. 550 (November, 1964), p. 25. For an informative chart comparing and contrasting the Soviet and American draft treaties of 1962, see *ibid.*, pp. 26–27.

of the five nuclear powers were included among the signatories to the test ban treaty; but even so its conclusion was a notable achievement.

In spite of these promising developments, the discussions in ENDC continued to be unproductive. By 1965 little was heard about general and complete disarmament, which both the Soviet and American proposals of 1962 had posited as the ultimate goal and which a resolution of the UN General Assembly in 1959, unanimously adopted, had declared to be "the most important issue facing the world today."

From September, 1964, until July, 1965, largely at the insistence of the Soviet Union, ENDC reverted to a standby status and the main forum for disarmament discussions became again the UN's Disarmament Commission. Thereafter ENDC resumed deliberations, and it has held one or two lengthy sessions each year. The General Assembly of the United Nations has encouraged its perseverance in its rather frustrating task. Late in 1966, the Assembly adopted a series of resolutions on disarmament, appealing to all states to take steps to conclude a treaty on the nonproliferation of nuclear weapons (ironically, some of the non-nuclear states blocked agreement on a nonproliferation treaty to which the United States and the Soviet Union seemed to have agreed), requesting the ENDC to give high priority to this matter, and calling for a conference of non-nuclear states. Since 1965 the General Assembly has been on record in favor of a world disarmament conference which would include representatives of Communist China On January 27, 1967, representatives of sixty countries signed a treaty banning weapons of mass destruction in outer space.

On July 1, 1968, at parallel ceremonies in Washington, London, and Moscow, representatives of 61 nations signed the treaty on the nonproliferation of nuclear weapons. Among the conspicuous non-signers were the Federal Republic of Germany, India, Japan, and Brazil — and, of course, France and Communist China. President Johnson hailed the treaty as "the most important international agreement since the beginning of the nuclear age."

Unhappily the prospects for really far-reaching agreements on disarmament and/or arms control seem as remote as ever; yet many students of international affairs believe with Nobel Peace Prize winner and veteran campaigner for peace, Philip Noel-Baker, that on "the making of a treaty of general disarmament, the future of civilized mankind depends."[27]

An Appraisal

While one must admit that the United Nations has failed to "settle," definitively, a single dispute brought before it, this is not to say that it has not relieved tensions in many crucial situations. That it has failed to achieve any of the three major objectives of the security provisions admits of less qualification.

Two points should be mentioned in defense of the UN's record of limited success in dealing with political disputes. (1) Few international disputes are really "settled," but they may be compromised, postponed, or otherwise prevented from leading to serious international crises, and with the passage of time may lose much of their explosive character. The UN can play, and has played, a useful role in "defusing" disputes that might otherwise lead to international explosions. (2) The United Nations encourages the parties to a dispute to "seek a solution by negotiation, enquiry, mediation, conciliation, arbitration, judicial settlement, resort to regional agencies or arrangements, or other peaceful means of their own choice" (Article 33 of the Charter). In other words, the role of the UN is an intermediary one, and only

[27] Article on "Peace" in *The Americana Annual, 1965* (New York: Americana Corp., 1965) p. 555.

Vicky in The London Daily News Chronicle

"Big Job for a Child Prodigy"

when all other procedures for peaceful settlement have been exhausted is the Security Council requested to invoke the more stringent provisions of Chapter VII of the Charter. Moreover, it is well to note again that the Council cannot act unless all the great powers are ready and willing to support its action.

Although the UN does not have many striking successes to its credit in the handling of political disputes, its services as a mediator have been valuable in several instances. The work of the UN Committee of Good Offices in Indonesia, the services of various UN commissions dealing with Greek frontier incidents, India and Pakistan, and Palestine, and the indefatigable labors of Count Bernadotte and Dr. Ralph Bunche in the delicate negotiations between Jewish and Arab spokesmen — all these deserve high commendation, much more than has yet been accorded. Although the efforts of other commissions and committees, such as the UN Temporary Commission on Korea and the Technical Committee on Berlin Currency and Trade, were less fruitful, they were nonetheless conscientious and zealous, and their limited results were due to "circumstances beyond their control." In all of the political disputes which have been discussed in this chapter, the UN played a useful and significant, if sometimes a peripheral and limited role. The value of the UN presence in such crisis areas as Kashmir, Korea, the Gaza Strip, West Irian, the Congo, and Cyprus can hardly be denied, although it is sometimes overlooked or denigrated.

In dealing with security problems, however, the UN has run into obstructions just as real as, and even more serious than, those faced in political disputes. The main security agencies of the Security Council — the Military Staff Committee, the Commission for Conventional Armaments, the Atomic Energy Commission, and the Disarmament Commission — prepared elaborate plans which the majority approved, but all of these plans encountered the great power deadlock that has frustrated every effort to implement the security provisions of the Charter and hampered international cooperation everywhere in the postwar period. If the failure to provide armed forces for the United Nations and to regulate and reduce armaments is particularly serious — as it certainly is — what shall be said of the complete impasse in the efforts to set up an effective system for the international control of atomic energy? Atomic control may well be the central problem in the international relations of our time. Even if the choice is not so inexorably between "one world or none," as many scientists tell us, or between "the quick and the dead," to use Bernard Baruch's phrase, the problem is still a crucial one. Until some answer is found to the question of the control of the power of the atom — an answer which, we can be sure, must be sought on the international planc — insecurity and ever-present danger will be the lot of the people of the world.

It would be unfair to blame the United Nations for this most tragic of failures on the international scene. The roots of this failure lie deeply embedded in nationalism, sovereignty, and nation-state psychology, and also in the perversities of the human race. The United Nations has made a thorough study of the technical and political requirements for the effective control of atomic energy; beyond that it cannot go unless the peoples of the world, or at least those of the great powers, are willing to support its efforts on their behalf.

SUGGESTIONS FOR FURTHER READING

See the list at the end of Chapter 14.

14 The United Nations: Economic, Social, and Organizational Issues

Overshadowing the political and security activities of the United Nations, in scope, achievement, and perhaps in ultimate significance, are its operations in economic and social fields. As stated in Article 1 of the Charter, the third major purpose of the UN is the achievement of "international cooperation in solving international problems of an economic, social, cultural, or humanitarian character, and in promoting and encouraging respect for human rights and fundamental freedoms." The UN is thus concerned not only with the maintenance of peace but also with promoting the conditions under which genuine peace will be possible. "In the long run, United Nations leadership in the struggle for world welfare holds the chief promise of creating the underlying conditions of social stability and human satisfaction essential to a lasting peace."[1]

The Economic and Social Council of the United Nations, the Council's commissions and specialized agencies, the Trusteeship Council, and the Secretariat are primarily concerned with work in these fields.[2] We shall here present a survey of that work under the following main headings: (1) economic questions; (2) social and cultural questions; (3) human rights and fundamental freedoms; and (4) problems of dependent peoples. Then, having completed our examination of the functioning of the UN, we shall note some of the criticisms that have been made of the UN structure and operation, and review actions taken and proposals made to strengthen the organization.

[1] Philip E. Jacob, "The United Nations and the Struggle for World Welfare," *Pennsylvania School Journal,* 1950, p. 60.

[2] For concise summaries, see the September issue each year of *International Conciliation.*

Economic Issues

The Charter of the United Nations specifically states that the UN shall promote "higher standards of living, full employment, and conditions of economic and social progress and development," and shall "employ international machinery for the promotion of the economic and social advancement of all peoples." General responsibility for implementing these ambitious goals rests with the General Assembly, and especially, under the General Assembly's overall discretion, with the Economic and Social Council. Almost all of the functional and regional commissions, specialized agencies, and special committees associated with ECOSOC are seeking in various ways to carry out the mandate of the Charter in economic and social fields.

General Factual Studies. The paucity of reliable statistics and other vital information on conditions in most of the countries of the world has been one of the greatest handicaps to intelligent planning and action. The UN is now helping to supply this information. Especially noteworthy are its general economic surveys. In January, 1948, it issued a report entitled *Salient Features of the World Economic Situation, 1945–47,* the first comprehensive world economic report to be published since before the war. Since 1949 the UN has put out an annual report on world economic conditions and, in addition, annual economic surveys of Europe, Asia and the Far East, and Latin America. Many agencies and commissions of the UN have also issued important studies. The Secretariat and the specialized agencies have published a number of studies in the field of technical assistance and economic development, and others are in preparation.

Finance and Trade. "A change of political dimension," declared the Secretary-General of the United Nations in July, 1964, has taken place "in the awareness of the need for a more organized international co-operation in the economic and financial field."[3] Evidence of this change may be found in the growing interest in the question of international liquidity, in the "strategic confrontation of commercial policies" in the General Agreement on Tariffs and Trade (GATT), and in the United Nations Conference on Trade and Development in 1964.

All countries must pay particular attention to their gold reserves and their holdings in major world currencies, notably American dollars and British pounds. The continuing strength of the dollar and the pound is a matter of concern to many nations, and especially to the United States and the United Kingdom. The United Kingdom has on several occasions exercised her drawing rights on the International Monetary Fund for currencies from the main trading countries,[4] and in late 1964 she received emergency short-term credits of $3 billion from the central banks of eleven leading financial nations ($1 billion from American sources). Emergency measures failed to solve the plight of the pound; in 1967 England announced a 14.3 per cent devaluation. Confidence in the dollar, somewhat shaken by American balance of payments difficulties despite some success in efforts to reduce the deficit, was challenged by the British devaluation and the temporary wave of gold-buying by those who expected the dollar to follow the pound. The governments of most major nations rallied to the support of the dollar. Clearly, however, the international monetary system is faced with a continuing crisis of major proportions.

Recent efforts to reduce trade barriers through multilateral negotiations under the auspices of GATT have been affected greatly by the United States Trade Expansion Act of 1962, which led to the "Kennedy round" of negotiations; General de Gaulle's veto of Great Britain's application for membership in the European Economic Community (EEC); differences between the United States and EEC, especially over prices of grain and other agricultural products; and the pressure of the developing countries for more favorable treatment and consideration. The response to the compaints of the developing countries has taken many forms. In 1963 a Programme of Action was adopted, and an Action Committee was appointed. In the following year a GATT International Trade Center was opened. The developing countries welcomed these and other steps by GATT to give greater recognition to their needs, but they still regard GATT as an asso-

[3] United Nations Press Release SG/ISM/110, July 16, 1964, p. 2.

[4] In August, 1961, she was authorized to draw upon the Fund for credits equivalent to $1.5 billion, the largest single drawing the Fund has ever authorized. In late November, 1964, she arranged to draw $1 billion from the Fund, in addition to the credits by the United States and ten other nations.

ciation weighted in favor of the developed nations and place greater reliance on the new machinery created by the United Nations Conference on Trade and Development.

This remarkable conference, which has staged two mammoth international conferences, in 1964 and 1968, attended by delegates and observers from some 120 countries, is described in Chapter 19. It features extensive attention to the interests and needs of the developing countries. Although representatives of these countries displayed an unusual degree of cohesion and common purpose, they were unable to obtain acceptance of their desire to create a new International Trade Organization as a specialized agency of the United Nations. The compromise agreement provided that the Conference should be established as an affiliate of the UN General Assembly, to meet at intervals of not more than three years, and that it should have a permanent Trade and Development Board of 55 members, with permanent committees on commodities, manufactures, and invisibles and financing related to trade, and such other subsidiary organs as might be deemed necessary.

Technical Assistance and Economic Development. In 1948 the General Assembly requested the Economic and Social Council and the specialized agencies to give particular attention to the problems of technical assistance and economic development in underdeveloped countries, and expressed the hope that the International Bank for Reconstruction and Development would make loans for such purposes. The Assembly made available to the Secretary-General the sum of $288,000 for 1949; this was intended to finance pioneering work in preparation for the operational program. The grants have risen substantially in more recent years.

1. *TAB, TAC, and TAA*. In a sense, the Economic and Social Council was forced into the assumption of leadership in this area by the fact that the specialized agencies of the UN had already undertaken so many independent activities that overlapping, serious gaps, and cross-purposes were beginning to appear. While these agencies were especially well qualified to do their particular jobs, some coordination had to be effected. Further impetus to the establishment of coordinating machinery came from President Truman's announcement of the Point Four Program in January, 1949. Consequently, the UN in 1949 created two new bodies: the Technical Assistance Board (TAB), consisting of the executive heads of the UN and of the specialized agencies; and the Technical Assistance Committee (TAC), composed of delegates from states with representation on ECOSOC. The General Assembly established a Technical Assistance Administration (TAA) as a separate branch of the Secretariat.

2. *Financing the Programs.* Under its regular program the UN has two main sources of funds for technical assistance: a relatively small item in its regular budget, and larger voluntary contributions to the United Nations Development Program (UNDP), which came into existence in November 1965, as a result of the merger of the Expanded Programme of Technical Assistance (EPTA) and the Special Fund. The annual budget of EPTA grew from $20 million in 1950 to $50 million in 1964. Its major fields of activity have been in agriculture, health services, education, resource surveys, and administrative improvement. The Special Fund, in the first five years of its existence (1959–64) contributed approximately $374 million to 421 approved projects in many countries, chiefly for pre-investment and feasibility surveys, technical education and training institutes, and applied research in the developing countries.

The problem of financing the economic development of underdeveloped countries, and not simply of giving them technical assistance, is difficult under any conditions, as the United States is discovering, and is par-

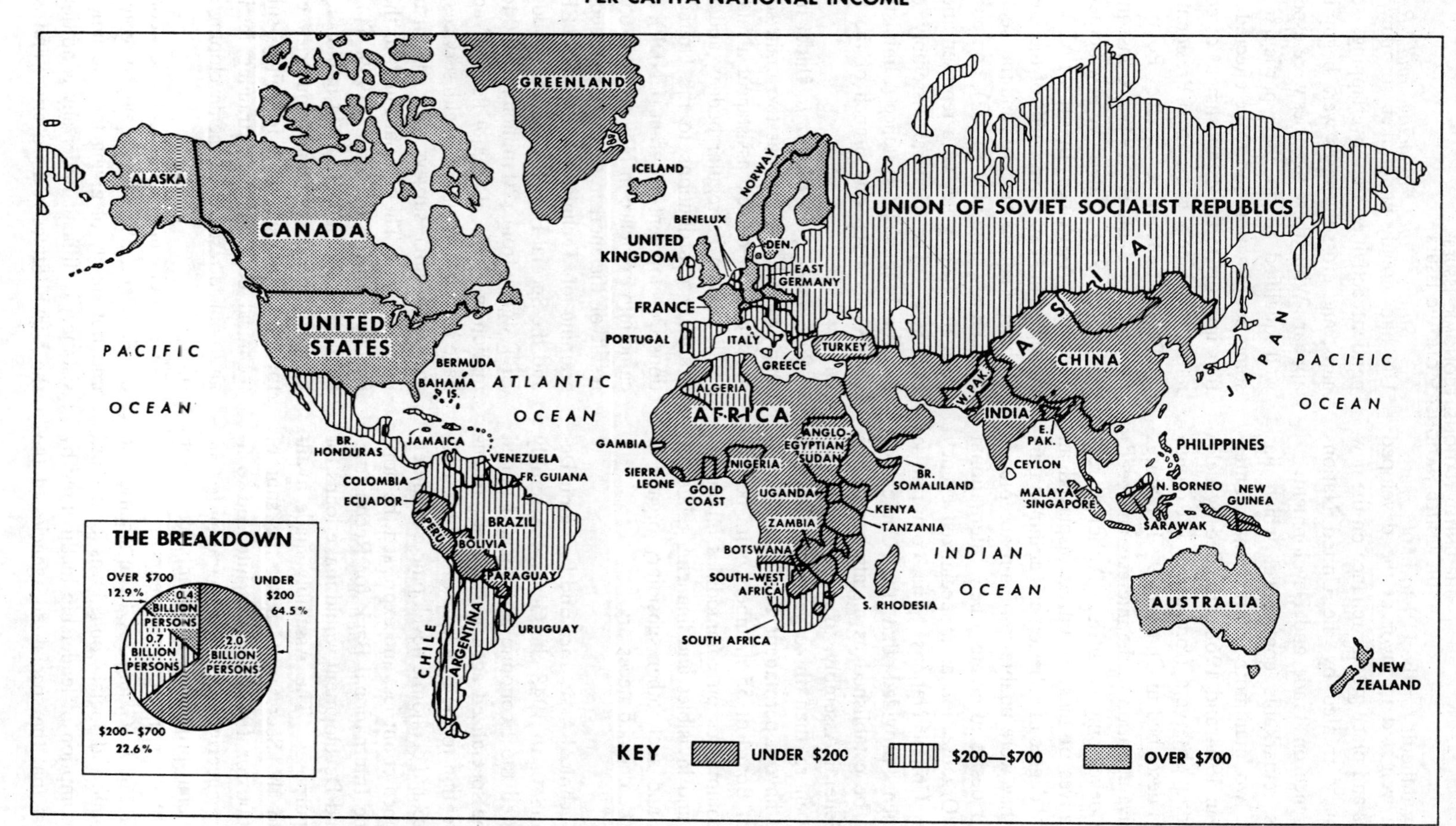
THE UNEVEN DISTRIBUTION OF THE WORLD'S INCOME
PER CAPITA NATIONAL INCOME
GREENLAND
ALASKA
CANADA
UNITED STATES
PACIFIC OCEAN
BERMUDA
BAHAMA IS.
ATLANTIC OCEAN
BR. HONDURAS
JAMAICA
VENEZUELA
FR. GUIANA
COLOMBIA
ECUADOR
BRAZIL
PERU
BOLIVIA
PARAGUAY
CHILE
ARGENTINA
URUGUAY
ICELAND
NORWAY
BENELUX
UNITED KINGDOM
DEN.
EAST GERMANY
FRANCE
PORTUGAL
ITALY
GREECE
TURKEY
UNION OF SOVIET SOCIALIST REPUBLICS
ASIA
CHINA
JAPAN
W. PAK.
INDIA
E. PAK.
CEYLON
PHILIPPINES
N. BORNEO
NEW GUINEA
MALAYA SINGAPORE
SARAWAK
ALGERIA
AFRICA
GAMBIA
SIERRA LEONE
GOLD COAST
NIGERIA
ANGLO-EGYPTIAN SUDAN
BR. SOMALILAND
UGANDA
KENYA
TANZANIA
ZAMBIA
BOTSWANA
SOUTH-WEST AFRICA
S. RHODESIA
SOUTH AFRICA
INDIAN OCEAN
AUSTRALIA
NEW ZEALAND
THE BREAKDOWN
OVER $700 12.9%
0.4 BILLION PERSONS
0.7 BILLION PERSONS
2.0 BILLION PERSONS
UNDER $200 64.5%
$200–$700 22.6%
KEY
UNDER $200
$200—$700
OVER $700

ticularly difficult for the UN to handle satisfactorily. The UN does not command sizable amounts of capital. The only organizations in the UN system which have the resources to make substantial loans are the International Bank and its affiliate, the International Development Association (IDA). The Bank makes loans only at commercial rates and with ironclad guarantees. Most of its loans, however, have been for purposes related to economic development. In recent years it has loaned well over half a billion dollars annually to developing countries. IDA, which extends "soft" loans, began operations only toward the end of 1960, and it has been handicapped by limited resources; but by mid-1966 it had loaned a total of more than $1.3 billion.

In 1957 another World Bank affiliate, the International Finance Corporation (IFC), was created to further economic development by investing in productive private enterprises in association with private investors in developing countries. Thus far, however, its investments and underwriting operations have involved an expenditure of only a few million dollars. The Capital Development Fund which began operations in 1968, has also not been able to obtain substantial financial resources.

The decade of the 1960's has been proclaimed by the UN as the "Decade of Development." In 1960 the General Assembly suggested that international assistance to underdeveloped countries be increased "so as to reach as soon as possible approximately 1 per cent of the combined national incomes of the economically advanced countries." This seems to be a modest goal which would hardly meet the capital needs of developing countries. Some countries, notably France, already contribute considerably more than one per cent of their national incomes to foreign assistance programs; but the total contributions of developed countries, including the United States, in foreign assistance still fall well short of one per cent.

3. *Studies on Financing and Related Problems.* While the UN is not prepared to assist substantially in the financing of economic development, it has been helpful in making studies bearing on the matter. In 1949 the Secretary-General issued a report, prepared by the Secretariat with the assistance of experts from all parts of the world, entitled *Methods of Increasing Domestic Savings.* Other related studies have dealt with international capital movements, relative prices of exports and imports in underdeveloped countries, conditions governing private investment in certain countries, the domestic financing of economic development, the formulation and execution of development projects, and the effects of price fluctuations and the rise in raw-material prices upon underdeveloped countries. Of particular importance was a 1951 report, *Measures for the Economic Development of Underdeveloped Countries,*[5] which analyzed at considerable length the capital requirements for increasing national income per capita by two per cent annually. It also recommended an International Development Authority in the UN, with power to make grants to underdeveloped countries.

4. *Technical Assistance Programs.* "The methods of technical assistance vary from simple, short-range ones, like the introduction of new seed strains, to infinitely complex ones, like the support of an operating mission authorized to reorganize the civil service system of a requesting government."[6] At times single experts may conduct a study in a particular country, but more frequently teams of two or more are sent. These "expert missions" are of three kinds: the survey mission, the advisory mission, and the operating mission. The survey mission is often an indispensable preliminary to any real work, but as it is expensive it is not likely

[5] UN Pub. 1951. II. B. 2.

[6] Marian Neal, "United Nations Technical Assistance Programs in Haiti," *International Conciliation,* No. 468 (February, 1951), p. 62.

to be sent unless the requesting government is clearly prepared to take further action. The advisory mission, like the survey mission, has proved to be readily acceptable to host governments. The operating mission sometimes encounters local resistance, for it may have to attempt basic social and economic reforms.

There are many approaches to technical assistance. These include regional projects in underdeveloped areas, the provision of experts, an extensive fellowship program, and training centers. In 1965 a United Nations Institute for Training and Research, supported by voluntary contributions from governments and private sources, was opened.[7]

The coordination of the many technical assistance programs is becoming increasingly serious and complicated. "The problem . . . is many-tiered coordination between EPTA and the Special Fund; between them and regular programs of the intergovernmental bodies; between international and bilateral assistance programs and between these programs and those of the host government; and coordination between technical assistance and sources of capital financing. Still another tier is the synchronization of regional activities with country and global programs."[8]

World Food Problems. "The rapidly increasing population of the world, together with the decreasing productivity of the soil," wrote Lord Boyd-Orr in 1949, "makes world famine as great a threat to our civilization as the atomic bomb."[9] Two-thirds of the people of the world do not get enough to eat. It is estimated that food production must be increased substantially if mass starvation is to be avoided. Such facts as these are of particular concern to the UN, especially to the Food and Agriculture Organization (FAO). During the postwar world food crisis the FAO played a significant role. Especially through the World Food Council and the International Emergency Food Committee it focused attention on the gravity of the crisis and on the need for coordinated action by national governments and international agencies. It supplied essential statistical and technical information, sent missions of experts to several countries, sponsored a series of conferences, and helped member states of the UN in a variety of other ways. It assumed responsibility for the World Agricultural Census of 1950, and was instrumental in drafting the International Wheat Agreement, to which most of the major wheat-producing countries have adhered. In 1960 it launched a Freedom from Hunger campaign.

The following year the United Nations and FAO established the World Food Programme (WFP) to "explore the possibilities of stimulating economic and social development through aid in the form of food." By the end of 1963, 53 countries had pledged about $90 million in commodities, services, and cash. This amount, especially the cash contributions, was well short of expectations. WFP is a worthwhile experiment which must still prove its feasibility and long-term value.

FAO plays a major role in the UN's technical assistance work; already it has aided in a variety of problems, such an animal and plant disease control, storage of grains, conservation and prevention of soil erosion, and fishery production and conservation. The regional commissions of the UN have set up joint working groups with FAO to eliminate bottlenecks in the production and distribution of food, fertilizers, and agricultural machinery. FAO has fostered such agencies as the International Rice Commission, the Indo-Pacific Fisheries Council at Bangkok, the General Fisheries Council for the Medi-

[7] See Arthur M. Cox and Karl Mathiasen, III, *The United Nations Institute for Training and Research* (Washington D.C.: The Brookings Institution, December, 1964), a mimeographed Brookings Staff Paper.

[8] "Issues Before the Eighteenth General Assembly," *International Conciliation*, No. 544 (September, 1963), pp. 165–166.

[9] "Science, Politics, and Hunger," *The Nation*, CLXIX (July 16, 1949), 61.

FOOD AND POPULATION

Distribution of the population of the world according to daily intake of calories (Recent)

Size of country in proportion to population

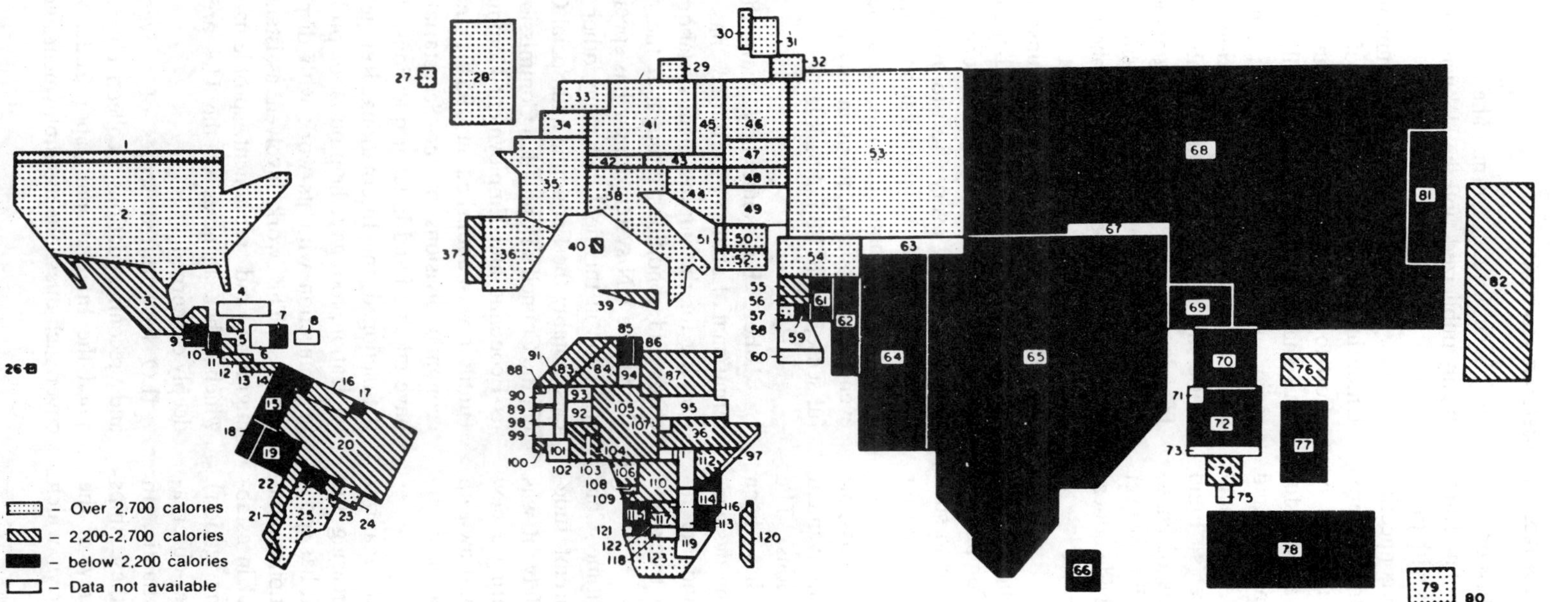

1. Canada - 2. United States - 3. Mexico - 4. Cuba - 5. Jamaica - 6. Haiti - 7. Dominican Republic - 8. Puerto Rico - 9. Guatemala - 10. El Salvador - 11. Honduras - 12. Nicaragua - 13. Costa Rica - 14. Panama - 15. Colombia - 16. Venezuela - 17. Guianas - 18. Ecuador - 19. Peru - 20. Brazil - 21. Chile - 22. Bolivia - 23. Paraguay - 24. Uruguay - 25. Argentina - 26. Hawaii - 27. Ireland - 28. United Kingdom - 29. Denmark - 30. Norway - 31. Sweden - 32. Finland - 33. Netherlands - 34. Belgium - 35. France - 36. Spain - 37. Portugal - 38. Italy - 39. Sicily - 40. Sardinia - 41. Germany, Fed. Rep. - 42. Switzerland - 43. Austria - 44. Yugoslavia - 45. Germany, Eastern - 46. Poland - 47. Czechoslovakia - 48. Hungary - 49. Romania - 50. Bulgaria - 51. Albania - 52. Greece - 53. U.S.S.R. - 54. Turkey - 55. Syria - 56. Lebanon - 57. Israel - 58. Jordan - 59. Saudi Arabia - 60. Yemen - 61. Iraq - 62. Iran - 63. Afghanistan - 64. Pakistan - 65. India - 66. Ceylon - 67. Nepal - 68. China, Mainland - 69. Burma - 70. Thailand - 71. Laos - 72. Viet-Nam - 73. Cambodia - 74. Fed. of Malaya - 75. Singapore - 76. China, Taiwan - 77. Philippines - 78. Indonesia - 79. Australia - 80. New Zealand - 81. Korea - 82. Japan - 83. Morocco - 84. Algeria - 85. Tunisia - 86. Libya - 87. United Arab Rep. - 88. Mauritania - 89. Gambia - 90. Senegal - 91. Mali - 92. Upper Volta - 93. Niger - 94. Chad - 95. Sudan - 96. Ethiopia - 97. Somalia - 98. Guinea - 99. Sierra Leone - 100. Liberia - 101. Ivory Coast - 102. Ghana - 103. Togo - 104. Dahomey - 105. Nigeria - 106. Cameroon - 107. Central African Rep. - 108. Gabon - 109. Congo (Brazzaville) - 110. Congo (Leopoldville) - 111. Uganda - 112. Kenya - 113. Ruanda-Urundi - 114. Tanganyika - 115. Angola - 116. N. Rhodesia - 117. S. Rhodesia - 118. Nyasaland - 119. Mozambique - 120. Madagascar - 121. S.W. Africa - 122. Bechuanaland - Basutoland - Swaziland - 123. South Africa.

Food and Agriculture Organization of the United Nations

terranean, and Forestry Commissions for both Latin America and Europe. The International Labor Organization deals with problems of agricultural production in connection with its manpower and technical training programs. The World Health Organization cooperates with FAO on many projects, for instance in anti-malarial campaigns and joint nutrition programs. Both FAO and WHO work with the Children's Fund (UNICEF) on nutritional aspects of child-feeding programs. FAO has a joint project with UNESCO to promote worldwide education on problems of "Food and People."

Transport and Communications. The Transport and Communications Commission of the UN gives particular attention to such problems as the coordination of sea and air safety activities, inland transport in Asia and Latin America, the simplification of passport and frontier formalities, and the improvement of road and motor-traffic regulations. The Inland Transport Committee has been markedly successful in securing the designation of international highways and the removal of restrictions on through truck and bus transportation.

The Inter-Governmental Maritime Consultative Organization has important functions in the field of maritime safety; it was given responsibility for administering a new convention on safety of life at sea, drawn up in 1948, and for all matters affecting international shipping.

The International Civil Aviation Organization is doing good work in increasing the safety of international air travel. It has sponsored a series of safety and operational regulations, and has been instrumental in establishing Loran (long-range aid to navigation) stations and in stationing weather-observation-rescue ships in the North Atlantic. In the winter of 1948–49 one of these ships rescued all the passengers and crew of the transoceanic plane *Bermuda Queen,* which had been forced down. The incident was highly publicized, and the UN was given due credit.

The International Telecommunication Union has devoted a great deal of time and effort to solving the difficult technical problems that are involved in the allocation of radio wave-length frequencies; the announced requirements of the nations of the world are three times the available supply. ITU has also tried to secure agreement to revised regulations for the transmission of international telegraph and telephone communications.

Another highly important but unspectacular service is the supervision and regulation of international mail. The Universal Postal Union is making every effort to assure uninterrupted postal communications, without which international business, and perhaps even international relations in any meaningful sense, would be impossible.

Labor. For some fifty years the International Labor Organization has been working for the improvement of labor standards and conditions throughout the world. Within the UN system it now has special jurisdiction in this field, but many other agencies, notably the Economic and Social Council, the Council's Population Commission and its Economic and Employment Commission (until it was abolished in 1951), and the economic divisions of the Secretariat also have taken a hand in labor questions. While it functioned, the International Refugee Organization, too, gave help on labor problems in connection with its work with displaced persons. This work involved assistance in migration and settlement, problems with which other agencies of the UN are still deeply concerned.

ILO has drafted scores of conventions and recommendations, collectively designated the International Labor Code, which cover such questions as employment and unemployment, conditions of employment, employment of women and children, vocational training, industrial health and safety, social security, industrial relations, maritime labor, immigration, freedom of association, and trade union rights. It is active in the field of assistance, providing experts, organizing training centers, seminars, and courses, exchanging technical information, and granting fellowships. Upon request by member states, ILO sends commissions of inquiry to look into particular problems. It investigates allegations of forced labor and violations of freedom of association, although it is not permitted to operate in Communist countries, where these violations are most likely to abound. It collects and makes available in publications such as the *International Labor Review* and the *Yearbook of Labor Statistics* a vast amount of information from all over the world. Its many tripartite committees, composed of representatives of governments, employers, and workers, work on matters of major concern to parent organizations.

Social Issues 1: General

In the Charter the UN is charged with promoting "solutions of international economic, social, health, and related problems" and "international cultural and educational cooperation." Thus the UN is vitally concerned with the furtherance of human welfare, social justice, and the aspirations of men for a better lot in life. We shall here discuss its work in social welfare and social defense, cultural activities, health problems, control of narcotic drugs, refugees and stateless persons, and aid to children.

Social Welfare and Social Defense. The Department of Social Affairs of the UN Secretariat, and especially its Division of Social Welfare, ECOSOC and its Social Commission, and a number of the specialized agencies are interested in such aspects of the social field as technical assistance for social development, social conditions and levels of living, social services, housing, town and country planning, community organization and development, family, youth, and child welfare, social defense and juvenile delinquency, rehabilitation of the handicapped, population, migration, and refugee questions, and social policy and development. The UN budget provides for advisory social welfare services, including "technical assistance in such special aspects as public welfare administration, social insurance, child welfare, and vocational rehabilitation." Aid to physically handicapped persons in several countries has been an especially popular phase of this work. Social defense, which is of particular concern to the Social Commission as well as to the Social Welfare Division of the Secretariat, includes programs for the prevention of crime, the treatment of offenders, the suppresson of prostitution, probation, the reduction of juvenile delinquency, and related questions.

In 1950 the Secretary-General issued a comprehensive report, at the request of ECOSOC, on housing and town and country planning. The Social Welfare Division now issues a regular bulletin on these subjects, and is doing a great deal of work in this field. The General Assembly authorized a tropical-housing mission, which in 1950 visited the countries of Southeast Asia to investigate "technical questions relating to housing for low-income groups in the humid tropics."

Community organization and development, to which housing and town and country planning are related, is regarded by the Secretary-General as "one of the most promising activities of the United Nations family of agencies." These activities are described in detail in a series of country monographs and reports of regional survey missions which were inaugurated jointly in 1952 by the Department of Social Affairs and the Technical Assistance Administration.

The UN has taken an active interest in continuing and extending the good work done by the League of Nations for suppressing the traffic in women and children. In 1949 the General Assembly approved a new convention relating to this subject, which had been prepared by the Social Commission and recommended by ECOSOC, but for various reasons a number of major states, including the United States and the colonial powers, have failed to ratify it.

In 1952 a general report on the world social situation, compiled by the UN Secretariat in cooperation with ILO, FAO, UNESCO, and WHO, was submitted to the General Assembly. At the request of the Assembly a supplementary survey of measures being taken to improve social conditions, entitled *International Survey of Programs of Social Development,* was issued in 1955. Additional reports are now issued periodically by the Secretariat, in cooperation with the specialized agencies most directly concerned.

Health Problems. With the establishment of the World Health Organization in 1948 a systematic effort to improve health conditions throughout the world was launched. Some of the activities of WHO have been dramatic and have received well-deserved acclaim — for example, the prompt action in dealing with the cholera epidemic in Egypt and the typhus outbreak in Afghanistan in 1949; others have been less spectacular though equally important.

As a specialized agency of the United Nations, WHO is the central directing and coordinating authority in international health work. It also provides advisory and public health services to member countries (124 countries were members in 1963), and central technical services. It has given major assistance to many countries in the fight against malaria, tuberculosis, poliomyelitis, venereal diseases, influenza, smallpox, leprosy, yaws, trachoma (an eye disease), filariasis (a disease caused by parasitic worms), bilharziasis (a disease communicated to man by water snails), and other communicable diseases. In some cases the results of the joint efforts have been most impressive. Malaria has been virtually wiped out in Europe and North America, and in many countries where it was once a prime killer it has been reduced spectacularly. WHO in cooperation with UNICEF has launched a long-term program aimed at its total eradication.

WHO has also given assistance to many countries in public health administration, maternal and child health, nursing, social and occupational health, public health education and training, mental health, nutrition, sanitation, dental health, the development of community water supplies, the rehabilitation of physically handicapped children and adults, and medical research. It administers health and sanitary regulations, maintains a medical library and an international center for the compilation and analysis of medical and health statistics from all countries, establishes international standards of purity in medicines in current use, and issues a number of publications.

In 1946 the General Assembly decided to assume the functions and powers of the League of Nations relating to the control of narcotic drugs. The matter was referred to the Economic and Social Council, which decided at its first meeting to establish a Commission on Narcotic Drugs. The Permanent Central Opium Board and the Supervisory Body, set up in 1925 and 1931 respectively, have continued to function, but they are now so closely affiliated administratively with the Commission on Narcotic Drugs that the three bodies may be said to constitute a single organ of control. Although ECOSOC and its Commission on Narcotic Drugs are the chief policymaking bodies in this field, the General Assembly has given increasing responsibility to WHO and to its Expert Committee on Drugs Liable to Produce Addiction.

Refugees and Stateless Persons. The termination of the International Refugee Organization in January, 1952, was largely a result of the insistence of the United States that since most of the refugees and displaced persons had been resettled or repatriated the burden of the care of the "hard core" refugees still remaining should be assumed by the individual countries concerned. But the United Nations continued to be interested. On January 1, 1952, a UN High Commissioner for Refugees opened an office in Geneva. He was empowered to assist only "stateless" persons, i.e., those persons who did not want to return to their own countries because of actual or feared social, religious, or political persecution and who had sought asylum in other countries; but he was also permitted to extend his "good offices" to certain other limited categories of refugees and displaced persons. While he has been able to be of assistance to refugees in non-Communist lands, he has only limited power and inadequate resources for providing for them.

From the beginning of the operations of its Preparatory Commission on July 1, 1947, until its termination, IRO performed a great and difficult service. Altogether it assisted in the resettlement of more than 1.6 million persons. The United States, in spite of the limitations of the Displaced Persons Act of 1948, received more than 150,000, Israel almost as many, and Australia more than 100,000; the United Kingdom and Canada also took large numbers. About 70,000 were repatriated, presumably all with their consent. Mrs. Franklin D. Roosevelt and others, in hot debates in the General Assembly and the Human Rights Commission, staunchly resisted the demand of the Soviet Union that former nationals of countries now behind the "iron curtain" be returned, regardless of their own feelings in the matter.

The largest numbers of refugees in IRO camps were in Europe, especially in Germany, but IRO also looked after refugees in other parts of the world. A special problem of great proportions, involving over one million refugees, was created by the conflict between Jews and Arabs over Palestine. IRO, WHO, UNESCO, UNICEF, the Conciliation Commission for Palestine (especially its Technical Committee on Refugees) and other UN agencies did what they could to deal with this problem. The main work, however, has been directed by the United Nations Relief for Palestine Refugees, established by the General Assembly in November, 1948, and by its successor organization, the United Nations Relief and Works Agency for Palestine Refugees (UNRWA), established in December, 1949. UNRWA's mandate has been extended several times, for the task with which it is charged, involving resettlement and rehabilitation as well as relief, is a long-range one. Numerous church groups and philanthropic agencies, such as the Red Cross and the American Friends Service Committee, also give substantial assistance, either through UNRWA or through their own field agencies.

As of October, 1966, over 11,000,000 persons, located in 80 countries and on every continent, were classed as refugees. The largest numbers were in India and Pakistan, just outside the borders of Israel (or within Israel's expanded borders after the brief Arab-Israeli war of June, 1967), in Hong Kong, in South Vietnam, in the United States (mostly refugees from Cuba), and in sub-Saharan Africa.

The whole question of the status of refugees and stateless persons calls for a new approach by the states of the world. Current practice, which is inclined almost to regard stateless persons as having no rights or even as having no legal existence at all — at a time when countless thousands have lost their national status through no fault of theirs — seems barbarous and outmoded. "Tasks of special concern include the issuance of travel documents, access to courts, social insurance benefits, the right to work, privileges of education, and the right to remain in a country of asylum."[10] The International Law Association, the UN, and a number of other official and unofficial agencies are taking a continuing interest in these questions. A resolution of the UN General Assembly in 1959, inaugurated the World Refugee Year, which served to call attention to refugee problems, to bring in contributions to UNRWA and other organizations engaged in refugee work, and to encourage national action.

Aid to Children. One of the brightest chapters of the UN story is the record of the United Nations International Children's Emergency Fund (UNICEF), established by the General Assembly in 1946 on a temporary basis to help to provide food, clothing, and medical aid for needy children in war-devastated countries, and placed on a permanent basis in October, 1953, as the United Nations Children's Fund. This agency is a true "international cooperative." It is supported by voluntary contributions of money, goods, and services from governments, private organizations, and individuals. It has launched ambitious programs, many in cooperation with WHO, for health services, mass health campaigns, maternal and child welfare and training, and child nutrition. It has provided supplementary feeding, usually through school lunches or at maternal and child welfare centers, for millions of children and expectant mothers. Through its efforts, in cooperation with WHO and the Red Cross in the Scandinavian countries, 50,000,000 European children were tested for tuberculosis and some 15,000,000 were vaccinated — "the largest single mass-immunization campaign ever undertaken."[11]

In 1964 UNICEF approved programs totaling $37 million to help children in 112 countries. In spite of its financial handicaps it planned to undertake new services, especially in family and child welfare, education, and vocational training, and it emphasized the need to take a broader approach to child welfare as an important part of overall economic and social development.

Several other UN departments, commissions, and specialized agencies, especially the Bureau of Social Affairs and its Social Welfare Division in the Secretariat, the Social Commission of ECOSOC, WHO, and FAO have also been concerned with child welfare.

Educational, Scientific, and Cultural Activities. The United Nations Educational, Scientific and Cultural Organization (UNESCO) seeks to stimulate a worldwide attack on illiteracy, raise educational standards, encourage fundamental education, foster scientific research and promote the dissemination of scientific knowledge, provide for the exchange of persons to promote cultural activities, improve facilities for mass communication, and in general promote international understanding. These goals are of course shared by the UN in general.

UNESCO estimates that 700 million people over the age of 15 are wholly illiterate, that 97 of the world's countries and territories have illiteracy rates higher than 50 per cent, and that in 20 others the rates are over 95 per cent. The organization has undertaken a variety of programs to reduce these rates. In 1965 work on pilot mass literacy projects planned by UNESCO began in eight countries. UNESCO has devoted major attention to fundamental education. It is assisting many countries in a major program to provide universal primary education for some 250 million children by 1980. Among the problems on which it is concentrating are the recruitment and training of teachers, the development of suitable teaching methods, and the provision of school buildings. It spon-

[10] *United States Participation in the United Nations: Report by the President to the Congress for the Year 1949*, Dept. of State Pub. 3765, International Organization and Conference Series III, 48 (May, 1950), p. 129.

[11] Jacob, p. 60.

sored a program for the examination and improvement of textbooks and other teaching materials, which revealed alarmingly low quality and a shocking amount of distortion and chauvinism in the texts to which the world's children are exposed.

To help raise educational standards throughout the world, UNESCO sends teams to various countries to plan with educational leaders of those countries long-term educational policies keyed to national development programs. It sponsors many international conferences on educational matters. In 1963 it established an Institute for Educational Planning in Paris.

In the social sciences UNESCO has sponsored conferences and research on social and religious problems, industrialization, urbanization, and other problems which contribute to misunderstandings between peoples and nations. It conducted a major study of the psychological tensions affecting international understanding, collaborated with various nongovernmental organizations in a study of the concepts of "democracy" and "liberty" as interpreted by peoples of different countries, and launched a series of comparative studies of cultures.[12]

In the natural sciences UNESCO is equally active. It has science offices in Uruguay, China, India, and Egypt. It has made a sizable grant to the International Council of Scientific Unions. It helped to establish the Institute of the Hylean Amazon, and has taken a special interest in the development of arid land. On January 1, 1965, it launched a program for the International Hydrological Decade to promote scientific research on ways to solve the world's water shortage. It has taken steps to promote science teaching at the elementary level in countries where this is almost nonexistent.

[12] **For an illuminating survey of this UNESCO project, see Otto Klineberg, *Tensions Affecting International Understanding: A Survey of Research* (New York: Social Science Research Council, 1950).**

UNESCO's cultural activities extend from theater, music, painting, sculpture, literature, architecture, and other arts to philosophy and creative thought generally. It has sponsored campaigns to preserve historic and natural sights and monuments, such as the ancient monuments threatened by the Aswan High Dam project in the U.A.R., and it has drawn up two universal copyright conventions.

Many countries have national commissions for UNESCO. The United States National Commission, in whose work many organizations participate, is associated with the State Department. It has held several large national conferences — usually attended by more persons than the international conferences of UNESCO itself — and has engaged in a variety of useful activities. UNESCO has been quite successful in securing the cooperation of nongovernmental organizations, international and national, and has encouraged the formation of international associations of political scientists and other professional groups.

It would be difficult to assess the results of its varied activities, for it works in the area of intangibles where the temptation to woolgather is great, and UNESCO has not always been able to resist temptation. Concerned with improving the cultural life of mankind, its work is by no means unrelated to the central problem of war or peace, for, in the oft-quoted words of the Constitution of UNESCO, "since wars begin in the minds of men, it is in the minds of men that the defenses of peace must be constructed."

Social Issues II: Human Rights and Fundamental Freedoms

In only a few parts of the world are human rights and fundamental freedoms really secure, and in large areas they still have little meaning. "The lot of the Chinese peasant, the Egyptian falleen [fellah], the South African native, the Latin American peon, the Russians' political prisoner demonstrates the contradiction between principle and practice which is the present overwhelming challenge to United Nations action in the struggle for human rights."[13] Spokesmen of the United Nations, as well as thoughtful leaders everywhere, are painfully aware of the barriers to progress. "Actually, all organs of the United Nations touch in greater or less degree upon this same subject of human rights, for it lies at the root of all the aspects of effective organized cooperation among nations in carrying out the United Nations Charter."[14] The UN is specifically pledged to promote "universal respect for, and observance of, human rights and fundamental freedoms for all without distinction as to race, sex, language, or religion."

Universal Declaration of Human Rights. Within the UN system the Commission on Human Rights has headed efforts toward this great goal. After two and a half years of painstaking labor the commission, under the able chairmanship of Mrs. Roosevelt, with frequent clashes between champions of the Western and the Soviet concepts of fundamental human freedoms, drafted a Universal Declaration of Human Rights, as a "common standard of achievement for all peoples and all nations." This declaration, the first of its kind in history, was approved by the Third Session of the General Assembly on December 10, 1948, by a vote of 48 to 0, with the six nations of the Soviet bloc, Saudi Arabia, and the Union of South Africa abstaining. The first part reaffirms the political and civil rights and freedoms embodied in the American Bill of Rights and other basic Western declarations of the rights of man. The second part enumerates the "newer economic, social and cultural rights and freedoms which have in the twentieth century come to be recognized as fundamental to man."[15] The declaration is merely a statement of principles, not a legally binding instrument; but it has become one of the best known of international documents, and it has often been referred to in resolutions of the UN, the specialized agencies, regional arrangements and other international organizations, and in national constitutions, legislation, and court decisions. It is a beacon light for all mankind, even though it has been honored more often in the breach than in the observance.

In 1963 the General Assembly designated 1968 — the twentieth anniversary of the adoption of the Universal Declaration of Human Rights — as the International Year for Human Rights. It asked the Commission on Human Rights to draw up "a programme of measures and activities representing a lasting contribution to the cause of human rights," and it urged all governments and all UN agencies to make special efforts during the UN Development Decade to promote respect for and observance of fundamental human rights.

Covenant on Human Rights. Having framed the declaration, the Commission on Human Rights then turned its attention to the even more difficult task of drafting an International Covenant on Human Rights. Unlike the declaration, the covenant, if approved by the General Assembly, would be submitted to the member nations of the UN as a treaty and would therefore be binding on all states that ratified it. At first the commission decided not to include economic, social, and cultural rights, although they had been in the declaration. The Soviet bloc demurred, but the United States, and to a

[13] Philip E. Jacob, "The United Nations and the Struggle for Human Rights," *Pennsylvania School Journal*, January, 1951, p. 200.

[14] *United States Participation in the United Nations, 1949*, p. 137.

[15] *United States Participation in the United Nations: Report by the President to the Congress for the Year 1948*, Dept. of State Pub. 3437, International Organization and Conference Series III, 29 (April, 1949), p. 131.

lesser extent the states of Western Europe, argued that while civil liberties lend themselves readily to judicial processes, social and economic rights entail the development of practical institutions and the making of appropriations to implement the kind of policy sponsored by UN agencies. After a number of shifts in policy the General Assembly in the fall of 1951 requested the commission to prepare drafts of two covenants, one on civil and political rights and the other on economic, social, and cultural rights, and to submit them to the 1952 General Assembly. The commission found the drafting a long and difficult process. Not until 1954 were the two covenants presented to the General Assembly. Since then they have been under consideration by the Assembly's Third Committee, and all efforts to obtain their adoption by the Assembly have been unavailing.

It is highly doubtful that a covenant or covenants on Human Rights will ever be approved or will be really implemented even if approved. Indeed, it may be wiser not to press for a covenant at all, but to rely upon the force of moral pressure and the constant reminder of the rights embodied in the Universal Declaration. No one who has followed the debates in the Human Rights Commission can fail to be conscious of the great distances which separate the nations in their views of what constitute human rights and how they should be enforced.

Convention on Genocide. Genocide is the destruction, in whole or in part, of a national, ethnic, racial, or religious group.[16] It has been a particularly barbarous aspect of the policies of certain supposedly "civilized" states in the twentieth century, notably of Nazi Germany. The General Assembly, in a resolution approved on December 11, 1946, declared it to be a crime under international law, and it instructed the Economic and Social Council to prepare a draft convention on the subject. Drafted in March-April, 1948, by the Ad Hoc Committee on Genocide set up by ECOSOC, the convention in slightly revised form was unanimously approved by the Assembly on December 9, 1948. The Assembly invited the International Law Commission "to study the desirability and possibility of establishing an international judicial organ for the trial of persons charged with genocide." In 1950 the commission reported that an international criminal court for this purpose was both desirable and possible.

The convention provides that five kinds of acts, aimed at the destruction of "a national, ethnic, racial, or religious group," are punishable as genocide. More specifically, these include: (1) killing members of a group because of their group affiliation; (2) causing bodily or mental harm to group members; (3) deliberately inflicting conditions on the group to bring about its physical destruction; (4) imposing measures to prevent births within the group; and (5) forcibly transferring children from one group to another. It also covers conspiracy or incitement to commit genocide, as well as complicity in the crime.

With its ratification by 23 states — three more than the required number — the convention came into effect on January 12, 1951. Ratifying states agree to implement the convention with whatever legislation may be necessary and to permit extradition of persons formally accused of genocide. Government officials as well as private individuals come within its provisions.

The United States has not ratified the Convention on Genocide. The Senate Committee on Foreign Relations has insisted upon certain interpretations of the convention, and the American Bar Association has taken a stand in opposition. Both groups appear

[16] Acts constituting genocide and other acts punishable under the Convention on Genocide are enumerated in Articles II and III of the convention.

to have doubts on the score of the effect on domestic laws and on the status of American court decisions. One American student, deeply concerned with human rights, has declared that "in America as elsewhere, the ghost of national sovereignty intrudes to scare off support for an *international* commitment to protect the rights of men. No one would dare to suggest that genocide be tolerated in this country. But we hesitate to obligate ourselves before the rest of the world to prevent it."[17] Some distinguished American opponents of ratification would say that the United States *is* obligated before the world by a multitude of constitutional provisions to prevent genocide within her borders, but hesitates to grant an international agency the right to police American territory.

In late 1950 the Assembly asked the International Court to hand down an advisory opinion on the question whether reservations to the proposed Convention on Genocide required the unanimous consent of the other parties before the accession containing the reservations could be accepted. By a margin of 7 to 5 the Court ruled that such unanimous consent was not necessary as long as the reservations were compatible with the spirit of the convention.

Freedom of Information. The problem of international guarantees of freedom of information and of the press has been another difficult one for the UN. In the spring of 1948 a UN Conference on Freedom of Information met in Geneva and formulated several draft conventions and recommendations. The General Assembly, ECOSOC, the Subcommission on Freedom of Information and of the Press, the Commission on Human Rights, and the Secretariat have given a great deal of attention to implementing these proposals. The General Assembly on May 19, 1949, against the opposition of the Soviet bloc and with thirteen abstentions, adopted the first international Convention on the International Transmission of News and the Right of Correction. It had more difficulty with the proposed Convention on Freedom of Information. In 1958 the Assembly voted to proceed with a discussion of a draft text prepared by a special committee, but the document has been bottled up in the Third Committee and may never be reported to the Assembly.

The evolution of the proposed convention into a document that contained so many restrictive governmental controls that it belied its title is a sad lesson in the limited prospects in our time for genuine freedom in this field. "While there is general agreement that freedom of information is 'the touchstone of all the freedoms to which the United Nations is consecrated,' there is a sharp division between the proponents of a free press and those of a controlled press."[18]

In 1960 the United States and three Latin American states submitted to the Assembly a draft Declaration on Freedom of Information. No action has been taken on this draft declaration, which has been criticized as an evasive and delaying proposal that will interpose further barriers to the Assembly's approval of the more binding convention.

Status of Women. In only a few countries do women have legal, political, economic, and social rights comparable with those of men; in fact, even the principle of equality is still rejected in large areas of the world. A great deal of data was presented in a report by the UN Secretariat on the political rights accorded to women throughout the world. ECOSOC, in transmitting this report to the General Assembly, recommended that

[17] Jacob, "The United Nations and the Struggle for Human Rights," p. 201.

[18] "Issues Before the Nineteenth General Assembly," *International Conciliation,* No. 550 (November, 1964), pp. 98–99.

information on this subject be circulated annually to members of the United Nations "until all women throughout the world have the same political rights as men." Its Commission on the Status of Women has as its first objective the extension of equal suffrage to women everywhere. Other goals are the better protection under national laws of the rights — including that of nationality — of married women, the extension of educational opportunities for women, the advancement of women in developing countries, the guarantee of equal pay for equal public services, and the increased participation of women in the work of the UN. In 1952 an international conference, held in New Delhi, considered some of these topics. In the same year the General Assembly adopted a Convention on Political Rights for Women.

Self-Determination and the Protection of Minorities.

The right of peoples and nations to self-determination has been a favorite theme of many of the Asian and African members of the United Nations during the discussions on human rights in recent years. They have argued that self-determination is a fundamental human right which should be recognized and supported by the United Nations. The so-called "colonial" states have resisted this campaign, not (according to their statements) because they oppose self-determination, but because they believe it to be a political principle rather than a personal human right and too fuzzy a concept to be formally endorsed without clarification and definition.[19]

At an early stage of its deliberations, in response to Assembly requests, the Commission on Human Rights gave considerable attention to the right of self-determination. In 1952 the Assembly adopted two recommendations of the commission on the principles of self-determination in non-self-governing territories. Three years later it considered, but did not act upon, recommendations for the establishment of a commission to consider important aspects of the problem of self-determination. In the following year, against the wishes of most of the developed countries, the Assembly voted to establish a commission to conduct a "full survey" of the status of the right of peoples and nations to "permanent sovereignty over their natural wealth and resources" and to make recommendations for strengthening that right. This commission reported to ECOSOC in 1960.

While expressing reservations over what seemed to them to be the excessive zeal of the "anti-colonial" members of the United Nations for the self-determination of peoples in non-self-governing territories, some "colonial" states argued that the same principle should be applied to "satellite" states in the Communist orbit and to minority groups within independent states. Both suggestions raise very delicate questions. The first lies largely outside of the province of the United Nations, and surprisingly little attention has been given to the second. Aside from the right of self-determination, not much progress, in fact, has been made toward insuring the protection of minorities within independent states, although presumably many of the rights promised in the Declaration of Human Rights and in the covenants apply to minorities as well as to all other groups. In 1947 a Subcommission on the Prevention of Discrimination and the Protection of Minorities, under the Human Rights Commission, began a thorough study of the problems of minorities to the end that the UN "may be able to take effective measures for the protection of racial, national, religious or linguistic minorities." The subcommission has studied various minority problems and has been largely responsible, through the Commission on Human Rights, for the preparations of

[19] "Issues Before the Fourteenth General Assembly," *International Conciliation*, No. 524 (September, 1959), p. 132.

important draft declarations and draft conventions on the Elimination of All Forms of Religious Intolerance and on the Elimination of All Forms of Racial Discrimination.

Racial Discrimination. The Charter of the United Nations calls for "fundamental freedoms for all without distinction as to race, sex, language, or religion." At its first session the General Assembly adopted a resolution condemning "religious and so-called social persecution and discrimination." The desire to hasten the end of racial discrimination was symbolized by the establishment of the subcommission whose work on minorities and discrimination is described above. In 1949 UNESCO inaugurated a major program of studies of racial discrimination which has attracted considerable attention and praise. The much-discussed "Statement on the Nature of Race and Race Differences, by Physical Anthropologists and Geneticists" was issued in June, 1951 by a group of scientists convened by UNESCO.

Over the years the General Assembly, ECOSOC, the Commission on Human Rights, and other UN agencies have adopted increasingly stronger resolutions against discrimination of all kinds and especially against racial discrimination in general and *apartheid* in South Africa in particular. In 1963 the General Assembly adopted unanimously a declaration prepared by the Commission on Human Rights on racial discrimination (South Africa abstained because of a specific reference to *apartheid*), and it has also been considering a draft convention of a legally binding nature. From its inception the Assembly has been critical of the racist policies of the government of South Africa, and it has passed numerous condemnatory resolutions on this subject. With the admission of large numbers of Asian and African states, criticisms of South Africa have been greatly intensified. In 1962 the Assembly established a special committee on *apartheid*. This committee has kept a continuing watch on developments in South Africa and has recommended strong measures against the South African government.

Social Issues III: Dependent Peoples

The provisions of the UN Charter relating to dependent peoples represent an advance over the corresponding section of the Covenant of the League of Nations. Perhaps the most notable difference lies in the scope of application. The Covenant brought the former colonies of Germany and Turkey under the Mandates Commission of the League, but it established no special position for the colonies and other non-self-governing territories of other states. The Charter, on the other hand, provides for a Trusteeship Council to perform functions much the same as those of the Mandates Commission, but in addition it asserts principles to be applied by member states to all their colonies. With the League, actual administration was in the hands of "mandatory states"; under the UN, while the direct administration is commonly in the hands of states singly or jointly as "administering authorities," the UN itself may take direct control, as it did in Eritrea.

International Trusteeship System. The UN Charter provided for an International Trusteeship System "for the administration and supervision of such territories as may be placed thereunder by subsequent individual agreements." Immediate responsibility for carrying out these functions in trust territories (except for strategic trust territories) was vested in the Trusteeship Council, which was established as a major organ of the UN. The Council was composed equally of states which administered trust territories and of states which did not. Territories could be placed under the trusteeship system by agreements approved by the "states directly concerned," and by the General Assembly or Security Council, depending upon their status as regular trust territories or "strategic areas." Three categories of trust territories were listed: (1) the old mandated areas as of the time of the San Francisco Conference of 1945; (2) territories taken from enemy states in World War II; and (3) other territories voluntarily placed under the trusteeship system by the states which administer them. No state chose to avail itself of the opportunity to subject its colonial administration to the supervision of the Trusteeship Council. All of the trust territories were therefore former colonies of Germany (lost in World War I) or of Italy or Japan (lost in World War II). Consequently the non-self-governing territories under the trusteeship system were in several ways less impressive than those which had no relation to the system: they were smaller in number (11 as compared with more than 60), in area (about one million square miles as compared with about eight million), and in population (less than 20,000,000 as compared with more than 200,000,000).

The pre-World War I Germany colony of South-West Africa is the only former mandated territory (disregarding those areas which have become independent states) which has not been placed under the International Trusteeship System as a trust territory. Although the Assembly has repeatedly recommended that this be done, South Africa, the administering authority, has refused to do so. For a time the South African Government submitted reports to the UN on its administration, but in 1949 it announced that no further reports would be forwarded; and it has consistently maintained that the status of South-West Africa was solely within its domestic jurisdiction. The matter was appealed to the International Court of Justice, which in July, 1950, held that South Africa continued to have international obligations concerning South-West Africa resulting from the mandate it assumed in 1920, and that the mandate could be modified only with the approval of the United Nations. It also held, however, that the Charter imposed no obligation on South Africa to place South-West Africa under trusteeship.

The Trusteeship Council supervised trust territories under the International Trusteeship System in three main ways: (1) by considering annual reports from the administering authorities, (2) by receiving and examining petitions, and (3) by sending visiting missions to the trust territories. For a time this Council was a fairly active organ, but at the height of its activity only the eleven territories shown in the chart below were associated with the International Trusteeship System:

Territories Supervised under the International Trusteeship System

Trust Territories	*Area (in Sq. Miles)*	*Population*	*Administering Authority*
Cameroons (British)	34,136	1,160,000	United Kingdom
Cameroons (French)	166,489	3,000,000	France
Nauru	9	3,432	Australia
New Guinea	93,000	1,000,000	Australia
Pacific Islands	687	85,000	United States
Ruanda-Urundi	20,500	3,960,000	Belgium
Somaliland (Italian)	194,000	1,266,000	Italy
Tanganyika	360,000	7,400,000	United Kingdom
Togoland (British)	13,041	383,600	United Kingdom
Togoland (French)	21,893	999,000	France
Western Samoa	1,130	78,000	New Zealand

By mid-1968 only two trust territories remained in the International Trusteeship System: the Australian-administered portion of New Guinea, and the Strategic Trust Territory of the Pacific Islands, administered by the United States. Thus the Trusteeship Council, even though it was a principal organ of the UN, was left with only limited and insignificant authority. It was greatly overshadowed by a Special Committee of the General Assembly, known after 1963 as the Committee of 24.

Trust Territory of the Pacific Islands. The one strategic trust territory, created in accordance with Article 82 of the United Nations Charter, consists of the Pacific islands of the Gilberts, Marshalls, and Marianas (except Guam), which were formerly a Japanese mandate. These islands extend over an ocean area of some 3,000,000 square miles but they have a total land area of only 687 square miles and a small population (approximately 85,000), forming at least eight different cultural groups. The United States is the administering authority for these islands, now known as the Strategic Trust Territory of the Pacific Islands. For the first three years or more of American supervision the territory was governed by naval authorities, with headquarters at Guam, which is geographically but not politically within the trust territory. Since then a civilian administration has taken over the supervision of the territory, and the capital has been transferred to Truk.

The islands are so widely scattered and there is so little feeling of unity that political independence is hardly feasible. Instead, emphasis has been placed on the establishment of local self-governing municipalities and the development of self-government on a regional basis.

According to the UN Charter, the functions of the United Nations relating to strategic areas are to be exercised by the Security Council. This body, however, has asked the Trusteeship Council to act for it in discharging the functions specified in Articles 87 and 88 of the Charter for strategic trust territories.

Non-Self-Governing Territories and the Committee of 24. Quite naturally, there has been a considerable difference of opinion about the responsibilities and authority of the United Nations with respect to non-self-governing territories other than trust territories — that is, the colonies and dependencies of the colonial powers. In general the countries possessing such territories — notably the United Kingdom, France, and Belgium — have tended to give a strict interpretation to Chapter XI of the Charter and to oppose substantive recommendations of the General Assembly on the grounds that they constitute intervention in matters exclusively within their jurisdiction; whereas non-administering states, and especially those which have recently emerged from a colonial status, have favored a broad construction of the provisions of Chapter XI.

When the member states of the UN were first asked to enumerate their non-self-governing territories under Chapter XI, 74 territories were so listed; after that the number declined, largely because many of the territories became independent states. Whether the UN must automatically accept unilateral declarations of independence is a point of controversy; but in practice it has been compelled to do so.

Under Article 73 (e) of the Charter, states possessing non-self-governing territories are obligated to submit regular reports to the UN, subject to such limitations as security and constitutional considerations may require. The states concerned are asked to supply information requested in a form approved by the General Assembly. This information is more limited in scope and detail than that required for trust territories, but it is nevertheless quite extensive. The Assembly was at somewhat of a loss as to what it could or should do with this information, but it worked out a procedure which proved to be reasonably satisfactory. A Special Committee on Information from Non-Self-Governing Territories was charged with examining the information submitted under Article 73 (e) and with making recommendations to the Assembly.[20] This committee was dissolved by a resolution of the General Assembly, adopted on December 16, 1963. Its functions were taken over by the Committee of 24.

There is real doubt whether Chapter XI was intended to create a system of accountability. The United Kingdom, France, and Belgium opposed the extension of the life of the Special Committee of the Assembly on the ground that the UN has no authority to create machinery of this sort. Whatever the limitations of Chapter XI, it is well to remember its broad significance. In the words of Ralph Bunche:

> One may still say that the obligations under Chapter XI are unique and a very great step forward over anything the world had yet seen. . . . The acceptance of the principle that the international community does have a proper concern for these territories and the right to devote its attention to them automatically removed them from the hidden realm of exclusive domestic jurisdiction. This was, even without raising the question of international accountability, a unique advance.[21]

By 1960 the de-colonization campaign in and outside of the UN was in full swing. It was symbolized by the emergence of many new nations, especially in Africa — 1960 was called "the year of African independence" — and by the adoption by the General Assembly, by a vote of 89 to 0, with 9 abstentions,[22] of a historic Declaration on the Granting of Independence to Colonial Countries and Peoples. A year later the Assembly, noting that not much progress had been made, created a Special Committee on the Implementation of the Declaration. Originally consisting of 17 members, its membership was increased to 24 in 1962.[23] The committee was directed "to carry out its task by employment of all means which it will have at its disposal within the framework of the procedures and modalities which it shall adopt for the proper discharge of its functions."[24] This is certainly the broadest mandate ever bestowed on any UN committee. The Committee of 24 "now stands as virtually the only United Nations body charged with the examination of colonial questions"; it has become in effect, but not in name, one of the major organs in the UN system.

In 1963 the Committee of 24 in outlining its program of future work agreed on a list of 64 territories deemed to be within its purview. It has devoted special attention to

[20] The United States submits information annually on American Samoa, Guam and the Virgin Islands. In 1952 she informed the UN that she would no longer transmit information on Puerto Rico, since a new constitution granting a full measure of self-government had entered into force in July. This unilateral notification was strongly criticized by some UN members.

[21] Quoted in Clyde Eagleton and Richard N. Swift, eds., *Annual Review of United Nations Affairs: 1950* (New York: New York University Press, 1951), pp. 149–150.

[22] The United States abstained in the voting on this declaration, a position which resulted in widespread criticism in the United States as well as in the newly emergent countries. The United States member of the General Assembly which considered the declaration in detail, Senator Wayne Morse, declared later that "but for . . . pressure from the British Government the United States would have voted in favor of the resolution." *The United States in the United Nations: 1960 — A Turning Point,* Supplementary Report, Committee on Foreign Relations, U.S. Senate, 87th Cong., 1st. Sess. (Washington, D.C.: Government Printing Office, February, 1961), pp. 20–21.

[23] The members of this important committee are: Afghanistan, Australia, Bulgaria, Chile, Ethiopia, Finland, India, Iran, Iraq, Italy, Ivory Coast, Madagascar, Mali, Poland, Sierra Leone, Syria, Tanzania, Tunisia, U.S.S.R., United Kingdom, United States, Uruguay, Venezuela, and Yugoslavia. It is obvious that the membership is heavily weighted in favor of the "anti-colonial" states.

[24] Paragraph 5 of General Assembly Res. 1654 (XVI), November 27, 1961.

several of these, notably Southern Rhodesia, South-West Africa, the territories under Portuguese administration, Aden and Southern Arabia, and British Guiana. Early in 1964 the committee created three subcommittees to deal with all territories on the preliminary list which had not been given special consideration. It realized that for the inhabitants of some of the smaller territories a "full measure of self-government," as advocated in a famous resolution of the General Assembly, adopted on December 15, 1960, would not necessarily mean national independence. This resolution specifically stated that according to circumstances, "A Non-Self-Governing Territory can be said to have reached a full measure of self-government by (a) Emergence as a sovereign independent State; (b) Free association with an independent State; or (c) Integration with an independent State."[25]

Organizational Issues

"The United Nations has already achieved the simplest criterion of success . . . it has made itself indispensable in the lives of nations."[26] This was the theme that echoed through the Opera House in San Francisco in June, 1955, when representatives of sixty states met to commemorate the tenth anniversary of the signing of the United Nations Charter. Yet about two years earlier, when the General Assembly had discussed the subject of Charter revision, twenty of the twenty-eight states which had expressed their views had gone on record in favor of amending the existing document.[27] These sentiments were by no means incompatible; they revealed general approval of the UN as a working reality, coupled with a rather widespread feeling that some changes in the operation of the organization would permit still more effective performance.

To the world at large the record of the UN has unquestionably been disappointing. Observers seem to forget the basic character of the UN — that it is an organization of sovereign states, that success in its vital political and security functions is dependent upon great power unanimity, and that it is sharply limited in its coercive power. They complain that states pursue national interests, national objectives, and national policies in an international organization — as though any state could possibly do anything else. Above all, they point to the veto in the Security Council, and they apparently believe that most of the failures of the United Nations could be summed up in that one word.

Because of the importance which the veto has assumed in the minds of many persons who deplore the shortcomings of the UN, and, indeed, because of the importance which it has actually possessed in the functioning of the Security Council, we shall first examine the veto, its origin and nature, its abuses, and the suggestions for its modification. After that we shall review some of the many proposals and actions designed to strengthen the UN.

The "Veto" in the Security Council

The voting procedure in the Security Council was the most sharply debated issue at the San Francisco Conference, and it has been the most generally criticized aspect of the UN's procedure ever since. Representatives of smaller powers in the UN have attacked the veto arrangement in every session of the General Assembly and they have introduced scores of resolutions to limit or eliminate the veto. Because its frequent use has tied the hands of the Security Council in many crucial matters, various devices for circumventing the Council have been employed.

The word "veto" nowhere appears in the

[25] General Assembly Res. 1541 (XV), December 15, 1960.

[26] United Nations Press Release SF/5, June 21, 1955, p. 1.

[27] "Issues Before the Tenth General Assembly," *International Conciliation,* No. 504 (September, 1955), p. 9.

United Nations Charter. While technically inaccurate, it has come into common usage. It refers to the voting procedure in the Security Council as laid down in paragraph three of Article 27, which reads as follows:

> Decisions of the Security Council on all other matters [that is, on nonprocedural matters] shall be made by an affirmative vote of seven members including the concurring votes of the permanent members; provided that, in decisions under Chapter VI, and under paragraph 3 of Article 52, a party to a dispute shall abstain from voting.

This means that any one of the five permanent members of the Security Council — China, France, the U.S.S.R., the United Kingdom, and the United States — can veto a decision on nonprocedural matters which all other members of the Council support. It should be remembered, however, that a negative vote by one of the Big Five is a veto only if this vote defeats an action which would otherwise have been approved.

Origin and Purpose. The wording of Article 27 was based directly on a voting formula proposed, be it noted, by Franklin Roosevelt and approved by Churchill and Stalin at the Yalta Conference in February, 1945. The formula included an informal agreement that a state should not vote on substantive matters relating to a dispute in which it was involved.

The Yalta formula was left essentially unchanged at San Francisco, in spite of scores of amendments proposed by almost every delegation except those representing the great powers. Britain, France, and the United States were as firm as the Soviet Union in insisting that the veto be incorporated, as agreed to at Yalta. Dr. Grayson Kirk, who served as Executive Officer of the Third Commission of the San Francisco Conference, which gave detailed consideration to the composition and role of the proposed Security Council, has described the "basic assumptions" on which their decision rested:

> Open as it is, on theoretical democratic grounds, to serious objection, this Council voting arrangement rests upon two basic assumptions to which the sponsoring powers attached great importance. The first was that in any enforcement action the permanent members of the Council would be those whose forces must necessarily bear the predominant burden. In consequence, it would be unrealistic to expect those Council members to allow their own forces to be committed to an action which they, or any one of them, opposed. The other argument was that the organization must depend for its strength upon the essential solidarity of the great powers. If this solidarity fails, then the security of enforcement arrangements will as surely fail.[28]

The only joint declaration of the great powers on the Yalta formula as embodied in Article 27 of the Charter was the "Statement by the Four Sponsoring Governments on Voting Procedure in the Security Council," issued during the San Francisco Conference.[29] This reaffirmed the Yalta formula with its denial of a right of veto in procedural questions; and it clarified the process to be used in determining whether the status of a question was to be shifted from substantive to procedural. The San Francisco understanding provided that the veto could be used to prevent this shift. Consequently a permanent member of the Council could use its veto power to keep a motion from being declared procedural (and as such exempt from the operation of the veto) and then use it again to defeat the substantive motion. Thus the statement validated the "double veto." It added, however, that "it is not to be assumed that the permanent

[28] "The United Nations Charter," *International Conciliation*, No. 413 (September, 1945), p. 468.

[29] The statement is printed in *The United Nations Conference on International Organization, San Francisco, California, April 25 to June 26, 1945, Selected Documents* (Washington, D.C.: Government Printing Office, 1946), pp. 751–754.

members, any more than the non-permanent members, would use their 'veto' power wilfully to obstruct the operation of the Council." The representatives of the United States placed special emphasis on this assurance.

Use of the Veto. UN experience with the veto has been wholly different from that envisioned in the joint statement issued at San Francisco. During the first two years, 1946 and 1947, the veto was used 23 times, 21 of these by the Soviet Union. Since then it has been employed less frequently, but the Soviet Union has resorted to it well over one hundred times.

In justice to the U.S.S.R. two considerations should be presented. The first is that, as Professor Padelford found, "the record plainly shows that the Soviet Union has no monopoly on negative voting." In 165 votes in the Security Council on substantive questions in 1946 and 1947, including the 23 vetoes, China voted "no" 27 times, France 23 times, Great Britain 29 times, the Soviet Union 24 times, and the United States 34 times. The votes of Britain, China, and the United States, and all but two of those of France, were not classed as vetoes because in each instance others of the Big Five — and usually all or most of the nonpermanent members of the Council — voted the same way; whereas in 21 of the negative Soviet votes no other permanent member voted with the U.S.S.R., and in all these instances the measures proposed would have been approved if the Russian representatives had not voted against them.[30]

The second consideration frequently advanced by spokesmen of the U.S.S.R., or of the Soviet bloc, is that the other permanent members of the Security Council, which are on the other side of the East-West split, can produce almost as many Soviet vetoes as they wish. Thus they can make the Russians appear even more obstructionist than they actually are, simply by forcing votes on issues which they know will not be approved by the Soviet Union but will be approved by every other great power and by most of the nonpermanent members of the Security Council. The Soviet Union vetoed Italy's application for membership three times before July 1, 1948, and presumably would have vetoed it thirty times if it had come up that often.

In practice, various methods have been employed to evade the veto and, in effect, to bypass the Security Council. One clear result has been to give enhanced importance to the General Assembly, where the power to veto does not exist. Article 12 of the Charter provides that the General Assembly may not consider a dispute with which the Security Council is seized; but the practice of removing matters from the agenda of the Council by a procedural vote has facilitated the reference of even political issues to the Assembly, as, for instance, the Greek frontier case in the fall of 1947, or, even more important, the Korean crisis three years later. Furthermore, another way out has been provided by the Uniting for Peace Resolution, by which a question can be transferred promptly from the Security Council to an emergency session of the General Assembly (unless a regular session is already in progress) if the Council is rendered impotent by the use of the veto power by a permanent member, as happened in August, 1950.

Undoubtedly, also, the difficulties in the

[30] Norman J. Padelford, "The Use of the Veto," *International Organization*, II (June, 1948), 231–232. Professor Padelford thus explains this important point: "It is clear from the record that when the Soviet Union finds its vital interests at stake there are now no other great powers generally inclined to stand with it. Therefore, the negative vote of the Soviet delegate usually becomes a sole veto, accompanied ordinarily only by the vote of whatever satellite holds a non-permanent seat on the Council. When other great powers, particularly the United States and Great Britain, find their national interests at issue they can usually persuade other permanent members to go along with them in casting a multiple negative vote sufficient to stop a proposal without the stigma of exercising a sole veto (or near-sole veto), or to join in introducing and passing a resolution more suitable to their desires." P. 233.

Security Council explain, in part at least, the steps taken outside the UN for individual and collective self-defense, as provided for in Article 51 of the Charter, and the increasing reliance on "regional arrangements" (Articles 52, 53, and 54 of the Charter). Indeed, as we have noted, Articles 51–54 of the Charter were inserted expressly to counterbalance the Yalta formula for voting in the Security Council, a precaution which has been justified by subsequent events.

The Conflict of Interpretations. The action of the Security Council in the Korean crisis of June, 1950, launched a vigorous debate on all aspects of the veto question. It will be recalled that the Council voted to recommend the use of military force against the aggression from North Korea, and that the vote was taken during the absence of the Soviet representative, Mr. Malik. The ensuing discussions, engaged in by both diplomats and scholars, involved the precise meaning of "concurring votes," the legal effect of absence, and the equivalence or nonequivalence of absence and abstention.

The Soviet Union took the position that the "affirmative vote of seven members including the concurring votes of the permanent members" meant the concurring votes of all five permanent members. Granted this interpretation, the action of the Council was obviously invalid. Most of the Western states, however, supported another interpretation. To them "the concurring votes of the permanent members" meant "the concurring votes of the permanent members that voted at all." Otherwise, they argued, any one of the permanent members could prevent the Security Council from functioning at all for as long as it chose to absent itself from the Council's meetings; and they cited Article 28 of the Charter, which states: "The Security Council shall be so organized as to be able to function continuously. Each member of the Security Council shall for this purpose be represented at all times at the seat of the Organization."

Despite considerable support for the position that abstention — or, to a lesser extent, absence — does not constitute a veto within the meaning of Article 27, paragraph 3, of the Charter, the realities of the situation at the time the formula was adopted would seem to direct that the meaning of the controversial phrase "concurring votes of the permanent members" should not be given anything but a strict and literal translation. The very fact that all great powers were so insistent on its being included would appear to indicate that its purpose was to preclude the taking of any substantive decision without the unanimous concurrence of the Big Five — all present and all voting affirmatively.

Admittedly, Russian obstructionism in the UN has been a persistent annoyance, and it certainly precludes the achievement of some of the goals set by the founders. But the point here is a purely legal one.[31] The lead-

[31] For discussions of the veto, see the cited writings of Leland M. Goodrich, Hans Kelsen, Myres S. McDougal and Richard N. Gardner, Norman J. Padelford, and Francis O. Wilcox and Carl M. Marcy. See also H. Field Haviland, Jr., *The Political Role of the General Assembly* (New York: Carnegie Endowment for International Peace, 1951); and Jiménez de Aréchaga, *Voting and the Handling of Disputes in the Security Council* (New York: Carnegie Endowment for International Peace, 1951). Two additional points with respect to the veto should be mentioned. Hans Kelsen calls attention to the fact that the English version of the Yalta Agreement reads "including the concurring votes of the permanent members," whereas the French version reads *"les voix des tous les membres permanents"* — the votes of all the permanent members. The Chinese, Russian, and Spanish versions agree with the French. It had been agreed at Yalta that all five versions would have equal validity. See Kelsen, *Principles of International Law* (New York: Rinehart, 1952), p. 180n. Second, the "Statement by the Four Sponsoring Governments on Voting Procedure in the Security Council," mentioned above, makes it difficult to believe that as of June 8, 1945, the governments of Britain, China, the Soviet Union, and the United States disagreed on the meaning of "concurring votes," for the statement says that "the first group of decisions [on substantive matters] will be governed by a qualified vote — that is, the vote of seven members, including the concurring votes of the five permanent members. . . ." *The United Nations Conference on International Organization*, p. 752.

ing Western states, themselves once the unyielding supporters of the principle of the great-power veto, seem ready to assert a principle of unanimity-except-one, at least on those issues on which they can agree. The dilemma is a truly distressing one, for the choice may become one between unanimity-except-one and the paralysis of the United Nations. On the one hand, perhaps minor crises may be weathered, much good work accomplished, and the future kept open by the well-meaning proponents of parliamentary legerdemain. On the other hand, effective security action in a major crisis will require unanimity in fact rather than in legal fiction; it was so recognized at Yalta, and it is true today.

The Financial Impasse

"In recent years the United Nations has been pursuing a precarious policy of financial brinkmanship. The gap between total liabilities and cash on hand reached $111,700,000 by the end of 1961."[32] Three years later the UN had $8 million in hand; no budget could be formally adopted because the General Assembly had been rendered almost inoperative over the constitutional issue of the obligations of member states to contribute an assessed share of the costs of peacekeeping operations; and several member states owed nearly $150 million on their assessments for the 1963 and 1964 regular budgets and for the peacekeeping operations in the Middle East and in the Congo.

Until the UN created UNEF in 1956, its financing was divided into two categories — a regular budget, and voluntary contributions by member and nonmember states; private groups and individuals also sometimes supported programs not financed out of the regular budget, including UNICEF, the Expanded Program of Technical Assistance, the Special Fund, and the Office of the High Commissioner for Refugees.

Article 17 of the UN Charter provides that the Assembly shall approve the budget of the organization and that the expenses "shall be borne by the members as apportioned by the General Assembly." Article 19 stipulates that a member may not vote in the Assembly "if the amount of its arrears equals or exceeds the amount of the contributions due from it for the preceding two full years." The scale of amounts varies from .4 of 1 per cent for some of the smaller and poorer nations to about 33 per cent for the United States (until 1956 the United States paid 39.79 per cent of the regular budget). "Twenty states now pay almost 90 per cent of the regular budget. The total assessment of fifty members amounts to little more than 3 per cent, and it will be some years before these members can make any significant contribution; at the same time they require a proportionally larger percentage of assistance from the organization. As far as the voluntary programs are concerned, the major burden falls on an even smaller number of states, with the United States alone paying between 40 and 70 per cent."[33]

This situation was alarmingly unbalanced and precarious, but it became infinitely worse when the UN undertook the peacekeeping operations in the Middle East in 1956 and in the Congo in 1960. The costs of UNEF were heavy enough — about $20,000,000 a year — but they were exceeded by the expenses of the Congo operation, which for about four years were considerably greater than the UN's regular budget. Furthermore, several members did not contribute to these costs, either because of alleged inability to pay or, as in the case of the Soviet Union and France, because they refused to recognize their obligation to pay for peacekeeping operations which were not decided upon in the Security Council, where the veto obtained. They persisted in this view even after the As-

[32] "Issues Before the Seventeenth General Assembly," *International Conciliation*, No. 539 (September, 1962), p. 184.

[33] "Issues Before the Sixteenth General Assembly," *International Conciliation*, No. 534 (September, 1961), p. 201.

sembly, in a resolution approved in 1960, declared that the costs of ONUC were "expenses of the Organization" within the meaning of Article 17, paragraph 2; and after the International Court of Justice, in 1962, had had handed down an advisory opinion endorsing the Assembly's position. The resulting constitutional crisis has reduced the General Assembly to impotence and threatens the future of the entire organization. After the "no-vote" Nineteenth Session of the General Assembly in late December, 1964, and early 1965, a Special Committee of 33 was created to attempt to find a way out of the constitutional and financial impasse; but even though the United States and the Soviet Union, whose views on the basic issues involved seem to be diametrically opposite, have showed a greater tolerance and flexibility, the basic dilemma remains.

Proposals and Actions to Strengthen the UN

Short of world government, proposals to strengthen the UN range all the way from a reorganization of the present structure without the Soviet Union to formal modifications of the voting procedure in the Security Council, with relatively minor changes in the Charter. Most of the plans for more basic revisions have come from unofficial organizations and influential private citizens in various countries; many of the less drastic changes have been advocated in the form of official proposals to the General Assembly.

Lie's Proposals. Trygve Lie, in his third annual report to the General Assembly in the summer of 1948, made some pertinent recommendations for the strengthening of the UN. In the first place, he declared that "nothing could contribute more to the effectiveness of the United Nations than a settlement" of the problem of the future of Germany. Second, he urged "fuller use of the existing powers of the Security Council for the settlement of international disputes and for the preservation of peace." Third, he called attention to the value of implementing Article 43 of the Charter by providing armed forces for the use of the Security Council. Fourth, he suggested that the UN should "begin a study of some of the problems involved in the control of bacteriological and lethal-chemical weapons." Fifth, he expressed the hope that the permanent members of the Security Council would not continue to exercise their veto powers to prevent the UN from moving "as rapidly as possible toward universality of membership." Finally, he asked members of the UN to give "all possible weight and support to the decisions of the General Assembly and of the Council, even though they be in the form of recommendations to the member states."

On June 6, 1950, Mr. Lie proposed a "Twenty-Year Program for Achieving Peace Through the United Nations," calling for the implementation of the following ten-point program: (1) "periodic meetings" of the Security Council, to be attended "by foreign ministers, or heads or other members of Governments," for the purpose of "consultation — much of it in private — in efforts to gain ground toward agreement on questions at issue, to clear up misunderstandings, to prepare for new initiatives that may improve the chances for definite agreement at later meetings"; (2) a renewed effort to achieve agreement on the international control of atomic energy; (3) a new approach to control of armaments of all sorts; (4) a new attempt to make armed forces available to the Security Council; (5) rapid progress toward universality of membership in the UN; (6) a sound and enlarged technical assistance program; (7) more vigorous use of the specialized agencies of the UN; (8) wider respect for human rights; (9) promotion of equality for dependent peoples; and (10) further development of international law. The only new proposal in this "Twenty-Year Program" was the first. The other points were reminders of oft-expressed aspirations rather than specific plans for action.

Uniting for Peace Resolution. The action of the UN in dealing with aggression in Korea has been described in a previous chapter. One of the results of that crisis was the adoption by the General Assembly, on November 3, 1950, of the so-called Uniting for Peace Resolution. The resolution contained five major provisions:

(1) It authorized the General Assembly to meet on short notice in an emergency in which the Security Council was prevented from acting, and to recommend appropriate collective measures, including the use of armed force when necessary.

(2) It established a fourteen-nation Peace Observation Commission to observe and report on dangerous situations in any part of the world.

(3) It asked all member states to maintain in their armed forces special elements which could be made available for United Nations service on call of the Security Council or the General Assembly.

(4) It established a fourteen-nation Collective Measures Committee to study and report on these and other methods for maintaining and strengthening international peace and security.

(5) It urged all United Nations members to renew their fidelity to the United Nations, honor its decisions, and promote respect for human rights and achievement of economic stability and social progress.

While the delegates of the Soviet bloc opposed most parts of the resolution — they supported provisions (2) and (5) — they did not offer a very determined resistance. Nevertheless, they did contend that some portions of the resolution were completely illegal.[34] Mr. Vyshinsky argued that Article 11 of the UN Charter imposed limits on the powers of the General Assembly and insisted that the changes proposed could properly be made only by amendment of the Charter. Nevertheless, the resolution was adopted by the General Assembly by a vote of 52 to 5, with 2 abstentions.

The Uniting for Peace Resolution was first invoked to convene a special emergency session of the General Assembly in 1956, in connection with the Suez crisis, and almost immediately again in the Hungarian crisis. While it has seldom been resorted to since 1956, it does seem to have some limited usefulness in those disputes which cannot be considered adequately in the Security Council because of great power disagreement; but given the reluctance of the majority of the members of the UN to get involved in peacekeeping operations and the General Assembly's constitutional crisis over the proper interpretation of Article 19 of the

[34] The legality of the Uniting for Peace Resolution seems to rest on the proper interpretation of Article 12, paragraph 1, of the Charter, which reads as follows: "While the Security Council is exercising in respect of any dispute or situation the functions assigned to it in the present Charter, the General Assembly shall not make any recommendation with regard to that dispute or situation unless the Security Council so requests." Authorities on the UN Charter differ widely on this point. Professor Leland M. Goodrich asserts: "From the point of view of law it is highly doubtful whether the General Assembly has the power to recommend enforcement measures while the matter is still on the agenda of the Security Council." "Development of the General Assembly," *International Conciliation,* No. 471 (May, 1951), p. 273. Professor Kelsen, on the other hand, has this to say: "The words while the Security Council is exercising the . . . functions . . . may be interpreted to mean: while a dispute or situation is still on the agenda of the Council. But it may also be interpreted to mean: while the Security Council is actually exercising its functions; so that when the Council because of the exercise of the veto right is reduced to inaction, it should not be considered as 'exercising' its functions. Article 12, paragraph 1, does not prevent the General Assembly to make [*sic*] a recommendation after the Security Council has made a recommendation in the same case. The competence of the Assembly to make recommendations is restricted only temporarily. The Council may lift this restriction by requesting the General Assembly to make a recommendation. Thus the purpose of this restriction, to avoid conflicts between the General Assembly and the Security Council, is not completely assured." Hans Kelsen, *The Law of the United Nations* (London, 1950), p. 217. See also Myres S. McDougal and Richard N. Gardner, "The Veto and the Charter: An Interpretation for Survival," *Yale Law Journal,* LX (February, 1951), 290–291.

Charter, it is doubtful that the resolution will prove to be a really effective instrument.

The other specific provisions of the Resolution have not been really implemented, although the Peace Observation Commission and the Collective Measures Committee were created and some efforts made to persuade member states to earmark units of their armed forces for possible UN service.

Charter Revision and Review. The Charter provides (Article 109, paragraph 3) that if a conference for the purpose of reviewing the Charter itself has not been held previously, the proposal to call such a review conference will be placed on the agenda of the Tenth Session of the General Assembly, "and the conference shall be held if so decided by a majority vote of the members of the General Assembly and by a vote of any seven members of the Security Council." Consequently, the question of the revision of the Charter was widely discussed in the two or three years prior to the convening of the Tenth Assembly in September, 1955. The foreign offices of most of the member states gave some consideration to technical aspects of the problem. Scholars, private organizations, and foundations in many countries carried on pertinent studies and made recommendations for amending the Charter along various lines.[35] The Ninth Session of the General Assembly instructed the Secretary-General to initiate preliminary studies.[36]

On July 28, 1953, the United States Senate established a special Subcommittee on the United Nations Charter under the Foreign Relations Committee. The subcommittee, headed by the chairman of the Foreign Relations Committee, collected basic documentation relating to the review of the Charter, initiated a series of staff studies, and held several public hearings.[37] In 1954 it held a series of five open hearings outside Washington — "the first attempt to take a májor question of foreign policy directly to the people of the United States for testimony and discussion."[38] On August 9, 1955, the subcommittee issued a rather noncommittal report, saying that "if a review conference is held it might profitably explore the twilight zone where national powers commingle to determine whether further clarification is desirable in our national interest."

Two years earlier, in August, 1953, Sec-

[35] For a specific and sweeping proposal for revising the UN Charter in the direction of a form of world government, with national disarmament as a prerequisite, see Grenville Clark and Louis B. Sohn, *Peace Through Disarmament and Charter Revision: Detailed Provisions for Revision of the United Nations Charter* (Preliminary print by the authors, 1953). One of the most thorough series of studies on major aspects of the United Nations system was sponsored by the Brookings Institution. See especially Francis O. Wilcox and Carl M. Marcy, *Proposals for Changes in the United Nations* (Washington, D.C.: The Brookings Institution, 1956).

[36] In accordance with instructions of the Ninth General Assembly of the UN, the Secretariat prepared "a comprehensive summary of the decisions of United Nations organs, together with related material, organized by Charter articles and presented in such a way as to throw light on questions of application and interpretation of the Charter which have arisen in practice." From the Preface by Secretary-General Hammarskjold to Vol. I in this series: *Repertory of Practice of United Nations Organs: Vol. I, Articles 1–22 of the Charter,* UN Pub. 1955. V. 2.

[37] U.S. Senate, Committee on Foreign Relations, Subcommittee on the United Nations, *Review of the United Nations Charter: A Collection of Documents* (Senate Doc. No. 87, 1954). Ten staff studies were published in 1954. They dealt with the following subjects: (1) "The Problem of the Veto in the United Nations Security Council"; (2) "How the United Nations Charter Has Developed"; (3) "The Problem of Membership in the United Nations"; (4) "Representation and Voting in the United Nations General Assembly"; (5) "Peaceful Settlement of Disputes in the United Nations"; (6) "Budgetary and Financial Problems of the United Nations"; (7) "Enforcement Action under the United Nations"; (8) "The International Court of Justice"; (9) "The United Nations and Dependent Territories"; and (10) "The United Nations and the Specialized Agencies."

[38] Alexander Wiley, "The Senate and the Review of the United Nations Charter," *The Annals* of the American Academy of Political and Social Science, CCXCVI (November, 1954), 161.

retary of State Dulles had announced that the United States would vote in favor of a review conference when the question came before the Tenth UN Assembly. This official American position never changed, although it had become apparent by 1955 that the United States viewed the prospect of a review conference with limited enthusiasm and even with some alarm. In the United States there was growing support for a point of view expressed by Ernest Gross, former Assistant Secretary of State and Deputy Representative at the United Nations, that a Charter review conference would almost certainly be of one of three types: it might be a "punctuation" conference, in which case it "would not seem worth the effort or expense"; it might be a "showdown" conference, which "would precipitate a break-up of the organization"; or it might be a "propaganda" conference, "a sort of peace conference in the cold war." Questions such as disarmament ("a major cold war issue"), domestic jurisdiction ("a major issue within the free world, embittering vast sections of it in connection with the 'colonial' issue and evoking controversy at each session of the General Assembly"), and membership ("involving differences in basic attitudes within the free world regarding the universal or selective character of the organization") were, in his opinion, "real issues"; whereas "questions of structure and procedure such as those involving the veto or changes in voting methods [might] be regarded either as false issues, or as real issues which are often given false weight in the balance of judgment about the United Nations."[39]

In testimony before the Senate Subcommittee on the Charter, on January 18, 1954, Secretary Dulles discussed "the more important Charter amendment issues which particularly concern the United States." These related to: (1) universality of membership; (2) security; (3) membership and voting in the Security Council; (4) voting in the General Assembly; (5) armaments; and (6) international law.

By 1955 the reluctance to hold the conference had become quite apparent. Secretary-General Hammarskjold in his annual report of that year suggested as a possible way out of the dilemma that there might be "valid arguments for a decision at the coming Assembly session in favor of holding a Charter review conference, while leaving until later the question of when it should be convened." The Tenth Assembly debated at some length the item on its agenda regarding a proposal to call a conference, but in the end it elected to adopt the suggestion of the Secretary-General. Thus a conference of this kind is scheduled, but it may well remain in a state of indefinite suspension, pending the coming of a more hopeful international atmosphere.

Dozens of suggestions for amending the UN Charter have been advanced. There is little likelihood, it seems, that any really significant revisions, even if recommended by a review conference, would be finally accepted; they would require adoption by a two-thirds vote of the members of the General Assembly and ratification by two-thirds of the member states of the UN, including all the permanent members of the Security Council. This rigid amendment procedure has dampened the enthusiasm of many who think the review conference should be held and that changes in the UN Charter should be made.

No amendments to the Charter were formally adopted by the General Assembly until 1963, when two structural proposals, to increase the membership of the Security Council from 11 to 15, and of ECOSOC from 18 to 27, were approved and submitted to the member states for ratification. They entered into force on August 31, 1965.

Much can be done in another way, however, through what may be called the process of informal amendment. In fact, many

[39] Ernest A. Gross, "Revising the Charter: Is It Possible? Is It Wise?" *Foreign Affairs,* XXXII (January, 1954), 203–216.

changes have already been brought about in this manner. Obviously the United Nations of today is not the United Nations of 1945. The basic premise on which it was founded — great power agreement — has proved to be invalid, profound changes have occurred in the general international situation, and the UN itself has evolved in ways not contemplated by its founders. In a staff study prepared for the Senate Subcommittee on the United Nations Charter, Francis O. Wilcox found that the Charter had been amended informally in the following ways: "(1) through the nonimplementation or nonapplication of certain provisions of the Charter; (2) through the interpretation of the Charter by various organs and members of the U.N.; (3) through the conclusion of supplementary treaties or agreements, such as the Headquarters Agreement of 1947 and the North Atlantic Pact; and (4) through the creation of special organs and agencies."[40] Much more can and doubtless will be done by this process of adaptation. Indeed, as Professor Clyde Eagleton pointed out, "many of the things which have been suggested for consideration by a conference could . . . be done by general acceptance, if that could be obtained."[41]

Future Prospects. Obviously the United Nations must find new methods of financing its activities, and it must find some more satisfactory way to deal with conflicting issues of authority and Charter interpretation. Above all, it needs more genuine cooperation and support from its members. The immediate problems of strengthening the organization can probably be solved within the framework of the Charter, with perhaps relatively unimportant procedural changes. In spite of the limitations imposed by the Charter there are still-unutilized opportunities for the expansion of the UN's usefulness. In his second annual report as Secretary-General, Dag Hammarskjold stated: "We have only begun to make use of the real possibilities of the United Nations as the most representative instrument for the relaxation of tensions, for the lessening of distrust and misunderstanding, and for the discovery and delineation of new areas of common ground and interest." The failure to develop these "real possibilities" led Carlos Romulo to warn that "The UN is dying,"[42] and Professor Hans Morgenthau to assert that "The UN of Dag Hammarskjold is dead."[43]

The United Nations: Review and Appraisal

The year 1965 marked the twentieth anniversary of the United Nations and was proclaimed by the General Assembly as "International Co-operation Year" (ICY). The theme ot ICY was "Peace and Progress Through Co-operation." As the year opened this theme seemed ironically inappropriate and utopian. The General Assembly was bogged down in an impasse over financial obligations which turned the Nineteenth Session into a "no-vote session" of an almost farcical character. The organization's financial impotence placed its future in jeopardy. In January Indonesia announced her withdrawal from the UN. In the major crisis situations which developed in early 1965, notably those in Vietnam and the Dominican Republic, the UN was either ignored or was permitted to play at best a peripheral role. Those with historical interests or memories wondered whether the UN would go the way of the League of Nations. In actuality, the League, which seemed to be in better condi-

[40] Francis O. Wilcox, "How the United Nations Charter Has Developed," *The Annals* of the American Academy of Political and Social Science, CCXCVI (November, 1954), 4.

[41] Clyde Eagleton, "Proposals and Prospects for Review of the Charter of the United Nations," in Clyde Eagleton, Conley H. Dillon, and Carl Leiden, *The United Nations: Review and Revision* (Marshall College, Huntington, West Va., 1954). p. 40.

[42] *Collier's*, July 23, 1954, pp. 30–33.

[43] *New York Times Magazine*, March 14, 1965.

tion than the UN after ten years of operation, was almost forgotten ten years later, whereas the UN, for all its travail, was still actively involved in the international life of a world in which the danger of global war, while ever-present, did not seem to be imminent.

The world, of course, had changed greatly since the San Francisco Conference of 1945. The hopes and expectations for great power cooperation in peace as in war proved to be illusory. By 1947 the cold war had begun; the division between Communist and non-Communist countries came to shape the entire thinking and approach of leaders and peoples, at least in the major countries. Yet gradually the stark bipolarity that marked the early postwar years gave way to a confused kind of multipolarity or polycentrism, characterized by divisions within both the Communist and non-Communist worlds, the emergence of the Third World of new nations of Asia and Africa as a major factor in the international scene, and more independent policies by states within as well as outside alliance systems. The atomic age began a few weeks after the San Francisco Conference; the space age, in 1957. More and more patterns of diplomacy and international relations generally seemed inappropriate or inadequate for the new age, and the United Nations seemed to be geared more for a pre-atomic than for an atomic era.

United Nations Membership, by Year, since 1945

Years	*New members*	*Number of members at end of year*
1945	Original members	51
1946	Afghanistan, Iceland, Sweden, and Thailand	55
1947	Pakistan and Yemen	57
1948	Burma	58
1949	Israel	59
1950–54	Indonesia (1950)	60
1955	Albania, Austria, Bulgaria, Cambodia, Ceylon, Finland, Hungary, Ireland, Italy, Jordan, Laos, Libya, Nepal, Portugal, Rumania, Spain	76
1956	Morocco, Sudan, Tunisia, Japan	80
1957	Ghana, Malaya	82
1958–59	United Arab Republic (Egypt-Syria), Guinea	82
1960	Cameroon, Central African Republic, Chad, Congo (Brazzaville), Congo (Leopoldville), Cyprus, Dahomey, Gabon, Ivory Coast, Malagasy, Niger, Somali Republic, Togolese Republic, Upper Volta, Mali, Senegal, Federation of Nigeria	99
1961	Sierra Leone, Syria (United Arab Republic), Mongolia, Mauritania, Tanganyika	104
1962	Burundi, Jamaica, Rwanda, Trinidad-Tobago, Algeria, Uganda	110
1963	Kuwait, Kenya, Zanzibar	113
1964	Tanzania (Taganyika-Zanzibar merged) Malawi, Malta, Zambia	115
1965	Gambia, Maldive Islands, Singapore Indonesia withdrew	117
1966	Indonesia returned Barbados, Botswana, Guyana, Lesotho	122
1967	South Yemen	123
1968	Mauritius, Swaziland	125

Adapted from table in "The Costs of World Peacekeeping," report by Hon. Barratt O'Hara and Hon. Peter H. B. Frelinghuysen, members of the United States Delegation to the Twentieth Session of the United Nations General Assembly, House Report No. 1404, 89th Cong., 2d Sess., March 31, 1966 (Washington, D.C.: Government Printing Office, 1966), p. 183.

"*Oh, do stop this feeling inferior just because you're not an Afro-Asian.*"

© *Punch, London*

Great changes were also occurring in the UN itself. One of the most obvious changes has resulted from a more than twofold increase in membership. The Charter of the UN was signed in June, 1945, by representatives of 50 nations, most of them in the Western world. Only four African nations were among the signatories. By late 1968 membership had risen to 125, more than half from Asia and Africa. The UN had therefore nearly attained universality in membership, but for various reasons several states, including Switzerland and both regimes in the divided countries of Korea, Vietnam, and Germany, were not members. China was represented by the Nationalist Government in Taiwan and not by the government which controlled the mainland.

Indonesia's withdrawal in 1965, the first case of its kind in UN history, aroused apprehensions and alarms, and unhappy memories of the effects of withdrawals from the League of Nations in the 1930's. Other states, however, showed no inclination to follow Indonesia's lead. "President Sukarno of Indonesia has frequently called for the formation of a new international organization composed of the 'New Emerging Forces' to oppose the 'Old Established Forces' currently, in his opinion, represented in the United Nations. In this appeal President Sukarno seems to have the support of the P.R.C. It is significant, however, that other 'neutralist' states, notably India, Yugoslavia and the U.A.R., have refused to seriously consider following Indonesia's lead in this respect."[44] In 1966, as a result of profound political changes inside the country, Indonesia rejoined the world organization.

Several important caucusing blocs or groups have emerged in the United Nations. The most easily identifiable are the Communist, the Asian-African, the Latin American, and the Western groups. Aside from the Communist, none of these groups really functions as a "bloc," except on certain issues of mutual interest. The Asian-African group, for example, may present a relatively solid front on such issues as colonialism, human rights, and economic development, but its growing size and disparate membership make it increasingly unwieldy as a caucusing group.

Perhaps because of the change in the size and character of membership, but also, undoubtedly, because of the changing character of international relations, the focus of concern in the General Assembly and other UN organs has changed from essentially cold war preoccupations to questions relating to decolonization, economic development, and human rights. Whereas the major Western powers have been inclined to stress the obligations and role of the UN in the maintenance of international peace and security,

[44] William M. Jordan, "Political Problems," in Richard N. Swift, ed., *Annual Review of United Nations Affairs, 1964–1965* (Dobbs Ferry, N.Y.: Oceana Publications, 1966), pp. 20–21. Until his untimely death in January, 1966, Mr. Jordan was Director of the Political Affairs Division of the UN Secretariat.

MEMBERSHIP OF CAUCUSING BLOCS AND GROUPS IN THE UNITED NATIONS, DECEMBER, 1962

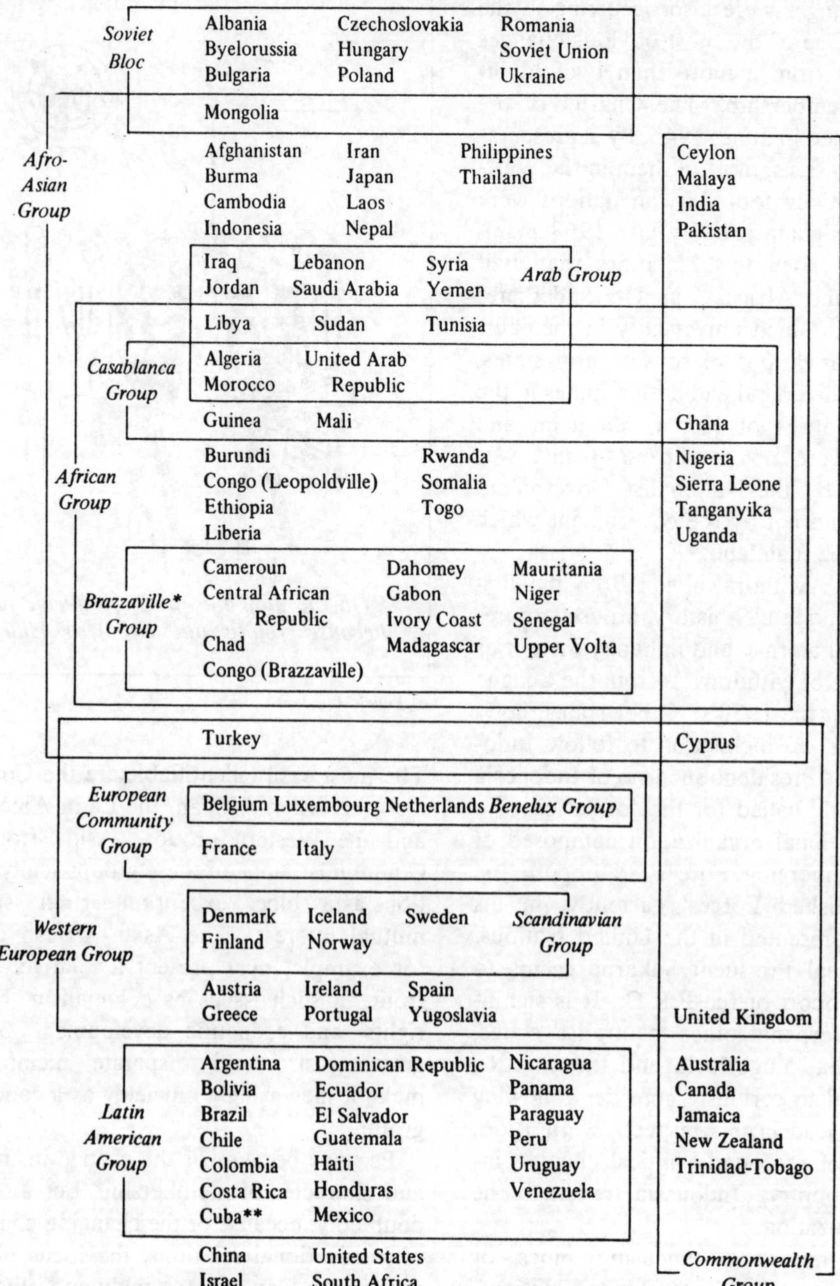

* The Brazzaville Group is also known as the African Malagasay Union, or AMU, Group.

** Despite the expulsion of Cuba from the Organization of American States at the Punta del Este Conference in January 1962, the Latin American Group has not followed this decision. Rather, the Group has evaded decisive action on the issue by not inviting Cuba to informal caucusing sessions.

Thomas Hovet, Africa in the United Nations (Evanston, Ill.: Northwestern University Press, 1963).

the new members from the underdeveloped world, most of whose foreign policies could be characterized as various forms of nonalignment, have preferred to concentrate as far as possible on the three other major purposes stated in Article I of the Charter: the development of friendly relations among nations, international cooperation, and harmonizing the actions of nations. Yet, beginning with the Suez crisis, the UN was involved in important peacekeeping operations, including the major commitment in the Congo, and it was continually engaged in one way or another with disputes or other situations which threatened the peace of the world.

Secretary-General U Thant warned that the UN should not "shy away from a timely and concerted effort to take on those problems of peace and security which are a primary responsibility of the United Nations under the Charter, for fear of failure."[45] Nevertheless, as the director of the Political Affairs Division of the UN Secretariat pointed out in 1965, "One salient characteristic of the UN in the past decade has undoubtedly been the acceptance of the view that the organization would have to function as a noncoercive international political body." Hence, "the basic issue still confronts the United Nations as to the effects to be given to efforts to eradicate the alleged 'remnants of colonialism' within the political context of 'neutralism' and 'nonalignment', as against provisions in the Charter regulating the use of force in international relations."[46]

Among the changes of an organizational nature, with larger implications, two may be given special mention. As the executive arm of the UN and the only agency empowered to make decisions and act upon them, the Security Council was generally recognized for some years as by far the most important organ in the UN system; but when the frequent use — or abuse — of the veto limited the Council's margin for action and when the 1950 Uniting for Peace Resolution broadened the Assembly's powers, a shift in the focus of authority from the Security Council to the General Assembly could be discerned. This shift became more obvious as representatives of many more new nations appeared, especially after the "package deal" of 1955 and the "year of Africa's independence" in 1960.

In recent years the Assembly has certainly been the most active of the UN organs. But the Assembly too has become less effective as its membership has mushroomed and as its work has been partially stymied by the disagreement over the financial obligations of some of its members. Moreover, the United States began to entertain doubts about the wisdom of giving too much emphasis to a body whose members might well pass resolutions of which the United States strongly disapproved. By 1965 these factors were producing a new emphasis on constituting what Professor Hans Morgenthau called a UN counterrevolution. Thus the precise relationship between the Council and the Assembly has varied over the years, and along with this change has gone a shift in the balance of forces in the entire organization.

A second noteworthy organizational change has been the growing importance and the larger role of the Secretary-General. This may be in part a matter of personality and temperament. The first Secretary-General, Trygve Lie, conceived of his role in a more limited sense than did his successor, Dag Hammarskjold; the third Secretary-General, U Thant, a retiring Buddhist and champion of nonalignment, while less forceful and activist than Hammarskjold, has nevertheless concerned himself in various international crises and has recommended firm action when he felt it to be necessary to maintain the prestige and advance the purposes of the United Nations. Article 99, which autho-

[45] Speech prepared for a Convocation at Queen's University (Kingston, Ontario), released as a statement on May 22, 1965; quoted in the *New York Times,* May 23, 1965.

[46] Jordan, pp. 17, 21.

rizes the Secretary-General to "bring to the attention of the Security Council any matter which in his opinion may threaten the maintenance of international peace and security," remained a dead matter until 1960, when Hammarskjold first invoked it to bring the Congo question to the attention of the Security Council. Since then the Secretary-General has been less hesitant to assert himself more positively, both within the UN and in dealing with international disputes in the name of the world organization.

There can be no question that the United Nations, for all the vicissitudes which it has experienced and for all the changes in the international environment since 1945, has been an active and useful participant in international life. Much of the world's work is done by its various organs, agencies, and commissions, and there is hardly an international question that does not come before it in one way or another. For the small nations, in particular, it has been, in the words of Hans Kohn, the "gateway to history." The UN gives them an entrée to national life, and a world stage and forum. For all of its members it has provided a means of promoting national interests and of engaging in various kinds of bilateral as well as multilateral diplomacy. It has often served as a safety valve, as a place where grievances may be vented. While it has not been markedly successful in bridging the gap between Communist and non-Communist, between aligned and nonaligned, or between developed and underdeveloped nations, it has brought together nations representing all of these groups and has provided an almost unique meeting-place for nations and peoples of diverse views and orientation. Much of its work has been unspectacular, and some of its less successful ventures have been the most highly publicized; but perhaps in the long run day-by-day efforts on many fronts and "quiet diplomacy" may prove to be more effective than spectacular performance.

There can be no question, however, that at the end of its first twenty years the United Nations was facing an unusually severe crisis of survival. In spite of frequent professions of support from many of the heads of government, the fact was that the more powerful nations gave the UN a rather low priority in their overall foreign policy. More and more the UN was being ignored and bypassed when particularly serious disputes and problems arose. This condition was frankly recognized by the Secretary-General, in an address which he prepared for delivery in May, 1965:

> For various reasons, the role of the United Nations has been ignored or avoided in the settlement of some recent disputes, thus causing profound uneasiness in the minds of those who maintain that the United Nations represents the world's best hope for peace.
>
> We are witnessing today, I feel, a definite reversal of the slow progress the United Nations has made toward world stability and world peace. A further drift in this direction, if not arrested in time, will mark the close of a chapter of great expectations and the heralding of a new chapter in which the world organization will provide merely a debating forum and nothing else.[47]

[47] *New York Times*, May 23, 1965.

Alexander in The Philadelphia Bulletin

"Why is the Doughnut Less Interesting?"

It must be conceded that the United Nations, for all its activities, is an inadequate instrument for collective security and an imperfect instrument for human betterment under present world conditions; and yet, as one top official of the UN has said: "It seems that we now have about as much United Nations as today's world is prepared to accept." Here is the root of the problem. Experience with the UN has shown that men and nations are not yet ready to create the only kind of international institutions that can offer any hope of proving adequate to the imperatives of the atomic age. Perhaps even more important, they have made little progress in developing the sense of community that is essential for the successful functioning of international political institutions, however carefully conceived.

But if the UN is not, and cannot be, the last best hope of anyone, it does serve mankind in highly important lesser ways. It will continue to be an occasional peacemaker in smaller disputes; a decompression chamber even for large quarrels; a forum for the views, right or wrong, of all nations; and a reminder, as nagging as a conscience, of the dream of world order. The UN, as Dag Hammarskjold used to say, only mirrors the world as it really is — its idealism and its baseness, its nobility and its savagery.[48]

Thus the basic failure of the United Nations, which has diverted attention from its very real achievements, is hardly chargeable to the world organization itself; it is inherent in the kind of national and international life that exists today. In a period when man's ideas and institutions are unequal to his scientific accomplishments and his social needs, the UN has not only survived but won acceptance and approval on an amazingly wide scale.

SUGGESTIONS FOR FURTHER READING

ALKER, HAYWARD R., JR. and **BRUCE M. RUSSETT.** *World Politics in the General Assembly.* New Haven: Yale University Press, 1965. Based on factor analysis.

ASHER, ROBERT E. *et al. The United Nations and Promotion of the General Welfare.* Washington, D.C.: The Brookings Institution, 1957. A detailed analysis by outstanding specialists.

BAILEY, SYDNEY D. *The United Nations; a Short Political Guide.* New York: Frederick A. Praeger, 1963.

BOWETT, D. W. *United Nations Forces: a Legal Study of United Nations Practice.* London, 1964.

CHEEVER, DANIEL S. and **H. FIELD HAVILAND, JR.** *Organizing for Peace: International Organization in World Affairs.* Boston: Houghton Mifflin Company, 1954.

CLAUDE, INIS L., JR. *Changing United Nations.* New York: Random House, 1967.

———. *Swords into Plowshares: The Problems and Progress of International Organization,* 3d ed. New York: Random House, 1964. One of the best texts in the field.

EICHELBERGER, CLARK M. *UN: The First Ten Years.* New York: Harper, 1955.

FALK, RICHARD A. and **SAUL H. MENDLOVITZ,** eds. *The United Nations.* New York: World Law Fund, 1966. Vol. III of a series entitled "The Strategy of World Order." Selections from articles and statements of leading authorities.

FELLER, A. H. *United Nations and the World Community.* Boston: Little, Brown and Company, 1952.

FORGAC, ALBERT T. *New Diplomacy and the United Nations.* New York: Pageant Press, 1965.

48 "The UN: Prospects Beyond Paralysis" *Time* Essay, *Time,* April 2, 1965, p. 27.

FRYE, WILLIAM R. *A United Nations Peace Force.* Dobbs Ferry, N.Y.: Oceana Publications, for the Carnegie Endowment for International Peace, 1957.

GOODRICH, LELAND M. *The United Nations.* London, 1960. Issued under the auspices of the London Institute of World Affairs.

GOODRICH, LELAND M. and ANNE P. SIMONS. *The United Nations and the Maintenance of International Peace and Security.* Washington, D.C.: The Brookings Institution, 1955.

GOODSPEED, STEPHEN S. *The Nature and Function of International Organization.* New York: Oxford University Press, 1959.

GORDENKER, LEON. *The UN Secretary-General and the Maintenance of Peace.* New York: Columbia University Press, 1967. A study of three UN Secretaries-General.

GREEN, JAMES FREDERICK. *The United Nations and Human Rights.* Washington, D.C.: The Brookings Institution, 1956.

HAVILAND, H. FIELD, JR. *The Political Role of the General Assembly.* New York: Carnegie Endowment for International Peace, 1951.

JACOB, PHILIP E. and ALEXINE ATHERTON. *The Dynamics of International Organization.* Homewood, Ill.: Dorsey Press, 1965.

JIMÉNEZ DE ARÉCHAGA, EDUARDO, JR. *Voting and the Handling of Disputes in the Security Council.* New York: Carnegie Endowment for International Peace, 1951.

LAUTERPACHT, H. *International Law and Human Rights.* New York: Frederick A. Praeger, 1950.

LAVES, WALTER and CHARLES THOMPSON. *UNESCO.* Bloomington: Indiana University Press, 1957.

LEFEVER, ERNEST W. *Crisis in the Congo: A United Nations Force in Action.* Washington, D.C.: The Brookings Institution, 1966.

LIE, TRYGVE. *In the Cause of Peace.* New York: The Macmillan Company, 1954. Reflections on the United Nations by the first Secretary-General (1946–53).

MACLAURIN, JOHN. *The United Nations and Power Politics.* New York: Harper, 1951. The UN and world tensions.

MITRANY, DAVID. *A Working Peace System: An Argument for the Functional Development of International Organization.* London, 1946.

National Studies on International Organization. New York: Manhattan Publishing Company, 1955–56. A series of volumes, sponsored by the Carnegie Endowment for International Peace, on national policies and attitudes toward international organization, particularly the UN. Twenty-five volumes deal with the experience of twenty-three countries with the UN (the U.S. study is in three volumes). Two concluding volumes were prepared by Maurice Bourquin and Robert MacIver.

NICHOLAS, H. G. *The United Nations as a Political Institution.* New York: Oxford University Press, 1959.

PADELFORD, NORMAN J. and LELAND M. GOODRICH, eds. *The United Nations in the Balance: Accomplishments and Prospects.* New York: Frederick A. Praeger, 1965. The essays in this volume, by leading specialists, originally appeared in a special issue of *International Organization,* XIX, No. 3 (Summer, 1965).

ROSNER, GABRIELLA. *The United Nations Emergency Force.* New York: Columbia University Press, 1963.

RUSSELL, RUTH B. *United Nations Experience with Military Forces: Political and Legal Aspects.* Washington, D.C.: The Brookings Institution, 1964. A Brookings Staff Paper.

SHARP, W. R. *International Technical Assistance.* Chicago: Public Administration Service, 1952.

SINGER, J. DAVID. *Financing International Organization.* The Hague, 1961.

STOESSINGER, JOHN G. *Financing the United Nations System.* Washington, D.C.: The Brookings Institution, 1964.

SWIFT, RICHARD N., ed. *Annual Review of United Nations Affairs.* Dobbs Ferry, N.Y.: Oceana Publications. A concise year-by-year review of the UN's work. Fifteen volumes, edited by Clyde Eagleton, then by Eagleton and Richard N. Swift, and more recently by Swift, covering the years 1949–1966, have been published.

Synopses of United Nations Cases in the Field of Peace and Security, 1946–1965. New York: Taplinger Publishing Company, for the Carnegie Endowment for International Peace, 1966. Synopses of 68 cases, compiled by Catherine G. Teng and Kay L. Hancock of the Carnegie Endowment.

TEW, BRIAN. *International Monetary Cooperation, 1945–52.* London, 1952.

United Nations Publications. See Appendix. Especially valuable and comprehensive: *Yearbook of the United Nations* (an annual volume), and *United Nations Chronicle* (official monthly magazine).

"United Nations: Then and Now," *International Studies,* VI (October, 1965). A publication of the Indian School of International Studies, New Delhi. Special issue in commemoration of UN's 20th anniversary.

VANDENBOSCH, AMRY and WILLARD N. [illegible]GAN. *The United Nations: Background, Organization, Functions, Activities.* New York: McGraw-Hill Book Company, 1952.

WADSWORTH, JAMES J. *The Glass House: The United Nations in Action.* New York: Frederick A. Praeger, 1965. By a former U.S. Permanent Representative to the UN.

WAINHOUSE, DAVID W. *Remnants of Empire: The United Nations and the End of Empire.* New York: Council on Foreign Relations, 1965.

WAINHOUSE, DAVID *et al. International Peace Observation: A History and Forecast.* Baltimore: The Johns Hopkins Press, for the Washington Center of Foreign Policy Research, School of Advanced International Studies, 1966. A series of excellent case studies of peace observation under the aegis of the League of Nations, Inter-American organizations, and especially the United Nations.

WATTS, V. ORVAL. *The United Nations: Planned Tyranny.* New York: The Devin-Adair Co., 1955. Advertised as "the only complete argument against the United Nations."

WHITE, LYMAN C. *International Non-Governmental Organizations: Their Purposes, Methods, and Accomplishments.* New Brunswick, N.J.: Rutgers University Press, 1951.

WIGHTMAN, DAVID. *Economic Co-operation in Europe.* New York: Frederick A. Praeger, 1956. A study of the Economic Commission for Europe.

WILCOX, FRANCIS O. and CARL M. MARCY. *Proposals for Changes in the United Nations* Washington, D.C.: The Brookings Institution, 1956.

PART FOUR

CONFLICT AND CHANGE IN THE POSTWAR WORLD

15 The Rebuilding and Reorientation of Europe

What Is Europe?

Europe is a civilization, a territorial unit, and an idea. It is the heartland of the civilization that developed from the Judaic-Greco-Roman-Christian tradition, which is conventionally known as Western civilization. But that civilization spread far beyond the confines of continental Europe, especially to the New World, to Australia and New Zealand. In many ways it was dominant in Asia and Africa throughout most of the so-called modern period of human history. Only now, as Arnold Toynbee observed, have the civilizations of the non-Western world begun to challenge as well as to respond to the Europe-centered civilization of the West.[1] Toynbee distinguished between Western Christian and Western Orthodox civilizations, the latter emerging in Southeastern Europe and finding its homeland in European Russia; but both had essentially the same origins, and much of the same character. Non-Western civilizations, especially Hindu civilization, were very different in origin, and frequently in spirit and in essence.

[1] See Arnold J. Toynbee, *The World and the West* (New York: Oxford University Press, 1953).

Geographically, to use a favorite expression of General Charles de Gaulle, Europe extends "from the Atlantic to the Urals." It covers an area of approximately 4,000,000 square miles, more than half of which is occupied by European Russia. It is only sixth in size among the continents, and may be described as simply the largest of the many peninsulas which jut from the vast Eurasian land mass. Its population, including European Russia, is about 600,000,000, less than the population of India and Pakistan. Politically, it is divided into 33 nation-states, including the miniscule "states" of Andorra, Liechtenstein, Monaco, San Marino, and Vatican City (which covers 108 acres!). Those with the largest population, and also the greatest influence, are the Soviet Union — the giant of Europe, as well as of Asia — West Germany, the United Kingdom, France, and Italy. The main geographic regions may be described as East Europe (the Soviet Union and Poland), Southeast Europe (Rumania, Hungary, Yugoslavia, Albania, Bulgaria, Greece, and European Turkey), Scandinavia (Norway, Sweden, Denmark, and Finland), Southern Europe (Italy, Spain, Portugal, plus the vest-pocket units of San Marino, Vatican City, and Andorra), Central Europe (East and West Germany, Czechoslovakia, Austria, Switzerland, and Liechtenstein), Western Europe (France, Belgium, the Netherlands, Luxembourg, and Monaco), and the British Isles (the United Kingdom of Great Britain and Northern Ireland and the Republic of Ireland). Certain "offshore islands," such as Iceland, Malta, and Cyprus, which are independent states, are often associated with Europe, in geographical as well as political terms.

As an idea Europe is a culture as well as a civilization, a way of life shaped by its cultural and religious heritage, its climate and topography, its historical experience, and its racial composition. This idea is invoked by advocates of a united Europe, who argue that Europe is one, even though it is divided into many racial, linguistic, and political units. The European idea has developed through the centuries, and it has given shape and character to the whole civilization of which Europe has been the center. It has been the lodestone of the great "Europeans" of the past and present.

Even in a physical sense the definitions of Europe may vary greatly, and in common parlance the meanings may be even more varied. Because Europe has ties with all the rest of the world, there has been, and still is, in a sense, a series of Europes overseas. Europe's ties with its daughter nations across the Atlantic and in the Southwest Pacific, and to a lesser degree with the peoples of the vast areas of Asia and Africa which were once under European rule, are still very extensive indeed. Europe extends to the Atlantic Community, to the Mediterranean world, and often far beyond. In this sense Europe is far larger than the continent itself.

In another common usage, Europe is smaller than the entire continent. Very often the term is used to refer to Europe outside of the Soviet Union, which occupies more territory in Asia than in Europe, or to non-Communist Europe, or to Western Europe. The latter use is particularly prevalent in Western Europe itself and in the United States and Canada; and to confuse matters still further, the term Western Europe, in these same areas, is often used to include all of non-Communist Europe. Moreover, since the emergence of the economic communities, reference is often made to "Little Europe," the Europe of the Six — France, West Germany, Italy, and the Benelux countries; and after the European Free Trade Association was formed in 1959, "Little Europe" was sometimes described as "Inner Europe," with the EFTA countries — the United Kingdom, Norway, Denmark, Sweden, Switzerland, Austria, and Portugal — constituting "Outer Europe."

Non-Communist Europe, in which West Germany, France, the United Kingdom, and Italy are the leading nations, constitutes one of the three or four great power centers of the world today. Its importance in power-political terms was clearly stated by Joseph C. Harsch in late 1964:

> Non-Communist Europe has 339.5 million people, against 190.7 millions for the United States and 230 for Russia. These 339.5 million free and boisterous West Europeans possess impressive quantities of many things. Their gold and currency reserves stand at $32.5 billion against just under $16 billion for the United States. They export $112.1 billion worth of goods every year against $21.4 billion for the United States. They move their goods abroad in 75.4 million registered tons of shipping against a mere 23.1 for the United States. They consume two-thirds as much electricity as does the United States, have almost as many motor vehicles of all kinds . . . and in 1962 made 99.6 million tons of steel against 89.2 million tons for the United States.
>
> If you were selecting the part of the world that might, if it chose, challenge the United States for leadership you would take Western Europe. It could even challenge the United States in nuclear military power. It is, in

fact, the only other part of the world which has all the necessary resources and wealth to build and sustain a military system as expensive as the Americans. It could outstrip Russia easily.[2]

What, then, is Europe? In his stimulating book on *Western Europe Since the War,* Professor Jacques Freymond wrote: "Attempts were made in vain to set frontiers to a continent that had never had precise boundaries. The undertaking was still more impossible in the twentieth century, when, by virtue of scientific and technological progress, diplomacy had been extended to the entire world and economic activities were even more inextricably entangled."[3] Europe, in short, is more and less than a territorial area, and even the territorial limits are subject to varying interpretations. After all, an ancient and complex civilization and culture cannot be confined to its heartland, and the heartland itself cannot be precisely defined.

Europe During World War II and the Immediate Postwar Years

The twentieth century has witnessed basic changes in Europe's world role. Until the late nineteenth century all the great powers were European. Their economic strength and cultural contributions, as well as their political and military might, gave them a dominant position in the world. Although World War I exposed grave structural and economic weaknesses and profoundly affected the pattern of world power, the nations of Western Europe, notably Britain and France, seemed to recover much of their old strength without great loss of prestige. Defeated Germany, after the low ebb of the 20's and early 30's, became resurgent under the Nazis; and Russia, under Bolshevist rule, gained enormously in strength and influence. On the eve of World War II these four states were unquestionably great powers, and even Italy, under Mussolini, was making an impressive bid for similar recognition.

After six years of war a wholly different picture emerged. The old balance of power was shattered. The nation which under the Nazis had been the strongest state in Europe in 1939 and had succeeded in achieving European and threatening world domination was a divided and occupied country. Italy had been liberated from the Fascist regime, but she was wrestling with serious economic and political problems. France, smashed by the Nazi *blitzkrieg* and smarting from the humiliation of defeat and collaborationism, was in a plight almost as serious of that of Italy. Britain, it soon became clear, had been fundamentally weakened by accumulated strains and the wartime efforts which overtaxed her resources, and she did not stage as rapid a recovery as had been expected. Only the Soviet Union was more powerful than ever, in spite of tremendous loss of life and destruction of property during the war. "The condition of Europe after the second world war," in short, "was without precedent in modern history."[4]

Immediately after the nonaggression treaty with Germany in August, 1939, Soviet troops occupied a large part of eastern Poland, and in June, 1940, the Baltic states of Esthonia, Latvia, and Lithuania. At the Yalta Conference of early 1945 Churchill and Roosevelt were faced with a Soviet *fait accompli* in Eastern Europe, and they had to be content with Stalin's signature on agreements for the "liberation of Eastern Europe," free elections in Poland and elsewhere, and similar pledges. In violation of the Yalta Agreements, the Russians reduced Poland, Czechoslovakia (after the coup of February, 1948), Hungary, Rumania, and Bulgaria to

[2] Joseph C. Harsch, "Don't Underestimate Europe," *New York Times Magazine,* November 11, 1964, p. 72. © 1964 by the New York Times Company. Reprinted by permission.

[3] (New York: Frederick A. Praeger, 1964), p. 214.

[4] *Major Problems of United States Foreign Policy, 1949–1950* (Washington, D.C.: The Brookings Institution, 1949), p. 93.

the status of satellite states. They virtually sealed off their zone in Austria. The Soviet Union stood astride Eastern Europe, and there was no comparable power alignment elsewhere on the continent.

Aside from the growing power of the Soviet Union — which is only in part a European state — the position of Europe had undergone a change so fundamental as to lead students of history to speak of "the passing of the European age."[5] In 1944 William T. R. Fox wrote that "the transition from the old, world-dominating Europe to the new, 'problem-Europe' is a central fact in the international politics of our time."[6] Europe still held a far more important place in world affairs than these statements suggest; but it is a fact, as Harold and Margaret Sprout pointed out, that "Central and Western Europe no longer enjoys a virtual monopoly of political power and world leadership."[7]

The decline of Europe did not begin with World War II. The war merely accelerated a deterioration which, though largely unperceived, had been in progress for several decades. Moreover, the recuperative powers of the continent were not sufficient to assure recovery from the vast dislocation and destruction of a second world war. It was suffering from a gigantic loss of capital; its earnings from capital investment had largely vanished; and on other invisible transactions, such as shipping and tourist trade, it had a net deficit instead of a favorable balance. This situation was not new, but Europe's ability to pay for its imports had seriously declined. Production was at a low level. The population was greater than before the war and was still rising. There were more mouths to feed, and not enough food to satisfy even minimum caloric requirements. The shortage of dollars abroad — the much-talked-about "dollar gap" — and of supplies at home produced inflationary pressures and a serious disequilibrium in the currencies of many countries. Europe was plagued by inconvertible currencies, currencies of varying degrees of stability, and many serious internal barriers to trade. Intra-European trade, which before the war had been a major factor in the life of the continent, fell off alarmingly. Severe winters and poor crops in 1946 and 1947 further complicated the problem of recovery.

To add to the economic woes there were grave political and moral weaknesses and ideological divisions. As the hopes for postwar cooperation among the great powers receded, the dictates of the cold war took priority over considerations of recovery and rehabilitation. The stricken continent, which needed to muster all its resources in an effort to survive, was rent in two between East and West, separated by an "iron curtain" which ran from Stettin on the Baltic to Trieste on the Adriatic and divided the Communist from the non-Communist world. Germany became the hottest spot in the cold war, the greatest bastion for both sides; and hopes for her unification — or even for a German peace settlement — seemed to fade away.

These developments seriously retarded the economic recovery of Europe, raised again the old problem of security against aggression, and prevented the distraught people of Europe from resuming their normal lives. The future of millions was jeopardized by the real or supposed imperatives of the cold war

Problems of Peacemaking

Before peace could be preserved in the postwar period it first had to be made. The major victors were in agreement on one point at least: there would be no general peace conference such as followed World War I. Instead, the heads of the governments of Great Britain, the Soviet Union, and the

[5] This is the title of a challenging book by Eric Fischer, published by the Harvard University Press in 1948.

[6] *The Super-Powers* (New York: Harcourt, Brace, 1944), pp. 12–13.

[7] *Foundations of National Power,* 2d ed. (Princeton, N.J.: D. Van Nostrand Co., 1951), p. 168.

United States—Churchill and Attlee, Stalin, and Truman — agreed at the Potsdam meeting of July–August, 1945, to create a Council of Foreign Ministers of five powers — the Big Three, plus China and France — "to continue the necessary preparatory work for the peace settlements." The Council, therefore, became the principal agency for peacemaking in Europe. Since all its decisions had to be unanimous, its success was conditioned on great power unanimity; but from the outset of its deliberations it was apparent that real unanimity was highly unlikely. The first meeting of the Council, held in London in September–October, 1945, came to a dead end on disagreement over the nations which should be allowed to participate in the peace negotiations.

Preparatory Work on the Early Treaties. The London impasse was seemingly broken at a conference of the foreign ministers of the Big Three in Moscow in December, 1945. They agreed to consider peace treaties with Italy, Hungary, Bulgaria, Rumania, and Finland before attempting the more difficult assignment of writing treaties for Austria and Germany. A compromise was worked out which seemed to reconcile the American desire to bring all belligerent members of the wartime United Nations into the peace negotiations with the Russian view that the great powers, through the Council of Foreign Ministers, should determine the terms of peace. According to this compromise, the preparatory work on each of the five treaties would be conducted by those victor nations which had in each instance signed the terms of surrender (the 4–3–2 formula); this meant that the Big Three, plus France, would draft the Italian treaty, the Big Three would draft the three Balkan treaties, and Great Britain and the Soviet Union would draft the treaty for Finland. Then the draft treaties would be considered at a general conference of all states which had participated in the European campaign against the Axis. The final treaties would thereupon be drafted by the Council of Foreign Ministers, with due heed to the recommendations of the conference.

In two lengthy sessions in Paris in 1946, from April 25 to May 16 and from June 15 to July 12, the Council of Foreign Ministers managed to supervise the preparation of draft treaties for the five states, after much debate and disagreement. The Italian peace treaty, in particular, posed many thorny problems. Among these were the disposition of Trieste, which Russia had promised to Yugoslavia but which Italy, backed by Great Britain, France, and the United States, wanted for herself; the disposition of the former Italian colonies of Libya, Eritrea, and Somaliland; French demands for small but strategically and economically important bits of territory on the Franco-Italian frontier; and Russian demands for very heavy reparations for herself and Yugoslavia. There were also serious problems in connection with the Balkan treaties, particularly the free navigation of the Danube and equality of economic opportunity in the Balkans.

Paris Conference, 1946. Having agreed at last on the terms of the draft treaties, the major powers issued invitations to a general conference to consider the proposed peace settlements. As the price of Russian cooperation the United States had been forced to agree to support the draft treaties as prepared by the Big Four — now France was included — and even to join in presenting some "suggested" rules of procedure which would further limit the scope and power of the general conference. These restrictions did not prevent a searching scrutiny of the draft treaties by the smaller powers. Some sixty articles on which the Big Four had been unable to reach complete argeement were submitted to the conference.

From July 26 to October 15, 1946, more than 1,500 delegates from twenty-one nations, meeting in the Luxembourg Palace in

Paris, examined the drafts article by article, both in committees and in plenary sessions. The fruits of these arduous labors were modest; "the possibility of arriving at generally accepted solutions by negotiation was ruled out both by the methods adopted and by the temper of the delegates."[8] Most of the recommendations on disputed points were passed over the strong opposition of Russia and the other participating Communist states. Foreign Minister Evatt of Australia, who tried to lead a revolt against the iron-handed control of the great powers, abandoned his efforts after a few weeks and left the conference.

Major Provisions of the Treaties. Although the Paris meeting was generally regarded as a failure, its recommendations were seriously reviewed by the Council of Foreign Ministers, and in some instances they were adopted, at least in modified form. Meeting in New York later in 1946, the Council agreed on the final terms of the five treaties. Its decisions on the major issues in dispute may be quickly summarized:

1. Trieste, with most of the Istrian Peninsula, plus a narrow strip of territory extending to the Italian border, was created as a Free Territory under the supervision of the Security Council of the United Nations. This "solution" pleased nobody, but it was the only compromise on which the Big Four could agree. Because of great power deadlocks the Security Council was unable to take the necessary steps for the creation of the Free Territory of Trieste. Thus, while theoretically the Free Territory of Trieste was internationalized, in reality Yugoslavia controlled Zone B and American and British forces administered Zone A, which included the city of Trieste. On the eve of the Italian elections in 1948 the United States, Britain, and France suddenly proposed that Trieste be returned to Italy; but this proposal too proved to be impossible of fulfillment. Obviously no real settlement could be achieved without the consent of both Italy and Yugoslavia. Relations between these two countries improved after the "Tito split" in 1948, but the Trieste issue remained at dead center for many months thereafter. At length, on October 6, 1954, after long discussions in London, representatives of Italy, Yugoslavia, Great Britain and the United States initialed a "Memorandum of Understanding" on Trieste.[9] According to this, the city itself and almost all of Zone A were given to Italy, and a slightly enlarged Zone B was awarded to Yugoslavia.

2. The boundary line between Italy and Yugoslavia was drawn roughly midway between the lines proposed by the Soviet Union and the United States.

3. There were no further major changes in the boundaries of postwar Italy, although Briga-Tenda and a few other small areas were ceded to France.

4. The question of the disposition of the Italian colonies was "solved" by postponing a solution and providing for a method of eventual settlement. The Italian peace treaty stipulated that if the Council of Foreign Ministers was unable to reach a decision within one year after the effective date of the treaty, the question should be referred to the General Assembly of the United Nations and the Assembly's decision should be regarded as binding. In spite of an eleventh-hour effort by Russia to convoke a meeting of the Council of Foreign Ministers to seek an agreement, the deadline of September 15, 1948, passed without a decision. Accordingly, the General Assembly took up the problem in the spring of 1949. The action of the Assembly has been described in Chapter 13.

5. Italian reparations were fixed at $260,000,000, most of which was to go to Greece and Yugoslavia. Some of this amount was to

[8] J. C. Campbell, *The United States in World Affairs, 1945–1947* (New York: Council on Foreign Relations, 1947), pp. 136–137.

[9] The text of this memorandum is given in the *New York Times*, October 6, 1954.

European Territorial Changes as a Result of World War II

come from current production, but such payments were not to begin until 1952, and they were not to be made if they imposed a serious strain on the Italian economy. Hungary, Bulgaria, and Finland were each to pay $100,000,000 in reparations, mainly to Russia. Bulgaria was to pay $25,000,000 to Yugoslavia and $45,000,000 to Greece.

6. All of Transylvania was assigned to Rumania, which in turn agreed to Russia's possession of Bessarabia and Bukovina.

7. Finland ceded the province of Petsamo to the U.S.S.R. and gave the Soviets a fifty-year lease on the Porkkala-Udd area.

8. With the approval of Russia, the Balkan treaties guaranteed the free navigation of the Danube, but all attempts to implement this pledge were later blocked by Russian maneuvers. The Big Four agreed to hold a conference to establish an international navigation authority for the Danube within six months after the treaties went into effect.

Such a conference was finally held in Belgrade, in July–August, 1948, almost a year after the effective date of the treaties.

Treaty Violations. Some two years after the cessation of hostilities, the peace treaties with Italy, Hungary, Bulgaria, Rumania, and Finland were finally declared to be in effect, as of September 15, 1947. Many of their provisions, however, have been deliberately violated, evaded, or ignored. Only lip service has been paid to the guarantees of freedom and independence for the peoples of Hungary, Bulgaria, and Rumania. The provision for the free navigation of the Danube went overboard when at the Belgrade conference in 1948 Russia and her satellites forced through a treaty which, while endorsing the principle, in reality completely subverted it. The Western powers refused to sign the treaty and instead strongly denounced it. In effect, the control of the Danube passed to the Soviet Union and the Soviet bloc, with only Yugoslavia disputing the Soviet position.

The Italian peace treaty, like the treaties with Bulgaria, Hungary, and Rumania, has become almost a dead letter. In late 1951 the United States, Britain, and France proposed to the Soviet Union and other interested nations that the treaty be revised, and that Italy be granted full sovereignty and admitted to the United Nations. Since Italy had cast her lot with the nations of Western Europe and the Atlantic Community, and since the primary purpose of the suggested treaty revision was to remove the limitations on the size of Italian armed forces, it is hardly surprising that the Russian reply was unsatisfactory.[10] Charging the Soviet Union with bad faith, and alleging that full independence and national defense were vital to her existence, Italy in effect repudiated most of the peace treaty, with the acquiescence and in many respects the strong encouragement of the Western powers.

Peace with Austria. Having disposed of five peace treaties, the Council of Foreign Ministers, meeting in Moscow in the spring of 1947, turned to even thornier problems — the treaties for Austria and Germany. There seemed to be real hope for a basic agreement regarding Austria. Technically it would not be a peace treaty, since Austria was regarded as a liberated and not an enemy state. She had been promised full independence in the Moscow Declaration of 1943.

Disagreement between the Soviet Union and the Western powers was complete on three major issues: (1) the claim of Yugoslavia to a portion of Austrian territory in southern Carinthia; (2) Yugoslavia's demand for $150,000,000 in reparations; and (3) the definition of German assets. The last issue was the most basic. The Potsdam Agreement, in a loosely worded provision, had assigned to the Soviet Union, as part of her share of German reparations, all German assets in the Soviet zone in eastern Austria. The U.S.S.R. argued that the provision embraced all property acquired by the Germans, through whatever means. Since Austria had been governed as a part of Germany from 1938 to 1945, this interpretation would deprive Austria of most of her properties and resources. The Western powers strongly opposed the Soviet interpretation.

Unable to agree at Moscow on these disputed issues affecting the Austrian treaty, the foreign ministers decided to establish a four-power Treaty Commission to meet in Vienna for the purpose of resolving the issues. The commission held 85 sessions in 1947, but it could not agree on a single one of the nineteen questions submitted to it. After futile efforts in 1947 and 1948, the Council of Foreign Ministers itself, meeting in May–June, 1949, seemed to make real progress on the Austrian treaty. The reparations issue was apparently settled by agreement of the

[10] For the texts of the statement of the three Western powers regarding Italy on September 26, 1951, and the Soviet note on Italy of October 11, 1951, see *Current History*, XXI (December, 1951), 362, 365–366.

Western powers to allow the Soviet Union extensive rights to the oil and shipping facilities in Austria and a cash payment of $150,000,000 over a six-year period in lieu of other "German assets," but attempts to implement the agreement were unsuccessful.

The deadlock over Austria was broken at long last as a result of a *volte-face* by Russia in 1955. On February 8 Molotov blandly announced that an Austrian treaty could be signed if "effective guarantees" against an *anschluss* could be secured. In April the Austrian chancellor, Julius Raab, pledged his country to a policy of neutrality, the Russians accepted the commitment, and the way seemed clear for an Austrian state treaty. After further negotiations the foreign ministers of the Big Four went to Vienna, and on May 15 they affixed their signatures to the treaty.[11] Austria was "re-established as a sovereign, independent and democratic state," with the same frontiers she had had before her forced union with Germany in 1938. She agreed not to "enter into political or economic union with Germany in any form whatsoever," or to "possess, construct or experiment with" any weapons of mass destruction. All forces of the Allied and Associated Powers and members of the Allied Commission for Austria would be withdrawn "in so far as possible not later than December 31, 1955." The treaty contained detailed provisions regarding claims arising out of the war, including the question of German assets. Thus Austria regained her independence in "the first major European settlement between East and West since the outbreak of the cold war."[12]

Peace with Germany. The Council of Foreign Ministers avoided any real consideration of a German peace settlement until 1947, when the central problems of a German treaty were considered at two meetings of the Council, the first in Moscow in March–April, the second in London in November–December. When they were over, the prospects for a treaty were as remote as before. The first item on the agenda at Moscow was the consideration of a two-volume report of the Allied Control Council in Berlin on the implementation of the Potsdam Agreements. The bitter debates on demilitarization, denazification, democratization, deindustrialization — "barbarous and not easily defined expressions which had been accepted at Potsdam"[13] — almost disrupted the conference. At the London meeting the Western powers wanted to discuss measures for the economic recovery of Germany, whereas the Soviet Union wanted to debate the establishment of a central German government and the collection of reparations. The complete failure of the London meeting marked the virtual end of four-power efforts to negotiate a treaty of peace with Germany. Henceforth "the German problem" was one of implementation of the Soviet policies in East Germany and of tripartite policies in West Germany.

All of the four former occupying powers are on record in favor of German unification and the conclusion of a peace treaty for a unified Germany at the earliest possible date. Nevertheless little or no progress has been made toward these professed objectives. At the Berlin conference of the foreign ministers of the Big Four in January–February, 1954, issues regarding Germany were discussed at length, but in the end all that the foreign ministers could report was "a full exchange of views on the Germany question." The heads of states of the same four powers, at their meeting in Geneva in July, 1955, frequently referred to German problems, which they agreed that their foreign ministers should discuss at a meeting in October. The foreign ministers, however, were unable to resolve the impasse; it was

[11] For the text of the Austrian state treaty, see the *New York Times,* May 16, 1955.

[12] *New York Times,* May 13, 1955.

[13] J. C. Campbell, *The United States in World Affairs, 1947–48* (New York: Council on Foreign Relations, 1948), p. 62.

obvious that more than "the Geneva spirit" was needed to produce agreement on concrete issues. A German peace treaty still seems to be remote, for it is bound up with many issues in dispute between the Soviet Union and the Western powers.

Thus the detailed agreement on Germany which emerged from the Potsdam Conference of July–August, 1945, spelling out the decisions reached at Yalta a few months before, was to shape the future of that nation in a way not realized at the time. Substantial portions of prewar Germany were transferred to the U.S.S.R. and to Poland, and the rest of the country was divided into four zones. Berlin, in the heart of the Russian sphere, also was divided into four zones and made the seat of a four-power Allied Control Council authorized to make decisions for Germany as a whole. The machinery for four-power cooperation in the governing of Germany was from the outset weakened by basic disagreements among the occupying powers, and it broke down completely in 1948, when the Soviet representatives ceased to attend the meetings of the Council. The occupying powers did cooperate after a fashion in certain matters, including the long-drawn-out and much-discussed War Crimes Trials at Nuremberg in 1945–46. Local governments were established in each of the four zones. In eastern Germany a program of sovietization was carried out from the beginning, with the Communist-dominated Socialist Unity Party as a convenient mouthpiece. In 1949 a "People's Democratic Republic" was proclaimed in the Soviet zone. The three Western occupying powers cooperated rather closely from the outset, although France was inclined to favor much harsher policies than either Britain or the United States and her position regarding the Saar, which she was occupying, caused frequent disagreements with her Western allies.

After 1947 Great Britain and the United States, with the increasing cooperation of France, concentrated their efforts on plans for the economic and political integration of the western zones of Germany. Tripartite conversations in June, 1948, led to agreement on a general plan for future action. It was the three-power program in West Germany that precipitated the crisis of 1948.

The Berlin Crisis of 1948. The first important move of Britain, France, and the United States was to carry out a much-needed currency reform in West Germany. The new currency was not introduced into Berlin until the Soviet Union had rejected proposals for quadripartite control of the circulation of eastern marks in the city and had instead announced a currency reform of her own. But the main Russian countermoves to the active cooperation of the other occupying powers were withdrawal from the Allied Control Council and the Berlin Kommandatura and the imposition of increasingly drastic restrictions on traffic between the western zones and Berlin. The reply of the Western powers was the famous "Berlin airlift." This afforded a convincing demonstration of the determination of the democratic states to remain in Berlin and not to give in to further Soviet pressures. As such it was a stimulus to the morale of the non-Communist world.

In July and August, 1948, the Western powers made joint representations to Moscow regarding the Berlin impasse. After many conferences the Russians agreed to end the blockade, but they soon declined to cooperate in implementing the agreement. Faced with this situation, the Western states referred the dispute to the Security Council of the United Nations; but the Council's efforts produced no solution.

Founding the West German State. During the negotiations in Moscow it had become apparent that the Soviet Union wanted the Western powers to postpone or cancel their plans for a West German state

Department of State

Germany Today

in return for the lifting of the Berlin blockade. This they refused to do, and after the failure of further efforts to reach an agreement with the Soviet Union they turned again to the task of doing the best they could with a divided Germany. In September, 1948, while the Berlin dispute was before the Security Council, a German parliamentary council met in Bonn, to draft a "provisional constitution" or "basic law" for a West German state, and the military governors of the three occupying powers began work on an occupation statute to define the limits within which the "basic law" must operate. In December these three states, plus the Benelux countries, agreed on a draft statute for an International Authority for the Ruhr, and a month later the three military governors established a Military Security Board to keep watch over German disarmament and demilitarization. In April, 1949, after the formal signing of the North Atlantic Pact, the foreign ministers of France, Great Britain, and the United States discussed all major problems relating to Germany and in a few days reached agreement on the terms of the occupation statute. On May 5 the "Basic Law of the Federal Republic of Germany," drafted by the Bonn parliamentary council of German leaders and approved by the military governors of the western zones, was promulgated.

These developments placed the Western powers in a more favorable bargaining position vis-à-vis the Soviet Union and apparently helped to persuade the Russians to agree to lift the Berlin blockade. This agreement was reached as a result of a series of conversations in New York City in February–March, 1949, between Jacob Malik and Philip C. Jessup, Soviet and United States representatives at the United Nations. After some weeks of negotiation through these and other channels, the four governments concerned announced an agreement to lift the blockade on May 12 and to hold a meeting of the Council of Foreign Ministers in Paris later in the same month.

Accordingly, from May 23 to June 20 the Council of Foreign Ministers met again, for the first time since December, 1947. It soon became apparent that no compromise was possible on the basic problem of the political and economic unification of Germany. The month of discussions produced only frayed nerves and minor agreements, mostly relating to Austria. The foreign ministers did agree to try again at some unspecified future date, and they promised that "the occupation authorities, in the light of the intention of the Ministers to continue unity of Germany, shall consult together in Berlin on a quadripartite basis."

West Germany and Western Europe. The Western occupying powers and the Soviet Union next proceeded to sponsor "democratic" governments in Germany. In September, 1949, the newly elected parliament of the Federal Republic of Germany established other organs and agencies of the new government. Theodor Heuss became president and Dr. Konrad Adenauer became chancellor. After these steps the three Western powers declared the military occupation of their zones to be at an end; civil government formally began with the promulgation of the Occupation Statute and the establishment of the Allied High Commission. In November the West German state was admitted to the Council of Europe, and in the Petersberg agreement with the Allied High Commission it promised to cooperate in the defense of Western Europe in return for a relaxation of the restrictions upon its freedom of action. These restrictions were further relaxed in 1950, especially as a result of the decision of the foreign ministers of the Western occupying powers to permit the creation of a West German foreign ministry and a mobile police force.

In November, 1951, the foreign ministers of Britain, France, and the United States, and Chancellor Adenauer approved the draft of a general agreement which, they announced, would be "a concisive step toward

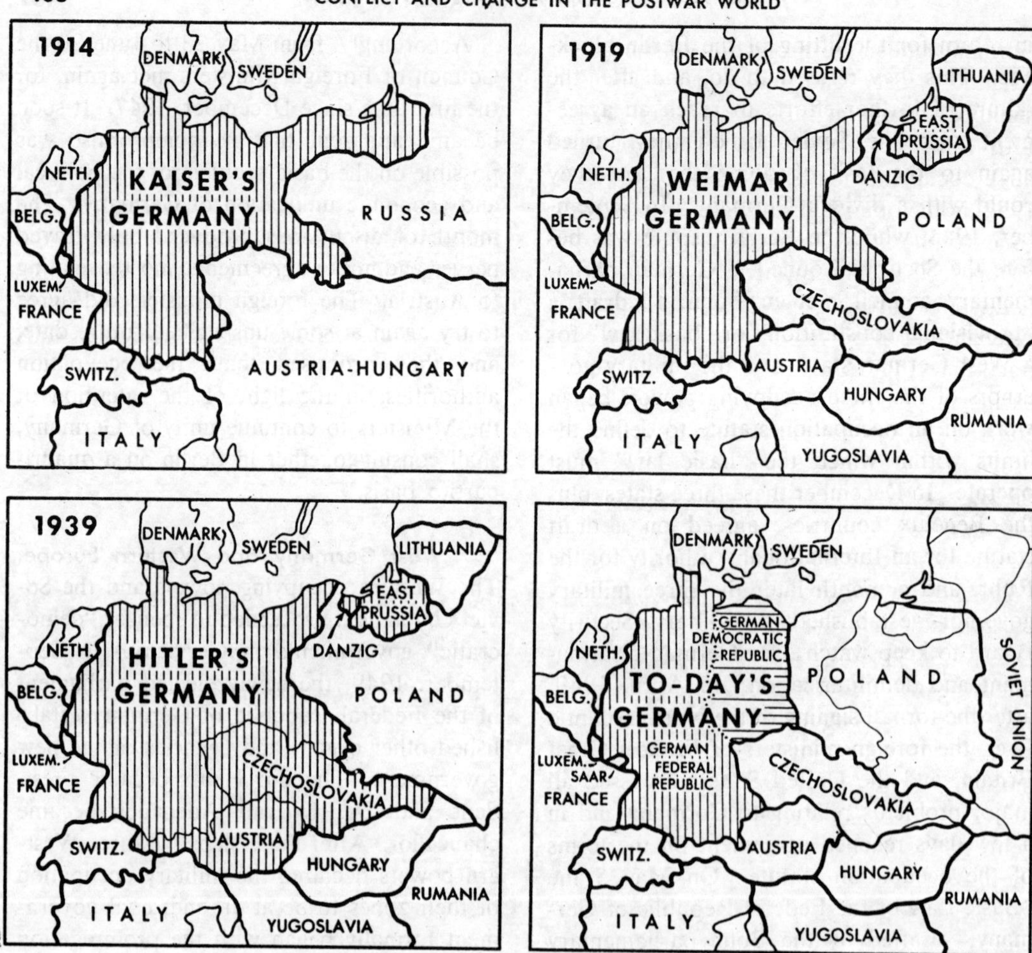

Four Stages in German History

the realization of the common aim of the three Western Powers and the Federal Government to integrate the Federal Republic on a basis of equality in a European community itself included in a developing Atlantic community."[14] They agreed, however, that the new arrangement would not enter into effect until a number of related conventions had been accepted and until the association of Western Germany with the proposed European Defense Community had been assured.

These matters were worked out in the spring of 1952 after the North Atlantic Council had agreed to the creation under NATO of a European army, including West German troops. On May 26 the three Western states and the West German state signed the "peace contract" which gave the Federal Republic of Germany virtual autonomy in both foreign and domestic affairs. On the following day the foreign ministers of the Benelux countries, France, Italy, and West Germany signed the treaty for the European Defense Community. Shortly afterwards an amendment to the North Atlantic Treaty was signed, extending the guarantees of the treaty to the European Defense Community. The effect of this amendment was to put

[14] The text of this important joint statement on Germany is given in the *Department of State Bulletin,* XXV (December 3, 1951), 891–892.

Germany under the protection of the North Atlantic Treaty and make her "a quasi-member of the larger alliance pledged to fight with it, if necessary."[15] The signing of these three documents made the week of May 25, 1952, in the opinion of the *New York Times*, "one of the most important weeks in the history of the Old Continent."

Despite strong opposition, Chancellor Adenauer secured full approval of the contract and the EDC treaty by the federal parliament; but with the refusal of the French National Assembly, in August, 1954, to approve the EDC treaty the agreements of 1952 became void. An alternative solution for the problems of European security and Western Germany's role in a reorganized Western Europe was embodied in the London and Paris agreements of October, 1954.[16] On May 5, 1955, almost ten years to the day after V-E Day, these agreements entered into effect, thus ending a decade of occupation and marking the emergence of West Germany as a sovereign state.[17]

The Western powers fully subscribe to the goal of Germany's ultimate unification, but they are also determined to help to make West Germany as viable a unit as possible and to associate her ever more closely with Western Europe and the Atlantic community. Russia loudly proclaims her desire for a united Germany, but certainly she does not envision a Germany integrated into the Western European community. At the "summit" conference in July, 1955, and at the Big Four foreign ministers conference in the following October, the Russians insisted that German reunification should be considered only in relation to the whole issue of European security. They organized their zone along Communist lines, and they have continued to maintain a strong presence and indirect control there. They are doing everything possible to ensure that the Germany of the future will be a state dominated by the Soviet Union.

East Germany. In October, 1949, as a countermove to the establishment of the Federal Republic in West Germany, the "German Democratic Republic" was proclaimed in East Germany, and the Soviet Union announced the end of the Soviet Military Administration and its replacement by the Soviet Control Commission. These steps involved little actual modification of Soviet controls over East Germany or over the East German Communist Party and government. In June, 1953, a Soviet civilian commissioner replaced the military commander in East Germany, and the severe policy of sovietization was moderated. When these measures were followed by the uprising in East Berlin on June 11, one of the most dramatic episodes of postwar history, the Soviets responded by ruthlessly suppressing the riots and severely punishing the defectors who were apprehended. In March, 1954, the Soviet Union declared that the German Democratic Republic was a sovereign state, and in September, 1955, the Soviet High Commission was replaced by an embassy; but Soviet troops remained in the area and the "Democratic Republic" continued to be a faithful satellite state.

Most of the non-Communist states do not recognize the East German Democratic Republic. The Soviet Union obviously regards it as a vital outpost of Soviet power in Central Europe, a shield against threats to the homeland, and a strategic position for control of the East European countries. Khrushchev repeatedly threatened to enter into a peace treaty with the East German government if the other former occupying powers would not accept that government and agree to Russia's terms for a German peace settlement. His successors have been more cautious in dealing with the German question, but presumably there has been no change in Russia's ultimate objectives.

[15] *New York Times*, May 25, 1952, p. E8.

[16] For the text of these agreements, see the *New York Times*, October 24, 1954.

[17] *New York Times*, May 6, 1955.

Berlin. One of the most delicate of all the questions arising from the continued division of Germany, and from "the tug and pull of international pressures" in that vital part of Central Europe, concerns the present and future status of the great city of Berlin. "The stakes in Berlin are high, and the duel between Eastern Communism and Western democracy has been increasing since 1945."[18] Like Germany west of the Oder-Neisse line, Berlin was divided into four zones by the occupying powers; and when the rift between the Soviet Union and the Western powers became complete by 1948, Berlin, like Germany, remained divided, a hostage to the fortunes of the cold war. The Soviet Union's closing of the land corridors into Berlin in 1948 showed how far it was prepared to go to bring the entire city under Communist control. The Allied "air lift," carried on at great risk and expense, showed the Western powers' determination to protect Berlin and to maintain it as an island of freedom inside the Soviet zone. Soviet and East German pressures on Berlin in 1961 and 1962, culminating in the sealing off of East from West Berlin and the signing of a "peace treaty" between Russia and the German Democratic Republic, precipitated one of the most serious crises of the postwar years.

As the center par excellence of cold war pressures and conflicts, Berlin "is one of the strangest governmental phenomena of modern times. Since 1945, it has been the 'capital' or 'headquarters' of eight major governmental units, including four occupation regimes (the former Allied Control Authority for Germany, the Allied Kommandatura, the Soviet Control Commission for Berlin, and the unilateral Soviet Control Commission for Germany); one German 'national government' (the East German Democratic Republic); and three metropolitan governments (the intital post-hostilities administration of the entire metropolis, the Government of West Berlin, and the East Berlin Government). In addition, there are four unilateral Allied occupation administrations, and twenty city boroughs."[19] Although Berlin has experienced an industrial boom, and although the West Berliners have shown great courage and the Western powers great determination, the future of the divided city, an enclave in a hostile Communist state, is dependent to an alarming degree on a basic improvement in East-West relations. The Berlin Wall, erected on Soviet orders in August, 1961, is not only a grim and ugly barrier between East and West Berlin, but also a standing reminder of the barriers which, even in the period of detente, still divide the Communist from the non-Communist world.

Potentially Germany is the most powerful state in Europe, aside from the U.S.S.R. It would make a great deal of difference whether a strong, united Germany associated herself with the Western powers or with the Soviet Union or followed a relatively independent course. In short, the future of Germany and the character of the institutions which she develops are matters of the gravest concern.

In view of the profound differences between the Soviet Union and the other former occupying powers, and between the governments that have come into existence in East and West Germany, Germany will probably remain divided, and will continue to be an area of conflicting pressures and interests. The peculiar status of Berlin, a divided enclave within the East German state, raises further complications and dangers.

Economic Recovery and Integration

Within three years of V-E Day the prospects for great power collaboration in peace as in war — pledged in the Moscow Declaration of 1943, in the United Nations Charter, and in many other solemn agreements — had become dim indeed. The refusal of the

[18] Elmer Plischke, *Contemporary Government of Germany* (Boston: Houghton Mifflin Company, 1961), p. 214.

[19] *Ibid.*, p. 215.

Soviet Union to participate in the Marshall Plan, or to allow any of the states within her orbit to participate, was a clear indication that the problems of European recovery could not be considered on a continental scale. Zhdanov's statement of October, 1947, that the Soviet Union would "bend every effort in order that this plan be doomed to failure" was in a sense an open declaration of war against the Marshall Plan and its sponsors.

Faced with a divided continent, the countries of Western Europe took up the tasks of recovery and rehabilitation and defense on a regional rather than a continental basis. Driven together by a common disaster and a common danger, their peoples have achieved an unprecedented degree of cooperation in the postwar period. Indeed, the closer "integration" of Western Europe — disregarding for the moment the exact meaning of this term and the limited progress in the direction of real union — has been one of the significant developments of recent years.

The problems which the nations of Western Europe had to face, individually and collectively, were basic ones. They included inflation, trade restrictions, balance of payments, the production and distribution of goods, the rebuilding of factories, the recovery of agriculture, the feeding and housing of an increasing population in an area with a reduced capacity to sustain existing numbers, the settlement of displaced persons, the replacement of destroyed materials, industrial unrest, political instability, and military insecurity. "But," said General George C. Marshall at a ceremony in 1950 marking the halfway point of the plan which bears his name, "slowly I learned that the most serious phase of rehabilitation was related to other considerations — political, moral, spiritual. These were less tangible, but far more difficult to deal with."

Benelux. The first major official step in the direction of closer integration in Western Europe in the postwar period was the formation of the Benelux Customs Union. As early as September, 1944, the governments-in-exile of Belgium, the Netherlands, and Luxembourg had signed a convention for the creation of such a union. The convention, as modified in March, 1947, entered into effect on January 1, 1948. It provided for the elimination of all customs duties between the participating states and for a uniform tariff schedule for imported goods. The ultimate objective was proclaimed to be a complete economic union.[20] In June, 1948, the foreign ministers of the Benelux countries set January 1, 1950, as the target date for the beginning of economic union. This date has been repeatedly postponed, for the difficulties have proved to be greater than expected. The attempts to harmonize the internal economic policies of the member states encountered serious obstacles — with the balance of payments problem as a major stumbling block — giving rise to a growing "conviction that these obstacles can be overcome only within a wider framework of economic union embracing France and western Germany," or even a much larger area. The Benelux countries "have concluded therefore that Benelux as originally planned is not enough, and that greater sacrifices of the interests of particular industries, as well as greater subordination of national interests, must be made the price for achieving greater economic advantages over a wider European area."[21]

[20] See Howard J. Hilton, Jr., "Benelux — A Case Study in Economic Union," *Department of State Bulletin*, XXIII (July 31, 1950).

[21] *Major Problems, 1949–50*, p. 414. Economic union is still the goal of the Benelux countries, and considerable progress is being made in this direction. A concise summary of the progress toward economic union is contained in *News Digest from Holland*, issued by the Netherlands Information Service, New York, June 20, 1955. See also John Goormaghtigh, "European Integration," *International Conciliation*, No. 488 (February, 1953), 79–83.

The European Recovery Program. All the nations of Western Europe developed national programs for recovery (for example, the Monnet Plan in France), but the major effort was made cooperatively through the Marshall Plan. The participants in the plan — probably the most ambitious program of economic cooperation in history — included all of non-Communist Europe except Spain, plus Iceland and Turkey. After Secretary of State George C. Marshall's famous address at Harvard on June 5, 1947, representatives of the sixteen participating states met in Paris to draft a program of joint effort for recovery and to consider the amount of outside assistance necessary. Molotov and a large delegation of advisers joined them for a few days and then left. Soon afterwards the Russian government announced its strong opposition to the whole idea of the Marshall Plan, which it charged was an American imperialist and anti-Soviet plot in thin disguise. At its insistence Czechoslovakia and Poland, which had indicated their intention to participate, withdrew their acceptance. These actions "set a seal to the breach between the west and the Soviet *bloc;* the history of Europe for years ahead was settled within these weeks."[22]

Undaunted by Russia's action, the foreign ministers of the West European states set up the Committee of European Economic Cooperation. After hard work through the summer of 1947, the committee issued a two-volume report[23] outlining a four-year program "similar in general scale to that achieved by the United States in the mobilization years 1940 to 1944." This report formed the basis of the planning which resulted in the European Recovery Program.

[22] Herbert Luethy, *France Against Herself* (New York: Frederick A. Praeger, 1955), p. 353.

[23] *Committee of European Economic Cooperation Report,* Dept. of State Pub. 1930, European Series 28 (Washington, D.C.: Government Printing Office, 1947). Vol. I contains the general report and Vol. II the technical reports.

OEEC. On April 16, 1948, after the United States Congress had passed the Foreign Assistance Act of 1948, which established the Economic Cooperation Administration (ECA), the CEEC adopted a Convention for European Economic Cooperation. In this convention the sixteen participating states agreed "to work in close cooperation in their economic relations with one another," with "the elaboration and extension of a joint recovery programme" as "their immediate task." To further these objectives the convention established the Organization for European Economic Cooperation.

OEEC, therefore, was the coordinating agency for this great experiment in cooperative action. Long before the Marshall Plan had passed into history, OEEC had demonstrated so convincingly that it met a continuing need that its members announced their intention to extend its life for an indefinite period. It remained in existence until 1961, when it was superseded by the Organization for Economic Cooperation and Development. Among its outstanding accomplishments were arrangements for the allocation of Marshall Plan funds among the various participating countries, the establishment of the Intra-European Payments Scheme, and, in general, unprecedented success in coordinating the economic programs and policies of member states. Its main efforts, aside from the preliminary task of organization, study, and exchange of views, were directed toward the increase of production and the expansion of trade.

The Payments Plan. One of the first tasks of OEEC was to propose and put into effect the Intra-European Payments Scheme. This complicated plan was incorporated in the Agreement for Intra-European Payments and Compensations, approved on October 16, 1948.[24] Through exhaustive analysis the

[24] See *Agreement for Intra-European Payments and Compensation* (OEEC, Paris, October 16, 1948), Part I.

experts of OEEC had sought to determine the contributions of the creditor countries and the drawing rights of the debtor countries. The Bank for International Settlements at Basle acted as a clearing agent for all transactions under the balance of payments plan. The sterling area was treated as a unit, and each country was obligated to provide all necessary information relative to its international transactions.

The payments scheme of 1948 was a major achievement and helped to pave the way for the even more ambitious European Payments Union, which came into existence in 1950. In its report to ECA on the first annual program, OEEC stated that "it is not too much to say that as a direct and immediate result of that scheme more than 800 million dollars worth of goods will move which would otherwise never have been made, or would have rusted or rotted away."[25]

Counterpart Funds. ECA aid was given largely in the form of outright grants, although some funds were earmarked for conditional grants, loans, and technical assistance. Countries receiving grants deposited in a special account amounts in their own currencies equivalent to the dollar grants of the United States. These deposits were known as counterpart funds, and could be spent only for basic recovery projects, upon approval of ECA. "In general, the 'counterpart' funds are to be used for (*a*) reconstruction, expansion, and modernization of industrial capacity, (*b*) stabilization of internal financial and monetary conditions, and (*c*) development and expansion of the productive capacity of raw materials."[26] "The governments reimburse themselves for the money they deposit in the counterpart funds by selling the dollar credits the United States advances them to those of their own citizens who require dollars to import goods from dollar countries."[27] This explains why people of the Marshall Plan countries paid in their own currencies for products made available by American aid grants.

ERP: An Appraisal. In its immediate objectives the Marshall Plan was a brilliant success. ECA reported that industrial and agricultural production in Europe had substantially increased; that inflation had been brought under control in all countries; that "a sustaining diet had been restored"; that real wages and living conditions had greatly improved; and that substantial progress had been made in removing quota restrictions, exchange difficulties, and other barriers to intra-European trade. It also reported, as "collateral facts" of great importance, that communism had been "rolled back throughout Western Europe"; that individual freedom and democratic institutions had been strengthened; that "cooperation for economic recovery has led to cooperation for military defense"; and that "institutions of European cooperation have been started and are growing in strength."[28]

In its long-range objectives, however, the Marshall Plan was less successful. Mounting production figures and optimistic statements from ECA and OEEC could not obscure the fact that Western Europe was not a viable economic unit and that its fundamental problems remained unsolved. Paul G. Hoffman, then administrator of ECA, who had made repeated pleas for "economic integration" in Western Europe, had to admit that "Western Europe's progress toward in-

[25] Organization for European Economic Cooperation, *Report to the Economic Cooperation Administration on the First Annual Programme, July 1, 1948–June 30, 1949* (Paris, 1949), Part I, Chapter 10, p. 2.

[26] "European Recovery," *International Conciliation*, No. 447 (January, 1949), p. 36.

[27] *Counterpart Funds* (Economic Cooperation Administration, March, 1950), p. iii.

[28] *The Marshall Plan: Where We Are and Where We're Going* (Economic Cooperation Administration, March, 1950), p. 1.

tegration has been disappointing." Yet the cooperative effort symbolized by the term "Marshall Plan" represented a great advance along the road to European unity. "When future historians look back upon the achievements of the Marshall Plan," declared Richard M. Bissell, Jr., formerly acting ECA administrator, "I believe they will see in it the charge that blasted the first substantial cracks in the centuries-old walls of European nationalism — walls that once destroyed will clear the way for the building of a unified, prosperous, and, above all, peaceful continent."[29]

The European Economic Communities. The most far-reaching measures for the economic integration of Western Europe have been taken in the efforts to implement the Schuman Plan, which led directly to the establishment of the European Coal and Steel Community and indirectly, a few years later, to the creation of the European Economic Community and the European Atomic Energy Community. This famous scheme may be described as an economic plan with a political purpose. By placing the entire production of coal and steel of the Benelux countries, France, Italy, and West Germany under a joint High Authority, and by creating political institutions of a partially supranational character as well, the Schuman Plan seemed to offer a means of getting to the heart of the Franco-German problem and of providing a remedy for some of Europe's basic maladies.

On April 18, 1951, nine months after the negotiations had opened in Paris, the foreign ministers of the six participating countries signed a draft treaty for the creation of a European Coal and Steel Community.[30] Several months elapsed before the parliaments of all the six countries approved the treaty. On August 10, 1952, the nine-man High Authority took office, with Jean Monnet as chairman.

Whether the European Coal and Steel Community was really "Europe's first supranational organization" is a matter of definition; in any event, it was a bold new experiment in integration. Some observers had thought that the rejection of EDC by France in 1954 would deal a fatal blow to the Community, but in fact the organization continued to press for further pooling of vital resources and for expansion of its activities.

On May 20, 1955, the governments of the Benelux countries sent formal proposals to France, Italy, and West Germany for new integrative moves "which may best be taken in the economic field." The Benelux memorandum proposed a conference for the purpose of beginning work on (1) a treaty on the pooling of transport, power, and atomic energy, (2) a treaty on general economic integration, and (3) a treaty defining the European institutions necessary to carry out the entire program. The foreign ministers of member states appointed a committee to study the problems raised by the integration plans, with Paul-Henri Spaak, Foreign Minister of Belgium, as chairman.[31] As a result of this initiative the member states of the Coal and Steel Community established two other institutions of a similar nature, the European Atomic Energy Community (Euratom) and the European Economic Community (the Common Market), both of which began to function as operating agencies in January, 1958. The three communities

[29] *Department of State Bulletin*, XXVI (January 14, 1952), 43. For an excellent appraisal of the Marshall Plan, see Harry B. Price, *The Marshall Plan and Its Meaning* (Ithaca: Cornell University Press, 1955).

[30] For the texts of the draft treaty and the accompanying documents, see *The Schuman Plan Constituting a European Coal and Steel Community*, Dept. of State Pub. 4173, European and British Commonwealth Series 22 (April, 1951).

[31] "The Benelux Proposals," *Bulletin from the European Community for Coal and Steel*, No. 8, (June, 1955), pp. 2–3.

have used interlocking machinery, and they have cooperated closely in all relevant phases of their activities.

The European Community. On April 8, 1965, representatives of the six member states of the three European communities, meeting in Brussels, signed a "treaty Establishing a Single Council and a Single Commission of the European Communities," to replace the executive bodies and councils of the existing communities, as a first step toward the eventual merger of the various communities into a single European community.[32] This historic treaty entered into force on July 1, 1967, as did a Common Market for cereals, pork, eggs, poultry, fats and oils, and a 5 per cent reduction in industrial tariffs (to 15 per cent of their 1957 level).[33] In commenting on this event Jean Rey, president of the new European Communities Commission, wrote:

> We are now entering a new phase. The customs union has been completed [actually the final tariff reductions were scheduled to take effect a year later]; work has begun on an economic union; the most important parts of the common agricultural policy have entered into force; the Kennedy Round has been satisfactorily settled; and the internal political crisis of 1965–66 has been satisfactorily overcome. Thus the three Communities, strengthened by the unification of their executive organs, can now begin work with increased authority and renewed dynamism on solidifying their internal structure and, if possible, on enlarging themselves by the admission of other countries.[34]

There were, however, serious political and economic problems, as the final report of the EEC Commission, covering the year ending on March 31, 1967, pointed out. "The half-way situation of the Community presents risks of imbalance if not rupture."[35] But at least, as M. Rey stated, "The merger of the three Communities has now begun."

The community approach is a significant new development in the long search for ways of achieving closer economic cooperation among the states of Western Europe. It provides an interesting and ingenious formula for avoiding the clash between the federal and the functional approaches to European integration. It emphasizes the pooling of activities in well-defined functional fields, but it has some supranational features. The major aim of the originators of the community approach was political, for they regarded it as a long step toward the ultimate goal of European union in a political as well as an economic sense. More recently, however, more cautious views have prevailed, and as a result the European communities have lost many of their supposedly supranational features. President de Gaulle has publicly advocated confederation rather than federation for Western Europe. Britain has officially held aloof from all movements and organizations dedicated to European federal union. The confederationalists have won out, at least for the time being. The European communities, however, form a nucleus for the closer economic integration of Western Europe, one of the significant developments of the postwar period.

The Military Defense of Western Europe

The problem of the military defense of Western Europe is a particularly difficult one. The chief assurance of the West European countries lies in the implication of the presence of American troops between them and the Russians, and in the protection af-

[32] See Gordon L. Weil, "The Merger of the Institutions of the European Communities," *The American Journal of International Law*, LXI (January, 1967), 57–65.

[33] For details, see *European Community*, No. 104 (July–August, 1967), pp. 3–7.

[34] Ibid., p. 3.

[35] Quoted in *ibid.*, p. 18.

forded by the "balance of terror" and American nuclear capability. The French, in particular, but many other Europeans as well, have been arguing that the United States might be an unreliable shield in the event of a Soviet attack, that the European countries should have more to say about their own defense, and that in any event the Soviet threat to Western Europe is no longer as immediate or as serious as it seemed to be two decades ago.

Because of the tensions created or symbolized by the divisions between East and West in the years 1947–49, the countries of Western Europe were driven by sheer necessity to make concerted efforts for defense and security, and since even concerted efforts would not provide a sufficiently formidable counterweight to Soviet power, they were eager to associate themselves with the United States in formal defense arrangements. The major defense organizations and military alliances to result from these efforts were the Western European Union and the North Atlantic Treaty Organization.

The Dunkirk and Brussels Treaties. Quite logically, Britain and France took the initiative in promoting common defense efforts in Western Europe. The first concrete step was directed not against the new danger, Russia, but against the old aggressor, Germany. On March 4, 1947, nearly seven years after the unforgettable evacuation of Dunkirk, British and French officials met in that city to sign a fifty-year treaty of alliance and mutual assistance.

In the year that followed the signing of of the Dunkirk Treaty relations between the East and the West rapidly deteriorated. With the Truman Doctrine, the breakdown of four-power negotiations on the German peace settlement, the Berlin crisis, Soviet opposition to the Marshall Plan, and other developments, the cold war began in earnest. The Communist coup d'état in Czechoslovakia in February, 1948, steeled the determination of Britain, France, and other countries to take further concerted measures for defense. British, French, and Benelux representatives met in Brussels to consider new security measures for Western Europe, and on March 17, 1948, they signed a fifty-year treaty of economic, social, and cultural collaboration and collective self-defense. The Brussels Treaty also set up a Consultative Council composed of the foreign ministers of the five participating states. Under the supervision of the council an elaborate pattern of committees and defense machinery was developed, including a permanent defense organization with headquarters at Fontainebleau.

The North Atlantic Pact. No amount of coordination could give the Brussels powers, by themselves, a satisfactory defensive posture. They did not have the resources in manpower, finances, or equipment to develop more than a skeleton organization. The next step, therefore, was the association of the countries of Western Europe with the United States in a security pact. On April 4, 1949, after many months of negotiations on military, diplomatic, and political levels, representatives of twelve nations — the Brussels Pact powers, Canada, Denmark, Iceland, Italy, Norway, Portugal, and the United States — signed the North Atlantic Treaty in Washington. In this notable document the major nations of the West, representing some 350,000,000 people, pledged themselves to strengthen "their free institutions," to "encourage economic collaboration," to "maintain and develop their individual and collective capacity to resist armed attack," and, most important of all, to consider "an armed attack against one or more of them in Europe or North America . . . an attack against them all."

In general, the North Atlantic Treaty Organization (NATO), as the elaborate structure of commands and committees which was created to implement the North Atlantic

Treaty is called, provides the essential framework for the concerted defense of the North Atlantic area, broadly defined. Most of the participants are European states, and the defense of Western Europe is *the* major concern of the organization. Its permanent headquarters were located in Paris, and SHAPE (Supreme Headquarters of the Allied Powers in Europe) was established nearby. SHAPE was the result of an important decision of the North Atlantic Council in September, 1950, to establish, "at the earliest possible date . . . an integrated force under centralized command, which shall be adequate to deter aggression and to ensure the defense of Western Europe." At a meeting in Lisbon in February, 1952, the council agreed to undertake more effective defense measures, but for various reasons the military programs of the European members never approached the proportions envisioned at Lisbon.

The "new look" in Russia after Stalin's death produced a more relaxed atmosphere in the non-Communist world and thereby further undermined support for greater sacrifices and expenditures for collective defense. The spectacular developments in nuclear warfare also raised serious questions regarding the feasibility of existing defense planning for Western Europe. Indeed, many people wondered whether in the atomic age Western Europe was defensible at all. Under these circumstances the gap between the actual programs and the defense effort needed to give Western Europe even a minimum degree of security remained disturbingly great.

In recent years NATO has been weakened in many ways as a result of such developments as the apparent lessening of the Soviet threat; the recovery of economic strength and confidence by most of the states of Western Europe; the divergent policies, interests, and priorities of members of NATO; and, above all, the independent stance assumed by France under Charles de Gaulle. The NATO countries have been bogged down in a confused debate about strategy, especially nuclear strategy. Britain has virtually opted out of the nuclear arms race, and France has become a nuclear power, although a relatively lesser one. A vexing question has concerned ways and means for the sharing of decisions regarding the use of nuclear weapons, when only three NATO members have nuclear capability and when one, the United States, has virtual monopoly of decision-making in this fateful area. There may be advantages in having only one instead of fifteen "fingers on the trigger," but what if the one finger belongs to a rather capricious and seemingly unreliable giant? France, in particular, wants real partnership in decision-making and in all other matters. She is also especially concerned with finding some means of satisfying West Germany's nuclear ambitions without allowing what British Prime Minister Harold Wilson described as "a German finger on the nuclear trigger," not to mention the dread possibility of a Germany armed with nuclear weapons. The United States, in an effort to resolve this difficult dilemma proposed a multilateral nuclear force (MLF), and the British countered with a less far-reaching proposal for an Atlantic nuclear force (ANF), but neither proposal found favor with the majority of NATO's members. The MLF idea, supported strongly by the United States and West Germany, proved to be something of a boomerang and had to be decently interred.

French opposition tactics in and toward NATO became so serious as to threaten the existence of the organization iself. By 1965 France had virtually ceased to cooperate in most NATO agencies, military and political. At General de Gaulle's insistence the major NATO military commands — SHAPE and the Central European Command — were removed from French soil. De Gaulle demanded a thorough reorganization of NATO, and at a press conference on September 9, 1965, he announced that by 1969, the twentieth anniversary of the signing of the North

Atlantic Treaty, France's commitments to NATO would cease to the extent that they subordinated France to the so-called integrationist NATO system. De Gaulle clearly regards NATO as an organization dominated by *les Anglo-Saxons,* especially the United States, and he believes that some other arrangements are needed to free Europe from excessive dependence on the United States and to give the nations of Europe "from the Atlantic to the Urals" a greater opportunity to work out their own destiny in their own way. Thus NATO is in disarray, but alternative arrangements are either inadequate or are being considered without general agreement.

The European Defense Community. With the attack on South Korea in June, 1950, the United States in particular became convinced that West German rearmament could no longer be avoided. Since a separate German army could not be tolerated, the only answer seemed to be to integrate German troops into a West European army. The idea was formally approved by the Consultative Assembly of the Council of Europe, meeting at Strasbourg in August, 1950—the same meeting at which the presence of German delegates signalized Germany's formal re-entry into the community of European states. A month later, at a meeting of the North Atlantic Council, Secretary Acheson suggested the organization of ten German divisions, to be placed under the operational control of the NATO commander in Europe. Unwilling to go along with this proposal, which seemed to revive memories of the German menace, French statesmen turned their thoughts to an alternative concept. Realizing that they must soon reconcile themselves with as much grace as they could muster to the idea of a sizable German force, they proposed the development of a European army simultaneously with that of the integrated North Atlantic force. This projected European Defense Community, a military counterpart of the Schuman Plan, became known as the Pleven Plan, after the French premier who proposed it.

In February, 1952, both the German Bundestag and the French National Assembly approved the negotiations for the European army, but both attached important conditions. The Germans agreed to rearm only if they were given almost complete independence and were fully accepted into the West European community and the North Atlantic Treaty Organization. The French, reflecting what the *New York Times* called "an abiding suspicion of the good faith of Germans in uniform," would consent to German rearmament only after West Germany had finally accepted the Schuman Plan and after the European Defense Community had actually been created. Soon afterwards the North Atlantic Council, in the historic meeting in Lisbon, approved the plan for a European Defense Community and agreed on "cross guarantees" between NATO and the community. Encouraged by these developments, the delegates working on a draft treaty completed their work, and in May, 1952, the treaty for the establishment of the community was signed by the foreign ministers of the six participating states.

Instead of becoming a reality, EDC was torpedoed by the very country whose representatives had first proposed it. Throughout 1953 and the first half of 1954 weak French governments showed a notable reluctance to press forward with EDC, and the general climate of opinion in France became increasingly unfavorable to the proposal. On August 30, by a vote of 319 to 264, the French National Assembly voted to kill the EDC Treaty. This action seemed to be a severe setback to the arrangements for the defense of Western Europe, to the efforts to deal with the growing problem of West Germany's place in the new Europe, and to the European community movement generally. It created something close to despair among the major states of the Atlantic Community, except France. The United States, in particular, seemed to be at a loss as to desirable next moves. Fortunately, however, the confusion was only temporary, and, under British initiative, a new approach was soon evolved.

The Paris Agreements: A New Approach. In the fall of 1954 the foreign ministers of nine states — seven of Western Europe, plus Canada and the United States — met in London to consider alternatives to EDC. Here Sir Anthony Eden made an explicit pledge of Britain's willingness to maintain forces on the continent of Europe, and on October 3 the delegates signed accords for the military and political association of the West German state with the other states of Western Europe. On October 23, in Paris, representatives of fifteen nations signed thirty separate treaties and agreements to implement the decisions of the London conference. These provided for ending the occupation of Western Germany and granting full sovereignty to the West German republic, the enlargement of the Brussels Treaty Organization into a Western European Union by the inclusion of West Germany and Italy, the admission of West Germany into NATO, and British, American, and Canadian guarantees for participation in the defense of Western Europe. France and Western Germany signed a separate agreement for the "Europeanization" of the Saar.

Instead of establishing a supranational organization for European defense, as the EDC Treaty proposed, the new agreements called for cöoperation and closer association on many fronts without approaching the sensitive issue of sovereignty. They provided a broad framework for the defense of Western Europe until more permanent arrangements became possible. In May, 1955, the London–Paris agreements entered into effect. On May 2 the North Atlantic Council met for the first time with West Germany as a member. Three days later the occupation of Germany formally ended, and Chancellor Adenauer proclaimed the beginning of a new era in German history. But the great issue of German unification remained unsettled.

The Political Integration of Western Europe

For those who believe with Clement Attlee that "Europe must federate or perish," concrete progress toward the political integration of Europe in the postwar period has been disappointing. Obviously, as long as the East–West split continues, the prospects for a real United States of Europe are fantastically remote. The only kind of integration that can take shape to the east of the "iron curtain" is integration by conquest and not by federation — a process not unknown to earlier periods. In Western Europe the movement toward unity has suffered serious reverses. On the surface it seems blocked by a revival of nationalism, symbolized by the rock-like figure of General de Gaulle. Underneath the surface, however, other currents are still strong.

We should not underestimate the cumulative effects of historical experience and postwar realities upon the peoples of Western Europe. The necessity of self-preservation has driven them and their governments closer together and has produced a great variety of cooperative plans and organizations. It may well be that as a result of this experience Western Europe is being in fact unified to a far greater degree than most persons realize. This is the conviction and the hope of many distinguished European statesmen and scholars, as well as of sympathetic observers across the Atlantic. In his message to Congress of March 6, 1952, on the Mutual Security Program for fiscal 1953, President Truman expressed the view that "Europe has moved faster toward integration in the last five years than it did in the previous 500." Although this sounded good, a bit of historical research would have disclosed that it meant very little.

The Idea of a United Europe. The idea of a United Europe is an ancient one. In the Roman Empire, the empire of Charlemagne, the universality of medieval Christendom, and the Napoleonic empire it came close to realization—usually, however, through conquest. Although the rise of national states resulted in the fragmentation rather than the unification of Europe, the idea persisted. In one form or another it has been advocated by many famous men from the time of Henry IV and the Duke of Sully to that of Winston Churchill and Jean Monnet. In the years between the two world wars, especially between 1922 and 1930, the idea of European federation received a great deal of attention and support. In 1923 Count Richard Coudenhove-Kalergi, an Austrian, perhaps the most persistent of the modern advocates of European unity, published *Pan-Europe,* the first of a number of challenging books and pamphlets from his pen. In October, 1926, the first Pan-European Congress, attended by some 2000 delegates, met in Vienna and organized the Pan-European Union, with Coudenhove-Kalergi as president. The movement received powerful support from the leading European statesmen of the mid- and late 1920's, notably Edouard Herriot and Aristide Briand of France and Gustav Stresemann of Germany.[36]

In a brilliant speech to the Assembly of the League of Nations in 1929 Briand invited all European members of the League to join in setting up a Union of Europe; and in the following year he submitted his famous "Memorandum on the Organization of a System of European Federal Union."[37] The memorandum aroused great interest but led to no concrete results. After 1930 the international situation rapidly deteriorated, and with it the hopes for European unity.

Postwar Movements. In the postwar period official and semi-official pressures for European federation have been powerfully manifest. In December, 1947, the United Europe movements in England and France, headed by Churchill and Herriot, joined with the European Union of Federalists, headed by H. Brugmans of the Netherlands, and the Independent League for European Co-operation, headed by Paul van Zeeland of Belgium, to create an International Committee of the Movements for European Unity and to issue a call for a Congress of Europe to be held at The Hague. Within a short time several other groups, notably the International Society for the United States of Europe and the European Parliamentary Union, agreed to send representatives to the Hague Congress.

The Congress at The Hague, in May, 1948, was the most important of the many meetings of unofficial organizations for European unity. More than seven hundred delegates from fifteen countries of Europe and observers from most of the rest, except Russia, and from Canada and the United States attended this notable conference. In his opening address Winston Churchill, who presided, declared that "we cannot aim at anything less than the union of Europe as a whole."[38] The Congress adopted a number of stirring resolutions,[39] and it established the International Committee of Movements for European Unity as a permanent agency to influence governments to act along the line of the Hague resolutions. In August this committee addressed a memorandum to

[36] The early projects for European unity have been described in a number of volumes. See, for example, Andrew and Francis Boyd, *Western Union: A Study of the Trend Toward European Unity* (Washington, D.C.: Public Affairs Press, 1949); Edith Wynner and G. Lloyd, *Searchlight on Peace Plans* (New York: E. P. Dutton & Co., 1944); Snyder D. Bailey, "United Europe: A Short History of the Idea," *National News-Letter* (1947).

[37] The full text of Briand's memorandum is printed in Boyd and Boyd, Appendix A, pp. 95–108.

[38] For the full text of this important speech, see the *New York Times,* May 8, 1948.

[39] The texts of the resolutions of the Hague Congress are given in full in Boyd and Boyd. Appendix H, pp. 159–164.

the Brussels Pact states, urging them to undertake the task of organizing a European Assembly. Pressure from the committee and expressions of approval from unofficial organizations helped to persuade the Brussels Pact states to establish a Committee on European Unity and to take the steps leading to the creation of the Council of Europe.

The Council of Europe. In July, 1948, Georges Bidault, then Foreign Minister of France, submitted a proposal to the Consultative Council of the Brussels Pact powers for the creation of a European Assembly "in which there would be represented, in addition to our Parliaments, those of the other States who wished to participate in this great and notable enterprise." Ernest Bevin of Britain rejected the proposal as premature, but he later agreed to the appointment of a special intergovernmental Committee on European Unity. The committee hammered out a compromise plan for a Council of Europe, with a Committee of Ministers, which should meet in private, and a Consultative Assembly, which should hold public sessions to discuss agenda approved by the Committee of Ministers. Britain was reluctant to endorse even this proposal; but at a meeting of the Brussels Consultative Council in January, 1949, Bevin joined the foreign ministers of the four other powers in a decision to establish a Council of Europe, as proposed by the Committee on European Unity, with headquarters in the Alsatian city of Strasbourg.

In March, 1949, representatives of ten nations — the Brussels Pact countries, Denmark, Ireland, Italy, Norway, and Sweden — met in London to draft a statute for the Council of Europe. The statute was signed and made public on May 5, 1949. While it marked the beginning of something like a parliament of Western Europe, that parliament is in reality a futile sort of thing, with no sovereign powers. The Consultative Assembly, which is the deliberative organ of the Council, is limited almost entirely to a consideration of matters referred to it by the Committee of Ministers and can only make recommendations to the Committee of Ministers. A statement issued by the foreign ministers who signed the statute expressly declared that "matters relating to national defense do not fall within the scope of the Council of Europe," and it implied that political matters were excluded as well. Moreover, in effect the main work of economic integration was largely outside its compass, since the OEEC Council and other bodies were already functioning in that field.

The second session of the Consultative Assembly, held in August–September, 1950, was highlighted by the adoption of a resolution, proposed by Winston Churchill, for the creation of a "unified European army," and by vigorous debates on the Schuman Plan. By taking a stand on a European army, or even by discussing the subject, the members of the Consultative Assembly were challenging and in a sense modifying the provision of the Statute that "matters relating to national defense" were outside the Council's jurisdiction.

At almost every subsequent meeting of the Consultative Assembly proposals for extending the Council's powers and activities have been advanced, usually without leading to concrete results. The Assembly has frequently considered problems of relations with new institutions and communities in Western Europe, either contemplated or actually in existence, and with the European federation, when and if it is established.

The Council of Europe has carried on a rather undramatic existence, but it has served as a useful forum for European opinion on a political level and it has given encouragement to other and bolder movements for West European cooperation. It is eager to expand its own powers and activities. Six of its members, including West Germany, have adhered to a European Convention of Human Rights and Fundamental Freedoms, which entered into effect in 1955. The Council has a small but competent secretariat at its headquarters in Strasbourg. Leading statesmen still come to the Council's sessions, and often they speak more frankly in the "House of Europe" than they are wont to do elsewhere.

Political Implications of the Schuman and Pleven Plans. When he outlined his proposal for a European Coal and Steel Community on May 9, 1950, French Foreign Minister Schuman declared: "By pooling basic production and by creating a new high authority whose decisions will be binding on France, Germany, and the other countries who may . . . join, this proposal will create the first concrete foundation for a European federation which is so indispensable for the preservation of peace."[40] Accordingly, when delegates from six West European nations met in Paris in June, 1950, to consider the Schuman Plan, their meeting was called "unique among international conferences. It was unique because its aim was unique. This aim was a pooling not only of power but of a measure of sovereignty . . . . it was to be the first real step, an unprecedented step, toward a federation of European nations."[41] Because of its bold and sweeping character, the Schuman Plan "captured the imagination as no other proposal has done since the war." It was the first major test of the willingness of the European nations to give up some of their sovereignty in fact as well as on paper.[42]

The Pleven Plan presented an even more searching test. In attempting to implement it the governments of the West European states, with the strong encouragement of the United States and of the Consultative Assembly of the Council of Europe, and in spite of British aloofness, agreed to create supranational political as well as military institutions. They expressed a hope that a single directly elected bicameral parliament, with the power "to levy taxes, administer a combined defense budget, and oversee management of coal and steel industries united under the Schuman Plan," could be established by January 1, 1955. This agreement was hailed at the time as "the most important move yet taken for a United States of Europe."

Even more significant was a decision by the Common Assembly of the European Coal and Steel Community, made at its first meeting in September, 1952. At the suggestion of the Council of Ministers, the Assembly decided to undertake the task of preparing a treaty which would create "a European political community," with "a common Parliament which, presumably, would have real powers and would be a further step toward a federation of the six states and possibly later of other states."[43] In 1953 the draft plan for a European federation was submitted to the respective governments. A new chapter in the long story of efforts toward European unity was thus opened.

Since 1953, however, the trend has been away from the federal approach. Since the defeat of EDC the plan for a European political community has been all but forgotten.

New Initiatives, 1956–63: The Treaty of Rome and the Grand Design. The defeat of the EDC in 1954 was a major setback to

[40] For the text of this statement, see *Department of State Bulletin*, XXII (June 12, 1950), 936–937. When representatives of France, the Benelux countries, West Germany, and Italy met in Paris to study the French coal-steel plan, the French proposed that the suggested joint high authority be responsible to a federal parliament chosen by the national legislatures of the participating states.

[41] Harold Callender, dispatch from Paris, *New York Times*, June 25, 1950, p. E3.

[42] In February, 1955, the head of the French Steel Federation stated publicly that Jean Monnet should pay more attention to coal and steel and less attention to politics. This remark revealed a basic lack of comprehension of the real nature and objectives of the organization which M. Monnet was serving so ably. "For the Coal and Steel Community is above all political. It does not aspire to offer Europe a federal constitution, but it does aspire to point the way toward something like a United States of Europe." Harold Callender, "Coal-Steel Pool Has Politics, Too," *New York Times*, February 28, 1955.

[43] *New York Times*, September 14, 1952, pp. E5; see also pp. E1 and E2.

the movement for European integration. When in the same year Jean Monnet, one of the great "Europeans," resigned his post as president of the High Authority of the European Coal and Steel Community, his action seemed to symbolize the disappointment of the "Europeans" over the resurgence of nationalism in most countries of Western Europe.

This reaction, however, was short-lived, and soon brilliant new initiatives looking toward further European integration were launched, with conspicuous success. In the years 1956–63 the European community idea, one of the most promising new departures in international cooperation, received fresh impetus with the Treaty of Rome of 1957 and the creation of the European Economic Community (EEC) and the European Atomic Energy Community (EURATOM) in 1958.

Like Robert Schuman and other progenitors of the Schuman Plan and the community idea, the supporters of the new communities were more concerned with political than with economic objectives. As Walter Hallstein, then president of the European Economic Community Commission, declared in an address in Cambridge, Massachusetts, in 1961: "We are not in business to promote tariff preferences, or to . . . form a larger market to make us richer, or a trading bloc to further our commercial interest. We are not in business at all; we are in politics."

For a few years the economic and to some extent the political work of the new communities seemed to be making real progress. "The Six began to weave a single economic fabric out of six separate and often different national economies. Under this common economic flag, the six member states appeared also to be moving in unison toward their common goal of genuine European political and economic unity. The centuries-old concept of enduring peace and prosperity on the Continent — the rewards of European unification — changed from an unattainable dream to an accessible reality."[44] A major breakthrough seemed about to occur when in August, 1961, the British Government announced its decision to enter into negotiations with the members of the Common Market on possible British adherence to the Treaty of Rome. At long last, it appeared, Britain was about to reverse her historic policy of aloofness from the European continent.

In 1961, also, the dynamic new American president gave many indications of his interest in European integration and Atlantic cooperation. To Europeans President Kennedy projected the image of a youthful, imaginative American in tune with the times and aware of the goals of the nations across the Atlantic. His call for an "Atlantic partnership" evoked favorable response in official, and especially unofficial, circles in many West European countries. This relationship, as one of his top advisers declared in December, 1961, would be a "partnership of freedom," and would require "the re-creation of a great central political force in Western Europe."[45] Thus a new Grand Design was advanced for Western Europe and the Atlantic Community.

Countervailing Trends, 1956–63. Even during the period of the new initiatives in 1956–63, progress toward closer unity in Western Europe was more apparent than real, and there were many trends and developments which were moving in the other direction. A marked resurgence of nationalism became increasingly manifest, and since 1963 it has dominated the European scene. In part this was a consequence of Europe's remarkable economic recovery. "The imperatives of war and privation that gripped Europe after World War II," wrote Drew Mid-

[44] Drew Middleton, "Europe Approaches Decisions on Unity," *New York Times,* January 10, 1964.

[45] Address of McGeorge Bundy, Special Assistant to the President for National Security Affairs, to the Economic Club of Chicago, December 6, 1961.

dleton in January, 1964, "no longer motivate European peoples. The European unity concept is in the background, replaced by a revival of nationalism. Peace and prosperity — and Europe has known a decade of it — encourage political lassitude and economic laissez-faire."[46]

In 1958 General Charles de Gaulle returned to power in France, and soon afterward the Fifth French Republic, with De Gaulle as a virtual dictator, came into being. He took strong measures to deal with pressing internal and external problems, including the war in Algeria. He demanded a tripartite directorate for NATO, and when Britain and the United States failed to agree to this, he became increasingly cool toward the alliance and publicly championed a new approach to European cooperation, based on greater independence from the United States, closer relations with the Soviet Union and the countries of Eastern Europe, Franco-German cooperation, and a *Europe des parties,* or a Europe of states not bound by supranational controls over sovereign nation-states. Obviously, in this Europe France would have a major voice. De Gaulle refused to support the Grand Design or to cooperate fully with the European communities and NATO, even though he did not go so far as to withdraw from these organizations. While disregarding the sensitivities of other states, he proclaimed his support of European cooperation — not federation — and he insisted that France still needed allies, but under new arrangements and on more equal terms.

In some respects De Gaulle spoke the language of a resurgent Europe. In others he was a lonely, if towering, figure in the European landscape, and many of his views were tolerated rather than accepted. Even in France there were reservations about his foreign policies, especially about his position on European unity and Atlantic cooperation. In 1963 he and another elder statesman, Konrad Adenauer, signed a treaty of friendship and cooperation, which seemed to reverse historic policies and to inaugurate a new era in Franco-German relations. This rapprochement, however, was limited by continuing suspicions, by Germany's ties with the United States, and by conflicting interests and policies; after Adenauer's retirement in 1963, it seemed to lose much of its spirit and impetus.

Other developments in the period 1956–63 also worked against any movements toward European unity. Although Britain was later to apply for membership in the Common Market, in 1959 she took the initiative in forming a rival organization, the European Free Trade Association — composed of Austria, Denmark, Norway, Portugal, Sweden, Switzerland, and the United Kingdom — which put Europe "at Sixes and Sevens." The Bay of Pigs fiasco in 1961 tarnished President Kennedy's image in Europe, and his meeting with Khrushchev in the same year, instead of lessening tensions and improving United States–Soviet relations, seemed to have the opposite effect. Before the end of the year the Berlin Wall had been erected, and Khrushchev had precipitated another crisis over Berlin. While he failed to carry out his threats when the United States and her European allies stood firm, his actions were a reminder of the perils of a divided Europe and the limitations of possible cooperation across the "iron curtain." The Cuban missile crisis of October, 1962, the most direct and dangerous confrontation between the United States and the Soviet Union in the postwar period, was another reminder of the precarious nature of the alleged détente. Paradoxically, the strong United States stand and the Russian failure to challenge it by force produced a widespread conviction in Western Europe that the Soviet Union had ceased to be a major threat to their security and independence. Hence many Europeans felt that they could continue to relax and concentrate on other

[46] *New York Times,* January 10, 1964.

matters, without making the sacrifices and new departures which only a crisis of survival could evoke.

Reverses since 1963: De Gaulle's Europe and the Resurgence of Nationalism. In most respects 1963 was a bad year for advocates of European unity, or even cooperation. It started with De Gaulle's closing of the European door on Britain and ended with a jerry-built compromise that only temporarily patched up a rift in EEC over agricultural and trade issues. By the end of the year only De Gaulle of the four leaders of the major Western nations was still in office. Prime Minister Harold Macmillan had given way to Sir Alec Douglas-Home, and a year later, as a result of a close election, a Labor Government, less interested in European integration, came into office; Adenauer had retired in West Germany, yielding with misgivings to Ludwig Erhard of his own party; and John F. Kennedy was dead of an assassin's bullets.

The following years saw a renewed emphasis on national self-interest. The Labor victory and the growing concern about England's economic and political future, in spite of apparent prosperity, generated a movement toward retrenchment and austerity in Britain. Erhard, after winning an independent mandate in West Germany, tended to concentrate on internal economic development and on evolving more positive, but not more cooperative, policies abroad. In his press conference of September 9, 1965, De Gaulle continued his assault on EEC and NATO. In many ways he challenged the basic arrangements for military security and economic cooperation in Western Europe. In other West European countries his approach, if not his manners or his obsession with French pride and grandeur, was more widely approved than would be apparent on casual investigation. This was particularly true of his views on the NATO alliance. As James Reston of the *New York Times* wrote in April, 1965: "The paradox of Europe is apparent in every Western capital today. Europe is celebrating 20 years of peace, but challenging almost every assumption of the alliance that made the peace possible." In a sense this questioning was a consequence of the successful efforts at West European cooperation and recovery, and of the "new look" in the Soviet Union. "The validity of the alliance is not being questioned because it has failed, but because it has succeeded in changing the balance of power and the tactics of the Soviet Union."[47]

As Reston noted, the assumptions underlying the NATO alliance and the organizations for West European cooperation are being increasingly questioned "in one capital or another, but mainly in Paris." The movement for European unity has been checked, and the countervailing trends toward a resurgence of nationalism are in the ascendency. Europe is, indeed, in disarray. This is as true of Eastern Europe as it is of the West. "On the surface, the NATO and Warsaw Pact alliances are still the forms within which Europe lives. Europe still clings to these old forms because it is not yet sure of what comes after them. Yet in truth there has not been such a period of political fluidity and uncertainty since the 18th century."[48]

That the disarray of alliances and the resurgence of nationalism are surface manifestations of more fundamental changes was also stressed in late 1964 by Knut Hammarskjold, Deputy Secretary-General of EFTA, in an address in New York:

> The fact is that Europe . . . is more fluid today than it has been since the Hundred Years War, which ended centuries ago. . . . The mixture is boiling and changing shape almost every day. The search for a crystallization of the mixture into newer and larger

[47] "Challenge to Alliance: A View of Europe's Attitudes on the Future of NATO," *New York Times*, April 12, 1965.

[48] Harsch, p. 90.

units still continues. . . . A struggle for power in a fluid Europe is now fully engaged. It is a struggle essentially between the old, but immensely strong, concept of nationalism and national sovereignty, and the newer concept of political and economic integration and the pooling of sovereignty. The new idea has many ardent and dedicated supporters and has already caught the imagination of men's minds on an enormous scale, but it still lacks the strong institutions which make nationalism so powerful. . . . There is no sign that the European melting pot is anywhere near being ready to crystallize.[49]

"Federate or Perish"?

In the twentieth century, and especially since the end of World War II, great changes have occurred in Europe and in Europe's position in world affairs. The countries which were at the heart of Western civilization for many centuries have been fundamentally weakened, and their political and economic progress since V-E Day has not obscured this underlying reality. Collectively, Europe is still a center of international life, but it is not the only, or even the most important, major center, and it is weakened by its own divisions and rivalries. Trends toward integration and cooperation have not won out over the deep-rooted forces of competing nationalisms. Above all, Europe is still split in twain by the Communist–non-Communist divide, although the division is not so sharp or so menacing as it was a decade and a half and more ago, in the heyday of the cold war. Polycentrism is strongly manifest on both sides of the "iron curtain," and contacts across ideological barriers are increasing. Europe's future depends as much upon the trend of world events as upon its own evolution. It needs an open rather than a closed world; it can survive only with difficulty if trends toward economic and political seclusion predominate for long.

Although some of the general observations in this chapter apply to Europe as a whole, we have concentrated our attention on non-Communist Europe, reserving for a later chapter the developments east of the "iron curtain." There a system of people's democracies has come into existence under varying degrees of Soviet domination. An exception to the pattern of Soviet domination appeared in 1948 when Tito of Yugoslavia asserted and made good an independent national communism. More consistent with Soviet policy than the acquiescence in Tito's "deviationism" was the ruthless suppression of the anti-Communist, anti-Russian, and pro-nationalist uprising in Hungary in late 1956.

More recently, however, the Soviet grip over Eastern Europe has visibly loosened, although it was fastened again on Czechoslovakia in August, 1968. The Warsaw Pact and COMECON still bind most of the countries of the area to the Soviet Union, but there are growing demands for a larger voice for the East European members. Albania has openly defied the Soviet Union, and has identified herself with the position of Peking vis-à-vis Moscow. Other East European states, notably Rumania, have been increasingly independent of the Soviet Union in their internal and external policies. The overthrow of Antonín Novotný in Czechoslovakia, early in 1968, and the subsequent trends toward "liberalization" "transformed Czechoslovakia into the most liberal of Communist states" and had a profound impact in most of Eastern Europe. A "big change" has set in in Eastern Europe, where polycentrism, still within the Communist framework, has replaced the former satellite system.

The countries of Western Europe have achieved a remarkable degree of economic recovery since the end of the Second World War, and they have taken a number of important steps in the direction of military and political as well as economic integration. The greatest contributions to economic recovery were made through and as a result of the Marshall Plan. This plan was dependent, of course, on generous assistance from the

[49] Quoted in *EFTA Reporter*, No. 110 (December 11, 1964), p. 1.

United States; but it also stimulated heroic concerted efforts by the participating nations.

In the postwar years the countries of Western Europe have moved forward more rapidly in the direction of cooperative efforts than at any previous period in their long history. Thousands of their people and scores of their political leaders have espoused the cause of unity, although few have really been able to think in truly supranational terms. A bewildering complex of agencies and organizations for West European cooperation has evolved, and the experience in common action on many fronts may lead to more binding association. But Western Europe is still a long way from effective unity,[50] and the prospects for real unity on an all-European, West European, or Atlantic Community basis seem remote indeed. The gap between the Council of Europe and a United States of Europe represents the distance between reality and idealism in the European scene today.

Almost without exception, the great spokesmen for European unity — men like Winston Churchill, Robert Schuman, Paul-Henri Spaak, Alcide de Gasperi, Konrad Adenauer, Jean Monnet and Walter Hallstein — have passed from the scene, or are politically inactive. A nationalist resurgence, as has been noted, has apparently overwhelmed, at least for the time being, the movement toward European unity. Europe remains divided; alliances on both sides of the "iron curtain" are in disarray; the Berlin Wall cuts not only through a city but also through the hearts of all aspirants for a united world; the formidable figure of De Gaulle looms over the West European scene; and in most of the major countries of Western Europe and the Atlantic Community lesser and more inward-oriented men have succeeded to leadership positions.

The measurement of Europe's progress toward integration must take account of more than the proliferation of organs and agencies; it must note possible changes in motivation as well. How much of the postwar willingness to venture toward unification has been due to temporary desperation brought on by the miseries of World War II? How much to the Communist threat? How much to please the rich uncle across the seas? How much to the idealism and vigor of a handful of European visionaries? How much to a deep belief in the good to be gained from expanded production, enlarged markets, cultural fusion, and all the other products and by-products of unification?

We should not underestimate the cumulative effects of historical experience and postwar realities upon the peoples of Western Europe. The necessity of self-preservation has driven them and their governments closer together and has produced a great variety of cooperative plans and organizations. It may well be that as a result of this experience Western Europe is being in fact unified to a far greater degree than most persons have yet realized. This is the conviction and the hope of many distinguished European statesmen and scholars, as well as of sympathetic observers across the Atlantic.

In late 1964 Joseph C. Harsch, an experienced observer of the European scene, wrote:

> Something else is happening besides disarray in Europe. Disarray is political, and on the surface. Down below, in the lives of the people, Europe continues to grow together. The movements of people among West European countries is now almost as free and easy as among the various American states. . . . The trend is still toward the free movement of people, money, and goods among the Europeans. When it is achieved,

[50] There is unfortunately much truth in Herbert Luethy's observations on "the fate of all European undertakings; they were never able to mature, but were always overtaken by a hurried new beginning in a totally different direction or using different methods; the result was that they were obscured or pushed to the sidelines, with the result that 'Europe' ended by resembling a chaotic building site on which a dozen half or quarter-finished buildings lay higgledy-piggledy, making the whole look astonishingly like a heap of ruins." *France Against Herself*, p. 359.

> there is bound to be some closer political association.[51]

A year later a distinguished American expert on foreign affairs, of European origin, made the same general observation:

> The present state of Europe does not seem to warrant an optimistic appraisal of Europe's potential for unification. Yet, the regressive trends of the present and even the dismal record of the past need not portend the shape of the future. While the high policies of Governments point in one direction, powerful forces push European countries towards one another. . . . The European masses have achieved an unprecedented mobility. Millions of Europeans travel, each year, from their domicile to some other or several European lands. The young seem to travel faster and more widely than their elders and to form, with greatest of ease, associations and attachments beyond their homeland's borders. Such that, at the grass roots level, a united Europe exists. The pressure of common needs and the pull of shared aspirations may, sooner than now seems likely, compel the rulers of the one-time Great Powers of Western Europe to exchange their precarious claim to an independent policy for a European one.[52]

The outlines of the new Europe are still not yet clear. There are countervailing tendencies and many cross-currents in the present maelstrom of European affairs. The European age may have passed into history, but Europe itself is again a formidable force in the world, from almost any point of view, and, if it does not fall prey to its own divisions and inherited rivalries, it may become even more formidable in the coming years. One can be sure that the new Europe, without divorcing itself from its past, will forge new patterns of continental and international association in the future.

SUGGESTIONS FOR FURTHER READING

ALBRECHT-CARRIÉ, RENÉ. *France, Europe and the Two World Wars.* New York: Harper, 1961.

ARON, RAYMOND. *Charles de Gaulle.* Paris, 1964.

———. *France Steadfast and Changing: the Fourth to the Fifth Republic.* Cambridge, Mass.: Harvard University Press, 1960. By one of France's leading publicists.

———. *The Great Debate; Theories of Nuclear Strategy.* Garden City, N.Y.: Doubleday & Company, 1965. A stimulating commentary on the nuclear debate, especially among NATO members.

BAILEY, SYDNEY D. *United Europe: A Short History of the Idea.* London, 1947.

BARACH, ARNOLD B. *The New Europe and Its Economic Future.* New York: The Macmillan Company, 1964.

BARRACLOUGH, GEOFFREY. *European Unity in Thought and Action.* Oxford, 1963.

BENOIT, EMILE. *Europe at Sixes and Sevens; the Common Market, the Free Trade Association, and the United States.* New York: Columbia University Press, 1961.

BLACK, C. E. and E. C. HELMREICH. *Twentieth Century Europe: a History,* 3d ed. New York: Alfred A. Knopf, 1966.

BOLLES, BLAIR. *The Big Change in Europe.* New York: W. W. Norton & Company, 1958.

BOYD, FRANCIS. *British Politics in Transition, 1945–63.* New York: Frederick A. Praeger, 1964.

BRENTANO, HEINRICH VON. *Germany and Europe; Reflections on German Foreign Policy.* New York: Frederick A. Praeger, 1964.

BRIERLY, CAROLINE. *The Making of European Policy.* London, 1963. Published under the auspices of the Royal Institute of International Affairs.

[51] Harsch, p. 82.

[52] Robert Strausz-Hupé, "Europe: Divided She Stands," *The Wharton MBA*, Fall, 1965, p. 11.

CALLEO, DAVID P. *Europe's Future; the Grand Alternatives.* New York: Horizon Press, 1965.

CAMPS, MIRIAM. *European Unification in the Sixties.* New York: McGraw-Hill Book Co., 1966.

———. *What Kind of Europe? The Community since De Gaulle's Veto.* New York: Oxford University Press, for the Royal Institute of International Affairs, 1965.

COLLIER, DAVID S. *Western Integration and the Future of Eastern Europe.* Chicago: Henry Regnery Co., 1964.

COLLIER, DAVID S. and KURT GLASER, eds. *Berlin and the Future of Eastern Europe.* Chicago: Henry Regnery Co., 1963.

COOK, DON. *Floodtide in Europe.* New York: W. W. Norton & Company, 1958.

COUDENHOVE-KALERGI, RICHARD. *Crusade for Pan-Europe.* New York: G. P. Putnam's Sons, 1943. By one of the first great crusaders for the Pan-Europe idea.

DENNETT, RAYMOND and AMELIA C. LEISS. *European Peace Treaties After World War II.* Boston: World Peace Foundation, 1954.

DIEBOLD, WILLIAM, JR. *The Schuman Plan.* New York: Frederick A. Praeger, 1959.

ELLIS, HARRY B. *The Common Market.* Cleveland: The World Publishing Company, 1965.

FELD, WERNER. *Reunification and West German-Soviet Relations.* The Hague, 1963.

FISCHER-GALATI, STEPHEN A. *Eastern Europe in the Sixties.* New York: Frederick A. Praeger, 1963.

FLEMING, DENNA F. *The Cold War and Its Origins, 1917–1960.* 2 vols. Garden City, N.Y.: Doubleday & Company, 1961. Vol. 1: 1917–50. Vol. 2: 1950–60. An important and provocative work.

FLORINSKY, MICHAEL T. *Integrated Europe?* New York: The Macmillan Company, 1955. For Western European cooperation without supranational features.

FRANK, ISAIAH. *The European Common Market.* New York: Frederick A. Praeger, 1961. A careful study.

FREUND, GERALD. *Germany Between Two Worlds.* New York: Harcourt, Brace, 1961.

FREYMOND, JACQUES. *Western Europe since the War: A Short Political History.* New York: Frederick A. Praeger, 1964. An historical essay by a noted Swiss scholar.

GOGUEL, FRANÇOIS. *France under the Fourth Republic.* Ithaca: Cornell University Press, 1952. A good analysis of French party politics in the early postwar years.

GRAUBARD, STEPHEN R., ed. *A New Europe?* Boston: Houghton Mifflin Company, 1964. A symposium by 26 European and American contributors, originally published in *Daedalus* (Winter, 1964).

GUNTHER, JOHN. *Inside Europe Today.* New York: Harper, 1961.

HAAS, ERNST. *The Uniting of Europe; Political, Social, and Economic Forces, 1950–1957.* Stanford, Calif.: Stanford University Press, 1958. A sophisticated analysis of the movement and process of European integration in a hopeful period.

HALASZ, NICHOLAS. *In the Shadow of Russia; Eastern Europe in the Postwar World.* New York: The Ronald Press Company, 1959.

HALLSTEIN, WALTER. *United Europe; Challenge and Opportunity.* Cambridge, Mass.: Harvard University Press, 1962. The William C. Clayton Lectures on International Economic Affairs and Foreign Policy, 1961–62, by a leading proponent of the European Community idea.

HEISER, HANS J. *British Policy with Regard to the Unification Efforts on the European Continent.* Leyden, 1959.

HOLBORN, HAJO. *The Political Collapse of Europe.* New York: Alfred A. Knopf, 1951.

HUGHES, H. STUART. *Contemporary Europe: a History,* 2d ed. Englewood Cliffs, N.J.: Prentice-Hall, 1966. A history of Europe since 1914.

IONESCU, GHITA, *The Break-up of the Soviet Empire in Eastern Europe.* Baltimore: Penguin Books, 1965.

ISENBERG, IRWIN, ed. *Ferment in Eastern Europe.* Bronx, N.Y.: H. W. Wilson Co., 1965.

JENSEN, FINN B. and INGO WALTER. *The Common Market; Economic Integration in Eu-*

rope. Philadelphia: J. B. Lippincott Co., 1965.

KISSINGER, HENRY. *The Troubled Partnership; a Re-Appraisal of the Atlantic Alliance.* New York: McGraw-Hill Book Company, for the Council on Foreign Relations, 1965.

KITZINGER, UNE W. *The Politics and Economics of European Integration; Britain, Europe, and the United States,* rev. ed. New York: Frederick A. Praeger, 1963.

KOHNSTAMM, MAX. *The European Community and Its Role in the World.* Columbia: University of Missouri Press, 1964.

LERNER, DANIEL and RAYMOND ARON. *France Defeats EDC.* New York: Frederick A. Praeger, 1957. A significant case study.

LICHTHEIM, GEORG. *The New Europe: Today and Tomorrow.* New York: Frederick A. Praeger, 1963.

LINDBERG, LEON N. *The Political Dynamics of European Economic Integration.* Stanford, Calif.: Stanford University Press, 1963.

LINDSAY, KENNETH. *Towards a European Parliament.* Strasbourg, 1958. A good account of the Council of Europe, published by the Secretariat of the Council.

LISKA, GEORGE. *Europe Ascendant; the International Politics of Unification.* Baltimore: The Johns Hopkins Press, 1964.

LUETHY, HERBERT. *France Against Herself.* New York: Frederick A. Praeger, 1955. A penetrating analysis by a Swiss journalist of the dilemmas facing France.

LUKACS, JOHN. *Decline and Rise of Europe; a Study in Recent History, with Particular Emphasis on the Development of European Consciousness.* Garden City, N.Y.: Doubleday & Company, 1965.

MADARIAGA, SALVADOR DE. *Portrait of Europe.* London, 1953. The diversity of Europe, and the obstacles to integration.

MERKL, PETER H. *Germany: Yesterday and Tomorrow.* New York: Oxford University Press, 1965.

MEYER, FRIEDRICH V. *The European Free-Trade Association; an Analysis of the Outer Seven.* New York: Frederick A. Praeger, 1960.

MIDDLETON, DREW. *The Atlantic Community: A Study in Unity and Disunity.* David McKay Co., 1965. By a seasoned American reporter.

———. *The Supreme Choice: Britain and Europe.* New York: Alfred A. Knopf, 1963.

MOORE, BEN T. *NATO and the Future of Europe.* New York: Harper, for the Council on Foreign Relations, 1958.

OPIE, REDVERS, *et al. The Search for Peace Settlements.* Washington, D.C.: The Brookings Institution, 1951.

PRICE, HARRY BAYARD. *The Marshall Plan and Its Meaning.* Ithaca: Cornell University Press, 1955.

ROBERTSON, A. H. *The Council of Europe.* New York: Frederick A. Praeger, 1956.

———. *European Institutions: Cooperation Integration, Unification.* New York: Frederick A. Praeger, 1959. Published under the auspices of the London Institute of World Affairs.

ROYAL INSTITUTE OF INTERNATIONAL AFFAIRS. *Britain in Western Europe; WEU and the Atlantic Alliance.* London, 1956. A report by a Chatham House study group.

SCHMITT, HANS A. *The Path to European Union, from the Marshall Plan to the Common Market.* Baton Rouge: Louisiana State University Press, 1962.

SCHOENBRUN, DAVID. *The Three Lives of Charles de Gaulle.* New York: Atheneum Publishers, 1966. A lively analysis by a well-known correspondent.

SCHRÖDER, GERHARD. *Decision for Europe.* London, 1964. By a former foreign minister of the Federal Republic of Germany.

SETON-WATSON, HUGH. *The East European Revolution,* 3d ed. New York: Frederick A. Praeger, 1956.

WILLIS, F. ROY. *France, Germany, and the New Europe, 1945–1963.* Stanford, Calif.: Stanford University Press, 1965.

ZURCHER, ARNOLD J. *The Struggle to Unite Europe, 1940–1958.* New York: New York University Press, 1958.

16 The Shifting Scene in Asia

The "revolt of Asia" may prove to be the most significant development of the twentieth century. Arnold Toynbee ventured the prediction that even the challenge of communism "may come to seem a small affair when the probably far more potent civilizations of India and China respond in their turn to our Western challenge. In the long run they seem likely to produce much deeper effects on our Western life than Russia can ever hope to produce with her Communism."[1]

Much of Asia is in the process of emerging into the modern era and of establishing an entirely new pattern of relations with the rest of the world. There has been, as Jawaharlal Nehru emphasized, "a certain historic change in the relationship of forces in Asia." Declining colonialism and rising nationalism are symptomatic of a new order of affairs. But the free nations of Asia are finding that independence is attended by a host of problems; they are beset from without by the repercussions of the cold war and of power diplomacy and from within by political divisions, by the clash between the old ways and the new, and by demands which they are in no position to fulfill. Although the revolution for national independence in Asia has been largely won, the more deep-rooted "revolution of rising expectations" has just begun. Already it is threatening to become "the revolution of rising frustrations." The masses of the people are beginning to be articulate — a development that has revolutionary implications for the world. The life conditions of the Asian peoples are still close to intolerable, and they are improving slowly, if at all. Unless life becomes better for the Asian masses there can be no peace in Asia or in the world. The effect of these tendencies — accentuated but not initiated by World War II — is certain to be that Asia will play a more active role in world politics, a role more commensurate with its size, its population, and its potential might.

Perhaps, as Robert Payne insisted, "the major task of our generation is the understanding of Asia, for Asia represents potentially the mastery of the world in manpower and resources."[2] We of the Western world are poorly prepared to seek this understanding. To us the history of the world is the history of Western civilization — an assumption which is a logical result of our formal education and conditioning but which never did make much sense. Actually, civilization began in the Orient, and for many centuries the rich cultures of Asia were far superior to those of the Western world. The tradition of

[1] *Civilization on Trial* (New York: Oxford University Press, 1948), p. 221

[2] Robert Payne, *The Revolt of Asia* (New York: The John Day Company, 1947), p. 290.

ancient greatness lingered long after the reality had gone, and has, in fact, never completely died out.

The people of the West are not yet fully conscious of either the extent or the revolutionary implications for their own society of the awakening of Asia. Students of international politics, in particular, can no longer concentrate on the Western state system to the exclusion of the rest of the world. They must now really study *world* politics. Unfortunately, for some time to come they will have neither adequate source materials nor experienced teachers in Asian studies.

The Asian Setting

Geography. Asia is the giant among the continents — so large that on the map Europe appears as hardly more than one of its several great peninsulas. Asia has one-third of the land area of the globe. From north to south it extends more than 5,000 miles, from well above the Arctic Circle to below the Equator, if we include the Indonesian chain of islands. From east to west it extends for more than 5,500 miles. Its coastline is some 35,000 miles in length.

Central Asia has been called "the roof of the world." It is an area of great tablelands and lofty mountain ranges, including the Himalayas, the highest on earth. It is also an area of vast desert and wasteland. It includes such remote lands as Sinkiang, the "pivot of Asia," Outer Mongolia, and the Central Asia portions of the U.S.S.R. These are the "inner frontiers of Asia."[3]

"Almost every known climate occurs in Asia, from the equatorial rainy type of Malaya to the ice field climate of Novaya Zemlya."[4] Sections of India receive some of the heaviest rainfall in the world, while several of the desert areas of the continent receive some of the lightest. Temperatures vary from extremes of 100° or more below zero in parts of Siberia to 120° and above in parts of India. Average temperatures range from around 0° to 80° or more.

For the student of international relations the continent of Asia may be regarded as consisting of five major areas: (1) Soviet Asia, (2) the Far East or East Asia, (3) Southeast Asia, (4) South Asia, and (5) Southwest Asia. "Southwest Asia" is probably better, although less widely used, than either "Near East," to which Americans are accustomed, or "Middle East," the favorite British designation, which Americans are beginning to use. There is some doubt whether Iran, for example, belongs in the "Near East" or whether Turkey can be placed in the "Middle East," but there is no doubt at all that both are in Southwest Asia. Even this more comprehensive designation can include the United Arab Republic, as it must, only by a certain amount of geographic license.[5]

Western students today are inclined to think of Asia as divided into two inharmonious parts: Communist Asia and non-Communist Asia. The area under Communist control embraces considerably more than half of the entire continent. On the map it appears as a huge mass resting in a bowl or crescent running from Turkey to Japan. Students of geopolitics may think of it in Halford Mackinder's terms as an expanded, more highly developed, and more militant

[3] See Owen Lattimore *et al., Inner Asian Frontiers of China* (New York: American Geographical Society, 1940); also Owen Lattimore *et al., Pivot of Asia* (Boston: Little, Brown and Company, 1950).

[4] George B. Cressey, *Asia's Lands and Peoples,* 3d ed. (New York: McGraw-Hill Book Company, 1963), p. 24. See also E. H. G. Dobby, *Monsoon Asia,* 2d ed. (London, 1962), Chapter 3, "The Climatic Environment."

[5] See G. Etzel Pearcy, "The Middle East — An Indefinable Region," Dept. of State Pub. 7684, Near and Middle Eastern Series 72 (June, 1964). The Indian government has announced that henceforth it will use the terms "East Asia" and "West Asia." There may be some uncertainty about where India herself fits in these two categories, but they are less relative than the conventional designations, which reflect geographical realities only when viewed from Europe.

Heartland pressing upon a steadily diminishing Inner Crescent or Rimland.

Many Asians will object to this Communist versus non-Communist division on the ground that it reflects the "two camps" or "two worlds" obsession of the West rather than the "many worlds in one world" philosophy of the East. Moreover, any reference to the East–West conflict, one of the standard clichés in the Western world, is likely to be misunderstood everywhere in Asia, for all Asians, Communist and non-Communist, belong to the East.

In many respects, however, the distinction between East and West has considerable validity. As an anonymous Indian official put it,

> It is more truly a distinction between peoples and governments preoccupied with the elementary needs of humanity, with food and freedom and peace — and peoples and governments preoccupied with the more complex aspirations arising out of the possession of vast power. It is the distinction, as one might say, between the spinning wheel and the atom bomb. This is what lies at the root of the protest against "power politics" that is so often to be heard in the east.[6]

The Social Pattern. In population, Asia comprises nearly three-fifths of the world. About two billion people live in the vast continent, mostly in China, India, Japan, Indonesia, and Pakistan. Asia has sparsely populated areas, as in the great deserts in the Arabian Peninsula and the Gobi Desert, and in the wastelands of northern Siberia; and it also has densely inhabited areas, as in Java and along the lower reaches of the Yangtze and Yellow rivers in China and the Ganges River in India.

The vast majority of the people of Asia are landless agricultural workers, living at the starvation level, illiterate, inarticulate, sunk in age-old poverty, torpor, superstition, and disease. Birth rates are still appallingly high and life expectancy is appallingly low. Asia's people are engaged in a bitter struggle for survival. There is not enough food for all; and if improved methods of health and sanitation are introduced without great increases in food production and without voluntary limitations on the size of families, the population, already increasing rapidly, will tend to expand so tremendously that many millions more will die of malnutrition and disease. Although demographic statistics are notoriously inadequate and inaccurate in Asian countries, even the most conservative estimates of future population growth in the already overcrowded parts give cause for alarm. In Japan some 100 million people are crowded into an area about the size of California, with limited natural resources and with only 15 to 20 per cent of the area in arable land. Although Japan has reduced its population growth rate to one per cent or less, the pressure of population on the land will become increasingly severe. The picture in China and India, already the most populous nations of the world, is almost equally depressing. Apparently China now has well over 700 million people, and India and Pakistan combined about 650 million; their populations are growing at the rate of about 2.5 per cent a year.

The widespread illiteracy in nearly all Asian lands is another serious problem. In some respects this is both the cause and the natural result of the deplorable living conditions, for until at least the barest rudiments of learning can be made available to the masses, with advanced training in technical and social fields for a substantial number of potential leaders, there is little hope for improvement. On the other hand, as long as the vast majority live at the subsistence level or below it, they can never have the opportunity, the incentive, or the vigor for even the most elementary kind of formal education.

These problems of poverty, illiteracy, dis-

[6] "India as a World Power," *Foreign Affairs*, XXVII (July, 1949), 550.

ease, and population pressure must be kept in mind if Asia is to be understood. These are the basic social facts. Most of the people are peasants in a relatively low stage of agrarian economy, subject to all the vagaries of nature and the oppression of landlords, moneylenders, and feudal masters. They cannot be expected to appreciate the blessings of "democracy" or the dangers of "communism." They will judge any political system by its apparent effects on their conditions of life. They may respond to nostrums rather than to reason, and they may listen to false prophets and demagogues who exploit their grievances and promise them better things. They represent "the hewers of wood and the drawers of water" who have been the victims of knaves and despots throughout history. Yet the power of these heretofore inarticulate masses is potentially greater than that of atom bombs and made more explosive by the fact that throughout large sections of Asia misery is on the increase.

Attitude Toward Change. These problems would be serious enough if they could be dealt with rationally and scientifically, with the full cooperation of native leaders, other governments, and international agencies. But any far-reaching changes in the life conditions of the Asian masses would tend to upset the existing social and political order, and would threaten the position of the privileged few who exercise a determining influence in most countries in Asia today. Almost nowhere is there a powerful and influential native middle class; instead, a great gulf intervenes between the rulers and the ruled, between those at the top of the social and political hierarchy and the uncounted millions who live on the edge of the abyss or in it. With some happy exceptions, the leaders of many Asian states are hostile to all attempts at social change.

It is hard for well-fed Occidentals, accustomed to a relatively stable political and social structure, to understand the cumulative ills which beset so much of Asia, especially when they are described in general terms. Perhaps a concrete illustration will be helpful. In June, 1951, at the height of the controversy over the proposed nationalization of the oil fields in Iran, an American correspondent wrote from Teheran:

> Iran today is sick with disease, with poverty, with governmental corruption and bureaucracy. Nine-tenths of its people live, almost literally, in the 15th century. Its 43,000 villages are owned by a few hundred families, and the average farm income is $50 a year. Between 80 and 90 per cent of the population is illiterate, and utterly ignorant of politics and the outside world.
>
> Hygiene, outside the large centers, is almost unknown. One baby in every three dies before he is a year old. In great areas of the country 88 per cent of the people have malaria.
>
> Politics, as the West knows it, hardly exists: Business and government are equally feeble, corrupt and slipshod. Provincial officials are appointed from Tehran, rule over people who never saw them before, and count it their right to line their pockets while the appointment lasts. A bloated bureaucracy stumbles helplessly through red tape, and it takes a letter ten days to cross the country.[7]

The events in Iran in mid-1951 were typical of what Sir Olaf Caroe called "that political malaise which turns men aside from reasonable action and disturbs the course of international planning."[8]

East Is East. Western students of international politics need to be reminded that the standards of values, the attitudes toward life, and the concepts of society of oriental peoples are often very different from those which

[7] Morley Cassidy, dispatch from Teheran, *Philadelphia Evening Bulletin*, June 11, 1951.

[8] *Wells of Power* (New York: The Macmillan Company, 1951), p. 190. Used by permission of the author, Macmillan and Company, Ltd., London, and St. Martin's Press, New York.

lie at the base of Western civilization. "Man and society have not been seen by East and by West through identical spectacles."[9] At the risk of making facile generalizations which are subject to all kinds of qualifications, it may be said that in the Orient a greater emphasis is placed on spiritual and nonmaterial values; that the oriental tradition has been one of group or collective behavior, with a definite subordination of the individual; that oriental customs and traditions, deeply rooted and often ages old, impose formidable obstacles to technological progress and social advance; and, in short, that a wholly different concept of the nature of man, his purpose in life, and his place in the universe prevails. The Confucianist concept of the Ta Tung, the Great Unity, the universal unity of man and nature, has meaning to most oriental peoples. It has little meaning for Occidentals.

Time, too, is one thing in the East, another in the West. The typical Chinese view, Graham Peck believed, is that "Man's position in time is that of a person sitting beside a river, facing always downstream as he watches the water flow past," whereas a characteristic Western view is that "Man faces in the other direction, with his back to the past, which is sinking away behind him, and his face turned upward to the future, which is floating down upon him."[10] Many of the attitudes of Asians toward world problems which Americans, in particular, regard as of the greatest urgency can be better understood if it is remembered that Asians are conditioned by what Robert Trumbull has called "an oriental consciousness of limitless time."

[9] Paul H. Clyde, "Post-War Government in the Far East," in Taylor Cole and John H. Hallowell, eds., *Post-war Governments in the Far East* (*Journal of Politics,* 1947), p. 484. See also Derk Bodde, "Dominant Ideas," in H. F. MacNair, ed., *China* (Berkeley: University of California Press, 1946), pp. 18–28; Hajime Nakamura, *The Ways of Thinking of Eastern Peoples,* edited by Philip P. Wiener (Honolulu, Hawaii: East-West Center Press, 1964), especially pp. 3–38; and Sidney Lewis Gulick, *The East and the West; a Study of Their Psychic and Cultural Characteristics* (Rutland, Vt.: Charles E. Tuttle Co., 1962).

[10] *Two Kinds of Time* (Boston: Houghton Mifflin Company, 1950), pp. 3–4.

The Heritage of the Past

The past weighs heavily upon the Asian present. That past is a long and varied one. It goes back to the most ancient of civilized societies. Perhaps the first of the world's civilizations were those in Egypt, Mesopotamia, Persia, the Indus Valley, and northeastern China. Those of India and China are today the world's oldest continuous civilizations, but they have somehow pretty much escaped the consciousness of Western man.

Culture Currents in Ancient Asia. From the beginnings of recorded history until the Renaissance, the Reformation, and other developments ushered in the modern — and European — era of history, Asia was the home of much of the civilization of the globe. Even the Greeks owed a great deal to the earlier cultures of Asia, and Hellenistic civilization reached its highest development in Egypt and Western Asia rather than in Greece. The debt of the Romans to Asia was more indirect, chiefly through the Greeks; but Western Asia formed an important part of the Roman Empire, and Asian influences — such as Christianity and Mithraism — had a profound effect on Rome. Indeed, all the great religions — Judaism, Buddhism, Zoroastrianism, Christianity, Mohammedanism — originated in Asia, and Hinduism and Confucianism, which perhaps should be regarded as systems of philosophy rather than as religions, also are products of Asia.

Of all the civilizations that developed in Asia, after the mighty empires of antiquity had passed from the scene, those which had the most lasting effect were the Arab-Persian, the Indian, and the Chinese. The Arab-Persian had roots deep in the past but it developed a conquering zeal after the rise of Mohammed in the deserts of Arabia in the late sixth and early seventh centuries. In the eighth and ninth centuries Baghdad became "the biggest intellectual center of the civilized world," where Greek, Hebrew, Christian, and Indian scholars mingled with their Muslim colleagues and thousands of precious manuscripts and books were collected. Later the Muslims drove across North Africa into Spain, and there established universities and other centers of culture. Islam eventually spread throughout most of North Africa and into Central and Southeastern Asia. From today the peoples of these areas, from Morocco to Pakistan, are overwhelmingly Muslim.

Indian civilization, the product of the fusion of many peoples and cultures over many centuries, reached out to put its mark on distant lands, especially in Central and Southeast Asia and in the Far East. Rulers of Indian Empires governed parts of Central Asia, and in turn strong men emerged from Central Asia to sit on Indian thrones. Southeast Asia has long been under Indian influence — it is still sometimes referred to as "Greater India" — chiefly as a result of the establishment of Indian colonies and the spread of Indian cultures and customs.

For many centuries, and to a marked degree even up to the present, Chinese civilization has dominated the Far East. Confucius, Lao-tzu, and Mencius — the greatest of Chinese philosophers — lived during the Chou dynasty, and the Chou passed into history two and a half centuries before the birth of Christ! By the time of the fall of the Han dynasty in 220 A.D., "China and its civilization had developed most of the main aspects which were to characterize them down into the twentieth century."[11] Early Chinese culture was by no means wholly isolated from other flourishing cultures elsewhere in Asia, or even from those which eventually arose in Europe; but it was basically self-satisfied and self-centered, and it had a peculiar concept of its relations with the rest of the world. While the richness of ancient Chinese culture was preeminently one of philosophy, it was also notable for its achievements in art and literature. It is significant that printing was developed in China centuries before the first book was printed in Europe.

Moreover, no one of the major civilizations of Asia was insulated from any of the others. An extensive trade between India and China, and between India and Western Asia, both by land and by sea, had developed by the third and second centuries B.C., and "there was regular maritime intercourse between India and the Far East at least as early as the first century A.D."[12] In the early centuries of the Christian era Buddhism began to spread to China and Southeast Asia, and, changed and adapted to the traditions of the native civilizations, it became the dominant religion of China, Japan, and Korea.[13] Later, during the nearly four and a half centuries that K. M. Panikkar termed "the Vasco da Gama epoch of Asian history," much of Asia fell under the domination of foreign powers, and the rest was isolated and backward, out of the stream of international life. Even between major areas, as between China and India and between China and Japan, relations were limited and unimportant.

The Impact of the West. From the sixteenth century to the present the impact of the West upon these ancient lands has been tremendous and — it should be confessed —

[11] Kenneth S. Latourette, *A Short History of the Far East* (New York: The Macmillan Company, 1946), p. 110. Used by permission of The Macmillan Company.

[12] Jawaharlal Nehru, *The Discovery of India* (New York: The John Day Company, 1946), p. 196.

[13] See Edward Conze, "Buddhism," in Guy Wint ed., *Asia: a Handbook* (New York: Frederick A. Praeger, 1966), pp. 303–306. See also C. P. Fitzgerald, "Religion in China," and Carmen Blacker, "Religion in Japan," in *ibid.*, pp. 308–312.

generally unfortunate for the Asians themselves.[14] While Christian missionaries were trying to save the souls of the people, and often their bodies as well, officials and traders from the West were extorting what wealth they could, with little concern for the welfare of the inhabitants. In the sixteenth and seventeenth centuries England gained footholds in India and attempted to win concessions in Japan and China. French missionaries and traders established contacts with Indo-China as early as the seventeenth century, but nearly three hundred years were to elapse before French Indo-China came into being. Portugal, too, early contended for possessions in the East, but managed to pick up and retain only small holdings in India and the island of Macao, near Hong Kong. Holland took over the East Indies, and in the seventeenth century won from the *shoguns* — who were leading Japan into isolation — concessions on Deshima Island in Nagasaki Bay, which became Japan's only window to the outside world.

China was open to foreign penetration in the nineteenth century through the Opium War of 1839–42 with Great Britain and the treaty concessions that followed. Soon after the middle of the century the "black ships" of Commodore Perry forced Japan to open her gates. Meantime Russia had long since pushed eastward. In the mid-nineteenth century she reached the Pacific and in 1860 founded Vladivostok as a military outpost. It is still her best port on the Pacific. In the same year she obtained the northern half of the island of Sakhalin from Japan. Russia's building of the Trans-Siberian Railway, begun in the 1890's and completed in 1905, was an engineering triumph comparable to the building of the first transcontinental railroad in the United States after the Civil War. Extending for 6,300 miles, nearly one-fourth of the circumference of the globe, the Trans-Siberian linked Europe with the Far East and the Pacific and did much to make the vast expanse of Siberia an effective part of the Russian realm.

India experienced the most intimate contact with the West, and in some ways the most disturbing one. Clive's defeat of the Nawab of Bengal at Plassey in 1757 traditionally marks the beginning of the British Empire in India. By the early nineteenth century British power had been consolidated there, and no serious challenge to that power arose until the years following World War I, when the Indian nationalist movement became an effective force. In India three civilizations — the Hindu, the Islamic, and the Western Christian, to adopt the terminology of Arnold Toynbee — have met. The encounter has led to a considerable degree of fusion and cross-fertilization, but it has also produced frictions and tensions on a mammoth scale.[15]

Almost all of Asia has been profoundly affected by the impact of Western technology and Western ideas. Both have made a deep impression, although both seem to be ill-adapted to the Asian scene. In a sense the nations of Asia have used the new strength which they acquired from the West to throw off the shackles of Western domination. Western ideas underlie the present Asian revolution. Above all, as Toynbee pointed out, the impact of the West gave the peoples of Asia "an idea, an ideal, a hope," and implanted in their minds the dream of the "possibility of a change for the better." If the West is reaping the whirlwind in Asia today, it should remember that it began to sow the wind many decades ago.

The Western student of international af-

[14] See K. M. Panikkar, *Asia and Western Dominance; a Survey of the Vasco da Gama Epoch of Asian History, 1498–1945* (New York: The John Day Company, 1954); and Claude A. Buss, *Asia in the Modern World* (New York: The Macmillan Company, 1964), Part II, "Impact of the West."

[15] See Arnold J. Toynbee, *The World and the West* (New York: Oxford University Press, 1953), which deals with "encounters between civilizations."

fairs must never minimize or forget the greatness of Asia's ancient past or the tribulations of its recent past. Today the people of Asia, and especially their leaders, are very conscious of these as their lands begin to stir after the lassitude and the foreign domination of the past. Although in some respects consciousness of the older past and loyalty to its customs, traditions, and superstitions rest with great weight upon the people of Asia, at the same time the legends of bygone ages give them a sense of pride, of achievement, and of confidence in themselves. Nehru expressed these same views in speaking of India:

> The tremendous inertia of age and size [has] weighed her down, degrading custom and evil practice have eaten into her, many a parasite has clung to her and sucked her blood, but behind all this lie the strength of ages and the subconscious wisdom of an ancient race. For we are very old, and trackless centuries whisper in our ears; yet we have known how to regain our youth again and again, though the memory and dreams of those past ages endure with us.[16]

Asia "Out of Control"

The Turn of the Century. For centuries political and social instability has been a constant feature of the Asian scene, and for at least the past three centuries external pressures, chiefly from the Western powers, have been generally present. At the beginning of the twentieth century, however, a kind of momentary political equilibrium existed. The major stabilizing element, perhaps, was British power. Strongly entrenched in India, Singapore, Hong Kong, and elsewhere, Britain's influence was felt from the Mediterranean to the Far East. In Southwest Asia she was cultivating close ties with the Arab world, ties which were to be exploited during World War I, when British and Arabs worked together to bring about the collapse of the decadent Ottoman Empire. India, though on the verge of a strong national awakening, was relatively tranquil under British rule. Most of Southeast Asia was under the control of the French and the Dutch. Russia was beginning to develop Siberia, but, as the Russo-Japanese War demonstrated, she was not strong enough to upset the equilibrium elsewhere.

In China the weak Manchu dynasty, which had barely survived the Taiping Rebellion of the mid-nineteenth century, was tottering; it held on a bit longer largely through the dynamic energy of the Dowager Empress, Tzu Hsi. China herself escaped extinction chiefly because of the rivalry of a number of great powers. Britain, France, Germany, and Russia all had major spheres of interest and special concessions. Japan was the only Asian power which had risen to first rank. Her easy defeat of China in 1894–95, her alliance with Great Britain in 1902, and, above all, her victory over Russia in 1904–5 won for her general recognition as a great power. Nevertheless, she had not yet embarked on a career of continental expansion.

World War I and Its Aftermath. World War I had an upsetting effect in the Far East and elsewhere in Asia, and the old equilibrium was never fully restored. Britain began to lose her dominant position there and with it the role on the world stage which she had played so effectively during the period of the *Pax Britannica*. The Russian Revolution had profound effects on Asia, and communism began to have a powerful appeal for Asian minds. Nationalism became an increasingly potent force, especially in the Near and Middle East and in India. China floundered in a revolution of many phases, and in the 1930's Japan embarked on a policy of military fascism at home and expansion and conquest on the mainland. Asia began to experience the full impact of the changes which had been gathering momentum for many decades. New stabilizing

[16] Nehru, p. 144.

forces did not develop to arrest the tendencies toward dislocation and disequilibrium.

The New Asia. The power equilibrium which prevailed throughout most of Asia at the turn of the century has been shattered beyond repair. Possibly the fundamental cause was the growing national consciousness of the Asian peoples and the growing weakness of the colonial powers. The more immediate cause was probably the actions of Japan, whose invasion of Manchuria in 1931 inaugurated a campaign of expansion on the mainland of Asia and set in motion a train of events which culminated in World War II. The Japanese slogan of "Asia for the Asians," although it proved to be a thin disguise for Japanese imperialism, had explosive effects which lasted long after the sun of Nipp had set in the waters of the Pacific. The defeat of Japan, however, had at least one major disturbing result: it upset the international balance of power in that part of the world and left a power vacuum in the Far East. Because China was too weak, and because Britain was unable to resume her historic role in the area, the Soviet Union and the United States, the two rival giants of the postwar era, were drawn into — or rushed to fill — this vacuum.

Over the past two decades the relative positions and influence in Asia of the United States, the U.S.S.R., and Great Britain have undergone profound changes. Briefly stated, the attractive power of the United States, which had steadily increased until the end of World War II, has noticeably declined. There are, of course, many reasons for this change, but the fact remains that for the United States the Asian "reservoir of good will" — as Wendell Willkie put it — has reached a new low. At the same time the United States has never before been so deeply involved in Asian affairs; her influence is considerable, even if her objectives and intentions are often misunderstood, and her policies and actions widely criticized.

For many years the Red Star rose steadily over the Asian continent. In a sense Russia has won, by design and by accident, the position in Asian affairs formerly held by Britain and aspired to by Japan. The Soviet leaders were diabolically clever in exploiting the prestige of success, the anti-colonial and anti-imperialist feelings of Asian peoples, and the weaknesses and injustices of native regimes. The Communist victory in China was a tremendous accretion in strength for the Communist world. As long as the Soviet Union and the People's Repuhlic of China were apparently working together to promote mutual ends, the prospects for the consolidation and spread of Communist power were impressive. The split between the two Communist giants, however, which has been an open one since the late 1950's, has destroyed the impression of Communist unity and suggests that in many respects China and Russia are now working at cross purposes, even as rivals, in non-Communist Asia. The effect of this momentous development has been to lessen the influence of the Soviet Union in Asia, although that influence is still great; in some parts of the continent, especially in South Asia, it seems to be growing.

The decline in the power and influence of Great Britain in the present century has been startling. Her position has been seriously weakened by her own internal difficulties, by growing competition from other states with larger populations and greater resources, and by the rising national consciousness in her former colonial possessions and elsewhere in Asia. Today the British Empire in the East, as elsewhere, has been virtually liquidated. But British political and economic influence in Asia remains, especially in those former colonial possessions which comprise the independent states of India, Pakistan, Ceylon, Malaysia, and Singapore, and which are members of the sterling area and the Commonwealth.

It would be difficult to assess the relative position and influence of the United States and the Soviet Union in Asia at the present time. The U.S.S.R. directly controls a substantial part of the entire Asian area, is linked by many ties to Asian Communist regimes, and has an obvious, though indeterminable, influence in non-Communist Asia. Her recent moves in the Middle East are elements of her bid for Asian supremacy. The United States, as the most powerful of the non-Communist states, the leading industrial nation, the chief purchaser of raw materials, and the main barrier to the further extension of Communist power, has great influence in non-Communist Asia from Japan and Korea to the shores of the Mediterranean. Both superpowers are aware that they are involved with a continent passing through a revolutionary new era.

Great changes have occurred in the power structure of Asia, and in consequence Asia today is, in Owen Lattimore's words, "out of control."[17] It is casting off its external restraints, with the exception of those being imposed by the semi-Asian power of Russia, and by the United States, and it has not yet developed effective controls of its own. Under present conditions there can be "no peace for Asia."

Although differences within Asia are so great that there is much basis for the contention that, to quote the title of a well-known book, "there is no Asia," the countries and the peoples of Asia have many things in common, and they are now beginning to share an unprecedented awakening. On certain matters most Asian spokesmen seem to be agreed. This agreement centers on demands for economic and social justice, political independence and anti-imperialism, the end of racial discrimination, the improvement of living conditions for the masses of the people, and freedom from any kind of outside domination. Asian leaders show an extreme sensitivity to pretensions of outside powers to make decisions affecting Asia without the full participation and agreement of the Asians themselves. In a statement on foreign affairs in the Indian Lok Sabha (House of the People) on September 17, 1953, Nehru declared in a typical outburst: "Somehow it is not realized by many of the great powers of the world that the countries of Asia, however weak they may be, do not propose to be ignored, do not propose to be bypassed, and certainly do not propose to be sat upon." The slogan "Asia for the Asians," even though it has been corroded by the use which the Japanese made of it, still exercises an almost irresistible appeal in Asia. The Communists use it with considerable success.

Asia is in revolt. Asian peoples are revolting against bondage to the past, against the old feudal relationships between rulers and ruled, against social and caste distinctions, against poverty and ignorance and disease, against foreign domination in any form. The immensity of their multi-faceted revolutions should escape no one. It is among the most powerful forces in the world today. The protest in Asia is not altogether against the West and colonialism; equally important is the resolution to end old and wretched ways of living. Not all Asians are misled into believing that the two revolutions are one and the same thing.

Nationalism in Asia

In his address to a joint session of the United States Congress on May 17, 1956, President Sukarno of Indonesia declared: "Nationalism may be an out-of-date doctrine for many in this world; for us of Asia and Africa, it is the mainspring of our efforts. Understand that, and you have the key to much of post-war history." Certainly nationalism is the most dynamic force in Asia today; yet in many ways it is foreign to the Asian scene. It has few roots in the history of that continent, and was, indeed, essentially an importation from abroad. "The origin of nationalism in Asia was in the nature of a rebound from the European imperialism of

[17] See Owen Lattimore, *The Situation in Asia* (Boston: Little, Brown and Company, 1949), pp. 3–13.

the last century."[18] The nation-state, developed in the Western world, has for the past three hundred years provided the dominant pattern of international organization; but as late as 1900 there was hardly a "nation" in all of Asia, unless the rising island kingdom of Japan, fast taking to Western political, military, and industrial techniques, may be regarded as an exception.

Nationalism in Asia is an increasingly potent force. It has led to the rise of many new states in the postwar period, from Israel to the Republic of the Philippines, and it has stimulated independence movements in nearly all colonial areas. It has been a significant force in re-emerged Japan, in war-torn China, in devastated and still-divided Korea, in somnolent Saudi Arabia, even in remote Nepal. It has been invoked with revolutionary effect by great leaders of the recent past, and it has been a source of unifying strength for present-day leaders. Its influence has by no means been confined to Asia. It has given enormous impetus to independence movements in Africa, and it is a power to be reckoned with in world affairs in general. Although similar in theory and effect to the nationalism of the Western state system, it also seems to be developing distinctive features of its own.

The "un-Asianness" of Asian nationalism is suggested in these penetrating observations by Paul M. A. Linebarger:

> Asian nationalism involves the application to a variety of non-European cultures of political concepts not indigenous to those cultures. . . . Though Asian nationalism functions in the modern world, it is derived from an identification on the part of Asians themselves with the image "Asian" projected to Asia by Europeans, whether in person or through mass communications, and by the further mimesis on the part of the Asians of the European concept "nationalism," for which neologisms have had to be created in most of the Asian languages concerned. The Asian nationalism which confronts the world today is, ideologically and emotionally considered, not an internal dynamic springing from the older pre-modern Asian cultures. It is instead an entirely valid response to massive Western emotional and spiritual demands.[19]

Until the present century the obstacles to the development of nationalism in Asia were many: spiritual and cultural traditions; ignorance, poverty, and provincialism; the rigid social and caste system in most countries; and the strong grip of foreign imperialism. But one of the most obvious signs of Asia's renaissance is the emergence of nationalism. This has affected, and is affecting, all sections of the continent. It has already revolutionized the internal conditions in many countries, and it has led to the appearance of many new states. It has made Asia a focal point in the cold war.

Sun Yat-sen believed that China would remain a "hypo-colony" and would be open to further indignities from foreign interests as long as she remained disunited and weak. To him nationalism was the cohesive force that was needed to build a strong state. He expressed a universally held view of leaders of Asian nationalism: that independence is a prerequisite of national development, of the solution of the economic and social problems of their countries, and of human dignity.[20] Hence the desire for independence

[18] B. R. Sen, "Nationalism and the Asian Awakening," *The Annals* of the American Academy of Political and Social Science, CCLXXXII (July, 1952), 110.

[19] "Asian Nationalism: Some Psychiatric Aspects of Political Mimesis," *Psychiatry*, XVII (August, 1954), 262. By permission of the William Alanson White Psychiatric Foundation, Inc.

[20] In an unsigned article in *The Voice of Free Indonesia* in the spring of 1946 Soetan Sjahrir, the theorist and technician of the Indonesian revolution, stated the reasons for this revolution: "So we resisted, not primarily because we were driven by hatred, resentment, or aversion to foreigners, but because we consider freedom as a *conditio sine qua non*, without which it is impossible for us to be ourselves, to form ourselves and our community. Freedom is the condition for human dignity." Quoted in Payne, p. 60.

was no less strong in countries which were experiencing the mellow imperialism of Great Britain and the United States than in those, like Korea, where all nationalistic tendencies were ruthlessly stamped out. An oft-repeated slogan, "Good government is no substitute for self-government," expressed this conviction. Nor were Asian nationalists impressed by the argument that their peoples were not ready for freedom and that they must therefore be patient.

In their immediate objectives the nationalist movements of Asia have been almost universally successful; but the transition from the struggle for nation-winning to the no less arduous task of nation-building has been difficult. Many Asian leaders and peoples are still in the colonial frame of mind; they seem still to be fighting the battle for independence rather than building sound political, economic, and social foundations for the new nations. But they are beginning to realize that independence is not an end in itself, and certainly not a panacea for all their ills. Asian nationalism must now be directed toward making independence meaningful.

Nationalism is, of course, always complex. The student must probe beneath the surface to the intangibles of the social system, the cultural pattern, national character, and many other basic factors. This basic approach is particularly important in the case of Asian nationalism, which not only has developed distinctive general characteristics but also has varied greatly from country to country. For these reasons a general commentary on Asian nationalism should be accompanied by a country-by-country analysis of nationalist movements and by a study of the careers of the great nationalist leaders of the past and present, such as Sun Yat-sen, Mustafa Kemal Pasha, Mahatma Gandhi and Jawaharlal Nehru, Aung San, Achmed Sukarno, Mohammed Hatta, and Soetan Sjahrir, Syngman Rhee and Kim Koo, and José Rizal and Manuel Quezon.

Japan. Japan was the first of the Asian countries to be influenced by modern nationalism, strongly flavored by traditional practices and beliefs.[21] Beginning in the second half of the nineteenth century her leaders built up a highly centralized state, with all the trappings of militarism, authoritarianism, and nationalism. They made every effort to inculcate loyalty to the emperor, and thus to the state and its real rulers. By building up with all possible speed a strong central government, based on industrial and military power, Japan was able to guard her sovereignty and gain recognition as a major power. In this process, "the relatively mild official type of state nationalism" of the nineteenth century turned into "virulent integral nationalism — once the government safety valve of expansionism had been opened."[22]

The rise of Japan to the unquestioned status of a great power after her surprising defeat of Russia in the war of 1904–5 stimulated nationalist movements elsewhere in Asia. This marked the beginning of the decline of foreign control over Asia and of the legend of the invincibility of the white man, and it heralded a new order of affairs for half the people of the world. If Japan had pursued different policies she might have become the recognized leader of Oriental aspirations for individual and national independence; instead, she evinced a brutal dis-

[21] Yoshida Shoin and a few of his disciples who became leaders of Meiji Japan espoused views which might be described as "nationalistic" or even "ultranationalistic" in the mid-nineteenth century, but even in Japan it would be a mistake to suggest that nationalism in the modern sense had much of an impact before the last third of the century. F. Hilary Conroy concluded: "In spite of the island setting, the emperor system, the blatant preachings of Nichiren (1222–1282) . . . the ambitious schemes of Hideyoshi (1590's) . . . and the antiforeignism of the Imperial party (1854–1867), there was at most 'national consciousness' in Japan before 1868." Moreover, "there was little nationalism in the leadership of the Restoration." "Japanese Nationalism and Expansionism," *The American Historical Review*, LX (July, 1955), 820–821.

[22] *Ibid.*, p. 829.

regard for the interests of her fellow Orientals. The potential leader of the new Asia offered hardly more than a new yoke for the old.

As a result of World War II and six and a half years of occupation Japan underwent a series of political, economic, and social changes which, on the surface at least, seemed to be truly revolutionary. On April 28, 1952, the Japanese peace treaty, signed in San Francisco in the previous September, went into effect, and Japan regained full sovereignty. The once-mighty Asian state re-entered the family of nations with firm promises of good intentions and peaceful aims. Japanese nationalism, it appears, is already reasserting itself. Thus far its manifestations have been of a relatively healthy kind, but some observers insist that no fundamental change in national character or national policy has occurred, and they even fear that "what has happened under MacArthur in Japan has paved the way for the resurgence of Japanese ultranationalism."[23] But "the base of economic discontent that could create the sort of public sympathy for ultranationalism that existed in the 1930's does not exist today."[24] Japan's remarkable economic progress has occurred during a period characterized by the avoidance of a large international role and of heavy defense expenditures. She is, however, beginning to take a growing interest in international affairs, without any evidence of a renewal of the desire to dominate other parts of Asia. In view of uncertainties at home and abroad "the conservative elite has found it difficult to shape a new set of nationalist goals that might replace the shattered symbols of Japan's prewar 'greatness' in the popular imagination."[25]

China. The obstacles to the growth of modern nationalism in China have been very great. The concept of China as one nation among many was foreign to Chinese tradition. To the Chinese theirs was a universal empire, the center of the universe, and all other countries were satellites. Individualism and patriotism meant very little. The family system, with its emphasis on obedience to the elder members of the larger family and on ancestor worship, was the important social fact. Confucianism strongly supported this system. It was a unifying influence for centuries, but it was wholly antithetical to modern nationalism. On the one hand, it taught a kind of universal humanism; on the other, by its famous concept of the five fundamental relationships, it emphasized filial duty and obedience. Illiteracy, desperate poverty, superstitions, isolation, and local rivalries virtually decreed that loyalty should be first of all to the family, then perhaps to the village or even to the province, but seldom to the state.

Some early evidences of a kind of negative nationalism can be found in the many protests against foreigners and against the Manchus. Positive Chinese nationalism, however, dates from the later years of Manchu rule and from the Revolution of 1911–12. Its most active promoters were students, intellectuals, and businessmen, and its greatest leader was Dr. Sun Yat-sen, "the Father of the Chinese Republic."[26] In the famous "Three Principles of the People," which he had enunciated in tentative form as early as 1904 and which he formulated in greater detail in 1924, Dr. Sun laid down the cardinal principles which China must adopt. These principles are usually translated as nationalism, democracy, and the people's livelihood; since Sun's death they have been subscribed to, at least in theory, by all im-

[23] Hessell Tiltman, "Japan: The Strictly Democratic 'Banzai!'" *The Reporter*, March 20, 1951, p. 19.

[24] Lawrence Olson, *Dimensions of Japan* (American Universities Field Staff, 1963), p. 401.

[25] *Ibid.*, p. 393.

[26] See two articles on Dr. Sun Yat-sen by Norman D. Palmer in *Current History*, XV (October and November, 1948), 193–198, 279–284. See also Lyon Sharman, *Sun Yat-sen: His Life and Its Meaning* (New York: The John Day Company, 1934).

portant factions in China, including the Communists. It is particularly significant that the first of the "Three Principles" was that of nationalism.[27] Dr. Sun described China as "a heap of loose sand" which needed the cement of nationalism to bind it together and give it the strength without which the Chinese people could not hope to escape foreign domination or divisive internal strife. As a guide for them he evolved his doctrine of the three stages of development: military rule, political tutelage, and constitutional government. The nationalism which Sun coveted was modern in pattern but devoid of imperialism and other excesses which marked Western nationalist movements; and it was based upon traditional Chinese virtues such as loyalty, filial piety, harmony, and peace, and was wholly compatible with internationalism.

Generalissimo Chiang Kai-shek, head of the Kuomintang and of the Nationalist government and the most powerful man in China during the two decades from the death of Dr. Sun Yat-sen to the end of World War II, appealed many times for national unity to gain support for the Kuomintang in its struggle first with Communists and war lords, then with the Japanese, and finally with the Communists again. In his book, *China's Destiny,* published in 1943, Chiang declared: "In order to enable China to pass from instability to safety it is necessary that education throughout the country focus on the concept of statehood, and place the ideology of nationalism before anything else."[28] Unfortunately for China and for the entire world as well, in the postwar period the Nationalist government was unable to provide a strong, efficient, and enlightened administration or to retain the support of the people. The Kuomintang, it seems, had lost its revolutionary spirit and had strayed from the paths charted by its founder, Dr. Sun Yat-Sen. It was increasingly unable to cope with the growing Communist challenge. In consequence, its leadership of the nationalist movement ebbed away.

Out of the chaos and confusion of the early postwar years, the Chinese Communists gradually emerged as the most potent force. Although in ideology and to an increasing degree in practice they were identified with the Soviet Union, which many Chinese viewed with deep suspicion, the Communists posed as champions of the national aspirations of their country. By endorsing the "Three Principles of the People," by advocating and to some extent effecting needed economic and social reforms, and by emphasizing the indigenous and nationalistic character of Chinese communism, while at the same time playing down the more radical phases of their program, the international aspects of their movement, and their ideological and other links with Moscow, the Chinese Communists won widespread support. Nominally, at least, they gave nationalism an important place among their principles. In his opening address to the Chinese People's Political Consultative Conference in September, 1949, which made the final plans for launching the "People's Republic of China," Mao Tse-tung declared: "Our nation will never be an insulted nation any more." Repeatedly the Chinese Communists have successfully invoked the popular slogans of nationalism, anti-foreignism, and anti-imperialism. Thus in China today the revolution has been diverted into Communist channels, and Chinese nationalism has been perverted to the service of other ends.

Indonesia. A strong nationalist movement developed in the Netherlands East Indies in the first decade of the twentieth century. The first important native party, called

[27] Norman D. Palmer, "Sun Yat-sen: Canonized Symbol," *Current History,* XV (November, 1948), 282.

[28] English translation by Philip Jaffe (New York: Roy Publishers, 1947), p. 462.

the Boedi Oetomo, was formed in 1908. Its character was thus described by Robert Payne: "The movement possessed no political credo. Essentially scholastic, it looked toward India, deriving strength not from the nascent Moslem nationalism but from Rabindranath Tagore's vision of a self-governing Asia at peace. The 'striving' was purely intellectual striving. . . . No one knew exactly what it was striving for."[29] Boedi Oetomo never became powerful, and by 1910 it had been eclipsed by a more militant party, the Sarekat Islam, which advocated political and social reforms and a vigorous Mohammedanism. Sarekat Islam was soon claiming more than 80,000 members and demanding complete independence for the Netherlands East Indies. During World War I it adopted a Socialist program.

The nationalist movement entered a more vigorous phase in 1927 with the formation of the Partai Nasional Indonesia. Its founder was a young Javanese engineer, Achmed Sukarno (or Soekarno), who may deservedly be called the father of modern Indonesian nationalism. His National Indonesian Party attempted to unite the many nationalist groups; the degree of his success may be measured by the stern measures taken by the Dutch to suppress the new party. But the suppression of even the most important nationalist organization did not end the efforts for independence. Other groups sprang up, demanding all kinds of reforms, including political freedom within or without the Dutch Empire.

The Dutch showed little understanding of the nature or strength of the native nationalist movements. To deal with them they relied largely on a policy of stern repression. Accordingly, "in the late twenties and early thirties a large section of the nationalist leadership, including Sukarno, Hatta, and Sjahrir, were transported into exile, many to the notorious Upper Digul concentration camp in New Guinea."[30] Nevertheless, the nationalist groups increased in strength and gradually began to coordinate their efforts more effectively. In late 1939, at the first All-Indonesian Congress in Batavia, the nationalist parties cooperated to press their demands for concrete steps toward independence and to promote a more widespread support for their activities.

The fall of Holland in 1940 seemed to open the way to a greater degree of independence for Indonesia; but the speedy Japanese occupation of the islands brought a bondage worse than the Dutch had ever imposed. The new conquerors, however, were successful in securing the collaboration of native nationalist groups. Many Indonesian leaders, including Sukarno and Mohammed Hatta, accepted positions under the Japanese, although after the war they insisted that they had collaborated only to moderate the enemy's policies toward the native peoples and that they had been in constant touch with underground movements of resistance.

Six weeks elapsed between Japan's surrender in August, 1945, and the first landings of British troops in the Netherlands East Indies. These weeks saw the birth of the Indonesian Republic, with Sukarno and Hatta as the moving spirits. Proclaimed on August 17, 1945, in a declaration signed by these two men, the republic was so firmly entrenched in popular support in Java and parts of Sumatra before the Dutch returned that it could not be destroyed. Sukarno became the first president of the Indonesian Republic and Dr. Hatta vice president. On October 7, 1945, Dr. Hatta announced that the five policies of the republic would be belief in God, nationalism, universalism, democracy, and social security. As Payne pointed out, these policies are very similar

[29] Payne, p. 26.

[30] Paul M. Kattenburg, quoted in Lawrence K. Rosinger, *et al.*, *The State of Asia* (New York: Alfred A. Knopf, 1951), p. 410.

to Dr. Sun Yat-sen's "Three Principles of the People," with belief in God and universalism added "as make-weights."

After extensive military operations the Dutch government, in the Linggadjati Agreement of March, 1947, extended *de facto* recognition to the republic, which presumably was to become one of the major units in a United States of Indonesia, loosely associated with the Dutch crown. Unfortunately, the pact was not implemented, and until mid-1949 relations between the Indonesian leaders and the Dutch ran the gamut from temporary periods of truce to armed hostilities or "police actions," as the Dutch described them.

The developments in Indonesia were brought to the attention of the Security Council of the United Nations, and the UN Good Offices Committee made determined efforts to effect a peaceful solution. A Round Table Conference at The Hague in the fall of 1949, after much difficulty, produced enough agreement among the Dutch, the Indonesian Republicans, and the Indonesian Federalists to proceed with plans to create a truly independent Indonesia. On December 27, 1949, in a simple ceremony, Queen Juliana of the Netherlands proclaimed the Republic of the United States of Indonesia a sovereign partner in a Netherlands Indonesian Union. Under these circumstances three hundred years of Dutch rule over the rich islands of the East Indies came to a peaceful rather than a bloody end, and a new state formally came into being.

The Indonesian Union did not last long, for Sukarno soon proclaimed Indonesia a unitary state, and relations with the Netherlands again became strained. Later they were broken off for three years (1960–63) over the West New Guinea issue, which on May 1, 1963, was taken over by Indonesia and became Indonesia's province of West Irian. In asserting Indonesia's claims to this area, in his measures against the new state of Malaysia and in his announcement of Indonesia's withdrawal from the United Nations, Sukarno posed as the spokesman of Indonesian nationalism. His policies, however, were reversed and he himself was relegated to the background by General Suharto and his associates, who took control atter the attempted coup of October, 1965. In this anticlimatic way the Sukarno era of Indonesian nationalism came to an end, and a new period of nationalism and nation-building began.

India. Although the revolt of 1857 was "the first organized expression of anti-foreign sentiment" in India,[31] the beginnings of nationalism as an effective political force date from the founding of the Indian National Congress in 1885.[32] The Congress soon became "the dynamic, consolidated expression of Indian nationalism." During its first and almost pre-national period, from 1885 to 1905, Congress membership was confined largely to Hindu intellectuals and professional men in Bengal. In its second phase, which lasted from 1905 to 1917, it spread over all of India and enlisted support from all social and industrial classes and from Muslims as well as Hindus. Indian nationalism in this period assumed a mystic and spiritual quality which it never lost.

In 1920 Gandhi launched a campaign of nonviolence and noncooperation, with which the British did not know how to cope. When violence and force were resorted to by some of his own followers, Gandhi called a halt to his campaign. From 1922 to 1924 he served the first of many prison sentences, and for some six years after his release he played

[31] Sen, p. 110.

[32] The Indian National Congress is not to be confused with the Indian Parliament. The Congress headed the movement for independence, and since 1947 it has been the major political grouping within the country. It has been closely identified with the government. Until 1967 more than two-thirds of the members of the Lok Sabha, the lower house of the Indian Parliament, were members of the Congress. It is now often referred to as the Congress Party.

little part in the nationalist movement, which in these years tended to emphasize Western approaches to nationalism. Gandhi and other important leaders of the Congress Party, such as C. R. Das and Rabindranath Tagore, deplored this trend. "Both Gandhi and Tagore subordinated the idea of nationalism, as representing the political power and economic mastery of the state, to the less materialistic and more spiritual conception that nationalism means the well-being, development and unity of its people."[33]

The publication of the Simon Report by an all-British Indian Statutory Commission in 1930 led to a resurgence of Indian nationalism. Gandhi, again taking active leadership of the movement, launched another campaign of civil disobedience and led a dramatic 170-mile "salt march" to the sea to make salt in defiance of British laws. In 1935 the British Government made further concessions in the Government of India Act, but these merely stimulated further nationalist feeling. Shortly before World War II, however, Gandhi and other spokesmen of an evolutionary course seemed to be regaining their influence, and the British Government eased the situation considerably by releasing thousands of political prisoners.

When the British Government declared, in September, 1939, that India was at war, Indian nationalists were split on the policies to be followed. In July, 1940, after the fall of France, the Congress Party announced that it could not "go the full length" with Gandhi in his pacifist views; but the British would not offer the concessions it demanded as the price of cooperation in the defense of India, and in October, 1940, it began a program of civil disobedience. Britain's promise of Dominion status after the war, made upon the recommendation of the Cripps mission of 1942, was rejected as inadequate; instead, in August, 1942, the All-India Congress Committee demanded that Britain "quit India" or take the consequences.

[33] Mary E. Townsend, with the collaboration of C. H. Peake, *European Colonial Expansion Since 1871* (Philadelphia: J. B. Lippincott Co., 1941), p. 412.

In the postwar period Indian nationalism achieved its objective of independence, but at the price of partition and the strains and stresses of emergent nationhood. Division was made inevitable by the rise of a Muslim nationalist movement, headed by Mohammed Ali Jinnah and the Muslim League. The governments of India and of the Muslim state of Pakistan now jealously guard their newly-won freedom; and, while they have not been successful in establishing satisfactory relations with each other, they seem determined to prove that their brand of nationalism is consistent with the objectives of the United Nations and with all movements toward greater international cooperation.

The Chinese attack on India in October, 1962, was widely interpreted in India as an affront to the Indian nation as well as a threat to India's security. Throughout the country the people responded to the call of their leaders to put aside domestic divisions, to accept greater sacrifices, and to unite in defense of the nation. For a few months after the Chinese assault, before apathy again began to set in, India was probably more truly a nation than she had never been in her entire history. Certainly the unexpected Chinese blow provoked the most impressive display of Indian nationalist feeling since independence.

Turkey. The evolution of the surviving fragment of the once-mighty Ottoman Empire into the vigorous Turkish Republic of today is one of the miracles of the "new nationalism." Much of the credit for this achievement goes to a single man, the hero of modern Turkey, Mustapha Kemal Pasha (1881–1938) or Atatürk ("Father of the Turks"), as he came to be called by a grateful people. For fifteen years, from 1923 until his death in 1938, Atatürk ruled with a benevolent but iron hand, emphasizing nationalistic uniformity, modernization, and Westernization in all phases of the life of the people. All foreign controls were gradually eliminated, by forceful means or subtle. The type of nationalism which Atatürk championed, in Eleanor Bisbee's words, aimed at "not an empire for the Turks, not subject lands to rule, not expansionism, but nationalism inside *Turkey*."[34] "Turkey for the Turks," was one of Atatürk's avowed objectives; and this has also been a part of his vast bequest to his successors.

More recently, Turkish nationalism has been manifest in sturdy resistance to Soviet threats and pressures, and in the assistance given to Turkish Cypriots. Both Turkey and Greece have gone to the brink of war several times because of their involvement in the disturbances on Cyprus, and strong nationalist feelings on both sides have frustrated all efforts to reach an amicable settlement of the Cyprus dispute.

Distinctive Characteristics of Asian Nationalism. Asian nationalism has differed from the nationalism of the Western world in several important respects, among which the following may be cited:

1. It has had more social and cultural overtones, and has been less predominantly a political creed. A traditional, cultural type of nationalism, linked with the religious and social attitudes of the past, has existed almost universally in Asia, and is still a major force. Perhaps Asian nationalism is the result of a conscious effort to adapt Western nationalism to the Asian scene without departing too far from the traditions of the past.

2. Nationalism in Asia has had a strong negative aspect, for, as we have noted, in origin it was a reaction against foreign rule and against colonialism and all that the term implied. It is often regarded as a necessary means for the achievement of national unity in the face of all the centrifugal forces of ignorance, superstition, localism, familistic and religious customs, local warlordism, and the like, which have tended to discourage unity and make resistance to foreign encroachments all the more difficult. Because of the occasional identification or collaboration of Asian nationalists with communism in recent years, it is particularly important to remember that, as Carlos Romulo said, nationalism in Asia has generally found expression in "a simple and straightforward freedom movement from colonial status, untainted either by the racialist and regionalist appeal of Japanese anti-Western propaganda or by the ideological appeal of communism."[35]

3. With the obvious exception of Japanese policies, and possibly of the Russian and Chinese as well, nationalistic movements in Asia have sought to avoid some of the worst tendencies of Western nationalism, such as those toward imperialism, racialism, and war. On the other hand, they have given rise to same particularly alarming manifestations, notably mob violence and fanaticism. Some tendencies of Asian nationalism seem likely to lead to national suicide and widespread anarchy rather than to national unity and independence.

4. Asian nationalism has been linked much more closely with movements for economic and social reform. Many Asian nationalists have been radicals in their internal policies. They have worked for social reforms as ardently as for freedom from foreign rule, although they have usually insisted that the latter was a prerequisite of the former. In his presidential address to the Indian National Congress in 1936 Nehru declared: "I work for Indian independence because the nationalist in me cannot tolerate alien domination; I work for it even more

[34] *The New Turks: Pioneers of the Republic, 1920–1950* (Philadelphia: University of Pennsylvania Press, 1951), p. 58.

[35] Carlos P. Romulo, "The Crucial Battle for Asia," *New York Times Magazine*, September 11, 1949, p. 13.

because for me it is the inevitable step to social and economic change."[36] Asian nationalists, therefore, are generally revolutionaries in the sense that they are proponents of drastic change and opponents of the status quo.

5. Perhaps most important of all, the Asian brand of nationalism is generally interpreted as being wholly consistent with cosmopolitanism, humanism, peace, and international cooperation. "We seek no narrow nationalism," declared Nehru at the opening session of the First Asian Relations Conference on March 23, 1947. "Nationalism has a place in each country and should be fostered, but it need not be allowed to become aggressive and come in the way of international development."[37] During his visit to the United States in the fall of 1949, Nehru stated in an address in Chicago on October 26: "Internationalism can only grow effectively when nationalism has achieved its objectives in countries which are struggling for freedom." A moving statement of this same fundamental point was made by Soetan Sjahrir, one of the greatest leaders of the Indonesian Republic, in a radio broadcast on the first anniversary of the proclamation of the republic:

> Our nationalism serves only as a bridge to reach a human level that nears perfection, not to gratify ourselves, far less to do damage to human intercourse. We keep firmly to our faith in humanity in general. We are no enemies of humanity. Our nationality is only one facet of our respect for humanity.[38]

Relation to Communism. To the people of the Western world communism appears to be antithetical to nationalism, for in theory it preaches an internationalism of the proletariat of the world and the withering away of the nation-state, but in practice it leads to the subordination of national interests — except those of the Soviet Union — to allegiance to a foreign power and to a world ideology. In Asia communism has been presented in a wholly different light. In that vast continent it has been linked with nationalism and anti-imperialism, with the widespread desire for land reform and social change, and with opposition to foreign rule and to native landlords, warlords, and "reactionaries."

The ideological association of communism and nationalism in Asia requires special emphasis. As J. C. Campbell stated: "Belief in dialectical materialism never blinded the Soviet leaders to the strength of nationalism in Asia. On the contrary, from the time of their coming to power they had had a carefully thought-out policy on nationalities and the colonial question." Lenin, Campbell reminds us, "set about planning a twofold attack on the citadels of capitalism through agitation for social revolution in the metropolitan countries and for national independence in their colonies. On coming to power the Bolsheviks announced themselves as champions of movements of national liberation."[39] The "Theses on National and Colonial Questions" adopted by the Third International — the Comintern — in 1920 spelled out the doctrine in detail. "It is the duty of the Communist International," read this important document, "to support the revolutionary movement in the colonies." The reasons for this doctrine were frankly proclaimed: "The revolution in the colonies is not going to be a Communist revolution in its first stages. But if from the outset the leadership is in the hands of a Communist vanguard, the revolutionary masses will not be led astray, but

[36] Quoted in Payne, p. 85.

[37] *Asian Relations.* A Report of the Proceedings and Documentation of the First Asian Relations Conference, New Delhi, March–April, 1947 (New Delhi, 1948), p. 26.

[38] Quoted in Payne, pp. 50–51.

[39] *The United States in World Affairs, 1948–1949* (New York: Council on Foreign Relations, 1949), pp. 264–265.

may go ahead through the successive periods of the development of revolutionary experience."

This doctrine has been repeated and elaborated many times, in one form or another, in resolutions of the Comintern and in speeches of Soviet leaders and of native Communist spokesmen in various Asian countries. Nowhere has it been more clearly presented, in a manner adapted to the situation in Asia, than in Mao Tse-tung's *On New Democracy,* a famous pamphlet published in 1940 which has been called "the most important Communist writing produced outside of the Soviet Union since before the Russian revolution." "The Chinese revolution," argued Mao, "can only be achieved in two steps: (a) new democracy; (b) socialism." The revolution "can never be achieved without the guidance of communism," which was also, of course, the ultimate, long-range goal. To anyone at all conversant with Marxist dialectics or with the Soviet vocabulary, the term "new democracy" will have a familiar ring. It is similar to the "people's democracy" of the satellite states of Eastern and Southeastern Europe, a "democracy" which is professedly a stage in the direction of communism. Along that road lies national subservience, not freedom; but to millions of people of Asia the "new democracy" seems to offer more than does the "capitalistic democracy" of the West, which in their minds stands for imperialism and exploitation.

Imperialism and Communism in Asia

While nationalism in Asia is becoming more powerful and more successful, colonialism, or imperialism, is declining — indeed dying. This is a development of vast importance to the areas of Asia that have recently achieved independence, to the former colonial powers that, with varying degrees of realism, are adjusting themselves to the inevitable, and to the world at large. The decline of imperialism has been in progress for some decades, but it reached the proportions of a collapse after the Second World War. Before 1939 Britain, France, and the Netherlands possessed vast empires in Asia; British imperial interests, in fact, extended from one end of the continent to the other. Today the great empires are gone, probably forever.

One form of imperialism, however, is definitely on the ascendant in Asia. This is Communist imperialism. For many decades tsarist Russia followed an imperialist policy in Asia, but this was mostly of the incorporative type, involving the absorption of peoples and territories into the expanding Russian domains. After the Revolution of 1917, the leaders of the Bolshevik regime repudiated imperialism — which Lenin described as the last gasp of a dying capitalist system — and appealed to the people of Asia as champions of anti-imperialism. It soon became apparent nonetheless that the Soviets were furthering their own ends through a subtle form of imperialism while posing as friends and liberators. In the Stalin era their techniques of expansion and control became more flagrant and more overt. World War II, and especially the defeat of Japan, created a situation in Asia which the Soviet leaders were not slow to exploit. There is much truth in the bitter statement of Dr. T. S. Tsiang, United Nations representative of Nationalist China, in 1949: "Even at the height of the nineteenth-century imperialism, no movement of imperial expansion can be compared to what Soviet Russia has achieved in Asia in recent years. Stalin has surpassed all the Ivans, Peters, Alexanders, and Nicholases of Russian history."[40]

This view found vigorous support at the Asian-African conference in Bandung, in April, 1955. Spokesmen of Turkey, Iran, Iraq, Pakistan, the Philippines, and even Ceylon backed a resolution so worded as to include condemnation of the "new colonial-

[40] Address before the First Committee of the General Assembly of the United Nations, November 25, 1949.

ism" of the Communists carried out by "force, infiltration and subversion," as well as of the older colonialism associated with Western powers. Naturally a conference attended by Chou En-lai, Nehru, Nu, Sastroamidjojo, and others who sought agreement rather than division did not endorse this resolution, but the energy with which the charge was pressed was a singular revelation of the strong anti-Communist sentiment among Asians themselves.

Since 1955 the successors of Stalin have tended to emphasize a policy of "peaceful co-existence" and the relaxation of international tensions. This was particularly the case during the Khrushchev era. Soviet pressures on non-Communist areas in Asia continued, but they were confined largely to economic, cultural, political, and propaganda offensives.

The U.S.S.R. has several clear-cut advantages in Asia. In the first place, Russia is an Asian as well as a European power, in some respects more Asian than European. She extends over the entire northern part of the continent, with a land frontier in Asia of more than 5,000 miles. Second, she is — or recently was — herself an underdeveloped country, and she provides for the still backward lands of Asia an experience in economic development which can presumably be a pattern for them.[41] Third, her ideology has always emphasized the importance of associating the Soviet Union with the aspirations of colonial peoples, and therefore has a peculiar appeal for those who identify imperialism with the capital states of the West. Fourth, even the Soviet brand of "democracy" seems more genuine and more desirable to the masses of Asia than people brought up in the Anglo-Saxon tradition of freedom can possibly imagine. Asians have never known freedom or political unity in the Western sense. To them bread means more than abstract political rights, and the propaganda of the Soviet Union about the economic freedom in the U.S.S.R. and about the equal treatment of all peoples, in contrast to the racial discrimination and economic stratification in capitalist states, has strong appeal.

The Communists have benefited from the decline in the power of the colonial nations in recent years, and from the efforts of these nations, especially the French in Indo-China and the Dutch in Indonesia, to block or sidetrack movements for independence. They have also benefited from some of the alleged failures and shortcomings of American policy in Asia, among which may be listed postwar policy toward China, support of the colonial powers in their efforts to restore their prewar positions, the apparent failure of Americans to understand or to sympathize with the native peoples of Asia in their struggles for freedom and a better lot in life, the alleged interest in the preservation of the status quo in a continent desperately crying for change, the evidences that the United States is trying to build up Japan as a kind of Far Eastern bastion, and the American military presence in Korea, Japan, Okinawa, Vietnam, and the China Sea. Such charges have been the stock-in-trade of Communist propagandists, and they have apparently made a considerable impression throughout Asia.

The Sino-Soviet rift has led to bitter rivalry of the two Communist giants for leadership in the Communist world and for influence in non-Communist countries and in Communist parties throughout Asia, and indeed throughout the world; but it has not blunted the edge of the Communist drive in Asia. If Soviet influence in Asia has waned, Chinese influence, and Chinese power and militance, have increased greatly. Since the late 1950's, and especially after the Chinese attack on India in late 1962, the Chinese shadow over non-Communist Asia, and especially over South and Southeast Asia, has been ominous. Even spokesmen of neutral-

[41] Lattimore, *The Situation in Asia*, pp. 79–83.

ist countries, including those in India herself, have been openly describing Chinese policies as imperialistic.

Communist power in Asia today is formidable, and the attraction of communism is very great. Soviet Asia and China encompass much of the continent, forming a huge Communist intrusion and focus of power. Communist-controlled regimes hold power in North Korea and North Vietnam, and Communist parties and fellow-travelers probe and scheme in almost every part of non-Communist Asia. Until late 1965 they were particularly numerous, active, and influential in Indonesia, but they have a considerable following in many other Asian countries, including India and Japan. Communists continue to infiltrate non-Communist parties and groups, and Communist-dominated movements are a constant threat to the weak regimes in various Asian states, notably in Laos and South Vietnam. Communism, presented more as a formula for giving oppressed peoples a better lot in life and for overthrowing oppressive regimes than as an international ideology, obviously appeals to impoverished and unsophisticated Asians who are beginning to enter the arena of political activity and influence.

Asian Political Systems

Politically, as well as racially, culturally, and geographically, Asia is a remarkably diversified area. Except for vest-pocket remnants of colonialism, such as Portuguese Timor, Hong Kong, and Macao, the entire continent is divided into independent states. The fact in itself is a startling and very new development, for until World War II most of the continent outside of the Soviet Union and China was under foreign rule. Communists were active in several parts of the continent outside of Soviet Asia, but except in China they seemed to be little more than a nuisance. Today Communist regimes control well over half of the land mass of Asia, and communism in various forms and guises threatens other parts of the continent as well.

Most of the new nations which emerged soon after the end of World War II began their careers as independent nations with various forms of democratic institutions, at least in name. Few of them were able to make democracy work. Since 1958, in particular, the erosion of democracy in the new states of Asia has assumed almost landslide dimensions. It is difficult to determine whether democracy failed in these states, or whether it was ever really tried. In any event, few if any Asian states today can be described as democratic, without stretching the term beyond all recognition. The possible exceptions include Israel, India, Malaysia, the Philippines, and Japan; but at best each of these states can be called an embryonic democracy, and in each of them democracy has very shallow roots and faces many formidable obstacles. While none of the new states is still a wholly traditional society, few if any — Japan is the possible exception — can properly be characterized as modern. Most if not all are therefore in various stages of transition. Most are under the control of authoritarian regimes, including various versions of "guided democracy."

A brief review of the prevailing political systems in Asia, on a country-by-country basis, may provide useful background information for an analysis of contemporary Asia and its place in world affairs. This review is valid as of 1968; the picture may change rapidly in future years, as in recent years.

Far East. According to the 1954 Constitution, the People's Republic of China, as Communist China is properly called, is "a peoples' democratic state led by the working class." It is in fact a totalitarian Communist dictatorship under the control of the leaders of the Chinese Communist Party. The other China, known popularly as Nationalist China and more accurately as the Republic of China, controls only the island of Formosa (Taiwan), most of whose population are native Taiwanese who have little voice in the government which controls them and which claims to be the rightful government for all of China. The Nationalist Government has various representative institutions, but it is in fact a one-party state, with the single important party — the Kuomintang — controlled by the indomitable Chiang Kai-shek. Japan is a constitutional monarchy with a parliamentary system which seems to be working rather well, although it is a recent innovation and an adaptation of a form of government imposed during the occupational period. The Democratic People's Republic of Korea, north of the 38th parallel, is a Communist state, while the Republic of Korea to the south has undergone many vicissitudes and many changes in government since the overthrow of Dr. Syngman Rhee in 1960. A constitution adopted in 1963 provided for a strong presidential system of democracy, but South Korea is in reality governed by a military junta, under General Chung Hee Park, the President of the Republic of Korea.

Southeast Asia. In Southeast Asia the political patterns are equally mixed. The Republic of the Philippines is a democracy of the presidential type, modeled in some measure after the American system. Indonesia, whose leaders proclaimed independence in August, 1945, and actually achieved it in December, 1949, is in name a republic. President Sukarno became chief of state in 1945, and in 1963 he was proclaimed president for life. An unabashed champion of "guided democracy," he steered a delicate middle course between the army and the Communists at home, pursued adventurous foreign policies, and retained his charismatic appeal to the Indonesian masses in spite of deepening economic problems. After the abortive coup of October, 1965, however, he was relegated to a subordinate position by the new military leaders who assumed control of the country.

As a result of the Geneva agreements of 1954 Vietnam was divided into two states. North Vietnam — known as the Democratic Republic of Vietnam — is a Communist state, under the domination of the veteran Vietnamese Communist, Ho Chi Minh. The non-Communist Republic of Vietnam in the south has experienced a sea of domestic and external troubles in trying to establish and maintain a viable state. From July, 1954, until November, 1963, she was governed by the increasingly dictatorial regime of Ngo Dinh Diem, who saved the country from imminent collapse only to resort to policies which left a tragic legacy. Since his overthrow and murder South Vietnam has had a variety of provisional governments, mostly dominated by various factions in the military, with politically-minded Buddhists and other groups as rival centers of power, or at least of disturbance, and with the Communist-dominated Vietcong maintaining a kind of rival government in large sections of the country outside of Saigon.

Cambodia is a constitutional monarchy dominated by the mercurial Prince Norodom Sihanouk, who resigned as king in order to run the country in a more direct and active way as chief of state and popular leader. Thailand, which has been independent for some 600 years, is a kingdom with some constitutional trappings. The country has generally been under the control of strongmen with military background and connections, notably General Pibul Songgram from 1948 to 1957, and Field Marshal Sarit Thanarat from 1959 to 1963. Since General Sarit's death his successor, General Thanom Kittakachorn, has continued the domestic and foreign politics of Sarit, with some relaxation of controls at home. Thailand is still pro-Western in orientation, is a member of SEATO, and is greatly concerned over her vulnerability to Communist pressures from the north. Laos is a constitutional monarchy with an hereditary ruler and a weak coalition government composed of representatives of the royalist, neutralist, and pro-Communist factions. Prince Souvanna Phouma, the neutralist leader became premier in June, 1962. The government is unstable, and the country is harassed by Communist-led rebels, the Pathet Lao, openly supported by North Vietnam and China.

Malaya became independent, as a parliamentary democracy, a federation, and a member of the Commonwealth, in 1957. In September, 1963, as a result of the merger of the Federation of Malaya, the self-governing state of Singapore, and the British colonies of North Borneo (renamed Sabah) and Sarawak, the Federation of Malaysia came into being. The new federation faced serious internal divisions — its mixed racial composition, with Chinese numbering about 43 per cent of the total population and Malays about 40 per cent, was a particular source of tension — as well as the bitter opposition and growing hostility of Indonesia. In August, 1965, Singapore, predominantly Chinese, was virtually forced out of the federation, and is now an independent state, a "reluctant republic," under the control of the People's Action Party, headed by Lee Kuan Yew. Malaysia, which kept the same name even after the exclusion of Singapore, for all its internal and external difficulties, seems to be one of the most stable and democratic states in Asia. After the political coup in Indonesia in late 1965, the Malaysia-Indonesia confrontation was virtually ended and diplomatic relations were resumed.

The Union of Burma also seems to be relatively stable, but the prospects for democratic government were dimmed, at least for the foreseeable future, when the second constitutional government headed by U Nu was suspended in March, 1962, and General Ne Win assumed control for the second time. Under the virtual dictatorship of Ne Win, with the Burma Socialist Program Party as a front for the Revolutionary Council dominated by the military junta, Burma is turning her back on most foreign ties and associations and is pressing forward along "the Burmese Way to Socialism."

South Asia. India and Pakistan, the two giants of South Asia, are both republics and members of the Commonwealth; but since they became independent in August, 1947, their political evolution has moved along very difficult lines. India is a parliamentary democracy, with a federal system, a written constitution, an indirectly elected president, and a bicameral parliament whose lower house is chosen directly by popular vote. The prime minister is the effective head of the government, and this office gained special status and prestige because Jawaharlal Nehru was the incumbent from even before independence until his death in May, 1964. India has successfully held four nationwide general elections, in 1951–2, 1957, 1962, and 1967. In the rural areas, where most of the people live, a new experiment in "democratic decentralization" known as Panchayati Raj is under way; it may provide a new pattern of local government, administration, and development for India and a model for other underdeveloped countries.

Pakistan, like India, was in form a parliamentary democracy from 1947 until 1958, although the parliamentary system was never really implemented. Pakistan did not get a constitution until March, 1956, and national elections were never held. In October, 1958, the feeble "parliamentary" system was suspended by "revolution." General Ayub Khan emerged as the key man in a regime dominated by the military. From 1958 until 1962 Pakistan was under martial law. In 1959 Ayub Khan introduced a system of "basic democracies," which apparently was designed to provide not only a more comprehensive program of administration and development throughout the country but also a framework for a new political system, a "democracy" better suited to Pakistan's peculiar needs and conditions. In June, 1962, a new constitution, promulgated by Ayub Khan, went into effect. Martial law was ended, a newly elected national assembly met, and Pakistan became a republic of the presidential type, with Ayub Khan as president. Elected president in 1960 by the "basic democrats," acting as an electoral college, Ayub was re-elected in 1965 for another five-year term by the same method, in spite of a strong challenge by the nominee of five opposition parties, Miss Fatima Jinnah, sister of Mohammed Ali Jinnah, the "Father of the Nation."

Ceylon, like India and Pakistan, is a member of the Commonwealth, and like India is a parliamentary democracy. It is still a Dominion, with a governor-general (a Ceylonese) nominated by the British crown. It is one of the few democracies in Asia with at least two important political parties, the United National Party and the Sri Lanka Freedom Party, both of which have controlled the government for long periods.

The mountain kingdoms of Nepal and Bhutan are traditional monarchies, or at least traditional oligarchies. Since he dissolved Nepal's only elected parliament in December, 1960, and at the same time dismissed and arrested the prime minister and abrogated the constitution, King Mahendra of Nepal has been in direct control of the government. In April, 1963, he promulgated a constitution providing for a system or "partyless Panchayat Democracy," and he appointed a cabinet to rule in association with a National Panchayat (council); but this form of "guided democracy" is a limited one, and effective power is still centered in the King. Bhutan, just emerging from its long period of isolation, is at best a semi-autonomous state, since India is largely responsible for its foreign relations and defense and provides Bhutan with an annual subsidy. Two great families, the Wangchuks and the Dorjis, dominate the country. The ruler, Jigme Dorji Wangchuk, is advised by a national assembly and assisted by feudal governors.

Southwest Asia. Afghanistan, which has ties with both South and Southwest Asia, is a constitutional monarchy of the traditional type, under King Mohammed Zahir Shah. For more than nine years Prince Mohammed Daud, a cousin of the King, was prime minister, but in March, 1963, Dr. Mohammed Yusuf was placed at the head of a cabinet in which no members of the royal family were represented. The new prime minister promised political and social reforms, a new constitution, and elections within two or three years. On September 19, 1964, a new constitution went into effect, and in 1965 elections were held. On October 30, 1965, Yusuf resigned, and was succeeded by Mohammad Hashim Maiwandwal.

Between 1961 and 1963 parliamentary government was suspended by the Shah of Iran, but in September, 1963, elections were held for the Majlis (the lower house of the parliament), and constitutional government was restored. Shah Mohammed Reza seems to be firmly in control and using his powers to carry out a "revolution from the throne."

Under the new constitution of 1961 Turkey retained her republican system, with an indirectly elected president. Recent governments have been weak coalitions, and there are disturbing signs that parliamentary democracy is not so firmly entrenched in Turkey as was generally believed.

The Israeli Republic is perhaps the leading example of democracy in Asia. In many respects, she is hardly an Asian state at all. She is headed by a president elected by the Knesset (Assembly) and a prime minister. Since she lost her veteran top leadership in 1963 with the death of President Ben-Zvi and the resignation of Premier David Ben-Gurion, she has been governed by weak coalition cabinets. Her continued existence is constantly challenged by the hostility of the surrounding Arab states.

The most persistent enemy and the spearhead of Arab hostility toward Israel is the United Arab Republic, most of whose territory is in Africa. This is ruled by Gamal Abdel Nasser, with the assistance of an executive council and a defense council. The U.A.R. was formed by a merger of Egypt and Syria in 1958, and the name has been preserved despite the secession of Syria in 1961. Her government and institutions have undergone revolutionary changes within the framework of Arab nationalism and socialism, as interpreted by Nasser.

For the first twelve years of independence (1946–58) Syria had a parliamentary government, which fell on evil days. From February, 1958, until September, 1961, she was a part of the United Arab Republic, but this experiment did not work well either, at least from Syria's point of view. Since then Syria has been seeking a satisfactory pattern of representative government, but she has had a series of weak coalition governments and the outlines of its future political order are not clear. In neighboring Jordan, contrary to many predictions, the hereditary ruler, King Hussein I of the Hashemite family, has continued in power, with a cabinet and a bicameral legislature, the lower house of which is directly elected.

Lebanon, in many respects the most advanced of the Arab states, has a population almost equally divided between Christians (mostly Maronite and Greek Orthodox) and Muslims (both Sunnite and Shiite). Seats in the unicameral legislature are divided among the religious communities on a proportional basis. According to custom the president of the republic is a Maronite Christian, the premier a Sunnite Muslim, and the speaker of the chamber of deputies a Shiite Muslim.

In Iraq the regime of Premier Abdul Karim al-Kassem was overthrown by a military coup in February, 1963, and a government dominated by the Baath Party and headed by Colonel Abdul Salam Mohammed Arif came into power. President Arifs's hold on the government was consolidated as a result of a second coup in November, 1963. His attempts to patch up differences with the U.A.R. produced a joint announcement in 1964 that Iraq and the U.A.R. would set up a "unified political command" which would be the supreme political authority for both states and which would prepare for a "constitutional union between the two countries within a maximum period of two years." On April 13, 1966, Colonel Arif was killed in a helicopter crash, and three days later his brother, Major General Abdul Rahman Arif, was elected president.

Saudia Arabia is a monarchy under the House of Saud. The real ruler during the last years of the reign of King Ibn Saud was his brother, Prince Faisal, who presided over the Council of Ministers. In early November, 1964, Faisal replaced his brother as king. Saudi Arabia shares the Arabian Peninsula with three smaller Arab states — Kuwait, Yemen, and Southern Yemen — and several lesser Sheikhdoms. The oil-rich sheikhdom of Kuwait is under the firm rule of the al-Sabbah family. A new constitution, promulgated in November, 1962, provided for a democratic system of government and in January, 1963, elections were held for the unicameral national assembly. Most of the members of the cabinet, however, belong to the al-Sabbah family.

From 1948 until his death in 1962, the Imam Saif al-Aslam Ahmad was the absolute ruler of the isolated and backward state of Yemen. Since then a royalist government headed by the new Imam and former Crown Prince, recognized by Saudi Arabia and Jordan, and a republican government, recognized quickly by the U.A.R. and the Soviet Union and eventually by the United States and many other countries, and also by the United Nations, have been vying for supremacy.

In December, 1967, the British pulled out

of Aden and surrounding territories in South Arabia, which became the People's Republic of Southern Yemen. The new state, with the finest and most strategically located natural port in Arabia, has one political party, the National Liberation Front, and a government headed by President Qahtan al-Shaabi. She is following a "neutralist" foreign policy oriented against the West.

Asia in World Affairs

"Asia is now, and will continue to be a veritable cauldron of confrontations. . . . Asia is faced with the prospect of not just one major confrontation that could lead to war, . . . but five, encompassing the world's and Asia's foremost powers. These are: (1) a clash between the national and ideological interest of the Soviet Union and Communist China; (2) the Sino-Indian conflict over borders and leadership in Asia; (3) the U.S.-Soviet competition over allies, influence, and strategic position in Asia; (4) the Sino-U.S. confrontation from Korea to Kashmir; and (5) the Indo-Pakistan confrontation over national survival and predominance in South Asia. There are many lesser confrontations, involving Malaysia v. Indonesia, North v. South Korea, Nationalist v. Communist China, North v. South Vietnam, and so forth, throughout Asia. There is hardly an area or a country on that continent, or its periphery, that is not involved today in a major or minor confrontation that could lead to war."[42]

Differences in Foreign Policy Orientation. With respect to foreign policy orientation, many different attitudes may be discerned among Asian leaders today. Communist China would keep peace in Asia and save the continent from "capitalist imperialism" by bringing the entire area under direct or indirect Communist control. Nationalist China and the Republic of Korea would, in Syngman Rhee's words, "make Asia safe for freedom" by winning back the mainland of China, unifying Korea, and forcing the "inevitable" showdown with the Communist world before it becomes too strong. Several Asian states have followed a policy of alignment, and have joined Western powers in regional security arrangements. This group of states includes Turkey, Pakistan, Thailand, and the Philippines. The largest of these states, Pakistan, has been entertaining growing doubts of the value of her allies and alliances, and in recent years has been veering toward a more independent policy. Japan, Korea, and Nationalist China have security arrangements with the United States, but Japan, the most important of these states, may well move toward a more independent position at the expiration of her security treaty with the United States in 1970, even if the treaty is renewed.

Iran and the Arab states of the Middle East combine an awareness of the Communist threat with bitter memories of past relations with Western powers. Their recollections of the Iranian oil dispute, the Suez Canal question, and the complex of issues involved in the Arab-Israeli hostility put them in no mood for close association with their former "oppressors."

Most of the non-Communist states of Asia belong to the so-called uncommitted world; they seek to occupy "middle ground between America and Russia" and to remain aloof from "power blocs"; they speak of "neutrality," "independence," and "nonalignment." India is the leading member of this group, and Nehru was for years its most eloquent spokesman. The Chinese attack on India forced that nation to resort to policies which previously would have been regarded as inconsistent with nonalignment, and even though officially she still adheres to a policy of nonalignment, her influence in other nonaligned states is no longer as great as it was.

[42] Thomas A. Rusch, "Confrontation Between India and Pakistan," a paper read at the inaugural meeting of Asian Studies on the Pacific Coast, San Francisco State College, June 17, 1966, pp. 2–3 (unpublished manuscript).

The nonaligned states form a united front only on certain issues. There are many de-degrees and variations of nonalignment, both between and within these nations, at different periods and under different circumstances.

Asia in the United Nations. All of the non-Communist states of Asia, except the divided states of Korea and Viĕtnam and the semi-autonomous kingdom of Bhutan, are members of the United Nations, which provides an important international forum for their activities. Several Asians have been presidents of the UN General Assembly; the Secretary-General and other top members of the Secretariat are, or have been, Asians; and many Asians serve, or have served, in key positions in virtually all UN agencies and organs, including the specialized agencies. The Asian-African Group is an especially important channel for Asian influence and activity in the United Nations. When it first came into existence in the early years of the United Nations as the Arab-Asian Group, it consisted wholly of Asian members, with the exception of Egypt, which in many respects is more Asian than African. India played the main role in bringing the group into existence, and was and perhaps still is its most influential member. At the present time there are more African than Asian members, which somewhat alters the group's orientation. The influence of the Asian members, including such important countries as Japan, India, Pakistan, and Turkey, is still great and would be much greater if the Asian states were not so disunited and if they could work out bases of cooperation such as the African states are attempting to do through the Organization of African Unity and other regional organizations.

The Great Asian Triangle. In the great Asian continent three states, Japan, China, and India, deserve special attention. At least two others, Indonesia and Pakistan, stand out prominently, Indonesia because she is by far the most populous state of Southeast Asia and Pakistan because she occupies a strategic position in the South Asian subcontinent.

Politically, if not geographically, India, China, and Japan form a great Asian triangle. At present these states are in a process of transition and the relations of each to the others are still in a state of evolution and flux. For a decade relations between India and Communist China seemed to be peaceful and cordial. After the Chinese suppression of the revolt in Tibet in 1959, the revelation of the border and other difficulties between India and China, and the Chinese attack on India in late 1962, the two states emerged as rivals rather than as collaborators. The present rulers of China are Communists who are attempting to remake that ancient land in the Communist image and to extend their influence by a "revolutionary strategy" abroad. The leaders of free India, on the other hand, have deliberately chosen the democratic way, and they have not hesitated to take strong measures against the Communists within their country. Nor are they unmindful of the two thousand miles of frontiers with Communist China, or of the nature and aims of world communism. Japan is being drawn irresistibly to develop closer contacts with Communist China. She wishes in particular to expand her trade with the Chinese mainland, and in time, no doubt, in spite of American pressures to the contrary, to regularize her diplomatic relations with Communist China. Japan and India have not had close relations in the past, but in the postwar period both have shown a desire for closer contacts as well as concern for the effects of competition in Southeast Asia and elsewhere for markets and raw materials. Certainly the interaction of the three great states which form the Asian triangle will have an important bearing on the future of Asia and the world.

Japan. World War II marked the end of the phenomenal rise of Japan, of her aspirations for domination of East Asia, and

— at least for the time being — of her status as a great power. When she surrendered in 1945, Japan had been driven out of most of the vast territory she had occupied, except in China; her navy and merchant fleet had been largely destroyed; most of her factories and many of her larger cities had been reduced to heaps of rubble; and her dreams of conquest had been shattered. From the fall of 1945 to the spring of 1952 Japan, confined once more to her four home islands, was an occupied country under the stern paternalism of General MacArthur and his successors. During this period the Japanese had an opportunity to re-establish a basis of economic strength and to learn the difficult art of democratic government. They proved to be more adept in the former than in the latter, although since the restoration of independence they have continued to progress along the lines charted during the occupation period. Japan's economic recovery has been spectacular, and her efforts to operate democratic institutions have met with some success. With the recovery of sovereignty, confidence, and economic strength, she has been taking an increasingly active role in world affairs, especially in economic and inter-Asian relations. Her security treaty with the United States has enabled her to postpone the difficult question of defense. In all probability, after the expiration of the treaty in 1970, she will continue to try to find security without undertaking a substantial defense program, and will try to maintain good relations with the United States and increase her influence in world affairs while at the same time entering into increasing trade and political relations with Communist China and perhaps also with the Soviet Union. In short, she is likely to adopt an "independent" policy that will lead to rather substantial changes in her political and international orientation.

China. The changes in China during the past generation have been even more profound than in Japan. From the Revolution of 1911–12, which overthrew the decadent Manchu dynasty, until 1949, when the Chinese Communists consolidated their victory on the Chinese mainland, China never had a government which exercised effective control over all her territory. The Nationalist Government of Chiang Kai-shek, which was established in Peking in 1928, might have achieved this objective if it had not been harassed by both the Communists and the Japanese, not to mention dissident war lords, and if it had not developed serious internal weaknesses. China emerged from World War II in such a debilitated condition that the Nationalist leaders were never able to establish the bases of control and power. In the civil war with the Communists that broke out with renewed fury in 1946 and 1947, the Nationalist Government was forced into continuous political and military retreat; and by the end of 1949 it had been forced from the mainland of China to refuge on the island of Formosa, where it maintains a precarious existence, still claiming to represent China and still dreaming dreams of returning to power on the mainland.

The Communist victory in China and the effective consolidation of Communist power in the world's most populous state since then have been among the most significant events in contemporary international relations. These developments have altered the world balance of power, as well as the balance inside the Communist orbit. They have introduced disrupting new factors into the Asian picture. Internal developments in China in recent years have presented a mixed and confused picture of considerable progress and great turmoil, as illustrated by the failure of the "Great Leap Forward" and by the excesses of the "Great Proletarian Cultural Revolution" and the Red Guards.

China is a more effective state than she has ever been in the modern era. That she is under Communist control makes her a more difficult and dubious member of the family of nations, as became clear when the Communist leaders of the "New China" in the late 1950's and early 1960's embarked on such militant and aggressive policies in foreign affairs as the attack on India, pressures on Indo-China, and intervention in such distant places as Africa and Latin America. Under the ambitious and ruthless direction of her new leaders China has developed formidable economic and technological strength, as illustrated by a rate of economic growth which cannot be accurately measured but which is obviously impressive, and by successful efforts to explode nuclear devices and lay the foundations for becoming a nuclear power. In the international relations of the future China is bound to play an increasingly influential role, and if recent courses of policy are continued she will be a disturbing factor in the international picture.

India. After she achieved independence in 1947, and to some extent even before this time, India emerged as perhaps the leading spokesman of Asia in world affairs, and her world-famous prime minister Jawaharlal Nehru, perhaps more than any other single person, was widely regarded as the voice of the new Asia. Nehru and other Indian leaders insisted that they did not seek any role of leadership for themselves and did not wish to form a coalition of Asian states, but that they sought to bring the new nations of Asia together to consider common problems, to promote common interests, and to renew old contacts with neighboring countries that had been almost wholly suspended with the coming of the Western powers. It is significant that India took the initiative in calling the Asian Relations Conference in 1947 and the Conference on Indonesia of 1949, both of which were held in New Delhi. She was also a leading member of the so-called Colombo powers (the others were Pakistan, Indonesia, Ceylon, and Burma), which convened the historic Asian-African Conference at Bandung in April, 1955.

India's influence in Asia is still as great as any other single Asian state, with the possible exception of Communist China, but it is relatively less than it was in the first decade of the post-World War II era. This is due to many factors. Since the Bandung Conference other Asian states, particularly Communist China, have been more active in the Asian scene, and many of these in addition to China, notably Japan, Indonesia, Pakistan, and Turkey, are not inclined to follow India's leadership or example unless this happens to coincide with their own conceptions of their national interests. In the early 1950's Japan, China, and Indonesia were adapting to new political systems and were still laying the bases of a new order. Today China and Japan have developed much greater power, and Indonesia is following a path rather divergent from India's.

The political and military and psychological humiliation that she suffered at the hands of the Chinese noticeably reduced India's prestige and influence in world affairs. This has been especially true among nonaligned states, and in Asia generally. The loss of her great leader, Jawaharlal Nehru, in May, 1964, deprived India of her chief international spokesman. The new leaders of India are relatively inexperienced, and most of them are quite unknown in international diplomacy. They have been forced to concentrate rather heavily on pressing domestic problems and on relations with neighbors and to eschew a larger international role. Yet the voice of India is still a powerful one, and it will be heard with increasing frequency in coming years.

The Sino-Soviet Split: Its Impact on Asia. One of the most significant developments in recent international relations has been the spread of polycentrism within the Communist world. Although the trend may perhaps be traced to the success of Yugoslavia in maintaining her political and economic independence as a Communist state even after she had been read out of the Cominform in 1948, it was most dramatically illustrated by the so-called Sino-Soviet split, which became public knowledge in the late 1950's and which has divided the entire Communist world and almost every Communist party. Some authorities believe that the split has gone so far as to be irreversible, that, in the words of Richard Lowenthal, "The Humpty-Dumpty of single-centered world Communism cannot be put together again." "We have thus been watching," wrote Lowenthal in October, 1964, "the disintegration of the original Leninist doctrine and the development of two 'Communist' powers and two 'Communist' ideologies in wholly different directions."[43]

In some respects friction between the Russians and the Chinese is "an old, old story."[44] The course of the Russian and Chinese revolutions of the twentieth century has been very different. Russia came under Communist domination in 1917, China not until 1949. For nearly a decade after the Communist victory in China, it seemed that the binding force of a Communist ideology had overcome differences in historical experience and in stages of economic and political development, as well as old sources of conflict. After Stalin's death, the Soviet claim to dominance over the entire Communist world came under increasing challenge. China, in particular, was no longer content to be simply a junior partner. Mao Tse-tung may well have regarded himself as the senior leader of world communism in the post-Stalin era. In any event, he and his associates began to rebel against the concept of Soviet hegemony over the international Communist movement, and they found increasing support in certain other Communist countries and in some Communist parties outside of the Communist orbit. The differences were not primarily ideological; they were rather a result of a struggle for leadership within the Communist world and for influence outside. Involved as well were personal rivalries and opposing views of the proper course of action to follow in dealing with the non-Communist world.

The Chinese became increasingly critical and distrustful of Khrushchev's policies of de-Stalinization, of détente and peaceful coexistence with the Western powers, including the United States, and of economic and political support of "bourgeois" regimes in the emerging nations of Asia and Africa. They also criticized specific actions and policies, notably Khrushchev's "retreat" under American pressure during the Cuban missile crisis of October, 1962, and his willingness to sign the nuclear test ban treaty with the United States (also signed by many other nations) in 1963. They accused the Russian leaders of being passive and negative toward "liberation" struggles and of using the theory of "peaceful transition to communism" to cover up their "cowardice." They insisted that the Communist victory could not be gained peacefully, but only through perpetual struggle, including armed struggle where necessary. The Russian response was that the Chinese leaders were dangerous "adventurists" who might provoke the West into nuclear attack at a time when the West was in disarray and when history was on the side of the Communists if they applied their growing strength to winning through unrelenting pressure and through the exploitation of "capitalist" weaknesses. They charged the Chinese with splitting the Communist world and with appealing to the peoples of underdeveloped countries on grounds of race and color. They were critical of the Chinese attack on India in late 1962, and they continued to provide India with economic and military assistance after the attack.

In the early years the People's Republic of China had been too dependent on the Soviet Union for political, military, economic, and technical assistance to challenge Soviet control of world communism. But behind the scenes friction was building up, and it burst

[43] "Communists of the World, Unite?" *New York Times Magazine*, October 25, 1964, p. 114.

[44] See John Paton Davies, Jr., "The Sino-Soviet Rift: An Old, Old Story," *The Reporter*, August 15, 1963.

out into the open in 1959–60. At this time the Soviet Union withdrew virtually all of her technical advisers from China, suspended much of her foreign aid to that country, and reduced her trade with China to a fraction of the 1959 figure of nearly $2 billion. Within the Communist world and without, the two Communist giants acted increasingly as rivals rather than partners, and they seemed to be concentrating more on their differences than on their common objectives vis-à-vis the non-Communist world. Harsh words were exchanged at international Communist gatherings, at national party conferences attended by "fraternal" delegates from other Communist states, and in official Soviet and Chinese organs. Indeed, the debate has become seemingly endless. Outside of the Communist orbit, the rivalry has set off a struggle for influence in the Communist parties of non-Communist countries, and in underdeveloped nations generally. This competition has even extended to Africa and Latin America. It has affected and nearly disrupted almost every Communist party in the world. In effect, it has led to the emergence of two Communist movements, not one.

In Asia the Sino-Soviet rivalry has been particularly fierce. It has been manifest in border disputes, in struggles for influence in Asian Communist parties, and in competing policies in South and Southeast Asia, which in a peculiar way have become main theaters of the Sino-Soviet conflict. The Soviet Union now seems to regard Communist China as the principal threat to her security and to her position in Asia.

Two sensational events in October, 1964, occurring almost simultaneously — the deposition of Khrushchev and the Chinese explosion of a nuclear device — appeared to improve China's position vis-à-vis its more powerful rival. "The Khrushchev ouster has substantially strengthened the Chinese position, weakened the position of the Soviet leadership, and increased the tendencies toward neutralism and polycentrism in many Communist parties."[45] The Chinese claimed that Khrushchev's fall was proof of their contention that he had been following wrong policies. His removal, however, did not lead to any marked improvement in Sino-Soviet relations. Premier Chou En-lai did go to Moscow in November, 1964, but apparently his visit did not lead to any basic agreements with the new Soviet leaders, who were later denounced by official Chinese organs for following a policy of "Khrushchevism without Khrushchev."

The growth of Chinese power, coupled with increasingly militant policies and actions, has at once heightened China's influence in non-Communist Asia and alarmed many of the leaders and peoples of other Asian countries. Since the armed attack on India, they feel insecure and the prospect of a militant neighbor armed with nuclear weapons has undoubtedly added to Asian apprehensions. Most Asians, however, seem to believe that various forms of nonalignment, backed perhaps, as in India, by more vigorous measures of defense, are still preferable to any more open stand in the face of a stronger and more aggressive China. They have to live under the Chinese shadow, and they obviously hope that the Chinese leaders will find outlets for their militancy in dealing with internal problems, and in their disputes with the Soviets and the United States and other Western powers. In spite of their belligerence in recent years, the Chinese leaders have usually acted cautiously when the odds have not seemed to be greatly in their favor; and they are still in no position to engage in direct conflict with either the Soviet Union or a major Western power, least of all the United States.

A Third Force?

As the strong winds of social change blow over Asia, the leaders of the many nations

[45] Harry Schwartz, "Sino-Soviet Conflict Enters New Phase," *New York Times*, December 20, 1964.

of this greatest of continents are becoming more and more conscious of their common problems and common needs. This is a development of revolutionary implications.

Perhaps the most concrete evidence of this tendency was the First Asian Relations Conference, which was held in New Delhi in the spring of 1947. Delegates from twenty-eight Asian countries and other political entities, including some of the republics of the U.S.S.R., attended this historic conference. "When the history of our present times is written," declared Prime Minister Nehru in his address of welcome at the opening session, "this event may well stand out as a landmark which divides the past of Asia from the future." The great Indian leader thus expressed the meaning of the new era for Asia: "A change is coming over the scene now and Asia is again finding herself. We live in a tremendous age of transition and already the next stage takes shape when Asia takes her rightful place with the other continents. . . . The countries of Asia can no longer be used as pawns by others; they are bound to have their own policies in world affairs." While giving due credit to the Western world for its contributions to human progress, Nehru also pointed to the apparent inability of the West to prevent recurrent wars. Delegate after delegate followed him to the rostrum to voice the identity of interests of the countries of Asia and to emphasize the importance of close collaboration among them.

Another conference in New Delhi, held in January, 1949, also had broad implications for future Asian unity, although it was convened to consider the Indonesian question. Delegates from nineteen countries, mostly from South and Southeast Asia but also including Australia, New Zealand, and Ethiopia, called for the withdrawal of Dutch troops from the areas under the control of the Indonesian Republic and for a transfer of sovereignty to a United States of Indonesia by January 1, 1950. At the same time the delegates were careful to emphasize that they were not seeking to align the East against the West. They decided not to establish a permanent organization, but agreed to consult more frequently and to cooperate more closely in the future.

History was made again in April, 1955, when representatives of twenty-nine countries of Asia and Africa met in Bandung, Indonesia, for the first Asian-African conference. The conference was sponsored by the Colombo powers — India, Pakistan, Ceylon, Burma, and Indonesia. The countries represented were rich in history and cultural traditions, but they were relatively weak in a power-political sense. They embraced more than half of the world's population, the vast majority of whom were colored. Their strongest bond was that for more than a century they had all experienced foreign domination or had lived in the shadow of the Western powers. They were also united in their belief that for them a new era had dawned, that henceforth they would count more heavily in the affairs of the world. In his address of welcome President Sukarno of Indonesia stated: "I hope this conference . . . will give evidence that Asia and Africa have been reborn, nay that a new Asia and a new Africa have been born." Other speakers echoed this theme. In spite of widespread apprehensions in the Western world, the Bandung Conference did not resolve itself into an anti-Western gathering; nor, in spite of the presence of Chou En-lai in a most affable mood, did it take a pro-Communist position. In fact, to Chou En-lai's face several delegates denounced communism as a new form of colonialism. The conference revealed that there is no such thing as an "Afro-Asian bloc" and certainly no alignment of East versus West. On almost every issue the delegates at Bundung showed many variations of viewpoint and emphasis. The final communiqué, couched for the most part in general terms, emphasized the importance of economic and cultural cooperation among nations, respect for human rights and the right to self-determination, and the promotion of world peace and cooperation.[46]

Writing in 1949 an eloquent spokesman of Asian aspirations, Carlos P. Romulo of the Philippines, expressed the view that Asia "is gradually assuming the role of a Third Force interposed between the two great powers, the United States and the Soviet Union" and "has emerged from her travail as the most dynamic region in the world today."[47] Unfortunately, as the events of the postwar period have revealed all too clearly, Asia has not "emerged from her travail" and the desire of many of her peoples and governments to remain aloof from the great-power struggle or to play the role of a "Third Force" has proved to be a rather unrealistic one. Asia has in fact been a theater of the cold war, and a cockpit of the Sino-Soviet controversy. It is, as has been noted, "a veritable cauldron of confrontations." Since the Bandung Conference of 1955 its divisions have been more obvious than its areas of agreement, its internal rivalries more marked than its cooperative tendencies. It is split into at least two Asias by the Communist–non-Communist divide. The Chinese attack on India in late 1962 shattered the pretensions of friendly cooperation between the two largest Asian states. Sukarno's erratic behavior cut him off from most of his Asian neighbors in Southeast Asia and from India. Asian differences have been apparent even at conferences in which Asian states have participated, such as the second conference of non-aligned nations, held in Cairo in October, 1964, and the preparatory meetings for the second Asian-African Conference, scheduled for 1965, but never held. Asian countries are too weak and disunited to be an effective "Third Force," even if they aspired to be — which in itself is a dubious assumption.

But there can be no doubt that leaders of non-Communist Asia share many of the same hopes. They believe that by removing the remaining bonds of colonialism, by raising the standards of living of the masses, by greater experience in self-government, and by self-help, mutual help, and help from the Western world, they will be able to stand on their own feet, resist the tides of communism, divert the demands for social change into constructive channels, and cope more effectively with the Four Horsemen of the Apocalypse — Conquest, Slaughter, Famine, and Death — which have ridden roughshod over Asia for countless centuries. They also believe, most strongly, that Asia has much to offer to the Western world and to humanity and that, as Nehru predicted, "the emergence of Asia in world affairs will be a powerful influence for world peace."

[46] For the text of the communiqué, see the *New York Times*, April 25, 1955.

[47] Romulo, p. 13.

SUGGESTIONS FOR FURTHER READING

BARNETT, A. DOAK. *Communist China and Asia.* New York: Random House, for the Council on Foreign Relations, 1960. An excellent survey of the internal situation and external orientation of the People's Republic of China.

———, ed. *Communist Strategies in Asia.* New York: Frederick A. Praeger, 1963.

BERGER, MORROE. *The Arab World Today.* Garden City, N.Y.: Doubleday & Company, 1962. One of the best general surveys.

BONE, RICHARD C., JR. *Contemporary Southeast Asia.* New York: Random House, 1962.

BORTON, HUGH. *Japan's Modern Century.* New York: The Ronald Press Company, 1955.

BROWN, DELMER M. *Nationalism in Japan: An Introductory Historical Analysis.* Berkeley: University of California Press, 1955. One of the most satisfactory studies of nationalism in an Asian country.

BULLARD, SIR READER WILLIAM, ed. *The Middle East: A Political and Economic Survey.* 3d ed. New York: Oxford University Press, 1958.

BUSS, CLAUDE. *The Arc of Crisis.* Garden City, N.Y.: Doubleday & Company, 1961. An interesting survey of the situation in "the arc of crisis" extending from Tokyo to the Khyber Pass.

———. *Asia in the Modern World.* New York: The Macmillan Company, 1964. A readable introduction to Asia, from the historical point of view, with particular emphasis on the period since 1939.

CRESSEY, GEORGE B. *Asia's Lands and Peoples; a Geography of One-Third of the Earth and Two-Thirds of Its People,* 3d ed. New York: McGraw-Hill Book Company, 1963. A standard work on the physical and political geography of all of Asia, including Soviet Asia and Southwest Asia (the Middle East).

DEBARY, WILLIAM THEODORE, ed. *Introduction to Oriental Civilizations.* Vol. I: *Sources of the Japanese Tradition.* Vol. II: *Sources of Indian Tradition.* Vol. III: *Sources of Chinese Tradition.* New York: Columbia University Press, 1958 and 1960. Valuable collections of source materials.

EDWARDES, MICHAEL. *Asia in the Balance.* Baltimore: Penguin Books, 1962.

———. *Asia in the European Age.* London, 1961.

FIFIELD, RUSSELL H. *The Diplomacy of Southeast Asia: 1945–1958.* New York: Harper & Brothers, 1958.

———. *Southeast Asia in United States Policy.* New York: Frederick A. Praeger, for the Council on Foreign Relations, 1963.

FISHER, CAROL ANN. *Middle East in Crisis; a Historical and Documentary Review.* Syracuse: Syracuse University Press, 1959.

FISHER, SIDNEY. *The Middle East, a History.* New York: Alfred A. Knopf, 1959.

FITZGERALD, C. P. *Revolution in China.* New York: Frederick A. Praeger, 1952.

FRYE, RICHARD N., ed. *The Near East and the Great Powers.* Cambridge, Mass.: Harvard University Press, 1951. Essays by specialists.

FURNIVALL, J. S. *Colonial Policy and Practice: A Comparative Study of Burma and Netherlands India.* Cambridge, England, 1948. A classic study of comparative colonial policy.

GINSBURG, NORTON, ed. *The Pattern of Asia.* Englewood Cliffs, N.J.: Prentice-Hall, 1958. A geographical survey emphasizing "the changing political and economic geography of Asia,"

HALL, D. G. E. *A History of South-East Asia.* New York: St. Martin's Press, 1955. A major work.

HALPERN, MANFRED. *The Politics of Social Change in the Middle East and North Africa.* Princeton, N.J.: Princeton University Press, 1963.

HAMMER, ELLEN J. *The Struggle for Indochina.* Stanford, Calif.: Stanford University Press, 1954.

HARARI, MAURICE. *Government and Politics of the Middle East.* Englewood Cliffs, N.J.: Prentice-Hall, 1962.

HARRISON, BRIAN. *South-East Asia: A Short History,* rev. ed. New York: St. Martin's Press, 1963.

HINTON, HAROLD C. *Communist China in World Politics.* Boston: Houghton Mifflin Company, 1966.

HOLLAND, WILLIAM L., ed. *Asian Nationalism and the West.* New York: The Macmillan Company, for the Institute or Pacific Relations, 1953. Based on documents and reports of the Eleventh Conference of the IPR, Lucknow, India, October, 1950.

HOSKINS, HALFORD L. *The Middle East: Problem Area in World Politics.* New York: The Macmillan Company, 1954. An excellent survey.

KAHIN, GEORGE MCT., ed. *Governments and Politics of Southeast Asia,* rev. ed. Ithaca: Cornell University Press, 1963.

———, ed. *Major Governments of Asia,* 2d ed. Ithaca: Cornell University Press, 1963. Several chapters each on the government and politics of Japan, China, Indonesia, India, and Pakistan.

KIRK, GEORGE E. *Contemporary Arab Politics: a Concise History*. New York: Frederick A. Praeger, 1961.

LAQUEUR, WALTER. *Communism and Nationalism in the Middle East.* New York: Frederick A. Praeger, 1956.

———. *The Middle East in Transition, Studies in Contemporary History.* New York: Frederick A. Praeger, 1958.

———. *The Soviet Union and the Middle East.* New York: Frederick A. Praeger, 1959.

LEE, CHONG-SIK. *The Politics of Korean Nationalism.* Berkeley and Los Angeles: University of California Press, 1963.

LENCZOWSKI, GEORGE E. *The Middle East in World Affairs,* 3d ed. Ithaca: Cornell University Press, 1962. An excellent survey, mainly on a country-by-country basis.

LEWIS, BERNARD. *The Middle East and the West.* Bloomington: Indiana University Press, 1964.

LINEBARGER, PAUL M. A., DJANG CHU, and ARDATH W. BURKS. *Far Eastern Governments and Politics,* 2d ed. Princeton, N.J.: D. Van Nostrand Co., 1956.

McLELLAN, GRANT S. *The Middle East in the Cold War.* Bronx, N.Y.: H. W. Wilson Co., 1956.

MATHEW, HELEN G., ed. *Asia in the Modern World.* New York: Mentor Books, 1963.

MYRDAL, GUNNAR. *Asian Drama: An Inquiry into the Poverty of Nations.* 3 vols. New York: The Twentieth Century Fund, 1968. A long-awaited work by a prominent Swedish economist, which reaches gloomy conclusions on conditions in and prospects for the countries of South and Southeast Asia.

NAKAMURA, HAJIME. *The Ways of Thinking of Eastern Peoples,* edited by Philip P. Wiener. Honolulu, Hawaii: East-West Center Press, 1964. A penetrating analysis by a Japanese scholar.

NEHRU, JAWAHARLAL. *The Discovery of India.* New York: The John Day Company, 1946. A remarkable and stimulating work.

NOLTE, RICHARD H., ed. *The Modern Middle East.* New York: Atherton Press, 1963.

PALMER, NORMAN D. *South Asia and United States Policy.* Boston: Houghton Mifflin Company, 1966. Deals mainly with the internal politics and foreign policies of India and Pakistan.

PANIKKAR, K. M. *Asia and Western Dominance.* New York: The John Day Company, 1954. A bitter analysis of "the Vasco da Gama epoch of Asian history" by a well-known Indian scholar-diplomat.

PAYNE, ROBERT. *The Revolt of Asia.* New York: The John Day Company, 1947.

PERETZ, DON. *The Middle East Today.* New York: Holt, Rinehart & Winston, 1963.

REISCHAUER, E. O. and JOHN K. FAIRBANK. *A History of East Asian Civilization.* Vol. I: *East Asia: The Great Tradition.* Vol. 2: *East Asia: The Modern Transformation.* Boston: Houghton Mifflin Company, 1960. One of the best modern surveys.

RIVLIN, BENJAMIN and JOSEPH S. SZYLIOWICZ, eds *The Contemporary Middle East: Tradition and Innovation.* New York: Random House, 1965.

ROMEIN, JAN. *The Asian Century.* Berkeley: University of California Press, 1962. By a leading Dutch historian.

ROSE, SAUL, ed. *Politics in Southern Asia.* London, 1963. Sophisticated essays by several authorities on aspects of politics in South and Southeast Asia.

SANSOM, SIR GEORGE. *The Western World and Japan.* New York: Alfred A. Knopf, 1950. An interpretative work that is much broader than its title indicates.

SCALAPINO, ROBERT A., ed. *The Communist Revolution in Asia: Tactics, Goals, and Achievements.* Englewood Cliffs, N.J.: Prentice-Hall, Inc., 1965.

SPENCER, WILLIAM. *Political Evolution in the Middle East.* Philadelphia: J. B. Lippincott Co., 1962.

STAMP, L. DUDLEY. *Asia; a Regional and Eco-*

nomic Geography, 11th ed. London, 1962. A standard work.

TOYNBEE, ARNOLD J. *The World and the West.* New York: Oxford University Press, 1953. Essays on encounters between civilizations.

VINACKE, HAROLD M. *Far Eastern Politics in the Postwar Period.* New York: Appleton-Century-Crofts, 1956. Good review of politics and international relations of China, Japan, Korea, and Southeast Asia since 1945.

WINT, GUY, ed. *Asia: a Handbook.* New York: Frederick A. Praeger, 1966. Basic information and comprehensive essays by more than 60 leading authorities.

YANAGA, CHITOSHI. *Japan Since Perry.* New York: McGraw-Hill Book Company, 1949.

ZINKIN, MAURICE. *Asia and the West.* London, 1951.

———. *Development for Free Asia,* rev. ed. New York: Oxford University Press, 1963.

17 Latin America in Search of a Future

More than North America, more than Europe, perhaps more than Africa, although certainly less than Asia, Latin America is a land of startling diversity. Much of it is flat and tropical, but much of it is rugged and bleak. It produces most of the world's bananas and much of the world's wool. Some of its people are rich, but most of them are desperately poor. It is the home of distinguished scholars and celebrated artists and at the same time a region of deplorable illiteracy. Some of its people know and cherish democracy, but most of them bear the scars of military dictatorship. Against "gentiles" Latin Americans present something of a common front, but at home they are highly partisan, within their states playing the great game of politics with furious words and occasional bloodletting. Yet Latin America is not all diversity. Most of the states have a common Spanish heritage and a common memory of the Wars of Independence, and they wage a common struggle against formidable natural handicaps. All have a common church, and all give at least lip service to the ideals of freedom. In varying measure all are aware of the overwhelming power of the "Colossus of the North," and many feel a heavy dependence on that power. It is difficult not to read either too much or too little into "Latin America."

Broadly speaking, the term "Latin America" is applied to all of the lands in the Western Hemisphere south of the United States, located in Central and South America and the Caribbean area. Often, however, the term is used more specifically to refer only to those states of the Western Hemisphere that possess a common background of Latin culture. In this narrower sense Latin America is made up of twenty republics: seven in Central America, three in the Caribbean, and ten in South America. It does not include the former British territories which have recently emerged as the newly independent states of Jamaica, Trinidad and Tobago, Guyana, and Barbados, or lands controlled by states outside the Western Hemisphere, such as French Guiana, Surinam, British Honduras, the Falkland Islands, and many small islands in the Caribbean. Nor does it usually include Puerto Rico, which, though primarily Latin in language and culture, is associated with the United States, and has, in fact, come to regard itself as a kind of "third force" with a mission to bring the United States and Latin America into closer ideological communion.

Since Latin America reaches into the northern hemisphere and excludes areas of the southern, it is not synonymous with South America. Neither is it the same as "Hispanic

America." That term is narrower in that its implications are Spanish and Portuguese; it leaves out Haiti, whose backgrounds are French, and Jamaica, Trinidad and Tobago, Guyana, Barbados, and the British possessions in the Caribbean. Hubert Herring suggested that to be logical, to take proper account of the native Indians, the Africans, and the Spanish and Portuguese, we should speak of "Indo-Afro-Ibero-America." "But," he added "for lack of a better term we fall back on 'Latin America.' "[1]

Latin Americans everywhere feel that they are "Americans." During the warm days of the Good Neighbor Policy people in the United States learned that their propensity to monopolize the term irritated Latin Americans. Had not Dwight W. Morrow won instant popularity in Mexico when he ordered the tablet reading "American Embassy" replaced by one reading "United States Embassy"? Were not all the inhabitants of the Americas really Americans? One sensitive North American authority on Latin American history proposed that his countrymen call themselves "United Staters"; and the term *estadounidenses* is not uncommon "south of the border." Ignoring possible complaints from Canadians and Mexicans, Latin Americans put the label *norte americanos* on citizens of the United States. Most of them still use it. Many others are coming to recognize the etymologic plight of the United States: "After all," as one "American" has pointed out, "each of the Latin American nations has a perfectly satisfactory name of its own. Its people are Cubans or Peruvians or Nicaraguans. If we use the name 'Americans' for ourselves, it is because we have no other name, and no slight to the other peoples on the continent is implied in its use."[2]

[1] Hubert Herring, *A History of Latin America* (New York: Alfred A. Knopf, 1955), p. 3.

[2] William L. Schurz, *Latin America* (New York: E. P. Dutton & Co., 1949), p. 9.

The Land

Latin America comprises more than half the land surface of the Western Hemisphere. Its nine and a half million square miles make it almost three times the size of the United States. It is larger than Europe and Australia combined, about three-fourths the size of Africa, and slightly more than half the size of Asia. It is shaped like a triangle, its widest point a little below the Equator. Seventeen of its twenty-four republics, occupying the bulk of the land mass, lie wholly within the tropics; six extend from the tropical zone into the temperate, with two of these — Argentina and Chile — lying almost wholly in the temperate zone; and one — Uruguay — lies wholly in the temperate zone. Its continental mass — South America — projects far to the east and south. The eastern coast of Brazil is twenty-six hundred miles east of New York City, and the southern tip of the continent is seven thousand miles from the southern borders of Texas and more than fifteen hundred miles nearer the Antarctic Circle than any part of Africa. This position removes South America from the main lines of east-west travel, leading it to be sometimes called the "neglected continent."

The dominant topographical feature of mainland Latin America is the mighty Andean chain, the backbone of the great cordilleran mass extending from Cape Horn to the Bering Strait. In the far south the Andean ranges are compact, scarcely a hundred miles in total width, but in Bolivia and Peru they widen to four hundred miles, then narrow again toward the Isthmus of Panama. This cordilleran backbone broadens into sprawling low mountains through most of Central America, then, in Mexico, divides into two flaring chains to form the borders of the great triangular Mexican plateau. For much of their four thousand miles in South America the Andes rise sharply out of the Pacific, leaving only a thin and hot coastal strip at a low elevation. They are very high, with

Russell H. Lenz with adaptation by Joan W. Forbes. Adapted by permission from The Christian Science Monitor © 1964 The Christian Science Publishing Society. All rights reserved.

Latin America

many peaks above twenty thousand feet, and for three thousand miles they offer only a few passes as low as twelve thousand feet. They hold many volcanoes, both dead and intermittently active. In addition to the Andes, South America has two large and rugged plateaus: the Brazilian Highlands, occupying much of southeastern Brazil and varying from two to three thousand feet in height; and the Guiana Highlands, much smaller in area than the Brazilian but covering southern Venezuela and parts of Guyana, Surinam, and French Guiana. In the Caribbean, Haiti and the Dominican Republic are mountainous, whereas Cuba is much less rugged.

The heart of South America is the Amazon basin of more than three million square miles, much of it almost uninhabited jungle. Far to the south lie the flat or rolling lands of southern Brazil, Uruguay, and the rich *pampas* of Argentina, the largest expanse of fertile soil in Latin America. The thousand-mile southern tip of the continent is a cold, windswept tableland.

Topography is always a major determinant of where people live. In temperate climates they may live at low elevations, as they do in Argentina, Chile, Uruguay, and southern Brazil. But much of Latin America lies in the tropics, where the heat may be intense at sea level. In all the Andean republics except Chile, most of the people live in mountain valleys or on plateaus; the coastal strips are too hot and the high mountains too cold. In a few instances, where trade seems to compel it, a city may rise on the hot and humid coast, as, for instance, Maracaibo, Venezuela, Barranquilla, Colombia, and Panama City. Most of the large cities in the tropics, however, are in upland country.

A number of other significant natural features must be mentioned very briefly. The Humboldt Current, flowing northward from the Antarctic, exerts a cooling effect as far north as Peru. The trade winds blow in from the Atlantic to give heavy rainfall to the tropical interior. West winds bring adequate moisture to the western slopes of Colombia and Ecuador and to central and southern Chile, but the intervening three thousand miles get little rain. Mexico receives a heavy rainfall on its eastern slopes, but the great plateau requires irrigation on such a scale that in some years the cost absorbs almost ten percent of the federal budget. The four most important rivers are the Amazon in Brazil; the Orinoco in Venezuela; the Plate system draining parts of Bolivia, Paraguay, Brazil, Uruguay, and Argentina; and the Magdalena in Colombia. For the most part the rivers of South American run in the wrong direction to be of great value to commerce. Moreover, many of them have obstructive rapids, but this condition often facilitates much-needed irrigation, and it provides a vast hydroelectric potential.

Latin America is rather poor in mineral resources, with some notable exceptions. Its greatest shortage is in good coal; its reserves appear to amount to less than 1 per cent of the world's total. It is rich in oil, with Venezuela being by far its leading producer, followed by Mexico, Colombia, Argentina, and Peru. Altogether it possesses about 21 per cent of the world's iron ore reserves. Brazil has been thought to have the largest, but Venezuela may now have taken first place. Chile is the leading copper producer, followed at some distance by Mexico and Peru, but her production is only about half that of the United States. Bauxite ore, the principal source of aluminum, is found in considerable quantity in Guyana, Surinam, French Guiana, and Venezuela and in lesser quantity in Brazil. Mexico has uranium deposits of undetermined importance. Mexico and Peru are important producers of lead and zinc. Bolivia is a large producer of tin, second in the world to Malaysia; it is, in fact, an often-named example of a one-product state, although in fact it produces a number of minerals.[3]

The weakness of the Latin American mineral position is neither in lack of diversity nor in uniformly low production. It is in

[3] Other minerals and their significant Latin American sources are as follows: nitrates — Chile; silver — Mexico, Peru, and Bolivia; gold — Mexico, Colombia, and Brazil; nickel — Brazil and Cuba; manganese — Brazil and Cuba; antimony — Bolivia and Mexico; chromium — Cuba; mercury — Mexico, Peru, and Brazil; beryllium — Brazil; tungsten — Bolivia, Peru, and Mexico; platinum — Colombia and Brazil; vanadium — Peru; quartz crystals — Brazil; diamonds — Brazil; and molybdenum — Mexico, Chile, and Peru.

the smallness of the production of a number of minerals essential to a balanced industrial economy. Furthermore, it must be remembered that the resources that we have been speaking of are distributed — quite unevenly — among many nations. Although oil revenues have long kept the government of Venezuela in an enviable financial position — among the very best in the world — only Brazil seems to have the mineral resources to justify the hope for broad industrialization.

Thus in many respects nature has not been kind to Latin America. True, she has given it enchanting islands, some of the world's best scenery, and scattered bits of "eternal spring," but she has also given it unconquerable mountains, unendurable jungle, tropical heat and tropical diseases, too few good rivers and harbors, too little good soil, and too little in mineral resources. She has made it hard, very hard, for peoples to become integrated, for nations to be governed, and for the common man to do well by his stomach and his mind.

The People

All sorts of theories have been advanced to explain the presence of human life in the Western Hemisphere when Columbus arrived in 1492. The one now accepted is that the Indians had come from Asia by way of the Bering Strait, at least ten thousand years before. Estimates put their number in the year 1500 at perhaps a million north of the Rio Grande and from 7.4 to 45 millions below it. In the course of their American development the best of these had progressed from the food-gathering stage of culture to the point where they knew something — in some cases a great deal — of agriculture, pottery making, weaving, metal working, road building, the use of stone for construction purposes, pictorial writing, mathematics, astronomy, and administrative organization. The vast majority of them, however, were in a far more primitive stage, and many of them were nomadic. None of them knew the use of the wheel. As of 1500 they were divided into a great many ethnic and linguistic groupings, the most advanced of which were the Aztecs of Mexico, and the Incas of the Peruvian area. The great Mayan civilization had already declined.

When, in the wake of Columbus, "Europeans lifted the curtain and revealed the American drama, warfare and conflict were the normal order from the Arctic Circle to Tierra del Fuego. Men were killing one another over hunting grounds, water-holes, river valleys, lake sites, flint beds, salt deposits, arable lands, and water for irrigation." In fact, "the dominating theme in the history of pre-Columbian America was the struggle for land and subsistence."[4] As the Indians appeared to possess vast treasure in precious metals, the invading white men soon convinced themselves that these backward red men desperately needed to be taken in hand and civilized. Speaking only of the Spanish colonies, overlooking the mestizo element that was important from the start, and disregarding what was at least lip service to Indian welfare by the Spanish government, one authority has had this to say of the white men's treatment of the Indians:

> And so they proceeded to civilize them. . . . with or without the consent of the Spanish government, the Indians were, to all intents and purposes, enslaved, and that by the time this enslavement was abolished, their debasement was, in most cases, such that it effectively prevented them from participating in the new order that arose after the Spanish yoke was overthrown. The leaders and inaugurators of the South American republics after 1821 were all creoles, and the governments they established took little cognizance of the native populations except to see to it that they remained in ignorance and poverty and that they constituted no threat to their domination. The justification for this

[4] Bailey W. Diffie, *Latin-American Civilization* (Harrisburg, Pa.: Stackpole Books, 1945), pp. 13, 12.

attitude, if indeed they thought any justification necessary, was that the Indians were utterly incapable of self-government, racially and intellectually.[5]

In the overall view the present population of Latin America, approximately 220,000,000, is made up of descendants of some 10,000,000 to 35,000,000 Indians, some 10,000,000 white immigrants (a 1950 estimate) or their descendants, and several million immigrant Negroes or their descendants. Some investigators put the number of white immigrants at closer to 15,000,000. As one writer remarked, "As a rule, Latin Americans lack a sense of numerical precision, with the result that the national statistical services are likely to suffer from a general disregard of accuracy."[6]

South America has 11 people per square mile, compared to 53 in the United States. Yet most of the people are crowded together on small farms, usually on the poorest soil, and, increasingly, into the coastal cities. The vast Amazon Basin, covering nearly one-third of all Latin America, is very sparsely inhabited, but Brazil, where most of the Basin is located, has two great cities — São Paulo and Rio de Janeiro — which have populations of between three and four million.

Miscegenation has produced a vast mestizo (white-Indian offspring) population and much smaller mulatto (white-Negro) and zambo (Negro-Indian) populations. These mixtures have cross-married; consequently Latin America now has an almost infinite variety of mixed strains. The largest number of immigrants of the republican period have come from Spain, Italy, and Portugal, but there has been considerable diversity in sources. Brazil has the largest Japanese group outside Asia, and the Latin American states collectively have received some 200,000 persons whom they list as "Turks" but who in fact are mostly Syrians. Argentina, Brazil, Cuba, and Uruguay have been the most attractive to Europeans.

If we classify the twenty-four republics of Latin America according to the largest single ethnic grouping, we have the following (the figure gives the percentage of the whole population in the largest group): white — Argentina (97), Uruguay (90), Cuba (73), Brazil (55), and Costa Rica (48); mestizo — Paraguay (95), El Salvador (92), Honduras (91), Mexico (70), Nicaragua (68), Venezuela (68), Chile (68), Panama (65), and Colombia (59); Indian — Ecuador (58), Bolivia (57), Guatemala (53), and Peru (46); Negroid — Haiti (100), Barbados (95); Dominican Republic (85), Jamaica (77), Trinidad and Tobago (40); and East Indian — Guyana (48). The figures do not reveal certain other significant aspects of the ethnic composition: that about 20 per cent of the population of Colombia and Venezuela is white, between 40 and 50 per cent of the people of Guatemala, Costa Rica, Peru, and Brazil are mestizo, 27 per cent of the population of Cuba and over 40 per cent of Guyana are Negroid, 28 per cent of the Mexican population is Indian, and 36 per cent of the population of Trinidad and Tobago is of East Indian origin.[7] Socially — not statistically — these ethnic terms must be used with the realization that "white" is much more broadly construed and that race consciousness is much less acute than among white *norte americanos*.

The significance of ethnic composition lies mostly in the relationship of the various groups to the stream of national life as charted by the dominant group. Indians frequently maintain an isolation or semi-isolation in part imposed by themselves and

[5] Paul Radin, *Indians of South America* (Garden City, N.Y.: Doubleday & Company, 1942), p. 305.

[6] Schurz, p. 64...

[7] These figures were drawn mainly from *1968 Reader's Digest Almanac and Yearbook* (Pleasantville, N.Y.: The Reader's Digest Association. 1967), pp. 61–248 ("Nations of the World")

in part imposed by the political and social order. Both Indians and mestizos have resented their subordinate status; their "demands for recognition . . . [have been] repeatedly voiced; sometimes peacefully, more frequently, violently. Today these demands have become more insistent and more coherent. . . . No stable peace and prosperity can ever come to the republics of this great region unless these demands are granted."[8] But, fortunately, something is being done. Some countries have abandoned their objective of becoming "Spanish" states and have recognized that they are, and always will be, mestizo states. Led by Mexico, virtually every Latin American state has undertaken some constructive action in behalf of the suppressed elements in its population. Many Catholic orders have assumed special responsibilities in this work, and the *apristas* in Peru have sought to make Indian welfare a basic concern of an international political party. The Inter-American Congress on Indian Life held in Mexico in 1940 adopted a body of resolutions that represented "a veritable charter of Indian rights for the guidance of the American republics in formulating their Indian policies." The Andean Indian Programme, launched by the UN and its specialized agencies in 1953 at the request of Bolivia, Ecuador, and Peru, is "probably the most ambitious and complex technical assistance program ever attempted by international organization."[9] Five international agencies are "here combined in a cooperative effort to raise the living standards of ten million people [virtually all Indians] and integrate them into the lives of their countries."

Although the overall rate of population growth in Latin America is probably the highest in the world, this area contains only about one-fifteenth of the world's people. In many Latin American countries a substantial proportion of the people congregate in or near a few large cities. The cities are the germinating centers of new ideas and of social change. Indeed, "the city is the only place where there is light in Latin America. . . . Beyond [it] is darkness, the endless stretches of land still unilluminated by the progress and change of this century."[10] The city is also the center of unrest and of radical movements, and most Latin American cities, including Rio, Caracas, Santiago, and Lima, have appalling slums.

The Historical Setting

The study of the historical background of the present-day Latin American states should include careful attention to the aboriginal culture, an analysis of the many influences of Spain and Portugal, an examination of the conflict of interests that led to independence, and a review of the struggles of the young republics for democracy and economic well-being. In this account we shall have to be very brief. Having already taken a quick look at the Indian natives, we shall now turn to the imprint of Spain, the winning of independence, and the trend of developments in the republican era.

The Imprint of Spain. At the time of the discovery of America "no part of Europe had suffered more from the shock of conquest or felt the impact of more diverse races and cultures than had the peninsula of Spain." To the extent that a "race" may be said to have evolved, it was "sober" and "robust," a people "endowed with endurance and tenacity, to whom the opportunity for wealth and adventure aboard made a peculiarly strong appeal"; and "the national temper displayed a hardness that sometimes amounted to cruelty, as well as a certain intellectual indolence which explains in part the exaggerated attachment to tradition."

[8] Radin, p. 306.

[9] See Agnese Nelms Lockwood, "Indians of the Andes," *International Conciliation*, No. 508 (May, 1956).

[10] Joseph Maier and Richard W. Weatherhead, eds., *The Politics of Change in Latin America* (New York: Frederick A. Praeger, 1965), p. 8.

Five centuries of almost constant warfare against the infidel Moors had "engendered a vigorous military spirit and love for an irregular and venturesome mode of life — together with something of a contempt for the less spectacular peacetime arts . . . [and] an ideal of religious solidarity that was easily transformed into intolerance and fanaticism."[11] All these qualities were to be displayed in the conquest and rule of the New World.

To Spanish America went soldiers to fight, adventurers to be thrilled, ambitious men to gain wealth and power, and priests to save souls. Although some of the colonizers were farmers or artisans, few of them took their wives along. Thus the Spaniards who sailed off to America were not prepared to build a sound agrarian society or establish a commerical order. They were eminently qualified, however, to fight heroically and victoriously against appalling obstacles posed by nature and the Indians, to explore a vast continent with courage and resolution unsurpassed in the history of adventure, to carry the flag and the cross into and across millions of square miles of jungle and mountain, to wrest fabulous wealth in gold and silver from almost inaccessible mines, and, in dealing with the Indians, to enslave, to exterminate, to convert, or to mate, as circumstances seemed to direct. They were qualified to build one of the most extensive empires that the world has ever seen. But they created only an empire and neither free men nor sturdy nations.

For about three centuries Spain ruled an American empire of more than six million square miles, and Portugal one of some three million square miles. The only suggestion of self-government appeared in the *cabildo abierto,* or open meeting of the town council, but this had only the shadow of the substance of the New England town meeting of about the same period. "Power, however benevolently intended, came from above,"[12] and there was no effort or intention to educate the people to share that power. Spanish rule remained a paternal autocracy to the end.

The economic pattern, too, was monopolistic. The colonies were to produce raw materials, particularly minerals, and they were to buy their manufactured goods in Spain. Commerce was rigidly controlled in the interest of the crown and of privileged merchants in the home country. But foreign traders — most of all the English — were far more concerned with what was possible than with what was merely legal. Contraband trade sprang up and grew to substantial proportions — eventually far outdistancing the legal trade. Although the restrictions were relaxed in the eighteenth century, and Spain's trade with her colonies soon more than doubled in volume, the colonists began to sense the possibilities in unrestricted trade. Here was a prime motivation to widespread evasion of the law and, in fact, to independence.

The pattern of social life in the colonies reflected both the Iberian mind and the American environment. The Spanish are a gregarious people, and it was natural that they should build an urban society. Some of their cities began as trading points, others as mining centers, and still others as seats of political and ecclesiastical authority. The great landholders preferred the glamour of the cities, often leaving their estates to be run by overseers, and the small landowners and the peasants lived in villages rather than on lonely farms as the English colonists so often did. The born-in-Spain Spaniards — the *peninsulares* — who held virtually all the high positions in state and church, stood at the head of the social hierarchy; next came the colonial-born full-blooded Spaniards, or creoles, often enterprising and wealthy; next

[11] Clarence H. Haring, *The Spanish Empire in America* (New York: Oxford University Press, 1947), p. 27.

[12] Robin A. Humphreys, *The Evolution of Modern Latin America* (New York: Oxford University Press, 1946), p. 30.

came the mestizos or persons of mixed blood, mostly farmers but frequently artisans or owners of small businesses; and at the bottom stood the Indians and Negroes and mixtures of the two races, almost altogether menial laborers. Since status was largely a matter of blood, tradition, and landholding, the social order tended to be a rather rigid one. More recently the emergence of a class of successful business and professional men has considerably modified the old pattern. In Brazil the color line is less distinct than in the United States, but it has by no means been erased.

Next to the monarchy the strongest institution was the Roman Catholic Church. It grew to be immensely wealthy and powerful, with bishops and archbishops at times defying governors and viceroys. It must be credited with most of the schooling and virtually all of the organized care of the sick and the destitute. It was the church and its orders that founded and maintained the universities that so early arose in Spanish America; and it was the church that did most to protect and civilize the Indians. Its influence was not all good, for it sought to enforce conformity of thought, if need be by the confiscation of property and the burning of heretics. It was at times ruthlessly acquisitive. Although itself an arm of the state, it endeavored ceaselessly to exalt its own power at the expense of the secular authority. It still possesses great strength in parts of Spanish America, and, as we shall later observe, it still commands fervent loyalty while at the same time it is bitterly attacked.

Briefly, the imprint of Spain on her American empire was in part that of the Spanish institutions. When these encountered a world of nature — or many worlds of nature — and a great Indian population totally outside the Spanish experience, the result was conflict, confusion, adaptation, and the emergence of a society which was neither Spanish nor Indian but Latin American. The creoles within this order were likely to be adventuresome, ambitious, too conscious of blood and position, arrogant, scornful of manual labor, and indifferent to the poverty and misery of those around them. The Indians and Negroes, resigned, plodding, and wretchedly poor, formed the mudsill of society. Between these two levels increasing millions of mestizos struggled for bread and manhood; underprivileged, politically illiterate, and too easily led, they would later form the "masses" of most of the Latin American republics.

The imprint of Portugal on her colony of Brazil was different in a number of particulars. Neither the state nor the church was quite so authoritarian. The mining economy was less important, the agricultural more important. As some historians have pointed out, the methods used in the colonization of Brazil more nearly approximated those of the English in North America than those of the Spanish in South America. Nevertheless Portugal gave her colonists few lessons in self-government, and only the fortunate circumstance of the long rule of a benevolent monarch gave Brazilians some preparation for governing themselves.

The Winning of Independence. The literature of the American Revolution, with its emphasis on the rights of man — to life, liberty, and the pursuit of happiness — made a stirring appeal to those Latin American thinkers who, notwithstanding discouragement from state and church, had already begun to yearn for greater political and economic freedom. Even more profound was the impact of the French Revolution. Francisco de Miranda, Mariano Moreno, Antonio Nariño, and the great Simón Bolívar knew the philosophy upon which French revolutionaries had sought to erect a republican France. Given the repressive colonial policy of Spain, and given the taste of a broader trade through British contraband practices and the relaxation of controls incident to Spanish involvement in the Napoleonic Wars, many restive minds in Latin

America were ready to break from the mother country when the opportunity came to them almost without their connivance.

Despite a few scattered, hopeless revolts and the agitation of some early advocates of Spanish-American independence, notably Francisco de Miranda and Antonio Nariño, the Spanish colonies in America were essentially loyal when Napoleon Bonaparte invaded Spain in 1808. In one important particular, however, the situation had changed from earlier days. The American-born Spaniards now outnumbered the *peninsulares*. Many of them were wealthy and educated, and since they did not have their forbears' loyalty to Spain, their first love was for the only home they had ever known and for the only land in which they might achieve personal ambitions. Consequently, when Napoleon set aside the Spanish king and put a Bonaparte in his place and Spaniards responded by organizing resistance in local councils or *juntas,* the creoles — or *Americanos,* as they had come to call themselves — for a time made common cause with the *juntas* in Spain and the loyal Spaniards in the New World by setting up American *juntas* to govern in the name of Ferdinand VII. They quickly sensed the fact that they had thereby put the colonies in an intermediate position between subordination to Spain and self-rule. Even before the restoration of Ferdinand in 1814 they had provided the stimulus and the leadership for isolated assertions of independence and for sporadic revolt. Within a short time the colonials had made frank resort to force, with the leadership of the forces of northern South America coming under Simón Bolívar and those of southern South America under José de San Martın and Bernardo O'Higgins.

By late 1825 the wars had been won, and South America had been freed from Spain. Mexico achieved her independence in 1821 with little fighting, and in 1825 Brazil became independent of Portugal with even less fighting. Spanish control of Santo Domingo was terminated in 1821. Haiti had asserted her independence from France in 1804. The breakup of Great Colombia into Venezuela, Colombia, and Ecuador in 1830 and the fragmentation of Central America by 1840 put the number of Latin American states at seventeen. The Dominican Republic resumed her independence in 1844 after twenty-two years of union with Haiti; Cuba won independence from Spain in 1898; and Panama achieved statehood in 1903 by secession from Colombia. With these developments the roll of the Latin American states which emerged from the Spanish and Portuguese empires in the New World was completed.

Republics without Democracy. The Latin Americans faced the problems of nation-building and state-building with far more optimism than circumstances warranted. Perhaps too much influenced by the example of the United States, they apparently believed that independence, a written constitution, and a republican form of government would at once bring them the stability and the prosperity that had been the good fortune of the English colonists in North America. But they reckoned without an awareness of many differences. Civil war soon became the norm almost everywhere. Bolívar himself in 1830, within a few months of his death, deplored the "anarchy" in Colombia, and declared himself "ashamed to say it, but independence is the sole benefit we have gained, at the sacrifice of all others."[13] Bloodshed, dictatorship, and poverty fell to the lot of most of the Latin American states to the end of the nineteenth century, and they remain the lot of many of them to this day.

By the year 1900 only three of the states of Latin America had shown some promise of political stability and progress toward democratic institutions. In Brazil, after a half-century of peace and development under

[13] Message to the Constituent Congress of the Republic of Colombia, January 20, 1830.

Pedro II, a bloodless revolution brought the monarchy to a close in 1889 and prepared the way for a federal republic. An excellent constitution was adopted in 1891, and by 1900 Brazil had begun a period of unsteady progress toward stability and prosperity. In Chile the reign of the *caudillos* virtually ceased with the adoption of the constitution of 1833; and the landed aristocracy took over the reins of power, giving Chile stability if not democracy. Argentina's early struggles between Buenos Aires and the provinces ended in 1861 with a victory for Argentine union, and under the leadership of a number of able presidents the country entered upon a long period of material progress and comparative tranquility. These three — Brazil, Chile, and Argentina — comprise the full role of those states of Latin America that by 1900 had moved perceptibly toward political maturity.

Four additional states entered the select list within the next few decades: Colombia, Costa Rica, Mexico, and Uruguay. Two of the older democracies — Argentina and Brazil — went under the heel of dictators and have since found it difficult to regain their constitutionalism. Chile has been so sorely beset by inflationary woes in the postwar years that her democracy has seemed to be at stake, but she has thus far survived. Colombia, which had entered upon a long period of democratic promise soon after the opening of the new century, succumbed in 1949 to bloody dissension and from 1953 to 1957 to a military dictatorship. Some 150,000 persons were reported killed in civil strife by late 1955.[14] With some brief interludes, Costa Rica has followed the path of constitutional government since 1902. In the years since her great revolution of 1910–20, Mexico has settled down to stable government under the qualified democracy of a one-party system. Uruguay in the first half of this century established herself as probably the most vigorous and progressive democracy in Latin America, but in recent years the nation has faced disrupting economic problems. Elsewhere, only here and there in recent years has a strong and able president momentarily brightened an otherwise dreary record of dictatorship and bad government. Some Cubans said that they had not had an honest president since Tomás Estrada Palma — their first one. Other Latin Americans may speak in much the same vein.

On the whole, Latin America seems to be almost as far from political stability as it was a century ago. In recent years, as in past decades, there has been a dreary succession of coups, revolts, civil wars, assassinations, and overturns of regimes, good and bad. Few Latin American states have had much experience in democracy. On the basis of evaluations by a number of specialists in 1945, 1950, and 1955, Professor Russell Fitzgibbon ranked Uruguay, Costa Rica, and Chile as the most democratic of the states south of the border, with Colombia, Cuba, Mexico, Brazil, and Argentina also well up on the list.[15] Uruguay, Costa Rica, Chile, and Mexico would still hold a relatively high rating, although democracy in each is subject to intermittent challenges and pressures. The delicate political arrangement designed to restore order to Colombia is so beset with problems that the prospects for democratic processes and stability can only be described as uncertain. Brazil and Argentina are under military rule, whose leaders promise economic reforms and an eventual resumption of more democratic practices. Castro's Cuba, of course, must be removed from the list of democratic states, unless it is described as a Latin American version of a "people's democracy" of the Communist type.

A classification issued early in 1964 gen-

[14] See the Latin American edition of *Time*, November 14, 1955, p. 34.

[15] "How Democratic Is Latin America?" *Inter-American Economic Affairs*, IX, No. 4 (Spring, 1956), 65–77. See also Russell H. Fitzgibbon, "A Statistical Evaluation of Latin-American Democracy," *The Western Political Quarterly*, IX, No. 3 (September, 1956), 607–619.

erously listed eight Latin American states — Brazil, Chile, Colombia, Costa Rica, Jamaica, Mexico, Trinidad and Tobago, and Uruguay — as democracies. Cuba, the Dominican Republic, Guatemala, Haiti, Honduras, Nicaragua, and Paraguay were classified as dictatorships, and the remaining Latin American states — Argentina, Bolivia, Ecuador, El Salvador, Panama, Peru, and Venezuela — were grouped together under the suggestive heading: "dictatorship sometimes, democracy other times."[16]

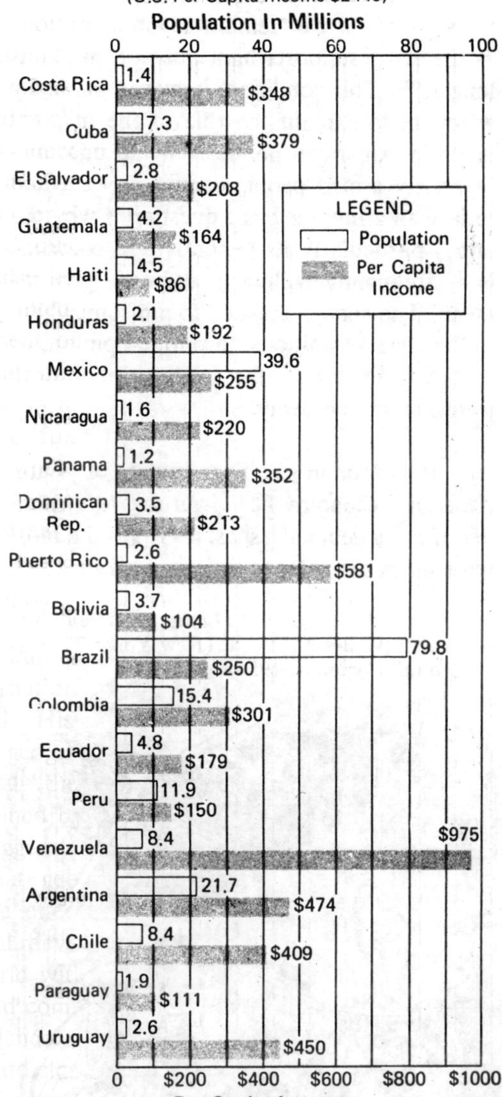

The Philadelphia Inquirer, October 18, 1965.

Current Problems

Government. Most of the states have a long record of political instability, corruption, and undemocratic practices. "Latin America," said Germán Arciniegas, "is synonymous with instability."[17] Nowhere in the world do the public leaders subscribe more passionately to the ideals of democracy, and perhaps nowhere else in the so-called free world does performance lag so far behind professions. While part of the discrepancy is to be accounted for by sheer demagoguery, some of it must be charged to conditions which make even an approximation to real democracy impossible. At times instability gives way to excessive stability: dictators put an iron grip on entire states and hang on until revolutions or death. Usually they bleed their victims for personal profit, but in some instances they have been well-meaning and financially honest men. They have sought to give "democracy" much more the meaning of "independence," of freedom from foreign domination, than of government by the people, and they have succeeded all too well. Dictatorship commonly falls to the lot of weak and backward states, with neither a middle class with a stake in law and order nor the slightest tradition of constitutional government; but the past few years have demonstrated that even progressive states with earlier promising records of constitutionalism may, for a time at least, be bound and gagged by a "strong man." This has happened in Argentina, Brazil, and Colombia.

The governments of most Latin American countries are "run by the generals, with the aid of the colonels and a few civilians." "Every president, whether soldier or civilian,

[16] *World Events* (a news publication of Silver Burdett in association with *Time* and *Life*), Special Map Issue: Vol. II, Issue 18, January 20, 1964.

[17] Germán Arciniegas, *The State of Latin America* (New York: Alfred A. Knopf, 1952), p. 355.

knows that he can remain in office as long as the army supports him, but not one hour longer."[18] This condition, however, is hardly adequate to explain the role of the military in Latin American politics. While unarmed or poorly armed people cannot be expected to face an army, the basic question is why the army, particularly its generals and colonels, is so frequently willing to defy the government. The answer must be found somewhere in the state's traditions, in public opinion, or in the character of the leadership of both government and army.

The Economy. The future of Latin America's economy has given rise to a number of hotly debated issues. Perhaps the most basic of these relates to the so-called Prebisch thesis, which derived its name from the distinguished Argentine economist Raul Prebisch, formerly Executive Secretary of the UN's Economic Commission for Latin America and later Secretary-General of the United Nations Conference on Trade and Development. It was contained in ECLA's *Economic Survey of Latin America, 1949,* published in 1951, and embraced in the following specific findings of the *Survey:* (1) The two-hundred-year-old industrial revolution has so far been concentrated in a few industrial centers (Great Britain, Western Europe, the United States, and Japan) and has had little effect on the peripheral areas. (2) Such improvements in productivity as have taken place in the peripheral areas have been largely confined to the industries producing raw materials for the industrial centers. (3) This has led to a situation in which most of the gains in productivity in the peripheral countries have been "exported" to the industrial centers, and have done little to advance the well-being of the people of the peripheral areas. (4) Unless some kind of positive action is taken, the long-run outlook is for a continuing deterioration of the relative position of the peripheral areas.[19]

These findings of the ECLA *Survey* said in effect that "the peoples of Latin America are caught in the inexorable workings of a process that condemns them to the role of second- or third-class citizens in the modern world economy," and they further carry the "implication . . . that only strong action by the governments of Latin American countries can break through this process and bring the fuller life these people so earnestly desire." In the opinion of Benjamin A. Rogge, a vigorous critic of the Prebisch thesis, the policies recommended in the *Survey* "would bring economic nationalism and a whole host

[18] Austin F. Macdonald, *Latin American Politics and Government,* 2d ed. (New York: Thomas Y. Crowell Company, 1954), p. 16.

Valtman in The Hartford Times

"I'd rather have them drink more coffee"

[19] This discussion of the Prebisch thesis is largely based on Benjamin A. Rogge, "Economic Development in Latin America: The Prebisch Thesis," *Inter-American Economic Affairs,* IX, No. 4 (Spring, 1956), 24–49.

of new tensions among the countries of the world," and they ran sharply counter to his conviction that "the best chance for economic development *cum* freedom will exist in a country whose government undertakes little more than the limited but very important task of creating an environment in which all the constructive forces of private initiative and private enterprise can be released for the tasks of economic progress."[20] Professor Rogge suggested that governments first concentrate on the traditional functions of government — "so necessary to economic development": the police force, the legal system, the monetary system, highways, education, and the like. When these have been brought to a high level of efficiency, the people should then decide what additional services they may ask of the government.

The Prebisch thesis really involves two issues: the fundamental nature of the Latin American economy of the future and the role of government in the promotion of national economies. Other important issues that have arisen relate to heavy or basic industries versus light or secondary industries, diversification versus specialization in agricultural production, the source of needed investment capital, the barriers to the investment of foreign capital, the limits of technical assistance, self-sufficiency in food production, and a new inter-American lending agency. Latin Americans themselves sharply disagree on the foreign aid policy of the United States as it relates to Latin America. Some contend that Uncle Sam is niggardly and that he helps only when he needs friends; others insist that his much greater aid to European and Asian countries is in behalf of the entire free world and that his generosity has been without parallel in history.

The mixed record of the Alliance for Progress since its inception in 1961 is an indication at once of the obstacles to and the possibilities of effective United States-Latin American cooperation in the economic development of the areas south of the United States border. Certainly even a vast infusion of outside aid cannot bring the underdeveloped states of Latin America into the modern world unless those states undergo fundamental economic, social, and political reforms. These reforms must come from within; they can hardly be imposed from without.

Social Changes; Budgets. With some notable exceptions, poverty and illiteracy are present to a marked degree in Latin American states. The two conditions are interrelated, and behind them lies a variety of causes: insufficient good soil; uncongenial temperature; lack of diversity in mineral resources; rugged terrain and poor communications; in many instances large Indian populations isolated by geography, traditions, or language, or all three; limited markets for local products; small national revenues for education, social welfare, and necessary services; a church-dominated school system that gives too little attention to liberal arts and technical education; a possible shortage of investment capital — although some observers deny this and point to the sizable investment (nearly two billion dollars) which Latin Americans hold in the United States; and the neglect of the welfare of the politically impotent masses. Whatever the causes, the consequences are national weakness and backwardness.

Critics of Latin America's achievements in education, health, and similar areas should be mindful of the fact that it is working with very little money. In 1950 the total national income of the twenty republics was about one-eighth that of the United States, and the per capita incomes were in about the same proportion. Although the average per capita income of the five highest-income countries (Venezuela, Cuba, Uruguay, Panama, and Argentina) was only about one-

[20] *Ibid.*, p. 24; and Benjamin A. Rogge, "The Role of Government in Latin American Economic Development," *Inter-American Economic Affairs*, IX, No. 3 (Winter, 1955), 65–66.

fifth that of the United States, it was four times that of the five lowest-income states (Bolivia, Peru, Ecuador, Paraguay, and Haiti). In 1953 the total of the twenty national budgets of Latin America amounted to less than $6 billion; the United States budget was nearly $75 billion.[21] Since then the disparities in both total and per capita income have increased rather than diminished. As late as 1964 only two nations in all of Latin America — Venezuela and Trinidad and Tobago — had a per capita income of more than $400, and in seven — Peru, Guatemala, Brazil, Ecuador, Paraguay, Bolivia, and Haiti — the per capita income was $150 or less. Some of the states of Latin America have smaller annual budgets than a few of the wealthier universities in the United States. Obviously government revenues are often woefully inadequate for doing what needs to be done.

Social Stratification. Latin America has a much better record than the United States in the matter of discrimination against nonwhites, "but after all of this has been said, it has to be added that Latin-American society has remained stratified, immobile, and, if a colonial expression may be used, divided into *castas.*" Compared with the United States, "there is noticeably less vertical mobility," and "the barrier made by wealth, race and occupation is markedly obvious in its effect upon social mobility."[22] There is, in addition, another source of stratification — that between urban and rural societies. Whether because of an instinctive rejection of the white man's values or because discrimination and suppression have left them only the security of ancient customs and isolated living, the Indians and many of the mestizos of Latin America have never caught the liberal creoles' enthusiasm for democracy, education, and money-making. In short, they have taken very little to what we call "Westernization." With an increasing number of exceptions, they have retained primitive ways and dress, kept to large plantations or to their own scanty patches of soil in the mountain valleys and jungles, accepted a Christian veneer for their pagan religions, and eschewed urbanization, schooling, and voting. They have trodden old trails with uncomplaining fatalism, turning aside only now and then to shed their blood for an ambitious *caudillo*. "The major single issue in the political destiny of Latin America is to bridge this gap between the rural Indian and mestizo community and the nation."[23] An important consequence of rural isolation has been that political leadership has been regional and personal — that the *caudillo* could become the undisputed master of a tiny region or a large one. There, where his word was law, he could sustain the central government or conspire to overthrow it.

The Church. Dissension — often bitter and at times bloody — has been occasioned by differences of opinion about the proper role of the Roman Catholic Church, by its propensity to take a hand in politics, and by its failure to exert a progressive social influence. The overwhelming majority of Latin Americans are Catholics, although one figure puts the "merely nominal Catholics" at 70 per cent of the whole number.[24] For a long time many Latin Americans remembered that the church had supported Spain in the South American Wars of Independence; and many Catholics, "nominal" and otherwise, have fought for the separation of church and state. Some states have made that separation; others have not. That church-state relations are still a subject of bitter controversy

[21] These figures have been compiled from tables in Herring, p. 776.

[22] Frank Tannenbaum, "Democracy and Rural Education in Latin America," in Ángel del Río, ed., *Responsible Freedom in the Americas* (Garden City, N.Y.: Doubleday & Company, 1955), p. 6.

[23] Tannenbaum, p. 11.

[24] *Hispanic-American Report,* VIII (August, 1955), 337.

is demonstrated by the oppression of Protestants in Colombia, the circumstances attending the fall of Perón in Argentina, and Guatemala's difficulties in drafting a new constitution.

The separation of church and state does not in itself take the Church out of politics. In Brazil, where separation took place more than half a century ago, the Catholic clergy openly campaigned for Eurico Dutra in 1945; the Catholic Electoral League openly opposed Café Filho, a Presbyterian, in the elections of 1950; and in August, 1953, Carlos Cardinal Vasconcelos, Archbishop of São Paulo, issued the following statement on a move in the Brazilian congress to enact divorce laws: "Should any Brazilian Government dare to institute divorce in Brazil, the people would have the right to oppose by armed resistance this attempt to undermine the foundation of Christian family life in this country."[25] In Brazil — where Protestants are stronger than in any other Latin American state, and where Protestantism "is growing faster than in any other country on earth"[26] — Protestants complain of the barriers against Protestant missionary activity in some parts of Latin America, and they "point to Catholicism's double standard — the demand for full freedom to convert the United States while attempting to deny freedom to Evangelicals [Protestants] and maintain a monopoly in Latin America."[27]

One authority on Latin American institutions has declared that "it is accurate to state that the Church in Latin America is not social-minded," that "even in the moral and ethical fields, Latin American Catholicism tends more to form than to content," that "the evidence indicates that the hierarchy in Latin America are more interested in the ritual of Catholicism than in any such social policies as might permit each individual an equal opportunity to develop his potentialities," and that "in those countries in which there are fewer Catholic churches and less demonstration of faith in the form of public ceremonials, the largest amount of progress toward democracy has been realized."[28] If these conclusions are correct, it is understandable that Latin American liberals should make strenuous protest and that the role of the church should offer divisive issues.

There is growing evidence that in some countries of Latin America the Church is developing a social conscience, and is making rather successful adaptations to the forces of social change. Indeed, the editors of a symposium on *The Politics of Change in Latin America,* published in 1964, maintained that the church in Latin America is "resilient and remorseful," that it is "the institution most receptive to the forces of change," and that it is "adjusting to these forces more rapidly than are the traditional elites."[29] This does not necessarily imply any marked propensity toward social reform, but, to the extent that it is valid, it does suggest either that the conventional treatment of the church as a citadel of social conservatism needs to be modified or that the attitude of the church has undergone a rather basic change.

American Influences. It seems correct to suggest that in two particulars the example of the United States may have been harmful to the newer republics of Latin America. One relates to government, the other to business.

The United States Constitution of 1787 provided Latin Americans with a pattern for republicanism, and from this document, as well as from the Declaration of Independence, they have freely borrowed words and phrases. But the Constitution established a federal system and separated state and

[25] Quoted in William S. Stokes, "Catholicism and Democracy in Latin America," in del Río, p. 374.

[26] *Hispanic-American Report,* p. 337.

[27] *Ibid.,* p. 337.

[28] Stokes, pp. 368, 366.

[29] Maier and Weatherhead, p. 6.

church, and the efforts to incorporate these two principles into their own political structures have given Latin Americans their most persistent internal issues. The Constitution also set up an elaborate system of checks and balances which Latin Americans have never really understood. In fact, the whole North American scheme of government assumed an experience in self-government which the Latin Americans totally lacked, and it related to a social and economic order quite unknown to them. The experience of Brazil suggests that San Martín and others may have been right in their preference for an evolutionary period under constitutional monarchs. Latin Americans had too long been steeped in the authoritarian tradition to shift smoothly into responsible democracy.

The spectacular prosperity of the United States appears to have done much to influence the economic thinking of Latin America since the Wars of Independence. For these lands the era of the "robber barons" has not yet ended. The correctives which asserted themselves in the United States — effective representative government, powerful labor organizations, a free press and free speech, public social welfare programs, a growing social conscience, and good public relations — have not been fully operative in Latin America. Until they are operative, many Latin Americans will misunderstand the free enterprise system, and for them it will remain a qualified blessing.

Communism. Although fascism is by no means entirely a nightmare of the past in Latin America, communism probably represents a more deadly threat to the democracies of the Western world than that ever posed by fascism. Unlike fascism, it marches under the banner of democracy and, again unlike fascism, it presumes no feeling of racial superiority and no divine appointment. Furthermore, "in the Latin American republics where exploitation of the masses is a commonplace whether by the foreign capitalist or by the national politician, the glittering promises of Communism are more persuasive and alluring than the realities of a none too successful democracy."[30]

Marxian communism found articulate leaders in Latin America during the decade of the 1820's, and with few exceptions its spokesmen were sincerely interested in bettering the conditions of the lower classes. About 1930, however, Latin American Communists fell under the influence of the Comintern, whereupon they lost their earlier patriotic character and became the agents of international communism. The evidence suggests that they have at one time or another achieved rather formidable strength in six Latin American republics.

In terms of membership, according to 1965 estimates of the United States Department of State, the largest numbers of Communists in Latin America were in Argentina (65,000), Mexico (50,000), Brazil (31,000), Venezuela (30,000), and Chile (27,500).[31] In three of these countries — Argentina, Brazil, and Venezuela — and in more than half of the Latin American states, the Communist Party is legally banned. Most of the Communist parties of Latin America, including those in Argentina and Chile, are pro-Soviet in their orientation, but in Brazil, Colombia, Mexico, and Paraguay there is an open split between pro-Soviet and pro-Chinese factions; in Cuba and Venezuela, for different reasons and under different circumstances, the Communists prefer to be "neutral" or to take "no stand" in the Sino-Soviet dispute, and in Ecuador and Peru they are too riven by internal factions to assume any well-defined external orientation.

Measured by votes, communism has won

[30] Graham H. Stuart, *Latin America and the United States*, 5th ed. (New York: Appleton-Century-Crofts, 1955), p. 88.

[31] *World Strength of the Communist Party Organizations*, U.S. Department of State, 1965.

its greatest victory in Brazil, and Latin America's best-known Communist is a Brazilian, Luis Carlos Prestes. After being outlawed in 1927, the Communists supported the Vargas dictatorship briefly after its rise in 1931 and then, after an unsuccessful revolt in 1935, remained inactive until 1945. After ten years in jail Prestes was released in 1945 and his party again legalized; in return, Prestes supported the Vargas nominee for the presidency. In the elections that followed, the Communist Party received more than 600,000 popular votes and won fourteen seats in the Chamber of Deputies. Prestes was elected to the Senate. The Communist vote rose to about 800,000 in 1947. Soon thereafter the party was dissolved by government action. From 1956 to 1964, during the troubled regimes of three mercurial presidents, Juscelino Kubitschek, Janio Quadros, and João Goulart, Communists again became active in the Brazilian scene; but in the spring of 1964 Goulart was overthrown by a military uprising, and the new government, headed by General Humberto Castelo Branco, was strongly anti-Communist and took quick measures to expel Communists from the Congress and other influential public bodies.

The Communists won their first Latin American cabinet posts in Chile. On instructions from Moscow the Chilean Communists backed the Radical Party in a Popular Front and gained a number of seats in the Congress in the 1937 elections and additional seats in the 1941 elections. As a reward for Communist support President Gabriel Gonzáles Videla appointed three of their number to cabinet posts in 1946. These men proved troublesome, and five months later he ousted them. When the Communists encouraged strikes in the copper mines in reprisal, Gonzáles Videla induced the congress to outlaw the Communist Party; and he broke off relations with the Soviet Union and Czechoslovakia and gave Tito's diplomats their passports. His successors, Carlos Ibanez and Jorge Alessandri, were usually able to keep the Communists under control. In 1964 Eduardo Frei, a Christian Democrat, won a landslide victory over the candidate put up by a left-wing coalition of Socialists and Communists. His election was hailed as a victory for moderate democratic socialism over communism that might set an encouraging pattern in Chile and elsewhere in Latin America.

The Communist Party in Argentina was outlawed in 1930 but was legalized in 1945 when dictator Perón saw its value in his diplomatic battle with the United States. The Stalinist wing became intermittently anti-Perón; much of its hostility to Perón arose from the rivalry of labor unions. Perón kept the Communist Party within view as part of the window dressing for his Third Position — neither communism nor capitalism but a third philosophy, *justicialismo* — but he never let it get out of hand. The post-Perón regimes have dealt roughly with both *peronistas* and Communists, at times charging that the two groups had joined forces.

The Communist Party in Mexico polled its largest vote in 1946 — about 40,000 — but its importance, though never great, has been out of proportion to its voting strength. The difference has been Vincente Lombardo Toledano, Latin America's Number One Communist intellectual and Number Two political leader. Toledano's influence has derived from his role in organized labor, his talents as a writer and orator, and his newspaper, *El Popular*. He organized Mexican labor into the CTM (*Confederación de Trabajadores Mexicanos*) and headed the CTAL (*Confederación de Trabajadores de la América Latina*), an inter-American labor organization which followed the Soviet lead throughout World War II. Unlike the tolerant Cárdenas (1934–40), later presidents have taken a strong position against the Communists. Partly because of the economic prosperity and the programs of social reform, the

Communists have lost much of their earlier strength in both labor and politics. In the presidential elections of 1964 Toledano eventually supported the successful candidate of the Institutional Revolutionary Party (PRI), Gustavo Díaz Ordaz.

The Communists in Cuba established themselves during the corrupt regime of Machado (1925–33), received nearly 200,000 votes in the elections of 1947, and then began to decline in number and influence. On regaining power in 1952 Batista moved against all Communist-front groups, driving their leaders from the country and closing their newspapers. He paid little attention at first to the "26 of July" movement, launched in 1956 by Fidel Castro, but on January 1, 1959, he was forced to flee from Cuba, and Castro assumed control of the island. There may be some doubt of the extent of Castro's commitment to communism prior to 1959 or of the Communist influence in this "26 of July" movement; but there can be little doubt of Castro's increasing espousal of the Communist approach after he came into power. In 1961 he openly proclaimed his allegiance to the Communist camp. Thus Cuba became the first Communist-oriented state in the Western Hemisphere and a center for the training of agents and the preparation of subversive activities in many other Latin American countries. Because of these developments, the OAS, on July 26, 1964, voted to impose both economic and diplomatic sanctions on Cuba, and all of its members except Mexico broke off relations with the Castro regime. But Cuba under Castro remains the head-center of Communism in Latin America.

Prior to Castro's victory in Cuba, the conquest of Guatemala was the supreme achievement of communism in Latin America. After several years of devious operations behind a variety of front organizations, the Communists elected Arbenz Guzmán to the presidency in 1950 and instituted a program of nationalization aimed primarily at the holdings of the United Fruit Company. Although the Communist regime was overthrown by Castillo Armas in 1954 — apparently with some United States support — and the beachhead of international communism destroyed, escaping Communists injected a subversive influence into the politics of other Central American states.

Elsewhere in Latin America communism has won some momentary prestige here and there, but it has nowhere assumed the proportions of a serious threat. It has achieved its greatest success where labor has been best organized, but as labor unions have gained some sophistication they have spurned the Communist line. The postwar prosperity, the technical assistance programs of the United Nations and the United States, and the opposition of Latin American dictators and democrats have substantially reduced the measure of the Communist threat. In recent years the OAS has taken a resolute stand against the operations of international communism, especially since two important reports in 1964 — one submitted by the Special Security Commission, the other by a five-nation investigating body — revealed that Communist subversion throughout Latin America was increasing and that Cuba was the head-center of subversive activities. The main defense against communism in Latin America probably lies more in the kind of social democracy symbolized by the Mexican Revolution and by President Eduardo Frei of Chile than in the anti-Communist efforts of Latin American dictators or the United States.[32]

The Social Mind. An intangible but major problem relates to what may be called a lack of social consciousness, to what one perceptive American who has lived many years in Latin America calls "insensitivity." It is revealed in comparative indifference to

[32] This point is strongly underscored in Charles O. Porter and Robert J. Alexander, *The Struggle for Democracy in Latin America* (New York: The Macmillan Company, 1961).

the welfare of the poor and the handicapped, in the tolerance of injustice and brutality when others are the victims, in placid acceptance of corruption, and in insistence on royal roads to everything, whether democracy, wealth, or position. More concretely, it is revealed in the luxurious officers' club in Caracas, hardly a rifle-shot from a hillside shantytown; in the boast of Mexicans that graft in the United States is penny-snitching compared with operations in Mexico; in the alleged remark of the late Rafael Trujillo, Dominican dictator, that it was a shame that his great administrative talents — which he undoubtedly had — should have to be wasted on "such a dinky little country"; in the fabulous jewels and wardrobe of Eva Perón; in indifference to the condition of public thoroughfares as long as walls can be built; and even in the fact that dogs on the streets are afraid of pedestrians. "A policeman in the United States or London," says a distinguished Latin American, "is a human being who helps an old lady across the street, a guardian angel for the children coming out of school, the protecting arm of the law. A policeman under a Latin American despot is a shady character not too far removed from the criminal, a man of dubious past who is handed a uniform and a revolver with orders to crush the opposition and maintain order by terror."[33]

Whatever its cause — whether an aspect of the authoritarian tradition, a narrow view of the capitalist creed, or merely the sense of futility with which the few on top regard the prospects of really doing something for so many who need so much — there has been little devotion to the common weal, and, socially as well as politically, most Latin American states have failed to be the melting pots out of which could come true nationalities.

Foreign Relations

The international relations of Latin American states involve, first of all, their relations with each other; second, their intra-Western Hemisphere relations, particularly those with the United States; third, their relations with Europe, parts of which stand in a special historical and cultural position; and, fourth, their role in the United Nations.

Intra-Latin American Relations. Most of the disputes between Latin American states have arisen from the "boundaries" inherited from the colonial period, when precision was unimportant. Although boundaries were generally defined during the early years of the republican period, some, mainly those in sparsely settled regions, remained unsettled until the appearance of some economic asset in the disputed area. Rubber led to the Acre crisis between Bolivia and Brazil; oil, together with cattle raising and the quebracho industry, led to the Chaco War between Bolivia and Paraguay; and oil figured in the long controversy over the Ecuadorian-Peruvian boundary.

Latin American states have fought three major wars among themselves. The Paraguayan War, 1865–70, with little Paraguay aligned against Argentina, Brazil, and Uruguay, was caused more by the ambitions of the Paraguayan dictator, Francisco López, than by any substantial issue. The War of the Pacific, 1879–83, with Chile fighting against Bolivia and Peru, had its origin in rivalry for the rich nitrate deposits of Tarapacá but eventually involved a complex of issues; by this war Bolivia lost her Pacific frontage. The Chaco War, 1932–35, fought between Bolivia and Paraguay, gave Paraguay title to most of the disputed Chaco region.

Other instances of hostility or friction have arisen from the efforts of Bolivia to secure access to the Plate and Amazon systems as a means of reaching the Atlantic with its commerce, of both Peru and Colombia to reach the Amazon, and of Chile to reach the Atlantic across Patagonia. Brazil has had boundary disputes with most or perhaps all of the

[33] Arciniegas, p. 387.

eight states on her borders, but sne has settled them by patience and good diplomacy rather than by war. Several bits of undefined boundary remain, but this fact apparently imposes no severe strain on good relations at present.

Ideological issues have rarely disturbed the relations of Latin American states with each other. Mexico was eyed with some distrust in her early years as a consequence of the conservative nature of the revolution which gave her independence from Spain; Argentina was something of an outcast during World War II when she persisted in collaborating with the Nazi regime in Germany; and Guatemala's neighbors gave a helping hand to Guatemalan elements conspiring to overthrow the pro-Communist regime of Arbenz Guzmán. Dictators have at times carried on personal feuds and at times supported their kind in other states. Commercial rivalry has more often led to eventual cooperation — as in the common front established for the marketing of coffee, sugar, cacao, and other products — than to serious friction.

Latin American countries do an increasing amount of business with each other. Trade within the LAFTA area — embracing Mexico and all of the states of South America except Bolivia — has increased substantially; in 1965 it was 60 per cent of the member states' total foreign trade.

The two strongest powers of South America, Argentina and Brazil, are noncompetitive in their economies; and their political relations are proper without being cordial. Nevertheless, a sort of rivalry exists, one more keenly felt by Argentines than by Brazilians. Argentina has long aspired to Latin American leadership, and she is at times annoyed by Brazil's unwillingness to regard this ambition seriously. Some of the smaller states bear grudges against each other, as Costa Rica and Nicaragua, and the Dominican Republic and Haiti. Bolivia and Ecuador are still smarting from what they regard as the rapacity of their neighbors.

Castro's seizure of power in Cuba in 1960 and his quixotic internal and foreign policies imposed new strains on intra-Latin American as well as United States-Latin American relations. In the early years of his regime, reactions to Castro varied greatly in other Latin American countries. To many people south of the border, and to some of the leaders of the Latin American governments and parties as well, Castro seemed to be bigger than life as a champion of social revolution and staunch defender of all Latin America against the perpetual threat of United States dominance. Gradually, however, as Castro turned Cuba into the first Communist-dominated "people's democracy" in the Western Hemisphere and as the evidence of Cuba's role in efforts at Communist subversion in many latin American states mounted, leaders of most of the Latin American governments turned away from Castro and joined in strong measures against him through the Organization of American States. But Castroism, if not Castro, still has a powerful appeal in most of Latin America, especially among radical groups.

When the Venezuelan government charged the Castro regime with aggression and subversive activities directed against Venezuela, the OAS Council, in December, 1963, appointed a five-nation investigating committee. This committee, after eight months' investigation, submitted a damning report, citing detailed evidence that the Castro regime was sending arms and trained agents into Venezuela and had tried to prevent the Venezuelan elections of December 1, 1963, and that it was training more than 1,500 subversives annually for operations elsewhere in Latin America. In July a Meeting of Consultation of the Ministers of Foreign Affairs of the member states of OAS declared, with Bolivia, Chile, Mexico, and Uruguay dissenting, that Cuba was an aggressor and voted to impose economic and diplomatic — but not military — sanctions in accordance with the Inter-American Treaty of 1947 (the Rio

Treaty). Eventually all of the members of OAS, except Mexico, broke off diplomatic relations with the Castro regime. At the same time many expressed the hope that Cuba could soon be brought back into the hemispheric community.

On the whole, the record of the Latin American states in getting along with each other is not a bad one. With few if any exceptions, every country has spilled far more blood in domestic strife than in international wars. For the generally peaceful character of interstate relations credit must be given to a number of factors: most of the boundaries are in unsettled or sparsely settled areas, few states have a munitions industry, Brazil — almost everybody's neighbor — has demonstrated diplomacy of a high order, and international organizations, especially the League of Nations and the Organization of American States, have often exerted a quieting influence. One writer has pertinently remarked that "Latin Americans have a strong juridical sense and international law is not a dead letter, as it largely is in the Old World."[34]

Copyright 1964 Herblock in The Washington Post.

"We're taking a new look at it."

Relations with the United States. Geography, common democratic ideals, and the consciousness of a common destiny, plus America's enormous economic and military strength, have made the United States the great power that matters most to Latin America. Conversely, the United States, despite her interludes of indifference and bad manners, has a historic and even a sentimental interest in Latin America, and, in addition, she has an awareness of the importance to herself of the population, the goods, the markets, and the military potential of Latin America. In different ways the two areas of the Western Hemisphere are dependent upon each other. Trade between them amounts to about \$3.5 billion a year in each direction. Americans have invested nearly \$10 billion in Latin America, which in turn has about \$2 billion invested in American enterprises.

American friendliness to Latin American independence was largely motivated by considerations of territorial security. But two other considerations also were important. One related to trade: the confidence that the new states would open their doors to the commerce of the world. The other related to the American feeling of a basic antagonism between monarchism and republicanism: much comfort could be found in the emergence of "sister republics" dedicated to representative government and helping to hold the line against autocratic monarchism.

The same set of national interests that produced America's benevolent neutrality during the Wars of Independence and her early recognition of the new states brought about the Monroe Doctrine. President Monroe's pronouncement, made on December 2, 1823,

[34] Schurz, p. 263.

was received with approval in Latin America, when it was noticed at all. The Doctrine languished for many years, during which "American influence was unimportant and even minute compared with that of Britain."[35] But during the 1850's "the principles of 1823 . . . grew steadily in popularity and . . . rose to the rank of a national dogma."[36] In the 1860's Secretary of State Seward invoked the Doctrine to frustrate Spanish occupation of the Dominican Republic and to end the French occupation of Mexico in support of Maximilian's empire. During the 1870's and 1880's, doubtless in consequence of its new status as a "national dogma," the Doctrine was interpreted even more liberally. President Grant declared that it denied the right of transfer of American territory from one European power to another, a principle asserted on many later occasions when such a transfer appeared imminent. Presidents Hayes and Garfield interpreted the Doctrine as denying the right of a European state to construct a trans-Isthmian canal, and as implying that the United States must have exclusive control of any such canal. In the 1890's President Cleveland went still further when in the name of the Doctrine he virtually compelled the arbitration of a boundary dispute between Great Britain and Venezuela. Cleveland's action won praise in Venezuela, Colombia, Brazil, and Peru, but it reaped suspicion and hostility in Mexico, Argentina, and Chile.[37] During the Spanish-American War the Doctrine was scarcely mentioned. Instead, to use the words of John Bassett Moore, the Americans justified their intervention as the exercise of the right to effect "the abatement of a nuisance."

The first instance in which the United States asserted a right to interfere in the affairs of a Latin American state occurred when the Platt Amendment of 1901 required Cuba to permit American intervention. The Monroe Doctrine was not invoked. But soon thereafter the United States intervened in the Dominican Republic, and on this occasion the Monroe Doctrine was advanced in justification. This use of the Doctrine had its origin in the so-called Second Venezuelan Affair. Although the affair was settled, it opened a question on the implications of the Monroe Doctrine: Since the United States was unwilling to allow European states to use force to collect lawful debts from Latin American countries, did she have an obligation to see that the defaulting countries paid their debts? With further defaulting in the unstable Caribbean area almost certain to occur, the question was by no means an academic one. The issue was taken to the Permanent Court of Arbitration, which in 1904 decided by a unanimous vote that the states which had used force to compel Venezuela to pay her debts had a right to payment before states which had not been so belligerently inclined. This, of course, put a premium upon the use of force in the collection of debts. The dilemma thus confronting the United States has been stated by Professor Bemis:

> Should the United States stand by with folded arms while non-American powers, backed in principle by a Hague Court decision, intervened and perhaps ensconced themselves in strategic positions from which in the future they might cut the Panama life-line and the security of the Continental Republic; or should it intervene itself to guarantee justice and responsibility in strategically located countries whose condition invited foreign intervention, and thereby run the risk of incurring by its own intervention the misunderstanding and animosity of the neighboring republics?[38]

[35] Dexter Perkins, *Hands Off: A History of the Monroe Doctrine* (Boston: Little, Brown and Company, 1941), p. 75.

[36] Dexter Perkins, "Monroe Doctrine," *Encyclopaedia of the Social Sciences* (New York: The Macmillan Company, 1937), X, 631. Used by permission of The Macmillan Company.

[37] Perkins, *Hands Off*, p. 188.

[38] Samuel F. Bemis, *The Latin American Policy of the United States* (New York: Harcourt, Brace, 1943), p. 152.

The occasion for an American decision was not long in coming. When the Dominican Republic defaulted on its foreign debts in late 1904, its president sought American intervention to forestall naval action by European powers. In February, 1905, a protocol was signed giving the United States control of Dominican customs and foreign debt payment. This began an American intervention that lasted until 1940, and included eight years of military occupation, 1916–24.

In December, 1904, President Theodore Roosevelt declared that "in the Western Hemisphere the adherence of the United States to the Monroe Doctrine may force the United States, however reluctantly, in flagrant cases of such wrong-doing or impotence, to the exercise of an international police power." In other words, if the Monroe Doctrine prevented European powers from chastising an American republic that deserved chastisement, then the United States herself must take the culprit in hand. This, in substance, was the Roosevelt Corollary, although it is usually dated from Roosevelt's more definitive statement of February 15, 1905.

The Roosevelt Corollary endured for twenty-five years. During that time the United States resorted to military occupation in four Latin American states: Cuba, the Dominican Republic, Haiti, and Nicaragua; it is impossible to state the number of interventions, for "intervention" is a term of diverse meanings. Included among these were certainly Roosevelt's Panama adventure, which, though antedating the Roosevelt Corollary, was in the spirit of the "Big Stick," and Woodrow Wilson's intervention in Mexico to establish constitutional government. The heyday of the Corollary was during the administrations of Theodore Roosevelt and William H. Taft (1901–13). Woodrow Wilson, too, was an interventionist — really the greatest of them all — but he had the vision of a genuine Pan-Americanism that, shared by his successors, inspired the liquidation of protective American imperialism and the emergence of the Good Neighbor Policy.

The Roosevelt Corollary was never really popular in the United States. It was clearly a justification of intervention, and, to repeat an earlier quotation from Dexter Perkins, "American rule over other peoples has always been rule with an uneasy conscience." The Latin American states grew increasingly hostile to the Corollary, and opposition sentiment at home grew increasingly vocal. Finally Frank B. Kellogg, President Coolidge's Secretary of State, requested Under Secretary of State J. Reuben Clark to make a study of the implications of the Monroe Doctrine. Clark reported in a confidential memorandum submitted in December, 1928: ". . . it is not believed that this [the Roosevelt] corollary is justified by the terms of the Monroe Doctrine."[39] President Hoover and Secretary of State Henry L. Stimson, determined to improve relations with Latin America, caused the Clark Memorandum to be published, and in notes sent to all Latin American governments declared that the American State Department would be guided by its principles. "In this sense, by June of 1930, the Roosevelt Corollary had been definitely and specifically repudiated."[40] But renunciation of the Corollary was not tantamount to a renunciation of intervention, for, as the Clark Memorandum suggested, intervention might be justified by the "doctrine of self-preservation." The demand of the Latin American states was for total renunciation.

At the Havana Conference of 1928 an unusually able American delegation, headed by former Secretary of State Charles E. Hughes, refused assent to a convention asserting the doctrine of unqualified nonintervention. The Americans argued that more attention to the *duties* of states would reduce the need for insistence on *rights*. "It was at Havana that

[39] J. Reuben Clark, *Memorandum on the Monroe Doctrine* (Washington, D.C.: Government Printing Office, 1930), p. xxiii.

[40] Perkins, *Hands Off*, p. 344.

the United States made its last defense of the interventions still unliquidated in the Caribbean."[41]

Herbert Hoover visited South America, promoted the settlement of the Tacna-Arica dispute, withdrew the last marines from Nicaragua, arranged for the military evacuation of Haiti, officially repudiated the Roosevelt Corollary, refused to support American bankers in El Salvador, and, outside of Central America — where America was bound by treaty — he declined to use nonrecognition as a sanction against revolutionary governments. Thus by the time of the inauguration of Franklin D. Roosevelt in March, 1933, the new Latin American policy of the United States had been well launched.

At the Montevideo Conference in late 1933 the American delegation, led by Secretary of State Cordell Hull, accepted the principle of nonintervention, subject to "the law of nations as generally recognized." Three years later, at the Buenos Aires Conference of 1936, the United States went all the way, agreeing with the other republics to "declare inadmissible the intervention of any one of them, directly or indirectly, and for whatever reason, in the internal or external affairs of any other of the Parties." Here was absolute nonintervention — so long and so ardently desired by Latin America. The Special Protocol Relative to Nonintervention, expanded to deny a right of collective intervention, became Article 15 of Chapter III of the Charter of the Organization of American States, drafted at Bogotá in 1948.

We cannot even list here the measures taken by the Roosevelt administration to promote the security, prosperity, and harmony of the Western Hemisphere. Roosevelt's Good Neighbor Policy symbolized a new spirit and a new approach in United States-Latin American relations. We can scarcely do more than suggest how, "determined henceforth to reconcile promises with deeds, the United States in typically Yankee fashion attacked the problem on all fronts — political, economic, and cultural."[42] Military occupation was everywhere terminated, the Platt Amendment was repudiated, tariff barriers were lowered through Secretary Hull's Reciprocal Trade Agreements Program, cultural exchange was promoted, trade was encouraged and enlarged, and health and education assistance was extended. "The greatest accomplishment in the political field," says Graham H. Stuart, "was the utilization of the Pan American Conferences to serve as effective agencies for cooperation among the twenty-one republics."[43] When World War II began, the American republics were prepared for unprecedented cooperation in the struggle against the Nazi menace; only Argentina and, to a lesser extent, Chile dragged their feet. After the war had been won the new spirit found expression in the strengthening and revision of the Inter-American System at Rio in 1947 and Bogotá in 1948.

The Inter-American Treaty of Reciprocal Assistance, adopted at a conference in Rio de Janeiro in September, 1947, was a multilateral security arrangement for the defense of the Western Hemisphere against any outside attack. At the Ninth International Conference of American States, held in Bogotá, Colombia, from March 30 to May 2, 1948, the Inter-American System was given more definite and comprehensive form by the establishment of the Organization of American States as a regional arrangement in accordance with the United Nations Charter. Much of United States-Latin American relations in recent years has been encompassed in the operation of the OAS, which is discussed in Chapter 20.

The Truman administration, pressed by the exigencies of the cold war and by frequent budgetary deficits, failed to follow through with the Good Neighbor Policy in a

[41] Bemis, p. 252.

[42] Stuart, p. 451.

[43] *Ibid.*, p. 451.

way to meet Latin American expectations, but its attitude was by no means one of indifference. The Eisenhower administration, using a Good Partner label, gave increased attention to technical assistance and encouraged trade and private investment.

It may be possible to explain the shift from Franklin D. Roosevelt's vigorous pro-Latin America policy to the less vigorous policies of Truman and Eisenhower in terms of personalities or simply in terms of the financial capacity of the United States. Perhaps more valid than either of these is the view that FDR believed that strength and unity in the Western Hemisphere, together with isolationist neutrality laws on the part of the United States, might permit the New World to sit out the war which the European dictators seemed intent on beginning. The postwar administrations, however, have felt compelled to fight for global peace and, in doing so, to abandon the hope that the peoples of the two Americas might build a peaceful world of their own. It is this shift, and not weakness within the Inter-American System, that led Professor Arthur P. Whitaker to speak of the decline of the idea of Western Hemisphere unity.[44]

During the Kennedy and Johnson administrations the relative neglect of Latin America by the United States was dramatically reversed. On March 13, 1961, a few weeks after he had entered the White House, President Kennedy, in an address at a reception for Latin American diplomats, proposed that the people of the Western Hemisphere "join in a new Alliance for Progress — *Alianza para Progreso* — . . . a vast new Ten Year Plan for the Americas." This bold proposal was given more tangible form by the adoption, in August, 1961, of the Charter of Punta del Este by representatives of all twenty of the members of the OAS who participated in the Punta del Este Conference. The drafters of the Alliance established the area's needs for outside funds during the ten-year period at $20 billion, and the United States formally pledged to provide "a major part" of this amount. It was assumed that the Latin American countries themselves would raise a much larger sum during the decade of the Alliance. The Alliance's program of achieving its ambitious objectives

> is to hitch the standard apparatus of U.S. aid — Agency for International Development, Export-Import Bank, Food for Peace, Peace Corps — to detailed development plans drawn up by countries and approved by review committees under supervision of the Organization of American States. This linkage is intended not only to keep all development activities in a given country going in the same direction but also to tie the disbursement of U.S. funds to adoption by the recipient countries of the social measures espoused by the Alliance and the "self-help" provisions, as the recommended land and tax changes are styled.[45]

As a vast cooperative program in economic, social, and political development, designed, as President Kennedy hoped, "to transform the 1960s into an historic decade of development," the Alliance for Progress, in the first years of its implementation, was a disappointment. The Alliance did not achieve the necessary cooperation, did not stimulate the necessary economic, social, and political reforms, and did not secure the necessary public and private financial support to offer solid ground for hope in its ultimate success. As an OAS panel of experts reported in 1962, Latin Americans were regarding the whole program "not in its true perspective as a multilateral cooperative effort, in which self-help plays the main role, but as a vast plan of aid by the United States." The United States financial contribution to the Alliance has been substantial. In the first three years of the Alliance program it amounted to slightly more than $3 billion.

[44] *The Western Hemisphere Idea: Its Rise and Decline* (Ithaca: Cornell University Press, 1954).

[45] "The Alliance for Progress," *The Morgan Guaranty Survey*, February, 1963, pp. 8–9.

By far the largest amount ($724.7 million) went to Brazil. Other major recipients were Chile, Colombia, and Mexico. On a per capita basis the chief beneficiaries were Chile, Bolivia, and Panama. In spite of this substantial infusion of foreign assistance, the impact of the Alliance on the Latin American countries was spotty, at best. Unless it is given increased support and momentum, it can hardly be expected to achieve its ambitious objectives.

However disappointing in its early phases, the Alliance for Progress represented a significant new approach by the United States to Latin America and laid the basis for "a vast cooperative effort," in President Kennedy's words, "to satisfy the basic needs" of the people of the Americas. On the whole, even though it raised apprehensions in many sensitive Latin American minds of a revival of American "imperialism," it was widely welcomed in Latin American countries.

United States efforts to work more closely with the countries and peoples south of the border were at once frustrated and handicapped by the course of events in Cuba and the Dominican Republic. Fidel Castro, as has been noted, appealed to many Latin Americans as an apostle of social change. He was able to capitalize on the strong anti-United States feelings prevalent in most parts of Latin America, particularly after the Bay of Pigs incident in 1961, often described as President Kennedy's greatest failure in foreign affairs, revived old fears of United States interventions in Latin America. Eventually — in part because of United States pressures, but also because of growing opposition to Castro's internal and external policies — most Latin American governments joined in condemning Castro's Cuba as an aggressor, and all except Mexico severed diplomatic relations with Cuba. Nevertheless, the new suspicions aroused by United States policy toward the Castro regime and the continuing appeal of Castroism to many Latin Americans created further strains in United States-Latin American relations. The reasons for this estrangement were to be found partly in the long-standing aversion to any "interventionist" United States policies or tactics anywhere in Latin America, and partly to differing assessments of the nature and seriousness of the Communist threat in the Western Hemisphere and the proper steps to deal with it.

President Johnson concluded that the danger to American citizens and the further danger of a Communist take-over in the upheaval in the Dominican Republic in early May, 1965, was so imminent that he could not wait to see what action the OAS would take to deal with the new emergency. In fact, he did not even inform the OAS, much less request permission, before dispatching American troops to Santo Domingo. Naturally, his unilateral action was sharply criticized in Latin American countries, as well as by Communist critics throughout the world. A Rio de Janeiro newspaper, the *Jornal de Brasil,* said that President Johnson's moves "represent the death certificate of the present structure of the inter-American system." Actually, at the strong request of the United States, the OAS became involved in the crisis rather quickly. Within a few days the Secretary-General of the OAS and a five-man peace mission representing the OAS were in Santo Domingo, and shortly thereafter the first contingents of an inter-American peacekeeping force, authorized at a special meeting of the foreign ministers of the OAS countries, arrived in the troubled island. Gradually this force, representing the first peacekeeping force to be organized by the OAS, took over increasing responsibilities in the Dominican Republic and enabled the United States Government to withdraw a large part of its military personnel from the island.

Thus, United States action was very shortly fused into a multilateral effort by the

OAS, and the United States was able to divest itself somewhat of unilateral responsibility for dealing with the Dominican crisis. But President Johnson left no doubt of his intention and willingness to act promptly in any similar crisis in Latin America. "The United States," he said, "will never depart from its commitment to the preservation of the right of all of the free people of this hemisphere to choose their own course without falling prey to international conspiracy in any quarter." This position, frequently referred to as the Johnson Doctrine, was sometimes interpreted as a new corollary to the Monroe Doctrine, almost as tough as the discarded Roosevelt Corollary of an earlier generation. Almost certainly it was not so intended, but was meant rather to be a clear acceptance of special United States responsibility in preventing any Latin American state from "falling prey to international conspiracy from any quarter." Whatever its justification, it was bound to be criticized in many Latin American quarters as a revival of "gunboat diplomacy" and to make cooperation between the United States and the countries of Latin America, through the OAS, in the Alliance for Progress, or unilaterally, more difficult.

Relations with Europe. Since winning their independence the Latin American states have been relatively unaffected by the power politics of Europe. The only exceptions have come when European politics spilled over into world politics in the two great wars of this century. During World War I eight of the republics declared war on Germany, five broke off diplomatic relations, and seven remained neutral. During World War II all twenty republics issued declarations of war, but those of Chile and Argentina came only when the collapse of the Axis was clearly in sight. Two of the republics, Brazil and Mexico, took part in the fighting. All twenty joined the League of Nations, but most of them lost faith in it before World War II. All have joined the United Nations, and some of them have played influential roles, as we shall presently see.

Latin America's estrangement from Spain lasted until the close of the nineteenth century. Since then, the common bond of Spanish culture has drawn them into a friendly relationship. This natural tie has been somewhat weakened by wide differences of opinion in Latin America on the virtues of the Franco regime in Spain.

The relations between Brazil and Portugal have always been cordial. Portuguese immigrants are exempted from the operation of the Brazilian quota system, and they are well received. In other ways the two countries have demonstrated their friendship by concessions to each other.

Until many of her interests were liquidated during World War II and the Perón regime, Great Britain was long the principal foreign investor in Latin America, and she remains important as both buyer and seller. The propensity of her nationals abroad to set up little Britains excludes them from close association with the local communities. The Latin Americans do not like this exclusiveness, but they do admire many of the fine qualities of the British. Argentina and Britain have a long-standing but seldom irritating difference of opinion on the ownership of the Falkland Islands.

Although Argentina and Mexico have unpleasant memories of French machinations, the political relations between Latin American states and France have been uneventful for a long time. A bit of high drama was provided in 1964, when President de Gaulle visited Mexico in March, and ten countries of South America in September and October. While his visits were a personal *tour de force* and were well received, his suggestions that France might provide an alternative to the United States in the Western Hemisphere did not register in Latin American minds. During the year France concluded several trade and aid agreements with Latin American countries, but there was, in fact, very little that France could offer Latin America. French trade does not approach the American or British, although at times it has been sizable. But French culture has traditionally held a powerful appeal for Latin Americans, overshadowing that of any other foreign country. This influence has extended to language, literature, art, the stage, architecture, and dress styles. Although losing some ground to Spanish influence and to nativist movements, it remains strong; and, as has often been remarked, Paris is the cultural capital of Latin America.

German relations with Latin America have been primarily economic. German firms made great inroads into Latin American trade before World War I, and then sought to regain their position after losing out entirely during the war. They succeeded pretty well, only to be cut off again during World War II; now they are making another successful effort to recover. German culture has never appealed to Latin Americans, but German military efficiency has been much admired, and German military missions were welcomed during the interwar years. German prestige suffered badly through Nazi intrigue and propaganda and the collapse of Hitler's empire.

Latin America in the United Nations[46]

The republics of Latin America were disappointed by the League of Nations. Many of them entered the organization with high expectations, hoping to find in it comparative security and a counterweight to the "Colossus of the North." But the League proved to have neither the universality in membership that they associated with security nor the willingness to interfere with inter-American relationships. Consequently, although all twenty republics were members at one time or another, they drifted away one by one during the Great Depression and the years when the Fascist states were defying the League with impunity.

The American republics began preparations for post-World War II organization as early as 1942 when their foreign ministers, meeting in Rio, directed the Inter-American Juridical Committee to prepare recommendations on postwar international organization. The committee formulated fourteen specific recommendations that emphasized universalism, the priority of "the moral law," the peaceful settlement of disputes, collective security, and the repudiation of all forms of imperialism. When the Latin Americans failed to get an invitation to the Dumbarton Oaks discussions or to be consulted by the United States State Department prior to Dumbarton Oaks, they utilized the Inter-American Conference on the Problems of War and Peace — held at Mexico City in February and March, 1945 — to re-formulate their views and to promote a number of actions to strengthen inter-American regionalism. The proposals adopted by the conference to improve the announced blueprint included an enlargement of the powers of the General Assembly, an extension of the jurisdiction of the "Court of Justice," the establishment of an agency charged with promoting "intellectual and moral cooperation among nations," a grant of "more adequate" representation to Latin America on the Security Council, and recognition of inter-American regionalism. The measures taken to strengthen the American regional system consisted of an agreement to conclude a hemispheric defense treaty (accomplished at Rio in 1947), a resolution to formalize the structure of the inter-American organization (accomplished at Bogotá in 1948), a deci-

[46] This discussion of Latin American participation in the UN is largely based on John A. Houston, *Latin America in the United Nations* (New York: Carnegie Endowment for International Peace, 1956).

sion to coordinate existing inter-American agreements for the pacific settlement of disputes (also accomplished at Bogotá in 1948), and a determination to support the admission of Argentina to the coming San Francisco Conference (this, too, was accomplished despite an earlier decision to exclude Argentina because of her pro-Axis leanings during the war). Thus, with their ranks closed, the Latin American republics hoped to make their influence felt at the UN organizational meeting where they would constitute two-fifths of the nations represented.

Despite their solidarity, the Latin Americans were unable to accomplish as much as they had hoped at San Francisco. Again and again they ran into the stone wall of great power agreement and had to give way. In contrast to their attitude within the League of Nations, they now espoused international regionalism. Their conversion had been effected by the liquidation of American imperialism, the unfolding of the Good Neighbor Policy, and perhaps most of all by the growing power of Communist Russia. They found themselves unable to achieve an open consolidation of forces with the United States, for the North Americans feared that to appear to ask favors for their regional system would put the Soviet Union in a good position to ask favors for her satellites. But the United States representatives remained loyal to inter-American regionalism and helped to gain for it the recognition that they and the Latin Americans desired — a recognition far more forthright than that contained in the Covenant of the League of Nations. The Latin Americans were primarily responsible for the addition of Article 51 to the Charter and for Chapter IV's assertion of the Assembly's right to discuss any question not on the agenda of the Security Council. Both were important victories.

The record of Latin American participation in the UN has been one of fairly consistent but by no means complete solidarity. The twenty republics which were original members of the UN, plus four new Latin American states, have been pursuing a deliberate policy of consultation and collaboration in support of principles common to all or most of them. They have been dedicated — more or less — to the principles of universality of membership, the juristic equality of states, anti-colonialism, the rights of dependent peoples, the social and cultural missions of the UN, the rights of women, freedom of information, the control of armaments, and financial assistance to underdeveloped areas. In many instances, however, their devotion to these principles has been subordinated to their resolution to forestall the expansion of Communist power.

The Latin Americans have allied themselves with United States spokesmen on virtually all issues related to the "cold war" and, indeed, on most political issues. Often the Latin Americans themselves have presented a solid front on underlying principles and ultimate objectives, but have broken ranks on matters of tactics or procedures. The Latin American–United States alignment has usually crumbled on issues related to assistance to underdeveloped areas. The North Americans have been unable or unwilling to commit themselves to the measure of financial assistance which the Latin Americans feel that they need and that they are entitled to in view of the vastly greater United States aid programs in behalf of Europe and Asia. Most of the southern republics have also feared that the efforts toward more freedom in commercial intercourse espoused by the United States would raise serious obstacles to the progress of their infant industries. On a number of issues, relating to colonialism, trade, economic development, and the rights of small states, the Latin American countries, or at least the majority of them, often voted with the Asian-African Group in the UN. "As far back as 1952 a keen observer of UN affairs called attention to this fact, and suggested that it symbolized 'the growing independence of countries usually included in the

"Anglo-American majority," ' and might in time lead to 'a new proven alignment.' "[47]

At the United Nations Conference on Trade and Development, held in Geneva in 1964, the Latin American states participated in the effective caucus of seventy-five developing nations in bringing pressure to bear on the developed nations to make substantial concessions to the needs of the underdeveloped majority. An important report by a distinguished Latin American economist, Dr. Raul Prebisch, entitled *Towards a New Trade Policy for Development*,[48] was a major working document for the conference. Dr. Prebisch was secretary-general of the conference, and he continued to serve in the same capacity when UNCTAD was established as a continuing agency, with a Trade and Development Board as its permanent organ.

Although the Latin American republics have failed to modify the great power concept on which the UN was founded, they have usually maintained such a solidarity among themselves, and they have commonly sent such able representatives to the various bodies of the UN, that they have at times exerted a decisive influence on the course of the UN policy. Their delegates have often been eloquent spokesmen for small states, for a system of law and justice, for the underdeveloped areas, and above all, for the non-Communist world. Unhappily, their governments, like most of those represented in the UN, have often failed to take action to implement the resolutions adopted in New York.

An Assessment. Collectively, Latin America would seem to possess a number of conditions that tend to increase its importance in international affairs. For one thing, it has a rapidly increasing population, more than that of Canada and the United States combined, and it has ample space for a great many millions more. Second, it is a large producer of raw materials that are in continuous demand, and it is at the same time an expanding market for a wide range of commodities and for foreign capital. Third, it is part — a very large part — of the most completely developed example of organized international regionalism, the Organization of American States, within which the members find substantial security, create new modes of international cooperation, and often achieve a common world policy. Fourth, again and again the states of Latin America, even the smallest and weakest of them, send statesmen of high talents into the councils of nations. This was true with the League of Nations, and it is now true with the United Nations. Fifth, the Latin American countries have caught the urge to industrialize and modernize. Aided by the assistance programs of the UN, the OAS, and the United States, they are developing industries, improving agriculture, building public works, and in various other ways seeking to improve the material basis of national life.

A New Role?

What does the future hold for the states of Latin America? For some of them the future would seem to be as gloomy as the past. It must be remembered, however, that many forms of assistance and encouragement that were unknown only a short time ago are now available. Many of the Latin American states are grasping their opportunities. Encouraged by their most perceptive leaders, by the United States, by the specialized agencies of the Organization of American States, and by the UN's Economic Commission for Latin America — ECLA is a magic term in Latin America — they have addressed themselves to their shortcomings in health, housing, education, highways, soil improvement, crop diversification, tax reform, industrialization, and a host of other areas.

Encouraging too is the fact that so many

[47] Norman D. Palmer, "The Afro-Asians in the United Nations," Chapter VI in Franz Gross, ed., *The United States and the United Nations* (Norman: University of Oklahoma Press, 1964), p. 143.

[48] UN Publication No. 64.II.B.4.

able Latin American statesmen, scholars, and journalists are speaking in behalf of a new order of affairs. Particularly hopeful are the efforts of the Inter-American Press Association, which since its organization in 1942 has taken a firm stand in defense of the freedom of the press. While United States journalists are still important in its work, it is "becoming more and more a Latin American organization." It has had the courage to decline grants from private foundations in the United States as well as to criticize the Department of State "for doing business with people like Perón" and for "unnecessarily befriending Latin American dictators who are enemies of the free press." It flatly condemned Colombian dictator Rojas Pinilla for his closing in 1955 of Eduardo Santos' great liberal newspaper *El Tiempo,* of Bogota.[49]

There are still other encouraging signs. One is the way in which foreign experts take to the countries in which they work: again and again the visiting North American encounters a countryman who is "sold" on this or that country and talks enthusiastically of its future. Another is the growing stream of North American tourists — something like four hundred thousand a year — who fly, sail, or drive southward to enjoy the striking beauty of Latin American lands and the hospitality of their people, and in doing so both receive and transmit ideas.

Although Latin America is making unquestionable progress in its economic development, the United States Department of State speaks unrealistically when it says that Latin America is "far from being a 'backward' or 'underdeveloped' area." And it is certainly inaccurate in citing Venezuela, which is first in the value of exports in Latin America and first in per capita income, as an "example" of Latin American countries on the march.[50] Nevertheless, progress is substantial even if poorly distributed.

The bustling economies of many Latin American states,[51] perhaps especially their present fervor for industrialization, public works, and technical assistance, evidently furnish the Department of State's warrant for its rhapsodical declaration that "the big news in our day is that Latin America's time has come" — that "once again one of the great land masses of the world has caught fire and is growing and developing at a rate that is sure to change completely its relationship to the rest of the world."[52] While one may question that America's good neighbors are aflame, he can hardly doubt that some of them are making the sparks fly, and that there is sound basis for the more restrained observation of John M. Cabot, former Assistant Secretary of State for Inter-American Affairs, that "the development of Latin America is today so rapid that it must in a short span strongly affect the balance of world economics and military power."[53]

Unhappily, most of the currently optimistic appraisals pertain only to the Latin American economies. They do not say — nor could they say — that democracy is about to bloom or even to bud. While it is certainly true that power in world affairs can be exercised by states ruled by dictators, the power desired by the great liberal leaders of the Latin American republics, like that of the true liberals of every state, is power consis-

[49] For a brief account of the Inter-American Press Association, see *Hispanic-American Report,* VIII (October, 1955), 449–451. See also Ronald Hilton, "Responsibility and Freedom in Communications Media," in del Río, pp. 256–262.

[50] *Objectives of U.S. Foreign Policy in Latin America,* Dept. of State Pub. 6131, Inter-American Series 51 (November, 1955), pp. 24, 23. The figures cited in the above paragraph have been taken from this same work, p. 23.

[51] For an annual review of economic developments in Latin America, see the special supplements in the *New York Times,* issued sometime in January of each year.

[52] *Objectives of U.S. Foreign Policy in Latin America,* p. 1.

[53] See *Toward Our Common American Destiny* (Fletcher School of Law and Diplomacy, n.d.), pp. 56–57. These remarks were originally made on October 4, 1953.

tently to pursue the objectives of peace and justice. This power their countries cannot have while despots rule.

Despite every effort that its states may make, it seems clear that Latin America will never be a region of great powers. Only Brazil appears to have the potential for such a status, and her political and economic maturity lies many decades in the future.[54] Of the two other large states, Argentina lacks the essential mineral resources and Mexico lacks both industrial minerals and good soil. But nearly every state does have the material resources to pursue hopefully the more laudable objective of a good life for its people. Reaching this objective calls for a helping hand from the United States, but it obviously also calls for a dedicated leadership that has all too frequently been lacking in Latin America.

SUGGESTIONS FOR FURTHER READING

ALBA, VICTOR. *Alliance without Allies: The Mythology of Progress in Latin America.* New York: Frederick A. Praeger, 1966.

ALEXANDER, ROBERT J. *Communism in Latin America.* New Brunswick, N.J.: Rutgers University Press, 1957.

———. *Latin American Politics and Government.* New York: Harper & Row, 1965.

ANDERSON, CHARLES W. *Politics and Economic Change in Latin America: The Governing of Restless Nations.* Princeton, N.J.: D. Van Nostrand Co., 1967.

BAILEY, NORMAN A., ed. *Latin America: Politics, Economics, and Hemispheric Security.* New York: Frederick A. Praeger, for the Center for Strategic Studies, 1965.

BEMIS, SAMUEL F. *The Latin American Policy of the United States.* New York: Harcourt, Brace, 1943.

BERLE, ADOLF A. *Latin America: Diplomacy and Reality.* New York: Harper & Row, for the Council on Foreign Relations, 1962. A thoughtful and provocative work.

BUSEY, JAMES L. *Latin America: Political Institutions and Processes.* New York: Random House, 1964.

CLARK, GERALD. *The Coming Explosion in Latin America.* New York: David McKay Co., 1963.

[54] For an excellent brief discussion of Brazil's "Problems and Promises," see Herring, pp. 734–741.

CLINE, HOWARD F. *The United States and Mexico.* Cambridge, Mass.: Harvard University Press, 1963.

EDELMAN, ALEXANDER T. *Latin American Government and Politics; the Dynamics of a Revolutionary Society.* Homewood, Ill.: Dorsey Press, 1965.

GORDON, LINCOLN. *A New Deal for Latin America; the Alliance for Progress.* Cambridge, Mass.: Harvard University Press, 1963.

GUERRANT, EDWARD O. *Roosevelt's Good Neighbor Policy.* Albuquerque: University of New Mexico Press, 1950.

HAMILL, HUGH M., ed. *Dictatorship in Spanish America.* New York: Alfred A. Knopf, 1965.

HERRING, HUBERT. *A History of Latin America.* New York: Alfred A. Knopf, 1955.

HOROWITZ, IRVING LOUIS. *Revolution in Brazil; Politics and Society in a Developing Nation.* New York: E. P. Dutton & Co., 1964.

HOUSTON, JOHN A. *Latin America in the United Nations.* Carnegie Endowment for International Peace, 1956. Has extensive tables on voting in the UN as well as a good bibliography.

LIEUWEN, EDWIN. *Arms and Politics in Latin America,* 2d ed. New York: Frederick A. Praeger, for the Council on Foreign Relations, 1961.

———. *Generals vs. Presidents; Neomilitarism*

in Latin America. New York: Frederick A. Praeger, 1964.

———. *U.S. Policy in Latin America; a Short History.* New York: Frederick A. Praeger, 1965.

MAIER, JOSEPH and RICHARD W. WEATHERHEAD, eds. *Politics of Change in Latin America.* New York: Frederick A. Praeger, 1964.

MARTZ, JOHN D. *Central America; The Crisis and the Challenge.* Chapel Hill: University of North Carolina Press, 1959.

———. *The Dynamics of Change in Latin American Politics.* Englewood Cliffs, N.J.: Prentice-Hall, 1965.

MATTHEWS, HERBERT. *The Cuban Story.* New York: George Braziller, 1961. A provocative, pro-Castro account of the Cuban Revolution.

MECHAM, J. LLOYD *A Survey of United States — Latin American Relations.* Boston: Houghton Mifflin Company, 1965

NEEDLER, MARTIN C. *Latin American Politics in Perspective.* Princeton, N.J.: D. Van Nostrand Co., 1963.

NEEDLER, MARTIN C. *et al. Political Systems of Latin America.* Princeton, N.J.: D. Van Nostrand Co., 1964. A country-by-country approach. Sixteen contributors.

NEHEMKIS, PETER. *Latin America: Myth and Reality.* New York: Alfred A. Knopf, 1964. Challenge to America's leaders in light of present conditions and the Alliance for Progress, which the author helped to formulate.

NYSTROM, JOHN W. *The Alliance for Progress, Key to Latin America's Development.* Princeton, N.J.: D. Van Nostrand Co., 1966. Searchlight Book #27.

PERKINS, DEXTER. *The United States and Latin America.* Baton Rouge: Louisiana State University Press, 1961.

PIKE, FREDERICK B., ed. *Freedom and Reform in Latin America.* Notre Dame, Ind.: University of Notre Dame Press, 1959.

PORTER, CHARLES O. and ROBERT J. ALEXANDER. *The Struggle for Democracy in Latin America.* New York: The Macmillan Company, 1961.

SCHMITT, KARL M. and DAVID D. BURKS. *Evolution or Chaos: Dynamics of Latin American Government and Politics.* New York: Frederick A. Praeger, 1963.

SCHURZ, WILLIAM L. *The New World: The Civilization of Latin America.* New York: E. P. Dutton & Co., 1964. A lively interpretation of the main features of Latin American civilization.

SCOTT, ROBERT. *Mexican Government in Transition.* Urbana: University of Illinois Press, 1965. A mature analysis of what has happened in Mexico in the past 50 years.

SEERS, DUDLEY *et al. Cuba: The Economic and Social Revolution.* Chapel Hill: University of North Carolina Press, 1964.

SILVERT, KALMAN. *The Conflict Society: Reaction and Revolution in Latin America.* New Orleans: Hauser Press, 1961.

STOKES, WILLIAM S. *Latin American Politics.* New York: Thomas Y. Crowell Company, 1959.

SZULC, TAD. *The Winds of Revolution; Latin America Today and Tomorrow.* New York Frederick A. Praeger. 1963. Stimulating observations by a first-class reporter.

TANNENBAUM, FRANK. *Ten Keys to Latin America.* New York: Alfred A. Knopf, 1962.

WHYTE, GEORGE. *The United States and Inter-American Relations; a Contemporary Appraisal.* Gainesville: University of Florida Press, 1964.

WOOD, BRYCE. *The Making of the Good Neighbor Policy.* New York: Columbia University Press, 1961.

18 Africa: The Wind of Change

Until the late 1950's most of Africa was under colonial rule, and, except in a negative sense, was not a significant factor in world affairs. Within a remarkably few years Africa has experienced a momentous awakening. More than 35 independent states have emerged in nearly all parts of the continent, and these new states have already made a profound impact on the United Nations and on international life generally.

In some respects the northern part of Africa, bordering on the Mediterranean, has been a part of the European realm for many centuries; but even here, once the traveler leaves the few cities along the seacoast, he enters a land scarcely known except to a few administrators and colonial experts. Aside from the Republic of South Africa, this is even more true of the continent south of the Sahara. Accurate information on most of Africa has been very spotty; and much of it is less than a century old.[1] Even today reliable data are hard to come by.

Thus Africa is still the "dark continent" — dark in two respects: the great majority of its inhabitants are Negroes and other dark-skinned peoples, and it is still largely unknown. Perhaps George H. T. Kimble was right when he wrote in 1951: "The darkest thing about Africa has always been our ignorance of it."[2]

Africa is a troubled continent, bubbling with conflicting forces and tribal, personal, and national rivalries. "The wind of change," to use a much-quoted phrase of former British Prime Minister Harold Macmillan, is still blowing strongly, if not steadily, over the vast continent and is affecting the whole picture of African life. Although the student of international relations is primarily interested in such matters as the changing patterns of colonialism and of nationalism, the emergence of new states, and Africa's growing role in world affairs, he must also look for the more basic forces which are transforming the face of Africa today. In the striking words and confused imagery of John Gunther: "Africa is like an exploding mass of yeast. Its fermentations are not merely political and economic, but social, cultural, religious. It is springing in a step from black magic to white civilization."[3]

As we read disturbing news from Algeria or the Congo, with "the spectacle of millions upon millions of people being transformed almost overnight from a primitive, tribal way of life to aggressive membership in modern

[1] Harry R. Rudin, "Past and Present Role of Africa in World Affairs," *The Annals* of the American Academy of Political and Social Science, CCXCVIII (March, 1955), 32.

[2] "Africa Today: The Lifting Darkness," *The Reporter,* May 15, 1951, p. 17.

[3] John Gunther, *Inside Africa* (New York: Harper, 1955), p. 3.

society,"[4] we wonder how in this age of international tensions and great social ferment Africa can be anything but a source of trouble. There is much justification for our apprehensions. Thousands of Africans have been uprooted from their old ways, and have not found their place in the new and changing society in which their destinies are now cast. "Yet all over the continent the Africans are on the move. They are people going somewhere, without being quite sure of the direction."[5] For all the instability, unrest, and uncertainty, the feeling of awakening is strong; "this continent seems united by a common surge of hope — just as, in the past, it must so often have seemed united by a common acceptance of despair."[6]

The Physical and Human Setting

Africa, second largest of continents, covers one-fifth of the land area of the globe. It is nearly four times the size of the United States. The Sahara alone, the largest desert in the world, is nearly as large as the United States; it operates in some respects as a sea — a sea of sand — dividing the African continent into two unequal parts. Geographically, historically, and to some extent culturally North Africa is much closer to Europe — and, through Islam, to the Middle East — than to Africa south of the Sahara. Most of Africa is a plateau, averaging some two thousand feet in height, and much of it is still relatively inaccessible land, in spite of the fact that its major cities are linked by air and in spite of a number of mighty rivers — the Nile in the east and northeast, the Zambesi in the southeast, the Congo in equatorial Africa, and the Niger and the Senegal in West Central Africa. Few natural harbors interrupt its sixteen-thousand-mile coastline.

By mid-1968 the population of Africa was about 300,000,000, and the annual rate of growth was around 2.3 per cent. The continent as a whole is rather sparsely populated, averaging perhaps 15 to 20 persons to the square mile; but "the population map of Africa shows every variation from the remarkable densities of the irrigated Nile Valley in Egypt to the uninhabited tracts of the Sahara, with such extremes often occurring in the closest proximity to one another."[7] While the Nile Valley in Egypt is by far the most heavily populated area, densities of more than 100 persons per square mile occur in a number of other parts, including the coastal regions of Tunisia, Algeria, Morocco, Nigeria, the southern and eastern coasts of South Africa, and the upper Sudan along the Nile Valley. Demographically, Africa certainly belongs to the Africans. According to most ethnologists, the three main racial groups are Hamites, Negroes, and "Bantus." The term "Bantu," which properly speaking is a linguistic and not a racial term, is applied rather generally to the great majority of the African peopes, dark-skinned but not Negroes, who live in Africa south of the Sahara. Some 900,000 persons of Indian origin live mostly in the Republic of South Africa and in East Africa. There are only about 6,000,000 Europeans in all of Africa; and about half of this relatively small number are in the Republic of South Africa. The rest are concentrated in white settler areas, mostly in East Africa. Nigeria, the largest African political unit in terms of population, has nearly 60,000,000 people, but fewer than 12,000 white Europeans.

Most of Africa belongs to what is referred to as the underdeveloped world, and most of the people are poor. In many parts the standards of living are among the lowest in the

[4] *Ibid.*, p. 3.

[5] Peter Abrahams, review of Oden Meeker, *Report on Africa* (New York: Charles Scribner's Sons, 1955), in the *New York Times Book Review*, August 22, 1954, p. 6.

[6] Basil Davidson, *The African Awakening* (London, 1955), p. 233.

[7] Robert W. Steel, "Africa: The Environmental Setting," *The Annals* of the American Academy of Political and Social Science, CCXCVIII (March, 1955), 7.

world, and per capita incomes among the smallest.[8] Millions of Africans are still hardly more than slaves — to their tribal chiefs, to their European masters, to their own ignorance and superstitions. Forced labor still exists in Portuguese Africa, and the conditions in mining areas and in native "reserves" in South Africa are hardly better than those of slavery. Life expectancy is low in most parts of the continent. The struggle against the diseases which afflict millions of Africans is dramatized by many records of striking successes, and by the labors of selfless men, of whom Dr. Albert Schweitzer was the best known.

Africa is deficient in several important resources, including oil, and large areas lack such essentials as an adequate water supply. It does have great sources of hydroelectric power, mostly untapped as yet, and it is the chief source of many vital materials. It supplies 98 per cent of the world's industrial diamonds, 80 per cent of the cobalt, 75 per cent of the sisal, 70 per cent of the palm oil, 50 per cent or more of the gold, 25 per cent of the manganese, and 20 per cent of the copper and tin. Furthermore, it has substantial amounts of uranium, especially in the Congo and in South Africa. Without the raw materials of Africa the Western world would be in a vulnerable position indeed. Furthermore, as John Gunther noted, "Africa is not only vital for what it already has, but is incomparably the greatest potential source of wealth awaiting development in the world."[9]

The cultural and social variations among the peoples of Africa are even more pronounced than their differences in political and economic status. Some still live in primitive tribal or subtribal groups, while others are sophisticated residents of cosmopolitan cities like Alexandria and Casablanca. Africans speak some seven hundred main languages, and belong to innumerable tribal and subtribal groupings. The people of Nigeria alone comprise at least 250 different tribal and linguistic groups. By almost any standards more than one-half of the people of Africa would be classified as pagans. About one-third are Muslims, mostly in North Africa and in West Africa as far south as the northern region of Nigeria, and their numbers are rapidly increasing. The 21,000,000 or more Christians include the Coptic Christians of the U.A.R. and Ethiopia.

The African Past

Very little is known of Africa's past, althought it was undoubtedly the home of some of the oldest human types. In fact, "recent discoveries in Uganda, Kenya and the Transvaal support the theory that Africa, and not Asia, was the cradle of the human race."[10] The original inhabitants may have been small, yellow-skinned men, resembling the Pygmies or the Bushmen who still exist in small numbers in remote parts; but black-skinned invaders from the northeast apparently pushed them southward. The one section in contact with existing civilizations since early times has been the area north of the Sahara. The Nile Valley, of course, was the center of one of the oldest of all civilizations, dating back more than five thousand years. Centuries before Christ, Phoenician traders skirted the coast of North Africa and established colonies, the most famous of which — Carthage — became the focus of a powerful empire which flourished for several centuries until it was destroyed by the Romans. Next to Egypt, the oldest center of advanced civilization in Africa, dating back to the third century B.C., was in what is now Ethiopia. Islam was introduced into North Africa by the Arabs between the seventh

[8] Naturally per capita income varies greatly, with the figures for Europeans being much higher than for Africans, even in the same parts of the continent.

[9] Gunther, p. 5.

[10] Vernon Bartlett, *Struggle for Africa* (London, 1953), p. 15.

and eleventh centuries A.D. Muslims from North Africa invaded southern Europe, and were not finally expelled until the late fifteenth century. Their expulsion almost coincided with the rounding of the Cape of Good Hope by Bartholomew Diaz in 1488 and Vasco da Gama's voyage to India in 1499. Thereafter, European contacts with Africa, which had been limited to settlements in North Africa and scattered landings along the northwestern coast, increased rapidly. These ventures were largely confined to the coastal strips, although the Dutch — ancestors of the present-day Boers or Afrikaners — colonized the Cape of Good Hope in the seventeenth century.

"Slavery was the ugly dominant note in African history for at least 250 years, roughly from 1562 to the early 1800's. It is impossible to underestimate the importance of this today in psychological and other realms."[11] Millions of Africans were seized and taken across the seas, by Arabs to the Middle East and by Europeans to the West Indies, the United States, and South America. Internal slavery continued to exist on a fairly large scale well into the nineteenth century.

Until little more than a century ago Africa south of the Sahara was "a coast, not a continent" as far as European knowledge of it was concerned.[12] Thereafter the interior was frequently explored, although Africa remained a relatively unknown continent, geographically as well as politically. In the first half of the nineteenth century the slave trade was finally ended, but in the second half the imperialist "scramble for Africa" took place. In the amazingly short space of a single generation, trickery and pressure resulted in the carving up of most of the continent among European powers. Great Britain and France got the lion's share, but substantial portions also went to Belgium, Italy, Portugal, Spain, and later Germany. The exploitation of the indigenous peoples by the imperial powers left a bitter legacy.[13] By 1912 only Egypt, Ethiopia, and Liberia were even nominally independent, and Egypt was under strong British influence, while the others were weak and backward. In spite of their defeat in the Boer War, the Boers in South Africa had attained a large measure of independence under British rule; but they too were of European stock and were already supporting the concept of "white supremacy" so strongly upheld by the rulers of the Republic of South Africa today.

Until relatively recently, therefore, the vast majority of the people of Africa lived quite isolated lives centered on remote villages or regions dominated by autocratic tribal chieftains or foreign rulers. The annexation of most of the continent by European powers in the late nineteenth century had the incidental effect of bringing the continent into the modern world. It is important to bear in mind how recently this emergence has occurred.

Patterns of Colonial Development

While certain similarities were present in the policies of the five European powers which controlled most of Africa, there were also striking differences in philosophy and objectives. Moreover, the territories of a single power were often in various stages of economic, social, and political development; and therefore the colonial power would follow a variety of practices in administering its territories.

British Africa. The official objective of British policy in Africa was "to guide the colonial territories to responsible self-government within the Commonwealth." No other colonial power stated this objective so unequivocally, or did so much to give it reality. The British, however, were faced with many complications and dilemmas in giving

[11] Gunther, p. 11.

[12] Margery Perham, quoted in Gunther, p. 12.

[13] Davidson, p. 60.

Africa in 1952

meaning to their pledge; some of these arose in Britain herself, and others in the colonial areas. They produced a rather marked discrepancy between British theory and practice in many parts of Africa.

It was by no means a coincidence that progress toward self-government was greatest in British West Africa — in the Gold Coast, Nigeria, Sierra Leone, and Gambia — where there were no substantial white settler communities.[14] In Nigeria, progress was delayed not so much by British resistance as by regional and tribal divisions within the colony. In East Africa the picture was entirely different and more disturbing. Especially in Kenya and the two Rhodesias, white minorities stood in the way of African advances toward self-government and constituted a special problem for Great Britain. In East Africa a third element — some 200,000 people of Indian origin — formed "a distinct layer wedged in between Europeans and Africans." The Central African Federation, created in 1953, a strange political arrange-

[14] See Don Taylor, *The British in Africa* (London, 1962).

ment that was not really a federation at all but a novel association of the self-governing colony of Southern Rhodesia and the protectorates of Northern Rhodesia and Nyasaland, was dominated by white settlers who numbered less than 200,000 as compared with more than 4,500,000 Africans. In all of British East and Southeast Africa, from Kenya to Bechuanaland, Swaziland, and Basutoland, only one African was a member of an executive council in 1952, and only 20 sat in legislative councils.

French Africa. With the exception of the island of Madagascar and the tiny colony of French Somaliland, all of the vast French empire in Africa was located in the western and northwestern parts of the continent. Algeria was classified as an Overseas Department, an integral part of metropolitan France, and therefore not a colony at all. Tunisia and Morocco were Associated States. French West Africa, French Equatorial Africa, French Somaliland, and Madagascar were Overseas Territories. French Togoland and Cameroons, which France held as trust territories, were known in the language of the "French Union" as Associated Territories. In *Afrique noire* — i.e., French Africa south of the Sahara — French rule was relatively moderate, and encountered little organized opposition. In French North Africa, inhabited largely by Moors, Berbers, and other peoples of Muslim faith, and by a substantial number of French settlers or *colons,* the situation was unhappily quite different. French difficulties in Tunisia and Morocco — and even in the Algerian Department as well — were constantly in the world's headlines.

Traditional French policy toward colonial areas may be summed up in the word "assimilation." At a conference in Brazzaville, the capital of French Equatorial Africa, in 1944, it was decided to abandon "assimilation" in favor of "closer association" in "one and indivisible French Union," a formula clearly designed to keep sovereign power as much as possible in French hands. Until a late date the French did not accept the goal of self-government for the peoples in their colonies; instead, they conferred on some of them what they regarded as an even greater boon: French citizenship. Under the constitution of 1946 all of the inhabitants of French Africa automatically became French citizens. The color bar was of little significance, except in a social sense. The emphasis was upon culture rather than color.

Belgian Africa. The Belgian Congo, one of the richest of colonial possessions, was eighty times as large as Belgium herself. Belgian colonial policy was a strange combination of enlightened and efficient paternalism and almost complete denial of social and political rights. A former governor-general of the Congo summed up the official policy in these words: "To dominate in order to serve." The Congo administration probably did more to improve the health and promote the welfare of Africans than any other colonial regime, but Africans were completely excluded from participation in government above the village level, and educational opportunities for them were highly restricted. If the Belgians thought at all in terms of self-government for the Congo, they obviously thought in long-range terms, and they did little to prepare for it.[15] Africans of the Congo congregated in large numbers in the

[15] Pierre Otis, Belgian representative on the United Nations Trusteeship Council, once stated that "the natives of Ruanda-Urundi, like those of the Congo . . . had no political aspirations and that if Colonial powers withdrew the result would be a return to savagery." Quoted in George Padmore, "Comparative Patterns of Colonial Development in Africa: 3, The Belgian System," *United Asia,* VII (March, 1955), 89. In an interview published in the *New York Herald Tribune* on November 25, 1951, the acting governor-general of the Congo predicted that some kind of electoral system providing "mixed black and white representative government" might come "in perhaps 20 to 30 years" and that self-government for the Congo might follow "in something less than 100 years." Less than a decade later the Congo became independent. See also H. A. Wieschoff, *Colonial Policies in Africa* (Philadelphia: University of Pennsylvania Press, 1944), p. 106.

urban centers. Although they were exposed to the vices and temptation which seemed to prevail generally in new industrial and commercial communities, they were not subjected to residential and social segregation, and they were probably far better off than most of their fellow Africans.

Portuguese Africa. Conditions in the two huge Portuguese possessions of Angola and Mozambique, and in the smaller territory of Portuguese Guinea, are generally the most backward in Africa. Forced labor still exists on a large scale; the Portuguese admit this and in fact condone it. They intend to make the Africans work, and to keep them under control indefinitely. If they ever need a safety valve for indigenous discontent or pressures, they think they have already devised one in the *assimilado* or *civilizado* system, which provides an opportunity for any inhabitant of a Portuguese territory to become assimilated or "civilized" by due process of law. "Once he becomes an *assimilado,* he assumes not only the privileges but the duties of full citizenship"; in effect, "he becomes a white man instead of black, no matter what his color."[16] In 1955 *assimilados* numbered only 30,000 out of more than 4,000,000 inhabitants in Angola and 4400 out of more than 5,600,000 in Mozambique.

Technically, Angola and Mozambique are integral parts of Portugal itself, with the rank of overseas provinces. They are administered under a highly centralized system, with virtually all decisions of importance being made in Lisbon. Since Portugal is ruled by authoritarian methods, it is hardly surprising that its overseas provinces should be governed in the same way. There are some redeeming features, including a relative absence of racial feeling. As compared with that of the former Belgian Congo the paternalism is less enlightened and less efficient.

[16] Gunther, p. 590.

Spanish Africa. Until 1956 Spain's most important possession in Africa was Spanish Morocco, across the Mediterranean from Gibraltar. Administered by the military in a way to keep it sealed off from the nationalist infection in adjoining French Morocco, it was "not only a feudal backwater, but the walled-off preserve of a grossly totalitarian dictatorship."[17] Thus insulated, the Moors got along with the Spaniards well enough. Dictator Franco's association with them has been close. Indeed, it was from Spanish Morocco that he led an army which was composed for the most part of Moorish soldiers to overthrow the Spanish Republic in 1936.

In 1956 Franco opened up this "walled-off preserve" in a surprising way by offering it to the emerging state of Morocco headed by Sutan Ben Youssef. The largest Spanish possession in Africa is unimportant Spanish Sahara, just below Morocco. Divided into two zones, Rio de Oro and Sekia el Hamra, its total area is slightly more than 100,000 square miles and its population about 75,000. Spain also retains some minute holdings in the northwest.

British and French Colonial Policies Compared. The pattern of colonial development in Africa was thus a most varied one. The greatest of the colonial powers, Great Britain and France, were willing to make more political concessions than Belgium, Portugal, or Spain. It is interesting to compare British and French colonial policy — the one based upon an increasing measure of self-government but open to serious criticism on the color issue, the other emphasizing "assimilation" and "association" and having much greater tolerance of people with colored skins. Two informed but somewhat contrasting views (both published in 1955) of the relative merits of these two policies will be presented here. In a comparison of

[17] *Ibid.*, p. 117.

colonial attitudes on "Colour and Culture," George Padmore wrote:

> The British colonial system provides the most flexible constitutional machinery for political evolution from colonial status to complete sovereign independence. Yet the racial relationship between French Europeans and the coloured colonial peoples in France and her overseas territories is easier and more tolerant than that of Britain and her colonies. The French judge a man by his culture; the British by the colour of his skin. . . . Politics apart, the French colonial officials are able to establish closer ties of personal friendship with the native elite than with the tribal Africans. . . . the Englishman gets on better with the more backward and primitive Africans. . . . Collectively, the natives in the French colonies are more repressed than those under British rule, but individually, educated Africans enjoy greater human dignity and suffer far less from colour bars and racial segregation under French rule.[18]

After his lengthy firsthand examination of conditions in all the major colonial areas John Gunther made this judgment:

> Taken all in all, British rule is the best. If I were an African I would rather live in a British territory than any other. The British do not give as much economic opportunity in some realms as the Belgians and perhaps not as much political and racial equality as the French in Black Africa, but the average African in British territory has more copious access to the two things Africans need most — education and justice. No doubt the British make blunders on occasion. But Great Britain is the only colonial power that has as its official policy the systematic training of Africans for self-government.[19]

By 1955 few self-conscious and articulate Africans were in a mood to make comparisons; to them, all colonial policies were fundamentally wrong. Their eyes were fixed on another goal, one declared in the final communiqué of the Asian–African Conference at Bandung in April, 1955: ". . . colonialism in all its manifestations is an evil which should speedily be brought to an end."

Nationalism in Africa

General Characteristics. Nationalism is perhaps the strongest force in Africa today, as it is in Asia, but its influence varies greatly from area to area. As in Asia, nationalism in Africa is an exotic product; "it is the end product of the profound and complex transformation which has occurred in Africa since the European intrusion"; it "is in one way or another a response to the challenge of alien rule, or of the intrusion of the disintegrating forces — and consequently the insecurity — of modernity."[20] It is largely a reaction against outside domination, against imperialism and colonization and all that these terms imply for peoples who have experienced their consequences for many years. In the words of a leading spokesman of African nationalism, Dr. Nnamdi Azikiwe of Nigeria, the aim is to achieve a "mental emancipation" from a servile colonial mentality.[21] It is hardly surprising that African nationalism should often vent itself in agitation against people with white skins. Here is one of the great dangers in African nationalism. As Elspeth Huxley warned, "if it becomes a bitter flood of hatred toward the whites, with their complete expulsion as its object, a welter of strife, misery, and failure lies in store for its inhabitants, and a great setback to the progress of the rest of the world."[22]

[18] "Colour and Culture: A Comparison of Colonial Attitudes," *United Asia,* VII (March, 955), 88.

[19] Gunther, pp. 885–886.

[20] James S. Coleman, "Nationalism in Tropical Africa," *American Political Science Review,* XLVIII (June, 1954), 407–408, 410. This is an unusually penetrating article on the motivating forces and major aspects of African nationalism.

[21] See Azikiwe's book, *Renascent Africa* (Lagos, Nigeria, 1937).

[22] Elspeth Huxley, "The Vast Challenge of Africa," *New York Times Magazine,* July 16, 1954, p. 18.

Many Africans believe that through the nationalist awakening they can not only achieve a greater degree of political freedom but also enhance their dignity and status as human beings. Too long, they contend, they have been second-class citizens in their own lands. A gnawing sense of inferiority and a growing resentment of European assumptions and manners of superiority — exacerbated because much of this is unconscious on both sides — account in large part for the efforts of Africans to assert their own identity in both a national and a personal sense. "The demand for 'identity' in the sense of acceptance as equals is indeed the basis of much African 'nationalism.' "[23]

The contemporary emphasis on cultural nationalism is widely reflected in current writings, in speeches by nationalist leaders, and in a growing number of studies by Africans of African history and life. "It has usually been accompanied by a quest for an African history which would in general reflect glory and dignity upon the African race and in particular instill self-confidence in the Western-educated African sensitive to the prejudiced charge that he has no history or culture. In short, there has emerged a new pride in being African."[24]

In Africa, as in Asia, most of the leaders of the nationalist movements are Western-educated persons, who have absorbed the revolutionary ideas of the West but have had to fight for a place in their own society and lands. James S. Coleman thus appraises the African version of this common phenomenon:

> . . . nationalism where it is most advanced has been sparked and led by the so-called detribalized, Western-educated, middle-class intellectuals and professional Africans; by those who in terms of improved status and material standards of living have benefitted most from colonialism; in short, by those who come closest to the Western World but have been denied entry on full terms of equality.[25]

African nationalism is not only a foreign importation; it has also been affected in many ways by external influences from the colonial powers themselves, from the United States, from the Soviet Union, from India, and more recently from Communist China. Political parties, labor organizations, and other associations and groups, as well as many individuals in the metropolitan countries, particularly Great Britain and France, have given a great deal of encouragement and support, directly or indirectly, consciously or unconsciously, to the political awakening of Africa. The British and French have been almost as successful, albeit quite unintentionally, in training the leaders of nationalism as they were in Asia. Contributions of a similar kind have been made by the United States, in spite of the not-too-successful efforts of official American spokesmen to steer a course between support of the colonial powers and anti-colonialism. As people of African descent, strongly conscious of the struggle for racial equality, it is not surprising that many American Negroes and Negro organizations have taken a special interest in Africa and Africans. Some of the important leaders of African nationalist movements, including Dr. Kwame Nkrumah and Dr. Nnamdi Azikiwe, former presidents of Ghana and Nigeria, and Peter Koiwange of Kenya, studied at American universities.

African nationalism is compounded of many factors; some of these are common to nationalism everywhere, and others arise from the peculiar conditions of the African environment and experience. James S. Coleman listed the following as factors which deserve analysis:

[23] Kenneth Robinson, "Colonial Issues and Policies with Special Reference to Tropical Africa," *The Annals* of the American Academy of Political and Social Science, CCXCVIII (March, 1955), 92.

[24] Coleman, p. 409.

[25] *Ibid.*, p. 414.

A. Economic
  1. Change from a subsistence to a money economy.
  2. Growth of a wage-labor force.
  3. Rise of a new middle class.

B. Sociological
  1. Urbanization.
  2. Social mobility.
  3. Western education.

C. Religious and Psychological
  1. Christian evangelization.
  2. Neglect or frustration of Western-educated elements.

D. Political
  1. Eclipse of traditional authorities.
  2. Forging of new "national" symbols.[26]

The influence of these factors is manifest in many parts of the continent, but there are also many variations in the character and intensity and results of nationalist movements. As Coleman pointed out, these variations are occasioned by such considerations as degrees of acculturation in different areas, the absence or presence of white settlers, the culture traits of various tribal groups and peoples, and differing colonial policies. "Nationalism is predominantly a phenomenon of British Africa, and to a lesser extent of French Africa."[27] It was relatively weak, or even non-existent except as a potential force, in the Portuguese, Belgian, and Spanish territories. It was strongly manifest in some of the independent states, notably the U.A.R. and the Republic of South Africa.

Some Western students of politics have emphasized the "differences between the new African political systems and the national states with which we are familiar,"[28] and between historical nationalism and the so-called nationalism of the new African independence movements. An American student of comparative politics and African affairs has observed:

> Africa's independence movements have . . . not been "nationalist" in the sense that European nationalist movements have been or still are today. . . . Africans have been so much preoccupied with gaining their own independence or, after its achievement, with the independence of the rest of Africa, that they have not yet had the time to think ahead to the problem of the most suitable forms of political organization for their growing communities, at least not in theoretical or conceptual terms. This failure to theorize about their own future institutions, however, does not mean that the leaders of independence drives want only to create nations on the conventional pattern, or to transfer mechanically to their countries the political institutions of Europe or America.[29]

Case Studies in African Nationalism: Nationalist movements in the following areas are particularly worthy of careful analysis: Egypt, South Africa, the former French North Africa, Kenya, Ghana, and Nigeria. While it is impossible to include here any detailed case studies, a few comments on the rise and characteristic features of the nationalist movements in these areas may be helpful.[30]

1. Egypt. Egyptian nationalism dates from the rise to power of the peasant leader Ahmed Arabi, "the founder of modern Egyptian nationalism," and the British occupation of Egypt in 1882. From 1882 until the 1954 Anglo-Egyptian agreements regarding the Suez Canal area and the Sudan, the main objective of Egyptian leaders was the removal of British controls. In 1918 the "first of the great nationalist parties of modern Africa," the Wafd, was founded. Under the

[26] *Ibid.*, pp. 411–412.
[27] *Ibid.*, p. 413.
[28] Herbert J. Spiro, *Politics in Africa: Prospects South of the Sahara* (Englewood Cliffs, N.J.: Prentice-Hall, 1962), p. 12.
[29] *Ibid.*, p. 13.
[30] Gunther's *Inside Africa* contains excellent accounts of the nationalist movements in Africa. The quotations in the following paragraphs are taken from this book, unless otherwise noted.

leadership of Zaghul Pasha, and, after Zaghul's death in 1927, of Nahas Pasha, the Wafd spearheaded the anti-British movement until World War II. In the post-war period the Wafd lost influence. In 1952 a coup engineered by General Naguib and Colonel Nasser forced King Farouk into exile, and laid the foundation for a modern nationalist state. Nasser, who soon dispensed with Naguib, became the spokesman for the "new Egypt." His unilateral action in nationalizing the Suez Canal in July, 1956, was regarded as motivated less by anti-British feeling or by concern for the national economy than by a desire to inflame Egyptian nationalism and to make a spectacular move to strengthen Egypt's position at the head of the Arab world. Egypt (now the United Arab Republic) has not only taken a leading role in the Arab League and the Arab–Israeli struggle, but it also "regards itself as a kind of mother and father to African nationalist movements everywhere," especially in the Muslim lands of North Africa.

2. *South Africa.* In most parts of Africa nationalism was a movement of black or other dark-skinned peoples against colonial rule and against the white domination. The outstanding exception is the Republic of South Africa, where "the equation is reversed. There are African nationalists, true, and they have an organization called the African National Congress. But it is *Afrikaner* (white) nationalism that counts in the Union, not African (black) nationalism." In a sense Afrikaner nationalism in South Africa had its origins in the settlement of this part of the continent by Boers (Dutch) and English. Even today these two white groups are often at odds. The main differences, however, are between whites and Africans, with the people of Indian origin as a further complicating factor. "The founder of South African nationalism as we know it today" was General Hertzog, who was prime minister of the Union from 1924 to 1939. "He believed in the 'two streams' policy," and was, "in a manner of speaking, the father of *apartheid,* even though this term was not invented until after his death." His predecessor and successor as prime minister, Jan Christian Smuts, although a fellow Boer and a believer in segregation, did not share Hertzog's hatred of the Africans.

In 1948, two years before Smuts died, the Nationalists triumphed in the first election "ever fought in South Africa largely on the racialist issue," and Dr. Daniel F. Malan formed "the first all-Afrikaner government in history." After another election in 1953 the Malan regime moved rapidly to consolidate its racialist rule, based on *apartheid* and white supremacy, in defiance of the world opinion, United Nations resolutions, and the vast majority of the people of the Union. When Malan retired in November, 1954, he was succeeded by Johannes G. Strijdom, whose racialism was even more pronounced than Dr. Malan's. From 1958 until his assassination in September, 1966, Prime Minister Hendrik F. Verwoerd, another arch-champion of *apartheid,* strengthened control over Africans in the so-called white areas and took various steps to concentrate most Africans in separate areas, called Bantustans. This policy has been continued by his successors.

African nationalism in South Africa is rigidly suppressed, but its representatives are active outside of the country. They can find encouragement in the mounting world criticism of the racialist policies of the South African government. Because of the criticism in Britain and other Commonwealth countries, South Africa withdrew from the Commonwealth in 1960, and became a republic in 1961. Thus in South Africa two nationalisms clash. One — that of the dominant white minority — is firmly entrenched. The other is weak inside the country, but because it represents, or claims to represent, the overwhelming majority of the population of South Africa, and because it is so strongly supported throughout most of Africa and to a lesser degree by world public opinion, it may well turn out to be the wave of the future. Thus a major question arises whenever the future is considered: Can rival nationalisms in South Africa reach some basis of coexistence without a prolonged struggle?

3. French North Africa. Tunisian nationalism dates back many years. As long ago as 1857 reform groups were active, and before World War II two patriotic organizations had come into being. The first real nationalist party, the Destour, was formed after World War I. A decade later the Neo-Destour party was organized by nationalists who were dissatisfied with the policies of the Destour group. This party became the spearhead of the Tunisian nationalist movement. From 1938 to 1954, along with other nationalist groups, it was officially outlawed, and many of its top leaders were imprisoned or exiled. It received powerful support from the *Union Générale des Travailleurs,* a non-Communist labor organization which Gunther described as "the best run and most powerful trade union organization anywhere in Africa above the Rhodesian Copper Belt." The leader of the *Union,* Farhat Hached, was murdered in December, 1952, allegedly by "a secret vigilante organization set up by *colons* and known as the Red Hand." The leader of the Neo-Destour was Habib Bourguiba, "an African nationalist of real stature."[31] After many years of exile and agitation Bourguiba was allowed to return to Tunisia in 1954, as a result of the far-reaching concessions which Mendès-France made to the demands of the Tunisian nationalists. In 1956 Tunisia attained independence, and in 1957 she became a republic, with Bourguiba as president. Bourguiba has often acted as a moderating influence on more rabid nationalists in North Africa, such as Gamal Abdel Nasser and Ahmed Ben Bella.

[31] See Lorna Hahn, "Elder Statesman of North Africa," *New York Times Magazine,* October 2, 1955.

The main nationalist party of Morocco, the Istiqlal, was founded in 1943. After the Casablanca riots of December, 1952, which were set off by the murder of Farhat Hached in Tunisia, the Istiqlal was driven under ground. It had centers in Tangier, New York, and Cairo. In 1953 the Sultan, Mohammed Ben Youssef, was deposed by certain pro-French Moroccan pashas. The real charge against Ben Youssef was that he was showing signs of supporting the Moroccan nationalist movement. His successor, Sultan Mohammed ben Moulay Arafa el Alaoui, became increasingly unpopular, and in 1955 the French were forced to bow to Moroccan demands for his deposition and for the return of the former Sultan. Ben Youssef returned to his throne in 1956 with French recognition of Moroccan sovereignty. In the following year Ben Youssef became King Mohammed V. After his death in 1961 his son succeeded him as King Hassan II. In December, 1962, a constitution, giving the king extensive powers, was approved in a referendum. Since 1963 King Hassan has encountered increasing difficulties with the Istiqlal Party and other political groups. In 1963, also, Morocco and Algeria became embroiled in armed conflict over disputed border territory. Although Morocco's troubles with Algeria, as well as domestic problems, were at least temporarily alleviated, the future course of nationalism inside Morocco and Morocco's relations with Algeria, Tunisia, and her neighbor to the south, Mauritania, are still uncertain.

The nationalist agitation in the adjoining areas of Tunisia and Morocco affected Algeria, even though this huge area was technically an Overseas Department of France. Late in 1954 the Algerian nationalists began an open rebellion, which ended only after a costly war with the French, bitter-end resistance of French settlers in Algeria, and civil strife between rival nationalist forces. The struggle for leadership within the dominant nationalist organization, the National

Liberation Federation (FLN) ended only in mid-1962, when Ahmed Ben Bella was elected premier of an independent Algeria. In the following year, after a constitution establishing a presidential one-party system of government was approved in a popular referendum, Ben Bella was elected President of the Democratic Republic of the People of Algeria. His radical policies at home and abroad created apprehensions among internal opposition groups and among almost all of his Arab and Muslim neighbors. He seemed to represent the radical nationalism of many of the emerging states of the new Africa.

In June, 1965, shortly before the scheduled opening of the second Asian-African Conference — which at the last moment was postponed to the following November and eventually postponed indefinitely — Ben Bella was overthrown by a coup led by the Vice Premier, Colonel Houari Boumedienne. The new leader was generally regarded as less radical and less pro-Nasser than Ben Bella, but he kept Algeria on a course based on socialism at home and nonalignment in foreign relations, strongly flavored by a strident brand of nationalism.

4. *Kenya.* Nationalism in Kenya became identified with the Mau Mau excesses against the white settlers in the highlands. Actually the Mau Mau revolt was only partly a product of extreme nationalism; it was also a reversion to a more primitive tribalism, and a bloody orgy against the whites. Most of its supporters belonged to the Kikuyu tribe. Long before the Mau Mau took matters into their own hands the Kikuyu had anti-British organizations. In 1922 the Kikuyu Central Association was formed, with Jomo Kenyatta, the best-known nationalist leader of East Africa, as secretary-general. When it was outlawed during World War II, it was succeeded by the Kenya African Union in 1944. Kenyatta was president of the KAU, and it was supported by most of the African political leaders of Kenya. This in turn was suppressed in June, 1953, because of the suspicion that it had instigated the Mau Mau terror. Kenyatta was brought to trial on the charge that instead of trying to suppress the Mau Mau, as he had agreed to do, he had really been the "manager" of the tribal terrorists. His trial, which lasted for five months, attracted worldwide attention and much sympathy for the cause of Kenyan nationalism. Kenyatta was found guilty and sentenced to seven years' imprisonment.

In 1960, while in exile, he was made president of the Kenya African National Union (KANU). Released two years later, he became minister of state for constitutional affairs and economic planning under a new constitution which he helped the British government to draft. In May, 1963, following elections in which KANU emerged victorious, he became Kenya's first prime minister, a position which he continued to hold after Kenya became independent on December 12, 1963. In 1964 Kenya became in effect a one-party state when the leading opposition party, the Kenyan African Democratic Union (KADU), merged with KANU. A strong nationalist with charismatic appeal, Kenyatta is also interested in a possible East African Federation with Uganda and Tanzania and in various movements in the direction of African unity.

5. *Ghana.* In the Gold Coast (now Ghana), according to Dr. Kwame Nkrumah, nationalism has a long history, but it had made little progress before World War II.[32] At the end of that war the United Gold Coast Convention, with Dr. J. B. Danquah as president, was organized. On Dr. Danquah's invitation Dr. Nkrumah returned to the Gold Coast after an absence of twelve

[32] See Kwame Nkrumah, "Gold Coast's Claim to Immediate Independence," *United Asia,* VII (March, 1955), 59–64. This article is adapted from Nkrumah's famous speech on the Motion for Independence, delivered before the Legislative Assembly of the Gold Coast in July, 1953.

years. The two, however, soon became political rivals, and the younger man prevailed over the older nationalist spokesman. In the following years, while Dr. Nkrumah was prime minister, steps were taken to make the Gold Coast "a sovereign and independent state within the Commonwealth," a goal achieved in 1957, when as Ghana she became the first black member of the Commonwealth. In 1960, following a constitutional plebiscite and a presidential election, Ghana became a republic, with Dr. Nkrumah as president.

As head of state, chief executive, and leader of the only recognized party, the Convention People's Party, Dr. Nkrumah governed Ghana in an increasingly arbitrary way and ruthlessly suppressed any internal opposition. He also emerged as a leading spokesman of the more radical brand of African nationalism and perhaps the most vocal advocate of genuine union among African states. He regarded himself as both an ardent African nationalist and a great internationalist. He was hailed as the "Osagyefo" ("Redeemer") and was made president for life. The cult of Nkrumahism seemed to be the national ideology of the country. But, as had happened to so many seemingly strongly entrenched leaders in other African states, on February 24, 1966, Dr. Nkrumah, while on a goodwill tour in Asia, was overthrown by the military, and the policies of the country took an entirely new turn. Dr. Nkrumah sought refuge in Guinea with his friend, Sekou Touré, who proclaimed him "the head of the state of Guinea and secretary general of the Guinean Democratic Party." Very little was heard of him after his sudden deposition.

6. Nigeria. In Nigeria, Africa's most populous nation, there emerged several rival nationalist movements, based on conflicting tribal and regional loyalties. In the Western Region Chief Obafemi Awolowo founded the Action Group in 1953, drawing its chief support from members of the Yoruba tribe. In the Eastern Region American-educated Dr. Nnamdi Azikiwe became the dominant leader of the National Council of Nigeria and the Cameroons, organized in 1947, and supported mainly by members of the Ibo tribe. The two nationalist parties were "flamingly antagonistic," and nationalism became "a kind of football." They soon had to take account of the emergence in the more backward but more populous Northern Region of another nationalist group, the Northern People's Congress, the organ of the area's chief religious and political leader, the Sardauna of Sokoto, and of the dominant Hausa tribe.

Independence for Nigeria was delayed not so much by British policy as by differences among the rival regions, parties, and tribes. In a conference in London in 1953, attended by Azikiwe, Awolowo, and a representative of the Northern Region, an agreement was reached with the British government, providing that each of the three main regions of Nigeria "may, if it wishes, become completely self-governing" within a central federation.

Internal differences continued to be so great that seven more years passed before Nigeria became independent, on October 1, 1960. Three years later she became a republic, with Dr. Azikiwe, who had become governor-general since independence, as president. Differences between the regions, tribes, and parties, and within some of the parties, continued, and indeed became so serious that in late 1964, following elections which were largely boycotted in the three southern regions (a fourth region was created in 1963), Nigeria seemed to be in danger of splitting up. This crisis was surmounted, but the fissiparous tendencies within the nation are still strong.

These tendencies became even more manifest in January, 1966, when a bloody military coup overthrew the existing regime, and led to the murder of some of the most prominent leaders of the country, including the political boss of the Northern Region, the

Sardauna of Sokoto; his follower in Lagos, Sir Abubakar Tafawa Balewa, the Prime Minister of Nigeria; the Finance Minister of Nigeria, Festus Okotie-Eboh; and the Prime Minister of the Western Region, Chief Samuel L. Akintola. The coup was engineered by younger officers, and was rather quickly suppressed by more senior leaders, led by the army chief-of-staff, Major Aguiyi-Ironsi, an Ibo. In July, following anti-Ibo riots in the north, a second army mutiny led to the murder of Ironsi and the establishment of a coalition regime representing the main regions, under Colonel Gowon, a Hausa, a northerner, and a Christian. In September and October, 1966, thousands of Ibos were massacred in the north, and more than a million were driven out of the Northern Region. On May 30, 1967, Colonel Ojukwa, an Ibo, proclaimed the Republic of Biafra in the former Eastern Region of Nigeria, where the majority of Ibos and much of the oil wealth of the country were concentrated. The Gowon regime attempted to crush this rebellion by force.

These events raised a huge question mark about Nigeria's future. They adversely affected Nigeria's political stability and integration, her economy, her foreign policy, and her international status. Potentially the most important state of Africa, Nigeria will have to overcome her serious internal divisions and tribal rivalries if she is to remain a state at all.

The Emergence of Africa

As late as 1955 most of Africa was still under the control of European powers. Britain was dominant in much of West, East and South Africa. In addition to important territories which she governed directly, such as the Gold Coast, Nigeria, Kenya and the Rhodesias, she supervised Uganda and Tanganyika as trust territories under the United Nations Trusteeship System, and the Sudan was a joint Anglo-Egyptian condominium. France was still in control of Morocco and Tunisia as well as of Algeria, which was technically a part of metropolitan France; and she governed vast tracts in East Africa, the area known as French West Africa, and French Equatorial Africa, as well as the island of Madagascar. Belgium seemed to be firmly entrenched in the Congo for an indefinite period, and she was the trust power for Ruanda and Burundi. Portugal controlled the vast areas of Angola and Mozambique, and smaller territories along Africa's west coast. Spain possessed the Spanish Sahara and other pockets in the northwestern part of the continent.

The only exceptions to this prevailing pattern of European rule were the ancient kingdom of Ethiopia, which Italy had occupied on two occasions, from 1895 to 1898 and from 1935 to 1941; Liberia, founded by freed American slaves in 1822, and an independent republic since 1847; the Union of South Africa, created shortly before World War I; and Egypt, recently freed of British influence and of the arbitrary rule of King Farouk. But Africa was on the verge of a vast political awakening, which in the next few years witnessed the emergence of independent states in most of the continent and thus drastically changed the map as well as the politics and international position of the second largest continent. In 1956 Morocco and Tunisia received their independence from France, though with some "interdependent links," and the Sudan was able to secure the end of the Anglo-Egyptian condominium. In 1957 the Gold Coast emerged as the independent state of Ghana, an event which marked the beginning of the end of British rule in Africa, and perhaps also the emergence of independent Africa as a powerful and often radical factor in the world. In the following year, after a plebiscite in the French colonies, Guinea elected to sever her political ties with France and to embark on an independent career, while the other African states of the "French Community" chose temporarily to retain their ties with France.

The year 1960 was truly the year of African independence. Within this year fifteen new states suddenly emerged, marking the end of the French empire in Africa and of the British empire in West Africa. Eleven of these fifteen new states were created in former French West Africa and French Equatorial Africa, and a twelfth — Madagascar, renamed the Malagasy Republic — was also a former member of the French Community. The other three were the Congo (Leopoldville) — so-called to distinguish it from the adjoining state of the same name, with its capital of Brazzaville — Nigeria, and Somalia. The Congo (Leopoldville) was the former Belgian Congo, an area which Belgium had done little to prepare for an independence that seemed to be many years away. Nigeria was of special importance, because she was the most populous state in all of Africa and appeared to be more stable and responsible and better prepared for independence than most of the new African states.

In the next six years thirteen more states were created in various parts of Africa — Sierra Leone, Cameroon, and Tanganyika in 1961, Algeria, Rwanda (as Ruanda was renamed), and Burundi in 1962, Kenya and Zanzibar (which later merged with Tanganyika to form a state known as Tanzania) in 1963, Malawi (formerly Nyasaland) and Zambia (formerly Northern Rhodesia) in 1964, the Gambia in 1965, and Botswana (formerly Bechuanaland) and Lesotho (formerly Basutoland) in 1966. By 1967 most of the continent was politically independent. The great exceptions were the Portuguese territories; South-West Africa, controlled by the Republic of South Africa; and Rhodesia (formerly Southern Rhodesia), whose unilateral declaration of independence was not recognized by Great Britain, or by any of the members of the OAU.

The emergence of Africa is thus a very recent development. Before 1955, as we have seen, almost the entire continent was under European control. Africa was therefore the last major stronghold of colonialism. Strong nationalist movements developed at a rather late date, and in many instances gathered momentum with amazing speed. A new Africa has emerged, an Africa of many independent states. In most of these new states the first years of independence have been rather rocky ones, and at times, as in Algeria or the Congo or Nigeria, it has seemed that a new nation was about to disappear in a maelstorm of internal troubles, civil war, and foreign intervention. The new Africa is still seeking its own identity, and is still searching for ways to achieve national survival, continental cooperation and unity, and a new international status. All of these developments are so recent that their full implications cannot yet be properly assessed.

Major Trends and Problems

As Africa emerges into the modern world, it is hampered by barriers of geography and of ignorance, by racial tensions and social dislocations, by the legacy of the past, by problems arising from the struggle for racial equality, economic betterment, and political independence, and by the effect of conflicts among the great powers and of the general international situation. We shall here attempt to summarize what seem to be the major trends and problems of the present time.

1. As in Asia, though to a lesser degree, nationalism is a major force in most of the continent. It is particularly strong in Egypt, Algeria, Kenya, Guinea, and Ghana. As we have already noted, it has often appeared in perverted forms, in association with such movements as the tribal blood cult of the Mau Mau in Kenya and the *apartheid* drive in the Republic of South Africa.

2. Africa was the last great stronghold of colonialism in the world, but that stronghold has been breached and largely overthrown. Whereas after World War II all but one-

tenth of the area of Africa and one-fifth of its people were ruled by Europeans, at present European colonialism is entrenched only in Angola, Mozambique, and smaller pockets in the northwestern and southern parts of the continent.

In their present frame of mind, few Africans will say anything good of colonialism; but it did bring many benefits to the "dark continent" and, more important still, it laid the basis for the educational, social, economic, and political advances which had to come before Africans could hope to be really free. "Colonialism has been the terrible though necessary hurricane which has swept away the old in preparation for the new."[33] It provided the "revolutionary stimulus" which was essential to bring about a new order of affairs. "The supplying of this revolutionary stimulus may be the only moral and material justification for colonial conquest: but it is a real one."[34]

3. A by-product of the present urge to nationalism and the anti-colonial feeling is a tendency to glorify Africa's pre-European past and to paint the era of European domination in the blackest colors. This tendency is perhaps a natural consequence of the determination of Africans to find the roots of their present institutions and practices in their own soil and culture. But the picture is greatly overdrawn, and leads to a gross distortion of the conditions of the past and the needs of the present. As Basil Davidson has pointed out, African nationalism "carries with it a tendency to see the pre-European past as pure, noble and independent; and the disintegration of tribal life as the entirely negative consequence of Europen presence. This romantic attitude . . . lies at the root of much of the obscurantism which is now at work within the nationalist movements of central and southern Africa."[35]

[33] Davidson, p. 189.
[34] *Ibid.*, pp. 237–238.
[35] *Ibid.*, p. 139.

4. Thus far communism has not been a significant force in African nationalist movements, and it would be an inexcusable error to ascribe the African awakening to Communist instigation.[36] Neither the Soviet Union nor Communist China maintains diplomatic missions in many African countries, although the number is growing year by year as both step up their activities in Africa. In some cases they have suffered at least temporary setbacks. Guinea, for example, reacted rather strongly against Soviet pressures, after some Western observers had practically written her off as a Soviet satellite. Burundi, which in 1964 seemed to be the head-center of Chinese Communist machinations in Africa, expelled the Chinese bag and baggage early in 1965. The Soviet Union and Communist China are often rivals; Africa, in fact, has become a theater for a strange kind of Communist cold war.

In very few African countries do local Communist parties have any real strength. No African state has gone Communist (Zanzibar may have provided a temporary exception), although the leaders of some states have flirted dangerously with the Communists and have consciously or unconsciously played the Communist game.

At the same time it would be folly to underestimate the potential influence of Communism in Africa. Africans have not experienced Communist imperialism, but they are all too familiar with the Western brand. In their struggle for freedom from Western

[36] Stuart Cloete, author of *The African Giant* (Boston: Houghton Mifflin Company, 1955), appears to hold a different view: "Behind all African unrest, though there is real cause for some of it, lies the sinister force of Communist propaganda and the Communist *agent provocateur*." Unless the white and black races can learn how to cooperate and unless a multi-racial society emerges in Africa, Cloete fears "a black tyranny in which Africa will be swept into the gaping mouth of the Eastern Communist Dragon." Review of Edmund Stevens, *North African Powder Keg* (New York: Coward-McCann, 1955), in the *New York Times Book Review*, November 27, 1955, p. 3.

domination they may be willing to turn to the Communists, who claim to champion the causes which mean so much to the Africans: freedom from imperial control, racial equality, freedom from economic exploitation. Few, if any, outstanding African nationalist leaders are Communists but some of the persons and organizations upon which they depend have been less discriminating. Communist agents and sympathizers are active in French North Africa, particularly in Tunisia and Morocco. Communist agents and sympathizers control the *Confédération Générale de Travail,* which is affiliated with the Communist-dominated International Federation of Trade Unions. Communist influence is strong in several African states, including the U.A.R., Algeria, Mali, Tanzania, and the Congo.[37] The Communists go out of their way to establish contacts with African students in England and on the continent of Europe. Large numbers of African students have studied in the Soviet Union (in the Patrice Lumumba or "Friendship" University and elsewhere), in China, and in the Communist countries of Eastern Europe. Communist agents are active in many parts of Africa. The Communists, in short, are always available, and they are not discouraged by the limited results which they have achieved up to the present time.

5. "By all odds the most serious problem on the continent is that of race."[38] This usually centers on the relations between the black Africans and their white rulers or the white settlers in various parts of the continent. The experience of the indigenous peoples of Africa with white peoples over several centuries has created a basic mistrust which has often led to hatred and to extremist movements for revenge. This mistrust is strengthened by current evidences of the same old attitude of superiority, which takes aggravated forms in the Republic of South Africa and Rhodesia and which poisons all efforts to establish a tolerable working basis for the "co-existence" of whites and blacks and for effective international cooperation in dealing with other African problems. "It is the color bar, above everything, that makes Africa boil with discontent. It is the root cause of African inferiority, which in turn leads to resentment and revolt; it warps the minds of white man and black man both."[39]

Black Africans are inclined to overcompensate for real or imaginary indignities inflicted by white peoples by an exaggerated emphasis on "negritude" and on what a perceptive Indian journalist called "the importance of being black."[40] The Communists try to exploit these racial feelings to win support in Africa and to stir up the latent hostility toward the white nations of the West. The Russians are somewhat handicapped in this approach because most of them belong to the white race. The Chinese have had some success in identifying themselves with the black Africans as fellow colored peoples. This note has apparently been employed to turn Africans away from the Soviet Union, as well as from the nations of the "capitalist" West. The emphasis on racialism seems to be increasing year by year. In 1964, for example, the London *Times* observed: "Events, and even more propaganda, have in the past year fed a widespread feeling that in the last resort the issue in Africa is a fight between the white race and the black."

6. Conflicts of culture values, occasioned by rapid change, the breakdown of the old institutions and loyalties, and the existence

[37] See Zbigniew Brzezinski, ed., *Africa and the Communist World* (Stanford, Calif.: Stanford University Press, 1963); and John K. Cooley, *East Wind over Africa: Red China's African Offensive* (New York: Walker & Company, 1965).

[38] C. L. Sulzberger, "Africa Makes a Start Toward a Better Day," *New York Times,* February 8, 1953, Sec. 4, p. 3.

[39] Gunther, p. 15.

[40] Frank Moraes, *The Importance of Being Black; an Asian Looks at Africa* (New York: The Macmillan Company, 1965).

almost side by side in some parts of Africa of communities with different cultural patterns and habits, are disruptive features of the present social environment. Writing in 1949, "a distinguished intellectual of the Gold Coast" described the nature of conflicts of this sort on one West African community; his words may be applied to much of Africa:

> We have seen the conflict of cultural values in monogamy versus polygamy; Christianity versus Tigare; matrilineal versus patrilineal inheritance; individualism versus traditional family obligations; elective municipal government versus tribal loyalties; in the discourtesy governing social relations in the new economic and governmental institutions; in the absence of social responsibility. . . in the ineffectiveness of moral and legal sanctions; and most prominently and obviously of all in increased crime, prostitution, juvenile delinquency, unbridled acquisitiveness, bribery and corruption, which are symptoms of a maladjusted society.[41]

7. One of the most obvious and fundamental results of the impact of the West and of the emergence of a new order in Africa has been what might be called the de-tribalization of society. African tribal life is incompatible with modern society; its evils include "ignorance, superstition, submergence of the individual, rigid conformity, unrewarding use of natural resources, poor food, bad health, spiritual dwarfing."[42] But it once provided a framework within which the African people could feel fairly secure, or at least one which they understood. Now, as Emory Ross has observed, "a wholeness, a oneness in African tribal life . . . is being fractured by a force and at a speed from without which has no historical parallel in such a large and primary human society."[43] The reasons for this tremendous social change are summarized by Daniel F. McCall:

> The super-imposition of outside authority, the intrusion of proseletyzing religions which attack the ideological foundations of tribal authority, the values of the market place superseding the values of the kinship system . . . all contributed to the decline in effectiveness of tribal organization. The necessity of meeting new situations for which there were no tribal precedents, the temporary or permanent loss of much tribal manpower to outside employment, the corruption of chiefs in their role of custodian of land, and the venality of many of them in spending such profits for personal use have further reduced the capacity of tribal organization to function.[44]

The tribal system is still strong in many parts of Africa. Its influence is everywhere manifest, directly or indirectly. Even in the more economically advanced areas Africans still often revert to tribal practices, if only as a reaction to the foreign influences which seem to be disrupting their old ways of life. But even in rural areas the tribal system is a sick institution, and in the growing urban centers it is an anomaly. "Nothing can save it whole."[45]

[41] Quoted in Davidson, p. 188.

[42] Emory Ross, "Africa's Need for Wholeness," in Harold R. Isaacs and Emory Ross, "Africa: New Crisis in the Making," *Headline Series,* No. 91 (New York: Foreign Policy Association, January–February, 1952), p. 58.

[43] *Ibid.,* p. 58.

[44] Daniel F. McCall, "Dynamics of Urbanization in Africa," *The Annals* of the American Academy of Political and Social Science, CCXCVIII (March, 1955), 153.

[45] Ross, p. 58. The grave implications of the de-tribalization of African society and the "social disintegration of the African native" are well expressed in the following words of Apa B. Pant, former Indian High Commissioner to East Africa: "The real problem of Africa . . . is the problem of creating new societies from the ruins of the tribal, primitive societies that inhabited Africa for centuries. As long as this problem of creating new patterns of life wherein the African will find a place of honour and scope for creative living is not solved, Africa would always present a question mark to the world. . . . The tribal life was a life of comparative peace and tranquillity. If there was disease or tribal warfare, the heart of the man was peaceful and contented whilst he lived and obeyed the rules of tribal life. Today, there

8. Urbanization and industrialization, with all their momentous consequences, are changing the face of Africa. All over Africa there is a mass movement from the rural areas to the towns and cities. "It is more than a mere change in numbers; it is a change in social relations."[46] According to one estimate, "by 1980 the majority of the whole African population will be town-dwellers."[47] In the long run the effects of this rapid urbanization should be generally beneficial. "The town is the door through which Africa is entering the modern world."[48] But there can be no doubt that, as in other parts of the world, the early effects of urbanization and industrialization are generally unfortunate. They are reflected in widespread social disintegration, a sense of rootlessness, and all the evils which usually exist in overcrowded new urban centers.

9. The future evolution of Africa and the relations of its various parts with each other and with the rest of the world, particularly with the Western world, are still complicated by the existence in many areas of "white settler communities." The white settlers were usually opposed to far-reaching concessions to African demands. They were understandably concerned over their own future and fate if and when the Africans take over. They are a major barrier to satisfactory relations between the European colonial powers and the majority of the inhabitants of their former African possessions. Only in former French North Africa and in the Republic of South Africa, at the extreme ends of the continent, are whites very numerous. Before independence Kenya was also "a white settlement state par excellence." Only some 4,000 of the 42,000 white settlers held land, but they controlled 24 per cent of the arable land. Some 5,500,000 Africans were excluded from these territories. The Mau Mau terror in Kenya was occasioned in large measure by bitterness over the conditions of white land settlement.

10. For more than three centuries European powers dominated most of Africa, and their impact was felt in a multitude of ways. It is still a major determining aspect of African life and development. In the new era of African independence can the relations between Africans and Europeans change from those of superiority–inferiority, domination–subordination, and fear–hatred to those of understanding–cooperation?

11. For a long time Asia has exerted a powerful influence on Africa, and today Africans are looking toward Asia as never before. The Indian connection with Africa has been particularly close. Thousands of Indians migrated to South and East Africa several decades ago. The work of Mahatma Gandhi among his oppressed fellow-countrymen of South Africa is well known. It was there that he initiated and tested his techniques of *satyagraha,* or nonviolent resistance, which he applied extensively and effectively in India after World War I. In Kenya, Tanzania, and Uganda thousands of Indians live and work, chiefly in the commercial field. Their presence adds another complication to the racial problems in these areas, but it also contributes greatly to the economic and political life. African na-

---

is certainly less disease and no tribal warfare. There certainly is more food available and cloth to protect man from want. But the safety and security of the tribal life has vanished and with it has also vanished the peace and tranquillity of the heart. The African today is first of all bewildered, then frustrated, and then angry to find himself a nobody in the social pattern of existence that has been built up around him, as it were, overnight. . . . If his society is now broken down, it is inconceivable that he should live without any privileges or securities in the new society." "Social Disintegration of the African Native," *United Asia,* VII (March, 1955), 96. Professor Vernon McKay has argued that "the word *tribalism* . . . is to some extent a trap for loose thinking," since "it is used to cover such widely varied phenomena." *Africa in World Politics* (New York: Harper & Row, 1963), p. 419.

[46] Davidson, p. 95.

[47] *The Times* (London), April 5, 1954.

[48] McCall, p. 160.

tionalists have gained hope and confidence from the successful outcome of the struggle for freedom in many parts of Asia; and in the United Nations and elsewhere leaders of the newly independent states of Asia are champions of African aspirations. Contacts between Africa and Asia are increasing year by year. The Asian-African Conference in Bandung in April, 1955, symbolized the special ties and interests that bind together the peoples of the two largest continents.

African Political Systems

On the pedestal of a statue of "Osagyefo" Kwame Nkrumah which stood in front of the Parliament House in Accra, the capital of Ghana, until it was pulled down after Nkrumah's overthrow in 1966, were inscribed these words: "Seek ye first the political kingdom, and all other things shall be added unto it." The search for "the political kingdom" has come to dominate the African scene in recent years. Not long ago most of the continent was under colonial rule, independence movements were feeble and unimpressive, and little political activity was permitted. Today politics has become an absorbing profession, or at least pastime. The very novelty of African politics has given it a special fascination, and has led to the quest for new political ideologies and new forms of political organization which will not be pale copies of Western models.

Political systems of various kinds, of course, existed even before the colonial period. Many of these were essentially tribal, and some were so embryonic in nature that they hardly provided a framework of government in the modern usage of this term. Traditional Islamic political systems penetrated large parts of the northern half of the continent, extending as far to the southwest as present-day Nigeria. In the colonial era most of Africa was divided and subdivided to suit the administrative convenience of the ruling powers, often in disregard of tribal or other historic divisions. The pattern of colonial administration, and Western political thought and ideas of the sovereign state system, largely determined the boundaries and to a considerable degree the political ideologies of the states which sprang into existence so rapidly in 1960 and thereafter.

All of the states of Africa are transitional societies. Some are still strongly traditional in tribal organization, social customs, or ruling oligarchy; others have modernizing regimes, but these usually provide a thin façade for traditional structures and may represent negativism more than achievement. Some of the new states are controlled by the same groups, and often the same leaders, that headed the independence movements, while several others have come under the control of military regimes; but these revolutionary groups and leaders are not necessarily well qualified to lead in the difficult tasks of nation-building. Only in Ethiopia does an ancient ruling house still predominate. Emperor Haile Selassie is essentially an autocratic ruler, even though he granted a constitution in 1955 and has sponsored certain limited reforms in his country. One of the most backward of African states, Ethiopia has taken on some of the panoply of modernization, and the Emperor has provided a home for a number of African organizations, including the United Nation's Economic Commission for Africa and the Organization of African Unity. In greater or lesser degree this strange mixture of traditionalism, transitionalism, and modernism characterizes most of Africa. There are still amazingly backward areas and regions, and some, such as the Portuguese possessions of Angola and Mozambique, and South-west Africa, under the control of South Africa, about which little is known. British political patterns, forms of government, law, and administration, and political idioms are still strongly apparent in Kenya, Tanzania, Uganda, the former Central African Federation, and in Ghana, Nigeria and elsewhere in former British West Africa. French influences, extending even more noticeably to the cultural realm, are still apparent in the vast areas which were once French North Africa, French West Africa, and French Equatorial Africa.

Aside from Ethiopia, monarchy still exists in only a few African states, notably in Morocco, in Libya, and in Burundi. In all of these states certain constitutional forms are observed, but the government is in fact subservient to the ruling monarch. When the Abboud regime collapsed in the Sudan in 1964, the last clearly military dictatorship in Africa passed from the scene. Until 1965, except in the Sudan, the military had not played the role in Africa that it has played and still plays in some Latin American and Asian states. Where it was an important factor it was usually an instrument of the civilian leaders. But in 1965–66 a series of military coups toppled civilian leaders and governments in several African countries, including such important states as Algeria, Nigeria, and Ghana. Militarism seems to have become a significant new factor in Africa.

The fact has often been noted that most of the states of Africa have systems in which a single party, and often a single leader, so dominates the political scene that significant opposition does not seem to exist. Opposition may in fact exist, but it may be so ruthlessly suppressed by the party in power that it can be carried on only clandestinely inside the country and more vigorously by exiles in various parts of the world. In some cases the opposition may be subsumed in a kind of national political front; this is the case in the U.A.R., Mauritania, and Kenya. In most African states the dominant party is easily identifiable — for example, the Neo-Destour Party in Tunisia, the National Liberation Front (FLN) in Algeria, the Democratic Party of Guinea (PDG) in Guinea, Ivory Coast Democratic Party (PDCI) in the Ivory Coast, and Senegalese Progressive Union (UPS) in Senegal, the Convention People's Party (CPP) in Ghana (before Nkrumah's deposition), the Tanzanian African National Union (TANU) in Tanzania, the Malawi Congress Party (MCP) in Malawi.

The one-dominant-party pattern is not universal in Africa, even allowing for the fact that in a number of countries other parties are tolerated only to preserve a democratic façade. A few of the more traditionally oriented states, such as Ethiopia and Libya, and some of the states which have recently come under the control of military regimes, do not permit political parties at all. Few, if any, examples of genuine multiple party states can be found.

In Nigeria, unhappily, each of the three major political groupings had a tribal and regional base, and represented tribal rivalries rather than national loyalties. The Northern People's Congress was the party of the Northern Region, the largest region in terms of area and population but the most backward economically; the National Convention, of the Eastern Region; and the Action Group, of the Western Region. Even before the military coup in January, 1966, the multi-party system was working rather badly. Since then the parties have only reinforced the divisions that have eventuated in civil war.

Uganda, which became an "independent sovereign state" only on October 9, 1963, with the Kabaka (ruler) of the Kingdom of Buganda, Sir Edward F. Mutesa, as president, had three main parties: the Uganda People's Congress, whose leader, Milton Obote, was prime minister; the Kabaka Yekka, whose delegates were appointed by the legislature of Buganda; and the Democratic Party, the main opposition party after the Kabaka Yekka entered a coalition government with the UPC. This situation came to an abrupt end in 1966. On February 22 Obote assumed all government powers, and two days later he suspended the constitution. After bloody fighting in Buganda in May the

Kabaka fled from the country, and Buganda was split up into four provinces.

The Republic of South Africa is sometimes called a two-party state, since there is an official opposition party, the United Party, with some 50 seats in the 160-member House of Assembly; but the members of this party, supported largely by whites of English descent in South Africa, like those of the dominant Nationalist Party, composed almost wholly of *apartheid*-minded Afrikaners, are chosen by white voters only in a country where whites constitute less than one-sixth of the total population, and they are almost as firm, if not as adamant, the Nationalists on the question of the maintenance of white supremacy.

When the ill-fated Central African Federation was formally dissolved on December 31, 1963, after ten years of troubled existence, Nyasaland emerged as the independent state of Malawi, with the Malawi Congress Party in control; Northern Rhodesia became the state of Zambia, with at least three parties having some real strength in the unicameral legislature; and Southern Rhodesia, renamed Rhodesia, became a self-governing British colony with almost-Dominion status. In Rhodesia, whose unilateral declaration of independence in November, 1965, has not been generally recognized, two parties, the Rhodesian Front Party and the United Federal Party, have significant strength; but these are European-dominated parties in a country where the Europeans comprise hardly 18 per cent of the total population.

As in most newly emerging countries, personal loyalties and personal leaders are of surpassing importance in the African states, most of which are not only one-dominant-party but one-dominant-leader states. In most African states a single, charismatic leader stands out above all others, although he himself may have succeeded a previous charismatic leader and may have around him others with aptitude, if not opportunity, for such leadership. The roster of these charismatic leaders is long. Current or recent examples are Nasser in the U.A.R., King Idris I in Libya, Habib Bourguiba in Tunisia, King Hassan II in Morocco, Mokhtar Ould Daddah in Mauritania, Léopold Senghor in Senegal, Modibo Keita in Mali, Sekou Touré in Guinea, William Tubman in Liberia, Felix Houphouet-Boigny in the Ivory Coast, François Tombalbaye in Chad, David Dacko in the Central African Republic, Kwame Nkrumah in Ghana, Emperor Haile Selassie in Ethiopia, Jomo Kenyatta in Kenya, Julius Nyerere in Tanzania, Dr. Hastings Banda in Malawi, Kenneth Kaunda in Zambia, and H. F. Verwoerd in South Africa.

Trends toward Unity and Disunity

Pan-Africanism in its various forms can trace its origins back for well over three-quarters of a century. Many of its early leaders or spokesmen were not Africans at all, except by descent, but were West Indian or American Negroes like William Du Bois and Matthew Garvey. Several Pan-African conferences were held prior to World War II, usually somewhere in Europe or in England. London was a center for Pan-African movements, and many future African leaders, including Kwame Nkrumah and Jomo Kenyatta, planned and dreamed of the new Africa while they were living in the British capital. After World War II, as the liquidation of the colonial empires in Africa reached landslide proportions and as the Africans gained political independence, the leaders of many of the new African states began to speak in terms of African unity as well as of national independence.

This was particularly true of Kwame Nkrumah, who emerged as a leading spokesman for the new Africa when his state, Ghana, became independent in 1957. Nkrumah was an unabashed champion of African unity; he favored a federal union of African states, or of as many African states as would join, and Ghana's constitution contained a provision whereby Ghana's sovereignty might be merged into a larger African union. Accra, the capital of Ghana, became the headquarters of various Pan-African movements and a sanctuary for exiled leaders of still dependent areas of Africa. George Padmore, a veteran fighter for Pan-Africanism, spent most of the last years of his life in the congenial environment of Accra. In 1958 two major all-African conferences, one official and one unofficial, were held in that capital.

Shortly after Guinea became independent, Nkrumah and Sekou Touré announced the formation of a Ghana-Guinea Union, even though the two states were separated by the Ivory Coast and even though Nkrumah and Touré could talk to each other only through an interpreter. When Mali separated from Senegal, a Ghana-Guinea-Mali Union was proclaimed. In other parts of Africa, too, notably in East Africa, steps toward larger union were seriously discussed.

While most of the new African states did not follow the federal course which Nkrumah championed, they did rather quickly form a number of important associations, for political or economic reasons. Perhaps the best known and most significant were the Union Africaine et Malagache (UAM), later officially named the Inter-African and Malagasy States Organization (IAMSO) and unofficially known as the Brazzaville Group, comprised of twelve former French colonies which are associated members of the European Common Market, and which maintain close economic ties with France; the so-called Monrovia Group, embracing the members of the UAM and seven other African states — Liberia, Sierra Leone, Togo, Nigeria, Tunisia, Somalia, and Ethiopia — dedicated to a more moderate political and economic course emphasizing cooperation among African states and with former colonial powers; and the more aggressive Casablanca Group — the U.A.R., Algeria, Morocco, Mali, Guinea, and Ghana.

Pan-Africanism may be said to have come of age in May, 1963, when leaders of thirty African states — all of the then independent states of the continent except South Africa, which was not invited, Togo, whose new government formed after the assassination of President Sylvanus Olympio in the preceding January had not yet been recognized by other African states, and Morocco, whose delegation abstained from active participation because of the presence of delegates from Mauritania, with which Morocco had a territorial controversy — meeting in Addis Ababa, signed a Charter for an Organization of African Unity. At this conference the two contrasting approaches to African unity were eloquently presented. Dr. Nkrumah advocated a radical and far-reaching program, embracing a "Union Government of Africa," with a common African citizenship, foreign policy, defense system, and currency. The more moderate view was expressed by many African leaders, including the prime minister of Nigeria and the presidents of Tunisia, the Malagasy Republic, and Tanzania. This view prevailed and was incorporated in the Charter of the OAU, which provided for an Assembly of heads of state and government, a Council of Ministers, a General Secretariat, and a Commission of Mediation, Conciliation, and Arbitration, and a number of special commissions. At Addis Ababa the African leaders also passed a series of resolutions, on such matters as colonialism, *apartheid* and racial discrimination, nonalignment, economic development, and disarmament, and set up a nine-member coordinating committee for the liberation of Africa with headquarters in Dar-es-Salaam, Tanzania, and a special fund to aid liberation movements. Since its establishment this committee has concerted the efforts to bring pressure to bear on Portugal and South Africa, and Dar-es-Salaam has become the center for leaders of independence movements in Mozambique and elsewhere.

After the formation of the OAU the Casa-

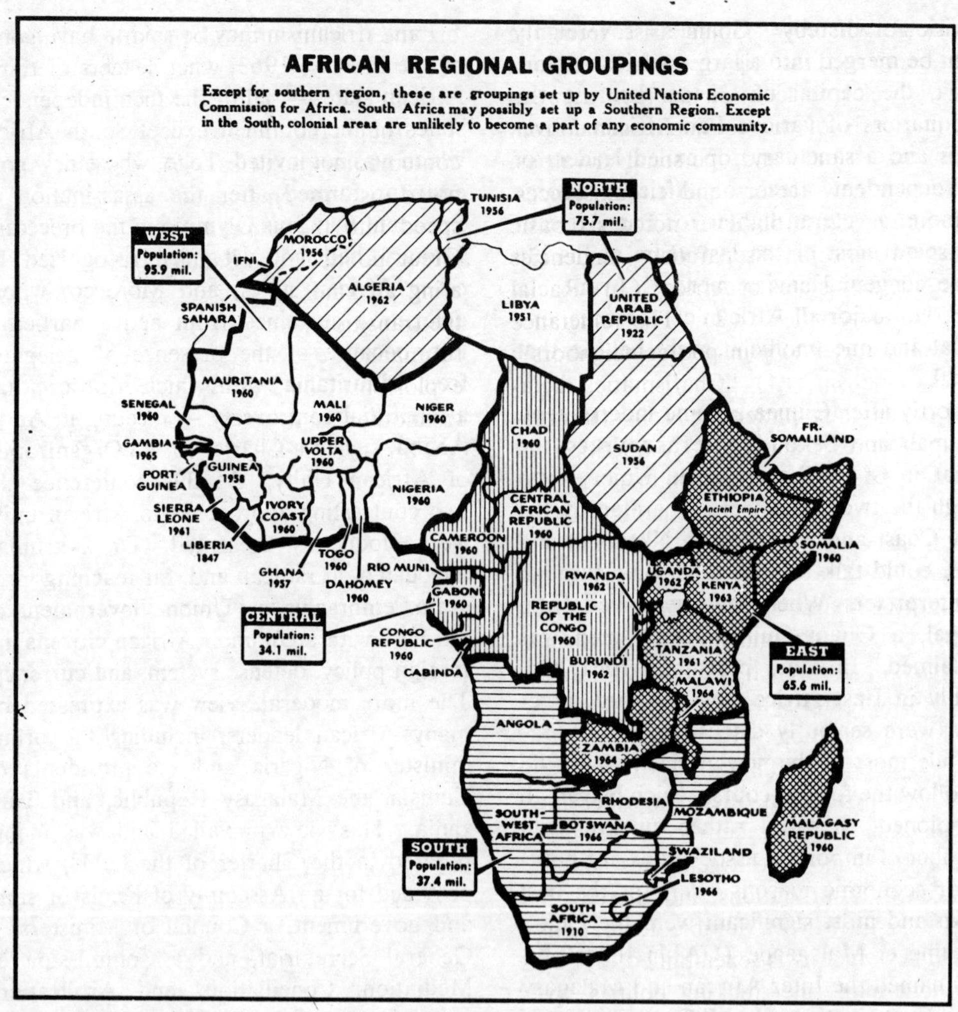

blanca group ceased to exist as a separate entity, and the Ghana-Guinea-Mali Union was dissolved. The UAM did not disband immediately, but its members decided to give up its political agencies, and to reconstitute themselves as the Afro-Malagache Union of Economic Cooperation. Thus OAU has become by far the most significant and comprehensive organization for African unity.

The difficulties as well as the prospects for African unity have been well illustrated in the progress of the OAU since its formation. It was slow in getting set up, and it is still hardly more than a skeleton organization. At the second meeting of the heads of African states, held in Cairo in 1964, the differences between the leaders were more marked than their areas of agreement. Its record in trying to help resolve the many territorial and other disputes among its members has been spotty. Since its members differed on Congo policy, its role in the whole Congo impasse has been equivocal. But its emergence and operations are important new developments in the African scene.

In spite of the strong emphasis on movements for African unity, recent events have highlighted the persistence of many factors making for disunity. Some arise from the geographic and historic division of Africa, and the relative lack of contact between different parts of the continent, some from continuing tribal and personal rivalries, some from new factors and circumstances. In 1961 an astute observer noted six basic factors promoting separatist tendencies among the new states of Africa: (1) "Racial and tribal diversities"; (2) "The reluctance of rich territories to join poorer neighbors"; (3) Nationalism; (4) "Charismatic, dictatorial leadership patterns"; (5) "International pressures"; and (6) "Competition for capital." The first factor facilitates the dismemberment of a state by placing "loyalty to race and tribe, or both, . . . before loyalty to country." The second was responsible for "Katanga Province's succession from the Congo, Gabon's unwillingness to be an integral part of a French Equatorial African confederation, and Senegal's discomfort over her close association with poorer and more populous Soudan." The third is two-dimensional, inasmuch as it offers "a wider focal point of loyalty than tribe, race or religion," while at the same time it generates animosities against other nations and thereby impedes "the growth of durable federations." The fourth factor is exemplified by one-party, one-man rule, making politics "personalized and rigid" and "the establishment of interterritorial federations more difficult." The fifth is illustrated by "the delivery of Belgian military equipment to Tshombe's forces and the dispatch of Soviet aircraft and trucks to assist Lumumba's army" and by the special "bonds of interest between the emergent African land and the former imperial power." The sixth hinders progress toward African unity by making those countries "which are most successful in finding the necessary capital to effect their plans" unwilling to share these advantages with their less fortunate neighbors. All of these factors are particularly disturbing because of "the fragility of modern African states."[49]

What Future for Africa?

Perhaps the most significant fact about contemporary Africa, as John Gunther noted, is "its emergence with exaggerated speed into the embrace of modern times." Great political and social changes are creating all kinds of stresses and strains. Will the transition take place in a relatively peaceful manner, or will Africa be convulsed with explosions from one end of the continent to another?

Three problems seem to rise above all others. One is the problem of economic and social development. As we have seen, the change from an essentially tribal or local basis of life to a more complex pattern, embracing a growing degree of urbanization and contact with the outside world, has been an upsetting one in many respects. It has caused widespread social disintegration. There is an obvious need for improved standards of living, for a more sweeping approach to the problem of mass illiteracy, for training in political skills and in political techniques, and for a concerted attack on disease and unsanitary habits and conditions.

A second problem is essentially political in nature. It concerns the capacity of the existing political units, most of which have emerged so recently and so suddenly, to preserve their newly won unity, to find satisfactory bases of cooperation with other African states, and to gain recognition in the world community. With only a few major exceptions, notably Angola and Mozambique, the age of political independence for Africa has dawned. From one end of the continent to the other, most of Africa is politically free. But many of the African states, old and new, are confronted with internal divisions and problems which are

[49] Donald S. Rothschild, "The Politics of African Separatism," *Journal of International Affairs,* XV (1961), 25–28.

so serious as to jeopardize their capacity to survive.[50] They have not yet worked out the outlines of their own political systems or the framework of their internal relations, not to mention their relations with other nations and with international agencies and organizations. Statesmanship of a high order will have to be displayed if the inevitable political changes of the coming years are to take place without violent eruptions and near-chaos.

The third main problem, that of color and race relations, vastly complicates the whole African situation. Here we have one of the most delicate and crucial problems in international relations, and Africa is a testing group for this issue. "If whites and blacks can learn to live together . . . Africa is saved. If not, it may be lost — to chaos, to civil war, to feudalism, or the Communists."[51] The need for cooperation and partnership between white and colored peoples is patent — without them none of the basic problems can be solved; but the obstacles in the way of satisfactory race relations are formidable indeed. They are psychological as well as political; they arise from ingrained prejudices as well as from historical experience. Only superlative forbearance and mental reorientation will suffice to cope with them.

The early years of the age of African independence have been difficult ones, and many hopes have already been dashed. It is very easy to view the contemporary African scene with almost unrelieved pessimism. Certainly evidences of chaos and of Communist penetration can easily be found. But this is, happily, an incomplete and one-sided view of the complex African scene. None of the new African nations has disintegrated into chaos — although some have seemed to be on the verge of dissolution — and none has come under Communist control (Zanzibar, as has been noted, was no more than a short-lived exception). The new Africa offers many grounds for hope as well as for apprehension and despair. In any event, whatever the future holds for Africa, African problems are impinging more and more upon the minds of men and the councils of nations. They can no longer be ignored by serious students of international relations.

[50] Within a period of less than eight months (July, 1965, to February, 1966) army leaders seized power and deposed civilian governments in seven African nations, including Algeria, the Congo, Nigeria, and Ghana.

[51] Gunther, pp. 886–887.

SUGGESTIONS FOR FURTHER READING

ADAM, THOMAS R. *Government and Politics in Africa South of the Sahara,* 3d ed. New York: Random House, 1965.

APTER, DAVID. *Ghana in Transition.* New York: Atheneum Publishers, 1963. A revised edition of a work first published by Princeton University Press in 1955, under the title *The Gold Coast in Transition.* A long final chapter covers the period from 1955 to 1963.

———. *The Political Kingdom in Uganda; a Study in Bureaucratic Nationalism.* Princeton, N.J.: Princeton University Press, 1961.

BRACE, RICHARD. *Morocco, Algeria, Tunisia.* Englewood Cliffs, N.J.: Prentice-Hall, 1964. An excellent short history of the Maghreb.

BRETTON, HENRY L. *Power and Stability in Nigeria: The Politics of Decolonization.* New York: Frederick A. Praeger, 1962. A systematic analysis of Nigerian politics.

BRZEZINSKI, ZBIGNIEW, ed. *Africa and the Communist World.* Stanford, Calif.: Stanford University Press, for the Hoover Institition on War, Revolution, and Peace, 1963. Six essays by specialists.

BUSIA, K. A. *The Challenge of Africa.* New York: Frederick A. Praeger, 1962. By one of the foremost African sociologists, and a political opponent of Dr. Nkrumah in Ghana.

CARTER, GWENDOLEN M., ed. *African One-Party States.* Ithaca: Cornell University Press, 1962. The political systems of Tunisia, Senegal, Guinea, Ivory Coast, Liberia, and Tanganyika.

———. *Independence for Africa.* New York: Frederick A. Praeger, 1960.

———. *The Politics of Inequality; South Africa since 1948.* New York: Frederick A. Praeger, 1958. A significant study.

CLOETE, STUART. *The African Giant.* Boston: Houghton Mifflin Company, 1955. Penetrating insights.

COLEMAN, JAMES S. *Nigeria: Background to Nationalism.* Berkeley: University of California Press, 1958.

COLEMAN, JAMES S. and CARL G. ROSBERG. *Political Parties and National Integration in Tropical Africa.* Berkeley: University of California Press, 1964.

COOLEY, JOHN K. *East Wind Over Africa: Red China's African Offensive.* New York: Walker & Company, 1965. By the North African correspondent of the *Christian Science Monitor.*

COWAN, L. GRAY. *The Dilemmas of African Independence.* New York: Walker & Company, 1964. Contains lengthy reference section, compiled by Annette Stiefbold.

DEGRAFT-JOHNSON, J. C. *African Glory: The Story of Vanished Negro Civilization.* New York: Frederick A. Praeger, 1953.

DVORIN, EUGENE P. *Racial Separation in South Africa; an Analysis of Apartheid Theory.* Chicago: University of Chicago Press, 1952.

FAGE, J. D. *An Introduction to the History of West Africa,* 3d ed. Cambridge, 1962. A revised version of a classic work, first published in 1955.

FERKISS, VICTOR C. *Africa's Search for Identity.* New York: George Braziller, 1966.

GOLDSCHMIDT, WALTER, ed. *The United States and Africa.* New York: Frederick A. Praeger, for the American Assembly, 1963. A survey of political, economic, and social conditions in contemporary Africa.

GUNTHER, JOHN. *Inside Africa.* New York: Harper, 1955. Most comprehensive survey of the postwar African scene. Outdated by rapid pace of events.

HAILEY, BARON WILLIAM MALCOLM. *An African Survey; a Study of the Problems Arising in Africa South of the Sahara,* rev. ed. New York: Oxford University Press, 1957. A classic work.

"Handbook on Africa," *Intercom,* Vol. 8, No. 3 (May–June, 1966), A special issue containing concise information on various aspects of contemporary Africa.

HANNA, ALEXANDER J. *European Rule in Africa.* London, 1961. Published for the Historical Association.

HANNA, WILLIAM J. *Independent Black Africa; the Politics of Freedom.* Chicago: Rand McNally & Co., 1964.

HAPGOOD, DAVID. *Africa: from Independence to Tomorrow.* New York: Atheneum Publishers, 1965.

HATCH, JOHN. *Africa Today — and Tomorrow,* rev. ed. New York: Frederick A. Praeger, 1964. The subtitle is: "An Outline of Basic Facts and Major Problems."

———. *A History of Postwar Africa.* New York: Frederick A. Praeger, 1965.

HODGKIN, THOMAS. *African Political Parties.* Baltimore: Penguin Books, 1961. By a leading authority.

HOVET, THOMAS. *Africa in the United Nations.* Evanston, Ill.: Northwestern University Press, 1963. Includes a detailed tabulation of voting records of African representatives.

HUGHES, JOHN. *Africa South of the Sahara.* New York: Longmans, Green & Co., 1961. A comprehensive survey by the Africa correspondent of the *Christian Science Monitor.*

———. *The New Face of Africa.* New York: David McKay Co., 1961.

JUNOD, VIOLANE I., ed. *The Handbook of Africa.* New York: New York University Press, 1963.

KENYATTA, JOMO. *Facing Mount Kenya.* London, 1953. A stirring book by the leading nationalist leader of Kenya.

KIMBLE, GEORGE H. T. *Tropical Africa.* Vol I: *Land and Livelihood.* Vol. II: *Society and Polity.* Garden City, N.Y.: Anchor Books, 1962. A detailed and comprehensive study.

KITCHEN, HELEN, ed. *A Handbook of African Affairs.* New York: Frederick A. Praeger, for the African-American Institute, 1964. A guide to contemporary Africa by the editor of *Africa Report.*

LEGUM, COLIN, ed. *Africa; a Handbook to the Continent,* 2d ed. New York: Frederick A. Praeger, 1966. Background information compiled by more than 40 authorities.

———. *Pan-Africanism: A Short Political Guide.* Frederick A. Praeger, 1962.

LEGUM, COLIN and MARGARET LEGUM. *South Africa: Crisis for the West.* New York: Frederick A. Praeger, 1964.

LEWIS, WILLIAM H., ed. *French-Speaking Africa; the Search for Identity.* New York: Walker & Company, 1965. Fifteen papers.

MCKAY, VERNON. *Africa in World Politics.* Baltimore: The Johns Hopkins Press, 1963. Perhaps the first comprehensive analysis of the international relations of the new African states.

———, ed. *African Diplomacy: Studies in the Determinants of Foreign Policy.* New York: Frederick A. Praeger, 1966. A collection of papers.

MBOYA, TOM. *Freedom and After.* Boston: Little, Brown and Company, 1963. By a leading African nationalist.

MEYER, FRANK S. *The African Nettle; Dilemmas of an Emerging Continent.* New York: The John Day Company, 1965.

MORISON, DAVID L. *The U.S.S.R. and Africa.* New York: Oxford University Press, 1964.

NASSER, GAMAL ABDEL. *Egypt's Liberation; the Philosophy of the Revolution.* Washington, D.C.: Public Affairs Press, 1955. An important statement by the leading Arab nationalist.

NKRUMAH, KWAME. *I Speak of Freedom: A Statement of African Ideology.* New York: Frederick A. Praeger, 1961. By one of the main spokesmen of African nationalism.

PADELFORD, NORMAN J. and RUPERT EMERSON, eds. *Africa and World Order.* New York: Frederick A. Praeger, 1963. Essays which originally appeared in a special issue of *International Organization,* entitled "Africa and International Organization" (Vol. XVI, No. 2, Spring, 1963).

Penguin Africa Library. Baltimore: Penguin Books. Described as "the most important and controversial collection of studies on modern Africa." Thirteen volumes had been published by the end of 1964.

RIVKIN, ARNOLD. *Africa and the West: Elements of Free-World Policy.* New York: Frederick A. Praeger, 1962.

———. *The African Presence in World Affairs; National Development and Its Role in Foreign Policy.* New York: Free Press of Glencoe, 1963.

ROTBERG, ROBERT I. *A Political History of Tropical Africa.* New York: Harcourt, Brace & World, 1965.

SEGAL, RONALD, ed. *Political Africa: A Who's Who of Personalities and Parties.* New York: Frederick A. Praeger, 1961. Contains information about more than 400 African political personalities and over 100 political parties.

SPIRO, HERBERT J. *Politics in Africa: Prospects South of the Sahara.* Englewood Cliffs, N.J.: Prentice-Hall, 1962.

STAMP, L. DUDLEY. *Africa: A Study in Tropical Development,* 2d ed. New York: John Wiley & Sons, 1964. Revision of a standard work, containing a detailed description of each region of Africa and each country.

TAYLOR, DON. *The British in Africa.* London, 1962.

THIAM, DOUDOU. *The Foreign Policy of African States: Ideological Bases, Present Realities, Future Prospects.* New York: Fredcrick A. Praeger, 1965. By the foreign minister of Senegal.

THOMPSON, VIRGINIA and RICHARD ADLOFF. *The Emerging States of French Equatorial Africa.* Stanford, Calif.: Stanford University Press, 1960. A detailed survey.

WALLERSTEIN, IMMANUEL. *Africa: The Politics of Independence.* New York: Vintage Books, 1961. A good political survey.

WATTENBERG, BEN. *The New Nations of Africa.* New York: Hart Publishing Co., 1963.

WIEDNER, DONALD L. *A History of Africa South of the Sahara.* New York: Random House, 1962.

WIESCHOFF, HANS A. *Colonial Policies in Africa.* Philadelphia: University of Pennsylvania Press, 1944.

ZARTMAN, I. WILLIAM. *Government and Politics in Northern Africa.* New York: Frederick A. Praeger, 1963. Includes the Sudan, Ethiopia, and Somalia.

———. *International Relations in the New Africa.* Englewood Cliffs, N.J.: Prentice-Hall, 1966.

19 Economic Nationalism versus Economic Internationalism

One of David Low's cartoons shows a group of weird figures representing "a disinflationary tendency at bay," "a sterling area ready for duty," "a severe repercussion practicing disinvestment," "an unrequited export serenading an off-shore purchase," "an over-all deficit bringing itself into equilibrium," and "a category of imports chasing a dollar equivalent"; and tucked away in one corner of the cartoon Low depicts his very bewildered self trying to think of some way of illustrating "an invisible import meeting an irreducible minimum output," and remarking: "Take it from me, people, making cartoons on economics these days is no joke."

Every student of international relations who is not a trained economist will share Low's trepidation in approaching the "jargon land" of international economics. Yet he must venture into this land, for today much of the subject matter of international relations is economic in character. This fact is reflected in current headlines, and in the amount of attention that is given to economic matters in every foreign office, in almost every major international organization, and in most international conferences. The student must try to see the implications of some of these economic concepts and to understand their relations to international problems, including basic issues of international cooperation and of peace and war. In the final analysis, perhaps, political considerations may outweigh the economic; political agreement may create conditions under which economic problems will fall into line. But, however strongly one may subscribe to the doctrine of the primacy of politics over economics, he must agree that it is difficult to make political sense out of economic nonsense. He must also admit that many of the tensions in today's world arise out of fundamental economic maladjustment and the "condition of deep structural change in international economic relations."[1]

Causes of Present Economic Disequilibrium

It is important to realize that our present economic disequilibrium is not simply a temporary phenomenon resulting from the troubled state of the postwar world. The disequilibrium, as P. T. Ellsworth wrote of one of its serious manifestations — the strong trend toward bilateralism in world trade — reflects "the basic imbalance trace-

[1] P. T. Ellsworth, *The International Economy: Its Structure and Operation* (New York: The Macmillan Company, 1950), p. 675. Used by permission of The Macmillan Company. For an elaboration of this point, see P. T. Ellsworth, *The International Economy*, 3d ed. (New York: The Macmillan Company, 1964), pp. 335–337, 402–409.

able not only to the war, but also to ten years of depression economics and to the longer-run influence of deep-seated secular change."[2] The halcyon days of free trade and the free market, of convertible currencies based on an international gold standard, have passed. In the twentieth century the old economic patterns have been shattered, along with the old political order of power. World War I was a major shock; but in the 1920's, at least, it seemed that a network of trade and finance, as well as a political pattern, had developed which would meet the needs of the new state of affairs. This network, however, was seriously disrupted by the worldwide depression of the 1930's, which gave a strong impetus to programs of national self-sufficiency and to other tendencies toward economic independence.

As a result of these and many other developments the decade of the 1930's was a period of growing economic nationalism. Its effects were political as well as economic. In the totalitarian states the efforts toward national self-sufficiency — a distinguishing characteristic of economic nationalism — were most strongly manifest. Perhaps the outstanding example was the policy of "autarchy" followed by Nazi Germany. Through strict economic controls of many sorts the Germans succeeded in linking the states of Central and Eastern Europe to the Nazi system and in orienting the economies of other states, including some in Latin America, to serve the needs of Germany. Besides currency and exchange controls, quotas, export subsidies, and other common devices of economic nationalism, the Nazis relied heavily on a barter system by which they sought to compensate for their lack of foreign exchange and to secure the materials needed for building up their war machine by the export of nonessentials. The economic nationalism of Nazi Germany, as reflected in her policy of autarchy, was one of the bases of her foreign policies and her military power. It lowered the standard of living of the German people and disturbed relations between Germany and other nations, but it did serve the political ends of the Nazi state. Here again, this time in a baleful way, the interrelationship of economics and politics may be clearly seen.

World War II delivered the *coup de grâce* to a system already severely weakened. Among its many consequences were major shifts in production and trade, changing economic as well as political relationships, the disruption of Europe's trading and financial system, strong price and currency fluctuations, a serious attrition of Britain's economic as well as political power, and a balance of payments problem. Another consequence was the frantic search for ways and means to free the channels of trade and finance, for without freedom in the movement of goods the essential expansion of world trade would be impossible in the face of the countervailing tendencies toward bilateralism, state trading, and preferences and restrictions of all kinds.

Current Problems of the International Economy

The international economy today is characterized by many sources of growth and strength and by many conditions of disequilibrium. In 1964 the increase in world trade among non-Communist countries was the largest in many years, and trade of the Communist countries with each other and with non-Communist states increased significantly. The "Kennedy Round" of tariff negotiations in 1964, under the auspices of GATT, led to further tariff reductions. At the same time it revealed fresh difficulties in reducing the barriers of international trade. It pointed up, for example, the restrictive as well as the liberalizing tendencies of the trade and tariff policies being followed by the European Common Market

[2] Ellsworth (1950), p. 688. See also Ellsworth (1964), pp. 330–339, 385–389.

and other regional trading groups, and it highlighted the dissatisfaction of the developing states with GATT, labeled a "rich man's club." Although total exports of Communist countries were estimated by the International Monetary Fund at $19.3 billion, and although some of the East European countries in particular showed a new interest in trade with the non-Communist world, East-West trade, hampered by special political and economic difficulties, remained at a rather low level. Trade between the United States and the Soviet Union and the states of Eastern Europe continued to be almost negligible, less than one per cent of total United States foreign trade.

The main trading nations and the main beneficiaries of the expanding world trade continued to be the industrially developed countries. This simple fact calls attention to perhaps the main economic disequilibrium in the world today, namely, the great and growing gap between the developed and the developing nations, sometimes referred to as the North-South problem. The gulf was dramatized at the United Nations Conferences on Trade and Development in 1964[3] and 1968. There representatives of the developing countries showed remarkable unanimity of approach, insisting that the powerful industrial nations must take more effective measures and provide greater assistance, through trade and tariff concessions, stepped-up foreign aid on easier terms, and more sympathetic and determined efforts generally, to help the majority of the world's states in meeting their grave problems of national development. Thus the matter of assistance to developing nations bulks large on the agenda of contemporary international economic relations. Yet all the time the gap between the "have" and "have-not" nations is widening, rather than narrowing. Unless some more effective means can be found to reverse this trend the attendant stresses in national economies and in the world economy and indeed in international affairs generally are bound to create an explosive world situation.

There is still considerable dissatisfaction with the amounts, types, conditions, and results of the aid that is currently being made available to the developing countries. It is apparently not enough to do the job, nor is it being handled well, either by donors or recipients. There is no general agreement on the relative merits of bilateral and multilateral aid, although there is a growing feeling that the amount of multilateral aid should be increased. Various UN agencies are working in this field, as is the Development Advisory Committee of the Organization for Economic Cooperation and Development, made up of the United States, Canada, Japan, the United Kingdom, and nine states of continental Western Europe. These states are also cooperating in a few international consortia, organized to give special attention and assistance to certain key developing countries, notably India and Pakistan.

The trend toward economic integration is another striking feature of contemporary international economic relations. The formation of the European Common Market (the European Economic Community), linking France, West Germany, Italy, and the Benelux countries in the third most important trading area in the world[4] has been a major new factor in the world economy. The development of EEC, its relations with the European Free Trade Association, the United States, the East European countries, the Soviet Union, and other states and regional trading blocs has had and will continue to have a profound impact on political as well as economic trends in international affairs. Other efforts at economic integration, in varying degrees and with varying re-

[3] See Kamal M. Hagras, *United Nations Conference on Trade and Development; a Case Study in UN Diplomacy* (New York: Frederick A. Praeger, 1965).

[4] See Isaiah Frank, *The European Common Market* (New York: Frederick A. Praeger, 1961).

sults, have developed in many parts of the world.

Since the abandonment of the gold standard, which gave stability and strength to the international economy in the nineteenth and early twentieth centuries, the international monetary system has been carefully regulated, with most currencies being pegged, directly or indirectly, to the two key currencies, the American dollar and the British pound. Because both the dollar and the pound have developed some alarming symptoms of weakness, there seems to be a growing feeling that major readjustments in the system are imminent.[5] For some years the United States has been facing a serious balance of payments and gold flow problem, and the pound has been threatened several times in recent years, notably in "the Great Bear Raid on Sterling" in the fall of 1964, which was checked only after the central banks of eleven nations hastily provided Britain with credits amounting to $3 billion. Lack of confidence in the pound is in part a reflection of the adverse effects on Britain of changing trade patterns in the Commonwealth, intensified international competition in world markets, difficulties arising as a result of the failure of efforts to bring Britain into the European Common Market, and the unsatisfactory rate of economic growth. Great Britain's decision in 1967 to devalue the pound had severe repercussions on world finance generally. Nations with weaker currencies, and with major foreign exchange problems, are resorting more and more to exchange controls and other devices which, however necessary because of the weakness of the economies of the states which resort to such nostrums, often have adverse effects on the delicate adjustment mechanisms of international trade and finance.

[5] See Sidney E. Rolfe, *Gold and World Power: the Dollar, the Pound, and the Plans for Reform* (New York: Harper & Row, 1966); and Robert Triffin, *Gold and the Dollar Crisis* (New Haven: Yale University Press, 1960).

In the present chapter we shall see how states are using nationalistic practices to defend and advance their own interests while at the same time professing to accept the ideal of economic internationalism. In examining this contradiction we shall review some of the evidences of contemporary economic nationalism and their underlying causes and implications; and we shall note the efforts to counteract this tendency through multilateral agreements for removing some of the barriers to world trade and for establishing the interconvertibility of currency.

Three areas of postwar relations are of particular importance: (1) trade and commerical policies; (2) procedures for the control of the international monetary system; and (3) international investments, both governmental and private. We shall also discuss some new patterns of economic aid and cooperation.

1. Postwar Economic Problems: Trade and Commercial Policy

The coming of the New Deal to the United States in 1933 effected a change in America's foreign economic policy featured by positive efforts to reduce the barriers to world trade. Undoubtedly the new policy expressed self-interest, but it was an enlightened self-interest, one which viewed American prosperity as inseparable from a sound international economy. Since the 1930's the United States has continued to pursue this policy, although not without reservations and contradictions.

The United States Trade Agreements Program. The results of American efforts of the past three decades to reduce the barriers to world trade have been impressive. The going has not been easy, for the United States has faced an unfavorable international environment, the insistence of most other nations — especially underdeveloped states — that temporary restrictive trade practices are necessary, the emergence of regional trading blocs, the growth of trade by the Sino-Soviet bloc, the opposition of powerful political and economic groups at home, and her own contradictory policies on such matters as agricultural and shipping subsidies.

The cornerstone of the American policy has been the reciprocal trade agreements program, a direct reversal of the policy laid down in the Smoot-Hawley Act of 1930. First enacted in 1934, with the vigorous sponsorship of Secretary Hull, and renewed many times since that date, the Trade Agreements Act was a direct and deliberate challenge to economic nationalism. Under the terms of the act, Congress authorized the President to enter into negotiations with other countries for the mutual reduction of tariff duties within certain defined limits.

By 1945 the United States had entered into bilateral agreements with some thirty states, all of them being given the most-favored-nation treatment,[6] and about half of them being granted the full 50 per cent reduction in American tariffs allowed by the Trade Agreements Act. In 1945 Congress authorized another reduction of 50 per cent, making it possible to lower the Smoot-Hawley rates by 75 per cent. In 1949 it approved a third cut of 50 per cent, thus bringing the minimum rates to 12½ per cent of Smoot-Hawley. In 1958 it acceded to President Eisenhower's recommendation for a long-term renewal of the act and broadened the authority of the President to lower tariff rates on a reciprocal basis. This authority was further broadened in the Trade Expansion Act of 1962, a new tariff measure which seemed to break fresh ground in the trade agreements field.[7] Armed with this new act, the Kennedy and Johnson administrations tried to sponsor bilateral and multilateral agreements for tariff reductions, for the removal of other barriers to world trade, and for greater concessions to developing countries. The sixth and most extensive round of trade negotiations, begun in Geneva in 1964 and conducted under the auspices of the General Agreement on Tariffs and Trade, was referred to as the "Kennedy Round," because the Trade Expansion Act of 1962, passed while Kennedy was President of the United States, provided the main theme and stimulus for this most ambitious effort in trade liberalization.

From the beginning of the American trade agreements program some of the good effects have been nullified by other actions. One of the original purposes had been to improve the export market for American agricultural products. When a number of farm organizations felt that the program was operating too slowly for them, they succeeded in inducing Congress to subsidize agricultural exports. Thus the Department of Agriculture was soon sponsoring what amounted to "dumping" abroad, a practice hardly consistent with the Department of State's program of promoting freer trade and economic internationalism. Under the "peril-point" and "escape clause" provision of the Trade Agreements Act, as amended, tariffs have been raised on certain imports in order to protect domestic producers. These in-

[6] As applied to tariffs, a state with a most-favored-nation status is entitled to ship goods into another country under a tariff rate as low as that granted by the importing country to the nation most favored. Therefore, when the importing country lowers the rate on a particular commodity brought in from any state, all states having a most-favored-nation agreement with the importing country are entitled to the new low rate on that commodity. When the new rate applies automatically, without the special *quid pro quo* conceded by the state which first received the new rate, the most-favored-nation clause is said to be *unconditional;* if it applies only when states receiving the new rate grant concessions equivalent to those of the first state granted that rate, then the most-favored-nation treatment is said to be *conditional*. The United States has always followed the most-favored-nation doctrine. She held to the *conditional* form until 1922; since then she has adhered to the *unconditional* form. The most-favored-nation clause is not limited to tariff agreements.

[7] Harry G. Brainard, "The Trade Expansion Act — 1962" in J. S. Ewing and F. Meissner, eds., *International Business Management* (Belmont, Calif.: Wadsworth Publishing Co., 1964).

creases have hurt major industries in other countries, and consequently have raised questions of the sincerity of American professions in foreign economic policy. However, all recent American Presidents have often refused to approve recommendations by the Tariff Commission for increases, and they have shown an awareness of the international implications of American foreign economic policy.

GATT and the ITO Charter. The United States has not depended entirely upon bilateral agreements in her efforts to reduce barriers to international trade. She took the lead in the drafting of the two most ambitious multilateral agreements of this kind since the close of World War II — the General Agreement on Tariffs and Trade (GATT) and the Charter of the International Trade Organization (ITO). She also played an active role in the United Nations Conferences on Trade and Development in 1964 and 1968.

At the time of the signing of the Anglo-American Financial Agreement of December 6, 1945, which provided for a loan of $3.75 billion to Great Britain, the Department of State issued a notable statement of American economic foreign policy, entitled *Proposals for Expansion of World Trade and Employment.*[8] In form it was a listing of matters which should be considered by a proposed International Conference on Trade and Employment. It was a clear statement of existing restrictions on international trade and of appropriate measures to release trade from some of them. World trade, it pointed out, was "kept small by four things": (1) restrictions imposed by governments; (2) restrictions imposed by private combines and cartels; (3) fear of disorder in the markets for certain primary commodities; and (4) irregularity, and the fear of irregularity, in production and employment. The *Proposals* discussed all of these problems and outlined steps for dealing with them. It expressed particular concern over tariffs and preferences, quantitative restrictions, exchange controls, subsidies, cartels, and state trading. It urged that whenever possible tariffs should be substantially reduced and tariff preferences eliminated by gradual steps. While it warned against quantitative restrictions, it recognized the possible necessity of imposing such restrictions during "the early postwar transitional period" to relieve "conditions of distress in the exporting country caused by severe shortages of foodstuffs and other essential products" and, above all, "as an aid to the restoration of equilibrium in the balance of payments." The *Proposals* reflected an awareness of both the possibilities and limitations of commodity agreements, and of measures for full production and full employment.

This important document was endorsed in a joint statement on commercial policy by Great Britain and the United States and copies were sent to all governments. At the same time the United States invited fifteen countries to participate in multilateral negotiations for the purpose of reducing tariffs and other barriers to world trade. All except the U.S.S.R. accepted the invitation. In February, 1946, the newly organized Economic and Social Council of the United Nations established a Preparatory Committee to draft a charter for a proposed International Trade Organization and to lay plans for an international conference on trade and employment. This committee accepted the *Proposals* as a basis for its work. Just before the first session of the Preparatory Committee, held in London in October–November, 1946, the United States issued a *Suggested Charter for an International Trade Organization.* This document, which was an elaboration of the *Proposals* of 1945, became the principal working paper at the London meetings of the Preparatory Committee, thus sup-

[8] Dept. of State Pub. 2411, Commercial Policy Series 79. Hereafter cited as *Proposals.*

plementing the *Proposals*. After extensive revisions the *Suggested Charter* was debated at the long second session of the committee, held in Geneva from April to September, 1947; and at the same time representatives of twenty-three nations engaged in negotiations to reduce trade barriers. The results of the Geneva discussions were embodied in two important documents: the General Agreement on Tariffs and Trade, and the draft Charter for an International Trade Organization.

The General Agreement on Tariffs and Trade was a multilateral convention incorporating the results of more than 120 sets of bilateral negotiations among twenty-three nations, embracing some 43,000 separate terms.[9] The resulting agreements affected more than three-fourths of the import trade of the participating nations and about one-half of total world imports. The general provisions of GATT established "for the first time a generally accepted international code of fair treatment in commercial relations." Its three major parts related to "Tariffs and Preferences," "Non-Tariff Trade Barriers," and "Procedural and Others Matters." Many of the provisions were almost identical with those of its companion document, the draft Charter for an ITO. This duplication was, of course, intentional; the assumption was that the provisions of the ITO Charter would automatically supersede the corresponding sections of GATT when and if the Charter entered into effect, but that by being incorporated into GATT these provisions would be put into effect promptly instead of being dependent on the creation of ITO. As events were to prove, this was a wise precaution. GATT was put into effect by France, the United Kingdom, the United States, and four other nations as early as January 1, 1948, and it has since been implemented by many other states. The ITO Charter, on the other hand, was not approved by the required twenty states.

The draft ITO Charter was considered at the United Nations Conference on Trade and Employment, held at Havana from November, 1947, to March, 1948. Attended by several hundred delegates from fifty-six nations, as well as by representatives from several international agencies and nongovernmental organizations, the Havana Conference was the largest and most significant economic conference of the early postwar period. The main struggle at Havana was not between Communist and non-Communist states — Czechoslovakia and Poland were the only "iron curtain" countries to send official delegates — but between those which sought to secure acceptance of the basic principle of freeing the channels of world trade and those which were more concerned with writing into the Charter exceptions to justify restrictive practices in their own particular cases. "The difficulties that confronted this conference largely reflected the clash of economic policies and philosophies."[10] As a result, the Charter, which already embodied numerous concessions and escape clauses, was further weakened — or mutilated.

Signed on March 24, 1948, by representatives of fifty-three nations, the Charter was a lengthy document of 106 articles, divided into nine chapters.[11] Its drafting was a major feat of economic statesmanship, and represented the culmination of many months of effort. Although it was so full of reservations as to seem almost meaningless, it at least pointed the way toward international

[9] See *General Agreement on Tariffs and Trade* (United Nations, 1947); *International Conciliation,* No. 434 (October, 1947); and *Analysis of General Agreement on Tariffs and Trade,* Dept. of State Pub. 2983, Commercial Policy Series 109 (November, 1947).

[10] J. B. Condliffe, *The Commerce of Nations* (New York: W. W. Norton & Company, 1950), p. 614.

[11] *Havana Charter for an International Trade Organization,* Dept. of State Pub. 3117, Commercial Policy Series 113 (March, 1948).

cooperation and out of the morass of trade restrictions which were already threatening to stifle international economic relations and to endanger world peace.[12] It deserved a better fate than it received. Not a single nation ratified the Charter — not even the United States, its major creator and most vigorous champion.

Implementation and Extension of GATT. With the ITO Charter on the shelf, the implementation and extension of the General Agreement on Tariffs and Trade assumed greater importance. GATT, too, encountered serious difficulties, but these did not prevent the general lowering of customs duties to which the participating nations were pledged. By July, 1948, GATT was in effect among twenty-two of the twenty-three original signatories. Chile, the one exception, adhered to the agreement early in 1949. Ten more nations joined the list of contracting parties and participated in a second round of tariff negotiations in a conference at Annecy, France, which dragged on from April to August, 1949.

The third in the series of international tariff conferences was held at the delightful English resort of Torquay from September, 1950, to April, 1951. At Torquay the trend toward bilateralism and trade restrictions of all sorts was more apparent than ever; since Torquay the difficulties have been accentuated, often by nations or groups of nations seeking to provide themselves with artificial protection against outside competion, especially from the United States. Such policies have been characteristic of the countries of the Commonwealth, of Western Europe, and of the underdeveloped areas. In extreme form they represent a departure from the spirit of GATT and the ITO Charter, and they demonstrate forcefully that many countries, even outside the Communist sphere, are adopting domestic economic and social policies which are inimical to international cooperation.[13] There is considerable truth in the contention of Michael L. Hoffman that "this thesis that stable international relationships must always be sacrificed to domestic social policy is the very essence of modern economic nationalism."[14]

In March, 1955, delegates from forty-four nations completed an intensive review of GATT in the light of its seven years of operations. Missing from the revised agreement which followed were the controversial provisions regarding full employment, commodity agreements, and cartels. The revised GATT continued the tariff truce, which covers more than three-quarters of the free world's trade, and it preserved the most favored-nation principle, subject to many exceptions. A separate protocol provided for an Organization for Trade Cooperation (OTC) to administer the General Agreement. In a special message to Congress in

[12] For a detailed explanation of the ITO Charter, and of the principles underlying it, by one of its champions, see Clair Wilcox. *A Charter for World Trade* (New York: The Macmillan Company, 1949).

[13] "Governments motivated by socialist and interventionist ideas conduct policies of 'welfare' and protection through tariffs, licenses, quotas, exchange controls, and many other welfare measures, all of which promote economic nationalism." Hans F. Sennholz, *How Can Europe Survive?* (Princeton, N.J.: D. Van Nostrand Co., 1955), p. 317. See also Ludwig von Mises, *Socialism* (New Haven: Yale University Press, 1951); F. A. Hayek, *The Road to Serfdom* (Chicago: University of Chicago Press, 1944); and Benjamin M. Anderson, *Economics and the Public Welfare* (Princeton, N.J.: D. Van Nostrand Co., 1949). The case for government planning and "welfare economics" is presented in John Maynard Keynes, *The General Theory of Employment, Interest, and Money* (New York: Harcourt, Brace, 1936); William H. Beveridge, *Full Employment in a Free Society* (New York: W. W. Norton & Company, 1945); Herman Finer, *The Road to Reaction* (Boston: Little, Brown and Company, 1945); and Alvin H. Hansen, *Economic Policy and Full Employment* (New York: McGraw-Hill Book Company, 1947).

[14] Dispatch from Geneva, *New York Times,* June 11, 1951.

April, 1955, President Eisenhower urged American participation in the OTC, and a year later he renewed his recommendation; but considerable opposition to OTC developed in the United States, and Congress failed to act on the President's request.

Agreement upon the terms of the new GATT and the extension of the American Trade Agreements Act for three years seemed to create a favorable atmosphere for another round of multilateral tariff negotiations. These negotiations were held in Geneva between January 18 and May 17, 1956, and resulted in nearly sixty bilateral agreements affecting some two billion dollars of trade at 1955 prices. The cooperative attitude of Great Britain, Western Germany, and Italy was largely responsible for the unexpectedly wide range of the final agreements, which were incorporated in protocols to GATT.

A fifth tariff negotiating conference under the auspices of GATT was held in Geneva from September, 1960, until the summer of 1961. In addition to another general round of tariff negotiations, affecting some 60,000 items and more than half of the world's trade, the GATT conference devoted a great deal of time to the special problems that had arisen as a result of the policies of the new European Economic Community, including renegotiations of "bound" rates of duty with members of EEC and negotiations with EEC for concessions in its new common external tariff.

The sixth round of tariff negotiations under GATT auspices, also held at Geneva in February–March and May–June, 1964, was the most highly publicized of all. As has been noted, it is often referred to as the Kennedy Round because the United States Trade Expansion Act of 1962 laid the basis for a consideration of more comprehensive trade and tariff agreements than had been possible before its passage. At Geneva representatives of 62 countries agreed on procedures to be followed in the actual negotiations of agreements in the Kennedy Round. Two issues which complicated the early stages of the discussions were the so-called tariff disparities problem, arising from the insistence of representatives of the EEC and several other countries that low rates of duty must be reduced by a smaller percentage than high rates, and a congeries of problems relating to agricultural products and national agricultural policies which seemed to conflict with the aims of the negotiations. Before the Kennedy Round talks began, the representatives to the conference gave special consideration to the special problems of developing countries, whose spokesmen argued that the GATT agreements discriminated against them and did not give due consideration to their special circumstances and needs.[15]

United Nations Conference on Trade and Development. While the governments of the developing countries were rather suspicious of GATT and rather disappointed at the results of the 1964 GATT negotiating conference, their interests were more fully considered and promoted at the United Nations Conference on Trade and Development (UNCTAD), held almost simultaneously (March 23 to June 16, 1964) with the GATT sessions, and in the same city.[16] Attended by representatives of some 120 governments, plus various regional organizations, UN agencies, and other international organizations, UNCTAD was one of the largest international conferences ever held. As the conference progressed, it came to be dominated by the spokesmen of the developing nations, numbering some 75, with the delegates of the industrialized states very much on the defensive. Thus the conference witnessed the emergence of what has been called "the

[15] For an excellent analysis of GATT, see Irving B. Kravis, *Domestic Interests and International Obligations; Safeguards in International Trade Organizations* (Philadelphia: University of Pennsylvania Press, 1963), Chapter 2.

[16] See Hagras, Chapters 5 and 6.

world's largest pressure group," which will certainly be a major new force in world affairs if it can preserve a significant degree of unity and cohesion. At the end of UNCTAD this group was able to wrest some concessions from the industrialized states, but it did not by any means gain all of its objectives. The conference approved a new charter of international economic relations, recommended to the General Assembly the establishment of permanent institutions to continue its work, and adopted several important resolutions. Its deliberations ranged over a wide field, embracing questions of aid to developing countries as well as trade matters.

At its Nineteenth Session, held later in the year, the UN General Assembly adopted a resolution[17] providing for the establishment of UNCTAD as a permanent body to meet at least every three years, with a secretariat and a Trade and Development Board to carry out the functions of UNCTAD between sessions. The board held its first meeting in New York in April, 1965. Representatives of 22 Asian and African, 9 Latin American, 6 Communist, and 18 industrially developed non-Communist states are board members. UNCTAD is therefore a going concern. It has a special affiliation with the United Nations, but it does not have the status of a specialized agency. It will apparently be the main agency through which the developing nations will seek to obtain a more widespread recognition of their special interests and needs and more substantial and appropriate assistance in dealing with their problems of trade and development. In 1968 it sponsored a second major world conference, held in New Delhi in February and March.

Regional Trading Blocs. The growth of regional trading blocs has been marked in recent years; it may "spell the beginning of the end for the kind of product-by-product and country-by-country tariff negotiations which was so usefully developed under the aegis of GATT." The most powerful of these blocs, the Soviet bloc, has been operating for some time, but in the past five or six years it has played an increasingly important — and increasingly disruptive — role in the world's markets. Obviously this development "poses a great many problems for the United States and for like-minded nations which are bent on preserving an open trading system based on the free choices of individual buyers and sellers." Moreover, "the power of the Soviet bloc to exert political influence on third countries, either by buying their products on an emergency basis or by threatening to cut off such buying, is a weapon of considerable economic and political potential."[18]

In Western Europe two major trading blocs have emerged, the European Economic Community and the European Free Trade Association. Although serious differences exist between them, both blocs profess certain common objectives and consist of nations which are associated with each other in other organizations. Thus the prospects for ultimate cooperation and perhaps even fusion are quite bright. At the opening of the GATT conference on September 1, 1960, F. T. Wahlen, Vice President of the Swiss Federal Republic, declared: "Since both E.E.C. and EFTA agree on a common objective, there should be no slackening in our efforts finally to achieve an integrated European trade system, compatible with the rules of GATT, committed to liberal foreign trade policies, so that our overseas partners will be able to preserve and steadily develop their share in European markets."[19]

[17] General Assembly Res. 1995 (XIX).

[18] The quotations in this paragraph are taken from "Recommendations for a New International Trade Policy for the United States," a statement prepared by the Committee on Commercial Policy of the United States Council of the International Chamber of Commerce, and adopted by the Council's Executive Committee in April, 1961.

[19] Quoted in *EFTA Bulletin,* I (October, 1960), 11.

Other regional trading blocs have been proposed in many other parts of the world, including Latin America, Southeast Asia, North Africa, West Africa, and the Middle East. A Central American Common Market is already in existence, and a Latin American Free Trade Association, has become a reality. In the former French Community areas of Africa the African-Malagasy Organization for Economic Cooperation has some of the characteristics of a regional trading association.

State Trading and the Communist Economies. According to one authority, the emergence of state-controlled foreign trade is "undoubtedly the most important international economic phenomenon of the twentieth century."[20] This greatly complicates the problem of economic cooperation among states, and introduces many other disturbing factors into the international picture.

What is called state trading comes about when the governments, not content with the control that comes from conventional regulatory devices, themselves engage in trade. Most governments do this in special circumstances and in particular commodities, and the total amount of foreign trade carried on by governments of non-Communist states is substantial. In fact, "A very substantial portion of today's world trade is carried on under state trading."[21] In the Soviet Union and in most controlled economic and political systems foreign trade is a monopoly of the government. Ironically, the United States — the country of "free enterprise" — is one of the top state trading countries. "The United States engages in state trading through the government's (1) disposal abroad of surplus commodities acquired in the process of supporting agricultural prices, (2) purchase abroad of goods and services under the 'offshore procurement' program, and (3) purchase abroad of strategic raw materials for stockpiling purposes."[22] So-called bulk purchasing agreements are used by many governments to obtain raw materials and other commodities important to their national economies. State trading is also a normal consequence of nationalization. Thus, when the nationalization of a particular industry takes place, a government marketing agency is usually set up to handle the selling of its products.

In Communist states trade is carried on by state-owned trading monopolies, which are usually stock companies set up to conduct foreign trade in particular commodities. These monopolies serve as both central selling agencies and central buying offices. They work within quantitative limits and on price schedules fixed by the government, and they surrender their profits to the government. All operations in a particular foreign country may be consolidated; "Amtorg" in the United States, for instance, executes the orders for all Soviet industries. In most state trading countries, however, the government itself conducts the negotiations and concludes the agreements, and then turns over to the monopoly the job of meeting the state's commitments. In the states within the Soviet bloc in Eastern Europe the Russians share control with the East European governments.[23] While monopoly states may prefer to do business with each other, they are usually pleased to trade with anybody as long as the terms are "right," just as nearly everybody else is. They need certain commodities from the democratic states, and they are sensibly willing to trade for them.

The activities of the Soviet trading bloc illustrate to an extreme degree the dilemmas which state trading creates for nations which

[20] M. Heilperin, *The Trade of Nations* (New York: Alfred A. Knopf, 1947), p. 106.

[21] Walter Krause, *International Economics* (Boston: Houghton Mifflin Company, 1965), p. 211.

[22] *Ibid.*, pp. 211–212.

[23] See Nicholas Spulber, *The Soviet Economy* (New York: W. W. Norton & Company, 1962), Chapters 6 and 14.

seek to promote an open trading system. It is difficult for individual entrepreneurs to compete with state trading associations, which operate within an artificial price system, which are not subject to the ordinary conventions of international trade in free world markets, and which subordinate economic to political considerations. "The familiar rules of the game developed among private-enterprise economies cannot realistically be applied to Soviet bloc trading. Concepts such as profit and loss, dumping, discrimination, and trade restrictions lose their customary meaning when applied to a state-directed flow of trade."[24] Above all, "wherever state trading exists . . . the use of economic power in furtherance of political power is a possibility."[25]

In his last public statement on international affairs Wendell Willkie warned: "If after the war the industrial and commercial life of most of the countries of the world is either state-owned or controlled, then the whole problem of the survival of a free economic system, even in the United States, will be complicated."[26] Willkie's warning has a prophetic ring, for the very situation he feared has eventuated, and free enterprise systems are at a peculiar disadvantage with such an order of economic affairs.

2. Postwar Economic Problems: Currency and Exchange Control

It is no mere coincidence that the period of relatively free movement of goods and services in the nineteenth and early twentieth centuries was also the period of the international gold standard. The latter was essential to the former, for the easy movement of goods calls for the easy movement of money. But the international gold standard could not survive the economic and political explosions which began in the second decade of the twentieth century. As Michael Heilperin pointed out, the gold standard was "the monetary system of an essentially peaceful world, where confidence reigned, trade was reasonably free, and capital movements between countries were regular."[27] It did not provide a mechanism for dealing with financial crises and basic disturbances in balance of payments. While it was partially revived in the 1920's, it disappeared — perhaps forever — in the economic blitz of the 1930's. Britain was forced to abandon it in October, 1931, in the midst of a major economic and political crisis. This step, together with the abandonment of free trade which soon followed, seemed to mark the end of an era. One immediate result was the general flight from the gold standard, chiefly by those countries in the Commonwealth and the sterling area whose currencies were linked to the British pound. In April, 1933, in the early days of the Roosevelt administration, the United States followed suit, and in 1934 the President reduced the gold content of the dollar so that it was valued at fifty-nine cents in relation to the old. It was later reduced to fifty cents. Thus the two most powerful currencies in the world, the pound and the dollar, were adversely affected by the economic troubles of the 1930's.

In recent years the general pattern has been one of growing monetary as well as economic nationalism, arrested but by no means checked by temporary improvements in the world economic picture, by the efforts of international agencies such as the International Monetary Fund, and by the policies of the United States and other major financial powers. A peaceful world needs monetary as well as economic stability; this stabil-

24 "Recommendations for a New International Trade Policy for the United States."

25 Carroll and Marion Daugherty, *Principles of Political Economy,* (Boston: Houghton Mifflin Company, 1950), II, 112.

26 *An American Program* (New York: Simon and Schuster, 1944), p. 19.

27 Heilperin, p. 58. See also Arthur I. Bloomfield, *Monetary Policy under the International Gold Standard: 1880–1914* (Federal Reserve Bank of New York, October, 1959).

ity can be attained only when international payments can be made easily, when exchange rates are stable, and when currencies are freely convertible. Obviously the present trend is in the opposite direction. Most nations feel compelled to impose exchange controls and husband their currency and their reserves. These attitudes are most prevalent in states which have accepted the principles of state planning and control of economic life and which are inclined to limit their international economic cooperation because of fear of adverse effects on their national programs. However necessary these measures may be in particular situations, it should be recognized that if pursued too intently they may seriously endanger human freedoms and world peace.

Balance of Payments Difficulties and Exchange Controls. Many of the present-day measures of monetary nationalism may be attributed to balance of payments problems. "Balance of payments" is the economist's term for the difference between what a nation receives for its exports and "invisible" items — another technical term to refer to income from shipping, investments abroad, tourist trade, etc. — and what it has to pay for its imports.[28] "The most difficult questions of international economic relations at the present time," asserts J. B. Condliffe, "are those connected with the balancing of payments between national economies."[29] Many nations today are having balance of payments difficulties — particularly those which are heavily dependent upon foreign trade, such as Great Britain and Japan. Faced with the necessity of importing much of the food to keep their people alive and most of the raw materials to keep their industries going, these countries are unable to pay for such essentials through their own exports of goods and services. These difficulties are all the greater because their own productive capacities were injured by the war, because many of their former markets have disappeared, and because of the growing embarrassments to foreign trade. In an attempt to protect their own interests they add to these restrictions through import rationing, exchange controls, bilateral clearing arrangements, and other devices. Their problems are also immensely complicated by the practices of other states, by the complete monopoly of trade and exchange in the countries of the Soviet bloc, and by the overwhelming economic power of the United States.

Bilateral clearing arrangements, like bilateral trade agreements, have proliferated in the postwar period. They can be justified only as a temporary and necessary deviation from the multilateral way. Condliffe has explained this point very well: "All the difficulties that arise in the trade relations between free and controlled economies are inherent in the adoption of bilateral clearing practices, since such practices must utilize discriminatory trade regulation as the principal balancing mechanism. . . . Bilateralism is necessarily a system of discrimination."[30]

Balance of Payments Problems and Gold Flow. From the period of World War I until recent years a major problem in international economic relations was summed up in the term "dollar shortage" or "dollar gap." The problem arose out of a single significant fact: that year after year the United States has exported more than she has imported and that the nations which have received her exports have not been able to obtain the dollars to pay for the

[28] ". . . a country's balance of international payments is a summary statement, or account, of all the transactions of its residents with the residents of the rest of the world." Ellsworth (1964), p. 249.

[29] Condliffe, p. 8.

[30] *Ibid.*, p. 745. See also Poul Nyboe Andersen, *Bilateral Exchange Clearing Policy* (Copenhagen, 1946); and Charles P. Kindleberger, *International Economics* (Homewood, Ill.: Richard D. Irwin, 1963), Chapters 4, 9, and 10.

American export surplus, i.e., the excess of exports over imports, which has created the "dollar gap." In no year since 1914 has the United States had an import surplus. From 1914 through 1948 the total American export surplus, mounting steadily and reaching staggering proportions after 1940, amounted to more than 100 billion dollars. Only a small amount of this surplus was paid for by gold or other capital movements; over two-thirds was financed by United States government grants and loans.[31]

Since the end of World War II the United States has poured out many billions of dollars, mostly in the form of grants and "soft" loans, to aid other countries in rehabilitation and recovery and to enable them to buy essential materials from the United States. The European Recovery Program represents the greatest single venture of this sort, but funds have been made available through many other channels and for many other purposes. The British loan of $3.75 billion, plus other credits to Britain, represent the largest extension of credit, as contrasted to outright grants. Outside of Western Europe the largest amounts of economic assistance, chiefly in the form of "soft" loans and surplus food shipments under Public Law 480, have been made available to India. Military spending, comprising the expenses for maintaining substantial American forces overseas and military assistance to many nations, now represents more than half of the total government expenditures abroad. United States private foreign investment, which now runs to about three billion dollars a year, is another substantial item in the balance of payments account.

[31] *The United States Balance of Payments Problem,* Dept. of State Pub. 3695, Commercial Policy Series 123 (December, 1949), pp. 1–6; and Joint Economic Committee, U.S. Congress, *Factors Affecting the United States Balance of Payments,* 87th Cong., 2d Sess. (Washington, D.C.: Government Printing Office, 1962). The present American gold stock was acquired mostly by direct purchases of gold between 1933 and 1940, particularly from Britain, France, China, and the Soviet Union.

H. E. Kohler in Die Zeit

"Buddy, can you spare a dime?"

The heavy United States Government expenditures overseas have usually more than offset the continuing export surplus. In fact, the United States has had an "unfavorable balance" in international payments in every year since 1949, with the exception of 1957; since 1958 the unfavorable balance has been approximately $3.5 billion a year. One of the consequences of this deficit in the overall balance of payments has been a considerable reduction in the gold reserves, which from a high point of $22.9 billion in 1957 (59 per cent of the free world total) fell below $12 billion in 1968. In January, 1961, three American financial experts, in a report prepared for the incoming President, John F. Kennedy, warned that "an outflow of gold in the amounts and at the rate of recent movements could impair or destroy the ability of the United States dollar to serve as a principal world currency and thus break down the international monetary system which has been slowly and laboriously built up during the past fifteen years, and which it is in the interest of all countries of the free world to maintain and strengthen."[32] Seven years later, in the wake of the devaluation of the British pound and the continued American imbalance of payments, accentuated by the war in Vietnam, the United States was faced with a "gold rush" abroad that threatened to impose an intolerable drain on her dwindling gold reserves, and the crisis in the international monetary system against which the financial experts had warned seemed to be at hand. Clearly drastic measures and an unprecedented degree of international cooperation would be required to restore confidence in the two great international currencies, the dollar and the pound, and in the international monetary system generally.

Exchange Rates and Controls. In the absence of the international gold standard, the problem of fixing exchange rates between the currencies of the various countries is a particularly difficult one. "In any circumstances — whether the exchange market is free or controlled, whether the clearing is multilateral or bilateral — this exchange rate is the most important single factor in the balancing of international payments. . . . All the international economic relations between trading countries come to focus in this ratio. . . . In theory and in practice this is the core of international economic relations."[33] Of all the exchange rates the dollar-sterling rate is the most important. The relations of these two major world currencies are as crucial as the relations between major powers, for they are the great powers of the world of international finance. When the pound was devalued, under strong American pressure, in September, 1949, it was dropped from \$4.03 to \$2.80. One immediate result was that since the dollar would buy more pounds, purchases in Britain and elsewhere in the sterling area by dollar countries were stimulated, whereas British purchases in the United States were discouraged. This was generally regarded as a desirable result, since Britain was trying to export more to the United States and to buy less from her, thereby earning more of the dollars which were desperately needed. The devaluation of the pound, followed by that of nearly all of the other currencies linked with the pound, had worldwide repercussions. The consequences of the British devaluation in 1967 were equally far-reaching, although the need to devalue the pound once again raised doubts about the long-term efficacy of such measures.

The International Monetary Fund. A major purpose of the International Monetary Fund (IMF), one of the institutions which emerged from the Bretton Woods Conference in 1944 and which is now associated with the United Nations as a specialized agency, is to help to stabilize international monetary relations. By adhering to the Articles of Agreement of the IMF, each member pledged itself to avoid restrictions on payments for current international transactions as well as discriminatory currency practices, except when the Fund finds such restrictions to be necessary on a temporary basis because the currency in question is

[32] From a report prepared for President Kennedy by Allan Sproul, Ray Blough, and Paul W. McCracken, submitted in January, 1961; in *The Morgan Guaranty Survey*, February, 1961, p. 10. "The lessening of the volume of dollars going abroad poses the threat of restricting the availability of capital in many foreign financial markets, reducing international trade, and of restricting development in some foreign countries. These possibilities point up the necessity for all of the countries of the free world to further seek long-term solutions to international monetary problems." *The Gold Situation*, seventeenth report by the Committee on Government Operations, U.S. House of Representatives, dated June 30, 1965 (89th Cong., 1st Sess., House Report No. 702), p. 27.

[33] Condliffe, p. 746. See also Krause, Chapters 4, 9, and 10.

scarce or because of the exigencies of "the postwar transitional period." Under certain conditions member states may draw upon the Fund for the purpose of tiding over temporary strains on their balances of payments. Members agree to abandon exchange controls "as soon as they are satisfied that they are able, in the absence of such restrictions, to settle their balance of payments in a manner which will not unduly encumber their access to the resources of the Fund."

Perhaps the Fund's signal contribution to facilitating international exchange was the creation of a new form of international monetary reserves, called Special Drawing Rights. After long negotiations, a compromise between the United States and French plans was adopted in September, 1967. This established the procedure whereby assets to supplement gold, dollars, and pounds — none of which exist in sufficient quantity to satisfy the needs of expanding world trade — may be created.

Clearly, the major objectives of the Fund have not been achieved; exchange controls and financial restrictions are still the order of the day. But to the extent of its limited capacities and resources the Fund is doing useful work. It has always been envisioned as an agency which would be really effective in dealing with long-term and not with emergency problems of currency stabilization and control. Its reports have consistently called attention to the long-run implications of the monetary policies being pursued by the nations of the world.[34]

ERP and EPU. More limited steps to deal with matters of balance of payments and currency convertibility on a regional basis were taken in connection with the European Recovery Program. The system of having drawing rights and contributions incorporated into the Intra-European Balance of Payments Scheme, formulated by OEEC, was an effective means of stimulating intra-European trade.[35] The Balance of Payments Scheme was, in turn, superseded by the more substantial European Payments Union in 1950. In each program the Bank for International Settlements at Basle acted as the agent. This is only the most recent of the many services which the Bank, originally established in 1924 in connection with the Dawes Plan for German reparations, has rendered in international monetary matters. EPU was able to provide a badly needed multilateral clearing mechanism for member countries; its efforts, however, were seriously hampered by the heavy deficits of some of its members and the strong surplus positions of others.[36]

3. Postwar Economic Problems: International Investment

Foreign investment has been one of the chief factors in the tremendous economic and industrial advances of modern times.[37] Until World War I Britain had made the greatest contribution in this field, and her overseas investments were sources of great economic and political strength. Even for some years after 1914–18 the serious deterioration in her economic position was not generally apparent. This was due in part to the fact that she was living on the accumulated resources of many decades of economic and financial supremacy. Only when a great percentage of British overseas investments was liquidated during World War II, and when Britain, once a great creditor nation, had become saddled with heavy foreign in-

[34] See Brian Tew, *The International Monetary Fund; Its Present Role and Future Prospects* (Princeton, N.J.: Princeton University Press, 1961).

[35] *Agreement for Intra-European Payments and Compensations* (Organization for European Economic Co-operation, Paris, 16 October 1948), Part I. See also "European Recovery," *International Conciliation*, No. 447 (January, 1949), pp. 49–56.

[36] Krause, pp. 280–281.

[37] For an excellent discussion of this development, see the chapter on "Investment and Enterprise" in Condliffe, pp. 320–359.

debtedness and a staggering balance of payments deficit, did the full magnitude of the change become apparent.

The lessons of the British experience in the nineteenth century may still be studied with profit, but those successes can hardly be repeated under the more difficult conditions of the twentieth century. "What the private capitalism of the London money market achieved in the half-century preceding the first World War," declared J. B. Condliffe, "was an impressive demonstration of economic development resulting from well-directed investment and skillfully-managed monetary policies. Any attempt to repeat that demonstration must now reckon with heightened economic nationalism and must therefore proceed by international agreement. This involves a larger measure of intergovernmental control so that foreign investment and trade must in the future proceed in a different political climate."[38]

Obstacles to International Investment. The political climate to which Professor Condliffe refers is generally unhealthy; and the problem of creating a healthy one for foreign investment is one of the gravest problems in international economic relations today. The obstacles are many. They are to be found in the conditions in countries which need foreign capital and in countries which could supply funds for capital investment; they are also to be found in the general international environment. In his *Report to the President on Foreign Economic Policies,* submitted in November, 1950, Gordon Gray listed the major obstacles as "present international tensions," "actions, or expressed unfriendly attitudes of other governments toward foreign capital, political instability, fear of government control, or expropriation," and "economic difficulties, particularly those resulting in exchange restrictions."[39] A Woodrow Wilson Foundation–National Planning Association Study Group reported in 1955, with reference to private foreign investment, that "an expansion in its volume and scope is not likely to occur automatically," for these reasons:

> The major economic and political obstacles to such expansion include the poor economic health of many national economies, the incalculability of the international economy, the cold war, and the profound social transformation of the underdeveloped countries. . . . The immediately apparent obstacles . . . are broadly of two kinds — those arising from competitive uses of capital and those unduly enhancing risks. The most important competition with which private American investment abroad has had to contend has been the alternative opportunities for investment at home. . . . The greatest obstacles . . . have been the high risks — over and above those traditionally considered to be normal business risks — which the private investor . . . recognizes as entailed in the commitment of capital funds in most parts of the world today.[40]

Private International Investment. International investment may be either private or public. In the United States, the chief source of funds, the former is regarded as "the most desirable method of development," in the words of the Gray Report; whereas in the countries which most need development funds the latter is preferred, for private investment is viewed with suspicion by governments which are still sensitive to any trace or hint of foreign interests — "imperialism!" — and which believe in the necessity of state planning of development projects.

Despite unsettled conditions abroad and

[38] *Ibid.*, p. 349.

[39] Gordon Gray, *Report to the President on Foreign Economic Policies* (Washington, D.C.: Government Printing Office, 1950), pp. 61–63, 72.

[40] *The Political Economy of American Foreign Policy*, pp. 332–333.

the plentiful opportunities for capital investment in the United States, American direct private foreign investment, including reinvested earnings, has increased from approximately $1.5 billion a year in the first four or five years of the postwar era, to about $2 billion annually in the decade 1950–60, and it is now more than $3 billion a year.[41] The cumulative total of United States private foreign holdings rose to over $66 billion in 1963. American industry's direct investment in other countries amounts to more than $40 billion. Of this amount one-third is invested in Canada, more than one-fourth in Western Europe, and nearly one-fourth in Latin America. Some $2 billion, representing earnings on foreign investments and operations, are returned to the United States each year. Of the $2.236 billion of investment in the Middle East and Asia in 1961, $1.6 billion was in the petroleum industry. Relatively small amounts were represented by other forms of investment in Asia, Africa, and the Middle East. Clearly private capital is not attracted by many types of badly needed development projects or to those countries whose political regimes and unstable economies make them poor risks for private enterprise.

British overseas private investment has averaged about $850 million annually in the past decade. Most of this has gone to the United States, to the nations of Western Europe, and to other members of the Commonwealth. About one-third has been invested in underdeveloped areas, mostly in Commonwealth countries and British possessions.

A great many suggestions have been made for encouraging the flow of private capital abroad.[42] The most common are investment treaties with countries in need of such capital, government guarantees of private investment against such grave risks as inconvertibility of currency and foreign expropriation, and a combination of investment treaties and government guarantees. In the former, the main commitments are made by potential recipient governments; in the latter, the governments of the capital-exporting countries make the commitments. In both instances private investors are the beneficiaries.

Development Financing. In the financing of economic development it is obvious that public funds must play the major role. At the present time, the two main public lending institutions providing loans to the underdeveloped countries are the International Bank for Reconstruction and Development (commonly referred to as the World Bank) and the Export-Import Bank. The International Bank was created, along with the International Monetary Fund, by the Bretton Woods Agreement of 1944; it was established to help to finance postwar reconstruction and develop the resources and productive capacities of the countries which need outside aid. Its operations in the sphere of development financing have been restricted by the difficult conditions which must be satisfied before it will make loans, and by the high rates of interest and terms of repayment, rather than by limited borrowing capacity on its own part. Nevertheless, over one-half of all World Bank loans, totaling some $3 billion, have been made to underdeveloped countries.[43] The Export-Import Bank, an agency of the United States government, is the main channel through which American public funds are loaned to foreign governments. Up to May 31, 1960, the Ex-Im Bank had loaned more than $5.5 billion to underdeveloped nations.

Several other international or national agencies offer loans for economic development on easier and more flexible terms than

[41] See Raymond F. Mikesell, ed., *U.S. Private and Government Investment Abroad* (Eugene: University of Oregon Books, 1962).

[42] See Raymond F. Mikesell, *Promoting United States Private Investment Abroad* (National Planning Association, 1957).

[43] See Krause, Chapter 18.

do the World Bank and the Ex-Im Bank. Among these are two affiliates of the World Bank, the International Finance Corporation, formed in 1956 to encourage private enterprise in less developed countries, and the International Development Association, established in the fall of 1960 to provide long-term, low-interest loans to developing countries, repayable in local currencies. The main United States agency for "soft" loans for economic development is the Development Loan Fund, established in 1957 and now administered by the Agency for International Development. Many other organizations and agencies provide technical and other forms of assistance to underdeveloped areas. Among these are the United Nations Development Program, the UN specialized agencies, the Economic and Social Council and its commissions, at least 35 international agencies outside the formal structure of the UN, and "probably 100 or more national agencies carrying out the bilateral programs of the industrialized free world nations."[44]

In the period 1954–59 fifteen industrialized nations made available nearly $18 billion in loans and grants to less developed countries. Two-thirds of the total amount was provided by the United States. The other large contributors were France (3.8 billion) and the United Kingdom (slightly over $1 billion). The Federal Republic of Germany advanced less than $275 million, and Japan only a little more than $50 million. Since 1959 the annual contributions of Germany and Japan have been substantially increased, and those of the United Kingdom have doubled.

Estimates regarding the total amount of foreign capital needed annually for economic development vary widely. Some authorities insist that the capacity of underdeveloped countries to utilize outside capital is extremely limited,[45] while others think that many billions a year can be used. Gray seemed to be thinking in terms of approximately two billions a year, mostly from American sources. The Rockefeller Board recommended an annual rate of two billion dollars in private foreign investment, plus a two-billion-dollar raw materials program. A United Nations memorandum on *Measures for the Economic Development of Underdeveloped Countries,* published in May, 1951, estimated capital requirements for underdeveloped areas at 19 billion dollars a year; even assuming an increase in domestic savings, this would mean annual deficits of "well in excess of $10 billion."[46] One economist computed that if the UN figures were scaled downward to take account of some neglected considerations, and if China were excluded, "the excess over current savings would then be within the range of $4.7 to $7.1 billion" per year.[47] FOA estimates of capital requirements ran in the neighborhood of four billion dollars a year for an initial period of four years. The United Nations Economic Commission for Asia and the Far East reported that Southeast Asia alone needed thirteen billion dollars over a five-year period. The Colombo Plan of Britain and the Commonwealth countries in South and Southeast Asia called for five billion dollars over the same period. Professor Seymour Harris, a well-known American economist, suggested some seven billion a year of overseas investment for an undesignated number of years.[48] An interdisciplinary

[44] "Special Report on Aid for Free World Growth," *Economic World,* August–September, 1960.

[45] For an excellent summary of this point of view, see Harlan Cleveland, "Problems of Economic Development in the Far East," Chapter II in John K. Fairbanks *et al., Next Step in Asia* (Cambridge, Mass.: Harvard University Press, 1949), pp. 25–47.

[46] U.N. Document E/1986, 3 May 1951, p. 79.

[47] Benjamin Higgins, "Development Financing," *International Conciliation,* No. 502 (March, 1955), p. 292.

[48] Cited in Ellsworth (1950), p. 842. See also Krause, pp. 512–514.

group of specialists at the Center for International Studies at the Massachusetts Institute of Technology, headed by Max F. Millikan, has estimated that the "capital inflow required per annum by underdeveloped countries" for the fifteen years, 1961–76, would range from over $5 billion to less than $3.5 billion, with private investment rising from one-third to more than one-half of the total amounts.[49] Many other estimates of this sort could be given; nearly all of them emphasize the continuing need for sizable funds for economic development.

In 1963 and again in 1964 the flow of capital from developed to developing countries amounted to approximately $9 billion. In 1965 it reached a record figure of almost $11 billion. There is considerable evidence that this amount, large as it is, is far from adequate. This point was strongly emphasized by representatives of the developing countries at the 1964 United Nations Conference on Trade and Development, and was concurred in by OECD, whose eleven members are the richest nations in the world. As development programs get under way, and, more important, as population increases in underdeveloped countries, the capital needs are greater and greater. The present amounts made available to these countries do not seem to be sufficient to offer any hope of achieving the objective, as stated in the cautious words of OECD, of "acceleration in the process of development in the less-developed nations."[50] "More finance is needed, and on terms more appropriate to the facts of life in underdeveloped countries."[51]

Patterns of Economic Aid and Cooperation

We cannot here examine the many projects in economic and financial cooperation, mutual aid, and technical assistance. Some relate to relief and rehabilitation, some to foreign private and public investment, some to national and international loans or grants, some to monetary and exchange stabilization, some to regional schemes of self-help, some to multilateral or unilateral technical assistance and advisory aid. It would be difficult to classify these projects and programs, or even to give them a common label. They differ greatly in sponsorship, mechanism, and immediate objectives. Many countries now have national programs of economic development. Most of these call for expenditures which can be realized only with outside assistance. Technical assistance under various UN agencies call for the use of limited funds subscribed by member states and spent under the guidance of experts of many nationalities. The World Bank is essentially an underwriting concern, arranging for foreign investment but itself providing only small amounts of capital. The Monetary Fund is in no sense an investment agency; its function is the stabilization of international exchange and the making of short-term loans to states with unfavorable trade balances.

Various programs for economic cooperation are being carried on in Latin America under the leadership of the Organization of American States. In the Organization for Economic Cooperation and Development, the European members of the earlier Organization for European Economic Cooperation are joined by the United States, Canada, and Japan in developing programs for the expansion of their own economies and those of underdeveloped countries. The Colombo

[49] Max F. Millikan and Donald L. M. Blackmer, eds., *The Emerging Nations: Their Growth and United States Policy* (Boston: Little, Brown and Company, 1961), pp. 156–157 (Table V on p. 156 and explanatory note on p. 157).

[50] See Andreas Freund, "Flow of Funds to Poorer Lands Is Termed Inadequate to Need," *New York Times*, January 15, 1965.

[51] George Woods, "The Development Decade in the Balance," *Foreign Affairs*, XLIV (January, 1966), 206–215. In this important article the President of the World Bank warned: "Unless the Development Decade . . . receives greater sustenance, it may, in fact, recede into history as a decade of disappointment." P. 206.

Plan is a spacious framework for cooperative self-help in South and Southeast Asia which seeks to enlist substantial outside capital.

The sterling area, "the largest multilateral trading area in the world," is a group of countries, in the Commonwealth and outside, which are bound together by the British pound and which cooperate with relatively few economic and financial restrictions within the area. The British Colonial Development Corporation makes capital and technical assistance available for projects of a productive or commercial nature in British dependencies. The *Fond D'Investissement pour le Developpement Economique et Social* has been the main agency for channeling even greater assistance to the states which have emerged in former French West and Equatorial Africa. In Western Europe, through the three existing communities, France, West Germany, Italy and the Benelux countries function almost as a single unit in some important activities of mutual concern. The European Coal and Steel Community involves essentially joint control over the coal and steel resources of the major industrial nations of Western Europe, notably Germany and France. The European Economic Community is a customs union which will eventually be virtually a free trade area, with a common external tariff and common policies in trading with other nations. Euratom is an association for the development of common policies and programs regarding the peaceful uses of atomic energy.

The European Payments Union was designed to provide a system of currency convertibility among the countries of Western Europe and thereby to stimulate intra-European trade. The Marshall Plan, one of the most ambitious programs of economic cooperation in history, provided for unilateral subsidies on a large scale, contingent upon certain demonstrations of self-help. The American Mutual Security Program is a comprehensive package that embraces the major foreign aid programs which the United States is now undertaking, including economic and technical as well as military assistance.

The final results of the host of aid programs are, of course, still speculative. These programs must be viewed with a number of sobering thoughts in mind. In the first place, even those which have been officially completed, like the Marshall Plan, have left many problems and succeeding plans in their wake, and it is still too early to attempt to measure their long-range achievements. Second, these plans assume a continuing political cooperation that may or may not be forthcoming, and an international climate that will permit concentration of extensive efforts and resources on basic problems of development and finance. Third, it remains to be seen how much they have been occasioned by the rise of the Communist threat, and how well they will fare in a period when relations between the Communist and the non-Communist worlds seem to be less ominous. Fourth, there is the very real question of the limits of the assistance which may be obtained from outside sources. Finally, we must not be too quick to take for granted a correlation between rising living standards and a passion for peace. To some extent we have been misled into such an assumption by the victories of Communist propaganda in underdeveloped areas, forgetting that literacy, industrialization, and improving — but still far from adequate — living standards are very likely to bring increased unrest, a widening of the gap between aspirations and possibilities, and an insistence upon all the theoretical rights of sovereignty, including the right to wanton nationalism.

There are also grounds for a more hopeful outlook. We seem to have in the making workable plans for economic development without the penalties of imperialism. The enlivened nationalism which may accompany the rise of economic levels may very well express itself in laudable social and cultural enterprises, and may prove to be wholly compatible with economic and political internationalism. The more general utilization of natural resources should prevent or delay the early exhaustion of the resources of some states. Increased productivity in certain areas will help to relieve the present disastrous imbalance of world trade, and will make possible higher standards of life for countless millions of people. Finally, new patterns of sympathetic cooperation may even become something of a norm for future generations.

Current Trends: A Summing Up

The dominant pattern today is one of economic nationalism rather than internationalism. It is apparent in trade restrictions, exchange controls, and obstacles to private foreign investment. It is most conspicuous in countries where state trading is the normal pattern. But there are some hopeful signs of better days to come. Many nations have subscribed to the principles of multilateral trade, currency convertibility, removal of exchange controls, and the stimulation of foreign investment. Although her own economic internationalism is somewhat qualified — even uncertain — the United States, perhaps largely because of her fortunate economic position, has taken the lead in urging concrete steps toward applying these principles. Her trade agreements program, her leadership in the negotiations leading to the General Agreement on Tariffs and Trade, her support of the economic agencies of the United Nations, her Mutual Security Program and numerous other programs of economic aid, involving many billions of dollars — these are but some of the more notable evidences of her sponsorship of economic internationalism. The United Nations, especially through the Economic and Social Council, the regional and functional commissions, the specialized agencies, and the economic offices of the Secretariat, is also exerting strong pressure for international economic sanity.

It is difficult to say how much of present-day economic nationalism is due to the general disequilibrium and to the serious problems confronting most countries, with the omnipresent necessity of imposing restrictions to cope with emergency situations, and how much is due to the trend toward state planning and control of economic life and the acceptance of philosophies which gravely jeopardize the hopes for economic cooperation. If the restrictive measures which most states now impose are not caused by temporary emergencies, but instead are to be a permanent feature of national economic policy, the prospects for a peaceful world are dim indeed.

The case for economic internationalism was forcefully stated by an American economist some years ago:

> Much has been granted, in the argument of this book, to the case for protection to stimulate economic development, for exchange controls as a weapon against capital flight, and for the use of import licensing as a device in times of emergency. Much scope is also given for the use of these measures in the provisions of the International Monetary Fund and of the proposed International Trade Organization. But if restrictive practices are required to deal with the pressures of exceptional severity, it is vitally important that their use be safeguarded, their necessity constantly reviewed, and their use abandoned when conditions permit in favor of arrangements which invoke comparisons of efficiency. To establish a pattern of trade restrictions as the probable permanent framework of future international economic relations would be to turn our backs on the hope of growing international cooperation, expanding world trade, and steadily improving standards of living and to guarantee the return of nationalism, intense trade rivalry, and the collapse of western unity.[52]

[52] Ellsworth (1950), p. 885.

Aside from the Soviet Union and the states of the Soviet bloc, the strongest tendencies toward economic nationalism are apparent in the policies of the underdeveloped nations and of those states which are experiencing serious balance of payments difficulties. The problem varies with the position and resources of the particular states. In underdeveloped countries the main need is for basic economic development; it is not for recovery, for that would imply a return to what never existed. In war-dislocated countries which once possessed considerable industrial development, the problem after World War II was recovery and rehabilitation, although this was complicated by what were apparently permanent shifts in the basic factors of economic power and in the channels of trade and finance. The nature of the need also varies according to regions; it is one thing in Western Europe, another in Asia. As Harlan Cleveland stated, "whereas the European economic problem is now to a considerable extent a trade and payments problem, the fundamental economic problem in the Far East is development."[53] Again we are faced with a familiar dilemma: nations that are trying to raise their economies above the present intolerably low levels and those that are trying to rebuild economies shattered by war and postwar equilibrium feel compelled to resort to devices of economic nationalism, whereas their only hope of ultimate success lies in the creation of a world in which economic internationalism prevails.

In the building of such a world the responsibility of the United States is particularly great. As President Truman declared in a famous address suggestive of Wilson's First Inaugural: "We are the giants of the economic world. Whether we like it or not, the future pattern of economic relations depends upon us. The world is watching and waiting to see what we shall do." Mr. Truman also underscored the interrelationship of political and economic policies: "Our foreign relations, political and economic, are indivisible. We cannot say that we are willing to cooperate in one field and unwilling to cooperate in the other."[54] In the wisdom of these words the question of the primacy of politics over economics, or of economics over politics, may be resolved; in reality the two are "indivisible" and inseparable, simply different aspects of the enduring problem of finding ways by which nations and peoples may live together peacefully in an interdependent world.

SUGGESTIONS FOR FURTHER READING

ALLEN, ROBERT L. *Soviet Economic Warfare.* Washington, D.C.: Public Affairs Press, 1960.

AUBREY, HENRY G. *United States Imports and World Trade.* New York: Oxford University Press, 1957. A thorough study.

BALASSA, BELA. *Trade Prospects for the Developing Countries.* Homewood, Ill.: Richard D. Irwin, 1964.

BALDWIN, ROBERT E. *et al. Trade, Growth, and the Balance of Payments.* Chicago: Rand McNally & Co., 1965. Essays in honor of Gottfried Haberler.

BASCH, ANTONIN. *Financing Economic Development.* New York: The Macmillan Company, 1964.

BAUER, P. T. and B. S. YAMEY. *The Economics of Under-Developed Countries.* Chicago: University of Chicago Press, 1957. A laissez-faire approach.

BELL, PHILIP W. *The Sterling Area in the Postwar World — Internal Mechanism and Cohesion, 1946–52.* London, 1956.

BERLINER, JOSEPH S. *Soviet Economic Aid:*

[53] Fairbank *et al.*, p. 32.

[54] Address at Baylor University, Waco, Texas, March 6, 1947; in the *New York Times,* March 7, 1947.

The New Aid and Trade Policy in Underdeveloped Countries. New York: Frederick A. Praeger, 1958. A significant work, even though it was written at an early stage of the Soviet economic offensive.

BLACK, EUGENE R. *The Diplomacy of Economic Development.* Cambridge, Mass.: Harvard University Press, 1960. Brief but illuminating observations by a former president of the World Bank.

BONNÉ, ALFRED. *Studies in Economic Development, with Special Reference to Conditions in the Underdeveloped Areas of Western Asia and India.* London, 1957.

BRAND, WILLEM. *The Struggle for a Higher Standard of Living; the Problem of Underdeveloped Countries.* New York: Free Press of Glencoe, 1958.

BUCHANAN, NORMAN S. and HOWARD S. ELLIS. *Approaches to Economic Development.* New York: The Twentieth Century Fund, 1955.

COPPOCK, JOSEPH D. *International Economic Instability; the Experience after World War II.* New York: McGraw-Hill Book Company, 1962.

CURZON, GERARD. *Multilateral Commercial Diplomacy: An Examination of the Impact of the General Agreement on Tariffs and Trade on National Commercial Policies and Techniques.* London, 1965.

DELL, SIDNEY. *Trade Blocs and Common Markets.* New York: Alfred A. Knopf, 1963.

DIEBOLD, WILLIAM, JR. *The Schuman Plan — A Study in Economic Cooperation, 1950–1959.* New York: Frederick A. Praeger, 1959.

ELLSWORTH, P. T. *The International Economy,* 3d ed. New York: The Macmillan Company, 1964.

GALBRAITH, JOHN K. *Economic Development.* Cambridge, Mass.: Harvard University Press, 1964. A brief personal statement by a well-known economist.

GALBRAITH, VIRGINIA L. *World Trade in Transition.* Washington, D.C.: Public Affairs Press, 1965.

GARDNER, RICHARD R., *Sterling Dollar Diplomacy.* New York: Oxford University Press, 1956.

HAGRAS, KAMAL M. *United Nations Conference on Trade and Development; a Case Study in UN Diplomacy.* New York: Frederick A. Praeger, 1965.

HARRIS, SEYMOUR. *International and Interregional Economics.* New York: McGraw-Hill Book Company, 1957.

HARROD, SIR ROY, ed. *International Trade Theory in a Developing World.* New York: St. Martin's Press, 1963. Proceedings of a conference held by the International Economic Association.

HEILPERIN, MICHAEL A. *Studies in Economic Nationalism.* Geneva, 1960. Publication No. 35 of the Institut Universitaire de Hautes Études Internationales.

HIGGINS, BENJAMIN. *Economic Development.* New York: W. W. Norton & Company, 1959. Especially good on development theories.

HOFFMEYER, ERIK. *Dollar Shortage and the Structure of U. S. Foreign Trade.* Amsterdam, 1958.

JOHNSON, HARRY G. *World Economy at the Crossroads; a Survey of Current Problems of Money, Trade, and Economic Development.* New York: Oxford University Press, 1966. By a leading Canadian economist.

KENEN, PETER B. *Giant Among Nations: Problems in United States Foreign Economic Policy.* New York: Harcourt, Brace, 1960.

———. *International Economics.* Englewood Cliffs, N.J.: Prentice-Hall, 1964. A brief but competent survey.

KINDLEBERGER, CHARLES P. *Economic Development,* 2d ed. New York: McGraw-Hill Book Company, 1965.

———. *International Economics,* 3d ed. Homewood, Ill.: Richard D. Irwin, 1963.

KRAUSE, WALTER. *Economic Development.* Belmont, Calif.: Wadsworth Publishing Co., 1961.

———. *International Economics.* Boston: Houghton Mifflin Company, 1965. A revision of *The International Economy,* published in 1955.

KRAVIS, IRVING B. *Domestic Interests and International Obligations; Safeguards in International Trade Organizations.* Philadelphia: University of Pennsylvania Press, 1963. Excellent discussions of GATT, the OEEC Code of Liberalization, the European Coal and Steel Community, and the Common Market.

LARY, HAL B. *Problems of the United States as World Trader and Banker.* New York: National Bureau of Economic Research, 1963. One of the most thorough analyses of the U.S. balance of payments problem.

LUBELL, SAMUEL. *Revolution in World Trade and American Economic Policy.* New York: Harper, 1955

LUTZ, FRIEDRICH A. *The Problem of International Economic Equilibrium.* Amsterdam, 1962.

MARCUS, EDWARD and MILDRED R. MARCUS. *International Trade and Finance.* New York: Pitman Publishing Corp., 1965

MEIER, GERALD M. *International Trade and Development.* New York: Harper & Row, 1963. Excellent bibliography, pp. 193–202.

MILLIKAN, MAX F. and W. W. ROSTOW. *A Proposal: Key to an Effective Foreign Policy.* New York: Harper, 1957.

MYINT, HLA, *The Economics of the Developing Countries.* New York: Frederick A. Praeger, 1965. By a noted Burmese economist who teaches at Oxford.

MYRDAL, GUNNAR. *Beyond the Welfare State; Economic Planning and Its International Implications.* New Haven: Yale University Press, 1960. Especially interesting on relation of trade and economic growth.

———. *An International Economy; Problems and Prospects.* New York: Harper, 1956. By a famous Swedish economist and sociologist and a former Executive Secretary of the Economic Commission for Europe. Especially good on underdeveloped areas.

———. *Rich Lands and Poor; the Road to World Peace.* New York: Harper, 1957.

POLK, JUDD. *Sterling: Its Meaning in World Finance.* New York: Harper, for the Council on Foreign Relations, 1956. A major study by a former Treasury official.

ROLFE, SIDNEY E. *Gold and World Power: The Dollar, the Pound, and the Plans for Reform.* New York: Harper & Row, 1966. An important study of a timely subject.

ROSSA, ROBERT V. *Monetary Reform for the World Economy.* New York: Harper & Row, for the Council on Foreign Relations, 1965. By a former Under Secretary of the Treasury.

ROSTOW, W. W. *The Stages of Economic Growth.* Cambridge, England, 1960. A much-discussed series of lectures.

SNIDER, DELBERT A. *Introduction to International Economics,* 3d ed. Homewood, Ill.: Richard D. Irwin, 1963.

SONNWALD, ROLF F. and JACQUES STOHLER. *Economic Integration: Theoretical Assumptions and Consequences of European Integration.* Princeton, N.J.: Princeton University Press, 1959.

STALEY, EUGENE. *The Future of Underdeveloped Areas,* rev. ed. New York: Harper, 1962. One of the best-known treatments of the subject.

TINBERGEN, JAN. *Central Planning.* New Haven: Yale University Press, 1964. A concise analysis by a leading authority.

———. *The Design for Development.* Baltimore: The Johns Hopkins Press, for the Economic Development Institute, 1958.

———. *International Economic Integration,* rev. ed. Amsterdam, 1965.

———. *Shaping the World Economy; Suggestions for an International Economic Policy.* New York: The Twentieth Century Fund, 1962. Far-reaching suggestions by one of the world's leading economists.

TRIFFIN, ROBERT. *Europe and the Money Muddle.* New Haven: Yale University Press, 1957. An overall view of Europe's currency problems.

———. *Gold and the Dollar Crisis.* New Haven: Yale University Press, 1960. A searching analysis.

World Economic Survey. A comprehensive annual survey of world economic conditions, with emphasis on international trade, payments, and production. Each volume also includes a special study of a major economic subject of particular current interest. Published annually since 1948 by the United Nations. Volumes until 1955 were entitled *World Economic Report.*

WOYTINSKY, W. S. and E. S. WOYTINSKY. *World Commerce and Governments; Trends and Outlook.* New York: The Twentieth Century Fund, 1955.

YOUNG, JOHN PARKE. *The International Economy.* New York: The Ronald Press Company, 1963.

20 The New Regionalism

The trend toward regionalism and regional arrangements is one of the most interesting developments in recent international relations. The Charter of the United Nations specifically recognized it; and the Vandenberg Resolution, adopted by the United States Senate on June 11, 1948, gave it strong endorsement.[1] It has reached its fullest development in the Western Hemisphere and in Western Europe, but it has also appeared elsewhere.

This trend is in part an outcome of the necessity of pooling national resources for protection in a divided and war-threatened world; but it is also an outgrowth of other pressures which are driving nations together in the present era. Indeed, it may indicate that the nation-state system, which has been the dominant pattern of international relations for some four centuries, is evolving toward a system in which regional groupings of states will be more important than the independent sovereign units. Perhaps, as Walter Lippmann said, "the true constituent members of the international order of the future are communities of states."[2]

In this chapter we shall examine the nature and implications of international regionalism and analyze the most important regional arrangements which are now in being or which are seriously contemplated. To gain some understanding of the limitations and possibilities of regional arrangements, we must also consider their relations to the United Nations.

The Use of Terms

At the outset a number of terms should be defined. Although these are defined today in a wide variety of ways, it will be necessary to indicate rather definitely how they will be used in the present chapter.

Because of the frequent use of "regions" to mean areas smaller than states, it is important to emphasize that in international relations a region is invariably an area embracing the territories of three or more states. These states are bound together by ties of common interests as well as of geography.

[1] Of the six objectives listed in this resolution, two (2 and 3) concerned regional arrangements. They recommended: (2) "progressive development of regional and other collective arrangements for individual and collective self-defense in accordance with the purposes, principles, and provisions of the Charter," and (3) "association of the United States, by constitutional process, with such regional and other collective arrangements as are based on continuous and effective self-help and mutual aid, and as affect its national security."

[2] Unpublished address on "The Atlantic Community," at a conference on "Regionalism and Political Pacts," Philadelphia, May 6, 1949. E. H. Carr shares this view. See *The Twenty Years' Crisis, 1919–1939*, 2d ed. (London, 1946), p. 231. UN Secretary-General U Thant has predicted that "in the seventies the world will witness four big powers — the United States of America, Europe, Russia and China."

They are not necessarily contiguous, or even in the same continent. The outstanding example of far-flung regionalism is the association of fifteen nations, on both sides of the Atlantic and in the Scandinavian and Mediterranean areas, in the North Atlantic Treaty. For the purposes set forth in the treaty these states, geographically so scattered, may be regarded as forming a real community of states. In other words, the countries of the North Atlantic Pact form an international region.[3]

At the San Francisco Conference in 1945 the Egyptian delegation introduced an amendment to the draft text of the United Nations Charter to limit the term "regional arrangements" by definition to "organizations of a permanent nature grouping in a given geographical area several countries which, by reason of their proximity, community of interests or cultural, linguistic, historical, or spiritual affinities, make themselves jointly responsible for the peaceful settlement of any disputes which may arise between them and for the maintenance of peace and security in their region, as well as for the safeguarding of their interests and the development of their economic and cultural relations."[4] B. V. Boutros-Ghali, a distinguished Egyptian scholar who has written one of the best studies of regional agreements, in general approved of this definition but proposed to revise it in several particulars, notably to attribute to a regional arrangement "the final aim of forming a distinct political entity."[5] Dr. E. N. van Kleffens, former Dutch Ambassador to the United States formulated this definition: ". . . a regional arrangement or pact is a voluntary association of sovereign states within a certain area or having common interests in that area for a joint purpose, which should not be of an offensive nature, in relation to that area."[6] This definition requires one qualification. The terms "arrangement" and "pact" should not be used synonymously. Although a "pact" is the usual means of bringing an "arrangement" into being, "pact" is a looser and more general term; it may relate to an understanding on a single, comparatively simple matter, requiring no administrative machinery of any kind. A real regional arrangement, on the other hand, cannot exist without fairly elaborate organization.

To point out that writers do not agree on a definition would simply be saying that "regional arrangement" has not yet become a technical term.[7] Such an arrangement must involve sovereign states, certainly more than two, and they must be engaged in a substantial common enterprise. Agreement is lacking on the geographical implications — if

[3] Admittedly this is stretching the concept of "region" well beyond its usual limits. One can understand the bewilderment expressed in the following lines, quoted in the *New York Times*, May 22, 1949. They were sung at the spring dinner of the Gridiron Club in Washington, D.C., on May 21, 1949, to the tune of "Far Away Places":

The old North Atlantic has spread quite a lot
To Italy from Maine.
There'll soon be no country that touches it not
With the single exception of Spain.
They call me a schemer, well maybe I am
But today I can follow the shore
Of our North Atlantic, all the way to Siam
There's no other ocean no more!

[4] *Documents of the United Nations Conference on International Organization, San Francisco, 1945* (United Nations, 1945), XII, 850; Document 533 (English), III/4/A/9, May 23, 1945.

[5] B. V. Boutros-Ghali, *Contribution à l'étude des ententes régionales* (Paris, 1949), p. 101.

[6] E. N. van Kleffens, "Regionalism and Political Pacts," *The American Journal of International Law*, XLIII (October, 1949), 669.

[7] Writers who would lay down special qualifications, such as Boutros-Ghali and Van Kleffens, believe that these are necessary if the term is to be used in any meaningful way. They feel that there is need of terminology to distinguish peaceful, voluntary, and effective multilateral collaboration from ventures that may be aggressive in purpose, wholly involuntary, without real means of implementation, bilateral in nature, or superficial in interests. Those writers who prefer a looser use of the term point out that the Charter makers carefully avoided a definition, and they insist that the proposed definitions make nothing illegal and change nothing, and that they are arbitrary, unrealistic, conflicting, and futile.

any — of any international region and on the degree of collaboration necessary to qualify as a regional arrangement. This inexactness in definition means that students of international relations may disagree on whether a true regional arrangement exists in a particular instance.

Several regional arrangements may exist within a given area, as is the case in Western Europe today. Such arrangements do not have to include all the states within the area immediately affected. A state may be excluded for political or ideological reasons (for instance, Spain) or it may choose to stay out because of fear of international entanglement and possible violation of neutral status (Switzerland, in most instances).

A regional arrangement may be primarily a military alliance, but it must be more than that. It must provide for collaboration in other respects, and it need not involve military matters at all. The North Atlantic Treaty Organization, for example, is primarily a military alliance, but it also has many other interests and purposes.

A "regional understanding" is quite different from a regional arrangement, for it may be entirely without machinery for the implementation of common policies. It suggests more of a common attitude than integrated or even concerted action. Nor should a regional arrangement be confused with "such vague, all-inclusive, and not too candid terms as 'orbit,' 'bloc,' or 'zone' — euphemisms for domination plain and simple."[8] Hence, as we shall point out later, the Warsaw Treaty Organization and the East European "bloc" within the Soviet "orbit" are not genuine regional arrangements.

Regional Arrangements before World War II

Many examples of regional arrangements prior to World War II have been cited by various commentators, but one may doubt that most of them would satisfy the tests now commonly imposed. Dr. van Kleffens, for example, specifically mentions the leagues and confederacies of ancient Greece; the treaty of 1856 giving neutral status to the Aaland Islands; the treaty of 1863 regarding the Ionian Islands; and the Congo Act of 1885. But it seems highly doubtful that any of these examples meets the requirements of Dr. van Kleffens' own definition of a regional arrangement.

Before World War I. Possible examples of regional arrangements in the century between Waterloo and World War I would be the Germanic Confederation and the limited regionalism in the inter-American, the Balkan, and the Baltic areas. "The great political unifications in Europe," noted Adolf Б. Drucker, "were preceded by economic 'regions,' just as such 'regions' survived the great dissolutions of political units." As examples of the former process he cited the German Zollverein, which prepared the way for the political unification of Germany, and economic arrangements in Switzerland, Italy, Austria-Hungary, the Scandinavian area, and the Iberian Peninsula, all of which preceded the coming of political unity. His second point is illustrated in the survival of "regional preferences in the economic intercourse of the Balkan States" after the dismemberment of the Ottoman Empire.[9] Moreover, to continue Drucker's analysis, "before 1914, world integration was proceeding steadily by means of regional policies expressed in customs unions, preferential relationships, 'open door' arrangements, long term commercial treaties interrelated through the most-favored-nation clause, monetary unions, and worldwide acceptance of the gold standard." In some cases these trends

[8] Robert Strausz-Hupé, *The Balance of Tomorrow* (New York: G. P. Putnam's Sons, 1945), p. 273.

[9] "Regional Economic Principles and Problems," in *Regionalism and World Organization* (Washington, D.C.: Public Affairs Press, 1944), pp. 102, 104.

toward economic regionalism resulted in the formation of true regional arrangements; most of them, however, were of a relatively minor and ill-defined character and led nowhere.

Between World Wars. A number of regional arrangements came into being in the interwar period (1918–39), although some were in embryonic form and were never fully organized. One of the most obvious examples was the Little Entente. "Composed of Czechoslovakia, Yugoslavia, and Rumania and created shortly after the conclusion of the war, it grew out of a series of bilateral mutual assistance treaties among the three countries. It gradually developed into a broader political organization and, after 1933, came to approximate a close diplomatic confederation with definite organizational structure."[10]

There were many other attempts through agreements to form groupings of states in Eastern Europe and the Balkan area, but with the possible exception of the Balkan Entente of 1934 these attempts did not lead to any real regional arrangements. The Five-Power Treaty signed by Belgium, England, France, Germany, and Italy in 1925 regarding the western frontiers of Germany — the most important of the seven Locarno pacts — seemed to lay the foundation for regional collaboration for a specific purpose; but it was not implemented to the extent necessary to bring a regional arrangement into effective operation. The most hopeful instance of developing regionalism was that embracing the republics of the New World.

The Commonwealth. Should the Commonwealth of Nations — in many respects the most effective of all international associations — be regarded as a regional arrangement? The answer must certainly be in the negative. The Commonwealth is too scattered, and its driving force is at times less practical than sentimental. The ties that bind its members are at once too loose and informal and too deep-rooted and traditional. While its members consult with each other regularly on many matters, they have deliberately avoided setting up elaborate machinery for Commonwealth cooperation. Not until June, 1965, did the Commonwealth prime ministers decide to establish a secretariat, and even this was done on a modest scale.

Nor should the British Empire, which has been reduced to bits and fragments, or the sterling area, both of which center in Britain, be classed as regional arrangements. The empire is not an association of sovereign states, and the pound sterling, for all its power in world affairs, is not a sufficiently cohesive force to bring a regional arrangement into being in the absence of formal organization and integrating purpose.

The Inter-American System. From its formal beginnings in 1889 the so-called Inter-American System had expanded rather steadily in both purpose and machinery prior to World War II, but it had not explicitly accepted the principles of common defense or close economic cooperation. Before 1939 inter-American collaboration had been present in many areas of interest: sanitation, public health, highways, international law, trade, agriculture, conservation, education, radio, child welfare, and others. As machinery existed for the promotion of these common interests, one may properly regard the Inter-American System as a regional arrangement, even before World War II. But since Pearl Harbor far-reaching changes have been made by way of formalizing its organization, expanding its interests, and elaborating its machinery. The Inter-American System is now international regionalism in its most advanced form. For that reason

[10] Ward P. Allen, "Regional Arrangements and the United Nations," *Organizing the United Nations*, Dept. of State Pub. 2573 (1946), pp. 5–6.

we shall examine it first among the present instances of regional arrangements.

Regional Arrangements in the Western Hemisphere

World War II brought unprecedented cooperation among the American republics. They made provision for common defense, the exchange of essential materials, and financial and cultural collaboration. The Inter-American Conference on Problems of War and Peace, held in Mexico City in 1945, laid the groundwork for the Rio Treaty of 1947 as well as for the Charter of the Organization of American States and other important agreements approved at the Bogotá Conference of 1948.

The Rio Treaty. A special Inter-American Conference for the Maintenance of Continental Peace and Security, held at Rio de Janeiro in August–September, 1947, drafted the famous Rio Treaty — the Inter-American Treaty of Reciprocal Assistance. This agreement not only provided for collective security in the Western Hemisphere but also furnished a pattern which was closely studied, if not actually copied, in the drafting of the Brussels Treaty of 1948 and the North Atlantic Treaty of 1949.

The heart of the Rio Treaty is Article 3, which closely resembles Article 4 of the Brussels Treaty and Article 5 of the North Atlantic Pact:

> The High Contracting Parties agree that an armed attack by any State against an American State shall be considered as an attack against all American States and, consequently, each one of the said Contracting Parties undertakes to assist in meeting the attack in the exercise of the inherent right of individual or collective self-defense recognized by Article 51 of the Charter of the United Nations.

The Rio Treaty is regarded as a collective security arrangement within the meaning of Article 51 of the United Nations Charter. That it was to fit into a larger community of interests is clearly stated in Article 26: "The principles and fundamental provisions of this Treaty shall be incorporated in the Organic Pact of the Inter-American System."

The Organization of American States. The Organic Pact or Charter of the Organization of American States, adopted at the Ninth International Conference of American States (the Bogotá Conference), provides the framework for a comprehensive regional organization. "It systematizes and integrates what was formerly a loose, informal and disorganized arrangement. . . . into a unified form of hemispheric organization."[11] The Charter is a lengthy document of 18 chapters and 112 articles. Article I states specifically: "The Organization of American States is a regional agency within the United Nations."

The Organization of American States — or, briefly, the OAS — is similar in structure to the United Nations in some ways and dissimilar in others. The Inter-American Conference, for example, resembles the General Assembly of the UN, although it meets much less frequently (a regular session is to be held every five years) and, unlike the General Assembly, it is formally designated as "the supreme organ." The Council is similar to the United Nations Security Council, but its powers in the field of security action and enforcement are more limited. It has twenty-one members, one from each state in the OAS; it is the central administrative and coordinating agency for the organization; it supervises the work of the Pan American

[11] Georgine L. Ogden, "The Organization of American States," *Columbia Journal of International Affairs,* III (Spring, 1949), 48. The Bogotá reorganization also involved a change in name. The Union of American Republics (until 1910 the International Union of American Republics) became the Organization of American States. Also in 1910, the Bureau of American Republics (formerly the Commercial Bureau of American Republics) became the Pan American Union. The name "Pan American Union" has never applied to the larger organization, but always to the central secretarial office.

ORGANIZATION OF AMERICAN STATES

The OAS as it will be when the "Protocol of Buenos Aires" is in effect

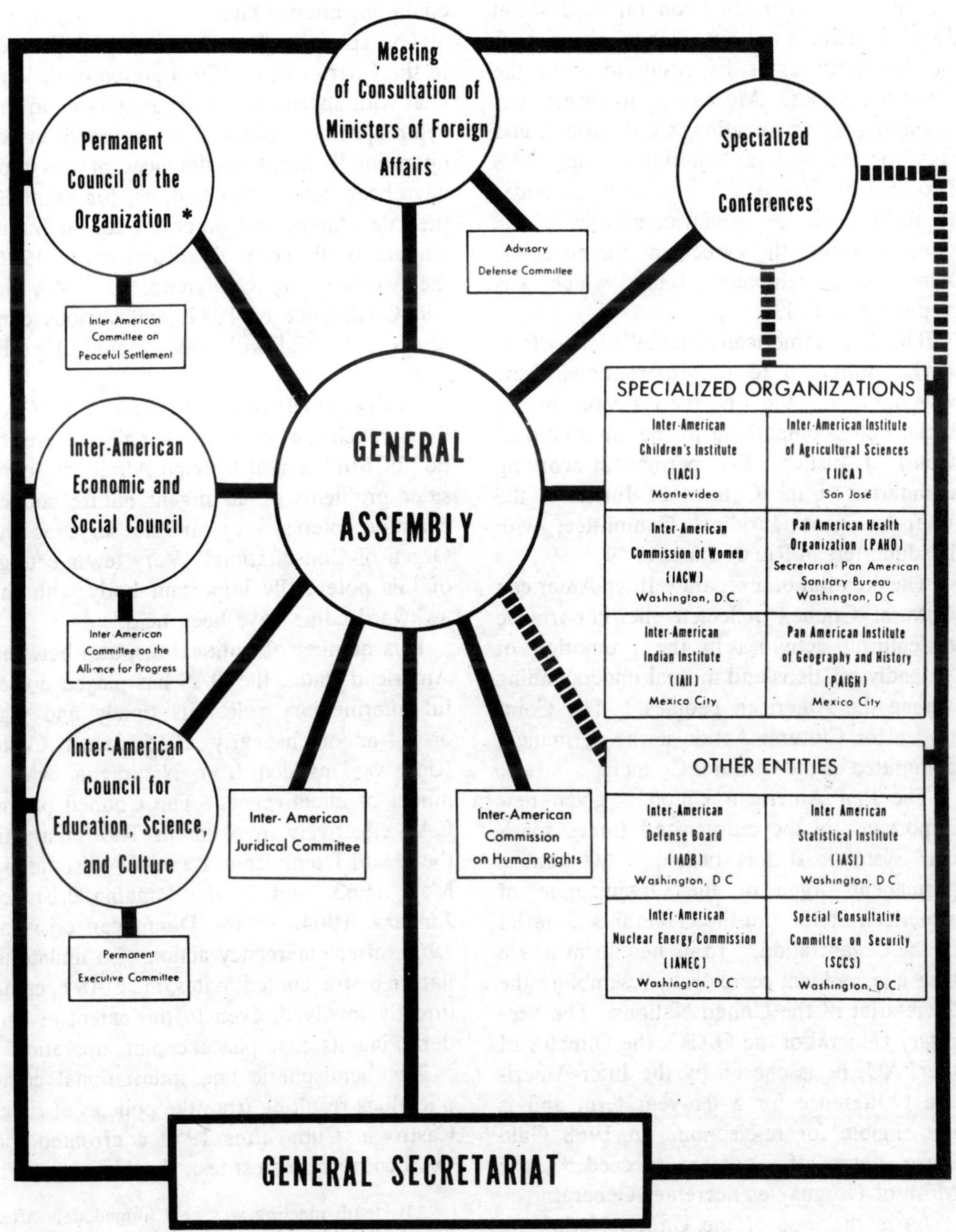

Pan American Union

Union, and has under its direct control the following organs: (1) the Inter-American Economic and Social Council; (2) the Inter-American Council of Jurists; and (3) the Inter-American Cultural Council.

The Inter-American Economic and Social Council, then, is not one of the major organs of the OAS, as is its counterpart in the United Nations. Moreover, it meets less regularly, its organization is less formal, and its program is less ambitious. The OAS Program of Technical Cooperation is under its jurisdiction. A special committee of the council drafted the agreement for an Inter-American Development Bank, which was approved in 1959.

The Inter-American Council of Jurists is to be compared to the International Law Commission of the UN; the OAS has no judicial body comparable to the International Court of Justice. The permanent working committee of the Council of Jurists is the Inter-American Juridical Committee, with headquarters in Rio de Janeiro.

The creation of a separate Inter-American Cultural Council reflected the importance of cultural activities in the promotion of "friendly relations and mutual understanding among the American peoples." The Committee for Cultural Action is the permanent committee of the Cultural Council.

The Pan American Union is given new importance in the reorganized Inter-American System. It has become "the central permanent organ of the Organization of American States and the General Secretariat of the Organization." In its new form it is a true international secretariat, resembling the Secretariat of the United Nations. The Secretary-General of the OAS is the Director of the PAU; he is chosen by the Inter-American Conference for a ten-year term and is not eligible for re-election. In 1968 Galo Plaza Lasso of Ecuador succeeded José Mora of Uruguay as Secretary-General.

As in the case of the United Nations, a number of specialized organizations are integrated into the OAS. These include the Pan American Health Organization, the Inter-American Institute of Agricultural Sciences, the Pan American Institute of Geography and History, and the Inter-American Telecommunications Office.

The specialized conferences provided for in the Charter of the OAS are convened "to deal with special technical matters or to develop specific aspects of inter-American cooperation." Many conferences of this type have been held in the past, as, for example, the Inter-American Conference for the Maintenance of Peace at Buenos Aires in 1936, the Mexico City Conference of 1945, the Rio Conference of 1947, and various conferences to deal with more technical problems.

At the request of any member of the OAS the Council may call a Meeting of Consultation of Ministers of Foreign Affairs "to consider problems of an urgent nature and of common interest . . . and to serve as the Organ of Consultation." Very few meetings of this potentially important body with the awkward name have been held.[12]

In a number of political disputes between American states, the OAS has played a useful intermediary role. Its timely and vigorous action in early 1955, when Costa Rica was invaded from Nicaragua, was a model of effectiveness. The Council of the OAS effectively invoked the Rio Treaty in the Haiti-Dominican Republic dispute in May, 1963, and in the Panama crisis of January, 1964. In the Dominican crisis of 1965, after emergency action of a unilateral nature by the United States, the OAS became directly involved, even to the extent of undertaking its first peacekeeping operation.

The hemispheric and international complications resulting from the policies of Fidel Castro in Cuba after 1959 confronted the OAS with its greatest test. In this instance it

[12] Its tenth meeting was held immediately after President Johnson dispatched American marines to the Dominican Republic in April, 1965.

was particularly handicapped by the general aversion in Latin America to "intervention" in any form or for any reason and by the widespread sympathy among the Latin American people for Castro and the principles of social revolution which they associated with his name. Eventually, however, every member of the OAS except Mexico severed diplomatic relations with the Castro regime. On January 31, 1962, the Foreign Ministers of the OAS, by a vote of 14 to 1, excluded Cuba "from participation in the inter-American system" because of Castro's alleged "alignment with the Communist bloc." This action was designed to exclude Cuba from OAS activities, but not to deprive her of membership in the organization.

In the Cuban missile crisis of October, 1962, the council of OAS, acting as the organ of Consultation under the Rio Treaty, adopted a resolution calling for the removal of the weapons and authorizing the establishment of a quarantine. When the Venezuelan government charged Cuba with efforts to subvert and overthrow it, the OAS Council, in December, 1963, appointed an investigating commission, and in July, 1964, after considering the commission's report, the Meeting of Consultation of Ministers of Foreign Affairs decided to impose additional diplomatic and economic sanctions on Cuba.

In November, 1965, a second Special Inter-American Conference was held in Rio de Janeiro for the purpose of reviewing the Charter of the OAS and of strengthening the Inter-American System. The conference adopted the so-called Act of Rio de Janeiro, calling for a special committee to draft a new charter, to be submitted to member governments and then to a third Special Inter-American Conference in Buenos Aires. Thus the entire Inter-American System is in the process of re-examination and overhaul.

As a result of the many agreements, especially the Charter of the OAS and the Rio Treaty, a comprehensive and coordinated pattern of regional agencies and arrangements has come into existence and is actively functioning in the Western Hemisphere.[13] A great deal of defense planning has been done, as was contemplated in the Rio Treaty, and the prompt and efficient action of the Council of the OAS in a number of instances has shown that it is capable of dealing with threatened breaches of the peace. Nevertheless, the most notable achievements of the OAS have been in the promotion of trade, public health, education, cultural exchange, and other pursuits of peace.

Central American Common Market and LAFTA. In June, 1958, representatives of five states of Central America — Costa Rica, Guatemala, El Salvador, Honduras, and Nicaragua — signed a Multilateral Treaty on Free Trade and Central American Integration. This treaty provided for the establishment of what is usually called the Central American Common Market. Two and a half years later a permanent Secretariat was established in Guatemala City. The treaty also provided for the creation of a Central American Economic Council and

[13] The OAS began to function shortly after the Bogotá Conference, although the Charter did not officially enter into effect until December 3, 1951, when Colombia became the fourteenth state to ratify. Twenty-one Latin American states and the United States participate in the work of the OAS. Canada is not a member, but may join if she chooses; in fact, the substitution of "States" for "Republics" in the name was made to permit her inclusion.

Perhaps it should be added that other ventures in regionalism have been projected in the Western Hemisphere. None of these aimed at general membership and none has ever had much prospect of success. The best known was Bolívar's scheme for a confederation to preserve freedom, harmonize the laws, and maintain peace. The most persistent effort has been made in Central America; indeed, the five "states" constituted a single federal republic from 1823 to 1839. Federative proposals were advanced in 1845, 1847, 1849, 1862, 1876, 1885, 1886, 1895, 1907, and 1921. An Organization of Central American States was set up in 1951, with headquarters in San Salvador. Dictator Perón of Argentina sought to embrace his neighbors in an economic union, but with varying degrees of coolness they repelled his overtures.

a Central American Bank for Economic Integration, which began functioning on May 8, 1961, at Tegucigalpa, Honduras. In March, 1964, an agreement to establish a Central American Monetary Union entered into effect. By that time nearly all of the internal duties in the Common Market area had been eliminated. The eventual goal is to establish a complete customs union and a common external tariff.

An important step toward the creation of a free trade area in most, or all, of Latin America was taken in June, 1961, with the establishment of a Latin American Free Trade Association (LAFTA), as a result of an agreement among Argentina, Brazil, Chile, Colombia, Ecuador, Mexico, Paraguay, Peru, and Uruguay. The main organs of LAFTA are a Permanent Executive Committee, a conference which meets annually and sometimes more frequently, and a secretariat. The Executive Committee is empowered to set up consultative commissions and to call on the UN's Economic Commission for Latin America and the Inter-American Economic and Social Council of the OAS for technical help. LAFTA has already proved to be an important organization for economic cooperation in Latin America. It is hoped that through its efforts a free trade area will be achieved in a period of not more than twelve years.

Caribbean Commission and Caribbean Organization. The Caribbean Commission, an outgrowth of the Anglo-American Caribbean Commission created in 1942, came into existence in 1948. Its members were France, the Netherlands, the United Kingdom, and the United States. Its central purpose was to promote the social and economic development of the Caribbean territories of the member states. Composed of sixteen representatives, four from each member state, the commission met twice a year and sponsored a series of conferences and educational, informational, technical assistance, and social programs. It had two auxiliary bodies, the West Indian Conference and the Caribbean Research Council.

In 1961 the Caribbean Commission was replaced by the Caribbean Organization, composed of the non-self-governing territories and possessions of the four members of the former Commission, namely the Netherlands Antilles, Surinam, British Guiana, the West Indies, the Virgin Islands, and Puerto Rico. France is also a member, but only because French Guiana, Guadeloupe, and Martinique are officially departments of France. When the West Indies became the independent states of Jamaica, and Trinidad and Tobago, and when British Guiana became the independent state of Guyana, they ceased to be members. The headquarters of the Caribbean Organization are in Puerto Rico. Its governing body is the Caribbean Council, composed of one delegate from each member. This body meets annually.

Regional Arrangements in Western Europe

Even the most casual view of the existing regional organizations among the states of Western Europe reveals a complex and confusing pattern. There are at least seven economic coordinating bodies which are wholly or substantially concerned with Western Europe. In addition to the major coordinating groups there are many other important organizations which are regional in character, such as the inter-Scandinavian economic bodies, and Franco-Italian and French-British economic groups. On the military side, the organs, agencies, and committees created in implementation of the Dunkirk Treaty, the Brussels Treaty, the North Atlantic Pact, and the Western European Union, to mention only the major defense arrangements, already overlap so seriously as to create many new problems in coordination of resources and effort.

Without making an arbitrary classification, we shall here first discuss the regional arrangements of a primarily economic character, then those whose functions are largely political or military. As we examined the background, evolution, and potentialities of these various arrangements in Chapter 15, our attention will now be given mostly to structure and inter-agency relationships.

The Benelux Union. "Benelux" is a term derived from the names of the three countries — Belgium, the Netherlands, and Luxembourg — which have combined to form a single customs union and now operate as a unit on many international issues. Benelux represented the first official action of West European countries toward integration, and it has pointed the way to more extensive moves in the same direction. The customs union has been created, but the economic union which was to follow is still in the planning stage.

The permanent Organization provided for by the Benelux Customs Union Convention of 1944, as supplemented by later decisions, consists of (1) the Conference of Cabinet Ministers; (2) the Council for Economic Union; (3) the Administrative Council on Customs Duties; (4) the Commercial Agreements Council; and (5) the General Secretariat, which has headquarters in Brussels. In May, 1955, the Conference of Cabinet Ministers approved a draft agreement for the establishment of an Inter-Parliamentary Benelux Council.

The organs and committees of the Benelux customs union have been operating successfully for several years. While the union is primarily an arrangement for economic cooperation among its members, political and cultural collaboration has led the representatives of the Benelux countries to take a common stand at many international conferences.

Organization for European Economic Cooperation. In many respects the Organization for European Economic Cooperation was the most elaborate regional arrangement in Western Europe. It was created by the Convention for European Economic Cooperation, signed in Paris on April 16, 1948 — less than two weeks after the United States Congress had passed the Foreign Assistance Act of 1948, which established the Economic Cooperation Administration. Representatives of sixteen nations, plus the Anglo-American and French zones of Germany and the Free Territory of Trieste, drafted the convention. West Germany and Spain later became regular members. Canada and the United States were associate members, and Yugoslavia was given the status of observer.

The functions of OEEC were "to promote consultation between the countries concerned, to consider measures and create the machinery necessary for European economic cooperation, especially in matters of trade, international payments and movements of labour."[14] The Organization was the main coordinating agency of the countries receiving Marshall Plan aid, and it proved to be so useful that it continued to exist for nearly a decade after the Marshall Plan officially came to an end in December, 1951. It also cooperated with many organs and agencies of other European organizations and of the United Nations.

OEEC headquarters in Paris directed an intricate organization. Its central organ, the Council, was composed of representatives of all member states, normally cabinet ministers or their deputies. Responsible to the Council was a Board of Management, which supervised the activities of such important operating units as the European Payments Union, the European Monetary Agreement, and the European Productivity Agency. An Executive Committee consisting of the representatives of seven member countries, elected an-

[14] Resolution 1 on the Functions of the Organization for European Cooperation. The text of this resolution is given in *Documents Relating to the North Atlantic Treaty*, Senate Document No. 48, 81st Cong., 1st Sess., April 12, 1949, pp. 76–82.

nually, assisted the Council. The secretariat was a true international civil service of some 600 members, headed by a secretary-general. The Organization also had a Customs Union Study Group and many technical and special committees.

Organization for Economic Cooperation and Development. Late in 1961 OEEC was replaced by the Organization for Economic Cooperation and Development, with the same members as OEEC, plus Canada and the United States as regular members. Whereas OEEC was "an organization predominantly oriented to European recovery and other intra-European problems," OECD was described as "a new outward looking organization," with three main functions: "(1) to achieve the highest sustainable economic growth and employment and a rising standard of living in member countries; (2) to contribute to sound economic expansion in non-member countries in the process of economic development as well as in member nations; (3) to work for an expansion of world trade."[15] OECD was envisioned as an agency with a double purpose. First, it would work for close economic cooperation among the states of Western Europe and between these states and Canada and the United States. Second, it would promote cooperative economic assistance by the nations of the Atlantic Community to the underdeveloped countries of the non-Western world. The advantages and disadvantages of this more integrated approach were equally obvious to all the nations concerned.

All the member states are represented on the OECD Council by permanent delegations. The Organization has a large secretariat headed by a secretary-general and two major committees, one concerned with development assistance to underdeveloped areas, the other with the reduction of barriers to trade and the flow of capital among member states and between these states and nonmember countries.

The European Communities. In international relations as in domestic affairs the term "community" has many meanings. In Western Europe, however, it has come to refer to a promising new approach to the obvious need for closer cooperation and association — an approach which seems to combine federal and functional, supranational and national features in a manner which is unique. Three communities of this type — which may be regarded as parts of the European Community that is in the process of creation — are already in existence: the European Coal and Steel Community, the European Economic Community, and the European Atomic Energy Community. A proposed European Defense Community barely missed becoming a reality in 1954.[16] The statute of a European Political Community has been drafted, and is presumably before the governments of the states which are members of the existing communities; but there seems to be little likelihood that it will be approved in the near future since it would have greater implications for the states involved.

Whatever the nature of the communities which are created, the ultimate purpose of all of them is to contribute to "the political construction of Europe," to use the language of a report on the activities of the European Economic Community in 1959. There is no general agreement on the precise form which "the political construction of Europe" should take. Some, like the proponents of the European Movement, favor a genuine federal union of Europe, or at least of Western Europe, whereas others, including General de Gaulle, think in terms of a loose confederation.

A beginning has already been made in associating the organs of the three existing communities more closely. They share a

[15] "Focus on Regional Organizations," *Intercom*, II (December, 1960), 16.

[16] See below, pp. 688–689.

Common Assembly and High Court and certain other organizations, and plans for a common executive authority are well advanced.

The initiative for the various steps toward the creation of the European Community has come from six nations — Belgium, France, Italy, Luxembourg, the Netherlands, and West Germany — which are members of all three of the functioning communities. These nations are often referred to as the "Inner Six," or as "Little Europe." Since other European states, for various reasons, have not been willing to embrace the community approach, serious differences have developed between them and the "Inner Six." Thus, while the evolution of the European Community, which is still more dream than reality, is an encouraging phenomenon on the European scene, there is concern lest the growing bonds among the nations of the "Inner Six" impede their closer association with other nations of Europe and the Atlantic Community.

1. European Coal and Steel Community. The draft treaty for a "European Coal and Steel Community," signed on April 18, 1951, provided for a federal type of organization, with four main organs: (1) a High Authority, advised by a Consultative Committee; (2) a Common Assembly; (3) a Council of Ministers; and (4) a Court of Justice.[17] The High Authority, set up in August, 1952, is a kind of board of directors of nine members, who are expected to act "in complete independence in the general interest of the community" and neither report to nor accept "instructions" from any government or organization. They may issue binding decisions and recommendations as well as advisory opinions. Among the extensive powers conferred on the High Authority are the right to tax private coal and steel producers, to levy fines for violations of its orders, and to borrow and lend. Member states pledge to use their police powers, if necessary, to enforce the directives of the High Authority. A Consultative Committee of from 30 to 51 representatives of producers, workers, and consumers, appointed by the Council of Ministers for two-year terms, advises the Authority.

An organ not originally contemplated by the initiators of the Schuman Plan, which led to the Coal and Steel Community, is the Council of Ministers. Composed of one minister from each of the six member nations, the Council serves as a direct link between the High Authority and the member states. "In many cases when an important decision is at stake, the High Authority may act only after having obtained the concurrence of the Council."[18] Another check upon the High Authority is the Common Assembly which meets once a year to consider the Authority's report and to question its members. By a two-thirds vote the Assembly may compel the members of the Authority to resign. This body is composed of 142 members, 34 from the Benelux countries and 36 each from France, Italy, and West Germany, chosen by the national parliaments. The Court of Justice has jurisdiction over appeals from decisions or recommendations of the High Authority by the Council of Ministers, a member state, or private coal or steel enterprises or associations. It also has the power to annul acts of the Assembly and of the Council of Ministers.

One may raise the question whether the ECSC has in fact retained its original character. The activities of the High Authority are severely limited by the controls which the Common Assembly, the Council of Ministers, the Court of Justice, and even in some respects the Consultative Committee exer-

[17] The texts of the draft treaty and accompanying documents were printed in *The Schuman Plan Constituting a European Coal and Steel Community*, Dept. of State Pub. 4173, European and British Commonwealth Series 22 (April, 1951).

[18] John Goormaghtigh, "European Coal and Steel Community," *International Conciliation*, No. 503 (May, 1955), p. 367.

cise over it; and at least the first two of these supervisory bodies seem to be subject to the governments of the member states to such a degree that the supranational character of the new European Coal and Steel Community may have been modified. Nevertheless, the ECSC represents a deliberate attempt to delegate sovereign powers for a carefully prescribed purpose.

2. European Economic Community. The European Economic Community, often called the Common Market, began its operations on January 1, 1958. A year later the first reductions in tariffs and import quotas went into effect. At the end of a transition period of 12 to 15 years, it is anticipated, the Common Market will become a reality. Even before that time a single external tariff will apply to imports from other countries, except Greece, Turkey, 18 African states, and 13 overseas territories which have a special relationship with the EEC.

The main organs of the EEC — a Council, a Commission, an Assembly, and a Court — are very similar to those of the ECSC. The Council is composed of one representative from each member state. "In regard to questions of major importance or those that pose political problems, . . . the authority of the Council is supreme."[19] The Commission, consisting of nine nationals from the member states, is the chief executive body. Like the High Authority of the ECSC, it is supposed to be an agency of the community, and independent of the member governments, but it has considerably less real authority than its prototype in the ECSC. As has been noted, the same Common Assembly and Court serve for all three of the existing European communities, with slightly less power and scope of operations for the two newer communities.

Also associated with the EEC are an Economic and Social Committee of 101 representatives chosen by the Council, a number of specialized committees, a European Investment Bank, a European Social Fund, and Development Fund for the Overseas Countries and Territories.

3. European Atomic Energy Community. Established simultaneously with EEC, Euratom is helping to develop nuclear energy as a source of power for European industries and homes. "Euratom maintains a common market in nuclear materials, conducts research programs, promotes the diffusion of technical knowledge and is setting up its own nuclear research center and university-level training center."[20] The main organs of Euratom are a Council of one representative of each member state, a Commission of five members, and the Common Assembly and Court of Justice. It also has an Atomic Agency, a Joint Nuclear Research Center, and an important Scientific and Technical Committee.

European Free Trade Association. The EFTA represents a second approach to economic cooperation in Western Europe. In November, 1959, representatives of seven European states — Austria, Denmark, Norway, Portugal, Sweden, Switzerland, and the United Kingdom — that were unable to accept the degree of political integration envisioned by the architects of the European communities met in Stockholm and signed a Convention for a European Free Trade Association (EFTA), which officially came into existence on May 3, 1960. EFTA is a free trade area and not a customs union. Its members — often called the "Outer Seven," in contrast to the "Inner Six" of the communities — have agreed to achieve free trade in industrial goods by abolishing tariffs and quantitative restrictions among the member states by January 1, 1970. They will not try to establish a common external tariff.

[19] Serge Hurtig, "The European Common Market," *International Conciliation,* No. 517 (March, 1958), p. 333.

[20] "Focus on Regional Organizations," p. 19.

The governing body of EFTA is the Council, composed of ministers from the seven member countries, whose decisions must be unanimous in most cases. A small secretariat, headed by a secretary-general, is located in Geneva. Several committees, dealing with customs, trade, and budgetary matters, have been set up by the Council.

Obviously the existence of two trading associations in Western Europe, so similar in some respects and so different in others, has created much confusion and many complications. Some critics of EFTA have charged that this organization was created as a rival to EEC. The members of EFTA strongly deny that they are opposed in any way to EEC. Indeed, they insist that, to use the words of F. T. Wahlen, Vice President of the Swiss federal government and Chairman of the EFTA Council in 1960, they wish to avoid "a permanent or even prolonged cleavage between the two groups," and that their "ultimate aim is the creation of a single market which would embrace all the members of the O.E.E.C."[21] By cooperation with the members of the "Inner Six" and other states in OECD, in GATT, and in other associations for international economic cooperation, they believe that they can avoid serious intra-organizational differences in the immediate future and achieve agreement on long-range common objectives. If and when Britain is admitted to EEC, other members of EFTA will also join, and EFTA will probably cease to exist.

The Brussels Pact and Western European Union. The Brussels Pact, signed in March, 1949, by the Benelux states, Britain, and France, was the first concrete expression of "Western Union," a term which has been used to label any and all proposals and steps looking toward the closer economic, military, and political integration of the countries of Western Europe. The pact was primarily a military arrangement.[22] It also provided for economic, financial, social, and cultural cooperation among the member states and for the coordination of all activities, including joint defense planning and operations, by a political agency — the Consultative Council. The Council is composed of the foreign ministers of the five participating states. In its early meetings the Council set up a Permanent Commission as a coordinating and consultative organ.

By 1954 the Brussels Treaty Organization's economic functions had been largely assumed by OEEC, and its military functions had been for the most part yielded to NATO. Shortly afterward, when the Consultative Assembly of the Council of Europe recommended that the social and cultural functions be transferred to the Council, it seemed that the Brussels Treaty Organization had served its purpose and would soon pass into history. Instead, before the end of the year it had been given a new lease on life.

When the foreign ministers of nine nations met in London in late September and early October, 1954, in an attempt to devise some alternative for the European Defense Community, which had just been killed by the French National Assembly, they decided to deal with the problem of German rearmament and Germany's place in Western Europe through NATO and an enlarged and strengthened Brussels Treaty Organization. They agreed that West Germany and Italy should be invited to accede to the Brussels Treaty. The expanded organization soon came to be known as the Western European Union (WEU).

The WEU Treaty fixed ceilings for troops and armaments of the seven member states

[21] Quoted in *EFTA Bulletin,* I (October, 1960), 3.

[22] For a detailed chart of the Brussels Treaty Defense Organization, see p. 17 of *Western Cooperation for Defense,* a publication (I.D. 998) of the Reference Division of British Information Services, New York, issued in June, 1950.

which could be changed only by unanimous vote of the Council of the WEU, consisting of representatives of the member governments. An Armaments Control Agency, supervised by a Standing Armaments Committee, inspects and reports on the observance or nonobservance of the troop and armaments ceilings. Germany is forbidden to maintain certain types of armaments, including atomic weapons, unless and until the WEU Council lifts the prohibition. Under the treaty the United Kingdom is pledged to maintain a minimum force on the continent of Europe, which cannot be withdrawn or even reduced without the consent of the other member states. Special agreements determine the maximum defense contributions of each WEU member to NATO. The WEU has very close relations with NATO, and also with the Council of Europe, whose Consultative Assembly serves also as the Assembly of the WEU.

In its revised form the WEU is serving many useful purposes. Not the least of its services, perhaps, is that it provides a meeting place for the United Kingdom and the members of the European communities, the "Inner Six." There is some question, however, regarding the future of the WEU amid the multiplicity of coordinating and sometimes overlapping European agencies and regarding its proper role in relations to NATO. It is "difficult for WEU to proceed confidently in a sphere of its own reserved functions. . . . Furthermore, the presence of higher, more inclusive levels, like NATO and the Council of Europe, and of the lower levels of bilateral negotiations detracts from the exclusive control of Western European Union over its most important interests."[23]

The Council of Europe. The Council of Europe held its first session in Strasbourg, France, in August–September, 1949. Since then it has been an operating entity of limited powers but of great potential significance. At present it has seventeen regular members — the WEU countries, Austria, Cyprus, Denmark, Greece, Iceland, Ireland, Norway, Sweden, Switzerland, and Turkey — and one associate member, the Saar. Its main organs are the Committee of Ministers and the Consultative Assembly.

The Committee of Ministers, composed of the foreign ministers of the participating countries, has far greater powers than the Consultative Assembly in both substantive affairs and internal organization. The Committee meets in private before the beginning of each session of the Consultative Assembly and "at such other times as it may decide." Its recommendations are not binding until ratified by the respective governments. Important conventions on legal, cultural, social, and technical questions have been ratified. The most notable of these is the European Convention on Human Rights, the only convention of its kind that has ever entered into force anywhere in the world. A European Commission of Human Rights and a European Court of Human Rights have been established to supervise the implementation of this historic agreement.

The Consultative Assembly is the deliberative organ of the Council of Europe. It consists of "representatives of each Member appointed in such a manner as the Government shall decide," which in practice has come to mean representatives of the parliaments of the member nations, from opposition as well as from governing parties. Representation ranges from three (Iceland, Luxembourg, and the Saar) to eighteen (France, the Federal Republic of Germany, Italy, and the United Kingdom). Members of the Assembly speak for themselves rather than for their countries.

The Assembly has a Standing Committee and committees on general affairs, economic questions, and legal and administrative mat-

[23] Ernst Haas and Peter Merkl, "Parliamentarians Against Ministers: The Case of the Western European Union," *International Organization,* XIV (Winter, 1960), 59.

ters. A secretariat, headed by a secretary-general and a deputy secretary-general, with headquarters in Strasbourg, assists the Committee of Ministers and the Consultative Assembly.

The Statute of the Council of Europe expressly stated that the Consultative Assembly could discuss only those questions which were approved by the Committee of Ministers. At its first session the Assembly rebelled against the "pale agenda" prepared for it and demanded the right to discuss some of Europe's fundamental problems. It proceeded to do exactly that. Furthermore, with the approval of the Committee of Ministers, it appointed a General Affairs (Political) Committee to consider ways and means of acquiring greater independence and thereby greater power and prestige.

Although the Council of Europe embodies only a limited form of European cooperation, it has served as a stimulus to many other movements. It provides a "general framework for European cooperation in all fields except national defense," which is specifically excluded from its jurisdiction.[24] It has close relations with the European communities and with OECD, as it had with OEEC. Its "main contribution," however, "has been in the realm of thought and opinion." The proceedings of the Consultative Assembly, in particular, have called attention to different trends of thought in and between European countries, and "they have helped to clarify the ways and means of seeking European unity."[25] In December, 1964, the Council agreed to adopt a more flexible attitude toward the Communist countries of Eastern Europe, and announced that it would welcome any move by these countries to join in technical discussions.

But while the Council of Europe has performed many useful services, it has not fulfilled the hopes of its founders. Instead of becoming the effective center of movements toward political unity in Western Europe, it has been virtually superseded by movements and organizations which are located elsewhere. It remains a vague aspiration instead of a living reality.[26]

The North Atlantic Community

Experience with regional arrangements in Western Europe, from Benelux to the Council of Europe, convinced many realists that the existing arrangements were too narrow in scope, geographically as well as politically. In other words, the basic problems of Western Europe seemed to be unsolvable within the geographical area between the Atlantic Ocean and the "iron curtain." More and more it came to be realized that the destinies of Western Europe are inextricably linked with those of a larger area, now commonly termed the Atlantic Community.

The North Atlantic Pact, signed in Washington on April 4, 1949, by representatives of twelve states, gave formal recognition to this broader community. These states had long been bound together by many ties. They shared the heritage of Western civilization. In a sense the Atlantic Ocean had become a broad highway which joined the states bordering on it, rather than a barrier which separated them. Walter Lippmann, who had been mindful of the Atlantic Community since World War I, declared in 1949:

> The Atlantic Ocean has never been a military frontier between Europe and the Americas; it has always been the inland sea of a neighborhood of nations closely connected with one another by geography, history and vital necessity. . . . The concept of the Atlantic Community is not an upstart idea. . . . The Atlantic Community has in fact existed

[24] "Focus on Regional Organizations," p. 24.

[25] *Western Co-operation in Brief,* a publication of the British Information Services, issued in September, 1960, p. 4.

[26] For a sympathetic but critical evaluation of the Council of Europe, see Kenneth Lindsay, *Towards a European Parliament* (Strasbourg, 1958).

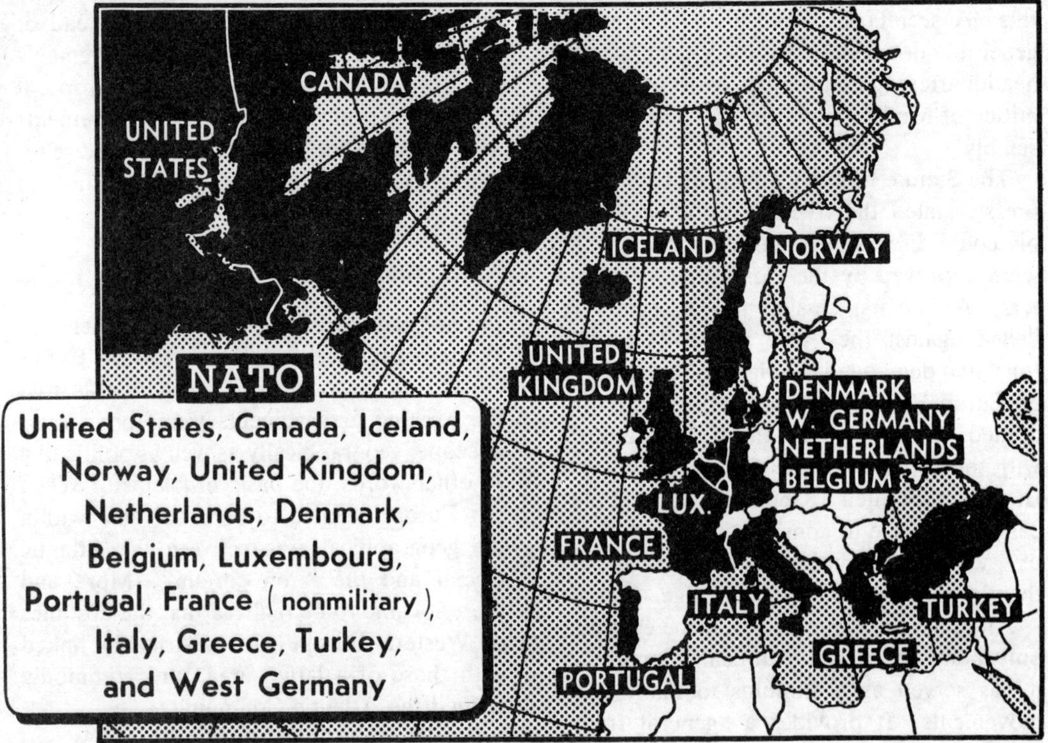

Joan W. Forbes. Adapted by permission from The Christian Science Monitor © 1967 The Christian Science Publishing Society. All rights reserved.

for more than thirty years. It has fought two great wars for its survival and its freedom. . . . April 4, 1949, is an important date in the history of the world, not because it creates new obligations but chiefly, in my view, because it marks the formal recognition of a new political entity which will play a great part in the history of the world . . . the common interest which has existed *de facto* is recognized *de jure*.[27]

North Atlantic Treaty Organization (NATO). The North Atlantic Treaty now binds together the major states of the Atlantic Community — the United States, Great Britain, France and Western Germany — and Canada, Italy, Portugal, Norway, Denmark, Iceland, the Benelux countries, Greece, and Turkey in a regional organization of great significance in world affairs.[28] The structure of NATO has undergone con-

[27] Address in Philadelphia, May 6, 1949. Lippmann himself was one of the first to emphasize this concept. In an editorial in *The New Republic* of February 17, 1917, on "The Defense of the Atlantic World," he wrote: ". . . on the two shores of the Atlantic ocean there has grown up a profound web of interest which joins together the western world. Britain, France, Italy, even Spain, Belgium, Holland, the Scandinavian nations, and Pan-America are in the main one community in their deepest needs and their deepest purposes. They have a common interest in the ocean which unites them. They are today more inextricably bound together than most even as yet realize." Thirty-two years later Lippmann listed as members of the Atlantic Community, in addition to the countries which he mentioned in his editorial of 1917 (which, be it noted, included *all* of the Latin American states), Canada, Ireland, Iceland, Portugal, and even Australia and New Zealand. See also Lippmann, *U.S. Foreign Policy: Shield of the Republic* (Boston: Little, Brown and Company, 1943), Chapter VII, "The Atlantic Community."

[28] Greece and Turkey were invited to join NATO in September, 1951. Western Germany became a member in May, 1955.

stant change and expansion to meet new international developments.

1. *NATO Civil Organization.* The North Atlantic Treaty provides for a directing Council, to be "so organized as to be able to meet promptly at any time." Originally the Council was composed of the foreign ministers of the member states, or their representatives; in 1951 the participating states agreed to add the defense, economic, and finance ministers to the Council whenever problems of direct interest to them were considered. Even earlier, in May, 1950, the foreign ministers had decided to create a permanent body of deputies. The deputies immediately undertook the task of planning for the military defense of Western Europe, an undertaking soon made more urgent than ever by the attack on South Korea, with its clear warning of the possibility of aggression elsewhere. As the activities of NATO expanded, the need for an agency with greater authority than the Council of Deputies became apparent. Accordingly, at its Lisbon meeting in February, 1952, the North Atlantic Council decided to establish a Permanent Council which would sit continuously at headquarters in Paris, and which would replace the Council of Deputies and certain other agencies which had been functioning in a semi-independent manner. The Permanent Council, composed of representatives of all the member states, is now "the focal point of NATO. Everything else depends on it and is linked to it."[29]

The NATO Council meets at the ministerial level two or three times a year, and once or twice a week at the level of permanent representatives. In December, 1957, the Council met for the first time at the level of heads of government. At all meetings the secretary-general of NATO acts as chairman. The presidency of the Council rotates annually in accordance with the alphabetical list of NATO members. All decisions of the Council must be taken unanimously — one of many reminders that NATO is not a supranational organization.

Many think of NATO as exclusively a military organization, yet in fact Article II of the North Atlantic Treaty calls for cooperation among member states on a wide front. Although the full potentialities of this article have not been realized, the Council has set up committees to direct activities in many fields — information and cultural relations, armaments, infrastructure, emergency planning, food and agriculture, industrial raw materials, and manpower planning. There are also committees of political and economic advisers, and planning boards for ocean shipping and for European inland surface transport.

NATO's secretariat has major divisions of political affairs, economics and finance, and production and logistics, as well as an office of the scientific adviser. Most of the secretariat staff work in NATO's new permanent headquarters in Brussels.

2. *NATO Military Organization.* Supervising the work of the NATO military organization, under the Permanent Council, is the Military Committee, assisted by a Military Representative Committee and a Standing Group, consisting of the Chiefs of Staff, or their representatives, of Britain, France, and the United States, who together form "the key military unit of the whole North Atlantic edifice." The Standing Group must integrate the plans of the component areas and develop an overall strategic concept and plan. As its name suggests, it meets continuously; its headquarters are in Washington.

The two major commands under NATO cover the European area (SHAPE) and the Atlantic Ocean area (SACLANT). There

[29] Michael L. Hoffman, dispatch from Geneva, *New York Times,* March 9, 1952. "A Series of jolts propelled NATO from its early madness of irresponsible committees into an organization which now, however primitive, points to the way ahead." Theodore H. White, *Fire in the Ashes: Europe in Mid-Century* (New York: William Sloane Associates, 1953), p. 308.

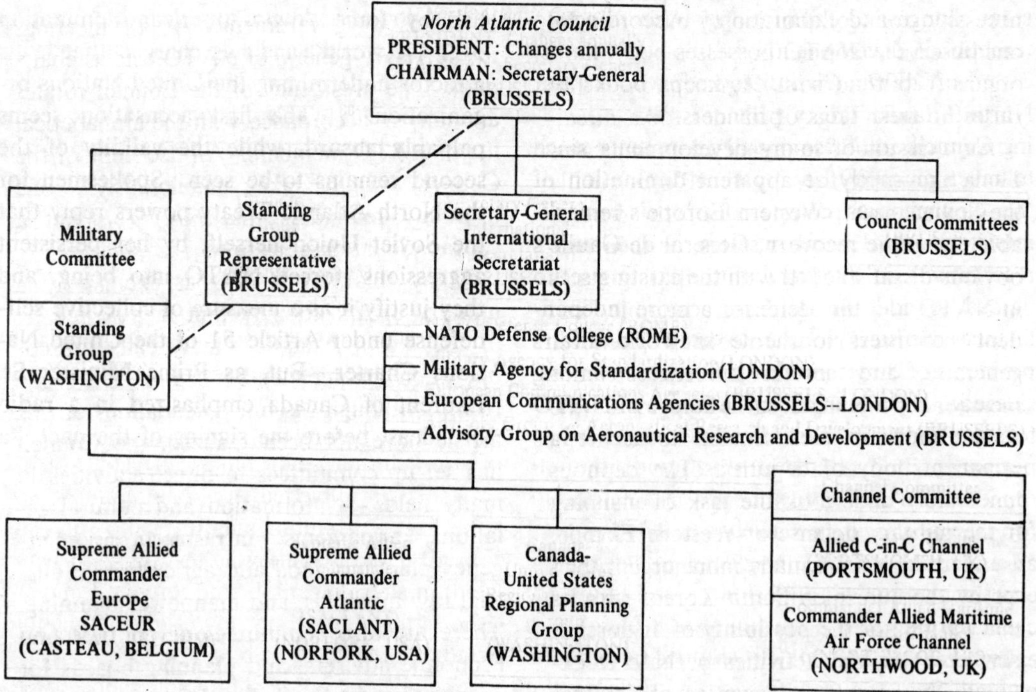

is also a regional planning group for Canada and the United States, with headquarters in Washington, and a Channel and Southern North Sea Command at Portsmouth, England, with a Channel Committee (CHANCOM) in London. The headquarters of SACLANT are in Norfolk, Virginia.

Of crucial importance in the planning of NATO's military experts is the defense of Western Europe. This is the direct responsibility of Supreme Headquarters Allied Powers in Europe (SHAPE), which directs the NATO forces in Europe under the command of the Supreme Allied Commander in Europe (SACEUR). One might say that the efforts of the nations of the free world to defend themselves by combined action are centered in SHAPE's headquarters at Casteau, in Belgium. In the SHAPE area there are four subordinate commands: Northern Europe (Kolsaas, Norway), Central Europe (Brunssum, the Netherlands), Southern Europe (Naples), and Mediterranean (Malta).

The ramifications of NATO are no more than suggested by a discussion of its major organs. To do full justice to the subject one should examine the organization and functions of the many subordinate agencies and commands and study the activities of the hundreds of individuals, military and civilian, drawn from all the member states, who are, after all, the moving force of NATO.[30]

NATO and the Atlantic Community. With the progress of plans for the coordination of the resources of the North Atlantic area for defense and other purposes, the outlines of a true regional arrangement in the Atlantic Community have taken form. Whether they can be filled in, especially in view of French noncooperation, remains to be seen. As the states which participate in NATO are discovering, it is difficult to reconcile conflicting interests and to establish common policies even when there is agreement on objectives and an awareness of the

[30] For the real nature and meaning of NATO, see White, Chapter XIII, "The Basin of Freedom," especially pp. 285–286, 316–317.

necessity for collaboration. According to one observer, "NATO possesses body, limbs, organs — but no soul. It keeps books but raises no fresh flags or banners."[31]

As a result of many developments since 1949, including the apparent diminution of the Soviet threat, Western Europe's remarkable economic recovery, General de Gaulle's obvious dissatisfaction with the existing setup in NATO and his desire for a more independent and prestigious role in world affairs generally, and certain differences among members of the alliance, the future of NATO is very much in question. In a sense, it has served its immediate purpose, even though it has not realized its potential, as envisioned by those who hoped to see it develop into far more than a military alliance.[32] Article 13 of the North Atlantic Treaty provided that "After the Treaty has been in force for twenty years, any Party may cease to be a party one year after its notice of denunciation has been given. . . ." In 1969 NATO will be twenty years old, and there are some apprehensions that General de Gaulle may invoke this article of the treaty and withdraw France from the organization completely. He has denied that this is his intention, but almost certainly if he is still in power in France, he will press his demands for a breakup of the integrated command structure of NATO and for major changes in the political structure. He has already (in 1966) insisted on the withdrawal of all foreign NATO forces and bases from French territory and for the removal of SHAPE, the Central European Command, and the NATO Defense College from France. NATO is thus faced with the prospect of carrying on without France, one of its key members, or of dismantling most of its integrated command structure.

The Soviet Union has bitterly denounced NATO as an aggressive coalition "to establish by force Anglo-American domination over the world" and has charged that it "is a factor undermining the United Nations organization."[33] The first accusation seems palpably absurd, while the validity of the second remains to be seen. Spokesmen for the North Atlantic Treaty powers reply that the Soviet Union herself, by her persistent aggressions, forced NATO into being, and they justify it as a measure of collective self-defense under Article 51 of the United Nations Charter. But, as Prime Minister St. Laurent of Canada emphasized in a radio broadcast before the signing of the pact, "a Security Treaty will not be fully effective if it is nothing more than a military alliance." NATO was clearly intended to be more than an anti-Soviet alliance; its founders were motivated by the desire to establish more satisfactory machinery for collaboration among the states of the Atlantic Community. In its larger context, to repeat Walter Lippmann's trenchant observation, NATO's chief significance is that "it marks the formal recognition of a new political entity" in a community of nations which

[31] *Ibid.*, p. 315.

[32] See Robert Pfaltzgraff, "NATO in World Politics," *Orbis*, IX (Summer, 1965).

[33] Official Text of U.S.S.R. Statement on North Atlantic Pact," *USSR Information Bulletin*, IX (February 11, 1949), 86, 87.

Yardley in The Sun (Baltimore, Md.)

"Unintentional Cupid"

"has in fact existed for more than thirty years." It is the most ambitious experiment in international regionalism yet launched.

Regional Arrangements in Eastern Europe

Tendencies toward regionalism have also appeared in Eastern and Southeastern Europe. The Little Entente of the 1920's and 1930's, though primarily a military defense agreement, led to organized cooperation in many fields. The Pan-Slav idea, frequently distorted and invariably vague, was often a stimulus to closer regional ties. Proposals for a Danubian federation, or for a Balkan federation, were advanced many times in the nineteenth century, and they have also been voiced in recent years. Even native Balkan Communist leaders, notably Dimitrov in Bulgaria and Tito in Yugoslavia, have openly advocated some kind of Balkan federation.

On February 28, 1953, representatives of Greece, Turkey, and Yugoslavia, meeting in Ankara, signed a treaty of friendship and cooperation, and on August 9, 1954, representatives of the same three countries, meeting at Bled, Yugoslavia, signed a defense treaty, modeled after the North Atlantic Treaty, and providing for a permanent council and a secretariat. The permanent secretariat was brought into being on November 7, 1954, by a supplement to the Treaty of Ankara. This organization has not overcome historic animosities and continuing differences among its three members, but it is potentially a significant association of a Communist state and two NATO members.

Cominform and Comecon. The East European bloc, consisting of the U.S.S.R., Poland, East Germany, Czechoslovakia, Hungary, Rumania, Bulgaria, and Albania, bound together by a network of nearly twenty bilateral treaties of mutual assistance,[34] concluded between 1943 and 1949, cannot be considered a true regional arrangement as we use the term here. It was clearly not a voluntary association; perhaps it should not be regarded as an association of states at all — certainly not one of free states. Moreover, the countries associated in it never even claimed to belong to a regional arrangement as recognized by the United Nations Charter.[35] Since 1949 the relations of the states of Eastern Europe with the Soviet Union and with each other have become more fluid and more diverse.

Still less could the Cominform — the Communist Information Bureau — be classified as a regional arrangement. This organization came into existence in September, 1947, under the sponsorship of the Soviet Union, for the announced purpose of defeating the Marshall Plan. It was basically a coordinating body for the Communist parties of Eastern Europe and therefore for the governments of the Soviet satellite states. It played a major role in the campaign against Tito after June, 1948, but after 1955, when the new leaders of the Soviet Union began to woo Tito instead of fulminate against him, it lost its *raison d'être*. It was dissolved in 1956. The widely heralded "Molotov Plan," announced as a substitute for the Marshall Plan in East Europe and directed by a Council for Mutual Economic Assistance, took form in January, 1949. The original members were Bulgaria, Czechoslovakia, Hungary, Poland, Rumania, and the Soviet Union. Albania joined in February, 1949, and East Germany in September of the fol-

[34] For a convenient listing of these treaties of mutual assistance and cooperation, from the Soviet-Czechoslovak Treaty of December 12, 1943, to the Polish-Rumanian Treaty of January 26, 1949, and the texts of some of them, see *Documents Relating to the North Atlantic Treaty,* Senate Document No. 48, 81st Cong., 1st Sess. (Washington, D.C.: Government Printing Office, 1949), pp. 102–115. For a detailed analysis of these East European treaties, see W. W. Kulski, "The Soviet System of Collective Security Compared with the Western System," *The American Journal of International Law,* XLIV (July, 1950), 453–476.

[35] Leon Govre, "The Eastern European Bloc and the United Nations Charter," *Columbia Journal of International Affairs,* III (Spring, 1949), 38–39, 46. See also Van Kleffens, p. 672, n. 10.

lowing year. At one time or another Yugoslavia, Communist China, North Korea, Mongolia, North Vietnam, and Cuba have participated as observers at sessions of the COMECON Council. Mongolia became a full member in 1962. By that time the other Asian countries and Albania had ceased to attend.

COMECON was supposed to be an economic organization linking the Soviet Union and the Communist states of Eastern Europe "for the purpose of providing mutual assistance, coordinating foreign trade, furnishing information about their economies, and exchanging views on common experiences. . . . In the first years of its existence, COMECON appears to have been simply another organization in the series of 'transmission belts' linking the Soviet Union with other Communist countries in East Central Europe. It appears to have supplemented the Communist Information Bureau . . . as another 'formal' link between Moscow and it European allies. . . . Presumably the organization was designed as an instrument of Soviet control over the East Central European economies in response to the Marshall Plan, the establishment of the Organization for European Economic Cooperation, and the division of Europe into two camps."[36] For some years the Soviet Union showed little interest in it. Its Council did not meet at all between November, 1950 and March, 1954. The secretariat, located in Moscow, had several hundred employees, but it did not become really active until 1957. At about this time, obviously reflecting changes in the personnel and policies of the Soviet Union and some of the East European states, COMECON was given a new lease on life, and its institutional structure and operations expanded rapidly in the following years. All of its more than twenty standing commissions were established in 1956 and subsequently. Even the charter of the organization was not made public until 1960, and its Executive Committee, replacing the Conference of Representatives of Member Countries, was not formed until June, 1962. It is still rather restricted and ineffective in its operations. Efforts to coordinate long-term exchanges of goods and economic plans of its members have run into many technical snags; but the greatest limitation arises from recent evidence that some of the East European states, notably Rumania, are trying to follow more independent trade policies with each other, with the Soviet Union and the rest of the Communist world, and with the countries of Western Europe.[37]

The Warsaw Treaty Organization. The Soviet response to the ratification of the Paris agreements of October, 1954, which provided the framework for associating a re-armed West Germany with the new Western European Union and with NATO, was to take the initiative in the establishment of a kind of East European rival to NATO. On May 11–14, 1955, leading Soviet and satellite figures, with an observer from Communist China, met in Warsaw for a "Conference of European Countries on Safeguarding Peace and Security in Europe." On May 14 they agreed to establish a unified command of their armed forces and signed a Treaty of Friendship, Cooperation and Mutual Assistance. According to its text, the treaty was "open to other states, irrespective of their social or Government regime," and would lapse "from the day . . . a collective security treaty comes into force." Article 4 contained the usual "an attack on one shall be regarded as an attack on all" provision, and Article 5 provided for a unified command. The main organ of the Warsaw Treaty Organization is the Consultative Political Commission, which may set up "any auxiliary

[36] Andrzej Korbonski, "COMECON," *International Conciliation*, No. 549 (September, 1964), pp. 4–5. See also Michael Gamarnikow, "COMECON Today," *East Europe*, March, 1964, pp. 3–9.

[37] See Harry Schwartz, "Comecon Tries Again," *New York Times*, January 21, 1966.

organs it considers necessary." Headquarters of the unified command, under a Russian general, are in Moscow, where each member state maintains permanent representatives on its general staff.

The signatories to the Warsaw Pact were the Soviet Union, Albania, Bulgaria, Czechoslovakia, East Germany, Hungary, Poland, and Rumania. Albania dropped out in 1961. The pact seemed to be effective as long as the Soviet Union dominated the East European area "through military might and political puppetry." It "provided the institutional framework for the stationing of Soviet troops" in East Europe.[38] It served Soviet purposes quite admirably for more than a decade.

> But now, as in NATO, the nature and rationale of the pact are challenged. Ceausescu's Rumania like de Gaulle's France is questioning the desirability of anything resembling military integration when a land war in Europe seems less and less likely and bilateral relations between countries of East and West seem to offer more beneficial possibilities. . . . Now the Soviets propose strengthening the pact to meet what they call a new NATO threat — the danger of West German "access" to nuclear weapons. Rumania for one agrees with the Kremlin on the need for revision, and proposes that the way to do it is to evolve as NATO is evolving, by increasing the responsibility of the individual members.
>
> This is the current crisis within the Warsaw pact: not a threat of breakup, but pressure for creation of a true alliance out of what was designed to be an institution of veiled Soviet control.[39]

The parallelisms between the Warsaw Treaty Organization and NATO are obvious, but in view of the relationship between the Soviet Union and the states of Eastern Europe it must be concluded that the WTO falls more appropriately into the discussion of the Soviet bloc and the satellite system in the following chapter.

Regionalism and Regional Arrangements in the Middle East

Two well-developed regional arrangements, very different in membership and in orientation, exist in the Middle East today. They are the Arab League and the Central Treaty Organization (CENTO). A third, the Regional Cooperation for Development (RCD), is limited in its operations but may become increasingly important.

The Arab League. The League of Arab States, usually referred to as the Arab League, may properly be regarded as the first and perhaps still the most comprehensive non-Western regional arrangement. All of the Arab states — Algeria, Iraq, Jordan, Kuwait, Lebanon, Libya, Morocco, Saudi Arabia, the Sudan, Syria, Tunisia, the United Arab Republic, and Yemen — are members. It was formed in 1945 with the benediction and indeed the active assistance of the British;[40] its primary objectives as stated in the Pact of the League of Arab States are "the strengthening of the relations between the member states, the co-ordination of their policies in order to achieve cooperation among them and to safeguard their independence and sovereignty."[41] The pact specifi-

[38] Peter Grose, "The Warsaw Pact Shows Its Age," *New York Times,* May 22, 1956.

[39] *Ibid.* The key demands of Rumania, as expressed quite bluntly by the Rumanian party chief, Nicolae Ceausescu, in a long speech on May 7, 1966, are "that the command of the pact be rotated among all member nations instead of being held permanently by a Soviet officer, and that the member nations be given a finger on the alliance's nuclear trigger, now held by the Russians alone." *Ibid.*

[40] See Judith Laikin, "British Influence on the Arab League," *Columbia Journal of International Affairs,* III (Spring, 1949), 102–104.

[41] The text of the Pact is given in B. V. Boutros-Ghali, "The Arab League, 1945–1955," *International Conciliation,* No. 498 (May, 1954), Appendix A. The basic documents of the League and information regarding the League's activities may be found in *The Arab World,* the official monthly magazine published by the Arab Information Center in New York.

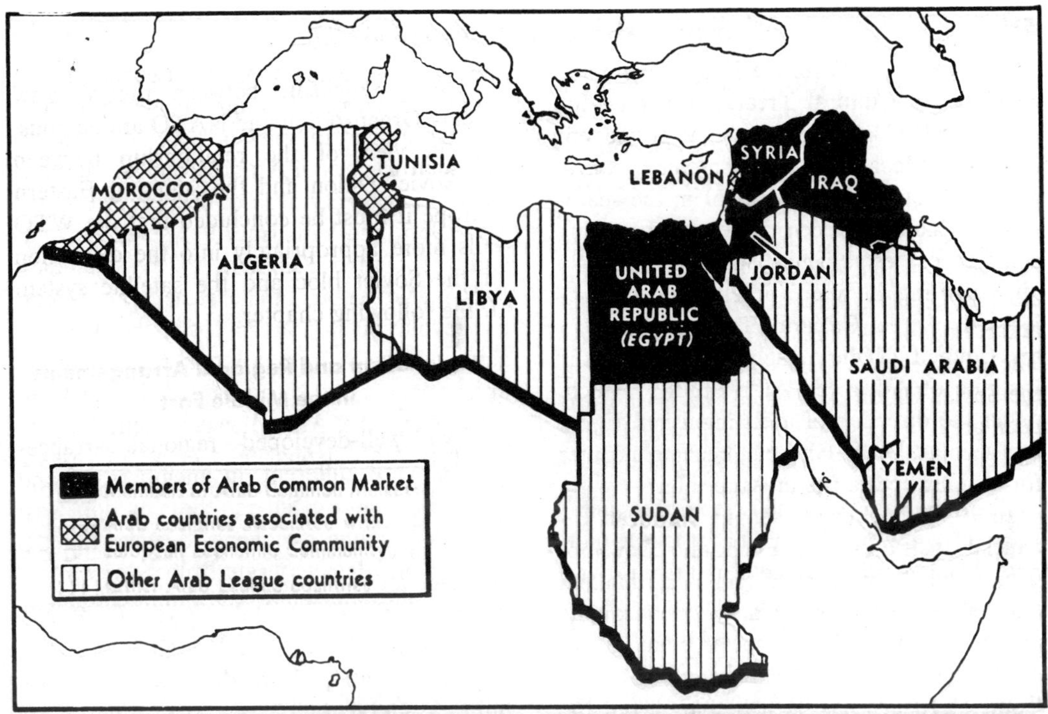

Arab Political and Economic Ties

cally referred to cooperation among the member states in economic and financial affairs, communications, cultural affairs, nationality and related matters, social affairs, and health problems.

The chief organ of the Arab League is the Council, composed of representatives of all member states. Decisions of the Council on security matters are not binding unless they are unanimous, and the League cannot enforce decisions which involve the "independence, sovereignty, or territorial integrity" of a member state. A state which in the opinion of the Council "is not fulfilling its obligations under the Pact" may be excluded from the League by the unanimous vote of all other member states.

Since its inception the headquarters of the League have been in Cairo. On March 22, 1960, the fifteenth anniversary of its formation, the League's handsome new building in Cairo was officially opened.

The League maintains a Permanent Observer at United Nations headquarters in New York, and has concluded formal agreements and informal arrangements with most of the specialized agencies of the UN. It also maintains information centers in several countries, including four in the United States.

Personnel from all members of the League compose the secretariat, although here, as in almost all other aspects of its organization and work, the League is dominated by Egyptians. Both of the secretaries-general have been Egyptians. The first, Abdul Rahman Azzam Pasha, who served until late 1952, was more responsible than any other person for keeping the organization intact and functioning. His successor was Mohammed Abdel Khalek Hassouna, a former Egyptian foreign minister. The major divisions of the secretariat are the political, legal, social, cultural, press and publicity, administrative and financial, and Palestine departments. The League has set up committees paralleling most of these departments.

In November, 1946, the League members concluded a Cultural Treaty, providing for a Cultural Committee with a permanent bureau and local branches in member states, and for a Cultural Department in the secretariat, which has been active in arranging conferences, establishing institutes, and in implementing in many other ways the objectives of the Cultural Treaty. In 1953 the Council of the League established the Institute of Advanced Arab Studies, which, under the direction of a distinguished Egyptian scholar, Dr. S. Ghorbal, became a center for training specialists in Arab affairs.

In 1957 the League set up the Arab Financial Institution for Economic Development (the Arab Bank), and a Permanent Council for Economic Unity to coordinate economic, financial, and social plans of the Arab states. A draft statute of an Arab Court of Justice has been prepared, but the League's members have shown no great interest in establishing such a court, which would help to implement the provisions of the pact relating to the pacific settlement of disputes between Arab states.

In 1950 representatives of the member states of the League drafted a collective security pact. With Iraq's ratification, announced on March 16, 1952, the pact entered into force. All of the members of the Arab League have now adhered to it. Officially labeled a Treaty of Joint Defense and Economic Co-operation, the pact provided for a Joint Defense Council under the control of the League Council, assisted by a Permanent Military Commission. These agencies have met infrequently since 1952. It has in fact been difficult to implement the treaty, "largely because of difficulties inherent in creating and equipping an army under the command of the Permanent Military Commission."[42] A complicating factor in the period 1955–58 was the willingness of one of the members of the League, Iraq, to enter into security commitments with non-League states. In spite of bitter opposition by Egypt and Saudi Arabia, Iraq joined with Turkey in a treaty of joint defense in February, 1955, and with Iran, Pakistan, Turkey, and the United Kingdom in the Baghdad Pact in November of the same year. After the revolution in Iraq in 1958, the new regime withdrew from all non-Arab defense arrangements but for a time stood somewhat aloof from the Arab League itself, largely because of a personal feud between Kassim and Nasser. During the Suez crisis of 1956 there seemed to be a strong possibility that the Arab collective security pact would be invoked; although the other members of the Arab League gave solid support to Egypt when Israel, Britain, and France resorted to force, that support did not extend to military intervention.

In addition to its defense agreements the 1950 treaty also provided for an Economic Council. In 1961 this council drafted an Economic Unity Pact, a plan for an Arab Common Market. To implement this pact, which went into effect in 1964, the five states which had signed the economic agreement — Iraq, Jordan, Kuwait, Syria, and the United Arab Republic — set up an Economic Unity Council. (Kuwait withdrew in 1965.)

The establishment of the Arab Common Market was in part a response to the European Common Market, which the more revolutionary Arab states regarded "as a form of neo-colonialism or commercial imperialism aimed to maintain European economic domination of developing countries." This attitude was modified in 1963 when three of the more conservative members of the Arab League — Lebanon, Morocco, and Tunisia — signed association agreements with the EEC "to keep open traditional markets for their produce."[43] New suspicions were aroused in 1964, when Israel also signed

[42] Boutros-Ghali, "The Arab League, 1945–1955," p. 392. The text of the treaty is given in Appendix B.

[43] See "Crisis Develops in Arab Market," *New York Times,* January 21, 1966.

an agreement of association with the EEC.

The Arab Common Market officially began its operations on January 1, 1965, and the Economic Unity Council became a permanent organization. If the pact is implemented as planned, which seems highly unlikely, the Arab Common Market will become fully operational after ten years, and it may lead to the creation of an Arab economic union. It may be regarded as another regional arrangement in the Arab world, closely affiliated with the Arab League.

Since its formation the Arab League has concentrated largely on political matters, and especially on questions relating to Palestine. It has pledged support to Arab peoples who have not yet gained independence — in Algeria until 1958 and in the Trucial Oman and other sheikhdoms of the Arabian peninsula — and it has asserted Arab claims to Palestine and its determination to defend that area against Jewish encroachments. It failed to prevent the creation of Israel in 1948 or to subdue the Israelis in the hostilities of 1948–49. While it has presented a united front on most matters relating to Israel, it has been hampered in other respects by deep-seated rifts and conflicting ambitions among the rulers of the Arab states. At one time or another President Nasser of the U.A.R. has been on bad terms with other Arab heads of state, including King Ibn Saud of Saudi Arabia, King Hussein of Jordan, General Kassim of Iraq, and Habib Bourguiba of Tunisia.

Too loose in organization, too much dominated by the U.A.R., too sharply divided by political and personal rivalries, and too much a hostile coalition against Israel, the Arab League has not been a strong regional arrangement. Nevertheless, it is a symbol of national revival in the Arab world, and it may herald a trend toward a larger political grouping in a strategically critical area. By such means as bloc voting and active participation in the United Nations and in the Asian-African Group in the UN it has emphasized the determination of the Arab states to remain free from foreign control and to consider certain common problems on a regional basis. "As a self-contained and effective unity," wrote David Courtney about the Arab League in the *Jerusalem Post* of June 19, 1950, "it has never existed; but it has existed, and still exists, as a formal attempt to create a common external policy out of a natural kinship among the Arab States." This statement is as valid today as it was in 1950.[44]

CENTO and RCD. In 1951 an Anglo-American plan for the establishment of a Middle East Command was stillborn, largely because of its curt rejection by Egypt. A hard look at the situation in the Middle East by the incoming Republican administration in 1953 led to United States encouragement of steps to develop the "northern tier" concept. The states of the "northern tier" from Turkey to Pakistan (except for Afghanistan) came together in a series of bilateral security pacts — notably the pacts between Turkey and Pakistan in August, 1954, and between Turkey and Iraq in February, 1955 — which became the multilateral Baghdad Pact when Britain adhered to the Turkey-Iraq Pact in April, Pakistan in September, and Iran in October, 1955. In November, 1955, the five members of the pact met in Baghdad and set up a formal organization, with a Council of Ministers, special committees for military planning, economic cooperation, communications and counter-subversion, and headquarters in Baghdad, with a secretariat headed by a secretary-general. For various

[44] "Even if the League becomes weaker, its prestige for the Arabs remains intact, not only because it is the first *non-Western* international organization, but because it symbolizes Arab unity to the people from Agadir to Aden." Boutros-Ghali, "The Arab League, 1945–1955," p. 433. See also J. S. Raleigh, "Ten Years of the Arab League," *Middle Eastern Affairs,* VI (March, 1955), 65–77.

reasons, notably a desire not to give unnecessary provocation to Saudi Arabia and Egypt, the United States decided not to join the Baghdad Pact, but it welcomed the signing of the pact, sent an observer to its original meeting, and agreed to full participation in the Economic and Counter-subversion Committees and to permanent liaison with the Military Committee. "It was in the pact but not of it, a participant for practical purposes but without the legal commitments."[45]

Iraq's adherence to the Baghdad Pact created a crisis in the Arab League, and strained relations between Iraq and Egypt. After the revolution in Iraq in 1958, and the establishment of a new government headed by Brigadier Abdul Karim Kassim, the West lost its only Arab ally, a loss which was dramatized by Iraq's withdrawal from the Baghdad Pact in March, 1959. The headquarters of the Baghdad Pact — or Baghdad-less Pact — were hastily moved to Ankara, and the organization was renamed the Central Treaty Organization.

CENTO has carried on under great difficulties. The defection of Iraq was followed by troubles in Turkey and Iran, and by new techniques on the part of the Soviet Union with which the organization was hardly prepared to cope. As a collective security pact CENTO is a weak arrangement, and the "northern tier concept" is still more dream than reality.

Pakistan has become increasingly dissatisfied with its alliances, and it has taken various steps, including the conclusion of several agreements with Communist China, which suggest that it is trying to develop a more independent foreign policy. But it still seems to be interested in maintaining close relations with its fellow-Muslim countries in the "northern tier." Occasionally its leaders advance, in rather general and long-range terms, a proposal for a confederation, or even a federation, of Pakistan, Afghanistan, and Iran. With Iran and Turkey, and largely at her instigation, Pakistan has set up a new regional organization, known as the Regional Cooperation for Development. RCD really grew out of the association of these three Muslim states in CENTO, but apparently it is regarded by its members as a separate organization. Pakistani spokesmen like to refer to it as "the first example of regional cooperation among developing nations."[46]

Regionalism and Regional Arrangements in Africa

So many political changes are occurring in the continent of Africa that it is difficult to determine even general trends. Amidst much talk about African unity, African "personality," and African federation, a multitude of new states has suddenly emerged, with attendant emphasis on nationalism, anticolonialism, and self-determination. These states vary greatly in historical experience and in orientation, and they are just beginning to develop patterns of cooperation for common interests. Many proposals for African regional associations have been discussed, and a few have actually taken organizational form.

Conference of Independent African States. In April, 1958, delegates of eight African states — Ethiopia, Ghana, Liberia, Libya, Morocco, the Sudan, Tunisia, and the United Arab Republic — met in Accra, Ghana, for the first Conference of Independent African States (CIAS). The delegates agreed on the necessity for establishing "machinery for consultation and cooperation," and they decided to hold a conference every two years. The permanent representatives of the participating governments at the United Nations were designated as the informal permanent council for CIAS. The second conference, held in Addis Ababa,

[45] John C. Campbell, *Defense of the Middle East,* rev. ed. (New York: Frederick A. Praeger, 1960), p. 61.

[46] See *Pakistan Affairs,* XVIII (April 16, 1965).

Ethiopia, in June, 1960, was attended by delegates of eleven independent African states and of five areas — the Mali Federation, Madagascar, Nigeria, Sierra Leone, and Somalia — whose dates for independence had been set. The conference recommended the establishment of a Council for African Economic Cooperation, a joint African Development Bank, and an African Commercial Bank.

Although it was loose in organization and in purpose, CIAS was for five years, in the words of an Ethiopian report, "the top level policy planning body in Africa."[47] Its work was hampered, however, by rivalries among the leaders of the new African states and by conflicting interests and orientation. These rivalries led to the emergence of two different, and in some respects conflicting, groups, the Casablanca and Monrovia Groups.

The Casablanca Group. In January, 1961, the heads of five neutralist states of Africa — Nasser of the U.A.R., Nkrumah of Ghana, Touré of Guinea, Keita of Mali, and King Mohamed V of Morocco — met in Casablanca, and proclaimed what they called the African Charter of Casablanca. The charter pledged its signers to "a policy of nonalignment." It called for a new African organization which "all independent African states" were invited to join. The organization would include an African Consultative Assembly, having a permanent seat and holding periodic sessions, a Joint African High Command, committees on political, economic, and cultural affairs, and a secretariat.

[47] See "Focus on Regional Organizations," p. 42. The Ghana Mission to the UN issued two useful documents on the CIAS, *Declarations and Resolutions of the First Conference of Independent African States*, and *Resolutions Passed by the Second Independent African States Conference at Addis Ababa*. A 144-page document on the second conference of the CIAS, with considerable background information, entitled *Second Conference of Independent African States*, was issued by the Ethiopian Mission to the UN.

The Casablanca Group was never a very active or very cohesive organization. Only Algeria and Libya, in addition to its original members, adhered to it in any way. It was hampered by its own militancy, and by the conflicting aims and ambitions of the leaders of the member states. After the Addis Ababa Conference of 1963, it was officially dissolved.

The Monrovia Group. Four months after the Casablanca meeting leaders of twenty African states — all of the states of the former French Community except Guinea, Mali, and Mauritania, plus Ethiopia, Liberia, Libya, Nigeria, Sierra Leone, Somalia, the Sudan, and Tunisia — came together in Monrovia, Liberia, in the first major conference of leaders of French-speaking and English-speaking African states. The conference was boycotted by the states of the Casablanca Group, but hope was expressed at Monrovia that the Casablanca states would join the Monrovia Group in subsequent conferences, and would participate in the establishment of an inter-African organization.

The Organization of African Unity. The Charter of the OAU, by far the most important and most comprehensive regional arrangement in Africa, was drawn up and approved at the Addis Ababa conference of the foreign ministers and the heads of state of thirty African states in May, 1963. It specified that the main organs of the new organization would be an Assembly of Heads of State and Goverment, which was to meet yearly; a Council of Ministers, composed of foreign ministers or other designated ministers, which was to convene at least twice yearly; a secretariat, headed by a secretary-general, which was located, at least temporarily, at Addis Ababa; and a Commission of Mediation, Conciliation, and Arbitration. The assembly was specifically authorized to create specialized commissions for social and

THE ORGANIZATION OF AFRICAN UNITY

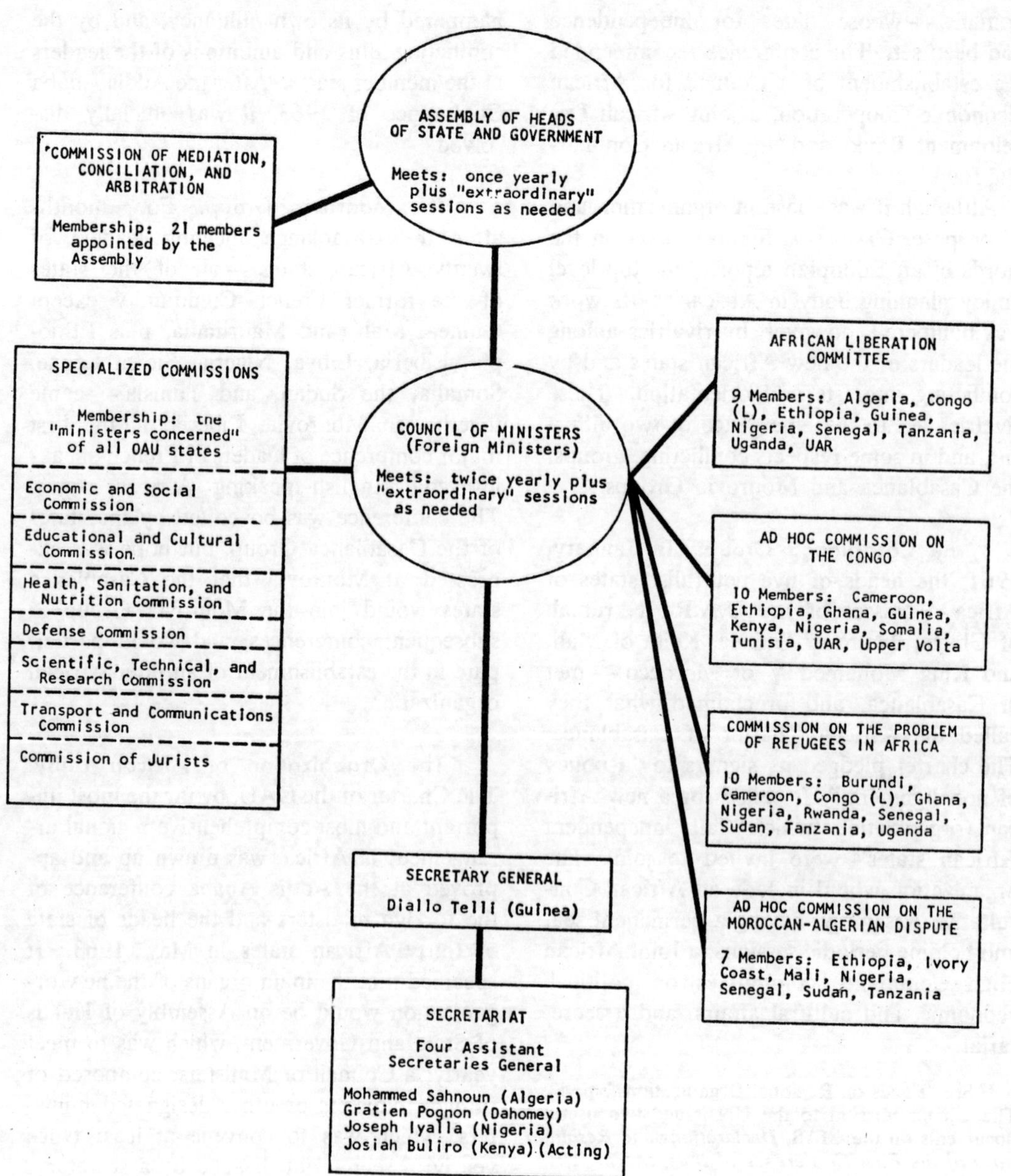

Department of State

economic affairs, for education and culture, for health, sanitation, and nutrition, for defense, and for technical and scientific affairs. The heads of state decided to create an economic committee to study the feasibility of an African common market, a common external tariff, and the harmonization and coordination of national development plans.

At the Addis Ababa meeting the assembly created an African Liberation Committee to coordinate aid from African states to national liberation movements in Africa, and to train volunteers to help the liberation movements. This unique committee, consisting of representatives of Algeria, the Congo (Kinshasa), Ethiopia, Guinea, Nigeria, Senegal, Tanzania, Uganda, and the United Arab Republic, operates from headquarters in Dar-es-Salaam, in Tanzania, which has become a center for efforts to provide tangible assistance to African liberation movements.

In 1963 the Council of Ministers established an Ad Hoc Commission on the Moroccan-Algerian dispute; in 1964, a Commission on the Problems of Refugees in Africa and an Ad Hoc Commission on the Congo. All of these commissions have held several meetings and have been actively functioning bodies. The five specialized commissions provided for in the OAU Charter, plus a Transport and Communications Commission, have discussed a wide variety of economic, social, and technical questions, and have initiated some practical programs in these fields. In addition to its annual meetings the Council of Ministers has held a number of extraordinary sessions. The main political concerns, as reflected in resolutions of the council and assembly, have included colonialism, South Africa's *apartheid* policy, the future of the Portuguese territories in Africa, Rhodesia, the Congo, African representation at the United Nations, and the political evolution of the OAU.[48]

The OAU is now a going concern; it is supported by every independent African state except South Africa and Rhodesia. Although its potential is very great, it is still functioning on a limited basis, and it is weakened by inadequate support from some of its members and by personal and national rivalries, which have threatened to disrupt the annual meetings of the Assembly of the Heads of State and Government.

The OCAM. Dissensions within the OAU and concern over the radical foreign policies being carried on by some African states, such as Ghana, led 13 French-speaking nations of Africa — Cameroun, the Central African Republic, Chad, the Congo (Brazzaville), Dahomey, Gabon, Ivory Coast, Malagasy Republic, Mauritania, Niger, Senegal, Togo, and Upper Volta — and Rwanda to meet at Nouakchott, the capital of Mauritania, on February, 1965, and to form a new organization, representing a "new moderate center of gravity for the continent's politics,"[49] designed the *Organisation Commune Africaine et Malagache.* In June, 1965, OCAM admitted the Congo (Kinshasa) to full membership, thus helping Premier Moise Tshombe to gain at least a partial acceptance by other African nations. At the same meeting the members of OCAM voted to boycott the meeting of the Assembly of Heads of State of OAU in the following September, because it was to be held in Accra, and to stay away from the second Asian-African Conference, scheduled to meet in Algiers in late June.

The Brazzaville Group. All of the French-speaking states of Africa except Mali and Guinea have joined in a major regional economic organization, known as the African-Malagasy Organization for Economic Cooperation (AMOEC). This organization, which aims specifically for cooperation in planning for economic development, exten-

[48] See "The Organization of African Unity," *Department of State Bulletin,* May 3, 1965.

[49] *Time,* June 4, 1965, p. 30.

sion of a customs union, harmonizing fiscal policies, and other measures of economic cooperation, also professes to have more general aspirations in the direction of political "integration." The first meeting of AMOEC was held in the spring of 1961 in Brazzaville, capital of the former French Congo, and its members are sometimes referred to as the Brazzaville Group.

The CCTA. Although AMOEC has been described as "Africa's only regional economic grouping,"[50] at least two other organizations, composed of African and West European states, are also primarily concerned with economic cooperation and development in Africa. One of these, the Economic Commission for Africa, is a regional economic commission of the United Nations. The other is the Commission for Technical Cooperation in Africa South of the Sahara (CCTA). Originally established in 1950 to promote economic cooperation among European governments with the most extensive colonial possessions in Africa — the United Kingdom, France, Belgium, and Portugal — it "has moved forward from the stage of being a colonial organization to that of constituting a regional association of African countries."[51] It is probably the only organization of a regional character in which the European colonial powers, South Africa, Rhodesia, and some Black African states — both French-speaking and English-speaking states — are associated at the present time. CCTA, which has headquarters in Lagos, Nigeria, has been a very active organization.[52] It has sponsored at series of technical meetings, has provided for the regular exchange of information through several permanent bureaus, and has encouraged scientific research and cooperation through its secretariat in Lagos and through associated agencies, including the Foundation for Mutual Assistance in Africa, the Scientific Council for Africa South of the Sahara, the Inter-African Research Fund, and the Inter-African Foundation for the Exchange of Scientists and Technicians. It works closely with the Organization for Economic Cooperation and Development, the Economic Commission for Africa, and the specialized agencies of the United Nations. At the Addis Ababa conference in May, 1963, the heads of African states agreed to maintain CCTA and to integrate its structure within the framework of the OAU.

[50] *Economic World,* III (June, 1961), 2.

[51] "Focus on Regional Organizations," p. 41.

[52] The CCTA Publications Bureau in London has issued several informative publications. See, for example, *Inter-African Cooperation,* Publication No. 60.

Regionalism in Asia and the Pacific Area

The obstacles to Asian regionalism are enormous. They include ideological and policy differences, political and personal rivalries, illiteracy, profusion or confusion of tongues, abject poverty, population differentials, localism, and mountain barriers, to mention only the more obvious. On the other hand, cooperation among the countries of Asia is facilitated by certain common features. Particularly noteworthy among these are the peculiarly supranational — almost non-national — character of nationalist movements, the imperative of common action to obtain necessary outside aid, something approaching a common standard of living, and the absence of a single dominant power.

Among the tangible evidences of Asian and Pacific regionalism are various proposals for some form of "Pacific Union," a number of mutual security pacts, notably SEATO, conferences sponsored by Asian countries such as the Colombo powers, the Colombo Plan, the Asian and Pacific Council, the Association of South-East Asian Nations, and the South Pacific Commission.

Asian Cooperation Without Regionalism: 1947–55. The Asian Relations Conference of March, 1947, described as "the first outward expression of the new awakening in Asia," was attended by representatives of most of the Asian states. Both Gandhi and Nehru were there. While intended primarily to effect an exchange of views on economic and cultural matters, it had some political significance. It set up a Provisional Council with Nehru as president, and approved the creation of an Asian Relations Organization, with headquarters in New Delhi. The organization never expanded beyond its skeleton status, although it has issued some publications and participated in a few conferences.

A resolution adopted unanimously by the nineteen states represented at the Asian Conference on Indonesia, held in New Delhi in January, 1949, recommended that the participating nations explore the possibilities of regional arrangements within their areas. Since Australia, New Zealand, China, and the states of the Arab League, as well as the countries of South and Southeast Asia, were represented, the meaning of "regional arrangements within their areas" was none too clear.

In many respects the Asian-African Conference at Bandung in 1955 was one of the most remarkable international gatherings in history, and seemed to mark the new role of Asia and Africa in world affairs. Its final communiqué expressed a desire for cooperation in economic, cultural, and other fields, agreement to establish liaison officers in the participating countries, and a hope for "prior consultation of participating countries in international forums." But it also affirmed specifically: "It is . . . not intended to form a regional bloc."[53]

"Pacific Union" and Asian Regionalism. The term "Pacific Union," like its better-known European counterpart, "Western Union," has many meanings. It has been used to refer to associations, most of them imaginary in nature, of Asian countries on a continental, regional, or localized basis, ranging from real federations to the loosest possible kind of cooperative action.

The most specific and geographically the most limited proposal for Pacific Union is for a Southeast Asia Union to promote the common political, economic, and cultural interests of the states of that area. Presumably such a union would eschew military commitments. It would attempt to assist the peoples of Southeast Asia to better their conditions of life and to prepare themselves for greater freedom and greater responsibilities, thereby, it is hoped, bolstering the region against persistent colonialism and the threat of mounting Communist pressures.

In 1950, the chief sponsor of a Southeast Asia Union, President Elpidio Quirino of the Philippines, invited countries of Asia interested in forming a union to a conference at Baguio to take the necessary first steps. The results of the Baguio Conference were limiting and disappointing. Delegates from seven scattered countries — Australia, Ceylon, India, Indonesia, Pakistan, the Philippines, and Thailand — agreed on a series of resolutions for regional cooperation in economic, social, and cultural programs, and exchanged views on matters of common interest; but largely on the insistence of India and Indonesia, the conference avoided altogether public declarations or commitments of a political nature. For political reasons, no official representatives from Indo-China, China, or Korea had been invited. The conference failed to accept a Philippine proposal for a permanent organization.

ASA, "Maphilindo," and an Asian Common Market. In January, 1959, the Prime Minister of Malaya, Tunku Abdul Rahman, while on a visit to the Philippines, officially proposed the establishment of an Association of Southeast Asia.[54] This pro-

[53] The text of the communiqué is given in the *New York Times*, April 25, 1955.

[54] See Tunku Abdul Rahman, "Malaysia: Key Area in Southeast Asia," *Foreign Affairs*, XLIII (July, 1965), 665–666.

posal was welcomed by the Philppines and shortly thereafter by Thailand as well, but it was coolly received by most of the other states of Southeast Asia, notably Indonesia and Burma, and it was denounced by Communist China as an offshoot of SEATO. In 1960 the three interested states set up a working group to lay specific plans for the formation of ASA — initials which spell a word meaning "hope" in all three main languages of its charter members — and in August, 1961, the orgànization came formally into being, for the announced purpose of establishing "a firm foundation for common action to further economic and social progress in Southeast Asia." Unfortunately, ASA became practically moribund within two years of its founding, although its secretariat remained in existence. When Malaysia was proclaimed in 1963, the Philippines, which laid claim to some territory on the island of Borneo that was part of the new state, refused to extend recognition. Since the establishment of diplomatic relations in 1966, ASA has been revived in somewhat different and enlarged form through the Association of South-East Asian Nations.

In August, 1963, the foreign ministers of Malaya, the Philippines, and Indonesia announced that they had drafted a declaration establishing "Maphilindo," an organization to promote closer cooperation among the three countries. The organization was doomed by the creation of the state of Malaysia, which the other two refused to recognize. The tension between Indonesia and Malaysia was so great that it led to the verge of war. Clearly President Sukarno's oft-proclaimed determination to "crush Malaysia" could hardly be reconciled with the announced objectives of "Maphilindo." Following the political change in Indonesia in late 1965 the "crush Malaysia" campaign was quietly shelved, in spite of Sukarno's protests, and the new Indonesian government took steps to establish diplomatic relations with Malaysia; but the kind of cooperation envisioned in the "Maphilindo" declaration has not yet been achieved.

At the nineteenth annual conference of the Economic Commission for Asia and the Far East, held in Manila in March, 1963, President Macapagal of the Philippines advocated the establishment of an Asian regional economic organization patterned after the European Economic Community. The new organization, it was thought at the time it was proposed, would include the major states of South and Southeast Asia, and also Australia, Japan, Hong Kong, and possibly Macao. Although there has been a continuing interest in an Asian and Pacific Common Market, and although a Philippine resolution at the ECAFE conference in 1963 stated that "The time is ripe for regional economic cooperation," the prospects for the establishment of an Asian counterpart to the European Common Market seem remote indeed.[55]

The Colombo Plan. In spite of its name, the Colombo Plan for Cooperative Economic Development in South and Southeast Asia is not an integrated plan at all. Rather, it is "the name given to the whole sum of the cooperative effort which the countries of South and South-East Asia, helped by member countries outside the region, are making to develop their economies and raise the living standards of their peoples."[56] It has some machinery, and it represents what is probably Asia's most advanced effort at regional cooperation, but it is not a true regional arrangement. Its main agency of cooperation is the Consultative Committee, which was set up at a meeting of the Commonwealth foreign ministers in Colombo in January, 1950.

After hasty preparation of development programs by the Asian members of the Con-

[55] See Artemio R. Guillermo, "Asian and Pacific Common Market," *The Asian Student,* May 11, 1963.

[56] *What Is the Colombo Plan?* British Information Services, New York, August, 1960.

sultative Committee, the Colombo plan was formally inaugurated on July 1, 1951. It still operates with a minimum of machinery and staff. Assistance is provided by the Technical Cooperation Scheme; coordination, by a council and by the Bureau for Technical Cooperation, located in Colombo.

The original members were the United Kingdom and the other Commonwealth countries, plus Malaya and British Borneo. It now has twenty-two members. Fifteen are states within the region: Afghanistan, Bhutan, Burma, Cambodia, Ceylon, India, Indonesia, Laos, Malaysia, the Maldive Islands, Nepal, Pakistan, the Philippines, South Vietnam, and Thailand. The remaining seven members are outside the region: Australia, Canada, Japan, New Zealand, South Korea, the United Kingdom, and the United States.

Since its formation the Colombo Plan has helped to channel billions of dollars in economic aid to the member countries of South and Southeast Asia, plus technical assistance worth some $400 million. The United States has been by far the largest contributor. Other major donors are the United Kingdom, Canada, Australia, New Zealand, and Japan. Under the Plan approximately 28,500 persons from the region have received technical training, and some 5,000 outside experts have been sent to the member states of the region. The Plan is also involved in three large joint regional schemes, namely the Indus River Basin and the Mekong River development programs, and the Asian highway scheme for a 30,000-mile network of all-weather roads running from Saigon to Istanbul.[57]

Pacific Pacts. Users of the term "Pacific Union" frequently mean a Pacific Pact, similar to the North Atlantic Pact. Supporters of such proposals are prompted by the desire to present a stronger front to the menace of communism in Asia, to establish a common defense plan and organization, and to associate the United States in such an undertaking. In July, 1950, the Committee on Foreign Affairs of the United States House of Representatives unanimously endorsed proposals for a mutual defense pact for the Pacific area, patterned after the North Atlantic Treaty, in which the United States would participate. In the following year the Truman administration took the initiative in launching "an overall system of Pacific Ocean collective security pacts." Three such pacts were concluded in 1951, with the Philippines, with Australia and New Zealand, (the ANZUS Pact), and with Japan; one in 1953, with the Republic of Korea; and one in 1954, with Nationalist China. Presumably these pacts were envisioned as the first steps in a widening network of Pacific security arrangements in which, it was hoped, other Asian nations, as well as Britain and France, would join. Until such time, however, as India, Indonesia, and other Asian states participate, and until the pacts bring about cooperation on a broader front, these agreements belong to the pattern of mutual defense arrangements of the free world, with the United States as the main link, rather than to the pattern of true Asian regionalism.

SEATO. After the Geneva truce agreements regarding Indo-China in 1954, the United States, Britain, France, Australia, New Zealand, the Philippines, Thailand, and Pakistan agreed to meet in Manila in early September to consider measures for concerted resistance to possible aggression or subversion in Southeast Asia. Out of this conference emerged the so-called Pacific Charter and the Southeast Asia Collective Defense Treaty.[58] Although the treaty provided for a minimum of machinery, and al-

[57] See Robert Stephens, "Aid Program That Works: Colombo Plan," dispatch from London, in the *Philadelphia Inquirer*, November 29, 1964.

[58] For the texts of the Pacific Charter and the Manila Treaty, see the *New York Times*, September 9, 1954.

though only two states of Southeast Asia adhered to it, it was immediately dubbed the Southeast Asia Treaty Organization (SEATO). The "treaty area" was designated as "the general area of Southeast Asia," and a protocol specifically extended the provisions of the treaty to the states of Laos, Cambodia, and South Vietnam. Unlike the North Atlantic Treaty, the Manila Treaty contained provisions for countering "subversive activities from without," but the provisions for action in the event of armed attack were more general than those of the North Atlantic Treaty. Each member of SEATO simply agreed that if an armed attack occurred it would "act to meet the common danger in accordance with its constitutional processes." The Manila Treaty also contained provisions for cooperation in strengthening "free institutions" and the promotion of "economic progress and social well-being."

Although the treaty provided only for a Council "so organized as to be able to meet at any time," the member states soon found it advisable, like the signatories to the North Atlantic Treaty, to establish more elaborate machinery. The Council meets at the ministerial level only once a year; at other times its work is carried on by Council representatives, aided by military and other advisers, at SEATO's headquarters in Bangkok. Until 1965, when Lieutenant General Jesus M. Vargas of the Philippines was appointed for a three-year term, the secretaries-general were Thais. SEATO has a number of special committees, notably a "watchdog committee" of experts on subversion, and a Committee on Information, Cultural, Education, and Labor Activities.

SEATO is a weak regional defense system, but some efforts are made through conferences, exchanges of views and information, training programs, joint military exercises, and other means to make it a useful instrument of collective planning. Its nonmilitary functions have expanded steadily, not only in counter-subversion but in such activities as cultural exchange, public health programs, and economic cooperation.

It was inevitable but unfortunate that SEATO should be compared with NATO. The contrasts between the two organizations are striking:

> NATO is a strong association of natural allies . . . bound together by firm commitments and by an elaborate organization. It has substantial forces at its command, and has evolved elaborate plans for united military and other action in the event of an attack on any of the member states. It has vigor and teeth. . . . SEATO, on the other hand, is a loose association which calls for little organization, for no unified command and for almost no unified military measures at all, and which has none of the automatic action provisions of the North Atlantic Treaty. . . . [Nevertheless,] the stumbling block is not in the treaty but in the capabilities and will of the member states, and even more in the attitudes of those who determine the policies of other Asian states.[59]

SEATO has never realized the hopes of its sponsors, and it has been severely criticized by leaders of the "neutralist" states, including the major states of South and Southeast Asia, India and Indonesia. Critics argue that the limited advantages which it offers as a collective security organization do not compensate for the disadvantages of alienating several important Asian nations. Its greatest test to date has come as a result of the growing Communist penetration of Laos and South Vietnam. In January, 1961, the SEATO Council met at the request of the United States to consider what action should be taken to meet the Communist challenge in Laos, but largely because of the reluctance of Britain and France the Council adjourned without taking any decisive stand. At a meeting in London in May, 1965, the majority of the members of the Council joined with the United States in declaring that resolute

[59] Norman D. Palmer, "Organizing for Peace in Asia," *The Western Political Quarterly,* VIII (March, 1955), 26.

defensive action had to be continued to defeat Communist aggression; but Pakistan, which had clearly been veering away from the SEATO alliance for some time and had been drawing closer to Communist China, expressed some reservations, and France, which was represented only by an observer rather than her foreign minister, flatly refused to endorse the resolution and openly expressed opposition to United States policy in Vietnam.

With such divisions among its members, SEATO is not now a viable alliance. Apparently its members cannot agree on common action to meet common dangers. It may still be a useful diplomatic device, and in time it may reverse the trends toward disintegration and instead may become a more effective instrument for cooperation and defense in Southeast Asia.

ASPAC. In June, 1966, a significant new regional organization, known as the Asian and Pacific Council (ASPAC), was organized at a conference at the Walker Hill resort, outside of Seoul, of representatives of nine Asian states — Australia, Japan, Malaysia, Nationalist China, New Zealand, the Philippines, South Korea, South Vietnam, and Thailand (Laos sent an observer). In a joint communique these representatives announced their "determination to preserve their integrity and sovereignty in the face of external threats." Some of them wanted to take a strong collective stand in support of South Vietnam, but this move was blocked by spokesmen of Japan and Malaysia. It was agreed that the new organization would give primary attention to the promotion of economic cooperation, and would be non-military, nonideological, and not anti-Communist. This might, it was hoped, provide a sufficiently flexible framework for enlisting the eventual cooperation, and perhaps the membership, of other Asian states.

Only a skeleton organization was agreed upon at the Seoul conference. The affairs of the organization are being handled by a standing committee in Bangkok, consisting of the ambassadors to Thailand of the member states, under the chairmanship of the foreign minister of Thailand, assisted by a small secretariat provided by Thailand. The committee headquarters will rotate from year to year. Once a year, at the capitals of the member states in rotation, a meeting will be held at the ministerial level.[60]

"ASPAC has a long and difficult way to go to achieve a permanent life because it is an association of nations with perhaps the greatest racial, religious, political, economic, cultural, and historical differences in the world." Nevertheless, its formation, on the initiative of South Korea and with the cooperation of other Asian non-Communist nations, "has added another piece to the gradually spreading mosaic of unity among non-Communist nations in this area."[61]

ASEAN. In August, 1967, representatives of Indonesia, Malaysia, the Philippines, Singapore, and Thailand, meeting in Bangkok, Thailand, adopted a declaration announcing the establishment of the Association of South-East Asian Nations (ASEAN). The avowed purposes of the new organization, which was in effect an enlarged version of ASA — although the member countries prefer not to refer to it in this way — were "to accelerate economic growth, social progress and cultural development in the region," "to promote active collaboration and mutual assistance . . . in the economic, social, cultural, scientific and administrative fields," and "to promote regional peace and stability." The machinery provided for in the ASEAN declaration consisted of an annual meeting of foreign ministers, a Standing Committee, "*Ad Hoc* Committees and Permanent Committees of specialists and officials on specific subjects," and "a National Secre-

[60] See Robert Trumbull's dispatch from Seoul, in the *New York Times,* June 16, 1966.

[61] Richard Halloran, "Non-Communist Asian Nations Unite to Offset Red Chinese," *Philadelphia Inquirer,* June 23, 1966.

tariat in each member country." ASEAN is essentially a new economic grouping in Southeast Asia. Presumably membership is open to other countries in the area, and even in South Asia as well. It may also become an agency to promote regional security.

South Pacific Commission. An interesting and little-known regional organization, modeled after the Caribbean Commission, exists in the South Pacific area. In February, 1947, representatives of the six states having major responsibilities in the South Pacific — Australia, France, the Netherlands, New Zealand, the United Kingdom, and the United States — signed an agreement in Canberra establishing the South Pacific Commission (SPC), a consultative and advisory body, with no executive powers and with political matters specifically excluded from its jurisdiction, to assist participating governments in matters relating to the economic and social development of territories embracing an area of some thirteen million square miles with a population of some 3,500,000 Micronesians, Melanesians, and Polynesians. The main agencies of the SPC, which has headquarters in Noumea, New Caledonia, are the Research Council, with three sections specializing in health, economic development, and social development; the Commission, composed of two commissioners from each member state, which usually meets annually; the South Pacific Conference, a unique body of delegates from the inhabitants of the territories and advisers which meets every three years; and a small secretariat. Although its powers are severely limited, the SPC has proved to be a useful agency "for personal contacts among the representatives of the different governments, territorial administrations, and native peoples" and for bringing "the island peoples into association with an international effort."[62]

The United Nations and Regional Arrangements

Regional arrangements were given more positive and detailed endorsement in the Charter of the United Nations than in the Covenant of the League of Nations. Woodrow Wilson viewed with suspicion the idea of regional arrangements and alliances; and the founders of the League feared that they would open the way for alliances and a return to the balance of power system which would, in the long run, be in substantial opposition to the League concept of collective security on a global basis.

At the San Francisco Conference the question of regional versus international organizations was debated at great length; indeed, it was "one of the knottiest questions"[63] with which the conference wrestled. According to an American expert who served on the Committee on Regional Arrangements of the Third Commission at the San Francisco Conference:

> . . . the approach of the various countries to the problem of regional arrangements may be said to have been conditioned in part by one or another of five points of view, all of which operated in favor of varying degrees of autonomy for regional or other limited arrangements within the general framework of the United Nations:
>
> 1. The desire of the American republics to safeguard the inter-American system;
>
> 2. The similar feeling on the part of the states of the Arab League . . . that the status of that League be preserved;
>
> 3. The wish of the U.S.S.R. to except from any restrictive control under the Char-

[62] Norman J. Padelford, "Regional Cooperation in the South Pacific: Twelve Years of the South Pacific Commission," *International Organization*, XIII (Summer, 1959).

[63] For a detailed report on this subject see *The United Nations Conference on International Organization, San Francisco, April 25–June 26, 1945. Report on the Action of the Conference on Regional Arrangements.* Submitted to the Governing Board of the Pan American Union by the Director General. Congress and Conference Series No. 48, (Washington, D.C.: Pan American Union, 1945).

ter the system of bilateral mutual assistance pacts;

4. France's concern over possible renewal of German aggression, leading her to seek freedom of action against ex-enemy states without the necessity of awaiting prior action by the Security Council;

5. The general uneasiness of the small states over the power granted the Security Council in the light of the Yalta voting formula.[64]

There was also strong objection, especially on the part of the United States and the Latin American republics, to the stipulation in the Dumbarton Oaks Proposals that a regional arrangement or agency could not take enforcement action without the express authorization of the Security Council of the new international organization. In view of the Yalta voting formula, this requirement seemed to imply that a single permanent member of the Council could block action under any regional arrangement.

In its final form the United Nations Charter devoted an entire chapter (Chapter VIII, Articles 52–54) to the subject of regional arrangements. In addition, Article 33 provided for "resort to regional agencies and arrangements" among the recommended procedures for the pacific settlement of disputes. As stated in Article 53, the authorization of the Security Council is not required before action is taken against an enemy state of World War II. An even more important exception is provided for in Article 51, which opens the way for a great variety of regional security arrangements outside the effective control of the United Nations.

The Charter does not attempt to define "regional arrangements or agencies"; it leaves the whole question of their character and purposes, and of their exact relations with the United Nations, very much up in the air. What it does have to say on regional arrangements is confined to the field of security. It is silent on the possible economic, social, and other potentialities of such groupings. Yet within the UN itself, as well as outside, the regional principle has been applied in these broader fields, as, for instance, in the regional commissions of the United Nations.

Proponents of regional security arrangements naturally insist that these devices are wholly consistent with the United Nations Charter and are necessary steps in regional or collective self-defense. The Charter specifically recognizes the right of nations to take action of this sort until and unless the United Nations is able to assert itself effectively in the maintenance of peace. But while these arrangements can be readily defended, there is real danger that they will deteriorate into military alliances *against* some country or countries, that they will provoke counter-measures — that they will, in short, increase international tensions and thereby accentuate the very evils they are presumably designed to prevent. There is much truth in this frank comment by Professor Leland M. Goodrich:

> It must be clearly recognized, however, that the world organization is not being strengthened by the multiplication and tightening of these regional security arrangements. On the most optimistic view they are to be regarded as temporary expedients and as possible aids in creating conditions which permit the rehabilitation of the global system. If the United Nations as an organization to maintain international peace and security becomes effective, such regional arrangements should decline in importance and be subordinated in operation to the responsible organs of the United Nations.[65]

Because of the limitations of the United Nations, the major non-Communist states

[64] Allen, p. 7. See also Arthur H. Vandenberg, Jr., ed., *The Private Papers of Senator Vandenberg* (Boston: Houghton Mifflin Company, 1952), pp. 186–198.

[65] "Regionalism and the United Nations," *Columbia Journal of International Affairs*, III (Spring, 1949), 19–20. See also Grayson Kirk, "The Atlantic Pact and International Security," *International Organization*, III (May, 1949), 239–251.

have increasingly tended to rely more on regional security arrangements than on the international organization. This trend has alarmed many supporters of the UN. Writing in a popular American magazine in 1954, Carlos Romulo of the Philippines contended that "the United Nations is dying" because member states are "more and more taking the great political issues outside the framework of the organization."[66] "In the name of regional arrangements," added another observer, "the United Nations has been placed in a position of inferiority, so that now the link between the regional arrangements and the world organization exist at the practical pleasure of the former."[67] This bypassing of the UN on vital issues greatly troubled Secretary-General Trygve Lie, and he frequently warned of the danger of the attrition of the UN and urged a reversal of the regional trend. His successors have taken the same position.

As Trygve Lie pointed out in February, 1948, regional arrangements can be "a very useful element in building a United Nations system of collective security provided they recognize the supremacy of the Charter."[68] This is an important point. Article 103 of the Charter states it clearly: "In the event of a conflict between the obligations of the Members of the United Nations under the present Charter and their obligations under any other international agreement, their obligations under the Charter shall prevail." Moreover, as Lie insisted in a memorandum of June 6, 1950: "Measures for collective self-defense and regional remedies of other kinds are at best interim measures, and cannot bring any reliable security from the prospect of war." Regional arrangements, in other words, have constructive possibilities only if they are truly a part of a larger pattern, centering on the United Nations — "the one common undertaking and universal instrument of the great majority of the human race."

Yet the balance between regionalism and universalism as illustrated by the relative role and effectiveness of regional arrangements and the United Nations, especially in the security field, seems to be clearly tilted in favor of the regional approach. Far from operating within the framework of the UN Charter, most regional arrangements have largely ignored or bypassed the UN. On the basis of his own extensive studies of regionalism, Professor Furniss concluded that "The United Nations has been placed in a position of inferiority so that now the links between regional arrangements and the world organization exist at the practical pleasure of the former."[69] Professor Inis L. Claude, Jr., after a detailed analysis of the relations between the UN and the Organization of American States, declared that "The development of the relationship between the OAS and the United Nations comprises the proposition that the original project of permitting and encouraging regional agencies to operate within a framework of the United Nations supervision and control has broken down."[70] In late May, 1965, Secretary-General U Thant

[66] "The UN Is Dying," *Collier's,* July 23, 1954, p. 30.

[67] Edgar S. Furniss, Jr., "A Re-examination of Regional Arrangements," *Journal of International Affairs,* IX (1955), 84. For a concrete example of the problems that may arise in the relations between the UN and a regional arrangement, see A. M. Rosenthal, "Guatemala Case Raises Issue of U.N.'s Future," *New York Times,* July 4, 1954, p. E4.

[68] The question may be raised whether this very cautious endorsement is really an endorsement at all. Mr. Lie showed a conspicuous lack of enthusiasm for regional security arrangements (including the North Atlantic Treaty), and many other UN officials and delegates have shared his restraint. Even if one approves of an arrangement like the North Atlantic Pact, it may be more realistic to confess that it came into being because of the obvious weakness of the United Nations as a security arrangement, and as a necessary substitute for a more desirable, but apparently unobtainable, protective system on the international plane.

[69] Furniss, p. 84.

[70] "The OAS, the UN, and the United States," *International Conciliation,* No. 547 (March, 1964), p. 63.

warned that the peacekeeping action by the OAS in the Dominican Republic, taken without reference to the UN, might set a dangerous, or at least embarrassing precedent. The action of the OAS in this instance was vigorously criticized by representatives of the Soviet Union, Cuba, and other nations in debates in the Security Council, and the presence of UN representatives in the Dominican Republic during the crisis of mid-1965 was openly resented and criticized by some OAS member states. In this case the UN and a regional organization were working at cross-purposes.

The co-existence of regional arrangements and a nearly universal world organization is a fact of contemporary international life. Both meet a real need in the area of interstate cooperation. In the words of Professor John C. Stoessinger:

> The record supports neither the "building-block theory" of regionalism nor the opposite contention that regional arrangements are necessarily antithetical to the principles of the United Nations Charter. Rather, the evidence shows that frequently the United Nations has been a second line of defense for regionalism, and that sometimes regional arrangements have served as backstops for the world organization. Certainly there is ample room for both types of political order-building on the international scene.[71]

The Balance Sheet of International Regionalism

The trend toward international regionalism is now an acknowledged feature of the international scene. It has achieved a new meaning and a new significance. While it has not in any real sense breached the barrier of the sovereign state system, it has provided the impetus and the machinery for much closer cooperation of states on the regional level.

In spite of the growing importance of international regionalism, as evidenced by the appearance of many new regional arrangements, very little attention has been given to this development by students of international relations. The exact nature of international regionalism is by no means clear. The same comment could be made of its significance and place in the international society of the present, and even more particularly of the future. As Edgar S. Furniss, Jr., pointed out, there is a great need "to rethink the concept of regionalism." It is important to explore its relations to the prevailing nation-state pattern; to looser arrangements between states through treaties, trade relations, alliances, etc.; to proposed unions and federations, on a regional or broader level; to larger associations of states such as the Commonwealth of Nations; and to universal organizations, notably the United Nations at the present time, but embracing also any other nearly universal associations which are now in existence or which may come into being in the future.

Professor Furniss has itemized six "perplexing difficulties" to which "the development of so many 'arrangements' since 1945 have given rise." The first is "the continuing confusion arising from the lack of precision in definition." A second difficulty arises from the "overlapping networks of agreements." A third difficulty is caused by the exclusion of certain states from regional arrangements in their areas or the refusal of other states to adhere to such arrangements. The fourth and fifth difficulties are that some so-called regional arrangements are preoccupied "with conditions inside the area as a means of attaining objectives outside the area," and, conversely, "that too much internal organization may lead to difficulties in linking the arrangements one with another and each with the United Nations." The sixth difficulty "concerns the relevance of such arrangements to the maintenance of peace and security in the light of the series of revolutions which have taken place in military

[71] *The Might of Nations: World Politics in Our Time,* rev. ed. (New York: Random House, 1965), p. 333.

technology since 1945."[72] The difficulties are indeed perplexing; they justify Furniss' insistence on the need for a fundamental rethinking of the meaning of regionalism and of the nature and place of regional arrangements in today's world.

If international regionalism is properly developed and is closely integrated into a more universal framework such as is provided by the United Nations, it can fill a real gap in the existing pattern of international society. Wrongly used, it will become nothing more than a camouflage, and a poor one at that, for military alliances, "blocs," and "orbits," and therefore will exercise a disturbing and destructive influence on international relations.

The multiplication of regional arrangements, especially in Western Europe, is already giving rise to problems of coordination and to apprehensions about the possibility of conflicting obligations. Hamilton Fish Armstrong warned that "the overlappings in a security system based on regions are evidently as troublesome as the gaps." But while problems of coordination are obviously great, such obligations should be complementary and not conflicting. Indeed, the thesis may be hazarded that the more regional arrangements a given state enters, the more secure is that state and the brighter are the prospects for peaceful international collaboration. Georges Scelle believed that "there is in this interlocking or interweaving of groupings a guarantee of peace. . . . If a state belongs to many different systems, it will be by that very fact restrained in its warlike inclinations by the very weight of each of the groups to which it belongs, and on the other hand will help neutralize the warlike inclinations of its partners by the care which it will take to safeguard its own associations."[73] Moreover, the experience and perspective gained in many cooperative endeavors on the regional level should contribute greatly not only to the successful functioning of regional arrangements but also to the development of that international climate of opinion without which all efforts at international cooperation are doomed to failure.

SUGGESTIONS FOR FURTHER READING

"The Atlantic Community," *Intercom*, Vol. 7, No. 2 (March-April, 1965). Contains concise information on NATO, OECD, and the major regional organizations in Western Europe.

BECKETT, SIR W. ERIC. *The North Atlantic Treaty, the Brussels Treaty and the Charter of the United Nations.* London, 1950.

BOYD, ANDREW and FRANCES BOYD. *Western Union: A Study of the Trend Toward European Unity.* Washington, D. C.: Public Affairs Press, 1949.

BOYD, ANDREW and WILLIAM MATSON. *Atlantic Pact, Commonwealth and United Nations.* London, 1947.

CANYES, MANUEL. *The Organization of American States and the United Nations,* 3d ed. Washington, D.C.: Pan American Union, 1955.

CHEEVER, DANIEL and H. FIELD HAVILAND, JR. *Organizing for Peace: International Organization in World Affairs.* Boston: Houghton Mifflin Company, 1954. Part Four: "Regional and Other Systems."

DEUTSCH, KARL W. *et al. Political Community in the North Atlantic Area: International Organization in the Light of Historical Experience.* Princeton, N.J.: Princeton University Press, 1957.

FENWICK, CHARLES G. *The Organization of American States; the Inter-American Regional System.* Washington, D.C.: Pan American Union, 1963.

"Focus on Regional Organizations," *Intercom,*

[72] Furniss, pp. 81–85.

[73] *Une crise de la Société des Nations* (Paris, 1926), p. 216.

Vol. 2, No. 8 (December, 1960). Basic information on some 25 regional organizations.

GRZYBOWSKI, KAZIMIERZ. *The Socialist Commonwealth of Nations.* New Haven: Yale University Press, 1964. Contains a detailed treatment of COMECON and the Warsaw Treaty Organization.

HAAS, ERNST. *The Uniting of Europe: Political Economic and Social Forces, 1950–1957.* Stanford, Calif.: Stanford University Press, 1958. A sophisticated interpretation of the process of European integration.

"Handbook on Africa," *Intercom,* Vol. 8, No. 3 (May–June, 1966). Contains information on 10 African regional organizations.

KHALIL, MUHAMMAD, ed. *The Arab States and the Arab League; a Documentary Record.* 2 vols. Beirut, 1962.

KISER, MARGARET. *Organization of American States,* 5th ed. Washington, D.C.: Government Printing Office, 1955.

LAWSON, RUTH C., ed. *International Regional Organizations: Constitutional Foundations.* New York: Frederick A. Praeger, 1962. Basic documents.

MACDONALD, ROBERT W. *The League of Arab States: a Study in the Dynamics of Regional Organization.* Princeton, N.J.: Princeton University Press, 1965.

NYE, JOSEPH S., JR. *International Regionalism: Readings.* Boston: Little, Brown and Company, 1968.

PALMER, MICHAEL, JOHN LAMBERT, *et al. European Unity: A Survey of the European Organization.* London, 1968.

PANIKKAR, K. M. *et al. Regionalism and Security.* New Delhi, 1948. A symposium, mostly on Asia.

"Regional Organizations: Their Role in the World Community," *Columbia Journal of International Affairs,* III (Spring, 1949).

Royal Institute of International Affairs. *Atlantic Alliance: NATO's Role in the Free World.* London, 1952.

———. *Britain in Western Europe — WEU and the Atlantic Alliance.* London, 1956. A Chatham House study group report.

———. *Defence in the Cold War: the Task for the Free World.* London, 1950.

———. *Documents on Regional Organizations Outside Western Europe, 1940–1949.* London, 1950.

SCHMITT, HANS A. *The Path to European Union.* Baton Rouge: Louisiana State University Press, 1962. From the Marshall Plan to the European Common Market.

SINGH, LALITA PRASAD. *The Politics of Economic Cooperation in Asia: a Study of Asian International Organizations.* Columbia: University of Missouri Press, 1966. Gives particular attention to ECAFE and the Colombo Plan.

STANLEY, THOMAS W. *NATO in Transition: the Future of the Atlantic Alliance.* New York: Frederick A. Praeger, for the Council on Foreign Relations, 1965.

STARKE, J. G. *The ANZUS Treaty Alliance.* London, 1966. Compares ANZUS with other regional security treaties, and suggests needed revisions.

STOESSINGER, JOHN C. *The Might of Nations: World Politics in Our Time,* rev. ed. New York: Random House, 1965. Contains good discussion of the relative roles of the UN and regional arrangements.

THOMAS, ANN WYNEN and A. J. THOMAS. *The Organization of American States.* Dallas: Southern Methodist University Press, 1963.

Union of International Associations. *Yearbook of International Organizations.* Brussels. Issued annually. Contains basic information regarding some 1500 intergovernmental and nongovernmental international organizations.

United Nations Conference on International Organization, San Francisco, April 25–June 26, 1945, *Report on the Action of the Conference on Regional Arrangements.* Washington, D.C.: Pan American Union, 1945. Congress and Conference Series No. 48.

WEIL, GORDON L., ed. *A Handbook on the European Economic Community.* New York: Frederick A. Praeger, 1965. A definitive reference work.

YALEM, RONALD J. *Regionalism and World Order.* Washington, D.C.: Public Affairs Press, 1965. A critical assessment of the record of regional and universal international organizations since 1920.

PART FIVE

FORMULATIONS OF THE NATIONAL INTEREST

21 The Foreign Policy of the Soviet Union

"In its distant objectives," asserts Edward Crankshaw, "the foreign policy of the Soviet Union is less obscure and more coherent than that of any other country in the world. The objectives embrace the ultimate victory of the world proletariat under the leadership of Moscow."[1] The goals of communism have been proclaimed, with some variations of emphasis, ever since Karl Marx and Friedrich Engels declared in the *Communist Manifesto:* "The Communists disdain to conceal their views and aims. They openly declare that their ends can be attained only by the forcible overthrowing of all existing social conditions." This program of world revolution distinguishes the Soviet Union from every other modern state — Soviet leaders and dialecticians never weary of expounding the unique character of their political order — and, understandably, it creates deep hostility between the "two worlds" and introduces a peculiarly dynamic and menacing element into all tendencies toward Soviet expansionism and imperialism.

Conditioning Factors. Soviet foreign policy, however, can hardly be summed up as the fanatical pursuit of a single goal, although this interpretation is popular in many circles. Instead, like the foreign policy of any state, it is inevitably shaped by a variety of factors: geographic and strategic considerations; historical and traditional policies; the general international situation; internal political problems; the elements of economic strength and weakness within the state; the morale of the people and the character of the leadership; and other equally basic conditions. At various stages in their brief tenure of power the Communist leaders of Russia have appeared to regard world revolution as an imminent and then as a remote expectation, as a goal to be placed in the forefront of their policies and then as one which can be relegated at least temporarily to the ideological closet. Moreover, as Barrington Moore, Jr., believed, there is some indication that world revolution has been transformed "from a goal into a technique." "If there is any central goal behind the policy of the Soviet leaders," he argued, "it is the preservation and extension of their own power, by any means whatever, rather than the spread of a specific social system or the realization of a doctrinal blueprint."[2]

[1] Review of Max Beloff, *The Foreign Policy of Soviet Russia,* Vol. II: 1936–1941 (Oxford University Press, 1949); *New York Times,* July 3, 1949.

[2] Barrington Moore, Jr., *Soviet Politics — The Dilemma of Power: The Role of Ideas in Social Change* (Cambridge, Mass.: Harvard University Press, 1950), p. 394.

Special Problems in Analysis. In any analysis of Soviet foreign policy two limitations should be borne constantly in mind. The first is that reliable information is very difficult to obtain and is indeed generally lacking. Even a casual perusal of some of the literature on the Soviet Union will reveal that on the whole the sources are scanty and unreliable, and that supporting evidence for many of the statements is quite unsatisfactory. Few important original documents are available; the press is government-controlled; public debate on foreign policy is practically nonexistent; the value of the reports of the foreign correspondents tolerated in the Soviet Union is necessarily lessened by the fact that these correspondents have little access to essential documents, and are not free to move about at will. Moreover, the strict censorship of an earlier era has now been replaced by self-censorship, in some respects an even more restrictive policy since correspondents know that misjudgment will bring expulsion.

A second limitation is that the Russians and in fact all Communists use familiar words and concepts in very unfamiliar ways. The Communists have posed a semantic problem which did not arise during the years of Fascist aggression. Mussolini boasted that he spat on the corpse of liberty, and Hitler sneered at democracy; but the Communists, who are equally contemptuous of liberty and democracy as understood in the non-Communist world, use these and other words in a wholly novel sense. Failure to understand this practice, as John Foster Dulles said, "explains why we so often agree with what Soviet leaders say and then find it difficult to reconcile their acts with what we thought they meant."[3] "Upside-down language" to use Sir Gladwyn Jebb's phrase, is the usual fare offered by Communist propagandists. It suggests that the slogans which George Orwell foresaw in his book *1984* are not so fantastic after all: "War is Peace," "Freedom is Slavery," and "Ignorance is Strength."

[3] "Thoughts on Soviet Foreign Policy," *Life*, June 3, 1946, p. 113.

Bases and Instruments

To what extent is Soviet foreign policy a continuation of tsarist policy, conditioned by the same geographic and strategic, historical and traditional factors? To what extent is it a product of Communist ideology, particularly of the Communist view of world revolution and inevitable conflict and of the Marxist-Leninist theory of international relations? To what extent is it shaped by international developments? by domestic events? by personalities? Who formulates it and how is it implemented?

A Continuation of Traditional Policies? To Communists this question seems meaningless. According to their doctrine the interests of Russian national policy and of world communism are identical. To non-Communists this is a hotly debated question on which all kinds of opinions have been expressed. Thus many historically minded observers point out that nearly all of the policies now followed by the Soviet Union are a natural and logical continuation of historic Russian policies.

From the time of Peter the Great, perhaps from an even earlier period, the leaders of Russia have sought to consolidate and develop the resources, human and natural, of their vast land mass, to acquire windows to the West, and to gain access to the oceans without abandoning their self-imposed isolation. Communist Russia shows the same tendencies to expansion, the same overzealous solicitude for her "fellow-Slavs," the same concern for Asia, although the motives may be different. Russian interest in the Balkans, in Poland, in Manchuria and Outer Mongolia, in the entire borderland area, is nothing new. It has often been pointed out that since 1939 the Soviet Union has expanded almost to the fullest extent of tsarist aspirations, with the one outstanding exception of the Turkish Straits.

There are also plenty of precedents for the present suspiciousness and aloofness of the Russian leaders, for their calculated obscurantism, for their isolationism and messianism, for their intolerance and autocratic tendencies, for strict control from above, and for persecution, purges, and slave labor camps. George F. Kennan once remarked that he could piece together lengthy excerpts from the observations in De Custine's *La Russie en 1839* and submit them, with only slight changes, to the State Department as a report on present conditions in the Soviet Union.[4]

We may conclude, therefore, that the foreign policy of the Soviet Union is in many respects a continuation of the policies of tsarist Russia, but that the Communist leaders of Rusisa, like the tsars, have had to make adjustments to the existing structure of international relationships.

When the Nazis attacked the Soviet Union in the summer of 1941, the war almost overnight ceased to be "the Great Imperialist War," and became instead "the Great Patriotic War." In that time of crisis the appeal of the Soviet leaders was to Russian nationalism and not to communism, to "Mother Russia" and not to Karl Marx. In 1956 David J. Dallin, a Russian-born opponent of the Communist regime and prolific writer on Soviet affairs, made this prediction:

> Today the old world-revolutionary trend, although dimmed and anemic, still prevails. As new tendencies crystallize, the two components of Soviet policy — Russian national interest and Communist *Weltanschauung* — will tend to become divorced in Soviet minds and actions. In the end the first must prevail, though not without grave internal crises.[5]

There are some observers who would take sharp issue with this analysis. Writing in the American journal *Foreign Affairs* in 1934, Karl Radek, then one of the most prominent of Russian spokesmen, stated that "to attempt to represent the foreign policy of the Soviet Union as a continuation of Tsarist policy is ridiculous. Bourgeois writers who do so have not grasped even the purely external manifestations of this policy."[6] To support his position Radek pointed out that the Soviet Union had not tried to seize the Dardanelles, or Port Arthur, or Dairen, and had maintained a uniformly friendly attitude toward Poland and the Baltic states. In view of the course that Soviet policy has taken since he wrote, his examples were singularly ill-chosen to support his thesis, and his own fate is a reminder that many old Bolsheviks could not themselves master the inner workings of the party machinery. In July, 1951, a group of Russian émigrés in the United States, including Alexander Kerensky, wrote in a letter to the *New York Times* that "to confuse Kremlin policies with historic Russia is to miss the heart of the threat confronting the world today." They argued that this confusion identified Stalin with the Russian people, and that this identification might be a fatal error; besides, the Bolsheviks had "created an entirely new species of state, unknown in the annals of human history" — "a party state" in which the people were "a powerless instrument."[7]

The Influence of Marxism-Leninism. The statement of the Russian émigrés tended to underestimate the continuing influence of basic factors and to exaggerate the unique qualities of the Soviet experiment; but it did call attention to another determining element. Something new has been added. The new element, of course, is communism. The

[4] An interesting summary of the observations of the Marquis de Custine was printed in the *Christian Science Monitor,* October 18, 1949.

[5] *The Changing World of Soviet Russia* (New Haven: Yale University Press, 1956), p. 350.

[6] 'The Bases of Soviet Foreign Policy," *Foreign Affairs,* XII (January, 1934), 194.

[7] *New York Times,* July 8, 1951, Sec. 4, p. 8.

leaders of the Soviet Union believe that communism represents the wave of the future, that capitalism will be destroyed by inner collapse and by external pressures, and that surely — though probably only after revolutions and other upheavals while capitalism is in its death throes — the dictatorship of the proletariat and the classless state will be established, leading, in turn, to the withering away of the state. The Marxist-Leninist theory of international relations assumes inevitable conflict between the Communist and non-Communist worlds; it regards imperialism as the last stage, the dying gasp, of capitalism (Lenin wrote a famous book on *Imperialism*); it emphasizes finality of ends and flexibility of means, astute timing of strategy and tactics, and the duality of morality and of standards between Communists and non-Communists; it stresses the either-or philosophy and the absolute impossibility of neutrality.

Stalin never wearied of repeating Lenin's dictum that "without revolutionary theory there can be no revolutionary movement." Many of the most widely circulated Communist writings, including most of the works of Marx and Lenin, are essentially theoretical treatises. They seem heavy and almost meaningless to the uninitiated, but they are carefully studied in Communist-dominated countries and accepted as gospel by the faithful. In a society in which theory and practice are so intertwined such works are of basic significance.

1. A Scientific Doctrine? The allegedly scientific character of Marxism-Leninism, the proclaimed infallibility of its Soviet interpreters, the doctrines of world revolution and inevitable conflict, and in fact its whole approach to international relations makes communism, when based on a strong state led by able and ruthless men, a constantly threatening force in the world. "Soviet diplomacy," insisted Eugene Tarlé, a noted Soviet historian, "is fortified with the scientific theory of Marxism-Leninism. This doctrine lays down the unshakable laws of social development." This doctrine, observed Gerhart Niemeyer, "is at the very core of the regime. It is the cement that holds its adherents together. . . . Marxist doctrine . . . motivates communists chiefly through the certainty of a communist destination of history and the dogma of party infallibility." Actually, as Niemeyer demonstrated, Marxism itself is "torn by an inner contradiction between social analysis and revolutionary will, scholarship and prophesy, rational and irrational elements." Moreover, "in Soviet policy making, one finds that the scientific-analytical elements of Marxism are indeed constantly present but are subjected to continuous re-interpretation, juggling of concepts and distortions of meaning in accordance with changing political intentions of the Party leadership. . . . The scientific part of the doctrine has been abandoned by continuous adaptation to changing political needs." There is no point, however, in trying to convince the Soviets of the irrationality of their doctrine. As Niemeyer says:

> Communist doctrine renders communist minds somewhat impervious to the results of empirical observation and scientific analysis. It makes it possible for them to overlook the inadequacies of the theories on which Soviet policies officially operate, and to ignore the evidence these theories fail to explain and coordinate. . . . The fear of inconsistency does not bother them. They can ride two horses at the same time and confidently await for a kind of dialectic Pegasus that will take off with them in a third direction. . . . Hence communist doctrine, with all its attendant features of semi-rationality, must be expected to continue as the political basis of the Russian regime.[8]

[8] "An Inquiry into Soviet Mentality," paper prepared for the Foreign Policy Research Institute, University of Pennsylvania. Published in revised and expanded form, with the same title, as Foreign Policy Research Institute Series No. 2 (New York: Frederick A. Praeger, 1956). See especially Chapter 2, "Soviet Doctrine." See also Czeslaw Milosz, *The Captive Mind* (New York: Alfred A. Knopf,

2. Inevitable Conflict or Peaceful Co-existence? The Communist doctrine of world revolution has been a major source of misunderstanding and apprehension. As Max Beloff has written:

> The basic inescapable relation of the Soviet state to other states is one of conflict. And for a full understanding of the Soviet attitude, it is necessary to realize that the conflict is one in which the outcome is a foreordained victory for the Soviet State and, with it, the international proletariat. To try to comprehend the Soviet outlook and to dismiss the inevitability of the world proletarian revolution is as idle as to try to comprehend the outlook of medieval man and to dismiss the reality of the Last Judgment.[9]

But does the doctrine of world revolution mean then that war is inevitable between the Communist and non-Communist worlds? Or is peaceful co-existence possible? The behavior of the Soviet Union and the pronouncements of her leaders provide no clear answer to this question. At certain periods, especially when the Soviet Union was interested in collective security and popular fronts to meet the menace of fascism, and during the years of wartime collaboration, the goal of world revolution seemingly faded into the background; at other times the Soviet leaders have appeared to be determined to press forward at all costs. It is little wonder that people who are not skilled in Marxist dialectics cannot fathom the intentions of the men in the Kremlin. Those men speak with many tongues.

Lenin once said: "We are living not merely in a state, but in a system of states, and the existence of the Soviet Republic side by side with imperialistic states for a long time is unthinkable. One or the other must triumph in the end. And before that end supervenes a series of frightful collisions between the Soviet Republic and the bourgeois states will be inevitable." Stalin himself later quoted this statement of Lenin with approval, and then added: "A peaceful victory over capitalism is not to be expected. In present circumstances, capitalism can only be overthrown by means of revolution which will take the form of protracted and violent struggle to the death." Yet Stalin at times took a wholly different tack. As early as 1921 he declared: "The basis of our relations with capitalist countries consists in admitting the co-existence of two opposed systems." In almost every one of the rare interviews which he granted to Westerners he reiterated this theme.[10] In his essay *Economic Problems of Socialism in the U.S.S.R.*, first published in 1952, Stalin expressed the belief that the capitalist countries were not likely to make war upon the Soviet Union because they realized that this would mean the destruction of capitalism. He also affirmed that "the Soviet Union itself would not attack capitalist countries." But, he added, the inevitability of wars between capitalist countries for markets and their desire to drive out their competitors were "stronger than the contradictions between the camp of capitalism and the camp of socialism." Stalin's self-proclaimed grand strategy was to prepare the way for the coming victory of the proletariat everywhere by exploiting and aggravating

---

1953); and Richard Crossman, *The God That Failed* (New York: Harper, 1949). "What must be realized is the continued psychological advantage which the belief in inevitable victory — in working with the inexorable laws of history and not against them — has conferred upon the Communist faithful, and above all the extreme flexibility in daily action which they have derived from the conviction of their own absolute righteousness." Max Beloff, *The Foreign Policy of Soviet Russia, 1929–1941* (New York: Oxford University Press, 1947, 1949), II, 392–393. In a lecture at the University of Pennsylvania on April 19, 1948, Professor Hans Kohn declared: "The Russians do not wish to conquer the world. They wish to save the world, in spite of itself. They must learn to understand that unfortunately, from their point of view, the world is beyond salvation by them."

[9] Beloff, II, 392.

[10] "Historicus," "Stalin on Revolution," *Foreign Affairs,* XXVII (January, 1949), 175–214.

the "three major contradictions which are already undermining the strength of the capitalistic system." These are: the contradictions between proletariat and bourgeoisie, between the imperialist powers themselves, and between the capitalist-imperialist powers and the colonial areas.

In the Khrushchev era the themes of peaceful co-existence and the reduction of tensions were strongly emphasized. Western observers spoke of a "thaw" and expressed the hope that this portended a real and continuing détente between East and West; at the same time they were puzzled by many statements and acts that were not calculated to foster peaceful co-existence and reduce tensions. This apparent contradiction did not exist in Soviet minds. Clearly peaceful co-existence means one thing to non-Communists and quite another to Communists, who regard it in fact as a form of struggle. This point was stressed in an analysis prepared in 1961 by Dr. Joseph Whelan of the Legislative Reference Service of the Library of Congress:

> How can such conduct in world affairs so patently aggressive be consistent with Khrushchev's often proclaimed intention of "peaceful co-existence"? The answer to this question which contrasts so sharply with our conception of "peaceful co-existence" goes to the heart of the Communist outlook on world politics. Khrushchev, like Lenin and Stalin, understands all human activity as a massive, cataclysmic and continuous struggle for life and power, an unending struggle destined to go on until communism triumphs as a new universal order. Normality in life is not a search for rational adjustments of social, economic, and political differences in society; it is a sustained, persistent assault on all other countries until they capitulate in defeat. Khrushchev conceives of world politics as a vortex of dynamic human struggle where force is exalted and power sanctified. He is committed to a strategy of continuous conquest of power. He adheres to a conception of international relationships, alien to American diplomatic traditions: that power relationships among nations are inherently conflicting, not adjustable, and thus it is irrational to view international politics in terms of maintaining the status quo or a particular harmony of interests; that the drive for power is a continuous factor in foreign relations and thus genuine peace between capitalism and communism is unthinkable; and that international politics, even in times of peace, is really a continuation of war by other means. To Khrushchev, therefore, genuine "peaceful co-existence," as we understand it, is impossible, and acquiescence in what we would term the status quo, unthinkable. To him, "peaceful co-existence" is in reality a form of advance; and the status quo, as he told Walter Lippmann, means simply the unimpeded progress of the march of communism.[11]

If there is any misunderstanding in the non-Communist world regarding the meaning of peaceful co-existence in the Communist vocabulary, this can only be attributed to wishful thinking and to a failure to believe that the Communists mean what they say. Khrushchev himself often indicated quite frankly the context in which he used the term. In a famous speech on January 6, 1961, for example, he declared: "Thus, the policy of peaceful co-existence, as regards its social content, is a form of intense economic, political, and ideological struggle of the proletariat against the aggressive forces of imperialism in the international arena."

In his "secret" speech at the Twentieth Party Congress in 1956, in which he denounced Stalin and reversed or reinterpreted a number of basic Soviet doctrines, Khrushchev specifically repudiated the thesis of the "fatalistic inevitability of war" and expressed confidence that the growth of Soviet power, augmented by the Communist bloc of states and the "zone of peace" of nonaligned states,

[11] *Khrushchev and the Balance of World Power*, an analysis prepared for Senator Hubert H. Humphrey by the Legislative Reference Service, Library of Congress, dated June 27, 1961 (87th Cong., 1st Sess., Document No. 66), pp. 15–16.

had become a "mighty force" capable of preventing "the imperialists from unleashing war." "If they try to start it," he added characteristically, "the world camp of socialism" would give them "a smashing rebuff . . . and frustrate their adventurist plans." In an article in the American journal *Foreign Affairs* in 1959, he repeated the theme of "no fatal inevitability of war." At the same time he charged that "Those in the West who believe that war is to their benefit have not yet abandoned their schemes," and he stated that because of this "it is so much the more necessary to continue an active struggle in order that the policy of peaceful co-existence may triumph throughout the world not in words but in deeds."[12]

The issue of inevitable conflict versus peaceful co-existence, therefore, may be somewhat clarified if we bear in mind the meaning of conflict in the Communist vocabulary and the difference between strategy and tactics. The Communists believe that conflict is the normal relationship between the two orders; but to them this does not necessarily mean an all-out global war. They pretend to see a wide no-man's-land between war and peace in which they can maneuver openly and clandestinely in preparing for the final collapse of the capitalist order. Furthermore, as Lenin interpreted history, it "does not have a 'victory or death' quality — there is no urge to seek a final dramatic showdown and a Götterdämmerung finale."[13]

3. *Strategy and Tactics.* Communist literature is replete with references to the importance of strategy and tactics, and to the possibility of frequently shifting policy without abandoning the ultimate goal. Stalin's conception of Communist strategy and tactics was "highly flexible" and rested on "a continual assessment of the status of forces in both the capitalist and the Socialist systems."[14] It is often difficult for a person schooled in neither military concepts nor Communist dialectics to decide when the Soviet Union is undertaking a tactical maneuver and when it is pursuing a strategic aim. It seems probable, however, that the frequent references to the possibility of peaceful co-existence fall within the realm of tactics rather than that of long-term strategy. Certainly in the Soviet view such statements do not negate or even conflict with the ultimate revolutionary goals. "One of the chief conditions to which tactics must be adjusted," according to Stalin, "is the ebb and flow of the forces favoring revolution. Aggressive tactics should be timed with a rising tide; tactics of defense, the assemblage of forces, and even retreat go with an ebbing tide."[15] It is highly important to gauge correctly the direction of the tide.

4. *The Shifting Balance and the Correlation of World Forces.* In his famous speech, "For New Victories of the World Communist Movement," delivered in Moscow on January 6, 1961, at a meeting of party organizations, Khrushchev said:

> Our era is an era of the struggle of two diametrically opposed social systems, an era of socialist revolutions and national liberation revolutions; an era of the collapse of

[12] Nikita S. Khrushchev, "On Peaceful Co-existence," *Foreign Affairs,* XXXVIII (October, 1959), 8–9. In this article Khrushchev maintained that "From its very inception the Soviet state proclaimed peaceful co-existence as the basic principle of its foreign policy." The next issue of *Foreign Affairs* carried a reply by George F. Kennan: "Peaceful Co-existence: A Western View," *Foreign Affairs,* XXXVIII (January, 1960), 171–190.

[13] Moore, p. 399. See also "X," "The Sources of Soviet Conduct," *Foreign Affairs,* XXV (July, 1947), 566–582; and Waldemar Gurian, "Permanent Features of Soviet Foreign Policy," *The Year Book of World Affairs, 1947* (London, 1947), I, 1–39.

[14] "Historicus," p. 205.

[15] *Ibid.,* p. 206. It was this point, among others, which George F. Kennan, the intellectual father of the "containment" policy, had in mind when he proposed a policy for meeting Soviet pressures in his famous article in *Foreign Affairs* on the "Sources of Soviet Conduct." Similar assumptions lay behind the frequent references of Secretary of State Acheson and other prominent American spokesmen to the necessity of creating "situations of strength."

> capitalism and of liquidation of the colonial system; an era of the change to the road to socialism by more and more nations; and of the triumph of socialism and communism on a world scale. . . . Comrades, we live at a splendid time. Communism has become the inevitable force of our century.

Again and again Khrushchev propounded the thesis that "the correlation of world forces" had shifted decisively, and irrevocably, to the "socialist camp." "All the world," he prophesied, "will come to Communism. History does not ask whether you want it or not." The West, he said, must recognize the central "fact" that the balance of world power had shifted, that the emergence of the "world system of socialism" had radically altered the distribution of power. In view of this "fact," he suggested at the Twentieth Party Congress in 1956, the doctrine of "capitalist encirclement," a favorite thesis of the Stalin era, was no longer applicable; and at the Twenty-first Party Congress, nearly three years later, he said: "The situation in the world has fundamentally changed. Capitalist encirclement of our country no longer exists."

Khrushchev's confidence was apparently based on the growth in the economic and military strength of the Soviet Union and the successes of the international Communist movement, even outside the Communist world, and on the difficulties which non-Communist countries of the West were experiencing in domestic affairs and in their dealings with one other, with the developing nations of the Third World, and with the Communist states. His assessment may have been quite erroneous, based more on images than on reality; but it nevertheless reflected an outlook and a state of mind that had to be weighed carefully in the international equation. As one Western student of Soviet affairs observed in 1961:

> Khrushchev's total image of the world as he sees it and his belief in the correctness and righteousness of his shifting balance thesis are the most critically relevant facts in world affairs today. . . . The image in Khrushchev's mind . . . is the favorable "correlation of world forces." To him, this *is* reality and as such *is* the basis for all decision making in the Soviet state. It provides the general conceptual framework for determining broad foreign policy lines. It is the most essential element in the entire Soviet foreign policy process.[16]

5. *"Socialism in One Country" and World Revolution.* In the struggle between Stalin and Trotsky which followed Lenin's death the major issue was Stalin's view that primary emphasis should be on building "socialism in one country" against Trotsky's view that the goal of world revolution should neither be subordinated nor shelved. With Stalin's victory the theory was reconstructed to fit the facts. Henceforth the Soviet Union would be regarded as the base for world revolution; there could be no conflict between the goal of building socialism in one country and that of world revolution. This dual objective was proclaimed by Stalin on innumerable occasions. The following statement is typical: "The goal is to consolidate the dictatorship of the proletariat in one country, using it as a base for the overthrow of imperialism in all countries. Revolution spreads beyond the limits of one country; the epoch of world revolution has begun."[17]

While Stalin was in power this concept was not seriously challenged. With the exception of Yugoslavia, all Communist states, including China, deferred to Moscow, and often boasted that they belonged "to the world socialist camp, headed by the Soviet Union." In the post-Stalin era, however, this interpretation is seldom advanced outside of the Soviet Union. The relations of Moscow with other Communist political regimes and of the CPSU with other Com-

[16] *Khrushchev and the Balance of World Power*, pp. 12–13. Italics in original.

[17] Quoted in "Historicus," p. 198.

munist parties have altered greatly. Moscow may still be the head-center of world communism, but it no longer exercises the dominance which it long enjoyed.

6. *Nationalism and Polycentrism in the Communist World.* The theory that communism is an international doctrine, appealing to the proletariat all over the world, has become increasingly unrealistic, as one Communist state after another, including the Soviet Union, has shown that it is not immune to the strong pressures of nationalism characteristic of the present age. Each Communist country is a nation-state as well as a member of "the world socialist camp", and nationalism has often been invoked in times of crisis within the Communist bloc as well as in relations with the non-Communist states. Indeed, these nationalist tendencies raise questions about how much of the ideological flavor and messianic drive of world communism remains. It is perhaps well to remember that while communism is an organized international conspiracy, with tentacles in most of the countries and regions of the world, it is also a movement which has established various national bases and is supported by formidable national power.

Growing nationalism within the Communist world has led to the emergence of a "second Rome" in the Communist movement; to manifestations of greater independence from the Soviet Union among the so-called satellite states of Eastern Europe; and to the phenomenon referred to as polycentrism, one of the most significant new developments in international relations. The Communist bloc is no longer a monolithic one. Russia is still by far the most powerful state in the Communist world, but it no longer receives the near-universal and unquestioning allegiance of Communist states or parties.

The growing rift between the Soviet Union and China has split the entire Communist world and most Communist parties. It is impossible to tell how deep-seated or how enduring this schism is, or what its consequences will be. It seems to stem from many causes, including historic rivalries and suspicions; competing national interests; differences in stages of economic, political, and ideological development; rivalry for leadership within the "world socialist camp"; disagreements over the proper interpretation of the gospel of Marxism-Leninism and over strategy and tactics, within and outside the Communist world. It may be more of a power struggle than a debate on the true interpretation of the faith. If so, the Chinese charges of Soviet "revisionism" and the Russian charges of Chinese "adventurism" may merely camouflage deeper issues. On the other hand, it is also possible, as many Western skeptics predict, that the dispute may be largely verbal fencing and shadow-boxing, and that Russia and China will bury their feud and unite again to achieve the worldwide victory of "socialism." Their differences seem to be less ideological than power-political, concerned with tactics rather than with strategy. The same may be true of Eastern Europe, despite the heartening degree of national self-assertion that now seems to be developing. In short, the Communist states may draw together again, for common aims and at the expense of those nations and peoples that do not wish to follow the Communist road to "salvation"; but for the moment, at least, polycentrism and not unity is the most obvious characteristic of the Communist world and the international Communist movement.

7. *Relations with the Third World.* Until the emergence of many new states in Asia and Africa in the post-World War II era, Soviet doctrine divided the world into two hostile camps — the "socialist camp," headed by the Soviet Union, and the "capitalist camp," led by the United States — and no "third road" existed. Now, however, the Soviets are very conscious of the existence of a Third World, the world of the emerging nations. There they seem to be

competing not only with the "capitalist" states of the West, but also with the other Communist giant, Red China.

For some time the Russian and other Communist parties seemed to be in agreement regarding "three large regions of global Communism, somewhat along the lines of a plan developed by the Italian Communist Party in 1956–57. According to this plan the Soviet sphere embraced Eastern Europe, Western Germany, Mongolia, North Korea, India, Pakistan, Afghanistan, and Iran; the Chinese sphere included North Viet Nam and the non-Communist countries of mainland Southeast Asia; and a sphere under the tutelage of the Italian Communist Party, the largest outside of the Communist bloc, encompassed Communist parties in North Africa, Greece, and Portugal. Most of the Western world, all of Africa south of the Sahara, much of the Middle East, and the important Southeast Asian state of Indonesia were not included in this demarcation."[18]

With the struggle between the Soviet Union and China extending to Communist parties in most of the countries of the world, the division of "regions of global Communism" seems to have become quite blurred. The Soviet Union and Communist China are directing a great deal of attention to the new states of Africa and Asia and to the older states of Latin America. They are using all the techniques of persuasion and coercion in their well-stocked arsenal: massive propaganda barrages, economic, political, cultural, and psychological offensives, appeals to local pride and prejudices, infiltration, subversion, and other weapons of political warfare. They play upon the appealing themes of independence, nationalism, peace, and nonalignment. They endorse and give support to "wars of national liberation."

> From the Soviet point of view the countries of Asia, Africa, and Latin America fall into three categories. The first category includes the dependent territories and territories in which, though they are independent states, a European minority rules over a non-European majority. . . . Here the aim of Soviet policy is to accelerate progress toward independence, or toward overthrow of European rule. The second category includes countries which are independent but allied to or closely associated with the West. . . . Here the aim of Soviet policy is to bring about a change of foreign policy, leading to the adoption of neutralism. The third category is composed of the independent neutralist states. . . . The aim of such states, in the Soviet view, should be to win "economic independence," which consists in the rupture of all significant economic ties with the West and the development of far-reaching links with the "socialist camp." . . . The aims of Soviet policy in the underdeveloped countries may be summed up as follows: to expedite colonies toward independence, independ allied countries toward neutralism, neutralist countries toward national democracies, and finally convert national democracies into people's democracies.[19]

The category of "national democracies" was a new one, first introduced into Communist terminology in the declaration issued at the close of the conference of representatives of 81 Communist parties, held in Moscow in November–December, 1960. Cuba may belong in this category, although it seems to have moved into the status of a people's democracy; Indonesia prior to 1965 seemed to be close to the status of a "national democracy," and from time to time Mali, Ghana, Guinea, and the U.A.R. have exhibited some of the distinctive features of this classification.

Ever since the Second Comintern Congress and the first Congress of the Peoples of the East, both held in 1920, the Soviet Union

[18] David J. Dallin, *Soviet Foreign Policy after Stalin* (Philadelphia: J. B. Lippincott Co., 1961), p. 459.

[19] Hugh Seton-Watson, "Soviet Foreign Policy in 1961," *International Relations,* II (October, 1961), 205, 206.

has been interested in "the colonial question" and has supported "wars of national liberation" in the dependent areas of Asia and Africa. Today most of the former colonies in these areas have gained political independence; but the Soviet Union still seeks to identify herself with the developing nations' programs for genuine economic and social freedom and to champion their inmost aspirations and hopes. Possibly one of her main aims is to undermine the Atlantic alliance, not only by exploiting fissions and weaknesses in the West, but also by piecemeal successes in Asia, Africa, and Latin America. In any event, the Soviet Union is a factor to be reckoned with in the Third World.

8. Consequences of Marxist-Leninist Theory. Soviet foreign policy may not differ fundamentally from that of tsarist Russia; but certainly, as Max Beloff stated, "an explanation of Soviet policy which dismisses the Revolution would seem to be an explanation which neither the facts nor Soviet writings warrant."[20] It would seem that Soviet activities about the borderlands of Russia since 1939, which have resulted in the annexation of some 400,000 square miles of territory, the establishment of satellite states in the Balkans and in Central Europe, and the extension of Soviet influence in Asia, could all be explained, on the one hand, as being motivated by a desire for security and for the prevention of encirclement by a hostile capitalist world or, on the other hand, as nothing more dangerous than an unusually successful application of the traditional expansionist policies of the tsars. Unfortunately, neither explanation seems quite adequate. It would be folly to overlook the treatment meted out to the satellite states and the many evidences that the Soviet appetite, sharpened by a revolutionary dynamism, is by no means satiated. This brings us again to the disturbing consequences of the Marxist-Leninist view of the world. These consequences were well stated by Barrington Moore, Jr.:

> Russian expansion can be explained very largely without references to Marxist ideological factors. For the most part, each step in Soviet expansion can be considered a logical move to counter a specific actual or potential enemy. . . . What, then, is there left for the Marxist ideological factor to explain? This much at least: the Marxist-Leninist tradition has made it very difficult to reach a *modus vivendi* with the Soviets. . . . A belief in the inherently aggressive tendencies of modern capitalism obviously excludes any agreement except an armed truce of undetermined duration.[21]

Additional Influences. A study of Soviet foreign policy must take note of a number of additional influences. Here we can mention and briefly comment on only four of these: "the existing structure of international relationships"; domestic conditions; personalities; and the structure of the government.

The Bolshevik regime in its early months seemed determined not to conform to the rules of the international game as laid down by capitalist powers. It gave abundant evidence of this feeling: repudiation of the national debt, publication of the secret treaties, and appeals to peoples of foreign states over the heads of their governments. But the Soviet Union has had to have many dealings with other nations and with international organizations. "On the whole," Barrington Moore stated, "Soviet policy has been characterized by a series of adjustments to the existing structure of international relationships, which the U.S.S.R. has been unable to overthrow and replace by a new world community of toilers' states."[22] Thus the Soviet leaders, though suspicious, reluctant, and in-

[20] Beloff, II, 390.

[21] Moore, p. 392.

[22] *Ibid.*, p. 405.

experienced participants in world politics, have resorted to alliances, measures of collective security, intervention, balance of power practices, and other standard techniques of Western diplomacy.

Although the Soviet leaders seem to exercise complete and unquestioned control over the Soviet sphere, they are nevertheless very sensitive to domestic happenings. The attention and effort they devote to internal propaganda offer ample evidence of this. They are determined that the Soviet Union shall have the powerful economic base which a modern great power must possess, and that public discipline and morale shall be equal to any demands. No careful interpretation of the sources of Soviet behavior in foreign affairs can neglect the implications of such internal developments as the New Economic Policy of 1921–28, the Stalin-Trotsky feud, the Five-Year Plans,[23] the liquidation of kulaks, the collectivization of agriculture, the political purges of 1936–38, the cultural purges in the postwar period, the agricultural crisis in recent years, and the "downgrading" of Stalin after 1956.

Although communism holds that the individual is important only as a member of a group, the role of personalities in shaping Soviet foreign policy has been very important. The leadership — including the revamped Presidium — has shifted from the "Old Bolsheviks" to new men, some of whom Stalin gathered around himself, while others have emerged only in the post-Stalin years. The "Old Bolsheviks" were trained in the school of bitter experience, whereas most of the younger group, said Bertram Wolfe, "never knew the wide dreams and humane ideals of the nineteenth century intelligentsia, the feverish disputation, hope and wretchedness of the tsarist underground, prison and exile, nor the 'heroic days' of the storming of the Winter Palace and the Kremlin." Instead, continued Wolfe, "they were wholly formed in the Stalinist fight for a monopoly of power . . . under the new régime of bureaucratic totalitarianism."[24] The growing importance of younger men may account for the "new look" in Soviet diplomacy, but the roles of individuals cannot be determined, at least now, as Theodore White makes clear in a forceful simile:

> Of all those areas which Russian secrecy guards, none is more jealously sheltered than the inner area of decision-making where personalities, ambitions, rivalries and emotions clash. . . . Like subterranean monsters, Russia's masters grapple with each other in the deep, beyond the range of sight and only an occasional stinking bubble breaking to the surface tells us that a struggle is going on at all.[25]

Stalin once remarked that "the Politburo is the highest organ not of the state but of the Party, and the Party is the highest directing force of the state." When it is remembered that the Communist Party of the Soviet Union is one of highly restricted membership, the power of the party, working through the Politburo (formerly Presidium), the Central Committee, and the Secretariat, becomes apparent. Not only is that power unchallenged, but the decisions are made in secret party meetings where "Russia's masters grapple with each other in the deep." Thus the Russian Communists have contrived a monopoly of power in a monolithic state. But they have not been able to "provide effective machinery for the orderly transmission of authority." After Lenin's death in 1924 the chief contenders for power

[23] For example, as Max Beloff stated, "the great internal readjustment known as the First Five-Year Plan provides the master-key to every aspect of Russian policy in the years immediately following 1929." I, 27.

[24] Bertram D. Wolfe, "A New Look at the Soviet 'New Look,'" *Foreign Affairs,* XXIII (January, 1955), 184–185.

[25] *Fire in the Ashes: Europe in Mid-Century* (New York: William Sloane Associates, 1953), pp. 324–325.

were Stalin and Trotsky, and the former won out only after a prolonged and bitter struggle. Stalin's death in 1953 unleashed a struggle among Beria, Malenkov. Molotov, Kaganovich, and Khrushchev.

"The abrupt end of Nikita Khrushchev's reign" on October 14, 1964, "marked, without any doubt, the beginning of a prolonged, complex, and turbulent struggle for power in the Soviet Union."[26] Three veteran Communist leaders assumed the top positions in the party and the state: Leonid Brezhnev as First Secretary of the CPSU, Aleksei Kosygin as premier, and Anastas Mikoyan as president. Some younger members of the Presidium, notably Nikolai Podgorny and Alexsandr Shelepin, both secretaries of the Central Committee, and at least two nonmembers of the Presidium, Marshal Rodion Malinovsky, the head of the armed forces, and Vladimir Semichastny, head of the secret police, seemed to wield special influence and power. In December, 1965, Mikoyan retired as president, and was succeeded by Podgorny. It was difficult to determine whether Podgorny had been promoted, or had been "kicked upstairs." Shelepin, in what appeared a definite demotion, gave up his post as vice premier of the government and chairman of the Committee for Party-State Control, although he continued to be a secretary of the CPSU.

Thus the leadership picture raises many questions. Will collective leadership again give way to a single dominant personality? If so, how will he assert his control and his "legitimacy"? Will the Soviet system be able to develop a procedure for the orderly transmission of authority, or at least one more clearly defined and less primitive that the recurrent "prolonged, complex, and turbulent struggle for power?"[27]

Soviet Diplomacy from Brest-Litovsk to San Francisco

The General Course. The Bolsheviks had no sooner seized power in 1917 than they faced the issue of survival. The making of a separate peace with Germany posed the first major test. The choice lay between a betrayal of revolutionary principles by making peace with an imperialist power and the continuation of a war that might well end in Russian defeat and the extinction of the Bolshevik regime. Lenin spoke for peace, and by a narrow margin he carried the day. Presumably he believed that some of the harshest features of the Treaty of Brest-Litovsk could be evaded; and he may have foreseen the defeat of Germany, with the consequent nullification of the entire treaty. The second test involved the Bolsheviks' capacity to maintain their regime against revolting anti-Bolsheviks, notably White Russians, supported by small Allied forces at several points. Even before succeeding in this effort they had in 1919 organized the Comintern and started it on its career of promoting communism outside Russia.

Many states, including the United States and most of the countries of Latin America, refused to recognize the new regime. Gradually, however, some states began to relent, and in 1922 the Soviet Republic was invited to the Genoa Conference. In the same year Russia and Germany, both outcasts in the family of nations, reached an agreement of friendship and trade in the Treaty of Rapallo, followed by a nonaggression pact in 1926 that foreshadowed a more famous agreement of the same kind in 1939. Meantime, in 1923 the Soviet Republic had joined other Socialist republics to become the Union of

[26] Severyn Bialer, "Twenty-four Men Who Rule Russia," *New York Times Magazine,* November 1, 1964, pp. 27, 104.

[27] "Two days after Stalin's death on March 5, 1953, the first list of post-Stalin leaders was made public by the Kremlin. It included twenty men who occupied all the key positions in the party and the government bureaucracy. . . . Only two (Mikoyan and Suslov) outlasted Khrushchev and are now in the front ranks of post-Khrushchev leadership." *Ibid.*, p. 27. This article, written shortly after Khrushchev's fall, listed "Twenty-four Men Who Rule Russia." It will be interesting to see how many of these men manage to stay on top of the Soviet power struggle in the coming years.

Soviet Socialist Republics. The new state was quite willing to make agreements with other countries: "It has been calculated that between 1920 and 1937 the Soviet entered into 234 bilateral and 57 multilateral international agreements of all sorts."[28] Many of these were nonaggression pacts. The Communist government had been recognized by most states by 1927, but American recognition did not come until 1933.

The victory of Stalin over Trotsky in intraparty politics inaugurated a long period of building a strong Russia at the cost of a program for immediate world revolution. Consequently, while concentrating on the first objective with a series of Five-Year Plans, the Soviet Union sought peace with other states through repeated proposals for disarmament, through support of the Kellogg-Briand Pact of 1928, through encouraging an anti-democracy campaign in 1935, and, after a dozen years of hostility, through joining the League of Nations in 1934 and for five years leading the movement for peace, disarmament, and collective security. As the aggressive intent of the Fascist states became clear, she proposed a multilateral Eastern pact of mutual assistance, she signed mutual assistance agreements with France and Czechoslovakia, and she urged strong action by the League to defeat aggression in Ethiopia and Spain. Whatever their motives, from 1934 until 1939 the Russians were the only powerful friends of collective security to be found in the world. But they were not powerful enough. Appeasement at Munich in 1938 destroyed whatever remaining confidence the Russians had in the British and the French, and thereby sowed the seeds of the Nazi-Soviet Pact of August, 1939. For almost a year Soviet leaders drew back into diplomatic seclusion, played a wait-and-see game, and, as later revelations showed, lent an ear to the simultaneous wooing of Germany and of Britain and France.

[28] Warren B. Walsh, "Soviet Foreign Policy from Petrograd to Yalta," in Stuart Gerry Brown, ed., *Great Issues* (New York: Harper, 1951), p. 262. See also T. A. Taracouzio, *War and Peace in Soviet Diplomacy* (New York: The Macmillan Company, 1940), pp. 315–342; and Michael T. Florinsky, "The Soviet Union and International Agreements," *The Political Science Quarterly*, LXI (March, 1946), 61–89.

Soviet Policies in the Middle East. In the early days of their power the Communists showed some signs of abandoning traditional Russian aspirations in the Middle East, but they soon responded to the attraction of geographical and strategic considerations. The new dream, like the old, was control of the Turkish Straits and access to the Mediterranean, a port in the warm waters of the Persian Gulf, and a safe and easy route to India.

The new Russia and the new Turkey remained on friendly terms for twenty years after World War I. Then, in 1939, the Soviet Union reverted sharply to the policy of the tsars. In 1945, after several years of deteriorating relations, she announced her intention of terminating the twenty-year-old treaty of friendship; and at the Potsdam Conference later in the same year she persuaded Britain and the United States to agree to seek a revision of the Montreux Convention of 1936, which had fixed the status of the Straits in a way pleasing to Turkey. Farther east, Persia had effected a withdrawal of Bolshevik penetration in 1921 by agreeing to permit Russian troops to move in if a third power tried "to use Persian territory as a base of operations against Russia." Later the Russians vainly sought an oil concession in northern Persia. After the signing of a nonaggression pact in 1933 relations remained unchanged until World War II. Russian and British troops moved into Iran (the name was changed in 1935) to frustrate Nazi designs; and at the conclusion of the Teheran Conference in 1943 Churchill, Roosevelt, and Stalin issued a statement thanking Iran for her cooperation during the war, pledging economic assistance, and affirming their desire for the continuance of the country's sovereignty and territorial integrity. Soviet-Afghan relations have generally been peaceful. The two states signed a treaty of alliance and friendship in 1921, a treaty of neutrality and nonaggression in 1926, and a commercial agreement in 1936. No Anglo-Russian frictions developed in Afghanistan during World War II, as they did in Iran.

In their early days the Soviets made a strong bid to win the support of the Muslims of the Near East for communism, but their propaganda was poorly suited to peoples still living under semi-feudal conditions. Soviet tactics thereupon shifted from preaching class struggle to inciting discontented minorities. Again the failure was almost total.

Soviet Policies in the Far East. By the Treaty of Peking of 1860 Russia picked up some 350,000 square miles of Chinese land in the Amur region which, added to her own northern areas, gave her a dominating position in northeastern Asia. She founded Vladivostok, also in 1860; she built the Trans-Siberian Railroad in the 1890's; she obtained concessions for the Chinese Eastern Railway in 1896; and she won control of Port Arthur and Dairen in two agreements of 1898. But by these thrusts she put herself at odds with the rising state of Japan as well as with Great Britain and other European powers with spheres of interest in China. The clash of the expansionist policies of Russia and Japan culminated in the Russo-Japanese War of 1904, which cost Russia heavily in prestige and territory. For some two decades thereafter her influence and activity in the Far East were at a low ebb. Japan even achieved a temporary foothold in eastern Siberia from 1918 to 1922 while the new Russian regime was weak, after which the Russians began to regain their strength in the area. When Japan sought to expand her influence from her bases in Korea and Manchuria in the early 1930's, the two states engaged in "semi-war" from 1933 until 1941, when a neutrality pact gave them a four-year truce. When the Soviet Union declared war on Japan in August, 1945, her troops occupied Manchuria with little opposition, placing her in a strong position to fill the power vacuum resulting from the complete defeat of Japan less than a week later. Moreover, she was then ready and willing to lend a hand to the Communists of China.

During the period of Soviet weakness, 1917–24, China tried to reduce the Russian pressure on her border areas, but she too was weak. Her great revolutionary leader, Sun Yat-sen, was in fact so disturbed over the steady deterioration of the Chinese Republic and the ineffectiveness of his own party, the Kuomintang, that he sought help from the outside. Rebuffed by the Western powers, he turned to Russia, which sent advisers and organizers. But Sun Yat-sen died in 1925, and two years later his successor, Chiang Kai-shek, broke the "First United Front," driving the Russian Communists not only out of the Kuomintang but out of the country as well. For the next decade Russian interference in China was slight and was largely confined to border areas. In 1935 the Chinese Communists offered to join with the Kuomintang in resisting Japanese encroachments, and for the next ten years relations between the Soviet Union and Chiang Kai-shek's government were outwardly placid, embracing a nonaggression pact and considerable material aid by Russia to China. Apprehensions raised by the Nazi–Soviet Pact of 1939 were relieved by the Nazi attack on Russia, but the Soviet–Japanese neutrality pact of 1941 left China alone in the war against Japan on the mainland of Asia. In one of the most controversial incidents of World War II, Roosevelt at the Yalta Conference acceded to Stalin's demand for an enhanced status for Russia in the Far East at the expense of China, and he later pressured Chiang Kai-shek into acquiescence. Nevertheless, the Soviet Union promised to respect Chinese sovereignty and to give moral and material support to the Nationalist Government.

Relations with Germany, 1939–41. The German occupation of Czechoslovakia in March, 1939, left few doubts regarding Hitler's intentions or the imminence of war. At this critical stage the Soviet leaders appear to have appraised their position something like this: We cannot count on the British and the French. We have left three possible courses: (1) Resist Germany and enter a war in which we may have no powerful allies and for which we are unprepared. (2) Do nothing, but let Hitler add Polish resources and manpower to his own and station his great war machine on hundreds of miles of the Russian border, poised for the long-advertised *Drang nach Osten.* (3) Collaborate with Hitler for the time being, thus avoiding immediate war, allowing us time for greater rearmament, giving us a buffer zone, and diverting to us some of the Polish potentials that would otherwise go to Hitler. This course will at the same time let the Axis states and the democratic states exhaust their strength against each other, precisely as each of those groups of states would willingly have us do with the other group.

On August 24, 1939, a joint communiqué announcing the Nazi-Soviet Nonaggression Pact stunned most of the world. Until June, 1941, the Soviet Union appeared to collaborate with Nazi Germany, but in fact relations soon became strained. Never trusting or complacent, the Russians continued the speedup of military and industrial preparations. Warnings poured into Moscow from many sources, including Britain, France, and the United States, that the Germans might be planning a surprise attack. This blow fell on Sunday, June 22.[29]

"The Strange Alliance." In a single day Hitler and the Communist propagandists transformed "the Imperialist War" into "the Great Patriotic War." Summoned by their leaders to rise in defense of "Mother Russia" — not, be it noted, to defend communism or promote world revolution — the soldiers and plain people of Russia responded magnificently to the challenge of the Nazi invaders. Churchill and Roosevelt instantly proclaimed support of Russia, and Stalin assured his countrymen of "loyal allies in the peoples of Europe and America." The United States alone sent more than eleven billion dollars in Lend-Lease aid to the U.S.S.R.

On the surface "the strange alliance" worked well; but we now know that relations were never easy or truly cordial. The Soviet Government gave little credit to its Western allies for the materials which it received, treated their representatives with coolness and restricted their movements, was almost pathologically secretive about its military needs, and refused to allow the Americans and British to use Russian airfields and other facilities freely. We also know now that the Soviets made a number of peace overtures to Germany in 1943 and 1944,[30] and that they were continually and consciously making plans for exploiting the postwar situation.

During the war several conferences of top-ranking leaders of Britain, Russia, and the United States were held, notably the meeting of the foreign ministers in Moscow in October, 1943, and the two conferences of Churchill and Roosevelt with Stalin, at Tehe-

[29] For a penetrating analysis of the background and causes of the German attack on Russia in June, 1941, see John A. Lukács, "The Story Behind Hitler's 'Biggest Blunder,'" *New York Times Magazine,* June 17, 1951.

[30] Walsh, p. 275. In the captured files of the German Foreign Office were secret documents relating to Nazi–Soviet peace overtures in 1943. The Russians themselves have repeatedly charged that the British and Americans secretly negotiated with the Germans between 1941 and 1943. In the fourth reply to the published documents on *Nazi-Soviet Relations, 1939–1941,* the Russians listed specific instances when, they alleged, British or American representatives met with German agents for the purpose of "betraying their Russian Ally." See "Falsifiers of History and Historical Notes," summarized in the *New York Times,* February 17, 1948.

ran in November–December, 1943, and at Yalta in February, 1945.[31] The avowed purpose of all these conferences was to agree on concerted measures for winning the war and for preparing for the peace that would follow. At Moscow Russia joined with Britain and the United States in announcing a determination to establish "a general international organization . . . for the maintenance of peace and security" after the war. At Teheran, Churchill, Roosevelt, and Stalin announced their "complete agreement" on plans for the defeat of Germany. At Yalta the three leaders agreed on common policies for the occupation and control of Germany, for establishing order in Europe and assisting peoples formerly under Nazi domination to regain their freedom, for Russia's entry into the war against Japan in return for major concessions in the Far East, and for convening a United Nations Conference to draft a charter for a new world organization.

Within two weeks after the Yalta Conference the Soviet Union began to violate the Declaration on Liberated Europe. In direct defiance of the spirit and letter of the Yalta Agreements, Vyshinsky undertook a mission to Southeastern Europe for the purpose of imposing Soviet-controlled regimes on the countries of that area. Shortly afterwards the Soviet Union showed an equally flagrant disregard of her commitments in the agreements on Poland and Germany. Instead of encouraging the formation of a "Polish Provisional Government of National Unity," she gave her full support to the Lublin regime which she had sponsored, and concluded with this regime a treaty confirming Poland's new western boundary, which the United States and Britain had refused to recognize. She also began to give every indication of ignoring her agreements regarding four-power control of Germany. Toward the end of his life President Roosevelt, who had gambled heavily on continued Russian cooperation in the post-war period, made several strong protests, including direct appeals to Stalin. They were ignored.

The Post-Yalta Shift: 1945–53

For at least eight years — until 1953 — postwar Soviet foreign policy was characterized by growing hostility to the West, by increasing tendencies toward noncooperation and isolation, by consolidation of the Soviet orbit, and by general intransigence. These tendencies were encouraged by Soviet reinterpretation of national interests, especially the means to security, and by the strong reaction of the leading states of the non-Communist world to Russian moves and techniques. They were undoubtedly also influenced by the re-emphasis on Marxist-Leninist doctrinairism and the subordination of all cultural and intellectual activity to the interests of the Communist Party.

Until 1947 or 1948 the general orientation of Soviet policy was somewhat obscured by the subtle and indirect means with which it was being forged, and by the tendency of non-Communist statesmen to confuse tactics with strategy. From 1948, when the Communists became more overt in their propaganda and policies both at home and abroad, until the death of Stalin in March 1953, the emphasis was clearly on conflict. During this period the cold war became "hot war" on a limited scale in Korea, and it threatened to erupt into total war at almost any moment. It is apparent now that the Soviet leaders were undertaking, as a conscious and deliberate policy, what Philip Mosely called a "post-Yalta shift from limited co-operation to an attitude of sharp rivalry."

Stalin's death was followed by evidences of a struggle for leadership and by the emergence of internal economic problems and of more flexible and cooperative policies within the Soviet orbit and toward non-Communist states. The repeated Soviet emphasis on the

[31] The texts of the official statements issued at the Moscow, Teheran, and Yalta Conferences, and the secret agreements made at Yalta, are printed in Ruhl J. Bartlett, ed., *The Record of American Diplomacy* (New York: Alfred A. Knopf, 1947), pp. 658–671.

theme of "peaceful co-existence," and the Soviet concessions which made possible truces for Korea and Indo-China, a state treaty for Austria, the renewal of discussions on disarmament and on the future of Germany, and the "summit" meeting in the summer of 1955, encouraged many observers to hope that the "new look" in Soviet policy presaged a happier era in international relations. But most seasoned observers warned that the "new look" was not so new after all, and that there was little evidence that the new leaders of the Soviet Union were following different objectives from those which were laid down by Lenin and Stalin and which had been pursued relentlessly with only an occasional shift in tactics.

The Renewed Emphasis on Marxist-Leninist Doctrinairism. The general intransigence of postwar Soviet foreign policy, its tendencies toward isolation, suspicion, and aloofness, and its strong anti-Western and particularly anti-American bias, may be explained as a reflection of the basic Marxist-Leninist interpretation of international relations—including inevitable conflict and "capitalist encirclement."

Statements of Soviet leaders support this interpretation. One of the earliest of these was Kalinin's address in Moscow early in 1945, in which he warned of the danger of "capitalist encirclement" after the war. Perhaps the most significant statement was Stalin's election speech of February 9, 1946, in which he rejected the idea of wholehearted cooperation with other countries and forcefully restated the Marxist-Leninist thesis that conflict was inevitable as long as capitalism survived.

In September, 1947, Zhdanov called upon Communists in all countries to lead the fight against the "imperialist aggressors," and proclaimed the now familiar thesis of the two camps, the "imperialist" camp headed by the United States and the "anti-imperialist" camp led by the Soviet Union. Early in 1949 the Soviet Ministry of Foreign Affairs declared in an official statement that the North Atlantic Treaty was convincing proof "that the ruling circles of the United States and Great Britain have adopted an openly aggressive political course, the final aim of which is to establish by force Anglo-American domination over the world, a course which is fully in accord with the policy of aggression, the policy of unleashing a new war pursued by them."[32] Pronouncements of this same tenor were particularly virulent in 1952. The effects of the renewed emphasis on Marxist-Leninist doctrinairism were even more marked on the domestic scene than in international relations. Apparently the Soviet leaders concluded that drastic measures were necessary to purify and strengthen the party, to rehabilitate the country, and to steel the Russian people to new endeavors and new sacrifices. "Stalin, it would seem, made an even greater mistake in allowing the Red Army to see Europe than in allowing Europe to see his Army."[33] The "iron curtain" was lowered from Stettin to Trieste and soon divided the Communist from the non-Communist areas in more than a territorial sense.

Contacts with the West were reduced to a minimum, and were in fact confined almost exclusively to a few officials. Western diplomats in the Soviet Union were restricted in their movements and allowed to see only certain Russian officials. A few newspaper correspondents led a lonely existence in Moscow and some of the satellite states, ever subject to expulsion at any moment or to arbitrary arrest and imprisonment.[34]

[32] The full text of this statement was printed in the *USSR Information Bulletin*, IX (February 11, 1949), 79–87.

[33] Sergius Yakobson, "Postwar Historical Research in the Soviet Union," *The Annals* of the American Academy of Political and Social Science, CCLXIII (May, 1949), 126.

[34] For official U.S. protests and other action in the Vogeler case, see issues of the *Department of State Bulletin* of January–March, 1950. Vogeler was released in 1951. For Vogeler's own story, see *I Was Stalin's Prisoner*, with Leigh White (New York: Harcourt, Brace, 1952).

Control of Cultural and Intellectual Activity. The same considerations led to cultural purges. Soviet leaders undertook to determine correct economics, correct mathematics, correct history, correct international law, correct biology, correct music, and correct art. By their decisions the greatest authorities in these and other fields were silenced or forced to recant. Among the victims of the Jovian displeasure of the party hierarchy were persons world famous in their special fields — Varga the economist,[35] Shostakovich the composer, Marr the linguistics expert, Alexandrov the historian-philosopher, and Orbeli the biologist. Other victims of the hierarchy's wrath were the Mendelian theory of heredity and, indeed, objectivity in every field. "Soviet scholars, the party insisted, were to be trusted, active Marxists, militant, partisan, and intolerant." A certain kind of "objectivity," however, was encouraged. "Partisanship in the proletarian world view," stated an official mouthpiece, "did not exclude objectivity in the study of facts, but on the contrary presupposed it, since the class interests of the proletariat do not contradict but coincide with the objective course of historical development."[36] The exact meaning of this "upside-down language" became even more elusive when, in 1948, "objectivism" was condemned as "an exaggerated attachment to facts."

In his capacity as "Politburo arbiter of intellectual production," Andrei Zhdanov frequently laid down the correct line for Soviet intellectuals. On many occasions he demanded that Soviet intellectuals beware of foreign influences and form an ideological front in support of the Communist Party and Marxist-Leninist doctrine.[37]

Scholars who worked in particularly dangerous fields tried to lessen their occupational hazards by adulation of the party leaders and by avoiding as far as possible any subject which might be remotely controversial. Some of the major works in history and allied fields were hardly more than propaganda tracts, useful only as proof of the mental straitjacket which even the greatest of Soviet thinkers had to wear. This stricture could be laid on such potentially important works as the three-volume *History of Soviet Diplomacy,* edited by V. P. Potiemkine. The difficulties of laying down the official party line are illustrated by the fate of the great multivolumed *Soviet Encyclopedia,* which was supposed to sum up all Communist knowledge and wisdom. The first edition took something like a quarter of a century to compile, and it is now proscribed because of its doctrinal "errors."

The Strategy of Peace. Ever since the Communists came into power in Russia they have insisted that they are the true friends of peace and that the leaders of capitalist states are "warmongers." They have used peace appeals as instruments of foreign policy to gain recruits for the Communist cause and to divert attention from acts which belie their profession of peaceful intentions."[38]

Three Soviet "offensives" of the postwar Stalin years deserve attention: (1) the "World Peace Movement" of 1949–50, (2) the Stockholm Peace Appeal of 1950, and (3) the mid-1951 offensive.

The World Peace Movement grew out of a series of "peace congresses" held in 1949–

[35] Varga made the mistake of concluding, on the basis of his research, that the capitalist economic system, especially in the United States, had shown unexpected vitality and strength during the war, and that its collapse was less imminent than had been supposed. See Frederick C. Barghoorn, "The Varga Discussion and Its Significance," *American Slavic and East European Review,* VII (October, 1948), 214–236.

[36] Yakobson, p. 127.

[37] *Ibid.*, p. 126; see also Percy Corbett, "Postwar Soviet Ideology," *The Annals* of the American Academy of Political and Social Science, CCLXIII (May, 1949), 45.

[38] See Leon Dennen, *The Soviet Peace Myth,* a pamphlet issued by the National Committee for a Free Europe, Inc., n.d.

50 in many cities of the world, including Paris, London, New York, and Mexico City. The sponsoring organization, called "Partisans of Peace," established an executive bureau in Paris, and through it succeeded in encompassing "virtually all important front organizations" through which the Communists were then "appealing for support to labor, women, youth, and other 'peace loving' people." The World Congress of the Partisans of Peace became "the leading overall Communist-front organization in the world."[39] Its World Peace Movement promoted three noteworthy enterprises. The first was an unsuccessful effort to incite strikes to close European ports to American shipments of arms under the Mutual Security Program. The second was an attempt to mobilize worldwide support for peace proposals similar to those introduced by the Soviet Union in the UN. The third enterprise was the Stockholm Peace Appeal, initiated at a meeting in Stockholm in March, 1950. The objective was to collect millions of signatures to a simple declaration against the use of atomic weapons. By August the congress claimed that nearly 275,000,000 persons had signed, including 1,350,000 Americans. Obviously, many haters of war signed the Appeal in good faith, too easily forgetful of Russia's atomic backwardness, her massing of terrible nonatomic weapons, and the Communist aggression then getting under way in Korea.

The peace offensive of mid-1951 directed friendly declarations to the Western world through radio, the press, and even the United Nations. It carried with it some relaxation of censorship, even to the extent of accepting a half-joking proposal for the publication in both Britain and the Soviet Union of an exchange of statements by spokesmen of the two countries. The Russian press also was permitted — or directed — to give full publicity to a not unfriendly exchange of letters between President Truman and "President" Shvernik of the U.S.S.R. As no deeds accompanied Soviet words and as the propaganda blasts were quickly resumed, the peace offensive was interpreted by most Western observers as an attempt to slow down Western rearmament and to enervate the Atlantic Community.

[39] "Delegates from World Congress of Partisans of Peace Refused Entry to U.S.," *Department of State Bulletin,* XXII (March 13, 1950), 400–401.

Soviet Diplomacy, 1945–53

The areas in which the Soviet Union is most interested and in which she can most effectively bring her diplomacy to bear are naturally those contiguous to her. Here she must erect her defense barriers or launch her threatened conquests, as the case may be. There are three or possibly four such areas. One is the Middle East, another the Far East, and another Germany. A fourth area, comprising the satellite states of Eastern Europe, is in a somewhat anomalous position, being neither in the Soviet Union nor apart from her. In the early postwar years all of these areas were the objects of intensive Soviet diplomatic activity and political pressures.

Pressures in the Middle East. For the first decade after World War II the Russians gained no major victories in the Middle East and in fact suffered some serious rebuffs; but they established contacts with various discontented groups and established the basis for the exploitation of grievances and frictions. Subsequently they scored some obvious successes in the Arab world, through arms deals, economic assistance, and propaganda campaigns.

The Turkish Straits. In 1946 the Soviet Union demanded a "new regime" for the Straits, one to be controlled by "Turkey and other Black Sea Powers." Turkey and the Soviet Union, she proposed, should "organize joint means of defense of the Straits." Well aware of the implications of the demands, the Turkish government, with the strong encouragement of Great Britain and the United States, rejected them. Instead, it joined the two Western powers in proposing a conference to revise the Montreux Convention. The Russians did not respond favorably to this suggestion, but they were unable to obtain a "new regime" for the Straits.

The Turks have shown a sturdy independence and a determination to resist Soviet pressures, and they are aware of the seriousness of the Soviet threat. Turkey was quite willing to associate with Western and other states in measures for collective self-defense, and was proud of the role that her troops played in resisting Communist aggression in Korea.

Iran. As the end of the war approached, the Soviet Union revealed her aims in Iran by three major moves. First, she revived the demand for an oil concession. In 1944 an Assistant Commissar went to Teheran to negotiate such a concession, but he returned to Moscow empty-handed. Second, she tried to stir up a revolt in the Iranian province of Azerbaijan and to set up a puppet regime there. Late in 1945, when the province proclaimed itself an autonomous state, Russian forces prevented the Iranian government from sending troops to suppress the revolt. Iran appealed to the Security Council of the United Nations. In April, 1945, the Soviet Union promised to withdraw her troops from all of Iran in return for the formation of a joint Soviet-Iranian oil company. With the departure of the Soviet troops the puppet regime in Azerbaijan collapsed, and the Iranian government re-established its authority. To Russia's deep chagrin the Majlis, after a delay of nearly a year and a half, refused to ratify the oil agreement.[40]

[40] Sir Olaf Caroe, *Wells of Power* (London, 1951), pp. 72–76; Harry N. Howard, "The Soviet Union and the Middle East," *The Annals* of the American Academy of Political and Social Science, CCLXIII (May, 1949), 184–186; George E. Kirk, *A Short History of the Middle East from the Rise of Islam to Modern Times* (London, 1948), pp. 262 ff.

With the assassination of Premier Ali Razmara in March, 1951, and the formation of a government headed by Mohammed Mossadegh, Iranian nationalism reached new heights of fanaticism. The chief object of attack was the Anglo-Iranian Oil Company, whose vast properties in Iran were expropriated. This situation gave the Russian Communists an excellent opportunity for their third move: to pose as champions of Iranian independence from Western imperialism. The Soviet Union officially remained aloof from the imbroglio, but her propaganda agencies gave full attention to the events in Iran.

After the fall of Mossadegh in 1953 and the settlement of the oil dispute, the political and economic situation in Iran greatly improved. The strong anti-Western feeling subsided, and the Tudeh (Communist) Party was outlawed. In 1955 Iran associated herself with Britain, Iraq, Pakistan, and Turkey in the Baghdad Pact. She was no longer a gaping hole in the "northern tier" of states that forms the Middle Eastern frontier of the Soviet Union.

Israel. The Soviet Union, at least until World War II, had posed as a friend and protector of the Arab world. She showed little sympathy for Zionism, holding that it was "a theocratic bourgeois doctrine, unworthy of support." With the emergence of the new Jewish state of Israel and its successful resistance to the Arab armies, however, the Soviet Union showed a willingness to abandon the Arabs and to embrace the cause of Israel. But Russian solicitude for Israel was short-lived. Soviet purges of early 1953 seemed to have a definite anti-Jewish cast; and in February the Kremlin severed diplomatic relations after the bombing of the Soviet Legation in Jerusalem. In more recent years Soviet anti-Semitism has led to attacks on Jews in "iron curtain" countries and to denunciations of Israel and Zionism as instruments of Anglo-American imperialism.

Involvement in East Asia. The Soviet Union, with almost no effort or cost, scored tremendous gains in East Asia in 1945. These came chiefly as a result of the Yalta Agreement, the occupation of Manchuria by Russian troops, the Sino-Soviet Treaty of August 14, 1945, and the power vacuum created by Japan's defeat, China's weakness and division, Britain's inability to resume her former position, and the speedy withdrawal and demobilization of the United States. Russia was not slow to profit from the virtual removal of the once formidable counterweights to her ambitions in East Asia. She obtained the concessions in the Far East which had been promised to her at Yalta and in the Sino-Soviet Treaty, but she soon violated many of the pledges she had made in return. In Manchuria she stripped the industrial plants, and withdrew her forces in such a way as to aid the Chinese Communists and frustrate the efforts of the Nationalists to occupy this vital area. Although she remained officially aloof from the civil war which began in China in 1946, at no time did she give aid and support solely and "entirely" to the Nationalist Government, as she had promised. When the People's Republic of China was proclaimed on October 1, 1949, Russia abandoned all pretense at impartiality and recognized the new regime with great fanfare on the following day.

In December, 1949, Mao Tse-tung visited Moscow, presumably for the first time. At the end of his visit, in February, 1950, the Soviet Union and China announced the signing of a Treaty of Friendship, Alliance and Mutual Aid, with two supplementary agreements, one confirming Russian rights in Manchurian railways and in Port Arthur and Dairen, with a pledge by the U.S.S.R. to abandon these areas by 1952, the other promising a Soviet credit of $300,000,000 to China.[41] As later modified, these agreements provided for Soviet withdrawal from the Changchun Railway in Manchuria, in accordance with the pledge of 1950, but they also stipulated that Soviet troops could remain in Port Arthur, contrary to the 1950 commitment, "until such time as peace treaties between the Chinese People's Republic and Japan and between the Soviet Union and Japan are concluded."[42]

At the end of the war Korea was divided at the thirty-eighth parallel into a northern zone occupied by the Russians and a southern zone occupied by the Americans. Because the two occupying powers could not agree on the unification of the country, the division was formalized by the establishment in 1948 of two rival regimes, the Democratic People's Republic in the north and the Republic of Korea in the south. By mid-1949 all occupation troops had been withdrawn. The attack a year later on South Korea from north of the parallel precipitated the gravest crisis of the early postwar period.

The precise roles of the Soviet Union and Communist China in Korea, and their relations with the Communist government of North Korea, cannot be determined. Presumably the Communist leaders of both countries participated in planning the attack of June, 1950, the Chinese intervention in November, and the general direction of the campaign against the United Nations forces. In Korea itself, after 1949, the Russians kept in the background.

The conclusion of a peace treaty for Japan was delayed until 1951 because of the inability of the Soviet Union and the United States to agree on either methods of procedure or treaty terms. The American position was generally supported by most of the non-Communist nations directly concerned. After the

[41] The texts of the Sino-Soviet treaty of February 14, 1950, and of the supplementary agreements were printed in the *USSR Information Bulletin,* X (February 24, 1950), 108–110. An official summary of the agreements of March 27 appears in the issue of April 14, 1950.

[42] The text of the Sino-Soviet communiqué of September 16, 1952, was printed in the *New York Times* of the same date.

problem of Chinese representation had been "resolved" by deciding to invite no delegation from China, the United States issued invitations to no less than fifty nations still theoretically at war with Japan to attend a conference at San Francisco on September 4, 1951, for the purpose of concluding a peace treaty with Japan. Russia caused a mild diplomatic surprise by accepting the invitation and sending a delegation headed by Deputy Foreign Minister Gromyko; but her delegates refused to sign the treaty.

When the Japanese peace treaty officially became effective, on April 28, 1952, the Soviet Government repeated its strong protests against the whole proceeding. It also objected to the security treaty between the United States and Japan, to the abolition of the Far Eastern Commission, and to all other logical corollaries of the new status of Japan. Russia and the Soviet bloc long refused to acquiesce in Japan's re-entry into the family of nations; in September, 1952, Malik cast the Soviet Union's fifty-first veto to keep Japan out of the UN.

East-West Competition in Germany. During the period of "the strange alliance" representatives of Britain, the Soviet Union, and the United States held several discussions on questions relating to Germany. Many important decisions were made at Yalta, and a comprehensive agreement on Germany was negotiated at Potsdam. The decisions at Yalta included the procedure for reparations payments, arrangements for the occupation of Germany, with each state to control a particular zone — with a French zone to be created out of the areas assigned to Britain and the United States — and an agreement in principle that Poland should get territories in East Prussia and Upper Silesia. Both Churchill and Roosevelt made it very clear at Yalta that in their opinion the final delimitation of the western frontier of Poland should be made at the peace conference, and the Potsdam Agreement contains a

Fischetti. Reprinted by Permission of Newspaper Enterprise Association.

"Are You Tryin to Start a War?"

clear statement to this same effect. Yet the Russians have insisted that Britain and the United States did accept the present western boundary of Poland.

The Potsdam Agreement covered the political and economic principles which were to govern the treatment of Germany, reparations claims and procedures, the disposal of of the German merchant marine, territorial changes in Eastern Germany, the trial of war criminals, and the orderly transfer of German populations (which actually became the forced uprooting and transportation of some eight million people). Disputes over the interpretation of the Potsdam Agreement began almost at once, and so did violations. The procedure for joint occupation and four-power collaboration in Germany, with the Allied Control Council as the coordinating body for the four zones and with the Kommandatura serving a similar function in the government of Berlin, proved to be unsatisfactory from the outset. No solution except the division of the defeated country, and of its capital, into separate zones seemed possible, and the occupying powers were faced from the beginning with the necessity of trying to make the best of a bad situation.

Basing their claim upon the secret understanding reached at the Yalta Conference by Churchill, Roosevelt, and Stalin that the figure of twenty billion dollars in reparations should be taken "as a basis for discussion," Soviet representatives insisted on this figure, particularly the amount of ten billions which they demanded for the U.S.S.R. In the absence of agreement the Soviet Union went ahead with heavy exactions, nominally at least for reparations, in the eastern part of Germany. The experiment with wholesale dismantling of plants and their removal to the Soviet Union proved to be so unsatisfactory and caused such hostile repercussions that after the summer of 1946 the Russians transferred to themselves the title to many German plants and operated them in Germany "as Soviet properties for the reparations account."[43]

Efforts of the occupying powers to agree on unified policies toward Germany in implementation of the Potsdam Agreement proved generally futile almost from the beginning. By the summer or fall of 1946 further attempts at coordinated action had been largely abandoned, and each side began to concentrate on consolidation and development of its area and on attempts to win the support of the German people against the other. Since 1947 the differences between the Soviet Union and the Western powers over Germany have been so great and so fundamental that no appreciable progress has been made in one of the most crucial sectors of the cold war. In Chapter 15 we described Allied policies in Western Germany, notably the steps to bring into existence a West German state and to associate it with Western Europe. Russia protested bitterly against every one of them and denounced the Western powers for the open violations of the Potsdam Agreement. Two of the Soviet measures of retaliation, or of unilateral action, were particularly significant. These were the Berlin blockade and the establishment of the "German Democratic Republic" in the Soviet zone, also described in Chapter 15.

[43] Franz L. Neumann, "Soviet Policy in Germany," *The Annals* of the American Academy of Political and Social Science, CCLXIII (May, 1949), 174–178.

Eastern Europe and the Satellite System. In the Declaration of Liberated Europe, agreed upon at the Yalta Conference in February, 1945, Stalin joined with Roosevelt and Churchill in the following pledge: ". . . the three Governments will jointly assist the people in any European liberated state or former Axis satellite state in Europe . . . to form interim governmental authorities broadly representative of all democratic elements in the population and pledged to the earliest possible establishment through free elections of governments responsive to the will of the people." A special Declaration on Poland promised that "the Provisional Government . . . should . . . be reorganized on a broader democratic basis."

Within a few weeks after the Yalta Conference, the Soviet Union had violated the pledges regarding the "liberated" former Axis satellite states in Eastern Europe and had begun the process of creating a Soviet orbit virtually sealed off from the outside world. There were obvious geographic, historic, and security reasons for the Soviet interest in this part of the world. Moreover, by their wartime policies the Allies had inadvertently facilitated Soviet designs there through the decision to launch a second front from Western Europe and through acquiescence in Russian demands that Soviet troops should occupy such key centers as Berlin and Prague. The "iron curtain" soon divided Eastern from Western Europe. Behind that curtain Soviet political influence was supreme.

Soviet Objectives in Eastern Europe. Among the many reasons for Soviet efforts to bring the states of Eastern Europe under complete domination, the following, at least, should be emphasized: (1) to dominate the buffer zone between the Soviet Union and the West, to establish "friendly" governments in the states in that area, and to indoctrinate and regiment the people so that they would be faithful satellites and dependable allies of the Soviet Union in the event of war; (2) to orient the countries of Eastern Europe toward the Soviet Union, instead of toward the Western world, politically, economically, culturally, and in every other respect, and to eliminate Western influences and ties; and (3) to make use of the economic resources of the area for rebuilding the Soviet economy and developing the economic strength which would be essential for the successful prosecution of another war.[44]

It should be noted that the policies followed by Russia in Eastern Europe could be interpreted either as security measures or as vital first steps for further Soviet expansion. Certainly the Soviet leaders did not regard this area as a bridge between East and West; they did everything in their power to destroy the bridge that already existed. The unanswered question was whether they regarded Eastern Europe as a security buffer zone or as a bridgehead.

The Pattern of Control. Between 1945 and 1948 local Communist organizations, with the direct and indirect assistance of the U.S.S.R. — and especially with the visible presence and occasionally the active intervention of the Red Army — gained complete control in Albania, Bulgaria, Czechoslovakia, Hungary, Poland, Rumania, and Yugoslavia. In all of Eastern and Southern Europe only Finland, Greece, and Turkey escaped the Communist shackles.

The pattern of control was strikingly uniform, varying only with local conditions such as the strength of opposing parties and of democratic institutions, the extent of popular resistance, and the popularity or unpopularity of native Communist leaders. It made little difference whether a state had been associated with the Axis or had fought on the side of the United Nations, or whether the political parties and their leaders had collaborated with or had opposed the Russians. In the end their fate was the same.

At first the Communists participated in "Popular Front" governments, but they joined with the "bourgeois" parties only to destroy them. With the assistance of the Red Army and Soviet political "advisers," native Communist leaders who had usually been trained in Moscow came into power through clever propaganda, economic and social reforms, and terrorism and intimidation. They secured key ministries, such as the ministry of interior and the ministry of information or propaganda. They saw to it that persons loyal to them occupied most of the important posts in the armed forces and in the police. With these two instruments in hand they moved swiftly to take over the press, the radio, and other organs of information, industry, and the labor unions. Thus firmly entrenched, they were in a position to undermine other parties and to take over the machinery of the state.[45]

[44] John C. Campbell, *The United States in World Affairs, 1947–1948* (New York: Council on Foreign Relations, 1948), pp. 450–451.

[45] An examination of the steps leading to the taking over of any one of the states of Eastern Europe would provide a case study in the pattern of control. For the general picture, see Hugh Seton-Watson, *The East European Revolution* (New York: Frederick A. Praeger, 1951); David J. Dallin, *The New Soviet Empire* (New Haven: Yale University Press, 1951); J. C. Harsch, *The Curtain Isn't Iron* (Garden City, N.Y.: Doubleday & Company, 1950); Campbell, pp. 444–452 ("Consolidation of the Soviet Bloc"); Dinko Tomasic, "The Structure of Soviet Power and Expansion," *The Annals* of the American Academy of Political and Social Science, CCLXXI (September, 1950), 32–42; Bogdan Raditsa, "The Sovietization of the Satellites," *The Annals,* CCLXXI (September, 1950), 122–134 (see especially the blueprint for the sovietization of Yugoslavia which Tito received from the Comintern on May 9, 1941, quoted

In the establishment of the "people's democracies" the Communists, Russian and native, won considerable popular support. They were adroit in their propaganda appeals, especially in exploiting the weaknesses of other parties and institutions, in disguising their own real motives, and in posing as champions of needed economic and political reforms and as enemies of exploitation, whether by favored groups within the countries or by foreign nations. They ended all surviving monarchies in that area, and identified their most formidable political rivals, the peasant or Social Democratic parties, with collaboration with the Axis, with corrupt and conservative groups, and faithless leadership. They attempted to woo the peasants of Eastern Europe by sponsoring land reforms, the nationalization of industries, and agricultural cooperatives.

Along with persuasion went ruthless terrorism. The opposition was intimidated and gradually liquidated, and opposition leaders were imprisoned or executed unless they had fled for their lives. War-crime and treason trials became vehicles for public "confessions," extracted by methods which combined medieval tortures with the diabolical application of modern techniques for breaking the human mind and spirit.

Even Communist parties in the satellite states were frequently "purged," especially after the Yugoslav defection in the summer of 1948. The peasant parties were greatly weakened by the arrest, exile, or defection of their leaders, and by their inability to resist those who controlled all the effective organs of power. After the Communists had been defeated in relatively free elections in Hungary in 1945, they saw to it that no more elections were held until the campaign of indoctrination and intimidation had made deeper inroads and until the peasant parties had been weakened or destroyed.

After the destruction or corruption of the peasant and "bourgeois" parties, the most formidable organized opposition to Communist rule in the satellite states came from religious groups, especially from those with ties with the West. "The Orthodox churches, by tradition and organization linked to the state authorities, were brought under control without great difficulty in Rumania and Bulgaria through the appointment of subservient church officials."[46]

In every one of these East European countries the Communists in control sought to dissolve Catholic organizations, to take over Catholic schools, and to destroy the influence of Catholicism. Hungary was the great test case. There the Communists struck at Jozsef Cardinal Mindszenty, the Roman Catholic Primate of Hungary. In December, 1948, Mindszenty was arrested on charges of treason against the state and of espionage and lesser crimes, and, after a farcical trial, was sentenced to life imprisonment.

The Coup in Czechoslovakia and the Tito "Split." By 1948 the only state in Eastern Europe which had managed to escape Soviet domination was Czechoslovakia, democracy's "show window" to the East, whose economic and political ties bound her closely with the West. She had made a treaty with the Soviet Union in 1943, and in the postwar period had followed a conciliatory policy toward her powerful neighbor, hoping and apparently believing that cooperation might be an alternative to Communist domination. Her hopes were in vain, and in February,

---

on pp. 124–126. Ferenc Nagy, *The Struggle Behind the Iron Curtain* (New York: The Macmillan Company, 1948) is an account of Soviet and Communist machinations in Hungary by a former prime minister. The sovietization of Poland is described in Stanislaw Mikolajczk *The Rape of Poland: Pattern of Soviet Aggression* (New York: Whittlesey House, 1948), and Arthur Bliss Lane, *I Saw Poland Betrayed* (Indianapolis: The Bobbs-Merrill Co., 1948).

[46] John C. Campbell, *The United States in World Affairs, 1948–1949* (New York: Council on Foreign Relations, 1949), p. 108.

1948, in a coup which reverberated throughout the world, Czechoslovakia too passed into the Communist camp.[47] For a few months the "iron curtain" revealed no rifts from Stettin on the Baltic to Trieste on the Adriatic.

Not long afterward, however, a major rift did appear in the apparently monolithic structure of communism. It was caused by the Kremlin's denunciation of the policies — or "heresies" — of the Communist leaders of Yugoslavia, first announced to a startled world by the Cominform on June 28, 1948. As shown in documents issued by both sides shortly after the Cominform announcement, the break had been in the making for some time. Instead of recanting abjectly, as erring Communists were expected to do, Tito and his associates complained of Soviet attempts to interfere in Yugoslav affairs and denied the "unjust fabrications" of the Russian Communist Party; at the same time they declared their loyalty to Stalin and the Soviet Union, and defended their policies as completely in accord with Marxist-Leninist doctrine. Furthermore, their position was endorsed by the Communist Party of Yugoslavia, although it was denounced without exception elsewhere in the Communist world.

Although the economic situation in their country became increasingly serious, the Yugoslav leaders showed no signs of weakening. Under these conditions they took a more conciliatory attitude toward the non-Communist states, but they continued to proclaim their allegiance to Communist principles.

The Coordination of Policies. The Tito "split" in 1948, and the increasingly effective measures of the nations of the North Atlantic Community to counteract Soviet threats and pressures, caused the leaders of Soviet Russia to renew their efforts to strengthen their hold over the satellite states. These efforts have been pressed as vigorously during the period of the "new look" as they were before 1953. In fact, in some respects they have been intensified. If the Soviet leaders had any thought of relaxing their hold, they must have abandoned it as a result of the great uprising in Berlin in June, 1953. The Soviet reaction to the Paris agreements of 1954 regarding Germany was the Warsaw Conference, which established a more elaborate kind of regional organization east of the "iron curtain." Three main agencies or instruments, in addition to the national Communist parties and Soviet representatives and "advisers," were utilized: (1) a network of treaties of mutual assistance and cooperation; (2) the Cominform; and (3) the so-called Molotov Plan and its Council for Mutual Economic Assistance.

1. The Soviet Treaty System. On December 12, 1943, a "Treaty of Friendship, Mutual Assistance, and Post-War Cooperation" between the Soviet Union and Czechoslovakia was signed in Moscow. This pact inaugurated a series of treaties between Russia and the states of Eastern Europe — with Yugoslavia (April 11, 1945), Poland (April 21, 1945), Rumania (February 4, 1948), Hungary (February 18, 1948), Bulgaria (March 18, 1948), and Finland (April 6, 1948). The treaty system was further extended by nearly twenty similar treaties

[47] For the background and details of the Communist coup in Czechoslovakia in 1948, see *The Coup d'Etat in Prague,* Supplement III (A) to Report of Subcommittee No. 5 on the Committee on Foreign Affairs of the United States House of Representatives on "The Strategy and Tactics of World Communism"; House Document No. 154, Part I. 81st Cong., 1st Sess. (Washington, D.C.: Government Printing Office, 1949). Also helpful: Dana Adams Schmidt, *Anatomy of a Satellite* (Boston: Little, Brown and Company, 1952); Albion Ross, "The Communist Way: How Czechoslovakia Was Taken Over," and Drew Middleton, "Soviet Push Westward Long in the Making," *New York Times,* February, 29, 1948; and Dana Adams Schmidt, " 'Coexistence' — A Lesson from History," *New York Times Magazine,* August 12, 1951.

among the Soviet-dominated European states themselves, beginning with the Yugoslav-Polish Treaty of March 18, 1946.[48]

2. The Cominform. In September, 1947, Communist leaders from nine European countries held an important meeting in Warsaw. Among them were two influential members of the Russian Politburo, Zhdanov and Malenkov. Zdanhov proclaimed the Soviet position on the Marshall Plan by declaring flatly that the Soviet Union would "bend every effort in order that this plan be doomed to failure." The principal decision of the conference was to establish a Communist Information Bureau, with headquarters in Belgrade, Yugoslavia. After the Tito "heresy," in July, 1948, these were hastily removed to Bucharest, Rumania.

The Cominform was nominally an organization of the Communist parties in the Soviet Union, in the Soviet satellite states of Eastern Europe, in France, and in Italy; but it seemed to be in many ways a revived Comintern, a kind of coordinating agency for the worldwide Communist movement. Its official organ, which bore the intriguing title *For a Lasting Peace, For a People's Democracy!* was full of news of Communist activities all over the world. Many major pronouncements of Communist policy first appeared in its pages.

After 1948 the Cominform headed the attacks on Tito as well as other campaigns of opposition to the heretic state. Its efforts were for the most part singularly ineffective, and it soon fell into disuse. As far as is known, it held no meetings after 1949. When the new leaders of the Soviet Union decided to court Tito instead of casting him into the outer darkness, the Cominform was deprived of its chief propaganda objective. In April, 1956, it was officially dissolved on the ground that it had "exhausted its uses" owing to the emergence of socialism from the confines of one country and to the "strengthening of many Communist parties in the capitalist, dependent and colonial countries."

3. East-West Trade and the "Molotov Plan." Historically, the chief markets of the states of Eastern Europe, particularly of Czechoslovakia and Poland, have been in Germany and to a lesser extent in Western Europe. Among the most significant early postwar agreements which were negotiated by countries on either side of the "iron curtain" were the trade agreements which Poland signed with France in December, 1948, and with Great Britain in January, 1949.

But the obstacles to a revival of East-West trade were many. The chief of these was undoubtedly the policy and outlook of the Soviet Union, which attempted — and with considerable success — to isolate the East European states from the West and to make them economic as well as political satellites of the U.S.S.R. By her trade pacts, her priority system, and her general policies the Soviet Union sought "to expand the trade of East European countries with one another and with the U.S.S.R. at the expense of trade with the West."[49] Apparently she hoped to integrate the economic systems of the orbit states and to develop a balanced regional economic unit under the leadership of an industrialized Czechoslovakia and Poland.

The term "Molotov Plan" came into general use after the countries of Eastern Europe had been directed not to participate in the Marshall Plan. Heralded as the Soviet answer to the Marshall Plan, it was designed to tighten the economic ties of the East European states with each other and with the Soviet Union. Actually it was hardly a plan at all; and since all of the states had adopted generally similar economic plans in the postwar period and had become oriented toward the Russian economy, a kind of "Molotov

[48] Campbell, *1947–1948,* p. 449; Campbell, *1948–1949*, p. 115.

[49] Laurie Sharp, "The Molotov Plan Rolls over Eastern Europe," *United Nations World, IV* (February, 1950), 57.

Plan" had been in existence for some time. The plan was given more definite form in January, 1949, by the creation of the Council for Mutual Economic Assistance (COMECON). The organization and activities of COMECON are described in Chapter 20.

Stalin's Last Statement. On the eve of the August, 1952, meeting of the Communist Party of the Soviet Union — the first since 1939 — Stalin issued a 25,000-word statement of views on basic economic and political questions. This statement, on *Economic Problems of Socialism in the U.S.S.R.*, was "Stalin's last and most significant theoretical work."[50] It was described by *Pravda* as "the greatest event in the ideological life of the Party and the Soviet people." It heralded what is now commonly spoken of as the "new look" in Soviet Russia. In it Stalin laid down some propositions on the prerequisites for the transformation of the Soviet Union from the existing "socialist" system to one of "complete communism," and others on the nature of international conflicts. While he reaffirmed many basic Communist theories, he did not hesitate to repudiate or to revise many concepts and propositions enunciated by Marx, Engels, Lenin, and himself. Rejecting the familiar interpretation of the inevitability of conflict between the "capitalist" and "socialist" worlds, he argued that in the existing situation, with the capitalist states virtually cut off from trade with Russia, China, and the Communist states, conflict among capitalist countries over markets was a stronger force than the "contradictions between the camp of capitalism and the camp of socialism." He reaffirmed the socialist theory of international relations: "In order to destroy the inevitability of wars, it is necessary to destroy imperialism." Later, while reasserting his belief that war between "capitalist" and "socialist" countries was not imminent, Stalin discussed ways to promote wars between "capitalist" states and to encourage "struggles for liberation" and for the "overthrow of capitalism."

[50] Wolfe, p. 195. Quotations in this section not otherwise credited were taken from Wolfe's article.

The "New Look" in the Post-Stalin Era

Developments and rumors in the fall of 1952 and the spring of 1953 convinced observers that the stage was being set for momentous changes in the Soviet Union. In the weeks following the Party Congress, reports of scandals, exposures, arrests, and purges filled the newspapers and created an air of tense expectancy in Moscow and elsewhere in Russia. "It was apparent to all in Moscow in February," reported Harrison Salisbury, "that great and sinister events were in the making"; there were "increasingly plain signs that something akin to dementia was taking hold of Stalin and that the country stood on the brink of a reign of terror. . . ."[51] But on March 5, 1953, the death of Stalin was announced. Whatever plot had been hatched for his removal — if any at all — now evaporated, and the transfer of power was made in an outwardly peaceful way.

Change in Leadership. Immediately after the announcement of Stalin's death the new leaders of the Soviet Union took their posts. Without exception, they had all been prominently identified with Soviet and party politics. They were either old associates of Stalin, like Beria, Molotov, Bulganin, and Voroshilov, or protégés of Stalin and products of the new Russian bureaucracy, like Malenkov and Khrushchev. Many observers concluded that Malenkov and Beria were the two top leaders. Some believed that the new leaders would inevitably be drawn into a power struggle from which would again emerge a single leader.

The two men whom the "experts" generally rated as the strong men in the new

[51] Harrison Salisbury, "Russia Re-Viewed," *The New York Times*, September 20, 1954.

regime soon lost out. Beria was the first to fall. On July 10, 1953, *Pravda,* the CPSU organ, announced that he had been dismissed from all of his posts. He had become "a bourgeois renegade and an agent of international imperialism." Nearly six months later, on December 23, *Izvestia,* official organ of the Soviet Government, announced that Beria had "confessed" to all the charges against him, and that he and six accomplices had been shot. Beria's fall seemed to consolidate Malenkov's position, but less than two years after Stalin's death the new premier was made the scapegoat for certain failures in Soviet policy, particularly on the domestic front. On February 10, 1955, he submitted his "request" to step down, saying that "lack of sufficient experience in local work" had led to his failure "to effect direct guidance of individual branches of national economy." In less than ten minutes the Supreme Soviet approved Malenkov's "request," and a short while later Bulganin was appointed premier. Malenkov retained his membership in the Presidium of the CPSU and was assigned the posts of deputy premier and Minister of Electric Power Stations.

After Malenkov's demotion most observers believed that Khrushchev held the real power and that Bulganin was hardly more than a figurehead.[52] This appraisal was strengthened by developments that brought Khrushchev more and more to the front. In 1958 he replaced Bulganin as premier, thus becoming the first Soviet leader since Stalin to hold the highest office in both the party and the government.

The Downgrading of Stalin. "The Stalin myth was dead as soon as his body was cold," and his successors "began immediately a fresh rewriting of history to cut him down to size — not to actual size, but to their own size, so that there could be some sense in their claim to individual or collective succession." For one-man dictatorship was substituted the "Leninist" practice of "collective leadership" and the revival of the party as an active political organism. At the Twentieth Party Congress, held in Moscow in February, 1956, the attacks on Stalin were openly pressed. In his opening report Khrushchev condemned the leader cult, and he mentioned Stalin's name only once in the course of a 50,000-word address. A few days later Mikoyan questioned the correctness of Stalin's *Economic Problems of Socialism in the U.S.S.R.* — a work which at the Nineteenth Party Congress in 1952 he had hailed as a masterpiece of Communist thought. He also praised a number of old Bolsheviks who had been purged during the Stalin era, referred sarcastically to Stalin's famous "Oath to Lenin," and called attention to Lenin's last testament, which contained some highly critical comments on Stalin. The Twentieth Congress closed with an address by Khrushchev in which, in the words of Philip E. Mosely, he depicted Stalin as a "bullheaded and uninformed meddler in military strategy" who was wrong in his nationality policy, stubborn in his Yugoslav policy, and addicted to fancying himself "an infallible genius."[53] After the Congress the anti-Stalin campaign was openly prosecuted, and most leaders in other Communist countries as well as in the Soviet Union soon joined in the chorus.

Change in Policies? The changes in Russia which followed the death of Stalin not only included changes in leadership but also seemed to involve changes in policies. The new leaders went out of their way to introduce a more flexible and relaxed note into their behavior and policies. In both domestic

[52] See articles by Harry Schwartz and Harrison E. Salisbury in the *New York Times,* February 9, 1955; also Philip E. Mosely, "Russia After Stalin," *Headline Series,* No. 111 (May–June, 1955), pp. 9–22.

[53] "Soviet Foreign Policy: New Goals or New Manners?" *Foreign Affairs,* XXXIV (July, 1956), 541. For the purported text of Khrushchev's address, see the *New York Times.* June 5, 1956.

Orr in The Chicago Tribune

The Red Napoleon — and His War Horse

and foreign affairs so many concessions and changes were made that they gave a "new look" to Soviet policy. All over the world troubled people wondered what these changes meant. How "new" was the "new look"? Was it simply a shift in tactics, such as had occurred on several earlier occasions, or did it portend a fundamental reorientation of Soviet policy?

The domestic changes included a new emphasis on consumer goods, a relaxation of many restrictions and controls, greater freedom of movement within the country, and deep concern with the general agricultural situation. Perhaps the greatest of all was a willingness to admit mistakes of policy and to reverse courses of action which had not proved to be successful.

In foreign policy the new regime relaxed in many respects: visas for the U.S.S.R. became easier to obtain; many restrictions on travel within the country were modified; hundreds of foreign nationals were released from arbitrary imprisonment; some Soviet-born wives of foreigners were allowed to leave the country; many of the annoying restrictions on foreign diplomats and correspondents were ended; official and unofficial delegations and visits by individual foreigners were encouraged, and those who came to Russia found a comparative affability. The Soviet Union agreed to a truce in Korea in 1953 and in Indo-China in 1954. After an originally negative reaction, she agreed to consider President Eisenhower's atoms-for-peace proposals, and in May, 1955, she herself advanced some significant new proposals on disarmament and the international control of atomic energy. In March, 1954, Molotov proposed a European security pact open to the United States, and he declared his country ready to consider adherence to the North Atlantic Treaty, which Communist propagandists had consistently damned as an association of "warmongers." Reversing her traditional policy, the Soviet Union contributed to the United Nations Technical Assistance Program and insisted that her technicians and resources should be drawn upon. She also embarked on a kind of Point Four program of her own, and entered into technical assistance agreements with a number of countries, including India, Iran, and Afghanistan.[54] Relaxing elsewhere, in 1956 she issued a stamp in honor of Benjamin Franklin, "Great American Public Figure and Scientist."

The overtures which the new Soviet leaders, at the risk of considerable humiliation, made to Tito in 1955 led to a basic reorientation of policy toward the former Communist "heretic." After many years of stalling, Russia suddenly invited Austrian leaders to Moscow to discuss the terms of the Austrian state treaty, and made concessions which in a short time cleared away the last remaining obstacles. Although she had consistently denounced the West German government as an illegal regime, and had bitterly resisted any and all moves to rearm Western Germany

[54] Alvin Z. Rubinstein, "Russia, Southeast Asia and Point Four," *Current History*, XXVIII (February, 1955), pp. 103–108.

and to associate her with Western Europe, in the early summer of 1955 the Soviet Union offered to recognize the West German government and invited Konrad Adenauer to Moscow. In June she agreed to a meeting at the "summit" with Britain, France, and the United States to consider crucial issues between the Soviet Union and the West. The meeting of Eden, Faure, Eisenhower, and Bulganin was held in Geneva in July, 1955; and while no agreement on details resulted it did lead to a frank exchange of views and helped to pave the way for more fruitful negotiations on several fronts.

The Twentieth Congress of the Communist Party of the Soviet Union in 1956 was "a significant landmark in the history of Soviet Communism." At this congress Khrushchev and other Soviet spokesmen "revealed an ideological flexibility and capacity for fresh maneuver in striking contrast with the rigidity of later-day Stalinism." They reformulated Communist doctrine in such a way as to facilitate cooperation with other countries, Communist and non-Communist alike, and with Socialist parties in Europe and Asia; they declared that "war is not fatalistically inevitable"; and they reaffirmed the thesis of peaceful co-existence as "a fundamental principle of Soviet foreign policy."[55]

Khrushchev often talked the language of peaceful co-existence and the reduction of international tensions. On occasion his actions fitted his words. In 1963 he joined with the United States in three much publicized agreements: to establish a "hot line" between Washington and Moscow, to cooperate with the United States in certain programs in outer space, and to sign the nuclear test ban treaty. With the possible exception of the Austrian state treaty of 1955 and the nuclear nonproliferation treaty of 1968, the test ban treaty was perhaps the most significant agreement which the Soviet Union was willing to conclude with the United States and other Western nations in the postwar years. It was speedily ratified by most of the nations of the world, with the conspicuous exceptions of Communist China and France, and it was hailed as a major breakthrough in the long and frustrating quest for an end to the nuclear arms race.

In many ways the post-Stalin "new look" seemed to be much more appealing and hopeful than the forbidding Soviet visage of the last years of the Stalin era. But the concessions in doctrine and in foreign policy have doubtless been occasioned less by purity of heart than by such factors as the crisis in Soviet leadership, serious economic problems, especially in agriculture, difficulties in the satellite countries, and the success of the policies of non-Communist states. The very real concessions regarding Austria may have been prompted by the changed situation in the satellite area, by a desire to prevent the rearming of Western Germany and her association with Western Europe, and by a hope of forcing American troops out of Europe and their air bases with them. The only other major concession — the signing of the nuclear test ban treaty — may have been prompted by Khrushchev's feeling that further atmospheric tests were unnecessary, at least for the time being, that the treaty might lead to a slowdown in the American development of nuclear weapons, and that it might help to mobilize world opinion against nuclear testing by China, France, or any other powers in future years.

All during the Khrushchev era the reality of the "thaw" and the "new look" was often belied by other Soviet actions which seemed quite incompatible with professions of belief in peaceful co-existence and the reduction of international tensions. In actuality, Soviet policy under Khrushchev alternated between a soft and a hard line, at different periods, on different issues, and in different parts of the world. Khrushchev constantly boasted of the shift in the world balance of forces in favor

[55] Merle Fainsod, "Russia's 20th Party Congress," *Foreign Policy Bulletin*, XXXV (May 1, 1956), 127.

of the "world socialist camp" and the Soviet Union, and of the formidable growth of Soviet economic and military power. In 1958–59 he threatened to precipitate a major crisis over Berlin. In 1960 he walked out of the Paris "summit" conference, allegedly in protest against the U-2 incident; he indulged in his famous shoe-waving exhibition in the General Assembly of the United Nations and advanced the disruptive "troika" proposal for the top direction of the UN; and he joined with Communist leaders from eighty other countries at the Moscow Conference in statements and resolutions which proclaimed a continuance of the relentless campaign against "capitalist-imperialism." In January, 1961, in what was perhaps his major speech on foreign policy, he reasserted his shifting balance thesis and warned that if the Western powers, whose "prestige and foreign political stock have never been so low . . . are stubborn, we will adopt decisive measures."

When President Kennedy met the Soviet leader in Vienna a few weeks after assuming office, the President was obviously disturbed and shaken by the encounter. At this meeting Khrushchev was anything but flexible and cooperative. In the following year his clandestine assistance to Cuba in building missile sites on that island led to perhaps the most serious and most direct confrontation between the United States and the Soviet Union in the postwar period. This time Khrushchev yielded, and for the rest of the Kennedy administration he seemed to have been chastened by the Cuban experience. But shortly after Kennedy's assassination, Khrushchev reverted to a hard line. This policy of ups and downs, of smiles and threats, of rapid shifts in strategy and/or tactics, was in fact the manner of his predecessors.

Most seasoned observers were agreed that the "new look" was in basic respects not so new after all. It was generally considered more a change of manners than a change of heart. While the new Soviet leaders have publicly downgraded Stalin, they have not deviated fundamentally from the principles which he laid down in his lastest significant statement.[56] In non-Communist countries there were many who shared the belief of Merle Fainsod that "the Khrushchev-Bulganin arsenal of intensive industrialization, diplomacy, trade, technical assistance, cultural penetration, and subversion is no less formidable than the cruder threats, pressure and bluster which Stalin employed in the period of the Berlin blockade and the Korean adventure."[57] On the other hand, the many evidences of changes in Soviet tactics in the post-Stalin era were welcomed as opportunities to deal with some acute problems, to reduce international tensions, and to lay the foundations for the kind of "peaceful co-existence" which would give new hope for mankind in the atomic age.

Polycentrism in East Europe. Since the death of Stalin most of the countries of Eastern Europe, with the notable exceptions of Albania and East Germany, have been characterized by a growing diversity, a growing "liberalization," a growing measure of autonomy in internal affairs, and a growing degree of independence for the Soviet Union. One can no longer speak of the East European "bloc" or "satellite states" without major qualifications. Many of the countries have developed patterns of trade, cultural exchange, and other relations with the West which the Soviet Union has viewed with marked disfavor; Albania has openly sided with China in the intra-bloc dispute between the two Communist giants; Poland, Rumania, Czechoslovakia, and to some extent Hungary have been following more liberal and more independent policies; and Yugoslavia has continued to be the most "independent" of any Communist state. In this

[56] Thomas P. Whitney, "What We Can Expect of the Russians," *New York Times Magazine*, May 22, 1955, p. 9.

[57] Fainsod, p. 127.

area de-Stalinization has assumed "the forms of de-satellization."[58] How far can this process go without incurring punitive action by the Soviet Union? In the minds of the peoples and leaders of the East European states, memories of the East Berlin uprising of 1953 and the Hungarian uprising of 1956 are still fresh and poignant.

1. East Germany. On June 17, 1953, hundreds of people in East Berlin staged an impromptu uprising which was crushed only when Russian tanks and troops were brought into action. The much-publicized photographs of Germans tearing up bricks from the streets to hurl at Russian tanks symbolized great courage, but courage alone could not change the situation in the Soviet Zone. "If anything has changed," read an informed report of March, 1954, "it is that the anti-Communist leadership has been so seriously weakend by arrests and executions that the population will be incapable of organized resistance for some time to come."[59] "The events of June, 1953, and the Soviet response have largely defined the nature of the relationship between the U.S.S.R. and the G.D.R. This implies a mutual, nearly

[58] Vaclav E. Mares, "East Europe's Second Chance," *Current History*, XLVII (November, 1964), 279; and Joseph Wechsberg, "Letter from Prague," *The New Yorker*, April 27, 1968.

[59] "East Germany After Berlin," *Current Germany*, I (March, 1954).

Zeichnung: Hicks (Copyright Die Welt)

"The main thing is that we firmly hold the strings in our hands!"

symbiotic dependence which neither side can in the foreseeable future be expected to abandon, and makes unreal any projects for the general unification of Germany on terms acceptable to both East and West."[60] In spite of an impressive degree of economic progress, East Germany has been characterized by an "air of sluggish instability," symbolized by "the single-minded determination" of its long-time leader, Walter Ulbricht, and by the building of the Berlin Wall in August, 1961. East Germany is heavily dependent on the Soviet Union, and is in many respects Russia's most faithful satellite. The twenty-year treaty of friendship and mutual assistance between East Germany and the U.S.S.R. was evidence that, in contrast to the growing de-satellization in most of Eastern Europe, the ties between the German Democratic Republic and the U.S.S.R. were being forged more tightly than ever. Ulbricht has always been a "Moscow man." "Yet he was no mere puppet, and the Russians need him as badly as he needed them."[61] The Soviet Union seems to regard East Germany as a vital anchor in the control of Eastern Europe, as an important leverage against West Germany, and as a guarantee that German reunification will be achieved only on the Russians' own terms.

2. *Yugoslavia.* Shortly after the death of Stalin the bitter Soviet attacks and organized pressures on Yugoslavia gave way to conciliatory gestures. Formal diplomatic relations were resumed, and trade between the two countries greatly increased. Russia supported a settlement of the Trieste question favorable to Yugoslavia. The climax of the Russian campaign to establish a new relationship with Tito came in May, 1955, when top Soviet leaders, headed by Khrushchev, Bulganin, and Mikoyan, made an official visit to Yugoslavia. On his arrival in Belgrade Khrushchev declared: "We sincerely regret what happened and resolutely reject the things that occurred. . . . For our part we are ready to do everything necessary to eliminate all obstacles standing in the way of complete normalization of relations between our states."

Possibly the Russians actually hoped to lure Tito back into the international Communist camp, but they certainly also had other and more immediate objectives in mind. In all probability they aimed to create a better situation in the satellite states, to encourage Yugoslavia to maintain a neutralist position, to weaken her ties with the West, and to undermine her alliance with Greece and Turkey. Like the almost simultaneous concessions on Austria, Germany, and disarmament, the Russian pilgrimage to Belgrade was hailed in non-Communist countries as a major reversal of Soviet policy.

The abolition of the Cominform in 1956, the more flexible tactical and ideological position of the new leaders of the Soviet Union, and the deliberate wooing of Tito effected at least a partial reconciliation. Since 1955–56 Yugoslavia's relations with the Soviet Union and other countries of Eastern Europe have generally improved.[62] At the same time she has maintained closer and more extensive relations with the West than any other Communist state. Ironically, Tito has emerged as one of the leaders of the "neutralist" countries, especially since his meetings with Nehru and Nasser and the first Conference of non-Aligned States, which was held in Belgrade in 1961. A corollary to a more independent foreign policy has been a greater degree of decentralization and liberalization. "But there is also no doubt that it

[60] Hans Rogger, "East Germany: Stable or Immobile?" *Current History,* XLVIII (March, 1965), 135–136.

[61] *Ibid.,* p. 136.

[62] In 1956 Edvard Kardejl, Vice-Premier of Yugoslavia, wrote in an American journal that relations with the Soviet Union had improved "greatly" and had become "stable and friendly." "Evolution in Jugoslavia," *Foreign Affairs,* XXXIV (July, 1956), 601.

[Yugoslav leadership] intends to accomplish these advances in individual and material well-being within a system that ensures the concentration of ultimate political decision-making authority in the hands of the Communist party."[63]

The Sino-Soviet Dispute: A Post-Stalin Phenomenon. For the first few months following Stalin's death, relations between the U.S.S.R. and Communist China seemed to be close, and there was little indication that China was reluctant to continue to accept a subordinate role in the Communist camp. In late September and early October, 1954, a Soviet delegation headed by Khrushchev, Bulganin, Mikoyan, and Shvernik visited Peking, supposedly to attend ceremonies commemorating the fifth anniversary of Communist China. One result was the signing of a series of "seven accords" dealing with Chinese-Soviet relations, the international situation, relations with Japan, Port Arthur, mixed Soviet-Chinese companies, technical assistance, and railroads.[64] Russia agreed to evacuate Port Arthur by May, 1955, to extend another long-term loan of $130 million, to sell her share in four joint Soviet-Chinese companies, to help China undertake fifteen heavy industry projects, and to build two railroads from Central China to the Russian border. She gave Red China her moral support but not a specific commitment regarding Formosa. The two countries expressed their "deep sympathy for Japan and the Japanese people" and urged Japan to "take the path of liberation from foreign dependence."

After 1955, however, signs of a developing rift between the two began to multiply. They were particularly apparent after Khrushchev denounced Stalin at the Twentieth Party Congress in 1956 and launched the de-Stalinization process. Mao Tse-tung was obviously not enthusiastic about the downgrading of Stalin — perhaps he saw in this move a challenge to the principle of individual leadership in Communist countries — and he may have expected greater recognition than he received of his new position as the senior leader of one of the most powerful Communist states. In 1960 the Soviet Union withdrew her technicians from China and virtually suspended her aid to that country, while at the same time stepping up assistance to India and other non-Communist states. The Russian leaders openly disapproved of the Chinese attack on India in October–November, 1962. With mounting frequency since 1963, the two Communist countries and their respective Communist parties have engaged in lengthy and vitriolic verbal exchanges and charges. They have competed openly at conferences of nonaligned countries and in various countries of Asia and Africa. They have vied with each other for support in Communist parties, inside and outside the Communist world. China has had some success in weakening Russia's influence in Asia, especially in East and Southeast Asia, and in gaining significant footholds or even a dominating influence in most Asian Communist parties. On the surface, at least, the Sino-Soviet dispute has reached the proportions of an open split, although, as noted previously, the two countries and parties still share common objectives. Their differences may turn out to be almost wholly those of tactics rather than of strategy, ideology, or long-range goals.

The nature of the dispute, and its implications, have been further examined in Chapter 16.

Soviet Foreign Policy since Khrushchev's Fall. With Khrushchev's sudden overthrow in October, 1964, speculation was

[63] Alvin Z. Rubinstein, "Yugoslavia's Opening Society," *Current History,* XLVIII (March, 1965), 179.

[64] For the text of the Soviet-Chinese Communist communiqué on the seven accords, see the *New York Times,* October 12, 1954.

79.8 billion dollars, almost half of all expenditures provided in the new U.S. budget, are earmarked for the Pentagon. At the same time expenditures for domestic social programs have again been cut, and taxes are rising. (From the newspapers)

Yuri Kershin in Pravda, February 1, 1968

"They have 'divided it up.'"

(The buzz saw reads "The Pentagon"; the sack reads "79.8 billion dollars")

Experience has condemned the Washington strategists who were just opening the way to "new shores" for Latin America, with the neo-colonial program "Alliance for Progress." The looting of the continent continues. (From the newspapers)

Yuri Kershin in Pravda, March 10, 1968

"New Shores . . . and New Robberies."

(The sign reads "Alliance for Progress")

Three Russian Views of American Policy

rife whether new leadership would portend any significant changes in Russia's domestic or foreign policy. Apparently Khrushchev was overthrown primarily because of internal power struggles and dissatisfaction with some of his domestic policies, although after his fall he was also criticized for inept and "undignified" diplomacy, for exacerbating the Sino-Soviet dispute, for alienating some influential Communist leaders in Eastern Europe, for blunders in dealings with underdeveloped nations, and for "softness" in his relations with the United States.

For a few weeks the new Soviet leadership, with Brezhnev, Kosygin, and Mikoyan in the top positions, seemed to be trying to reverse the trend in Sino-Soviet relations. Premier Chou En-lai came to Moscow with a large delegation some three weeks after Khrushchev's downfall to participate in the first top-level talks between Russian and Chinese leaders in many months. Apparently, however, these talks led nowhere, and shortly afterward the Chinese attacks on the Soviet Union were resumed. The new Soviet leaders were charged with following a policy of "Khrushchevism without Khrushchev."

Within a few weeks, also, the new Soviet leadership seemed to abandon a conciliatory tone and revert to a much harder line in its dealings with the United States and most Western countries. It tried to play off Paris against Washington, and it welcomed De Gaulle's suggestion for a settlement of the German question "among Europeans." In general the new leadership was more "opportunist" than Khrushchev was. It sought to weaken the Western alliance, to regain Russia's influence in the Third World, and to reassert her position in the Communist World.

Regardless of increasing military failures, the American aggressors are continuing the escalation of the criminal war against the Vietnamese people, and sinking ever deeper into the swamp of this imperialist adventure. (From the newspapers)

Kukryniska in Pravda, February 9, 1968

"In the swamp of the 'dirty' war."

Whether these were differences in basic policy or in approach would become clear only with the passage of time. Six months after Khrushchev's fall, a distinguished German authority on Communist affairs wrote:

> In fact, there has been a marked shift both in the immediate priorities and in the style of Soviet relations with the outside world. It has not been announced or explained: on the contrary, the new men have reacted against the Khrushchevian style of basing Soviet diplomacy on grandiose, comprehensive concepts, and have preferred to make their adjustments quietly and with a minimum of verbal fuss. But in substance, they have shifted the emphasis of their relations with Communist China from direct opposition, in terms of ideology and power politics, to indirect competition for influence on the anti-Western, revolutionary-nationalist government and movements of the underdeveloped world. At the same time, in their relations with the West, they have transferred their main effort from direct approaches to the United States aiming at a major *détente* to indirect maneuvers for exploiting the disagreements within the Western alliance.[65]

Clearly, as this authority noted, "the new tactics of Khrushchev's successors have been much more successful against the West than against Communist China." In style they indicated a hardening of the Soviet line, and in priorities they suggested that the struggle against imperialism and the promotion of national liberation would be placed ahead of efforts toward peace. Whatever the situation within the Communist world, the Soviet Union under the new leadership was obviously still dedicated to the achievement of its long-proclaimed world objectives, which boded no good for those who stood in the way.

[65] Richard Lowenthal, "The Soviets Change Their Foreign Policy," *New York Times Magazine*, April 4, 1965, p. 30.

SUGGESTIONS FOR FURTHER READING

BARGHOORN, FREDERICK C. *The Soviet Cultural Offensive; The Role of Cultural Diplomacy in Soviet Foreign Policy*. Princeton, N.J.: Princeton University Press, 1960. By an American political scientist and former press attaché in the U.S. Embassy in Moscow.

———. *The Soviet Image of the United States: A Study in Distortion*. New York: Harcourt, Brace, 1950.

BELOFF, MAX. *The Foreign Policy of Soviet Russia, 1929–1941*. 2 vols. New York: Oxford University Press, 1947–49. Vol. I covers 1929 to 1936; Vol. II covers 1936 to 1941. Scholarship of a high order.

———. *Soviet Policy in the Far East, 1944–1951*. New York: Oxford University Press, 1953.

BERLINER, JOSEPH S. *Soviet Economic Aid: The New Aid and Trade Policy in Underdeveloped Countries*. New York: Frederick A. Praeger, for the Council on Foreign Relations, 1958. A detailed study by an American economist.

BRZEZINSKI, ZBIGNIEW K. *The Soviet Bloc: Unity and Conflict*, rev. ed. Cambridge, Mass.. Harvard University Press, 1967. Particular emphasis is given to the impact of the Sino-Soviet dispute.

CARR, EDWARD H. *German-Soviet Relations Between the Two World Wars, 1919–1930*. Baltimore: The Johns Hopkins Press, 1951.

———. *A History of Soviet Russia*. 4 vols. New York: The Macmillan Company, 1950, 1953, 1955. These volumes cover the period from 1917 to 1924.

CRANKSHAW, EDWARD. *The New Cold War: Moscow v. Peking*. Baltimore: Penguin Books, 1963.

DALLIN, ALEXANDER, ed. *Soviet Conduct in World Affairs; a Selection of Readings*. New York: Columbia University Press, 1960.

———. *The Soviet Union at the United Nations; an Inquiry into Soviet Motives and Objectives*. New York: Frederick A. Praeger, 1962.

DALLIN, DAVID J. *The Changing World of Soviet Russia*. New Haven: Yale University Press, 1956.

———. *The New Soviet Empire*. New Haven: Yale University Press, 1942.

———. *The Rise of Russia in Asia*. New Haven: Yale University Press, 1949.

———. *Soviet Foreign Policy after Stalin*. Philadelphia: J. B. Lippincott Co., 1961. Soviet foreign policy during the period 1953–60, by a noted expert.

———. *Soviet Russia and the Far East*. New Haven: Yale University Press, 1948.

FISCHER, LOUIS. *The Soviets in World Affairs*, 2d ed. 2 vols. Princeton, N.J.: Princeton University Press, 1951. First published in 1930.

GARTHOFF, RAYMOND. *Soviet Strategy in the Nuclear Age*, rev. ed. New York: Frederick A. Praeger, 1962. An analysis of Soviet military doctrine.

GOLDMAN, MARSHALL. *Soviet Foreign Aid*. New York; Frederick A. Praeger, 1967. Particular attention to Soviet economic assistance to other Communist countries, and to Afghanistan, India, Indonesia, and the U.A.R.

GOLDWIN, ROBERT A., GERALD STOURZH, and MARVIN ZETTERBAUM, eds. *Readings in Russian Foreign Policy*. New York: Oxford University Press, 1959. Articles by 19th and 20th century authors.

GOODMAN, ELLIOTT R. *The Soviet Design for a World State*. New York: Columbia University Press, 1960

HUDSON, G. F., RICHARD LOWENTHAL, and RODERICK MACFARQUHAR, eds. *The Sino-Soviet Dispute*. New York: Frederick A. Praeger, 1961.

HUNT, R. N. C. *The Theory and Practice of Communism*, rev. ed. New York: The Macmillan Company, 1952

KENNAN, GEORGE F. *Soviet Foreign Policy, 1917–1941*. Princeton, N.J.: D. Van Nostrand Co., 1960. A brief survey by a leading American writer on Soviet affairs, a former diplomat.

KULSKI, W. W. *The Soviet Regime: Communism in Practice.* Syracuse: Syracuse University Press, 1955.

LEDERER, IVO, ed. *Russian Foreign Policy; Essays in Historical Perspective.* New Haven: Yale University Press, 1962.

MACKINTOSH, J. M. *Strategy and Tactics of Soviet Foreign Policy.* New York: Oxford University Press, 1962.

MCLANE, CHARLES B. *Soviet Strategies in Southeast Asia: An Exploration of Eastern Policy under Lenin and Stalin.* Princeton, N.J.: Princeton University Press, 1966.

MAGER, N. H. and JACQUES KATEL, eds. *Conquest Without War.* New York: Simon and Schuster, 1961. Mainly a collection of writings and statements of Stalin and Khrushchev.

MAMATY, VICTOR S. *Soviet Russian Imperialism.* Princeton, N.J.: D. Van Nostrand Co., 1964.

MOORE, BARRINGTON, JR. *Soviet Politics — The Dilemma of Power.* Cambridge, Mass.: Harvard University Press, 1950. A painstaking and balanced account.

MOORE, HARRIET L. *Soviet Far Eastern Policy, 1931–1945.* Princeton, N.J.: Princeton University Press, 1945. A sound review.

MOSELY, PHILIP E. *The Kremlin and World Politics.* New York: Random House, 1960. Twenty-five essays by a noted authority on Russian foreign policy during a period of two decades.

NIEMEYER, GERHARD. *An Inquiry into Soviet Mentality.* Foreign Policy Research Institute Series No. 2. New York: Frederick A. Praeger, 1956.

RUBINSTEIN, ALVIN Z., ed. *Foreign Policy of the Soviet Union,* 2d ed. New York: Random House, 1966.

———. *The Soviets in International Organizations; Changing Policy Toward Developing Countries.* Princeton, N.J.: Princeton University Press, 1964.

SETON-WATSON, HUGH. *The East European Revolution.* New York: Frederick A. Praeger, 1951. A readable account of the sovietization process.

SHARP, SAMUEL L. *Soviet Foreign Policy: A 50-Year Perspective.* New York: Atherton Press, 1966.

SHULMAN, MARSHALL. *Stalin's Foreign Policy Reappraised.* Cambridge, Mass.: Harvard University Press, 1963. Emphasizes the "remarkable continuity" in the Kremlin's view of the world.

THORNTON, THOMAS PERRY. *The Third World in Soviet Perspective.* Princeton, N.J.: Princeton University Press, 1964. A selection of Soviet writings.

WALSH, EDMUND J. *Total Empire: The Roots and Progress of World Communism.* Milwaukee: The Bruce Publishing Co., 1952.

ZAGORIA, DONALD S. *The Sino-Soviet Conflict, 1956–1961.* Princeton, N.J.: Princeton University Press, 1962.

22 The Foreign Policy of the United States

Americans like to think of their country as the goddess of liberty, holding high the torch of freedom as a beacon light to all the peoples of the world. Communist propagandists point to that same America as a ruthless imperialist power trying to prop up her rotten system by exporting her troubles to the rest of the world and to force all other nations to accept her dictates. Some friendlier critics speak of her as a reluctant dragon with brute strength but with little mind or imagination. All these images are stereotypes. The interesting thing about them is not that they misrepresent or obscure the real United States but that they all appraise her in terms of foreign policy.

By history and by experience, by temperament and by inclination, Americans are ill-prepared to accept the heavy responsibilities and commitments in world affairs which their country has assumed in recent years. The transition has been made too suddenly, and the tempo of events has accelerated too rapidly, for the evolution of a satisfactory policy for the "long pull." Moreover, the state of the world has been such that a really satisfactory foreign policy is probably impossible.

After some preliminary observations, we shall center our discussion on the period since 1945. But first something must be said about the factors conditioning American foreign policy, the basic principles of that policy, and the nature of the national interest.

Factors Conditioning American Foreign Policy

The foreign policy of the United States, like that of any state, is shaped largely by geographical and historical considerations, by her political and social system, by her economic strength and military power, by her relative power position, by the policies of other states, and by the world environment. The following observations on American foreign policy, made in 1949 by an anonymous but "important United States statesman who has much to do with shaping this policy," point to its basic setting and nature:

> United States foreign policy is the sum total of the aspirations and reactions of the American people, with relation to world affairs, as they are channelled up through the executive branch of the Government and through Congress.
>
> This policy is necessarily fluid. It is by its essential quality neither static nor the conscious decision of one man or of one group of men. As public sentiment changes, the color of American policy changes. . . .
>
> In foreign affairs nations cannot pursue static objectives. The whole subject is dynamic. Diplomacy must operate in a fluid medium. Some objectives cannot ever be

attained — like perfection. Some problems cannot ever be permanently "solved." We must learn to live with them. The important thing is motion toward given objectives.[1]

National Characteristics. American national characteristics have always had a decided bearing on foreign policy. In foreign as in domestic affairs "some clues as to how the American people *will behave and should behave* must be sought in the total complex of conditions and factors which make American society what it is or what it is becoming."[2]

Many of the strengths and weaknesses of the American character may be traced to the efforts to give reality to "the American dream" of democracy as "a system in which every man had the same rights as any other, where formal class lines did not exist and where any citizen could rise to the heights permitted by his abilities and his labors";[3] to the intermingling of many races and peoples in that vast "melting-pot" that is America; and to the expansion across a great continent with little opposition. These experiences have given strength and vitality to the American experiment; they have made it possible to develop a society possessing great economic and political strength based on the principles of democracy and liberty. On the negative side, these same characteristics may account for the qualities which Thomas Bailey and others have noted in their analyses of the attitudes of the American people toward foreign affairs — their "spirit of spread-eagleism"; their bumptiousness and exaggerated confidence in themselves; their "blind optimism," which together with their idealism tends to give them a false picture of the world and to lure them into moral crusades; their inability to grasp the intimate relationship between foreign policy and military power and between foreign and domestic affairs; their selfishness and shortsightedness; their immaturity and inexperience; their caprices and fluctuations in mood, which create uncertainties abroad regarding American intentions and determination; their apathy and ignorance with respect to foreign affairs; their xenophobism and xenophilism; their provincialism and isolationism, or at best their very tentative internationalism.[4]

In his well-known study, *The American People and Foreign Policy,* Professor Gabriel Almond called attention to and carefully documented the instability of mood which characterizes the American people in their reactions to developments in foreign affairs, especially to crisis situations.[5] In such situations Americans are inclined to swing from one extreme to another, although possibly these swings seem even greater than they actually are because spokesmen for more extreme views make much more noise than do those in "the silent center." This phenomenon is illustrated in American reactions to the frustrating dilemmas that the United States has faced in Vietnam. Very vocal groups which might be labeled interventionist demanded a major escalation of the mili-

[1] Quoted by C. L. Sulzberger, in the *New York Times,* October 20, 1949.

[2] Robert K. Carr *et al., American Democracy in Theory and Practice: The National Government* (New York: Rinehart, 1951), p. 951. Italics in original.

[3] "Making Foreign Policy in a Nuclear Age: 2. Challenges to U.S. Foreign Policy," *Headline Series,* No. 172 (August, 1965), p. 34.

[4] See Thomas Bailey, *The Man in the Street: The Impact of American Public Opinion on Foreign Policy* (New York: The Macmillan Company, 1948); Gabriel Almond, *The American People and Foreign Policy* (New York: Harcourt, Brace, 1950); Lester Markel, ed., *Public Opinion and Foreign Policy* (New York: Harper, 1949).

[5] Professor Almond isolated six "potential movements of opinion and mood which may have significant effects on foreign policy": withdrawal–intervention; mood–simplification, from "unstructured moods in periods of equilibrium to simplification in periods of crisis"; optimism–pessimism; tolerance–intolerance; idealism–cynicism; and superiority–inferiority. See Almond, Chapter III, "American Character and Foreign Policy."

tary effort, while equally vocal groups which might be described as neo-isolationist demanded complete United States withdrawal from Vietnam. Official American policy and majority public opinion were concerned with steering a more cautious course between these extremes. Both interventionists and neo-isolationists were united in criticizing official American policy and in demanding quick "solutions" to the kind of situation in which such "solutions" were not possible. Both were therefore equally unrealistic.

Many close observers of American foreign policy, especially those who are familiar with the experience of other nations, are highly critical of the alleged American "intoxication with moral principles" and the tendency to regard power politics as something which can and should be avoided. These points are stressed — perhaps overstressed — in Hans Morgenthau's *In Defense of the National Interest* and to a lesser extent in George F. Kennan's *American Diplomacy, 1900–1950.* Morgenthau held that these attitudes have continued into the postwar period and account for the "stultification of mind" and "paralysis of will" which he believed have characterized recent American foreign policy. The "four intellectual errors of American postwar policy," in his opinion, are Utopianism, legalism, sentimentalism, and neo-isolationism.[6] Kennan decried "our [American] general ignorance of the historical processes of our age and particularly . . . our lack of attention to the power realities involved in given situations." According to him, "the most serious fault of our past policy formulation" lies "in something that I might call the legalistic–moralistic approach to international problems. This approach runs like a red skein through our foreign policy of the last fifty years."[7]

There is unfortunately much truth in these strictures; but they are by no means the whole or even the major part of the story, and they reflect a misunderstanding of American history and American character, and of the role of moral concepts and legal principles in international affairs. While it may be well to be reminded by devotees of *realpolitik* that American tendencies to go off on moral crusades and to expect to avoid the "contamination" of power politics are dangerous, these same critics do a great disservice by underestimating the strong and healthy influence of idealism in foreign policy and by overlooking one of the major forces which has actuated the United States in her dealings with other nations.

Domestic Policies and Pressures. The Task Force on Foreign Affairs of the Hoover Commission referred to "the disappearance of the line of demarcation which hitherto has existed between domestic and foreign problems."[8] Many Americans are becoming more conscious of the interconnection between domestic and foreign affairs, and of the effects of the one upon the other; but "for the present," as a study of the Brookings Institution pointed out, "the people of the United States frequently show an unwillingness to support wholeheartedly specific foreign policies advocated by their government when this requires a substantial modification of domestic policies, sometimes to the detriment of local or personal interests. The result is that the government often adopts domestic policies that are incompatible with

[6] Hans J. Morgenthau, *In Defense of the National Interest* (New York: Alfred A. Knopf, 1951). See especially pp. 28–33, 91–138, 229–242. Morgenthau described three forms of Utopianism: Wilsonianism, isolationism, and internationalism.

[7] George F. Kennan, *American Diplomacy, 1900–1950* (Chicago: University of Chicago Press, 1951), pp. 88, 95.

[8] *Task Force Report on Foreign Affairs,* Appendix H. Prepared for the Commission on Organization of the Executive Branch of the Government. January, 1949 P 38.

its stated foreign policies."[9] The heavy burdens which the military budget and the foreign aid programs now impose upon the American economy would seem to indicate that this is an age when foreign policies are of primary importance. On the other hand, the influence of the country abroad depends primarily upon the strength of the internal political, economic, and social structure. Moreover, the position of the United States on many international issues is often shaped by domestic pressures, even to the detriment of the national interest.[10] This is probably true of many aspects of postwar China policy. On a lesser issue, one can sympathize with the attitude of a British statesman who, when asked for his views on the partition of Ireland, replied that he never interfered in American domestic politics!

Among the strongest internal pressures whose effects are not always conducive to the formation of rational foreign policies are those from organized minority groups, especially from what Thomas Bailey calls the "hyphenate organizations."[11] These groups form powerful voting blocs, as members of Congress are well aware. One can argue that so great is the Jewish-American influence in this country that the entire American position on the Palestine issue was framed largely to conform to the demands of this minority group. Religious and other organizations are sometimes equally effective. The position of the United States toward the civil war in Spain was certainly influenced by the strong Catholic support of General Franco; in this case, however, there were other organized pressures, perhaps equally potent, which took an opposite view. While America cannot play her proper role in the world if her policies are determined by pressure groups within, it is certainly true that most of the hyphenate organizations are sincerely concerned with national interests, and that the successful intermingling of peoples of many nationalities has given the United States one of her greatest sources of strength.

Pressure tactics are by no means confined to ethnic and religious groups. Probably the best financed and most persistent of all pressure groups are those which speak for bankers, farmers, manufacturers, organized labor, and veterans' organizations. Lesser groups — professional, educational economic, cultural, and others — also raise their strident voices to demand foreign policies to conform to their convictions or their interests.

Constitutional Handicaps. Under the best of conditions a democratic state, especially one of the federal type, labors under rather severe handicaps in the conduct of its foreign relations. Today's conditions impose particular strains on the United States. The Constitution itself and Supreme Court decisions, such as *Missouri v. Holland,*[12] have centered authority over foreign affairs in the central government and have restricted state action which might contravene foreign commitments, and they have given the President primary responsibility for the conduct of foreign relations. Nevertheless, the federal-state dichotomy can still produce embarrassments, and in actual practice the principle of the separation of powers and the deliberate vagueness of the Constitution have led to serious friction between the executive and the legislative branches.[13]

[9] *Major Problems of United States Foreign Policy, 1947* (Washington, D.C.: The Brookings Institution, 1947), p. 28.

[10] "History does not forgive us our national mistakes because they are explicable in terms of our domestic policies. . . . A nation which excuses its own failures by the sacred untouchableness of its own habits can excuse itself into complete disaster." Kennan, p. 73.

[11] See Bailey, Chapters II and III.

[12] 252 U.S. 416 (1920).

[13] See Edward S. Corwin, *The President's Control of Foreign Relations* (Princeton, N.J.: Princeton University Press, 1917), *The President: Office and Powers* (New York: Oxford University Press,

Party Cooperation and Administrative Coordination. Differences between the President and Congress are, of course, most likely to occur when the President's party is not in control of Congress. On these occasions the President may find his treaties and his appointments obstructed by the Senate and his requests for appropriations blocked by one or both Houses. This political handicap has been only partially overcome by an attempt to bring the two major parties to an informal agreement that partisan politics end "at the water's edge," or, in other words, that they strive for "bipartisanship" in foreign policy.

Begun during World War II when Roosevelt took two Republicans into his cabinet, and repeatedly urged by Senator Arthur H. Vandenberg, bipartisanship in foreign policy has an off-and-on record. President Eisenhower early appealed for it, but, with a narrow Republican majority in the Eighty-third Congress, an actual minority in the Eighty-fourth, and at times the opposition of Senate Republican leader William F. Knowland, he had little choice. Indeed, without it hardly one of the major items of his legislative program would have been approved. After February, 1965, President Johnson received more support in the Congress for his policies on Vietnam from Republican members of the Congress than he did from members of his own party, even though he used all his great political skills to cultivate his fellow-Democrats in the Congress. Even the Senate majority leader and the chairman of the Senate Foreign Relations Committee publicly expressed views on Vietnam which were considerably at variance with administration policy, and some of the bitterest critics of the actions of the United States in Vietnam were Democrats. Thus on a number of major issues of foreign policy in recent years the administration would have been unable to carry out its announced policies without bipartisan support. But bipartisanship is a vague term, with many possible interpretations;[14] and back of it lies the warning of Senator Vandenberg that it must not become "an iron curtain behind which specious unity would stifle traditional American debate."[15]

Moreover, the President, elected by a different constituency from the Congress, has no assurance that the members of his own party will follow his lead or will even abide by the party platform. Only when he has a large majority in the Congress can he count upon the members of his own party for support. Even when his special duties and powers in foreign policy are acknowledged, the President may run afoul of congressional insistence that the proposals he is making relate primarily to domestic rather than to foreign affairs. This difficulty is common at times when the line between internal and foreign policies is hard to draw and when powerful domestic interests have to be considered in almost every issue of foreign affairs. Agricultural, shipping, and trade policies may be cited as examples.

Another problem is to achieve the effective cooperation of the multitude of departments and agencies having functions related to foreign policy. When it is realized that the Task Force on Foreign Affairs of the Hoover Commission found within the Executive Branch alone "59 departments, agencies,

---

1940), and *Total War and the Constitution* (New York: Alfred A. Knopf, 1947); *Task Force Report on Foreign Affairs*, pp. 46–48, 125–134; Daniel S. Cheever and H. Field Havlland, *American Foreign Policy and the Separation of Powers* (Cambridge, Mass.: Harvard University Press, 1952); Richard E. Neustadt, *Presidential Power* (New York: John Wiley & Sons, 1960); and James N. Rosenau, *National Leadership and Foreign Policy* (Princeton, N.J.: Princeton University Press, 1964).

[14] Richard C. Snyder and Edgar S. Furniss, Jr., *American Foreign Policy: Formulation, Principles, and Programs* (New York: Rinehart, 1954), pp. 497–500; Cecil V. Crabb, Jr., *Bipartisan Foreign Policy: Myth or Reality?* (New York: Harper, 1957), pp. 217–220.

[15] Radio broadcast of October 4, 1948; in the *New York Times*, October 5, 1958.

commissions, boards, and interdepartmental councils under the President, of which the work of at least 46" involved "some aspects of the conduct of foreign affairs," it is obvious that American foreign policy is conditioned by the efficiency of each of these agencies and particularly by the degree of coordination with which they operate. While we cannot here discuss the structure and operation of these forty-six bodies — even of the Department of State and the Foreign Service[16] — we shall consider briefly the most common devices for coordination, especially the interdepartmental committee. The Foreign Affairs Task Force found that "in the foreign affairs field 33 such committees were sufficiently important to warrant special study. Over 20 or two-thirds of these were created since the end of World War II."

The most important of the high-level interdepartmental committees is the National Security Council, which is a cabinet-level advisory committee charged with the coordination of foreign, military, and domestic policies. First established in the National Security Act of 1947 as a coordinating agency within the "National Military Establishment," it was transferred to the Executive Office of the President two years later. Administratively the huge Central Intelligence Agency is responsible to the President through the National Security Council. The NSC is composed of the President, who is the chairman, the Vice President, the Secretaries of State and Defense, the Director of the Office of Emergency Planning, and such other agency heads and senior officials as the President may invite. It usually meets once a week, and on other occasions at the discretion of the President. Its meetings are invariably attended by many senior advisers, such as the Director of Central Intelligence, the Chairman of the Joint Chiefs of Staff, and the Special Assistant to the President for National Security Affairs.

Constitutionally speaking, the Secretary of State is the President's chief adviser in foreign affairs. He has usually, but not always, functioned in this capacity. Some presidents, such as Roosevelt and Kennedy, have in effect been their own Secretaries of State, at least in crisis situations. Others have relied on a variety of persons in official or unofficial positions for advice on foreign policy matters. President Johnson seemed to rely almost equally on the Secretary of Defense, his Special Assistant for National Security Affairs, and the Secretary of State, and sometimes he has seemed to give almost equal weight to the advice of other officials in the White House Office or elsewhere in the Executive Office of the President, of key members of the Congress, and even of persons outside official circles

[16] On the Department of State and the Foreign Service, see: *The Administration of Foreign Affairs and Overseas Operations.* A Report Prepared for the Bureau of the Budget, Executive Office of the President by the Brookings Institution (Washington, D.C.: Government Printing Office of the President, by the Brookings Insti-*Service* (New York: Holt, 1948); Commission on Organization of the Executive Branch of the Government, *Foreign Affairs, A Report to the Congress* (Washington, D.C.: Government Printing Office, February, 1949), and *Task Force Report on Foreign Affairs,* Appendix H (Washington, D.C.: Government Printing Office, January, 1949); *The Department of State, 1930–1955: Expanding Functions and Responsibilities,* Dept. of State Pub. 5832 (Washington, D.C.: Government Printing Office, 1955); William Y. Elliott *et al., United States Foreign Policy: Its Organization and Control* (New York: Columbia University Press, 1952); Arthur W. Macmahon, *Administration in Foreign Affairs* (University, Ala.: University of Alabama Press, 1955); James L. McCamy, *Conduct of the New Diplomacy* (New York: Harper & Row, 1964); Elmer Plischke, *Conduct of American Diplomacy,* 3d ed. (Princeton, N.J.: D. Van Nostrand Co., 1967); Snyder and Furniss, *American Foreign Policy;* Graham H. Stuart, *The Department of State: A History of Its Organization, Procedure and Personnel* (New York: The Macmillan Company, 1949); *Toward a Stronger Foreign Service,* Report of the Secretary of State's Public Committee on Personnel, Dept of State Pub. 5458, Department and Foreign Service Series 36 (Washington, D.C.: Government Printing Office, June, 1954); Burton M. Sapin, *The Making of United States Foreign Policy* (New York: Frederick A. Praeger, 1966).

whose opinions he especially respected. The result of these procedures of coordination and administration is decision-making by consensus, which has obvious advantages and disadvantages.

Problems of coordination between Washington and American embassies, consulates-general, consulates, and special missions overseas are accepted as a normal feature of modern diplomacy. Every day the State Department sends or receives some 3000 telegrams and thousands of other messages, dispatches, and reports. In a foreign country the American ambassador, as the chief representative of the United States and head of the "country team," supervises the activities not only of a large group of Foreign Service Officers and other diplomatic and consular personnel, but also of representatives of the United States Information Agency, the Central Intelligence Agency, the A.I.D. Mission and the Military Assistance Advisory Group in countries receiving economic and military assistance, and other departments and agencies of the American government. In 1965, for example, 31 American agencies had representatives in Britain.

Not only is it important to coordinate the activities of all United States agencies involved in foreign policies and operations, it is also necessary, or at least desirable, to consult friendly governments, especially allied governments, on all major issues before decisions are made. Failure to do this can have unfortunate consequences. The abrupt cancellation of the Skybolt missile project in 1962 without consultation with the Conservative government in Great Britain placed the British Government in a most embarrassing and vulnerable position, for it was planning to rely on the Skybolt for its missile defense; and the subsequent agreement of President Kennedy and Prime Minister Macmillan at Nassau, made without consulting General de Gaulle, was regarded as an affront, thus further exacerbating Franco-American relations and perhaps influencing De Gaulle's decision to "veto" Britain's application for membership in the European Economic Community. The American decision to intervene in the Dominican Republic in mid-1965 was taken without real consultation with the other members of the OAS, and was widely interpreted as a violation of the OAS Charter. Whatever the justification for this move, there can be no doubt that it strained the relations of the United States with her sister nations to the south.

Principles of American Foreign Policy

It is often asserted that the United States has no foreign policy; but such an analysis is at best a superficial one, as any student of American diplomacy, not to mention any member of the much-abused State Department, should know. Broadly speaking, the United States, like any other state, has to have a foreign policy, or foreign policies. This was a matter of supreme importance in the early days of the republic, and it has become so again. Even in the period of American history when foreign affairs were regarded as relatively unimportant — indeed, as something of a luxury — there were certain basic policies to which the United States adhered. In fact, some of these have become traditional.

The fundamental principles of American foreign policy have been stated in general terms on innumerable occasions. Such statements are so general as to be virtually meaningless, hardly more than pious platitudes. A more profitable approach is to study the history of American diplomacy. No one can read any of the standard texts in the field without reaching the conviction that there are certain underlying concepts and principles which have played an important part in America's foreign policy throughout all, or most, of her history. The most basic of these, according to one authority, are those of security, expansion, and neutrality. Nathaniel Peffer believed that "the fixed points" in American foreign relations are isolationism, the Monroe Doctrine, freedom of the seas, and the Open Door.[17] Bemis held that the following principles are "foundations of American foreign policy": (1) sovereign independence; (2) continental expansion; (3) avoidance of the ordinary vicissitudes and ordinary combinations and collisions of European politics; (4) the noncolonization principle; (5) the no-transfer principle (no transfer by one European power to another of any possession in the Western Hemisphere); (6) freedom of international trade; (7) self-determination of peoples; (8) freedom of the seas for neutral ships in time of war, and freedom of navigation of international rivers; (9) the right of expatriation and the wrong of imprisonment; (10) nonintervention; and (11) a feeling of anti-imperialism.[18]

As Bemis pointed out, these principles were firmly established and generally accepted in the early days of the republic, and they have been governing principles throughout most of America's history as an independent nation. Since World War I, however, some of them have obviously been substantially modified. Freedom of seas for neutral ships in time of war, for example, antedated the development of submarine warfare. The principle of continental expansion is a matter of historical record. And the United States is now involved in European, and indeed in world, politics to a degree that might have appalled the Founding Fathers. Nevertheless, present American foreign policy is influenced by traditional principles as well as by current interests and conditions. However much one may question statements of fundamental principles, they are useful guides for a study of American diplomacy, and for an understanding of current American policies and attitudes.

Before World War II. The Monroe Doctrine and other important statements from the period when John Quincy Adams served his country so ably as Secretary of State (1817–25) were largely reformulations of policies which had already been put into practice with reasonable consistency. The Founding Fathers believed that the United States should and must remain aloof from the power struggle in Europe, but they were deeply concerned with any threats to the European balance. They wanted to steer clear of "entangling alliances" — the phrase is Jefferson's, not Washington's — and of "the ordinary vicissitudes of her [Europe's] politics" — the phrase is Washington's. But from Washington to Wilson American presidents were insistent upon all the rights of neutrals. "About the historic problem of neutral rights," as Professor Bemis has observed, "has been gathered a major part of the history of American diplomacy."[19] Since the earliest days of the republic, moreover, the promotion and protection of trade — and therefore an active participation in at least some aspects of world affairs — have been paramount interests of the United States.

Beginning in 1898 the United States embarked on a bolder course in international affairs and assumed more sweeping commitments beyond her borders, especially in the Far East and Latin America. This was the springtime of the Open Door and the Indian summer of Manifest Destiny. Admiral Mahan succinctly described American foreign policy in the first decade of the twentieth

17 *America's Place in the World* (New York: The Viking Press, 1945), p. 32.

18 Samuel Flagg Bemis, "The Shifting Strategy of American Defense and Diplomacy," *The Virginia Quarterly Review*, XXIV (Summer, 1948), 321–335

19 Samuel Flagg Bemis, *A Diplomatic History of the United States*, 3d ed. (New York: Holt, 1950), p. 99.

century as "participation in Asia, a sphere of influence in the Caribbean, and continued nonparticipation in Europe."[20] At about the same time the political system of the nineteenth century, based upon a Europe with an apparently stable balance of power, with Britain as the continuous holder of the balance, began to reveal those serious rifts which led to its almost complete collapse in two world wars. With the coming of the First World War the United States was faced with the full implications of her new position in a changing political order. Probably the "world structure of power" was such that she could not have escaped eventual involvement in the struggle; in any event, she did participate, and her President, Woodrow Wilson, tried to turn the bitter lessons of the war into constructive ventures in international cooperation and into higher standards of international conduct. His famous "Fourteen Points" and his many other public utterances reflected that idealism, that "intoxication with moral abstractions" or "pernicious abstractions," which many students of American policy deplore.

In the years following 1920 American foreign policy became more and more divorced from reality. The United States was in the "ambiguous position of being a major power, unwilling to act as such, yet inevitably exerting on international relations the influence of a major power. . . . The policy line consequently fluctuated between an avoidance of commitments, an insistence on freedom of action, and an effort to establish universal principles of international conduct."[21] Bemis has called this "the Fool's Paradise of American history," during which "American foreign policy degenerated into five postulates: isolationism, anti-imperialism, disarmament, neutrality, pacifism."[22] Above all, it was the period of isolationism, which reached its peak — or its nadir — in the neutrality legislation of the 1930's. Although the exponents of this policy, or lack of policy, tried to defend it by asserting that it represented a return to the first principles of American diplomacy, in reality it was very different in character from early American "isolationism." Hans Morgenthau made this point very effectively: "For the realists of the first period, isolation was an objective of policy, and had to be striven for to be attained. For the isolationists of the interwar period, isolation was a natural state, and only needed to be left undisturbed in order to continue forever. Conceived in such terms, it was the very negation of foreign policy."[23]

The Roosevelt Administration and After. The first reactions in the United States to the march of aggression in the 1930's came in efforts to withdraw into a storm cellar that did not exist. The cool reception of Roosevelt's "quarantine speech" in 1937 was an indication of the state of the American mind. In the two years or so prior to Pearl Harbor, however, Roosevelt took one bold step after another in support of Britain and against the Axis powers, while America was supposedly neutral. He believed that such steps were essential to the national interest, and he tried to educate the American people to the imperatives of the situation; but he did not — perhaps could not — take the people into his full confidence in justifying his actions. In a sense, therefore, as both his defenders and his critics, for different reasons, have pointed out, he "deceived" the American people.[24]

[20] Quoted in William G. Carleton, *The Revolution in American Foreign Policy, 1945–54* (Garden City, N.Y.: Doubleday & Company, 1954), p. 5.

[21] *Major Problems of United States Foreign Policy, 1950–51* (Washington, D.C.: The Brookings Institution, 1950), p. 30.

[22] Bemis, "Shifting Strategy," pp. 330–331.

[23] Morgenthau, p. 29.

[24] For bitter attacks on Roosevelt's pre-Pearl Harbor policies, see H. E. Barnes, ed., *Perpetual War for Perpetual Peace* (Caldwell, Idaho: The Caxton Printers, 1953); Charles A. Beard, *Presi-*

On the whole, the isolationism of the inter-war years finds only a feeble echo today, and one of the outstanding characteristics of the American reaction to the postwar world is the general acceptance of full American participation. While the trend of events was the great educator in the realities of world affairs, Franklin D. Roosevelt contributed much by his ability to dramatize and popularize the principles of American political action. "Prior to World War II," wrote Senator Arthur Vandenberg in 1951, "the oceans were virtual moats around our continental bastions. All this changed progressively at Pearl Harbor and thereafter. It became very obvious to me that this was a different world in which we had to sustain our own freedoms."[25]

Before undertaking a more detailed examination of American foreign policy since World War II, we shall first observe the nature of that paramount consideration, "the national interest," after which we shall note the general course of postwar policy and the conditions under which it has been pursued. Then we shall be ready to review the significant decisions and measures in America's recent foreign policy.

What Is the National Interest?

The foreign policy of every country is at all times presumably designed to promote the national interest. But what is the national interest?[26] And by what standards and by whom is it to be determined? Hamilton and Jefferson at times differed sharply on these questions. Franklin D. Roosevelt believed that he was acting in the national interest in the months prior to Pearl Harbor, but Charles A. Beard and other critics have charged that he was not. According to Morgenthau, Hamilton correctly foresaw and Wilson did not that the national interest was the maintenance of the European balance of power. Today, to continue Morgenthau's analysis, the "vital objective" — that is, the national interest "sharpened to meet particular inter-national situations" — of American foreign policy in Europe and Asia in "the restoration of the balance of power by means short of war."[27]

---

dent Roosevelt and the Coming of the War (New Haven: Yale University Press, 1948); George Morgenstern, *Pearl Harbor, the Story of the Secret War* (New York: The Devin-Adair Co., 1947); F. R. Sanborn, *Design for War: A Study of Secret Power Politics, 1937–1941* (New York: The Devin-Adair Co., 1951); Charles C. Tansill, *Back Door to War: The Roosevelt Foreign Policy, 1933–1941* (Chicago: Henry Regnery Co., 1952); and R. A. Theobald, *The Final Secret of Pearl Harbor: The Washington Contribution to the Japanese Attack* (New York: The Devin-Adair Co., 1954). Thomas A. Bailey, who is generally sympathetic with Roosevelt, speaks of the President's deception in a different sense: "Franklin Roosevelt repeatedly deceived the American people during the period before Pearl Harbor. . . . He was faced with a terrible dilemma. If he let the people slumber in a fog of isolation, they might well fall prey to Hitler. If he came out unequivocally for intervention, he would be defeated in 1940. . . . If he was going to induce the people to move at all, he would have to trick them into acting for their best interests, or what he conceived to be their best interests. . . . This is clearly what Roosevelt had to do, and who shall say that posterity will not thank him for it?" *The Man in the Street*, pp. 11–13.

[25] Letter to a Princeton University student, February 26, 1951; in Arthur W. Vandenberg, Jr., ed., *The Private Papers of Senator Vandenberg* (Boston: Houghton Mifflin Company, 1952), p. 577.

[26] A volume published by The Brookings Institution makes a helpful distinction among national interests, objectives, policies, and comments: "Stated broadly, *interests* are what a nation feels to be necessary to its security and well-being; *objectives* are interests sharpened to meet particular international situations; *policies* are thought-out ways of attaining *objectives;* and *commitments* are specific undertakings in support of *policy.*" Again: "*National interests* reflect the general and continuing ends for which a nation acts." *Major Problems, 1950–1951*, pp. 24n., 383. Italics in original.

[27] Morgenthau, p. 201; see also pp. 14–18, 23–28. Morgenthau's book is a particularly provocative study of the concept of national interest. For different points of view, see "The Idea of National Interest in 1950," a series of articles by Fred H. Harrington, William Carleton, George A. Lundberg, Ruhl J. Bartlett, Harry Elmer Barnes, and

This kind of analysis by no means clearly defines national interest; in fact, it illustrates rather the temptation to define it in terms of particular theories and of generalities. The warning of George F. Kennan is quite apposite: "The national interest does *not* consist in abstractions." Indeed, in most cases, as Charles Burton Marshall observed, "the question . . . is not whether, but how, to serve the national interest. That involves the question of what is the national interest in a particular situation." Moreover, "there are many national interests, not just one. The difficulties arise in the conflict of one interest with another; for example, in the clash of the interest in peace with the interest in preserving national institutions."[28]

Yet the concept of national interest is a very useful one which policy-makers should never forget. It helps to place foreign as well as domestic policy in the framework of national policy, and it is a much-needed antidote to political shortsightedness and partisanship. Fred H. Harrington said that "the concept of American national interest in the diplomatic field centers around economic forces, strategic patterns, and moral judgments with reference to the proper role of the United States in world affairs."[29] While it may be true that "despite changed meanings, *national interests* are the constants rather than the variables of international relations,"[30] it is likewise true that developments at home or abroad require a continual reassessment of these interests. Instances of such developments are the transition from an agricultural to a predominantly industrial economy in the United States, and the repercussions of World War II and of postwar Soviet foreign policies.

The most searching investigation of the concept of national interest is still Charles A. Beard's *The Idea of National Interest,* first published in 1934. Beard summarized many views of the national interest, but concluded that there were two major concepts — which he called the Jeffersonian and the Hamiltonian — and that each was based upon a sound conception of the national interest. Throughout most of American history these concepts have provided a useful guide in the formulation of foreign policy, but by the third decade of the twentieth century they had become outmoded. In the concluding paragraph of his important study Beard said:

> Evidently, then, the two inherited conceptions of national interest are in the process of fusion and dissolution. A new conception, with a positive core and nebulous implications, is rising out of the past and is awaiting formulation at the hands of a statesman as competent and powerful as Hamilton or Jefferson.[31]

No such statesman has yet appeared, and no such clear formulation of the national interest as that provided by Hamilton and Jefferson has been made for modern America. In view of the heavy international commitments of the United States and of the growing importance of foreign policy, the need for a correct appraisal of the national interest is a matter of particular urgency. Doubt-

---

Allan B. Cole, in *American Perspective,* IV (Fall, 1950), 335–401; address by George F. Kennan on "The National Interest of the United States," delivered at the Centennial Conference on International Understanding at Northwestern University, January 30, 1951 (reprinted in the *Illinois Law Review,* March–April, 1951); Norman D. Palmer, ed., "The National Interest — Alone or with Others?," *The Annals* of the American Academy of Political and Social Science, CCLXXXII (July, 1952); and Charles Burton Marshall, "The National Interest," in Robert A. Goldwin *et al.,* eds., *Readings in American Foreign Policy* (New York: Oxford University Press, 1959).

[28] Marshall, pp. 665–666.

[29] Fred H. Harrington, "Beard's Idea of National Interest and New Interpretations," *American Perspective,* IV (Fall, 1950), 345.

[30] *Major Problems, 1950–1951,* p. 383.

[31] *The Idea of National Interest* (New York: The Macmillan Company, 1934), pp. 552–553. Used by permission of The Macmillan Company.

less it will have to be related to a broader framework and it will be subject to more variables than ever before. Moreover, it will have little meaning unless it represents a widespread consensus and unless it is applied to specific policies. It is also well to remember that the national interest "involves, not only military security and the American economy, but also a defense of American values."[32]

The Setting and Course of Postwar Policy

Before World War II the United States had only intermittently played a central role in world affairs. She emerged from the war as one of the two "superpowers," i.e., as one of the two major actors on the international scene. Much of her postwar foreign policy has centered around her efforts to adjust to her new position and to the realities of the postwar world. For this role she was largely unprepared, and the imperatives of the nuclear age have made her task even more complicated.

Like all other states, the United States has not yet been able to grasp the full implications of the nuclear and the space age, or to develop satisfactory policies for the radically changed "human situation," to use a favorite expression of Arnold Toynbee. She has also not been able to evolve satisfactory policies for dealing with two other major developments of the postwar period: the growing power of the Soviet Union and the incessant challenge of world communism; and the virtual end of the colonial age with the emergence of more than sixty new nations, mainly in Asia and Africa.

In the postwar years the United States has entered into formal military alliances with old friends in Western Europe and Latin America and with new friends in the Asian area, but all of these alliances have been subject to increasing stresses. Because of the unsatisfactory state of the relations between Communist and non-Communist states, between "have" and "have-not" nations, and between members of alliance systems, the postwar era has been one of protracted conflict. Nuclear weapons have imposed a "balance of terror," mitigated only by peripheral successes in efforts at international cooperation and by a growing realization of the interdependence of nations and peoples. Thus the United States, in common with other nations, is still engaged in a quest for ways to bring peace and security to a troubled world.

Postwar American foreign policy may be divided into five main periods, of unequal duration. The first lasted for about a year and a half after V-J Day. It was marked by the emergence of the United Nations, by peacemaking efforts following the end of armed hostilities, and by cooperative programs of postwar rehabilitation and reconstruction, especially in war-devastated areas. This was the "honeymoon" period, when the United States was still under the influence of a series of illusions about the nature of the postwar world and the possibilities of great power cooperation. But in late 1946 and early 1947 she faced the fact of a divided world and took the leadership in formulating policies which conformed more closely to existing realities. Her New Departure in foreign policy was highlighted by the Truman Doctrine, by the policy soon to be characterized as that of "containment," by the Marshall Plan, and by the North Atlantic Treaty, which marked the end of American abstention from formal military commitments with European nations and the beginning of a new emphasis on military alliances and alliance diplomacy. In this period the Soviet explosion of an atom bomb in 1947, the Communist coup in Czechoslovakia in February, 1948, and the Communist victory in China in 1949 symbolized the growing strength and militancy of the Communist powers.

Communist aggression in late June, 1950, ushered in the third period, that of the Korean War, which coincided in time with the

[32] Harrington, p. 344.

last years of the Truman administration. Economic considerations were subordinated to military preparedness, and American policies in Western Europe and the Far East were subjected to searching criticism and reexamination. A fourth period began in 1953 when the long era of Democratic occupancy of the White House and the even longer rule of Joseph Stalin in Russia came to an end. During the eight years of the Eisenhower administration the United States sought simultaneously to develop "situations of strength" and to work for a peaceful world. The new Soviet leaders gave hints of a desire to follow more flexible and conciliatory policies, and hopes rose for the reduction of international tensions and a reversal of the drift toward war.

In January, 1961, a fifth period was signaled by the beginning of the Kennedy administration. The youthful President, representing "a new generation" of leaders, created a new and more favorable image of the United States abroad; and while that image was somewhat tarnished by early foreign policy reverses and failures it took on additional luster in the later months of the Kennedy administration. This was demonstrated by the success of the President in his personal contacts with leaders of other states and in his travels abroad; by his astute diplomacy in the confrontation with the Soviet Union over the issue of Soviet missiles in Cuba in October, 1962; and by the worldwide grief after his assassination in late November, 1963. His successor, Lyndon B. Johnson, was less successful in his foreign relations. Although he worked heroically to convince other nations and peoples that he was prepared to take any measures and make any sacrifices to advance the cause of international cooperation and world peace, he encountered increasing opposition and frustration in his international endeavors. After the sharp escalation of the military operations in Vietnam, beginning in February, 1965, American policies were viewed with growing suspicion by many friendly countries, including formal allies, as well as by inveterate critics of these policies; and the military intervention in the Dominican Republic in mid-1965, whatever the justification, aroused fresh suspicion and opposition in most of the countries of Latin America.

In our brief survey of postwar American foreign policy we shall discuss some of the major aspects of the five periods we have outlined. Later we shall select for somewhat more thorough examination two broad areas of policy: first, the emerging patterns of security, with particular reference to military assistance programs and alliance diplomacy; and secondly, relations with the Third World of the developing nations of Asia and Africa, with special attention to economic assistance programs.

Postwar Illusions and Frustrations. "As autumn, 1944, approached," wrote Cordell Hull in his *Memoirs,* "my associates and I began to wonder whether Marshal Stalin and his Government were commencing to veer away from the policy of cooperation to which they had agreed at the Moscow Conference." Hull asked the American Ambassador to the Soviet Union, Averell Harriman, to "estimate the present trend of Soviet policy so that we might decide how to meet this possible change in Russian attitude." Harriman made a somewhat gloomy reply. The reason for the change, he believed, was "that when the Russians saw victory in sight they began to put into practice the policies they intended to follow in peace."[33]

In his State of the Union message of January, 1945, President Roosevelt said: "The nearer we come to vanquishing our enemies the more we inevitably become conscious of differences among the victors." The President and his top associates were fully informed of the limited nature of Russian co-

[33] *Memoirs of Cordell Hull* (New York: The Macmillan Company, 1948), II, 1459–1460.

operation during the period of "the strange alliance,"[34] and long before the end of the war they began to have mounting doubts about the behavior and the intentions of the spokesmen of the Soviet Union. But despite these and many other evidences that Roosevelt and other top American leaders foresaw difficulties with the Soviet Union, there can be little doubt that they allowed their optimism to triumph over their growing doubts. They confused what they believed had to be with what was actually possible, and thus they based their policies upon a number of false assumptions.[35] Perhaps the most serious of these was that the Soviet Union would not revert to her earlier suspicion and noncooperation based on the concept of "inevitable conflict." Great power unity was patently vital to the postwar world, for without it the United Nations could never live up to the great expectations placed in it, satisfactory peace treaties could not be agreed upon, and the great powers would engage in a costly and dangerous rivalry which would retard economic rehabilitation and recovery, put peace in constant jeopardy, and imperil the whole political and social order.

In the months following V-J Day the United States was primarily concerned with such matters as peacemaking, occupation policies, economic rehabilitation and recovery, and cooperation with the United Nations. In short, she had to face grave problems arising from the war and from the legacy of war, and she sought to help lay the foundations for a peaceful world order. In the fall of 1946 she reached agreement with other Allied powers on the terms of peace treaties for Italy, Hungary, Bulgaria, Rumania, and Finland, but not on treaties for the major defeated powers, Germany and Japan, or on an Austrian state treaty. She accepted new burdens in the occupation of Germany and Japan as well as of Korea and Austria. By participating in UNRRA, and tnrough direct loans, grants, and other forms of assistance, she accepted a major responsibility for the economic rehabilitation of the world; but not until the evolution of the European Recovery Program in 1947–48 did she develop a coordinated program of foreign assistance.

The United States took an active part in the United Nations from the beginning; she played a major role in setting up the various organs and agencies of the UN and in launching the world organization as a going concern. She exerted a moderating influence in a long series of political disputes, beginning with the Iranian crisis in the early part of 1946; and she assumed the leadership in working out a plan for the international control of atomic energy.

In the occupation of Germany the United States shared responsibility with Great Britain, the Soviet Union, and France. Against the background of the Casablanca declaration for "unconditional surrender," the heritage of the Morgenthau Plan for the pastoralization of Germany, dissensions within the American government and among the wartime allies on the proper policies to be followed, the Yalta Declaration regarding Germany, and the Potsdam Agreement, the formulation of satisfactory policies was an almost impossible task. It was made even more difficult by the many erroneous assumptions which handicapped American policy-makers in the early postwar period, the reluctance of the American people and the Congress to undertake consistent and long-term commitments in Germany or elsewhere, the confused and chaotic situation in Germany herself, and the uncooperative and in fact antagonistic policies of the Russians.

In many areas of policy the United States made substantial progress; but she was un-

[34] The difficulties of Anglo-American cooperation with the Soviets are recounted by the head of the U. S. Military Mission in Moscow, 1943–45, in John R. Deane, *The Strange Alliance* (New York: The Viking Press, 1947).

[35] Sumner Welles, *Where Are We Heading?* (New York: Harper, 1946), pp. 100–106.

able to formulate satisfactory policies for dealing with two of the most significant developments of the postwar period: Soviet aggressive tactics, especially in Europe, and the revolution in Asia. On almost every issue and in almost every part of the world, relations between the Soviet Union and the Western powers were characterized by basic disagreements and frequent deadlocks — in Eastern Europe, in Germany, in the United Nations, in most sessions of the Council of Foreign Ministers.[36] Soviet intransigence and noncooperation came as a particular shock to the American people, who were not aware of the wartime friction until the real story was released with the lifting of censorship. They clung to the belief that all the major powers would cooperate for the common good; and they also clung to their illusions about the nature of communism, even though Soviet words and deeds had made it clear that the leaders of Communist Russia had deliberately reverted to doctrinaire Marxism-Leninism.[37]

During the early postwar years American policy-makers showed little understanding of the nature of the Asian revolution, whereas the Communists were clever in capitalizing on anti-Western, anti-colonial, and anti-imperialist feelings, and in linking communism with native nationalist movements. For many reasons the United States became identified in Asian eyes with reaction and imperialism. In China she backed the losing side in the civil war which broke out soon after V-J Day and which ended only with the complete victory of the Chinese Communists in 1949. In Korea, American aspirations for the unification of the entire country were frustrated, in spite of repeated attempts to reach agreement with the Soviet Union on the basis of the Cairo Declaration. The United States could take credit for implementing her promise of independence for the Philippines, although the alarming political and economic deterioration of this "showcase of democracy in Asia" raised grave new problems. The one area in Asia where United States policy was truly impressive in the immediate postwar period was occupied Japan, but there General MacArthur, as Supreme Commander for the Allied Powers, ran virtually a one-man show, and the United States in effect assumed chief responsibility for the peaceful evolution of a nation with a record anything but peaceful and democratic.

The New Departure. In the latter part of 1946 the United States began to show signs of awakening to the nature of the Soviet threat and of heading toward a firmer policy. The New Departure in foreign policy was dramatized on March 12, 1947, when the President delivered his "Truman Doctrine" speech. In this speech Mr. Truman called for a program of aid to Greece and Turkey, and he emphasized the broad implications involved." "I believe that it must be the policy of the United States," he declared, "to support free peoples who are resisting attempted subjugation by armed minorities or by outside pressures." Thereafter a prime object of American foreign policy was to be the "containment of Soviet power," to use an expression first popularized by George F. Kennan, then director of the State Department's Policy Planning Staff. More and more it became recognized that the United States was involved in a cold war which might at any time shift into a hot war. Even the European Recovery Program, first suggested in Secre-

[36] For a series of illuminating case studies in the difficulties of negotiating with the Soviet Union, see Raymond Dennett and Joseph E. Johnson, eds., *Negotiating with the Russians* (Boston: World Peace Foundation, 1951). This book contains ten chapters by Americans who took a leading part in the negotiations which they describe.

[37] This was made particularly apparent by Stalin's speech of February 9, 1946, in which, as General Deane stated, he "reaffirmed the doctrine of Marx and Lenin and exhorted his people to extraordinary efforts in preparation for the inevitable wars which must be expected so long as the capitalist system exists." Deane, p. 320.

tary of State Marshall's Harvard speech less than three months after the enunciation of the Truman Doctrine, was regarded by many as primarily designed to build up Western Europe against Russia, although it had strong and obvious economic motivations. There were other major landmarks in the evolution of an American policy designed to protect the United States by building up "situations of strength" throughout the non-Communist world. They included: the Rio Treaty of 1947; strong approval of the Brussels Pact in early 1948; the Vandenberg Resolution in mid-1948; the Berlin airlift in 1948–49; the North Atlantic Treaty of 1949; encouragement of efforts toward economic, military, and political integration in Western Europe; cooperative endeavors with Britain and France to coordinate occupation policies in Germany, to bring into existence a West German state, and to associate that new state with Western Europe; and contributions to the rearming of the nations of Western Europe and the North Atlantic Community and to coordinated defense planning through the Mutual Defense Assistance Program and central planning in SHAPE (Supreme Headquarters Allied Powers in Europe).

In the Far East the situation was far less satisfactory. In 1949 American forces were withdrawn from Korea, but the country remained weak and divided, at the mercy of great power rivalries and Communist encroachment. The American occupation of Japan had passed its point of maximum effectiveness, and there was strong pressure to terminate it, even though many of the long-range objectives had not been achieved. In Indo-China the French were engaged in protracted warfare with Communist-led Vietnamese nationalists. Here the United States was faced with the double dilemma of maintaining satisfactory relationships with an indispensable ally of the Atlantic Community whom she did not wish to weaken in any way but whose colonial policies she could not approve, and of identifying herself with independence movements without undermining her European ally and without playing into the hands of the Communists.

The greatest dilemma of all stemmed from the developments in China. America's China policy satisfied no one. Against the wishes of the administration and particularly of the State Department, Congress insisted on continuing aid to the Nationalists, although that aid was inadequate and was made even less effective by the confusion into which the Nationalists had fallen. The fact was that the situation in China had deteriorated beyond hope of salvage and that it was a serious reverse for American policy. On October 1, 1949, the Central People's Government of the People's Republic of China was proclaimed, and before the end of the year the remnants of the Nationalist forces had taken refuge on Formosa. Confronted by bitter attacks from critics at home and abroad, the recognition of the new regime in China by several non-Communist states, including India and Great Britain, the arrest, imprisonment, trial and eventual deportation of Angus Ward, the United States Consul-General in Mukden, Manchuria, and other evidences of the anti-American orientation of the leaders of the new China, the United States attempted to reassess her entire Far Eastern policy. Little progress had been made before the Communist attack on South Korea changed the whole picture.

The Korean War and the Great Debates. With the attack on the Republic of Korea in late June, 1950, the cold war gave way to open aggression and direct military action by a Russian satellite. It was widely feared that the Korean War marked the beginning of a new and more dangerous phase of Communist imperialism, which might lead to similar attacks in other parts of the world and eventually to World War III. The intervention of the Chinese Communists in late October and early November added to these fears. The response of the United States was to take the leadership in United Nations action to deal with the aggression, to commit the bulk of her regular armed forces to the operation, to undertake a major defense effort which called for substantial increases in her armed forces and the production of more and better weapons, to coordinate her many programs of foreign aid and military assistance into a single Mutual Security Program in which the accent was heavily on military aid, to enter into security pacts with Japan, the Philippines, Australia, and New Zealand, to take the initiative in the preparation of a Japanese peace treaty (signed on September 8, 1951, by representatives of 48 nations), and in many other ways to strengthen herself and to assume the leadership of the growing alliance of free nations against Communist imperialism.

Most Americans agreed with their leaders that there was no other path which they could take without gravely endangering national security. Nevertheless, the new American steps and the basic decision which prompted them were not taken without grave misgivings about their possible effects, both upon the American economy and upon the prospects for peace. Vigorous debates were staged on the correct policy to be followed vis-à-vis the Soviet Union and on such issues as the Truman Doctrine, the Marshall Plan, the North Atlantic Pact, Chinese relations, American commitments in Western Europe, the Korean War, and the Mutual Security Program. Two of the "great debates" were particularly significant and aroused widespread interest. One centered on policies toward Western Europe, the other on policies in the Far East.

The first debate was touched off in December, 1950, at a time when the military situation in Korea was most alarming, by a radio address by former President Herbert Hoover. Mr. Hoover's convictions were well summarized in his declaration that "the foundation of our national policies must be to preserve for the world this Western Hemisphere Gibraltar of Western Civilization."[38] His criticisms came at a time when the administration was preparing to cooperate with the other members of the North Atlantic Treaty Organization in plans for the defense of Western Europe and to station more American troops in that area.

The debate which Mr. Hoover initiated seemed to probe to the fundamentals of American foreign policy and America's proper role in the world. Did American frontiers extend only to the Western Hemisphere and the defensive shield from Britain to Formosa, or were they also in Europe and on the mainland of Asia? Could the United States depend on her allies, particularly on the countries of Western Europe? Could Western Europe be defended anyway? Could the American economy stand the strain of a staggering military budget and global aid programs? On these and similar questions Mr. Hoover and Senator Robert A. Taft differed fundamentally from the supporters of the administration.

On January 5, 1951, in a 10,000-word address to the Senate of the new Eighty-Second Congress, Senator Taft attacked the administration's foreign policies, especially the plans to send more armed forces to Europe. He charged that the President had already exceeded his constitutional authority by ordering American troops into action in Korea without the approval of Congress, and that "the President has no power to agree to send troops to fight in Europe." Taft's view received considerable support in the Senate, but the pendulum began to swing in the other direction after General Eisenhower's address to a special session of Congress and his radio report to the nation in early February. On April 4, the second anniversary of the signing

[38] For the text of Mr. Hoover's speech of December 20, 1950, see the *New York Times*, December 21, 1950. The *Times* gave an excellent "blow-by-blow" account of the entire course of the "great debate" from December, 1950, to April, 1951.

of the North Atlantic Pact, the Senate approved a resolution pledging that the United States would station in Europe "such units of our armed forces as may be necessary and appropriate to contribute our fair share," with an amendment providing that no ground troops should be added to the four divisions in Western Europe except with Congressional approval. The result of this phase of the foreign policy controversy was a clear-cut victody for neither the Truman administration nor its critics, although popular and Congressional opinion sided heavily with the administration.

Hardly had the echoes of "the great debate" begun to fade away before they were succeeded by an even greater debate. A week after the Senate's passage of the troops-for-Europe resolution President Truman removed General of the Army Douglas MacArthur from all his Far Eastern commands. This action provoked a political and emotional explosion in the United States, "in an atmosphere that was already heavy with bitterness over foreign policy."[39] When MacArthur returned to the United States, for the first time in fourteen years, he was greeted as a hero rather than as a repudiated and deposed commander. He received the signal honor of being invited to state his views before a joint session of Congress, and on April 19, before a packed chamber and crowded galleries, with most of the American people gathered around radio or television sets, he made one of the most memorable and dramatic addresses in American history. Denouncing the Administration's policy in the Korean War as "appeasement," MacArthur urged that the United Nations forces in Korea should be "permitted to destroy the enemy build-up bases north of the Yalu" (i.e., in Manchuria); he also urged "the removal of restrictions on the forces . . . on Formosa, with logistical support to contribute to their effective operations against the Chinese mainland," a tighter economic blockade, and a naval blockade of the China coast "to prevent the Chinese Reds from getting succor from without."

Two major issues soon emerged in the early stages of the second great debate: (1) the reasons and the circumstances of General MacArthur's dismissal; and (2) the fundamental bases and assumptions of the Far Eastern policy of the United States, especially with respect to China and to the Korean War. The second issue — Far Eastern policy — had broad ramifications, affecting as it did the most criticized and the least successful phase of American foreign policy in the postwar years. Allied with this were questions of the relations of the United States with other countries and of the relative importance of Europe and Asia in American policy and strategy.

The exhaustive hearings which followed clarified a number of important points, added to the confusion about others, and led to certain announced modifications in the administration's Far Eastern policy, especially with regard to the admission of Red China into the UN and to the question of Formosa. Quite understandably, the reaction in the free world to *l'affaire MacArthur* was one of bewilderment and alarm. Among the nations that looked to the United States for leadership and assistance there were many that were concerned lest the policies MacArthur advocated, which to them seemed much too provocative and too likely to increase the danger of global war, should in the end be forced upon the administration by a critical and insistent public opinion. They must have wondered whether the United States was not too irresponsible and too disunited to be relied upon in the long, tough struggle with Communist imperialism.

The Eisenhower Administration. The future course of American foreign policy was determined more in the national party conventions in June and July of 1952 than by

[39] *New York Times,* April 15, 1951, p. E1.

the presidential election of November 4. The nomination by the Republicans of General Dwight D. Eisenhower instead of Senator Robert A. Taft was in effect a vote of confidence in the basic principles of President Truman's foreign policy. The same was true of the nomination of Governor Adlai E. Stevenson by the Democratic convention.

On January 20, 1953, for the first time in twenty-four years, a Republican President entered the White House. Many people in Western Europe and in Asia were apprehensive. Somehow they seemed to think that the Republicans were more "warlike" than the Democrats; they had grave doubts about the policies of the General become President; and they were rather suspicious of his Secretary of State, John Foster Dulles. But the President's Inaugural Address seemed reassuring.

The first evidence of the "positive" foreign policy promised by the Republicans came with President Eisenhower's message on the State of the Union, February 2. Two pronouncements in particular suggested that the administration had in mind some drastic tactical changes within the framework of the older policies. The Seventh Fleet would no longer prevent the Chinese Nationalists on Formosa from attacking the Chinese Communists on the mainland; and Mutual Security aid to Western Europe would be conditioned upon the earnestness of the efforts of the European states to effect a closer integration. These decisions did not abate the considerable anxiety among the allies of the United States in the Far East and Europe; for a time all of them continued to fear an enlargement of the Korean War into World War III. As the early weeks of the Eisenhower administration came to a close, however, it became clear that American foreign policy would remain essentially unchanged. Here and there a little "positive" emphasis had been added, but the soldier-President had shown no disposition toward recklessness in word or deed.

A number of events in the course of 1953 appeared to offer new hope for the lessening of international tensions. On March 3 Stalin died, and the new leaders of the Soviet Union began to follow more flexible and conciliatory policies. On July 27, after more than three years of fighting, the Korean War was brought to an end by the signing of a truce agreement, although subsequent efforts to agree on a political settlement were unproductive. In September a sweeping victory for Adenauer in the elections in West Germany augured well for the defense of Western Europe. In December, in an address before the General Assembly of the United Nations, Eisenhower proposed a world pool of atomic materials for peaceful purposes, which somewhat countered the alarm felt earlier in the year when the Russians announced they had exploded a hydrogen bomb.

The year 1954 was one of conferences, with Mr. Dulles setting new records as a traveling Secretary of State. At the Berlin conference in February the foreign ministers of the Big Four made another effort to consider a peace settlement for Germany; but even in the relaxed atmosphere of the "new look" they were unable to reach agreement. Instead, they agreed to sponsor a conference at Geneva to consider problems relating to Korea and Indo-China, with Communist China invited to attend. The United States was cool to the whole idea, and Mr. Dulles went to Geneva for only a few days. No progress at all was made on the Korean issue, but after weeks of negotiation agreements for a truce in Indo-China were signed. The United States refused to be a party to the Geneva settlement, for she feared that the terms compromised Indo-Chinese independence and gave the Communists an entering wedge in Southeast Asia.

After Geneva the United States took the initiative in calling a conference in Manila, where in September representatives of eight nations signed the Southeast Asia Collective Defense Treaty. Subsequently this treaty was given institutional form, through the establishment of the Southeast Asia Treaty Organization (SEATO), with headquarters in Bangkok. The treaty was bitterly denounced by Russia and Communist China and disapproved by India and other "neutral" nations.

In 1953 the United States entered into a security treaty with the Republic of Korea, and in 1954 with Pakistan and the Republic of China. She welcomed, and to some extent instigated, the conclusion of the Pact of Mutual Cooperation between Pakistan, Iran, Iraq, Turkey, and the United Kingdom (the Baghdad Pact) in February, 1955.

In Western Europe a fundamental objective of American policy was imperiled when the European Defense Community Treaty was rejected by the French National Assembly on August 30. But here, too, the loss was at least partially recouped. With Mr. Dulles taking a back seat, and with Sir Anthony Eden making an explicit declaration of the willingness of Great Britain to maintain troops on the Continent, the delegates of nine nations signed an accord in London to integrate West Germany politically and militarily with Western Europe, to expand the Brussels Treaty to include West Germany and Italy in a Western European Union, and to assure the West German government of full sovereignty in the near future. The decisions at the London conference were incorporated into a series of thirty separate treaties and agreements, signed in Paris on October 23 by representatives of fifteen nations. When these entered into effect in 1955, in spite of Soviet efforts to prevent their ratification, they created a broad framework for West European cooperation. President Eisenhower felt that the hopeful aspects of the "new look," which had at long last led to Soviet agreement to an Austrian state treaty, warranted his going to Geneva to participate in the "summit" conference of July, 1955. He scored a personal triumph at the conference, and he electrified the other participants, and the world at large, by his novel proposal for "open-skies" inspection — a proposal which was promptly frowned upon by the Soviet spokesmen. On the thorny question of German reunification the four heads of state could only agree that their foreign ministers would meet later in the year to discuss the problem. To no one's surprise, this meeting broke up in a complete deadlock.

In 1956 the American presidential elections, which resulted in the re-election of President Eisenhower by a thumping majority, virtually coincided with the height of both the Hungarian and Suez crises. In these crises the policies of the Eisenhower administration were put to the test, and the results were not very satisfactory. In spite of all the talk about the liberation of satellite peoples and winning the cold war, the American reaction to the ruthless Soviet actions in Hungary, as to the East Berlin uprising of June, 1953, was confined largely to strong condemnation of the Soviet Union, vocal sympathy with the victims of Soviet despotism, and some assistance to refugees who managed to escape. This policy of "verbal dynamism" but relative inaction was accepted reluctantly by the majority of the American people, for they did not wish to run the risk of all-out war with the Soviet Union, however much they might favor a vigorous anti-Communist policy.

Nasser's dramatic announcement of his intention to nationalize the Suez Canal Company was made only a week after Secretary Dulles' sudden retraction of the tentative offer to assist Egypt in building the Aswan High Dam. The seizure of the canal prompted Britain, France, and Israel to resort to force. President Eisenhower threw his full support behind the successful efforts of the United Nations to secure a speedy cease-fire and the withdrawal of the Anglo-French-Israeli forces from Egyptian soil. In the process the United States found herself in the unaccustomed position of voting with the Soviet Union and most of the "neutral" nations against her major NATO allies.

The Suez crisis of 1956, with its demonstration of British and French weakness, left a kind of power vacuum in the Middle East, and raised apprehensions in the Western world that the Soviet Union would seek to take advantage of the fluid situation. In January, 1957, in an effort to guard against such a development, President Eisenhower asked Congress to give him authority to provide economic aid and military support to any nation of the Middle East threatened by communism which requested such aid. After two months of debate, Congress gave him this authorization in a joint resolution. The key provision read: "the United States regards as vital to the national interest and world peace the preservation of the independence and integrity of the nations of the Middle East. To this end, if the President determines the necessity thereof, the United States is prepared to use armed forces to assist any such nation requesting assistance against armed aggression from any country controlled by international communism." This so-called Eisenhower Doctrine was poorly adapted for the kind of covert infiltration and plotting that constituted the real threats in the Middle East. It was invoked in 1958 when President Eisenhower, at the request of the outgoing president, Camille Chamoun, sent American marines into Lebanon to help avert civil war, presumably incited by outside parties. Fortunately the American forces were withdrawn in a few weeks without becoming involved in serious hostilities, but there was a widespread feeling that the Eisenhower Doctrine had not emerged from the experience with flying colors. Soon thereafter, in fact, it became a dead letter.

In June, 1957, the United States Senate approved the Atoms-for-Peace Treaty, based on Eisenhower's proposal of 1953 and already ratified by nine nations, including the Soviet Union. This step, and the work of a subcommittee of the United Nations Disarmament Commission, raised the hopes of a reversal of the arms race; but other developments soon discouraged all but the most hardy optimists. Among these were three Russian achievements in 1957: the test-firing on August 26 of the first successful intercontinental ballistic missile; the launching on October 4 of the first man-made earth satellite, "Sputnik"; and the launching a month later of a much heavier earth satellite carrying a live dog.

For the first six years of the Eisenhower administration Secretary of State John Foster Dulles dominated the making and conduct of American foreign policy. Few Secretaries of State were more praised and more blamed. Illness forced Dulles to resign in the spring of 1959, but in a sense, the Dulles era had ended before his resignation. The policies with which his name was indelibly associated — such as "liberation," "massive retaliation," and "brinkmanship" — had often proved to be impractical and had aroused a storm of criticism from friends as well as foes of the United States. The United States in the late 1950's began to assume a more flexible approach in her relations with the Soviet Union, with "neutral" nations, and with allied countries.

The Kennedy and Johnson Administrations. Eisenhower was forced to bequeath to his younger successor many unresolved problems, which Mr. Kennedy tackled with vigor and confidence. The new administration brought the Democratic Party back to the White House, with many fresh faces and fresh ideas. In his campaign, especially as a result of his debates with Mr. Nixon, in the weeks between his election and his inauguration, and in his eloquent Inaugural Address, Mr. Kennedy created a favorable image at home and abroad. That image never faded, in spite of some errors and reverses in both domestic and foreign affairs.

The first appraisals of the international

scene by the new President and his untried team were sobering. Ten days after taking office President Kennedy declared in his State of the Union message: "No man entering upon this office . . . could fail to be staggered upon learning . . . the harsh enormities of the trials through which we must pass in the next four years. Each day the crises multiply. Each day their solution grows more difficult. Each day we draw nearer the hour of maximum danger. . . . I feel I must inform the Congress that our analyses over the last ten days make it clear that — in each of the principal areas of crisis — the tide of events has been running out and time has not been our friend."

The following months seemed to confirm this analysis. In Asia the Chinese Communists were becoming more militant, and the situation in Laos was such that the United States was forced to accept a compromise arrangement that clearly spelled future trouble. In the Congo, which, as the President said in his State of the Union message, was "brutally torn by civil strife, political unrest, and public disorder," Americans were involved in the United Nations' efforts to restore peace and order. In Latin America the Communist threat was growing. In 1961 Castro openly proclaimed his identification with communism. President Kennedy had to face the fact that a Communist base had been established ninety miles off American soil, and that the appeal of Castroism would offer keen competition to his new approach to "the other Americas," the Alliance for Progress. In Europe, as he noted in his State of the Union message, "our alliances are unfulfilled and in some disarray." A new challenge developed over Berlin during the year, and grew particularly menacing in August, when the Communists built the Berlin wall. In his meeting with Khrushchev in Vienna, Kennedy was disturbed to find the Soviet leader dogmatic and unyielding.

But probably the most disheartening reversal experienced by President Kennedy was the "Bay of Pigs" fiasco of April, 1961. The circumstances leading to this "perfect failure," as Theodore Draper described it, are now a twice-told tale, although many of the details are still unclear. Sometime during the Eisenhower administration American hostility toward the Castro regime led to a decision to train and otherwise assist Cuban refugees for an eventual landing in Cuba. When he assumed office, Kennedy was faced with a program which was well advanced, largely in the hands of the Central Intelligence Agency. Despite apprehensions, he allowed the plans to go forward. At no time did the commitment of the United States include all-out military support for an armed invasion, but obviously many Cuban refugees assumed that the United States would not allow their venture to fail. When the invasion was attempted, almost everything went wrong; and while the invaders were dying or being taken off to prison, the United States gave logistic but no real military support. It was probably the most frustrating experience of Mr. Kennedy's tenure in the White House. After the failure of the invasion, he bitterly reproached himself for letting events develop as they did and for deferring too much to military and intelligence advisers, against the dictates of his own judgment.

The experience left him a sadder and wiser man. A year and a half later, when the second Cuban crisis came, he showed that he had learned much from his previous Cuban lesson and from his other tests since entering the White House. This time the test was in many ways a much more serious one, for it involved the most direct confrontation between the United States and the Soviet Union in the postwar years. Thanks to the President's firmness and Khrushchev's unwillingness to challenge American power close to American shores, the crisis was averted by astute diplomacy and a limited display of power. The Soviet missiles were withdrawn from Cuba, although the ties between Castro and the Soviet Union remained strong. In the diplomatic field it was perhaps Kennedy's finest hour.

Another positive step was taken in late July, 1963, when representatives of the United States, the United Kingdom, and the Soviet Union, meeting in Moscow, reached agreement on a nuclear test ban treaty, covering all but underground tests. This agreement was signed in Moscow on August 5, and was soon adhered to by more than one hundred nations. Although many Americans expressed apprehensions regarding this agreement, it was generally hailed as a significant effort — unhappily almost unique — to reverse the nuclear arms race. Apparently Kennedy regarded it as one of the most significant achievements of his administration. It was one of several agreements which the United States concluded with the Soviet Union in 1963.

In the same year President Kennedy made a triumphal visit to West Germany. Berliners, who welcomed him enthusiastically as their friend and protector, hailed his moving speech, delivered after he had seen the Berlin wall. Relations with NATO allies increasingly raised perplexing issues. General de Gaulle's curt "veto" of the British application to join the Common Market, made at a press conference in January, 1963, was a reminder of the difficulties of breathing new life into NATO and into movements for European integration. American proposals for a multilateral nuclear force for NATO, presumably intended as a formula for giving other members of the alliance some role in the use of nuclear weapons while leaving the power of final decision in the President of the United States alone, were strongly opposed by De Gaulle, and were given only lukewarm support by most of the other NATO members. Only West Germany welcomed the American initiative.

On visits to Latin America President Kennedy had an opportunity to see the first fruits of the Alliance for Progress, and the warm receptions accorded him revealed that the President and his program had captured the imagination of the Latin Americans.

In Southeast Asia the uneasy truce in Laos continued, but in South Vietnam the situation deteriorated alarmingly with Ngo Dinh Diem's increasingly arbitrary rule and, in November, his overthrow and assassination. As political instability and disruption spread and Viet Cong infiltration and encroachments mounted, the United States became more deeply committed to South Vietnam.

The assassination of the young American President in late November, 1963, raised new fears and alarms throughout the non-Communist world. As a new and vigorous leader in world affairs, a spokesman for the new generation in many lands, Kennedy had been perhaps more successful than any other member of his generation in projecting his image on the world scene. His successor, Lyndon B. Johnson, promised to carry on the Kennedy policies abroad as well as at home, but he was much less successful in his foreign policy than in his domestic efforts. Despite a desire to convince the whole world, including the Communists, of his goodwill and readiness to go anywhere and do anything to advance the cause of peace, he knew few successes in the foreign field, and he felt obliged to devote much of his time to the steadily escalating operations in Vietnam.

Even before the presidential election of November, 1964, the situation in South Vietnam had worsened and the American commitment had expanded. In August the President ordered bombing attacks on North Vietnamese coastal bases in retaliation for attacks on American warships in the Gulf of Tonkin, and later in the month his authority was reinforced by a Congressional joint resolution, passed by 416–0 in the House and 88–2 in the Senate, approving any action which he might deem necessary in the Vietnamese crisis. When the crisis became even more serious, he often cited this resolution as a partial answer to congressional critics of his escalation policies.

During the presidential campaign of 1964, however, Johnson favored a much more moderate and cautious policy in Vietnam than did his Republican opponent, Senator Barry Goldwater; and his overwhelming victory seemed to give reassurance that the United States would not be "trigger-happy." His actions in Vietnam and the Dominican Republic in 1965 led some domestic as well as foreign critics to charge that he was changing to a harder line.

In February, 1965, because of the growing strength of the Viet Cong and the mounting evidence of North Vietnamese infiltration and even commitment of regular forces south of the seventeenth parallel, President Johnson ordered the continuous bombing of military installations in North Vietnam, coupling this order with a standing offer to cease the bombings as soon as the North Vietnamese "stopped doing what they are doing" in South Vietnam, and expressing a willingness to negotiate at any time. After February, 1965, the struggle in Vietnam became a vir-

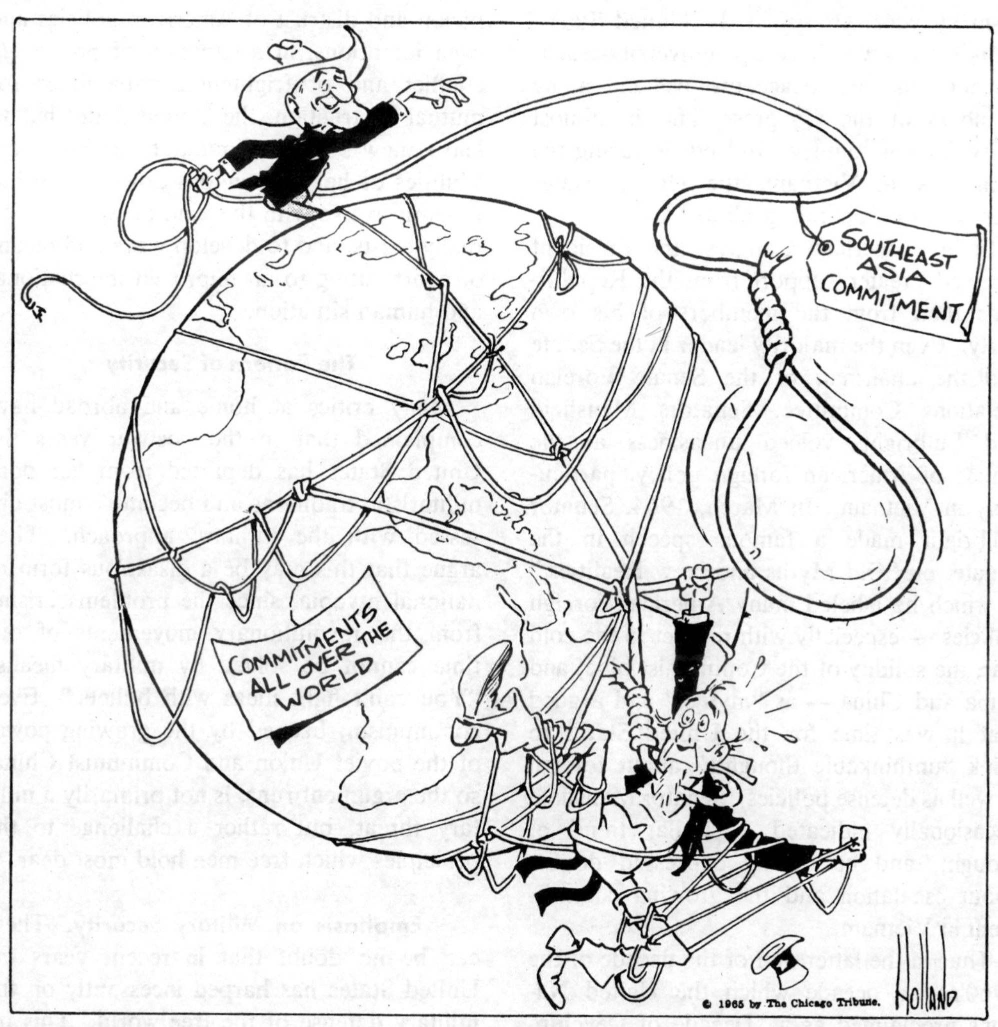

Holland in The Chicago Tribune

Enough Rope Already

tual war, to which increasing numbers of American troops were committed.

Support for the escalation of the struggle and the American determination to stay in Vietnam as long as necessary to prevent a Communist takeover of the whole country was strong and steady in the United States, and strong, if not always steady, in several other countries, including such surprising quarters as Britain under a Labor government and India; but American policies in Vietnam came under a constant fire of criticism by vocal groups in the United States, including many college and university teachers and students, peace groups, and many members of the Congress, and in almost every foreign country. Indeed, in facing the grim task in Vietnam, the United States seemed to be operating almost alone.

In the American Congress the President received greater support from the Republicans than from the members of his own party. Even the majority leader in the Senate and the chairman of the Senate Foreign Relations Committee, Senators Mansfield and Fulbright, voiced uneasiness at the course of American foreign policy, particularly in Vietnam. In March, 1964, Senator Fulbright made a famous speech in the Senate, on "Old Myths and New Realities," in which he labeled many American foreign policies — especially with respect to the cold war, the solidity of the Communist bloc, and Cuba and China — as "myths," and argued that it was time for the United States to think "unthinkable thoughts" about foreign as well as defense policies. Senator Mansfield occasionally indicated a similar trend of thought, and he openly expressed doubts about escalation and the growing commitment in Vietnam.

Thus in the latter half of the decade of the 1960's — a decade which the United Nations proclaimed as a "Decade of Development" — the United States was still trying to evolve policies which would best contribute to her own security and to world peace. Yet, as John F. Kennedy said in his State of the Union message in 1961, "Each day the crises multiply," and "Each day the solution grows more difficult." The "transcendent goal" of the United States, said Secretary of State Rusk in 1962, is "a peaceful world community of free and independent states, free to choose their own future and their own system so long as it does not threaten the freedom of others." Faced with the growing threat of Communist China, with alliances in disarray, with widespread suspicion and distrust of American policies and even intentions, in a situation of protracted conflict and of frightening capabilities for mutual destruction, the United States has to learn anew both the limitations and the possibilities of her tremendous power. She has to learn to live with the kind of world which really exists, and to develop ways and means of contributing to an improved international and human situation.

The Pattern of Security

Many critics at home and abroad have complained that in the postwar years the United States has departed from her nonmilitaristic traditions and become almost obsessed with the military approach. They argue that this may be a disastrous form of national myopia, since the problems arising from the revolutionary movements of our time cannot be solved by military means: "You can't fight ideas with bullets." Even communism, backed by the growing power of the Soviet Union and Communist China, so the argument runs, is not primarily a military threat, but rather a challenge to the principles which free men hold most dear.

Emphasis on Military Security. There can be no doubt that in recent years the United States has harped incessantly on the military defense of the free world. This indicates no desirable order of priority, but a recognition of real and present dangers. At the close of World War II American military forces were demobilized at a rapid rate under pressure to "bring the boys home" and to give tangible evidence of confidence in the good faith and good intentions of other states. By the end of 1946 the American armed forces had been reduced from nearly 12,000,000 men to hardly more than 1,500,000. "We didn't demobilize," said Bernard Baruch, "we scuttled and ran." As the dimensions of this error became apparent, and as the hopes for a peaceful and cooperative world faded, the United States felt impelled to strengthen her defense establishment, to encourage and assist other free nations to rearm, and to enter into bilateral and multilateral security agreements with many other states.

The annual budget figures reflect America's reaction to the trend of world events, including the rapid demobilization after the end of World War II, the vast rearmament effort after the outbreak o. the war in Korea in June, 1950, and the continuing heavy expenditures for defense since 1952. Since that date defense expenditures have never been less than 50 per cent of total federal expenditures. Between 1952 and 1961 defense expenditures fluctuated between \$40 and \$51 billion, and since 1962 they have never fallen below \$50 billion. Because of the escalating costs of the war in Vietnam, defense expenditures soared to over \$55 billion in 1966, and to approximately \$70 billion in 1967. Estimated expenditures for defense for 1968 were \$76.5 billion and for 1969 \$79.8 billion. The bulk of these expenditures was allocated to the armed forces and other activities of the Department

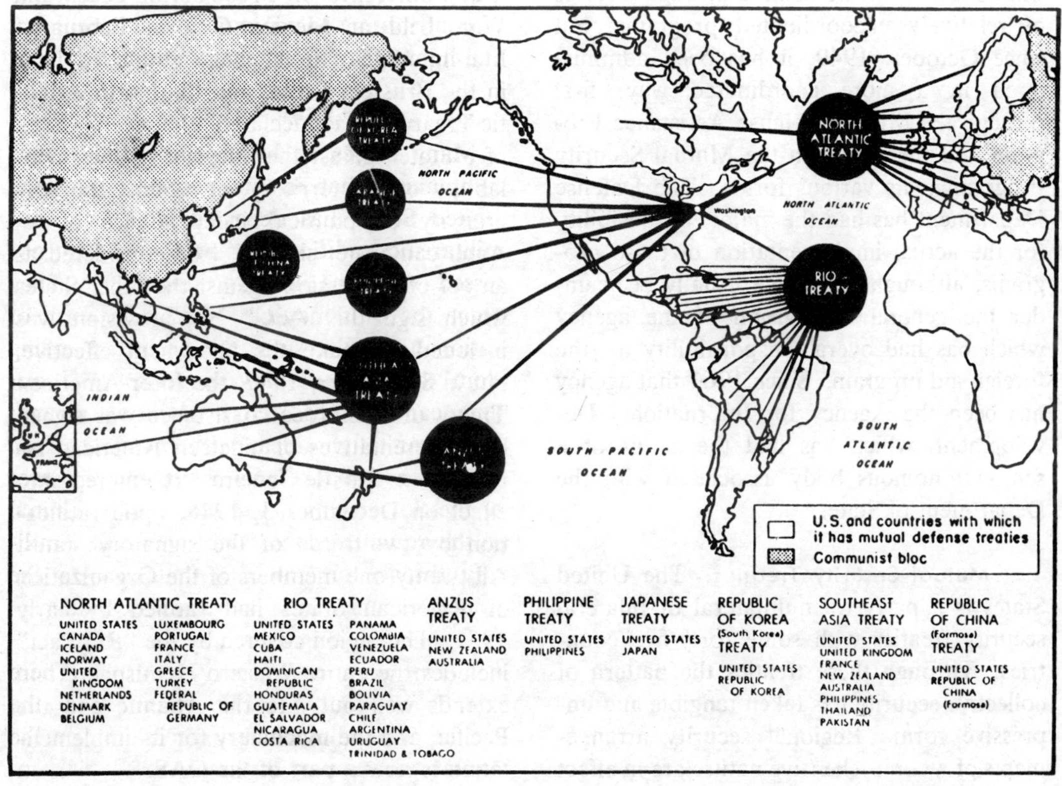

Department of State

United States Collective Defense Arrangements

of Defense, but also included outlays for military assistance programs, the Atomic Energy Commission, and certain "defense-related activities."

Military Assistance. National security, conceived in military terms alone, involves more than the maintenance of a strong defense establishment; it also includes military assistance to other friendly nations. The value of this military aid, mostly in the form of grants, between 1945 and 1964 was approximately $34 billion. Some $16 billion in military assistance was made available to countries of Western Europe, nearly $11 billion to countries in the Far East and Pacific areas, and about $5.6 billion to countries in the Near East (including Greece and Turkey) and South Asia. Until 1949 this assistance was extended through a series of relatively uncoordinated programs; but since October, 1949, it has been administered in a more coordinated way, first through the Mutual Defense Assistance Program and then through the Mutual Security Program in its various forms. The Defense Department has had the major responsibility for the actual implementation of these programs, although they have usually been under the general supervision of the agency which has had overall responsibility for the foreign aid program. Since 1961 that agency has been the Agency for International Development, which has had the status of a semi-autonomous body associated with the Department of State.

Mutual Security Treaties. The United States is a party to multilateral or bilateral security treaties with some forty-five countries. Through these treaties the pattern of collective security has taken tangible and impressive form. Regional security arrangements of a comprehensive nature are in effect in the Western Hemisphere and in the North Atlantic area. In another vital part of the world, the Far East and Southeast Asia, no similar arrangements have been possible; but the United States is associated with seven other nations — Great Britain, France, Australia, New Zealand, Pakistan, Thailand, and the Philippines — in the Southeast Asia Collective Defense Treaty (the Manila Treaty); she has joined with Australia and New Zealand in the so-called ANZUS Pact (1951); and she has entered into bilateral security agreements with Japan (1960, replacing an earlier security treaty of 1951), the Republic of Korea (1955) and the National Government of China (1954).

The Rio Treaty. The pattern for the regional security arrangements which were authorized by Article 51 of the United Nations Charter and which have proliferated in the postwar period was suggested in the Act of Chapultepec, drawn up at the Inter-American Conference on Problems of Peace and War, held at Mexico City in February–March, 1945. In language employed later in the Brussels Treaty and the North Atlantic Treaty, the act declared "that every attack of a State against the integrity or the inviolability of the territory, or against the sovereignty or political independence of an American State, shall . . . be considered as an act of aggression against the other States which sign this Act." No provision was included to make the agreement effective, but in September, 1947, the Inter-American Treaty of Reciprocal Assistance was signed by representatives of nineteen American republics at Rio de Janeiro. It entered into effect on December 3, 1948, upon ratification by two-thirds of the signatory states. All twenty-one members of the Organization of American States had ratified by early 1951. The region covered by the "Rio Pact" includes the entire Western Hemisphere and extends well out into the Atlantic and the Pacific; and the machinery for its implementation is now a part of the OAS.

The North Atlantic Treaty. In his Truman Doctrine speech in March, 1947, as has been noted, the President had declared: "I believe that it must be the policy of the United States to support free peoples who are resisting attempted subjugation by armed minorities or by outside pressures." This was clearly a statement of principle, not a specific program of action; but it was applied immediately to justify aid to Greece and Turkey, and it has since been invoked in support of many other programs of military and economic aid. It was this principle that underlay American participation in the North Atlantic Treaty Organization (NATO) and the passage of the Mutual Defense Assistance Act.

In NATO the United States is associated in a regional security arrangement with the United Kingdom, France, West Germany, Italy, the Benelux countries, Norway, Denmark, Portugal, Greece, Turkey, Canada, and Iceland. The signing of the North Atlantic Treaty by the United States was an epochal event. Article 5 declared that each of the parties to the treaty, in the event of an armed attack against one or more of them, "will assist the Party or Parties so attacked by taking forthwith, individually and in concert with the other Parties, such action as it deems necessary, including the use of armed force, to restore and maintain the security of the North Atlantic area." Except for the French alliance of 1778, this marked the first major long-term commitment into which the United States had ever entered with any state of Western Europe. But in another sense it was simply the formal recognition of a commitment which had in effect already existed for many years and which had been generally recognized by the American people in the postwar period. NATO is now one of the cornerstones of American foreign policy, even though, largely as a consequence of the policies and actions of De Gaulle, its command structure has been weakened and its fate after 1969 is uncertain.

The Manila Treaty. The Southeast Asia Collective Defense Treaty is a much weaker instrument than the Rio Treaty or the North Atlantic Treaty, not so much because of the provisions of the treaty itself as because of the difficulties in developing a satisfactory plan of defense in a weak and dangerously exposed part of the free world. Only two states of Southeast Asia — Thailand and the Philippines — are parties to the treaty; Communist China, India, Indonesia, and Burma are opposed to the concept on which the treaty rests; the Western signatories — France, Great Britain, and the United States — are far away and are handicapped by the continuing suspicion of colonialism and imperialism; and the remaining states — Australia, New Zealand, and Pakistan — have only peripheral interests in Southeast Asia.

In structure, too, the Southeast Asia Treaty Organization is weaker in its military aspects than either the OAS or NATO. The treaty itself "followed the pattern of the Australia, New Zealand, and Philippines treaties rather than the NATO model. That is to say, instead of declaring an attack upon one to be an attack upon all, it stated that an attack upon one would be recognized as dangerous to the peace and safety of the others."[40]

Mr. Dulles was quite right in opposing the initials SEATO to designate the new security arrangement, for they would suggest comparison with NATO, and by no stretch of the imagination is SEATO an Asian NATO. Nevertheless, it represented the maximum amount of cooperative planning for defense of Southeast Asia that was possible under existing circumstances.

Alliance Diplomacy. Through various mutual security arrangements the United States is associated with her Latin American neighbors, the major states of Western Europe, and such important Asian nations as Japan and Pakistan. These arrangements

[40] Julius W. Pratt, *A History of United States Foreign Policy* (Englewood Cliffs, N.J.: Prentice-Hall, 1955), p. 750.

are basically military alliances, presumably for common purposes and against common dangers; but they also have larger dimensions and implications. They link the United States by special ties with most of the major non-Communist nations, and they provide a forum for the exchange of views and for the formulation of common policies. Indeed, in the postwar period alliance diplomacy has been a major aspect of the foreign policy of the United States.

On the whole, her alliances have been a source of strength to the United States, and have contributed to the defense of the "free world" against possible Communist or other aggression. But in recent years references to these as "alliances in disarray" have been all too apposite. This has been especially true of NATO, the most important of them all.

The North Atlantic Treaty was signed at a time when the states of Western Europe were weak, economically and politically as well as militarily, and when the threat from the Soviet Union was thought to be particularly great. Since 1949 Western Europe has made a remarkable economic recovery, and the Russian threat has apparently become less imminent. Many members of the alliance, aware of their reliance on the United States for protection in the event of a nuclear war, are not certain that the United States, for all her professions, would come to their aid if the Russians attacked (would she risk the destruction of New York for the sake of London or Paris?), and they have increasingly chafed at the virtual American monopoly of atomic weapons and the decision-making authority to use such weapons. Within NATO a great many problems have developed, all the way from tactical matters to questions of broad national and international policy.

General de Gaulle, in particular, has been openly dissatisfied with NATO in its present form. Apparently he feels that it is too much dominated by *les Anglo-Saxons* and that France would do better to seek security through her own strength, including some nuclear capability, and through bilateral security arrangements. The North Atlantic Treaty contained a provision that after the treaty had been in force for twenty years, any member could withdraw one year after giving due notice. Thus 1969 may be a crucial year for NATO. Whether France withdraws or not, there will surely be demands for a thorough reconsideration of the organization, purposes, and operations of NATO, in the light of changing national interests and the general international situation. This will be a real test for alliance diplomacy.

The Rio Treaty, as administered through OAS, seems to be in reasonably good health; but it is hardly adapted to deal with the dangers of political infiltration and subversion from within and outside the hemisphere, and it is in many ways an unnatural alliance, given the preponderance of United States power and influence and Latin American suspicions of the American colossus. These suspicions have been enhanced by the "Bay of Pigs" incident and other actions against Castro, and by the unilateral United States intervention in the Dominican Republic, even though eventually most of the leaders of the Latin American states became disillusioned with Castro, and the OAS was brought into the Dominican picture promptly after United States troops landed. For the United States the Rio Treaty is a part of a larger relationship with the republics of Latin America — a relationship which is still as important, as fluctuating, and as sensitive as it has been for many years.

From the beginning SEATO has been a weak and unnatural alliance. It has been further weakened by the lukewarm support of some of its members and the open non-cooperation of some, notably France; by the strained relations among some of its members; by the hostility of important Southeast Asian states, notably Indonesia, North Vietnam, and Cambodia; and by its inability to be of much assistance in dealing with the Communist pressures in Laos and Vietnam. If the United States feels that SEATO can and should be strengthened — and her attitude is ambivalent — prompt action is called for.

The security treaties with Australia and New Zealand, the Philippines, the Republic of Korea, and the Republic of China do not presently call for major efforts of alliance diplomacy; but in each case the precise value of the arrangement and its influence on the relations of the United States and the signatory state or states are by no means clear. Many difficulties in United States–Philippine relations have developed because of the American naval and air bases in the Philippines and incidents involving Filipinos and American military personnel. The 1960 treaty was more acceptable to Japan than the 1951 treaty, signed at the same time as the peace treaty, but many vocal groups in Japan are demanding a revision, or even the abrogation, of this treaty at the earliest possible date, which presumably could be in 1970.

Thus none of the alliances with which the United States is associated is in a really flourishing condition at the present time. Possibly such alliances have served their purposes, or are of rather dubious value under present conditions. In any event, the United States obviously must look to its alliances and evolve new policies for their revision, revitalization, or supersession by more satisfactory diplomatic and military arrangements and techniques.

American Foreign Assistance Programs

World War II cost the United States about 40 billion dollars in the form of lend-lease expenditures. Since then she has spent more than 100 billion dollars on foreign aid programs. There seems to be little prospect that these will be discontinued in the foreseeable future; in fact, they seem to have become, as President Eisenhower stated in his message to Congress on April 20, 1955, "an integral part of our foreign policy."

The American foreign aid programs developed as emergency measures to deal with emergency situations. Only with the growth of the Marshall Plan did they lose their unsystematic and emergency character, and only more recently have they become part of a continuing and long-range policy. This evolution has occurred in the face of determined efforts to shelve the whole program of foreign aid.

The Five Phases. The period of large-scale American foreign assistance since 1941 may be divided into five phases. The first covered the years from the passage of the Lend-Lease Act in March, 1941, to the abrupt termination of this "weapon of victory" upon the cessation of hostilities in August, 1945. The second, lasting until the effective launching of the European Recovery Program in 1948, embraced American relief to war-torn areas and special credits to individual countries for reconstruction. The third began with the passage of the Foreign Assistance Act of 1948, "the first systematic attempt to deal with the problems of postwar reconstruction on a wider geographical basis." The Communist attack on South Korea in late June, 1950, marked the beginning of the fourth phase, one in which the emphasis was shifted from recovery to rearmament. This emphasis was apparent in the Mutual Security Act of October, 1951, "which combined the various types of assistance programs into a single scheme, worldwide in scope and based primarily on security considerations." The first appropriations for Point Four were made during this phase, and the Development Loan Fund was inaugurated. Certain events in 1953, notably the death of Stalin and the "new look" in Russia and the truce in Korea, seemed to promote a healthier international atmosphere; these naturally had an effect upon the American foreign aid program. In this phase em-

EVOLUTION OF U.S. ECONOMIC AID PROGRAMS

PROGRAM	PERIOD	OBJECTIVE
THE WAR YEARS Lend - Lease	1941 – 1945	Aid to our Allies in the Common Struggle
POST - WAR RELIEF UNRRA, Civilian Supplies British Loan, etc.	1946 – 1948	Emergency Food, Shelter, Clothing ; First Recovery Steps
MARSHALL PLAN European Recovery Program	1948 – 1951	Restoration of Industrial and Agricultural Production in Europe
"POINT IV" Technical Assistance	1950 – 1961	Transfer of Technical Skills and Knowledge to Underdeveloped Countries
DEFENSE SUPPORT Korean War, Indo - China, The Global Cold War	1952 – 1961	Assistance to Countries with Heavy Defense Burdens, or to those making Specific Contributions to the Common Defense
START OF DEVELOPMENT LOANS Development Loan Fund	1958 – 1961	Loans for Projects in the Less Developed Economies
THE DECADE OF DEVELOPMENT	1962 –	Support to Country Social and Economic Development Efforts

Department of State

phasis shifted from Europe to Asia, and from military to economic assistance.[41] The advent of the Kennedy administration in 1961 ushered in a new phase, during which the American foreign aid program was related to a "decade of development," with emphasis on selective assistance to certain countries, on self-help efforts, and on relatively larger contributions by other economically advanced countries. The Foreign Assistance Act of 1961 created the Agency for International Development and, in amended form after the annual Congressional scrutiny and debate, provided the framework for a more coordinated economic assistance program during the Kennedy and Johnson administrations.

Lend-Lease. The passage of the Lend-Lease Act was certainly one of the most unneutral steps ever taken during time of war by a so-called neutral. It made available to countries resisting Nazi aggression the resources of the United States. Of the total of $49.1 billion of gross assistance under lend-lease (there were about $7.8 billion in reverse lend-lease) Great Britain received $29 billion and the U.S.S.R. $10.8 billion. Only two other countries received more than a billion dollars of aid under the program: France ($2.6 billion) and China ($1.3 billion).

Early Postwar Assistance. Apparently the United States hoped to wind up her aid program after the war and to transfer the problems of financing postwar reconstruction to new international agencies and to private enterprises. Instead, the conditions resulting from the war and the deterioration of relations between the Soviet Union and the Western powers forced her to embark on a series of uncoordinated emergency measures on a variety of fronts. Large grants were

[41] The quotations in this paragraph are from William Adams Brown, Jr., and Redvers Opie, *American Foreign Assistance* (Washington, D.C.: The Brookings Institution, 1953), p. 543.

made for the termination of lend-lease operations, for postwar relief through UNRRA (United Nations Relief and Rehabilitation Administration) and international refugee organizations, to areas occupied by American forces, and to China (directly and through UNRRA),[42] and to the Philippines. The largest single item was a loan to Britain of $3.75 billion, but substantial credits were also made available for post-lend-lease operations, for surplus property disposal, and for loans by the Export-Import Bank. During this phase gross foreign assistance amounted to $14.5 billion, exclusive of nearly $500 million for interim aid to certain European countries while the Marshall Plan was taking shape and for aid to Greece and Turkey, which continued beyond this phase.

The European Recovery Program. The ERP was the most ambitious peacetime undertaking that the United States has ever assumed in foreign affairs. No other venture in American foreign policy has been more carefully planned, more actively debated, or more strongly implemented. The nature of the program and its contribution to European recovery are described in Chapter 15. Here we shall consider it as the major undertaking during the third phase of American foreign assistance programs, when economic rehabilitation was the dominant theme.

In a commencement address at Harvard University, on June 5, 1947, Secretary of State George C. Marshall proposed the idea that developed into the European Recovery Program. The Communist coup in Czechoslovakia in February, 1948, helped to persuade many Congressmen that the United States must strengthen the free countries of Europe, and the signing of the Brussels Treaty in March, 1948, afforded evidence that the leading nations of Western Europe were determined to defend themselves and to deserve American aid. On April 3, 1948, President Truman signed the Foreign Assistance Act, which authorized an expenditure of $5.3 billion for the European Recovery Program, $463 million for China, $275 million for Greece and Turkey, and $60 million for the International Children's Emergency Fund. It also provided for the establishment of an Economic Cooperation Administration, separate from but with close relations with the State Department. ECA special missions were soon established in each of the participating countries, which, in turn, signed bilateral aid agreements with the United States (except for Switzerland) and established the Organization for European Economic Cooperation (OEEC), with headquarters in Paris, to coordinate their recovery efforts and work closely with ECA.

In this manner the European Recovery Program was launched. It was conceived as a four-year program, with gradually decreasing appropriations; the total expenditure was estimated to be in the neighborhood of $17 billion. When the program came formally to an end, on December 31, 1951, the actual expenditures — made or committed — amounted to about $11 billion; but additional commitments had in the meantime been made for the rearmament of Western Europe and for the coordination of defense efforts in the North Atlantic Community. These called for many billions more. The shift in emphasis was reflected in the scale of the President's recommendations for fiscal 1952, when he asked for $1.65 billion for economic aid to Europe and for $5.24 billion for military assistance. For fiscal 1953 the amounts requested were $1.8 billion and $4.145 billion, respectively.

In its immediate objectives the Marshall Plan was generally a decided success. Quite possibly it helped to save Western Europe from economic collapse and from Communist conquest from within and from without. Moreover, it helped to restore hope and confidence in a crucial part of the free world. But when it was over Western Europe could

[42] For a comment on UNRRA, see p. 317n.

hardly be regarded as a viable economic or political unit or as in a position to defend itself. The economies of most of the countries could not sustain a major defense effort, and the political situation in many was still unstable. The strength of the Communists in France had declined only slightly, and in Italy they had actually increased in numbers; and "neutralism" and apathy and defeatism were still widespread.

Before it was fused into the Mutual Security Program, the Marshall Plan had become largely a program of economic mobilization for defense. In its early stages the economic aspects were paramount, but the critical international situation, especially after the attack on the Republic of Korea in June, 1950, made these attempts rather unrealistic; and the focus of the Marshall Plan was shifted from recovery to rearmament. There is considerable basis for Theodore White's conclusion: "Though the Marshall Plan continued in name down to 1952, historically it came to its end the week the Communists attacked in Asia."[43]

The Mutual Defense Assistance Program. On July 25, 1949, the day on which he signed the instrument of ratification of the North Atlantic Treaty, President Truman sent to Congress a request for legislation authorizing a program of "military aid to free nations." The Mutual Defense Assistance Program which followed was largely a program of military aid to the countries which participated in the North Atlantic Treaty Organization, with some economic aspects, and with some peripheral military and economic aid to Greece and Turkey (not then members of NATO) and to countries of the Far East and other parts of Asia.

According to the provisions of the act, the appropriation for military aid to NATO countries could be made available only when each country requesting assistance had signed a bilateral agreement with the United States and when the President had approved "recommendations for an integrated defense of the North Atlantic area." These formalities were not completed until January 27, 1950, when eight bilateral agreements were signed and the President announced his approval of the "strategic concept" worked out by the foreign and defense ministers of the North Atlantic countries.[44] In March the first assignment of airplanes and other military equipment under the MDAP left the United States.

In June, 1950, the President asked Congress for another billion dollars for the second year of MDAP. This time very little serious opposition was encountered in Congress. "The alternative to military assistance," declared a report of the Senate Foreign Relations and Armed Services Committees, "is the abandonment of freedom and the confession of weakness which the Soviet Union would not be slow to interpret as an invitation to aggression."[45] The attack on South Korea in late June seemed to prove that these were not idle words. Appropriations for MDAP were vastly expanded before the end of 1950, and when this program was made a part of the Mutual Security Program in the following year, the appropriations for military aid to Western Europe were more than five times as great as the previous annual figures under MDAP. For other areas the sums for military assistance were stepped up proportionately.

[43] *Fire in the Ashes: Europe in Mid-Century* (New York: William Sloane Associates, 1953), p. 70.

[44] For the President's statement and the texts of the Mutual Defense Assistance Agreements with Belgium, Denmark, France, and Italy, see *Department of State Bulletin*, XXII (February 6, 1950), 198–211. The agreements with Luxembourg, Norway, the United Kingdom, and the Netherlands were printed in the two subsequent issues of the *Bulletin*.

[45] *Mutual Defense Assistance Act Extension,* Senate Report 1853, 81st Congress, 2d Sess., June 21, 1950, p. 26.

The Point Four Program. The first announcement of the Point Four Program was made in President Truman's Inaugural Address of January 20, 1949. It soon became clear, however, that, as James Reston once said, "the speech preceded the policy." The administration took several months to work out the details of a program of a very modest sort, *after* the President's address. Hence, although it had its inception during what we have called the third phase of postwar foreign assistance, the implementation of Point Four began early in the fourth phase.

The Act for International Development (Title II of the Economic Assistance Act of 1950) was the first legislative step to implement the Point Four Program. Despite the fact that the United States was by that time spending some $400 million a year on various forms of assistance to underdeveloped areas,[46] the act was "a significant milestone in the evolution of American world policy."[47] For the first time, "technical assistance" had become a major foreign policy. The act declared the purpose was to "aid the efforts of the peoples of economically underdeveloped areas to develop their resources and improve their working and living conditions by encouraging the exchange of technical knowledge and skills and the flow of investment capital to countries which provide conditions under which such technical assistance and capital can effectively and constructively contribute to raising standards of living, creating new sources of wealth, increasing productivity and expanding purchasing power." It authorized participation in both bilateral and multilateral "technical cooperation" programs, and directed the President to set up machinery for administration and coordination, including an advisory board with representatives of private industry.

The administration continued to tailor its requests for Point Four to the dimensions which Congress would tolerate; but both within and without the government there was a strong feeling that the United States should raise her sights in this area of foreign policy, both because the needs of the underdeveloped countries were great and because American national interests would best be served by a truly bold program of aid.[48] Yet, despite the Gray Report of November, 1950, which declared that the new and "promising" economic measures "have not been pressed with the vigor that the situation requires, and they have not been fused into a sufficiently effective program," and the International Development Advisory Board's insistence in March, 1951, that a program of aid to underdeveloped areas was an essential part of the American defense effort as well as a necessary contribution to the promotion of more stable economic conditions in the world, Congress preferred to give priority to defense measures and military assistance, and to regard Point Four as an impractical, long-range scheme which had small relation to the existing emergency.

The Mutual Security Program. In the spring of 1951 President Truman proposed the consolidation of the foreign aid programs. He asked for $8.5 billion for the fiscal year ending June 30, 1952, with

[46] See address of Samuel P. Hayes, Jr., on "Point 4 Program after Korea," made in Baltimore, Md., January 23, 1951; printed in *Department of State Bulletin,* XXIV (February 5, 1951), 225–226.

[47] Richard P. Stebbins, *The United States in World Affairs, 1950* (New York: Council on Foreign Relations, 1951), p. 96.

[48] See, for example, Dewey Anderson and Stephen Raushenbush, *A Policy and Program for Success,* No. 1 in the Bold New Program Series of the Public Affairs Institute (Washington, D.C., 1951); James P. Warburg, *"Point Four": Our Chance to Achieve Freedom Without Fear* (Author's Publ., 1949); and *United States Policy for Foreign Economic Development,* a report by a seminar on "Economic Policies for Under-developed Areas" of the World Affairs Council of Philadelphia, supplement to *World Affairs Councilor,* II (May, 1951).

Herblock; Copyright, 1952, The Washington Post

"You mean these aren't enough?"

nearly $7 billion allocated to Europe. The Mutual Security Act of October 10, 1951, enabled the President to make the integration he had recommended. He appointed W. Averell Harriman as Director for Mutual Security, and Harriman, on January 15, 1952, announced the organization of the new Mutual Security Agency (MSA). This agency, located in the Executive Office of the President, exercised general supervision over all the foreign aid programs. The responsibility for the actual operation of the Technical Assistance Program devolved largely upon the State Department and that of the military aid programs upon the Department of Defense.

The objectives of the Mutual Security Program included those of the later phases of the ERP, with their emphasis on economic aspects of rearmament, the military objectives of the MDAP, and the technical assistance objectives of the Point Four Program. While it cannot be said that new objectives were included — except perhaps that of coordination — the new program made possible a broader and more intensified approach, as, for instance, greatly expanded economic aid and technical assistance in the Far East and an enlarged program in Latin America.

The integration of foreign assistance programs which had been promoted by the Mutual Security Act of 1951 was carried still further by Reorganization Plan No. 7 of August, 1953, which consolidated a number of agencies into the Foreign Operations Administration. The change was essentially an administrative one, with the projects directed by FOA still labeled the Mutual Security Program. Harold E. Stassen was director of FOA until it was terminated on June 30, 1955; during those twenty-two months he directed the expenditure of approximately $8.7 billion of which $6.3 billion went to military assistance and direct forces support.

On the conclusion of his service as director, Mr. Stassen submitted to the President a brief overall report on some of the major aspects of the Mutual Security Program under FOA.[49] Of particular interest was the change "from preoccupation mainly with building of military defenses to the aim of creating an economic base capable of both supporting necessary defense efforts and also of yielding a growing measure of economic progress and advance in human dignity and well-being." Of almost equal significance was "the shift in program emphasis from Europe to the less developed areas of the world." Mr. Stassen pointed out that "the arc of free Asia" was "the area offering the

[49] *Report to the President on the Foreign Operations Administration,* June 30, 1955.

most urgent challenge and the greatest opportunity for constructive action," but he noted that increased attention was also being given to Latin America, the Near East, and Africa. Other major developments listed by Mr. Stassen were: the suspension of all economic aid to the Marshall Plan countries; building "additional strength" in Spain, Yugoslavia, and Berlin; the development of the technical cooperation program into "a powerful instrument for meeting forthrightly a broad range of problems involved in achieving economic progress by democratic means"; and the realization that the program "has become in fact an integral part of our total foreign policy and national security system."

When FOA came to an end, the foreign economic assistance and technical assistance programs were returned to the State Department, with somewhat enhanced status. They were put under the International Cooperation Administration, with a director directly responsible to the Secretary of State. This administrative arrangement continued during the remaining years of the Eisenhower administration. In 1957 the Development Loan Fund was created, and soon became a major source of assistance to underdeveloped countries.

Programs for International Development. In 1961 the new Kennedy administration was responsible for substantial changes in the foreign assistance program. In March, in a special message to Congress, President Kennedy called for major United States participation in a "decade of development." He said that the fundamental task of foreign aid "is to help make an historical demonstration that in the twentieth century, as in the nineteenth — in the southern half of the globe as in the north — economic growth and political democracy can develop hand in hand." He announced that "special attention" would be given "to those nations most willing and able to mobilize their own resources," and he called for a special program of assistance to the countries of Latin America as a major feature of a new "Alliance for Progress." Among the proposed new features were a more unified administration and operation, increased emphasis on development loans on a long-term basis at low interest rates, greater participation by other economically advanced countries, and a clearer distinction between economic and military aid. The Foreign Assistance Act of 1961 provided the framework for the program, and it created the Agency for International Development to replace the International Cooperation Administration as the main economic agency.

In 1963 David E. Bell was appointed Administrator of the Agency of International Development. He discharged the difficult and arduous duties of this office with conspicuous success, even in the eyes of most members of Congress, until he resigned in 1966 to join the Ford Foundation. In the same year President Kennedy asked General Lucius Clay to head a White House committee — bearing the suggestive name of the Committee to Strengthen the Security of the Free World — to take a "hard look" at the foreign aid program. While the Clay committee concluded that continued foreign assistance was in the interest of the United States, it charged that the United States was "attempting too much for too many," and it made many specific as well as general criticisms of the foreign aid program. This rather critical report may have accounted in part for the action of Congress in making the first sizable reduction in foreign aid appropriations. Whereas President Kennedy originally asked for an appropriation of $4.945 billion, the eventual appropriation, not approved until December 30, was only $3 billion.

By 1962 the shift in aid from Europe to Asia had become clearly evident. Whereas in 1946 the major recipients of United States foreign aid were France and the United

AGENCY FOR INTERNATIONAL DEVELOPMENT

PROPOSED A.I.D. PROGRAM

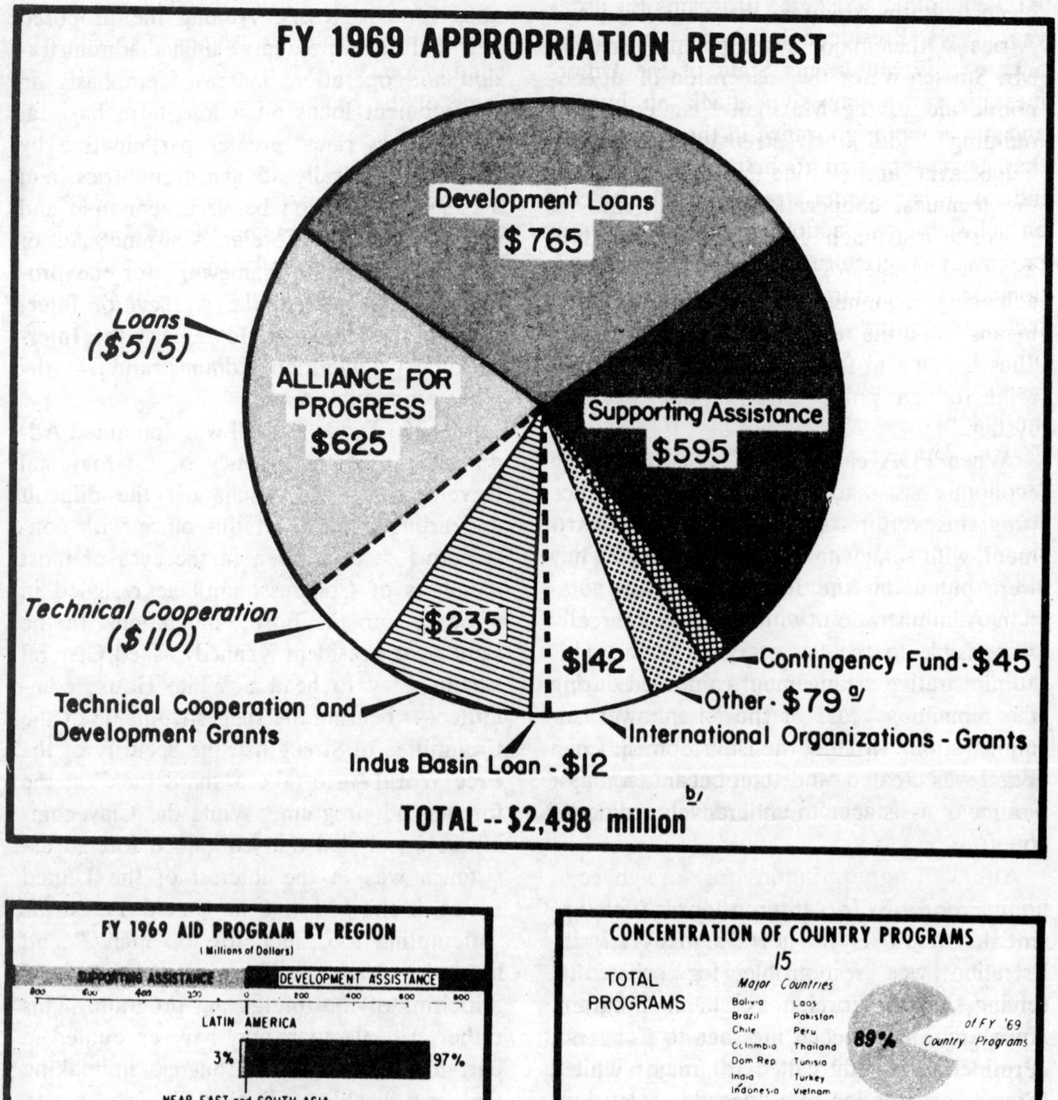

FY 1969 APPROPRIATION REQUEST

Development Loans
$765

Loans
($515)

ALLIANCE FOR PROGRESS
$625

Supporting Assistance
$595

Technical Cooperation
($110)

$235

$142

Contingency Fund - $45

Other - $79 a/

Technical Cooperation and Development Grants

International Organizations - Grants

Indus Basin Loan - $12

TOTAL -- $2,498 million b/

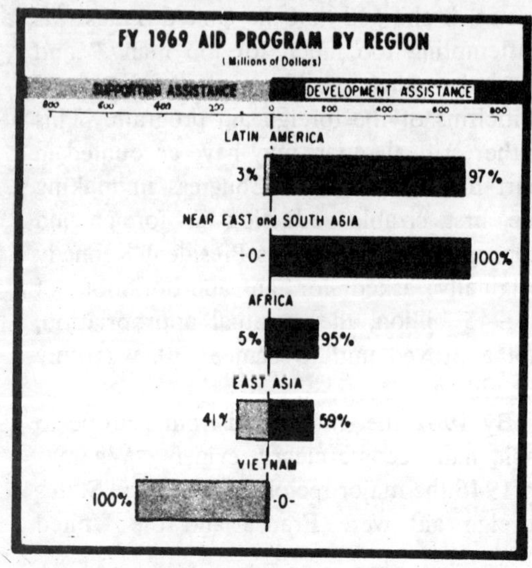

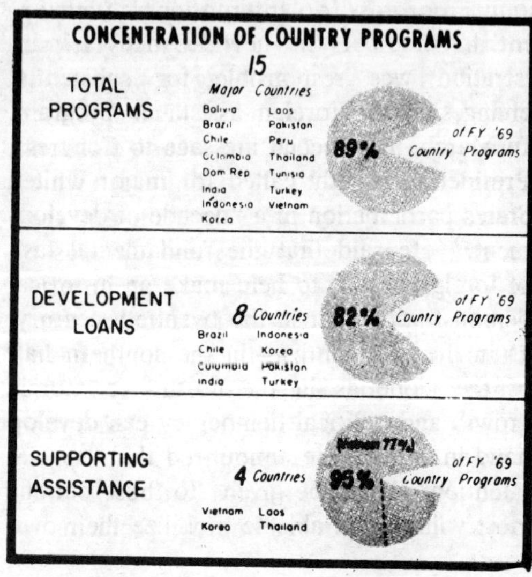

Department of State

Kingdom, in 1962 India and Pakistan were at the top of the list.

In his request for some $2.5 billion for AID economic assistance programs for fiscal year 1967, President Johnson — in pursuance of his call in his State of the Union message for a "massive attack on hunger and disease and ignorance in those countries that are determined to help themselves" — indicated that greater stress would be placed on self-help, on "action, not promises," on progress in agriculture, health, and education, on the resources of America's private sector, on more generous assistance from other free world countries, on new arrangements for channeling more assistance through multilateral agencies, and on programs to deal with direct or indirect Communist aggression, especially in Southeast Asia. He requested — but did not receive Congressional approval for — authorization of the aid program for a period of five years, subject to annual appropriations of funds. He indicated that military and economic assistance programs were being proposed in separate legislation, and that more than 90 per cent of direct country assistance was being programmed for just 20 countries and 84 per cent of development loans for only 8 countries.

Although appropriations for foreign economic assistance now run to hardly three-tenths of one per cent of the Gross National Product, there is a growing opposition to foreign aid programs in the United States. Apparently Americans are weary of shouldering even the relatively small burden which foreign assistance imposes on them, and they are critical of the conduct and dubious of the value of such programs, either in terms of American national interests or in terms of their contribution to the economic development of underdeveloped countries. It is increasingly difficult for the administration to obtain Congressional approval of the reduced requests for foreign aid appropriations; and in the meantime the problems of the developing countries multiply, and their development efforts falter.

The New Partnership

We have examined some of the factors conditioning American foreign policy and some of the principles which have governed it. We have seen that most of these principles were formulated early in the American experience, and that they have stood the test of time and of changing conditions much better than is generally realized. Since the turn of the century, however, some have had to be abandoned and others reformulated and re-examined. In this period vast changes have occurred in the world political pattern, and the United States has moved, somewhat haltingly and reluctantly, into a position of great power and responsibility. There is ample evidence for concluding that she has not yet learned how to act like a great power or how to wield such tremendous responsibility; that she has not yet adjusted herself to her new world position; that she is still handicapped by illusions and concepts which were acquired in a far different era. Perhaps it is not surprising that her motives and intentions are not always understood abroad; she does not fully understand them herself. She still is trying to formulate policies which will be truly in the national interest, and she is beginning to realize that good intentions and lofty statements of principle are no substitute for concrete policies closely geared to determined objectives.

A friendly English critic, J. B. Priestley, expressed the anxiety of many observers when he wrote in 1947:

> America now bestrides the world; she is the colossus of our time. Whatever is said and done in the United States may easily change the lives of unnumbered millions thousands of miles away. . . . It is clearly a terrible responsibility. But where, except in occasional speeches, is America's sense of responsibility? . . . Congressmen who have never given a morning's serious thought to

world problems hurry to register votes that may ruin half a continent. Columnists in search of a scoop casually blast the plans of half a dozen countries. Private feuds that we in Europe know nothing about shape our lives.

The most powerful government on earth seems to have no continuing policy, no tradition to guide it, and is clearly swayed by what is largely an irresponsible sensation-loving press and an electorate that can be stampeded like cattle. Imagine our feelings. It is like being locked in a house with a whimsical drunken giant.[50]

So startling is this image that most Americans might have difficulty in recognizing themselves in it; but they must admit that Priestley's misgivings have some basis in fact. They should realize that apprehensions of this sort have been frequently voiced in unofficial circles in almost every other country of the non-Communist world. Even in official quarters the same doubts and fears have been expressed, although in more restrained and diplomatic language. One may suspect that the real source of perturbation lies in the unwelcome realization by the peoples of other free nations that they are heavily dependent on the United States for economic well-being, political stability, and military protection. Quite understandably, they do not care to feel like poor relations of a "whimsical drunken giant" or even of a sober, reliable giant. The United States, for her part, still seems to expect gratitude and appreciation for the tremendous outlays she has made to assist other countries, when she should realize that gratitude is a rare commodity on the international market and that the real justification for her aid programs must be sought in the realm of national self-interest, with humanitarian considerations an important but nevertheless subordinate motivation.

The Hoover Commission's Task Force on Foreign Affairs called attention to two characteristics of the international position of the United States which call for recognition and implementation. The first is that "the objectives and policies of the United States are today by necessity fundamentally positive in nature rather than negative or declaratory as in the past" and that even a policy with so many negative aspects as the Truman Doctrine "requires positive commitments in terms of dollars and personnel." The second prime characteristic is "the cooperative nature of our foreign relations"; even the major issues between the two giants of the modern world, the Soviet Union and the United States, "are not bilateral but involve many countries."[51] Many Americans are still unwilling to face the full implications of these observations, but the majority are apparently beginning to accept them as among the unavoidable conditions of international life.

More than a generation ago Woodrow Wilson declared: "We are participants, whether we would or not, in the life of the world. The interests of all nations are our own also. We are partners with the rest." Many years of disillusionment and another world war were required before the American people realized and accepted the import of Wilson's words. Now, "for the first time in its history," said one historian of American diplomacy who became a member of the United States Senate, "the United States has been striving to live up to the responsibilities of world leadership"; and he added: "This is the single most important fact in the world today."[52]

[50] "You Worry the World," in *Magazine of the Year,* October, 1947; quoted in Harold and Margaret Sprout, *Foundations of National Power,* 2d ed. (Princeton, N.J.: D. Van Nostrand Co., 1951), p. 415.

[51] *Task Force Report on Foreign Affairs,* p. 37.

[52] Gale W. McGee, "American Foreign Policy: Using the Past to Move Forward," *The American Scholar* (Summer, 1950), p. 209.

SUGGESTIONS FOR FURTHER READING

ACHESON, DEAN. *Power and Diplomacy*. Cambridge, Mass.: Harvard University Press, 1958. The William L. Clayton Lectures on International Economic Affairs and Foreign Policy.

ALMOND, GABRIEL. *The American People and Foreign Policy*. New York: Harcourt, Brace, 1950. One of the best studies of American public opinion and foreign policy.

America in Crisis Series. New York: John Wiley & Sons. Paperback volumes.

American Assembly Series. Englewood Cliffs, N.J.: Prentice-Hall. Most of these paperback volumes deal with issues of American foreign policy.

BAILEY, THOMAS A. *A Diplomatic History of the American People,* 6th ed. New York: Appleton-Century-Crofts, 1958. First published in 1940. One of the most widely used texts.

BARTLETT, RUHL, ed. *The Record of American Diplomacy,* 2d ed. New York: Alfred A. Knopf, 1950. An excellent collection of documents covering the entire history of American foreign policy.

BELL, CORAL. *The Debatable Alliance; an Essay in Anglo-American Relations*. New York: Oxford University Press, 1964. Issued under the auspices of the Royal Institute of International Affairs.

———. *Negotiation from Strength; a Study in the Politics of Power*. London, 1962.

BELOFF, MAX. *The United States and the Unity of Europe*. Washington, D.C.: The Brookings Institution, 1963.

BEMIS, SAMUEL F. *A Diplomatic History of the United States,* 4th ed. New York: Holt, 1955. A comprehensive text.

———. *The Latin American Policy of the United States*. New York: Harcourt, Brace, 1943. Especially good on the doctrine of absolute non-intervention as developed by Latin American jurists.

BLOOMFIELD, LINCOLN. *The United Nations and U.S. Foreign Policy*. Boston: Little, Brown, and Company, 1960.

BLUM, ROBERT. *The United States and China in World Affairs*. New York: McGraw-Hill Book Company, 1966. One of a series of volumes on the same theme, published for the Council on Foreign Relations. All of the volumes in this series are recommended.

BOWIE, ROBERT R. *Shaping the Future; Foreign Policy in an Age of Transition*. New York: Columbia University Press, 1964. By a former chairman of the State Department's Policy Planning Staff.

CAMPBELL, JOHN C. *American Policy Toward Communist Eastern Europe: the Choices Ahead*. Minneapolis: University of Minnesota Press, 1965.

CARLETON, WILLIAM G. *The Revolution in American Foreign Policy, Its Global Range*. New York: Random House, 1964. Good general survey of postwar U.S. foreign policy.

COOMBS, PHILIP H. *The Fourth Dimension of Foreign Policy; Educational and Cultural Affairs*. New York: Harper & Row, for the Council on Foreign Relations, 1964. By a former Assistant Secretary of State for Educational and Cultural Affairs.

Council on Foreign Relations. *The United States in World Affairs*. Annual volumes. Published by Harper for the Council.

ELLIOTT, WILLIAM Y. *et al. The Political Economy of American Foreign Policy*. New York: Holt, 1955. Report of a Study Group sponsored by the Woodrow Wilson Foundation and the National Planning Association.

EPSTEIN, LEON. *Britain — Uneasy Ally*. Chicago, University of Chicago Press, 1954.

FEIS, HERBERT. *The China Tangle*. Princeton, N.J.: Princeton University Press, 1953.

———. *Foreign Aid and Foreign Policy*. New York: St. Martin's Press, 1964.

FINLETTER, THOMAS K. *Foreign Policy; The*

Next Phase, the 1960s, 2d ed. New York: Harper, for the Council on Foreign Relations, 1960.

FULBRIGHT, J. WILLIAM. *The Arrogance of Power.* New York: Random House, 1966. A criticism of American interventionism, especially in Latin America and Asia.

———. *Old Myths and New Realities.* New York: Random House, 1964. A critical and widely discussed commentary on American foreign policy, by the chairman of the Senate Foreign Relations Committee.

GELBER, LIONEL M. *America in Britain's Place; the Leadership of the West and Anglo-American Unity.* New York: Frederick A. Praeger, 1961.

GOLDWIN, ROBERT A. *Beyond the Cold War; Essays on American Foreign Policy in a Changing World Environment.* Chicago: Rand McNally & Co., 1965.

GOLDWIN, ROBERT A. *et al.,* eds. *Readings in American Foreign Policy.* New York: Oxford University Press, 1959.

GRAEBNER, NORMAN A. *Cold War Diplomacy; American Foreign Policy, 1945–1960.* Princeton, N.J.: D. Van Nostrand Co., 1962.

GRISWOLD, A. WHITNEY. *The Far Eastern Policy of the United States.* New York: Harcourt, Brace, 1938.

GUERRANT, EDWARD O. *Roosevelt's Good Neighbor Policy.* Albuquerque: University of New Mexico Press, 1950.

HAHN, WALTER and JOHN C. NEFF, eds. *America's Strategy for the Nuclear Age.* Garden City, N.Y.: Doubleday & Co., 1960.

HOROWITZ, DAVID. *The Free World Colossus; a Critique of American Foreign Policy in the Cold War.* New York: Hill & Wang, 1965.

JACOBSON, HAROLD K. *America's Foreign Policy.* New York: Random House, 1960.

KENEN, PETER B. *Giant Among Nations; Problems in United States Foreign Economic Policy.* Chicago: Rand McNally & Co., 1963.

KENNAN, GEORGE F. *American Diplomacy, 1900–1950.* Chicago: University of Chicago Press, 1951. A small volume with a great impact.

———. *Realities of American Foreign Policy.* Princeton, N.J.: Princeton University Press, 1954.

KERTESZ, STEPHEN D., ed. *American Diplomacy in a New Era.* Notre Dame, Ind.: University of Notre Dame Press, 1961.

KISSINGER, HENRY A. *The Necessity for Choice; Prospects of American Foreign Policy.* New York: Harper & Row, 1961.

———. *Nuclear Weapons and Foreign Policy.* New York: Harper, for the Council on Foreign Relations, 1957.

———. *The Troubled Partnership; a Reappraisal of the Atlantic Alliance.* New York: McGraw-Hill Book Company, for the Council on Foreign Relations, 1965.

KLEIMAN, ROBERT. *Atlantic Crisis; American Diplomacy Confronts a Resurgent Europe.* New York: W. W. Norton & Company, 1964.

LIEUWEN, EDWIN. *U.S. Policy in Latin America; a Short History.* New York: Frederick A. Praeger, 1965.

LIPPMANN, WALTER. *The Cold War: A Study in U.S. Foreign Policy.* New York: Harper, 1947. Reprinted articles taking issues with the "containment" policy.

LISKA, GEORGE. *The New Statecraft; Foreign Aid in American Foreign Policy.* Chicago: University of Chicago Press, 1960.

LYONS, GENE M., ed. *America: Purpose and Power.* Chicago: Quadrangle Books, 1965.

MASTERS, ROGER D. *The Nation Is Burdened: American Foreign Policy in a Changing World.* New York: Alfred A. Knopf, 1967. A thoughtful analysis, emphasizing the national interest approach.

MAY, ERNEST, ed. *The American Foreign Policy.* New York: George Braziller, 1963.

MORGENTHAU, HANS J. *In Defense of the National Interest: A Critical Examination of American Foreign Policy.* New York: Alfred A. Knopf, 1951.

OSGOOD, ROBERT. *Ideals and Self-Interest in*

America's Foreign Relations. Chicago: University of Chicago Press, 1953. A "national interest" interpretation.

PEETERS, PAUL. *Massive Retaliation; the Policy and Its Critics.* Chicago: Henry Regnery Co., 1959.

PERKINS, DEXTER. *The American Approach to Foreign Policy.* Cambridge, Mass.: Harvard University Press, 1952.

———. *America's Quest for Peace.* Bloomington: Indiana University Press, 1962.

PRATT, JULIUS W. *America's Colonial Experiment.* Englewood Cliffs, N.J.: Prentice-Hall, 1950. A survey of American colonialism and imperialism.

RANSOM, HARVEY H., ed. *An American Foreign Policy Reader.* New York: Thomas Y. Crowell Company, 1965.

RAPPAPORT, ARMIN, ed. *Issues in American Diplomacy.* New York: The Macmillan Company, 1965. 2 vols. Vol. 1: The Formative Years to 1895. Vol. 2: World Power and Leadership since 1895.

ROSS, HUGH. *The Cold War: Containment and Its Critics.* Chicago: Rand McNally & Co., 1963. The Berkeley series in American history.

ROSTOW, WALT W. *The United States in the World Arena; an Essay in Recent History.* New York: Harper, 1960. By a key adviser to Presidents Kennedy and Johnson.

RUSTOW, DANKWART A., ed. America's Role in World Affairs Series. Englewood Cliffs, N.J.: Prentice-Hall. A projected series of 11 volumes, the first of which were published in April, 1967: Rupert Emerson, *Africa and United States Policy,* and John D. Montgomery, *Foreign Aid in International Politics.*

SEABURY, PAUL. *Power, Freedom and Diplomacy: The Foreign Policy of the United States of America.* New York: Random House, 1963. A sophisticated analysis of basic themes in American foreign policy.

SPANIER, JOHN W. *American Foreign Policy since World War II,* 2d ed. New York: Frederick A. Praeger, 1965.

STEEL, RONALD. *The End of Alliance: America and the Future of Europe.* New York: The Viking Press, 1964.

STRAUSZ-HUPÉ, ROBERT, JAMES E. DOUGHERTY, and WILLIAM R. KINTNER. *Building the Atlantic World.* New York: Harper & Row, 1963.

STRAUSZ-HUPÉ, ROBERT *et al.* *A Forward Strategy for America.* New York: Harper & Row, 1961.

TANNENBAUM, FRANK. *The American Tradition in Foreign Policy.* Norman: University of Oklahoma Press, 1955. A vigorous polemic against *realpolitik* and balance of power thinking.

THOMPSON, KENNETH. *Political Realism and the Crisis of World Politics; an American Approach to Foreign Policy.* Princeton, N.J.: Princeton University Press, 1960.

WELLES, SUMNER and DONALD MCKAY, eds. *The American Foreign Policy Library.* Cambridge, Mass.: Harvard University Press. Highly competent studies by leading specialists. Authors and titles as follows:

BRINTON, CRANE. *The United States and Britain,* rev. ed. 1948.

BROWN, W. NORMAN. *The United States and India and Pakistan,* rev. ed. 1963.

CLINE, HOWARD F. *The United States and Mexico,* rev. ed. 1963.

DEAN, VERA M. *The United States and Russia.* 1947.

FAIRBANK, JOHN K. *The United States and China,* rev. ed. 1958.

GALLAGHER, G. F. *The United States and North Africa.* 1963.

GRATTAN, C. H. *The United States and the Southwest Pacific.* 1961.

HUGHES, J. J. *The United States and Italy.* 1953.

MCKAY, DONALD C. *The United States and France.* 1951.

PERKINS, DEXTER. *The United States and the Caribbean.* 1947.

POLK, WILLIAM R. *The United States and the Arab World.* 1965.

REISCHAUER, EDWIN O. *The United States and Japan*, rev. ed. 1957.

SAFRAN, NADAV. *The United States and Israel*. 1963.

SCOTT, F. D. *The United States and Japan*, rev. ed. 1950.

SPEISER, E. A. *The United States and the Near East*, rev. ed. 1949.

THOMAS, L. V. and R. N. FRYE. *The United States and Turkey and Iran*. 1951.

WHITAKER, ARTHUR P. *The United States and South America: The Northern Republics*. 1948.

———. *The United States and Argentina*. 1955.

WOLFF, R. L. *The Balkans in Our Time*. 1956.

WESTERFIELD, BRADFORD. *The Instruments of America's Foreign Policy*. New York: Thomas Y. Crowell Company, 1963.

WOLF, CHARLES, JR. *United States Policy and the Third World*. Boston: Little, Brown and Company, 1967.

WOLFERS, ARNOLD, ed. *Alliance Policy in the Cold War*. Baltimore: The Johns Hopkins Press, 1959.

23 The Foreign Policies of Great Britain, France, and Other States

The Soviet Union and the United States — the order is alphabetical — are the two superpowers in the world today. Great Britain is perhaps the next most influential state, with worldwide interests and commitments. Britain is, however, declining in relative importance and is reducing her international commitments. France has declined greatly in power and prestige, but she still plays a major role in Western Europe, in the NATO alliance (at least in a negative sense), in Africa, and in world affairs generally. General de Gaulle's every effort seems to be designed to restore the grandeur and glory of his beloved France. The military power of Germany and Japan, not long ago the most powerful states of Europe and Asia, is no longer formidable; but both Germany — or, rather, West Germany — and Japan have experienced a remarkable economic resurgence in recent years, and they have re-emerged as major powers.

India's potential is far greater than her power-in-being. The same is true of Communist China, even though the Chinese Communist army is probably the largest in existence today and China is developing a nuclear and thermonuclear capability. Nevertheless, Indian and China, by far the most populous nations in the world, are playing important roles in world affairs. In recent years, especially since the humiliating reverses at the hands of China in October–November, 1962, and the death of Jawaharlal Nehru in May, 1964, India's influence has waned, and she has been reducing her international activities; but she is still the giant of non-Communist Asia and of the entire underdeveloped world outside of the Communist orbit. Communist China has become a particularly disturbing force, because of her militant actions and policies at home and abroad.

For special reasons Korea — that is, the Republic of Korea — Turkey, the Republic of China on Taiwan, and South Vietnam have formidable military establishments, far out of proportion to their economic capabilities; but none of these countries could be regarded as a major power.

A number of other states, not in the great power category, are important regional powers. Examples are Argentina, Brazil, and Mexico in Latin America, Italy in Europe, the United Arab Republic in the Arab world, and Indonesia in Southeast Asia. Other "middle powers," such as Canada and Pakistan, are of special importance, even though they are overshadowed by larger states in the same geographical area. No African state has yet emerged into a position of unquestioned leadership, although several of them, notably the U.A.R. under Nasser and Ghana under Dr. Nkrumah, have apparently aspired to such a role. In time the influence of the largest of the African states, Nigeria, may increase; but this can come about only if Nigeria is able to lay firmer foundations for national existence and to overcome internal divisions and secessionist threats. Many militarily and economically weak states, through the United Nations and regional groupings, because of strategic locations or the possession of valuable raw materials or natural resources, and as a result of other special circumstances, may exercise an influence out of proportion to their actual power.

In the present chapter we shall review the foreign policies of Great Britain and France, and more briefly those of Communist China and of India. We shall then discuss the policies being pursued by the "reemergent powers," Germany and Japan; and finally we shall consider the general nature of the foreign policies of the lesser powers.

The Foreign Policy of Great Britain

"The general character of England's foreign policy," wrote Sir Eyre Crowe in his famous Memorandum of 1907, "is determined by the immutable conditions of her geographical situation on the ocean flank of Europe as an island state with vast overseas colonies and dependencies, whose existence and survival as an independent community are inseparably bound up with the possession of preponderant sea power." Because of these underlying factors, as well as her historical traditions, he argued, Britain "has a direct and positive interest in the maintenance of the independence of nations, and therefore must be the natural enemy of any country threatening the independence of others, and the natural protector of the weaker communities."[1] In particular, Britain sought to maintain a balance of power on the continent of Europe — a policy which had become so well established as to be "an historical truism." Sir Eyre could then also declare that England "champions the principle of the largest measure of general freedom of commerce," a policy dictated alike by enlightened self-interest and by the desire to be on friendly terms with other nations.

Traditional Bases of British Policy

Geography, sea power, trade, balance of power, imperial interests — these have been the traditional bases of British foreign policy, and every British statesman of the past few centuries has been conscious of them. On the whole British diplomacy has sought with considerable skill and finesse to promote the interests of Britain in the light of these underlying realities, and it has done so with a continuity that is one of the outstanding characteristics of British foreign policy.

Geography, Sea Power, and Trade

This fortress built by Nature for herself
Against infection and the hand of war,
This happy breed of men, this little world,
This precious stone set in the silver sea,
Which serves it in the office of a wall,
Or as a moat defensive to a house,
Against the envy of less happier lands.
— *King Richard II*

One may feel on reading these famous lines from Shakespeare that times have changed. Admittedly, the weapons of our day have modified Britain's geographical advantage of earlier years, but they have by no means obliterated it. It is still a factor of prime importance. But England's insularity

[1] "Memorandum on the Present State of British Relations with France and Germany," dated January 1, 1907. For text, see G. P. Gooch and H. Temperley, *British Documents on the Origins of the War, 1898–1919* (London, 1926–38), III, 402–407, 419–420.

did more than provide her with "a moat defensive" behind which she could develop the sturdy institutions of freedom; it also drove her people into their historic alliance with the sea — to naval supremacy, to foreign trade, and to empire.

One of the principal roles of British sea power has been to keep the sea lanes open, so that the island people could carry on their vital trade, especially the export of finished goods and the importation of raw materials and foodstuffs, without which survival would have been impossible. Before World War II Britain normally imported about half of her food and exported about twice the percentage of domestic production that the United States did. The attempts of the Germans in two world wars to blockade the British Isles were almost fatal reminders of the degree of Britain's dependence on outside sources of supply. Trade is indeed the lifeblood of Britain, and it is no mere coincidence that its promotion and protection have always been major concerns of British policy.

Balance of Power. A central aim of British foreign policy from the time of Henry VIII and Cardinal Wolsey to the present has been to prevent the domination of Europe by a single power. Of all the foreign policies of Britain, this has generally been regarded as one of the most basic and most enduring. For this purpose England intervened in continental affairs again and again, usually in support of the state or coalition of states which was prepared to resist the dominant power of the day. Occasionally short-sighted leaders, or those with special axes to grind, gave support to the stronger European states rather than to the weaker, and thus contributed to an upsetting of the balance of power.

Despite these apparent lapses of time, the main outlines of this historic policy are clear. England has viewed with ever-watchful suspicion any state which threatened to upset the balance of power; at crucial moments she has intervened on the continent with all her might — against France under Louis XIV and Napoleon, and against Germany under William II and Adolf Hitler. For centuries Britain and France had been the best of enemies, but under the altered conditions of the nineteenth century they began a cautious friendship and collaboration in many ways; and in the twentieth century the blood of Englishmen and Frenchmen has flowed in a common cause on many a battlefield. During this period Germany and not France threatened to upset the balance in Europe.

In the heyday of the balance of power policy England regarded herself as the holder of the balance in Europe rather than as an active participant in European power politics. This was wholly in keeping with her longstanding dualism of approach to continental affairs — that is, her concern with the affairs of Europe and at the same time her desire to remain aloof from them. Britain is no longer in a position to act as balancer, and indeed the present state of world politics offers little hope for those who would restore the old system. Two factors, in particular, in addition to the attrition of British power and prestige, prevent such a restoration. In the first place, as we have noted, Europe is no longer the only major theater where balance of power considerations are predominant. *World* politics are now really all that the term implies. A policy of balance of power is especially difficult to follow on a worldwide scale. Second, the balance of power in Europe has been so completely destroyed that there is no European state, or effective coalition of states, with which Britain could ally herself in order to restore it. In earlier times one of the conditions of Britain's balance of power policy on the Continent was the existence of such a state or of such a power grouping.

Imperial Interests. Great Britain was long the greatest of imperial powers. As the center of an empire "on which the sun never sets," the little island off the northwest coast of Europe played a role in world affairs which would have been inconceivable in the absence of colonies and dependencies far from home. The preservation of a vast empire, with the maintenance of lines of communication to all its parts and to the countries of the Commonwealth, was a cardinal aim of British foreign policy. Britain's statesmen have perforce thought in imperial terms, and many of her finest sons have served her well in far-off corners of the earth. Today very little of the once mighty empire remains, but Britain still has worldwide interests by virtue of her role in the Commonwealth, the sterling area, the Colombo Plan, SEATO, CENTO, and other associations.

The Decline of British Power

As we look back upon the last quarter of the nineteenth century we can see that in spite of the pomp and glory Britain's power in world affairs was already beginning to decline. The main causes for this decline, which has reached such serious proportions in the present century, are to be found in developments over which Britain had little control. Technological advances, for instance, operated to modify her insularity, reduce her naval preeminence, and diminish her industrial advantages. The rise of the United States and Japan signified that new and powerful non-European rivals had appeared to challenge Britain's political, commercial, and naval supremacy. The unification of Germany under Bismarck and her ambitious ventures under William II not only revived the old threat to the European balance of power but also introduced another economic and naval competitor for Britain. England still followed a balance of power policy, Sir Edward Grey's protestations to the contrary notwithstanding, but after the "splendid isolation" of the 1890's had lost its splendor, England vigorously sought allies — first Japan and next France and Russia. It should be noted, however, that England then became involved in the balance of power system in a less desirable role, for she ceased to be a balancer and instead consistently threw her weight onto one scale of the balance.

The world of the *Pax Britannica* was on the whole a stable and peaceful one, and the major stabilizing factor was British power, both visible and invisible. The decline of that power was gradual, and its full implications were not clearly perceived until after the Second World War. But since 1945 there have been numerous indications that British statesmen have become conscious of it and that, while they have sought to capitalize as much as possible on Britain's past influence and prestige, they have also faced the need of retrenchment and readjustment in foreign as well as in domestic affairs.

Even the fundamental bases of British foreign policy have been greatly weakened, and almost every one of the traditional British policies is gravely challenged today. Facts of geography — presumably the most immutable of all the factors conditioning a nation's power — have changed in significance. England's position as an island kingdom in a strategic location with respect to Europe and the trade routes of the world, blessed by favorable climate and valuable natural resources, is still of vital importance; but in the age of air power the Channel is an inadequate moat, and the development of atomic and hydrogen bombs makes England a peculiarly vulnerable base instead of an impregnable fortress. Her historic position of relative isolation from the European continent is changing to one of increasing involvement in West European affairs. She still possesses significant sea power, but she has lost command of the sea. Furthermore, for three-quarters of a century she has been at a growing disadvantage in competing for the markets of the world. In the postwar period she has increased her exports to a record level, but she has achieved this at the greatest sacrifice and under the most adverse conditions. Her income from investments overseas, one of her main sources of economic strength in the nineteenth century, has seriously declined as a result of the forced liquidation of a substantial part of her foreign holdings. Her basic industries — notably coal, steel, and textiles, which made her "the workshop of the world" — have lost their primacy. Many of the former elements of overseas strength have been seriously weakened, with a consequent deterioration of Britain's total position in world affairs. Even the value of the few vital bases and strategic points still under British control — including Hong Kong and Gibraltar — is far less than formerly.

On January 16, 1968, in a historic statement in the House of Commons, Prime Minister Harold Wilson announced that Britain would reduce her military spending, withdraw her military forces from East of Suez (except for a small garrison in Hong Kong) by the end of 1971, and cease to maintain military bases outside of Europe and the Mediterranean. The implications of this decision for Britain, for the United States, for the non-Communist countries of Asia, and for the world balance of power could not be immediately determined, but they were bound to be very great. In a sense this decision was forced on Britain by her inability to maintain her previous commitments and by the fact, as Prime Minister Wilson said on January 16, that for the past several years "we have been living beyond our means." "But few who listened could honestly believe that what was happening was other than the tide of history. By making the final decision to relinquish her role as world keeper of the peace, Britain was only recognizing the disappearance of empire and the power it once gave this tiny island."[2] "We are recognizing," said the Chancellor of the Exchequer, Roy Jenkins, in a TV address to the British people after Mr. Wilson's announcement in the House of Commons, "that we are no longer a superpower." Obviously Britain has decided to face "the facts of life" and to "search for a post-imperial role in the world."[3] As an American columnist observed, she will continue to "think big," but "in a very small way."[4]

Britain and Postwar Europe

The British Labor Government, which was in power from 1945 to 1951, was severely criticized for its apparent reluctance to cooperate with the nations of Western Europe. The Conservative government, which was in power from 1951 to 1964, while it may have been less doctrinaire and somewhat more sympathetic in its approach to European affairs, cooperated with the nations of Western Europe only to a limited degree and avoided association with all plans for real integration. Nevertheless, in the postwar period Britain has worked with unusual intimacy with European states economically, militarily, and, to a lesser extent, politically. In general, in her recent relations with Western Europe she has been the proponent of functionalism or inter-governmentalism, rather than of federalism. This position explains her wholehearted cooperation in arrangements such as the Brussels Pact and the OECD in contrast to her cautious attitude toward the Council of Europe and her early refusal even to discuss the Schuman Plan.

Western Union. In January, 1948, Foreign Secretary Ernest Bevin delivered his famous "Western Union" speech, which seemed to herald a new British orientation toward Europe. He made the most solemn pledge of cooperation with the countries of Western Europe that any responsible British statesman had ever uttered. But while Brit-

[2] Anthony Lewis, "Abroad, End of Empire," *New York Times,* January 21, 1968.

[3] "New Role in a Post-Imperial World," *New York Times,* December 24, 1967.

[4] Joseph C. Goulden, "Britain 'Thinks Big' in a Very Small Way," *Philadelphia Inquirer,* January 18. 1968.

ain's words were bold, her acts were cast in the old orthodox mold. Western Union, at least in British eyes, took the form of machinery for defense and for the social, economic, and cultural collaboration set up in implementation of the Brussels Treaty. This important agreement, signed on March 17, 1948, by representatives of the United Kingdom, France, Belgium, Luxembourg, and the Netherlands, was essentially a military alliance.

The European Recovery Program. In the evolution and administration of the European Recovery Program (ERP), Britain showed leadership as well as a willing spirit in working with the other European countries which shared the aid. She cooperated fully in the Organization for European Economic Cooperation (OEEC), which was set up in 1948 to implement the Marshall Plan. As the largest trading country in the program and the chief recipient of aid, Britain deserved particular credit for her part in drafting the Intra-European Payments Scheme in 1948, which set up Europe's own "Little Marshall Plan" to promote intra-European trade.

The Schuman Plan. The British reaction to the Schuman Plan for pooling the coal and steel production of France, Germany, and perhaps other countries, proposed by the French foreign minister on May 9, 1950, disclosed the limits of the Labor government's willingness to cooperate in real European integration. In spite of British aloofness, a blueprint for the European Coal and Steel Community was worked out in 1950 and 1951 by representatives of the Benelux countries, France, Italy, and West Germany; and in August, 1952, the Joint High Authority, the central directing agency of the new community, began to function. The British Government immediately appointed a permanent delegation to the new Authority, and since 1952 it has maintained close liaison with the community. On December 21, 1954, it signed an "Agreement of Association between the United Kingdom and the European Coal and Steel Community," which was clearly designed to "help to promote a growing association between the United Kingdom and the Community" without in any way limiting Britain's freedom of action.

The Council of Europe. British representatives participated in the drafting of the Statute for the Council of Europe under the supervision of the Consultative Council of the Brussels Pact and in all the meetings of the various organs of the Council. From the outset they favored a council of governments, with limited power, whereas the French wanted an assembly of prominent persons who could vote as they chose and envisaged the Council as a body which might eventually pave the way for real political union in Western Europe. In general, the British attitude prevailed. British pressure was partially responsible for the defeat, on November 23, 1950, of a proposal before the Consultative Assembly for a federal Europe. As Churchill later said in so many words, Britain had no intention "to be merged in a Federal European system"— "we are *with* them, not *of* them."

EDC and the Paris Agreements. After some preliminary hesitation Britain gave support to the concept of a European Defense Community. In April, 1954, she signed an agreement with the states to be associated in EDC, pledging "all possible support" and "close cooperation." Arrangements were announced for political and military liaison between the United Kingdom and the Defense Community. "Her Majesty's Government," an accompanying British declaration asserted, "have no intention of withdrawing from the Continent of Europe so long as the threat exists to the security of Western Europe and of the European Defense Community." This significant pledge was a strong one, but it was in line with Britain's policy of liaison but not participation.

When the French Assembly killed the EDC Treaty, Britain thereupon took the lead in devising an alternative formula for European security and for dealing with the Franco-German problem. The result was the London-Paris agreements of October, 1954, which substituted for the abortive EDC a looser kind of association which went well beyond the Brussels Treaty but which fell far short of the creation of a common defense force such as was envisioned in the EDC Treaty. On September 29 British Foreign Minister Eden pledged that Britain would continue to maintain forces on the continent of Europe and, except in the event of "an acute overseas emergency," would undertake "not to withdraw these forces against the wishes of the Brussels Treaty powers." Some British and American commentators hailed the pledge as a reversal of historic British policy toward the European continent. This interpretation may well be questioned. Later developments heralded more clearly the emergence of a new pattern of relations between Britain and continental Europe.

Britain, EFTA, and the Common Market. When the six countries of "Little Europe" agreed to form a European Economic Community (the Common Market), in a treaty signed in Rome in March, 1957, effective January 1, 1958, the British position was similar to its approach to the Coal and Steel Community. Unwilling to accept some of the commitments required of members of the Common Market, Britain took a leading role in the formation of an association of the "Outer Seven" — Austria, Denmark, Norway, Portugal, Sweden, Switzerland, and the United Kingdom — which officially came into existence on May 3, 1960. While the members of the European Free Trade Association (EFTA) professed to desire close cooperation between their organization and the Common Market, increasing differences arose in the relations between the two associations. In 1961 a variety of reasons led Britain to change her attitude toward EFTA and the Common Market. Among these factors were the successful operation of the Common Market, the victory of the "confederationists" over the "federalists" within the organization, Britain's serious economic difficulties, a desire to strengthen her economy by tapping the huge market of a European free trade area, and "a profound rethinking in Britain about the nation's place in the world."[5] On August 2, 1961, Prime Minister Macmillan announced in the House of Commons that Britain would seek membership in the European Common Market, and would join if she could get satisfactory concessions, especially concessions to the other members of the Commonwealth, the other members of EFTA, and British farmers. Negotiations between Britain and the Common Market countries were involved and prolonged, but the British decision to seek such association presaged important new directions in British foreign policy. Instead of her long-standing position of isolation or at least standoffishness — a policy sometimes described as that of liaison but not participation — Britain had deliberately decided, in the words of Prime Minister Macmillan, "to play our role to the full and use the influence we have for the free development of the full life of Europe." "Our rightful place," he said, "is in the vanguard of the movement toward the greater unity of the free world. We can lead better from within than from outside."

But Britain was destined not to take her place among the countries of Western Europe. In January, 1963, in a historic press conference, French President de Gaulle announced that France had "vetoed" Britain's

[5] Edwin L. Dole, Jr., "Britain's Bid to the Six," *New York Times,* August 6, 1961, p. E4.

application for entry into the Common Market, on the ground that Britain was not yet ready to be a fully participating member. This action came as a shock to the British and was regarded as a rude rebuff, even by those Englishmen who did not favor the application to EEC. Thereafter Britain reverted to a more cautious European policy — a position which was strengthened when the Labor Party won a narrow majority in the general election of October, 1964, and when it increased its electoral margin in another general election on March 31, 1966. But in 1967, still under a Labor government, Britain applied again for admission to EEC, only to be checkmated again by French resistance.

A further complication was introduced by growing concern over Britain's heavy military commitments, to NATO as well as east of Suez, and by the threats to the NATO alliance posed by General de Gaulle's noncooperative attitude and policies. While France was drastically reducing her commitments to NATO, the British continued to remain steadfast in their support of the alliance.

Britain and the Atlantic Community

The strengthening of ties among the nations of the North Atlantic Community, appearing to escape some of the limitations and embarrassments of Western Union, has appealed strongly to many Englishmen. Professor Robbins, for one, saw great possibilities in this larger association:

> . . . on the basis of the Atlantic Pact, there has been achieved a grouping which, if developed and suitably consolidated, may yet arrest the tide of advancing barbarism. . . . It is a grouping which can be sufficiently strong. . . . It is a grouping within which we ourselves can whole-heartedly cooperate without fear of destroying existing connections. . . . It is a grouping within which it is possible to solve the age-long problem of Germany. . . . It is a grouping, moreover, which corresponds to the main area of our spiritual solidarity. . . . Any attempt at supra-national organization on a lesser basis than this must necessarily be backward-looking.[6]

Perhaps, as Ernest Bevin once said, in British eyes "the Atlantic Community offers a reasonable and workable alternative" to European unity. One wonders whether the idea does not appeal to Britain because it gives her an excuse for her lukewarm support of all movements for real European unity, because the larger community is such a loosely organized one that it does not force Britain into binding commitments, and because it enlists the military power of the United States and Canada and perhaps of Latin America. The North Atlantic Treaty Organization provides the kind of collaboration in which the British believe they can participate without major reservations. It is extensive and calls for a large degree of cooperation without requiring any surrender of sovereignty or any commitments that might be interpreted by the British as conflicting with their existing obligations to the Commonwealth.

Britain's Relations with Other Great Powers

France. Franco-British relations were embittered early in World War II when the French collapse left the British army in the desperate position from which it was rescued only by the miracle of Dunkirk. Later French collaboration with the Nazis created a widespread feeling in Britain that the French had betrayed the cause of freedom. There were additional clashes during the war, and since 1945 there have been others. Many Frenchmen viewed with suspicion the doctrinaire nationalism and dogmatism of the British Labor government. They were apprehensive about British policy in Germany, fearing

[6] Lionel Robbins, "Towards the Atlantic Community," *Lloyds Bank Review*, New Series, No. 17 (July, 1950), pp. 13–14.

that Britain would again fail to appreciate the danger of a revived German state. Britain adopted an "austerity" program, an example which France, for political and perhaps for temperamental reasons, could not emulate. The French, deprived of British markets for wine and other so-called luxury items, charged that Britain was preserving her "austerity" at the expense of other countries; and the British countered with the declaration that France was not deserving of extensive outside aid until she had shown a willingness to try some "austerity" herself and a greater ability to manage her own affairs. British financial policies often affected France adversely. A prime example of this was the devaluation of the British pound in September, 1949, an action which the French resented on the ground that Britain had not given other countries enough time or aid to cushion the shock.

During the war the British had frequent difficulties in working with the proud and aloof General Charles de Gaulle, the leader of the Free French movement, and since *le grand général* has been President of the Fifth French Republic he has insisted on equality of treatment with Britain to a degree sometimes inconsistent with reality.

For some years the most recurrent source of French distrust of Britain was the official British attitude toward the closer integration of Western Europe. To the French the British gave the impression of holding aloof instead of working as partners in an area where cooperation was most vital. Because of this attitude French negotiators often preferred to work out the details of any far-reaching proposals without British participation, and to hope that when the blueprints were ready the British would cooperate. This policy at times paid dividends. Since about 1961, however, a curious partial reversal of roles has taken place. In general France, under De Gaulle, has become less enthusiastic about West European integration and cooperation with other NATO countries, whereas the British, even under Labor governments, have become more concerned with such cooperation. This, among other developments, has imposed new strains on Franco-British relations, but on the whole these relations have survived the retrenchments of the British and the frigidity and aloofness of De Gaulle.

Germany. As one of the four occupying powers in Germany, Britain was compelled to give a great deal of attention to German affairs. On the whole, she cooperated closely with the United States and France in the administration of Western Germany, in the Allied Control Council and the Berlin Kommandatura, in the establishment of an International Authority for the Ruhr, and in the steps leading to the formation of the West German state. With respect to such matters as reparations, punitive measures of control, the level of industry, and German disarmament, she usually took a position less intransigent than that of the French, with their long memories of German aggression, and less indulgent than that of the Americans, who seemed to be more concerned with getting Germany off the backs of the American taxpayers than with the danger of renewed German aggression. Faced with heavy overseas commitments, and with limited manpower and financial resources, the British were reluctant to maintain strong occupation forces in Germany and to bear the costs of occupation. Nevertheless, in general the basic decisions regarding Western Germany were worked out amicably on a three-power basis. Britain cooperated in the steps which made the Federal Republic a sovereign state, and she still maintains troops in Western Germany, in fulfillment of NATO commitments.

The Soviet Union. British policy toward the Soviet Union in the postwar period has been based upon realism, modified somewhat by wishful thinking about the possibilities of Soviet cooperation with the West. Even in responsible circles in Britain the United States was for a time criticized about as much as the Soviet Union, and many Englishmen became apologists for Russia's behavior and policies. As the "honeymoon period" gave way to the cold war, most Englishmen, including the majority of Laborites, took a more realistic and less hopeful view of the character and intentions of the Russian leaders; but the Socialist doctrinairism and anti-American proclivities of the left wing of the Labor Party are still strongly manifest. The Conservative position toward Russia was always more reserved, but Conservatives and Laborites alike are agreed that every effort should be made to cooperate with the Soviet Union and with other Communist regimes. While they seem to have recognized that their destinies are inseparably linked with those of their sister nations of the Western world, the British people still believe that they can exert a salutary modifying influence on the two rival giants of the postwar era. British governments, whether Laborite or Conservative, have continued to promote a fairly extensive trade with Russia and the other countries of the Soviet bloc. Nevertheless, Britain of course remains one of the great bulwarks of the free world.

The United States. Bismarck once said the supreme fact of the nineteenth century was that Britain and the United States spoke the same language. At the Conservative Party Conference in Blackpool, in October, 1954, Churchill said that he had always thought that "the growth of ever-closer ties with the United States . . . is the supreme factor in our future"; and in the following month, speaking at the Lord Mayor's banquet in London, he declared: "The whole foundation of our existence stands on the alliance and friendship, and, if I may say so, an increasing sense of brotherhood, with the United States."

The British are fully aware of the contributions of the United States to Britain's survival before, during, and after World War II. Conversely, fair-minded Americans will never forget the magnificent spirit of the British when they stood alone in 1940 and 1941, their long years of austerity, and their tremendous contributions to the cause of freedom everywhere. The ties of a common heritage and tradition, a common language (or a reasonable facsimile thereof), common foes, and common interests are very strong.[7] Americans as well as Englishmen respond to Wordsworth's vow that

> We must be free or die, who speak the tongue
> That Shakespeare spake . . .

For all "the ties that bind," Britain and the United States have often been poles apart in point of view, however much they have agreed on fundamentals. Criticism of one by the other sometimes approaches the dimensions of a favorite indoor sport; generally speaking, it is without particular malice and is apparently based upon the assumption that one has a special right to criticize his friends. This "antagonism" has, of course, a long historical background; but it has been accentuated by differences and misunderstandings in the postwar period. Among the many recent sources of friction the following may be noted:

(a) The abrupt suspension of Lend-Lease immediately after hostilities ceased in August, 1945, came before Britain could begin her postwar readjustment, and put her in a difficult financial position. This unexpected move aroused a great deal of resentment.

[7] When Churchill stepped down as prime minister in April, 1955, an American radio network honored him in a special program. On this, an American newscaster with several years of service in Britain declared that it was his observation that Englishmen in general regarded Roosevelt as a greater man than Churchill, but that Americans commonly regarded Churchill as the greater.

(b) The suspicion in the United States of Socialist programs in Britain, especially when a Labor government has been in power, is reciprocated by a distrust in England of allegedly conservative or even reactionary tendencies in the United States.

(c) It has been difficult for the British to reconcile themselves to their new and lesser position in world affairs. It is natural that a people who formerly occupied an enviable posion among nations should chafe under the realization that they must reconcile themselves to a very different international role, in a world in which less experienced nations, notably the United States and the Soviet Union, command greater influence and power.

(d) In the past some Americans criticized the British for their apparent reluctance to cooperate in steps toward the real political and economic integration of Western Europe. The British thought, even though they usually kept their sentiments to themselves, that criticism of this sort ill became a nation across the Atlantic whose political and economic policies often hindered effective European cooperation. More recently, Britain has shown more interest in closer association with Western Europe, and the United States has shown a greater awareness of the problems as well as the potentialities of closer European integration.

(e) The two nations have on occasion followed opposing foreign policies, especially vis-à-vis the Communist states. The British have repeatedly expressed alarm about America's Russian policy, especially during the heyday of the cold war. They favor an increase in East-West trade and a more conciliatory policy toward the Soviet Union and Communist China. Some official and much unofficial American thinking seems to be inclined in the same direction, but clearly in these areas, especially in China policy, differences between the United States and Britain persist. Britain announced her willingness to recognize the new regime in China as early as January, 1950, whereas the American Government, strongly influenced by certain segments of American public opinion, has thus far refused to extend recognition to the Chinese Communist Government, or even to support that Government's claims to representation in the United Nations.

(f) Although the United States has frequently been accused by anti-colonialists of supporting the colonial powers or of herself following colonial or neo-colonial policies, the British still criticize American policy as having been essentially unsympathetic to their aims and dilemmas in colonial and former colonial areas.

(g) When Nasser nationalized the Suez Canal Company in July, 1956, Britain and the United States differed strongly on the proper course to follow. The differences led to a major break when the United States publicly disapproved of the intervention of the British and French in Egypt, following Israel's invasion of the Sinai Peninsula. The whole complex of Middle East issues, at a time when British influence in the area is decreasing while that of the United States and the Soviet Union is increasing, places a severe strain on the unity of the Western alliance.

(h) Britain viewed with considerable disfavor and alarm the growing American involvement in Vietnam. Critics of America's Vietnam policies were particularly vocal in unofficial circles. Although the Labor Government of Harold Wilson showed a surprisingly sympathetic understanding of the compulsions of American policy in Vietnam, despite the fire of its own left wing, it insisted that no military solution was possible in Southeast Asia and publicly criticized American escalation of the conflict in Vietnam, particularly the bombing of targets in Hanoi and Haiphong.

(i) The disruptions of World War II have accentuated differences in economic philosophy and in trade and financial policies. Indeed, as a study prepared by the Brookings Institution emphasized, "almost all aspects of Anglo-American economic relations have been characterized by persistent differences of opinions."[8]

Britain and the Middle East

For many decades the Middle East has been an area of special concern to Great Britain. The primary consideration, historically speaking, has been the safeguarding of the route to India and the Far East. This became especially crucial after the completion of the Suez Canal in 1869. It also accounts in large part for the traditional British objective of preventing Russian domination of the Turkish Straits, which would place the Russian bear in the path of the British lion in the eastern Mediterranean. Until World War I Britain sought to preserve the Ottoman Empire as a stabilizing factor in the Middle East. But internal decay and revolt, the alliance with Germany and active participation in the First World War, and the changing world situation proved fatal to the tottering empire of the sultans.

The Arab States and Israel. During World War I, in the McMahon correspondence and other pledges, Britain entered into special relations with the new Arab states, while in the Balfour Declaration she encouraged Zionist aspirations for a Palestine homeland. No amount of finesse could convince Arabs and Jews, long-time enemies, that Britain's commitments to them could be reconciled. Undoubtedly British policy made possible the eventual creation of an independent Jewish state, but in the period immediately preceding Britain had been generally regarded as strongly pro-Arab in sympathies. Toward the end of the Second World War she actively encouraged the formation of the Arab League.[9]

From the early 1880's until 1923 Egypt was virtually a British protectorate. After 1923 the British hold was progressively weakened as a result of both British consent and Egyptian nationalist agitation, and the Anglo-Egyptian Treaty of 1936 officially ended the protectorate. During World War II British forces occupied Egypt against the wish of the Egyptian Government, and much bitterness developed. In the postwar years relations deteriorated still further. The main issues in dispute concerned the treaty rights of Britain with respect to the Suez Canal, the status of the Anglo-Egyptian Sudan, and the settlement of claims arising from the stationing of British troops in Egypt during the war. In February, 1953, Britain and Egypt reached an agreement which provided for the right of the Sudanese to determine their future status — some form of federation with Egypt or complete independence — after a transition period not to exceed three years.[10] Twenty months later, in October, 1954, an agreement provided for the complete evacuation of British forces from the Suez Canal base by June 18, 1956, for the efficient maintenance of the base by Britain and Egypt, and for the right of Britain to return to the base in the event of an armed attack by an outside power on any country that was a party to the Treaty of Joint Defense between the Arab League States or on Turkey.[11]

[8] *Anglo-American Economic Relations,* a Problem Paper prepared by the International Studies Group of the Brookings Institution for a Seminar on Problems of United States Foreign Policy held at the University of Pittsburgh, April 5–10, 1951 (Washington, D.C.: The Brookings Institution, 1951), p. 38.

[9] See Judith Laikin, "British Influence on the Arab League," *Columbia Journal of International Affairs, III* (Spring, 1949), 102–104.

[10] The text of the Sudan agreement is contained in Appendix C of *The Sudan, 1899–1953* (ID 1179), published by the British Information Services.

[11] For the main articles of the Anglo-Egyptian agreement of October 19, 1954, and for an excellent factual summary of the whole course of Anglo-Egyptian relations, see *The Background of Anglo-Egyptian Relations* (ID 735, Revised), published by the British Information Services in November, 1954.

British withdrawal from Egypt has not improved Anglo-Egyptian relations. On the contrary, many policies of the Nasser regime have disturbed the British: leadership of the Arab campaign against Israel, encouragement of anti-British moves in Jordan, acceptance of arms shipments from Communist countries, assistance to the anti-French agitation in North Africa, broadcasts over Radio Cairo attacking Western imperialism and urging the people of Africa to revolt, and the Egyptian nationalization of the Suez Canal. Anglo-Egyptian relations of course became particularly tense when the British and French invaded Egypt in the latter part of 1956, and during the Middle East crisis of mid-1967.

With other Arab states Britain's relations have varied from very close, as in the case of Jordan and Iraq — former British mandates — to relatively distant, as in the case of Saudi Arabia. Relations with both Jordan and Iraq have cooled somewhat in recent years. British pressures upon Jordan to join the Baghdad Pact, along with many other factors, led to anti-British demonstrations in Jordan and to the dismissal, in early March, 1956, of the long-time British leader of the Arab Legion, General John Bagot Glubb — ' Glubb Pasha." Some British officers, however, still serve with the Arab Legion, the British Government is continuing its subsidy to the Legion, and King Hussein's wife is English.

One of the first changes in foreign policy made by Abdul Karim Kassem after he assumed control of Iraq in July, 1958, was to take Iraq out of the Baghdad Pact, with which Britain was associated. When Kassem announced his intention to annex Kuwait after the British relinquished their special ties with that oil-rich sheikhdom in the summer of 1961, British troops were sent to Kuwait to guard against an Iraqi invasion — which, however, did not materialize.

The main source of Arab dissatisfaction with Great Britain, as with the United States, is her support of the Jewish state of Israel. Britain joined with the United States and France in May, 1950, in a pledge of assistance to either Israel or the Arab states in the event of aggression. Nevertheless, when Israel sent troops into the Sinai Peninsula in late October, 1956, Britain and France invaded the Suez Canal area and fought Egyptians, not Israelis. To be sure, the British did bring pressure upon Israel to withdraw Israeli forces from Egyption soil; but this did little to lessen the intense resentment against Britain in the Arab world. Britain, like the United States, has not been able to resolve the dilemmas occasioned by the tragic state of Arab-Israeli relations.

Britain and Cyprus. On her forced withdrawal from the Suez Canal area and the weakening of her position elsewhere in the Middle East, Britain's power in the area centered on the island of Cyprus. In 1955 and 1956 this crown colony became a major problem for the British. In the face of growing agitation and terrorism between the Greek and Turkish communities, the British imposed martial law on the island, while at the same time they promised the Cypriotes eventual freedom to decide their own destiny. In 1960 Cyprus became a republic, with Archbishop Makarios as president. The new nation became a member of the Commonwealth, and Britain retained her military bases on the island. Very shortly, however, independence, and even survival, were threatened by a flare-up of violence between Greek and Turkish Cypriots; Cyprus became a cockpit of civil war and international tension, especially between Turkey and Greece. The British contributed troops and financial support for the UN peacekeeping mission which was sent to the island.

Iran and the Persian Gulf Area. The main considerations of present British policy in the Middle East are those of oil and strategy. Britain is heavily dependent on the oil supplies of Iraq and the Persian Gulf area (Iran, Kuwait, etc.), and the British financial stake in Iranian and Iraqi oil is tremendous. The Anglo-Iranian Oil Company represented the largest single overseas enterprise in which the British Government was directly involved. The crisis over the nationalization of the Iranian oil fields in 1951 was one which called for the greatest tact and diplomacy. Britain's blockade of Iran after the seizure of the Anglo-Iranian's holdings led to the virtual collapse of the oil industry in Iran. Within Iran the political and economic situation deteriorated rapidly. At length, after the unbalanced Mossadegh had been ousted by groups loyal to the Shah, and with the assistance of American mediators, notably Herbert Hoover, Jr., a settlement of the oil dispute was reached in August, 1954.[12]

The closing of the rift between Britain and Iran, following closely upon Britain's agreement with Egypt on the Suez Canal base, vastly improved the atmosphere in the Middle East. In November, 1955, Britain joined Turkey, Iraq, Iran, and Pakistan in signing the Baghdad Pact, and she has continued her association with Turkey, Iran, and Pakistan in this pact, now known as the Central Treaty Organization. Britain is still vitally concerned with the preservation of her interests in the Middle East, but her prestige and power in that area have sharply declined, especially since her withdrawal from Aden and adjacent territories in late 1967 and her decision of January, 1968, to withdraw her military forces from the Persian Gulf area, as well as from the Far East, by the end of 1971.

Britain, the Commonwealth, and the Dependencies

Sir Winston Churchill once stated in a classic phrase that he had not become His Majesty's First Minister in order to preside over the liquidation of the British Empire; and he often criticized Mr. Attlee and the Labor government for their alleged willingness to hasten the loosening of imperial and Commonwealth bonds. The "liquidation" of empire has been a phenomenon of the postwar years. Most of the former British colonies are now independent states, and most are members of the Commonwealth.[13] In 1948 Burma formally "opted out" of the Commonwealth, as did the Sudan in 1956, former British Somaliland in 1960, the Southern Cameroons in 1961, and the Maldive Islands in 1965. Ireland left the Commonwealth in 1949, and the Republic of South Africa in 1961.

In 1947, with British aid, a compromise solution was reached whereby India was divided into the Union of India and Pakistan, both of which became Dominions in the Commonwealth. In February, 1948, Ceylon also was given Dominion status. In the spring of 1949 the prime ministers of the Commonwealth countries agreed on a formula under which India could become a republic and still remain in the Commonwealth. This formula was later applied to many other new members of the expanding Commonwealth, whose focus, geographically and demographically, was increasingly shifting from Britain and the older members to the newer members in Asia and Africa.

As of mid-1968 the members of the Commonwealth were: Australia, Barbados, Botswana, Canada, Ceylon, Cyprus, Gambia,

[12] The texts of the statements issued in Teheran and in London on August 5, 1954, are given in the *New York Times,* August 6, 1954.

[13] "The word 'Commonwealth' has been used in British official documents to refer to the dependent overseas territories as well as to the independent nations. The word 'Empire' is avoided by nearly everyone save Conservatives; the official phrase is 'Dependent Overseas Territories.' Even the word 'Dominion' is now sparingly employed, perhaps because it still carries a slight connotation of dependent status. Finally, even the designation 'British' in connection with the Commonwealth is now officially avoided." *Major Problems of United States Foreign Policy, 1950–1951* (Washington, D.C.: The Brookings Institution, 1950), pp. 202n.–203n.

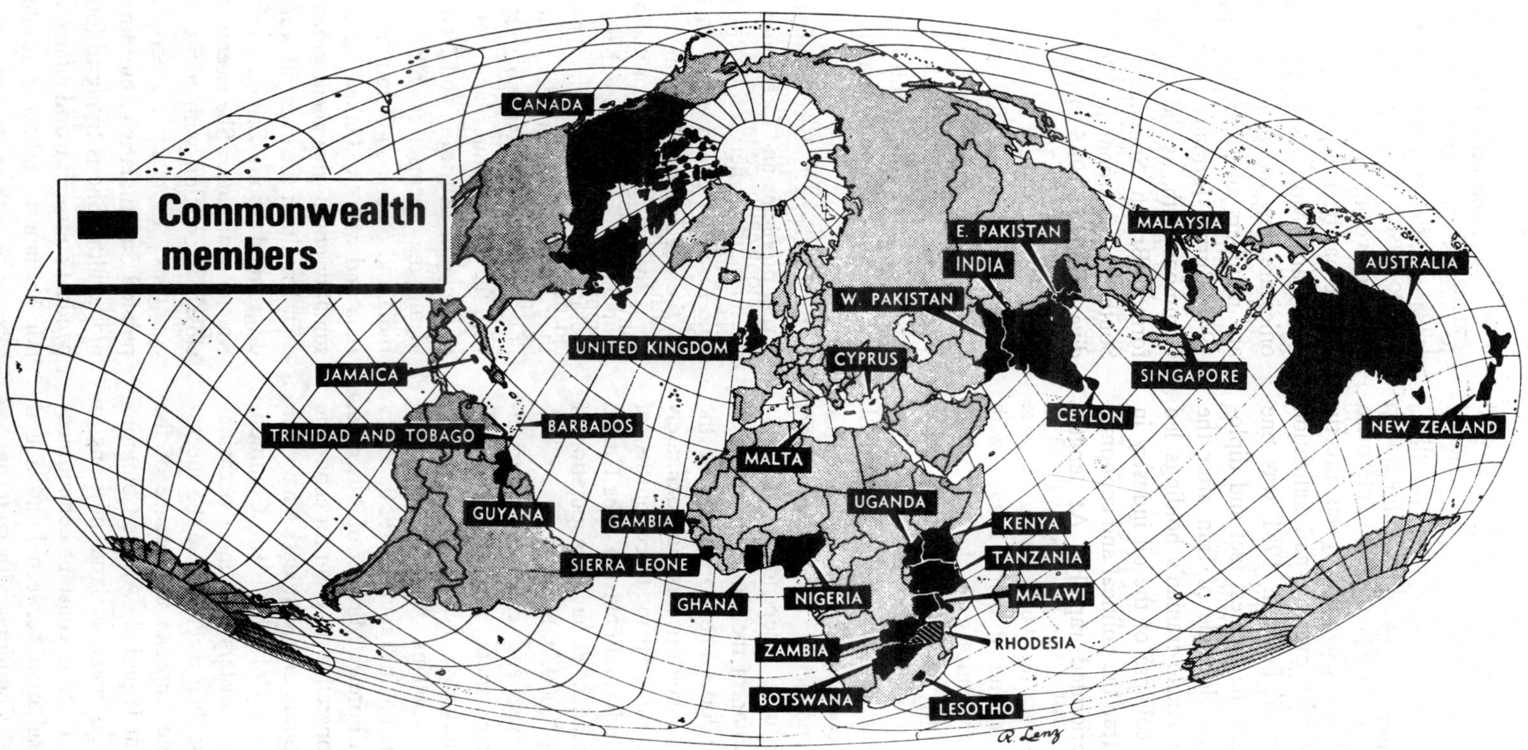

Russell H. Lenz. Reprinted by permission from The Christian Science Monitor

Ghana, Guyana, India, Jamaica, Kenya, Lesotho, Malawi, Malaysia, Malta, Mauritius, New Zealand, Nigeria, Pakistan, Sierra Leone, Singapore, Tanzania, Trinidad and Tobago, Uganda, the United Kingdom, and Zambia. More than half of the member states had achieved their independence in the previous five years. In population the member states ranged from Barbados with 245,000 people to India with more than two thousand times that number, and in area from Barbados with 166 square miles to Canada with over 3,850,000.

The United Kingdom still has dependencies scattered over the world, ranging in size from Gibraltar and Pitcairn Island, with hardly 2 square miles each, to the British Solomon Islands, with 11,500 square miles, in population from Pacific islands with no permanent inhabitants to Hong Kong with 3,800,000 people, and in degree of control from areas completely administered from London to virtually independent states.

The population of the United Kingdom is about 55,000,000. The population of the Commonwealth countries is approximately 760,000,000, more than three-fourths of whom live in India and Pakistan. The United Kingdom dependencies have a population of approximately 7,000,000.

Since the new and enlarged Commonwealth has taken shape, the Commonwealth foreign ministers have met frequently to discuss common problems. At the first meeting, held in Colombo in January, 1950, Percy Spender, then Foreign Minister of Australia, outlined a cooperative program for economic assistance to South and Southeast Asia which later became the Colombo Plan. Commonwealth prime ministers also meet occasionally; in a sense their meetings are the successors to the old Imperial Conference of the pre-World War II period. All the Commonwealth members maintain large missions in London, and there is constant communication and consultation between London and the capitals of Commonwealth countries.

Of the concentric circles linking Britain to various other states, that embracing the members of the Commonwealth is of first importance. On this point both major parties and most of the British people are agreed.

In spite of continued collaboration, however, all is not well within the Commonwealth. Its bonds have definitely weakened, and its future is uncertain. Its focus — at least demographically — has shifted to Asia. The vast majority of the people of Commonwealth countries now live in newly independent lands where the memories of British imperial rule are fresh and where suspicion of Western imperialism in any and every form is still pronounced. Relations between certain members of the association, notably between India and Pakistan, are gravely strained, and the centrifugal tendencies within the Commonwealth have grown stronger.

Britain herself, beset with mounting internal problems and faced with the necessity of husbanding her resources, is no longer able to act as effectively as in former years as the regulator of Commonwealth affairs, or as the guardian and protector of the Dominions. More and more these countries are looking outside the Commonwealth, or to their own resources, rather than toward London. Canada has many interests in common with the United States, and these are growing in strength. Australia and New Zealand are identifying themselves more closely with India and other non-Communist countries of Asia and with the United States, which presumably could give them greater protection than Britain in the event of war. Pakistan is disgruntled about Britain's position in the Kashmir dispute. She seems to aspire to closer association with non-Commonwealth countries. In many respects, as has been pointed out, India is *in* but not *of* the Commonwealth. She is trying to follow an independent course in world affairs, and she does not hesitate to follow a similar course in Commonwealth matters as well.

The Commonwealth has become an increasingly heterogeneous association, whose members have many differing and often conflicting policies and interests. The withdrawal of South Africa posed new problems for Britain, but in the long run it may prove to have strengthened rather than weakened the Commonwealth itself. Although vast changes are occurring within it and its future is uncertain, the Commonwealth has been probably the most successful of all international groupings. It will undoubtedly continue to exert a major influence in world affairs.

Britain Today and Tomorrow

Whatever may be the opinion of others, the British are by no means convinced that their future is behind them, that henceforth they must reconcile themselves to the status of a third-rate insular power and to the loss of their exalted position. Britain must continue to think in world terms, even though she is no longer, in a real sense, a world power. She cannot exist without allies, without markets abroad, without substantial imports of foodstuffs and raw materials. Her position, if not her survival, is likewise dependent on her relations with the Commonwealth, the sterling area, the Arab world, the North Atlantic Community, especially the United States, Western Europe, and, in a very special and vital sense, the Soviet Union and the Communist world. Her general objective is to retain as much of her former prestige and power as possible, to husband her limited resources and apply them where they will carry the greatest weight. Her worldwide interests are sometimes conflicting and contradictory, but they inevitably bend her efforts in the direction of international collaboration. British capacity to appraise the realities of international politics and to distinguish permanent bases of policy was reflected in an observation made by Harold Macmillan on June 15, 1955, in his first address in the House of Commons after his appointment as foreign minister: "After a long Russian winter of ice and snow the sun is beginning to come out, but I say that it is a good rule in setting out upon an expedition, if I may change the metaphor, to keep one's base secure. We have a sound base, and it is based upon a triple partnership of the British Commonwealth and Empire, the United States, and the peoples of Free Europe."

The Foreign Policy of France

Geographically, culturally, and politically France has occupied a central position throughout the history of Western civilization. For some decades before World War II, however, the French position was being steadily weakened, although this fact was often obscured by astute diplomacy and by the prestige of former greatness. Perhaps not until the collapse of 1940 were the flaws in French politics and society, and the basic weakness in France's power position, exposed mercilessly for all the world to see. Since the war, with major outside assistance, especially through the Marshall Plan, the French have made a rather impressive economic recovery and have repaired many of the visible wounds of war. Under General Charles de Gaulle, who has presided over the destinies of the Fifth French Republic, they have also made a remarkable political and psychological recovery. General de Gaulle aspires to restore France to a leading position among the nations and, in spite of France's relatively weak position in comparison with some more powerful states, he has made notable progress toward his ambitious goal.

Quite understandably, it is difficult for Frenchmen, realists though they are, to face present realities and to reconcile themselves to their changed position in the world. Even within the older European political system France was being outstripped in industrial and military power, as well as in population, by a unified and militaristic Germany, with Britain and Russia often exercising a decisive influence on European affairs. Now the very system of which France was a part has collapsed, perhaps forever, and to an unprecedented degree the destinies of France rest in the hands of other powers, which are either non-European, like the United States, or European in only a peripheral sense, like Britain and the Soviet Union. But De Gaulle is determined that for all her weakness the destinies of France shall be directed by Frenchmen, and that present "subordination" shall be ended.

Foreign and native historians have often called attention to the existence of at least two Frances: (1) authoritarian France, the France of the *ancien régime,* the France which looks to the "man on horseback," the France of the church, the army, and big business; and (2) republican France, the France of the Revolution, a liberal, democratic France, strongly entrenched in the middle class and the "common people." Perhaps one should add a third France, namely Socialist France; but Left-Center parties have lost heavily to the Communists. Added to France's divided tradition has been her demographic decline: second among European states in population in 1850, she was fourth in 1900 and she is fifth today. Moreover, she has failed to keep pace industrially and to achieve a sound political or social structure. In consequence, her foreign policy has at crucial times been cautious and vacillating or bold in statement but ineffective in action. Her situation has improved remarkably during the De Gaulle era, but many of the policies of *le grand Charles* have aroused strong opposition at home and abroad, and the future of France after the great leader has gone remains quite uncertain.

In restrospect it is clear that France never fully recovered from the "victory" of World War I. This struggle sapped her resources and destroyed many of her finest sons, whose leadership and services have been sadly missed. In the interwar period she realized quite clearly that she would be unable to find security by herself; therefore she sought it in alliances and collective security. But she failed to revive the prewar alliances with Britain and Russia, and when the aggressors began to march she sacrificed security to "peace." Her failure to act when German troops moved into the Rhineland in 1936 may be regarded as a turning point, and the capitulation at Munich two years later exposed her physical and psychological weakness and unpreparedness. A weak and distracted France entered the Second World War, and the mood of appeasement created the atmosphere for the collaborationism of the Vichy regime. For five bitter years, while the fate of the free world hung in the balance, France in effect was blotted out as an independent state. But the voice of France was not wholly stilled. The French of the Resistance and the Free French showed that the spirit of France had not been entirely crushed or corrupted; they established the basis for France's attempts to recover from the crushing blow to her pride and to her position in world affairs. But the wartime experience was a shattering one, psychologically as well as materially, and it still haunts the French as a nightmare that cannot be forgotten.

Conditioning Factors of Postwar Policy

It was not easy for the French to recover from the effects of the Vichy experience and to readjust themselves to a new and difficult world. Four new factors, in particular, as Saul K. and Irina Padover pointed out, had to be taken into account: "The primary factor was France's own reduced importance. The second was the decline of Europe in general and of Germany in particular. The third was the emergence of the Soviet colossus as the foremost continental power. The fourth was the appearance of the United States as the prime force in Western Europe."[14] These four factors condemned

[14] Saul K. Padover and Irina Padover, "France: Setting or Rising Star?" *Headline Series,* No. 81 (May–June, 1950), p. 55.

France to play a lesser role in Europe, at a time when other countries in other parts of the world were emerging to dominate the international stage; and in an age of declining colonialism the French gradually lost, none too gracefully, most of their overseas possessions and became involved in a bloody, costly, soul-rending, and futile struggle in Algeria.

"The period of French history between 1945 and 1958," observed Raymond Aron, "had three particular features: first, the material, demographic, and economic recovery of the nation; second, the colonial wars from Vietnam to Algeria, leading to what is called either the loss of the empire or the emancipation of the Asian and African peoples; third, the permanent political crisis of the Republic, symbolized in the eyes of foreign observers by the instability of its successive governments."[15]

For a few months after the end of World War II France, striving to recover from the physical and moral devastation of the wartime years, was under the firm control of the wartime leader of the French government-in-exile, General de Gaulle, who called for a policy of "grandeur" even in the face of French demoralization and weakness, at home and abroad. In January, 1946, De Gaulle resigned rather than make any basic compromises in his lofty policies. The governments which followed, with some fifteen different premiers in the next eight and a half years, attempted to compensate for the reverses in Indochina and elsewhere in the French Empire and for internal instability and weakness by assuming the leadership in movements toward West European cooperation, a policy which among other objectives was designed to further economic recovery and to keep a reviving West Germany from following an independent course that might threaten French interests and influence even more than association with an ancient enemy. In those years France participated in the Marshall Plan and joined both the Brussels Pact and the North Atlantic Treaty Organization. Her leaders sponsored the most imaginative proposals for the integration of Western Europe, notably Bidault's proposal in April, 1948, for the creation of an elected European Assembly, Schuman's bold proposal of May, 1950, for the pooling of Europe's resources of coal and steel, and Pleven's proposal in October, 1950, for a European Defense Community. Bidault's ideas led to the Council of Europe, a far weaker body than the European Political Community which the champions of European unification favored. The Schuman Plan resulted in the organization of the European Coal and Steel Community, and eventually to the creation of two other outstanding communities, the Common Market and the European Atomic Energy Community. The Pleven Plan was rejected by the French Assembly in 1954. It was perhaps symbolic of French divisions and weakness of leadership that the proposed EDC was killed through the actions of the representatives of the very country that had first officially advanced it.

In June, 1954, "seven years of centre government and ten years of M.R.P. [*Mouvement Républicaine Populaire*] control of foreign and imperial affairs" came to an end. "The 'continuity of French policy' had tied itself into a Gordian knot which it had become necessary to cut."[16] The man who assumed control at this critical juncture was Pierre Mendès-France, who apparently believed that he had a mission to reduce France's commitments overseas, to rescue the country from the dilemmas centering on the EDC Treaty, and to try to do something about the serious economic and political impasse at home. Dynamism succeeded "im-

[15] Raymond Aron, "France Has a Glorious Future, If —," *New York Times Magazine,* October 9, 1960, p. 27.

[16] Herbert Luethy, *France Against Herself* (New York: Frederick A. Praeger, 1955), p. 460.

mobilism," and after many months of indecision France had a government which seemed to be able and willing to act. Mendès-France fulfilled his pledge of a truce in Indo-China within a month; he extended a pledge of "internal sovereignty" to Tunisia; he acted as gravedigger for EDC; he won French approval of the London and Paris agreements of October, 1954, including the Saar compromise; he steered a constitutional reform through the Assembly; and he tackled a host of internal problems. In foreign affairs, at least, it may be that his acts raised France's prestige at the price of a weakening of her position within the French Union and in Europe. Mendès-France appealed to the people as no other premier in the postwar period, but he could not long carry the Assembly with him. In February, 1955, he gave way to a middle-of-the-road government headed by Edgar Faure. Dynamism, at least temporarily, came to an end.

De Gaulle and the Fifth French Republic. Three years later, after continued internal and external troubles, France turned again to General de Gaulle, who became premier with virtually unlimited powers in May, 1958, after an uprising in Algeria had threatened the foundations of the Fourth Republic. A few months later a constitutional referendum in France and her colonies led to the establishment of the Fifth French Republic, of which De Gaulle was elected president, and to virtual autonomy for French-speaking areas of French West and Equatorial Africa, all of which, with the notable exception of Guinea, voted to continue their close ties with France. De Gaulle's policies of "grandeur" and "glory" at least temporarily restored order and confidence in the divided country, and prepared the way for drastic changes in internal and external policies. "France is not really herself," he wrote in his memoirs, prepared during his long years of retirement, "unless in the front rank. Only vast enterprises are capable of counterbalancing the ferments of dispersal which are inherent in her people. . . . In short, to my mind, France cannot be France without greatness."[17]

Many of De Gaulle's acts and policies were in keeping with his reputation as a haughty and difficult person to deal with, and as a man who had exaggerated ideas about France's real power and world position. He imposed drastic fiscal and economic reforms which would have brought down any weaker government, and he shouldered the enormous problem of ending the war in Algeria and working out a formula that would satisfy the majority of the Algerian people and protect French interests as well.

Rejecting the supranational approach so ardently championed by such prominent Frenchmen as Robert Schuman, Georges Bidault, Jean Monnet, and Maurice Schuman, De Gaulle advanced a plan for a European confederation, composed initially of the six countries of "Little Europe" already associated in three existing communities. Instead of the concept of European federation, which he branded as "unrealistic," he offered "the alternative of organized cooperation between states, which would probably grow toward a confederation."[18] In January, 1963, he vetoed Britain's application for membership in the European Economic Community (the Common Market), and later he adopted a policy of noncooperation, amounting virtually to a boycott, toward the EEC. Apparently he envisaged a looser association than NATO, and a European grouping in which France would play a leading role. To achieve these goals, he advocated an independent policy for the states of Western Europe — meaning a policy of independence from the United States; he inaugurated a new era in Franco-German cooperation and rapproche-

[17] Charles de Gaulle, *War Memoirs.* Vol. I, *The Call to Honour, 1940–1942* (New York: The Viking Press, 1955), p. 3.

[18] News conference, September 9, 1965.

Peb in The Philadelphia Inquirer, June 26, 1966

Le Grand Design

ment, which was particularly marked during the last years of the Adenauer era in West Germany; and he took various steps to improve relations with the Soviet Union. All this, and much more, were parts of his "grand design" to restore French prestige, to give France a position of greater equality with Britain and the United States within the Western alliance and of leadership in Western Europe, and to lay the foundations "of a European entente between the Atlantic and the Urals."[19]

[19] See Edgar S. Furniss, Jr., "The Grand Design of Charles de Gaulle," *Proceedings of the Institute of World Affairs,* Fourteenth Session (Los Angeles: University of Southern California, 1963), pp. 98–111.

Toward NATO and his NATO allies De Gaulle followed a policy of increasing unilateralism and noncooperation, which caused extreme irritation and endless friction within NATO and which eventually threatened the very existence of the alliance itself. Shortly after he assumed power in 1958, in a secret note to President Eisenhower (with a copy to British Prime Minister Harold Macmillan), he proposed that the United States, Britain, and France should "create a tripartite organization to take joint decisions on global problems."[20] When this proposal was

[20] This note has not been made public, but a fairly detailed summary and comment was published in David Schoenbrun, *The Three Lives of Charles de Gaulle* (New York: Atheneum Pub-

not accepted, he began a deliberate policy of independence and of disinvolvement from NATO ties and obligations. In 1959 he withdrew French naval forces in the Mediterranean from NATO's command; and in 1964 he took the same action with regard to French naval forces in the Atlantic. By 1965 he was demanding the reorganization of the NATO alliance and the virtual dissolution of the whole NATO command structure. An immediate consequence was the forced removal from French soil of the headquarters of two major integrated commands — the Supreme Headquarters, Allied Powers in Europe (SHAPE) and the Central European Command — together with all American and other foreign military bases in France. The French Government based these sweeping demands on a desire "to reclaim the complete exercise of its sovereignty on French territory," and a conviction that NATO "does not fulfill, as far as it is concerned, the conditions prevailing in the world at present, which are fundamentally different from those of 1949 and of the following years."[21] In these and other respects De Gaulle's main motivation, as Dirk Stikker, former Secretary-General of NATO once declared, was "French nationalism, pure and simple."[22] "For us," stated De Gaulle in a news conference on September 9, 1965, "it is a matter of keeping ourselves free of all subservience. Thus, so long as we consider the solidarity of the Western peoples necessary for the possible defense of Europe, we will remain the allies of our allies. But at the expiration of our present commitments — that is, at the latest in 1969 — we shall end the subordination which is described as integration, which is provided for by NATO and which puts our destiny in the hands of foreigners."

In other respects, too, De Gaulle has followed independent policies, regardless of the disapproval of France's friends and allies. He went ahead with unilateral development of atomic bombs. In spite of strong pressures and protests he authorized atomic tests in the French Sahara, and later in the Pacific, and he has made France an atomic power, although of lesser status than the atomic giants, the United States and the Soviet Union. He adopted an attitude of "the greatest reserve" toward what he scornfully called "the United, or Disunited, Nations." He extended recognition to Communist China, and he was outspoken in his criticism of American policy and actions in Vietnam.

De Gaulle's policies have had the effect of increasing French influence and prestige, of ending the colonial era of modern French history, of giving a greater degree of political stability and strength to a divided country, of improving relations with West Germany and the Soviet Union, of creating stresses and strains in relations with the United States and the United Kingdom, of jeopardizing the future of the European Economic Community and of the other West European communities, and of virtually disrupting the NATO alliance and of placing its future in jeopardy after 1969. De Gaulle has managed to retain his personal prestige even while imposing greater austerities on the French people and carrying out many unpopular domestic and foreign policies; but the narrow margin of his victory in the French presidential elections of December, 1965, indicated that his popular support was not so

---

lishers, 1966), pp. 295–300. On August 13, 1966, the text of President Eisenhower's reply to De Gaulle's letter was made public for the first time by Senator Henry M. Jackson, chairman of the Senate Subcommittee on National Security and International Operations. An accompanying State Department memorandum contained quotations from De Gaulle's letter, and summaries of correspondence between the two leaders. See Drew Middleton, "Key De Gaulle Letter Made Public in U.S.," *New York Times*, August 15, 1966.

[21] From a note sent by the French Government to the governments of the United States and other NATO countries, March, 1966; text in the *New York Times*, March 13, 1966.

[22] Dirk Stikker, *Men of Responsibility; a Memoir* (New York: Harper & Row, 1966), p. 368.

great as it had seemed to be and that any major reverses or new threats to the delicate political equilibrium which he was able to maintain could bring the De Gaulle era to an end. In any event, even De Gaulle cannot go on forever — he was 78 years of age on November 22, 1968 — and it is hard to picture what France will be like when his towering personality has been removed from the scene.

For all his efforts to "save France," De Gaulle was still faced with some problems which even he seemed unable to resolve, and he staked his reputation on his ability to succeed where so many others had failed. When he took charge of the destinies of France in 1958, Guy Mollet, a leading Socialist and former premier, remarked: "Frenchmen expect miracles of De Gaulle. But can he work miracles?" The answer seems to be that he has already worked many lesser miracles, and that if he cannot work the greater ones that must be performed if France is to emerge with a hopeful future from her present years of travail, in all probability no other Frenchman can.

The Foreign Policy of Communist China

Like Sun Yat-sen and Chiang Kai-shek, the leaders of Communist China play upon the ancient themes and national aspirations and anti-foreign feelings of the Chinese people; but their basic policies, particularly in foreign affairs, are also conditioned by "the immutable premises and assumptions of Marxism-Leninism." The characteristically Chinese egocentric view of the world and of the superiority of the Chinese to all other peoples, has given even Marxism-Leninism a typically Chinese cast. Mao Tse-tung is regarded as the greatest living exponent of true communism, and "the thought of Mao Tse-tung" is the prevailing philosophy of the New China. Not surprisingly, therefore, the foreign policy of Communist China is a mixture, in uncertain proportions, of Han imperialism, Chinese nationalism, and "the revolutionary strategy" of Mao Tse-tung. The major aspects were summarized in 1950 by Henry R. Liberman, able Far Eastern correspondent of the *New York Times,* in a single sentence: "The Chinese Communists appear on the whole to be guided by their basic alliance with the Soviet Union, a deep suspicion of the West, a special sensitivity about 'imperialist encroachment' on their borders, and a desire to extend the Communist revolution whenever and wherever they can."[23] This summary is still valid, with the one significant exception that the "basic alliance with the Soviet Union" has given way, at least on the surface, to a growing split between the two Communist giants — a split which broke out into the open in the late 1950's and early 1960's, and which has become one of the major factors in contemporary international relations.

Major Aspects of Foreign Policy

Through a variety of techniques and approaches the rulers of Communist China are trying to consolidate their internal position and to gain a more favorable position abroad. Most of all they are concerned with assuming a leading role in Asian affairs. They appeal to their fellow-Asians as leaders of the "anti-imperialist bloc" and of "liberation" movements, as models for dealing with the serious political, economic, and social problems of Asia, as champions of Asia's new role in the world, and as leaders of the "peace movement." They have won the allegiance or at least substantial support of Communist parties in most of the countries of non-Communist Asia, and they have penetrated areas as distant as Africa and Latin America; but in these areas they have had to compete with the Soviet Union, the Western countries, and indigenous non-Communist leaders and regimes, and they have suffered a series of reverses in distant lands and even

[23] Dispatch from Hong Kong, in the *New York Times,* November 5, 1950.

in neighboring Asian countries. The strong reaction against the Communists in Indonesia, following the political changes of late 1965, was widely interpreted as a blow to Chinese hopes and plans. In Vietnam, however, the continued civil war in the south, the growing involvement of North Vietnam, and the heavy commitments of the United States without much hope of a speedy achievement of announced goals, may be regarded as a boon to the Chinese Communists. "War by proxy" is a favorite game for Communists, and the benefits to the Chinese Communists of "fighting to the last Vietnamese" and of keeping the United States bogged down in the Vietnamese morass are tempered only by the threat of a major American military presence so close to their own borders.

Upon the proclamation of the Central People's Government of the People's Republic of China, on October 1, 1949, the new regime invited recognition by other governments. By early 1960 it had established diplomatic relations with 33 countries, including 19 non-Communist states. The United States steadfastly refused to recognize the regime. Not until 1954 did Communist China begin to play a role in world diplomacy, although her spokesman appeared before the Security Council in November, 1950, and her representatives negotiated from 1951 to 1953 on a truce in Korea. She achieved a new status, however, with representation at the Geneva Conference in early 1954 and full participation in the Asian-African Conference at Bandung in April, 1955. In both meetings, and particularly at Bandung, Chou En-lai, the Foreign Minister of Communist China, took a leading part. In June, 1954, Chou joined with Prime Minister Nehru of India in a joint declaration of the "five principles" of peace.

To gain support abroad, as at home, the Chinese Communists have resorted to the "carrot and stick" technique. They have used strong-arm methods and vituperation along with conciliatory gestures and honeyed words. Prominent among their devices have been international conferences, cultural delagations and guided tours, mass movements and drives, peace appeals and campaigns, threats and blackmail, campaigns to coerce the Chinese people and to stir up hatred for America, friendship associations, mass liquidations and purges, and an unending barrage of propaganda on many fronts. They sent troops into Korea and Tibet in 1950, and into India in 1962. In the spring of 1959 they ruthlessly suppressed an uprising in Tibet. They have stationed large numbers of troops along India's Himalayan frontier and along the border of North Vietnam, as well as in Fukien province opposite Taiwan, and at several points along the borders with the Soviet Union. They insist that they will never rest until Taiwan, the refuge of "the Chiang Kai-shek bandit gang," is under their control. They have made special efforts to develop close contacts with overseas Chinese and with other Asian countries; but, as Robert Scalapino has observed, "more direct confrontations of Chinese and foreign authority are developing, raising new problems and apprehensions. The Sino-Indian border problem is an especially significant example."[24]

Relations with Soviet Russia

Perhaps the chief basis of collaboration between the Chinese and Russian Communists has been the fact that they are bound together by a common body of doctrines and beliefs, stemming from the same sources and directed toward the same general ends. During two periods in the past thirty years the Soviet Union appeared to be making a major effort to give firsthand direction to the Chinese revolution. The first period was from 1923 to 1927, when Russian advisers went

[24] "United States Foreign Policy: Asia," prepared for Committee on Foreign Relations, U.S. Senate, by Conlon Associates (Washington, D.C., November 1, 1959), p. 136.

to China at the invitation of Dr. Sun Yat-sen. One of these, Michael Borodin, was probably the most influential man in China during these years, with the exception of Dr. Sun himself. The second period is, of course, the first decade of the postwar era, when the leaders of Communist China proclaimed their devotion to the Soviet Union, and all the organs of propaganda praised Russia.

Mao Tse-tung went to Moscow in December, 1949, probably for the first time, for the alleged purpose of participating in the celebration of Joseph Stalin's seventy-first birthday. He remained about two months. One major result of his visit was the signing, on February 14, 1950, of a "Treaty Regarding Friendship, Alliance and Mutual Aid Between the Soviet Socialist Republics and the Chinese People's Republic." The two countries pledged to "undertake jointly all necessary measures at their disposal to prevent any repetition of aggression and violation of peace on the part of Japan *or any other state which directly or indirectly could unite with Japan in acts of aggression.*" The powerful Communist states agreed to "cooperate with each other in all important international questions" and "to develop and strengthen economic and cultural ties between the Soviet Union and China." In other agreements Russia made a number of concession to China in the Far East and promised a loan over a five-year period "to the amount of 300 million American dollars."[25] There has been much speculation about the possibility of secret agreements between the two countries, or secret codicils to the treaty of February 14. In all probability the costly gamble in Korea increased Communist China's dependence on the Soviet Union. It was significant that the willingness of the Chinese Communists, as well as the North Koreans, to discuss a cease-fire in Korea was first suggested not by a Chinese spokesman but by Mr. Malik, in a broadcast sponsored by the United Nations.

In the fall of 1954 a delegation of Soviet leaders, headed by Bulganin and Khrushchev, visited China. On October 11 a joint communiqué announced that "seven accords" had been reached.[26] In these the two governments proclaimed a "complete unity of views both in the sphere of the growing multilateral cooperation between the two states and in questions relating to the international situation." They seemed to embody real Soviet concessions to China, and they undoubtedly helped to raise the prestige of "New China" in Asia.

Beginning in the late 1950's, evidences of strains in the Sino-Soviet alliance became apparent. It was well known that Stalin had a rather low opinion of the strength of China and of the quality of Chinese Communist leadership, and that the Chinese people disliked and distrusted Russians — including Russian Communists. After Stalin's death the Chinese Communist leaders seemed to have doubts about his successors, and, in any event, they regarded Mao Tse-tung as the elder statesman of the entire Communist world. They disapproved of the de-Stalinization program and of the emphasis on "peaceful co-existence" and the denial of the inevitability of conflict which characterized the Khrushchev era. After thousands of Russian technicians in China were withdrawn in 1960 and most Soviet aid to China ceased, the Chinese Communist leaders expressed more openly their disapproval of Russian leadership and policies. They accused the Soviet Union of departing from the correct principles of Marxism-Leninism and of following "revisionist" policies. The Soviet leaders, in turn, accused the Chinese of "adventurism" abroad, and they criticized such important Chinese internal poli-

[25] For the text of the Sino-Russian Treaty and the two supplementary agreements, see the *New York Times,* February 15, 1950. The italics above have been added.

[26] The text of the communiqué announcing the "seven accords" is given in the *New York Times,* October 12, 1954.

cies as "the great leap forward" and the establishment of the communes. Apparently the struggle was more over tactics than over basic strategy or ultimate goals. It was less of an ideological contest than a struggle for leadership in the Communist world and for support among Communist parties and non-Communist leaders and groups in the Third World of underdeveloped nations.

The nature and significance of the Sino-Soviet split cannot be assessed with any degree of confidence or accuracy. It may indeed not prove to be as serious or as enduring as it now appears. But, together with the developments in Eastern Europe and elsewhere, it has destroyed the myth of a monolithic Communist world, and it has produced the still almost incredible phenomenon of polycentrism in the international Communist movement. It is a phenomenon to be watched carefully, in its various manifestations and convulsions.

The Revolutionary Strategy of Mao Tse-tung

The Chinese Communists seem to believe that the revolutionary strategy of Mao Tse-tung has worked admirably at home and provides the proper base for achieving their goals abroad.[27] This strategy is obviously a militant one, although it may be pursued by moderate as well as aggressive tactics, in accordance with the Chinese assessment of the realities of given situations. Temporary setbacks will in no way change the long-range strategy; this will come only as a result of successful constraint of Chinese probes and "adventurist" actions beyond the territorial confines of China and of significant changes in the leadership and conditions within China herself.

In September, 1965, a memorandum prepared by Marshal Lin Piao, Chinese Minister of Defense and one of the most influential spokesmen of Communist China, was made public[28] and immediately attracted worldwide attention. In this memorandum Lin Piao, with obvious reference to the successful tactics of enveloping the cities of China from the countryside, described the Western world as the cities and the non-Western world of underdeveloped nations as the countryside, and predicted that, as in China, the countryside would eventually engulf the cities. This was simply a restatement of militant Chinese doctrine, but it attracted special attention because of the conciseness of its formulation, its authorship, and the continuing uncertainty regarding the real nature of Chinese intentions and of the leadership struggle obviously going on inside China in the waning years of the Mao Tse-tung era.

There can be little doubt that Communist China will be an increasingly important and increasingly disturbing factor in international relations in the coming years. She looms as a major threat to world peace, not only because of her militant and revolutionary doctrine but also because of her growing military and economic power. In October, 1964, she exploded her first nuclear device. Since then she has been developing a nuclear and weapons-carrying capability. A militant China, with an arsenal of atomic and hydrogen bombs, will be a formidable force to reckon with in future years.

It seems quite certain that the Chinese Communists believe the gospel they preach, that they are convinced they are riding "the wave of the future," and that they will resort to any techniques to further their aims. By open propaganda, by direct military action, by clandestine infiltration, by open and disguised support of Communist parties and rebellious groups in other Asian countries,

[27] Tang Tsou and Morton H. Halperin, "Mao Tse-tung's Revolutionary Strategy and Peking's International Behavior," *American Political Science Review*, LIX (March, 1965), 80–99; and "Maoism at Home and Abroad," *Problems of Communism*, XIV (July–August, 1965), 1–13.

[28] For the text of this memorandum, see the *New York Times*, September 3, 1966,

and by constant preaching of their "either-or" doctrine, they will continue to exploit every weakness in the armor of their opponents, particularly in the vulnerable countries of Southeast Asia. With or without the Soviet Union they will wage "the holy struggle of world revolution."

The Foreign Policy of India

Measured in power-political terms India is far from being a power of the first rank. To be sure, she is the second most populous state in the world and the most populous of the non-Communist states; but one may question whether her huge population, in its present state of economic and social backwardness, constitutes a real element of strength. India has some important natural resources and is now the third most industrialized state in Asia, but she is nonetheless in an early stage of industrial development; about 80 percent of her people live in villages and depend upon agriculture for a livelihood. She occupies an area of considerable strategic significance, and the Indian subcontinent as a whole enjoys the protection of some formidable natural barriers, notably the Himalayas and the sea.

India's present influence in Asian and world affairs is greater than a brief analysis of factors of weakness and of strength would indicate. This is due in part to the quality of her leaders and the prestige they gained during the struggle for independence, to her strategic position, to her membership in the Commonwealth, and to the distinctive traditions and characteristics of her foreign policy; but it is due primarily to the nature of the present world struggle, and to India's role as a leading spokesman of the so-called uncommitted world.

The roots of India's foreign policy are to be found in the civilizations which developed there over many centuries, particularly in the Hindu, Buddhist, and Muslim views of life and patterns of thought, the heritage of British policies, the independence movement and the position taken by the Indian National Congress on foreign affairs, and the influence of Gandhian philosophy, including the Gandhian principles of nonviolence and the importance of ends as well as means.

More recently India's policies have been shaped by the circumstances under which she achieved her independence, including the voluntary abdication of the British and the bloodshed and dislocation which accompanied partition, by internal weaknesses and divisions, by difficulties with her nearest neighbor, Pakistan, by the postwar developments in Asia — notably the emergence of many new independent nations and the Communist victory in China — and by the world environment in which she has had to carry on her domestic and foreign policies.[29]

Until August, 1947, India was under British rule, and the major decisions of her foreign policy, officially speaking, were made in Whitehall or in the governor-general's palace in New Delhi. But long before 1947 spokesmen of the Indian independence movement were taking an active interest in foreign policy. India was a member of the League of Nations, and prominent Indians participated in many international and Commonwealth conferences. From its inception in 1885 the Indian National Congress evinced an interest in foreign affairs. In the 1930's resolutions of the Congress on foreign affairs showed an acute concern with developments in China, the struggle against imperialism, the Spanish civil war, Japan's aggression in China, the rise of fascism, and the cause of world peace. At its Madras session in 1927 it passed resolutions which are still referred to as reflecting basic foreign policies of independent India. Another strong element of continuity in policy was provided by Jawaharlal Nehru himself; for a longer period

[29] For a comprehensive review of major aspects of Indian foreign policy, see Norman D. Palmer, *South Asia and United States Policy* (Boston: Houghton Mifflin Company, 1966).

than any other world statesman he was the voice of a nation's foreign policy.

Among the major facets of Indian foreign policy have been a strong opposition to racial discrimination and to imperialism; an emphasis on the basic economic, social, and political development of nations rather than upon communism or upon power politics; an insistence that, to use Nehru's words, "the countries of Asia, however weak they might be, do not propose to be ignored, do not propose to be by-passed, and certainly do not propose to be sat upon"; an emphasis on a policy of independence or nonalignment; an interest in the United Nations and in other efforts at international cooperation; a desire to avoid being involved in the cold war and a particular aversion to regional security pacts (witness the Indian reaction to the Manila Treaty of 1954); and a deep concern for all efforts which tend to reduce international tensions and to promote "peaceful co-existence." Some observers, at home and abroad, have criticized these professions as being naive or annoyingly moralistic in tone, with little relation to India's actual policies. Some have even charged that Nehru's India actually followed pro-Communist policies in foreign affairs, and they point to the rather favorable Indian climate of opinion regarding the Soviet Union, the strong Indian denunciation of security measures by the United States and other non-Communist nations, the apparent unwillingness in India even to admit the reality of the Soviet-Communist threat, and the policies of India toward Communist China between 1954 and 1959, which at times amounted almost to courtship and which emphasized reliance on such professions of peaceful intentions as peace pledges and the "five principles" of the Nehru-Chou declaration of June, 1954.

Since the Chinese attack in late 1962, India's foreign policy has become increasingly pragmatic and realistic. She has continued to adhere officially to a policy — which is perhaps more of an approach than a policy — of nonalignment, but it has been nonalignment with a difference. With the death of Jawaharlal Nehru in late May, 1964, Indian foreign policy, in the less experienced hands of Lal Bahadur Shastri and Mrs. Indira Gandhi, tended to concentrate on the improvement of relations with near neighbors, with marked success as far as Nepal, Burma, and Ceylon were concerned, but with no success whatever in India's relations with her largest neighbors, Pakistan and China. Her relations with the Soviet Union and the United States have generally become closer. She has received substantial economic aid from both the superpowers. The Soviet Union has for some years provided her with weapons and military equipment, including assistance in building factories for the manufacture of MIG fighter planes in India, and the United States extended emergency military assistance in the immediate aftermath of the Chinese attack and continued a limited program until the outbreak of Indo-Pakistan hostilities in the fall of 1965.

That "neutralist" India is not unaware of security considerations is indicated by the attention given to maintaining an adequate military establishment and to guarding her frontiers. This has been particularly apparent since the abrupt turn for the worse in Sino-Indian relations, when India discovered that Communist China, far from being a friendly Asian neighbor, was a hostile and threatening presence.

India's relations with Pakistan are a matter of the deepest concern. These relations have been strained ever since the partition of the subcontinent in 1947. While the agreement on the use of the waters of the Indus River Basin in 1960, after years of negotiations under the aegis of the World Bank, removed a major source of conflict between the two countries, relations have deteriorated since that time, to the point of armed hostilities in September, 1965. There is little prospect for a basic improvement in these relations until the Kashmir dispute is resolved and until the two countries learn to work together with greater understanding and cooperation.

The Nehru government was profoundly disturbed when Chinese troops were sent to Tibet in 1950, but for some years, particularly between the signing of the Sino-Indian agreement regarding Tibet in April, 1954 (which incorporated the *Panchsheel*, the five principles of peaceful co-existence), and the uprising in Tibet nearly five years later, Indian policy toward China was presumably based on the *Panchsheel* and on the assumption that China was a friendly neighbor. Chinese moves in Tibet and along India's northern borders in 1959 precipitated a major crisis in Sino-Indian relations, which turned into a threat to India's security with the armed invasion of October–November, 1962. The attack came as a traumatic shock to India, and caused a searching reappraisal of India's foreign policies and her whole approach to problems of national security and external relations.

As the most influential member of the so-called neutralist group of nations, India is especially interested in developing the closest possible ties with other Asian and African nations which share her point of view. India disclaims any desire to act as a leader in Asia, but she is a leading champion of Asia's claims to a greater place in world affairs, and her actions suggest that she is not always averse to taking the initiative. India was the main organizer and is now a leading member of the powerful Asian-African group in the United Nations. She has repeatedly played a leading role in conferences of Asian states, including the one at Bandung in April, 1955, certainly the most significant international conference ever held in Asia and the first conference of its kind in history. She is the giant of the Third World of non-Communist, nonaligned, and underdeveloped states.

Crockett. Copyright 1966 by The Washington Star. Reprinted with permission.

Germany and Japan: Renascent Powers

Germany. We have called the Federal Republic of Germany and Japan powers of uncertain status. Before World War II they were among the great powers of the world. As a result of their military defeat, they ceased to exist as independent states and for several years were under the occupation of the victorious powers. The occupation of Japan officially ended in 1952, and that of West Germany in 1955. Both countries have experienced a remarkable economic resurgence and both are again playing major roles in foreign affairs, but Germany is still a divided country, and Japan is still shrinking from assuming the major responsibility for her own security.

The Federal Republic of Germany formally came into existence in September, 1949, but until the British, American, and French occupation officially ended in 1955 her powers in foreign relations and certain other respects were somewhat limited by the Occupation Statute. Even before 1955, however, she was permitted to establish diplomatic relations of a limited nature with non-Communist states, to participate in the

European Recovery Program, to become a member of the Council of Europe, to join in the defense of Western Europe (with certain restrictions), and in other ways to exercise more and more control over her own destinies.

In the Soviet zone of Germany a "German Democratic Republic" was proclaimed in 1949. From its inception it has been under Communist domination, and the voice of East Germany is the voice of Moscow. Its actions can be understood only in relation to Soviet policies in the East European area and to the gyrations of the world Communist movement.

West Germany, with her large population, her industrial resources and "know-how," and the energy of her people, is potentially the most powerful state in Europe west of the Soviet Union. In fact, she may already have achieved that status. Since the London and Paris agreements of October, 1954, went into effect, she has been affiliated both with NATO and the Western European Union. She has identified herself increasingly with Western Europe, and her long-time chancellor, Konrad Adenauer, was one of the great "Europeans" of the postwar era. She is a member of the "Inner Six" of "Littl Europe," along with her former enemy, France, and is therefore an active participant in the Coal and Steel Community, Euratom, the Common Market, and many other organizations and agencies of West European cooperation. German spokesmen have been quite vocal on such questions as German rearmament, German unification, West European cooperation, and their desire for a greater role in the affairs of Western Europe.

In many respects Germany is the focal point of the cold war. While her own future depends in large measure on the nature of the relations between Russia and the West, it may also be said that the outcome of the misnamed East-West conflict depends to a considerable degree on the future of Germany. One of the central points of that conflict is the city of Berlin, physically surrounded by the territory of the East German "Democratic Republic." The "governmental status and structure" of Berlin "during the postwar years . . . has been one of the most unusual and complex in modern times,"[30] and a source of continuing disagreement, threatening at times to flare up into a major crisis between the Soviet Union and the three major Western powers.

Whether Germany remains divided or is reunited, whether she leans toward the East or toward the West or retains a fairly independent position, whether she emerges again as a menace to world peace and freedom or moves in the opposite direction, whether she becomes "bridge or battleground" — on these issues much of the world's future depends.

Japan. In September, 1951, most of the nations which had participated in the war against Japan, except India and the countries of the Soviet bloc, signed the Japanese Peace Treaty, which went into effect in the following April, when Japan regained her sovereignty and independence. Since then she has become an important factor in world affairs, although she has been handicapped by her recent past, her heavy dependence on foreign trade, her reluctance to undertake even minimum security measures, and internal political divisions. She is by far the most highly industrialized state of Asia, and has become the third most productive nation in the world. She has had remarkable success in checking the rate of population growth. In external relations she is especially concerned with problems of foreign trade and with relations with Communist China and the Soviet Union, with the other mem-

[30] Elmer Plischke, *Contemporary Government of Germany* (Boston: Houghton Mifflin Company, 1961), p. 242.

bers of the Asian-African Group in the United Nations, and with the United States. Her experience with the United States during the decade of occupation, her heavy dependence on American markets, the American base on Okinawa, and the continuing presence of American troops in Japan have been and to some extent still are frequent sources of irritation and conflict; but on the whole her relations with her major enemy during World War II are reasonably friendly.

A resurgent Japan can become a powerful force for peace or for conflict. In spite of the dislocation and shock caused by many years of war and occupation, she is still potentially one of the major nations of the world. The great unanswered questions seem to be: (1) Have her people and her leaders really abandoned the dreams of a Greater East Asia under Japanese rule and the ideas of military fascism, and are they sincerely dedicated to establishing a peaceful, democratic — or at least constitutional — state? (2) Can Japan, now reduced to her four home islands, find the necessary markets abroad and develop a sufficiently high level of productivity to sustain a population of more than 100,000,000 at a reasonable standard of existence?

The Foreign Policies of Lesser Powers

As the "realists' like to emphasize, this is a great-power world, and the major decisions in world affairs, including the ultimate decisions on war or peace, are being and will continue to be made by the most powerful states. This is not to imply, however, that all of the other states, in which the majority of the world's people live, are nothing but pawns or satellites of the few great powers. Some may indeed be in this unhappy situation, but on the whole the lesser powers — a term which embraces both middle and small powers — have a far from negligible influence. With some exceptions, they have not been markedly successful in maintaining neutrality or even real independence; but they have been able to force major powers to consider their interests by developing common patterns of actions in regional and universal groupings, notably in the United Nations, and they have been a positive and sometimes decisive force.

Great-Power–Small-Power Relations. As the negotiations which preceded the drafting of the United Nations Charter revealed, there are considerable differences in the attitude of the great powers towards the lesser ones. Great Britain, the Soviet Union, and the United States were in agreement on the necessity for the veto in order to protect their interests, but they had varying concepts of the role of the lesser powers in the new international organization. In general, the Soviet Union wanted the UN to be definitely and almost exclusively a great-power show, whereas Britain and the United States favored more consideration of the rights and interests of the lesser powers. The policies which these countries have since followed reflect this difference in view.

Few states, whatever their size or power, can hope to follow a policy of neutrality under present world conditions. Those which have been most successful have been Switzerland, Sweden, Ireland, and perhaps Afghanistan. But in each case it may be demonstrated that neutrality was a policy that was made possible by peculiar and probably temporary conditions. However zealous a state may be in refraining from making any international commitments which are likely to compromise its neutrality, the danger of involvement because of circumstances beyond its control is ever present.

This does not mean, of course, that a state must choose sides in every power struggle, or that it cannot preserve a measure of independence of action. It may be true, as E. H. Carr insisted, that "the small country can survive only by seeking permanent association with a great power";[31] but many of the lesser powers will not admit this and are seeking other roads to survival. In many respects these states are right in believing that to analyze the present international situation in terms of a conflict between "two worlds" is shortsighted and dangerous. Surely not all of international relations revolve around the exigencies of the cold war. India, Indonesia, and other Asian countries, for example, are consciously trying to follow a policy of remaining aloof, a policy which they call "nonalignment."

States in a buffer zone are faced with a limited number of choices. They can ally themselves with a major power, they can become satellites of a major power, they can attempt to maintain a tenuous neutrality, or they can try to play one major power off against another as a means of preserving as much freedom of action as possible. Norway, Greece, and Turkey have cast their lot with the Western powers; the East European states live within the shadow of the Soviet Union; Sweden is trying to follow a neutral course; Iran seems to be interested in exploiting her bargaining position.

To overcome individual weakness some of the lesser powers have joined in cooperative efforts for defense, economic development, and other purposes, sometimes in concert with one or more great powers and sometimes by themselves. Through such groupings they are able to exert a greater influence on major powers and on world affairs in general. The Arab states of the Middle East, weak and torn by internal dissensions and dynastic feuds, have tried to present a united front through the Arab League and through bloc voting and other concerted action in the United Nations, especially on the Palestine question. A Muslim bloc could have considerable influence, since it would speak for states which occupy a strategically important position and possess the chief oil reserves of the world. India gains added influence through her position in the Asian-African Group in the United Nations and as a spokesman for the "uncommitted world." The many new African states, individually weak and inexperienced in world affairs, and often at odds with each other, have considerable impact on world opinion through their activities as a sub-group of the Asian-African Group in the UN, through various regional groupings, and in many other ways.

The Latin American states exert a powerful influence on the foreign policy of the United States, especially through the OAS and other agencies for inter-American cooperation. Most of the smaller states of Western Europe play an active part in the many organizations for economic, political, and military cooperation which have come into existence in that area. The Commonwealth is not, strictly speaking, a regional grouping, but undoubtedly its members speak with greater authority in world affairs because of their participation in it.

Lesser-Power Influence. Lesser powers are natural champions of all forms of international cooperation, for it is clearly in their interest to preserve the peace and to exert a moderating influence on the great powers.[32] They find the greatest opportunities in the United Nations. In spite of the dominating position of the great powers, the lesser states are represented in all organs and agencies of the UN, their spokesmen are listened to with respect, and often they are able to act as intermediaries between major powers. In

[31] *Conditions of Peace* (New York: The Macmillan Company, 1942), p. 58. Carr argued here that modern warfare and changing world conditions have destroyed the effective independence of small states. See specially pp. 52–58.

[32] In the words of Martin Wight, "not burdened with particular concrete interests, small powers are able to be conscious of a universal interest." *Power Politics* (London: Royal Institute of International Affairs, 1949), p. 50.

this way they make a truly great contribution to the peaceful settlement of disputes, as well as to the smoothing of ruffled tempers. Nor should the influence of individual statesmen from lesser states be minimized. Anyone who has followed the activities of the UN over the years must be impressed by the leadership of Evatt of Australia, Spaak of Belgium, Pearson of Canada, Rau, Madame Pandit, and Krishna Menon of India, Entezam of Iran, Padilla Nervo of Mexico, Belaúnde of Peru, Fraser of New Zealand, Romulo of the Philippines, and other spokesmen of the lesser powers.

The middle powers are in a position to exercise a great influence on the major powers and on the course of world affairs, and they are becoming more aware of their potentialities. Usually they possess a regional superiority which gives them effectiveness in a wider area. India's position in South and Southeast Asia has already been mentioned. Australia is especially concerned with security arrangements in the western and southwestern Pacific, with collaboration with the states of South and Southeast Asia, and with the future position of Japan. She took the lead in the development of the Colombo Plan, and an Australian represented the entire Commonwealth on the Allied Council for Japan. Argentina and Brazil are competitors for primacy in South America; and Argentina, in particular, has on occasion challenged the policies of the United States in Latin America.

At least two other states which should be classed as middle powers do not possess regional superiority, for they are too close to great powers, but they do have an influence out of proportion to their independent power. These states are Canada and Italy. Canada has close ties with both the United Kingdom and the United States; politically she is associated with the Commonwealth, but geographically and economically she is linked more closely with her North American neighbor. She is an important member of NATO, and although not affiliated with OAS she participates wholeheartedly in measures for hemispheric defense and cooperation. Italy is a vital bastion of the free world. She occupies a central position with regard to both Western Europe and the Mediterranean area. Her policies and indeed her destinies are tied to those of the other states of Western Europe.

Those peculiar hybrids, Spain and Yugoslavia — the one a Fascist state which survived a world war for the extinction of fascism, the other a Communist state outside the "iron curtain" — may perhaps also be considered as middle powers. Possibly Turkey and Pakistan should be added, too. Spain occupies such a strategic position with respect to Atlantic, Mediterranean, and West European defense that she can hardly be ignored, in spite of her internal weaknesses and the bad odor of the Franco regime. Yugoslavia is willing to exploit her unnatural position and is finding her very vulnerability a source of strength. Turkey maintains a sizable and efficient army, and seeks defense against Russia through cooperation with the West in NATO and through direct, if circumspect, relations with her giant neighbor. Pakistan is rather overshadowed by her larger neighbor in the Indian subcontinent, but in terms of population she is the fifth largest nation in the world, and the first or second largest Muslim state. She has a strong military establishment, and she is an influential, if disgruntled, member of both SEATO and CENTO.

One other observation should be made about the role of the lesser powers in world affairs. This is the real contribution that they are making in "sweetening" international relations and in calling attention to first principles. One shudders to think what the level of international life would be if the world were partitioned among a few superpowers. Smaller states have no monopoly on morality and justice and spiritual values, and often they cloak selfish and shortsighted ends in the mantle of principle, as do great powers; but because their possibilities of survival are so dependent on the avoidance of conflict between great powers, and because they are more likely to be pawns rather than victors in a power struggle, for their own well-being they often appeal to higher principles of conduct and action.

SUGGESTIONS FOR FURTHER READING

ALLEN, HENRY C. *Great Britain and the United States; a History of Anglo-American Relations (1783–1952)*. London, 1954. A detailed and provocative historical review.

ARNOLD, GUY. *Towards Peace and a Multiracial Commonwealth*. London, 1964.

ARON, RAYMOND. *France Steadfast and Changing: the Fourth to the Fifth Republic*. Cambridge, Mass.: Harvard University Press, 1960.

BARNETT, A. DOAK. *Communist China and Asia: Challenge to American Policy*. New York: Harper, for the Council on Foreign Relations, 1960. A detailed examination of the internal and external policies of Communist China.

BELL, CORA. *The Debatable Alliance; an Essay in Anglo-American Relations*. London, 1964. Chatham House Essays, 3.

BERKES, ROSS N. and MOHINDER S. BEDI. *The Diplomacy of India; India's Foreign Policy in the United Nations*. Stanford, Calif.: Stanford University Press, 1958.

BORTON, HUGH, ed. *Japan Between East and West*. New York: Harper, for the Council on Foreign Relations, 1957.

BOYD, R. *Communist China's Foreign Policy*. New York: Frederick A. Praeger, 1962.

BRANDT, WILLY. *The Ordeal of Coexistence*. Cambridge, Mass.: Harvard University Press, 1963. By the well-known former Mayor of West Berlin and leader of the Social Democratic Party of West Germany, who has served as foreign minister of the Federal Republic.

Britain in Western Europe. Royal Institute of International Affairs, 1956. A report by a Chatham House study group.

BULLARD, SIR READER. *Britain and the Middle East from Earliest Times to 1963*, 3d rev. ed. London, 1964.

CHAKRAVARTI, P. C. *India's China Policy*. Bloomington: Indiana University Press, 1961.

CHURCHILL, WINSTON S. *The Second World War*. 6 vols. Boston: Houghton Mifflin Company, 1948–53.

CRANKSHAW, EDWARD. *The New Cold War. Moscow v. Pekin*. Baltimore: Penguin Books, 1963.

DAS GUPTA, J. B. *Indo-Pakistan Relations, 1947–1955*. Amsterdam, 1958.

DUTT, V. P. *Communist China's Foreign Policy*. Bombay, 1964.

EARLE, EDWARD M., ed. *Modern France: Problems of the Third and Fourth Republics*. Princeton, N.J.: Princeton University Press, 1951.

EPSTEIN, LEON D. *British Politics in the Suez Crisis*. Urbana: University of Illinois Press, 1964. A case study of a controversial episode in recent British foreign policy.

ERIIS, HENNING. *Scandinavia: Between East and West*. Ithaca: Cornell University Press, 1950.

FITZSIMONS, M. A. *The Foreign Policy of the British Labour Government: 1945–1951*. Notre Dame, Ind.: University of Notre Dame Press, 1952.

FOX, ANNETTE BAKER. *The Power of Small States; Diplomacy in World War II*. Chicago: University of Chicago Press, 1959.

FRANKS, SIR OLIVER. *Britain and the Tide of World Affairs*. New York: Oxford University Press, 1955.

FRYE, RICHARD N., ed. *The Near East and the Great Powers.* Cambridge, Mass.: Harvard University Press, 1951. Essays by specialists.

FURNISS, EDGAR S., JR. *France: Keystone of Western Defense.* Garden City, N.Y.: Doubleday & Company, 1954. Doubleday Short Studies in Political Science, 3.

———. *France, Troubled Ally; De Gaulle's Heritage and Prospects.* New York: Harper, for the Council on Foreign Relations, 1960.

GLAZEBROOK, G. P. DE T. *A History of Canadian External Relations.* Oxford University Press, for the Canadian Institute of International Affairs, 1951.

GORDON, J. K., ed. *Canada's Role as a Middle Power.* Toronto, 1966. Issued by the Canadian Institute of International Affairs.

GOUTOR, JACQUES R. *Algeria and France, 1830–1963.* Muncie, Indiana: Ball State University, 1965.

GRIFFITH, WILLIAM E. *The Sino-Soviet Rift.* Cambridge, Mass.: The M.I.T. Press, 1964. A careful analysis, with documentation.

GROSSER, ALFRED. *French Foreign Policy under De Gaulle.* Boston: Little, Brown and Company, 1967. An objective study by a distinguished French political scientist.

HALPERIN, MORTON. *China and the Bomb.* New York: Frederick A. Praeger, for the Council on Foreign Relations, 1965.

HAMILTON, W. B., KENNETH ROBINSON, and C. D. W. GOODWIN, eds. *A Decade of the Commonwealth, 1955–1964.* Durham, N.C.: Duke University Press, 1966. In this massive book 25 scholars — British, American, Indian, Canadian, Nigerian, and Pakistani — examine various facets of a remarkable period of change in the Commonwealth.

HANREIDER, WOLFRAM F. *West German Foreign Policy, 1949–1963: International Pressure and Domestic Response.* Stanford, Calif.: Stanford University Press, 1967.

HINTON, HAROLD C. *Communist China in World Politics.* Boston: Houghton Mifflin Company, 1966. A comprehensive and informative treatment. Excellent background for more recent developments in Communist China's foreign policy.

JENNINGS, SIR IVOR. *Problems of the New Commonwealth.* Durham, N.C.: Duke University Press, 1958. By one of the leading authorities on Commonwealth affairs.

KARUNAKARAN, K. P. *India in World Affairs, August 1947–January 1950.* Calcutta, 1952. *India in World Affairs, February 1950–December 1953.* London, 1958. First two volumes in a series issued by the Indian Council of World Affairs.

KULSKI, W. W. *De Gaulle and the World: The Foreign Policy of the Fifth French Republic.* Syracuse: Syracuse University Press, 1966.

KUNDRA, J. C. *Indian Foreign Policy, 1947–1954; a Study of Relations with the Western Bloc.* Groningen, 1955.

LENCZOWSKI, GEORGE E. *The Middle East in World Affairs,* 2d ed. Ithaca: Cornell University Press, 1956. An able political and diplomatic survey.

LERNER, DANIEL and RAYMOND ARON, eds. *France Defeats EDC.* New York: Frederick A. Praeger, 1957. An informative case study.

LEVI, WERNER. *Modern China's Foreign Policy.* Minneapolis: University of Minnesota Press, 1953.

LINDSAY, MICHAEL. *China and the Cold War; a Study in International Relations.* Melbourne, 1955.

LUETHY, HERBERT. *France Against Herself.* New York: Frederick A. Praeger, 1955. A brilliant analysis by a Swiss political commentator.

MACNAIR, HARTLEY F. and DONALD F. LACH. *Modern Far Eastern International Relations,* 2d ed. Princeton, N.J.: D. Van Nostrand Co., 1955.

MACRIDIS, ROY C., ed. *Foreign Policy in World Politics.* Englewood Cliffs, N.J.: Prentice-Hall, 1958. Contains articles by specialists on the foreign policies of 10 important countries.

MENDEL, DOUGLAS H. *The Japanese People and Foreign Policy; a Study of Public Opinion in Post-Treaty Japan.* Berkeley: University of California Press, 1961.

MIDDLETON, DREW. *The Supreme Choice: Britain and Europe.* New York: Alfred A.

Knopf, 1963. Thoughtful observations by an experienced American journalist.

MORGENTHAU, HANS J., ed. *Germany and the Future of Europe.* Chicago: University of Chicago Press, 1951. A series of lectures by experts.

NEHRU, JAWAHARLAL. *India's Foreign Policy; Selected Speeches, September 1946–April 1961.* Delhi, 1961. An excellent collection of the most important speeches on India's foreign policy, by its main architect.

NICHOLAS, HERBERT. *Britain and the U.S.A.* Baltimore: The Johns Hopkins Press, 1963. The Albert Shaw lectures for 1961 at the Johns Hopkins University.

NORTHEDGE, FREDERICK SAMUEL. *British Foreign Policy: The Process of Readjustment, 1945–1961.* New York: Frederick A. Praeger, 1962.

OLSON, LAWRENCE A. *Dimensions of Japan.* New York: American Universities Field Staff, 1963. A collection of reports prepared for the AUFS by a perceptive observer.

PALMER, NORMAN D. *South Asia and United States Policy.* Boston: Houghton Mifflin Company, 1966. Deals largely with the foreign policies of India and Pakistan, and with U.S.–South Asian relations.

PATTERSON, GEORGE N. *Peking versus Delhi.* London, 1963. Rather critical of India's border claims.

RAJAN, M. S. *India in World Affairs, 1954–56.* Bombay, 1964. Vol. 3 of a series issued under auspices of the Indian Council of World Affairs.

RAMAZINI, ROUHOLLAH K. *The Foreign Policy of Iran: A Developing Nation in World Affairs.* Charlottesville: The University Press of Virginia, 1966.

REYNOLDS, P. A. *British Foreign Policy in the Inter-War Years.* London, 1954.

ROBERTS, HENRY and H. G. WILSON. *Britain and the United States: Problems in Cooperation.* Harper, for the Council on Foreign Relations, 1953.

SCHWARTZ, BENJAMIN. *Chinese Communism and the Rise of Mao.* Cambridge, Mass.: Harvard University Press, 1951. The best analysis in English of the evolution of Chinese Communist foreign policy.

SETON-WILLIAMS, M. V. *Britain and the Arab States: A Survey of Anglo-Arab Relations, 1920–1948.* London, 1948. A factual summary by countries, plus chapters on the Arab League and Arab nationalism.

STRANG, WILLIAM S. *Britain in World Affairs; the Fluctuations in Power and Influence from Henry VIII to Elizabeth II.* New York: Frederick A. Praeger, 1961.

TALBOT, PHILLIPS and S. L. POPLAI. *India and America: A Study of Their Relations.* New York: Harper, for the Council on Foreign Relations, 1958. Based on the work of two study groups, one Indian, one American.

WARD, A. A. and G. P. GOOCH. *Cambridge History of British Foreign Policy, 1783–1919.* 3 vols. Cambridge, Mass.: Harvard University Press, 1922–23.

WILMOT, CHESTER. *The Struggle for Europe.* New York: Harper, 1952.

WOLFERS, ARNOLD. *Britain and France Between Two Wars.* New York: Harcourt, Brace, 1940.

WOODHOUSE, CHRISTOPHER M. *British Foreign Policy since the Second World War.* New York: Frederick A. Praeger, 1962.

YOUNGER, KENNETH. *Changing Perspectives in British Foreign Policy.* London, 1964.

ZAGORIA, DONALD. *The Sino-Soviet Conflict, 1956–1961.* Princeton, N.J.: Princeton University Press, 1962.

PART SIX

THE FUTURE OF THE WORLD COMMUNITY IN THE NUCLEAR AND SPACE AGE

24 The Atom and Space: International Implications

Early on the morning of August 6, 1945, an American B-29 dropped a single bomb on the Japanese city of Hiroshima. The blinding flash of the explosion a few seconds later was followed by the appearance of a mushroomed-shaped cloud which soon towered for miles over the doomed city. Some 150,000 people were killed or wounded — and many of the latter were to die in agony from radiation effects — and 75 per cent of the buildings of the city were destroyed or badly damaged. A short time later the President of the United States, in a broadcast heard around the world, announced that "the basic power of the universe" had been unleashed against Japan.

In this dramatic and apocalyptic way the people of the world learned that the atomic age had begun. In a single moment, it seemed, problems of international conflict and cooperation, of war and peace, had become questions of the future of mankind, even of its survival. Since Hiroshima, the hydrogen bomb and experiments with bacteriological and chemical weapons have improved the techniques of mass destruction to the point where the atom bomb itself is hardly more than a conventional weapon. Since Hiroshima, too, many efforts have been made to adjust man's thinking and institutions to the imperatives of the atomic age, but these efforts have fallen far short of the dimensions of the crisis. "Truly," wrote Paul-Henri Spaak, one of the world's wisest statesmen, in 1955, "our imagination is not in step with our era."[1]

Shortly after the atom bombs were first used against Japanese cities an American physicist wrote:

> We find ourselves with an explosion which is far from completely perfected. . . . It is conceivable that totally different methods may be discovered for converting matter into energy since it is to be remembered that the energy released in uranium fission corresponds to the utilization of only about one-tenth of one per cent of its mass. Should a scheme be devised for converting to energy even as much as a few per cent of the matter of some common material, civilization would have the means to commit suicide at will. . . . Here is a new tool for mankind, a tool of unimaginable destructive power. Its development raises many questions that must be answered in the near future. . . . These questions are not technical questions; they are political and social questions, and the an-

[1] Paul-Henri Spaak, "The Atom Bomb and NATO," *Foreign Affairs*, XXXIII (April 1955), 359.

swers given to them may affect all mankind for generations.[2]

Since these words were written great progress has been made in harnessing new sources of nuclear energy, but almost no progress has been made in dealing with the political and social questions which the new discoveries raise. As Albert Schweitzer stated in his address in Oslo on November 4, 1954, on his receipt of the Nobel Peace Prize: "Man has become a superman . . . because he is in command . . . of latent forces in nature," but he "is not elevated to that level of superhuman reason which must correspond to the possession of superhuman force."

No competent analysis of international relations in the second half of the twentieth century can ignore the consequences of the availability, for the first time in history, of "power without limit" — power for the benefit or for the destruction of mankind. The unseen atom has become perhaps the greatest force in the world.

The Advent of the Atomic Age

Hiroshima's day of doom, August 6, 1945, marked the world debut of the atomic bomb, but it was not the birthday of the atomic age. That birthday was December 2, 1942, when, "amid the greatest wartime secrecy," a small group of scientists, gathered on a squash court underneath the west stands of the University of Chicago's abandoned football stadium, watched the lighting of "the first atomic fire on earth." Dr. Arthur H. Compton directed the project, and Dr. Enrico Fermi captained the scientific team which designed and built the atomic furnace (which Fermi called a "pile" but which has since become known as a nuclear reactor). The experiment proved that splitting the atom could start a self-sustaining chain reaction, and it demonstrated practically that an atom bomb could be made.

For some years scientists had been conducting experiments which suggested that a controlled chain reaction was possible. Einstein, in his famous formula $E = MC_2$, had advanced the startling theory that energy could be converted into matter. The splitting of the atom, however, with the consequent release of atomic energy, was the work of many scientists. Fermi's epoch-making experiments at the University of Rome in 1934 led directly to the discovery of uranium fission, apparently first produced by O. F. Hahn and Fritz Strassman in Germany about 1938. Lise Meitner and O. R. Fritsch learned of this discovery before they were exiled from Germany in 1938, and Niels Bohr received the news from them. In January, 1939, both Fermi and Bohr came to the United States, and Bohr communicated word of the achievement to physicists in Princeton and elsewhere. Fermi had accepted a post at Columbia University, where, on January 29, 1939, he and some of his new colleagues directed the first splitting of the uranium atom in the United States.

Fermi, Bohr, and other exiled physicists learned that a special institute had been created in Berlin for work on an atom bomb. They understood the grave consequences if the Nazis should perfect such a weapon ahead of the free world. They induced the most famous of the scientist-exiles in America, Albert Einstein, to write a now-historic letter to President Roosevelt, stressing the urgency of investigating the possibilities of developing an atomic bomb.[3] It was perhaps ironic that one of the great champions of peace, and even of pacifism, should have been the man to urge the American President to undertake "probably the greatest calculated risk in history" in order to develop a

[2] Henry De Wolf Smyth, *Atomic Energy for Military Purposes* (Princeton, N.J.: Princeton University Press, 1945), pp. 224, 226.

[3] See Ralph E. Lapp, "The Einstein Letter that Started It All," *New York Times Magazine*, August 2, 1964.

weapon of unprecedented capabilities for human destruction. The risk was taken, and the atomic age was the result.

On August 13, 1942, the "Manhattan District" was officially established in the Army Corps of Engineers to carry on the special project, with Major General Leslie R. Groves in charge. Canadian and British scientists were enlisted to aid the American and exiled European scientists. At Chicago, as we have noted, the first nuclear chain reaction was achieved in December, 1942. At Los Alamos, New Mexico, Dr. J. Robert Oppenheimer directed a group of scientists, including Fermi and Bohr, in designing and building the first bomb. Other research centers were established at Oak Ridge, Tennessee, and elsewhere. The first atom bomb ever to be tested was exploded not over Hiroshima but at Alamogordo, New Mexico, on July 16, 1945.[4] It was remarkable that a project of such dimensions, eventually involving an expenditure of more than two billion dollars and the labor of some 300,000 workers, could be undertaken and completed in full secrecy during a major war.

Nearly three months before the Alamogordo test proved that the atom bomb would actually work, and on the day that the United Nations Conference on International Organization met in San Francisco, Secretary of War Henry L. Stimson, one of the few top political officials aware of the nature and significance of the Manhattan Project, and Major General Groves went to the White House to deliver a memorandum to President Truman. Apparently Mr. Truman had known nothing about the bomb plans before the death of Roosevelt called him to the highest office in the land. Now, on April 25, 1945, nine days after he had become President, he learned from Mr. Stimson's memorandum that within four months the United States would in all probability possess "the most terrible weapon ever known in human history," one with which "modern civilization might be completely destroyed."

From the day of Stimson's "enlightening presentation of this awesome subject" until he left the White House nearly eight years later, President Truman was involved in a series of decisions regarding the development and control of the atom bomb and even more fearful weapons of mass destruction. The decision to drop the bomb on Hiroshima and Nagasaki was his to make, and he made it upon the advice of his most trusted advisers. Disagreement over the military and moral justification of that decision continues to this day.

Congress, at President Truman's request, established an Atomic Energy Commission to supervise all work relating to experimentation in the use of atomic energy for military and peaceful purposes. Although most of this work was carried on in secret, the commission's chairmen, particularly David E. Lilienthal and Lewis L. Strauss, along with many outstanding atomic scientists, were involved in a series of controversies, public as well as private, over the decisions and acts of the AEC. The division of opinion on the desirability of proceeding with experiments on the hydrogen bomb — a division reflecting the opposing positions taken by J. Robert Oppenheimer and Edward Teller — and the decision of the AEC to bar Dr. Oppenheimer from access to certain classified information added dramatic highlights to the postwar atomic story.

In the spring of 1946 a committee headed by Dean Acheson produced the so-called Acheson-Lilienthal Plan for an international atomic development authority, and at the first

[4] Dr. Oppenheimer later stated that the following words from the *Bhagavad-Gita* "wrote themselves on his mind when the first atom bomb turned night into day over the New Mexico desert": "If the radiance of a thousand suns were to burst into the sky, that would be like the splendour of the Mighty One . . . . I am become Death, the destroyer of worlds." Alfred Friendly, "The Tragedy of a Great Scientist," *Sunday Standard* (New Delhi), March 12, 1967 (an article reprinted from the *Washington Post*).

meeting of the United Nations Atomic Energy Commission the American representative, Bernard Baruch, submitted a proposal modeled on the Acheson-Lilienthal Plan. In spite of vigorous Soviet opposition the American plan, in revised form, was accepted by the majority of the members of the commission and later approved by the General Assembly. Nearly eight years later, in December, 1953, in an address to the General Assembly, President Eisenhower advanced a proposal for the pooling of atomic resources for peaceful uses. After considerable hesitation the Soviet Union agreed to discuss this atoms-for-peace plan, and a subcommittee of the Disarmament Commission studied it in some detail. Late in the summer of 1955 an international conference on the peaceful uses of atomic energy, attended largely by scientists, was held in Geneva. Hopes rose that the nations which had made the greatest progress in the development of nuclear weapons — the United States, Great Britain, Canada, and the Soviet Union — would cooperate in searching for some means of international control, in sharing their atomic resources with other nations, and in utilizing atomic energy for peace rather than war. At the same time, however, the atomic powers were adding to their stockpiles of atomic and perhaps also of hydrogen bombs, and they were pressing forward with experiments in the development of even more powerful instruments of destruction.

The United States enjoyed a monopoly of atomic bombs until 1949, a condition which many Western statesmen — including Winston Churchill — regarded as the chief deterrent to Soviet aggression and the chief shield for Western Europe. On September 23, 1949, all complacency arising from the American monopoly was shattered by President Truman's announcement that Russia had recently exploded her first atomic bomb. Although this development had been expected, calculations had fixed the likely date much later. Britain became the third member of the "nuclear club" on October 3, 1952; France, the fourth member on February 13, 1960; and China, the fifth on October 16, 1964. Thus in the first two decades of the atomic age five states had joined the "nuclear club," and questions regarding the "*n*th nation problem" and nuclear proliferation moved to the forefront of international concern.

The Hydrogen Bomb

Even before they knew that the Soviet Union had made a successful atomic bomb, a number of American scientists led by Edward Teller, some high military officials, and a few key members of Congress, notably Senator Brien McMahon, had begun to agitate for initiating work on a new bomb — a "super-bomb" much more powerful than the atom bomb. The suggestions of Teller, McMahon, and others who shared their views were strongly opposed by Chairman Lilienthal of the Atomic Energy Commission and by many outstanding American scientists, notably J. Robert Oppenheimer and James B. Conant. For a long time the proposals were coolly viewed by the White House. The explosion of an atomic bomb by the Soviet Union changed the attitude of many American policy-makers. Since the Russians had made the atomic bomb so quickly, there was no reason to doubt that they were already at work on the H-bomb, or that they could make it if it could be made at all. It became apparent at once that if the United States and the Western world were to keep the strategic initiative, they would have to do more than outmanufacture the Soviet Union in atomic bombs. On January 31, 1950, four months after he had revealed the Russian atomic explosion, President Truman announced that he had "directed the Atomic Energy Commission to continue its work on all forms of atomic weapons, including the so-called hydrogen or super-bomb."

The President's momentous decision met with "somber, overwhelming approval" in the United States. Almost all of the top atomic scientists, however, whether they approved of the President's decision or not, agreed that the development of the superbomb would raise new threats to civilization and human survival.[5] Soon after the President's announcement Albert Einstein, in a sense the father of the atomic bomb, declared:

> The hydrogen bomb appears on the public horizon as a probably attainable goal. . . . If successful, radioactive poisoning of the atmosphere, and hence annihilation of any life on earth, has been brought within the range of technical possibilities.

Thus with mixed emotions the United States entered the fateful race to develop the H-bomb. Encouraged by the administration and utilizing a combination of government resources and private scientific skills, the directors of the project achieved concrete results in an amazingly short time. On November 1, 1952, tests at Eniwetok in the western Pacific included what were described as "experiments contributing to thermonuclear reactions." It was later announced that the prototype of the H-bomb exploded at this time was in the megaton range (a megaton is the equivalent of 1,000,000 tons of TNT). The 1952 tests demonstrated beyond reasonable doubt that the dreaded H-bomb could be made.

Less than a year later, on August 8, 1953, Premier Malenkov revealed that Russia too had the H-bomb secret. Shortly before his announcement scientific instruments outside Russia had indicated that the Soviets had indeed "tested a weapon or device of a yield well beyond the range of regular fission weapons and which derived a part of its force from the fusion of light elements." This development was even more momentous than the news of Soviet success in making an atom bomb in 1949.

The first explosion of an actual hydrogen bomb occurred in March, 1954, during tests sponsored by the United States Atomic Energy Commission in the vicinity of Bikini atoll in the Pacific. On March 1 "a very large thermonuclear device" was exploded. It was described as "the most devastating explosion man has ever produced," and apparently generated an unexpectedly powerful force of 15 to 20 megatons, which would make it a blast 750 to 1,000 times more powerful than that of the atomic bomb that had been dropped on Hiroshima.[6] Even more ominous than the immediate effects — "blast, heat, immediate nuclear radioaction" — were those of "residual radioactivity," popularly known as the "fall-out." In 1955 the Atomic Energy Commission reported that as a result of the H-bomb explosion of March 1, 1954, "about 7,000 square miles of territory downwind from the point of burst was so contaminated that survival might have depended upon prompt evacuation of the area or upon taking shelter and other protective measures."[7]

[5] Appalled by the potential destructive power of the H-bomb, a group of American physicists, led by Hans A. Bethe and Samuel K. Allison, issued a statement on February 4, 1950, which took the rather enigmatic position that "there can be only one justification for our development of the hydrogen bomb, and that is to prevent its use." The statement continued: ". . . the thermonuclear reaction on which the H-bomb is based, is limited in its power only by the amount of hydrogen which can be carried in the bomb. Even if the power were limited to 1,000 times that of a present atomic bomb, the step from an A-bomb to an H-bomb would be as great as that from an ordinary TNT bomb to the atom bomb. . . . New York, or any other of the greatest cities of the world, could be destroyed by a single hydrogen bomb.

"We believe that no nation has the right to use such a bomb, no matter how righteous its cause. This bomb is no longer a weapon of war, but a means of extermination of whole populations. Its use would be a betrayal of all standards of morality and of Christian civilization itself."

[6] On October 30, 1961, the Soviet Union exploded a 50-megaton bomb, "the largest man-made explosion in history."

[7] The report of the AEC on the effects of hydrogen bomb explosives was printed in the *New York Times*, February 16, 1955.

American newspapers were prompt to point out that 7,000 square miles covered an area almost as large as the state of New Jersey, or of Connecticut and Delaware combined. Thus with a relatively few H-bombs it appeared that the major centers of population and industry in any country could be destroyed. A British physicist calculated that ten or twenty well-directed bombs could make "organized life impossible" in Britain; and most scientists apparently considered that if he erred at all it was in overestimating the number of bombs that would be required to produce this fearful result.

In 1954, therefore, the hydrogen bomb age actually arrived. Twenty months after the Bikini explosion the Soviet Union exploded a bomb which the chairman of the United States Atomic Energy Commission described as "in the range of megatons," meaning that it was a true hydrogen bomb.[8] Nearly twelve years later, in June, 1967, China tested a hydrogen bomb, and France was preparing for a similar test.

The hydrogen bomb is often referred to as a three-stage weapon — a fission-fusion-fission bomb. The initial explosion comes from a powerful fission bomb, made of either uranium 235 or plutonium. This explosion provides a temperature of several hundred million degrees, which causes the fusion of a mixture of the heavy varieties of hydrogen, namely deuterium or tritium. The fusion process releases neutrons of such energies that they are capable of splitting the nuclei of the normally nonfissionable uranium 238. "Thus the main explosive force of the hydrogen bomb comes not from fusion of hydrogen but from the fission of the cheap and abundant uranium 238."[9]

The hydrogen bomb, therefore, is not just a more powerful atomic bomb. "Thermonuclear weapons," declared a member of the United States Atomic Energy Commission in November, 1955, "represent an entirely new kind of power. Their potential destructiveness is so different from the destructiveness of 'A' bombs that these new weapons do not belong to the same category — not by any stretch of the imagination. . . . the atmospheric contamination that results from large thermonuclear explosions is serious. In fact, it is so serious that it could be catastrophic. A sufficiently large number of such explosions would render the earth uninhabitable to man. That is a plain fact."[10] The Soviet announcement less than a week later gave added significance to these gloomy words.

Scientists appear to be doubtful whether there are in fact any foreseeable limits to the potential power of thermonuclear weapons. Some even argue that for better or for worse the hydrogen bomb age holds out the prospect of "power without limit." The production of the hydrogen bomb, they point out, "now makes it certain that the most dreaded weapon of all — the cobalt bomb — can also be successfully built." The cobalt bomb would consist of a hydrogen bomb encased in a shell of cobalt instead of steel; when vaporized in the explosion, the cobalt would be "transformed into a deadly radioactive cloud 320 times more powerful than radium."[11] In 1950 Albert Einstein said that such a bomb could produce so much radioactive poisoning that it could annihilate all life on earth.

Reports of other nuclear weapons, which represent what has sometimes been called "the third generation" of atomic weapons, have been current for some years. In 1960 Thomas E. Murray, former member of the

[8] The announcement of "the largest explosion thus far in the U.S.S.R." was first made on November 23, 1955, by Chairman Lewis L. Strauss of the U.S. Atomic Energy Commission, and was confirmed three days later in an official Soviet statement. See the *New York Times,* November 24 and 27, 1955.

[9] William L. Laurence, in the *New York Times,* November 18, 1955.

[10] Address by Thomas E. Murray at Fordham Law School dinner, New York, November 17, 1955; in the *New York Times,* November 18, 1955.

[11] William L. Laurence, in the *New York Times,* April 7, 1954.

United States Atomic Energy Commission, in a letter to both presidential candidates, Vice President Nixon and Senator Kennedy, urged resumption of underground testing in order to develop "a radically new type of nuclear weapon" before the Russians did. Some nuclear scientists speculated that Dr. Murray was talking about a "neutron bomb" — a kind of small mobile nuclear reactor capable of spewing out lethal nuclear rays. In September, 1964, Premier Khrushchev told a group of visiting Japanese parliamentarians that the Soviet Union had a "monstrous" and "terrible" new weapon which could be "a means of the destruction and extermination of humanity." At the time Western scientists thought that Mr. Khrushchev was referring to either a hydrogen bomb in the 100-megaton range or a cobalt bomb.

In addition to the frightening possibilities resulting from the development of thermonuclear weapons and from experiments with radioactive poisons, equally unpleasant prospects are present in the field of chemical and bacteriological warfare. Although poison gas was not used during World War II, new and more deadly types were developed during wartime and in the postwar period. Biological weapons are apparently of great variety and potency. "Fungi, bacteria, rickettsiae, viruses and toxic agents" may be used with devastating effect against human beings and other living organisms.[12] Over thirty diseases are considered to have significant military potentialities; these include anthrax, botulism, tularemia, psittacosis, and pneumonic plague.[13] Bacteriological agents can be introduced into the water supply, sprayed from the air, or directed against enemy populations in many other ways difficult to guard against. Moreover, unlike the atomic and H-bombs, they can be produced easily and inexpensively in small laboratories and by small states. As early as 1947 Rear Admiral Zacharias summed up the significance of chemical and bacteriological warfare: ". . . there are today in the arsenals of several of the great powers other absolute weapons, chemical, biological, and climatological, more devastating than the atom. They are capable of exterminating the last vestige of human, animal and even vegetable life from the face of the earth. They are being manufactured at this moment."[14]

Herblock; Copyright, 1952, The Washington Post

"Pardon Me, Mister"

Dealing with "The Basic Power of the Universe"

The problems of world politics which occupy the attention of statesmen and nations today are not basically different from those of a somewhat earlier time, but the background against which they have to be considered has changed fundamentally. Since

[12] Ansley J. Coale, *The Problem of Reducing Vulnerability to Atomic Bombs* (Princeton, N.J.: Princeton University Press, 1947), p. 97.

[13] Hanson W. Baldwin, *The Price of Power* (New York: Harper, 1948), p. 73.

[14] Ellis M. Zacharias, "Absolute Weapons More Deadly Than the Atom," *United Nations World* (November, 1947), p. 13.

the end of World War II, a change far more basic than the deteriorating state of great power relations has occurred. "In 1945," wrote C. L. Sulzberger a decade later, "it was a question of peace. Now it is a matter of humanity's survival."[15] As Kenneth Boulding observed: "We live in a society with a positive possibility of irretrievable disaster — a possibility which grows every year. This is a very uncomfortable society to live in."[16] In Toynbeean terms, "Man's acquisition of this degree of command over non-human forces had made it impossible for him any longer to evade the challenge of two evils [war and class conflict] which Man himself had brought into the World in the act of providing himself with a new species of society."[17] Thus mankind, in Toynbee's view, confronted "an unprecedented human situation."

In the light of all available evidence it seems apparent that the atomic age has indeed uncovered ample grounds for the most optimistic hopes and for the darkest despair. Both scientists and students of politics and society tend to be appalled by the appearance of frightful instruments of destruction at a time when man is still patently incapable of developing social institutions commensurate with the needs of the new age. "We have found that the men who know most are the most gloomy," declared eight world-famous scientists in 1955. Hanson W. Baldwin, after a careful appraisal of the world political-strategic situation, had earlier come up with this melancholy observation:

> The face of tomorrow is a bleak visage; we are embarked upon a 'time of troubles' . . . We have opened for all time the lid of Pandora's box of evils. We cannot push the genii back into the box. We may not like it, but we must face it.[18]

In general, the atomic age has thus far accentuated the negative. Men are more deeply concerned with the dangers of atomic warfare than they are entranced by the prospects of atomic plenty. They are making some efforts to adjust to the new era, but as yet their political and social orientation, like their policies, has not crossed the threshold of the new age. Their words suggest that they are aware of the dilemmas which face them, but their acts suggest that they are either unwilling or unable to take the stern measures which the new era demands. The policies which seem practicable are inadequate, and those which seem adequate are impracticable. It is imperative that we think realistically and soberly of the policies which are both adequate and possible, and of the political and social implications of the great technological advances of our age.

In this chapter we shall examine existing trends and possible developments in those areas most relevant to our study of international politics: (1) problems of strategy; (2) problems of national policy and international action; (3) the peaceful uses of atomic energy; and (4) the dilemma occasioned by the incompatibility of atomic science and pre-atomic concepts of interstate relations.

Strategy for the Atomic Age

While the fundamental principles of war have changed but little through the centuries, tactics and strategy have been altered as a result of new weapons and new threats to the balance of power. Each of the major technological developments in the art of warfare has given at least temporary advantage to the offensive. In the past, techniques of defense gradually caught up with those of offense, although wars became deadlier and

[15] *New York Times*, June 20, 1955.

[16] "After Civilization, What?" *Bulletin of the Atomic Scientists*, October, 1962, p. 4.

[17] Arnold J. Toynbee, *A Study of History* (New York: Oxford University Press, 1954), IX, 467–468.

[18] Baldwin, p. 317.

costlier as a result of improved weapons. Today those who are responsible for the protection of nations and of peoples seek desperately to provide that protection in an age of weapons of mass destruction. If war comes, how can they find adequate defense when guided missiles can paralyze vast areas and kill millions of people? Short of the abolition of war or effective control of weapons of mass destruction, what defense is possible? Even minimal armed forces and armaments, an extensive warning system, and preparations for national mobilization and civil defense impose staggering burdens and threaten to turn free nations into garrison states.

The Strategy of Defense

Nations have maintained conventional types of armed forces, partially, no doubt, owing to inertia and to bondage to outmoded methods and concepts of warfare; hence the familiar observation that states seem always to be preparing for the last war rather than for the next. But the need for conventional types of forces is still great. Even in an atomic war, not all action would be carried out by technicians engaged in directing super-bombs to predetermined targets. Furthermore, some men hope that the wars of the future will be limited ones, if wars there must be. American monopoly of the atom bomb may have averted a military showdown in the early postwar years, but it was not used by the United Nations forces in Korea, where combined units of the army, navy, and air force, armed with nonatomic weapons, fought an old-fashioned type of war under unfavorable conditions. In addition to their regular functions, in fact, regular units of the armed forces are now expected to undertake certain special tasks, so that while the need for certain types of units and weapons has decreased new assignments have been added. These include training in guerrilla warfare and in counterinsurgency, as well as in the use of the most sophisticated weapons and the most complicated aspects of political-military strategy.

Great offensive emphasis is now placed on the development of unconventional weapons and effective methods of delivery by piloted planes or guided missiles; defensive emphasis is on early warning systems, interception devices and techniques, target dispersion, duplication of key equipment, and variety of armaments. Effective integration of the armed services has become imperative. "The true meaning, tactically, of the technological revolution and of total war," wrote the distinguished military analyst of the *New York Times* in 1948, "is just this: it has forced a 'shotgun marriage' or rather an atomic-bomb marriage, of all the fighting services, and a grudging but growing recognition that military force is indivisible and that all forms of it are interdependent, not independent." "Functional definitions of service responsibilities are not easily established in the atomic age," he continued, "and will tend to become more and more blurred as weapons develop."[19]

National safety and national survival may well depend upon the ability to withstand a sudden, devastating surprise attack with atomic weapons, to launch an immediate and effective counterattack, to mobilize military and national resources so that the entire nation becomes a giant war machine, to sustain severe losses on the home front as well as among the military forces for an indefinite period of time, and to undertake operations from overseas bases and to coordinate these with actions of allies. While much depends on the development of strong military forces in being, even more depends upon the ability of the entire nation to gear itself for war. As General Eisenhower stated in 1948 in his final report as Army Chief of Staff, "the military establishment is only the cutting edge of the national machine through which de-

[19] *Ibid.*, p. 179.

structive force would be applied against an enemy." Supremely important, as General Eisenhower recognized, are the intangibles of national morale and the moral and spiritual reserves of a people.

While nations should work for peace in every possible way, they must at the same time give prime attention to problems of immediate national security. Even in peacetime this necessity now imposes acute strains on national budgets. Most expenditures are devoted to the maintenance of military forces and equipment in being, to research and development of new weapons, and to facilities and techniques of military defense. Less attention is being given to reducing vulnerability to atomic attack. This is in part due to the nature of the problem, for no real protection seems possible. All that can be hoped for is that precautionary measures will help to reduce the number of casualties and the extent of the destruction, especially to vital military and industrial installations. In general these relate to dispersal, decentralization, the preparation of underground shelters, the construction of buildings which incorporate heat-, blast-, and radiation-resisting features, civil defense, and disaster relief. Thus far, however, no nation has really done much to prepare itself against the hazards of atomic warfare, aside from emphasizing military preparedness.

In the United States, for example, federal, state, and local authorities appear to be working at cross purposes in the vital field of civil defense, and efforts to rally strong public support have been largely futile. In truth, the measures which are called for may impose impossible demands on the people, and may even be antithetical to the objectives of a free society. "Any major measures to minimize casualties — such as relocation of population . . . or deep underground construction of all urban buildings — would require a revolutionary interference by the government in individual choices, a revolution for which public support can hardly be envisaged."[20] Crowded cities would be prime targets for atomic bombs, especially if they are also vital industrial centers; but while there has been much talk about the need for de-urbanization in the United States — perhaps for esthetic and moral as well as for military reasons — very little has been done in this direction.

"The political, economic and psychological problems are so major," stated Hanson W. Baldwin, "that compulsory de-urbanization can safely be termed 'impossible'; at least in peacetime." But Baldwin believed that gradual decentralization should be encouraged. Specifically, he suggested decentralization through city planning, slum clearance, zoning laws, suburban "green belts," the dispersion of military installations to non-urban areas, and the decentralization of city administrations and of hospital, police, and fire-fighting facilities. He stressed the need for a restudy of power and communications systems, the breaking of transportation and communications bottlenecks, emergency radio communications systems, new water supply and purification systems, more buildings above ground of steel girders and concrete and at least "pilot underground plants" and stockpiles, a "coordinated and integrated civilian defense home front defense scheme," and evacuation plans for every major city. As for the nation's capital, the general nature of his recommendations is indicated in this terse statement: "Washington must both disperse and dig."[21] While these measures are less drastic than compulsory de-urbanization, they raise some of the same difficulties and problems, and very little progress is being made in implementing them. Apparently the United States is prepared militarily to wage atomic war and to act immediately in the event of attack; but, short of a miracle, if an atomic war comes, it will find Ameri-

[20] Coale, p. 62–63.

[21] Baldwin, p. 263. For his discussion of "Dispersion and Centralization," see pp. 252–265.

cans psychologically and physically unprepared.

The Limits of Deterrents

The major non-Communist states have pursued security through policies of "containment," "building situations of strength," "mutual security," "defense through deterrents," or "stalemate through deterrent strength." These interrelated policies carry no guarantee of even minimal security, but they are the best that statesmen can devise when the policies which they would like to follow seem to be out of the question. Present measures are based on the assumption that the best hope for security in a divided world is to be strong enough to resist by force threats to the peace and to make aggression and war unprofitable for the would-be aggressor.

The present deterrent-strength point of view has been voiced again and again by statesmen of the Western world and by writers on military strategy. As early as March 31, 1949, in an address at the Massachusetts Institute of Technology, Churchill pointed to the deterrent effect of the American monopoly of the atomic bomb. "I must not conceal from you . . . the truth as I see it," he said. "It is certain that Europe would have been communized like Czechoslovakia and London under bombardment some time ago but for the deterrent of the atomic bomb in the hands of the United States." After the Soviet Union was known to possess both the atomic and the hydrogen bomb, Churchill continued to place his faith in deterrent power. In a debate on defense policy in the House of Commons on March 1, 1955, he declared:

> Unless a trustworthy and universal agreement upon disarmament, conventional and nuclear alike, can be reached and an effective system of inspection is established and is actually working, there is only one sane policy for the free world in the next few years. That is what we call defense through deterrents. . . . All deterrents will improve and gain authority during the next ten years. By that time, the deterrent may well reach its acme and reap its final reward.

A year earlier Churchill had sought to reassure those who were concerned about the contradiction of a peace-loving state following a policy of this sort. "Peace is our aim," he asserted, "and strength is the only way of getting it. . . . We need not be deterred by the thought that we are trying to have it both ways at once. Indeed, it is only by having it both ways at once that we shall get a chance of getting anything of it at all."

American spokesmen have been less eloquent but no less forceful in championing the policy of "defense through deterrents." For example, speaking in Washington on October 12, 1955, the Secretary of the Air Force, Donald A. Quarles, said: "The road to peace is long and tortuous, and meanwhile we must maintain our strength at the ready." Although a potential aggressor may have the capacity to launch an atomic attack, continued Mr. Quarles, "we would be no less secure so long as we maintain the power to retaliate decisively. This proposition creates a stalemate through deterrent strength, which I believe is, paradoxically, our best hope of peace."

The student of international politics may wonder how long a "stalemate through deterrent strength" may be expected to last, and whether deterrents really deter. The strategy of deterrents has many disadvantages; it seems to run counter to the lessons of the past and the hopes for the future. Certainly, as Quincy Wright argued, "while the fear of retaliation is an important deterrent, it may not suffice to prevent war if power political rivalries continue with mounting tensions." Fear of retaliation is "a slender reed to lean upon."[22] Even if it helps to prevent war in

[22] Quincy Wright, *Problems of Stability and Progress in International Relations* (Berkeley: University of California Press, 1954), pp. 330, 312.

the immediate future, "a world in which two or more states were sitting on powder kegs powerful enough to destroy every major city on earth will be a world of half peace at best."[23] Indeed, as Wright warned, "efforts to achieve national security by exclusive reliance on either military superiority or a military balance are likely to achieve ruin for all."[24]

It may well be, as Winston Churchill has said, "that we shall, by a process of sublime irony, have reached a stage where safety will be the sturdy child of terror, and survival the twin brother of annihilation." If so, it is indeed a gloomy prospect, but one far less gloomy than that of atomic catastrophe, and one which at least holds out the hope that "somehow, something good will come of ill." The American authors of *The Hydrogen Bomb* summed up the situation in these words:

> Possession of the thermonuclear bomb holds no answer in itself and shows no way to a decent future. It simply prevents an immediate end to the future. The United States, certainly along with its allies, was caught in the unhappy stalemate President Eisenhower described in his memorable speech to the U.N. on benign uses of atomic energy. Yet it is inescapable that two atomic colossi are doomed for the time being "to eye each other malevolently across a trembling world." It can only be said that better this than a single atomic colossus — the Soviet Union — eyeing a trembling world.[25]

A strategy for the atomic age must deal with more than deterrents and "massive retaliation." Even if a major atomic war is averted, it by no means follows that there will not be localized wars or that the nations of the free world will not be faced with threats to their security by limited wars and "creeping aggression." One writer asserts that "the struggle between the free and Communist worlds will go on. . . . The era of strategic deadlock is less likely to see a peaceful world than a busily vicious one, boiling with limited wars. These will not necessarily be little wars. The only limitation is on the use of the ultimate strategic weapons against the Russian and American homelands." This situation has given rise to what has been called "the strategy of the double deterrent," which calls for a "tactical deterrent" as well as a "strategic deterrent," for responding to less-than-atomic threats with less-than-massive retaliation.[26]

The nth-Nation Problem

Only two countries should really be called atomic powers; the same two are the only nations possessing a stockpile of hydrogen bombs. Britain, an early member of the "nuclear club," has virtually dropped out of the atomic arms race, although she possesses a formidable nuclear arsenal. Two other countries, however, have forced their way into the club, even though the original members were reluctant to admit them and even though they are, as it were, Class B members. France under General de Gaulle insisted on making her own atomic bombs and early in 1960 began nuclear testing in the Sahara. By mid-1964 France claimed to have between 80 and 100 atom bombs of about the 20-kilatron range, and she was preparing for hydrogen bomb tests in the Pacific. China

[23] William T. R. Fox, in Bernard Brodie, ed., *The Absolute Weapon: Atomic Power and the World Order* (New York: Harcourt, Brace, 1946), p. 196.

[24] Wright, p. 330.

[25] James R. Shepley and Clair Blair, Jr., *The Hydrogen Bomb* (New York: David McKay Co., 1954), p. 228.

[26] During the Johnson-McNamara era in the United States a new doctrine of controlled and limited strategic warfare was developed. See Chester Ward, "The 'New Myths' and 'Old Realities' of Nuclear War," *Orbis*, VII (Summer, 1964), 275–291; and *Statement of Secretary of Defense Robert S. McNamara before the House Armed Services Committee on the Fiscal Year 1966–67 Defense Program and 1966 Defense Budget*, February 18, 1965.

gave notice of her success in the nuclear field by exploding a nuclear device in the Takla Makan Desert in Sinkiang in mid-October, 1964. Since then she has conducted further nuclear tests, and on June 17, 1967, she detonated a hydrogen bomb.

The development of nuclear weapons would seem to have added to the already disproportionate power of the major states of the world, especially the superpowers. There is, however, another important consideration. Uranium and thorium can be found in many places, including the territories or possessions of many lesser powers — Australia, Belgium, Czechoslovakia, Portugal, and South Africa, for example. Nuclear research is being carried on in many laboratories, and significant progress is being made in Holland, India, and elsewhere, as well as in the leading atomic-power states — the United States, the Soviet Union, Britain, France, Canada, and China. In the course of the proceedings of the International Conference on the Peaceful Uses of Atomic Energy, held in Geneva in the summer of 1955, it was disclosed that scientists of many countries were generally cognizant of the advances that had been made in the new field and had in fact made significant contributions of their own. These developments seemed to confirm the earlier view of observers that small states would soon be able to manufacture atomic weapons and would thereby be able to make aggression costly for even the most powerful state.[27] With the rapid progress in atomic research this point of view has been expressed more frequently. The atom bomb has been called "the great equalizer." Bernard Baruch harked back to a favorite saying of the American West: "Smith & Wesson makes all men equal." The same analogy was employed also by C. L. Sulzberger in 1954:

> The day is bound to come when not only Superpowers and Great Powers but also smaller nations will have access to atomic weapons and will regard them as conventional. The international balance has already altered as weak countries with large deposits of fissionable material have assumed new importance. It will alter again when little lands possess arms capable of blowing up the world. For the atom bomb will then become, among nations, the "equalizer" that the six-shooter was in the days of our own Wild West.[28]

A year later Thomas J. Hamilton declared that "so many countries now possess the capacity to split the atom that the pattern of the industrial revolution will not be repeated. . . . Such countries as India, Sweden, and Norway are now challenging the right of the pioneer atomic countries to dominate the new economy that is to be built on atomic reactors."[29]

Thus the diffusion of nuclear weapons, which the United States, the United Kingdom, and the Soviet Union have striven to prevent, is already under way. This creates the so-called *n*th-nation problem, which raises new dangers of the dispersion of atomic weapons among many countries. In 1965 one commentator wrote that besides the five nuclear powers "twenty-four additional countries — had they initiated nuclear programs by 1960 — could already or very soon be members of the nuclear club."[30] As a matter of fact, any nation

[27] See, for example, Jacob Viner, "Implications of the Atomic Bomb for International Relations," *American Philosophical Society Proceedings*, XC (January 29, 1946), 55.

[28] Dispatch from Paris, *New York Times*, November 20, 1954.

[29] "U.N. Debate Reflects Atom's Growing Role," *New York Times*, October 23, 1955.

[30] S. L. Harrison, "*N*th Nation Challenges: The Present Perspective," *Orbis*, IX (Spring, 1965), 159. Another estimate, made in 1959, suggested that eleven states, in addition to the United States, the United Kingdom, the Soviet Union, and France, had the technical capacity to embark on a nuclear weapons program in the near future, that eight others had the necessary technical skills but were handicapped by a shortage of scientific per-

which possesses one or more nuclear reactors can produce the basic materials for the manufacture of atomic bomb, although relatively few nations have the resources to become important atomic powers. Nuclear reactors are now in operation in at least fifty countries. While they are presumably being used for peaceful purposes, there is almost no way to prevent their secret use for military ends as well. Furthermore, reactors are no longer necessary for obtaining materials needed to make atomic bombs. "Rapid progress is being made in ultracentrifuge technology that may provide a cheaper way to separate explosive uranium 235 from ordinary uranium."[31] West Germany, Japan, the Netherlands, and perhaps other countries are already well along with experiments with the centrifugation process, which can produce fissionable materials much more easily and more cheaply than nuclear reactors. Before restrictions on their distribution were imposed by various bilateral agreements, centrifuges had been sold to Brazil, the U.A.R., China, and Cuba, and many other countries were interested in obtaining them.

In the foreseeable future, therefore, many nations will be able to make atomic weapons. Thus time is the ally of unrestrained nuclear diffusion, with all its attendant dangers.[32] This raises grave problems of strategy, and even graver problems of national and international policy. "The fundamental problem," as a distinguished American atomic physicist wrote in 1965, "is that the nuclear superpowers continue to rely on nuclear weapons as a major ingredient of their military forces, and that the threat of the use of nuclear weapons remains one of the main components in the conduct of international relations. . . . In the long run, the problem is one of restraint: self-restraint, on the part of the nonnuclear powers and the nuclear powers as well, and the development of those mutual restraints which come under the heading of international law and order."[33]

There are, however, definite limitations to the nuclear potential of the lesser powers. The capacity for waging effective atomic warfare still rests in the hands of a few states, at present only two. This capacity rests upon a complex economy and technology; it requires vast expenditures and constitutes a heavy drain upon both manpower and finances; it calls for elaborate early warning systems, costly civil defense measures, the maintenance of armed forces capable of fighting with both atomic and conventional weapons, quantities of effective carriers for nuclear weapons — whether long-range jet bombers or long-range and even intercontinental guided missiles — atomic-powered submarines, surface ships equipped to launch guided missiles, extensive and expensive research, both basic and applied, and other weapons, carriers, and techniques which only the major states can acquire or maintain. "It, therefore, seems unlikely," concluded Quincy Wright, "that under conditions of power politics any small state would have both the capacity and the opportunity to equip itself with atomic weapons. . . . Small states in a jungle world would assume suicidal risks if they attempted to defend themselves by atom bombs."[34]

Nevertheless, nuclear proliferation is one of the real threats in the international scene today, and efforts to prevent it may well prove to be abortive. The impact of the nuclear nonproliferation treaty cannot yet be adequately assessed. Some spokesmen of

sonnel, and that six or more were "probably economically capable" but lacked industrial resources and skilled manpower. Howard Simons, "World-Wide Capabilities for Production and Control of Nuclear Weapons," *Daedalus,* Vol. 88, No. 3 (Summer, 1959), 395.

[31] "Five Nuclear Powers . . . Now," *New York Times* editorial, January 10, 1965.

[32] See Harrison, pp. 169–170.

[33] Bernard T. Feld, "The Nonproliferation of Nuclear Weapons," *Bulletin of the Atomic Scientists,* December, 1964, pp. 5, 6.

[34] Wright, p. 313.

nonnuclear states argue that their countries should develop an independent nuclear capability, and that the members of the "nuclear club" have no right to try to confine its membership to the present select group. A minimum condition for agreement to a ban on nuclear proliferation, according to some of them, would be a willingness on the part of the atomic powers, especially the United States and the Soviet Union, to cease their production of nuclear weapons and to destroy a substantial part of their existing nuclear arsenals. As for bacteriological and chemical warfare, which seems to be within the capacity of small as well as of great powers, the potentialities are as frightening as they are obscure.

Policy for the Atomic Age: Specific Proposals

Many proposals have been advanced in support of a particular approach to a general policy for the atomic age. Nine of these have achieved some popularity. They may be listed as follows: (1) the abolition of war; (2) the establishment of some form of world government; (3) general disarmament; (4) the establishment of effective controls for atomic energy; (5) an agreement of major powers not to use atomic weapons; (6) an agreement of states possessing atomic energy production facilities to terminate all experiments with weapons of mass destruction; and (7) an agreement by the United States and the Soviet Union to scrap all existing stockpiles of nuclear weapons; (8) an agreement for the nonproliferation of nuclear weapons; and (9) a guarantee of protection against nuclear attack by the nuclear giants.

The first three of these proposals are general in nature, whereas the remaining relate specifically to atomic weapons. Proposals for the abolition of war, for world government, and for general disarmament have been made again and again. Since 1946 the United Nations, chiefly through its Atomic Energy Commission and later its Disarmament Commission, and since 1962 the Eighteen-Nation Committee on Disarmament, has been trying to secure agreement on plans for the international control of atomic energy — the fourth of the proposals — as well as on other steps toward disarmament and arms control. These efforts are analyzed in some detail in Chapter 13. The last five proposals, more limited in nature, call for some attention.

Proponents of an agreement to "ban the bomb" argue that, as a result of formal agreement and informal understandings, poison gas, though it was manufactured in quantity and in more and more deadly forms, was not used to any extent during World War II, and that there seems to be a good prospect that bacteriological warfare can be averted in the same way. Why, then, cannot nuclear weapons be so regarded or rather disregarded?

The answer to this question is painfully obvious. There may be some arguments in favor of obtaining a clear pledge by the atomic powers that they will never use the fearful weapons in their possession, but this pledge may be of little value in the event of a global war. It may, in fact, embarrass and handicap peace-loving nations that wish to live up to their commitment at a time when their survival is threatened by an enemy who has already violated a similar commitment. The Einstein-Russell statement of July, 1955, emphasized the illusory nature of this "solution." "Whatever agreements not to use H-bombs had been reached in time of peace," the statement read, "they would no longer be considered binding in time of war, and both sides would set to work to manufacture H-bombs as soon as war broke out, for, if one side manufactured the bombs and the other did not, the side that manufactured them would inevitably be victorious."[35] In time of war all promises, vows, and com-

[35] For the text of this statement, see the *New York Times,* July 10, 1955.

mitments might give way to the urge for national survival.

During the H-bomb tests at Bikini in March, 1954, some Japanese fishermen within the range of the fall-out following the explosion suffered grave injury. This misadventure led to an outburst of anti-American feeling in Japan and became an international incident. It also led to renewed demands from many parts of the world, and most strongly from India, that further experiments of the kind be suspended pending an international agreement on disarmament. Support for this demand came from those concerned with the moral and political issues involved, and from those who feared that the experimental explosion of increasingly powerful atomic weapons would result in huge casualties. Speculation about the radiation and other effects of bigger and better blasts ran the gamut from confidence in scientific controls to science-fiction pictorial representations of the earth in fragments. A combination of risks too great to take and growing pressure from many quarters have curtailed nuclear tests, at least for the time being. On October 31, 1958, the United States announced a voluntary moratorium on testing, and was joined by the Soviet Union four days later. This unofficial moratorium lasted until September 1, 1961, when the Soviets resumed testing (leading the United States to follow suit with underground testing on April 25, 1962). After protracted negotiations a nuclear test ban treaty was approved by the United States, the U.S.S.R., and the United Kingdom at a conference in Moscow in the summer of 1963. This historic treaty was signed by the foreign ministers of the three main atomic powers on August 5, 1963, and officially entered into force on October 10. It was soon adhered to by over a hundred states. The treaty was a limited one, for it did not cover underground testing and it avoided "the controversial issues of on-site inspection, control posts, and international control bodies"; but it was "the most encouraging and most widely hailed brake on the arms race and on the proliferation of nuclear weapons."[36]

A variation of these two approaches calls not only for agreements to refrain from using nuclear weapons and from making further tests but also for the destruction of all existing stockpiles. Sometimes this proposal has come from rather surprising sources. Communist China, for example, has refused to take part in disarmament discussions or even to sign the nuclear test ban treaty; but her announcement of the explosion of a nuclear device in mid-October, 1964, contained a proposal for a world summit conference to discuss "the question of the complete prohibition and thorough destruction of nuclear weapons." Some of the supporters of this proposal have urged the United States to take the initiative in this gesture of faith, regardless of the action of the Soviet Union. A leading spokesman for this point of view, C. Rajagopalachari, veteran leader in India's struggle for independence and a former governor-general of independent India, has taken this position. In a letter to the *New York Times,* printed on December 26, 1954, he argued that "it is possible yet to save mankind . . . through tremendous courage — courage against one's own fear. . . . Salvation consists in unilateral action, in courage and in the fundamental faith that the good ultimately triumphs." Having laid down this philosophical premise, Rajagopalachari issued a call: "Let each not wait for the other but unilaterally let us throw all atom bombs in the deep Antartic and begin a new world free from fear." The United States — "she who committed the mistake first" — should lead the way. "She is morally big enough to do it. . . . If America does it, the whole world will rally round her as men rally round a hero or a god." And

[36] "Issues Before the Nineteenth General Assembly," *International Conciliation,* No. 550 (November, 1964), pp. 28–29.

what would the Soviet Union do if the United States by this act of faith gave her virtual monopoly of nuclear weapons? Rajagopalachari was ready with his answer: "It would be impossible for the party that lags to use this dreadful weapon thereafter." Apparently this would be impossible because of "the secret power of the good."

In 1967 the United States and the Soviet Union achieved a rare degree of cooperation in drafting a proposed treaty for the nonproliferation of nuclear weapons, which was referred to the Eighteen Nation Disarmament Committee in Geneva and to the spring session of the Twenty-second General Assembly of the United Nations, in the hope that it would be recommended to all nations and approved by at least the majority of them. Some countries had serious reservations about the treaty, even though they were in favor of its objectives. India, for example, held that the proposed treaty was a one-sided affair, for the nuclear giants were asking other nations to foreswear nuclear arms permanently while they themselves would make no concessions to reduce their own nuclear stockpiles or cease the manufacture of nuclear weapons. India also argued that she had to keep a nuclear option open in the event of further trouble with Communist China, which obviously would not adhere to the nonproliferation treaty.

In March, 1968, the United States, the Soviet Union, and Britain agreed to sponsor a joint resolution, to be referred to the Eighteen Nation Disarmament Committee and the UN Security Council, agreeing to defend any nation renouncing nuclear weapons from atomic attack. This commitment made the proposed nuclear nonproliferation treaty more attractive to many countries, although some expressed grave doubts regarding the credibility of the nuclear guarantee. On July 1, 1968, representatives of the United States, the Soviet Union, the United Kingdom, and 58 other countries signed the treaty in parallel ceremonies in Washington, London, and Moscow. Nonsigners included the two lesser nuclear powers, France and Communist China, and a number of other important states, including West Germany, Japan, Brazil, and India, which had serious reservations regarding the treaty. Thus, in spite of widespread adherence to the nonproliferation treaty, the problems of the prevention of the spread of nuclear weapons and of effective guarantees remained largely unresolved.

Some of the proposals for meeting the present crisis would require profound changes in international relationships, while others would deal more specifically with vital areas of danger. While some appear to hold no promise of effectiveness, others, however plausible they may be, seem unattainable in anything like the foreseeable future. Where, then, does this leave us? Surely, short of efforts to attain the unattainable, or of reliance on faith and religion and the power of good, something can be done to deal with the conditions which underlie present anxieties and to enable nations to live together without atomic war while on the "plateau of suspense." This will have to be more than a "new look" in Soviet foreign policy and more than bold proposals by the friends of peace. In part men must learn to live with their problems, even with those created by the advent of the nuclear era. But new measures will have to reinforce the more conventional approaches, and in fact are already doing so. These may be less dramatic than the proposals we have been examining, but some of them are even now being tested and implemented as they prove to be feasible. In the opinion of Quincy Wright, "relative security must be sought in political processes for changing opinions and conciliating differences." Wright sees grounds for hope in "peaceful means of education, discussion, and negotiation for modifying the opinions and intentions of both Russians and Americans so that they will better relate their needs to the changing conditions of the world."[37] We shall return in the following chapter to the subject of a path to the future.

Peaceful Uses of Atomic Energy

On August 6, 1955, ten years to the day after the bombing of Hiroshima, a United Nations-sponsored International Conference on the Peaceful Uses of Atomic Energy opened in Geneva. For two weeks delegates and observers from seventy-two nations, including the Soviet Union and other Communist states, exchanged views on the implications and possibilities of atomic power. For a decade the emphasis had been upon using that power to develop more powerful weapons of destruction, but at Geneva it was upon using the new source of energy for human betterment. There could be no question of the potential significance of the conference, especially since scientists from the "iron curtain" countries were also there. It "could be history's most portentous gathering," declared C. L. Sulzberger of the *New York Times.* "We are on the verge of unmapped revolutions. Over unending centuries, sources of power have been limited and costly. . . . Now energy is about to become almost limitless and free."[38] His colleague William L. Laurence, science editor of the *Times,* agreed with this interpretation:

> . . . nuclear energy . . . offers the greatest promise in history to increase greatly the world's food supply, to prolong life, to conquer disease, and, in general, to create a better life for the world's millions everywhere. . . . Unlike coal and oil, which are expected to be exhausted in less than a century, nuclear fuels, uranium and thorium, are expected to last thousands of years. And scientists are confident that within a decade or so they will learn how to use the lighter elements, such as "heavy hydrogen" and lithium, now used in the hydrogen bomb, as vast sources of controlled power. When this secret has been mastered — and progress in this direction is already being made — man will have fuels enough to last him for as long as the sun itself will keep life going on this planet.[39]

The first International Conference on the Peaceful Uses of Atomic Energy had been made possible not only by great advances in atomic research but also by certain developments in the political realm. The Geneva Conference could not have been held on the same scale and with the same frankness if the "new look" had not produced a greater degree of cooperation on the part of the Soviet Union, and if the earlier "summit" conference had not helped to clear the atmosphere for meetings on the nonpolitical and scientific level. Other conferences of the same magnitude were held in 1958 and 1964, in Geneva, and meetings on special aspects of the general subject of atomic power for peaceful uses are being held with increasing frequency.

In the meantime, research continues and significant discoveries are being made. Some of these pertain to fundamental research — for example, the discovery in October, 1955, of a new atomic particle, the antiproton, created from energy generated in the world's most powerful atom-smasher, the bevatron, in Berkeley, California. Other discoveries relate to applications of basic knowledge — for example, nuclear reactors which produce great quantities of heat, electricity, and radioactive substances, and atomic-powered submarines. "Man-made radioactive elements . . . open virtually limitless vistas as the most powerful agents for the treatment of disease, and a 'searchlight' into the living labyrinth of many of nature's most vital processes."[40]

[37] Wright, pp. 330, 331.

[38] Dispatch from Geneva, *New York Times,* August 8, 1955.

[39] Dispatch from Geneva, *New York Times,* August 7, 1955.

[40] William L. Laurence, dispatch from Geneva, *New York Times,* August 7, 1955.

In December, 1953, in an address to the General Assembly of the United Nations, President Eisenhower advanced a proposal for the pooling of atomic resources, under the aegis of the UN, for peaceful purposes. This atoms-for-peace proposal was widely discussed in the United Nations and throughout the world. In addition to the Geneva meeting, its fruits to date have been the encouragement of research in many countries and the sharing of the results, and the establishment of the International Atomic Energy Agency in 1957. Although it has less authority and scope than the United States proposed for it, the IAEA is playing a central role in serving as an international clearinghouse for nuclear materials for peaceful uses and for information on significant trends and developments in the field of atomic research and on their possible applications in such fields as agriculture, industry, and medicine. About eighty countries are associated with the Agency. The leading atomic powers and the leading uranium producers have semipermanent membership on the board of governors. The emphasis on the use of atomic energy for constructive purposes is helping to right the imbalance that existed during the first decade of the atomic age, which, born in wartime, tended to give priority to the development of nuclear weapons.

Wisdom out of Extremity?

Within one post-Hiroshima decade, wrote C. L. Sulzberger in 1955, "the entire world power relationship has altered."[41] The failure to achieve satisfactory peace settlements with the major defeated nations, the growing split between the Communist and non-Communist worlds, the rise of sensitive new nations afflicted with bitter memories and unstable economies and governments, the pressures of nationalism and of "the revolution of rising expectations," and other developments created more than enough crucial issues and problems to test the capacities of statesmen and institutions. The advent of the nuclear age made the era of transition infinitely more trying, for unprecedented power had emerged at a time of unprecedented political, moral, and spiritual crisis. It seemed to be difficult, as Bertrand Russell wrote a few years ago, "to persuade mankind to acquiesce in its own survival."

The atomic age burst suddenly upon the world, and its implications cannot be fully assessed for many decades. Sir Winston Churchill stated in March, 1955, that with the appearance of the hydrogen bomb "the entire foundation of human affairs was revolutionized and mankind placed in a situation both measureless and laden with doom." Two months later Aneurin Bevan, not Churchill's greatest admirer, flatly declared: "The hydrogen bomb has completely revolutionized international relationships." It would be more accurate to say that the hydrogen bomb has revolutionized the conditions under which international relations must henceforth be carried on, but that it has not yet revolutionized international relationships. In due time — unless disaster wins the race — the fundamental changes in technology may lead to equally fundamental changes in political and social institutions and in international relations. But so far in the atomic age the state system, which has been around for a long time, is still the dominant pattern of international relations, and many pre-atomic problems are being dealt with — or are not being dealt with — in the old pre-atomic ways. Political leaders, foreign ministers, and diplomats carry on pretty much as usual. They may move around more rapidly, and they may pay more attention to popular pressures and to scientific developments, but their methods and, in many cases, their mental orientation, have not changed a great deal.

In our study of international relations we must pay particular attention to existing

[41] Dispatch from Paris, *New York Times,* June 20, 1955.

practices and approaches, but we must never forget the vast changes in the world scene and in the "human situation" resulting from the startling developments in the nuclear field. In the words of the late Senator Brien McMahon, who labored mightily to make his fellow-Americans aware of the full implications of the atomic age: "It is our solemn obligation, I think, to lift our eyes above the lesser problems that seem to monopolize our time and to discuss and act upon what, by any standard, is the supreme problem before our country and the world."

Despite the persistence of traditional procedures and attitudes in high places, one of the encouraging notes of the present day is the growing awareness of the significance of the changes that are occurring, and a growing earnestness in the search for policies and outlooks which will be practical and adequate in the atomic age. On the other hand, the magnitude of present dangers has encouraged pessimism and cynicism; it has induced in some a state of resignation and in others a feeling of panic; it has led nations to give priority to measures of national security and defense at the expense of positive contributions to the improvement of living standards throughout the world and to human relations; it has aggravated ideological and other basic differences between nations, and has made real accommodation and real improvement in the international atmosphere difficult. And the uninvited guest present at all deliberations is the unseen but powerful atom. It may yet, indeed, "revolutionize international relationships." Perhaps the growing recognition of both the promise and the danger will light the way out of the present darkness. In the same article in which he voiced the lament that "truly our imagination is not in step with our era," Paul-Henri Spaak wrote in a more hopeful vein:

> Around the atomic bomb is being built a whole strategy, a whole policy, perhaps even, in outline, a philosophy. Out of our very extremity may come wisdom, out of the frightening means of destruction may come the means of assuring peace. What men in the past have sought to make prevail by persuasion, by appealing to humane feelings, may in the end be achieved because the insensate machine inexorably imposes it. Technical progress may indirectly produce moral and social progress. If so, what an extraordinarily crooked road it would have been that led toward the good![42]

The Space Age — Its International Implications

Mankind had hardly begun to accustom itself to the atomic age when another vast new dimension was added by the advent of the space age. The birthday of the space age was October 4, 1957, when the Soviet Union successfully launched the first man-made satellite. Known as Sputnik I, this 184-pound satellite moved in an orbit ranging from 125 to 560 miles above the earth's surface until it burned out three months after its launching. A month after Sputnik I was launched, a second Soviet satellite, more than six times heavier and carrying a live dog, followed, traveling between 140 and 1021 miles above the earth until it burned out in mid-April, 1958. By that time three small United States satellites, Explorer I, Vanguard I, and Explorer III, had been successfully orbited. Vanguard I, weighing only 3.25 pounds, was expected to stay up at least 200 years. The first heavy American satellite was an Atlas missile weighing about 8800 pounds; launched on December 18, 1958, it remained aloft for about 20 days. Other Soviet and American satellites followed in rapid succession.

The launching of Sputnik I caused a worldwide sensation. The space age, with all its untold possibilities, had begun. Even in its first decade it witnessed dramatic feats that would have staggered the imagination of a science fiction writer a few years before.

After pioneering with Sputnik I, the Soviet

[42] Spaak, p. 358.

Partymiller in The York (Pa.) Gazette and Daily

It's later than we think.

scientists next turned their attention toward the moon. On September 12, 1959, the Soviets launched a rocket which two days later crashed on the surface of the moon. In early October of the same year the Soviet Union put a satellite into orbit around both the earth and the moon, and a few days later cameras in this satellite took and relayed back to earth the first photographs ever obtained of the far side of the moon.

Probing interplanetary space, in May, 1961, a Soviet satellite passed within 60,000 miles of Venus after a flight of more than 50 million miles. Late in October an American satellite — Mariner II — was launched with Mars as its target some six months later. Like the Soviet satellite this scored a near miss. Conceivably interplanetary travel might be possible with present technology. Interstellar travel would not, until and unless some major new breakthrough in technology and space engineering occurred.

Man-made objects had conquered space. The next step was for man himself to enter the space age by riding in satellites of his own making. Again the Russians led the way. On April 12, 1961, Major Yuri Gagarin of the Soviet Union was launched into space in a five-ton satellite spaceship and, after making one orbit of the earth at altitudes ranging from 110 to 187 miles, landed in Soviet territory 108 minutes later. The United States, which had also been preparing for the same feat, sent two astronauts, Alan B. Shepard, Jr. and Virgil I. Grissom, on suborbital flights on May 5 and July 21, 1961; but before American astronauts could duplicate Gagarin's achievement another Russian cosmonaut, Gherman Titov, had surpassed it. On August 6–7, 1961, Titov made 17 orbits around the earth, and covered a distance of 435,000 miles in a little over 25 hours.

The United States finally put a man in space on February 20, 1962, when Colonel John Glenn made three orbits around the earth, and traveled some 81,000 miles in just under five hours. By mid-1963 four Russians and four Americans had made orbital flights. Time in space, number of orbits, and miles logged increased rapidly, and as spacecraft became more sophisticated new exploits were attempted. Walks in space, the docking of capsules, and difficult manuevers advanced the skill and knowledge that would be required for the conquest of space.

Both the United States and the Soviet Union have embarked on fantastically expensive and complicated programs to land men on the moon, as well as projects for manned explorations in interplanetary space. "Within our foreseeable future," wrote an American scientist in 1963, "there are likely to be colonies of men on the moon, living and extracting water and minerals to support further explorations into space."[43]

Thus within a few years after the advent of the space age various kinds of satellites were orbiting the earth, several manned spacecraft flights had been successfully made, satellites had been sent to and around the moon, Venus, and Mars, and projects to send men to the moon or even beyond were being launched with every confidence of success. Truly the sky was no longer the limit.

The probes into outer space were gigantic triumphs of technology and human ingenuity, and opened up new sources of knowledge and new vistas for human endeavor.[44] The many cooperative space programs which were carried out during the International Geophysical Year (an 18-month period from July, 1957, through December, 1958) demonstrated that the opportunities for peaceful cooperation of nations in outer space were tremendous. Satellites, manned or unmanned, could be used for weather forecasting, for astronomical observations above the earth's atmosphere, and for worldwide radio, television, and telephone communications. In 1962 a privately owned American enterprise put the first communications satellite — Telstar — into orbit, and thereby enabled the United States to take the first step "toward achieving a revolutionary new global communications system in space."[45] Cooperation in this field has been impressive. By 1964 a number of communications satellites were in orbit, and eighteen nations were involved in interim arrangements for multilateral ownership and management of a global system being developed by the United States Communications Satellite Corporation, a private undertaking.[46] All members of the International Telecommunications Union were eligible for membership. The value of such transcontinental communications facilities was dramatically demonstrated in 1964 when millions of people in many parts of the world watched the Olympic Games in Tokyo on live telecasts.

Other examples of multinational cooperation in space research and operations could be cited. The Soviet Union has participated in some of these and has cooperated with the United States in exchanging satellite weather data, and data on space biology and space medicine, as well as in other ways.[47] There is even some prospect of cooperation between the two leaders in "the race for space" in the major endeavor of sending manned spacecraft to the moon and in any programs which may follow this gigantic achievement.

Many unmanned satellites are now orbiting the earth, and there is every prospect that

[43] Franklin Pierce Huddle, "National Materials Policy" (unpublished article, 1963).

[44] *New York Times*, July 11, 1962.

[45] *Ibid.*, July 25, 1964.

[46] See *The Next Ten Years in Space, 1959–1969* (Washington, D.C.: Government Printing Office, 1959).

[47] U.N. Document A/AC.105/C.1/L.6, 21 April 1964.

manned satellites can also be kept aloft for almost any length of time. In fact, it has been suggested that "a manned satellite could be equipped to be completely and permanently independent of the earth."[48] The possible uses of manned and unmanned space satellites and space stations are virtually limitless. They can add new dimensions to the existence of earthbound human beings, and they can also threaten man's existence.[49] Space ships, satellites, and stations can be used for launching or directing guided missiles, for providing an attack warning and reconnaissance system, for applying new methods of weather prediction and communications to military purposes. Space war above the planet, and even missile launching bases on the moon, are not wholly fantastic possibilities. Some commentators have spoken in terms that sound like a new kind of geopolitics — space geopolitics — and have declared that "the race for space" is a race for the control of man's future. "Of one thing we may be sure," wrote General James M. Gavin in a widely read book, written at the very beginning of the space age, "the nation that first achieves the control of outer space will control the destiny of the human race."[50] Shortly after he learned of astronaut Gordon Cooper's flight into space on May 15, 1963, Senator Stuart Symington remarked: "As has been well said, once those who controlled the ground controlled the world; and then those who controlled the sea; and now the air; and tomorrow the leaders of this universe will be those who control space."[51]

These considerations have lent urgency to the evolving of international agreements on the use of space. "After the first Sputnik went into orbit in October 1957, the subject of outer space came down to earth, and men began to think in terms of how best to ensure its rational peaceful utilization."[52] In this effort the United Nations General Assembly and many other UN committees and agencies have played a major coordinating role. The first formal request for General Assembly consideration was made by the Soviet Union on March 15, 1958. The Secretary-General of the United Nations called for an agreement that "outer space, and the celestial bodies therein, are not considered as capable of appropriation by any State," and for "an assertion of the over-riding interest of the community of nations in the peaceful and beneficial use of outer space."[53]

In late 1958 the Thirteenth Session of the General Assembly established an ad hoc committee of eighteen nations (five of its members — the U.S.S.R., Poland, Czechoslovakia, India, and the U.A.R. — did not participate in its deliberations) to consider problems relating to the peaceful uses of outer space. In December, 1959, the Fourteenth Session transformed this committee into a larger Committee on the Peaceful Uses of Outer Space. This committee and its two major sub-committees — the Legal, and the Scientific and Technical Sub-Committees — have been very active since they began functioning in 1961. They were largely responsible for two important resolutions of the General Assembly. The first, adopted in December, 1961, incorporated the principles that international law applies to outer space and to celestial bodies and that both are free for exploration and are not subject to appropriation by any nation. Then on December 13, 1963, the General Assembly agreed on a

[48] Article on "Satellite, man-made" in *The Columbia-Viking Desk Encyclopedia* (New York: Dell, 1965), p. 1635.

[49] See Lincoln P. Bloomfield, ed., *Outer Space: Prospects for Man and Society* (Englewood Cliffs, N.J.: Prentice-Hall, 1962), a volume prepared for the American Assembly.

[50] *War and Peace in the Space Age* (New York: Harper, 1958), p. 248.

[51] Broadcast over Radio Station KFUO, St. Louis, May 15, 1963.

[52] "Issues Before the Fourteenth General Assembly," *International Conciliation*, No. 524 (September, 1959), p. 26.

[53] General Assembly, Official Records, 13th Session, 1958, Supplement No. 1A, p. 3.

Declaration of Legal Principles Governing the Activities of States in the Exploration and Use of Outer Space. Many states, including both the United States and the Soviet Union, have announced their acceptance of the principles embodied in this declaration, which has been hailed as a possible first step in the development of a comprehensive code of space law. The object of all of these efforts is of course much broader than to achieve a code of space law. As the General Assembly's ad hoc committee on the peaceful uses of outer space declared in its report of July, 1959, in an unexpected burst of eloquence, the fundamental objective is to gain acceptance of the proposition that "space activities must to a large extent be an effort of Planet Earth as a whole."[54]

The international implications of the space age are obviously enormous. Peaceful cooperation in outer space could give new dimensions to the human story and could contribute to peaceful cooperation on earth as well. An "outer space race for national beachheads in the universe,"[55] or a concentration on military space programs rather than on the peaceful uses of outer space, could be costly and even disastrous for the human race. In any event, international relations must henceforth deal with the activities of nations and other organized groupings beyond as well as on the earth.

SUGGESTIONS FOR FURTHER READING

ARON, RAYMOND. *The Great Debate: Theories of Nuclear Strategy,* translated by Ernst Pawel. Garden City, N.Y.: Doubleday & Company, 1964.

BEATON, LEONARD and JOHN MADDOX. *The Spread of Nuclear Weapons.* Studies in International Security, No. 5. New York: Frederick A. Praeger, for the Institute for Strategic Studies, 1962. A consideration of the present situation and future prospects, with a discussion of "nine leading cases."

BIORKLUND, ELIS. *Atomic Policies, 1945–54.* Princeton, N.J.: D. Van Nostrand Co., 1955.

BLAKETT, P. M. S. *Military and Political Consequences of Atomic Energy.* London, 1948. Published in the United States in 1949 under the title *Fear, War and the Bomb.* A highly controversial book.

BLOOMFIELD, LINCOLN P., ed. *Outer Space: Prospects for Man and Society.* Englewood Cliffs, N.J.: Prentice-Hall, 1962. Papers prepared for the 20th American Assembly.

BRODIE, BERNARD, ed. *The Absolute Weapon: Atomic Power and World Order.* New York: Harcourt, Brace, 1946.

BUCHAN, ALASTAIR, ed. *A World of Nuclear Powers?* Englewood Cliffs, N.J.: Prentice-Hall, 1966. Papers prepared for an International Assembly on Nuclear Weapons, held in Toronto, Canada, in June, 1966.

BURCHARD, JOHN E., ed. *Mid-Century: The Social Implications of Scientific Progress.* Cambridge, Mass.: The Technology Press, and New York: Wiley, 1950. Speeches and discussions at Mid-Century Convocation of M.I.T., March 31, April 1 and 2, 1949.

BUSH, VANNEVAR. *Modern Arms and Free Men.* New York: Simon and Schuster, 1949.

COALE, ANSLEY J. *The Problem of Reducing Vulnerability to Atomic Bombs.* Princeton, N.J.: Princeton University Press, 1947. Report prepared for the Committee on Social and Economic Effects of Atomic Energy of the Social Science Research Council.

COUSINS, NORMAN. *Modern Man Is Obsolete.* New York: The Viking Press, 1945.

GAVIN, JAMES M. *War and Peace in the Space Age.* New York: Harper, 1958.

GOLDSEN, JOSEPH M., ed. *Outer Space in World Politics.* New York: Frederick A. Praeger, 1963. Thoughtful essays by Karl Deutsch,

[54] U.N. Document A/4141, 14 July 1959, p. 28.

[55] Pierre J. Huss, "U.N. Code on Space Claims Could Rank as Vital Treaty," *Philadelphia Inquirer,* November 15, 1964.

Klaus Knorr, Thomas Schelling, Gabriel Almond, and others.

GOLOVINE, M. N. *Conflict in Space: A Pattern of War in a New Dimension.* London, 1962.

HASKINS, CARYL. *The Scientific Revolution and World Politics.* New York: Harper & Row, for the Council on Foreign Relations, 1964.

LAPP, RALPH E. *Man and Space: The Next Decade.* New York: Harper & Row, 1961. A distinguished scientist and writer on atomic energy places space research in scientific and historical perspective.

MASTERS, DEXTER and KATHERINE WAY, eds. *One World or None.* New York: McGraw-Hill Book Company, 1946. A collection of essays by outstanding scientists and others.

ODISHAW, HUGH, ed. *The Challenges of Space.* Chicago: University of Chicago Press, 1962. Based on a special issue on outer space of the *Bulletin of the Atomic Scientists*, May–June, 1961.

OGBURN, WILLIAM F., ed. *Technology and International Relations.* Chicago: University of Chicago Press, 1949.

RAMO, SIMON, ed. *Peacetime Uses of Outer Space.* New York: McGraw-Hill Book Company, 1961.

ROSENCRANCE, R. N., ed. *The Dispersion of Nuclear Weapons: Strategy and Politics.* New York: Columbia University Press, 1964. Contains a comprehensive annotated bibliography.

SCHWARTZ, LEONARD E. *International Organizations and Space Cooperation.* Durham, N.C.: World Rule of Law Center, Duke University, 1962.

SHEPLEY, JAMES R. and CLAY BLAIR, JR. *The Hydrogen Bomb.* New York: David McKay Co., 1954.

SHILS, E. A. *Atomic Bombs in World Politics.* London, 1948.

SLESSOR, SIR JOHN. *Strategy for the West* New York: William Morrow & Co., 1954

SMYTH, HENRY DE WOLF. *Atomic Energy for Military Purposes.* Princeton, N.J.: Princeton University Press, 1945. The official report on the development of the atomic bomb.

The Next Ten Years in Space, 1959–1960. Washington, D.C.: Government Printing Office, 1959. A summary of thinking by government experts on the national space program.

WENDT, GERALD. *Atomic Energy and the Hydrogen Bomb.* New York: McBride Company, 1950.

WIESNER, JEROME B. *Where Space and Politics Meet.* New York: McGraw-Hill Book Company, 1965. By a former scientific adviser to President Kennedy.

WRIGHT, QUINCY. *Problems of Stability and Progress in International Relations.* Berkeley: University of California Press, 1954. Especially Chapter 20, "The Atomic Bomb and World Politics."

25 The International System in Transition

At a time when man's scientific and technological achievements have almost dwarfed the wildest predictions of science fiction writers, his progress in evolving satisfactory political, economic, and social patterns and institutions has been alarmingly limited. Nowhere is the lag more obvious than in international relations, which by and large are still carried on in ways that would be familiar to students and diplomats of the pre-atomic age. This would not be a particularly noteworthy or serious situation if the old ways were still effective, of if they served the needs of the new era; but there is increasing evidence that they are not adequate and that new patterns and approaches are urgently needed.

There are many indications that we are living in a period of systematic change, which will lead to new and radical shifts in international relationships. Possibly, as Max Lerner has suggested, "we are witnessing the beginning of the end of classical world politics," which was characterized by a world of nation-states, based on the concept of sovereignty, applying the principles of the balance of power, with war as a frequent result of the internal failures and external pressures.[1] If so, many of the vestiges of the "classical" system are still with us, and the system as a whole exhibits an astonishing capacity for survival and persistence under rapidly changing world conditions.

It may well be that the nation-state system, with its concept of sovereignty, is an anachronism in today's world; yet it is already taking new forms and has become worldwide in scope. But it is doubtful that it will ever again be as dominant or as all-inclusive as it appeared to be in the Western world in the nineteenth and early twentieth centuries. What kind of international system will emerge after the nation-state system ceases to be the dominant form of institutionalized life is by no means clear, especially in the present era of cross-currents and countervailing pressures and trends.

All this is simply another way of saying that this is an era of transition, when old patterns and institutions are proving to be increasingly inadequate to modern needs but when few satisfactory substitutes have yet stood the test of practical application. "We

[1] Max Lerner, *The Age of Overkill: A Preface to World Politics* (New York: Simon and Schuster, 1962), p. 10.

are still," wrote former UN Secretary-General Dag Hammarskjold in 1960, "in the transition between institutional systems of international co-existence and constitutional systems of international co-operation."[2] The former emerged from and are quite compatible with the nation-state system; together with the normal channels of diplomacy, they provide the main mechanisms through which the nation-states conduct affairs today. Meanwhile, innumerable proposals for developing the latter have been prepared, but few have advanced beyond the experimental, or even the blueprint, stage. National sovereignty, with all that it implies, still blocks the way to effective "constitutional systems of international cooperation," even though sovereignty has lost much of its former significance and meaning and even though much of the international relations today can be carried out effectively only if the nation-states will accept limitations on their freedom of action in their own interest as well as in the interest of the world community as a whole. Thus the world is in an early stage of the transition to which the former UN Secretary-General referred, although it must be remembered that he was speaking only of formal systems, structures, and institutions, which usually lag far behind the underlying changes in national and international life.

Technological developments, which have opened up new vistas of human progress, have added to "the world-wide insecurity which is the fate of modern man." The consequences of this dilemma are well summarized by Reinhold Niebuhr:

> Our problem is that technics have established a rudimentary world community but have not integrated it organically, morally or politically. They have created a community of mutual dependence, but not one of mutual trust and respect. Without this higher integration, advancing technics tend to sharpen economic rivalries within a general framework of economic interdependence; they change the ocean barriers of yesterday into the battlegrounds of today; and they increase the deadly efficacy of the instruments of war so that vicious circles of mutual fear may end in atomic conflicts and mutual destruction. To these perplexities an ideological conflict has been added, which divides the world into hostile camps.[3]

Just why is mankind again at the old familiar crossroads? What is the enemy that must be defeated before man can regain hope for that "better world"? Is the answer in political or politico-economic terms, such as aggression, capitalism, communism, nationalism, or sovereignty? Or is it in social terms, such as illiteracy, overpopulation, poverty, or racial discrimination? Or is it in more personal terms, such as corruption, greed, immorality, irreligion, or just plain human nature? Or it is a composite of many or all of these?

The vital issue is the capacity of men to devise a regime of peace that also carries with it some assurance of security and well-being. Each generation poses the issue anew — each in its own set of concrete terms. If we may believe the lessons of history, once the present impasse has been resolved we shall pass on to new names and new threats of aggression. It is more sensible to ask if the repetition will ever cease than to ask if the present threat will be the last. We know that there is seldom finality in history.

Old issues have a new urgency. The human situation has drastically changed in many vital respects. As Toynbee has pointed out, for the first time in history man has at his disposal the knowledge and the facilities

2 Dag Hammarskjold, *Perspectives on Peace, 1910–1960* (New York: Frederick A. Praeger, for the Carnegie Endowment for International Peace, 1960), p. 65.

3 "The Illusion of World Government," *Foreign Affairs*, XXVII (April, 1949), 379.

for providing a decent standard of livelihood for virtually the entire human race. He also has at his disposal, again for the first time in history, "power without limit," capable of destroying countless millions of people, entire nations, and even civilizations. Conditions and problems which in the past have led to breakdown of the international system, to recurrent tensions and frequent wars, still exist; they have, in fact, been intensified by the acceleration in the pace of events, by the expansion of the theater of international relations to embrace the whole world, and all the world's peoples, to a degree never known before, and by the untold dangers, as well as the untold promise, of the nuclear and space age.

On the enlarged screen on which international relations are played these days, everything seems to be magnified beyond normal size. The outlook is clearly for continued instability and unrest, and for continued social, economic, and political tensions. These are normal characteristics of international life, especially in a transitional era. Today, however, they assume more frightening proportions because of the deepening impact on all phases of individual and group behavior, because of the ideological and other chasms which divide men and nations, because of the "snowball" effect of events in all parts of the world, and because of the existence, for the first time in human experience, of almost unlimited capacities for destruction. "Today we are faced with the potentially lethal combination of nuclear weapons against which there is no defense and international tensions from which there seems to be no respite."[4] How can peace, security, and well-being be attained and preserved in such a dangerous age?

In this concluding chapter we shall essay five very broad and very difficult tasks. First, we shall consider some of the likely changes in the patterns and factors of national power; second, we shall review some of the problems that beset the international community and impair or destroy good relations among states; third, we shall analyze some of the reasons why these problems arise and persist; fourth, we shall evaluate some general approaches to peace; and fifth, we shall attempt a preview of some likely trends in the years immediately ahead, and their impact on the nature of the international system.

[4] Charles E. Osgood, "Psychological Aspects of Policy Problems in a Nuclear Age," *Canadian Psychologist,* X (1960), 97.

Changes in Patterns and Factors of National Power

Power will continue to be a central theme in the study and practice of international relations. It should be remembered that power assumes many forms, both tangible and intangible, and that international relations is more than a crude power equation. In any event, the relative weight and significance of the factors of power may vary greatly at different periods and under different circumstances.

The Balance of Power. What of the concept of the balance of power, which, as noted, has been one of the main operational mechanisms or regulators of the nation-state system? Many observers insist that the whole concept is outmoded in the nuclear age and under existing world conditions; that the balance of power worked more or less effectively when international relations were confined largely to European powers that played the game of diplomacy and war according to recognized and generally observed rules; and that the same kind of game cannot be played effectively on the world stage, with larger numbers of actors, and with an absence of a balancer or even of a balance. But one gets the impression that a great deal of attention is still paid to balance of power considerations, whatever the professions to the contrary and however irrelevant these considerations may be under conditions of systemic change.

Geography and Geopolitics. Geographic factors of power, long considered to be relatively stable and relatively constant factors, obviously have to be reappraised in the light of the bewildering developments in communications and transportation. Major breakthroughs of the pre-atomic era, such as the telephone, electricity, the internal combustion engine, the automobile, the airplane, radio, television, changed the significance of geographic factors; and the same has been even more true in the nuclear and space age. We are now concerned with the nature of the Van Allen Belt or even with the texture and atmospheric conditions of the moon as well as with the geographic features of the earth's landscape. Geopolitics as conceived by Rudolph Kjellén or Sir Halford Mackinder or Major General Karl Haushofer seems outdated in the age of supersonic planes, guided missiles, and space explorations; but geopolitical principles, featuring the application of geographic considerations to political and national problems and policies and the relationship between space and power, are still carefully considered by responsible political leaders and students of international affairs. Geopolitics — and geostrategy — still have a significant application at local, regional, and global levels, as they will, no doubt, in time have beyond the terrestrial sphere.

Population Changes. Recent population growth figures and projected trends have already been cited. They are indeed alarming, at least at present and foreseeable states of economic and technological advance. For the world as a whole, population is increasing at the highest rate in human history. The population explosion is a relatively recent development; if continued unabated it may prove to be the greatest single threat to world peace and to human survival Moreover, the world's demographic map is changing rapidly in ways that are already having profound effects on international relations and will almost certainly be more marked in the future. With the exception of Latin America, where the population is probably growing faster than that of any other region, the demographic center of gravity is shifting more and more from the Western to the non-Western world. This is a fact of great political as well as economic significance.

In general, population growth rates are less and life expectancy figures are higher in the more developed countries. Hence, they face a growing problem of aged people, while underdeveloped countries have the problem of providing food, employment, and healthful outlets for the energies of a young and rapidly increasing population. Shifting age groups within the population may decisively affect a population's productive capacity and its military power. The import of these projections is that areas of higher living standards and more democratic institutions must face the prospect of an increasing disadvantage in one of the important elements of national power. On the other hand, the underdeveloped countries, with assistance from the more developed nations and from international agencies, must succeed in mobilizing more effectively their economic resources to satisfy, as well as profit from, their youthful populations.

Raw Materials and Natural Resources. Judgments on natural resources are necessarily tentative, partly because later discoveries may completely change the picture, partly because present calculations of reserves may be in error, and partly because scientific advances may well reduce the worth of some currently known resources and enhance the utility of others. In respect to the foremost of all natural resources — fertile soil — it may be assumed that progressive states will make its preservation one of the prime objectives of national policy. Less developed states will in many instances add immensely to their agricultural production through their own energies and through technical assistance programs and the use of more fertilizers, new seeds, and improved techniques. Indeed, the more effective application of known techniques and new discoveries may eventually bring into profitable use vast areas of land now completely unproductive. Perhaps the same general analysis will apply to forestry and animal husbandry. But the diligence of governments and the skill of scientists are unlikely to alter the specialization of areas in a wide range of agricultural products or the continued dependence on foreign sources for essential raw materials which are either nonexistent in particular countries or in short supply.

The extent and distribution of the world's mineral resources have been discussed in an early chapter on the elements of national power. In the present stage of international politics, perhaps the most significant observation to be made is that the states of the Western world now possess a substantial margin of superiority in the production of most of the essential minerals, but that Eastern Europe and Asia contain resources of such magnitude that they already sustain enormous military power and that the differential in productivity may be expected to decrease and perhaps disappear altogether. The conclusions to be derived from this observation, however, must be tempered by the consciousness of a great many unknown factors. The accuracy of present calculations of reserves and the discovery of additional reserves are perhaps not the most important of these, even if, as we are told, Africa possesses "mountains of coal and uranium, vast deposits of copper and iron, [and] outcroppings of diamonds and precious metals,"[5] and the polar regions have unmeasured riches. Technological factors may prove to be of decisive importance, involving the use of substitutes, the development of synthetics and alloys, the utilization of inferior ores, the harnessing of water power, the exploitation of the energy-producing potentialities of the atom, and the use of solar and tidal energy. These may alter the import of present resources. Furthermore, consideration must be given to reserves of essential minerals, as well as to industrial productivity.

Economic Disparities. The disparities between the "rich" and the "poor" nations are staggering, and there is some question whether the gap is being closed. Figures on Gross National Product may be cited by way of example.[6] In 1950 one country, the United States, accounted for an incredible 46.4 per cent of the GNP of all the nations of the world. The Soviet Union was next, with 9.5 per cent, closely followed by Britain with 8.1 per cent; but India had only 3.3 per cent, Italy 2.1 per cent, and Pakistan 0.7 per cent. Thus the United States stood out as an unrivaled giant in the economic world. If present trends continue, there will be some relative loss, but she will still be far ahead of her nearest rivals. In 1975, for example, it is estimated that the United States will have 33.0 per cent of the total world GNP, and the Soviet Union 18.2 per cent, while West Germany, China, and Japan will have increased their relative standing, and Britain and France will have declined (to 4.2 and 3.7 per cent, respectively). India will have only 2.1 per cent of the total world GNP, and Pakistan only 0.4 per cent.

Thus, while the relative position of certain nations, especially the Soviet Union, will increase, some developed nations, including the United States, will suffer a relative decline and the position of the most underdeveloped states may be no better than it was two decades ago (it may even be worse relatively, although not absolutely). Translated in terms of GNP per capita, the projected figures for 1975 are $3550 for the United States, $2900 for West Germany, $2600 for

[5] Theodore H. White, "Africa Is Next," *Harper's Magazine,* February, 1952, p. 38.

[6] These figures are taken from Bruce M. Russett, *Trends in World Politics* (New York: The Macmillan Company, 1965), p. 110.

Canada, between $1000 and $2000 for Czechoslovakia, Belgium, Britain, France, the Soviet Union, the Netherlands, Venezuela, and Japan, in that order, and as low as $85 for India and $75 for Pakistan. Present trends will probably not continue, and many other factors may intervene to change these projections. Moreover, it is hard to translate 1975 figures into purchasing power or other meaningful equivalents. But there can be no doubt that while per capita GNP will increase markedly in almost every developed country, it may not rise in some of the least developed states, where the need for a substantial increase is particularly crucial.

Technological Advances. We may confidently and fearfully expect increased efficiency in the science of killing — atomic devices, hydrogen bombs, guided missiles, faster planes, super-schnorkels, lethal gasses, bacteriological weapons, and so on. Whether or not we reach push-button or space-platform or interplanetary warfare, we can be sure that as long as states believe that their security is at stake they will give high priority to the means of defense. But there may be other areas of technological advance somewhat less directly but just as surely playing their roles in international relations.

What, for instance, would happen to "oil politics" if atomic energy supplants oil as motive power? What would be the political consequences if medical advances remove the population restraints in presently congested areas? Or if they extend life expectancy to eighty or a hundred years? What if revolutionary agricultural techniques provide the Indians and the Chinese with all the food they want? What if rain-making, the de-salting of ocean water, and the use of rumored new fertilizers add enormously to the arable surface of the earth? What if synthetic rubber drives natural rubber from the market and so afflicts great areas with poverty? What if other synthetics create like havoc among the growers of wool, flax, silk, and hides? What happens if our scientists present us with the long-threatened capsule diet? What are the political implications of a universal language? of a far more general distribution of newspapers, magazines, radios? indeed, of improved standards of living everywhere? What may come of more efficient techniques of propaganda? of the recently developed satanic techniques or chemicals for extorting confessions from innocent persons? What may be the effect of giant international cartels? of more powerful weapons of economic warfare?

Clearly there will be a vast increase in the amount of energy available to man, and a great change in the relative importance of the various sources of energy. Human and animal energy, in the present as in the past, is still the most common form over the world as a whole, but it seems remote from a future in which almost inexhaustible sources of energy will be made available by harnessing the atom and the rays of the sun.[7] This may indeed revolutionize man's ways of living and hence his social, political, and international relationships.

While one may view with apprehension an increase in man's ability to destroy, he should also bear in mind the probability that the science of the future will also enlarge man's capacity for good. The purposes to which he puts the tools of tomorrow will be determined not by the tools themselves but by the objectives he had in mind.

Military Power. For the time being at least, the nuclear-nonnuclear divide creates even greater disparities than usual in military might. Perhaps a better test of relative military power would be the potential rather than the actual power-in-being, measured by economic and technological capacity, politi-

[7] See Palmer C. Putnam, *Energy in the Future* (Princeton, N.J.: D. Van Nostrand Co., 1933); and B. C. Netschert and S. H. Schurr, *Atomic Energy Applications; a Preliminary Survey* (Baltimore: The Johns Hopkins Press, 1957).

cal capabilities, and other basic indices of national power. On this basis the relative position of today's superpowers is likely to remain unchallenged, although this could be changed if other nations develop effective nuclear power or if Communist China continues to combine militant internal and external policies with a growing nuclear arsenal.

Obviously, major new developments in weaponry or in other devices for destruction could change the picture considerably, but fortunately the prospect of developing a "Doomsday Machine" or some other "absolute weapon" seems to be remote. The dangers lurking in the present "Age of Overkill" and in the military use of space are disturbing enough.

Diplomacy, Leadership, and Morale. Among the intangible factors of national power special attention has been given to diplomacy, leadership, and morale. Diplomacy is still and doubtless will remain the normal way of conducting formal relations between states and of transacting much of the world's official business. But diplomacy now has to be practiced on a worldwide basis; it involves non-Western nations and actors; its scope has expanded in far more than a geographical sense; and as practiced by totalitarian states and by many of the newly emergent nations it seems to differ from its traditional forms. In all probability diplomacy will continue to play its normal role, but with larger dimensions, less precision, and perhaps less prestige. It will undoubtedly be affected by the systemic change which appears to be under way in international relations, although not fundamentally until the nature and impact of that systemic change become more apparent.

Leadership has always been a vital factor in human affairs, and will continue to be so, even in the vastly impersonal age of the computer and organization man. Future years may see fewer towering figures in top political positions, but leadership, collective or individual, will shape the course of events and the destinies of nations. The study of political leadership and of political decision-making will remain one of the most rewarding and fruitful areas of investigation and analysis.

Morale will be no less important a factor in the future than it has been in the past, and it will probably receive considerably more attention. Governments realize its importance, and they are trying to promote it by increased concern with the problems of all segments of the population, by extensive propaganda activities, and by mass education.

Underlying Changes. In addition to changes in the elements of national power, we must contemplate the virtual certainty of political changes of a fundamental character. Just what they will be is anybody's guess. Even within the framework of the existing international system great changes are clearly under way, and one can speculate endlessly on the probable consequences of various trends and events. For instance, what would be the effect if Pakistan, or the countries of the Arab League, or an independent North Africa should give effective leadership to the 230 million people of the Muslim world? Or if the Middle East should go Communist? Or if India should abandon her policy of nonalignment and take a vigorous stand one way or the other? Or if the Chinese and the Russians should together undertake large-scale aggression? Or if Japan should disappoint the hope of the West in her nascent democracy? What possibilities are there for dynamic nationalism in various parts of the world? Will the challenge of economic development be met? Is nazism really dead? Can Germany be peacefully reunited? Will American foreign aid continue? If so, will it bring returns of progress and harmony or of parasitism and acrimonious charges of favoritism? Can the American economy stand the strain? Is it possible that Americans may lose at home at least some of the freedoms they now feel are imperiled from abroad?

Beyond and underlying all such questions lie the prospects of even more fundamental changes of a systemic nature. The political pattern of the world is clearly in a state of transition. Its inadequacies have been obvious for some time. They have been frequently pointed out by statesmen and scholars, and have been dramatized by breakdown of the system under conditions of crisis and stress. Actually, the attainment of something like a harmonious world order implies basic changes in political relationships, but in working toward that end we shall have to cope with conditions quite different from those of today. The need for basic reorientation is apparent, and there is no lack of proposed "solutions" and panaceas. But there is little agreement on the actual steps which should be taken, and even less willingness to undertake even those steps which are generally agreed to be necessary. One of the burning questions in international relations is to what extent, in the interests of human survival and progress, can and will man shape the course of events rather than be a helpless victim of them.

Problems of the International Community

In an address in New Delhi in April, 1967, U Thant, Secretary-General of the United Nations, listed the following as "the four basic problems confronting mankind today": "problems of a political or ideological nature" and "tensions arising out of differences in political or ideological beliefs"; "problems of an economic and social nature," especially "tensions generated by discrepancies in economic and social status of peoples"; "problems connected with race or the problems of color," notably "tensions generated by racial discrimination in many parts of the world"; and "problems connected with the legacy and remnants of colonialism."[8]

[8] Address at the inauguration of the Centre of Applied Politics, New Delhi, April 12, 1967.

For purposes of convenience we shall refer briefly to eight problems, all of which could be classified under the general categories which U Thant itemized. These are: (1) war; (2) nationalism; (3) sovereignty and the nation-state system; (4) population pressures; (5) trade and development; (6) imperialism and colonialism; (7) race and color; (8) ideological universalism.

1. War. War has been a recurring phenomenon throughout human history, and there is no reason to believe that it will disappear, however crude and unproductive and dangerous it may be. At times, under certain conditions and for certain peoples and purposes, it may even have been a useful instrument of international conduct. Until more acceptable alternatives are developed, it may continue to be resorted to for positive or negative reasons — to achieve some goal, to right some injustice, to defend from abuse or attack. War may also be an unintended consequence of pyramiding national rivalries and international tensions. In the absence of an effective world authority, it may come as a result of the anarchy of the existing state system. A period of transition, in particular, is always a dangerous one.

The real peril springs from the nature of modern war and from the revolution in weaponry. The returns of war have declined, while the costs and dangers have increased. Even a minor war, limited in scope, area, and weapons, may develop into a major threat to the peace of the world and the survival of men and nations. Hence a great deal of effort is being made not so much to prevent minor wars, although this effort too is persistent, as to prevent them from escalating into larger conflicts. The overriding concern is to avert World War III, which would be a total war fought with incredibly destructive weapons. "Mankind, *for the first time in its history,*" wrote Raymond Aron in his classic little book *On War,* "is preparing for a war it does not want to fight."[9] Hence it may be said that atomic war is the greatest danger facing mankind today. Man's fate hinges on his success in resolving the underlying political, economic, social, and psychological problems that could unleash a nuclear holocaust.

2. Nationalism. Without repeating the more detailed analysis of nationalism in our first chapter, we may venture a number of observations to emphasize the importance of nationalism in the problems of the international community. First, nationalism has positive values of great importance. In addition to its familiar role in the liberation of nations, it has often provided the motivation for unified action by the people of a state toward praiseworthy objectives. It has been a significant force in promoting representative government. In brief, one might say that, by supplementing compulsion, self-interest, moral obligation, religious duty, and other forces, nationalism has added enormously to the constructive potentialities of modern states.

Second, it must be admitted that nationalism has often gone beserk, producing excesses in both domestic and foreign policies. On the home front, excessive nationalism may lead to ill-advised economic practices, militarism, intolerance, and repression. Civil liberties and cultural freedom may be straitjacketed in the name of national unity. On the international front, nationalism that has run riot has repeatedly eventuated in hatreds, economic strife, expansionism, imperialism, aggression, and long and bloody wars. A too-exuberant nationalism, laying claim to an exalted destiny, clashes head-on with other too-exuberant nationalisms or with the security considerations of peace-minded states. Not without reason. it has often been damned as the foremost warmaker of the past few centuries. To paraphrase Rabindranath Tagore, while it has often been a blessing, too often it has been a curse.

Third, one must recognize and accept the indisputable fact that nationalism, whatever its virtues and its viciousness, is so deeply implanted in the minds of men that it is a major force to be reckoned with in all our hopes and blueprints for a more perfect world. It is a living, emphatic reality, whether in ancient Britain or newborn Israel, in democratic France or Fascist Spain, in wealthy United States or impoverished Haiti, in huge Canada or tiny El Salvador, in progressive Uruguay or primitive Paraguay, in populous China or unpopulous Australia, in Protestant Germany, Catholic Italy, Hindu India, or Islamic Egypt. Good or bad, it will not quietly dissolve before the mutterings of theorists or the pontifical resolutions of international conferences. On the contrary, it will persist through the foreseeable future; sentiment and tradition will try to sustain it even should it cease to be the priceless tool that it now is for the implementation of national policy.

Finally, nationalism has heretofore performed vital functions, and it neither can nor should be obliterated until the functions are no longer needed, or until some better mechanism has been devised to carry out the functions that are still deemed essential. Nationalism gives the state unity and effectiveness; it contributes the spiritual quality which makes the state a going concern. Without it the state becomes weak and decadent, a potential victim to more vigorous states. But whereas a sensible nationalism is indispensable to the state system — and at present we have no other system — an aggressive nationalism may be madness loose in the world The immediate task is to make aggressive nationalism patently disastrous to the states which are likely to indulge in it, not to attempt to extirpate nationalism root and branch. In the fullness of time some more

[9] Raymond Aron, *On War*, translated by Terence Kilmartin (Garden City, N.Y.: Doubleday & Company, 1959), p. 162. Italics in original.

powerful force may arise to assume its functions. Pending that day, nationalism must figure in all our calculations.

3. Sovereignty and the Nation-State System. Sovereignty sets up barriers to international action and cooperation. Pleading their sovereignty or taking refuge behind it without using the term, states are technically justified in refusing assent to common action. The United Nations Charter, like conventional international law, presupposes that states may be expected to assume responsibilities without their express assent but that they cannot be compelled to undertake any positive act of collaboration with other states. Consequently, sovereignty is often pointed to as the great impediment to helpful international action.

Another important disservice of sovereignty is its tendency to freeze the status quo. Called into play by nationalism, it provides the legal justification for the refusal to right obvious wrongs. In the world of sovereign states there is always the danger that only by force can states be brought to effect the adjustments which ever-changing conditions of life seem to make desirable for the greater good. In short, the nation-state system, based on the principle of sovereignty, tends to develop a rigidity that often leads to tensions, at times to violence, and too frequently to full-scale war.

In all fairness, however, sovereignty must be appraised with the realism that we applied to nationalism. Despite all the obstructionism that provincial minds can squeeze from it, sovereignty, like nationalism, will and should remain a bulwark of the state until such time as the protective functions of the state are in fact as well as in theory assumed by a supranational organization or organizations. For the problem is not so much sovereignty, per se, as the nation-state system itself, in which sovereignty resides. This system is becoming increasingly anachronistic in an interdependent world, when few problems can be resolved without formal or informal cooperation at sub-national and supranational levels. As has often been noted, nation-states are still the main actors in international relations; they set the boundaries within which international cooperative undertakings may be carried on, and they possess a kind of veto power over all movements toward truly supranational practices and institutions.

4. Population Pressures. The alarmingly rapid growth of the world's population, especially in countries and among peoples which can least afford a population explosion, has raised the specter of widespread famines. Some economists and demographers say that the difficulty is not too many people but too little food; or that the world's food-producing capacity is adequate to sustain several times its present population, and therefore that the problem is not the social one of overpopulation but the technical one of production and transportation, the political one of restraints on trade and migration, and the economic one of distribution and land tenure.

Population pressure may affect international relations in a number of ways. Its most direct and obvious effect is to provide a semblance of validity for expansionism, as it did with Germany and Japan in the 1930's. But it may also impose a condition of dependence on other states, and it usually carries with it low standards of health and sanitation, high illiteracy, and absence of effective democracy.

Overpopulation is, of course, most pressing in Asia. There the rate of increase threatens permanently to outrun the increase in the production of food or exchangeable equivalents. Emigration offers no hopeful solution. These people cannot go anywhere in large numbers, and they could be assimilated only very slowly even if the utmost efforts were made.

Yet there are some grounds for a tempered optimism. Almost for the first time in history conscious efforts on a fairly large scale are being made in the field of family planning. Some of the most important of the underdeveloped countries, including India and Pakistan, have developed family planning programs as an integral part of their total planning efforts. These measures have been strongly supported by the Population Commission and other agencies of the United Nations, and by aid-giving nations and organizations. At the World Population Conference in Belgrade, Yugoslavia, held in 1965 under the auspices of the United Nations, family planning programs in many countries were reported on and discussed, and the whole problem was analyzed in great detail. But it is a far cry from these modest beginnings to a "balanced modernization of the world's backward areas," through which, it has been suggested, "a solution to problems of overpopulation may be reached."[10] And in the meantime the pressure of population grows ever greater and more threatening.

5. Trade and Development. No nation is self-sufficient today, either economically or politically. Economic interdependence is an even more obvious fact of international life than is political interdependence. Nations must look outside their own borders for essential raw materials and other products, and for markets for their goods and services. All nations must trade in order to survive, and the great majority, which are underdeveloped, must also have substantial technical and developmental assistance from the more developed states.

[10] Stephen W. Reed, in Ralph Linton, ed., *Most of the World* (New York: Columbia University Press, 1949), pp. 152–153. See also Harold L. Geisert, *World Population Pressures* (Washington, D.C.: Research Project, George Washington University, 1958); Joyce O. Hertzler, *The Crisis in World Population; a Sociological Examination, with Special Reference to the Underdeveloped Areas* (Lincoln: University of Nebraska Press, 1956); and Philip M. Hauser, "World Population Problems," *Headline Series,* No. 174 (December, 1965).

These vital aspects of the international economy were highlighted by the two United Nations Conferences on Trade and Development, held in 1964 and 1968, which were among the largest and most significant international conferences of the postwar years. They led to the formation of a special organization, and they focused attention on the problems of trade and development encountered by underdeveloped nations and on the economic relations between the developed and developing nations — the so-called North–South problem.

International trade today is hampered by all kinds of artificial barriers and restrictive national policies. Among these are many that are related to and characteristic of economic nationalism, which we have discussed in some detail in Chapter 19. From the overall point of view, the pursuit of policies designed to promote the economic well-being of one state without concern for the welfare of other states has four main weaknesses. In the first place, it often means waste and higher prices, for artificial trade barriers may nullify the economies of more efficient production elsewhere. Second, if it calls for a favorable balance of trade it probably weakens other states and injures the welfare of their nationals. Third, through the discriminations that it imposes it engenders resentment and all sorts of international tensions. Fourth, it probably means the development of the warmaking potential of the state pursuing such a policy.

For the practicing state, economic nationalism offers two principal gains: it brings more profit to protected industries and higher wages to workers in those industries, and it may add to the state's military capacity through the promotion of self-sufficiency. On the other hand, the curtailment of imports may mean an inadequate stockpiling of essential commodities that have to be imported. Devotion to the idea of a favorable balance of trade may also mean the early depletion or exhaustion of natural resources.

Much has been written in behalf of economic internationalism, and, indeed, it seems to be a prerequisite of a peaceful world. It must be recognized, however, that the road to economic internationalism is strewn with formidable obstacles which will not disappear before the sound reasoning of internationally minded economists. Even when it is granted that a free or relatively free world economy would operate to the advantage of all states, it does not follow that it would profit all groups in a state, or every state at a given stage of economic development.

Economic nationalism is by no means the whole of the world's economic problem. Some states are poor in resources, and no amount of economic internationalism can offer substantial relief. Other states desperately need technical assistance and investment capital. Now that peoples everywhere have become more articulate and more assertive, no one can sensibly expect peace in the future as long as poverty — and disease and illiteracy — afflict hundreds of millions of human beings. If it seems unduly optimistic to assume that people who are decently fed and cared for are lovers of peace, we can at least have the assurance that constructive action toward the alleviation of poverty is progress toward the solution of one of the world's most harassing problems.

Unfortunately that progress has been disappointingly slow. The Decade of Development, which began in 1960 with high hopes, seems to be ending in frustration and disillusionment, as was often emphasized by delegates to the United Nations Conference on Trade and Development in 1968. It is now apparent that economic development is a more comprehensive and multi-faceted problem than was generally realized. It calls for far greater efforts and commitments than are now being made, either in the developing countries themselves or in developed states, which are devoting far less of their resources and their attention to the problem than is obviously required.

6. Imperialism and Colonialism. The heyday of imperialism and colonialism is long since past, and we may now be in the "post-imperial age." Nevertheless, those who live in the new states of Asia, Africa, and elsewhere in the world still have vivid memories of the recent colonial past, and they harbor deep suspicions of the actions and motivations of the former colonial powers and their allies, notably the United States. For them only one phase of imperialism, which might be called the territorial phase, has ended. Colonialism, they insist, is still very much alive, and has taken new and often even more insidious forms, which they often group under the generic term of "neo-colonialism." Colonialism is still regarded by the people in the new states as one of their major problems and concerns. This view is forcefully and insistently advanced at almost every opportunity. In national politics, at international conferences, in the agencies of the United Nations, and at every other public forum spokesmen of the newly independent nations denounce "colonialism in all its manifestations," to use the language of the joint communiqué issued at the close of the Asian-African Conference at Bandung in 1955. As more and more new states have become members, colonial issues, real or imaginary, have often dominated the proceedings of various UN bodies; almost every issue has been given colonial overtones. The famous Declaration on the Granting of Independence to Colonial Countries and Peoples,[11] pushed through the United Nations General Assembly in December, 1960, was a product of the preoccupation of the majority of the UN's new members with colonial issues and of their concern lest colonialism in new and more threatening forms again overwhelm them. They hoped that the Special Committee of Seventeen, which the General Assembly established to check on the implementa-

[11] General Assembly Res. 1514 (XV), 14 December 1960.

tion of the declaration, would become, "in effect, the General Assembly's 'overseer' of decolonization."[12]

The Communists have of course skilfully capitalized on this continuing sensitivity to "colonialism in all its manifestations," and have sought to gain greater influence in the underdeveloped world by posing as champions of anti-imperialism. This position was adopted many years ago, and all the changes on the theme have been rung by Communist propagandists ever since. The emergence of most of Asia and Africa into independent nationhood has given them new "targets of opportunity" in pressing the anti-colonial campaign. The Chinese Communists have joined the Russians in this game, even while they are accusing the Russians of themselves becoming the tools of capitalists and imperialists. On the whole, the charges of imperialism are levied against the white nations of the Western world, and not against Communist countries or against colored nations and peoples.

Even in the "post-imperial age," imperialism cannot be dismissed as a stage that has completely disappeared. It is significant that the Secretary-General of the United Nations, himself a citizen of a particularly sensitive and suspicious new state, should have listed "problems connected with the legacy and remnants of colonialism" as one of the "four basic problems confronting mankind today."

7. Race and Color. Problems of race and color undoubtedly are complicating factors in international relations, and they may indeed be among the most difficult to deal with in future years. Some observers, including Arnold Toynbee, have warned of the danger of growing conflict between the white and the colored races. Certainly this conflict already exists. It is one of the decisive factors in the minds of the leaders and peoples of the colored nations of the world, particularly in Africa, where race and color are all mixed up with feelings of anti-colonialism and with suspicions of the white nations of the West. The Chinese Communists have tried, apparently without much success, to further their own ends in Africa and to combat the influence of both the United States and the Soviet Union — two white nations — by appealing to Africans as fellow-members of the colored races. The main gravamen of the charges of the Black African states against South Africa is that the white peoples of that country, numerically small but politically and economically predominant, are following a policy of unabashed official discrimination against the majority of the people of the area, who are black. Black African leaders accuse the Western nations of favoritism toward South Africa not only because of economic reasons, but also because of ties of race and color.

Because of the unresolved problems of race relations and the undoubted discrimination against the approximately one-tenth of the population which happens to be Negro — a discrimination gradually being mitigated by governmental policies and the combined efforts of Negro and white Americans alike, but still very real and very pervasive — the United States is vulnerable to charges of racial discrimination within its own borders. These charges are used with telling effect in anti-American propaganda aimed at colored peoples.

Undoubtedly race and color consciousness and prejudices do affect international relations and behavior. They are by no means confined to white peoples. They exist within almost every state — a reading of the matrimonial advertisements in Indian newspapers is revealing in this respect — and they affect the attitudes of colored peoples toward each other as well as toward peoples with white skins.

[12] "Issues Before the Seventeenth General Assembly," *International Conciliation*, No. 539 (September, 1962), p. 63.

Indictments of "racial discrimination" have been made too uncritically by nonwhite peoples, and they have been received too credulously by many sympathetic white people. They are in part conscious or unconscious propaganda designed to arouse and consolidate resistance to imperialism and colonialism. Rather than white versus yellow or white versus black, the alignment has actually been strong versus weak. For a time Hitler threatened to enslave most of a white Europe and Japan a large part of yellow Asia; and black nations have been known to hold white nations in subjection, as the story of Haitian-Dominican relations discloses. Generally speaking, the powerful states have been the white states and the weak states the colored ones. Inevitably white people came to feel "superior." Inevitably, too, yellow and black people came to explain their exploitation in terms of color rather than of weakness. The coincidence of white with strength and of yellow or black with weakness gives an undeniable plausibility and even some validity to charges of racial discrimination.

8. Ideological Universalism. By this term we mean the urge or drive to extend a given body of related beliefs throughout the world. It is motivated by the desire to make a particular ideology secure by making it universal. The impulse toward universalism has probably been felt by everyone whose brain has been disturbed by an idea, but we are here concerned only with those beliefs that are supported by instruments of national policy. Not every venture in widespread conquest, of course, has been prompted by the effort to implant or compel a way of thinking worthy of the name of ideology. Thus one may well doubt that Alexander the Great, Julius Caesar, Genghis Khan, or even Kaiser William II aspired to anything like ideological universalism. They may be written off as seekers after power and glory. On the other hand, it seems hardly correct to restrict the term to recent times, as some writers prefer. The spreading of Mohammedanism by the sword, the Thirty Years' War, and the early Napoleonic Wars appear to have brought rather fundamental values into conflict, with much of the world at stake.

However one may feel about the newness of basic ideological issues, he will doubtless concede that not all modern wars have involved an antagonism of ideologies. But it is significant that ideologies have become more important in war at the same time that war has tended to become total war. What is the relationship? Which is cause and which is effect?

Total war has been a factor — but only one of many — in making war increasingly ideological in nature. But it is also true that the presence of ideological issues has tended to promote total war, and this fact is of far greater moment to our generation. To say that one's ideology is at stake is to say that his way of life hangs in the balance. All the institutions and traditions that he cherishes may be torn from him and hateful ones may be put in their place. Add to this total stake the fact that mechanized warfare requires vast manpower and woman power in the production line, and the result is the entire adult population committed both emotionally and vocationally to war — that is, to total effort.

Ideological universalism is in itself no threat to the proponents of any particular ideology, for it may remain an unimplemented aspiration; but it becomes a threat when it is supported by aggressive designs and great military power. With certain qualifications, democracy is an unaggressive ideology, although those who urge preventive war would make it aggressive. One wonders, also, about the implications of the Wilsonian slogan that "the world must be made safe for democracy" or of the frequent assertions by democratic "hard-liners" that communism must not only be checked but also must be destroyed, along with the main citadels of its power. Fascism, whether of the German, the Italian, or the Japanese variety, was potently aggressive, but even now it is difficult to determine how much ideology was involved in its messianic appeals.

Not long after the close of World War II the "strange allies" of that war became the leaders of a bipolar world locked in a protracted conflict which first assumed the form of a cold war In recent years the ideological aspects of the conflict, although they still remain as underlying realities, seem to have become somewhat obscured as a result of changing world conditions, especially the emergence of a high degree of polycentrism, within as well as outside the Communist orbit.

Moscow and Peking may be rival Romes of international communism, but both the Chinese and the Russians insist that their object is the worldwide victory of communism, which they regard as "inevitable." Their differences are either internal or concern means rather than ends. Because the Russians command more formidable power, their policies and tactics are of the greatest immediate concern; but because the Chinese are more militant and because they seem to be growing rapidly in strength and influence, they are a particularly disturbing factor in contemporary international relations. The big question is whether the Chinese as well as the Russians will be content with an ideology without universalism, or, if not, whether they will pursue their objectives by means which will not threaten the peace of the world.

There is considerable debate today on the role of ideology in international relations. An interpretation which has gained widespread acceptance is that this is perhaps the most ideologically impregnated age in history, that never have ideological factors been of greater significance. In recent years, however, ideology has seemed to be less central to the foreign and domestic policies of nations, even Communist nations. Pragmatism rather than ideology seems to be the most conspicuous feature of these policies. But those commentators who speak of "the end of ideology" are certainly going too far.

Finally, let us venture a few observations about ideology and ideological universalism in the context of changing world conditions. 1. In theory, ideologies are rarely susceptible to compromise, although it does not follow that co-existence is impossible. That depends on the depth of the urge to universalism as well as upon the price tag of realization — whether the opposing military power makes the cost prohibitory. Something like a balance of power may effect a standoff or a spatial compromise. 2. If the Western community of states denies to communism the right to universalism, it must be willing to accept less than universalism for its own ideology. 3. An aggressive ideology, powerfully supported, must be guarded against on a thousand fronts, for its devices may be both completely ruthless and incredibly ingenious. 4. Democratic states must be on constant guard lest they sacrifice their distinctive liberties in the effort to combat repugnant ideologies. The loss may come through the laws themselves, as some conservative Americans believed to be the case in Socialist Britain, or it may come through the growing intolerance of public opinion, as evidenced by McCarthyism and witch-hunts in the United States. 5. Since ideological war between powerful states would almost certainly mean total wars, they should be avoided until the last honorable alternative has been exhausted; they should be prepared against with the knowledge that they will be total wars and that, if they come, they must be fought with an awareness of total stakes.

The Persistent "Why?"

The world is and always has been troubled to the people of any given time, often only to have the next generation look back longingly at "auld lang syne." Regretfully, the candid historian must declare his judgment that "the good old days" never were and that "the bright new tomorrow" will never be.

But to say that our problems will always be with us, is not to say that they will always be the same problems. We shall shed some of the old ones and gain — if gain is the word — some new ones. All of man's better impulses drive him toward "solving" the "problems" of his own day; often he fails, rarely does he succeed; frequently he is able to reduce their severity, to cut them down to manageable proportions. He then must learn to live as he can with what remains. Perhaps time will remove or modify them; perhaps a later generation will wage the fight more successfully, winning an inch here and an inch there.

The problems of international relations which we have listed and reviewed are only some of the major and obvious ones. To continue our analysis, we shall raise questions about the responsibility of man himself and some of his works for the inability of states to live together in peace and with a greater measure of cooperation. Here again the list is selective, not exhaustive.

Man Himself? The easiest and most obvious explanation for the ills of mankind is to blame man himself. Man has often proved himself capable of rising to heights that are "little lower than the angels," to use a Renaissance phrase, but too often he has descended to the animal level of existence. Throughout human history, with many exceptions to be sure, he has been unable to order his social relationships in a peaceful way. Moral sense, it seems, appeared only with *homo sapiens,* but even then at first it only glimmered. In a famous work of a generation ago, Professor James H. Breasted contended that "the dawn of conscience" came only about 5,000 years ago.[13] There has always been a wide and obvious gap between the ethical and religious codes to which men professed to adhere and human behavior, especially group behavior. War has been such a recurrent phenomenon at almost all periods of history, under many different political and social systems, that it is often alleged that "man is war" — an allegation, incidentally, that is strongly refuted by most modern psychologists and other students of human behavior. In his group actions man is usually even more irrational and violent than in his individual role in society; this is of course particularly true under conditions of stress and tension. At such times, which are all too frequent man often resorts to violent means in order to resolve differences, even if these means are likely to be self-defeating and may lead to disastrous consequences.

This situation was bad enough in past decades and centuries, but it is all the more alarming today, when the normal dangers of group relationships are magnified manyfold. As Walter Millis pointed out, "there are latent forces in all the peoples — the forces of hatred, of suspicion, of thirst for personal power, of nationalist ambition, always standing ready to convert even a minor contretemps into a major catastrophe."[14] This is the kind of escalation that is particularly to be feared in today's world. Will man be able to find ways to deal with inevitable tensions and conflict situations without resorting to means that may bring about his own destruction?

Is It These? The search for causes of the world's ills might be further extended. Let us note a few more of these very briefly, if only to show that they cannot be regarded as getting down to basic causes.

The real culprit cannot be any particular country, for the same country may have been aggressive at some periods in its history and

[13] See James H. Breasted, *The Dawn of Conscience* (New York: Charles Scribner's Sons, 1934).

[14] Walter Millis, *An End to Arms* (New York: Atheneum Publishers, for the Center for the Study of Democratic Institutions, 1965), pp. 253–254.

pacific in others. It cannot be the nation-state and its corollaries of nationalism and sovereignty, for conflicts among political and social groups were frequent before the evolution of the peculiar forms of political organization and behavior that have prevailed for the last few centuries. It cannot be any particular form of government, for governments of every kind have at times been aggressive. To be sure, modern totalitarianisms, notably fascism, have been especially prone to stir up trouble. Communism, linked to the power of the Soviet Union and Communist China, raises new and perhaps greater dangers. If these modern totalitarian systems and ideologies are now basic causes of international friction, something new and alarming has been added to the world's problems.

Nor can the real offender be armaments, for these are more of a product of international suspicions and rivalries than a cause of war, and unilateral disarmament may actually increase the danger of conflict. It cannot be diplomacy, for that is only an instrument of policies, good and bad. It cannot be illiteracy, for the great wars have been among the most literate states. It cannot be industrialism, for wars are by no means peculiar to the industrial era or to industrialized countries. It cannot be capitalism, for this system has been associated with unprecedented progress and freedom and internationalism as well as with economic rivalries among nations and human exploitation. It cannot be imperialism, for instead of proving to be the final desperate stages of capitalism, as Lenin predicted, imperialism has given way to concepts of trusteeship and national freedom; and today, when imperialism, except perhaps in certain forms, is dying, and is everywhere on the defensive, the threat of war remains. It cannot be race, for wars have rarely had an interracial character. It cannot be religion, for no great war of the past three centuries has been provoked by primarily religious factors. It cannot be poverty, for the wealthy states are precisely those which have done the bloodiest fighting.

If we have not yet found the common denominator in all the instances of conflict among states, it seems that we must accept one or the other of two conclusions: either that the common denominator is something we have not yet listed, or that there is none and that even basic causes differ from conflict to conflict.

The second seems to be a more realistic, if somewhat unsatisfactory, conclusion. It would be so much simpler if we could point the finger at the nation-state system or at communism, monarchy, poverty, or the like, and then get down to the business of eradicating it; it would be even simpler to say that man is inherently and unchangeably vicious, for then we could give up. Instead, we are dealing with a complex of human nature and external realities. To encourage us, however, we have the solid facts that within the past two generations moral judgments have extended to war itself, and that today we are tackling the problem with more earnestness and experience than ever before. To that extent we have already progressed beyond our forefathers.

Approaches to Peace

The archives and libraries of the world contain many thousands of proposals of alternatives to war and of approaches to peace.[15] A few of these have been tested by time and experience; most of them are no more than paper plans. Some emphasize an attack on the underlying causes of war; others stress methods of peaceful settlement of international disputes; still others concentrate on the development of various types of security systems, with the object of making aggression unprofitable through the concerted action of peace-loving states. Some are based on relatively simple formulas or panaceas; others call for a many-sided ap-

[15] For an analysis of hundreds of peace plans, see Edith Wynner and Georgia Lloyd, *Searchlight on Peace Plans* (New York: E. P. Dutton & Co., 1944).

proach. Some seek to improve the existing state system; others seek to replace this system with some form of world government or other supranational institutions. Some represent a unilateral, others a regional, and still others a nearly universal approach. Some call for the creation of new institutions or the strengthening of existing ones; others stress the need for changes in the minds or hearts of men, especially of those in the seats of power. Some give priority to disarmament, others to security. Some place heavy reliance on methods of moral suasion, others on the organization of force. Some are based on the development of international law, others on laying the foundations of a true international community, still others on upholding concepts of international morality. Some place faith in treaties for the outlawry of war, for nonaggression, for neutralization, for cooling-off periods, for conciliation, for arbitration, for the nonproliferation of nuclear weapons; others place no trust in such treaties, unless they are of the self-executing variety, and emphasize performance rather than promise.

Five of the many general approaches to peace may be called (1) the institutional, (2) the functional, (3) the curative, (4) the step-by-step, and (5) the many-fronts approaches. These are not exclusive of each other, but the terms suggest the line of greatest emphasis. We shall note here some of the merits and the limtations of each.

The Institutional Approach. The number of international organizations in existence at the present time is truly staggering. We have already observed some of the deficiencies of many of them, as well as the difficulties of coordination that have arisen. There is probably excessive confidence in the efficacy and potentialities of institutions in dealing with problems of war and peace. On the slightest provocation, whether on the national, regional, or universal level, a new institution or organization is created. The most outstanding and comprehensive of these today is, of course, the United Nations. Others of especial importance, which are basically political but are also comprehensive in character, are the North Atlantic Treaty Organization and the Organization of American States. There are no truly supranational institutions in existence at the present time; the three functioning West European communities — the European Coal and Steel Community, the European Economic Community, and Euratom — are probably the closest approximations.

Institutions of many types are obviously needed, and they serve a highly useful purpose. Without them the world's work could not be done. They also provide invaluable experience in international cooperation. They supplement the normal channels of diplomacy and of contact between nations in an important way. But for all their merits, they are, after all, merely instruments, and their value depends upon the way in which they are used. Something more than instruments is needed if peace is to be preserved. If a multiplicity of organizations could achieve this goal, war would be as dead as the dodo.

Most of the plans for world government, whether limited or universal in scope, call for the creation of institutions of a supranational character.[16] In fact, the institutional approach to peace relies mostly on structure and form, on the establishment of a wide variety of political institutions, some of a far-reaching character, to deal with the problems that beset the world. Some "institutionalists" would revise the United Nations Charter in such a way as to transform that organization into a United States of the

[16] See *Revision of the United Nations Charter*. Report of the Committee on Foreign Relations on Resolutions Relative to Revision of the United Nations Charter, Atlantic Union, World Federation and Similar Proposals. Senate Report No. 2501, 81st Cong., 2d Sess., September 1, 1950 (Washington, D.C.: Government Printing Office, 1950). See also Grenville Clark and Louis Sohn, *World Peace Through World Law* (Cambridge, Mass.: Harvard University Press, 1960).

World. Others would leave the UN more or less as it is, but would have as many of its members as possible join in establishing a separate federal structure with real power. The Atlantic Union Committee would form a federal union of the democracies of the Atlantic Community; conceivably this might be a first-big step toward a larger federation, but the Atlantic Union itself would be the nucleus of the Western world. Federal Union, Inc. — the organization headed by one of the true pioneers in the world government movement, Clarence Streit — is at present devoting most of its efforts to supporting the Atlantic Union proposal, although it advocates a larger and larger union as conditions permit. The United World Federalists take a more universal approach; they would include even Russia and other Communist states in their original union. One organization, centered at the University of Chicago, drafted a proposed constitution for a world federal union, and another, with offices in Washington and elsewhere, made plans for a convention to draft a world constitution. World government associations of a similar sort exist in Britain, the Commonwealth countries, Western Europe, and many other places.

Proponents of world government render a genuine service by calling attention to distant objectives and by acting as gadflies to those who have the responsibility for the relations of states. They are, of course, vulnerable to charges of impracticality and of oversimplification of international issues. They tend to place too much hope in new institutions and constitutions, and to overlook the fact that before these instruments can be effective "there are foundations to be fortified and sturdier foundations to be laid."[17]

The Functional Approach. The so-called functional approach also gives considerable emphasis to institutions and organizations, but, as the term suggests, it is concerned more with the encouragement of international functional agencies, particularly those having primary economic or social objectives, or both, rather than political ones. The premise on which this approach seems to rest may be stated as follows: Cooperation between nations is extremely difficult to achieve on the political level, for on this level matters of national pride and prestige, of balance of power and power politics in general, are of first importance; on the other hand, nations are willing to work together in the wide area of economic, social, and technical activities, and such cooperation is not only valuable in itself but also helps to create the atmosphere and to forge the ties that bind nations and peoples together. The argument here is that it is more important to create common interests and interdependence than it is to establish security organizations or federal parliaments. As one exponent of this point of view put it, "The only means through which political cooperation can ultimately be achieved is through gradual expansion of the existing areas of cooperation until the circles overlap and common national interests render closer political cooperation essential."[18]

Like proponents of world government,

[17] Edwin D. Dickinson, *Law and Peace* (Philadelphia: University of Pennsylvania Press, 1951), p. 134.

[18] Philip E. Jacob, "The United Nations and the Struggle for World Welfare," *Pennsylvania School Journal,* October, 1950, p. 60. A functional approach to international relations has been strongly championed by David Mitrany, especially in his book *A Working Peace System,* first published in 1943. This study is indispensable for anyone who wishes to explore the possibilities of the functional approach. E. H. Carr also sees more hope in the growth of international functional agencies than in those of a basically political nature. His views on this subject are developed most fully in *Conditions of Peace* (New York: The Macmillan Company, 1942) and in *Nationalism and After* (New York: The Macmillan Company, 1945), See also "The Functional Approach to Peace," Chapter 17 in Inis L. Claude, Jr., *Swords into Plowshares; the Problems and Progress of International Organization,* 3d ed. (New York: Random House, 1964).

though in a different sense, the "functionalists" are open to charges of ostrichism. The political field is the main area of international conflicts, and precisely for this reason it is the vineyard in which the serious student of international politics must labor. He cannot eliminate political problems by trying to ignore them. It is all very well to promote health and sanitary measures, better agricultural methods, respect for human rights and fundamental freedoms, and the like; but these steps by themselves will not resolve serious international disputes or build a peaceful world order. DDT and the Universal Declaration of Human Rights are fine and worthwhile, but they are not substitutes for security.

The institutional and functional approaches are not incompatible. Both would operate to a great extent through organizations. One stresses political, the other economic, social, cultural, humanitarian and other nonpolitical aspects. Organizations like the United Nations, the North Atlantic Treaty Organization, and the Organization of American States have agencies that are concerned with all phases of international life. The European communities seem to represent an attempt to fuse the political and the functional; or perhaps it would be more accurate to say that they seek to achieve political ends through agencies which are essentially functional but which provide a base for further political development in the form of federation.

The Curative Approach. Nor is the so-called curative approach wholly divorced from the institutional and functional approaches. It, too, usually envisions the creation of organizations to fulfill its objectives. Many of these objectives are political, but more are nonpolitical and seem particularly adapted to a functional treatment. This approach is essentially a long-term one. It calls for the eradication of — or at least a frontal attack upon — basic economic and social and political evils or handicaps, such as poverty, hunger, famine, disease, illiteracy, racial and caste discrimination, and human oppression and misery, wherever they may be found. This is the purpose of many of the activities of the United Nations and of technical assistance and economic development programs of a bilateral and multilateral nature.

In the long run the curative approach should be the most fruitful of all, but in more immediate terms it cannot be concentrated upon to the exclusion of the others. It is one of the anomalies of our age that a great country like the United States spends many billions on military preparedness and on military assistance programs and only a few hundred millions on technical assistance and economic development projects; that the total United States financial contribution to the United Nations since the inception of the world organization has been less than the cost of two months' operations in Vietnam in 1967 or 1968; that a great but underdeveloped country like India, faced with the vast problem of making her newly won independence meaningful for the mass of her people, devotes between one-fourth and one-third of her total budget to military purposes; that the total costs of the economic and social activities of the United Nations to date have been less than the cost of one modern aircraft carrier. Yet these anomalies exist because every state feels compelled to give first priority to national security and other immediate concerns. Perhaps this is as it should be; for peace must be safeguarded in order to allow time and opportunity for the curative approach to make itself felt. The waiting time is bound to be a long and dangerous one.

The Step-by-Step Approach. Perhaps the most hopeful of all approaches to peace, although a less exciting and imaginative one than blueprints for a new world order, is the gradualist approach, working from where we are to where we would like to be. There is much wisdom in the following observations by a seasoned British diplomat:

> . . . it is well to recognize the limits of human endeavor; to realize that the business of government is not an academic exercise; to reconcile oneself to the fact that there are no neat and final solutions, that international affairs are a fabric without much of a pattern, and that diplomacy is most often, as von Moltke said of strategy, a succession of expedients; to suspect that bold initiatives, imaginative gestures, stirring leads and elaborate blueprints of policy, so beloved of those who are free of responsibilities of government, are seldom of the stuff of practical statesmanship in international relations.[19]

The advantage of the step-by-step approach is that it works within the limits of the possible, without losing sight of the ultimate objective; the great drawback is that it may be too unplanned, that it may in fact not be an approach at all but rather a resigned acceptance of various trends, which may be leading in the wrong direction, that it may be too halting and ineffective, and that it may be overwhelmed by time and events. It is the approach to "peace by pieces," which may in time lay the foundations for a stronger world order. "The effort to build a cooperative world order," Senator J. William Fulbright once said, "must consist not in the drafting of blueprints and grand designs but rather in the advancement of a great many projects of practical cooperation — projects which, taken by themselves, may be of little importance, but which, taken together, may have the effect of shaping revolutionary new attitudes."[20] Such an approach has the virtue of practicality and feasibility, but there is a real question whether it will achieve the larger results to which Senator Fulbright referred.

The Many-Fronts Approach. Obviously the approaches to peace are many. There is no single key, and possibly all of them together cannot unlock the door to a peaceful world. Reinhold Niebuhr has said that "the trustful acceptance of false solutions for our perplexing problems adds a touch of pathos to the tragedy of our age"; yet Professor W. Friedmann holds that "one of the few fortunate developments of recent international politics is a healthy distrust of panaceas."[21] In approaching the problem of war and peace there is much to be said for concentrating on a few of the major issues and approaches, but without losing sight of the others. Even some of those who seem to put all their eggs in one basket are by no means unmindful that other baskets may be useful too. Thus a conference on world government in 1951 went on record in support of this view: "The approach to peace must, therefore, consist of two major parallel actions: the cooperative planning and building of a structure in which mankind could live at peace; and the cooperative planning and carrying out of an effective war upon those social and economic evils which arouse men to a sense of injustice and move them to violence."[22] The foremost living historian of civilizations past and present has raised two great issues for question and comment:

> Can we find a middle way in international affairs between the old anarchy of independent states jostling against each other — an anarchy which, I believe, cannot go on much longer in its old form — and the extreme opposite regime of a world peace imposed by some single Power on all the rest? . . . And can we find some middle course not only in the arena of international politics, but also in the social field, between the old

[19] Lord William Strang, *Britain in World Affairs* (New York: Frederick A. Praeger, 1961), pp. 18–19.

[20] "Approaches to International Community," address at the Pennsylvania State University, March 6, 1965.

[21] *An Introduction to World Politics* (Toronto, 1951), p. 56.

[22] From the preamble of report of the Economic and Social Commission of the Fourth Annual Congress of the World Movement for World Federal Government, held in Rome in April, 1951; quoted in *Freedom and Union,* VI (June, 1951), 28.

inequality of classes, leading to subterranean class warfare, and a social revolution leading to the forcible abolition of class, which is the programme for which Communism stands? . . . I believe that the discovery of middle ways of negotiating these two great questions of war and class is the supreme need of the world at present.[23]

The changing world situation seems to require the many-fronts approach, both to deal with a vast range of current problems, many of which seem to offer no hope for immediate solution, and to build eventually a sounder international system. As one student has observed, "We must maintain a pluralist approach so as to be able to adapt to the unexpected; we must have several possible alternatives and 'keep our options open.'"[24]

The Future of the World Community

It seems hardly necessary to emphasize the role of idealism in the lives of men. It is "the light on the horizon," "the dream of tomorrow," "the promises men live by." It is faith and hope and courage. It supplies the drive in the efforts toward a better world. Yet fifty centuries of recorded history have shown the limits within which idealism must operate; "experience," marking the possible as against the impossible, the practicable as against the impracticable, provides an equally necessary realism. He who has read history cannot avoid the conclusion that the rule of slow and uneven change will prevail in international relations as it has done for so long in all concerns of political life. "Peace by mechanism" is impossible. The answer is not that simple. The Bok Peace Award contest of 1923 drew out 22,165 plans. There must be quite a gap between making plans and making peace. Moreover, the problem is not just to preserve the peace, important as this undoubtedly is; it is to build the kind of world which will make the peace worth preserving, a world in which the many, and not just the privileged few, will have a real and vital stake.

If a better world is not to be reached by some ingenious scheme of international organization, what then? Are we never to attain it, or are we to await some super-ingenious scheme? The answer, as we have given it before, is that we may hope for progress on many fronts, but we must expect and prepare for disappointments and setbacks too. As for a magic formula, we shall here at least avoid the inconsistency of offering one. Instead, we shall offer some speculations about the probable course of international relations for the foreseeable future.

1. The nation-state system will continue to be the dominant pattern of international relations, and states will continue to be the main actors on the world stage. As in the past, there will be frequent changes in power relationships among states and groups of states. Other actors, including sub-national and supranational groupings, unofficial as well as official, will play an increasingly active and influential role. The conflicting trends toward the independence and the interdependence of states will become more and more apparent. The prospect is for increased change and instability within the system as the political patterns of the world fail to keep pace with technological progress and economic needs. As has been noted, some observers believe that we are experiencing a period of systemic change which will evenuate in the supersession of the nation-state system by another more adequate for modern times. There is nothing sacrosanct about the nation-state system, which has flourished in the Western world for only a few centuries, and which has become world-wide only in recent decades; but for the immediate future there is no ready substitute for it, and in all probability it will prevail, in one form or another.

[23] Arnold Toynbee, "The Study of History in the Light of Current Developments," *International Affairs*, XXIV (October, 1948), 564.

[24] Bruce M. Russett, "The Ecology of Future International Relations," *International Studies Quarterly*, XI (March, 1967), 30.

2. International relations will broaden and deepen and become more meaningful to larger numbers of people, as contacts increase and horizons expand. They have already expanded far beyond the confines of the Western state system to become international in fact as well as in name. While continuing to focus on political relations, especially the political relations of nation-states and of regional groupings, they have embraced economic, cultural, and other mutual concerns, and unofficial as well as official relations across national borders — in fact, they now encompass the whole gamut of international life. Through new techniques of analysis, ranging all the way from systems theory to content analysis and simulation techniques, their expanding dimensions are being subjected to more precise and more searching exploration. Indeed, the revolution in the study of international relations is hardly less startling than the radical changes that have occurred in the international situation in recent years.

3. Within the framework of the present system all states will continue to regard as their ultimate defense their own strength and that of their trusted allies. Only there can they find full loyalty to their own special interests. And there, protected by sovereignty, they will cultivate their strength until and unless a new order of affairs makes it abundantly clear that their destinies are secure in other hands. No such assurance has yet appeared.

4. States will continue to pursue security through military establishments, defensive alliances, and collective security arrangements. Many such power alignments will be ad hoc in nature. Others, based upon a fundamental community of interests, will achieve a relatively permanent character. Those which prove to be most enduring will have to be based on something more than security considerations.

5. For a long time to come states will aspire to a position where they can mobilize more power than their prospective enemies. In other words, they will remain conscious of the balance of power and seek to tip the balance in their own favor. They will do this in spite of international organizations and the elaboration of techniques for the peaceful settlement of disputes.

6. States will continue to place chief reliance for the settlement of their differences upon conventional diplomacy. Through this means they will foster trade, protect their nationals, and, as in the past, in many ways bring a degree of cooperation among states. They will privately and quietly resolve most disputes before these reach a serious stage.

7. For the time being, at least, and probably for the foreseeable future, the ideological components of international relations have been submerged and to some extent defused. The main champions of ideological universalism today, the Communists, have been weakened by internal rivalries and dissensions, and Communist as well as non-Communist states, with a few possible exceptions (Communist China being the great question mark), seem to have sublimated their ideological drives and preoccupations to more immediate needs and to more pragmatic policies. This situation may not last long — ideological factors are potentially still strong — but while it does, it will give a new look to international relations.

8. The United Nations will continue to provide a forum for the oratory and debates of the spokesmen of national states. It will pursue its vast programs of international cooperation, making some gains that states will be loath to forego. It will do particularly good work in social, cultural, and humanitarian fields, and it will achieve some successes in its economic work. It will be less effective in dealing with political problems. Through judicious operation it may establish norms for the relations of states and so enlist a supporting world opinion. It will have to earn respect and authority; it cannot legislate them.

9. Functional organizations will continue to gravitate toward the United Nations. Whether affiliated with the UN or not, they will direct international cooperation in many activities, drawing states closer together, often preventing differences from becoming conflicts, and do much to make cooperation a habit.

10. International law will be expanded and made more systematic. Individuals may be made clear subjects in theory, but states will continue to be the chief "persons" in international law. Some gains may be made in improving the legislative, judicial, and executive functions of international organizations, but powerful states will retain a nullifying power in fact.

11. Regional groupings of states will continue, and the number may increase. With the right kind of leadership, these groupings can be made to serve local and regional interests and at the same time buttress the United Nations. A more powerful United Nations would not necessarily make them useless.

12. Technical assistance and economic development programs, however sponsored, will do much to elevate standards of living and rates of literacy. They will contribute to economic interdependence and to the removal of psychological barriers between states. They may modify the problem of overpopulation. At the same time they will doubtless continue to be too limited in scope to deal with the vast needs of the underdeveloped countries and areas of the world.

13. Individuals and groups will continue the use of pressure devices of all kinds to achieve their own objectives. Some men will persist in subordinating the common good to the selfish ends of profit, power, or personal aggrandizement; we shall always be plagued with warmongers, profiteers, militarists, racists, monarchists, anarchists, Communists, robber barons, would-be messiahs, appeasers, peace-at-any-pricers, and a host of other vultures and crackpots. Some men will always be willing to join forces to sacrifice a larger society to achieve the "self-expression" of a smaller group, with the integrating denominator being race, language, geography, political or economic ideology, or something else. Some of these will be "good" men, others "bad" men, but who is to judge?

14. Other individuals will carry on the fight for the ostensible ends of peace and goodwill. They will give their time and money for the things they believe in, some giving a lifetime of service to a single cause, others giving momentary ecstasy to a succession of causes *du jour*. They will continue to band themselves together into innumerable societies to promote every conceivable and many inconceivable aspects of international relations. Some will act selfishly, others unselfishly; together they will do some harm, but they will do much good. Often they will act with too little information, too little realism, too much theory, too much optimism. Collectively, they will add much to the world's awareness of its great problems and to the resolution of people everywhere to support programs of constructive action.

15. International relations will undoubtedly continue to be characterized by instability, tension, complexity, and paradox. They have not been adjusted to the needs and imperatives of the nuclear and space age — an age marked by a "revolution in energetics, in communications, in industrial and agricultural productivity, in life expectancy and population growth." "In our time," wrote the editor of the *Bulletin of the Atomic Scientists*, "international life proceeds on two separate levels. One is the traditional level — the interplay of separate and conflicting national interests; the other, the newly important level of international cooperation in the prevention of nuclear war and in full utilization of science and technology for the common benefit of mankind."[25] There is an

[25] Eugene Rabinowitch, "New Year's Thoughts 1965," *Bulletin of the Atomic Scientists,* XXI (January, 1965), 2.

urgent need to weaken "the divisive forces operating on the traditional level of power politics" and to strengthen the "cohesive forces" and emphasize "common interests and cooperative efforts." But unhappily "this is not the direction that mankind has been traveling lately," and one of the all-important questions in contemporary international relations is whether, and how, this direction can be reversed.

If this preview of the world of tomorrow seems to mean that we and our descendants will still confront grave problems in the relationships of peoples, that we shall have little more to blame than the nature of man and his physical world and the institutions he has created, that new factors will certainly enter to modify or accentuate our difficulties, and that the road to peace is tortuous and altogether uncertain, then we must recognize that we have been given the lot of man in all ages. The history of mankind is a story of trial and error, and the most inspiring part of it is the persistence of good men in good causes. The outlook is gloomy, but by no means hopeless.

A basic assumption of all these speculations is that there will be no thermonuclear war. This assumption may unhappily prove to be incorrect. If so, all predictions will be erroneous, for no one can possibly foresee the kind of situation which would exist after World War III. In all probability the present international system would be completely shattered, and new forces and circumstances would shape the new order that emerged from the ashes.

For the present "top priority must . . . be given to the transitional problem of keeping the future open until men can make the fundamental adaptation necessary to civilized life in the atomic era."[26] The problem is one that will tax the abilities of men and the vitality of political institutions. It means that the future holds in store challenges and anxieties, opportunities and perils, such as men have seldom if ever experienced in other "times of trouble."

In helping to meet "the challenge to man's future" the student of international relations needs all of the technical skills and methodological competence, on the one hand, and all the wisdom and insights, on the other, that he can muster. His teacher is the entire world, in all its bewildering multiplicity. As he broadens his approach to the world scene he must also be conscious of the other worlds beyond — the worlds that, for example, lie hidden in the power of the atom and in the vastness of interplanetary and interstellar space. In this unfolding and expanding universe international relations have come of age, or at least have taken on new and more challenging dimensions.

SUGGESTIONS FOR FURTHER READING

ADLER, MORTIMER. *How to Think About War and Peace.* New York: Simon and Schuster, 1944.

ARON, RAYMOND. *On War,* translated by Terence Kilmartin, Garden City, N.Y.: Doubleday & Company, 1959.

BECKER, CARL. *How New Will the Better World Be?* New York: Alfred A. Knopf, 1944.

BOWLES, CHESTER. *The New Dimensions of Peace.* New York: Harper, 1955. Reflections on the nature and significance of the major revolutions of our time.

BRINTON, CRANE. *From Many One.* Cambridge, Mass.: Harvard University Press, 1948.

BROWN, HARRISON, JAMES BONNER, and JOHN WEIR. *The Next Hundred Years: Man's Natural and Technological Resources.* New York: The Viking Press, 1957.

BRYN-JONES, DAVID. *The Dilemma of the Idealist.* New York: The Macmillan Com-

[26] Bernard Brodie, *The Absolute Weapon: Atomic Power and World Order* (New York: Harcourt, Brace, 1946), p. 202.

pany, 1950. On reconciling personal ethics with the conflict of states.

CARR, EDWARD H. *Conditions of Peace.* New York: The Macmillan Company, 1942.

CHASE, STUART. *The Most Probable World.* New York: Harper & Row, 1968.

CLARK, GRENVILLE and LOUIS SOHN. *World Peace Through World Law.* Cambridge, Mass.: Harvard University Press, 1960.

CLAUDE, INIS L., JR. *Swords into Plowshares; the Problems and Progress of International Organization,* 3d ed. New York: Random House, 1964. Especially Chapters 11–17, dealing with "Approaches to Peace Through International Organization."

CURTIS, LIONEL. *World Revolution in the Cause of Peace.* New York: The Macmillan Company, 1949.

DICKINSON, EDWIN D. *Law and Peace.* Philadelphia: University of Pennsylvania Press, 1951.

FALK, RICHARD A. and SAUL H. MENDLOVITZ, eds. *Toward a Theory of War Prevention.* World Law Fund, 1966. Vol. I in a series entitled "The Study of World Order."

FRIEDRICH, CARL J. *Inevitable Peace.* Cambridge, Mass.: Harvard University Press, 1948.

GELBER, LIONEL. *Reprieve from War: A Manual for Realists.* New York: The Macmillan Company, 1950.

HAMMARSKJOLD, DAG. *Perspectives on Peace, 1910–1960.* New York: Frederick A. Praeger, 1960.

HOFFMAN, PAUL G. *Peace Can Be Won.* Garden City, N.Y.: Doubleday & Company, 1951. The prescription is production, armaments, allies, and propaganda.

KAPLAN, MORTON. *The Revolution in World Politics.* New York: John Wiley & Sons, 1962.

KOHN, HANS. *Living in a World Revolution.* New York: Pocket Books, 1965. Reflections by an eminent historian of nationalism and the modern world scene.

———. *The Twentieth Century.* New York: The Macmillan Company, 1949.

LASSWELL, HAROLD D. *The World Revolution of Our Time.* Stanford, Calif.: Stanford University Press, 1952.

LERNER, MAX. *The Age of Overkill: A Preface to World Politics.* New York: Simon and Schuster, 1962. An analysis of the contemporary world, in terms of "the passing of classical world politics."

LIE, TRYGVE *et al. Peace on Earth.* New York: Hermitage House, 1949.

MCCLELLAND, CHARLES A. *Nuclear Weapons, Missiles, and Future War: Problems for the Sixties.* San Francisco: Chandler Publishing Co., 1960. A volume in the Chandler Studies in International and Intercultural Relations.

MANGONE, GERARD. *The Idea and Practice of World Government.* New York: Columbia University Press, 1951.

MILLIS, WALTER and JAMES REAL. *The Abolition of War.* New York: The Macmillan Company, 1963. Based on the assumption that "it is today possible, for the first time, to think about a world without war."

MITRANY, DAVID. *A Working Peace System.* Chicago: Quadrangle Books, 1966. A classic exposition of the functional approach to international relations, first published in 1943.

MORGENTHAU, HANS J. *Scientific Man vs. Power Politics.* Chicago: University of Chicago Press, 1946. It is dangerous to believe that science can solve our political problems.

MYRDAL, GUNNAR. *Asian Drama: An Inquiry into the Poverty of Nations.* 3 vols. New York: The Twentieth Century Fund, 1968.

NIEBUHR, REINHOLD. *Moral Man and Immoral Society.* New York: Charles Scribner's Sons, 1946.

NORTHROP, F. S. C. *The Taming of the Nations.* New York: The Macmillan Company, 1952. A plea for cultural tolerance as the approach to peace.

OSGOOD, CHARLES E. *An Alternative to War or Surrender.* Urbana: University of Illinois Press, 1962.

Peace on Earth; Pacem in Terris. New York: Pocket Books, 1965. A report on the proceedings of the International Convocation on the Requirements of Peace, held in New York in 1965.

PUTNAM, PALMER C. *Energy in the Future.* Princeton, N.J.: D. Van Nostrand Co., 1953.

RUSSETT, BRUCE M. *Trends in World Politics.* New York: The Macmillan Company, 1965.

SCHECHTER, BETTY. *The Peaceable Revolution.* Boston: Houghton Mifflin Company, 1963.

THANT, U. *Toward World Peace: Addresses and Public Statements, 1957–1963.* New York: Thomas Yoseloff, 1964

THOMPSON, KENNETH. *The Moral Issue in Statecraft: Twentieth-Century Approaches and Problems.* Baton Rouge: Louisiana State University Press, 1968.

TOYNBEE, ARNOLD J. *Civilization on Trial.* New York: Oxford University Press, 1948.

———. *A Study of History.* 12 vols. New York: Oxford University Press, 1935–61.

WALLACE, VICTOR H., ed. *Paths to Peace: A Study of War Its Courses and Prevention.* Melbourne University Press, 1957.

WRIGHT, QUINCY, WILLIAM E. EVAN, and MORTON DEUTSCH, eds. *Preventing World War III: Some Proposals.* New York: Simon and Schuster, 1962.

WYNNER, EDITH and GEORGIA LLOYD. *Searchlight on Peace Plans: Choose Your Road to World Government.* New York: E. P. Dutton & Co., 1944. Digests of hundreds of peace plans.

APPENDIX

Countries of the World

Area, Population, and Membership in Selected Organizations

	AREA IN SQUARE MILES	POPULATION (1967 OR 1968 ESTIMATES)	MEMBERSHIP: LEAGUE OF NATIONS	UNITED NATIONS	ORGANIZATION OF AMERICAN STATES (OAS)	NORTH ATLANTIC TREATY ORGANIZATION (NATO)	ORGANIZATION OF AFRICAN UNITY (OAU)	COUNCIL OF EUROPE	ORGANIZATION FOR ECONOMIC COOPERATION AND DEVELOPMENT (OECD)	ARAB LEAGUE	COLOMBO PLAN	GENERAL AGREEMENT ON TARIFFS AND TRADE (GATT)	COUNCIL FOR MUTUAL ECONOMIC ASSISTANCE (COMECON)
Afghanistan	251,000	15,500,000	•	•							•		
Albania	11,100	1,900,000	•	•									
Algeria	919,592	12,000,000		•			•			•			
Andorra	175	12,000											
Argentina	1,072,067	22,800,000	•	•	•								
Australia	2,967,741	12,000,000	•	•							•	•	
Austria	32,374	7,300,000	•	•				•	•			•	
Belgium	11,781	9,500,000	•	•		•		•	•			•	
Bhutan	18,000	800,000									•		
Bolivia	424,162	3,800,000	•	•	•								
Botswana	222,000	576,000		•			•						
Brazil	3,286,470	88,000,000	•	•	•							•	
Bulgaria	42,823	8,300,000	•	•									•
Burma	261,789	25,500,000		•							•	•	
Burundi	10,747	3,200,000		•			•					•	

	AREA IN SQUARE MILES	POPULATION (1967 OR 1968 ESTIMATES)	MEMBERSHIP										
			LEAGUE OF NATIONS	UNITED NATIONS	ORGANIZATION OF AMERICAN STATES (OAS)	NORTH ATLANTIC TREATY ORGANIZATION (NATO)	ORGANIZATION OF AFRICAN UNITY (OAU)	COUNCIL OF EUROPE	ORGANIZATION FOR ECONOMIC COOPERATION AND DEVELOPMENT (OECD)	ARAB LEAGUE	COLOMBO PLAN	GENERAL AGREEMENT ON TARIFFS AND TRADE (GATT)	COUNCIL FOR MUTUAL ECONOMIC ASSISTANCE (COMECON)
Cambodia	69,898	6,300,000		•							•		
Cameroon	183,570	5,250,000		•			•					•	
Canada	3,851,809	20,000,000	•	•		•			•		•	•	
Central African Republic	240,535	2,000,000		•			•					•	
Ceylon	25,332	11,600,000		•							•	•	
Chad	490,733	3,400,000		•			•					•	
Chile	292,256	8,800,000	•	•	•							•	
China (Communist)	3,691,506	750,000,000	} •										
China (Nationalist)	13,885	13,000,000	}	•									
Colombia	439,512	18,500,000	•	•	•								
Congo (Brazzaville)	132,000	850,000		•			•					•	
Congo (Kinshasa)	905,562	16,000,000		•			•						
Costa Rica	19,650	1,500,000	•	•	•								
Cuba	44,218	7,900,000	•	•	•							•	
Cyprus	3,572	600,000		•				•				•	
Czechoslovakia	49,371	14,300,000	•	•								•	•
Dahomey	43,483	2,400,000		•			•					•	
Denmark	17,150	4,800,000	•	•		•		•	•			•	
Dominican Republic	18,703	3,750,000	•	•	•							•	

	AREA IN SQUARE MILES	POPULATION (1967 OR 1968 ESTIMATES)	MEMBERSHIP: LEAGUE OF NATIONS	UNITED NATIONS	ORGANIZATION OF AMERICAN STATES (OAS)	NORTH ATLANTIC TREATY ORGANIZATION (NATO)	ORGANIZATION OF AFRICAN UNITY (OAU)	COUNCIL OF EUROPE	ORGANIZATION FOR ECONOMIC COOPERATION AND DEVELOPMENT (OECD)	ARAB LEAGUE	COLOMBO PLAN	GENERAL AGREEMENT ON TARIFFS AND TRADE (GATT)	COUNCIL FOR MUTUAL ECONOMIC ASSISTANCE (COMECON)
Ecuador	109,483	5,400,000	•	•	•								
El Salvador	8,260	3,000,000	•	•	•								
Ethiopia	471,776	23,000,000	•	•			•						
Finland	130,119	4,700,000	•	•					• *			•	
France	211,207	50,000,000	•	•		•		•	•			•	
Gabon	103,300	470,000		•			•					•	
Gambia	4,361	340,000		•			•					•	
Germany (East)	41,816	17,500,000	} •										
Germany (West)	95,929	60,000,000	}			•		•	•			•	
Ghana	92,100	7,800,000		•			•					•	
Greece	50,944	8,600,000	•	•		•		•	•			•	
Guatemala	42,042	4,800,000	•	•	•								
Guinea	94,925	3,700,000		•			•						
Guyana	83,000	660,000		•									
Haiti	10,714	4,660,000	•	•	•							•	
Honduras	43,277	2,400,000	•	•	•								
Hungary	35,919	10,200,000	•	•									•
Iceland	39,770	197,000		•		•		•	•				
India	1,262,275	520,000,000	•	•							•	•	
Indonesia	735,268	110,000,000		•							•	•	
Iran	636,367	25,000,000	•	•									

* Finland has special status

	AREA IN SQUARE MILES	POPULATION (1967 OR 1968 ESTIMATES)	MEMBERSHIP: LEAGUE OF NATIONS	UNITED NATIONS	ORGANIZATION OF AMERICAN STATES (OAS)	NORTH ATLANTIC TREATY ORGANIZATION (NATO)	ORGANIZATION OF AFRICAN UNITY (OAU)	COUNCIL OF EUROPE	ORGANIZATION FOR ECONOMIC COOPERATION AND DEVELOPMENT (OECD)	ARAB LEAGUE	COLOMBO PLAN	GENERAL AGREEMENT ON TARIFFS AND TRADE (GATT)	COUNCIL FOR MUTUAL ECONOMIC ASSISTANCE (COMECON)
Iraq	173,250	8,400,000	•	•						•			
Ireland	27,136	2,880,000	•	•				•	•				
Israel	7,993	2,650,000		•								•	
Italy	116,304	53,000,000	•	•		•		•	•			•	
Ivory Coast	124,502	4,000,000		•			•					•	
Jamaica	4,232	1,850,000		•								•	
Japan	142,727	100,000,000	•	•					•*		•	•	
Jordan	37,737	2,000,000		•						•			
Kenya	224,960	9,650,000		•			•					•	
Korea (North)	46,540	12,500,000											
Korea (South)	38,004	30,000,000									•		
Kuwait	6,178	470,000		•						•		•	
Laos	91,428	2,800,000		•							•		
Lebanon	4,015	2,500,000		•						•			
Lesotho	11,716	976,000		•									
Liberia	43,000	1,100,000	•	•									
Libya	679,536	1,700,000		•			•			•			
Liechtenstein	62	19,300											
Luxembourg	999	335,000	•	•		•		•	•			•	
Malagasy Republic (Madagascar)	226,657	6,300,000		•			•					•	
Malawi	46,066	4,100,000		•			•					•	

* Japan has special status

	AREA IN SQUARE MILES	POPULATION (1967 OR 1968 ESTIMATES)	MEMBERSHIP: LEAGUE OF NATIONS	UNITED NATIONS	ORGANIZATION OF AMERICAN STATES (OAS)	NORTH ATLANTIC TREATY ORGANIZATION (NATO)	ORGANIZATION OF AFRICAN UNITY (OAU)	COUNCIL OF EUROPE	ORGANIZATION FOR ECONOMIC COOPERATION AND DEVELOPMENT (OECD)	ARAB LEAGUE	COLOMBO PLAN	GENERAL AGREEMENT ON TARIFFS AND TRADE (GATT)	COUNCIL FOR MUTUAL ECONOMIC ASSISTANCE (COMECON)
Malaysia	128,400	9,400,000		•							•	•	
Maldive Islands	115	98,000		•									
Mali	463,947	4,700,000		•			•						
Malta	122	320,000		•								•	
Mauritania	398,000	1,100,000		•			•					•	
Mauritius	720	760,000		•									
Mexico	761,600	47,000,000	•	•	•								
Monaco	370 acres	24,000											
Mongolia	604,247	1,200,000		•									•
Morocco	174,471	14,000,000		•			•			•			
Muscat and Oman	82,000	650,000											
Nauru	8.1	5,560											
Nepal	54,362	10,300,000		•							•		
Netherlands	13,967	12,500,000	•	•		•		•	•			•	
New Zealand	103,736	2,700,000	•	•							•	•	
Nicaragua	50,193	1,750,000	•	•	•							•	
Niger	489,190	3,500,000		•			•					•	
Nigeria	356,669	59,000,000		•			•					•	
Norway	149,280	3,800,000	•	•		•		•	•			•	
Pakistan	365,529	120,000,000		•							•	•	
Panama	29,576	1,500,000	•	•	•								
Paraguay	157,047	2,100,000	•	•	•								
Peru	496,222	12,400,000	•	•	•							•	

	AREA IN SQUARE MILES	POPULATION (1967 OR 1968 ESTIMATES)	MEMBERSHIP										
			LEAGUE OF NATIONS	UNITED NATIONS	ORGANIZATION OF AMERICAN STATES (OAS)	NORTH ATLANTIC TREATY ORGANIZATION (NATO)	ORGANIZATION OF AFRICAN UNITY (OAU)	COUNCIL OF EUROPE	ORGANIZATION FOR ECONOMIC COOPERATION AND DEVELOPMENT (OECD)	ARAB LEAGUE	COLOMBO PLAN	GENERAL AGREEMENT ON TARIFFS AND TRADE (GATT)	COUNCIL FOR MUTUAL ECONOMIC ASSISTANCE (COMECON)
Philippines	115,740	34,000,000		•							•		
Poland	120,359	32,000,000	•	•									•
Portugal	35,510	9,300,000	•	•		•			•			•	
Rhodesia	150,333	4,400,000										•	
Rumania	91,699	19,200,000	•	•									•
Rwanda	10,169	3,200,000		•			•						
San Marino	24	18,000											
Saudi Arabia	873,972	8,000,000		•						•			
Senegal	76,124	3,600,000		•			•					•	
Sierra Leone	27,925	2,500,000		•			•					•	
Singapore	225	1,900,000		•							•		
Somalia	246,155	2,500,000		•			•						
South Africa	471,819	18,400,000	•	•								•	
South Yemen	117,000	1,250,000		•						•			
Spain	194,883	31,900,000	•	•								•	
Sudan	967,491	14,000,000		•			•			•			
Swaziland	6,705	385,000		•			•						
Sweden	173,665	7,900,000	•	•				•	•			•	
Switzerland	15,941	6,000,000	•						•				
Syria	71,498	5,400,000		•						•			
Tanzania	362,844	10,600,000		•			•					•	
Thailand	198,455	32,000,000	•	•							•		
Togo	21,853	1,700,000		•			•					•	
Trinidad and Tobago	1,980	1,000,000		•	•							•	

	AREA IN SQUARE MILES	POPULATION (1967 OR 1968 ESTIMATES)	LEAGUE OF NATIONS	UNITED NATIONS	ORGANIZATION OF AMERICAN STATES (OAS)	NORTH ATLANTIC TREATY ORGANIZATION (NATO)	ORGANIZATION OF AFRICAN UNITY (OAU)	COUNCIL OF EUROPE	ORGANIZATION FOR ECONOMIC COOPERATION AND DEVELOPMENT (OECD)	ARAB LEAGUE	COLOMBO PLAN	GENERAL AGREEMENT ON TARIFFS AND TRADE (GATT)	COUNCIL FOR MUTUAL ECONOMIC ASSISTANCE (COMECON)
Tunisia	63,378	4,800,000		•			•			•			
Turkey	301,380	32,000,000	•	•		•		•	•			•	
Uganda	91,134	7,800,000		•			•					•	
Union of Soviet Socialist Republics	8,649,489	235,500,000	•	•									•
United Arab Republic	386,872	30,200,000	•	•			•			•			
United Kingdom	94,213	55,000,000	•	•		•		•	•		•	•	
United States	3,615,210	200,000,000		•	•	•			•		•	•	
Upper Volta	105,869	5,000,000		•			•					•	
Uruguay	68,536	2,800,000	•	•								•	
Vatican City	109 acres	1,000											
Venezuela	352,143	9,300,000	•	•	•								
Vietnam (North)	61,293	18,500,000											
Vietnam (South)	66,897	16,500,000									•		
Western Samoa	1,097	135,000											
Yemen	75,290	5,000,000		•						•			
Yugoslavia	98,766	20,000,000	•	•					•*				
Zambia	290,587	4,000,000		•			•						

* Yugoslavia has special status

Sources consulted: *The Americana Annual 1968* (New York: Americana Corporation, 1968), p. 549; *Britannia Book of the Year 1967* (Chicago: Encyclopaedia Britannica, Inc., 1967), pp. 442–443, 636–638; *1968 Reader's Digest Almanac and Yearbook* (Pleasantville, N.Y.: The Reader's Digest Association, 1967), pp. 61–249; Walter Mallory, ed., *Political Handbook and Atlas of the World* (New York: Harper and Row, for the Council on Foreign Relations, 1968); U.S. Bureau of the Census, *Statistical Abstract of the United States: 1967* (Washington, D.C.: Government Printing Office, 1967), pp. 862–864.

The Ten Largest Nations

In Area

Rank	*Area in Sq. Mi.*
1. U.S.S.R.	8,649,489
2. Canada	3,851,809
3. China (Communist)	3,691,506
4. United States	3,615,210
5. Brazil	3,286,470
6. Australia	2,967,741
7. India	1,262,275
8. Argentina	1,072,067
9. Sudan	967,491
10. Algeria	919,592

In Population
(1967 or 1968 estimates)

Rank	*Population*
1. China (Communist)	750,000,000
2. India	520,000,000
3. U.S.S.R.	235,500,000
4. United States	200,000,000
5. Pakistan	120,000,000
6. Indonesia	110,000,000
7. Japan	100,000,000
8. Brazil	88,000,000
9. West Germany	60,000,000
10. Nigeria	59,000,000

Materials for the Study of International Relations

For Ready Reference

Zawodny, J. K. *Guide to the Study of International Relations.* San Francisco: Chandler Publishing Company, 1966. An invaluable annotated reference manual.

Abstracts of Important Literature, and General Digests and Chronologies

Chronology of International Events. Royal Institute of International Affairs, London.

Current Thought on Peace and War; a World Affairs Digest on Current International Issues. Institute for International Order, New York.

Deadline Data on World Affairs. New York.

Facts on File; a Weekly World News Digest. Facts on File, Inc., New York.

International Political Science Abstracts (Documentation Politique Internationale). Basil Blackwell, Oxford, England.

Keesing's Contemporary Archives. Bristol, England.

Peace Research Abstracts Journal. Peace Research Institute, Clarkson, Ontario, Canada.

Atlases and Gazetteers

The Columbia Lippincott Gazetteer of the World, edited by Leon E. Seltzer. New York: Columbia University Press, 1952.

Cosmopolitan World Atlas, rev. ed. Chicago: Rand McNally and Company, 1963.

Encyclopaedia Britannica World Atlas. Chicago: Encyclopaedia Britannica, Inc., 1959.

Goode's World Atlas: Physical, Political and Economic, 12th ed., by J. Paul Goode, edited by Edward B. Espenshade, Jr. Chicago: Rand McNally and Company, 1964.

Hammond's Ambassador World Atlas. Maplewood, N.J.: C. S. Hammond and Company, 1954.

Illustrated Atlas of Today's World. Chicago: Rand McNally and Company, 1962.

National Geographic Atlas of the World, 2d ed. Washington, D.C.: National Geographic Society, 1966.

Rand McNally Commercial Atlas and Marketing Guide, 87th ed. Chicago: Rand McNally and Company, 1956 (Centennial Edition).

The Times Atlas of the World, edited by John Bartholomew. Mid-century edition, 5 vols. London: The Times Publishing Company, 1955–59. Also available in a one-volume edition, published in 196[illegible]

Worldwide Encyclopedia of the Nations, edited by Moshe Y. Sachs. 5 vols. New York: Harper and Row, 1967.

Paperback Series on World Affairs[1]

America in Crisis Series. New York: John Wiley and Sons.

The American Assembly Series. Englewood Cliffs, N.J.: Prentice-Hall.

American Problems Series. New York: Holt, Rinehart, and Winston.

Anvil Series. Princeton, N.J.: D. Van Nostrand Company.

Area Studies in Economic Progress. Chicago: Scott, Foresman and Company.

Asian Civilization Series. Englewood Cliffs, N.J.: Prentice-Hall.

Chatham House Essays. New York: Oxford University Press.

Contemporary Civilizations Series. New York: Holt, Rinehart, and Winston

Crowell Comparative Government Series. New York: Thomas Y. Crowell Company.

A Culture Area in Perspective Series. Boston: Allyn and Bacon.

Culture Regions of the World Series. New York: The Macmillan Company.

Foreign Relations Series. River Forest, Ill.: Laidlaw Brothers.

Ginn Studies in Depth Series. Boston: Ginn and Company.

Global Culture Series. Webster, Kansas: McCormick-Mather Publishing Company.

The Global History Series. Englewood Cliffs, N.J.: Prentice Hall.

The Hammarskjold Forums. Dobbs Ferry, N.Y.: Oceana Publications.

Hoover Institution Studies. Stanford, Calif.: Hoover Institution on War, Revolution, and Peace.

Interim History Series. New York: Facts on File.

The Modern Nations in Historical Perspective Series. Englewood Cliffs, N.J.: Prentice-Hall

The Modern World Series. New York: Oxford University Press.

The New York Times Byline Books. New York: Atheneum Press.

Our Widening World Area Studies Series. Chicago: Rand McNally and Company

Oxford Social Studies Pamphlets. New York: Oxford University Press.

Penguin African Library. Baltimore, Md.: Penguin Books.

Praeger Paperback Series: International Affairs; Geography; Economics and Development; Area Studies; Military Affairs; Non-Western Studies; Studies in World Communism; etc. New York: Frederick A. Praeger.

Problems in Asian Civilization. New York: D. C. Heath and Company.

Problems in European Civilization. New York: D. C. Heath and Company.

Public Affairs Pamphlets. New York: Public Affairs Pamphlets.

Scholastic World Affairs Multi-Texts. Englewood Cliffs, N.J.: Scholastic Magazines.

Searchlight Books. Princeton, N.J.: D. Van Nostrand Company.

Vista Books. New York: Viking Press.

Visual Geography Series. New York: Sterling Publishing Company.

The Walker Summit Library. New York: Walker and Company.

World Affairs Atlas Series. New York: Frederick A. Praeger.

World Culture Series Study Guides. New York: Taplinger Publishing Company.

World University Library. New York: McGraw-Hill Book Company.

Zenith Books. Garden City, N.Y.: Doubleday and Company.

Textbooks and Selected Readings (Published since 1955)

ATWATER, ELTON. *World Affairs: Problems and Prospects*. New York: Appleton-Century-Crofts, 1958.

ATWATER, ELTON, KENT FORSTER, and JAN S. PRYBYLA. *World Tensions: Conflict and Ac-*

[1] Source: H. Thomas Collins, "Paperback Series on World Affairs," *The Bulletin of the National Association of Secondary School Principals*, No. 315 (January, 1967), pp. 117–138, 140, 142, 144.

commodation. New York: Appleton-Century-Crofts, 1967.

BALL, M. MARGARET and HUGH B. KILLOUGH. *International Relations.* New York: The Ronald Press Company, 1956.

CEFKIN, J. LEO. *Background of Current World Problems.* New York: David McKay Company, 1967.

CLEMENS, WALTER C., JR., ed. *World Perspectives on International Politics.* Boston: Little, Brown and Company, 1965.

CRABB, CECIL. *Nations in a Multipolar World.* New York: Harper and Row, 1968.

DEUTSCH, KARL. *The Analysis of International Relations.* Englewood Cliffs, N.J.: Prentice-Hall, 1968.

DUCHACEK, IVO. *Conflict and Cooperation Among Nations.* New York: Holt, Rinehart and Winston, 1960.

FLEISS, PETER J. *International Relations in the Bipolar World.* New York: Random House, 1968.

FRIEDMANN, WOLFGANG. *An Introduction to World Politics,* 3d ed. New York: St. Martin's Press, 1956.

GOLDWIN, RICHARD, ed. *Readings in World Politics.* New York: Oxford University Press, 1959.

GREENE, FRED. *Dynamics of International Relations: Power, Security, and Order.* New York: Holt, Rinehart and Winston, 1964.

GYORGY, A. and H. S. GIBBS, eds. *Problems in International Relations,* 2d ed. Englewood Cliffs, N.J.: Prentice-Hall, 1962.

HAAS, ERNST and ALAN S. WHITING. *Dynamics of International Relations.* New York: McGraw-Hill Book Company, 1956.

HARTMANN, FREDERICK H. *The Relations of Nations,* 3d ed. New York: The Macmillan Company, 1967.

———, ed. *World in Crisis: Readings in International Relations,* 3d ed. New York: The Macmillan Company, 1967.

HERZ, JOHN. *International Relations in the Atomic Age.* New York: Columbia University Press, 1962.

HILL, NORMAN L. *International Politics.* New York: Harper and Row, 1963.

HOLSTI, K. J. *International Politics: A Framework for Analysis.* Englewood Cliffs, N.J.: Prentice-Hall, 1967.

KULSKI, W. W. *International Politics in a Revolutionary Age,* 2d ed. Philadelphia: J. B. Lippincott Company, 1968.

LANYI, GEORGE A. and WILSON C. MCWILLIAMS, eds. *Crisis and Continuity in World Politics: Readings in International Relations.* New York: Random House. 1966.

LERCHE, CHARLES O., JR. *Principles of International Politics.* New York: Oxford University Press, 1956.

LERCHE, CHARLES O., JR. and ABDUL A. SAID. *Introduction to World Politics.* Englewood Cliffs, N.J.: Prentice-Hall, 1962.

LIJPHART, AREND, ed. *World Politics: The Writings of Theorists and Practitioners, Classical and Modern.* Boston: Allyn and Bacon, 1966.

MILLER, LINDA B., ed. *Dynamics of World Politics: Studies in the Resolution of Conflict.* Englewood Cliffs, N.J.: Prentice-Hall, 1968.

MILLS, LENNOX and CHARLES H. MCLAUGHLIN. *World Politics in Transition.* New York: Holt, 1956.

MORGENTHAU, HANS J. *Politics Among Nations; the Struggle for Power and Peace,* 4th ed. New York: Alfred A. Knopf, 1967.

OLSON, WILLIAM C. and FRED A. SONDERMANN. *The Theory and Practice of International Relations,* 2d ed. Englewood Cliffs, N.J.: Prentice-Hall, 1966.

ORGANSKI, A. F. K. *World Politics,* 2d ed. New York: Alfred A. Knopf, 1968.

PADELFORD, NORMAN and GEORGE A. LINCOLN. *The Dynamics of International Politics.* New York: The Macmillan Company, 1962.

RENOUVIN, PIERRE and JEAN-BAPTISTE DUROSELLE. *Introduction to the History of International Relations.* New York: Frederick A. Praeger, 1967.

RIENOW, ROBERT. *Contemporary International Politics.* New York: Thomas Y. Crowell Company, 1961.

SCHLEICHER, CHARLES P. *International Relations: Cooperation and Conflict.* Englewood Cliffs, N.J.: Prentice-Hall, 1962.

SCHUMAN, FREDERICK L. *International Politics: The Western State System and the World Community,* 7th ed. New York: McGraw-Hill Book Company, 1969.

SCHWARZENBERGER, GEORG. *Power Politics: A Study of International Society,* 3d ed. London, 1964.

SPANIER, JOHN. *World Politics in an Age of Revolution.* New York: Frederick A. Praeger, 1967.

SPIRO, HERBERT J. *World Politics: The Global System.* Homewood, Ill.: Dorsey Press, 1966.

SPROUT, HAROLD and MARGARET SPROUT. *Fountains of International Politics.* Princeton, N.J.: D. Van Nostrand Co., 1962.

STOESSINGER, JOHN G. *The Might of Nations: World Politics in Our Time,* rev. ed. New York: Random House, 1965.

STOESSINGER, JOHN G. and ALAN F. WESTIN eds. *Power and Order: Six Cases in World Politics.* New York: Harcourt, Brace and World, 1965.

TOMA, PETER A. and ANDREW GYORGY, eds. *Basic Issues in International Relations.* Boston: Allyn and Bacon, 1967.

VAN DYKE, VERNON. *International Politics,* 2d ed. New York: Appleton-Century-Crofts, 1966.

Periodicals (A selected list)

Africa Digest, London
Africa Quarterly, New Delhi
Africa Today, New York
African Affairs Quarterly, London
African Forum, New York
African Recorder, New Delhi
African Review, Accra
American Behavioral Scientist, Princeton, N.J.
American Journal of International Law, Washington
American Political Science Review, Washington
American Slavic and East European Review, New York
Américas, Washington
Annals of the American Academy of Political and Social Science, Philadelphia
Annals of the Organization of American States, Washington
Asian Review, London
Asian Survey, Berkeley, Calif.
Atlantic Community Quarterly, Washington
Atlantic Studies, Boulogne-sur-Seine, France
Aussenpolitik, Stuttgart
Australian Outlook, Melbourne and Sydney
Behind the Headlines, Toronto
Bulletin of the Atomic Scientists, Chicago
Canadian Journal of Economics and Political Science, Toronto
Challenge, Los Angeles
China Quarterly, London
China Review, London
Chronique de Politique Étrangère, Brussels
Contemporary Review, London
Current Digest of the Soviet Press, New York
Current History, Philadelphia
Department of State Bulletin, Washington
Diplomatist, London
Disarmament and Arms Control, New York
East Europe, New York
East West Digest, Richmond, England
Eastern World, London
Economic Development and Cultural Change, Chicago
Economist, London
Europa-Archiv, Bonn
European Digest, London
External Affairs Review, Wellington, N. Z.
Far Eastern Economic Review, Hong Kong
Far Eastern Survey, New York
Foreign Affairs, New York
Foreign Service Journal, Washington
Freedom and Union, Washington
Global Digest, Hong Kong
Headline Series of the Foreign Policy Association, New York
India Quarterly, New Delhi
Inter-American Economic Affairs, Washington
Intercom, New York
International Affairs, London
International Affairs, Moscow
International Conciliation, New York
International Development Review, Washington
International Journal, Toronto
International Organization, Boston
International Relations, Athens
International Relations, London
International Review Service, New York
International Studies, New Delhi
International Studies Quarterly, Denver, Colo.
Journal of Asian Studies, Ann Arbor, Mich.
Journal of Central European Affairs, Boulder, Colo.
Journal of Commonwealth Political Studies, Leicester, England
Journal of Conflict Resolution, Ann Arbor, Mich.
Journal of Development Studies, London
Journal of International Affairs, New York
Journal of Modern African Studies, London

Journal of Peace Research, Oslo
Journal of Politics, Gainesville, Florida
La Communità Internazionale, Rome
La Revue des Deux Mondes, Paris
Latin American Report, New Orleans
Middle East Forum, Beirut
Middle East Journal, Washington
Middle Eastern Affairs, New York
Minority of One, Passaic, N.J.
Modern Asian Studies, Cambridge, England
New Times, Moscow
Orbis, Philadelphia
Pacific Affairs, Vancouver
Pakistan Horizon, Karachi
Peace Information Bulletin, London
Political Quarterly, Edinburgh
Political Science Quarterly, New York
Political Studies, London
Politique Étrangère, Paris
Politique Internationale, Paris
Relazioni Internazionali, Milan
Review of International Affairs, Belgrade
Review of Politics, Notre Dame, Ind.
Revue Française de Science Politique, Paris
Revue Internationale d'Histoire Politique et Constitutionelle, Paris
Revue Politique et Parlementaire, Paris
Round Table, London
Russian Review, New York
Slavic and East European Review, London
Soviet Periodical Abstracts, White Plains, N. Y.
Soviet Press Translations, Seattle, Wash.
Soviet Studies, Glasgow
Swiss Review of World Affairs, Zurich
United Asia, Bombay
United Empire, London
UN Monthly Chronicle (See also section on "United Nations Publications")
United Nations News, London
Western Political Quarterly, Salt Lake City
World Affairs, London
World Affairs, Toronto
World Affairs, Washington
World Affairs, Wellington
World Affairs Interpreter, Los Angeles
World Affairs Quarterly, Los Angeles
World Federalist, The Hague
World Politics, Princeton, N. J.
World Today, London
Zeitschrift für Geopolitik, Hessen, West Germany

League of Nations Publications

The most comprehensive listing of League publications is Hans Aufricht, *Guide to League of Nations Publications* (New York: Columbia University Press, 1951). Also highly useful are Marie J. Carroll, *Key to League of Nations Documents Placed on Public Sale, 1920–1929* (Boston: World Peace Foundation, 1930), plus four supplements which bring the *Key* through 1936; and Arthur Breycha-Vauthier, *Sources of Information: a Handbook on the Publications of the League of Nations* (London, 1939).

Some League publications are now available through the United Nations. Catalogues of these publications are no longer in print. Inquiries may be addressed to Sales and Circulation Section, United Nations, New York.

United Nations Publications

Next to the United States Government, the UN is the largest publisher in the world. Not only is its range of operations incredibly broad but it also has five official languages — Chinese, English, French, Russian, and Spanish — and some of its publications are issued in all of these. In order to facilitate the identification of published materials, two sets of symbols have been worked out. One is the Document Symbol, which indicates the organ involved, the date, and possibly other relevant information. The other is the Sales Number. Every UN publication except the United Nations Treaty Series, the Official Records, and the various periodicals carries this number. It is usually placed on the inside front cover or on the reverse of the title page. It is given with title entries in UN catalogues, and it should be used in ordering.

Some knowledge of the Document Symbol is indispensable to readers who need to find their way around among UN publications, and it should be used in giving citations. A United Nations Document Index is issued monthly, and an annual index is published for each volume. Since 1963 it has not included publications of specialized agencies, which issue their own catalogues. Number 43 of this series (ST/LIB/SER.D/43), dated September, 1952, and entitled *Consolidated List of United Nations Documents Index Series*, contains 31 pages of symbols. Useful guides are Carol C. Moor and Waldo Chamberlin, *How to Use United Nations Documents* (New York: New York University Press, 1952); and *United Nations Document Series Symbols* (as of November 15, 1955), published by the United Nations in 1956 (1956. I. 4).

In 1955 the United Nations Secretariat published a very comprehensive and well-indexed catalogue under the title, *Ten Years of United Nations Publications, 1945 to 1955: A Complete Catalogue.* Supplementary catalogues have been issued from time to time. These catalogues do not list the publications of the International Court of Justice and the specialized agencies, which have separate publication programs. Inquiries about these should be addressed to the agency concerned. Certain descriptive publications dealing with the activities and achievements of the specialized agencies are included in the United Nations publications program.

The majority of the publications of the United Nations fall under two main categories: (1) Secretariat Studies and Reports. This group is itself divided into seventeen categories, some of which are in turn divided. (2) Official Records. These comprise the proceedings of the General Assembly, the Security Council, the Economic and Social Council, the Trusteeship Council, the Atomic Energy Commission, and the Disarmament Commission.

Special mention should also be made of the following: (1) The United Nations Treaty Series. Treaties and agreements entered into by member states of the UN are published in accordance with Article 102 of the Charter. This series is, in effect, a continuation of the League of Nations Treaty Series of 205 volumes. (2) Annual reports and year books. The most valuable of these for general purposes is the huge *Yearbook of the United Nations,* a comprehensive and authoritative survey of all UN activities. In 1964, for example, in addition to the *Yearbook of the United Nations 1963,* the following year books were published: *Statistical Yearbook 1963; Commodity Survey 1963; Economic Survey of Asia and the Far East 1963; Yearbook of National Accounts Statistics 1963; Yearbook of International Trade Statistics 1962; World Economic Survey 1963; Demographic Yearbook 1963; Economic Survey of Europe 1963.* (3) United Nations mimeographed documents. Certain classes of mimeographed documents may be purchased by annual subscription. These include documents of the General Assembly and its committees, the Security Council, the Economic and Social Council and its committees and commissions, the Trusteeship Council, the International Law Commission, and the Disarmament Commission. (4) Periodicals. The United Nations issues a large number of periodicals, mostly of a specialized nature. A comprehensive and attractive general periodical is the *UN Monthly Chronicle,* the most valuable single general source of current information about the UN and its activities. The *Chronicle* was preceded by the *United Nations Weekly Bulletin,* August, 1946 through December, 1947, the *United Nations Bulletin,* January, 1948 through June, 1954, and the *United Nations Review,* July, 1954 through April, 1964. Among the more specialized periodicals are economic bulletins for Europe, for Latin America, and for Asia and the Far East, several statistical journals, and the *United Nations Documents Index.* (5) *A Bibliography of the Charter of the United Nations* (1955. I. 7), a comprehensive worldwide bibliography citing more than 2900 books, pamphlets, periodicals, articles, and government reports which cover the history of the Charter, comparisons made between the Charter and the Covenant of the League, and specific chapters and articles of the Charter. (6) *Repertory of Practice of United Nations Organs* (1955. V. 2), a summary in five volumes of the decisions of the UN organs from the beginning of their functioning to September 1, 1954, together with related material, organized by Charter articles. (7) *Documents of the United Nations Conference on International Organization, San Francisco, 25 April to 26 June 1945.* Volumes I–XV were published in 1945–46 by the UN Information Organizations (London and New York) in cooperation with the Library of Congress. Volumes XVI–XXII were published by the UN in 1954–56. (8) Publications of the International Court of Justice and the specialized agencies. Each of these agencies has an extensive publication program. The ICJ, for example, publishes a yearbook; reports of judgments, advisory opinions, and orders; pleadings, oral arguments, and relevant documents; a yearly basic catalogue of publications; press communiqués; etc.

Publications of Other International Organizations; OAS as an Example

Each of the many hundreds of international governmental and nongovernmental organizations issues lists and indexes of its voluminous publications, including official records. The *Yearbook of International Organizations* (*Annuaire des organisations internationales*), published every two years in English by the Union of International Associations (Brussels), supplies information on the structures, officials, activities, and publications of most of these organizations. The *Yearbook* is divided into the following sections: I, United Nations; II, European Community; III, Other Inter-Governmental Organizations; IV, Non-Governmental Organizations. A particularly useful collection of articles, documents, and bibliographies relating to various European organizations is the *European Yearbook* (*Annuaire Européen*), published annually under the auspices of the Council of Europe.

The publications of the Organization of American States may be cited by way of example. The Pan American Union, General Secretariat of the OAS, maintains a broad publication program, including the Official Records of the various OAS organs and agencies, in a combination of English and Spanish editions. Its books, pamphlets, and serials are commonly issued in English, Spanish, Portuguese, and French. They relate to a wide range of national and international interests in the Western Hemisphere. Some are elementary and impressionistic, others technical and highly specialized. Many are beautifully illustrated, and all are priced as low as possible.

In addition to many separate works dealing with the sessions and actions of the several organs of the OAS, commerce and industry, agriculture, health, education, geography, history, travel, national and international law, housing and planning, statistics, and the social sciences, the PAU issues four serials of interest to students of international relations: *Américas,* an illustrated monthly magazine devoted mostly to nonpolitical aspects of life in the Americas; *Annals of the Organization of American States,* a quarterly containing official documents of the OAS; *Inter-American Review of Bibliography,* a quarterly containing articles, book reviews, bibliography of recent books and pamphlets, news, and other notes; and the not-quite-annual *American Juridical Yearbook,* a survey of developments in inter-American law. The PAU offers an attractive "Depository Subscription' to all publications — books, booklets, reports, and periodicals.

United States Government Publications

The Government Printing Office in Washington issues a vast amount of material concerned with international relations. This includes a great many annual reports of government agencies as well as specialized papers and reports on the work of various committees and commissions and on the international conferences in which the United States has participated. The Government Printing Office issues many special subject catalogues of its publications. These are being constantly revised and reissued with a continuance of the same catalogue number. The *Monthly Catalog of United States Government Publications* is a guide to current publications. For a helpful list of representative publications of the Government Printing Office, see the appendix to the annual *United States Government Organization Manual* and Everett S. Brown, *Manual of Government Publications, United States and Foreign* (New York: Appleton-Century-Crofts, 1950). Elmer Plischke, *American Foreign Relations: A Bibliography of Official Sources* (Bureau of Governmental Research, University of Maryland, 1955) is particularly useful: A list of unofficial bibliographies, collections of documents, and periodicals is given in the appendices.

The Department of State issues various guides to publications, bibliographies and lists of materials (including selections for basic reference collections in international affairs and foreign relations), chronologies, diplomatic papers (including the *Foreign Relations of the United States* series), treaties and agreements and information concerning treaties, materials on international conferences and organizations (including an annual report by the President to the Congress on *United States Participation in the United Nations*), digests of international law, information on diplomatic and consular missions and officials, various "series" of publications (the bulk of State Department publications), periodicals, press releases, and certain special publications. In April, 1965, the Historical Office of the State Department issued a convenient 17-page listing of *Major Publications of the Department of State: An Annotated Bibliography* (Dept. of State Pub. 7843, General Foreign Policy Series 200).

Two serials, in particular, are indispensable for the student of international relations and foreign policy. The *Foreign Relations of the United States,* prepared in the Historical Office of the Department, is a documentary collection which began in 1861 under a somewhat different name and which has now reached more than 220 volumes. Except for a few special issues the materials included are now approximately fifteen years behind publication date, a delay that is caused by inadequate editorial assistance and shortage of funds rather than by any kind of statute of limitations, as many persons assume. For an enlightening discussion of this series and of the screening involved, see E. R. Perkins, "Foreign Relations of the United States," *Department of State Bulletin,* XXVII (December 22, 1952). The other essential serial is the *Department of State Bulletin* itself, begun in 1939 and issued weekly on a subscription basis. It is a useful source for news, official statements on policy, and current documentary materials.

Special volumes of the *Foreign Relations* series include several supplements on World War I; thirteen volumes on the Paris Peace Conference, 1919; two volumes on Japan, 1931–1941; and collections of documents on the Soviet Union, 1933–1939 and on several summit conferences during World War II. Among the more substantial publications of the Department of State since World War II are *Documents on German Foreign Policy, 1918–1945* (four volumes); *Nazi Conspiracy and Aggression* (eight volumes and two supplements); *Trial of the Major War Criminals Before the International Military Tribunal, Nuremberg* (thirty-seven volumes); *Germany, 1947–1949: The Story in Documents; Nazi-Soviet Relations, 1929–1941; Postwar Foreign Policy Preparation: 1939–1945; United States Relations with China, with Special Reference to the Period 1944–1949* (the China White Paper); *The United Nations Conference on International Organization, San Francisco, California, April 25–June 26, 1945: Selected Documents;* and *American Foreign Policy, 1950–1955: Basic Documents* (two volumes).

Much pertinent material is also published by other departments and agencies of the United States government. Particular attention is called to the publications of the Defense and Commerce Departments, and the Agency for International Development (a semi-autonomous agency within the Department of State). Much material is listed under the predecessors of AID: the International Cooperation Administration, the Foreign Operations Administration, the Mutual Security Agency, and the Economic Cooperation Administration.

Congressional publications are an increasingly valuable source of information on foreign affairs. These include the proceedings of the Senate and the House of Representatives (published in the *Congressional Record*), hearings, reports of committees, staff studies, materials printed as public documents, and the texts of bills and treaties. Two useful compilations of documents on foreign policy are *A Decade of American Foreign Policy: Basic Documents, 1941–1949,* Sen. Doc. No. 123, 81st Cong., 1st Sess. (Washington, D.C.: Government Printing Office, 1950), and *Review of the United Nations Charter: A Collection of Documents,* Sen. Doc. No. 87, 83d Cong., 2d Sess. (Washington, D.C.: Government Printing Office, 1954). Of special importance also is *United States Foreign Policy: Compilation of Studies,* prepared under the direction of the Committee on Foreign Relations, U.S. Senate, Sen. Doc. No. 24, 87th Cong., 1st Sess. (Washington, D.C.: Government Printing Office, 1961).

INDEX

(Abbreviations—"n.," footnote; "q.," quoted)